# Environmental Crime

# Environmental Crime
# A Reader

**Edited by Rob White**

**WILLAN**
PUBLISHING

Published by

Willan Publishing
Culmcott House
Mill Street, Uffculme
Cullompton, Devon
EX15 3AT, UK
Tel: +44(0)1884 840337
Fax: +44(0)1884 840251
e-mail: info@willanpublishing.co.uk
website: www.willanpublishing.co.uk

Published simultaneously in the USA and Canada by

Willan Publishing
c/o ISBS, 920 NE 58th Ave, Suite 300,
Portland, Oregon 97213-3786, USA
Tel: +001(0)503 287 3093
Fax: +001(0)503 280 8832
e-mail: info@isbs.com
website: www.isbs.com

First published 2009

ISBN 978-1-84392-512-5 paperback
      978-1-84392-511-8 hardback

British Library Cataloguing-in-Publication Data

A catalogue record for this book is available from the British Library

FSC
Mixed Sources
Product group from well-managed
forests and other controlled sources
Cert no. SGS-COC-2482
www.fsc.org
© 1996 Forest Stewardship Council

Typeset by GCS, Leighton Buzzard, Bedfordshire, LU7 1AR
Project managed by Julia Willan
Printed and bound by T.J. International Ltd, Trecerus Industrial Estate, Padstow, Cornwall

# Contents

# List of abbreviations

| | |
|---|---|
| ACF | Australian Conservation Foundation |
| AECEN | Asian Environmental Compliance and Enforcement Network |
| AFP | Australian Federal Police |
| AHC | Australian Heritage Commission |
| AMSA | Australian Maritime Safety Authority |
| ANZECC | Australian and New Zealand Environment Conservation Council |
| AQIS | Australian Quarantine Inspection Service |
| ARF | ASEAN Regional Forum |
| ASEAN | Association of Southeast Asian Nations |
| BAN | Basel Action Network |
| BKSDA | Provincial Office for Natural Resources Conservation |
| BOD | biochemical oxygen demand |
| C&D | construction and demolition |
| CAA | Clean Air Act |
| CARE | Citizens Against Ruining our Environment |
| CCG | Centre for Conservation and Government |
| CERCLA | Comprehensive Environmental Response, Compensation and Liability Act |
| CFC | chloroflurocarbons |
| CI | Conservation International |
| CID | Criminal Investigation Division |
| CITES | Convention on International Trade in Endangered Species of Wild Fauna and Flora |
| CSCAP | Council for Security Cooperation Asia Pacific |
| CSS | Central Statistics Service |
| CWA | Clean Water Act |
| DC | desire-for-control |
| DCA | Department for Constitutional Affairs |
| DEFRA | Department for the Environment, Food and Rural Affairs |
| DEP | Department of Environmental Protection |
| DFE | design for environment |
| DFID | Department for International Development |

| | |
|---|---|
| DFO | Department of Fisheries and Oceans |
| DOJ | Department of Justice |
| EC | European Community |
| ECOSOC | United Nations Economic and Social Control |
| ED | enforcement disincentive |
| EEZ | Exclusive Economic Zone |
| EGAT | Electricity Generating Authority of Thailand |
| EIA | Environmental Investigation Agency |
| EJ | Environmental Justice |
| ELAC | Environmental Legal Assistance Centre |
| EMS | environmental management systems |
| EPA | Environmental Protection Agency |
| EPCRA | Emergency Planning  and Community Right to Know Act |
| ESF | Environmental Strike Force |
| FAO | United Nations Food and Agriculture Programme |
| FBI | Federal Bureau of Investigation |
| FCI | Forest Civil Investigators |
| FLEGT | Forest Law Enforcement, Governance, and Trade |
| FPO | Forest Practices Officers |
| GA | General Assembly |
| GAO | General Accounting Office |
| GATS | General Agreement on Trade in Services |
| GBRMPA | Great Barrier Reef Maritime Park Authority |
| GM | genetically modified |
| GMO | genetically modified organisms |
| GDP | Gross Domestic Product |
| GNP | Gross National Product |
| GW | Global Witness |
| HMC&E | Her Majesty's Customs and Excise |
| HSE | Health and Safety Executive |
| IBAMA | Brazilian Institute for Environment and Renewable Resources |
| IBRD | International Bank for Reconstruction and Development |
| IDEA | Integrated Data for Enforcement Analysis |
| IEN | Indigenous Environmental Network |
| IEP | Illinois Environmental Protection |
| IESB | Institute for Social and Environmental Studies of Southern Bahia |
| IMPEL | European Network on the Implementation and Enforcement of Environmental Law |
| INECE | International Network for Environmental Compliance and Enforcement |
| ISO | International Organization for Standardisation |
| IUCN | International Union for Conservation of Nature |
| JSB | Judicial Studies Board |
| LGEEPA | General Law on Ecological Balance and Environmental Protection |
| LRFT | live reef fish trade |
| MAV | Municipal Association of Victoria |
| MAVUS | methodology for assessing the vulnerability of sectors |

| | |
|---|---|
| MEA | multilateral environmental agreements |
| MFU | Maritime Fishermen's Union |
| MRA | market reduction approach |
| NASA | National Aeronautics and Space Administration |
| NGO | non governmental organization |
| NIMBY | not in my back yard |
| ODS | ozone-depleting substances |
| OECD | Organization of Economic Cooperation and Development |
| OMB | White House Office of Management and Budget |
| OTIS | Online Tracking Information System |
| PAH | polycyclic aromatic hydrocarbons |
| PCB | polychlorinated biphenyl |
| PIC | Pesticides in International Trade |
| PNG | Papua New Guinea |
| PNP | Philippines National Police |
| POP | persistent organic pollutant |
| PPM | parts per million |
| PROFEPA | Federal Prosecutorial Service for Environmental Protection |
| PRP | primarily responsible party |
| PVC | polyvinylchloride |
| RCA | Conservation and Recovery Act |
| RCMP | Royal Canadian Mounted Police |
| RCRA | Resource Conservation and Recovery Act |
| RECAP | Reporting for Enforcement and Compliance Assurance Priorities |
| RIIA | Royal Institute of International Affairs |
| RILO/AP | Regional Intelligence Liaison Office of the World Customs Union |
| RTZ | Rio Tinto Zinc |
| SIC | standard industrial classification |
| SLAPP | Strategic Litigation Against Public Participation |
| SLATS | Statewide Landcover and Tree Survey |
| SLE | Suez-Lyonnaise |
| SSSI | Sites of Special Scientific Interest |
| Stats SA | Statistics South Africa |
| SWOP | Southwest Organizing Project |
| TAC | total allowable catch |
| TAM | traditional Asian medicine |
| TCE | trichloroethylene |
| TEC | transnational environmental crime |
| TRI | toxic chemical release inventory |
| TSCA | Toxic Substances Control Act |
| UAE | United Arab Emirates |
| UCE | Urban Environment Conference |
| UHF | ultra high frequency |
| UNECE | United Nations Economic Commission for Europe |
| UNEP | United Nations Environment Programme |
| UNODC | United Nations Office of Drugs and Crime |
| USAID | United States Agency for International Development |
| VIF | variance inflation factor |

WCO       World Customs Organisation
WPF       World Food Programme
WTO       World Trade Organisation

# List of figures and tables

**Figures**

**Tables**

# Acknowledgements

We have made every attempt to obtain permission to reproduce material in this book. Copyright holders who we may have inadvertently failed to acknowledge should contact Willan Publishing.

We are very grateful to the following for permission to reproduce material in this volume:

**Part One**
**1.** The authors and Sage Publications for Mark Halsey and Rob White, 'Crime, ecophilosophy and environmental harm', in *Theoretical Criminology* (1998), 2(3), pp. 345–371; **2.** The authors and the Southern African Journal of Criminology for F.J.W. Herbert and S.J. Joubert, 'Criminological semantics: conservation criminology – vision or vagary?', in *Acta Criminologica* (2006), 19(3), pp. 88–103; **3.** The author and Sage Publications for Rob White, 'Environmental issues and the criminological imagination' in *Theoretical Criminology* (2003), 7(4), pp. 483–506; **4.** The authors and Sage Publications for Michael J. Lynch and Paul B. Stretesky, 'The meaning of green: contrasting criminological perspectives', in *Theoretical Criminology* (2003), 7(2), pp. 217–238; **5.** The author and Sage Publications for David R. Simon 'Corporate environmental crimes and social inequality: new directions for environmental justice research', in *American Behavioural Scientist* (2000), 43(4), pp. 633–645; **6.** The authors and *Social Justice* for Penny Green, Tony Ward and Kirsten McConnachie, 'Logging and legality: environmental crime, civil society, and the state', in *Social Justice* (2007), 34(2), pp. 94–110; **7.** The authors and *Social Justice* for David O. Friedrichs and Jessica Friedrichs, 'The World Bank and crimes of globalization: a case study', in *Social Justice* (2002), 29(1–2), pp. 13–36; **8.** The author and Sage Publications for Ted Benton, 'Rights and justice on a shared planet: more rights or new relations?', in *Theoretical Criminology* (1998), 2(2), pp. 149–175; **9.** The author and the American Society of Criminology for Piers Beirne, 'For a nonspeciest criminology: animal abuse as an object of study', in *Criminology* (1999), 37(1), pp. 117–147; **10.** The author and *Social Justice* for Christopher Williams, 'An environmental victimology', in *Social Justice* (1996), 23(4), pp. 16–40; **11.** The author and *Social Justice* for Sharon Stephens, 'Reflections on environmental justice: children as victims and actors', in *Social Justice* (1996), 23(4), pp. 62–86;

12. The author and Oxford University Press for Mark Halsey, 'Against 'green' criminology', in *British Journal of Criminology* (2004), 44(4), pp. 833–853.

**Part Two**
**13.** The author and *Environmental Health Perspectives* for Charles W. Schmidt, 'Environmental crimes: profiting at the earth's expense', in *Environmental Health Perspectives* (2004), 112(2), pp. A96–A103; **14.** The author and the Sydney Institute of Criminology for Rob White, 'Environmental crime in global context: exploring the theoretical and empirical complexities', in *Current Issues in Criminal Justice* (2005), 16(3), pp. 271–285; **15.** The author and *Social Justice* for Alan A. Block, 'Environmental crime and pollution: wasteful reflections', in *Social Justice* (2002), 29(1–2), pp. 61–81; **16.** The authors and The Society for the Study of Social Problems Inc. for Robin Saha and Paul Mohai, 'Historical context and hazardous waste facility siting: understanding temporal patterns in Michigan', in *Social Problems* (2005), 52(4), pp. 618–648; **17.** The author and *Social Justice* for Déborah Berman Santana for 'Resisting toxic militarism: Vieques versus the U.S. Navy', in *Social Justice* (2002), 29(2), pp. 37–47; **18.** The author and Springer Science and Business Media for David N. Pellow, 'The politics of illegal dumping: an environmental justice framework', in *Qualitative Sociology* (2004), 27(4), pp. 511–525; **19.** The author and The University of California Press for Raquel Pinderhughes, 'The impact of race on environmental quality: an empirical and theoretical discussion', in *Sociological Perspectives* (1996), 39(2), pp. 231–248; **20.** The author and Blackwell Publishing Ltd. for Daniel Brook, 'Environmental genocide: Native Americans and toxic waste', in *American Journal of Economics and Sociology* (1998), 57(1), pp. 105–113; **21.** The authors and The Australian Institute of Criminology for Rebecca Tailby and Frances Gant, 'The illegal market in Australian abalone', in *Trends & Issues in Crime and Criminal Justice No. 225* (2002); **22.** The authors and Blackwell Publishing Ltd. for John L. McMullan and David C. Perrier, 'Lobster poaching and the ironies of law enforcement', in *Law and Society Review* (2002), 36(4), pp. 679–720; **23.** The author and Oxford University Press for Reece Walters, 'Crime, bio-agriculture and the exploitation of hunger', in *British Journal of Criminology* (2006), 46(1), pp. 26–45; **24.** The authors and Springer Science and Business Media for Michael J. Lynch and Paul Stretesky, 'Toxic crimes: examining corporate victimization of the general public employing medical and epidemiological evidence', in *Critical Criminology* (2001), 10, pp. 153–172.

**Part Three**
**25.** The author and Elsevier for Duncan Brack, 'Combatting international environmental crime', in *Global Environmental Change* (2002), 12, pp. 142–147; **26.** The author and Taylor & Francis Ltd. for Lorraine Elliot, 'Transnational environmental crime in the Asia Pacific: an 'un(der)secutitized' security problem?', in *The Pacific Review* (2007), 20(4), pp. 499–522; **27.** The author and the Sydney Institute of Criminology for Kevin Tomkins, 'Police, law enforcement and the environment', in *Current Issues in Criminal Justice* (2005), 16(3), pp. 294–306; **28.** The authors and Conservation International Foundation for Anita Sundari Akella and James B. Cannon, 'Strengthening the weakest links: strategies for improving the enforcement of environmental laws globally'

(2004), pp. 1–34 (Washington, DC: Center for Conservation and Government); **29.** The author and the Sydney Institute of Criminology for Robyn Luise Bartel, 'When the heavenly gaze criminalises: satellite surveillance, land clearance regulation and human-nature relationship', in *Current Issues in Criminal Justice* (2005), 16(3), pp. 322–329; **30.** The author and Sage Publications for Jacqueline L. Schneider, 'Reducing the illicit trade in endangered wildlife: the market reduction approach', in *Journal of Contemporary Criminal Justice* (2008), 24(3), pp. 274–295; **31.** The author and the American Society of Criminology for Paul B. Stretesky, 'Corporate self-policing and the environment', in *Criminology* (2006), 44(3), pp. 671–708; **32.** The author and Taylor & Francis Ltd. for Helena Du Rées, 'Can criminal law protect the environment?' in *Journal of Scandinavian Studies in Criminology and Crime Prevention* (2001), 2, pp. 109–126; **33.** The author and Oxford University Press for Paula de Prez, 'Excuses, excuses: the ritual trivialisation of environmental prosecutions', in *Journal of Environmental Law* (2000), 12(1), pp. 65–77; **34.** The Controller of the HMSO on behalf of Parliament for House of Commons, Environmental Audit Committee, 'Environmental Crime and the Courts', pp. 1–24; **35.** The author and the Texas Law Review Association for David C. Fortney, 'Thinking outside the 'black box': tailored law enforcement in environmental criminal law', in *Texas Law Review* (2003), 81(6), pp. 1609–35; **36.** The authors and Koninklijke BRILL NV for Nicholas Dorn, Stijn Van Daele and Tom Vander Beken, 'Reducing vulnerabilities to crime of the European waste management industry: the research base and the prospects for policy', in *European Journal of Crime, Criminal Law and Criminal Justice* (2007), 15(1), pp. 23–36.

# Introduction: Environmental crime and eco-global criminology

*Rob White*

Our world is in peril. Global warming, oil spills, massive numbers of extinctions, reduction in bio-diversity, toxic environments, disappearance of the Arctic ice, poisonous water, unbreathable air, burning of garbage, clearfelling of forests, the list goes on as to how planetary wellbeing is being destroyed and diminished in so many different ways. Most of what is happening is directly attributable to negative human intervention and the systemic imperatives, and unnatural consequences, of the global capitalist political economy.

Harm is being perpetrated across the earth, although the intensity and form it takes varies depending upon specific region and specific populations (White 2008a). Sometimes these harms are acknowledged in the law as criminal offences. In many cases, they are not. They are simply part of the 'normal' way of doing things, an attitude and a practice that will only lead to disaster for all.

From the very beginning, then, the notion of 'environmental crime' will necessarily be contentious. For police and law makers, it will usually be defined in conventional terms, as those acts or omissions that formally constitute a breach of criminal law (Situ and Emmons 2000). For many others, however, environmental crime is best described not in terms of 'legality', but in terms of new concepts of eco-justice (see for example, Beirne and South 2007; see also United Nations Environment Programme 2007). The ways in which environmental harm can be conceptualised are illustrated in Figure 1 which describes three broad approaches to the understanding of environmental issues.

Different philosophies, values and perspectives give rise to very different conceptions of what the problem is, and how best to respond to it.

As is evident from both objective changes in world conditions and academic engagement in this area, environmental crime is a topic of growing international interest and importance. This Reader provides a general introduction and overview of the shape and content of green/environmental criminology at this juncture in time by presenting key articles in the field.

The link between environmental issues and criminology finds its expression in environmental or green criminology, itself a development that has arisen from advances and concerns from outside the field as such. In this relatively new area of research and scholarship the concern is to stretch the boundaries of mainstream criminology to accommodate issues of global significance, while also utilising the insights of conventional criminology, to illuminate ways in which

## Conventional criminology

Legal conceptions of harm as informed by laws, rules and international conventions.

Key issue is one of legality, and the division of activities into legal and illegal categories.
- Illegal taking of flora and fauna – which includes activities such as illegal, unregulated and unreported fishing, illegal logging and trade in timber and illegal trade in wildlife.
- Pollution offences – which relates to issues such as fly-tipping (illegal dumping) through to air, water and land pollution associated with industry.
- Transportation of banned substances – which refers to illegal transport of radioactive materials and the illegal transfer of hazardous waste.

## Ecological perspectives

Ecological wellbeing and holistic understandings of interrelationship between species and environments.

Key issue is that of sustainability, and the division of social practices into benign and destructive from the point of view of ecological sustainability.
- Problem of Climate Change – in which the concern is to investigate those activities that contribute to global warming, such as the replacement of forests with cropland.
- Problem of Waste and Pollution – in which the concern is with those activities that defile the environment, leading to things such as the diminishment of clean water.
- Problem of Biodiversity – in which the concern is to stem the tide of species extinction and the overall reduction in species through application of certain forms of human production, including use of genetically modified organisms.

## Green criminology

Justice conceptions based upon notions of human, ecological and animal rights and egalitarian concerns.

Key issue is weighing up of different kinds of harm and violation of rights within the context of an eco-justice framework.
- Environment rights and environmental justice – in which environmental rights are seen as an extension of human or social rights so as to enhance the quality of human life, now and into the future.
- Ecological citizenship and ecological justice – in which ecological citizenship acknowledges that human beings are merely one component of complex ecosystems that should be preserved for their own sake via the notion of the rights of the environment.
- Animal rights and species justice – in which environmental harm is constructed in relation to the place of nonhuman animals within environments and their intrinsic right to not suffer abuse, whether this be one-on-one harm, institutionalised harm or harm arising from human actions that affect climates and environments on a global scale.

**Figure 1** Three approaches to conceptualising environmental harm
*Source*: White 2008b

to understand and respond to environmental harm (White 2008a: 3). The terms 'green' criminology and 'environmental' criminology are themselves somewhat contentious and ambiguous insofar as each is associated with particular political perspectives and analytical fields of enquiry. For present purposes, they are held to be interchangeable and to only refer to that research and scholarship that is concerned with environmental issues. Another formulation of this type of study – namely, eco-global criminology – will be discussed further on.

This Introduction provides a brief history of where we have been in terms of published work on environmental crime, and where we are heading. It also provides an explanation for which articles have been included in the Reader and which have not.

## Environmental crime: the story so far

The study of environmental crime or harm has expanded considerably in the last decade or so. Several journals have published special issues, dealing specifically with green or environmental criminology themes – such as *Social Justice, Current Issues in Criminology*, and *Theoretical Criminology*. Recent anthologies such as *Issues in Green Criminology* (Beirne and South 2007), and *Green Criminology* (South and Beirne 2007) have provided a forum for the bringing together of commissioned essays and reprinted articles that overall constitutes a substantial and growing body of work in this area.

The expansion of scholarly interest and academic study within criminology on environmental matters is also associated with the development of new ways in which to articulate the issues. For example, recent books such as *Crimes Against Nature* (White 2008a), *Global Harms* (Sollund 2008), *Defining Environmental Justice* (Schlosberg 2007) and *Environmental Justice and Environmentalism* (Sandler and Pezzullo 2007) not only offer new insights into the nature of justice, crime and harm, but they find voice to do so through the use of new terms and new concepts by which to describe the world around us. The language of green or environmental criminology is thus developing in the same moment that it approaches the study of harm in exciting, novel and critical ways. The question of language is further addressed in the chapter following this Introduction.

Globalisation, and the challenges that this presents for criminology as a field, specifically the study of environmental issues, is increasingly being acknowledged (Aas 2007; Van Dijk 2008; Larsen and Smandych 2008). This is evident in recent work that looks at transnational criminology, and asks the question of how to undertake comparative work that is at one and the same time sensitive to regional differences, yet able to make generalisations about specific types of criminal (and crime control) activities (Sheptycki 2008). Differences between, and the need for, global criminology as well as comparative international criminology have also been noted (Friedrichs 2007).

The intention of this Reader is to provide a selection of the most thoughtful, provocative and insightful articles on environmental crime to date. It contains a general introduction and overview of key articles in the emerging area of green or environmental criminology. The focus for the collection is environmental crime, itself an ambiguous concept, and one that has been defined in the broadest terms to include environmental harms of many different kinds (as indicated in Figure 1).

The articles reprinted in this Reader span a wide range of concerns – from issues of pollution, illegal disposal of waste and logging, through to prosecution of specific environmental offences and crime prevention as this pertains to trade in endangered species. The book includes articles that challenge existing conceptualisations of environmental crime and human rights, as well as those that provide insight into what the 'greening' of research and scholarship means for criminology as a field. The Reader draws upon work from many different sources and from many different disciplines and perspectives.

Decisions about what to include and exclude from this Reader were subject to the normal space constraints. In compiling the material, well over 100 articles and book chapters were initially chosen. The list covered the more conventional discussions of environmental harm such as pollution and the disposal of toxic waste; it also included a wide range of material from areas such as socio-legal studies, environmental management, regulation theory and practice, and environmental reform. These topics were narrowed down to a specific focus on environmental harms and crimes, and the responses to these.

A distinction can also be made between environmental crime, and crimes associated with the environment. For the purposes of the present book, it was decided that the main focus should be with the former, since the key concern is with crimes against nature (in its various manifestations). The latter includes what has been described as eco-terrorism or ecosabotage, acts that are sometimes committed by environmental activists involved in specific campaigns (e.g. tree spiking, damaging earthmoving equipment), and which, in themselves, are legally defined as criminal (Martin 1990; Amster 2006). These are crimes committed on behalf of, or in defense of, the environment, rather than crimes against the environment. There is nevertheless an important connection between the two sorts of activity, and each type of 'crime' calls forth major arguments over definition and what are deemed to be appropriate social responses.

Finally, for the sake of length and pragmatics, it was decided to only include those articles published in refereed journals, rather than book chapters. Of the refereed articles, the final list includes those that were the most substantive, interesting, useful, provocative and well written. This helped to reduce the size of the list, while building into the process a modicum of quality control. The exception to this was the inclusion of a useful extract from a UK House of Commons Report on environmental crime and the courts.

The Reader links the exploration of environmental issues with the core concerns of criminology – conceptualisations of crime, the dimensions and dynamics of crime, and the enforcement and prevention of crime. The Reader is divided into three sections reflecting these themes.

The first section, 'Conceptualising Environmental Crime', includes articles that challenge existing paradigms, that reject emergent ones, and that confirm the importance of dealing with environmental harms and victimisation in a systematic and theoretically informed manner. In essence, environmental crime is defined variably by different authors, but in ways that include reference to transgressions against humans, transgressions against environments, and transgressions against nonhuman animals. This selection provides a spectrum of offerings from a variety of sources. The ideas, too, reflect different emphases on what is deemed to be important, what is considered to be harmful, and what the meaning of crime is in different social, political and cultural contexts.

The second section, 'Dynamics of Environmental Crime', is more empirically and substantively grounded as the analyses turn to specific instances of harm and criminal activity. Issues range from lobster and abalone poaching through to pollution and the generation of toxic waste. What these articles demonstrate is that very often specific types of environmental harm cannot be separated from the fact that the harm is also specific to very particular groups of people. In other words, environmental harm frequently involves the simultaneous exploitation of particular bio-spheres, of particular plants and animals, and of the poorest, most vulnerable sections of the human community. Environmental crime and ecological injustice take place within certain historical and social contexts. One consequence of this is the phenomenon of differential victimisation, where different species, bio-spheres and human population groups are disproportionately subject to criminal and/or harmful activities.

The third section, 'Environmental Law Enforcement', explains how contemporary interest in green or environmental criminology has extended to questions of how best to respond to environmental harm. Certainly the law, including criminal law, is an important consideration in this regard. Yet, as much of the literature demonstrates, environmental crime rarely commands much more than trivial treatment, and very light-handed penalties when cases do actually make it into court. Much more needs to be done in terms of environmental policing and investigation, in prosecution of environmental crimes, and in developing suitable sentencing regimes that most appropriately address instances of environmental harm. Developing innovative and alternative forms of environmental crime prevention are also part of a systemic response to widespread problems.

The more one ponders the issues, the more one realises just how much further we need to go. Indeed, the transnational nature of much environmental harm – in terms of perpetrators (such as transnational corporations and organised criminal syndicates); transference (such as cross-national movement of polluted air and water) victimisation (such as universalising effects of climate change); and of social conflict (such as increasing tensions and conflicts over goods, water and other resources) – demands new ways of analysing and responding to environmental issues. This Reader thus provides a summary of where we have been before as well as providing a platform for work that needs to be done into the future.

## Towards an eco-global criminology

Eco-global criminology refers to a criminological approach that is informed by *ecological* considerations and by a critical analysis that is *global* in scale and perspective. Based upon eco-justice conceptions of harm, it considers transgressions against environments, nonhuman species and humans. One consequence of global trends, for example, is an expected upsurge in social conflict. These conflicts include those pertaining to diminished environmental resources, to the impacts of global warming, to differential access and use of nature, and to friction stemming from the cross-border transference of harm.

Intervention on environmental matters will require criminologists to be part of the policy and implementation process (in areas such as framing new laws, instituting environmental law enforcement, developing environmental crime prevention methods and taking part in environmental regulation). How we interpret and respond to global developments depends upon how we define environmental harm, how we envisage the protection of human, ecological and animal rights, and how we understand the power and interests that underpin recent trends and issues.

A major issue for eco-global criminology is that it must ultimately consist of a criminology of the South, as well as the North (see for example Cifuentes and Frumkin 2007). That is, it must be inclusive of researchers, scholars, activists and writers from non-Western, non-Christian and less developed countries as well as those from the metropoles of the USA, Europe and the UK. The ingrained political and analytical biases of the dominant strands of criminology need to be acknowledged (Marshall 2008; see also Connell 2007), and a more globally

---

Analysis of specific types and instances of environmental harm
- Disposal of hazardous waste
- Illegal fishing, logging and trade in wildlife
- Pollution and degradation of environments

Conceptual modelling of environmental harm
- Spatial and temporal dynamics of harm
- Transference of harm
- Agents, perpetrators and causes of harm, including organised crime

Intervention strategies and environmental law enforcement
- Audit of environmental enforcement and regulatory agencies
- Analysis of inter-agency collaboration
- Capacity building, including amongst police and the judiciary

Technologies and techniques to deal with environmental harm
- Environmental forensics across diverse areas
- Satellite and remote sensing surveillance
- Situational and social crime prevention

Comparative research and global networks
- Joint research on specific issues (e.g. policing of illegal fishing)
- Comparative research (e.g. dealing with toxic waste)
- Sharing of expertise and data (e.g. environmental disasters)

---

**Figure 2** Research areas of eco-global criminology

inclusive dialogue generated if we are to adequately build upon our understanding of environmental crime and to develop capacity to respond to it.

A dedicated research agenda informed by eco-global criminological considerations would consist of several interrelated prongs, each of which entails development of specific research projects. Figure 2 provides examples of some of the tasks that lie ahead. What is clear from this is that while much has been achieved in the area of green criminology over the past ten years or so, there is much, much more that is yet to be done.

The theoretical perspectives and empirical studies in this Reader are presented in the hope that they will stimulate continuing and further work across the spectrum of topics revealed in the articles and as signposted under the rubric of eco-global criminology. The urgency of the task should not be underestimated, as we experience the world radically changing before our very eyes. Criminology has much to offer in addressing environmental crime. For this to happen, though, the time to 'see, judge, act' is now.

## References

Aas, K. (2007) *Globalization and Crime*. Los Angeles: Sage.

Amster, R. (2006) 'Perspectives on Ecoterrorism: Catalysts, Conflations, and Casualties', *Contemporary Justice Review*, 9(3): 287–301.

Beirne, P. and South, N. (eds) (2007) *Issues in Green Criminology: Confronting harms against environments, humanity and other animals*. Devon: Willan.

Cifuentes, E. and Frumkin, H. (2007) 'Environmental Injustice: Case Studies from the South', *Environmental Research Letters*, 2: 1–9.

Connell, R. (2007) Southern Theory: The global dynamics of knowledge in social science. Sydney: Allen and Unwin.

Friedrichs, D. (2007) 'Transnational Crime and Global Criminology: Definitional, Typological, and Contextual Conundrums', *Social Justice*, 34(2): 4–18.

Larsen, N. and Smandych, R. (eds) (2008) *Global Criminology and Criminal Justice: Current issues and perspectives*. Peterborough, ON: Broadview Press.

Marshall, I. (2008) 'The Criminological Enterprise in Europe and the United States: A Contextual Exploration', in N. Larsen and R. Smandych (eds) *Global Criminology and Criminal Justice: Current issues and perspectives*. Peterborough, ON: Broadview Press.

Martin, M. (1990) 'Ecosabotage and Civil Disobediance', *Environmental Ethics*, 12: 291–310.

Sandler, R. and Pezzullo, P. (eds) (2007) *Environmental Justice and Environmentalism: The social justice challenge to the environmental movement*. Cambridge, MA: The MIT Press.

Schlosberg, D. (2007) *Defining Environmental Justice: Theories, movements, and nature*. Oxford: Oxford University Press.

Sheptycki, J. (2008) 'Transnationalisation, Orientalism and Crime', *Asian Criminology*, 3(1): 13–35.

Situ, Y. and Emmons, D. (2000) *Environmental Crime: The criminal justice system's role in protecting the environment*. Thousand Oaks, CA: Sage.

South, N. and Beirne, P. (eds) *Green Criminology*. Aldershot: Ashgate.

Sollund, R. (ed.) (2008) *Global Harms: Ecological crime and speciesism*. New York: Nova Science Publishers.

United Nations Environment Programme (2007) *Global Environment Outlook*. New York: UNEP.

Van Dijk, J. (2008) *The World of Crime: Breaking the silence on problems of security, justice, and development across the world*. Los Angeles: Sage.

White, R. (2008a) *Crimes Against Nature: Environmental criminology and ecological justice*. Devon: Willan.

White, R. (2008b) 'The Criminalisation of Environmental Harm', *Criminal Justice Matters*. London Centre for Crime and Justice Studies, King's College.

# Studying environmental crime: key words, acronyms and sources of information

*Diane Heckenberg**

## Introduction

*Dealing with environmental harm will demand new ways
of thinking about the world...*

Language shapes the way we think, understand and describe the world. In describing something, we categorise it, using the medium of language, in an attempt to provide a coherent interpretation for others of what it is we are trying to understand ourselves. Yet, as pointed out in the Introduction to this Reader, *environmental crime* is in itself an ambiguous concept. Consider, for example, the following questions:

What is an environmental 'crime' in the twenty-first century, as distinct from the twentieth century?
How do we adequately describe 'environment' in a global context?
How does environmental justice differ from ecological justice?
How do we make sense of the barrage of acronyms that confront us in this field?

Terms mean different things to different people and, over time, are often subject to alteration or enhancement in the light of new knowledge or a particular social context. This collection of words and acronyms is a guide to meaning, not absolute definitions. It is designed to give readers a general idea of some of the terms they will encounter in the study of environmental harms, laws and regulations. We would hope to develop and expand on this list over the coming years.

*Postgraduate student in the School of Sociology and Social Work at the University of Tasmania.

## Key Words

| Words | Explanation |
| --- | --- |
| Anthropocentric | Refers to a human-centred view of the world which privileges humans over all other life forms |
| Biocentric | Refers to a species-centred view of the world which views humans as just one of a number of beings on the earth, all of which have the same rights and all of which should be valued equally |
| Biodiversity | Refers to the variety and number of plants, animals, fungi and bacteria within a particular environmental space |
| Bio-imperialism | Refers to the way in which the basic means of life of humans is being reconstituted and reorganised through global systems of private ownership, often dominated by transnational corporations |
| Bio-piracy | Refers to the appropriation, mostly by those in the developed world, of the traditional knowledge, technologies and genetic resources of Indigenous peoples and those living in developing countries |
| Bio-security | Refers to the protection of people, animals and ecological systems from the transference of pests and diseases across national and international borders |
| Brown issues | Refers to those environmental issues that impact urban life, for example air pollution and disposal of toxic wastes |
| Built environment | Refers to significant sites of human habitation and residency including urban and rural areas, areas of cross-over such as major regional concentrations of people, commuter suburbs, zones etc |
| Chlorofluorocarbons | Also known as CFCs. A family of nontoxic, nonflammable chemicals containing carbon, chlorine and fluorine. Used in the manufacture of aerosol sprays, as solvents and to facilitate cooling in refrigerators and air conditioners. Known to damage the ozone layer. |
| Conservation criminology | Concerned with natural resource and wildlife management and protection |
| Deep ecology | Views humans as one component of an intricate web of life that includes plants, animals, mountains and rivers, with rights of their own and whose existence is not simply for human pleasure |
| Differential victimisation | Refers to the disproportionate effect of environmental harms on particular groups based on ethnicity and class. For example the siting of toxic dumps near people of colour, people in poverty and Indigenous communities |

| | |
|---|---|
| Dioxins | Refers to the generic term for a group of environmentally persistent toxic chemicals that can concentrate in body fat and accumulate as they move through the food chain |
| Eco-centric | An eco-centric perspective that considers issues of social justice to be as important as, and inextricably bound to, issues of ecology. While there is an explicit recognition that humans need to impact upon or utilise nonhuman nature in order to survive, there also exists the realisation that humans need to develop ecologically sustainable ways of satisfying their basic needs |
| Eco-crime | Refers to intentional acts of harm against the natural environment including ecocide (destruction of the environment on a large scale); geocide (destruction of the earth) and eco-terrorism (terrorism in support of ecological, environmental or animal rights causes) |
| Eco-feminism | Refers to attempts to connect feminism (a social movement that focuses on issues pertaining to the oppression and rights of women) with ecological perspectives (that focus on various aspects of nature, and the relationship between humans, the biosphere and animals). A key concern is the commonalities between gender oppression and environmental degradation |
| Eco-global criminology | Refers to a criminological approach informed by ecological considerations and by a critical analysis that is global in scale and perspective. Based upon eco-justice conceptions of harm, it considers transgressions against humans, nonhumans and environments |
| Ecological citizenship | Acknowledges that human beings are one component of citizenship-complex ecosystems that should be preserved for their own sake via the notion of the rights of the environment. It means present generations ought to act in ways that do not jeopardise the existence and quality of life of future generations. It also means we extend the moral community to include nonhuman nature |
| Ecological justice | An approach to the conceptualisation of harm within green or environmental criminology. Refers to the relationship of human beings generally to the rest of the natural world and includes concerns relating to the health of the biosphere, and more specifically plants and creatures that also inhabit the biosphere. The main concern is with the quality of the planetary environment (that is frequently seen to possess its own intrinsic value) and the rights of other species (particularly animals) to a life free from torture, abuse and destruction of habitat |

| Ecological sustainability | Refers to forms of production and consumption that maximise ecological wellbeing and biodiversity as foundations of the nature–human relationship. See also *Sustainable Development* |
|---|---|
| Ecology | A science concerned with the complex interactions of non-human nature, including its abiotic components (air, water, soils) and its biotic components (plants, animals, fungi, bacteria) |
| Eco-rights | Refers to the reconceptualisation of rights to include expanded notions of environmental and community rights, particularly around the concepts of 'common good', 'common property' and sustainable environments |
| Eco-socialism | Refers to attempts to link Marxist analysis (that focuses on the political economy of class societies) with ecological perspectives (that focus on various aspects of nature, and the relationship between humans, the biosphere and animals). A key concern is the simultaneous exploitation of humans and of nature by dominant or ruling classes, usually via transnational corporations |
| Eco-terrorism | This is a disputed term, sometimes also referred to as eco-sabotage. It refers broadly to violent or illegal acts, such as tree spiking or damaging laboratories, in support of environmental or animal rights causes. It is sometimes erroneously applied to legitimate social protests, non-violent forms of civil disobedience, and illegal activity that is obtrusive but not violent (such as tree sitting to protest against logging) |
| Environmental crime | Refers to environmental harms that are deemed to be illegal according to the law. These include acts or omissions related to illegal taking of flora and fauna, pollution offences and transportation of banned substances such as radioactive materials |
| Environmental criminology | Refers to a concern with environmental issues from a criminological perspective (see *Green Criminology*). Also may refer to a crime prevention approach which seeks to diminish opportunities for crime by changing physical aspects of the environment through social, architectural and planning initiatives (see *Green Criminology*) |
| Environmental harm | Refers to a wide variety of injuries and degradations linked to the use, misuse and poor management of the 'natural environment', including such things as pollution, toxic waste and the killing of plants, soils and animals. Environmental harm can be conceptualised as involving acts and omissions that are both 'legal' and 'illegal'. Defining harm is ultimately about values and priorities and not just what the law says it is |

| | |
|---|---|
| Environmental Impact Assessment | Also known as an EIA. Refers to a process of identifying and predicting the potential environmental impacts (beneficial and adverse) of proposed actions, policies, programmes and projects prior to decision-making |
| Environmental justice | An approach to the conceptualisation of harm within green or environmental criminology. Refers to the distribution of environments among peoples in terms of access to and use of specific natural resources in defined geographical areas, and the impacts of particular social practices and environmental hazards on specific populations (e.g. as defined on the basis of class, occupation, gender, age, ethnicity). The concern is with human beings at the centre of analysis and the focus is on human health and wellbeing and how these are affected by particular types of production and consumption |
| Environmental Management System | Also known as an EMS. Refers to a form of 'self-regulation' in which individual firms or industry groups take on the role of regulating how specific processes are to be organised, with the intention of designing environmentally friendly systems of production |
| Environmental Protection Agency | Also known as EPA. An agency responsible for regulating environmental issues |
| Environmental Regulation | Refers to the general method used to control environmentally destructive activities and to limit the damage done. It involves monitoring, enforcement and compliance. Prosecution of environmental crime is generally reserved as a last resort |
| Environmental victimisation | Refers to the social processes by which specific forms of harm are caused by 'acts' (e.g. dumping of toxic waste) or 'omissions' (e.g. failure to provide safe drinking water), leading to the presence or absence of environmental agents (e.g. poisons, nutrients) that are associated with human injury |
| E-waste | Abbreviation for electronic waste. Refers to obsolete, discarded electronic goods such as computers, monitors, televisions, mobile phones and printer cartridges, frequently exported from developed countries to developing countries, for the purpose of dismantling and recycling parts, which are often toxic |
| Fly tipping | Refers to the dumping of household or commercial rubbish in private or public areas |
| Genetically Modified Organisms | Also known as GMOs. Refers to the creation of biological entities through alteration of the genetic makeup of cells, |

| | |
|---|---|
| | usually by the insertion, removal, or manipulation of individual genes |
| Green criminology | Also known as *Environmental criminology*. Broadly refers to the study by criminologists of environmental harms, environmental laws and environmental regulations. Within green criminology the three broad approaches to the conceptualisation of environmental harm are *environmental justice* (main focus is on humans), *ecological justice* (main focus is on the environment) and *species justice* (main focus is on animals) |
| Green issues | Refers to wilderness areas and conservation issues relating to logging practices, ozone depletion, acid rain and loss of wildlife |
| Greenwashing | Refers to the practice of putting a particular 'corporate spin' on environmental issues and problems. Much of it has to do with image-making, and hence is heavily tied up with public relations and the manipulation of ideas through the mass media |
| Intergenerational equity | The principle of intergenerational equity asserts that future generations have the right to environments that are the equal in terms of quality and amenity to that of the present generation |
| Natural environment | Refers to an environment as close as possible to its natural state, such as wilderness, oceans, rivers and deserts. Although human beings may be present or traverse it, it is often seen as distinctive and 'separate' *per se*. See also *Built environment* |
| Not in my backyard | Also known as NIMBY. Refers to a political stance that environmentally destructive activities should not occur in ones own local area. Derivatives include NIABY (not in anyone's backyard) and NOPE (not on planet earth) |
| Persistent Organic Pollutants | Also known as POPs. Chemicals that remain intact in the environment for long periods, become widely distributed geographically, accumulate in the fatty tissue of living organisms and are toxic to people and wildlife. POPs circulate globally via air and water and are detrimental to human health and the environment |
| Precautionary Principle | Refers to the idea that official action be taken to protect people and environments in cases where there is scientific uncertainty as to the nature of the potential damage or the likelihood of risk. |
| Resource colonisation | Refers to the practice of direct appropriation of lands, plants and animals as 'property' (including intellectual property as in the case of patents). It also occurs |

|  |  |
|---|---|
|  | through displacement of existing systems of production and consumption (such as a subsistence economy) by those that are based on commodity production |
| Smart regulation | A particular strand of environmental regulatory theory which argues that the best way to regulate environmental activity is to bring together a wide diversity of methods and actors in order to foster compliance in relation to the goal of 'sustainable development' |
| Social regulation | Refers to the process by which a society, via the state or private agencies, monitors and shapes how human activity is to be carried out in relation to specific political, economic and social agendas (which are, in turn, reflective of particular social interests) |
| Speciesism | Refers to the practice of discriminating against nonhuman animals because they are perceived as inferior to the human species. In other words, privileging human viewpoints |
| Species Justice | An approach to the conceptualisation of harm within green or environmental criminology that is represented by those who wish to include consideration of animal rights within the broad perspective. In specific terms, concepts such as *speciesism* may be invoked |
| Strategic Lawsuits Against Public Participation | Also known as SLAPPS. The term SLAPP refers to a civil lawsuit filed against private individuals or organisations, usually by large corporations, which has the effect of intimidating an individual from engaging in particular behaviour believed to be detrimental to the SLAPP filer |
| Sustainable Development | Refers to that form of economic development that attempts to minimise environmental damage within the context of existing systems of production and consumption. See also *Ecological sustainability* |
| Think Tanks | Refers to organisations that are oriented towards propagating particular research and ideas that are in the interests of their funders, usually corporations |
| Transnational environmental crime | Refers to crime that is global in scope and that reflects environmental socio-economic processes and trends associated with crime globalisation. Includes things such as illegal trade in wildlife, the international transfer of toxic waste and the black market in ozone depleting substances |
| Universal victimisation | Refers to the fact that some types of environmental harm affect all people regardless of geography or social status, for example global warming |
| White issues | Refers to the impact of new technologies, for example genetically modified organisms, food irradiation, and pathological indoor environments |

## Acronyms

The following list includes some of the more widely used acronyms describing the global organisations, agreements, conventions and programs associated with environmental issues. Descriptions have been sourced from respective websites.

| BAN | Basel Action Network<br>http://www.ban.org/ | A global organisation focused on confronting the global environmental injustice and economic inefficiency of toxic trade (toxic wastes, products and technologies) and its devastating impacts |
| --- | --- | --- |
| BioNET | Biodiversity Action Network<br>http://www.bionet-intl.org/ | An international not-for-profit initiative dedicated to promoting taxonomy, especially in the biodiversity rich but economically poorer countries of the world. Established in 1993, they are committed to maintaining biodiversity in the earth's natural ecosystems |
| CAN | Climate Action Network<br>http://www.climatenetwork.org/ | A worldwide network of over 365 Non-Governmental Organisations (NGOs) working to promote government and individual action to limit human-induced climate change to ecologically sustainable levels |
| CBD | Convention on biological diversity<br>http://www.cbd.int/ | An international treaty to sustain the rich diversity of life on earth. The main goals of the Convention are the conservation of biological diversity, the sustainable use of its components, and the fair and equitable sharing of the benefits from the use of genetic resources |
| CITES | Convention on International Trade in Endangered Species of Wild Fauna and Flora<br>http://www.cites.org/ | An international agreement between governments that focuses on protecting endangered species through limiting trade. It aims to ensure that international trade in specimens of wild animals and plants does not threaten their survival |

| CMS | Convention on the Conservation of Migratory Species of Wild Animals http://www.cms.int/ | An intergovernmental treaty, concluded under the aegis of the United Nations Environment Programme, concerned with the conservation of wildlife and habitats on a global scale. Also known as the Bonn Agreement |
|---|---|---|
| CorpWatch | http://www.corpwatch.org/ | Part of a diverse global movement for human rights, social justice, environmental sustainability, peace, corporate transparency and accountability. Investigates and exposes corporate violations of human rights, environmental crimes, fraud and corruption around the world |
| FAO | Food and Agriculture Organisation of the United Nations http://www.fao.org/ | An international organisation dedicated to defeating hunger. Serving both developed and developing countries, FAO acts as a neutral forum for nations to meet, negotiate agreements and debate policy. It helps developing countries and those in transition to modernise and improve agriculture, forestry and fisheries practices and ensure good nutrition for all |
| G8 | Group of Eight http://www.g8.utoronto.ca/ | Previously G7. A forum that brings together the governments of eight industrialised nations – Canada, France, Germany, Italy, Japan, United Kingdom, United States and Russia. The European Union is also represented but cannot host or chair the G8. The group holds an annual summit that deals with the major economic and political issues facing their own countries and the international community as a whole. The term G8 refers to both the eight member states and the annual summit meeting |

| GATS | General Agreement on Trade in Services http://www.wto.org/ | A treaty of the World Trade Organisation (WTO), created to extend the multilateral trading system to the service sector, in the same way the GATT applies to trade. Established on 1 January 1995, it is the first multilateral Trade Agreement to cover trade in services |
|---|---|---|
| GATT | General Agreement on Tariffs and Trade http://www.wto.org/ | A treaty, not an organisation, GATT was the outcome of the failure of negotiating governments to create the International Trade Organisation (ITO). From 1948 to 1994, the GATT provided the rules for much of world trade. A key objective was the reduction of barriers to international trade. The World Trade Organisation (WTO) replaced GATT in 1994, as the organisation overseeing the multilateral trading system |
| GAW | Global Atmosphere Watch http://www.wmo.int/ | A worldwide system established by the World Meteorological Organisation (a UN agency). Monitors the composition of the atmosphere, provides high quality observations for the scientific community, governments and international organisations; and organises scientific assessments in support of formulating environmental policy |
| Greenpeace | Greenpeace International http://www.greenpeace.org/international/ | A global campaigning organisation that acts to change attitudes and behaviour, to protect and conserve the environment and to promote peace. Key concerns include climate change; defending the world's oceans; protecting the world's ancient forests; working for disarmament and peace; creating a toxic free future and campaigning for sustainable agriculture |

| GSN | Global Services Network http://www. globalservicesnetwork.com/ | A global interactive online community consisting of leaders in business, government and academia. Participants are dedicated to building global support for the liberalisation of international services trade, through multilateral negotiations under the auspices of the World Trade Organisation (WTO) |
| --- | --- | --- |
| ICC | International Chamber of Commerce http://www.iccwbo.org/ | An international business organisation, championing the global economy as a force for economic growth, job creation and prosperity |
| IDA | International Development Association http://www.worldbank.org/ | A section of the World Bank devoted to helping the poorest countries to reduce poverty. Provides interest-free loans and grants for programs that boost economic growth, reduce inequalities and improve people's living conditions |
| IFC | International Finance Corporation http://www.ifc.org/ | A member of the World Bank Group that provides investments and advisory services to build the private sector in developing countries |
| IFOAM | International Federation of Organic Agriculture Movements http://www.ifoam.org/ | Worldwide umbrella organisation for the organic movement, uniting more than 750 member organisations in 108 countries |
| IMF | International Monetary Fund http://www.imf.org/ | An organisation of 185 countries working to promote international monetary cooperation and exchange rate stability. Facilitates the balanced growth of international trade, and provides resources to help members in balance of payments difficulties or to assist with poverty reduction |

| INECE | International Network for Environmental Compliance and Enforcement http://www.inece.org/ | A global network of environmental compliance and enforcement practitioners. Key concerns include raising awareness of compliance and enforcement; developing networks for enforcement cooperation; and strengthening capacity to implement and enforce environmental requirements |
| INTERPOL | International Criminal Police Organisation (ICPO) http://www.interpol.int/ | The world's largest international police organisation, with 187 member countries. Facilitates cross-border police cooperation, and supports and assists all organisations, authorities and services whose mission is to prevent or combat international crime |
| IPEN | International POPs Elimination Network http://www.ipen.org/ | A global network of more than 600 public interest non-government organisations (NGOs), working together for the elimination of persistent organic pollutants (POPs) |
| ISO | International Organisation for Standardisation http://www.iso.org/iso/ | An international standards setting body headquartered in Switzerland. Comprises representatives from the standard-setting bodies of approximately 157 countries. Develops, publishes and promulgates international proprietary, industrial and commercial standards |
| MDGs | Millennium Development Goals http://www.undp.org/mdg/ | Eight non-binding goals to be achieved by 2015, drawn from the actions and targets in the Millennium Declaration and adopted by 189 nations during the UN Millennium Summit in September 2000. Each of the eight goals responds to a major development challenge facing the world: |

|  |  | 1 eradicating extreme poverty and hunger |
|  |  | 2 achieving universal primary education |
|  |  | 3 promoting gender equality and empowering women |
|  |  | 4 reducing child mortality |
|  |  | 5 improving maternal health |
|  |  | 6 combating HIV/AIDS, malaria and other diseases |
|  |  | 7 ensuring environmental sustainability; and |
|  |  | 8 developing a Global Partnership for Development |
| OECD | Organisation for Economic Cooperation and Development http://www.oecd.org/ | An organisation that brings together the governments of countries around the world. Aims to support sustainable economic growth; boost employment; raise living standards; maintain financial stability; assist other countries' economic development; and contribute to growth in world trade |
| PAN | Pesticide Action Network http://www.pan-international.org/ | A network of over 600 participating non-governmental organisations, institutions and individuals in over 90 countries working to replace the use of hazardous pesticides with ecologically sound and socially just alternatives |
| TRIPS | Trade-related aspects of Intellectual Property http://www.wto.org/english/tratop_e/trips_e/intel2_e.htm | An international agreement administered by the World Trade Organisation. The agreement requires members to adopt fair and equitable procedures to ensure adequate protection of intellectual property rights in their sovereignty. Besides the general obligations, the agreement also provides for provisional measures and criminal procedures if needed |

| UNDP | United Nations Development Program http://www.undp.org/ | A global network advocating for change and connecting countries to knowledge, experience and resources that help people build a better life. The network also links and coordinates global and national efforts to reach the Millennium Development Goals |
|------|-------------------------------------------------------|--------------------------------------------------------------------------------------------------------------------------------------------------------------------------------------------------------------------------------------------------------------|
| UNEP | United Nations Environment Program http://www.unep.org/ | The institution most directly responsible for coordinating the response to environmental concerns within the United Nations. UNEP works with a wide range of partners to provide leadership and encourage partnership in caring for the environment, by inspiring, informing, and enabling nations and peoples to improve their quality of life without compromising that of future generations |
| WBCSD | World Business Council for Sustainable Development http://www.wbcsd.org/ | A CEO-led global association of some 200 companies dealing exclusively with business and sustainable development. Provides a platform for companies to explore sustainable development, share knowledge, experiences and best practices, and to advocate business positions on these issues in a variety of government and non-government forums |
| WEDO | Women's Environment and Development Organisation http://www.wedo.org/ | An international organisation that advocates for women's equality in global policy. Working in key global forums such as the United Nations, WEDO advocates for and seeks to empower women as decision makers to achieve economic, social and gender justice, a healthy, peaceful planet and human rights for all |

| | | |
|---|---|---|
| WEF | World Economic Forum<br>http://www.weforum.org/ | An international organisation committed to improving the state of the world by engaging leaders in partnerships to shape global, regional and industry agendas. Meets annually in Davos, Switzerland, bringing together and facilitating dialogue among world leaders in business, politics, academia and civil society |
| WFP | World Food Program<br>http://www.wfp.org/ | The United Nations frontline agency in the fight against global hunger. Key objectives include saving lives in refugee crises and other emergencies, improving nutrition and quality of life of the world's most vulnerable people at critical times in their lives, and enabling development by helping people build assets that benefit them directly and promote the self-reliance of poor people and communities |
| WHO | World Health Organisation<br>http://www.who.int/ | The directing and coordinating authority for health within the United Nations. Provides leadership on global health matters, shaping the health research agenda, setting norms and standards, articulating evidence-based policy options, providing technical support to countries and monitoring and assessing health trends |
| WIPO | World Intellectual Property Organisation<br>http://www.wipo.int/ | A specialised agency of the United Nations. Dedicated to developing a balanced and accessible international intellectual property (IP) system, which rewards creativity, stimulates innovation and contributes to economic development while safeguarding the public interest |

| WSSD | World Summit on Sustainable Development http://www.un.org/events/wssd/ | A United Nations conference held in Johannesburg in 2002 that brought together world leaders in government, business, UN agencies, civil society, and multilateral financial institutions. A key objective of the summit was to discuss and review all aspects of sustainable development. The outcome was various non-binding communal goals – for example, the World Health Organisation, through its involvement in the WSSD process, is working towards the ultimate goal of making health more central to sustainable development |
| --- | --- | --- |
| WTO | World Trade Organisation http://www.wto.org/ | A global organisation that deals with the rules of trade between nations at a global or near-global level. The WTO also administers the General Agreement on Tariffs and Trade (GATT), the General Agreement on Trade in Services (GATS) and the agreement on Trade-related Intellectual Property Rights (TRIPS) |
| WWF | World Wide Fund for Nature http://www.panda.org/ | A global organisation focused on conservation of the environment as a whole. Key concerns are stopping the degradation of the world's natural environment and building a future in which humans live in harmony with nature, by conserving the world's biological diversity; ensuring that the use of renewable natural resources is sustainable; and promoting the reduction of pollution and wasteful consumption |

# Part I

---

# Conceptualising Environmental Crime

## Introduction

The concept of crime is in itself ambiguous and contentious. Writers have long argued over which acts or omissions ought to be criminalised, and how best to ascertain which social harms should be defined wrongs. Criminology is founded upon the idea that what constitutes 'crime' is a profoundly social process: crime is defined differently in different countries; a criminal is not 'made' until they have been apprehended, prosecuted and convicted of an offence; and law reform ensures that what is criminal today may well be legal tomorrow (and *vice versa*).

To speak of 'environmental crime', therefore, is to acknowledge some kind of specificity in the act or omission that makes it distinctly relevant to environmental considerations. Yet, as with crime generally, there is much dispute over what gets defined as environmental harms, and in particular what ends up in the legal statutes as a 'crime' *per se*.

The intention of this section on 'conceptualising environmental crime' is to explore some of the theoretical and philosophical discussions and debates relating to the study of environmental crime. The first three readings, by Halsey and White (Reading 1), Herbig and Joubert (Reading 2), and White (Reading 3), challenge us to think carefully about how our assumptions about the world shape perceptions of harm, wrongdoing and crime. Halsey and White, for example, explicate three philosophical positions – the anthropocentric, biocentric and ecocentric – in order to demonstrate the very different implications that each holds for conceptualising harm as well as for environmental regulation and law enforcement. Herbig and Joubert assert that criminology has been too reluctant and slow to appreciate 'conservation' issues and that the time to act is well and truly upon us. White argues that a criminological imagination is one that takes the everyday and commonplace (such as drinking water) and makes it problematic. Green criminology needs to engage with defining the problems, regulating the harms and responding to the issues.

The next few readings deal explicitly with the question of power. Lynch and Stretesky (Reading 4), for instance, make a strong argument for linking green criminology to social justice, and in so doing reject corporate definitions of the problem. It is the powerful, and especially the transnational corporations, that are the key source of environmental wrongdoing. This theme is also reflected by Simon (Reading 5), who likewise makes the case that powerful companies, often acting in collusion with state departments, enact the worst forms of environmental harm as a matter of normal business practice. Green, Ward and McConnachie (Reading 6) explore this further in their discussion of both legal and illegal logging practices. In either case, great damage to environments can be perpetrated, and frequently the perpetrators are the same in each case. The role of global institutions such as the World Bank in causing environmental catastrophes is examined in the next reading by Friedrichs and Friedrichs (Reading 7). The exploitation of natural resources is seen to go hand in hand with exploitation of poor people, living in less developed countries.

The challenge to conventional ways of viewing crime and criminology continues in the next group of papers. Benton (Reading 8), for example, argues that taking into account the rights and interests of nonhuman animals demands new ways of thinking about relationships generally on a global scale. In a similar vein, Beirne (Reading 9) asserts that it is vital that criminology tackle questions of animal abuse seriously. The call for a nonspeciesist criminology is a demand for viewing harms against the nonhuman as worthy of considered and considerable human attention. The question of who exactly is harmed, and how environmental victims are constituted is the main concern of Williams (Reading 10). The development of an analytical framework whereby we can understand environmental victimisation as a complex social phenomenon is crucial to Williams' contribution in this area. Moving from general victimology to specific types of victimisation, Stephens (Reading 11) urges us to view environmental harm as especially important when it comes to children, including the unborn, all of whom are placed at risk by particular kinds of environmentally damaging behaviour.

This section concludes with a paper by Halsey (Reading 12) that presents a theoretical argument against green criminology as a distinct area of study. In doing so, Halsey critically scrutinises some of the accepted perspectives and conceptualisations associated with environmental or green criminology. As with all of the readings in this section, the key point is to contest the conventional, to appreciate the philosophical underpinnings of what it is that we do, and to suggest some ways in which to move forward the study of environmental crime.

# 1. Crime, ecophilosophy and environmental harm*

*Mark Halsey and Rob White*

### Abstract

This article sketches out three broad philosophical frameworks relating to the human/environment nexus – the anthropocentric, biocentric and ecocentric perspectives. It is argued that acknowledgement of these different perspectives is essential in any analysis of environmental harm. To illustrate the importance of an 'ecological imagination', each philosophy is considered in relation to the regulation and use of old-growth forest.

**Key Words** ecocentrism • ecophilosophy • environmental harm • sustainable development

### Introduction

Historically, notions of 'harm' have been central to the formation of conduct norms of all social groups. As such, the social construction of this concept along with the laws that uphold its various meanings have been, and continue to be, significant objects of criminological analyses (Feinberg 1984; Hagan 1985; Ashworth 1991). Generally speaking, criminologists tend to frame their definitions of harm in two ways: a legal-procedural approach establishes the parameters of harm by referring to practices which are proscribed by the law; a socio-legal approach, on the other hand, conceives harm in terms of damaging practices which may or may not be encapsulated under existing criminal law. The work of Tappan (1947) is characteristic of the former, in that it privileges the criminal law in the definition of what constitutes serious social injury. In contrast, the second approach has facilitated the investigation of phenomena such as white-collar crime and denial of human rights by the adoption of conceptions of harm which are not limited to definitions solely generated by the state (Cohen 1992).

The rightful object of criminological inquiry is an important conceptual and political issue. This is especially so in the area of environmental harm, given

---

*From *Theoretical Criminology* (1998), 2(3): pp. 345–371.

that many of the most serious forms of environmental harm in fact constitute 'normal social practice'. Indeed, similar in orientation to the pathbreaking work of Sutherland (1949) on white-collar crime, and Schwendinger and Schwendinger (1975) on issues relating to racism, sexism and imperialism, we would argue that adequate analysis of environmental harm demands that the criminological gaze extend well beyond mainstream conceptions and legal definitions. This is because there exists a considerable disjuncture between what is officially labelled environmentally harmful from the point of view of criminal and civil law, and what can be said to constitute the greatest sources of harm from an ecological perspective (Halsey 1997a). Criminal acts such as 'sea dumping' or 'trading in endangered species', for example, have a relatively negligible impact on the natural environment. By contrast, there are profound, long-term adverse environmental effects flowing from such *legitimate* practices as using longlines and drift-nets to catch fish, injecting cyanide and arsenic into the earth to mine precious metals, or destroying non-human nature in the course of building freeways. Indeed, many conventional, and legal, forms of human production and interaction do far worse things to the natural environment than those activities deemed illegal (Breuer 1978; Neville 1990; Conacher and Conacher 1994; Kirkpatrick 1994).

Despite this situation and, more significantly, despite a central concern with the way in which various types of 'harm' are constructed and legislated against, criminologists and/or environmental law scholars have generally remained silent on these issues. There are important exceptions to this, with some writers now addressing issues such as the limits of the law in prosecuting environmental crime, bioregional and ecocritical analyses of environmental harm, and a theoretical reconstitution of environmental degradation as a form of violence (Franklin 1990; Seis 1993, 1996; Birkeland 1995; Cassell 1995).

Nevertheless, to date instances of harming the environment have usually been subsumed under the broader categories of 'white-collar' and 'corporate' crime which cast environmental harm as something that results from the particular actions of specific companies (Ermann and Lundman 1982; Hills 1987; Grabosky and Sutton 1989; Gunningham 1993; Poveda, 1994; Adler 1996; Corlett 1996). The scope of these studies is somewhat limited, however, in that environmental harm is by no means reducible to the (negligent) actions of corporations nor the individuals within them. People who drive to work each day, reside in dwellings which undermine the natural waterflows of the land, or who consume non-recyclable products, all contribute to environmental problems *en masse*. This suggests that environmental harm is in fact ubiquitous – a structural or systemic phenomenon – rather than exclusively contained within the operations of specific corporate giants or certain 'careless' individuals.

More generally, much of the work undertaken in the area of environmental crime exhibits two fundamental shortcomings. First, commentators on the whole have accepted uncritically the definitions of environmental crime as decreed by the state. This detracts attention away from a consideration of those social practices which are legal, but environmentally disastrous (Halsey 1997a). A second difficulty is the failure to explicate what the plethora of legalized (if regulated) ecologically destructive activities means for current approaches to environmental regulation (Grabosky and Braithwaite 1986; Albrecht and Leppa 1992; del Frate and Norberry 1993; Downs 1993; Gunningham *et al.* 1995). This is particularly important to consider at the present time, given that much regulation in fact represents a *facilitation*, rather than diminishment, of environmental harm (Halsey 1997b).

We want to argue that the continued existence of so many legal yet ecologically destructive practices demands a different kind of response. Specifically, these practices indicate the importance of examining the regulation of socio-ecological conduct within the context of broader philosophical perspectives on the nature of human–environment interaction. Accordingly, the aim of this article is to outline three philosophies (anthropocentric, biocentric and ecocentric) which generally underpin our understandings of the relationship between humans and the environment, and to show their relevance to analysis of environmental harm. To illustrate the concrete applications and effects of each philosophy for particular kinds of social practice, we consider the main tenets of each philosophy in relation to a contemporary instance of ecological harm – namely, clearfelling old-growth forest. We do so in order to facilitate a clearer understanding of how each perspective:

1 conceives of environmental problems;
2 depicts the role of humans in the production of such problems; and
3 approaches the issue of environmental regulation.

Our concern, then, is to demonstrate how different philosophical perspectives shape varying definitions of crime, and the nature of what are deemed to be appropriate responses to environmental issues.

## Human beings and the environment

Whether viewed from a practical or theoretical standpoint, the 'legalities of harm' essentially function to define the boundaries of acceptable citizenship and the nature of criminal conduct. In turn, ideas about acceptable citizenship – especially those traversing the human–environment nexus – emanate from very specific, if primarily implicit, notions of what 'being human' means and the relationship between the human and non-human.

Although the philosophies employed to explicate the nature of the relation between the 'social' and the 'natural' worlds are numerous (Tokar 1988; Dobson 1990, 1991; Eckersley 1992), an analytical distinction can be made between three broad approaches to human–environment interaction – what we refer to as the anthropocentric (human-centred), the biocentric (species-centred) and the ecocentric (socio-ecological centred) (see Figure 1.1). Our concern here is not to explicate these approaches in detail, but rather to provide a broad overview of their main elements. As will be demonstrated below, each philosophy conceives of the relationship between human beings and the environment in a different way, and this in turn has major implications when it comes to defining and responding to instances of environmental harm.

| | Anthropocentric | Biocentric | Ecocentric |
|---|---|---|---|
| **Conception of human beings** | Biologically, mentally and morally superior to all other entities | Morally and ethically equal to all other entities | Socially and ethically responsible for the integrity of non-human entities |
| **Conception of natural environment** | Instrumental use | Intrinsic value | Dialectical relationship |
| **Ideological basis for activity** | Self-interest | Biotic-interest | Socio-environmental interest |
| **Main objective of social world** | Maximization of economic freedom in commodity production/consumption | Self-realization based on Gaian biological and ecological concerns | Meeting of collective human needs by maintaining ecosystemic stability |
| **Structure of decision-making** | Highly centralized organs of power | Reliance on expertise | Participatory democracy |
| **Primary indicator of human well-being** | Economic success | Spiritual awareness | Socio-ecological well-being |
| **Favoured environmental strategy** | Sustainable development Economically efficient use of resources | Righteous management Mass preservation of wilderness | Bioregionalism Ecological balance |
| **Type and role of environmental laws** | State-administered laws informed by principles of liberalism and neo-classical political economy | Centrally administered laws informed by the idea of moral equivalence of all species | Communally-administered laws informed by bioregional concerns and related to wider global conditions |
| **Socio-environmental outcomes** | Deepening social inequality Extensive ecological problems | Maintenance of social inequality No significant ecological problems | Social justice Ecological sustainability |

**Figure 1.1** Perspectives on human beings and the environment

## Anthropocentrism

The anthropocentric perspective emphasizes the biological, mental and moral superiority of *humans* over all other living and non-living entities. As Eckersley puts it, anthropocentrism is:

> the belief that there is a clear and morally relevant dividing line between humankind and the rest of nature, that humankind is the only or principal source of value and meaning in the world, and that non-human nature is there for no other purpose but to serve humankind. (1992: 51)

Non-human nature is therefore viewed *instrumentally* – as something to be appropriated, processed, consumed and disposed of in a manner which best suits the immediate interests of human beings. The integrity of non-human entities (e.g. plants, micro-organisms, waterways, soils, air) is of concern only insofar as these stand to benefit the human race. This means that because people are held to be *separate from* rather than part of the world's ecosystems, there is relatively little consideration given to the idea that human welfare is wholly dependent on the long-term survival of *non*-human entities. Where limits to intervention are perceived (e.g. number of people versus carrying capacity of the land), reliance on human ingenuity and technological invention is seen as the most appropriate way to guarantee the continued exploitation of nature (e.g. biogenetic research in relation to food production).

The ideological basis for human activity in a strictly anthropocentric world is self-interest. Preservation of the self translates here into the quest for maximum individual liberty which, in turn, is viewed as a function of the relative capacity of individuals to compete successfully (against each other) for material resources.

The social structure of decision-making is one characterized by highly centralized organs of power, involving both nation-states and transnational corporations. Large bureaucratic organizations – capable of controlling human and non-human nature at local through to international levels – function to ensure that non-human nature is subordinated to human ends and desires as shaped and defined by the profit requirements of capitalist markets or the dictates of a central ruling body (as opposed to social and ecological needs). With the philosophy of anthropocentrism influencing such matters as what is called 'productive', which events constitute a 'crisis', and what should be conceived as socially, politically, culturally and ecologically 'significant', the ruling institutional apparatuses tend to focus on those indicators which reflect the level of human well-being as measured in narrow economic terms (e.g. GNP, GDP, stock market trends). In other words, in an anthropocentric world, very little, if any, time is given over to developing sets of indicators capable of explicating the impact that human activity has on non-human nature, unless this is relevant to immediate economic interests or longer-term economic prospects (for example, in Australia, the newly formed National Pollution Inventory and the State of the Environment reports deal with environmental impacts primarily as these affect the *human* population).

Decisions concerning the environment are made according to which outcomes will best secure narrowly defined economic outcomes. Usually such decisions are made at the expense of securing the long-term stability of social and ecological systems. A typical example would be a government that allows a coal-mining company to operate in previously untrammeled areas in order that they might generate social and economic 'benefits' for 'the nation' (with 'nation', here, conceived in terms of the collective strength of human economic capacities). Where anthropocentrism is dominant, scant attention is paid to the fact that such ventures secure a 'resource' which, when used by millions of human beings on a day-to-day basis (in transport, power stations, oil refineries), contributes immensely to the processes of ecological harm (e.g. global warming, destruction of habitat).

The favoured environmental strategy of anthropocentrism is neo-environmentalism or *sustainable development* (see World Commission on Environment and Development 1990). Such a philosophy seeks to reconcile the contradiction between 'rational' behaviour (i.e. satisfaction of biological and social needs through the consumption and accumulation of material goods) and the fact that such behaviour at the collective level, if left unregulated, will lead to 'irrational' outcomes (e.g. depletion of bio-diversity, fouling of waterways, degradation of arable land). Human beings continue to be placed at the centre of sustainable development, that is, nature is once again conceived as something to be exploited (and, on occasions, preserved) solely for human ends. The emphasis, however, is on the careful *management* of resources. Forests, for example, are managed in a manner that will best accommodate the human desire for wood, furniture, paper products and so on. Setting aside pockets of wilderness for other species is seen as important, but only insofar as these help to satiate 'spiritual' and aesthetic needs, or help to alleviate political pressures from environmentalists which threaten the social stability of the system as a whole. The fact that native forest is being harvested outside these areas in a manner which might dramatically impact upon biodiversity is ultimately cast as unproblematic, or simply the 'price that must be paid' to meet human demands.

Sustainable development in essence translates into a form of 'green capitalism'. That is, the aim of such development is to operate within the context of global capitalist markets, rather than to challenge the logic of these forms of production and consumption in and of themselves. Suggested economic measures within this framework include pollution taxes and depletion quotas relating to industrial use of the environment, and more generally putting an economic value on the natural landscape and on animal life (for examples see Elkington and Burke 1987; Pearce 1989; Daly and Townsend 1993). In other words, the idea of sustainable development is to integrate the environment directly into market based cost benefit analyses (Jacobs 1993: 62–70).

Where anthropocentrism dominates, environmental laws tend to be developed in accordance with the principles of liberalism and neo classical political economy. Under this philosophy, the primary aim of these statutes is to facilitate, privilege and rationalize the *human* benefits (as defined by and organized through capitalist market relations) which flow from the exploitation and protection of the natural environment. The market is seen as an important regulator in its own right, and in some cases it is more preferable to rely on the market than the criminal law for adequate environmental protection. It is argued that: 'Profit and environmental protection, far from being mutually exclusive, can be part of the same package' (Grabosky 1994: 434). While there may be some recognition of the capacity or tendency of capitalism to damage the environment, the ideal legal and criminal justice response is nevertheless framed in terms of ensuring collaboration with, rather than prosecution of, the key offenders. Furthermore, regulation is usually fostered by promoting a company or firm on the basis of its 'environmentally sound' business practices or production methods. Under anthropocentrism, the purpose of environmental regulation is to contain instances of specific environmental harms (e.g. oil spills), rather than to eradicate structural problems (e.g. reliance on fossil fuels).

An example of environmental legislation enacted solely for human benefit at the expense of ecological well-being would be those laws and statutes which facilitate the supply of fresh water to the agricultural industry for the irrigation of crops. In the Australian state of Victoria, for example, it has been shown that irrigation uses up to 75 percent of the water in the country's largest river each year, thus dramatically depleting the oxygen content of the water. This, in turn, has led to extensive outbreaks of toxic algae resulting in the poisoning of native aquatic animals and contaminated water supplies on a continent which has long been recognized as the driest on earth. In this case, the short-term needs of fruit growers and farmers have been elevated above those of longer term ecological, and social, well-being.

The socio-environmental implications of building a society around strictly anthropocentric principles are profound. Anthropocentrism in the current age has manifested itself as an integral part of the accumulation of capital, that is, it is essential to those social systems which attempt to 'naturalize' the domination of humans by humans (capital over labour) and the domination of non-human nature by humans (capital over the natural environment). At the social level, the privileging of the market in the pursuit of ways to maximize profit has been intertwined with such practices as racism, patriarchy, economic exploitation and imperialism (Bookchin 1986, 1994; Pepper 1993; O'Connor 1994). Ecologically, the collective impact of this philosophy has led to the global destruction of non-human ecosystems, with potentially disastrous conquences for humans and non-humans alike. Yet, most of the practices informed by an anthropocentric perspective continue unabated. As legally sanctioned or regulated activities they are presented as legitimate and good, not only for the owners of wealth and the holders of power, but for the majority of people on the planet.

### Biocentrism

Biocentrism, or as it is variously referred to, 'biocentric equality' or 'biological egalitarianism', can be described as:

> The intuition ... that all things in the biosphere have an equal right to live and blossom and to reach their own individual forms of unfold-ing and self-realisation within the larger Self realisation ['where "Self" stands for organic wholeness']. This basic intuition is that all organisms and entities in the ecosphere, as parts of the interrelated whole, are equal in intrinsic worth.
>
> (Devall and Sessions 1985: 67)

33

Biocentrism views human beings as simply 'another species' to be attributed the *same* moral worth as such organisms as, for example, whales, wolves and birds. As a logical corollary of this, human beings 'should be concerned about resources for all living species' (White 1994: 32), that is, the satisfaction of human desires must not impinge upon the ability of other species to realize their *'vital* needs' (Devall and Sessions 1985: 70 (emphasis in original)). The question of who decides what constitutes these vital needs has been the source of much contention both from within the different biocentrist schools of thought and from other philosophical perspectives (Bookchin 1994). The important point is that biocentrists hold that non-human species have *intrinsic* value, that is, they possess a moral worth and will continue to have moral worth no matter how insignificant human beings conceive their existence or 'use value' to be.

The ideological basis for activity in a biocentric world is the preservation and realization of all species. Preservation of the human self, here, means instituting forms of conduct that will foster the interests of the larger Self (which includes non-human nature).

Conceptually, much of the biocentric literature in effect reduces the *social* to the *biological*. Darwinian notions of evolution, incorporating ideas of 'survival of the fittest', are unproblematically transposed into the realm of human affairs. The logic of the biocentrist position goes something like this: all life forms are morally interchangeable with one another in terms of their 'intrinsic worth'; life itself proceeds by way of evolutionary struggle (although the historical time frame for *biological* change is seldom analyzed); humans are implicated in the ongoing struggle between and within species for (biological) survival; when any species, including human beings, comes up against 'natural limits', then 'Nature' will through various biological means reduce its population to the 'carrying capacity' of a particular region (Bookchin 1994). Concepts of evolutionary biology tend to be recast into a 'social Darwinian' framework, one which both legitimates and explains a hierarchy of human experience in which some sections of the world's population are worse off than others. Given the 'intrinsic worth' of all species in the context of Darwinian 'natural selection', the substantive differences among (and, especially, premature deaths of) human beings are not a moral problem, and indeed may ultimately foster a more healthy environment for greater numbers of life forms. Particular kinds of social harm can thus be viewed as beneficial, to both species in general and the human 'species' in particular, insofar as they lead to a significant reduction in population numbers.

In an ideal biocentric world, decision making would be directed at the adoption of styles of living which are 'simple in means, rich in ends' (Devall and Sessions 1985: 68). The organization of society (regarding such issues as best technologies, population size, housing, education, work, health) should be derived by observing the workings of non-human nature. For this to occur, social development would thus require, for a certain period of time at least, that decisions be overseen by those with certain 'expertise'. Under biocentrism, 'expertise' is attached to those individuals who possess a natural or biological affinity with nature (such as ecofeminists), or, alternatively, with those who 'understand' the workings of non-human nature (such as sociobiologists, ecologists, geologists, physicists, chemists and the like). Human pursuits should ideally be directed by an understanding of 'Gaian Truth'. Roughly translated, Gaia means 'Mother Earth' and can be understood as 'a complex entity involving the earth's biosphere, atmosphere, oceans, and soil; the totality constituting a feedback or cybernetic system which seeks an optimal physical and chemical environment for life on this planet' (Lovelock in Dobson 1991: 266).

Decisions concerning the environment would, in accordance with the central principles of biocentrism, be made according to which outcomes are most likely to foster the widest possible diversity of life, both non-human and human. For example, the desire of biocentrists to ease the pressure placed on non-human nature by overpopulation has led the more radical elements to declare:

> If radical environmentalists were to invent a disease to bring human population back to sanity, it would probably be something like AIDS ... the possible benefits of this to the environment are staggering ... just as the Plague contributed to the demise of feudalism, AIDS has the potential to end industrialism.
>
> (*Earth First* journal, quoted in Dobson 1990: 64)

Under this scenario, such things as famine, disease, floods and earthquakes, are viewed 'favourably' because each potentially hastens the death of millions of people who – under biocentrism – are considered as 'the cancerous growth[s] of the human hordes' (Tokar 1988: 35).

It should, of course, be noted that not all biocentrists are in favour of such approaches to the population issue, nor are all biocentrists oblivious to the political and economic origins of ecological problems, and nor are all – nor indeed any – biocentrists supporters of the holocaust or recent programmes of genocide (East Timor, Cambodia, Rwanda). However, it is essential to realize that most, if not all, of the key thinkers of biocentric persuasion (Malthus, Naess, Devall, Sessions, Lovelock, Manes, Erlich, Foreman, Wilson) are virtually silent about how best to deal with any unrest or social injustice which may result from implementing their ideas (Tokar 1988; Dobson 1990; Pepper 1993; Bookchin 1994). For example, the biocentric quest to preserve vast tracks of land and wilderness raises serious issues for those presently making their livelihood in such areas. Similarly, biocentric commentators (usually well-to-do white Anglo Saxon males) who insist that war, mass starvation, widespread disease, entrenched poverty and the like should be met by policies of *non*-intervention – on the basis that the planet is overpopulated and that such measures are Gaia's method of 'dealing with the problem' – need to acknowledge the arguments of those who say that pressure on Gaia could also be reduced through such *humane* efforts as decentralization of economic activity, redistribution of goods and services, valuing indigenous forms of knowledge and producing for direct consumption rather than profit. In other words, the interplay between human rights and 'biotic' rights, and the political and economic dimensions contained therein, are issues which remain problematic in biocentric thought.

The favoured environmental philosophy of biocentrism is 'reverence for non-human nature' or what John Muir long ago termed 'righteous management' (Devall and Sessions 1985: 145). In most instances, such management – also known as 'biocentric ecological management' – translates into an agenda which advocates the mass preservation of wilderness, protection of (endangered) non-human species and restoration of disturbed areas towards 'pristine condition' (Devall and Sessions 1985: 131–59). If biocentrism were to dominate political forums, then environmental laws would be equated to a set of centrally administered ethics, which derive their form from the 'laws of nature'. The key role of such 'laws' would be to 'reiterate' biological and ecological laws, regardless of the penalties to be paid by significant sections of the human population.

The social and environmental implications of biocentrism are considerable – not the least of which is the concern given to overcoming the domination of nature by human beings, which has led to a distinct lack of theoretical and practical concern for the multifarious ways in which human beings dominate and subjugate each other. In other words, it is not enough to simply declare 'equality between species', 'subservience to natural laws' and 'reverence for nature' as antidotes to ecological ills – for social phenomena such as malnutrition, lack of education, patriarchy and imperialism all play a decisive role in determining the nature and extent of ecological destruction. The roots of the environmental crisis, in other words, are to be found in the political and economic systems which humans have developed and of which they are a part.

### Ecocentrism

Ecocentrism is based on the idea that: 'humans and their activities are inextricably integrated with the rest of the natural world in communal or communal-like arrangements' (Steverson 1994: 71–2). Accordingly, this philosophy:

> views humankind as part of a global ecosystem, and subject to ecological laws. These, and the demands of an ecologically based morality, constrain human action, particularly through imposing limits to economic and population growth. There is also a strong sense of respect for nature in its *own* right, as well as for pragmatic 'systems' reasons.
>
> (Pepper 1993: 33)

On this account, ecocentrism 'refuses to place humanity either above or below the rest of nature' (Tokar 1988: 41). However, the unique capacity for human beings to develop and deploy methods of production which have global consequences, means that humans also have an explicit responsibility to ensure that such production methods do not exceed the ecospheric limits of the planet. Moreover, this responsibility is a responsibility that extends to human *and* non-human life. This means that:

> an ecocentric perspective will seek to choose the course, that minimise[s] ... harm and maximise[s] the opportunity of the widest range of

organisms and communities – *including ourselves* – to flourish in their/
our own way. This is encapsulated in the popular slogan 'live simply so
that others [both human and nonhuman] may simply live'.

(Eckersley 1992: 57 (parentheses in orginal))

Ecocentrism therefore attempts to strike a balance between the instrumental
and intrinsic conceptions of non-human nature espoused by anthropocentrists
and biocentrists respectively. That is, while there is an explicit recognition that
human beings – as living, breathing components of the natural world – need
to impact upon or utilize non-human nature in order to survive, there also exists the realization that human beings need – in the interests of future human
generations and the well-being of non-human nature – to develop ecologically
sustainable ways of satisfying their basic needs. Under ecocentrism, the idea
that the destruction of non-human nature is, ultimately, the destruction of that
which sustains human nature, is ascribed absolute validity. In short, there is
a specific acknowledgement of the *dialectical* nature of the relation between
human action and non-human processes.

In addition to the concern for the way in which certain *social* arrangements
impact on non-human ecosystems, ecocentrists are also concerned with
the way in which certain (human induced) ecological problems impact on
human well-being. Ecocentrism therefore considers issues of *social justice* to
be as important as – and inextricably bound to – issues of ecology. So, for
instance, ecocentrists would be concerned to abolish not only those political
and economic relations which lead to the domination and exploitation of
ecosystems, but also those relations of production which are premised upon
the domination and exploitation of human beings. In short, developing non-
exploitative relations between human beings (while retaining maximum
cultural diversity) is viewed here as equally as important as developing non-
exploitative relations between the human realm and non-human nature.

The ideological basis for activity in an ecocentric world is an ecologically
informed 'self interest' or what can be termed 'socio-environmental interest'.
Here, there is an explicit realization that human interests at the individual
and collective levels (such as freedom from want) can only be maintained
over the longer term via activities which work *with* non-human nature
rather than against it. There is, in other words, a dual commitment to meet
collective *needs* (as opposed to reified desires) and an attempt to maintain
ecosystemic stability. As such, material interests which are fulfilled via the
unsustainable commodification of non-human nature would be viewed as
logically incompatible with the objective of sustaining human life over the
longer term. That is, without the continued existence of certain basic elements
(clean air, non-toxic seas and fertile lands) the idea of 'human interests' would
be impossible for the simple reason that those who conjour such interests
would be unable to inhabit such an environment. The ecocentric perspective
thus acknowledges that social relations play a decisive role in determining the
nature and extent of both ecological destruction and human misery. Hence,
the solutions to environmental harm reside in the social, not the biological.
This requires analysis and action which is to a certain extent 'anthropocentric'
insofar as it expresses a commitment to securing the conditions for human

well-being, by concentrating on the social relations underlying current environmental practices.

Ideally, decision-making in this framework would be based upon the principles of participatory democracy. The notion of centralized bodies (whether comprised of capitalist corporations, state politicians or environmental experts) acting as the absolute arbiter over such issues as education, environmental planning, production methods or housing is anathema to the philosophy of ecocentrism. Rather, ecocentrists advocate a grass-roots (or localized) level of decision-making where 'right' and 'wrong' are calculated in terms of which actions would be most likely to support the principles of bioregionalism and non-violence. Bioregions, according to Sale, are 'distinguishable by particular attributes of flora, fauna, water, climate, soils and landforms [and] by the human settlements and cultures those attributes have given rise to' (quoted in Pepper 1993: 191). In terms of scale, bioregionalism emphasizes 'region' and 'community' rather than those of 'state', 'nation' and 'world'. Similarly, matters of economic life are conceived in terms of 'conservation', 'stability', 'self-suffiency' and 'cooperation' (Pepper 1993: 186). Worldwide environmental problems are recognized, but the answer to these problems requires a constant movement between local initiative and global solidarity.

For ecocentrists, then, decisions concerning the environment should be made according to which outcomes are most likely to support the long-term integrity of human life *and* non-human nature. The 'five basic assumptions' underlying an ecocentric perspective are that: '1) Everything is connected to everything else; 2) The whole is greater than the sum of its parts; 3) Meaning is context dependent; 4) Process has primacy over parts; [and] 5) Humans and non-human nature are one' (Merchant 1990: 59–60). From these basic tenets it can be deduced that any one decision taken at any point on the earth by a particular individual, community or nation which concerns any aspect of the environment, has implications (however small) for the ongoing quality of non-human environs of all those other individuals, communities and nations around the globe. This means that the decision to, say, clearfell massive areas of forest in one part of the world, will decrease the level of biodiversity existing on earth *as a whole* (and not simply for the human and non-human inhabitants of the region where the clearfelling takes place).

Such a philosophy (which stresses the interrelatedness of human and non-human life in its many dimensions) seeks to locate the origins of environmental damage in the relations of domination that exist throughout various cultural, political and economic practices. Thus, while the conservation and preservation of wilderness areas is viewed as important, ecocentrists 'are also concerned with the health, safety and social needs of human beings and the use of resources on a daily basis'. In other words, this perspective takes into account 'the human dimension and the social responsibilities involved in trying to resolve the ecological crisis' (White 1994: 35–6). Thus, ecocentrism in relation to, say, the effect of mass irrigation on certain river systems, would pay equal attention to the interplay between:

1 those who use irrigation for their crops (i.e. farmers);
2 those who consume the products (cereals, cotton, fruits) made available by such irrigation (i.e. consumers); and
3 the particular forces which compel certain sectors (such as agriculture) to undermine the fertility of land and river sytems (i.e. politico-economic relations).

This perspective therefore holds that securing the conditions for human well-being means – *at one and the same time* – securing the conditions which allow for ecological well-being (i.e. for the well-being of non-human entities as well).

An important aspect of ecocentric philosophy is that it challenges mainstream 'or anthropocentric notions of *human needs* in its construction of the relationship between human welfare and environmental sustainability. Indeed, the central question of politics would become precisely that of what constitutes human needs, and how they are to be satisfied (Deacon 1983; Pepper 1993). As part of this process, it is clear that new patterns of production, based upon new environmental ethics, must be central to the ecocentric project. This is already reflected in both general philosophical discussions of 'green economics' (Frankel 1987; O'Connor 1994), and in descriptions of alternative approaches to economic development which in one way or another represent attempts to respond to the social and environmental consequences of capitalism (Skins 1992; Pepper 1993).

For ecocentrists, environmental laws should be symbolic of the inter-relationship between the conditions of social justice and the conditions which allow for ecosystemic well-being. Such norms would, ideally, take the form of a communally administered set of ethics and rules of behaviour. What constitutes 'environmentally sound conduct' would depend very much on the particular bioregion which human beings happen to inhabit, and the relationship of these to wider global processes and conditions. There would be a wide variety of specific legal and political strategies, based upon a core ecocentric ethic revolving around socio-environmental interests.

To this point, we have briefly sketched out three competing philosophies concerning the relationship between human beings and the environment. In the next section we discuss how the assumptions underpinning each approach can lead to very different conceptions of and responses to environmental harm. The practice of clearfelling old-growth forest will be used for illustrative purposes. We want to know how each of the three perspectives deals with issues such as the conflicting calls for the maintenance of biodiversity, the preservation of forestry jobs, the social desire for wood products and the pressure from various groups to conserve old-growth forest. On what basis are judgements made regarding environmental harm and how do these differ in practical application?

**Defining environmental harm: clearfelling old-growth forest**

The clearfelling of old-growth forests has been a highly contentious issue in recent years in Australia, marked by significant political protests and social conflicts. In 1992, the *National Forest Policy Statement* – drafted and signed by all states and territories except Tasmania – offered the following definition of old-growth forest:

> Forest that is ecologically mature and has been subject to negligible unnatural disturbance such as logging, roading and clearing. The definition focuses on forest in which the upper stratum or overstorey is in the late mature to over mature growth phases.
>
> (Commonwealth of Australia 1992: 49)

For most eucalypt species, the terms 'late mature' and 'overmature' (old-growth) denote trees in excess of 150 years old. Nationally, eucalypt forest covers about 25.6 million hectares. Of this, 20.953 million hectares is regrowth (i.e. forest recovering from previous severe disturbance such as logging) and 4.652 million hectares (18 per cent) is thought to be 'unlogged' or subject to 'negligible human disturbance' (i.e. old-growth). Of the 25.6 million hectares of extant eucalypt forest, the forest industry has access to about 14 million hectares or 56 percent of the total area. However, when eucalypt forests occurring on private land (such as those owned by pulp and paper mills) are taken into consideration, a further 7 million hectares are available for wood-production purposes. This means that 82 percent of all remaining eucalypt forests (21 million hectares) is potentially subject to commercial exploitation (Lunney 1991: 8).

Of the 4.6 million hectares of extant old-growth forest, 91 percent (4.186 million hectares) is open to commercial exploitation. In other words, only '9 per cent (418,000 hectares) of all remaining unlogged eucalypt forest is in conservation reserves' (Resource Assessment Commission (RAC) 1992a: 145 (parentheses added)). Presently, 'six forest groups have less than 10 per cent of their remaining unlogged area in conservation reserves' (RAC 1992a: 145).

Viewed in isolation, 4.16 million hectares of extant old-growth forest appears to be a reasonably large area of forested land. However, Australian unlogged eucalypt forests represent only about 5 percent of such forests existing just over two centuries ago (see Milledge in Joss 1994: 14). In 1787 (the year preceding European settlement), approximately 10 percent or 70 million hectares of Australia's 768 million hectare land mass was covered by forest. A little over 200 years later, forests cover about 4.5 percent (34,313,000 hectares) of the continent's total land area. This means that Australia has about 50 percent less forest than it did 200 years ago and that approximately 65 million hectares (or 95 per cent) of the original (old-growth) eucalypt forests no longer exist (RAC 1990: 7; Lunney 1991: 5–6; Joss 1994: 6).

Viewed in isolation, the 34 million hectares of forest occurring on Australian soil sounds significant. However, this apparently 'large' figure appears quite meagre when compared to the forested areas of such countries as the USSR (792 million hectares), Brazil (357 million hectares), Canada (264 million hectares) and the USA (195 million hectares) which collectively exhibit 'more than half the world's forests' (RAC 1990: 7). In terms of maintaining vital ecological processes, however, it is not simply the gross area of forested territory which is important. Rather, it is how much of this area has remained relatively free from human disturbance. From the above mentioned figures, it is apparent that very little of Australian eucalypt forest falls into this category. And yet, it is precisely this kind of forest – old-growth – which continues to be clearfelled.

In Australia, articles of sufficient ecological significance, such as old-growth forest, can be (and have been) nominated for inclusion in the Register of the National Estate. This Estate is designed to function as a record of 'those places being components of the natural and cultural environment of Australia that have aesthetic, historic, scientific or social significance or other special value for present and future generations' (Delahunt *et al*. 1991: 245). In order to be eligible for register on the National Estate, articles must satisfy at least one of eight criteria set out by the Australian Heritage Commission (AHC). Significantly, old-growth forests satisfy no less than four of these criteria, which include:

> A.2 Importance in maintaining existing processes or natural systems at the regional or national scale.
>
> B.1 Importance for rare, endangered or uncommon flora, fauna, communities, ecosystems, natural landscapes or phenomena, or as wilderness.
>
> C.1 Importance for information contributing to wider understanding of Australian natural history, by virtue of their use as research sites, type localities, reference or benchmark sites.
>
> D.1 Importance in demonstrating the principal characteristics of the range of landscapes, environments or ecosystems, the attributes of which identify them as being characteristics of their class.
>
> (RAC 1992a: 140)

In the light of these criteria, we wish now to detail the significance of old-growth forests from the point of view of the three philosophical perspectives outlined earlier.

### Anthropocentric

An anthropocentric perspective (see criterion C.1) views old-growth forests instrumentally, that is, as a means to satisfy the demands of *human* beings. At the scientific level, old-growth forests become an important means by which to establish a domain of 'natural controls' from which to 'measure' the nature and extent of the numerous effects and impacts of human activity on the natural environment (Adair *et al*. 1979: 2.13). A common example of this is where old-growth forests are used to discern which elements (soil structure, composition of micro-organisms, foliage cover, plant life) need to be present in what proportions for a forest to function as an effective water catchment, that is, in order to yield a supply of clean water for human use.

An anthropocentric approach to conservation means that only the most 'sensitive' areas are likely to be preserved. 'Sensitive area' here indicates forest, which, if damaged, would have direct adverse consequences for humans. For instance, 'Research in the Melbourne Metropolitan Water Board catchments has shown that water yields decrease after old-growth forest is replaced by regrowth forest, and these decreases are likely to be maintained for at least 120 years' (Wilderness Society 1985: 11). Such potential long term effects help to explain the strict controls surrounding the use of forest in water catchment areas as opposed to the distinct lack of regulatory mechanisms governing the use of old-growth forest outside these areas (Halsey 1997b). In most cases, however, the conservation of specific natural sites simply reflects political machination and ideological pragmatism, rather than genuine concern about ecological matters (e.g. being sold to the public as places for human 'spiritual renewal').

Economically, the philosophy of anthropocentrism requires that forests be exploited for their commercial potential and that the production methods used be those which incur the least cost to producers. Under anthropocentrism, every facet of the old-growth forest plays a crucial role in the economic equation. For example, the decomposing logs lying on the forest floor which normally provide the necessary nesting and protective sites for numerous non-human species, are woodchipped or burnt by forest industry operations. This is necessary in order to gain ease of access to, and encourage the growth of, 'new' trees which will themselves be subject to 'thinning' (for pulp and paper products) after about 40 years, and clearfelling for saw- and pulp logs after approximately 80 years.

In the battle between environmental damage, and profits, anthropocentrism privileges the latter. The method of production that best suits the economic requirements of producers is *clearfelling*. It is this method of production that brings a measure of 'economy' to logging operations in the more remote forest areas. This technique clears over 90 percent of the trees from areas (coupes) ranging in size from 10 to 60 hectares. From an economic point of view, this harvesting method is considered indispensable even though there is strong evidence that it results in mass simplification and fragmentation of habitat (Halsey 1997b). The decisive factor from an anthropocentric perspective is that clearfelling allows for vast tracts of previously inaccessible forest to be felled swiftly and cheaply by way of exporting the 'residue' of these operations to international paper markets. Presently, Australia logs around 77,500 hectares of old-growth eucalypt forest annually – clearfelling is used in over 90 percent of instances.

From the point of view of regulation of environmental activity, the anthropocentric view is premised upon the notion of 'sustainable development'. In practice, this means that legislative efforts are generally directed towards either 'exploitative' or 'protective' laws (Frawley 1994). The first refers to instances where the aim of legislation is to facilitate the extraction and processing of particular resources (e.g. laws relating to the conditions whereby companies are guaranteed long term access to particular geographical sites for the purposes of commercial activity such as mining, forestry or farming). The second type of legislation is directed at conserving particular natural resources through prohibiting overuse or overextraction of particular resources (e.g. imposition of quotas on logging or fishing), or dealing with conflicts between certain industries (e.g. farming and mining) or between certain industries and specific population groups (e.g. mining companies and indigenous people). The central point of such regulatory strategies is that human production and consumption is still privileged over long term ecosystemic well-being, and profit maximization remains the basis of the legislation.

To illustrate this more clearly, it is useful to briefly outline the Australian approach to the regulation of forestry. Existing legislation in this country uniformly fails to reflect global ecological concerns. To the contrary, the legal armature plays a key role in facilitating the continued destruction of old-growth eucalypt forest by upholding laws which make clearfelling and woodchipping economically viable in forests that would otherwise be uneconomic to log (see, for example, National Association of Forest Industries 1995). In most instances, regulation of forestry activities is the responsibility of the various states and territories. However, the single most important piece of legislation relating to the continued woodchipping and clearfelling of old-growth forest is presently administered by the Federal Government in the form of the Export Control (Unprocessed Wood) Regulations as stated under the Export Control Act 1982. Arguably, it is the power flowing from this legislation which has seen the ecological harm occurring in Australia's native, old-growth forests become legally entrenched.

Under such legislation, the issuing of woodchip export licences presently allows for over 5 million tonnes (5.251 million tonnes in 1996) of hardwood chips from Australia's native forests to be sold annually to overseas markets. In conjunction with legislation such as Victoria's Forests (Timber Harvesting) Act 1990 designed to 'incorporate provisions for government guarantee of long term supply of hardwood logs to industry on a regional sustainable yield basis' (RAC 1992b: V28), and the various pulpwood concessions such as Tasmania's Huon Valley Pulp and Paper Industry Act 1959, the Export Control Act provides the forest industry with the opportunity to log Australia's more remote forests (such as old growth) in an 'economic' manner (Wilson 1991: 290). Specifically, the Act allows the vast amount of 'waste' (i.e. old-growth habitat trees and decomposing logs) accumulated from logging activities in these forests, to be exported as woodchips – a practice which earns the industry (and the Federal Government) in excess of $400 million a year. In crude terms, then, an anthropocentric approach to the regulation of forestry activities in Australia holds current operations to be anything other than environmentally criminal.

### Biocentric

Biocentrism (see criterion B.1) views old-growth forests (and the organisms which dwell within them) as having intrinsic worth, whereby such forests have a significance independent of any value placed on them by human beings. The role of science, according to biocentrism, is to study the ecological constitution of old-growth forests in order that they be preserved for *non-human* entities. In relation to the preservation of non-human species (see criterion B.1), biocentrists consider old-growth forests to be significant because they are suitably diverse in structure and age as to provide the *only* habitat for certain forest dependent species (Scotts 1991: 148; Wilson 1991: 295). Such diversity in age and structure ensures, for example, the existence of trees capable of shedding large portions of their bark. This 'wasted matter' – if allowed to accumulate at the base of the tree over an extended period of time – 'provides reservoirs of invertebrate prey ... (and) ... protection from predation for species that use ... the exposed tree surfaces' (Dickman 1991: 132).

Diversity in structure and age also allows for diversity in the species capable of inhabiting old-growth forest. In southeastern Australia, for instance, a selection of fauna:

> that find optimum habitat for foraging or nesting or both in old-growth Eucalyptus forest include: Tiger Quolls, Greater Gliders, Yellow-tailed Black Cockatoos, Superb Parrots, Powerful Owls, Sooty Owls, Satin Fly-catchers, Australian King-parrots, Diamond Pythons, Carpet Pythons, Tree Goannas and Spotted Tree Frogs.
>
> (Scotts 1991: 151)

The features unique to old-growth forests function as an integral means by which to maintain diversity within and between the species inhabiting a given forested area. This is important given the fact that 'maximum genetic diversity optimises the chances a species can withstand changes in the environment' (Suzuki 1990: 157). Accordingly, old-growth forest is *the* means through which certain non-human species maximize their chances of survival.

In terms of conservation, biocentrism demands that there be *no* human impact on old-growth forests. From this perspective, such ecosystems are considered too fragile to tamper with. More importantly, biocentrism holds that human beings – as 'just another species' – do not have the ethical right to alter the 'natural' integrity of these forests. This philosophy, in other words, invokes a view of preservation founded on the absolute sanctity of all that exists within old-growth forests. For instance, because decomposing logs are known to play an important role in the survival of ground-dwelling forest species (Dickman 1991: 127; Scotts 1991: 149), any individual or company wishing to use such logs for fire wood or woodchips is held to be on dubious ethical ground and runs the risk of being labelled ecologically insensitive.

Under biocentrism, it becomes anathema to conceive of old-growth forest in economic terms. There is no sense in attempting to ascribe economic value to something which has intrinsic value. The use of old-growth forest for profit whether this be through the sale of wood or as a result of corporatized 'wilderness experiences' – is forbidden.

From a biocentric perspective, regulatory legislation should be directed first and foremost to preserving the natural environment, particularly those sites identified as being 'wilderness'. The operational concepts here are those of biodiversity and species integrity, whereby selected areas or regions are deemed to be of such ecological significance that little or no human contact should be allowed. The rationale behind such legislation is that human beings are simply one of a multitude of species, and they do not have an ethical right to engage in activities which are destructive of 'natural' habitats and ecosystems. Regulation in this framework is not premised upon the needs of human beings (or companies) per se; rather, expert intervention is required to

44

ensure a rough equality in life chances for all manner of species, regardless of the immediate needs of specific human population groups (e.g. those who make a living from or depend upon natural resources such as forests and fish). In the context of old-growth forest, biocentrism might advocate legislation which specifically forbids the disturbance of tree hollows as these are particularly crucial to the long-term survival of certain arboreal (tree-dwelling) animals. The fact that these hollows also help to ensure a steady supply of grain-eating birds which often wreak havoc on the crops planted by humans, is viewed as unproblematic under the philosophy of biocentrism.

The goal of biocentric regulation, in other words, is the preservation and diversification of non-human life irrespective of the *social* cost. In crude terms, biocentrism espouses the idea that *all* human action is in some sense environmentally criminal.

### Ecocentric

From an ecocentric perspective (see criterion A.2), old-growth forests are seen to be crucial to the long term survival of humans *and* non-humans. Ecocentrism therefore attempts to strike a balance between questions of economics and questions of bioethics – between the need to utilize resources for human survival, and the need to develop rules which facilitate the benign use of the ecosphere.

At the scientific level, ecocentrism seeks to understand the impact of current production methods on the forest ecosystem in and of itself, and how this, in turn, affects the needs of human beings. In doing so, public or local knowledge of the impacts of forest use may be viewed with the same degree of legitimacy as that of 'empirical scientific research' carried out in affected areas. Most importantly, ecocentrism invokes the 'precautionary principle' in all decisions concerning human use of old-growth forest. This principle states that 'where there are threats of serious or irreversible environmental damage, lack of full scientific certainty should not be used as a reason for postponing measures to prevent environmental degradation' (Commonwealth of Australia 1992: 49). Ecocentrism would therefore argue that there be a moratorium placed on the clearfelling of old-growth forest as there is still limited knowledge on the long term effects of this practice.

An ecocentric perspective derives its rationale for conservation of old-growth forests via four fundamental and interrelated propositions. These are:

1 The greater the diversity between and within species inhabiting an old-growth forest the greater the forest's ability to withstand disturbance and thus maintain its overall old-growth status;

2 maintaining old-growth status maximizes 'energy flow; conservation and cycling of nutrients; and regulation of water flow' (Scotts 1991: 151);

3 such processes are integral to the long term well-being of human and non-human life forms; and

4 the only way to ensure the continued existence and integrity of old-growth ecosystems is to place such forests beyond the scope of intensive human activity and impact.

45

The importance of this last point has been emphasized by the Australian Conservation Foundation (ACF). As stated by this body:

> The recognition of old-growth forest as a complex ecosystem encompasses the dynamic nature of forest ecosystems and acknowledges that extant old-growth forests are the physical results of past ecological processes. Consequently, the conservation of *current* ecological processes becomes an essential aspect of providing an environment for the development and maintainence of future old-growth forests.
> (quoted in RAC 1992a: 147 (emphasis added))

Accordingly, from an ecocentric position, ensuring the preservation of biocentric values (such as providing for the widest possible spectrum of species within a forested area), becomes integral to maintaining long-term human needs (such as the continued existence of clean air, unpolluted rivers and fertile soils). More than this, conservation of old-growth forest, under the ecocentric view, is conceived to be the conservation of the ecosystemic processes essential to *all* life. To seriously disturb the last remnants of such forest would, according to this perspective, be to place at serious risk the most basic elements required for human and non-human survival.

In relation to matters of economy, ecocentrism explicitly acknowledges the need for human beings to utilize certain aspects of old-growth ecosystems for survival. However, ecocentrism advocates methods of production which privilege the long-term requirements of ecosystemic well-being over short-term economic demands. Accordingly, ecocentrism would vehemently oppose the clearfelling and woodchipping of old-growth forest even where this leads to the generation of many millions of dollars. This philosophy would advocate the decentralization of forest industries and the adoption of selective logging techniques which leave the forest ecosystem intact. The central idea here is that no amount of money can buy, produce or replicate an old-growth ecosystem that has taken millions of years to evolve and which plays a vital role in the continued well-being of human and non-human entities. Unlike biocentrism, ecocentrism advocates that those workers displaced from worksites or industries which have been shut down due to their inherently anti ecological nature (clearfell forestry, open-cut mining, nuclear power plants) be granted the resources (shelter, education, food) to move into jobs which are ecologically benign.

The regulatory concern of ecocentric approaches is to ensure that a reasonable balance is achieved between human need and ecological health. Legislation should be directed at empowering people in the context of enhancing their ability to extract and consume natural resources in a socio-ecological way. The emphasis is on participation in production and consumption activities in a manner which acknowledges the limits of environmental systems – at the local, regional and international levels. Specific regulatory laws might include attempts to ban activity which has clearly destructive consequences from an ecological perspective (such as clearfell logging). More positively, it would include the promotion of methods which recognize human interests in the use of natural resources (e.g. wood products), and the simultaneous need for humans to employ practices which minimize environmental harm (e.g. selective logging). What makes ecocentric legislation 'ecocentric' is the priority given to ecological considerations, rather than economic, in the assessment of community good. Legislation thus is framed by the limits of ecology (of which human beings are an integral part), instead of instrumental goals relating to economic growth and wealth accumulation.

From the point of view of the philosophical perspectives presented earlier, it is clear that the anthropocentric approach predominates when it comes to the actual definition and regulation of forestry activity. From both a biocentric and an ecocentric perspective, this is clearly problematic. As alluded to earlier, humans not only need ecosystems such as old-growth forests to purify the water they drink, filter the air they breathe and enrich the soils they use, but they also require the survival of those organisms (both invertebrate and vertebrate) that make these life-sustaining processes possible from the outset. In the anthropocentric framework, the lack of concern with core environmental questions, and ecosystemic limits, translates into activity which is profoundly destructive, yet legal.

## Concluding remarks

The intention of this article has been to highlight the importance for criminology of theorizing about human beings and the environment in a manner which acknowledges profoundly different perspectives on this relationship. Our concern has been to provide an indication of the necessity to not only examine more closely specific issues of environmental harm (regardless of whether or not such activity is deemed to be legal), but also to question the very assumptions upon which judgements are made regarding the definitions and responses to such harm. This kind of work represents simply the preliminary stages of a longer-term process of reconceptualizing the nature of crime – a process which needs to provide a more sophisticated and practically relevant understanding of the relationship between human need and environmental processes than hitherto has been the case.

The article has attempted to sketch out three broad philosophical frameworks relating to the human–environment nexus – the anthropocentric, the biocentric and the ecocentric. Community and academic commentary on each of these perspectives has been extensive. However, generally they have received little discussion or notice within mainstream criminological circles or in legal studies debates over environmental regulation. As demonstrated in this article, such discussions are central, and indeed crucial, if we are to unpack the environmental and human dimensions (and costs) of much existing economic activity. The challenge ahead is to further refine our understanding of the human–environment relationship, including environmental harm – to, in essence, develop an 'ecological imagination' regarding crime and crime control.

## References

Adair, D.S., A.G. Tharno and W.I. Thomas (1979) *The Threat to the Forests: A Submission to the Australian Senate Standing Committee on the Social Environment Concerning the Impending Manjimup Wood-Chip Project from the Campaign to Save Native Forests (WA)*. Perth: The Environment Centre.

Adler, F. (1996) 'Offender Specific vs. Offense Specific Approaches to the Study of Environmental Crime', in S. Edwards, T. Edwards and C. Fields (eds) *Environmental Crime and Criminality: Theoretical and Practical Issues*. New York: Garland Publishing.

Albrecht, H. and S. Leppa (eds) (1992) *Criminal Law and the Environment*. Finland: Forssan Kirjapaino OY.

Ashworth, A. (1991) *Principles of Criminal Law*. New York: Oxford University Press.

Birkeland, J. (1995) 'Cultures of Institutional Corruption and the Natural Environment', in J. Bessant, K. Carrington and S. Cook (eds) *Cultures of Crime and Violence*. Melbourne: La Trobe University Press.

Bookchin, M. (1986) *The Modern Crisis*. Philadelphia, PA: New Society Publishers.

Bookchin, M. (1994) *Which Way for the Ecology Movement*. San Francisco, CA: AK Press.

Breuer, G. (1978) *Air in Danger*. London: Cambridge University Press.

Cassell, P. (1995) 'Social Theoretical Reflections on Australia as a Culture of Violence', in J. Bessant, K. Carrington and S. Cook (eds) *Cultures of Crime and Violence*. Melbourne: La Trobe University Press.

Cohen, S. (1992) *Against Criminology*. London: Transaction Publishers.

Commonwealth of Australia (1992) *National Forest Policy Statement: A New Focus for Australia's Forests*. Perth: Advance Press Ltd.

Conacher, A.J. and J. Conacher (1994) *Rural Land Degradation in Australia*. Melbourne: Oxford University Press.

Corlett, J.A. (1996) 'Corporate Responsibility for Environmental Damage', *Environmental Ethics* 18(2): 195–207.

Daly, H. and K. Townsend (eds) (1993) *Valuing the Earth*. Boston, MA: MIT Press.

Deacon, B. (1983) *Social Policy and Socialism: The Struggle for Socialist Relations of Welfare*. London: Pluto Press.

Delahunt, A., A. Mednis and R. Purdie (1991) 'The National Estate, Forests and Fauna', in D. Lunney (ed.) *Conservation of Australia's Forest Fauna*. Mosman: Royal Zoological Society of New South Wales.

del Frate, A.A. and J. Norberry (eds) (1993) *Environmental Crime: Sanctioning Strategies and Sustainable Development*. Canberra: United Nations Interregional Crime and Justice Research Institute, Rome/Australian Institute of Criminology.

Devall, G. and B. Sessions (1985) *Deep Ecology*. Salt Lake City, UT: Gibbs Smith.

Dickman, C. (1991) 'Use of Trees by Ground dwelling Mammals: Implications for Management', in D. Lunney (ed.) *Conservation of Australia's Forest Fauna*. Mosman: Royal Zoological Society of New South Wales.

Dobson, A. (1990) *Green Political Thought*. London: Unwin Hyman.

Dobson, A. (ed.) (1991) *The Green Reader*. London: Andre Deutsch Limited.

Downs, T.M. (1993) 'The Responsible Corporate Officer Doctrine in State Environmental Crimes', *White Collar Crime Reporter* 7(9): 1–8.

Eckersley, R. (1992) *Environmentalism and Political Theory*. London: UCL Press.

Ekins, P. (1992) *A New World Order*. London: Routledge.

Elkington, J. and T. Burke (1987) *The Green Capitalists*. London: Gollancz.

Ermann, M. and R. Lundman (eds) (1982) *Corporate and Governmental Deviance*. New York, NY: Oxford University Press.

Feinberg, J. (1984) *The Moral Limits of the Criminal Law: Harm to Others*. New York: Oxford University Press.

Frankel, B. (1987) *The Post Industrial Utopians*. Cambridge: Polity Press.

Franklin, N. (1990) 'Environmental Pollution Control: The Limits of the Criminal Law', *Current Issues in Criminal Justice* 2(1): 81–94.

Frawley, K. (1994) 'Evolving Visions: Environmental Management and Nature Conservation in Australia', in S. Dovers (ed.) *Australian Environmental History: Essays and Cases*. Melbourne: Oxford University Press.

Grabosky, P. (1994) 'Green Markets: Environmental Regulation by the Private Sector', *Law and Policy* 16(4): 419 48.

Grabosky, P. and J. Braithwaite (1986) *Of Manners Gentle: Enforcement Strategies of Australian Business Regulatory Agencies*. Melbourne: Oxford University Press.

Grabosky, P. and A. Sutton (eds) (1989) *Stains on a White Collar*. Sydney: Century Hutchinson.

Gunningham, N. (1993) 'Thinking About Regulatory Mix: Regulating Occupational Health and Safety, Futures Markets and Environmental Law', in P.N. Grabosky and J. Braithwaite (eds) *Business Regulation and Australia's Future*. Sydney: Robert Burton Printers.

Gunningham, N., J. Norberry and S. McKillop (eds) (1995) *AIC Conference Proceedings: Environmental Crime*, no. 26. Canberra: Australian Institute of Criminology.

Hagan, J. (1985) *Modern Criminology*. New York: McGraw Hill.

Halsey, M. (1997a) 'Environmental Crime: Towards an Eco Human Rights Approach', *Current Issues in Criminal Justice* 8(3): 217–42.

Halsey, M. (1997b) 'The Wood for the Paper: Old-growth Forest, Hemp and Environmental Harm', *Australian and New Zealand Journal of Criminology* 30(2): 121–48.

Hills, S. (ed.) (1987) *Corporate Violence*. New Jersey: Rowman and Littlefield.

Jacobs, M. (1993) *The Green Economy*. London: Pluto Press.

Joss, K. (1994) *Sustaining Our Forests*. Sydney: self published.

Kirkpatrick, J. (1994) *A Continent Transformed*. Melbourne: Oxford University Press.

Lunney, D. (1991) 'The Future of Australia's Forest Fauna', in D. Lunney (ed.) *Conservation of Australia's Forest Fauna*. Mosman: Royal Zoological Society of New South Wales.

Merchant, C. (1990) 'Environmental Ethics and Political Conflict: A View from California', *Environmental Ethics* 12(1): 45–68.

National Association of Forest Industries (1995) *Green Gold: Growth Opportunities for the Australian Forest Sector*. Canberra: National Association of Forest Industries.

Neville, S. (ed.) (1990) *The Australian Environment*. Melbourne: Australian Conservation Foundation.

O'Connor, M. (ed.) (1994) *Is Capitalism Sustainable?: Political Economy and the Politics of Ecology*. New York: Guilford Press.

Pearce, D. (1989) *Blueprint for a Green Economy*. London: Earthscan Publications.

Pepper, D. (1993) *Eco Socialism: From Deep Ecology to Social Justice*. New York: Routledge.

Poveda, TG. (1994) *Rethinking White Collar Crime*. London: Praeger.

Resource Assessment Commission (RAC) (1990) *Australia's Forest and Timber Resources: Background Paper No.1*. Canberra: Australian Government Publishing Service.

Resource Assessment Commission (RAC) (1992a) *Forest and Timber Inquiry Final Report*, Vol. 1. Canberra: Australian Government Publishing Service.

Resource Assessment Commission (RAC) (1992b) *Forest and Timber Inquiry Final Report*, Vol. 2B. Canberra: Australian Government Publishing Service.

Schwendinger, H. and J. Schwendinger (1975) 'Defenders of Order or Guardians of Human Rights?', in I. Taylor, P. Walton and J. Young (eds) *Critical Criminology*, pp. 113–46. London: Routledge & Kegan Paul.

Scotts, D. (1991) 'Old-Growth Forests: Their Ecological Characteristics and Value to Forest Dependent Vertebrate Fauna of South East Australia', in D. Lunney (ed.) *Conservation of Australia's Forest Fauna*. Mosman: Royal Zoological Society of New South Wales.

Seis, M. (1993) 'Ecological Blunders in US Clean Air Legislation', *Journal of Human Justice* 5(1): 58–81.

Seis, M. (1996) 'A Native American Criminology of Environmental Crime', in S. Edwards, T. Edwards and C. Fields (eds) *Environmental Crime and Criminality: Theoretical and Practical Issues*. New York: Garland Publishing.

Steverson, B. (1994) 'Ecocentrism and Ecological Modeling', *Environmental Ethics* 16(1): 71–88.

Sutherland, E. (1949) *White Collar Crime*. New York: Dryden Press.

Suzuki, D. (1990) *Inventing the Future*. Sydney: Allen and Unwin.

Tappan, P. (1947) 'Who is the Criminal?', *American Sociological Review* 12: 96–102.

Tokar, B. (1988) 'Exploring the New Ecologies: Social Ecology, Deep Ecology and the Future of Green Political Thought', *Alternatives* 15(4): 31–42.

White, R. (1994) 'Green Politics and the Question of Population', *Journal of Australian Studies* 40: 27–43.

Wilderness Society (1985) *Woodchipping: The Real Impact*. Hobart: Forest Action Network & The Wilderness Society.

Wilson, B. (1991) 'Conservation of Forest Fauna in Victoria', in D. Lunney (ed.) *Conservation of Australia's Forest Fauna*. Mosman: Royal Zoological Society of New South Wales.

World Commission on Environment and Development (1990) *Our Common Future*. Melbourne: Oxford University Press.

# 2. Criminological semantics: conservation criminology – vision or vagary?

*F.J.W. Herbig and S.J. Joubert*

## Abstract

Traditionally, criminological research worldwide has focused on the more conventional or salacious or higher profile type crimes in society, especially those involving a readily identifiable victim. Crime categorisation and classification have developed commensurate with this tendency, a fact that is corroborated by, and reflected in generic criminological parlance; thereby, it is argued, undermining focused and dedicated intervention and mitigation in the conservation/natural resource sphere. This paper, by unravelling and coalescing current dichotomies and the chiefly spurious doggerel which is historically associated with the study of natural resource crime and deviance, therefore alludes to the development and delineation of a viable, parsimonious and mutually exclusive crime category that will effectively encapsulate conservation crime and criminality. Existing (i.e. conventional) crime categories are assessed and those terminologies purporting to represent and embrace the natural resource crime remit that is evaluated. Contemporary natural resource crime semantics or aphorisms are, furthermore, evaluated and ambiguities that have been undermining the formation, until now, of an unbiased conservation crime category with its own unique identity as a vanguard to an appropriately captioned and innovative conservation criminology, revealed. Within the delineated parameters and ambit of the conservation crime/criminology field a non-esoteric and integrated schematic which is aimed at augmenting written submissions, is, furthermore, drafted. Conservation crime/criminology as developed and presented in this paper, underscores the significant contribution this field of criminology can make in comprehending the illegal manipulation and exploitation of natural resources, thereby expanding and enhancing its theoretical constructs and implementing justice through holistic intervention strategies.

*From *Acta Criminologica* (2006), 19(3): pp. 88–103.

## Introduction

Criminology has incontrovertibly through the years contributed significantly towards understanding and addressing the quandary of conventional crime and criminality in society, but has barely begun to consider the questions and challenges raised in the conservation sphere. The extent and seriousness of natural resource crime have, it is submitted, only recently, together with a growing global awareness of conservation issues, begun, albeit cautiously, to receive focused attention from criminological scholars. It has by no means received, it is furthermore submitted, full acknowledgement as a field of study in criminology.

Promoting such indifference is indubitably the fact that natural resource crime issues in the criminological context have traditionally been viewed myopically and dealt with under diverse and nebulous captions, including aphorisms such as ecological crime, green crime and/or environmental crime. Such esoteric terminologies have undermined the delineation of lucid and unambiguous parameters with regard to this form of criminality, and have clearly served to sideline focused and dedicated intervention and mitigation in this sphere.

Contemporary natural resource crime parlance has, furthermore, it would seem, prevented the formation of a suitably captioned and innovative conservation criminology, depriving it, as it were, of its own unique identity. This paper will, therefore, by unravelling and coalescing current dichotomies and the chiefly spurious doggerel, which is historically associated with the study of natural resource crime and criminality, allude to the urgent need for the development, formulation and recognition of a viable, parsimonious and mutually exclusive crime category that will effectively encapsulate conservation crime and criminality. Thus a crime category that will essentially be capable of embracing most, if not all, forms of illegal natural resource manipulation. A sound argument will be presented for the use of the criminological discipline as a vehicle to appreciate as well as mitigate humankind's indiscretions towards natural resources. Conservation criminology should, it will be argued, be categorised within its own remit as an adjunct of the mainstream criminological field, which will facilitate its management in a manner similar to other forms of serious crime in society. Conservation crime should be founded on the contention that natural resource perturbation needs to be comprehended and managed within the sphere of criminology, and that a post-modern criminology relevant to the next century should have the intellectual breadth and constitutional space to embrace conservation and social issues holistically as related projects.

Through the establishment of an authentic and innovative conservation crime category as a vanguard to an unpretentious, unified and tenable conservation criminology, this phenomenon, it is submitted, will steadily gain recognition as a formal derivative of the mainstream criminological treatise, consolidate research efforts, and promote interest in this field whilst simultaneously broadening criminological frontiers and amplifying its gamut.

## Why classify crime?

Apart from the essentially macro reasons for crime classification already alluded to in the preceding section, the purpose and function of crime classification can be seen as a process whereby an overview of the various types of crime is undertaken, permitting the analysis and understanding of a particular group of crimes, revealing underlying crime commonalities, and, in essence, facilitating a concentrated insight into them. Stevens (1990: 148–9) maintains that knowledge of specific crimes is crucial in order to detect, combat and prevent them, and entails, according to Naude (in Stevens 1990: 148–9), the ordering of given facts into certain classes on the basis of their similarities or common features. Classification can, therefore, be seen as an aid to describe and explain a fixed phenomenon in the community in order to diagnose, clarify and predict it, and furthermore, to serve as a foundation for the treatment and prevention of the specific phenomenon. The converse would, naturally, also be true, namely that crimes, which are ambiguously classified, do not receive the attention that they deserve, subsequently being inadequately addressed as, it is submitted, is currently the case with natural resource (conservation crime). It would certainly seem that the failure to classify and/or recognise conservation crime as a distinct crime category until now has resulted in much of civic society, not in the least criminological scholars as well as a wide spectrum of compliance functionaries, remaining largely unreceptive of or 'ignorant' with regard to natural resource crime and criminality. The manifestation of this indifference resulting in the intensification of the general societal perception that natural resource issues are trivial and/or less relevant than other contemporary forms of crime. The situation with regard to conservation crime is, therefore, very much a case of, if one does not have a target, one will hit it every time! Similarly, by not clearly classifying, until now, natural resource crime issues as a separate germane and tenable crime category with its own unique identity, crime in this sphere has been rendered extremely difficult to measure, and making it near to impossible to manage.

## Crime classification requirements

According to Van Heerden (in Du Preez, Marais and Botha 1990: 98–9), crime classification should in order to be effective, embrace the following constructs: Uniform criteria, comprehensiveness, simplicity and unambiguousness, durability, feasibility and applicability. Aspirant crime classifiers should, however, remain cognisant of the fact that the parameters of certain forms of crime are still evolving and that the issue of crime classification in these identified instances should proceed with circumspection.

## Contemporary crime categories

A perusal of the criminological literature reveals nothing more than a plethora of divergent viewpoints and approaches to the issue of crime classification/ categorisation. Although it is beyond the scope of this paper to present a meticulous exposition of the vast miscellany of crime classification perspectives, it has been deemed prudent to examine some of the more customary trends, specifically with a view to underscoring the imprudence of not addressing natural resource crime classification more prominently hitherto.

While far from exhaustive, Stevens (1990: 149–153) exemplifies a number of different methods and approaches to the issue of crime classification, which, amongst others, include:

**Bonger's classification**, which refers to economic, violent, sexual and political crimes;

**Stumpfl's classification**, which refers to heavy and light criminality, crimes committed at an early and late age, conflict and habitual crimes;

**Carey's classification**, which refers to violent crimes, conventional and professional crimes, political crimes, crimes against the social order and white-collar crime;

**Schafer's 'life trend' typology**, which refers to occasional criminals, habitual criminals, abnormal criminals and conventional criminals; and

**Reid's typology**, which refers to violent crimes, property crimes, business crimes, organised crime and terrorism.

Glick (1995: 34–5) states that the Federal Bureau of Investigation divides crime into two categories, namely Part I and Part II crimes. Part I crimes encompass the more serious offences against persons and property (known as index crimes or felonies) and Part II the less serious types of offences.

Damonse (2002) mentions that the South African Police Service also classifies crime into two main categories, namely Category A and Category B crimes. Category A crimes, according to Damonse (2002), embrace more serious type offences such as murder, rape, armed robbery, aggravated assault and stock theft, whilst Category B crimes include less important offences such as traffic violations, drunk and disorderly conduct, environmental crimes and the contravention of a host of provincial and municipal regulations and by-laws.

According to Hirschowitz, Buwembo, Serwadda-Luwaga and Nasholm (1998: 8–9), Statistics South Africa (Stats SA), formerly known as the Central Statistical Service (CSS), divides crime into two main categories, each with various subclasses, utilising the following United Nations compatible terminology:

**Household crimes**, which are crimes committed against people living and/or eating together and sharing resources. This category is further divided into violent household crimes and non violent household crimes; and

**Individual crimes**, which are crimes that affect a single person rather than an entire household. This category can be further divided into violent incidents and non violent incidents.

Prior to its name change in 1998, the CSS classified crime into six main categories. This classification was known as the Code-list of Crimes and was composed as follows (South Africa 1998):

**Class A**: State security and good order (e.g. terrorism);
**Class B**: Social life (e.g. child abuse);
**Class C**: Personal relationships (e.g. murder and assault);
**Class D**: Property (e.g. burglary, theft);
**Class E**: Economic affairs (e.g. crimes in factories); and
**Class F**: Social affairs (e.g. traffic offences).

The categories of crime alluded to above, although far from being exhaustive, provide an adequate representation of the crime classification/categorisation ventures traditionally found in the criminological milieu. Crystallising out of this classification ensemble is the fact that crime classification is anything but harmonised, and that natural resource (conservation) crime is only marginally addressed in certain classification/categorisation attempts. If and where it is suggested, it is, to say the least, done in a nebulous manner, failing dismally, it is submitted, in singular and/or in mutual format to sufficiently recognise the nexus and synergy between the natural and human resource components inherent in conservation crime. In so doing it effectively renders conservation crime issues insipid, sidelining this form of crime and criminality in favour of those more conventional and visible (sensationalistic) types of crime. Subsequently these categories fall far short of accommodating the entire ambit and/or essence of natural resource crime and do not, therefore, negate the need for the formation of a separate and feasible conservation crime category.

## Towards conservation crime as a seceded crime category

Before the issue of crime classification/categorisation can be addressed in earnest within the context to this paper, it is necessary to examine and evaluate the existing and more commonly used terminologies which portray natural resource crime/vitiation issues, so as to elucidate the motivation for selecting *conservation criminology* as the most representative expression for the scientific study of the phenomenon at hand.

### The Sage Dictionary of Criminology

In order to at the outset gain objective input concerning the popular idiom pertaining to natural resource crime, it was deemed beneficial to consult a recent influential publication in this regard. McLaughlin and Muncie (2001, s.v. 'environmental criminologies') refer readers seeking more information about environmental criminologies to the sections dealing with the Chicago School of Sociology, Geographies of Crime, and Social Ecology. Invariably these sections provide succinct expositions of the relationship between environmental factors within, specifically, urban communities and crime, but do not in any way define or even address natural resource crime issues. The publication, furthermore, makes no mention of the popular expression 'Green' crime and seems to imply that natural resource crime (in any form) does not warrant a place between its covers, or in the criminological literature for that matter. It can, therefore, be regarded as extremely inadequate, not only for those seeking elucidation for natural resource crime semantics, but also as a criminological aid within a post-modern society where natural resource crime is rapidly becoming an important global social and global economic concern.

### Environmental criminology

Although the above term might, at face value, seem to adequately describe the study of criminality directed at the natural environment, it is in fact quite the opposite. In criminological circles environmental criminology refers to a growing field, which explores how actual criminal events involve an interaction between motivated individuals and the surrounding social, economic, legal and physical environment (Brantingham and Brantingham 1998: 31). According to South (1998: 212), the term 'environmental' within criminology is still principally employed in studies of 'place' and the spatial patterning of crime. The focus is, therefore, on understanding the criminal event and how it relates to individual motivation, to victims and targets, and to the legal, social, psychological, and social milieu. The original or traditional context in which the term has been, and still is predominantly being used, has, it is submitted, led to it acquiring 'ownership' of the axiom, and, furthermore, that the interchangeable usage thereof can quite easily lead to unnecessary confusion and uncertainty.

### Ecological criminology

As with the previous truism, ecological criminology is, according to Brantingham and Brantingham (1981: 13) and Van Heerden (1988: 177), primarily associated with the study of spatial patterns of crime in an urban context. Williams and McShane (1999: 54) corroborate this sentiment be postulating that an ecological study allows researchers to transcend individuality and, through the collection of social data, gain a sense of the characteristics of large groups of people. Once again, it is submitted, that 'ownership' of the term has, due to its conventional usage, been 'claimed' by this denotation.

### Green criminology

Although often referred to as green criminology, specifically in the USA (South and Beirne 1998: 147), the use of this term to collectively describe the study of crime impacting negatively on natural resources can, at least, be considered disingenuous. Firstly, green crime/criminology might easily and incorrectly be associated with the so-called 'greenies' or 'bunny huggers', expressions often used to describe the fanatical, overzealous and activist conservation fringe, and immediately conjures up images of the militant environmentalist group, Greenpeace. Conservation criminology purports to be well balanced and does definitely not favour any particular shibboleth within the natural resource/ conservation realm. Secondly, conservation criminology deals with a more focused range of issues than those traditionally and simplistically labelled 'green issues', inter alia, animal rights, animal abuse/cruelty, ecological spirituality, and eco-feminism (Agnew 1998: 177–9). Swanepoel (1997: 48) even talks of green environmental criminology, confirming as it were, the ambiguity of these terms and illustrating that a combination of already vague and non-specific terms does nothing to promote a focused approach to the issue at hand.

Conservation criminology, as will be argued in the subsequent section, unambiguously deals with, amongst others, the dynamics and nexus between humans and (biotic/abiotic) natural resources on the receiving environment (as a casualty/victim), and the extent to which natural resource crime encroaches or impacts on the limits of acceptable change with regard to any particular natural resource, or a collection of such resources.

### Conservation crime/criminology

For several reasons, some already alluded to above, the study of natural resource crime from a criminological perspective is considered most appropriately explicated by the term conservation criminology. This expression is proffered as the most acceptable, for amongst others, the following reasons, which can best be articulated by examining existing crime categories, such as violent crime, sexual crime, etc. Violent crime, as in the case of sexual crime, property crime, white-collar crime, and the like, are all crimes usually directed at and/ or impacting, in some or other way, on another human being or beings. These crimes are, however, not classified as human or people crimes but rather in terms of the inherent element contained therein, such as violence, sexual undertones, its organised nature etc. The consequences or repercussions of these crimes on the victims' family unit, occupational environment or even the community are not really recognised as a factor when categorising or classifying these crimes.

If one then looks at natural resource crime, the effect of the crime on the ecology or the natural environment *per se* should not be seen as the critical issue when attempting to classify such criminality, thereby omitting the essentially restrictive words, green, ecological and environment. It should rather, as in the case of the more conventional examples cited above, be based on the central intrinsic theme coursing through the various forms of such criminality, whether it be biotic marine resource, terrestrial or aquatic crime, or crimes involving abiotic natural resource contamination. The core component/central theme running through natural resource crime and criminality is conservation, and a classification or categorisation conducted along these lines will, therefore, be in accordance with conventional generic classification attempts. Armed robbery, assault, murder, and so forth, are to violent crime what herpetological (reptile) crime, abalone poaching or smuggling, intentional pollution, etcetera, is to conservation crime/criminology.

As the term violence then encompasses the conduct and negative consequences of such crime, so the term conservation crime embodies the various criminal activities associated with natural resource effacement and illegal manipulation, and unambiguously identifies the pivotal theme inherent therein. In the light of the foregoing, it then logically follows that natural resource crime should be classified/categorised as conservation crime, and the study thereof termed conservation criminology.

## Definition of conservation crime/criminology

Having looked at the semantical issues surrounding the terminologies used to describe natural resource crime, it is perhaps prudent at this point to provide a definition of conservation crime. Conservation crime can be defined as 'any intentional or negligent human activity or manipulation that impacts negatively on the earth's biotic and/or abiotic natural resources, resulting in immediately noticeable or indiscernible (only noticeable over time) natural resource trauma of any magnitude'. For obvious reasons conservation crime can, therefore, be considered the vanguard to conservation criminology.

## Constituents of conservation crime/criminology within existing crime categories

Owing to the fact that conservation crime deals with so many diverse facets of the natural resource/human interface, it is reasonable to assume that sections thereof will fall within the ambit of other crime categories. Virtually without exception, the (conventional) crime categories expounded upon previously cannot be considered mutually exclusive, unless they are defined so broadly so as to render them largely ineffective for anything but the most superficial categorisation exercise.

In order to progress towards the identification and delineation of functional conservation crime/criminology parameters, it is necessary at this point to examine the precedence and concentration of conservation crime issues within existing and commonly used crime categories. An in-depth perusal of current crime categories reveals that conservation crime, as previously defined, can, to a larger or lesser extent, fall within the following existing crime categories:

- White-collar crime;
- Corporate crime;
- Organised crime;
- Invisible crime; and
- Property (economic) crime.

### White-collar crime

According to Conklin (2001:77), white-collar crime can be defined as 'any illegal act, punishable by a criminal sanction, that is committed in the course of a legitimate occupation or pursuit by a corporation or by an otherwise respectable individual of high social standing'. Conklin (2001: 78) goes on to list the following as major forms of white-collar crime: Deceptive advertising, antitrust and/or securities violations, mail and wire fraud, tax fraud, bribery of political officials, unsafe workplace conditions, production of dangerous products, environmental law violations, embezzlement and employee theft; and expense account fraud. Environmental law violations, according to this author, encompass crimes such as air pollution, and the dumping of toxic waste. Authors such as Glick (1995: 317–319) and Schmalleger (1996:

342), corroborate Conklin's submission that white-collar crime embraces environmental issues, but similarly, go little further than identifying pollution as the offence dominating this sphere. Although evident from the foregoing that white-collar crime encompasses an eclectic variety of crimes, it is not only clear that natural resource crime and criminality overlap to a certain extent with white-collar crime, but also that it gravitates decidedly towards environmental pollution of some or other kind. Conservation crime, in the context of certain pollution issues, therefore, falls within the parameters of white-collar crime and visa versa. It should, however, be borne in mind that not all environmental pollution crimes can be classified as white-collar orientated/ motivated and that indeed many, if not most, pollution crimes would not be able to be classified under this category. For example, littering by the general populace, which can be regarded as a distinct source of pollution, can generally be considered insignificant when compared to, for example, intentional toxic waste disposal, but on a global scale these insignificant amounts can reach gargantuan proportions, but could most definitely not be categorised as white-collar criminality. The conservation crime/criminology category then, in terms of mutual exclusivity, is thus only to a negligible degree impinged upon by the category white-collar crime.

## Organised crime

Hagan (in Stevens 1990: 161) is of the opinion that organised crime includes any group of individuals whose primary activity involves violating criminal laws to seek illegal profits and power by engaging in racketeering activities and, when appropriate, engaging in intricate financial manipulations. Organised crime can, therefore, be seen as an umbrella term encompassing divergent gang activities, such as blackmail and conspiracy, illegal gambling, drug trafficking, organised theft, and so forth. Organised criminal activities could also, for example, include conspiring to illegally dispose of hazardous waste, which is essentially a white-collar crime and simultaneously a conservation crime. It could even be extended to the committing of rapacious crimes such as kidnapping, robbery and/or murder (Glick 1995: 325; Stevens 1990: 162), many of which could, it is submitted, more prudently be classified as violent crimes.

One of the most prominent examples of organised gang activity in the conservation criminology domain would be that of abalone or rock lobster poaching on the Cape's south-western seaboard. Syndicates working in an organised, criminally proficient, but often confrontational and violent manner, illegally exploit large quantities of these marine commodities for export to the Far East, where tremendously high prices are realised (Hauck 1999: 213–220; Naudè 2002: 28). The question can, however, be raised as to when is crime categorised as organised, and when is it not? If gang or syndicate activities are directed at, lets say murder, for perhaps some or other fiscal gain, when is such a crime categorised as a violent crime, and when is it categorised as organised crime? When does a gang/syndicate qualify for status as a gang or syndicate? How many characteristics of any particular crime must be present before it can be categorised in that particular crime category – where is the line drawn, and what are the deciding criteria, if any?

The precincts of this category of crime are thus, to say the least, ambiguous and could, depending on the angle of interpretation, violate the categorisation parameters of most existing crime categories. The organised crime category is, due to the vagueness and ambivalence mentioned above, consequently not considered to overlie the category conservation crime/criminology to anything but the slightest degree.

### Invisible crime

Davies, Francis and Jupp (1999: 3) are of the opinion that, amongst certain others, green crimes fall within this category of crime. South (in Davies *et al.* 1999: 3) suggests that green crimes, which include the pollution of the environment by industrial organisations (white-collar crime?) extend across international boundaries, and raise important issues regarding enforcement, regulation and control at the end of the 20th century. This author cites, as an example of (invisible) green crime, the increase in the smuggling of toxic waste and chlorofluorocarbons (CFCs), rumoured to destroy the earth's ozone layer. Davies *et al.* (1999: 4–5) maintain that the commonality of invisible crimes is firstly, that they are all infractions of the law, and secondly that the criminal acts are not transparent or readily observable. The gist of this category is that certain crimes exhibit degrees of invisibility (an inherent weakness of the approach?) and that these degrees can be judged against a number of characteristic features, to whit, no knowledge, no statistics, no theory, no research, no control, no politics, and no panic. In terms of this category's overlap with conservation crime (or visa versa) there seems to be several issues raised that could apply to the conservation crime phenomenon. Much, if not most, conservation crime is committed clandestinely, with the result that there is little civic knowledge or awareness of the crime phenomenon itself. Because of this lack of knowledge there is little (albeit growing) appreciation for conservation deviance in both the political and public arenas, reinforcing the notion that natural resources are infinite and unyielding.

Furthermore, little research has historically been done with regard to this form of deviance and subsequently inadequate theory has been generated. Control has also traditionally been neglected, with most policing efforts being channelled towards the more conventional crime issues in society. Notwithstanding the foregoing, various crimes, many listed elsewhere in this paper, are included under the caption invisible crimes, most of which, it is submitted, could just as easily, and perhaps more prudently, have been categorised under existing crime categories, for example, cybercrime/computer crime, employee theft, and/or unsafe working conditions as white-collar crime. It seems, therefore, that crimes were included in this category for speculative and superficial rather than utilitarian reasons. Most crimes can, however, considering that degrees of invisibility apply, be classified as invisible, and even highly visible crimes could from time to time be committed invisibly as well as visa versa. Murder, rape, child or spouse abuse in addition to certain property crimes, to name but a few, are often committed surreptitiously as well as hesitantly reported and could, therefore, just as easily be incorporated in this category. Conversely, this category might just as well have been approached, it is submitted, from the angle of degrees of visibility as opposed to degrees of invisibility. For this reason, conservation crime is not considered to be encroached upon by this essentially quasi-category and, furthermore, that the value of this categorisation attempt is negated by its generality and concomitant oversimplification.

### Property (economic) crime

Natural resources, such as wild animals, fish and plants are tangible commodities found in nature, which in essence belong to no one yet to everyone, and it seems logical to assume that their illegal exploitation could subsequently be regarded as a form of property crime. According to Kidd (1997: 108) and Snyman (1991: 477), however, wild animals and birds (and by implication therefore, also wild plants and fish) are regarded as a *res nullius*, i.e., things that belong to nobody although they can be the subject of private ownership. These authors are of the opinion that aforementioned things cannot be stolen unless they have been caught and are in private (legal) ownership (a *res in commercio*). Kidd (1997: 108) maintains that wild animals within the confines of a properly fenced off and protected area, a game farm for example, are the property of that landowner until such time as the animal escapes from the fenced area. In terms of the common law, if an animal escapes from such a refuge and, therefore, is no longer under the physical control of a person (the crux of the matter being this *animus domini*) it is no longer protected from being hunted, killed or captured by any other person (Kidd 1997: 108). The category property crime does, therefore, overlap to a certain degree with the conservation crime category, but because, by far the majority of natural resources (both biotic and abiotic) occur in the natural environment, which is unfenced and beyond the possibility of physical control, the category conservation crime is only violated by the category property crime to an infinitesimal extent.

### Conservation crime as a (viable) crime category

Bearing in mind what has already been recorded in this paper, it would be expedient at this stage to provide a detailed exposition of the conservation crime/criminology category so as to unambiguously demarcate, and place on record, the parameters of this phenomenon. Conservation crime/criminology, as the definition implies, covers a wide range of conservation-related deviance. The subsequent exposition of this crime category, which can best be embodied by means of a schematic representation, should, however, demystify any ambiguities that might exist and attempt to depict and fuse the complexities of this crime category in a pragmatic, succinct, integrated, and lucid manner.

As can be seen from a scrutiny of the above representation, conservation crime is essentially divided into two chief constituents, namely biotic and abiotic natural resources, representing, in essence, the entire natural world. The biotic (organic) natural resource component is further broken down into two subcomponents, namely crimes involving natural faunal resources

**Figure 2.1**  Conservation crime/criminology

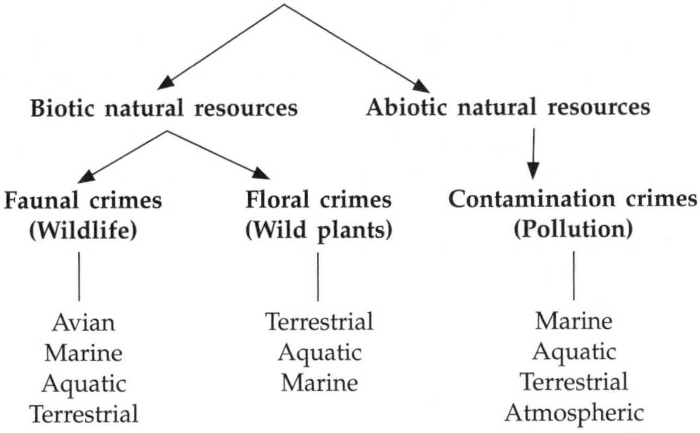

Biotic natural resources     Abiotic natural resources

Faunal crimes    Floral crimes    Contamination crimes
(Wildlife)     (Wild plants)     (Pollution)

| Faunal crimes (Wildlife) | Floral crimes (Wild plants) | Contamination crimes (Pollution) |
|---|---|---|
| Avian | Terrestrial | Marine |
| Marine | Aquatic | Aquatic |
| Aquatic | Marine | Terrestrial |
| Terrestrial | | Atmospheric |

(wildlife) in their various locales, and crimes involving natural floral resources (wild vegetation/plants), in the various milieus in which they exist. The term wildlife does not, according to *The South African Pocket Dictionary* (2001, s.v. 'wildlife'), include plants/vegetation and refers only to wild animals as a collective, hence the distinction in the above schematic. The abiotic (inorganic) natural resource component consists of only one adjunct, namely crimes involving natural resource contamination.

The chief components of this model are, however, in no way mutually exclusive and a crime committed in respect of abiotic natural resources can thus also impact on the biotic environment (and visa versa), whilst nevertheless remaining firmly within conservation milieu constructs, transcending as it were, other crime categories in this very important respect. The above categorisation captures adequately, it is submitted, the quintessence of conservation criminology and can suitably embrace most, if not all, conservation-related deviance.

## Conclusion

In this treatise the current and historical situation regarding the categorisation/ classification of natural resource crime has been appraised. Various semantic issues regarding the categorisation of natural resource criminality were discussed, and the established application of the terms used to portray natural resource crime subsequently found to be punctuated with inadequacies.

A lack of paradigm direction and focus regarding natural resource crime were established to be present, calling for the formation of a feasible framework to address this phenomenon in a consolidated and coherent manner. It has been unequivocally established that natural resource crime overlaps to a small degree with existing crime categories, but also that none of these categories are themselves mutually exclusive, and that many are in fact superficial and vague. In terms of the violation of crime category parameters, certain existing crime categories impinge on the newly formed category (with its bottom line being the conservation of natural resources) to a negligible degree, subsequently making this new category seem almost pristine.

The development of this innovative and germane conservation crime template, which embodies the underlying dynamics of natural resource crime, will hopefully serve to eliminate confusion about what qualifies, and what does not qualify as, conservation crime/criminology, i.e. conferring upon it its own unique identity, and to assist in streamlining, focusing and promoting the study of this particular phenomenon. Therefore, in the final analysis, contributing to the mitigation of the gratuitous manipulation and destruction of our fragile natural resources.

## References

Agnew, R. (1998). The causes of animal abuse: A Social Psychological Analysis. *Theoretical Criminology* 2(2): 177–209.

Brantingham, P.J. and Brantingham, P.L. (eds.) (1981). Introduction: The Dimensions of Crime, in *Environmental Criminology*, Beverly Hills: Sage: 7–26.

Brantingham, P.J. and Brantingham, P.L. (1998). Environmental criminology: From theory to urban planning practice. *Studies on crime and crime prevention*, 7(1): 31–60.

Conklin, J.E. (2001). *Criminology*. 7th edition. Boston: Allyn and Bacon.

Damonse, J.G., Inspector, South African Police Services. (2002). Personal interview. 27 May, Malmesbury.

Davies, P., Francis, P. and Jupp, V. (1999). *Invisible Crimes. Their Victims and their Regulation*. Newcastle: University of Northumbria.

Glick, L. (1995). *Criminology*. Needham Heights, MA: Allyn and Bacon.

Hauck, M.B. (1999). Regulating marine resources in South Africa: The case of the abalone fishery, in *Environmental Justice and the Legal Process*. J. Glazewski and G. Bradfield (eds.). Cape Town: Juta: 211–228.

Hirschowitz, R., Buwembo, P., Serwadda Luwaga, J. and Nasholm, H. (1998). *Victims of Crime Survey*. Pretoria: Statistics South Africa.

Kidd, M. (1997). *Environmental Law. A South African Guide*. Kenwyn: Juta.

McLaughlin, E. and Muncie, J. (2001). *The Sage Dictionary of Criminology*. S.v. 'Environmental Criminologies'. London: Sage.

Naudé, B. (2002). Crimes against the environment. *Acta Criminologica* 15(3): 21–38.

Schmalleger, F. (1996). *Criminology Today*. Englewood Cliffs, NJ: Prentice Hall.

Snyman, C.R. (1991). *Criminal Law*. 2nd edition. Durban: Butterworth.

South Africa. (1998). Central Statistical Service. *Crimes: Prosecutions and convictions with regard to certain offences. CSS Report No. 00 11 01 (1995/96)*. Pretoria: Government Printer.

South, N. (1998). A green field for criminology? A proposal for a perspective. *Theoretical Criminology* 2(2): 211–233.

South, N and Beirne, P. (1998). Editors' Introduction. *Theoretical Criminology* 2(2): 147–148.

Stevens, R. (1990). Classification of specific types of crime, in *Criminology*. M.G.T. Cloete and R. Stevens (eds.). Halfway House: Southern: 148–168.

Swanepoel, G. (1997). The illegal trade in rhino horn as an example of trade in an endangered species. *Acta Criminologica*, 10(2): 47–57.

*The South African Pocket Oxford Dictionary of Current English*. 2001. (8th impression.) S.v. 'wildlife'. Cape Town: Oxford University Press.

Van Heerden, T J. (1988). *Introduction to Police Science*. Pretoria: University of South Africa.

Williams III, F.P. and McShane, M.D. (1999). *Criminological Theory*. 3rd edition. Upper Saddle River, NJ.: Prentice Hall.

# 3. Environmental issues and the criminological imagination*

*Rob White*

## Abstract

This article provides an exploration of how the criminological imagination can provide particular insights into the nature of environmental issues. To illustrate the contribution of criminology to such discussions, the article provides a case study of the social, political and economic dynamics surrounding the provision of drinking water. The article demonstrates the complexities in determining the character, extent and impact of environmental harm. It furthermore identifies diverse and at times competing approaches to environmental regulation and to the prevention of environmental harm.

**Key Words** ecological justice • environmental criminology • environmental justice • environmental regulation • drinking water

## By way of introduction: key questions

Given the pressing nature of many environmental issues, criminologists now view environmental crime and environmental victimization as topics requiring concerted analytic and practical attention (see, for example, Williams 1996; Halsey 1997a; South 1998). Indeed, as a field of sustained research and scholarship, environmental criminology necessarily incorporates a range of theoretical perspectives and strategic emphases. It deals with a wide range of environments (e.g. land, air, water) and issues (e.g. fishing, pollution, toxic waste). It involves conceptual analysis as well as pragmatic intervention on many fronts, and includes multi-disciplinary strategic assessment (e.g. economic, legal, social and ecological evaluations). It involves the undertaking of organizational analysis, as well as the investigation of 'best practice' methods of monitoring, assessment, enforcement and education regarding environmental protection and regulation. Research in this area must also evaluate local, regional, national and global domains and how activities in each overlap.

---

* From *Theoretical Criminology* (2003), 7(4): pp. 483–506.

But environmental criminology also demands more than simply talking about the environment in general and what needs to be done to protect or preserve it. It requires investigating particular trends and issues and, regardless of whether we agree with answers, asking hard questions (see Wright Mills 1959). More than this, too, investigating environmental issues from a criminological perspective requires an appreciation of how harm is socially and historically constructed. In turn, this necessitates understanding and interpreting the structure of a globalizing world; the direction(s) in which this world is heading; and how diverse groups' experiences are shaped by wider social, political and economic processes. Thus this area of criminology is at once basic and exceedingly complex.

On the one hand, what happens in and to our 'natural' and 'built' environments affects us in quite personal ways; what we eat and drink, and the circumstances surrounding how we do so, directly affects our health and well being. At the same time, far from involving only private matters, these issues raise, in the words of C. Wright Mills questions of 'social structure' (1959: 8). As this article demonstrates through the case study of water, environmental harm occurs on both local and global levels; this harm is linked to major changes now taking place in the international domain. For water, arguably at the centre of life, is at present undergoing social reconstitution, its exchange value increasingly dominating its use value; in other words, the commodification of nature needs to be examined (White 2002). Simultaneously, for criminologists, a critical study of water also raises queries relevant to the larger tasks of criminology itself. First, what exactly is the character, extent and impact of environmental harm? Second, what responses are or should be taken to address such harm? Neither question is simple or straightforward, although this article's goal is to suggest ways of responding to both.

### Defining environmental harm

This first question raises problems of definition and explanation. To define what constitutes environmental harm implies a particular philosophical stance on the relationship between human beings and nature. What is 'wrong' or 'right' environmental practice depends on the criteria used to conceptualize the values and interests represented in this relationship, as reflected in anthropocentric, biocentric and ecocentric perspectives (see Halsey and White 1998). Within the realm of eco-philosophy, numerous competing claims and explanations have been offered about the source of the problem. From overpopulation to industrial model of production, human nature to patriarchy, capitalism to lack of an environmental ethic, myriad reasons have been cited for why environmental degradation occurs.

Meanwhile, in discipline-specific terms, debates still occur about the proper object of criminological attention: how and under what conditions should an act or omission be conceived as environmental 'crime' per se? A strictly legalistic response focuses on the central place of criminal law in defining criminality. Thus, as Situ and Emmons suggest, 'An environmental crime is an unauthorised act or omission that violates the law and is therefore subject to criminal prosecution and criminal sanctions' (2000: 3). However, other writers propose that, as with criminology in general, the concept of 'harm' ought to encapsulate activities that may be legal and 'legitimate' but nonetheless have detrimental impacts on people and environments (Sutherland 1949; Schwendinger and Schwendinger 1975).

Within environmental criminology, this broader conceptualization of crime or harm is often deemed essential for evaluating the systemic, as well as particularistic, nature of environmental harm. For example Halsey (1997a, 1997b) identifies social practices that are legal but environmentally disastrous, like the clearfelling of old growth forests. A wider conception of the problem is also vital in developing a critique of existing regulatory measures designed to manage (or, as some argue, to facilitate) harm. For example, Seis (1993) contends that US legislation intended to protect air quality is actually based on counter-ecological principles. As such, this legislation necessarily fails to protect and enhance air quality. The problem is not with the lack of criminal or civil law or enforcement powers, but with anthropocentric assumptions built into the legislation.

### Responding to environmental harm

Analysis of responses to environmental harm also takes multiple forms. For instance, one approach is to chart existing environmental legislation and to provide a sustained socio-legal analysis of specific breaches of law, the role of law enforcement agencies and the difficulties and opportunities of using criminal law against environmental offenders (see del Frate and Norberry 1993; Gunningham *et al.* 1995; Heine *et al.* 1997; Situ and Emmons 2000). For others, the key focus is not criminal sanctions as such, but regulatory strategies that could be utilized to improve environmental performance. Here the main concern is with varying forms of 'responsive regulation' (Ayres and Braithwaite 1992; Braithwaite 1993) and 'smart regulation' (Gunningham and Grabosky 1998). These approaches attempt to recast the state's role by using non-government, and especially private sector, participation and resources in fostering regulatory compliance in relation to the goal of 'sustainable development'. Increasingly important to these discussions is the perceived and potential role of third-party interests, in particular non-government environmental organizations, in influencing policy and practice (Gunningham and Grabosky 1998; Braithwaite and Drahos 2000; O'Brien *et al.* 2000).

Other writers are more sceptical of such perspectives and developments, arguing that key elements of such strategies dovetail with neo-liberal ideologies and practices (especially the trend towards de-regulation of corporate activity) in ways that do not address systemic environmental degradation (White 1999; Snider 2000). Furthermore, in terms of restructuring class relationships on a global scale, reforms in environmental management and regulation are perceived as closely linked with efforts made by transnational corporations to further their hegemonic control over the planet's natural resources (see Goldman 1998a, 1998b; Pearce and Tombs 1998; White 2002). In this type of analysis, political struggle and the contest over class power is viewed as central to any discussion of environmental issues. Issues of gender, ethnicity and race are important to these discussions as well, but are incorporated into a specifically eco-socialist understanding of capitalism and nature (see Pepper 1993; O'Connor 1994).

Whether at the level of definition or redress, then, discussions of environmental harm have an onion-like character. There are layers of complexity to unpeel, and important ideological differences that emerge over whether the core of the system is worth preserving or beyond redemption. Consequently, themes of analytical complexity and value judgement are central to this discussion. While trying to incorporate these themes, the next section of the article briefly describes recent developments pertaining to the use and management of drinking water. This analysis is by no means definitive or comprehensive. My intention is merely to survey this issue for illustrative purposes, rather than to provide an in-depth investigation. Last, I consider conceptual and political implications arising from these matters. Here, political economy and issues of environmental justice, corporate interests, strategic action and social power are key to showing how harm can be defined in relation to water and struggles over water as a resource.

## Drinking water

Water is vital to human life. Yet thousands of human lives are lost each day, week and month due to inadequate supply and the poor quality of drinking water in many parts of the world. Clear social and environmental harms are associated with existing practices related to the production, consumption and management of fresh water reserves. As such, what we drink, and the conditions under which we drink, is a topic deserving the close attention of environmentally oriented criminologists.

### The trend towards water market privatization

In recent years, drinking water has been increasingly valued for its 'exchange value' rather than 'use value': it is not the usefulness of water that counts but its saleability as a commodity. Key international organizations, including the World Bank, the International Monetary Fund and the World Trade Organization, have fostered this concept of water as an economic resource. More specifically, such thinking has been actively promoted by organizations like the World Water Council (a platform for major water firms), the Global Water Partnership (initiated by senior World Bank staff) and Business Partners for Development (an industry/World Bank promoter of privatization). The protection of this natural resource on behalf of private companies is presently sought through the extension of corporate bill of rights protection to water (as well as education, health services and utilities) via the General Agreement on Trade in Services (GATS) currently being negotiated through the World Trade Organization. Such neo liberal 'free trade' provisions are intended precisely to allow the commodification of an ever growing range of goods and services (many of which are essential to human well being) and to facilitate the entry of private sector interests into previously state-owned and state-regulated spheres.

The financial attraction of privatizing and commodifying drinking water is perfectly understandable. First, it is obviously a basic requirement of human life; water is always needed and, therefore, marketable. Second, restricted quantities of clean water make it a particularly valuable property for those who own and control it. For example, the global consumption of water is doubling every 20 years, more than twice the rate of human population growth. According to the United Nations, more than 1 billion people on earth already lack access to fresh drinking water. If the current trends persist, by 2025, the demand for fresh water is expected to rise by 56 per cent more than is available at present (Hausman *et al.* 2001). The actual scarcity of fresh, clean water means that there are lucrative profits to be made by privatizing water (and water-intensive industries), and delivering it only to those who can pay for it.

The role of the World Bank and the International Monetary Fund has been crucial to the processes of commodification and privatization of drinking water (see South African Municipal Workers Union 2001). Thus, for example, water privatization and full cost recovery policies have been imposed as conditions for IMF loans in more than 12 African countries (such as Angola, Benin, Guinea-Bissau, Niger, Rwanda, Sao Tome, Senegal and Tanzania). The result has been that water is now less accessible and less affordable and that, in some cases, people are resorting to unsafe water sources. In Ghana, to take one example, 'the results of forcing the poor to pay "market rate tariffs" for water means that most people can no longer afford water at all. Only 36 per cent of the rural population have access to safe water and just 11 per cent have adequate sanitation within the existing system.' (SAMWU 2001: 22). It was the local World Bank resident representative in Ghana who actively pushed for the leasing, over 10–25 years, of two large urban water systems to supply several million residents; five multinational corporations bid for the contracts (Bond 2001a). Good quality water is consequently being sold on the basis of 'willingness to pay' rather than 'ability to pay'.

Similar stories are told about countries like Angola, where there is an agreement that water prices should rise regularly so that the company delivering water can make a 'reasonable' profit (SAMWU 2001). Over a two-year period in Chile, the two most important water plants were sold to private interests and then resold at higher prices (Hall 1999). Closer to home for this author, similar developments regarding water have occurred in Australia. For example, the Sydney Water Board was corporatized by the New South Wales (state) government in the early 1990s. This led to a markedly different environment for water supply and maintenance. As Archer explains:

> The main function of the old Water Board was to manage Sydney's massive water supply system on behalf of its citizens; to make sure there would be enough for the future while keeping a watchful eye on water quality and things of that nature ... Its principal responsibility to the people of Sydney was to provide safe drinking water. The new Sydney Water Corporation [created in 1993] was given more important things to do. Its first priority was not the provision of safe water, its first priority was profit. In common with all corporations its number one objective

was to make money. That remains the fundamental operating principle of Sydney Water even after the catastrophe that occurred in July, August, and September of 1998.

(1998: 22)

In order of priority, the duties of the Managing Director are described as being running a successful business, protecting the environment in its operations and promoting public health by supplying safe drinking water.

Corporatization – that is, the management of state agencies and bodies as for-profit institutions – is frequently linked to the future privatization of such bodies or, at the least, to the farming out of selected operational activities to private sector businesses. This is happening with drinking water as it is with other goods and services such as telephone services, electricity grids, banking services, health services and education. For instance, the corporatization of Sydney Water also included the 'out-sourcing' of four water treatment plants to private operators.

Privatized water concessions have sprung up in cities on every continent (see Hall 1999). In every region of the world, the great majority of these concessions are run by one of the two biggest French groups – Vivendi (previously known as Generales des Eaux) and Suez-Lyonnaise (SLE) – with a smaller number, particularly in Africa, run by the third French group SAUR. SLE is the largest water company in the world outside France, while Vivendi is larger inside France. SLE has bought into US water resources companies, and water treatment companies in the USA, Chile, Italy and Germany. There are a smaller number of water concessions held by one of the UK companies – Thames Water, Anglian Water, United Utilities – but they lag behind the French transnational water companies in market dominance (Hall 1999). While there are at least nine internationally active water companies in the world market, effectively only four or five control the bulk of water contracts (Public Services Privatization Research Unit 1996). According to Vivendi projections on the future extent of privatization, the company believes that in 2010, over 80 per cent of water will still be in public sector hands in Asia, the USA and central and eastern Europe, and about 65 per cent of western Europe and Africa. Only in Latin America will the public sector share dip below 50 per cent (Hall 1999). In Australia, the water corporations recently joined together to form the Water Services Association of Australia in order to consolidate their authority and power. Collectively, the Association members now exercise control over 80 per cent of Australia's water supplies (Archer 2001). The track record of these transnational water companies is less than impressive. For example, they have been implicated in bribery scandals, price gouging and supply of poor quality water (see Public Services Privatization Research Unit 1996; Vassilopoulos 1998a: 13).

### Service and quality issues

According to the South African Municipal Workers Union (2001), more than 5 million people, most of them children, die each year from illnesses caused from drinking poor quality water. In many countries around the world, developed and less developed, there have been major outbreaks of disease. A few illustrative examples follow.

### South Africa

The impoverished township of Alexandra (near Johannesburg) is home to an estimated 300,000 people crammed into about five square kilometres of mainly squalid housing. In January 2001, there was an outbreak of cholera spread by the Jukskei River that cuts through the township. As part of a national epidemic, deaths were reported in four of South Africa's nine provinces. The reason for this is that nearly seven years after the formal end of racial apartheid, most South Africans still had to rely upon untreated water. At the epidemic's epicentre in deep rural KwaZulu-Natal, the outbreak was preceded by destitute people, who could not afford the US$7 connection fee, having their piped water cut off. For the 17 years before, water had been supplied free by the apartheid regime (Bond 2001b).

### USA

The US Centre for Disease Control and Prevention revealed that in 1993 more than a million people in the USA became ill and 900 died from drinking contaminated water (Archer 1998). In April 1993, 400,000 residents of Milwaukee, Wisconsin, fell ill with waterborne cryptosporidiosis, the gastroenteric disorder caused by Cryptosporidium which passed undetected through the city's modern water treatment plant (Archer 1998). Yet, in 2001, US President George W. Bush cancelled a health regulation that would have reduced allowable levels of arsenic in US drinking water from 50 parts per billion (ppb) to 10 ppb. In 1993, the World Health Organization set 10 ppb as the recommendation limit for arsenic in drinking water. The European Union adopted 10 ppb as a mandatory standard for arsenic in drinking water in 1998. The (US) Environmental Protection Agency estimated that cutting allowable arsenic from 50 to 10 ppb would prevent 1000 bladder cancers and 2000 to 5000 lung cancers during a human lifetime (Massey 2001).

### Canada

In 2000, seven people died and 2700 were poisoned in the town of Walkerton, Ontario. This has been blamed on privatization of testing, in which the town's water testing for Esherichia coli was outsourced to a local firm that failed to do the testing (Bond and Bakker 2001). What happened in Walkerton has been directly linked to government efforts to slash red tape in areas such as environmental protection through active endorsement of deregulation (see Snider 2002). In British Columbia, in 1996, there were more than 12,000 cases of water-borne illnesses caused by Cryptosporidium associated with human activities and livestock (Archer 1998).

### Australia

In a report commissioned by Sydney Water in 1992, consultants Dwyer Leslie 'conservatively' estimated that, as a direct result of 'current water quality', Sydney consumers experienced 'continuously occurring events' which caused 'between 4280 and 13,780 illness days per year; and 100 deaths per year'

(Archer 1998: 10). On three separate occasions in 1998, more than 3 million Sydney residents were forced to boil their water before drinking it due to the detection of the parasitic protozoa, Cryptosporidiurn and Giardia, to levels considered to be a health hazard to whomever drank it (White 1998). In the state of Victoria, a 1994 government study of country water supplies reported that more than 700,000 consumers were drinking polluted water. 'More than two thirds of Victorians are supplied with water that does not meet basic health guidelines', the report said (Archer 1996: 16).

Many of these incidents and events were preventable. In most cases they are attributable to changes in the tariffs placed upon drinking water (issues of access and affordability); changes in the philosophy of water management (from public need to commercial profitability); changes in operational practices (linked to corporatization and privatization, and away from structures that allow greater public scrutiny and accountability); and changes in quality control practices. Privatization is often accompanied by loss of jobs in the water services industry and increases in prices. For example, this is precisely what happened in the case of the corporatization of Sydney Water (see Vassilopoulos 1998b). Thus the shift in service orientation of the major provider of water (towards commercial interests), coupled with the privatization of specific functions (again, involving commercial considerations), had immediate ramifications on the service produced.

Another dimension to issues surrounding water supply is that of the relationship of alternative markets to the main water market. For instance, a water crisis may engender a shift among a proportion of the captive market to pursue alternative sources of clean water. For those who have the capacity to pay, it is possible to buy bottled water, another form of water commodity that is itself a source of profit for the companies involved (see Archer 1996, 2001). Even in relatively advantaged market circumstances, it is therefore possible that a segment of the buying population will turn away from the main provider. The demand in this case is fostered by the lack of apparent quality of the mass provided commodity. It also hinges on the ability, and perceived necessity, of a substantial number of people to purchase their commodity (which they buy for its use value) via other means. In this regard, note that Vivendi bought US Filter for over $6 billion in April 1999, giving the former a major presence in water-related products, including bottled water, and also a strong position for expansion into municipal utility services of water supply and sewerage. This also strengthened Vivendi's position in other markets, including bottled water in Latin America (Hall 1999).

## Political resistance

Despite these trends, commodification of drinking water and the privatization of its ownership has encountered resistance. For instance, in the South African township of Mpumalanga, near Durban, local residents engaged in concerted struggles against recent water initiatives. Residents are now required to pay a flat rate for their water services. Durban UniCity has tried to attach water meters to each private pipe and to charge for water from public taps. In response, 'the Mpumalanga community reacted with a vengeance, ripping up meters and chasing the contractors away. Running battles were fought with police' (Bohmke 2001: 22). In April 2001 the new UniCity council began installing water meters once more:

> Again residents have resisted fiercely, ripping up the water meters. Ten thousand people have attended rallies; the speeches are hot and the demand steadfast: free essential services for the poor. But the repression has also been harsher than ever. The army has been called in and meetings have been 'banned'.
>
> (Bohmke 2001: 22)

Interestingly, the leaders of this 'resistance' include former foes: a former activist with the ANC and a former member of the Inkatha Freedom Party.

State repression against water protesters has occurred in other parts of South Africa, too. On 26 September 2001, police opened fire on protesting residents in Tafelsig, Cape Town, who had mobilized to prevent 1800 households' water supplies being cut off by the Cape Town UniCity council. Most people affected by the water cuts were unemployed, pensioners or disabled; therefore, they could not afford to pay the more than R400 (A$100) to have their water reconnected. They would have had to pay an additional meter reconnection penalty of R125 (Dixon 2001).

Resistance in Ghana has grown more organized, surfacing in the formation of the Ghana National Coalition Against the Privatization of Water in 2001. The CAP is campaigning to ensure that the right to water is explicitly guaranteed under the constitution, and that the ownership, control and management of water services stay in public hands (Vanderpuye 2001). Perhaps they could take heart from events in Bolivia, where consumers and union leaders halted a World Bank-prescribed water privatization project. These protests culminated in an eight-day blockade and state of siege in April 2000 that claimed at least six lives before the Bolivian government was forced to cancel the deal. The protests began in response to stiff price hikes, with families earning the minimum wage of less than US$100 per month faced with water bills of $20 or more (Shallat 2001).

Public concern about drinking water issues has led some jurisdictions explicitly to consider new regulatory initiatives. For example, in the Canadian province of British Columbia, a recent government report outlines a series of measures meant to reassure the public that something will be done to address public fears (Government of British Columbia 2001). Among other things, these include the setting of state/region-wide and/or site-specific standards for drinking water sources (e.g. to include maximum allowable levels for specified substances that cannot be readily removed by conventional water treatments), and the stronger enforcement of Safe Drinking Water Regulations (including minimum standards for tap water quality monitoring and public reporting by water providers). It is clear that unease among the public at large over reported incidents of water contamination, with resultant deaths and illness, have forced some governments to reconsider the regulatory and policy framework under which water services are provided. The official inquiry into the contamination of the water supply in Walkerton was followed by a second inquiry into the safety of Ontario's drinking water generally. A key finding of the first inquiry was that re-regulation (but not necessarily public ownership of collective resources) is the remedy, and that deregulation and downsizing had gone too far (see Snider 2002). In the end the actual extent of government intervention, and the enforcement of quality and service standards, is an empirical question warranting further evaluation. On a conceptual level, though, it is more than apparent that issues of regulation cannot be divorced from the central questions of ownership, control, management and private/public sector involvement.

## Themes and issues for environmental criminology

One cannot take a specific environmental issue and expect that, on its own, it will encapsulate every aspect of criminological theory and practice. Nevertheless the example of drinking water provides an entry point for developing an analytic framework that is conceptually generic, beginning to address trends and issues evident when studying other examples relevant to environmental criminology as well.

### Environmental justice

Analysis of environmental issues proceeds from the assumption that, indeed, someone or something has been harmed. In this regard, a distinction is sometimes made between 'environmental justice' and 'ecological justice'. Environmental justice refers to the distribution of environments among peoples (Low and Gleeson 1998) and the impacts of particular social practices on specific populations. The focus of analysis is on human health and well-being, and on how these are affected by particular types of production and consumption. Here we can distinguish between environmental issues that affect everyone, and those which disproportionately affect specific individuals and groups (see Williams 1996). Again, water is a basic human requirement; people who have been affected by poor water quality in the advanced capitalist countries represent a broad cross-section of the population. In this sense, the periodic water crises are non-discriminatory in terms of class, gender, ethnicity and other social factors. This creates a basic 'equality of victims' since environmental problems – among them ozone depletion, global warming, air pollution and acid rain (Beck 1996) – threaten everyone in the same way.

Nevertheless, as discussion of water management in South Africa and other African nation-states demonstrates, some people are more likely than others to be disadvantaged in gaining access to quality water. In this instance, capacity to pay for water services or bottled drinking water creates and reflects significant social differences in how people relate to their environments. Often, particular class differences are intertwined with ethnic or 'race' differences as well. It is poor people of colour, rather than 'white' people (regardless of income), who are likely to suffer from bad water quality and services, in part due to their location in particular 'black' neighbourhoods (as opposed to 'white' suburbs).

Thus patterns of 'differential victimization' are evident with respect to the siting of toxic waste dumps, extreme air pollution and access to safe clean drinking water, among other manifestations of this problem.

Another dimension of differential victimization relates to the subjective disposition and consciousness of people involved. Specific groups who experience environmental problems may not always describe or see the issues in strictly environmental terms (see, for examples, Williams 1996). The unequal distribution of exposure to environmental risks, whether this involves the location of toxic waste sites or proximity to clean drinking water, may not always be conceived as an 'environmental' issue or 'problem'. For instance, Harvey (1996) points out that overlapping poverty, racism and desperation occasionally leads to situations where, for the sake of jobs and economic development, community leaders actively solicit the relocation of hazardous industries or waste sites to their neighbourhoods.

### Ecological justice

Ecological justice refers to the relationship of human beings, more generally, to the rest of the natural world. Here, analysis concentrates on the health of the biosphere, especially on plants and creatures that inhabit the biosphere (see Benton 1998; Franklin 1999). The main concern is with the quality of the planetary environment (frequently envisioned as having its own intrinsic value) and the rights of other species, particularly animals, to life free from torture, abuse and destruction of habitat. Insofar as poor quality drinking water, and diminished clean water resources, are attributable to social practices like disposal of agricultural, urban and industrial effluents into water catchments and river systems, not only humans are affected. Indeed local natural environments, and non-human inhabitants of both wilderness and built environments, can be harmed by human practices that destroy, re-channel or pollute existing fresh water systems. Thus how humans interact with particular environments presents immediate and potential risks to everything within them. For example, the practice of clearfelling old growth forests directly affects many animal species by destroying their homes (see Halsey 1997b).

### Commodification of nature

None of this is politically neutral: often 'choices' that result in environmental victimization of human beings and animals stem from systemic imperatives to exploit the planetary environment through commodification. In other words, how human beings produce, consume and reproduce themselves is socially patterned in ways that are dominated by global corporate interests (see Athanasiou 1996; Beder 1997; White 2002). And, thus, the privatization of water services illustrated above suggests both the dominance of neo-liberal ideology as a guiding rationale for further commodification of nature, and the concentration of decision making in state bureaucracies and transnational corporate hands. Overseeing this transfer from public to private sectors, and from conceptions of public need and accountability to notions of commercial viability and confidentiality, are institutions of global capitalist governance like the World Trade Organization, the World Bank and the International Monetary Fund (Goldman 1998a). Yet not all environmental harm or crime is perpetrated by the 'big players' (corporations, nation-states, multilateral economic institutions). Personal practices at an individual level can also be harmful (such as inappropriate disposal of left-over house paint). But, structurally, the most harmful forms of environmental destruction and degradation are clearly linked to those with the power to generalize such activity across wide geographical expanses and human domains.

The commodification and transformation of nature into a specifically capitalist nature (O'Connor 1994) simultaneously involves the exploitation of human beings as workers and consumers. In the example of drinking water, the profit-motive is inextricably linked to preoccupation with ways to make the 'production' process more efficient. This can be achieved by reducing the size of the water services workforce, increasing its productivity and manipulating wages, conditions and hours of work to best suit companies. It means putting more money into public relations and advertising, and less into maintenance, research and workplace improvements (see Archer 1998, 2001). Meanwhile, citizens and residents are treated as 'clients' who will only receive the service if they pay for it and accept the terms of the contract underpinning the sale of the commodity. The obligation is on the consumer to adhere to the prescriptions of the provider; the primary accountability of the company is to its shareholders.

Production and consumption practices are socially constructed, and ultimately this occurs through the machinations and lens of the dominant classes. For example, work- and home-related pressures (both material and cultural) reinforce reliance on capitalistically produced consumer goods and services like pre-cooked meals, ready-made clothes, bottled water; in other times, these goods would have been produced by family members themselves (see White 2002). Thus the power of capitalist hegemony manifests itself through certain forms of production and consumption becoming part of a taken-for-granted commonsense. The transition from one kind of consumption (such as provision of drinking water on the basis of need and use-value) to another kind of consumption (drinking water supplied on the basis of capacity to pay and exchange-value) may involve disruption and social unease since it challenges what came before. Hence, concerted campaigns surface materially to prepare the ground for commodification of water (e.g. by running down state-owned services prior to sale) and ideologically to sell the idea (e.g. through propaganda regarding the advantages of `free trade' in services, or talk of WTO agreements over which individual nation states ostensibly have little control). Environmental and ecological injustices are rationalized as the way things have to be in the new globalized system of trade and governance. Dissent may be tolerated, but only insofar as it does not challenge the core imperatives for economic growth, nor the generalized power of transnational capital to set the agenda.

From the point of view of environmental criminology, analysis of the nature of environmental harm has to encompass both objective and subjective dimensions of victimization (see Williams 1996). It also has to locate the processes of environmental victimization within the context of the wider political economy. That is, the dynamics of environmental harm cannot be understood apart from consideration of who has the power to make decisions, the kinds of decisions that are made, in whose interests they are made and how social practices based on these decisions are materially organized. As demonstrated above, issues of power and control also have to be analysed in light of global economic, social and political developments.

## Environmental regulation and prevention of harm

But what is to be done? Writings on this subject have approached environmental regulation, and the prevention of environmental harm, in the following ways. For one thing, interest has burgeoned in the area of corporate regulation (see, for example, Haines 1997; Braithwaite and Drahos 2000). At a theoretical level, much of this 'regulation' literature presents regulation on a continuum from direct control by the state through voluntary compliance on the part of companies and individuals. One suggested model of regulation is based on the notion of a regulatory pyramid, with persuasion the favoured approach at the base moving to coercion at the pinnacle (Ayres and Braithwaite 1992; Grabosky 1994, 1995). Fundamentally, the argument has been that the most effective regulatory regime is one that combines a range of measures; most of these measures presume that targeted institutions and groups are interested in participating or complying (see Braithwaite 1993; Gunningham and Grabosky 1998).

In contrast to approaches that highlight notions like effectiveness, efficiency and 'win/win' regulatory strategies, other writers have examined the nature of regulatory trends in recent decades through the lens of class analysis. For instance, when it comes to corporate harm and wrongdoing, a broad tendency under neo-liberalism towards deregulation (or, as a variation of this, `self regulation') has lately been noted. On the other hand, surveillance and use of harsher punitive measures in the case of conventional street crimes have intensified (see White 1999; Snider 2000). The first represents a major retreat of the state in the area of corporate regulation, while the second suggests a major offensive against the working class, poor people and people of ethnic minority backgrounds, especially young marginalized people. Importantly, the shift away from use of coercion in the area of corporate regulation has severe ramifications for those touting the pyramid regulatory theories: the pyramid only 'works' if there is the possibility, and reality, of hard-edged sanctions at the top. If these do not exist, by definition, the pyramid loses regulatory effectiveness.

### Capitalism, the state and neo-liberalism

When it comes to environmental regulation, and even if only through the absence of state intervention, the role of government remains central. Again, the general trend at present has been away from direct governmental regulation towards 'softer' regulatory approaches. For example, Snider (2000) describes that in Canada, despite policy directives specifying 'strict compliance', a permissive philosophy of 'compliance promotion' has reigned. Given that mainstream regulation literature offers a theoretical justification for enlisting private interests through incentives and inducements, it is not surprising that persuasion is favoured at a practical level. But, more than seeing this as simply a reflection of a new regulatory ideology, it is essential to consider the financial and political environment within which regulators are forced to work. For example, while never before in history have there been so many laws pertaining to the environment, it is rare indeed to find extensive government money, resources and personnel put into enforcement and compliance activities. Rather, such monies are usually put in the service of large corporations as a form of state welfare designed to facilitate and enhance the business climate and specific corporate interests.

The extensive links between capital and the state are manifest in overlapping financial and ideological agendas regarding the privatization and commodification of nature. The translation of social and environmental problems into economic and legal issues has meant that state action depends on a combination of political and jurisprudential considerations. For instance, governments that are materially and ideologically supportive of corporatization and privatization tend to avoid undermining these processes by intervening heavily in private corporate affairs. Neo-liberalism is oriented precisely towards less, rather than more, government regulation of corporate activity. This process has recently accelerated since governments are trying to attract and be on good terms with international capital so as to boost local investment and commodity production.

But what happens when specific cases of environmental harm become so apparent that, politically, they cannot simply be ignored? Once a problem like the Sydney water crisis has been identified, the conditions of privatization themselves can serve to deflect action away from dealing adequately with the problem's source. Thus, for example, appeals to 'commercial confidentiality' may appear as a way to evade close public scrutiny of operational practices and financial arrangements. Moreover, specific contractual conditions may open the door to protracted litigation over who is responsible for which facet of the production process, and who is responsible for the overall maintenance and improvement in water quality (versus those who simply operate the installations). In the end, the prosecution of selected individuals and corporations on specific offences tends to be the exception that makes the rule. Specific instances of environmental harm, as in the case of water quality issues, are subject to myriad legal considerations ranging from the nature of commercial contracts through to criminal responsibility. And, of course, the legal system is a strategic arena in which capital is particularly adept at defending its interests.

### Defending corporate interests

The corporate arsenal not only includes positive state action on behalf of selected business interests (via welfare handouts such as tax incentives, and through mobilization of police protection of property that enables profit making to occur, as with the installation of water meters). It also includes particular uses of the law as an offensive weapon. For instance, civil court action by companies in the form of what has been described as 'Strategic Lawsuits Against Public Participation' (SLAPPs) have been directed against environmentalists, individual citizens and community groups. The point of such suits is not to 'win' in the conventional legal sense, but to intimidate those who might be critical of existing or proposed developments (see Beder 1997). If they cannot be criminalized, at least environmentalists can be sued. Either way, the point is to de-legitimate and to silence the critics of both state and capitalist economic agendas.

At the centre of changes in environmental regulation has been a movement towards 'corporate ownership' of the definitions, and responses to, environmental problems. Again, this has taken different forms. One sort of response has been concerted efforts to 'greenwash' environmental issues. This has involved the spending of billions of dollars on public relations and advertising to portray companies as essentially environmentally benign (see Athanasiou 1996; Beder 1997; Hager and Burton 1999). The activities of international financial institutions like the World Bank (as well as individual firms and companies) are re-dressed in ways that convey the message that 'sustainable development' is happening, and that global power-brokers are doing what needs to be done to protect the environment. This belies actual environmental harms perpetrated by many of these institutions and by specific businesses that, cumulatively, are doing great damage to the global environment. It also ignores the cumulative effect of practices that ensue from the logic of economic growth, expanded consumption of resources and the further commodification of nature (as in the example of drinking water).

Another type of response has been to adopt the language of 'environmental management systems' (EMS) and to assert that regulation is best provided by those industries and companies directly involved in production processes. This occurs at both particular firm levels and when it comes to the setting of international standards for environmental management. EMS has various dimensions including environmental valuation and risk analysis, product design, corporate culture and environmental awareness, and supply and waste chain management (see Kirkland and Thompson 1999). For my purposes here, though, the crucial point is that, while EMS is seen by some (especially proponents of 'smart regulation' strategies) as progressive and a positive step forward in environmental regulation, embedded in EMS ideology are several assumptions that imply 'more of the same' rather than system transformation. For example, Levy (1997) observes that EMS does address some of the worst environmental excesses (i.e. real material consequences of production practices in specific cases). But he argues that on ideological and symbolic levels, EMS serves primarily to construct products and companies as 'green' and to legitimize corporate management as the primary societal agent responsible for addressing environmental issues. Consequently, decisions to adopt EMS can be seen as part of a political, practical and ideological response to the threat to corporate hegemony posed by environmental movements.

The key message of EMS is that corporations have the 'know-how', through technical means and managerial strategies, best to protect the environment. As Levy (1997) points out, and as echoed in the 'smart regulation' literature (see Gunningham and Grabosky 1998), EMS is presented as a win–win opportunity in which the potential structural conflicts between profit maximization and environmental goals are avoided. This provides yet another cover to circumvent governmental regulation; at the same time, the supposed benefits of EMS have not been demonstrated empirically. Yet much the same has been argued, optimistically, about the 'standards' put forward by the International Organization for Standardization (ISO). The 'ISO 14000', concerning environmental impacts, is a private sector initiative that allows for the state to divulge itself of regulatory functions; simultaneously, this initiative removes regulation and standards-setting from democratic participation, putting these beyond the reach of citizens and social movements (Wall and Beardwood 2001). From this, it becomes apparent that issues of who or what regulates, and who controls the process, are central to any discussion of how best to respond to environmental harm.

## Struggles over the global commons

I have argued that the overall direction of movement on environmental issues requires understanding the strategic location and activities of transnational capital as supported by hegemonic nation-states on a world scale. At the same time, informed analyses of political economy also opens the door to identifying strategic sites for protest on the part of those fighting for environmental and ecological justice.

### Different levels of analysis

Capitalist globalization, bolstered via neo-liberal state policy, has increased the potential scope of environmentally destructive activities. Nevertheless, different fractions of capital have divergent orientations to the environment depending on their market focus – for example, public relations firms, newly emerging environmental protection industries and/or forestry companies. International competition among capitalist sectors and among communities for access to healthy resources, including clean water, has also intensified because the natural resource base has shrunk. In this competition, the dominance of western capital has been sustained partly through 'environmental regulation' itself: ironically, this has sometimes been used as an entry card to new international markets. For example, markets may be protected through universalizing environmental regulation (developed in and by the private sector, and later enforced by governments in the form of preferred contracts, and business legal requirements) that themselves advantage the high-technology companies of the advanced industrialized countries (Goldman 1998a, 1998b). The largest companies are most likely to be capable of being environmentally 'virtuous'; they also have disproportionate influence when it comes to redesigning the rules of international standardization through environmental management (see also Haines 2000).

In addition, it has been argued that the cleaning up of old dirty industries and the re-writing of property laws in accordance with new international standards of environmental management and trade liberalization (particularly in the Third World and Russia) is a precursor to capitalist penetration and exploitation of nature (Goldman 1998a). To see environmental regulation in this light is to acknowledge the economic rather than ecological rationale behind the actions of global regulatory bodies like the WTO, IMF and World Bank. The undemocratic character of these institutions stems in part from the fact that 'regulation', in this instance, is about facilitation of the exploitation of nature and human beings, not about human interests and needs. Ultimately the appeal of 'smart regulation', which has found corporate expression in EMS and other global remedies like ISO 14000, lies in adhering to an 'ecological modernization' framework that represents economic and environmental interests as compatible. This is represented as a needed step beyond the 'standard view' of environmental management (see Harvey 1996) that has proved to be woefully and obviously inadequate to address environmental problems, especially where scientific and popular concerns can no longer be ignored or avoided. But, in practice, the emphasis remains on efficiency and effectiveness and the outcome ensures corporate sector 'ownership' of environmental responses.

In light of these developments, it is important that environmental criminology analyse issues of definition of harm and of regulation at different levels of abstraction. A specific firm, industry or event can be examined relative to various proactive and reactive measures put into place either to forestall environmental harm or to minimize negative publicity in relation to such harm. Investigation also must target broader political economic developments like the appropriation of natural resources and specific market opportunities, and the systemic consequences of neo-liberal policies and practices for environmental protection and preservation.

Both in terms of definitions of harm and responses to harm, then, further critical work is needed to unpack the material and ideological implications of the entrenchment of particular management models like EMS. Specifically, we need to examine their applications at local and global levels and how they serve to reinforce private sector control over regulatory and management processes. We also need to be wary of how the disappearance of criminality and coercion in regard to environmental regulation, and the trend towards favouring persuasive, self-regulating and co-operative strategies, also entails an ideological shift from environmental and social harm to enhanced 'environmentally friendly' production. Such enhancements collectively degrade the global ecological commons.

However, acts of destruction and discourses of absolution themselves generate counter-hegemonic resistance, sometimes in unlikely places. For instance, Snider (2002) describes how the inquiry into water issues in Ontario gave voice to opposing groups and thus to alternative ways of seeing and understanding the issues. The inquiry strengthened some voices of resistance and exposed the threats to social life posed by neo-liberalism. While not transformative in its recommendations (calls for fundamental change, i.e. public ownership, were not on the agenda), this case did present a progressive opening for reasserting public accountability in relation to essential services.

On another front, it is important to expose the track record of environmental vandals as part of a larger public accountability process. This can be done in relation to specific practices, as in the case of companies supplying poor or contaminated water. It can also be achieved by highlighting the overall negative practices and reputation of a particular company. Thus, for example, shares in Vivendi International plunged on the stock market in July 2002, due to concerns about its accounting practices and the downgrading of its bonds to 'junk' status by the credit-rating agency Moody's. But this downfall itself resulted from exposing efforts made by Vivendi's chief executive to spend US$100 billion transforming a water utility into a rival of huge telecommunications groups like AOL Time Warner.

### Different types of strategic action

The quest for environmental and ecological justice requires reacting against undemocratic decision making locally and globally, as well as against the imposition of a global capitalist economic agenda. Of necessity, resistance to the systemic forces that underpin global environmental destruction are fraught with difficulties, tensions and divisions. Furthermore the core philosophies, ideologies, policies and organizational structures of community groups and environmental movements vary greatly. For instance, green movements diverge over choices of tactics and strategies; goals and objectives; key philosophy; and concepts of environmental problems themselves. Simultaneously proposed solutions range from individualistic approaches urging spiritual change through to calls for collective action. Specific group orientations include 'soft green' approaches supportive of sustainable development through 'hard green' approaches calling for ecological sustainability. Thus major political issues divide a broad spectrum of green movements, affecting whether action will be taken in collaboration with or against capitalist institutions (see, for example, Goldman 1998b). This means that not only capitalist institutions but processes of reform and transformation (involving complicated questions of legislative change, and legal and illegal forms of activism) demand critical investigation by environmental criminologists.

Not coincidentally, those who wish to protest aspects of government policy or companies that do damage to the environment are increasingly likely to be dealt with under state public order provisions that show zero tolerance for street activism as well as street crime. Political dissent itself has been subject to a process of criminalization through myriad laws intended to curb 'anti-social behaviour' in public spaces. As illustrated by the case of South African demonstrators protesting water commodification, the coercive apparatus of the state is frequently directed at those who wish to protect environments, rather than at those who control and degrade them. A major concern for environmental criminologists should be the rise in paramilitary policing directed against popular movements (see, for example, McCulloch 2001). How and under what circumstances environmental issues are fought often implicates the state in maintaining dominant institutional arrangements. Of course, the criminal justice system has no small role to play in this process (see Haines 2000).

In the post-11 September 2001 world, is it even possible that the 'war on terrorism' will bring state mobilization against environmental activists? This may happen through granting enhanced police powers for surveillance and intervention, and through renewed political acceptability for closely monitoring 'suspect' individuals. Given that green propaganda and activity is sometimes directed against specific corporations, including transnational water companies, might this, too, become newly defined as somehow 'terrorist'? Meanwhile, wider-ranging questions need to be asked about the state's role in privately owned or run essential services like water utilities that may be the target of future terrorist attempts. In sum, public interest and protection must be linked with public ownership and accountability.

## Conclusion

This article raised numerous concerns relevant to environmental criminology. Fundamentally, I have been arguing that criminologists need to examine these issues in ways that incorporate the growing complexity and multi-dimensionality of this area. By way of illustration, I used a case in point of drinking water. This is an issue that, while apparently straightforward, actually entails layers of ambiguity and contestation. Thus, water can be used to demonstrate the range of considerations that need to be taken into account when investigating other specific issues, too, that involve defining and responding to environmental harm.

I also reviewed environmental actions and resistance, both from the perspective of corporate and state sectors and from that of green activists. Here, again, it is essential critically to scrutinize developments from multi-dimensional and often complicated angles to discern when 'reform' means managing rather than redressing problems, and when democratic participation becomes simultaneous occasions for demonization and criminalization.

Finally, despite the use of coercive measures, ideological campaigns and efforts to co-opt and divide environmental movements, it is clear that ordinary people continue to react against environmental degradation in their lives, whether toxic waste, oil spills and/or bad drinking water. Clever corporate greenwashing and the hesitancy of nation-states to limit corporate interests cannot hide the material basis of continuing protests against environmental destruction. Most relevant here, though, is that our criminological imagination contribute to these struggles by rethinking how new global relationships can diagnose, deter, prevent – and indeed, sometimes criminalize – ongoing environmental harms.

## References

Archer, J. (1996) *The Water You Drink: How Safe Is It?* Sydney: Pure Water Press.
Archer, J. (1998) *Sydney on Tap.* Sydney: Pure Water Press.
Archer, J. (2001) *Australia's Drinking Water: The Coming Crisis.* Sydney: Pure Water Press.
Athanasiou, T. (1996) *Divided Planet: The Ecology of Rich and Poor.* Boston, MA: Little, Brown & Company.

Ayres, I. and J. Braithwaite (1992) *Responsive Regulation: Transcending the Deregulation Debate*. New York: Oxford University Press.

Beck, U. (1996) 'World Risk Society as Cosmopolitan Society? Ecological Questions in a Framework of Manufactured Uncertainties', *Theory, Culture, Society* 13(4): 1–32.

Beder, S. (1997) *Global Spin: The Corporate Assault on Environmentalism*. Melbourne: Scribe Publications.

Benton, T. (1998) 'Rights and Justice on a Shared Planet: More Rights or New Relations?', *Theoretical Criminology* 2(2): 149–75.

Bohmke, H. (2001) 'Former Rivals Unite to Fight ANC Attacks', *Green Left Weekly*, 9 May, p. 22.

Bond, P. (2001a) 'Ghana: Sharpening Hydro Class Struggles', *Green Left Weekly*, 30 May, pp. 21–22.

Bond, P. (20016) 'South Africa: Welcome to the "New" Johannesburg', *Green Left Weekly*, 28 February, p. 13.

Bond, P. and K. Bakker (2001) 'Canada: Blue Planet Targets Commodification of World's Water', *Green Left Weekly*, 18 July, p. 22.

Braithwaite, J. (1993) 'Responsive Business Regulatory Institutions', in C. Coady and C. Sampford (eds) *Business Ethics and the Law*. Sydney: Federation Press.

Braithwaite, J. and P. Drahos (2000) *Global Business Regulation*. Cambridge: Cambridge University Press.

Del Frate, A. and J. Norberry (eds) (1993) *Environmental Crime: Sanctioning Strategies and Sustainable Development*. Rome: UNICRI/Sydney: Australian Institute of Criminology.

Dixon, N. (2001) 'South Africa: Anti-Cut Off Activists Shot', *Green Left Weekly*, 10 October, p. 22.

Franklin, A. (1999) *Animals and Modern Cultures: A Sociology of Human–Animal Relations in Modernity*. London: Sage Publications.

Goldman, M. (1998a) 'Introduction: The Political Resurgence of the Commons', in M. Goldman (ed.) *Privatizing Nature: Political Struggles for the Global Commons*, pp. 1–19. London: Pluto Press in association with Transnational Institute.

Goldman, M. (1998b) 'Inventing the Commons: Theories and Practices of the Commons' Professional', in M. Goldman (ed.) *Privatizing Nature: Political Struggles for the Global Commons*, pp. 20–53. London: Pluto Press in association with Transnational Institute.

Government of British Columbia (2001) *Drinking Water Protection Plan: A Discussion Document*. Vancouver: Government of British Columbia.

Grabosky, P. (1994) 'Green Markets: Environmental Regulation by the Private Sector', *Law and Policy* 16(4): 419–48.

Grabosky, P. (1995) 'Regulation by Reward: On the Use of Incentives as Regulatory Instruments', *Law and Policy* 17(3): 256–79.

Gunningham, N. and P. Grabosky (1998) *Smart Regulation: Designing Environmental Policy*. Oxford: Clarendon Press.

Gunningham, N., J. Norberry and S. McKillop (eds) (1995) *Environmental Crime, Conference Proceedings*. Canberra: Australian Institute of Criminology.

Hager, N. and B. Burton (1999) *Secrets and Lies: The Anatomy of an Anti-Environmental PR Campaign*. New Zealand: Craig Potton Publishing.

Haines, F. (1997) *Corporate Regulation: Beyond 'Punish or Persuade'*. Oxford: Clarendon Press.

Haines, F. (2000) 'Towards Understanding Globalisation and Control of Corporate Harm: A Preliminary Criminological Analysis', *Current Issues in Criminal Justice* 12(2): 166–80.

Hall, D. (1999) *The Water Multinationals*. London: Public Services International Research Unit, University of Greenwich.

Halsey, M. (1997a) 'Environmental Crime: Towards an Eco Human Rights Approach', *Current Issues in Criminal Justice* 8(3): 217–42.

Halsey, M. (1976) 'The Wood for the Paper: Old Growth Forest, Hemp and Environmental Harm', *Australian and New Zealand Journal of Criminology* 30(2): 121–48.

Halsey, M. and R. White (1998) 'Crime, Ecophilosophy and Environmental Harm', *Theoretical Criminology* 2(3): 345–71.

Harvey, D. (1996) *Justice, Nature and the Geography of Difference*. Oxford: Blackwell.

Hausman, T., D. Hazen, T. Straus and K. Fish (2001) 'Exposing the News that Didn't Make the News', *Australian Options* 25: 9.

Heine, G., M. Prabhu and A. del Frate (eds) (1997) *Environmental Protection: Potentials and Limits of Criminal Justice*. Rome: UNICJRI.

Kirkland, L.H. and D. Thompson (1999) 'Challenges in Designing, Implementing and Operating an Environmental Management System', *Business Strategy and the Environment* 8: 128–43.

Levy, D. (1997) 'Environmental Management as Political Sustainability', *Organization and Environment* 10(2): 126–47.

Low, N. and B. Gleeson (1998) *Justice, Society and Nature: An Exploration of Political Ecology*. London: Routledge.

McCulloch, J. (2001) *Blue Army: Paramilitary Policing in Australia*. Melbourne: Melbourne University Press.

Massey, R. (2001) 'United States: Arsenic from Your Tap', *Green Left Weekly* 23 May, p. 24.

O'Brien, R., A. Goetz, J. Scholte and M. Williams (2000) *Contesting Global Governance: Multilateral Economic Institutions and Global Social Movements*. Cambridge: Cambridge University Press.

O'Connor, J. (1994) 'Is Sustainable Capitalism Possible?', in M. O'Connor (ed.) *Is Capitalism Sustainable?: Political Economy and the Politics of Ecology*, pp. 152–75. New York: The Guilford Press.

Pearce, F and S. Tombs (1998) *Toxic Capitalism: Corporate Crime and the Chemical Industry*. Aldershot: Dartmouth Publishing Company.

Pepper, D. (1993) *Eco-Socialism: From Deep Ecology to Social Justice*. New York: Routledge.

Public Services Privatization Research Unit (1996) *The Privatisation Network*. London: PSPRU.

Schwendinger, H. and J. Schwendinger (1975) 'Defenders of Order or Guardians of Human Rights?', in I. Taylor, P. Walton and J. Young (eds) *Critical Criminology*, pp. 113–46. London: Routledge & Kegan Paul.

Seis, M. (1993) 'Ecological Blunders in US Clean Air Legislation', *Journal of Human justice* 5(1): 58–81.

Shallat, L. (2001) 'Consumer Challenges to Corporate Might', in *Corporate Citizenship in the Global Market*. Internet: Consumers International Website [http://www.consumidoresint.cl].

Situ, Y. and D. Emmons (2000) *Environmental Crime: The Criminal Justice System's Role in Protecting the Environment*. Thousand Oaks, CA: Sage Publications.

Snider, L. (2000) 'The Sociology of Corporate Crime: An Obituary (or: Whose Knowledge Claims Have Legs?)', *Theoretical Criminology* 4(2): 169–206.

Snider, L. (2002 ) 'Zero Tolerance Reversed: Constituting the Non-Culpable Subject in Walkerton', paper presented at Annual Meetings, Canadian Law and Society Association, Vancouver, 31 May.

South, N. (1998) 'A Green Field for Criminology', *Theoretical Criminology* 2(2): 211–34.

South African Municipal Workers Union (SAMWU) (2001) 'Union "Mourns" on World Water Day', SAMWU statement on World Water Day, reprinted in *Green Left Weekly* 28 March, p. 22.

Sutherland, E. (1949) *White Collar Crime*. New York: Dryden Press.

Vanderpuye, F. (2001) 'Ghana: Campaign Intensifies against Water Privatisation', *Green Left Weekly* 20 June, p. 20.

Vassilopoulos, J. (1998a) 'Water Companies' Criminal Record', *Green Left Weekly* 2 September, p. 13.

Vassilopoulos, J. (1998b) 'Sydney Water Crisis due to Corporatisation', *Green Left Weekly* 12 August, p. 13.

Wall, E. and B. Beardwood (2001) 'Standardizing Globally, Responding Locally: The New Infrastructure, ISO 14000, and Canadian Agriculture', *Studies in Political Economy* 64: 33–58.

White, R. (1998) 'Environmental Criminology and Sydney Water', *Current Issues in Criminal justice* 10(2): 214–19.

White, R. (1999) 'Criminality, Risk and Environmental Harm', *Griffith Law Review* 8(2): 235–57.

White, R. (2002) 'Environmental Harm and the Political Economy of Consumption', *Social Justice* 29(1–2): 82–102.

Williams, C. (1996) 'An Environmental Vietimology', *Social Justice* 23(4): 16–40.

Wright Mills, C. (1959) *The Sociological Imagination*. New York: Oxford University Press.

# 4. The meaning of green: contrasting criminological perspectives*

*Michael J. Lynch and Paul B. Stretesky*

**Abstract**

Previous discussions of green criminology have not defined the meaning of the term 'green'. Here we investigate alternative definitions of this term, focusing attention on two contrasting definitions. One definition is aligned with corporate interests and emerged through corporate redefinitions of green environmentalism; we provide examples of the 'green' criminology that resulted. We then offer a contrasting environmental justice definition. This alternative concept highlights common elements in social movements concerned with environmental justice while emphasizing these movements' commitment to simultaneously incorporating race, class and gender-oriented issues into green criminology.

**Key Words** corporate crime • criminological theory • defining crime • environmental justice • green crime

## Introduction

Criminologists have recently taken up the challenge of creating a 'green criminology' (e.g. Groombridge 1998; Lane 1998; South 1998; see also, Lynch 1990). Their efforts have important implications for reorienting the study of violations of criminal laws, ethics and crime. The purpose of this article is to expand on previous studies and to clarify the meaning of 'green'. An issue of *Theoretical Criminology* devoted to the topic of green criminology emphasized applications of this idea but offered little direction in terms of defining this key concept. For instance, in the previous issue, Groombridge noted that 'it is not possible simply to adopt a "green" perspective without bringing with it theoretical and methodological issues, *though these cannot be pursued here*' (1998: 253, emphasis added). In the same issue, South stated that 'it would be valuable, *at some other point*, to outline what these [green criminological theories] might look like but *such an elaboration is not the aim of this exploratory article ...*' (1998: 212, emphases added).

---

* From *Theoretical Criminology* (2003), 7(2): pp. 217–238.

As these authors implied, it is essential to define the meaning of the term 'green' in the process of forging a green criminology. We take the view that green crimes, like other crimes, are social constructions influenced by social locations and power relations in society (on social construction, social locations and definitions of environmental crimes see Seager 1993: 59). With respect to power issues, we examine the meaning of the term green as it has been influenced by two distinct groups: corporate actors and environmental justice activists/movements influenced by considerations of gender, race and class-based inequities.

To keep our approach manageable, we highlight a human-centered orientation and purposefully omit discussion of non-human and natural rights perspectives (for discussion see Benton 1998; Beirne 1999; with respect to green theory see Dobson 1991: 235–70). Rather, our goal here is to sketch the main issues and anchoring points needed to construct a definition of green criminology that recognizes the influence of existing corporate power structures and the achievements of the environmental justice movement (concerned as the latter has been with issues of gender, race and class discrimination).

To realize this task, this article proceeds in four sections. First, we review issues relating to the social construction of crime. Second, we examine implications for the social construction of green criminology from a 'top-down' perspective that has kept existing corporate power interests in mind. Third, we look at the construction of green from a 'bottom-up' approach that entails analyzing different types of environmental justice movements and perspectives. Fourth, drawing on both the 'bottom-up' and 'top-down' approach, we present two opposing definitions of green criminology and an argument about which one – for criminology – is preferable.

## The social construction of crime

Quinney (1970) popularized the idea that crime is a social construction that reflects societal power relations. For the most part, acts defined as crime are behaviors predominantly undertaken by relatively powerless social actors. However, the process of constructing crime is also subject to legitimation constraints (Wolfe 1977) and rules defining 'fair play' (Ryan 1981). Consequentially, *some* of the behaviors of the powerful will also be defined as criminal. Similarly, the interests of relatively powerless groups will sometimes be favored in the political process of constructing crime. In short, law-making processes contain mechanisms whereby law is legitimized because it appears capable of representing the diverse interests of both the powerful and powerless. Law is also a repository of the collective consciousness capable of transforming and controlling a variety of actions that threaten the health and well being of society's citizens. The construction of crime is also a contested arena with respect to identity construction. Consequently, while law primarily represents the interests of the powerful, it also contains mechanisms that allow it to appear to control the behavior of the powerful. This view of law and its relationship to power relations and the process of constructing crime helps to explain how laws designed to control the behavior of the powerful, such as environmental laws, are possible. Simultaneously, though, the overall impact of law and the construction of crime reinforce existing power relationships.

The social construction of crime is a political process that is affected by images of crime as reported in the news media (Surette 1997), and as depicted in popular magazines and popular culture venues like television, movies, comics and music videos (see Quinney 1979; Newman 1990; Lynch and Krzycki 1998). In addition, crime is constructed via the efforts of moral entrepreneurs and moral crusaders to expand the meaning of what ought to be considered crime. These kinds of activities have impacted the definition of both street crime (Schwendinger and Schwendinger 1970; Brownstein 1999) and corporate crimes (Nader 1965). The social construction of crime does not involve images and definitions alone: in addition, it can involve actions and behaviors that act as illustrative symbols as well as the behavior of law enforcement agencies.

## The corporate deconstruction of green

Like other crimes, the very definition of green crime is influenced through collective processes that mediate the behaviors of individuals and groups. Corporations play an important role in the social construction or meaning of the term green. This influence has become increasingly clear in the contemporary context. For instance, the 1990s was supposedly the decade of the environment. By the late 1980s, media and scholarly pundits predicted that the environment would become a major political issue over the following decade, reawakening people's environmental consciousness and fostering widespread political activism aimed at environmental protectionism reminiscent of the early 1970s. In reality, this prediction proved inaccurate. While a variety of grass-roots environmental movements gained some support during the 1990s, others were influenced by corporate memberships and donations (Karliner 1997). During the 1990s, World Resources Institute, National Audubon Society, Conservation International, World Wildlife Fund and National Wildlife Federation received donations from corporations well known as polluters including Waste Management, Cargill, Chevron, Dow, DuPont, Ford, Motorola and Scott Paper (Karliner 1997).

Indeed, the involvement of corporations in environmental movements facilitated the decline of renewed interest in the environment. According to Faber and O'Connor, one result of corporate environmentalism was to 'reestablish corporate discipline over social movements' (1993: 17). In large part, then, the limited success of the green movement can be tied to the transformation of the ideological basis and symbolism the public has come to associate with the term green. The corporate transformation of the idea of green during the 1990s is important because it demonstrates the ability of corporations to influence the social construction of green and to influence popularly based political movements through the use of mass media. Corporate constructions of green have led to widespread reinterpretations of what it means to 'be green' and to take a 'green' position. For instance, corporations that release cancer-causing substances into the environment in amounts that meet established regulatory limits are praised as 'exemplary environmental citizens' even though their production practices are often non-sustainable, exploitive and even criminal in some countries.

## Corporate reconstruction of 'green'

The popular base of the environmental movement was rapidly reconstructed in the 1990s in definitional rather than behavioral terms as corporations manipulated and remade the term green. Corporations' ability to 'appear green' was accomplished through massive public relations and advertising campaigns and reflected the immense resources at their command (Stauber and Rampton 1995). In a nutshell, the corporate redefinition of the word 'green' presented the public with a mild, less radical and de-politicized environmental vision along with less drastic responses (stressing consumption rather than production issues) to environmental issues. The environmental responses crafted by corporations were also easily accessible to the general public: consumers could become 'green' simply by altering their purchasing behavior, i.e. by buying 'green' products from companies that claimed to be green. By 'appearing green', then, corporations were able to defuse and redirect support for environmental issues and movements (Karliner 1997). In short, corporations correctly observed that a growing public concern with environmental issues had generated conditions under which a broader segment of the population wished to join green-based movements.

There is nothing inherently threatening to corporations about popular environmental movements. However, green movements are particularly radical in that they argue for changes in production practices, limits on growth and corporate power and economic redistribution as viable policy responses (Dobson 1991). Consequently, increasing public support for radical environmental positions posed a threat to corporations' abilities to engage in 'business as usual'. In response, corporations crafted two responses. The first was to make small environmental concessions to appease the public's concerns (Karliner 1997): for example, McDonald's Corporation bowed to pressure to eliminate the use of styrofoam. Second, corporations engaged in public relations campaigns. Again, in the case of McDonald's, the corporation appeased the public's desire for strengthened environmental protectionism through media campaigns designed to make them 'appear green' in supposedly sharing consciousness similar to that held by the public (Stauber and Rampton 1995). This green media/advertising campaign, still in the process of development and recently broadened to include the Internet, classroom TV and classroom teaching materials on environmental matters, has done much to alter perceived public meanings of the term green (Turner 1970; Mander 1972). Especially important is the fact that this transformation depoliticized the idea of being green.

Corporate use of advertising to affect environmental consciousness is not a new strategy (Stauber and Rampton 1995). Since the early 1970s, environmentalists have documented the appearance of green imagery in corporate media campaigns designed to convince people that specific businesses or sectors were environmentally friendly (Mander 1972). Commonly referred to as 'greenwashing' (Greer and Bruno 1997), this practice was designed to head off the development of a people's environmental movement. As Karliner (1997) argues, corporations have successfully employed this strategy as a response to popular environmentalism. Consumers have been encouraged to 'think' and 'buy' green, and to associate green practices with specific corporate advertisements rather than with environmentally friendly production practices. Corporations create and feed these 'green' images to the public through advertising and public relations campaigns (Stauber and Rampton 1995; on the theory and use of advertising generally, see Averill 1996; Ohmann 1996). For example, Chevron Corporation, well known for its environmentally destructive practices (Karliner 1997), developed an environmental advertising program that included a TV commercial featuring its attempts to save endangered species. Chevron summarizes these projects, such as its effort to save the El Segundo Blue butterfly, on its 'educational' webpages (http://www.chevron. com/community/education):

> The El Segundo Blue is a tiny butterfly on the Endangered Species List, whose habitat once spanned 36 square miles south from downtown Los Angeles. Urban development shrunk its habitat to two small acres, including land within Chevron's El Segundo refinery. To compound the problem, encroaching weeds were choking out the wild buckwheat plants on which the butterfly feeds. In response, the company fenced off the area, retained an entomologist, started eliminating marauding weeds and cultivating additional buckwheat seedlings to ensure the survival of the El Segundo Blue butterfly.

A television commercial devoted to this issue depicts the blue butterfly 'happily' flying around its 'habitat', and the role Chevron played in 'saving' this species from extinction. The purposeful corporate gaze of the commercial does not allow viewers to see that the protected area in question is a Chevron-owned field that sits on top of its oil refinery operations in El Segundo, alternatively described by environmentalists as a 'barbed wire fenced compound atop the United States' largest underground oil spill' (Karliner 1997: 168). Not surprisingly, Chevron's website fails to mention its role in creating the conditions that endangered the existence of this butterfly. And cleverly, Chevron's description of the responsible culprits points to other sources: weed encroachment and urban development. Obviously, Chevron has not changed its behavior to establish conditions that would save the El Segundo Blue. However, Chevron did use its resources to hire an environmental specialist and a public relations group to transform Chevron's minimal efforts into a seemingly 'green' consciousness.

Yet, despite corporations' ability to affect popular cultural meanings associated with 'being green', the ability of green movements to define themselves has not been destroyed. Here we employ two broad, contrasting referents for the term 'green', each with different implications for shaping a green criminology. One definition of green is the corporate construction that, if used, has the potential to severely limit green theoretical perspectives in criminology. The other is a social movement view that creates an alternative theoretical and cultural understanding helpful in analyzing environmental crimes. It is to this view that we now turn.

## The environmental justice construction of green

Environmental justice (EJ) definitions of green have important implications for green criminology. To be sure, equally significant differences among various EJ and green movements also prohibit us from developing a specific or fixed green theory of crime. Environmental crises vary over time as do reactions to these events. For example, the same person may find that joining a class-based movement is the best solution to environmental injustice in the workplace and joining a race-based movement is the best solution to environmental injustice in his/her neighborhood community. Moreover, justice claims relating to the environment are far from new (Taylor 2000: 521), meaning that the construction of 'green' likewise varies across time, social groups and group intersections. For this reason, the environmental justice movement has expanded into a broad set of perspectives and agendas, each based on different definitions of the environmental problem. Consequently, one finds commonalties among environmental justice movements, as discussed below, and diverse strategies for redressing environmental harms. To illustrate both such commonalties and differences, three environmental justice movements are examined below: ecofeminism; the struggle against environmental racism; and red-green movements.

### Ecofeminism

The US ecofeminist movement began in the 1970s as a combination of feminist, environmental and justice movements (Daly 1978; Griffin 1978; Merchant 1980). Ecofeminists criticized capitalist profit-growth orientations and its patriarchal nature, advocating subsistence as an alternative (Plant 1989; Epstein 1993; Mies 1993). For many ecofeminists the domination and exploitation of nature is related to the domination and exploitation of women (Merchant 1980, 1996). Patriarchal structures produced and reproduced the exploitation of women and nature and were ultimately responsible for the impending ecological crises. For example, Mies (1993) argued that women are more concerned with survival and subsistence than men; in her view, it was predominantly men who have promoted growth, technology, science and progress as solutions to ecological and economic crises.

Ecofeminism also argues that women have a unique social location from which to address the ecological crisis. According to Epstein, an ecofeminist solution would be simple:

> Patriarchy must be replaced with egalitarian forms of social organization in which men and women have equal power, and by a vision of social ecology wherein the natural environment is treated with respect insofar as it should be sustained rather than manipulated and destroyed.
>
> (1993: 145)

This can be achieved by reorienting cultural values and returning to smallscale local economies and grass-roots democracy (Mies 1993). While some ecofeminists reject class-based environmental justice movements because they place too much emphasis on the economic realm, they recognize the importance of economic oppression (see Dobson 1992; Mellor 1992). Gibbs (1995) states that both gender and class-based concerns have increased women's participation in anti-toxic movements.

### Environmental racism

The movement against environmental racism simultaneously advocates environmental justice and the elimination of racial discrimination in environmental decisions, actions and policies. This struggle emerged from the civil rights movement as a new 'master frame used to mobilize activists who want to link racism, injustice, and environmentalism in one frame' (Taylor 2000: 514). This movement's primary concerns include equality in environmental regulation enforcement, the siting of polluting industries and waste sites and the elimination of products and production processes that largely affect communities of color (e.g. African-Americans, Latinos, Asians, Pacific Islanders and Native Americans). The movement also connects issues of distributive justice (e.g. how environmental hazards are distributed across diverse races) to issues of productive justice (what and how things are produced). While the short-term goals involve race-linked theory and action, the long-term goal is the elimination of exposure to dangerous products or practices for all (Bullard 1990).

Hundreds of grass-roots groups found in every state and representing a multitude of racial and ethnic groups have organized to oppose environmental racism (see Bullard 1990, 1993; Bunyan 1995; Taylor 2000). While racially and ethnically diverse, these groups share similar perspectives rooted in both productive and distributive justice. For instance, organizations like the Indigenous Environmental Network and the South African Exchange Program on Environmental Justice formally state that they support basic rights to a clean environment regardless of race. From an environmental justice perspective, then, being green is ultimately related to ending racial oppression and discrimination.

### Red-green movement

The red-green movement relates economic oppression to environmental degradation. Red-greens assert that capital restructuring has externalizing costs that harm the environment and public health (O'Connor 1998). In a class society, these externalized cost and environmental problems are more likely to impact the working class and the poor. In this way, capitalism exploits working class labor and environments (see Engels 1968 [1845]).

For red-greens, the current process of production is exploitative in many ways (O'Connor 1998). One important form of exploitation involved private forms of production that removed workers from decisions concerning how things are produced and related forms of environmental damage. Commoner's (1987 [1971]) solution involved local public control over the forces of production. According to Commoner, this solution needs to be based on ecological and economic grounds, and he advances 'ecological socialism' as a method of simultaneously eliminating environmentally destructive, unsustainable production practices and the exploitative mode of production. As Foster notes:

> ... the battle over [a sustainable environment] is as much a class struggle as it is an ecological one. If [for example] forest product workers find their jobs threatened, this has far less to do with the struggle of environmentalists to preserve the [environment] than to the efforts of capital and the state to promote profits at the expense of both workers and the environment.
>
> (1993: 11)

For Commoner, the green revolution must also be red – i.e. it must also occur in the workplace. Commoner's influence on left-green politics has led to various local and regional coalitions that fight against workplace and community toxic pollution and push, radically, for the development of non-polluting technologies rather than less polluting technologies. According to O'Connor, Commoner's ecological socialism is 'beautiful in its simplicity [advocating] that pollution regulation, pollution licenses, and so on, are not needed if pollution is not produced in the first place' (1998: 283).

## Shared orientations of green movements

The diverse environmental justice movements discussed above advocate many similar policies that link their views (Faber 1998). For instance, ecofeminists are clearly against environmental racism and red-greens were among the many organizations that protested against the World Trade Organization's support of undemocratic, non-sustainable and exploitative practices. In short, it is simplistic to view green environmental movements as having only distinct, mutually exclusive emphases. Environmental justice movements may not be identical but they are not unique either. Indeed at a broader level, environmental justice movements share three common orientations: (1) the politics of being green; (2) the multi-issue basis of green theory and the inclusion of a theory of oppression in green theoretical perspectives; and (3) the appeal to historically situated theory and understanding. We review these points of compatibility below.

### The politics of being green

Any group or organization that claims to be concerned with environmental justice must have a legitimate political plan of action that outlines the need for broad structural reforms to address *environmental injustice*. This is common to environmental justice movements although the exact form of political action and theory espoused across groups varies. For some, political orientation and policy are grounded in class-based theory (O'Connor 1998). Other groups begin with race or gender-based perspectives; still others take positions that are nature-based (see Benton 1998). Despite these differences, though, environmental justice organizations are dedicated to democratic participation. As a result, the environmental justice movement is often organized along local lines and localized issues. These issues can, and most often do, have global implications capable of generating larger-scale movements (Hofrichter 1993). For instance, a multi-racial environmental justice movement composed of thousands of community members successfully prevented Shintech Corporation, a multinational petrochemical company, from placing the world's largest polyvinyl chloride (PVC) plant in Convent, Louisiana.

For some greens, local democratic forms of organization are the ultimate aim (e.g. Native Americans' ecological movements). For others, local organizations are used to assist broader political, social and economic movements (e.g. red-greens and some ecofeminist groups). However, in each case, environmental justice movements are founded on grass-roots forms of organization.

### Multi-issue character and a shared focus on oppression

Green environmental justice movements should not be seen as monolithic entities solely concerned with environmental problems.[2] Environmental issues are clearly an integral part of these movements, but they are also frequently concerned with a wide range of issues that, in turn, are connected to social and economic theories concerning the nature of society, human interaction and oppression. For example, as Rafael Pandam of the Confederation of Indigenous Nationalities of Ecuador writes:

> When we indigenous peoples talk about the environment, we are not just talking about the trees, rivers and butterflies. We are also talking about human beings. Likewise, when we talk of human rights, we are not just talking about the right to free speech. We are talking about the political, economic, social and cultural rights of all peoples, and their rights to sustainable development which fulfills the basic needs of human rights.
> (cited in the Center for Economic and Social Rights 1994: ix)

Thus environmental justice movements adhere to a theory of human oppression that links environmental harms and human justice (Dobson 1991). For example, red-greens examine the connection between class/economic oppression and environmental harms; 'EJ' greens connect environmental injustices with the subordination of racial/ethnic and native peoples (e.g. environmental racism); ecofeminists link environmental harms with broader structures and situations responsible for gender oppression (e.g. ecofeminism). Thus, environmental oppression is important because of its connection to other forms of oppression that are part of social, economic and political systems. This focus on oppression is closely connected to the historical dimension of the green theoretical position.

### The historical perspective in environmental justice

The third element common to green environmental justice movements is their historical orientation: in short, history is an important part of a green theoretical view for each of these movements. This is not to say that each movement views history in precisely the same way. For example, for red-greens, an historical dimension is captured in the process of class struggle (O'Connor 1998); for eco-feminists, the role of patriarchy and women's struggles for equality comprise the dimension of history and conflict that need to be addressed; for EJ greens, history is the story of the struggle over self-determination and against the external imposition of forces that generate systems of racial and ethnic subordination. Thus, history provides one portion of the theoretical framework within which political struggles for environmental justice (equity) are understood. Emphasizing the importance of this historical dimension, James O'Connor has noted that:

> Environmental history is the culmination of all previous history. Further, it should be seen as the study of how human agency shapes and modifies 'nature' and constructs and builds environments and spatial configurations, and how natural and cultural environments both enable and constrain human material activity; and, conversely, how human activity both enables and constrains cultural development and 'nature's' economy.
>
> (1998: 51–2)

In this view, environmental history is the study of nature itself, the interaction of nature with society, and the laws, myths and perceptions humans construct and apply to nature (Worster 1988). This history is both limited by the peculiarities of the particular place or places studied (O'Connor 1998: 54) and simultaneously connected with the history of other places (O'Connor 1998: 55).

In sum, while green movements certainly differ among themselves, commonalities are also easy to discern. Yet academic analyses have often emphasized differences over points of commonality, making it more difficult to perceive – and to act upon – environmental groups' shared aims and goals.

## Constructing green crime: implications for green criminology

Another important issue that points us back toward the task of developing a green criminology, is that environmental justice movements take different approaches depending on how they define the term 'green'. Accordingly, we turn now to demonstrating the quite disparate approaches to green criminology that emerge depending on whether one adopts a corporate or environmental justice construction of the term, 'green'.

### The environmental justice perspective

From an environmental justice (EJ) perspective a green crime is an act that (1) may or may not violate existing rules and environmental regulations; (2) has identifiable environmental damage outcomes; and (3) originated in human action. Some of these acts are sanctioned through criminal law while others amount only to civil, technical and/or administrative violations. Specific acts such as illegal polluting and toxic chemical dumping fit neatly within the traditional definition of crime (South 1998). In some instances, however, green crimes may not be a 'violation of any existing form of law' (Frank and Lynch 1992: 82) even though they result in, or possess the potential to result in, environmental and human harm. Examples of these latter behaviors include, but are not limited to, timber-clear cutting, vivisection, the sale of unnecessary and dangerous pesticides and pharmaceuticals banned in developed nations but lacking legal regulation in Third World countries (Frank and Lynch 1992: 82, 86–95) and race or class-related hazardous waste siting decisions.

To focus on acts not defined as illegal may disturb some criminologists. However, to understand crime it is necessary to investigate the processes involved in creating crime including: (1) identifying contested behaviors that are not defined as crimes and the reasons why this choice was made; (2) the content and organization of law and the enforcement mechanisms created to uphold law; (3) the activities of law enforcers; (4) the interplay of corporate and public interests; (5) conflicting scientific evidence on environmental harms (Fagan and Lavelle 1996; Steingraber 1998) and (6) media images (Stauber and Rampton 1995). Crimes are constantly made and unmade through acts of social construction and deconstruction (Brownstein 1999). Therefore it is important to understand *which* behaviors become the focus of law and *why*. For example, why is it that laws designed to 'protect everyone' from environmental harms often fail to be enforced in minority and lower-class communities? Is the differential enforcement of these laws across communities with different residential characteristics tied to the power of a community's residents? Answering these questions requires investigating how differential enforcement advantages the corporations that create the environmental harms in question.

A central concern in this analysis, then, is how overlapping forms of race, class and gender inequities affect the social construction of environmental laws. For example, a green criminology could examine how gender inequality relates to forms of female victimization caused by green crimes. For instance, why are there no special enforcement procedures designed to protect women against forms of environmental harm that enhance the risk of breast cancer, one of the most rapidly increasing health risks for women over the past three decades (Steingraber 1998)? Race or class issues may also be brought into play through research suggesting that race and income are important determinants in predicting the lax enforcement of environmental crimes against corporations (Lavelle and Coyle 1992; Friedrichs 1996; Simon 1999). In short, in the environmental justice perspective, enforcement processes favor the powerful over the powerless in terms of both the construction and application of laws.

Consequently, from this perspective, many green crimes result from structures and hierarchies that exclude women of color from full economic participation. For instance, the 'harvesting' of rain forests is always a form of class oppression; the greatest benefit accrues to those who own the means of production. In the process, trees are transformed into commodities while the economies of forest peoples are destroyed. When these activities occur in underdeveloped regions or nations, race enters the analysis insofar as the natural resources of native people are taken over and dominated by predominantly European-owned industries and markets (Mendez 1989; Karliner 1997). Finally, gender becomes an issue when rain forest harvesting disrupts native systems of gathering and agricultural production controlled by women, thereby destroying women's traditional productive roles (Mies 1993).

From this, several general components of an environmental justice definition of green crime can be deduced. First, this definition focuses attention on acts that, whether or not defined as illegal, should nonetheless be considered criminal. Second, an environmental justice perspective considers relations of power in the construction and application of environmental laws. Third, power is defined specifically with consideration not only to traditionally recognized notions of class but also to gender and race-based hierarchies. As discussed above, solutions to these problems would be radical, necessarily involving the elimination of social and economic inequalities. But this brings us to the corporate view: how does it compare?

### Constructing green crime: a corporate perspective

From a corporate standpoint, a green crime encompasses 'unauthorized acts or omissions that *violate the law* and are therefore *subject to criminal prosecution* and *sanctions*' (see Situ and Emmons 2000: 3, emphases added). This is a very precise, exact and limiting definition of what can be considered a 'crime'. Some criminologists have preferred this type of definition because they see it as 'value free'. Yet, by referring to law as though value free, criminologists tend to avoid responsibility for defining crime and investigating how power differentials affect the nature of law and its enforcement. But given this view of crime as law-based, how would a green criminology influenced by a corporate perspective interpret environmental crimes that fall outside the law? Because environmental harms are perceived as involving only illegal acts, targeting minority communities as waste sites or overselling pesticides to farmers may, as a result of this definition, be seen as standard and 'above the law' business practices.

Moreover, a corporate perspective on defining green crime would argue against the majority of cross-cultural studies of environmental harms. For example, few international laws define green crimes; in addition violations of environmental laws that carry criminal (or civil) liability in one country may not be considered criminal outside that country's boundaries. For example, an Ecuadorian Amazon tribe recently filed a billion-dollar class-action lawsuit against Texaco claiming the company dumped 10 million gallons of toxic wastewater and crude oil into unlined pits over a 20-year period harming the people, culture and environment of Ecuador. Texaco admits to dumping and causing the damage. Their defense: they are required to comply with deep well injection regulations in the United States; however, because this practice is preferred but not required in Ecuador, Texaco's behavior ought not be considered criminal outside American borders (Texaco 1999: 15–16).

By focusing only on violations of criminal law, a corporate definition of green crimes also constrains the number of victims that can be studied.

The environment, for example, is only a victim when a specific statute has been violated. The same applies to human or animal victims.[3] In addition, the corporate definition of being green is closely tied to economic outcomes. When the economic benefits of environmentally damaging actions outweigh associated civil liabilities, corporate actions are justified as good business practices in a highly competitive global economy. These practices are also justified by an elaborate cost–benefit science (e.g. integrated pest management; see, generally, Higley and Pedigo 1996). When justifying environmental damage, corporations argue that our standard of living cannot be sustained or improved without risk to some people and the environment; that damage to non-human species can be repaired and managed; and that the economic benefits of environmental damage outweigh its costs (see Guilder 1993). However, some people question whether corporations accurately assess these costs. For example, corporations have externalized or socialized the most costly forms of environmental damage they produce. This causes them to under-estimate the real costs of environmental damage. Further, calculations of the economic costs of human beings are usually minimized in these calculations (Higley and Pedigo 1996).

In contrast to an environmental justice view, a corporate view of green criminology does not specifically address inequities of race, class and gender. These hierarchies are seen as 'natural' and beyond the scope of corporations to create, maintain or change. Thus, when faced with evidence that minorities and lower class persons are more likely to live in polluted areas, corporations respond that this is their choice. A corporate green criminology emphasizes the individual-level decisions people make that places them in proximity to hazardous waste sites. It fails to comprehend that a persistent pattern of racial proximity to hazardous waste sites, for instance, implicates the need for structural rather than individual-level explanation.

Green corporatism also incorporates a particular position on liability. Legally, environmental standards typically employ the ideas of limited and excusable liability (e.g. under Title VI of the Civil Rights Act of 1964; see Mank 1999). These standards are much different than those criminologists typically encounter (strict liability), and one might wonder how the use of a lesser legal stand for criminals with greater economic power and a stricter legal standard for those with less can be justified. Finally, green corporatism has also supported limited policy responses to the enforcement of environmental laws. One such strategy has been the self-policing and self-reporting of violations of law. Controversies remain about whether this approach works to control corporate deviance. What we know is that self-policing has improved profits (Rebovich 1998).

In sum, the agenda of a corporate green criminology is immensely different than one informed by an environmental justice perspective. Green corporatism denies the need to look at power relations while EJ greens see these relations as fundamental to analysis and action. Power, then, is the key issue that separates these opposing stances toward green criminology.

## Toward a green criminology

Having contrasted two views on the term green, we need to address three additional questions: is a green criminology necessary? If so, which of the views reviewed above should be its basis? Finally, what are the basic issues that must be encompassed in an alternative perspective? Certainly many existing criminological views are capable of addressing environmental harms and crimes. However, the discussion of environmental crimes, laws and harms is absent from the vast majority of criminological approaches.[4] In general, criminologists have often left the study of environmental harm, environmental laws and environmental regulations to researchers in other disciplines. This has allowed little room for critical examination of individuals or entities who/which kills, injures and assaults other life forms (human, animal or plant) by poisoning the earth. In this light, a green criminology is needed to awaken criminologists to the types of major environmental harm and damage that can result from environmental harms; the conflicts that arise from attempts at defining environmental crime and deviance; and the controversies still raging over possible solutions, given extensive environmental regulations already in place. In other words, a whole range of crimes have tended to be neglected, thereby painting a limited picture of contemporary crime and its proportions.

The purpose of a revitalized green criminology, then, is to redirect attention toward serious and widespread environmental harms that, even more than ordinary crimes, threaten human life and community. In our view, this can only be accomplished by a green criminology grounded in environmental justice principles. Along with Dobson (1991), we argue that being green implies more than holding values favoring environmental protection: it also entails a political stance wherein it is acknowledged that solutions to environmental degradation may require substantial economic and political reorganization.

This being said, though, a green theoretical perspective is more of a guideline than a set of axioms or rules; no rigid theoretical structure emerges as a by-product of this article's argument. Yet several 'guiding principles' are important in helping to develop an ongoing green perspective. One is that environmental harm is a consequence of the primacy of the economic sphere over other social structures and issues. Consequently, economic interests play an integral role in determining which or whether environmental harms will be treated as crimes, and which ones will be accepted or justified as 'normal'.

Another important principle is that in an alternative green perspective, the environmental harms least likely to become the focus of law – both in terms of legal prohibition and/or active social control and enforcement efforts – are those that have the greatest direct impact on economically disenfranchised and oppressed groups. These environmental harms include those most likely to affect the lower classes, minority racial and ethnic groups and women. Because these politically and economically marginalized groups have little power, they are less likely to be able to defend and protect their interests, or to have others act on their behalf. Environmental oppression becomes a routine aspect of their economic and political oppression.

Finally, an alternative green criminology ought to draw on both structural and subjective explanations and understandings (see Groves and Lynch 1990) as a matter of course. In terms of structural considerations, green criminology employs a political economic frame of reference that addresses race, ethnicity, class and gender structures and their relationship to the definition, nature and distribution of environmental harms. But, in terms of subjective understandings, green criminology also needs to be sensitive to how group memberships (i.e. an individual's race, ethnic, gender and class identity and consciousness) affect the emergence and goals of social movements aimed at transforming social structures in an effort to reduce multi-dimensional environmental harms

A wide variety of harms, laws, systems of regulation, definitional debates and so on can be analyzed, and evaluated, from this point of view. From an alternative green perspective, one that draws on environmental justice considerations, the specifics of such analyses will no doubt vary according to the contextual elements of particular problems. In some cases, race will be more important than class or gender; in other cases, ethnicity; sometimes a complex relationship of overlapping social factors will affect how green-influenced analyses of crime ought to proceed at levels that may be local, regional or global in scope.

## Conclusion

Our objective in this article was to clarify the meaning of the term green on the assumption that doing so affects how an evolving green criminology can be envisioned. To make this discussion manageable, the above analysis was limited to human-centered green perspectives. This does not deny or overlook the influence that animal and other species-oriented perspectives have also had on green movements. We have simply omitted these perspectives because our focus here was on human-initiated harms and consequences, leaving others the task of developing green definitions of crime that affect other species. Thus this article highlighted the role played by power differentials, including gender and racial as well as class-based inequities, in the social construction of green crimes and laws (or lack of laws). In this regard we emphasized the idea that green movements seek to move beyond law to identify harms associated with green crimes.

Last, we examined and contrasted corporate and environmental justice perspectives since each leads to different definitions and implications of the term green. Here we explored shared commitments across green movements. These shared commitments were included to identify points of convergence ripe for unifying green perspectives founded on race, class and gender theorizing. Race, class and gender-based green perspectives take various forms and origins of inequality and power as a point of departure for theorizing and action. This focus is compatible with environmental justice definitions of green but incompatible with corporate definitions of green.

The green movement had its origins in radically situated theories of inequality. Each endeavors to demonstrate that addressing inequality is a useful strategy for defending people and the environment from harm. This view of inequality is opposed by corporate greens who argue that greater corporate freedom will remedy the situation. Consequently, this analysis emphasizes that how one defines the term 'green' has important implications for developing a green criminology. At present, two options appear available. The first is the corporate path with its emphasis on reduced self-regulation, greater corporate control, a reduction in law and a greater reliance on forms of power useful for influencing law and its enforcement. This is by no means new, and the results have been less than successful (take, for example, Texas state policies under George W. Bush). This option, which emphasizes legal definitions, has resulted in less legal protection for those who are the victims of corporate green crimes. Therefore, to escape this dilemma and fulfill the ambitions previously outlined by those who have proposed a green criminology, only one viable option remains: the more radical environmental justice definition of green outlined above.

In selecting one or the other of these options, criminologists clearly make a value judgment, supporting the present problematic attitude toward criminal justice or pointing toward an alternative understanding of green crimes. We believe that a green criminology points toward the logical necessity of taking the latter path: choosing the former eliminates the distinction between a green approach and more widely accepted methods of investigating corporate or even street crime, thereby calling into question the rationale for green criminology itself.

However, more work remains to be done than was possible in the purview of this article toward elaborating more precisely what a green criminology would look like. No doubt some critics will respond that greens are more different than similar; that only violations of criminal law ought to count; that we have left out specific groups; that our view is not 'objective'. But this journal has allowed an important discussion to begin, one that endeavors to redefine how environmental crimes are perceived and understood. In our view, this discussion should be open and public, allowing numerous sides to forward views and to be assessed by a broader audience. Whether or not this debate has a large or small impact on environmental crime research, its importance is undeniable, underlining the need for not only a sociological (as C. Wright Mills put it) but a vibrant and responsible criminological imagination as well.

## Notes

1 *Time* recently suggested that British Petroleum and one of its top executives Sir John Browne are 'unexpectedly green' (Kluger 2001: 36). Browne recently remarked, 'we [British Petroleum] use compliance with the law as a minimum and then go beyond that' (cited in Kluger 2001).

2 The tendency to interpret the goals of environmental movements in a narrow manner can also be seen with respect to environmental justice movements. These movements tend to be mischaracterized as being concerned only with the distribution of environmental hazards across diverse races and classes. That movement, however, is also about social inequality that arises from the production process. Hofrichter states that 'environmental justice is about *social transformation* directed toward meeting human needs and enhancing the quality of life – economic equality, health care, shelter, human rights, species preservation, and democracy – using resources sustainably' (1993: 4, emphasis added).

3   Corporations spend a good deal of effort denying they have caused serious human-environmental injury. As evidence they point to their own studies – or studies funded by associations they support financially – to provide the scientific evidence needed to undermine legal standards of proof of environmentally linked victimization in any *specific* instance (Stauber and Rampton 1995; Fagan and Lavelle 1996; Karliner 1997) – even when large-scale patterns exist, simple defenses are mounted. For instance, the corporation's lawyers argue that executives, though possibly aware of production-associated risks, did not intentionally target specific individuals or groups to harm. Legally, the lack of such intention separates these behaviors from ordinary crimes. Moreover, in many instances the injured parties have placed themselves at risk.

4   A search for several words related to this topic (i.e. green, environment, Superfund, toxic, EPA, environmentalism) returned less than 15 journal articles in the *Criminal Justice Periodical Index* over a 12-year period. In short, even during a period of heightened environmental concern marked by growing scientific evidence of the devastating effects of environmental pollution on humans (e.g. Gibbs 1995; Steingraber 1998), criminologists avoided addressing environmental harms.

## References

Averill, Gage (1996) 'Global Imaging', in R. Ohmann (ed.) *Making and Selling Culture*, pp. 203–23. Hanover, NH: Wesleyan University Press.

Beirne, Piers (1999) 'For a Nonspeciesist Criminology: Animal Abuse as an Object of Study', *Criminology* 37: 117–18.

Beirne, Piers and James Messerschmidt (1995) *Criminology*. San Diego, CA: Harcourt Brace.

Benton, Ted (1998) 'Rights and justice on a Shared Planet: More Rights or New Relations', *Theoretical Criminology*, 2(2): 149–75.

Brownstein, Henry (1999) *The Social Reality of Violence and Violent Crime*. Boston, MA: Little, Brown.

Bullard, Robert (1990) *Dumping on Dixie*. Boulder, CO: Westwood.

Bullard, Robert (1993) 'Anatomy of Environmental Racism and the Environmental Justice Movement', in R. Bullard (ed.) *Confronting Environmental Racism: Voices from the Grassroots*, pp. 15–39. Boston, MA: South End Press.

Bunyan, Bryant (1995) 'Issues and Potential Policies and Solutions for Environmental Justice', in B. Bunyan (ed.) *Environmental Justice: Issues, Policies, and Solutions*. Washington, DC: Island Press.

Cavanaugh, P.T. (2000) *Title VI Guidance Comments (August 24, 2000 Memo to the EPA)*. Washington, DC: The Chevron Companies.

Center for Economic and Social Rights (1994) *Rights Violations in the Ecuadorian Amazon: The Human Consequences of Oil Development*. New York: Center for Economic and Social Rights.

Chambliss, William and Robert Seidman (1982) *Law, Order and Power*. Reading, MA: Addison-Wesley

Chambliss, William and Marjorie Zatz (1994) *Making Law: The State, the Law, and Structural Contradictions*. Bloomington, IN: Indiana University Press.

Commoner, Barry (1987 [1971]) *The Closing Circle: Nature, Man, and Technology*. New York: Alfred A. Knopf.

Daly, Kathleen (1994) *Gender, Crime and Punishment*. New Haven, CT: Yale University Press.

Daly, Mary (1978) *Gyn/Ecology: The Metaethics of Radical Feminism*. Boston, MA: Beacon Press.

Dobson, Andrew (1991) *The Green Reader: Essays toward a Sustainable Society*. San Francisco, CA: Mercury House.

Dobson, Andrew (1992) *Green Political Thought*. London: Routledge.

Engels, Friedrich (1968 [1845]) *The Condition of the Working Class in England*. Trans. W.O.H.a.W.H. Chaloner. Stanford, CA: Stanford University Press.

Environmental Protection Agency (1999) 'Agency Launches New Compliance Incentive Program for Industrial Organic Chemical Sector', *Environmental Protection Agency Audit Policy Update* 4 (Spring): 6.

Epstein, Barbara (1993) 'Ecofeminism and Grass-Roots Environmentalism in the United States', in R. Hofrichter (ed.) Toxic *Struggles: The Theory and Practice of Environmental Justice*, pp. 144–52. Philadelphia, PA: New Society Publishers.

Faber, Daniel (ed.) (1998) *The Struggle for Ecological Democracy: Environmental Justice Movements in the United States*. New York: Guilford Press.

Fagan, Daniel and Marianne Lavelle (1996) Toxic *Deception: How the Chemical Industry Manipulates Science, Bends the Law, and Endangers Your Health*. Secaucus, NJ: Birch Lane.

Faber, Daniel and James O'Connor (1993) 'Capitalism and the Crisis of Environmentalism', in R. Hofrichter (ed.) *Toxic Struggles: The Theory and Practice of Environmental Justice*, pp. 12–23. Philadelphia, PA: New Society Publishers.

Frank, Nancy and Michael J. Lynch (1992) *Corporate Crime, Corporate Violence*. Albany, NY: Harrow & Heston.

Friedrichs, David (1996) *Trusted Criminals*. Belmont, CA: Wadsworth.

Foster, John (1993) 'The Limits of Environmentalism without Class: Lessons from the Ancient Forest Struggle in the Pacific Northwest', *Capitalism, Nature, Socialism* 4: 11–41.

Gibbs, Lois (1995) *Dying from Dioxin: A Citizen's Guide to Reclaiming Our Health and Rebuilding Democracy*. Boston, MA: South End Press.

Gidicks, A. (1993) *The New Resource Wars: Native and Environmental Struggles against Multinational Corporations*. Boston, MA: South End Press.

Greer, Jed and Kenny Bruno (1997) *Greenwash: The Reality behind Corporate Environmentalism*. New York: Apex Press.

Griffin, Susan (1978) *Woman and Nature*. New York: Harper & Row.

Groombridge, Nic (1998) 'Masculinities and Crimes against the Environment', *Theoretical Criminology* 2(2): 249–67.

Groves, W Byron and Michael J. Lynch (1990) Reconciling Structural and Subjective Approaches to the Study of Delinquency. *Journal of Research in Crime and Delinquency* 27(4): 348–75.

Guilder, George (1993) *Wealth and Poverty*. San Francisco, CA: ICS Press.

Higley, Leon C. and Larry Pedigo (eds) (1996) *Economic Thresholds for Integrated Pest Management*. Lincoln, NE: University of Nebraska Press.

Hofrichter, Richard (1993) *Toxic Struggles: The Theory and Practice of Environmental Justice*. Philadelphia, PA: New Society Press.

Karliner, Joshua (1997) *Corporate Planet*. San Francisco, CA: Sierra.

Kluger, Jeffrey (2001) 'A Climate of Despair', *Time 9* April: 30–6.

Lane, Pauline (1998) 'Ecofeminism Meets Criminology', *Theoretical Criminology* 2(2): 235–48.

Lavelle, Marianne and Marcia Coyle (1992) 'Unequal Protection: The Racial Divide in Environmental Law', *National Law Journal* 21 September: S1S11.

Lynch, Michael J. (1990) 'The Greening of Criminology: A Perspective for the 1990s', *The Critical Criminologist* 2: 11–12.

Lynch, Michael J. (1996) 'Class, Race, Gender and Crime', in M.B.S.a.D. Milovanovic (ed.) *Race, Class. Gender and Criminology*. New York: Garland.

Lynch, Michael J. and Lenny Krzycki (1998) 'Popular Culture as an Ideological Mask: Mass Produced Popular Culture, the Remaking of Popular Culture Messages, and Criminal Justice Related Imagery', *Journal of Criminal Justice* 26: 321–36.

Mander, Jerry (1972) 'Ecopornography: One Year and Nearly a Billion Dollars Later, Advertising Owns Ecology', *Communication Arts* 14: 45–56.

Mank, Bradford (1999) 'Title VI', in M. Gerrard (ed.) *The Law of Environmental Justice*, pp. 23–68. Chicago, IL: American Bar Association.

Mellor, Mary (1992) *Breaking the Boundaries: Toward a Feminist, Green, Socialism*. London: Virago.

Mendez, Chico (1989) *Fight for the Forest People*. London: Latin American Bureau.

Merchant, Carolyn (1980) *The Death of Nature: Women, Ecology and the Scientific Revolution: A Feminist Reappraisal of the Scientific Revolution*. New York: Doubleday/Anchor.

Merchant, Carolyn (1996) *Earthcare: Women and the Environment*. London: Routledge.

Messerschmidt, James (1993) *Masculinities and Crime*. Lanham, MD: Bowman & Littlefield.

Messerschmidt. James (1997) *Crime as Structured Action: Gender, Race and Class in the Making*. Thousand Oaks, CA: Sage.

Mies, Maria (1993) 'The Need for a New Vision: The Subsistence Perspective', in M.M.a.V Shiva (ed.) *Ecofeminism*, pp. 297–324. Atlantic Highlands, NJ: Zed Books.

Milovanovic, Dragon (1997) *Postmodern Criminology*. New York: Garland.

Nader, Ralph (1965) *Unsafe at Any Speed*. New York: Grossman.

Newman, Graeme (1990) 'Popular Culture and Criminal Justice: A Preliminary Analysis', *Journal of Criminal Justice* 18: 261–74.

O'Connor, James (1998) *Natural Causes: Essays on Ecological Marxism*. New York: Grossman.

Ohmann, Richard (1996) 'Knowing/Creating Wants', in R. Ohmann (ed.) *Making and Selling Culture*, pp. 224–38. Hanover, NH: Wesleyan University Press.

Plant, Judith (1989) *Healing the Wounds: The Promise of Ecofeminism*. Philadelphia, PA: New Society Press.

Quinney, Richard (1970) *The Social Reality of Crime*. Boston, MA: Little, Brown.

Quinney, Richard (1979) *Criminology*. Boston, MA: Little, Brown.

Rebovich, Donald (1998) 'Environmental Crime Research: Where We Have Been, Where We Should Go', in M. Clifford (ed.) *Environmental Crime: Enforcement, Policy and Social Responsibility*, pp. 341–54. Gaithersburg, MD: Aspen Publishers.

Ryan, William (1981) *Equality*. New York: Vintage Books.

Schwartz, Martin and Dragan Milovanovic (1996) *Race, Gender, and Class in Criminology*. New York: Garland.

Schwendinger, Herman and Julia Schwendinger (1970) 'Defenders of Order or Guardians of Human Rights', *Issues in Criminology* 5: 113–46.

Seager, Joni (1993) 'Creating a Culture of Destruction', in R. Hofrichter (ed.) *Toxic Struggles: The Theory and Practice of Environmental Justice*, pp. 58–66. Philadelphia, PA: New Society Publishers.

Simon, David (1999) *Elite Deviance*. Boston, MA: Allyn & Bacon.

Situ, Yingyi and David Emmons (2000) *Criminal Law and the Environment*. Thousand Oaks, CA: Sage.

South, Nigel (1998) 'A Green Field for Criminology? A Proposal for a Perspective', *Theoretical Criminology* 2(2): 211–33.

Stauber, John and Sheldon Rampton (1995) Toxic *Sludge is Good for You!* Monroe, ME: Common Courage Press.

Steingraber, Sandra (1998) *Living Downstream: A Scientists's Personal Investigation of Cancer and the Environment*. New York: Vintage.

Surette, Ray (1997) *Media, Crime, and Criminal Justice*. Belmont, CA: Wadsworth.

Tavlor, Dorceta (2000) 'The Rise of the Environmental Justice Paradigm', *American Behavioral Scientist* 43: 508–80.

Texaco (1999) *Texaco Inc.'s Memorandum of Law in Support of Its Renewed Motions to Dismiss Based on Forum Non Conveniens and International Comity*. United States District Court Southern District of New York, 93-CIV. 7527 (JRS).

Turner, Thomas (1970) 'Ecopornography or How to Spot an Ecological Phony', in G. De Bell (ed.) *The Environmental Handbook: Prepared for the First National Environmental Teach-in*, pp. 263–8. New York: Ballentine Books.

Wolfe, Alan (1977) *The Limits of Legitimacy: Political Contradictions of Contemporary Capitalism*. New York: Free Press.

Worster, David (1988) 'Doing Environmental History', in D. Worster (ed.) *The End of the Earth*, pp. 1–5. Cambridge: Cambridge University Press.

# 5. Corporate environmental crimes and social inequality: new directions for environmental justice research*

*David R. Simon*

In a 1997 article, Szasz and Meuser note that environmental justice research may have 'excluded' certain questions of import. Among the topics they list as neglected are (a) the place of the upper class in environmental research and (b) the lack of both a global and a historical perspective. This article represents a furtherance of suggestions concerning their proposed agenda. Specifically, the article examines patterns of environmental crime among the largest multinational corporations, both in the United States and around the world, as well as the environmental deviance committed by the federal government. This examination demonstrates that environmental crimes are part of an entire pattern of criminal activity that takes place within a political economy dominated by large corporations and upper-class stockholders. The article closes with suggestions for research into these patterns.

Szasz and Meuser (1997) note that environmental justice research may have 'excluded' certain questions of import (p. 114). Among the topics they list as thus far neglected are (a) the place of the upper class in environmental research and (b) the lack of both a global and a historical perspective. This article represents a furtherance of suggestions concerning their proposed research agenda. First, however, it is necessary to establish a theoretical context in which such research can take place.

Specifically, the place of many upper-class behaviors in environmental concerns involves the commission of environmental and other deviant offenses. As noted below, environmental corporate crimes are but a portion of an entire genre of corporate crime. Ever since Sutherland (1949), numerous criminologists have pointed out a form of differential association among these corporate executives and firms, making certain deviant and illegal practices routine (Simon 1995, p. 35 and following; Simon 1999, pp. 50-90; Simon and Hagan 1999, pp. 20–23, 40–43). As noted below, a number of illegal and deviant acts have become institutionalized practices among certain industries that pollute, dump toxic waste, and make environmental crime victims of various global minorities.

---

* From *American Behavioral Scientist* (2000), 43(4): pp. 633–645.

Thus, it is members of the upper class who are the CEOs and leading stockholders of the nation's largest industrial corporations, those very firms most frequently charged with various corporate violations including environmental harms. Moreover, numerous studies demonstrate that globally (Ridgeway and St. Clair 1998; Simon 1999, pp. 183–188), nationally (Blumberg and Gottleib 1989; Gedicks 1993), and locally (Gedicks 1993; Hurley 1995; Pulido 1996), upper-class business owners have consistently opposed certain environmental regulations, approved of those that benefited them economically, and used others as a form of social control of the lower and working classes (Taylor 1997, 1998).

Moreover, as demonstrated below, environmental crime is part of an entire pattern of criminal behavior in which many of these industrial giants engage with alarming frequency. The patterns of corporate wrongdoing and their relationship to environmental deviance are in need of further research. Thus far, environmental crime anthologies (Clifford 1998; Edwards, Edwards, and Fields 1996) have largely overlooked the social power context in which environmental deviance occurs.

Second, concerning the global context of environmental inequalities, most large American environmental polluters are transnational in scope. Not only do these firms commit environmental offenses within the United States, but many exhibit a disturbing pattern of international environmental wrongdoing. Moreover, anecdotal evidence indicates that these same international corporations commit a wide variety of criminal offenses. Likewise, extant research on environmental inequalities has focused on those offenses against environmental law that affect oppressed minorities within the United States. Such offenses, I will contend, represent a small portion of a much more widespread pattern of global victimization of the poor and peoples of color. Further knowledge of a more inclusive context of corporate criminality holds the promise of providing a much richer picture concerning global corporate criminal activity and its relationship to environmental offenses. Much evidence indicates that environmental law violations are what sociologists term 'socially patterned' (Simon 1995, p. 6). That is, these crimes are not merely random or accidental. They are examples of institutionalized behaviors that take place among a number of organizations in the same industry or agencies of government. As is explored below, these patterned 'green crimes' are, in turn, related to other patterns of corporate criminal violations.

Finally, any further environmental inequality research must include the role of government, both nationally and globally. As will be argued, government is frequently a major environmental polluter and, at times, engages in acts of environmental deviance in consort with major industrial corporations. This state-corporate crime (Simon 1999, pp. 303–328) is frequently well hidden and largely unresearched. Suggestions for further inquiry are made below. I begin with an agenda for domestic corporate crime research.

## Criminogenic corporate patterns, environmental crime, and the missing upper class

Corporate crime rates are not evenly spread across all industries. Some industrial groups are much more corrupt and criminogenic than others. Thus, Clinard (1979) found that 60% of all corporate offenses prosecuted by the Department of Justice between 1974 and 1976 occurred in just three industries: petrochemicals, pharmaceuticals, and automobile manufacturing. All three of these industries contain long-established patterns of criminal activity.

Patterns of deviant behavior in these industrial sectors fit C. Wright Mills's (1956, pp. 343–361; Simon 1999, pp. 50–90) description of 'the higher immorality,' an institutionalized insensitivity to right and wrong. If this depiction is correct, firms in the above-mentioned industries not only engage in the frequent violation of environmental laws; they also (with alarming frequency) regularly violate other white-collar crime laws as well.

General Electric (GE) represents perhaps the quintessential case study of these criminogenic patterns. Currently, GE is named by the Environmental Protection Agency (EPA) as a primarily responsible party (PRP) in more than 80 hazardous waste sites in need of cleanup in the United States (*Congressional Quarterly* 1998, p. 549). More than this, GE has a long-standing criminal record in many other areas dating back decades (Simon 1995, p. 35 and following).

Although the exact extent of petrochemical hazardous waste is difficult to determine, there are suggestive statistics. There are some 1,200 chemical firms operating some 11,500 production facilities. The 50 largest industrial organic chemical firms account for nearly 90% of all shipments, and the 50 largest agricultural chemical firms account for slightly more than 90% of all shipments. The 50 largest inorganic chemical firms account for roughly three fourths of all shipments. One study by Booz Allen concluded 'that these three industrial segments are the major source of petrochemical industry hazardous waste' (Barnett 1994, p. 19).

Three electronics firms, including GE and Westinghouse, were also identified in the EPA's Clean Water Project as PRPs at Superfund sites (hazardous waste sites in need of cleanup). Westinghouse is identified as a PRP at 90 EPA Superfund sites. Ford and General Motors, two automotive firms, are identified as PRPs at 19 and 21 Superfund sites, respectively (Barnett 1994, p. 21). Consistent with the higher immorality, there is evidence that major chemical corporations, including DuPont, Union Carbide, and others, have hired organized criminal syndicates to illegally dispose of hazardous waste in New York, New Jersey, and other locations (*ABC News* 1988; Rebovich 1992, pp. 64–76). In a number of states, mob-connected garbage haulers obtained permits and set themselves up as solid-waste disposers. Landfill owners were then bribed to sign for shipments that were never received, while the actual shipments were dumped illegally in sewers, in waterways, or into the ocean (Albanese and Pursley 1993, pp. 325–326).

The hiring of organized criminal syndicates to perform various services for corporations and the federal government, especially the CIA, has a long and sordid history. The Mafia was hired by naval intelligence during World War II to secure the New York docks from potential threats from Nazi submarines, to plan the invasion of Sicily and Italy, and to run the military government in Italy after the Allied victory. Moreover,

- The CIA has been linked to the furtherance of drug trafficking for the past 50 years, including the French connection heroin route (1950), the Golden Triangle opium production (1950–1970s), and Afghan heroin production and Latin American cocaine traffic (1980s). There is some evidence that the CIA played a role in spreading crack cocaine sales in African American and other minority communities in the 1980s.

- The CIA hired organized crime figures in the 1950s and 1960s to assassinate Fidel Castro.

- Organized crime money and/or electioneering favors were used by the Kennedy campaign in 1960, Nixon in 1968, and Reagan in 1980 to win election to office.

- Organized crime has provided finance capital to major corporations in various business ventures, especially building casinos, prevented unions from forming or helped unions win recognition, and provided arson services to slumlords and banks. Likewise, organized crime syndicates and numerous large banks, investment houses, jewelry exchanges, and check-cashing services have conspired together to launder drug money (Simon 1999. pp. 2–3, 77–80, 292–296).

In short, organized criminal syndicates have proved useful to corporate, labor, and political elites for the past 50 years, sometimes for antienvironmental purposes in the pursuit of profit.

Consistent with Clinard's (1979) findings, the majority of environmental violations by U.S. corporations are found in only a few industries: petrochemicals, petroleum, automobiles, and electrical products. These corporations are members of oligopolistic industries that are heavily concentrated, wherein four or fewer firms control 50% or more of a market. The corporations in these industries have some important common characteristics.

1 Their boards of directors contain upper-class executives from the largest banks and insurance companies. Many of the directors sit on more than one corporate board. They are thus interlocked (Simon 1999, pp. 16–24).

2 They are among the 500 largest industrial firms that sponsor 90% of the nation's network television programs.

3 They are among those corporations that spend the most money (hundreds of millions per election cycle) to lobby Congress and back political candidates.

4 Some are annually among the 100 largest defense contracting firms. A number of them have been involved in waste-disposal scandals at federally owned facilities, sometimes aided and abetted by the federal government.

5  They are among the largest 500 industrial corporations that make 80% of all after-tax profits in manufacturing. Many of the firms involved in environmentally polluting industries also own other firms in other industries. Philip Morris, for example, which owns Marlboro cigarettes, also owns Kraft Foods, Tang, Oscar Meyer, Jell-O, Miller Beer, Post cereals, and Maxwell House coffee. Monsanto, which makes herbicides, insecticides, and fertilizers, also makes pharmaceuticals, NutraSweet, and soap (Ridgeway and St. Clair 1998, pp. 82, 130).

6  They are among the largest 500 corporations that make 90% of all profits involved in U.S. foreign trade (Simon 1999, p. 20 and following).

7  A number of large chemical firms have been guilty of hiring organized criminal syndicates to dispose of toxic waste.

8  The victims of illegal hazardous waste disposal tend to be the most poor and powerless populations in both the United States and around the world.

One reason why corporate crimes of all types flourish within certain industries is that the mainstream press underreports both individual incidents of crime and the seriousness of such violations. In 1994 alone, 6 of the top 10 *Project Censored* stories were ecologically related (Curran 1995), and this pattern has been consistent since Carl Jensen (1993) began the project. Consider just a few of *Project Censored's* 1997 summary of its top 200 stories for the past 20 years:

• In 1976, a story related that 500,000 people annually in the world's poorest nations were poisoned by pesticides. By 1995, the United States had exported 58 million pounds of banned pesticides and prescription drugs to the world's poorer nations.

• Another censored story related that Mobil Oil had for years done business with Zimbabwe, a major human rights violator embargoed and condemned by most of the world's nations. In 1996, Mobil continued to do business with Zimbabwe, and Texaco had illegally done business with Haiti, a major global drug-trafficking and rights-violating nation.

• In the 1970s, baby formulas made by Nestle and Bristol Meyers were advertised by giving free samples to mothers in poor nations and with promises of modernization and increased social status. These formulas caused the deaths of 35,000 Third World infants and numerous cases of brain damage in part because of a lack of facilities to boil the water that was mixed with the formulas. By 1995, despite international boycotts, formula manufactures still advertised their products, which by then had contributed to more than 1 million infant deaths per year in poor nations (Jensen 1997, pp. 37–39, 52–53).

Thus, because companies like GE and Westinghouse also own major media outlets, news stories of GE's criminal violations are consistently given short shrift by mainstream media. The lack of stories is also accompanied by vigorous public relations efforts that function to cover up environmental harms (Ridgeway and St. Clair 1998, pp. 135–152; Stauber and Rampton 1995; see below).

What all this means is that corporate violators of ecological criminal laws are part of an entire political economy, a macro environment over which they exert considerable control. Part of this environment concerns the global political economy in which such transnational corporations operate. Often, corporate violations are international in scope and involve not just violations of hazardous waste laws but corruption statutes as well.

The problem of environmental destruction thus represents one of the most dangerous contradictions of giving priority to the value of accumulating wealth without regard to the means of doing so. Environmental problems also represent the outgrowth of an international system of nations in which corporations have been allowed to set priorities without regard to the welfare of individuals, especially the poorest and most powerless individuals in Third World nations, Third World workers, and poor men, women, and children around the globe.

## Global patterns of environmental victimization

The victimization of non-elites by environmental harms is a global pattern, one that especially strikes people of color. *Environmental racism* is the term used to describe the victimization of people of color by corporate polluters. Various studies have established that minorities in the United States are at considerable risk from such victimization (Bullard 1994, p. 6 and following; Parenti 1995, p. 112; Rosen 1994, p. 225).

Likewise, there are a large number of toxic-waste problems that are exported to foreign countries, many of which have involved the illegal bribery of officials of foreign governments. The advanced nations of the world generate about 400 million tons of toxic waste annually; 60% comes from the United States. A shipment of toxic waste leaves the United States every 5 minutes every day of the year. The vast majority of America's internationally exported toxic waste, 80%, is sent to Canada and Britain (Cass 1994, p. 2). The EPA requires U.S. companies to provide onsite disposal facilities for toxic waste, which cost upward of $30 million and take years to build. However, such waste can be dumped in Third World nations for a fraction of the cost, sometimes for as little as $20 a ton (Cass 1994, p. 7). In 1991, an internal memo written by one of the World Bank's chief economists advocated that the World Bank encourage 'more migration of dirty industries to the Less Developed Countries' (Rosen 1994, p. 226), thus giving credence to those who believe that environmental racism is an intentional policy. European nations also export toxic waste to the world's poorer nations.

At times, multinational corporations have provided handsome financial rewards to the recipient nations. For example, Guinea-Bissau, which has a gross national product of $150 million, will make $150 million to $600 million over a 5-year period in a deal to accept toxic waste from three European nations.

Typically, bribes are paid to Third World government officials to establish toxic waste dumps in their countries. Third World participation in the waste dumping of advanced nations has generated a host of scandals.

- In April 1988, five top government officials in the Congo were indicted after they concluded a deal to import 1 million tons of chemical waste and pesticide residue, receiving $4 million in 'commissions' from a firm specializing in hazardous waste disposal. The total contract was worth $84 million.

- After dumping toxic waste in Nigeria and Lebanon, in 1988, Italy agreed to take back some 6,400 tons. What's more, Nigeria recalled its Italian ambassador and arrested 25 people when it discovered some of the waste was radioactive. To complicate matters, Italian dock workers in 10 port cities have refused to handle the waste. Italy has pledged to ban further toxic exports to the developing world and plans to spend $7 billion a year to clean up its own toxic dumps at home. The Italian government has also sued 22 waste-producing firms to force them to turn over $75 million to pay for transporting and treating incoming waste.

- In 1987, Weber Ltd., a West German waste transporter, found a Turkish cement plant willing to accept 1,500 tons of toxic-waste-laden sawdust for about $70 a ton. Instead of being burned, the sawdust waste sat in the open air for nearly 16 months, slowly leaking poison into the ground. A newspaper reported the sawdust contained lethal PCBs, and a scandal ensued. Under pressure form the governments of Turkey and West Germany, Weber finally agreed to transport the waste back to West Germany. Normally, Weber charges its customers $450 to $510 a ton to dispose of waste in Germany. With Third World costs of $110 per ton or less, the amount of profit involved is substantial.

- In late 1991, three South Carolina metal smelting firms contracted with a waste disposal firm to send waste containing life-threatening levels of cadmium and lead to Bangladesh. Once in that country, the waste was used to make fertilizer used by Bangladeshi farmers (Brooks 1988; Cass 1994; Leonard 1994, p. 9; *Newsweek* 1988).

Closer to home, there are currently about 1,800 maquiladora plants owned by multinational firms along the U.S.-Mexican border. Of 600 plants owned by America's *Fortune* 500 firms, only 91 have thus far complied with Mexican law requiring that waste generated by American corporations be transported to the United States for disposal (Kelly 1993).

On both sides of the U.S.-Mexican border, there have been reports of deformed fish, increased cancer rates, and a doubling of typhoid and infectious hepatitis and other problems, including birth defects (Kelly 1993, pp. 13, 16–17; Wolkomir 1994, pp. 27, 30).

Finally, in 1995, it was learned that Shell Oil's parent firm paid the Nigerian military to use force against environmental protestors and that Shell offered bribes to witnesses at the trials of murdered protestors to testify against environmental activists (Ridgeway and St. Clair 1998, pp. 22–23; Simon 1999, p. 191). Taken collectively, all of this indicates that the global 'waste industry is one of the most corrupt industries in the world' (Jensen 1993, p. 57). Most of its victims include the least powerful people on the face of the earth, poverty-stricken people of color, most of whom are powerless to resist the environmental deviance of multinational firms (Bullard 1994, p. 6 and following). Moreover, many times the federal government has covered up and at other times been a coconspirator in the violation of environmental and other laws.

## The government as polluter

According to Helen Caldicott (1992), 'The U.S. government is the nation's chief polluter' (p. 7). Thanks to large campaign contributions and other forms of political influence, the federal government has all but become an ally of major polluters and their upper-class stockholders. Federal facilities discharge almost 2.5 million tons of toxic and radioactive waste annually without reporting it. The Government Accounting Office estimates that 95% of U.S. government toxic pollution is exempt from the government's own reporting procedures. At Department of Defense weapons plants alone, there are 14,401 potentially contaminated dumpsites.

Various agencies of the U.S. government are named as PRPs at 8% of the Superfund sites, but this estimate is considered very conservative because the federal government is exempt from EPA regulations in more than 90% of cases. It is estimated that 60 million Americans live within 50 miles of one of the military-related nuclear waste storage sites. Almost every U.S. domestic military facility

> works with hazardous materials and generates toxic waste through such activities as the production, cleaning, and use of weapons, explosives and rocket fuels, vehicles, aircraft, and electronic equipment. Substances like PCBs, dioxin, heavy metals, and cyanides are emitted directly into the air, soil, and ground water. (Ridgeway and St. Clair 1998, p. 108)

Likewise, more than half of the 10.5 billion pounds of toxic chemicals released into the air, soil, and water are not covered by EPA regulations (Caldicott 1992, p. 7).

Aside from the government's own abysmal record of polluting the environment, the EPA itself has demonstrated an alarming degree of corruption, misfeasance, and malfeasance. A 1992 Environmental Research Foundation report concludes that the EPA often opposes congressional attempts to pass environmental laws and spends more time trying to figure out how to exempt corporations from its regulations than it does regulating them (Jensen 1993, p. 56).

## 'Regulatory capture'

The EPA faces a daunting task in regulating an industry with a long criminal record. Given its past activities, it was inevitable that the waste industry would corrupt the EPA, and that is exactly what has happened. In 1992, the Environmental Research Foundation issued a report on the EPA's failure to adequately regulate the waste industry. Among the report's findings: (a) The EPA, more frequently than not, opposes congressional attempts to pass tougher environmental regulations; (b) the EPA devotes more of its resources (time and money) to attempting to exempt corporations from its regulations than it does enforcing them; and (c) the agency's efforts at enforcement are frequently so weak that environmental groups must bring it under court-ordered deadline before such efforts are considered for administrative signature. All this, however, is the tip of a dirty iceberg spanning much of the EPA's 25-year history.

- The EPA's most important scandal, 'sewergate' occurred in 1983 when the agency was accused by congressional critics of multiple violations of ethics and law. These violations included having a cozy relationship with regulated firms, including personal assurances of nonenforcement of environmental laws; agreeing to sweetheart deals with firms that allowed polluting industries to avoid full payment of clean-up costs; and manipulation of site clean-up timetables to benefit Republican candidates in congressional districts (Szasz 1986, pp. 205–206). After EPA administrator Ann Gorsuch Burford refused to turn over Superfund files (because they were 'enforcement sensitive'), the Justice Department refused to prosecute her and asked a federal court to uphold its refusal. The federal judge ordered that the matter is resolved, and before a case could be brought, Burford, Rita Laval, and dozens of other EPA officials resigned. Laval stood accused of harassment of a dissident employee, perjury, and conflict of interest. This scandal began a long history of EPA corruption.

- In 1983, Representative James Flora accused the EPA of awarding a clean-up contract to a company that had, 1 month earlier, been charged by EPA with clean-up violations. Attorney James Sanderson, a former consultant to EPA administrator Ann Burford, represented the company, Chem Waste Management Inc. (Rebovich 1992, p. 6).

- In 1988, officials from industry met secretly with officials of the White House Office of Management and Budget (OMB) to discuss pending EPA regulations. The OMB allowed the executives to suggest revisions in the regulations, and the EPA subsequently made the necessary changes in those regulations (Jensen 1993, p. 57).

- In 1994, an EPA employee wrote an internal memo charging that Monsanto had lied to the EPA concerning the toxic effects of Agent Orange by falsifying scientific studies on the carcinogenicity of dioxin. The employee, rather than being praised for exposing a scandal, was harassed by the EPA and was threatened with termination. The EPA quietly closed the case on the issue of Monsanto's falsification of findings (Freeman 1994, p. 5).

Today, there are 20 high-ranking former EPA administrators that have left the agency and become millionaire waste-industry executives, giving rise to charges of a revolving door between the EPA and the hazardous waste management industry. The situation reflects what Harold Barnett (1994, p. 45 and following) terms 'regulatory capture,' meaning that the EPA is now dominated by the very industries it is supposed to be regulating. According to the Environmental Research Foundation, the EPA, like many federal regulatory agencies, is 'more concerned with the interests of the parties [it] is supposed to be regulating than [it] is with the public interest' (Jensen 1993, p. 56).

Environmental polluters and toxic-waste management firms work not infrequently with the federal government in making pollution problems worse. In 1992, David Leroy, head of the Federal Office of the Nuclear Waste Negotiator, offered various Native American tribes at the National Congress of American Indians $100,000 each, 'no strings attached, just to consider' storing hundreds of canisters of highly radioactive waste on their reservations. Likewise, from the 1950s through the 1970s, Gulf Oil, with the aid of the Atomic Energy Commission, recruited young Hopi and Navajo men to work in their uranium mines. These workers were never advised as to any potential health risks, nor were they provided any protective clothing or gear, even though the firms knew of the carcinogenic risks of working with radioactive materials. Many of these workers have now contracted a range of illnesses, including cancer, but few have received any compensation (Ridgeway and St. Clair 1998, p. 105).

This corporate-government alliance is cemented in a myriad of ways, most important perhaps though various forms of legal and illegal graft, collectively known as lobbying and campaign financing. In the 1994-1995 election cycle alone, some 4,016 political action committees (PACs) registered in Washington, D.C., gave more than $391 million to the Republican and Democratic parties. Only $42 million of this came from labor PACs; the rest came from corporate entities. Much of this money came from industries responsible for the nation's environmental problems: agriculture industry PACs, defense industry PACs, and so on (Simon and Hagan 1999, pp. 13–14). From 1987 to 1996, the tobacco industry alone gave more than $30 million to members of Congress and their national party committees (Lewis 1998, p. 108).

Lobbying is the other skid-greasing tool of corporate America and many foreign interests. Some 90 Washington lobbying firms employing about 10,000 people now spend about $1.2 billion per year to influence federal policy. Their main effort is aimed at preserving the $170 billion in corporate welfare (Ridgeway and St. Clair 1998, pp. 136–137). Many of these lobbyists are defeated members of Congress, or former members of the U.S. Trade Representative Office. This is what DiMaggio and Powell (1983) describe as the breeding ground for coercive isomorphism among organizations in the same field (p. 149).

A chief tool used by the environmentally related companies is 'greenwashing,' the use of public relations to transform a corporate polluter into a seemingly ecologically friendly firm. Nearly all firms claim to be dedicated to environmental protection, and there are 42 public relations firms that engage in greenwashing to convince the public that such is the case. Greenwashing begins with contributions to environmental causes (e.g., saving dolphins, planting new trees) and moves to such practices as fashioning a message that indicates a company is environmentally concerned, discrediting and co-opting environmental journalists, and downplaying the degree of environmental destruction taking place. These tactics are accompanied by the writing of environmental legislation by lobbyists. Taken together, campaign contributions and lobbying ensure that corporate firms maintain a political environment friendly to their interests. Given all these realities, it is clearly time for a new research agenda in the field of environmental crime and justice.

## Conclusion: research agenda for ecological crime

The above discussion allows for some important conclusions concerning patterns of environmental crime and the place of those patterns within the structure of the American political economy (Simon 1995, p. 42–54). Further research in this area needs to focus on the interrelationships between environmental/hazardous waste violations and other forms of corporate and political crime. Specifically,

1 What additional violations of corporate crime laws are exhibited by the various chemical and other firms that have been convicted of multiple violations of hazardous waste and other environmental laws?

2 What are the specific relationships between the firms convicted of numerous violations of various environmental laws and the EPA?

3 What influence do powerful petrochemical and other firms frequently convicted of environmental criminal violations have on Congress and on the executive branch of the federal government?

4 What patterns of criminality exist in which government agencies and corporations violate environmental laws in a coconspiratorial fashion?

5 Reportage by the media of environmental racism and other green crimes has been slanted in favor of corporate polluters and governmental agencies (Rosen 1994, p. 224), and frequently these crimes have been dramatically underreported (Curran 1995; Jensen 1993; Rosen 1994, pp. 228–229). Studies are needed to ascertain when and if victims of ecological crimes are viewed in an objective light by the press. In addition, at what point does the mainstream media become concerned enough about environmental crimes to give them major and/or sustained attention?

6 Finally, in the structural sense, what corporate interlocks exist between firms in environmentally related fields and other sectors of American capitalism, especially finance capital sectors (multinational banks and insurance firms)?

Such research would aid in answering key questions concerning the distribution of power within the American political economy, the emerging nature of the higher immorality (including its international patterns), and the degrees of harm caused by various forms of environmental crime.

This article has described a set of institutionalized deviant behaviors among some corporate fields that are environmentally related. It has argued that such firms use a variety of political and media influences to persuade the public that they are actually environmentally concerned. Frequently, the government itself acts as a coconspirator in environmental crimes. In addition, these firms are interlocked with other segments of corporate America in understudied ways. These realities alone indicate that a new research agenda for environmental deviance is needed.

Finally, it is important for criminologists to study patterns of ecological crime as a way of empirically testing major criminological theories. Two dominant theoretical notions regarding organizational offenses are differential association and neo-Mertonian anomie theory (Messner and Rosenfeld 1994). Differential association holds that criminal activity and the methods of committing it are learned as socially approved behaviors. How and why such behaviors are learned within the petrochemical and related industries are important in assessing the role of organizational culture and the organizational environment in causing ecological crime.

Neo-Mertonian anomie theory focuses on the overall macro cultural and institutional structure in which environmental violations take place. Messner and Rosenfeld (1994) have correctly argued that America's social structure involves institutional dominance by business institutions and cultural values that emphasize individualism, achievement, competition, and the fetishism of money. This overarching social structure creates a climate in which ends (especially profit and power) are emphasized over means (lawful business practices). Thus, the values associated with the American Dream result in pressures on both individuals and organizations to achieve material success while neglecting the means of doing so (i.e., engaging in criminal activity). Ecological crime provides something of a laboratory for testing and refining these two theories of organizational criminal behavior. Likewise, the study of the context in which environmental crime takes places promises to enrich the environmental justice movement as well.

## References

*ABC News.* (1988). Sons of Scarface: The new mafia [documentary].

Albanese, J. S., & Pursley, R. D. (1993). *Crime in America: Some existing and emerging issues.* Englewood Cliffs, NJ: Prentice Hall.

Barnett. H. (1994). *Toxic debts and the Superfund dilemma.* Chapel Hill: University of North Carolina Press.

Blumberg, L., & Gottlieb, R. (1989). *War on waste: Can America win its battle with the garbage.* Covelo, CO: Island Press.

Brooks, J. (1988, July 17). Waste dumpers turning to West Africa. *New York Times,* p. 1.

Bullard, R. D. (Ed.). (1994). *Unequal protection: Environmental justice and communities of color.* San Francisco: Sierra Club Books.

Caldicolt, H. (1992). *If you love this planet: A plan to heal the Earth.* New York: Norton.

Cass, V. (1994, November). *The international toxic waste trade: Who gets left holding the toxic trash bag?* Paper presented at the 1994 meeting of the American Society of Criminology.

Clifford, M. (Ed.). (1998). *Environmental crime.* Baltimore. MD: Aspen.

Clinard, M. B. (1979). *Corporate crime*. Washington, DC: Government Printing Office. *Congressional Quarterly*. (1998, 19 June), p. 549.

Curran, R. (1995, March 29–April 4). Too hot to handle. *Sun Francisco Bay Guardian*, pp. 15–17.

DiMaggio, P., & Powell, W. (1983). The iron cage revisited: Institutional isomorphisrn and collective rationality in organizational fields. *American Sociological Review*, 48, 147–160.

Edwards, S., Edwards, T. & Fields. C. (Eds.). (1996). *Environmental crime and criminality*. New York: Garland.

Freeman, A. (1994, July/August). Bad chemistry at EPA. *Multinational Monitor*, p. 5.

Gedicks, A. (1993). *The new resource wars: Native environmental struggles against multinational corporations*. Boston: South End.

Hurley, A. (1995). *Environmental inequalities: Class, race, and industrial pollution in Gary. Indiana, 1845–1980*. Chapel Hill: University of North Carolina Press.

Jensen, C. (1993). *Censored: The news that didn't make it – and why*. Chapel Hill, NC: Shelburne.

Jensen, C. (and the *Project Censored* Staff). (1997). *Twenty years of* Project Censored. New York: Seven Stones.

Kelly, M. (1993, October). Free trade and the politics of toxic waste. *Multinational Monitor*. pp. 13–20.

Leonard, A. (1994, September). Dumping Pepsi's toxic waste. *Multinational Monitor*, pp. 7–10.

Lewis, C. (1998). *The buying of Congress*. New York: Avon.

Messner, S., & Rosenfeld, R. (1994). *Crime and the American dream*. Monterey, CA: Brooks/Cole.

Mills, C. W. (1956). *The power elite*. New York: Oxford University Press.

*Newsweek*. (1988, November 7), p. 68.

Parenti, M. (1995). *Democracy for the few* (6th ed.). New York: St. Martin's.

Pulido, L. (1996). *Environmentalism and economic justice: Two Chicano struggles in the Southwest*. Tucson: University of Arizona Press.

Rebovich, D. J. (1992). *Dangerous ground: The world of hazardous waste crime*. New Brunswick, NJ: Transaction.

Ridgeway, J., & St. Clair, J. (1998). *A pocket guide to environmental bad guys*. New York: Thunder's Mouth.

Rosen, R. (1994, Spring). Who gets polluted: The movement for environmental justice. *Dissent*, pp. 223–230.

Simon, D. R. (1995). *Social problems and the sociological imagination*. New York: McGraw-Hill.

Simon, D. R. (1999). *Elite deviance* (6th ed.). Needham Heights, MA: Allyn & Bacon.

Simon, D. R., & Hagan, F. (1999). *White-collar deviance*. Needham Heights, MA: Allyn & Bacon.

Stauber, J. C., & Rampton, S. (1995). *Toxic sludge is good for you*. Monroe, ME: Common Courage.

Sutherland, E. H. (1949). *White-collar crime*. New York: Holt, Rinehart & Winston.

Szasz, A. (1986). The process and significance of political scandals: A comparison of Watergate and the 'sewergate' episode at the Environmental Protection Agency. *Social Problems*, 33, 200–217.

Szasz, A., & Meuser, M. (1997). Environmental inequalities: Literature review and proposals for new direction in research and theory. *Current Sociology*, 45, 99–120.

Taylor, D. E. (1997). American environmentalism: The role of race, class and gender in shaping activism, 1820–1995. *Race, Gender and Class*, 5(1), 16–62.

Taylor, D. E. (1998). The urban environment: The intersection of White middle class and White working class environmentalism, 1820–1950s. *Advances in Human Ecology*, 7, 207–292.

Wolkomir, R. (1994, May). Hot on the trail of toxic dumpers and other eco-outlaws, Texas style. *Smithsonian*, pp. 26–37.

# 6. Logging and legality: environmental crime, civil society, and the state*

*Penny Green, Tony Ward and Kirsten McConnachie[1]*

This article considers how criminologists can best analyze the crime and harm involved in the destruction of forests around the world. Although 'illegal logging' as conventionally defined is undoubtedly a major form of transnational organized crime, the boundary between 'legal' and 'illegal' logging is ambiguous and conceptually unsatisfactory. We illustrate this point with a number of examples, focusing in particular on the highly destructive but generally lawful practices of the timber industry in Tasmania. Drawing on recent work on state crime, we argue for a definition of crime as behavior that is both deviant, in the sense that it is subject to, and significantly affected by, social processes of censure and sanction, and 'criminal' in the sense that it violates normative standards that we as criminologists endorse. We argue that in some situations (such as the Tasmanian case) the role of civil society in defining, censuring, and sanctioning deviant behavior is more significant than that of the state; however, the role of civil society in defining and censuring 'illegal logging' must itself be subject to critical scrutiny.

## Illegal logging as a major transnational crime

A significant part of the timber trade involves a world market in what are effectively illegal and stolen goods, worth up to $15 billion a year, for which the E.U. (including the U.K.), the U.S. and Japan are the main markets (House of Commons Environmental Audit Committee 2006: 10).

The evasion of laws and regulations designed to protect the natural environment – 'environmental crime' – is nothing new. Illegal trade in endangered species, illegal, unregulated, and unreported fishing and whaling, illegal dumping of hazardous waste, much of the aquaculture industry in Latin America, and the smuggling of ozone-depleting substances flourish around the globe. Illegal logging and the illegal trade in timber and timber products are almost certainly

* From *Social Justice* (2007), 34(2): pp. 94–110.

the most economically significant international environmental crime. As an illegal trade, precise quantification remains illusive, but a U.N. report (UNECE and FAO 2005: 13–15), citing a study commissioned by the U.S. paper industry, estimates that eight to 10% of global production and a similar proportion of trade is illegal, with the total value of 'suspicious' timber products at up to $23 billion per annum.[2] The World Bank has estimated that in the tropical forests alone, 5,000 square kilometers of forests – an area the size of the island of Bali – were being illegally logged each year during the early 1990s (Canister 1999). Figures from a range of NGOs and environmental research institutes suggest that over 50% of all logging in certain vulnerable regions is illegal. A World Bank-commissioned study (Contrems-Hermosilla 2001) reported that 80% of logging in Brazil was illegal in the late 1990s, as was 80 to 90% of forest clearance in Bolivia and 94% of logging in Cambodia (there is now a ban on all log exports, ITTO 2005: 45). The Indonesian government:

> estimates that approximately 2.8 million ha [one hectare (ha) equals 2.47 acres] of forests are being cut down and the resulting logs and forest products smuggled each year. It also predicts that at such a rate the country would lose all of its forests in the next 20 years (ITTO 2005: 45).

In Russia, levels of illegal logging are believed to vary widely between regions, with suggestions that as much as 70% in the far east and 100% in the Caucasus is illegal (Ottisch et al. 2005). The International Tropical Timber Organisation (ITTO 2004) estimates the trade in stolen timber between East and Southeast Asian countries is worth U.S.$2.5 billion annually.[3] China is now the world's largest consumer of illegal timber, with Indonesia the largest tropical supplier (Telepak and EIA 2005).

The consequences can be devastating: illegal and unsustainable legal logging contributes to deforestation (directly and by opening forests up to other destructive activities), destroying the world's greatest reservoirs of biodiversity, threatening species such as the great apes in equatorial Africa and orangutans in Borneo, and hastening climate change (Barraclough and Ghimire 1995; Dudley et al. 1995). It is directly implicated in 'natural' disasters such as landslides (e.g., the recent devastating landslides in the Philippines) and flooding. Recent floods and landslides in Indonesia and Thailand (Independent, May 28, 2006) have been widely blamed on illegal logging. Producer countries lose legitimate tax revenue, estimated by the World Bank (2002: 14) to be $15 billion annually. These practices also fuel and fund civil wars.[4]

## Problematizing illegality

The exploitation of forests is subject to a wide variety of laws: customary laws; international laws relating to trade, human rights, the environment (notably CITES, the Convention on the International Trade in Endangered Species); national and local laws relating to land tenure, human rights, exports, conservation, wildlife and forestry; and the terms of licenses or concessions for the logging of specific areas. There are, however, serious problems in accepting 'legality' as a criterion of criminality, or as a basis for measures to curb the damaging aspects of the timber trade.

Most tropical forests are owned by states, and logging is legal when it conforms to the terms of concessions granted to logging companies; but these legally defined property rights are based on the expropriation of land from its indigenous inhabitants (Ginting 2005; Colchester 2006). As Nancy Lee Peluso (1991: 11) writes with reference to Indonesia:

> The law defines and determines the boundaries of criminality, but customary laws, practices, and beliefs, or unfavorable material conditions often confound the enforcement of contradictory state laws. Under such circumstances, the enforcement of the state's law becomes a crime in the eyes of the people, an impingement either on ... their 'moral economy' ... or simply on the perceptions people have of what is right ...

Not only is the legitimacy of state law often contested, but contradictory laws may also exist within the same state. For example, the regulation of forestry in Indonesia was decentralized after the fall of Suharto, and now involves a complex combination of national laws, regulations, and licenses issued by local authorities, and legally recognized customary land rights that entitle peasant communities to royalties on timber felled (Smith *et al.* 2003).

Further ambiguities arise from forest laws, some of which are 'poorly written and confusing' (Brack *et al.* 2002: 15), while others are 'difficult to obtain [and] difficult to analyse' (quoted in *Ibid.*: 55). Ambiguous legislation makes the identification and quantification of illegal activities particularly difficult.

Lack of effective enforcement also compounds ambiguity. In Papua New Guinea (PNG), for example, most logging is licensed, and thus claimed by the government and industry advocates to be legal (ITS Global 2006). However, a recent report found that virtually all PNG logging was unlawful, primarily because companies fail to obtain 'informed consent' from the indigenous owners of forests or to ensure a sustainable timber yield. As the major Indonesian environmental NGO WALHI (Friends of the Earth Indonesia) argues:

> illegal logging is connected to, and dependent upon, 'legal logging.' This is so because of the misuse of the permits which are issued by government officers, bribed police and military officers, usually with support of economically and politically powerful interests. A technical focus on 'illegal logging' fails to target the real criminals, those behind the operations. Instead it risks targeting poor people who have no financial alternative, and are often forced to participate in the logging operations (WALHI 2003).

Smith *et al.*'s (2003) research in Kalimantan (Indonesian Borneo) confirmed this relationship. Local officials authorized timber companies to fell far higher volumes of timber than could realistically be extracted from authorized areas, providing a cover for timber felled outside those areas. Moreover, legal logging provides the industrial facilities that illegal logging needs, and provides a means of 'laundering' illegal timber (Ginting 2005).

Finally, even unambiguous legality is no guarantee of sustainability. A recent report from an alliance of Dutch NGOs (Milieudefensie *et al.* 2006) provides many examples from around the world (including Tasmania, discussed below). In Russia, some logging permits positively *require* companies to carry out ecologically destructive logging – requirements that, ironically, are often flouted because compliance would be unprofitable (*Ibid.: 28–29*).

The international regulation of the timber trade – such as it is – predictably focuses on legality rather than sustainability. The E.U. Commission justifies this aspect of its FLEGT (Forest Law Enforcement, Governance, and Trade) scheme on the grounds that:

> an immediate requirement for sustainability has proven not only difficult to define, but beyond the abilities of many forest owners and managers to meet. Legal compliance, which forms an essential component of many sustainable forestry definitions, should be a more achievable target ... (E.U. Commission 2004: 1).

Though true enough, this ignores the almost equally ambiguous nature of legality (Savcor Indufor Oy 2004). Under the FLEGT program (Council Reg. 2173/2005), imports of timber from countries that have entered into 'partnership agreements' with the E.U. (no such agreements have yet been signed) are subject to licensing and independent third-party verification. The scheme is open to evasion by imports via third countries (for example, China, whose voluminous plywood exports to the E.U. commonly use illegally sourced veneers) (Stark and Sze 2006).

## State crime theory and environmental harm

The problems surrounding the concept of legality in the context of logging resonate with those encountered in the study of state crime. Since most serious crime (torture, war crimes, genocide, and corruption) is carried out – like much illegal or destructive logging – by or with the complicity of states, how can we use the criminals' own definition of 'crime'? In a seminal article, Herman and Julia Schwendinger (1975) argued that criminologists should study not state-defined crimes, but violations of human rights, and based their definition on the underlying justification of human rights (i.e., to secure for all human beings the fulfillment of certain basic needs), rather than the legal definitions articulated in various international instruments.

An enquiry into why millions of human beings are denied even the most basic rights to security and subsistence (Shue 1996), though obviously important, takes us into realms that have little relation to conventional criminological subject matter. In an earlier contribution to this journal (Green and Ward 2000), we proposed that state crimes, for criminological purposes, should be defined as actions by state agencies that not only violate human rights, but also violate norms with which the agency in question was under significant pressure to conform. These pressures need not take the form of institutional law enforcement, but could come from domestic civil society, international organizations, other states, or, in many cases, from transnational networks involving all these elements (Risse *et al.* 1999). State crime, in other words, is *organizational deviance* by state agencies that involves the violation of human rights.

If we extend this definition to environmentally harmful activities such as unsustainable logging, we can readily see, as our case study of Tasmania will illustrate, that some strictly *legal* forms of logging nevertheless violate norms to which there is significant pressure to conform, particularly from domestic and transnational civil society. The legality of such activities, far from rendering them innocent, can be seen as an indication of state collusion, thus bringing the activities of logging companies within the concept of 'state-corporate crime' (Kramer 1992). In this context, more problematic is the use of 'human rights' as the normative element of a definition of 'crime.' In many instances, unsustainable logging entails catastrophic consequences for human rights, as when lives and livelihoods are swept away by landslides. A concern for human rights, however, does not capture why many Tasmanians (including one of the present authors) feel such outrage at the destruction of the island's forests. That outrage seems, rather, to reflect a sense that the forests have intrinsic value, not reducible to their utility for human beings.

When we say that forests have intrinsic value, we do not mean that such value resides, in some mysterious way, within the ecosystem independently of human perception. Rather, we mean that the perception of human beings of their environment is inherently value-laden. Certain perceptions of the environment constitute, in themselves, reasons to value aspects of that environment and to seek preservation of them.[5] Clearly, not everyone perceives or values the natural environment in the same way. According to Halsey (2004: 839), for example,

> forest administrators generally perceive a newly felled coupe as a thing of great beauty, since it represents the opportunity for 'new' forest structures to emerge (where each stand of trees will be incessantly managed to maintain the same height, age, and density).

The administrator's perception, shaped by a particular economic practice, gives salience and value to the land cleared for planting rather than the destruction of old trees that dismays the environmentalist or tourist.

As Halsey (2004) argues, these differences in the ways in which forests are perceived (or, as Halsey prefers, discursively constructed) raise important issues about the ethical foundations of 'green' criminology. We plan to discuss those issues in a future paper. Here it is sufficient to say that while we do not align ourselves with any particular strand of 'green' politics, it is our perception of the intrinsic value of old-growth forests, as well as concern for the human consequences of their destruction, that leads us to perceive the destruction of such forests as a harmful act potentially worthy of criminological investigation. What makes it a crime, however, is not merely that perception, but that in many instances it is subject to socially significant processes of censure and sanction. The focus of this article is on those processes, and particularly the role of civil society, or more specifically, of national and transnational nongovernmental organizations (NGOs).

## Civil society

Broadly speaking, we can categorize four primary operational roles that civil society organizations adopt or undertake: norm-setting, transmitting information, social action, and policing and enforcing norms. We shall focus briefly on policing and enforcing here, first by providing examples of the type of work civil society organizations have done to police and enforce norms in relation to illegal logging.

At the most passive end of the spectrum, some organizations merely restate existing norms, relying on other actors – usually a state – to actually do the enforcement. For example, it is comparatively common for concordats or agreements to be adopted that outline the commitment of parties to fighting illegal logging, but fail to impose or outline concrete mechanisms for doing so, and certainly offer no avenue for enforcement. 'Memorandums of agreement' have been adopted recently between NGOs and national governments in Cameroon (World Resources Institute 2005; *Post* 2005) and in Indonesia.

A more active form of engagement sees civil society taking action within existing policing and enforcement structures. For example, one of the largest environmental NGOs in Indonesia, WALHI, has pursued a number of legal actions to ensure enforcement of environmental norms, and also has successfully pursued an amendment to the Indonesian Constitution to recognize the right to a healthy environment as a basic human right.[6] This constitutional amendment supplements national legislation that also claims a healthy environment as a right and authorizes NGOs as having sufficient standing to bring suit in protection of this right.[7]

A more proactive approach to policing and enforcement of the timber industry is exemplified in the work of the Environmental Investigation Agency (EIA). The EIA describes itself as 'committed to investigating and exposing environmental crimes' (www.ela-international.org) and works almost entirely outside conventional structures. The EIA has employed hidden cameras and surveillance techniques to access the information it releases through national or international media channels to pressure political actors to effect change. A 'success story' on the organization's website details the undercover techniques that elicited the evidence for a report identifying key 'timber barons' in Indonesia.[8]

These methods are often very effective. For example, in 2002, the Malaysian Industry Minster stated publicly that the government was 'forced to take action' to restrict timber imports by accusations by environmental watchdogs that Malaysia was operating as a laundering center (Agence France Presse 2003). Such successes have created an increasingly prominent space for academic analysis to explore civil society roles and activities.

Without detracting from the achievements and potential of the non-state sector, we would suggest that the prevailing perception of civil society as a positive transformative force is founded on a set of assumptions that require critical interrogation. For example, the work of EIA, just described, raises some serious questions about the legitimacy and authority of surveillance by unelected and unaccountable private actors. Even a cursory exploration of NGO materials and publicity reveals that most organizations seek to effect change through existing political and legal structures. NGO engagement with governments can produce extremely ambiguous relationships. EIA/Telepak, for example, seems to have benefited to some extent from the conflict between central and local government in Indonesia. According to Brown and Luttrell (2004: 10), they have good relations with the central government's Ministry of Forests, which finds them a useful source of information about what is going on at the local level.

Tensions between different aspects of the NGOs' work are most evident when they are contracted by governments and aid donors to act as 'Independent Forest Monitors.' A U.K.-based NGO, Global Witness (GW), formerly played this role in Cambodia and Cameroon, being partly funded in both cases by the U.K.'s Department for International Development (DFID). The donor states and institutions clearly hoped to channel the campaigning energies of GW into assisting the regulation of timber companies and into disciplining the state agencies that were supposedly regulating them (Assembe Mvondo 2004; Brown and Luttrell 2004). The result in both cases was a very tense relationship between the monitors, the government, and the industry. After a period of 'very profound conflict and hostility,' the Cambodian government terminated GW's contract in 2003, subsequently appointing a private-sector firm, SGS, as an independent monitor (Brown and Luttrell 2004: 8). In Cameroon, GW was replaced by another NGO (REM, Resources Extraction Monitoring) after it decided not to bid for a further contract in view of the revised terms of reference laid down by the government (Global Witness 2005). A report prepared for DFID (Brown and Luttrell 2004) discerned a tension between GW's advocacy and monitoring roles, concluding that the negative tone of GW's reports did not encourage 'progressive' approaches to logging. Whatever the merits of these criticisms, they indicate the likely pressures donors will place on NGOs undertaking similar work in the future. The report also points out that the leverage GW possessed was largely dependent on conditionalities imposed as part of Structural Adjustment Programs and that such coercive pressures from donors are not favored under current poverty-reduction strategies (*Ibid.*: 30).

## State organizational goals

Illegal or unsustainable logging can be seen as a form of state-corporate crime to the extent that it arises 'from a mutually reinforcing interaction' between state agencies and corporations, each of which is pursuing its organizational goals (Kramer and Michalowski 2000: 28). As Ascher (1999) shows in a series of case studies of developing countries, the contribution of deforestation to state organizational goals is complex and varied. Policies of reckless deforestation (and other forms of natural resource wastage) serve a variety of state goals, including raising revenue, the distribution of patronage and subsidies in exchange for political support, and financing industrial development. Ascher (*Ibid.*: 257) identifies three important clusters of political motives in most of his case studies: competition between different state agencies to control natural resources and spending; 'the creation of rent-seeking opportunities that permit government officials to gain political support and policy cooperation of key actors outside of government'; and the evasion of accountability through circuitous financial maneuvers beyond the ken of the general population.

We would argue that an analysis of deforestation as an outcome of state crime can be applied to the developing countries studied by Ascher and to advanced democracies. To illustrate this, we now turn to a case study of the Australian state of Tasmania.

## Logging in Tasmania

For over 30 years, Tasmania has pursued a policy of eradication in respect of its greatest natural resource: the exotic old-growth forests of eucalyptus, myrtle, sassafras, leatherwood, and celery-top pine. The destruction of these unique rainforests through clear-felling and napalm – first removing all saleable timber, and then destroying the remainder to make way for short-rotation tree crops – in the interest of corporate profit has been carried out with the enthusiastic complicity of successive Tasmanian governments, both Labor and Liberal (the current Labor Premier of Tasmania, Paul Lennon, is a member of the industry-funded Forest Protection Society). The billion-dollar forestry industry manages one-third of Tasmania's landmass, but employs fewer than 8,000 people.

The corporate wealth of logging giant Gunns Ltd. (which controls over 85% of the state's logging, is the world's largest hardwood woodchip exporter, and is worth over one billion dollars) has not trickled down into the state's economy. Tasmania remains the poorest of Australia's eight states and territories. The rise of Tasmania's forestry industry has been called a 'dark tale of corporate greed and government connivance' (Flanagan 2004). Two current directors of Gunns were involved in a 1989 scandal in which another director attempted to bribe a Labor Member of Parliament (MP) to cross the floor to avert a Labor-Green Senate majority. When the Liberals regained power in 1991, they introduced punitive laws that criminalized environmental protests. Extraordinarily, these were later repealed because they were said to infringe on National Competition Policy by unfairly advantaging Tasmania's forest industries (Pritchett 2001). Gunns is also the Tasmanian Labor Party's biggest financial donor.

Over 90% of Tasmanian hardwood timber is turned into woodchips each year – that is, five million tons of Tasmanian native forest – and then sold to paper mills in Japan, South Korea, and China. The Wilderness Society (an important Tasmanian NGO) has estimated that this figure represents over 70% of Australia's total woodchip exports (Wilderness Society 2001). Between 1996 and 2000, the forestry industry replaced 62,831 ha of native forest with plantations and farmland (86% on plantations). In the year up to June 2005, Tasmania's native forest estate was reduced by 8,000 ha (representing a 3.1%

loss of native forest area since 1996) (FPB 2005). This amounts to one of the highest rates of land clearing in the developed world (Milieudefensie *et al.* 2006: 10).

### Regulation or regulatory capture

The logging industry in Tasmania is almost wholly self-regulated. According to the Forest Practices Authority (formerly Forest Practices Board),

> The Tasmanian forest practices system is based on a co-regulatory approach, involving responsible self-management by the industry, with independent monitoring and enforcement by the FPA. Self-management is delivered by Forest Practices Officers (FPOs), who are employed within the industry to plan, supervise, and monitor forest practices (Forest Practices Authority 2006).

Of 152 FPOs, only two work for the FPA; the other 150 FPOs are employed by either Gunns or Forestry Tasmania – the very industry they are employed to police. As for the 'independent' FPA, in 2005 its five-member board included the director of Private Forests Tasmania, the director of Forestry Tasmania,[9] and a local mayor (a former forester and investor in the forest industry) whose brother sits on the tribunal hearing complaints about forestry practice and whose son-in-law was a former employee of Gunns.

Anyone wishing to log in Tasmania has to complete a Forest Practices Plan, but under self-regulation an employee of a timber company is able to draw up the plan, certify it, and then be responsible for ensuring that their logging complies with the rules of the Forest Practices Code. Of 149 reports of alleged forest law breaches in 2004–2005 (an average of less than one notice per FPO per year), there were no prosecutions and only 22 fines (totaling a mere $75,750) (FPB 2005). Tasmanian forester Bill Manning, testifying before a Senate committee in 2003, described the culture of the industry as one of 'bullying, cronyism, secrecy and lies' and suggested an industry in 'regulatory freefall' (Senate 2003: 501). Manning was the only FPO, apart from the Chief FPO employed by the FPB between 1990 and 1999. He issued 100 tickets for breaches of the Forest Practices Code; none resulted in prosecution. Forestry Tasmania was exempt from prosecution for the first 10 years of the Forest Practices Act (i.e., until 1995).

> I have witnessed the most appalling deterioration in management of Tasmania's forests, especially state-owned forests. This has been driven by the forest industry's professional foresters through their total dominance of representation on the Forest Practices Board and the Forest Practices Advisory Council. This domination of the regulatory bodies has led to the Forest Practices Board being simply a rubber stamp to be used by industry and government and for it to be doubly abused as the mouthpiece for defending the most appalling forest practices (Senate 2003: 501).

Manning faced a campaign of intimidation and harassment by the regulatory authority;[10] in fact, his authority to issue notices was removed immediately following his first notice against Forestry Tasmania.

## State organizational deviance

In pursuit of its organizational goals of protecting the profit-making and employment capacity of the forestry industry and the financial support that Gunns provides to Tasmania's Australian Labor Party, the Tasmanian government has not only sanctioned the regulatory capture of the Forest Practices Board/Authority and squandered Tasmania's greatest natural resource, but is has also fostered a set of explicitly deviant practices that (when labeled by civil society) have resulted in concealment, denial, and redefinitions. Evidence of state organizational deviance includes the following:

- The industry's aggressive methods of clear-felling and logging of old growth and rain forests, though consistently supported by Tasmania's Labor government, is opposed by a majority of the public.[11]

- Tasmania violates standards accepted by other Australian states. No other state permits industry to rely almost entirely on logging native forest (old growth, re-growth, and rainforest).[12]

- Tasmania is the only state in Australia that offered its corporatized forestry department – Forestry Tasmania – exemption from a raft of regulations and laws. These include: the Freedom of Information Act (lifted in 2006), the Threatened Species Act, the Environmental Protection and Biodiversity Conservation Act, and Tasmania's own Resource Management and Planning System.

- Business confidentiality demands made by Gunns have resulted in the suppression (from 2001) of figures relating to the volume of wood chipped. The last figures published by the Australian Bureau of Statistics in 2000 revealed the highest volume of wood ever chipped in Tasmania (almost 5.5 million tons) (Macken and Chenowith 2001).

- The Tasmanian government has sanctioned killing of endangered and protected species such as the wombat and ring-tailed possum (Flanagan 2004).

- A systematic practice within the forest industry is the failure to map forest types that are rare and endangered because it complicates decision-making in the forest practices system. In 2003, this led to the 'accidental destruction' of Australia's largest tree (Wilderness Society 2003).

- The government and industry ignore scientific advice, e.g., by drastically reducing the streamside reserves recognized by their own forest practice code (Finlayson 2002).

- Between 1985 and 1995, Forestry Tasmania was able to breach the FPA with impunity in the knowledge that it was exempt from prosecution.

## Civil society policing the Tasmanian forest industry

In this regulatory vacuum, civil society (the Wilderness Society, Greenpeace, etc.) has mounted vigorous campaigns to publicize environmental destruction, to regulate the industry, and to preserve Tasmania's environmental heritage. The power of NGOs has been particularly visible in Tasmania, where mass campaigns, public protest,[13] rallies, and other actions have transformed an ostensibly local issue into a national and international one. A notable success has been the ability to influence international markets. In June 2005, after a sustained mass e-mailing campaign, Mitsubishi Paper Mills – a huge Japanese corporation – informed Greenpeace of its intention to purchase only woodchips sourced from 'second growth forests of environmentally benign and reclaimed wood.' The Nippon Paper Group (2005) soon followed suit, calling for public comment to assist in formulating their philosophy and policy on raw materials procurement.

### Gunns versus civil society

In December 2004, Gunns Ltd. sued The Wilderness Society, five of its staff, and 14 other conservation groups and individuals, including two Green MPs. The writ alleged that the defendants had unlawfully conspired to interfere with Gunns' business and claimed A$6.3 million in damages. These supposedly unlawful activities included media statements, the lobbying of shareholders, customers, and governments, and protest actions. After two versions of the statement of claim were struck out, a third version was lodged in August 2005, in which the damages claimed rose to $6.9 million (Ogle 2005: 7; White 2005: 6). This, too, has now been struck out (*The Age*, August 28, 2006). It remains to be seen whether Gunns will make a fourth attempt to sue.

While the chilling effect of this 'SLAPP' (Strategic Litigation Against Public Participation)[14] on free speech is worrying, it is something of a backhanded compliment to the NGOs that the amount claimed by Gunns is more than 90 times the annual fines for unlawful forest practices leveled by FPA. In other words, even assuming that Gunns' claim may be considerably inflated, the informal sanctions imposed by civil society are vastly more significant than any formal sanctions imposed by the state.

Logging in Tasmania thus presents an excellent example of contested definitions of deviance. From the perspective of Gunns, and its allies in Tasmanian civil society, such as the Forest Protection Society and Timber Communities Australia, the deviants are the Wilderness Society and other campaigners, whose activities the Federal Minister of Forestry has labeled 'akin to treason' (Clark 2005). From the perspective of the environmentalists, Gunns and the Tasmanian government are violating widely accepted environmental norms. In situations like this, what counts as 'crime' depends upon the standpoint that criminologists choose to adopt (Cain 1990). We make no apology for adopting an environmentalist standpoint.

## Conclusion

Illegal logging presents a range of important, theoretical, epistemological, and methodological questions for criminology, particularly for those interested in state and state-corporate crime. There can be little doubt that NGOs have made significant gains in the 'fight against forest crime.' Tasmania clearly challenges Gorm Rye Olsen's (1995) thesis that 'environmental NGOs have outplayed their role as pressure groups in relation to the states of the rich countries.'

Yet successes, particularly in countries such as Indonesia and Malaysia, generally take the form of promoting stricter enforcement of existing rules, or in modest reforms to existing legal structures (e.g., upgrading of big-leafed mahogany and ramin under the Convention on International Trade in Endangered Species of Wild Fauna, and the Flora and Forest Law Enforcement, Governance and Trade proposals). What they have yet to do is to articulate a clear set of alternative norms of sustainability and environmental justice (see Lynch and Stretesky 2003; White 2003). Labeling illegal loggers as 'criminals' and shaming governments into doing something about it essentially depends on accepting existing definitions, even while recognizing their inadequacy (in terms of wider questions related to sustainability and environmental protection). Some of the most recent NGO literature (Ginting 2005; Colchester 2006; Milieudefensie *et al.* 2006) shows a clear awareness of the need to move beyond legal definitions. The boundary between deviant and legitimate forest practices remains ill defined and contested, but that only adds to its criminological interest.

## Notes

1   We would like to thank Arturo Laurent for his excellent research assistance, and the Royal Institute of International Affairs for their invaluable website (www.illegal-logging.info) through which many of the documents cited here can be obtained.
2   This is 'an upper-bound estimate,' arrived at by using trade values for products that are mostly consumed in their countries of origin where prices are lower (Seneca Creek Associates and Wood Resources International 2004: 21).
3   Subsequently, however, ITTO (2005: vii) reported rising prices for Asian timber due to a 'crackdown' on illegal logging.
4   See Ellis (1999) on Liberia, Global Witness (2002) on Sierra Leone, Global Witness (2003) on activities of the Burmese regime, and Global Witness (2005) on activities of the Khmer Rouge near the Thai border.
5   This interdependence of perception and value is a key theme in the philosophy of John McDowell (1998). We are indebted to Kathleen Lennon for her exegesis of McDowell's work (Lennon 2007).
6.   See www.eng.walhi.or.id/ttgkami/prof_walhi_eng/#Achievements (accessed July 8, 2006): Indonesian Constitution Article 28(H): 'Every person shall have the right ... to enjoy a good and healthy environment': unofficial translation at www.us-asean.org/Indonesia/constitution.htm (accessed July 8, 2o06).
7   Environmental Management Act Article 5(1): 'every person has the same right to an environment which is good and healthy.'

pectedEnvironmental Crime: A Reader

8 For Telepak's somewhat sensationalist account of their 'mission:' see www.eia-international.org and www.ecocrimes.org (accessed July 8, 2006).
9 Forestry Tasmania is a 'Government Business Enterprise' that manages Tasmania's one million hectares of state forest and produces about three million tons of timber a year (www.forestrytas.com.au).
10 At www.christinemilne.org.au/500-parliament_sub.php?deptItemID=18.
11 Over 65% of the Australian population (and 69% of Tasmanians) want an end to the clearfelling of old-growth forests (Wilderness Society 2001).
12 Rather than encouraging diversification in forest products, Tasmania is almost entirely dependent on woodchip exports.
13 One effective protest saw four environmentalists abseiling from the lower deck of *The Spirit of Tasmania III* on its maiden voyage out of Sydney Harbor. They carried a banner, 'Woodchipping the Spirit of Tasmania;' which neatly, and with identical lettering, covered the ship's name (Bonyhady 2004).
14 SLAPP is a term used by White (2005) and was originally coined by two U.S. authors, George Pring and Penelope Canan (cited by Ogle 2005: 10, who notes that one Australian NGO was sued for applying the term to litigation against it).

## References

Agence France-Presse (2003) 'Malaysia to Ban Indonesian Logs from June: Minister.' May 13. At www.earthisland.org/borneo/news.html.
Ascher, William (1999) *Why Governments Waste Natural Resources: Policy Failures in Developing Countries*. Baltimore: Johns Hopkins University Press.
Assembe Mvondo, Samuel (2004) *Stakeholder Perspectives: Consultation Synthesis Report*. London: Global Witness.
Barnett, Thomas (1990) *The Barnett Report: A Summary of the Report of the Commission of Inquiry into Aspects of the Timber Industry in Papua New Guinea*. Hobart-Asia-Pacific Action Group.
Barraclough, Solon L. and Krishna B. Ghimire (1995) *Forests and Livelihoods: The Social Dynamics of Deforestation in Developing Countries*. London: Macmillan.
Bonyhady, Tim (2004) 'Woodchipping the Spirit of Tasmania.' At www.utas.edu.au/arts/imaging/bonyhady.pdf.
Brack, Duncan, Chantal Maijnissen, and Saskia Ozinga (2002) *Controlling Imports of Illegal Timber: Options for Europe*. London: Royal Institute of International Affairs/FERN.
Brown, David and Cecilia Luttrell (2004) *Review of Independent Forest Monitoring*. London: Overseas Development Institute.
Cain, Maureen (1990) 'Realist Philosophy and Standpoint Epistemologies or Feminist Criminology as a Successor Science.' L. Gelsthorpe and A. Morris (eds.), *Feminist Perspectives in Criminology*. London: Sage.
Callister, Debra (1999) *Corrupt and Illegal Activities in the Forestry Sector: Current Understandings, and Implications for World Bank Forest Policy* (draft for discussion). Washington: World Bank.
Clark, Nick (2005) 'Row Has Loggers Spitting Chips.' *The Mercury* (June 29).
Cohen, Stanley (2001) *States of Denial*. Cambridge: Polity.
Colchester, M. (2006) *Justice in the Forests: Rural Livelihoods and Forest Law Enforcement*. Bogor Barat, Indonesia: CIFOR.
Contreas-Hermosilla, Arnoldo (2001) *Law Compliance in the Forestry Sector: An Overview*. Washington, D.C.: World Bank.
Dudley, N., J.P Jeanrenaud, and F Sullivan (1995) *Bad Harvest? The Timber Trade and the Degradation of the World's Forests*. London: Earthscan.
Ellis, Steven (1999) *The Mask of Anarchy: The Destruction of Liberia and the Religious Dimension of African Civil War*. New York: NYU Press.
Environmental Investigation Agency (EIA) (2007) At www.eia-international/org/.
E.U. Commission (2004) 'Why the Focus on Legality Rather Than Sustainability?' *FLEGT Briefing Note* No. 4. At www.fcghana.com/afleg_ghana/FLEG/4_legality_vs_sustainability_en.pdf.
Finlayson, B. (2002) *Report to the Friends of the Blue Tier on Proposed Logging Operation in the Blue Tier Northeastern Tasmania*. Match 26; at www.bluetier.org/articles1/finlayson2.htm.
Flanagan, Richard (2004) 'The Selling Out of Tasmania.' *The Age* (July 22).
Forest Practices Authority (2006) At www.fpa.tas.gov.au/.
FPB (Forest Practices Board) (2005) *Annual Report on Forest Practices*. Hobart Tasmania: Forest Practices Authority (March 26); at www.fpa.tas.gov.au/.

Forest Trends (2006) *Logging, Legality and Livelihoods in Papua New Guinea: Synthesis of Official Assessments of the Large Scale Logging Industry*, Vol. 1. Jakarta: Forest Trends.

Friends of the Earth (2004) 'International Environmental Groups Unite Against Australian Corporate Assault on Free Speech.' Media Release, February 23; March 26; at www.foe.org. au/media-releases/2005-media-releases.

Gillespie, Alistair (1997) *International Environmental Law, Policy and Ethics*. Oxford: Oxford University Press.

Ginting, Laura (2005) 'Does Legalizing Logging Operations Promote Sustainability or Shouldn't We Be Concerned About Destructive Logging?' *World Rainforest Movement Bulletin* 98: 4–7.

Global Witness (2005) *IFM in Cambodia and Cameroon: Comparing Terms of Reference*. London: Global Witness.

Global Witness (2003) *A Conflict of Interests: The Uncertain Future of Burma's Forests*. London: Global Witness.

Global Witness (2002) *The Logs of War: The Timber Trade and Armed Conflict*. FAFO Report 379. September 1, 2006; at www.fafo.no/pub/rapp/379/379.pdf.

Global Witness (1995) *Thai–Khmer Rouge Links, and the Illegal Trade in Cambodia's Timber-Evidence Collected January–May 1995*. May 31, 2006; at www.globalwimess. org/reports/download. php/00079.pdf.

Green, Penny and Tony Ward (2004) *State Crime: Governments, Violence and Corruption*. London: Pluto Press.

Green, Penny and Tony Ward (2000) 'State Crime, Human Rights, and the Limits of Criminology.' *Social Justice* 27,1: 101–115.

Halsey, Mark (2006) *Deleuze and Environmental Damage: Violence of the Text*. Aldershot: Ashgate.

Halsey, Mark (2004) 'Against "Green" Criminology.' *British Journal of Criminology* 44: 833–853.

House of Commons Environmental Audit Committee (2006) *Sustainable Timber. Second Report of the Session 2004–5 (HC 607)*. London: The Stationery Office.

ITS Global (2006) *Whatever It Takes: Greenpeace's Anti-Forestry Campaign in Papua New Guinea*. Melbourne: ITS Global.

ITTO (International Tropical Timber Organisation) (2005) *Annual Review and Assessment of the World Timber Situation*. Yokohama: International Tropical Timber Organization. March 27; www.itto.or.jp.

ITTO (International Tropical Timber Organisation) (2004) *Annual Review and Assessment of the World Timber Situation*. Yokohama: International Tropical Timber Organization. March 27; www.itto.or.jp.

ITTO (International Tropical Timber Organisation) (2002) *Achieving the ITTO Objective 2000 and Sustainable Forest Management in Brazil*. Report for the International Tropical Timber Council, Yokohama. March 27; at www.itto.or.jp/live/PageDisplayHandler?pageId=9.

IUCN (World Conservation Union) (2004) *Draft International Covenant on Environment and Development*. Third edition. Cambridge: IUCN. March 27; www.iucn.org/themes/law/ pdfdocuments/EPLP3lEN_rev2.pdf.

Kramer, R.C. (1992) 'The Space Shuttle Challenger Explosion.' Kip Schlegel and David Weisburd (eds.), *White-Collar Crime Reconsidered*. Boston: Northeastern University Press: 215–242.

Kramer, R. and R. Michalowski (1990) 'State-Corporate Crime.' Quoted in J.R. Aulette and R. Michalowski (1993), 'Fire in Hamlet: A Case Study of State-Corporate Crime;' K.D. Tunnell (ed.), *Political Crime in Contemporary America: A Critical Approach*. New York: Garland: 171–206.

Lennon, Kathleen (2007) *Reason Constituting Perception*. Paper presented at the University of Hull.

Lynch, M.J. and PB. Stretesky (2003) 'The Meaning of Green: Contrasting Criminological Perspectives.' *Theoretical Criminology* 7,2: 217–238.

Macken, J. and N. Chenoweth (2001) 'Forests Under the Gunns.' *Financial Review* (July 20).

McDowell, John (1998) *Mind, Value and Reality*. Cambridge, MA: Harvard University Press.

Milieudefensie, Greenpeace Netherlands, ICCO, ICCN Netherlands Committee, NCIV, and WWF (2006) *Legal Forest Destruction: The Wide Gap Between Legality and Sustainability*. Amsterdam: Milieudefensie, Greenpeace Netherlands, ICCO, ICCN Netherlands Committee, NCIV, and WWR March 27; at www.illegal-logging.info/papers_Legal_Forest_Destruction.pdf.

Ministry of Forests and Wildlife (Cameroon) and World Resources Institute (2002) *Cooperation Agreement*. Yaoundé: Ministry of Forests and Wildlife (Cameroon) and World Resources Institute.

Nippon Paper Group (2005) July 17; www.np-g.com/e/news/news0506l70l.html.

Ogle, G. (2005) *Gunning for Change: The Need for Public Participation Law Reform*. Hobart: The Wilderness Society.

Olsen, Gorm Rye (1995) 'NGOs and the International Environment in the 1990s.' *Centre for Development Research Working Papers* 95,4. Denmark: Centre for Development Research.

Ottisch, Andreas, Alexander Moiseyev, Nikolai Burdin, and Lauma Kazusa (2005) *Impacts of Reduction of Illegal Logging in European Russia on the E.U. and European Russia Forest Sector and Trade.* Joensuu, Finland: European Forest Institute.

Peluso, Nancy Lee (1991) *Rich Forests, Poor People: Resource Control and Resistance in Java.* Berkeley: University of California Press.

*Post* (2005) 'Cameroon; Gov't, WRI Renew Convention on Forest Management.' *The Post* (Lusaka, June 21).

Pritchett, Sarah (2001) *Politicians, Gunns and Money.* March 27; at www.directorytasmania.com/pgm.*html*.

Risse, Thomas, Stephen Roppe, and Kathryn Sikkink (eds.) (1999) *The Power of Human Rights: International Norms and Domestic Change.* Cambridge: Cambridge University Press.

Savcor Indufor Oy (2004) *Impact Assessment of the EU Action Plan for Forest Law Enforcement. Governance and Trade (FLEGT).* Helsinki: Savcor Indufor Oy.

Schwendinger, Herman and Julia Schwendinger (1975) 'Defenders of Order or Guardians of Human Rights?' Ian Taylor, Paul Walton, and Jock Young (eds.), *Critical Criminology.* London: Routledge and Kegan Paul: 113–146.

Senate (Commonwealth of Australia) (2003) *Proof Committee Hansard. Rural and Regional Affairs and Transport References Committee. Reference: Plantation Forests Industry.* Wednesday, October 8. Canberra: Parliament House.

Seneca Creek Associates and Wood Resources International (2004) *'Illegal' Logging and Global Wood Markets: The Competitive Impacts on the U.S. Wood Products Industry.* Washington, D.C.: American Forest and Paper Association.

Shue, H. (1996) *Basic Rights.* Second edition. Princeton: Princeton University Press.

Smith, J., K. Obidzinski, A. Subarudi, and I. Suramenggala (2003) 'Illegal Logging, Collusive Corruption and Fragmented Governments in Kalimantan, Indonesia' *International Forestry Review* 5,3: 293–302.

Stark, Tamara and Sze Pang Cheung (2006) *Sharing the Blame: Global Consumption and China's Role in Ancient Forest Destruction.* London: Greenpeace International.

Telepak and EIA (2005) *The Last Frontier.* Telepak, EIA: London.

UNECE (U.N. Economic Commission for Europe) and FAO (Food and Agriculture Association) (2005) 'Forest Products Annual Review 2004-5.' *Timber Bulletin* LVIII.

WALHI (2003) 'Statement to the RIIA Meeting on Dec. 2, 2003: A Memorandum on Industrial Logging Is the Solution to Indonesia's 'Illegal Logging' Problem.' At www.illegallogging.info/sub_approach.php?approach_id=19andsubApproach_id=85.

WALHI (1992) *Violated Trust: Disregard for the Forests and Forest Laws of Indonesia.* The Indonesian Environmental Forum (WALHI), Jakarta.

Ward, Tony (2004) 'State Harms.' Paddy Hillyard, Christina Pantazis, Dave Gordon, and Steve Tombs (eds.), *Beyond Criminology: Taking Harm Seriously.* London: Pluto Press.

White, Rob (2005) 'Stifling Environmental Dissent: On SLAPPS and Gunns.' *Alternative Law Journal* 30,6: 268–273.

White, Rob (2003) 'Environmental Issues and the Criminological Imagination.' *Theoretical Criminology* 7,4: 483–506.

Wilderness Society (2003) 'Logging Program Will Destroy More Giant Trees and Undermine Tourism Potential of Tasmania's Styx Valley.' At www.wilderness.org.au.

Wilderness Society (2001) 'Opinion Poll Backs Tasmania Together Plan on Old Growth Forests.' At www.wilderness.org.au/campaigns/forests/tasmanial/20010911_mr/.

World Bank (2002) *A Revised Forest Strategy for the World Bank Group.* Washington, D.C.: World Bank.

World Resources Institute (2005) 'News Release WRI, Cameroon Agreement Cuts Down Illegal Logging.' At www.wri.org/biodiv/newsrelease_text.cfm?NewsReleaseID=318.

# 7. The World Bank and crimes of globalization: a case study*

*David O. Friedrichs and Jessica Friedrichs*

## Introduction

The basic issue addressed in this article can be concisely stated: are the policies and practices of an international financial institution (the World Bank), arising in the context of an accelerated globalization, usefully characterized as a form of crime and a criminological phenomenon? What kinds of strategies and actions are available in response to the harm caused by these policies and practices?[1] International financial institutions such as the World Bank are key players in an increasingly globalized capitalist system. The claim that capitalism itself is a criminal enterprise is, of course, an enduring thesis of Marxist thought (e.g., Buchanan 1983).[2] Moreover, some contemporary critics of globalization – as a transnational expansion of capitalist free markets – seem to suggest that globalization per se is a criminal enterprise that ought to be challenged on every level. We do not propose to pursue such sweeping claims here. Rather, we address the narrower claim that at least some of the policies and practices of the World Bank can be validly characterized as criminal. To support our case, we provide a case history of a World Bank-financed dam in Thailand.

## A perspective on globalization

The policies and practices of international financial institutions such as the World Bank, the World Trade Organization, and the International Monetary Fund can only be understood in the context of the notion of 'globalization.' The invocation of that term has become ubiquitous and the literature on globalization has expanded exponentially in the recent era, although its meaning is far from settled (Chase-Dunn *et al.* 2000; Dunne 1999: 20; Hay and Marsh 2000).[3] The term 'globalization' has been in wide use since the 1960s (Busch 2000: 22). In one sense, globalization is hardly a new phenomenon, if one means by it the emergence of international trade and a transnational

---

*From *Social Justice* (2002), 29(1–2): pp. 13–36.

economic order.[4] Yet globalization has become a buzzword of the transition into the era of the new century due to the widely perceived intensification of certain developments (Mazlish 1999: 5).[5] It is not simply an economic phenomenon, although it is most readily thought of in such terms.[6] Globalization also has important political and cultural dimensions (Chase-Dunn *et al*. 2000; Mazlish 1999: 7).[7] The phenomenal growth in the importance and influence of transnational corporations, nongovernmental organizations, intergovernmental organizations, international financial institutions, and special interest groups is a conspicuous dimension of contemporary globalization (Mazlish 1999; Shapiro and Brilmayer 1999; Valaskakis 1999).[8] Ordinary people lose control over their economic destiny (Greider 1997). World markets increasingly overshadow national markets, barriers to trade are reduced, and instant tele- and cyber-transactions are becoming the norm (Blackett 1998; Chase-Dunn *et al*. 2000; Jackson 2000; Scheuerman 1999). In the broadest possible terms, globalization today refers to the dramatic compression of time and space across the globe.

We accept here the view that globalization as a phenomenon is endlessly complex, is characterized by various contradictory tendencies and ambiguities, and is best seen as a dynamic process as opposed to a static state of affairs (McCorquodale with Fairbrother 1999: 733).[9] The contemporary discourse on globalization is quite contentious, characterized by claims about the effects of globalization that are often directly at odds with each other (Busch 2000). On the one hand, certain aspects of globalization – such as increasing global communication and interaction – are surely inevitable. On the other hand, the mission and policy choices of international financial institutions, in relation to the globalized economy, are hardly preordained and are very much open to challenge. Some commentators argue that globalization has basically increased living standards in much of the world, and that countries experiencing a rise in standards of living have done so by linking up with a globalized economy (Amsden 2000; Easterlin 2000; Zakaria 1999). No one should dispute the claim that there are many 'winners' in the move toward an increasingly globalized economy. However, we strongly agree with those who allege that the winners are disproportionately wealthy multinational corporations and the losers are disproportionately poor and disadvantaged peoples, especially indigenous peoples in developing countries (Frank 2000).[10] Globalization contributes to an overall increase in economic inequality, fostering impoverishment and unemployment for many (Carrasco 1996; George 2000; Kahn 2000b; McCorquodale with Fairbrother 1999: 747; Shapiro and Brilmayer 1999: 2).[11] It has been characterized as a new form of the ancient practice of colonization (Dunne 1999: 22).[12] Richard Falk (1993) argues that the logic of globalization is dictated by the well-being of capital rather than of people. Altogether, globalization is affecting human society in many different ways.[13]

Globalization has many dimensions, but the following are most pertinent to the thesis of this article:

1   The growing global dominance and reach of neoliberalism and a freemarket capitalist system that disproportionately benefits wealthy and powerful organizations and individuals;

2  The increasing vulnerability of indigenous people with a traditional way of life to the forces of globalized capitalism;

3  The growing influence and impact of international financial institutions (such as the World Bank), and the related relative decline of power of local or state-based institutions; and

4  The nondemocratic operation of international financial institutions, taking the form of globalization from above instead of globalization from below.

## The role of the World Bank in a global economy

The international financial institutions that play such a central role in contemporary globalization have become prime targets for criticism for their policies and practices in the global economy. These international financial institutions include the World Trade Organization, the International Monetary Fund, and the World Bank. Each entity has a different key mission, with the World Trade Organization primarily focused on fostering trade, the International Monetary Fund on maximizing financial stability, and the World Bank on promoting development (Stiglitz 2001). Of course, these institutions have many ties with each other, and the lines of demarcation between their activities can become quite blurred. Collectively, much evidence suggests that they have acted principally in response to the interests of developed countries and their privileged institutions, rather than in the interests of the poor (Phillips 2000; Sjoberg *et al.* 2001; Smith and Moran 2000; Stiglitz 2001), In this article, we focus principally on the activities of one of these institutions, the World Bank, because it played a key role in the particular case addressed here.

The World Bank (formally, the International Bank for Reconstruction and Development, or IBRD) was established at the Bretton Woods Conference in 1944 to help stabilize and rebuild economies ravaged by World War II. Eventually it shifted its focus to an emphasis on aiding developing nations (Johnson 2000). The Bank makes loans to governments of its member nations and to private development projects backed by the government. Projects are supposed to benefit the citizens of the country receiving Bank loans, which are made at a favorable rate of interest. The World Bank (2000) generally claims to contribute to the reduction of poverty and improved living standards in developing countries. Today the Bank is a large, international operation, with over 10,000 employees, 180 member states, and annual loans of some 30 billion dollars (Finnegan 2000: 44). Historically, the World Bank itself has been the principal source of information about its operations and programs; inevitably, such internally generated information can be strongly suspected of being self-serving (Rich 1994).

The World Bank was established (along with the International Monetary Fund) at the behest of the dominant Western nations, with little if any real input from the developing countries (Kapstein 1998/1999: 28). It is disproportionately influenced or manipulated by elite economic institutions and has been characterized as an agent of global capital (Greider 2000b: 15). In the developing countries, it deals primarily with the political and economic elites of those countries, with little direct attention to the perspectives and needs of indigenous peoples, a practice for which it has been criticized by U.S. senators (Caulfield 1996: 227; Rich 1994: 145). It has had a record of lending money to ruthless military dictatorships (engaged in murder and torture), after having denied loans to democratic governments overthrown by the military (Rich 1994: 99). It favors strong dictatorships over struggling democracies because it believes that the former are more able to introduce and see through the unpopular reforms its loans require (Caufield 1996: 209). Borrowers of money from the World Bank typically are political elites of developing countries, and their cronies, although the repayment of the debt becomes the responsibility of people in these countries, most of whom do not benefit from the loans.[14] In this reading, then, the privileged benefit disproportionately from dealings with the World Bank, relative to the poor.[15]

## Criminology and crimes of globalization

Most criminologists have paid little if any attention to the phenomenon of globalization and international financial institutions such as the World Bank, although some prominent criminologists have called for more attention to globalization as a new context within which crime must be understood.[16] Progressive or critical criminologists – writing in journals such as *Social Justice* and *Crime, Law, and Social Change* – have been especially attuned to the relevance of an evolving global economy to understanding crime and criminal justice issues.[17] A criminology of the 21st century must address immensely consequential forms of crime being committed in an evolving new global order.

If we claim here that it is useful to view at least some of the activities of the World Bank as criminal, an operative definition of crime must be established. First, we adopt the view that a valid definition of crime need not be limited to those actions clearly defined as crime by state law.[18] Some attempts to define crime have broken completely with a legalistic framework, on any level.[19] A core argument of those who reject the purely legalistic definition of crime is that criminologists should not restrict their study of crime to that which is defined by state law as crime, insofar as state-defined crime is ideologically biased and fails to address a wide range of objectively identifiable forms of harm.[20]

That powerful entities (including international financial institutions) are in a strong position to influence national (and international) law has long been recognized (Passas 1999: 401). In an increasingly globalized world, we need to adopt conceptions of crime that transcend limitations of traditional state-based law. Crime itself is increasingly a transnational or global phenomenon. Nikos Passas (2000: 17–18) offers the following definition of transnational crime: '...cross-border misconduct that entails avoidable and unnecessary harm to society, is serious enough to warrant state intervention, and is similar to other kinds of acts criminalized in the countries concerned or by international law.' Such a definition offers a specific starting point for a conception of crime that transcends the limitations of conventional, legalistic definitions within a state-based context. For our purposes here, if international financial institutions adopt policies and practices that violate the provisions of international human rights accords and covenants, they may be said to be complicit in a form of crime. The United Nations International Covenant on Economic, Social, and Cultural Rights (1966), for example, holds that:

> All peoples have the right of self-determination. By virtue of the right they freely determine their political status and freely pursue their economic, social, and cultural development ... In no case may a people be deprived of its own means of subsistence (United Nations 1966: 225)

Because they are not states, international financial institutions such as the World Bank are not technically bound by this U.N. covenant, but the states to which they have made loans have generally ratified the covenant (Stark 2000: 536–537). Even if these states have done little, if anything, to enforce the economic covenant, willful failures by the international financial institutions and the states to comply with these standards may be regarded as crimes in terms of the conception offered above. Accordingly, if the policies and practices of an international financial institution such as the World Bank result in avoidable, unnecessary harm to an identifiable population, and if these policies lead to violation of widely recognized human rights and international covenants, then crime in a meaningful sense has occurred, whether or not specific violations of international or state law are involved. The failure to characterize the forms of harm perpetrated by international financial institutions as crime tends to dilute the seriousness of such activity.

## Extending crime typologies to encompass crimes of globalization

The most readily recognized categories of criminal activity include violent personal crime, conventional crime, organized crime, professional crime, and public order – or victimless – crime. Although Sutherland's call for more attention to white-collar crime was not widely embraced for several decades, for some time now the categories of corporate crime and occupational crime have been accepted in some form by professional criminologists, the media, and the public. The senior author has argued elsewhere that certain hybrid or marginal types of white-collar crime – such as state-corporate crime, finance crime, technocrime, enterprise crime, contrepreneurial crime, and avocational crime – merit wider recognition (Friedrichs 1996). Although in one sense state crime (e.g., genocide) and political white-collar crime (e.g., accepting bribes) have been long recognized, these forms of crime have been largely slighted by criminologists and viewed by the public and the media as fundamentally disconnected from 'the crime problem.' A number of criminologists have recently called for more attention to state crime in particular as a significant criminological phenomenon (e.g., Friedrichs 1998; Ross 1995; Kauzlarich and Kramer 1998; Green and Ward 2000). The form of crime addressed here does not fit neatly into any of the existing categories, however. It incorporates elements of state crime, political white-collar crime, state-corporate crime, and finance crime, in particular.[21] In addition, it suggests the need to adapt existing, widely adopted typologies of crime to encompass such activities, prospectively labeled global or transnational state-finance crime. Such crime involves cooperative endeavors between international financial institutions, transnational corporations, and state or political entities that engage in demonstrably harmful activities in violation of international law or international human rights conventions.

If some of the policies and activities of the international financial institutions are specifically characterized as a form of crime, this provides a conceptual framework for systematically exploring parallels and differences, as well as interconnections, with other forms of crime. It facilitates the application of criminological knowledge to this form of crime and contributes to the development of a truly globalized criminology.

## A case study: the dam at Pak Mun (Thailand)

> The villagers are not against development. We are against violating rights. We're against organizations using their power over the governments of the people so that the people don't have a place to live or food to eat – Mae Sompong, villager affected by Pak Mun Dam (in Vienchang 2000: 49)

From December 2000 to April 2001, the junior author lived intermittently at the Assembly of the Poor Pak Mun (Moon) dam protest village just outside Ubon Ratchatani, Northeastern Thailand.[22] During this time, she acted as a participant-observer in daily village meetings, various protests, and marches throughout the country. She interviewed five villagers in great depth about their experiences with the dam. Interviews were also conducted with local Energy Generating Authority of Thailand officials, World Bank representatives, international and Thai non-governmental organization workers involved in dam or development issues, and Thai academics researching the subject. As an observer, she noted the daily futility of fishing in the Mun River, as well as the severe economic hardship faced by the villagers. Statistics and other data related to the issue were obtained from the 'World Commission on Dams Report for 2000,' the *Bangkok Post* newspaper, International Rivers Network publications, and World Bank sources. At the time of the protest, Thai academics as well as World Bank and government officials were becoming increasingly aware of the need to weigh affected villagers' concerns as heavily as environmental and socioeconomic data. In the following case study, dam-affected villagers present their concerns about the Pak Mun project. Factual data supports their claims. The project history covers the environmental and socioeconomic damage caused by the dam, and the protest history outlines the villagers' response to the dam. The entire study centers on the role and responsibility of the World Bank in this controversy.

### History of the project

The World Bank became involved in hydropower dam projects in the late 1970s and 1980s as part of structural adjustment policies that fostered production industries. The World Bank approved the Pak Mun dam loan in 1991 to support a shift in Thailand's economy toward export-oriented industrialization (Tyler 2000: 14, 23). Classified as a large dam, it was originally slated to produce 150 megawatts of energy; since its completion in 1994, however, it has not generated more than 40 megawatts over a given peak period. Construction costs soared from an original estimate of U.S. $135 million to an actual cost of U.S. $233 million (World Commission on Dams 2000). The World Bank contributed a $23 million loan and was involved in many facets of the project from the beginning (Tyler 2000: 14). The Electricity Generating Authority of Thailand (EGAT) oversaw the project and consulted with the Thai government throughout construction. Among the original goals of the dam were energy generation, irrigation for nearby farmland, and an increase in fisheries, but the latter have been adversely affected. More important, the entire process, from loan to construction to operation, took place without input from the many fishing communities along the river. Today, these villagers have lost their livelihood and community due to the dam's destruction of the river ecosystem.

The Mun River is a large tributary of the mighty Mekong River, which snakes through much of Southeast Asia. For generations, villagers living in the rural plateau area of Northeast Thailand along the Mun River sustained their communities through fishing, using fish to barter for rice from farmers nearby. Villagers depended on the complex system of rapids, watershed, and forest for everything in their lives. Yet when TEAM, a World Bank-approved group, conducted the first Environmental Impact Assessments (EIAs) for dam construction in 1982, villagers were not even made aware of the impending plans. One villager did not learn of the dam until 1985, when the construction plans that would affect her entire community and future were announced on the radio (Vienchang 2000: 18). Early on, the villagers were concerned about the effect the dam would have on their livelihoods, but government officials and EGAT and World Bank representatives never addressed their concerns (Ibid.). The EIA itself has been highly criticized. Dams by nature create detrimental effects on the watershed environment surrounding a river, including flooding farmland with reservoirs, submerging natural forests, and preventing the natural migration of fish upstream. In the case of Pak Mun, these issues were magnified by the lack of proper EIAs and pre-construction studies, and the push to complete the project quickly regardless of villagers concerns.

*Environmental Damage*: The EIA at Pak Mun was carried out in 1982 when the World Bank accepted EGAT's proposal to allow TEAM to conduct the studies. Since the consultants were chosen and hired through the Office of Environmental Planning and Policy, a Thai Government body, the developer institution can apply pressure to ensure the EIA is to their liking (Vallabhaneni 2000: 8). This issue, compounded with simple logistics, made for problematic EIAs in the case of Pak Mun. Logistically, the EIA discovered that the original dam site would flood a large portion of national forest, so they proposed to move the dam a few kilometers upstream and lower the dam's overall height. They saw no reason to conduct a new EIA after making these changes because any changes based on environmental concerns alone were considered a major accomplishment within the bank. After completion, the dam's new position was discovered to have serious effects on river life.

First, the dam still flooded a portion of forestland (community forest), violating the bank's own policies on the destruction of cultural property. The World Commission on Dams (2000) report – an independent global evaluation of dams – estimates that at least 40 edible plants, 45 mushroom species, and 10 bamboo species harvested by locals for subsistence and household meals were lost. These plants, overlooked by almost all EIA reports, provided income at local markets and had medicinal usages (*Ibid.*: 4).

From previous dam experiences, the EIA TEAM group knew the stagnant water created by the dam's reservoir would affect the health of local people. Therefore, the EIA made provisions for parasitic river fluke mitigation, but fewer than 30% of the plans for monitoring the disease have been implemented (Vallabhaneni 2000: 10). Water plants such as hyacinth, which choke up the river, have collected around the dam site and villagers living in the area are experiencing adverse health effects when they use the river. Traditionally, villagers used river water for most of their daily needs – drinking, bathing, and washing laundry – but today the villagers complain of skin rashes whenever they try to use it.

The blasting of the river's natural rapids, particularly a large one named Geng Supurr that now trickles by uneventfully, is another major concern of the villagers. The World Commission on Dams (2000) reports that more than 50 of Pak Mun's natural rapids have been permanently submerged. Villagers know that the rapids are responsible for oxygenating the water and serve as pools of energy for the fish system. The blasting of rapids around the dam site was extremely questionable since the rapids are technically part of protected forest. The rapids were known to be the habitats of some 20 species of fish, but since no baseline data on fish populations were collected, we cannot be sure of the economic loss due to decline in fish (*Ibid.*: 4).

The severe decline in fish population that has plagued the surrounding community and ecosystem since the dam's completion was the most devastating effect on the Mun River environment. Peak fish migration, when fish swim upstream to spawn, takes place at the start of the rainy season (May to July), a period in which the dam's flood gates are rarely opened (*Ibid.*). Due to the blockage of the dam, fish species have declined in the last few years from the 265 species recorded in the Mun watershed before 1994 to only 96 species found upstream of the dam. Therefore, the dam has affected 169 species of fish, with 56 vanishing through extinction. The annihilation of the way of life of these indigenous fishermen, who depended on the abundant fish for food and income, followed. According to the Project for Ecological Recovery, the number of families obtaining income from Mun River fisheries has declined by 75% and the average daily fish catches for family subsistence have decreased by 30% (Vallabhaneni 2000: 9). One villager remembers being able to catch 40 to 50 fish, weighing many kilograms, just by laying her nets in the river only a few years ago. The junior author's observation of villagers in 1999 found them spending an entire day fishing, only to come home with two tiny fish. The World Commission on Dams Report (2000: 7) notes that the 1981 EIA produced inadequate baseline information because studies should have covered different seasons over a two-year timeframe and natural fluctuations in abundance of fish should have been monitored. Socioeconomically, the study should have identified the dependency of the local population on fisheries.

*Social Harm*: For fishermen who had relied on the river their entire lives, the environmental damage created by the dam was dramatic. The problems were compounded by the Thai government, EGAT, and the World Bank's unjust handling of resettlement issues. The World Bank's operational directive on involuntary resettlement stresses that potential resettlement issues should be dispatched with early in the evaluation process. Yet qualitative issues of right to livelihood, sustainable economy, and community structure can often be manipulated to suit the project design, since they are inherently much more difficult to define. At Pak Mun, the physical resettlement of villagers who lost their land to flooding was appraised and compensation was supplied to those affected, but the figures regarding the meaning of 'affected' are hotly disputed. World Bank reports claimed 989 families would lose some land and housing, but only 200 would have to resettle because of the dam (Vallabhaneni 2000: 12). The World Commission on Dams (2000: 3) reported on predictions that the dam and reservoir would affect 31 villages, with a direct impact on 241 households. Yet it found that 1,700 households actually lost a house, land, or both. Their figures are much higher because they account for houses affected by the loss of fishing income upstream and downstream of the dam. Beyond flooding and loss of income, the overflow of water from the dam has surrounded some villages, creating difficulties for transportation, farming, and general access through their communities. Further, those building and funding the dam have made culturally insensitive arrangements for those truly dislodged by it. For example, in Ban Hoi Hay, a strip of 11 houses built as 'compensation' along a patch of highway far from the river, the one-room houses, which are stacked up on stilts, fail to provide for the traditional Thai family (including extended relatives) living under one roof. Water, previously obtained from the nearby river, now comes through unreliable pipes, leaving the villagers without options if the supply is disrupted.

### History of the protest

Villagers along the river witnessed the disintegration of their communities as fish populations declined and difficulties in finding basic sustenance mounted. Able-bodied family members, including young children, left school and the community to find work in big cities like Bangkok. With little formal education, the employment choices of the former fishermen were limited to the most undesirable jobs, such as searching through landfills for recyclable materials. Dissatisfied villagers demanded more for the loss of their land and houses, and after participating in the Assembly of the Poor protest for 99 days in Bangkok, they received some monetary compensation. Yet, as villagers told the junior author, the money was destructive to their community because they were not familiar with managing it. Without land for planting rice or rivers to fish, it was useless. The ideology guiding World Bank development projects such as dams that export energy is that they create a better, more secure future for villagers. Yet, without consultation, villagers are rapidly thrust into a money economy in areas not structured to absorb new employees, such as the rural northeastern area of Thailand around the Mun River.

As the money ran out, villagers became more aware of the struggles they faced due to the lack of fish, inundated farmland, and disintegrating communities. A group of over 5,000 people came together in March 1999 to set up a protest community beside the dam. Between then and March 2000, various villagers from nearby dams came to protest alongside them, and four protest villages were created in response to other dam issues. Instead of compensation, villagers demanded that the dam gates be opened to allow fish to spawn in the river.

Throughout the process, the government marginalized and often misled villagers on the future. The original announcement of the dam, one villager recalls, claimed they would be able to plant two or three rice crops a year (instead of the typical one), although this dam never had irrigation capabilities (World Commission on Dams 2000: 1). No villagers the junior author spoke with remember being warned of the negative consequences. Villagers who spoke out against the dam early on (in the form of protest) were physically attacked and restricted by government-hired neighbors.

> The World Bank, you have a lot of money, but wherever you invest there is destruction. I want you, if you are building, or developing, or investing in some underdeveloped country, I want you to see the humanity, to not violate the rights of people, to not violate the environment of those who live with nature. You adversely affect their lives, their communities, and cause their culture to crumble. What you have done already, you must fix. Whatever you have destroyed of ours, you must cure it. (Mae Sompong, villager affected by Pak Mun dam, in Vienchang 2000: 48.)

*A Postscript*: On July 17 2000, Thai police under Prime Minister Chuan Leekpai forcibly removed Assembly of the Poor protesters from the area around Government House in Bangkok and arrested 200 of them (South-East Asia Rivers Network 2000). The villagers responded with a mass hunger strike and both parties met on numerous occasions to discuss the opening of the dam gates, with no resolution. By spring of 2001, a new prime minister had been elected and talks seemed more promising. On May 26 2001, Prime Minister Thanksin Sninawarta promised to open the Pak Mun gates for a four-month trial period, to determine the impact on fishing. Although representatives from the World Bank visited the dam site and protest village in the spring of 2000, the World Bank has played no role in addressing villagers concerns to date.

## The World Bank and crimes of globalization

The World Bank has been criticized for being paternalistic, secretive, and counterproductive in terms of any claimed goal of improving people's lives.

Specifically, it has been charged with being complicit in policies with genocidal consequences, with exacerbating ethnic conflict, with increasing the gap between rich and poor, with fostering immense ecological and environmental damage, and with the callous displacement of vast numbers of indigenous people in developing countries from their original homes and communities (Rich 1994: xii 16, 30, 93 151). Critics claim that many of the less-developed countries that received World Bank loans are worse off today in terms of poverty, and that the severe austerity measures imposed on borrowing countries, deemed necessary to maximize the chances of Bank loans being repaid, most heavily affect the poorest and most vulnerable segments of the population (Johnson 2000).

The most favored World Bank project has been the building of dams, but even its own experts concede that millions of people have been displaced because of these projects (Caufield 1996: 12, 73). In many of these projects, resettlement plans have been nonexistent – violating the Bank's own guidelines – or have been inadequately implemented. In a notorious case from the 1970s, in which anti-dam protesters in Guatemala were massacred by the military, the World Bank report on the project failed to directly mention the atrocity (*Ibid.*: 207–208; 263). Given such circumstances, claims of criminality have been leveled against the World Bank. At a 1988 World Bank meeting in Berlin, protesters called for the establishment of a Permanent People's Tribunal to try the World Bank (and the International Monetary Fund) for 'crimes against humanity' (Rich 1994: 9). An American anthropologist characterized the forced resettlement of people in dam-related projects as the worst crime against them, short of killing them (Caufield 1996: 262). An American biologist characterized the World Bank's report on the environmental impact of one of its dam projects in a developing country as 'fraudulent' and 'criminal' (Rich 1994: 11–12). These allegations are certainly applicable to the Pak Mun dam discussed here.

The World Bank's complicity in the crimes outlined above is best understood in terms of its criminogenic structure and organization. The historical charge of its charter called upon it to focus on economic developments and considerations, not the other consequences of its policies and practices (*Ibid,*: 199). Throughout its history, it has thus avoided addressing or taking a strong stand on human rights issues (Caufield 1996: 206). Its focus on a less than well-defined mission of promoting 'long-term sustainable growth' has served as a rationale for imposing much short-term suffering and economic losses (Rich 1994: 189). This orientation has led the World Bank to adopt and apply somewhat one-dimensional economic models to its project-related analyses, with insufficient attention to many other considerations and potentially useful insights from other disciplines (*Ibid.*: 195). Once the projects are initiated, they tend to develop a momentum of their own that often marginalizes or negates any real adjustments in response to reports indicating negative environmental or social effects (Vallabhaneni 2000: 11). The underlying incentive structure at the Bank encourages 'success' with large, costly projects. Bank employees are pressured to make the environmental (as well as social) conditions fit. Like other international financial institutions, the World Bank is structured so that it rewards its personnel for technical proficiency rather than for concerning themselves with the perspectives and needs of the ordinary people of developing countries (Bradlow 1996: 75).[23]

In terms of their career interests, World Bank officials are rewarded for making loans and moving large amounts of money, rather than relative to any human consequences of these loans. Furthermore, World Bank personnel have not been held accountable for the tragic human consequences of their projects (Rich 1994: 91, 307). All of these institutional factors contribute to a criminogenic environment.

Insofar as the World Bank is not a signatory to international human rights treaties, it has manifested relatively little concern with human rights abuses (Bradlow 1996: 63). International financial institutions are, however, subject to the imperatives of international law, and at a minimum are obliged to insure that they do not exacerbate conditions impinging on human rights. Most of the countries with which they have dealings have ratified the U.N.'s Economic Covenants, and accordingly should be bound by its provisions.

Our claim is not that the World Bank adopts policies or makes loan-related decisions with the intent or objective of causing harm. The case can be made that at least some World Bank policymakers sincerely hope to achieve positive results, to foster development and reduce the scope of poverty (Caufield 1996; Rich 1994). Furthermore, voices within the World Bank during the recent era have questioned or challenged some World Bank policies and practices that appear to have had harmful consequences. Policies are being examined now through the Bank's internal departments that will more clearly define the Bank's influence (or lack of it) after a project has been completed. This influence may be monetary, such as providing compensation for mistakes made. It may also be based on leverage to pressure governments to take responsibility for a project, leverage that propelled these projects from the start. However, many critics – and even the former chief economist of the World Bank, Joseph Stiglitz (2000; 2001) – contend that the policies and practices of the World Bank and other international financial institutions have adopted the interests of the advanced industrialized nations and the Wall Street financial community as their highest priority. Without checks in the Bank's procedures, it can continue to encourage, fund, and assess development projects that do not support the goals of a country's people (yet continuously prop up powerful government and big business). Ideologically, the World Bank creates and contributes to the general concept of 'development' by funding only a certain kind of development. For the past 50 years, the World Bank has invested in large, export-oriented projects such as pipelines and dams that cause severe environmental upheaval and penalize the very people they claim they wish to help: the poor.

A characteristic of significant forms of white-collar crime (including much corporate crime) is that the harm involved is a consequence, not a specific objective, of certain policy choices and practices. As with other forms of white-collar crime, the harmful (or illegal) activity associated with the crimes of international financial institutions occurs within the context of productive, legal activity; it is a byproduct of efforts to achieve gain, avoid loss, or advance some other legitimate organizational objective, with such objectives taking precedence over other considerations. Legitimate organizations do respond at times to claims that they are engaging in harmful (or illegal) activities, as in the case of the World Bank. Yet such responses may simply be cynical (purely for public relations purposes), strategic (to maximize chances of achieving major objectives), political (in deference to internal coalitions, or as necessary compromises), or sincere (authentically concerned with pursuing the most morally and ethically defensible policies). With organizations such as the World Bank, a complex combination of responses is surely involved.

In sum, we do not contend that the specific intent and purpose of the policies of the World Bank is to do harm. However, we hold that the World Bank's mode of operation is intrinsically criminogenic and that it functions undemocratically; its key deliberations are carried out behind a veil of secrecy and it is insufficiently accountable to any truly independent entity. At a minimum, the World Bank is criminally negligent when it: (1) fails to adequately explore or take into account the impact of its loans for major projects on indigenous peoples; (2) adopts and implements policies specifically at odds with the protocols of the *Universal Declaration of Human Rights* and subsequent covenants; or (3) operates in a manner at least hypothetically at odds with international and state law.

## The social movement against international financial institutions

The anti-globalization movement has targeted the World Bank, the WTO, and the IMF. The movement includes a broad range of constituencies – 'an effervescent and troublesome cauldron of peasants, women, environmentalists, human rights activists, indigenous people, religious activists, and other individuals' (Rajagopal 2000: 539). Each has a somewhat different agenda. Some protesters have invoked the notion of 'crime' in an attempt to characterize the activities of the international financial institutions.[24] In general, though, the anti-globalization protests in Seattle, Washington, D.C., Prague, and Quebec have been animated by a concern with the alleged harmful consequences of globalization and the activities of the international financial institutions, rather than with claims of criminality. Our premise is that successfully imposing a label of 'criminal' on some activities of international financial institutions could broaden the appeal of the anti-globalization movement and lend support to the case for formally adjudicating these claims in an appropriate international body.

The anti-globalization protest movement may have influenced international financial institutions to undertake internal reforms and to incorporate matters such as poverty and environmental protection into their agendas (Gitlin 2000; Rajagopal 2000). Evidence from recent news stories suggests that protests in Seattle, Washington, D.C., and elsewhere have had an impact.[25] Globalization and its effects were the top agenda item in the Millennium Meeting of world leaders at the United Nations in September 2000 (Crossette 2000b).[26] It remained to be seen, however, whether the powerful nations of the world would seriously attempt to address the criminality inherent in the activities of the international financial institutions, or would principally direct their efforts toward deflecting and confronting protests against such activity.


## Conclusion

Globalization, as defined here, is an increasingly important dimension of the context within which crime of all types occurs. We have argued that the World Bank can be viewed as engaging in a noteworthy form of criminal activity and that it is necessary and useful to view some of its policies and practices this way. Raising consciousness about the criminal dimensions of the activities of international financial institutions ideally fosters the application of comparative criminological frameworks to these phenomena and directs activist responses to it on behalf of those most harmed by present trends.

The term 'globalization' is elusive and multifaceted; although globalization is a real and dramatic intensification of existing international patterns, we need not accept its current direction as inevitable. Critics of present global developments call for the development of popular accountability on the part of national and global institutions, for more public control over these institutions, for a true internationalism, and for just alternatives to the criminal activities of international financial institutions (Crossette 2000a; Frank 2000: 16 19; Hutton and Giddens 2000; Lenusch 2000: 10). Ideally, external pressures on international financial institutions such as the World Bank will lead to substantive internal reforms, or to the demise of such institutions.

What is the role of law in responding to the crimes of globalization? Although law and legal forms play a central role in facilitating the global exchange of persons, capital, and culture, the place of justice in this world order is not clear (Silbey 1997). Advancing human rights demands its own law, one that is independent of national law and sometimes deliberately at odds with states (Teubner 1997; Williams 1990: 660). A movement on behalf of indigenous peoples seeks to establish a universal declaration of such rights, quite independent of the law established by conquering colonial powers. The United States (along with other leading Western powers) has claimed a commitment to human rights and has challenged other countries on human rights issues, but this posture is hypocritical given its own dismal historical record on the implementation of such rights (Hahnel 2000: 41). In a parallel vein, global business and finance engage in hypocrisy by campaigning against many forms of regulatory law in Western developed nations, while calling for adherence to 'the rule of law' in developing nations (Greider 1997: 34). The World Bank's perspective on law has been market-focused and has failed to recognize the protection of human rights and of settled indigenous communities as legitimate purposes of law (McCorquodale and Fairbrother 1999: 755).

In one interpretation, the rule of law can play a role in allowing the disadvantaged to protect themselves from abuse (*Ibid.*: 753). Law can thus serve a positive function by insisting that human rights be incorporated into government policies and those of international financial institutions, demanding the inclusion of human rights in international treaties, and requiring transnational corporations to conduct themselves in line with international human rights law (*Ibid.*: 766). Legal prohibitions could be imposed on World Bank loans for projects with demonstrably harmful consequences (Greider 2000a). Americans have the sovereign power to reform legislation at state and national levels, to impose codes of conduct on corporations, and to impose rules on U.S.-based transnationals (Greider 2000b). Law, then, can be seen as part of the problem or part of the solution in connection with the oppressive and exploitative dimensions of globalization.

This account of the suffering of the Pak Mun dam protesters documents the criminality claim directed at the World Bank; it also serves as a cautionary tale for a globalized future. Demonstrably harmful policies and practices of the World Bank can be appropriately labeled as crime, more fully understood by applying a criminological perspective, and responded to by activist protest and engagement.

## Notes

1 This article was inspired by a juxtaposition of the authors' intellectual and activist concerns. The senior author was influenced by the progressive political initiatives that emerged in the 1960s and by activist experiences during that era (i.e., the Civil Rights campaign in Mississippi in 1964 and antiwar protests from 1965 on). His most recent intellectual, or scholarly, interests have focused on white-collar crime, state crime, state/corporate crime, genocide, and elite deviance. The junior author has been strongly influenced by a summer in China and eight months living in Thailand (with trips to Cambodia and Laos). During her time in Thailand, she lived among and became actively involved with anti-dam protesters, landfill scavengers, and traditional fishermen. She has participated in anti globalization demonstrations in Washington, D.C., and Philadelphia, and has produced an honors thesis on the ACORN antipoverty movement, with which she worked.

2 Recently, in the context of his magisterial exploration of the role of law in a globatized world, Boaventura de Sousa Santos (1995: 359) has called for bringing historical capitalism to trial before a world tribunal, to be held accountable for its complicity in the massive violation of human rights.

3 For an especially broad, current survey of the issues surrounding globalization, see Held and McGrew (2000).

4 In the most inclusive sense, globalization is many centuries old, going back at least to the 15th century voyages of discovery and the gradual emergence of a world economic system (Hay and Marsh 2000; Valaskakis 1999). If one adopts a more restrictive conception of globalization, to refer to the establishment of formal, international institutions to coordinate international trade, finance, and economic activity, such institutions were established in the first half of the 20th century (Thurow 2000). In another interpretation, globalization truly begins from the 1970s on, with the ending of the cooperative economic system established by the Bretton Woods Conference after World War 11, and with the liberalization of world financial markets (Hay and Marsh 2000: 14, *fn.* 2).

5 Theorists of globalization are somewhat divided on the extent to which recent developments do or do not establish a fundamentally new institutional order in the world (Dunne 1999: 18). For a thorough discussion of globalization very much in line with our own views, see Greider (1997). In the final section of the book, Greider (1997: 335) observes, '... the global system tears at the social fabric – upending the peasantry in Thailand, attacking the social state of Germany, suppressing human freedoms on behalf of commerce in Indonesia or China, threatening the foundations of social cohesion of Japan, deepening the social deterioration in the United States and elsewhere.'

6 Chase-Dunn *et al.* (2000: 78) observe that '*economic globalization* means greater integration in the organization of production, distribution, and consumption of commodities in the world economy ... *Political globalization* is conceptualized as the institutional form of global and interregional political/military organizations (including 'economic' ones such as the World

Bank and the International Monetary Fund) and their strengths relative to the strengths of national states and other smaller political actors in the world-system.'

7 Globalization leads to homogenization, polarization, and hybridization, with the cultural consequences of globalization being diverse and complex (Holton 2000; Mazlich 1999).

8 One commentator suggests that the most striking feature of contemporary globalization is the runaway quality of global finance, which appears remarkably independent of traditional constraints of information transfer, national regulation, industrial productivity, or 'real' wealth in any particular society, country, or region (Appadurai 1999).

9 Among the most pertinent general questions and themes pertaining to globalization are: (1) Can poorer countries be helped without compelling them to raise standards on wages, working conditions, and the environment? (2) Can high wages and full employment be maintained in more affluent countries without hindering the economic development of poorer countries? (3) Is protectionism – in either the richer or the poorer countries – ever justified? (4) Can the inherent conflict between economic growth and environmental protection be satisfactorily resolved? (5) Is the notion of effective international regulation of corporations and investors realistic? (6) Should the World Trade Organization, the World Bank, and the International Monetary Fund be reformed or abolished? (Landy 2000: 13).

10 Critics of globalization must be sensitive to paternalistic attacks on policies and practices that appear to be repugnant in Western terms, but that may be experienced as a 'lesser evil' by poor people in developing countries. For example, conditions in developing country sweatshops producing products such as upscale clothing for affluent Americans are often miserable, with wages of 60 cents an hour, but the alternative for sweatshop laborers may be no work, or even more oppressive working conditions, such as prostitution (Kristof and WuDunn 2000; Kaufman and Gonzalez 2001). It does not necessarily follow from consciousness of such realities, however, that one should refrain from exposing and criticizing policies and practices that are inherently unjust and harmful.

11 The World Bank itself reports that the number of people living on less than a dollar a day had increased to 200 million in the 1990s, and that over 80 countries suffered a decline in per capita income in the recent era (Levinson 1999: 21).

12 Silbey (1997: 219) regards 'globalization as a form of postmodern colonialism, where the worldwide distribution and consumption of cultural products removed from the contexts of their production and interpretation is organized through legal devices to constitute a form of domination.' McDonald's is an especially conspicuous symbol of this new form of domination. Similarly, Santos (1998) suggests that globalization is best thought of as the imposition of the agendas of particular entities and countries upon the rest of the globe, rather than authentic globalization. Neumann (2000: 89–90) observes, 'our current global system is a process of colonization. It not only creates organizations like the WTO that replace national sovereignty with corporate interests, it also displaces human ways of relating to each other and substitutes monetary relationships in which human worth is measured in dollars.'

13 A number of presidents of sociological associations have recently used their presidential addresses to call for more sociological attention to globalization and to some of the harms attendant to it. Susan Silbey (1997: 209), in a Presidential Address to the Law & Society Association, called for a sociology of globalization. She observed, 'while it is clear that law occupies a prominent place in the global society – because most of the global exchange of persons, capital, and culture is managed through legal forms – it is not clear where the place of justice is in this new world order.' Francesca M. Cancian (1996), in a Presidential Address to the Pacific Sociological Association, called for a sociological commitment to reducing inequality, a renewal of the commitment of earlier sociologists to social reform, and a more activist research agenda addressing nonacademic audiences and their concerns. Too much present sociology, she stated, follows a pure science model. Evelyn Glenn (2000: 16), in a 1999 Presidential Address to the Society for the Study of Social Problems, noted the great impact of globalization on social existence and the need for sociologists to address new forms of inequality that result, with justice now having to be challenged on a transnational level. Glenn highlighted the role of supranational entities such as the World Trade Organization, the World Bank, and the International Monetary Fund in contributing to conditions of deprivation and inequality on a global scale: '… [T]he new global economy is contributing to new forms of race, class, and gender inequality by widening economic disparities, displacing people from land which provided selfsufficiency and eroding accustomed ways of life that can't be addressed in a strictly domestic context. Struggles for economic justice and human rights thus need to be moved to the transnational level.' Pamela Roby (1998), in her 1997 Society for the Study of Social Problems Presidential Address, also argued that sociologists must become actively engaged in promoting movement toward a just world.

14 As Noam Chomsky (2000: 29) has observed, 'debt is not valid if it's essentially imposed by force. The Third World debt is odious debt.'

15 For Caufield (1996: 338), 'there is much truth in the saying that development – at least in the monopolistic, formulaic, foreign-dominated, arrogant, and failed form that we have known – is largely a matter of poor people in rich countries giving money to rich people in poor countries.'

16 Freda Adler (1995), in her 1995 Presidential Address to the American Society of Criminology, observed that new paradigms are called for within the global village and in the information age. Margaret Zahn (1999), in her 1998 Presidential Address to the American Society of Criminology, calls for criminology to expand it scope, testing its propositions in new contexts. She noted that the international community requires increasing attention, and that it has established standards based on principles of human rights that may transcend national laws. William McDonald (1997: 7) has called for a global criminology, separate from a comparative and international criminology. He suggests that 'the phrase, global criminology, should be reserved for ... the study of crime and justice problems related to the compression of the globe.' Mark Findlay (1999), in *The Globalization of Crime*, argues that the globalized economy of today has produced a new context within which the issue of crime must be understood.

17 Recent issues of *Social Justice*, for example, have explored the intersections between globalization, neoliberalism, militarism, crime, and criminal justice (Weiss 2000; Kirk and Okazawa-Rey 2000). Ian Taylor (1999), writing in a recent issue of *Crime, Law, and Social Change*, argues that the rise of the (free) market society provides a new context for a critical criminology.

18 The familiar term 'crime' has been defined in quite different ways, and an ongoing debate within criminology has focused on the most appropriate way to define this key term. E.H. Sutherland's (1940) conception of white-collar crime – incorporating violations of civil and administrative, as well as criminal law – was one influential challenge to more traditional legalistic definitions of crime.

19 Herman Schwendinger and Julia Schwendinger (1970, 1977) and Larry Tifft and Dennis Sullivan (1980,1998) have promoted a humanistic conception of crime – as social harm, as a violation of human rights – while Stanley Cohen (1993) has characterized crime somewhat more narrowly as directly harmful violations of widely recognized human rights. Still others – e.g., Raymond Michalowski and Ronald Kramer (1987) and David Kauzlarich, Ronald Kramer, and Brian Smith (1992) – have advanced conceptions of crime based upon United Nations codes or international law.

20 Conservative and mainstream criminologists have largely dismissed or ignored this call for an alternative approach to defining crime, but even some of those with a progressive orientation contend that stretching the definition of crime as broadly as the Schwendingers propose to do is either counterproductive and unhelpful, or transforms criminology into a moral crusade (Cohen 1993; Green and Ward 2000). Braithwaite (1985) has criticized humanistic definitions of crime as irrelevant to people who do not share the applicable morality.

21 State-corporate crime is crime committed as a cooperative endeavor between the state and private-sector corporations, such as exploitation by multinational corporations in developing countries. Finance crime is crime committed on behalf of, or in the context of, major financial institutions, such as frauds by thrifts and manipulations of securities markets.

22 The pronunciation of the river is Pak Moon, although in most of the literature it is spelled Pak Mun.

23 In the case of Thailand, the government elite adopted a policy to deliberately undermine rural peasants. 'The World Bank supported this strategy with development loans to finance infrastructure – roads, dams, electrical generation – and the industrialization of agricultural production' (Greider 1997: 352).

24 Conversely, a small number of protesters in Seattle engaged in vandalism and were accordingly accused of engaging in criminal activity. In response, an activist collective communique states: 'We contend that property destruction is not a violent activity unless it destroys lives or causes pain in the process. Private property, especially corporate private property, is in itself infinitely more violent than any action taken against it' (Neumann 2000: 91).

25 For example, some headlines include the following: 'World Trade Officials Pledging to Step Up Efforts Against AIDS: Growing Sensitivity to Criticism as Protests Ebb' (Kahn and Kifner 2000); 'World Bank Criticizes Itself over Chinese Project Near Tibet' (Sanger and Kahn 2000); 'World Bank Cites Itself in Study of Africa's Bleak Performance' (Kahn 2000c); and 'I.M.F. Is Expected to Ease Demands on Debtor Nations' (Kahn 2000d).

26 U.N. Secretary General Kofi Annan (Crossette 2000b: 4) observes, 'it has been said that arguing against globalization is like arguing against the laws of gravity. But that does not mean we should accept a law that allows only heavyweights to survive. On the contrary: We must make globalization an engine that lifts people out of hardship and misery, not a

force that holds them down.' It is not unreasonable to suppose that the concerns expressed by Mr. Annan, and surely shared by many world leaders, have been influenced or activated by the protests. Yet some anti-WTO activists have expressed concern with the U.N.'s own vulnerability to manipulation by corporations and other elite powers (*Ibid*.). The U.N. is certain to be buffeted by countervailing pressures on the globalization issue in the years ahead.

# References

Adler, Freda (1995) 'Our American Society of Criminology, the World, and the State of the Art – The American Society of Criminology 1995 Presidential Address.' *Criminology* 34: 1–9.
Amsden, Alice H. (2000) 'Ending Isolationism.' *Dissent* (Spring): 13–16.
Appadurai, Arjun (1999) 'Globalization and the Research Imagination.' *International Social Science Journal* 160: 229–238.
Blacken, Adelle (1998) 'Globalization and Its Ambiguities: Implications for Law School Curricular Reform.' *Columbia Journal of Transnational Law* 37: 57–79.
Bradlow, Daniel D. (1996) 'The World Bank, the IMF, and Human Rights.' *Transnational Law & Contemporary Problems* 6: 47–90.
Braithwaite, John (1985) 'White Collar Crime.' R.H. Turner and J.F. Short, Jr. (eds.), *Annual Review of Sociology*. Palo Alto, CA: Annual Reviews, Inc.: 1–25.
Buchanan, Allen E. (1983) *Marx and Justice: The Radical Critique of Liberalism*. Totowa, NJ: Rowman & Littlefield.
Busch, Andreas (2000) 'Unpacking the Globalization Debate: Approaches, Evidence and Data.' Colin Hay and David Marsh (eds.), *Demystifying Globalization*. New York: St. Martin's Press: 21-48.
Cancian, Francesca M (1995) 'Truth and Goodness: Does the Sociology of Inequality Promote Social Betterment?' *Sociological Perspectives* 38: 339–356.
Carrasco, Enrique R. (1996) 'Critical Issues Facing the Bretton Woods System: Can the IMF, World Bank, and the GATT/WTO Promote an Enabling Environment for Social Development?' *Transnational Law & Contemporary Problems* 6: i–xx.
Caufield, Catherine (1996) *Masters of Illusion: The World Bank and the Poverty of Nations*. New York: Henry Holt & Co.
Chase-Dunn, Christopher, Yukio Kawano, and Benjamin D. Brewer (2000) 'Trade Globalization Since 1795: Waves of Integration in the World-System.' *American Sociological Review* 65: 77–95.
Chomsky, Noam (2000) 'Talking 'Anarchy' with Chomsky.' *The Nation* (April 24): 28–30.
Cohen, Stanley (1993) 'Human Rights and Crimes of the State: The Culture of Denial.' *Australian and New Zealand Journal of Criminology* 26: 97–115.
Crossette, Barbara (2000a) 'Making Room for the Poor in a Global Economy.' *New York Times* (April 16): 4.
(2000b) 'Globalization Tops 3-Day U.N. Agenda for World Leaders.' *New York Times* (September 3): A1.
Dunne, Tim (1999) 'The Spectre of Globalization.' *Indiana Journal of Global Legal Studies* 7: 17–34.
Easterlin, Richard A. (2000) 'The Globalization of Human Development.' *The Annals* 570: 32–48.
Falk, Richard (1993) 'The Making of Global Citizenship.' Jeremy Brecher, John Brown Childs, and Jill Cutler (eds.), *Beyond the New World Order*. Boston: South End Press: 39–52.
Findlay, Mark (1999) *The Globalization of Crime: Understanding Transitional Relationships in Context*. Cambridge, U.K.: Cambridge University Press.
Finnegan, William (2000) 'After Seattle.' *The New Yorker* (April 17): 40–51.
Frank, Ellen (2000) 'Global Democratization: Spotlight on the United States.' *New Politics* 8: 14.
Friedrichs, David O. (1996) *Trusted Criminals: White Collar Crime in Contemporary Society*. Belmont, CA: Wadsworth Publishing Co.
Friedrichs, David O. (ed.) (1998) *State Crime*. Volumes I and II. Aldershot, UX.: Ashgate/ Dartmouth.
George, Susan (2000) 'Carte Blanche, Bete Noire.' *Dissent* (Winter): 13–15.
Gitlin, Todd (2000) 'Shouts Bring Murmurs, and That Works.' *Washington Post* (April 16): B 1.
Glenn Evelyn (2000) 'Citizenship and Inequality: Historical and Global Perspectives.' *Social Problems* 47: 1–20.
Green, Penny J. and Tony Ward (2000) 'State Crime, Human Rights, and the Limits of Criminology.' *Social Justice* 27,1: 101–116.
Greider, William (2000a) 'Global Agenda.' *The Nation* (January 31): 11–16.

— 2000b 'Time to Rein in Global Finance.' *The Nation* (April 24): 13–20.
— 1997 *One World, Ready or Not: The Manic Logic of Global Capitalism.* New York: A Touchstone Book.
Hahnel, Robin 2000 'Globalization: Beyond Reaction, Thinking Ahead.' *New Politics* 8: 31–42.
Hay, Colin and David Marsh (eds.) (2000) *Demystifying Globalization.* New York: St. Martin's Press.
Held, David and Anthony McGrew (eds.) (2000) *The Global Transformations Reader.* Cambridge, U.K.: Polity Press.
Holton, Robert (2000) 'Globalization's Cultural Consequences.' *The Annals* 570: 140–152.
Hutton, Will and Anthony Giddens (2000) 'Is Globalization Americanization?' *Dissent* (Summer): 58–63.
Jackson, John H. (2000) *The Jurisprudence of GATT and the WTO.* Cambridge, U.K.: Cambridge University Press.
Johnson, Bryan T. (2000) 'The World Bank Does Not Provide Effective Development Programs.' Laura K. Egendorf (ed.), *The Third World – Opposing Viewpoints.* San Diego, CA: Greenhaven Press: 116–122.
Kahn, Joseph (2000a) 'Globalization Unifies Its Many-Striped Foes.' *New York Times* (April 15): A7.
— (2000b) 'Globalization: Unspeakable, Yes, But Is It Really Evil?' *New York Times* (May 7): A4.
— (2000c) 'World Bank Cites Itself in Study of Africa's Bleak Performance.' *New York Times* (June 1): A9.
— (2000d) 'I.M.F. is Expected to Ease Demands on Debtor Nations.' *New York Times* (June 30): C2.
Kahn, Joseph and John Kifner (2000) 'World Trade Officials Pledging to Step Up Effort Against AIDS.' *New York Times* (April 18): Al.
Kapstein, Ethan B. (1998/1999) 'A Global Third Way: Social Justice and the World Economy.' *World Policy Journal* 15: 23–35.
Kaufman, Leslie and David Gonzalez (2001) 'Labor Standards Clash with Global Reality:' *New York Times* (April 24): Al.
Kauzlarich, David and Ronald C. Kramer (1998) *Crimes of the American Nuclear State: At Home and Abroad.* Boston: Northeastern University Press.
Kauzlarich, David, Ronald C. Kramer, and Brian Smith (1992) 'Towards the Study of Governmental Crime: Nuclear Weapons, Foreign Intervention, and International Law.' *Humanity & Society* 16: 543–563.
Kirk, Gwyn and Margo Okazaw-Rey (2000) 'Neoliberalism, Militarism, and Armed Conflict: An Introduction.' *Social Justice* 27,4: 1–17.
Kristof, Nicholas D. and Sheryl Wu Dunn (2000) 'Two Cheers for Sweatshops.' *New York Times Magazine* (September 24): 70–71.
Landy Joanne (2000) 'Symposium on Globalization: Hard Questions for the Left.' *New Politics* 8: 12–13.
Lemisch, Jesse (2000) 'A Movement Begins: The Washington Protests Against IMF/World Bank.' *New Politics* 8: 5–11.
Levinson, Mark (1999) 'Who's in Charge Here?' *Dissent* (Fall): 21–23.
Mazlish, Bruce (1999) 'A Tour of Globalization.' *Indiana Journal of Global Legal Education* 7: 5–16.
McCorquodale, Robert, with Richard Fairbrother
— 1999 'Globalization and Human Rights.' *Human Rights Quarterly* 21: 735–766.
McDonald, William F. (ed.) (1997) *Crime and Law Enforcement in the Global Village.* Cincinnati, OH: Anderson Publishing Co.
Michalowski, Raymond J. and Ronald C. Kramer (1987) 'The Space Between the Laws: The Problem of Corporate Crime in a Transnational Context.' *Social Problems* 34: 34–53.
Neumann, Rachel (2000) 'A Place for Rage.' *Dissent* (Spring): 89–92.
Passas, Nikos (2000) 'Global Anomie, Dysnomie, and Economic Crime: Hidden Consequences of Neoliberalism and Globalization in Russia and Around the World.' *Social Justice* 27,2: 16–44.
(1999) 'Globalization, Criminogenic Asymmetries, and Economic Crime.' European *Journal of Law Reform* 1: 399–423.
Phillips, Peter (2000) 'Seattle Awakens Working People to the Dangers of Globalization.' *Social Policy* (Spring): 34–40.
Rajagopal, Balakrishnan (2000) 'From Resistance to Renewal: The Third World, Social Movements, and the Expansion of International Institutions.' *Harvard International Law Journal* 41: 529–578.
Rich, Bruce (1994) *Mortgaging the Earth: The World Bank, Environmental Impoverishment, and the Crisis of Development.* Boston: Beacon Press.

Roby, Pamela Ann (1998) 'Creating a Just World: Leadership for the Twenty-First Century.' *Social Problems* 45: 1–20.

Ross, Jeffrey Ian (ed.) (1995) *Controlling State Crime*. New York: Garland.

Sanger, David E. and Joseph Kahn (2000) 'World Bank Criticizes Itself over Chinese Project Near Tibet.' *New York Times* (June 27): A7.

Santos, Boaventura de Sousa (1995) *Toward a New Common Sense: Law, Science, and Politics in the Paradigmatic Transition*. New York: Routledge.

Scheuerman, William E. (1999) 'Economic Globalization and the Rule of Law.' *Constellations* 6: 3-25. Schwendinger, Herman and Julia Schwendinger.

— (1977) 'Social Class and the Definition of Crime.' *Crime and Social Justice* 7: 4–13.

— (1970) 'Defenders of Order or Guardians of Human Rights?' *Issues in Criminology* 5: 123–157.

Shapiro, Ian and Lea Brilmayer (eds.) (1999) *Global Justice*. New York: New York University Press.

Silbey, Susan S. (1997) 'Let Them Eat Cake': Globalization, Postmodern Colonialism, and the Possibilities of Justice.' *Law & Society* 31: 207–235.

Sjoberg, Gideon, Elizabeth A. Gill, and Norma Williams (2001) 'A Sociology of Human Rights.' *Social Problems* 48: 11–47.

Smith, Jackie and Timothy Patrick Moran (2000) 'WTO 101: Myths About the World Trade Organization.' *Dissent* (Spring): 66–70.

South-East Asia Rivers Network (2000) 'Thai Government Denying Human Rights! Arrest of 200 Villagers at Government House.' E-mail Transmission (July 17).

Stark, Barbara (2000) 'Women and Globalization: The Failure and Postmodern Possibilities of International Law.' *Vanderbilt Journal of Transnational Law* 33: 503–571.

Stiglitz, Joseph (2001) 'Globalization and Its Discontents.' Henry George Lecture. University of Scranton (April 26).

— (2000) 'The Insider.' *The New Republic* (April 17–24): 56–61.

Sullivan, Dennis and Larry Tifft (1998) 'Criminology as Peace-Making: A Peace-Oriented Perspective on Crime, Punishment, and Justice That Takes into Account the Needs of All.' *The Justice Professional* 11: 5–34.

Sutherland, Edwin H. (1940) 'White Collar Criminality.' *American Sociological Review* 10: 132–139.

Taylor, Ian (1999) 'Criminology Post-Maastricht.' *Crime, Law & Social Change* 30: 333–346.

Teubner, Gunther (1997) 'The King's Many Bodies: The Self-Deconstruction of Law's Hierarchy.' *Law & Society Review* 31: 763–788.

Thurow, Lester (2000) 'Globalization: The Product of a Knowledge-Based Economy.' *The Annals* 570: 19–31.

Tifft, Larry and Dennis Sullivan (1980) *The Struggle to Be Human: Crime, Criminology and Anarchism*. Sanday, Orkney, U.K.: Cienfuegos Press.

Tyler, Christopher (2000) *The Pak Mun Dam: A Case Study of a Large Development Project in Thailand*. Honors Thesis. State College: The Pennsylvania State University.

United Nations (1966) *International Covenant on Economic, Social, and Cultural Rights*. Reprinted in Walter Laquer and Barry Rubin (eds.), Human Rights Reader. New York: New American Library (1989): 225–233.

Valaskakis, Kimon (1999) 'Globalization as Theatre.' *International Social Science Journal* 160: 153–164.

Vallabhaneni, Snigdha (2000) *Inertia of Change in the World Bank: The Pak Mun Dam Project as a Case Study*. Honors Thesis. Providence, Rhode Island: Brown University.

Vienchang, Mae Sompong (2000) *Voice of the River: One Thai Villager's Story of the Pak Moon Dam*. Jessica Friedrichs, Sofia Olson, Kaia Peterson, and Lydia Shula (eds.). Translated by David Streckfuss and Arunee Chupkhunthod. Koen Kaen, Thailand: CIEE.

Weiss, Robert P. (2000) 'Introduction: Criminal Justice and Globalization in the New Millenium.' *Social Justice* 27,2: 1–15.

Williams, Robert A., Jr. (1990) 'Encounters on the Frontiers of International Human Rights Law: Redefining the Terms of Indigenous Peoples' Survival in the World.' *Duke Law Journal* 1990: 660–704.

World Bank (2000) 'The World Bank Provides Effective Development Programs.' Laura K. Egendorf (ed.), *The Third World – Opposing Viewpoints*. San Diego, CA: Greenhaven Press, Inc.: 107–115.

World Commission on Dams (2000) *Pak Mun Case Study Final Report – Executive Summary*. At www.dams.org/studies/th/thfinalscopesect3-4.htm.

Zahn, Margaret A. (1999) 'Thoughts on the Future of Criminology – The American Society of Criminology 1998 Presidential Address.' *Criminology* 37: 1–15.

Zakaria, Fareed (1999) 'After the Storm Passes.' *Newsweek* (December 13): 40.

# 8. Rights and justice on a shared planet: more rights or new relations?*

*Ted Benton*

## Abstract

It is now widely recognized that members of other animal species and the rest of non-human nature urgently need to be protected from destructive human activities. This article evaluates the case for extending the moral and legal scope of rights as a strategy for achieving these aims. It suggests that we require a more pluralistic approach to the moral standing of non-human beings – i.e. one which does not depend entirely on the discourse of rights and its cognates – and that moral argument and legal reform need to be pursued in the context of a wider movement for far-reaching structural changes in social and economic life.

**Key Words** animal rights • environment • human rights • liberalism • social reform

Outrage against 'modern', 'industrial' destruction of nature is not new (see, for example, Gould 1988; Pepper 1996). The romantic movement of the 19th century expressed a predominantly aesthetic revulsion against the reductionism of modern science's representation of the natural order, and against its destructive consequences (see Soper 1995). The 19th century also saw the beginnings of legislative reform aimed at the improvement of environmental conditions in the urban industrial centres. In part this was motivated by middle-class fears of both contageous disease and social unrest. In his classic work on *The Condition of the Working Class in England* ([1845] 1969), Engels wrote:

> I have already referred to the unusual activity which the sanitary police manifested during the cholera visitation. When the epidemic was approaching, a universal terror seized the bourgeoisie of the city. People remembered the unwholesome dwellings of the poor, and trembled before the certainty that each of these slums would become a centre for

---

\* From *Theoretical Criminology* (1998), 2(2): pp. 149–175.

the plague, whence it would spread desolation in all directions through the houses of the propertied class.

(p. 97)

Among 19th-century commentators Engels was quite typical in seeing direct connections between questions of environmental degradation, on the one hand, and poverty, class power and social order, on the other. One of my themes in what follows is that much of our contemporary environmental concern has become too detached from central questions about the nature of our society and its continuing injustices.

In our own century, the period since the early 1960s has been marked by an unprecedented explosion in both popular and official concern about our increasingly destructive relation to the non-human world. In the US, writers such as Rachel Carson (1962), Barry Commoner (1972) and Murray Bookchin (1991) were prominent among those who successfully roused public anxiety about the threat posed to both wildlife and human health by chemical poisoning of the environment. But the changes to which these writers drew attention were international in scope. The shift to intensive agriculture, and the associated concentrations of industrial capital in pesticides, fertilizers, agricultural machinery, food processing and distribution was, likewise, an international process. It brought with it profound scenic, ecological and socio-economic transformations of the countryside, as well as changes in dietary habits and divisions of labour in the home (see, for example, Shiva 1989; Conway and Pretty 1991; Goodman and Redclift 1991). These changes in the countryside coincided with the growth of 'commuter villages', and also an increase in leisure uses of the countryside on the part of urban dwellers. However, urban expectations of the 'rural idyll' were soon dashed as they encountered the reality of an industrialized agriculture promoting landscape homogeneity, crop monocultures and a poisoned, inhospitable countryside. These direct experiences of environmental degradation fuelled an unprecedented expansion of locally based social movement organizations, some focussing exclusively on rural issues, or seeking greater protection for wildlife and their habitats, others concerned with issues of public access.

Meanwhile, seemingly authoritative 'elite' groupings such as the Club of Rome put alarm about human impacts on finite planetary 'life-support systems' onto an emergent global political agenda (Meadows and Meadows 1974). From the early 1970s there was a growing consensus among the world's scientific and political leaderships that prospects for world 'development', and even human survival itself were deeply threatened by prevailing patterns of resource use, population growth and pollution. However, there was no consensus at all about the kinds of change demanded by this recognition. Questions of power, wealth and poverty again became inextricably linked with the environmental agenda, but now posed at a global level. While national government representatives struggled to protect their particular interests within internationally negotiated regimes for environmental regulation, grass-roots social movement organizations extended their vision to include the global character of the environmental threat posed not just by changes in agriculture and food production, but by other industrial sectors

– energy, transport, weapons production, waste disposal and so on. These new organizations themselves played a crucial part in capturing the attention of the media and thereby the wider public. People were made aware of the ecological disasters flowing from the wreckage of oil tankers, the chemical explosion at Bhopal, the desertification of parts of Africa, the destruction of the tropical moist forests, the nuclear disaster at Chernobyl and the ecological dimension of modern warfare, most especially during the Gulf war.

Significantly, media images of these disasters included both the human death and suffering they entailed, together with poignant coverage of the 'innocent' non-human victims – the oiled sea birds, the myriad living denizens of the rain forests, the fish deaths resulting from chemical spillages and so on. In this way, growing public awareness of environmental problems became intertwined with a growing sensibility to the suffering of non-human beings. From the high-profile campaigns against whaling, seal culling, and the fur trade, through to the rise of anti-vivisection and animal welfare activity, awareness has been growing of the moral issue of human relations with non-human species. The quite striking intensity of the emotional tone of some of this social movement activity may be linked to a growing, and quite central cultural contradiction in our civilization. On the one hand, we understand more vividly than ever before the complexity of the social and mental lives of other animal species, our evolutionary kinship with them and our economic, spiritual and ecological interdependence with them – many of us have direct experience of this through the practice of pet keeping, and all of us through powerful and sophisticated media coverage. On the other hand, intensive agriculture and associated animal 'husbandry' regimes increasingly reduce living animals to the status of engineered factors of production, whilst the use of animals in scientific research and product testing similarly underlines their status as mere instruments of human purposes. Only a pervasive practice of concealment and cultural schizophrenia keeps at bay the explosive implications of this contradiction (Thomas 1983).

Much of the public concern which has been aroused in the last three decades or so has been directed towards the existing power structure. To some extent businesses have been targeted, either directly, or indirectly, by the mobilization of consumer pressure. However, most environmental campaigning has been aimed at governments and the mainstream political parties, in the hope of environmentally friendly legal reforms. By some measures this strategy has been very successful. In most countries of the economically 'developed' world there are high levels of environmental regulation. Most have environmental ministries, procedures for vetting and, if necessary, banning the use of toxic substances in industry, legal liability on the part of public and private bodies for environmental damage, various public health measures, including provisions for health and safety at work, planning law governing the siting of environmentally hazardous installations and provisions for 'environmental impact assessments' in the case of large-scale development proposals. So far as animal welfare is concerned the situation is much more uneven as between different legislatures, but many countries now require minimum standards of animal welfare in intensive regimes and in research labs, outlaw cruel treatment of captive animals and outlaw at least some cruel sports. The

National Environmental Policy Act 1970, in the US played an exemplary role in prompting legislation elsewhere, whilst among the European countries, a crucial role has been played by the European Union, which has seen environmental protection as an important resource to bolster its own legitimacy. European law on the environment has been very influential in forcing the pace of national legislation, both among those countries already within the Union, and also among aspirant members to the East.

However, the sheer quantity of environmental legislation may not be the best measure of the success of the environmental movement. Questions need to be asked about the content of the legislation – does it adequately address the causes of the abuses it is designed to control? Does it enable unambiguous assigning of legal responsibility? Are the penalties it imposes an adequate deterrent? Are there adequate systems of inspection, monitoring and detection? Is enforcement rigorous and uncompromising? Above all, is the legislation effective in protecting non-human nature to the extent and in those respects that public concern requires? As we shall see, there are strong reasons for being less confident about the answers to these questions than the advocates of 'environmental reformism' might wish.

Nevertheless, the extension of well-established legal principles and precedents to offer protection to non-human species as well as to aspects of the human environment has many attractions. This approach does not appear to require deep-level institutional or cultural change, and is continuous with relatively successful reform strategies carried through by oppressed or exploited human groups. The discourse of universal rights and justice found its substantive expression in the revolutionary constitutions of America and France in the 18th century, and has by now acquired near universal moral authority, notwithstanding some cultural relativist and communitarian philosophical scepticism. Since World War 2, movements for national liberation on the part of former European colonies, as well as the nationalist opposition to Soviet domination, asserted their claims in the form of moral rights – in these cases to national sovereignty and self-determination. The emancipatory struggle of black Americans began with efforts to exercise civil and personal rights formally already possessed in the American constitution, but soon became a struggle for new rights and recognitions – including rights to assert a distinctive cultural identity. The subsequent 'second wave' feminist movement likewise moved from demands for equal rights towards more self-assertive claims for the recognition of difference (see, for example, Gilligan 1982).

## Rights for nature

When Singer ([1975], 1990), one of the pioneers of the contemporary animal liberation movement, explicitly situated the claim for animal liberation as the logical next step beyond these other causes, he was able to draw upon the considerable store of 'moral capital' already accumulated by those movements:

I argue that there can be no reason – except the selfish desire to preserve the privileges of the exploiting group – for refusing to extend the basic principle of equality of consideration to members of other species. I ask you to recognise that your attitudes to members of other species are a form of prejudice no less objectionable than prejudice about a person's race or sex.

(p.v)

As we shall see, the claim that animal liberation had a moral authority comparable with that assigned to the various human liberation movements turned out to be very contentious. But Singer's utilitarian grounding for animal liberation also came in for criticism for failing to accord animals sufficient protection. For utilitarians, the moral character of an act (or moral rule) is determined exclusively by its consequences. So, while Singer succeeds in arguing for equal consideration of human and animal suffering and welfare in the calculation of the consequences of actions, it still remains possible that human benefits may outweigh harms to animals in any particular case. It might, for example, be possible to justify causing suffering to animals in medical experiments if it could be shown that the overall total suffering of both humans and animals would be thereby reduced.

The leading exponent of this line of criticism, and of the alternative rights view has been Tom Regan ([1984] 1988). In his 'deontological' approach, the rightness or wrongness of acts is not simply a matter of their consequences. Some acts are inherently wrong, even if it can be shown that a balance of benefits might accrue from their being committed. Individual humans, for example, have inherent value, and are entitled to respectful treatment. Here, Regan draws implicitly on the near universal moral authority of human rights, as moral claims which override considerations of mere utility. But Regan extends the category of beings who have inherent value beyond the boundaries of the human species. If some non-humans have those qualities in virtue of which we assign inherent value to humans, then it is illogical and unjust to refuse to recognize inherent value, and so rights, in their case too. Regan's case for animal rights is a powerful one, but it does have both conceptual and practical limitations, to which I will return. Some other writers (most notably, Stone 1988) have taken the notion further, including trees, rivers, mountains and ecosystems as bearers of moral rights, and therefore as deserving of legal standing. Again, there is much to be said for such a strategy, but its conceptual and practical problems are still more serious than those surrounding Regan's much more limited extension of the idea of rights beyond the species boundary.

So, when ecological destruction and the abuse of other species became major public issues, it was not surprising that the social movements which had brought them to public attention presented their case in the language of rights and justice. Equally, it is unsurprising that the moral claims being advanced should take the practical form of pressure for legal recognition. But it is important here to distinguish two quite distinct ways in which the morality of rights and justice might be deployed in the pursuit of protections for non-human nature.

### Anthropocentrism or ecocentrism?

The key division here concerns whether we justify the protection of non-human beings, processes, relations and so on in virtue of their own inherent value, or, alternatively, whether we justify such protection on the basis of its actual or possible benefit to humans. The latter, 'anthropocentric' justification for environmental protection was already well established long before the current wave of ecological concern. If, in the case of human rights, we consider such formulations as 'life, liberty and the pursuit of happiness' it is clear that they embody a set of assumptions about the basic conditions for human flourishing. Each individual is to be protected from invasions on the part of other individuals or public bodies which threaten those basic conditions. Liberal conceptions of rights, most authoritative in the West, have emphasized liberty of conscience, of speech and a range of civil liberties, at the expense of the more material and bodily conditions of well-being. These latter have been advanced as extensions to the earlier liberal rights agenda as welfare rights, employment rights and so on, by social democratic political traditions, and as rights to bodily integrity and autonomy, reproductive rights and so on by the women's movement. Once the environmental movement establishes its case for full recognition of the ecological conditions for human well-being, then the addition of environmental rights appears as a logical further extension of the list. The rights of consumers to safe food, of citizens to clean air and unpolluted water and of workers to safe and healthy working conditions and so on, are already enshrined in law in most countries. Legal recognition of these rights may be institutionalized in a number of different ways. Individual citizens or interest groups may have the right to indict private or public bodies for causing environmental damage, or alternatively, statutory bodies may be set up with the legal responsibility to monitor and if necessary prosecute on behalf of the public. In other cases, environmental rights may be recognized in planning and development control procedures, and in the responsibilities of local authorities. In this sort of approach, the links between environmental protection and wider issues of human rights and socio-economic justice can be readily made.

However, from the standpoint of the animal liberation and rights movements, and the 'deeper' end of the ecological movement, there is a fundamantal flaw in this approach to environmental rights. The criticism is not so much that its practical effectiveness is questionable, but rather that its metaphysical and moral foundations are too limited. Advocates of 'deep ecology' (see, for example, Devall and Sessions 1985; Naess 1989) argue for a relational view of the world in which all beings are defined by their interconnections with one another. Special pleading on behalf of humans makes no sense in this perspective, so that inherent value is to be recognized in all of nature. Human supremacy is to be replaced by a principle of 'biospheric egalitarianism'. The animal rights perspective is much less radical than this in its implications, since it includes only a relatively small category of sentient beings into the charmed circle of bearers of inherent value. Nevertheless, Regan and those who think like him insist that non-human animals have value in themselves, and not in virtue of any relation to human interests. From both these perspectives then, environmental protection pursued as an augmentation of human rights

156

is open to criticism for its anthropocentrism. Rights are attributed to human individuals or groups only, and non-humans only benefit contingently and indirectly.

Though the committed activists of deep ecology and animal rights organizations constitute a small minority of the populations of the liberal democracies, they both express and crystallize a much more pervasive shift of moral sensibilities in relation to the non-human world. That moral concern should be extended beyond the boundaries of our own species, and that non-human beings should be recognized as having value in their own right, not merely as components in an expanded conception of human flourishing, are moral precepts now widely shared (see, for example, Agnew, pp. 177–209, this issue). Such a non-anthropocentric value framework does, indeed, involve a radical shift away from the dominant western traditions of moral and legal thought.

Of course, this shift is not without its opponents. One fairly standard objection to it rests on a secular view of value as the product of human social practices of valuing – things or persons or their attributes are held to be valuable only in so far as there is a human normative frame within which they are assigned value. This seems to rule out the idea of things having inherent value, independently of some such human normative system.

### In defence of a non-anthropocentric ethic

There are, broadly, three ways in which this sort of objection to a non-anthropocentric value orientation might be countered. One is to appeal to a higher order source of value in a divine being, creator of, or immanent within both human and non-human nature. Such an appeal is coherent with much deep ecological emphasis on spirituality, and may well have its place within a diverse and tolerant culture. However, to make such beliefs the basis of a 'green' legal order would be to abandon the libertarian impulse which has so far sustained the argument for extending rights across the species boundary. Moreover, to make concern for non-human nature dependent upon a specific set of religious or spiritual beliefs would be to restrict unnecessarily the potential breadth of appeal of a non-anthropocentric ethic.

The remaining two lines of defence for non-anthropocentric ethics are secular in character. The first is that adopted by the main tradition of animal rights advocacy. This begins with the claim which underlies the notion of human rights: that human individuals are inherently valuable – that they are the autonomous source of their own value. If we ask in virtue of what are human beings credited with inherent value, then the answer provided by the Kantian 'rights' tradition includes such attributes as the capacity to make choices, personal autonomy and the ability to act purposively. Such beings stand in need of rights in so far as they are liable to suffer harm with respect to the exercise of these basic powers and potentials.

The advocates of animal rights offer both theoretical reasons and empirical evidence for thinking that at least some categories of non-human animals are sufficiently psychologically complex for such concepts as autonomy, preference, benefit, harm, intention and cognates to be applicable to them. In Regan's terms, such beings are 'subjects of a life'. If this is so, then there are no good grounds for limiting our attribution of inherent value, and therefore of rights to human individuals only. To continue denying rights to non-humans which share the basic qualifying conditions for rights holding, whilst recognizing basic rights for humans is therefore, as we have seen, a form of 'speciesist' discrimination – an injustice. A powerful supporting argument is the reminder that many human individuals (small infants, victims of severe addictions, severely psychologically damaged or disabled individuals) may lack some or all of the full list of qualifying conditions for basic rights, or may satisfy them only to some limited degree. By comparison with these humans, at least some non-human animals may possess a fuller complement of autonomy, purposive behaviour and related capacities. If we do not deny basic rights to such undeveloped, damaged or disabled humans, what grounds are there for denying rights to comparable non-humans?

The third strategy for defence of the non-anthropocentric approach is to concede the secular argument which links value with human practices of valuing. This implies a significant departure from the deep ecological position, but it retains the non-anthropocentric moral orientation of deep ecology by marking an important distinction among such human practices of valuing. In brief, it is both possible, and quite familiar, to value other beings in virtue of their usefulness to us, or, alternatively, in virtue of what they are. Other beings may figure as means to our purposes, or, alternatively, as 'ends in themselves'. One can value someone or something for their own sake. This does not imply belief in the supernatural, nor need it necessarily be the case that the being valued has 'subject of a life' status. This is, broadly, the sort of approach I advocate. It is inclusive of the rights view where that can be applied, but it is also open to alternative ways of grounding moral concern for beings (both living and non-living) to which the attribution of rights makes little sense. To make clear why such a broader and more open-textured moral orientation to non-human nature is required, I need to explore in more depth both the strengths and the limitations of the rights view.

## The limits to rights

The 'subject of a life' argument for animal rights is, to my mind, a powerful and convincing one. There is plenty of room for disagreement about the empirical differences between animal and human behaviour, and the basis for imputing subjective states across the species boundary. It is also very questionable how comparable damaged or undeveloped humans are with fully competent members of other species. Regan's inclusion of these within the single category of 'moral patients' is a crucial, but quite contestable step in his argument. Nevertheless, it still seems to me that the broad outlines of the rights view can be sustained in the face of such considerations. However, it is significant that most of the debate about the moral status of animals has focussed on whether or not they satisfy the appropriate criteria for rights-bearers. In all this it is rather taken for granted by the advocates of animal rights that the key to giving practical protection to the interests of non-human animals is to get them recognized as rights-holders. That this assumption seems uncontroversial is a testimony to the current moral authority of the discourse of human rights, from which the argument for animal rights draws. But there does exist a long and important tradition of criticism of the morality of rights. This is most strongly associated with the socialist tradition, with its *locus classicus* in Marx's 'On the Jewish Question' ([1843] 1975). It may well be that the current (but probably temporary) decline in currency of socialist beliefs is part of the explanation for the uncritical acceptance of the discourse of rights. However, recent feminist work also includes significant scepticism about rights (see Benton 1993: Ch. 4, which also contains an extended version of the following argument), as does much of the work of communitarian political philosophers.

Part of my purpose here is to bring together some of the key arguments of this legacy of radical criticism of (liberal) rights, and to explore their continuing relevance, both to the defence of human interests, and to the protection of non-human nature. So, I have thus far been happy to agree with Regan and the other advocates of animal rights that extending rights to members of (some) other species is conceptually plausible, and, indeed, morally required to the extent that we attribute basic rights to humans themselves (which, again, I do). But, given that it makes sense to attribute rights to members of at least some non-human species, there are still some remaining problems for a rights-based approach to the protection of non-human nature. These can be summarized in the form of three questions. The first is: *can* the morality of rights, and its legal enactment, work as well for animals as it does for humans? The second is: *how far* beyond the species boundary can the morality of rights be stretched? The third is: given the significant *failures* of moral and legal rights to protect vulnerable humans, what grounds are there for thinking it might do better in the case of animals? The answer to this third question will plunge us into the issues posed by the radical tradition of scepticism about rights.

Let us deal with these questions in turn.

### Rights and the species boundary

One obvious limitation inherent in the carry-over of rights to non-human animals is that by nature they are not equipped to enjoy, or suffer from deprivation of, many of the basic goods which human rights seek to protect: not only freedom of religion and conscience, but also the full range of what we recognize as civil liberties. Given the deeply ingrained mind/body dualism in western cultures, and the priority given to capacities associated with the psychological dimension of well-being in the liberal tradition, this might make animal rights seem a very limited and trivial affair. It probably sustains the widespread disdain for the very idea of animal rights. However, two (slightly cross-cutting) considerations are relevant here. One is that for many other animal species there is good evidence of considerable psychological complexity, including a wide range of shared emotional capacities and vulnerabilities, together with often powerful and sophisticated social dispositions (see Beirne 1998). Many kinds of relation between humans and animals as 'companions' and 'servants', and a whole range of (ab)uses of animals as experimental subjects would be impossible if this were not true. It follows from this that animals may be vulnerable to suffering on many dimensions not reducible to the pleasure/pain calculus, and so stand in need of protection from physical confinement, social isolation, boredom, anxiety, stress and so on. The other consideration is that if the case for animal rights does serve as a foreground to the significance of bodily needs for health, adequate nutrition, physical freedom, bodily autonomy and integrity and so on, then this may serve as a reminder of the centrality of the bodily dimensions of human need and vulnerability, relatively neglected in the liberal tradition of thinking about rights.

Still on the theme of how well the moral framework of rights carries across the species boundary, it is commonly argued that there is no real comparability between the liberation struggles which take place among human groups and the case for animal rights (see, for example, Rose 1991). Sometimes the point being made is that the comparison demeans and trivializes the quest for human emancipation (implicitly assuming the lesser moral standing of non-human animals). However, there is another respect in which the two sorts of social movement are not comparable. This is that campaigns for animal rights or liberation are always and necessarily fought by human groups on behalf of animals, never by the animals themselves. By contrast, campaigns for the emancipation of specific groups of humans, whilst they often include non-members of the aggrieved group, can never acquire full legitimacy unless the claims they make are at some stage endorsed by those groups on their own behalf. But the point can be made more strongly than this. Once a movement for self-emancipation gains momentum, processes of social and political learning and dialogue often bring about deep changes in the content of the emancipatory project itself. This can lead to quite sharp mutual alienation between would-be supporters of such movements and in-group activists. Both the emancipatory movement of black Americans between the 1950s and the end of the 1960s and the 'second wave' feminist movement displayed this sort of dynamic. At a certain point, black activists came to reject integration on the terms of the dominant 'white' culture, and forged a distinctive black American cultural identity with associated radicalizations of the emancipatory political project. Similar shifts from the pre-eminence of liberal and socialist visions towards radical feminist insistence on the specificity and irreducibility of gender oppression, and on a revaluation of feminine identity, took place during the course of 'second wave' feminism.

One distinctive feature of these emancipatory movements, then, is the emergence of the claim to self-definition, the claim to be the author of one's own emancipatory project, the rejection of any form of paternalism, however sincere or well meant. There is, here, a duality in the structure of human emancipatory rights claims: a (second order) right is claimed to active participation in the definition of the *content* of the agenda of (first order) rights. This duality is missing in the case of the rights of non-human animals: so far as is known, no other species on earth has the necessary psychological and communicative equipment to be self-defining in the way that human emancipatory struggles are (but we should be cautious about this, bearing in mind the now discredited 'scientific' case against the fully human status of both women and non-European races by opponents of their emancipatory claims).

There are several important consequences here. One is that in formulating the protections to which non-human animals are entitled, we are dependent on our (human) beliefs as to their nature, and their vulnerabilities, as well as to what is to count as 'flourishing' for them. In the absence of articulate communication with other species, such beliefs can never be endorsed by them, and must remain very much dependent on our interpretation of their behavioural responses to various treatments. Since both lay and scientific beliefs about (especially the psychological dimensions of) animal natures are very variable, subject to change through time, and always controversial, the risk that well-meant legislation might actually impose suffering as an unintended consequence is considerable. This point is, in fact, just one aspect of a broader issue posed by the extension of rights to other species. This is that the underlying logic is one which assigns moral protection on the basis of similarity, or commonality of attributes between humans and other animals. It cuts against the grain of such a strategy to make out the full case for a contrary principle of moral regard for what is 'other', or different.

A second consequence of the necessarily 'paternalistic', or once-removed character of animal rights claims is that any attempt to give practical, institutional form to a legal recognition of their rights would necessarily involve their interests being 'represented' vicariously. The normal interaction between client and legal representative is ruled out in the nature of the case, and in the absence of any unequivocal rules by which to weight conflicting human and animal rights and interests, justice is likely to be, at best, both very rough and somewhat partial. This is not, of course, to deny that partial and rough justice is better than no justice at all.

Thinking back to the case for animal rights itself, these considerations point to a strong disanalogy between rights claims as they figure in human liberation struggles, where the subject of such claims is centrally involved in pressing them, and rights claims as they are claimed on behalf of beings, human or otherwise, who are deemed to possess less than full personal and moral agency. We might distinguish, on this basis, 'active' rights, associated with moral agency, and 'passive' rights, associated with the status of what Regan calls 'moral patients'. Moral patients are entitled to (passive) rights in virtue of their character as 'subjects of a life', and they stand in need of rights precisely because of their lack of full moral agency: they are particularly vulnerable to exploitative and oppressive treatment. This distinction does, I think, preserve the core of the argument for recognizing non-human beings as bearers of rights, whilst confirming strongly held intuitions that animal rights and human liberation struggles such as those against racism, homophobia, patriarchy and imperialism are not fully comparable.

### The scope of rights

This takes us to a consideration of the second of the three main problems with the rights approach which I distinguished above: the question of how far this approach is able to take us across the species boundary. Those animals sufficiently like humans to be considered as 'subjects of a life', and which are either systematically included in human social practices (such as horse-racing, farming, scientific research and pet keeping) or are liable to more sporadic and contingent encounters with dangerous humans (such as hunters and badger baiters) may, then, derive potential benefits from the extension of rights to cover their conditions of life. However, this leaves entirely unprotected the vast majority of individuals and species of non-human animals, plants and ecosystems. This is more than just a boundary problem. It may be open to dispute whether, for example, fish are subjects of a life in the relevant respects, but this can be addressed by a generous application of the necessary criteria, just in case they are. The point is, wherever the cut-off point is placed, many non-human beings will fall on the wrong side of it. To leave this vast array of beings in the moral wilderness, subject to whatever destructive projects humans may unleash on them, runs strongly counter to the emergent moral sensibility towards non-human nature. New forms of moral and legal – not merely prudential – restraints on human destructiveness in nature seem to be required – and these need to cover more than our closest evolutionary kith and kin.

One possible strategy here is to extend the moral purchase of rights and justice beyond psychologically complex mammalian relatives to include other forms of animal and plant life and even non-living beings such as lakes, rivers and mountains. Stone (1974), among others, has seen no good reason why, for example, trees should not have legal standing, independently of the human groups who might be aggrieved by their destruction. Such an extension of the range of beings who could be said to be bearers of rights would involve weakening the criteria by which individuals are credited with being 'subjects of a life', or, alternatively, pluralizing the qualifying conditions: perhaps the applicability of such concepts as benefit and harm, needs, interests or some notion of self-sustaining structural identity might be called upon. However, this sort of strategy is difficult to defend against the charge of arbitrariness. Moreover, the difficulties associated in the case of psychologically complex non-human animals with evaluating their needs and interests without the help of linguistic communication are multiplied as we move out to even more distant animal and plant species and non-living beings. Not only must it seem arbitrary which beings do and do not count as rights-holders, but also what their substantive rights should be and how they should be weighted in relation to others.

A deep-ecological response here might be to argue that the very project of extending moral considerations to non-human animals and the rest of nature is implicitly anthropocentric, in that it seeks to include non-human nature within what is after all a human social practice. For leading exponents of deep ecology (see, for example, principles three to five of the eight 'basic principles', or 'platform' of deep ecology listed in Devall and Sessions 1985: 70) the implication of our recognition of inherent value in non-human nature is to limit our interactions with it to a minimum. Beyond such interventions as are indispensable to the meeting of our vital needs, we should withdraw from nature as much as possible. Authoritative normative regulation of human conduct in relation to non-human nature would then be required only for those dimensions of nature with which we indispensably interact. However, there are some difficulties with this. One is that human geographical spread and technological powers clearly now are global in their reach. No part of the biosphere has been unaffected by the intended or unintended consequences of human activity. Where this impact has been at its least, this is often due to deliberate restraint, in recognition of the special ecological or aesthetic value of an area. In this sense, all of the biosphere falls within human society. What we recognize as 'wilderness' is generally affected by human activity to some degree, and remains less severely transformed than the rest of the biosphere because of agreed normative restraints, or because of the practical difficulties or economic costs of exploiting it. In short, it is now too late for a strategy of minding our own business and leaving nature to itself. Either what is vulnerable to human destructiveness in non-human nature will continue to be destroyed, or it will be protected by some form of effective normative restraint of human activity. Moreover, for such normative restraint to be both effective and consistent with civil liberties will require further extension and consolidation of spontaneous popular moral sentiments which respect and value non-human nature. Such moral sentiments flourish best in the context of active engagements of non-destructive kinds with the rest of nature, rather than a withdrawal of contact.

This brings us back directly to the question of rights and justice. If there are conceptual difficulties in the way of grounding the case for authoritative norms restraining human destructiveness by extending the concepts of rights and justice, what alternatives do we have? I will make a start in the direction of answering this question in a rather indirect way. Above, I distinguished three questions posed by the extension of rights across the species boundary. The third of these questions acknowledged that the assertion of rights has not been an unqualified success in its primary application to humans. If it has failed to protect humans in respect of their basic interests, why should we suppose it will succeed in this for non-human animals, let alone the rest of nature?

## The radical critique of (liberal) rights

The radical case against rights has four strands or themes. The first draws attention to the ways in which severe inequalities in power and wealth may undermine the capacity of the impoverished and powerless in society to exercise such rights as they are legally assigned. Such rights may be little more than an empty formality, serving merely to legitimate persisting de facto inequalities. The second strand addresses the liberal tradition's conceptualization of the individual subject, or citizen as the paradigm bearer of rights. The third strand also takes issue with the individualism of liberal notions of rights, but now with regard to the range of harms from which individuals are held to stand in need of protection. Rights typically impose duties on identifiable individual agents (or the sovereign power conceived as an individual) to refrain from infringement of certain basic interests of the rights-holder. But what of the many sources of harm to basic interests of individuals which are located in established social and economic structures and practices, pervasive environmental transformations and technical innovations? Such everyday risks can rarely if ever be assigned to any particular individual agency, so they stand outside the scope of rights as they are generally understood in the liberal tradition. The fourth strand in the radical critique of rights is in many ways the most fundamental. It calls into question why we need rights in the first place. The idea of universal and basic human rights is, after all, very much a modern invention. At its most radical, this strand of criticism of rights argues that rights are only needed to protect individuals from their neighbours because something has gone deeply wrong in society. Competitive, egoistic individuals, acting under conditions of scarcity are impelled to invade one another's basic interests unless restrained by a firmly enforced framework of rights. I will explore the implications of each of these strands in the radical critique in a little more detail.

### Rights, formal and substantive

The first strand in the radical critique focusses on the implications of the formal recognition of rights in contexts of severe social and economic inequality. The liberal tradition, in particular, emphasizes rights such as freedom of opinion, property, equality under the law and so on. However, where these rights require resources, or an appropriate context for their exercise, many individuals may not benefit at all. The law protects property of the beggar no less than that of the millionaire, but this is no help to the beggar. In fact, if the property rights of the millionaire constitute a barrier to redistributive policies to help the beggar, then property rights actually harm the interests of those who are most vulnerable. To respond to this kind of problem, a radicalization of the liberal rights tradition is available. Rights should be defined not formally, or negatively, as 'non-interference' rights, but substantively, or positively, as entitlements to the necessary resources to enable people to exercise them. This is one important argument leading beyond civil liberties to a more extensive provision of welfare, social and economic rights. However, well meant and enabling as these extensions have been in those (mainly European) societies where they have been at least partially implemented, they remain limited in their scope, and vulnerable to adverse shifts in the balance of political power (witness the consequences of the recent ascendancy of the new right).

If it is the case that large sectors of the human populations of societies whose polities implement liberal rights remain unprotected in their basic interests – if many go homeless, lack secure sources of income necessary for the meeting of material needs, suffer coercive and unsafe working conditions, cannot afford adequate health care and so on – why should we suppose that extending liberal rights to non-human nature will do much good? Non-human beings, lacking the capacity to act on their own behalf, and dependent on humanly constructed juridical institutions to take action on their behalf are even less well placed than the least advantaged human groups to win concessions from the wealthy and powerful.

### The individualism of rights

The second theme in the radical critique of rights focusses on the individualism of liberal rights. In the version of this line of argument which

I wish to advocate here, the objection is not to the moral priority which the liberal tradition gives to individuals (as against collectivities, such as ethnic groups). This is common ground with most radical traditions. The point is, rather, that the liberal tradition has tended to work with a rather narrow and inadequate view of individual human nature and of the associated conditions of human well-being or flourishing. For socialist critics of the liberal tradition the complaint has been that liberals do not afford sufficient priority to the meeting of bodily needs for food and shelter. A society in which there are prisoners of conscience is clearly one in which human rights are not fully recognized, but, on this argument, so is one in which people freeze to death on the streets for lack of housing access. Both socialist and communitarian critics add to this that liberals are inclined to under-recognize the extent to which the character of the social and cultural 'embedding' of individuals is constitutive of their identity. So, for example, the implementation of welfare rights through 'targeted' and means-tested benefits may fail to recognize the individual's cultural requirement for personal recognition and autonomy. The emergence of environmental sensibilities adds yet another dimension to this theme in the radical critique of liberal rights. Our concept of human individual well-being has to be expanded to include the environmental, as well as the social and cultural 'embedding' of each person. Unpolluted water, fresh air, uncontaminated food, access to a rich and diverse physical environment and other conditions would all be included in any comprehesive characterization of the conditions for human well-being. It is important, here, to notice the interconnectedness of the environmental, bodily, and social dimensions of well-being both with one another and with psychological and cultural–political ones. A politically very important example is the close tie between cultural identity, especially for many indigenous peoples, and social practices which link them with distinctive biotopes – whether tropical moist forest or arctic tundra. As we saw above, one response to such arguments as these might be an (anthropocentric) enrichment of the concept of human rights to include cultural, economic and environmental dimensions. However, as the first strand in the critique reminds us, it is one thing to proclaim a right, but quite another to live in a society which enables one to exercise it.

But how relevant is this second strand in the critique of rights to any proposed extension of rights to non-human beings? Although it is true that the cultural and identity-sustaining dimensions of human relatedness to their environments are probably absent in the case of non-human species, nevertheless, the material dependence of non-human populations on often highly specific habitats is even more evident than in the human case. Bodily needs are no less pressing, and for most of those animal species subjected to domestication, there is a complex set of social needs and dispositions. If it is accepted that the liberal-individualist conception of rights is too limited in its view of human well-being, then the same criticism applies to its extension to non-human beings. However, though this line of criticism might have force against the most influential versions of liberal-individualist rights theory, there is no reason a priori why the agenda of rights should not be extended to cover the protection of bodily, social, cultural and environmental dimensions of well-being. The advocates of rights are usually reluctant to accept such 'catch all' extensions of rights, however, as they threaten to undermine the central purpose of rights claims – namely, to give unequivocal priority to some interests over others. Rights are held to work only if they can be used as a kind of 'trump card' in cases of conflicting interests. However, there are also historical and sociological reasons why radicalization of rights has been limited in theory and even less in evidence in practice. In modern history, the enunciation of liberal rights has been closely associated with the emergence of capitalist economic relations and the social and political institutions which have sustained and regulated them. In these societies, the pre-eminence of property rights, together with the political and economic power of the class of capital owners has constituted a bulwark against extensions of substantive and universal environmental, bodily and socio-cultural rights. Where private capital disposes over the opportunities of most individuals to obtain income, decides the terms under which that income is earned in physical spaces owned also by capital, such extensions of rights for non-capital owners can only be at the expense of an erosion of the property rights of the owners of capital.

The theoretical possibility remains open that an expanded view of rights, informed by a multi-layered radical critique of the liberal view of (human and non-human) well-being could be both developed as part of an argument for radical social and economic change, and implemented in the course of attempts to realize such radical change. Of course, any such project would need to be tempered by a full recognition of the dreadful costs of any sacrifice of personal and civil liberties justified in the name of either social and economic justice, or environmental protection. The historical experience of projects for radical change in our own century suggests that in the absence of full civil and political rights, the material, social and ecological dimensions of well-being fare badly too!

### Rights and unattributable harms

So far, then, the critique of rights turns out to be a critique of specifically liberal views of rights, and of their implementation in radically unequal societies. The prospect remains open of a radicalization of rights alongside egalitarian social change as a way of realizing the so-far unredeemed promises of liberal rights. The third strand in the radical critique of rights is also related to the individualism of liberal views of rights. In this line of criticism, however, the problem has to do with the liberal tradition's characteristic ways of thinking about the sources of harm to which individual rights-holders are vulnerable. These sources are, typically, other individual citizens, and the sovereign power, also conceived on the model of a super-individual. There are at least three pervasive sorts of hazards to individuals' basic interests which are very difficult if not impossible to reduce to this individualist model. First, there are consequences of acts of commission or omission on the part of large private organizations – transport disasters, chemical plant explosions, the break-up of oil tankers and the like. In these cases, it is notoriously difficult to pin down criminal responsibility. In UK law, for example, it is necessary for the prosecution to identify individuals within the organization whose duties included responsibility for whatever is defined as having caused the incident

(Benton 1993: Ch. 4). This means that firms with no clearly defined policy on environmental protection or health and safety, or which contract out or delegate such responsibilities are more likely to escape prosecution. Alternatively, blame may be placed on the shoulders of an overworked, exhausted and untrained employee who functions as a convenient scapegoat. The second sort of hazard is embedded in everyday life, and especially in routine working life. Pedestrians, cyclists and motorists themselves, for example, run considerable risks of death or injury in road accidents. Many occupations, such as mining, building, nuclear reprocessing and so on carry health risks that are well known. The statistical evidence reveals stark differences in chronic sickness and early death as between the social classes. There is strong evidence that the combination of material deprivation and emotional stress related to unemployment or threat of it is also a serious health hazard (Benton 1991). Finally, persistent consumption of chemical toxins, and exposure to pathogenic organisms as a result of water pollution and changes in the food production and processing system can be seen as a colossal 'experiment' whose long-term consequences are unknown.

These hazards share many characteristics with a third class of risks which are often represented as 'natural disasters': floods, droughts, hurricanes, epidemics, earthquakes and so on. In these sorts of case, injuries and fatalities are often concentrated in space and time, and there is a readily identifiable physical or biological causal mechanism at work. Nevertheless, or perhaps even because of this, there is a common tendency to see such hazards as part of 'normal' life, as something you just live with as part of the 'package' of living where you do, or of participating in a particular 'given' mode of life. However, in many cases there are available technologies or feasible organizational strategies for avoiding or radically reducing the impact of such disasters. The extent of suffering, usually at its greatest among the poor and relatively powerless, is very much linked to failures on the part of public authorities to give the necessary priority to preventative or damage-limitation strategies. Increasingly, what appear as natural disasters are really caused by complex interactions between human social and economic practices and causal mechanisms in nature (a category of hazard rather misleadingly characterized by Beck (1992), Giddens (1994) and others as 'manufactured' risk). For example, global climate change is thought to have as one of its consequences an increase in the incidence and unpredictability of extreme weather events. Both droughts and floods are also often attributable to localized ecological effects of such changes as upland deforestation and over-exploitation of dry-land ecosystems, processes which themseves often have complex and far-reaching causes in global economic and political institutions.

What is common to both my second and third sorts of hazard is that the identification of either individual or even corporate responsibility seems in the nature of the situation ruled out. Beck (1992) gives the term 'organized non-liability' to this state of affairs, though it seems to me that it is much more widespread than is suggested by his limitation of it to an important class of high-profile risks associated with advanced technologies. However, as Beck puts it, when everyone pollutes, no-one pollutes. The difficulty faced by a strategy of extension of the apparatus of rights to deal with this is that rights cannot be enforced if no one can be identified as responsible for their infringement. Perhaps the most that a rights approach could achieve in the face of all this would be to launch a moral indictment of a whole way of life and of those powerful institutions and social groups which are committed to sustaining it.

### Why do we need rights?

Now I turn to the fourth strand in the radical critique of rights. This line of argument poses the very fundamental question: why does anyone need rights at all? In other words, what conditions of life make authoritative norms to protect individuals in their basic interests necessary? Lukes (1985) has distinguished four such conditions: scarcity (in relation to desires); lack of full mutual benevolence between humans; plurality of values; and lack of complete knowledge. Since our discussion is concerned with the plausibility and effectiveness of extending the morality of rights and justice beyond the species boundary, we have to consider these conditions, likewise, in a species-transcendent way. At its most radical, the critique of rights (and justice) has focussed on the first two of these conditions, and argued that both are artificial consequences of the institutional arrangements of modern capitalist societies. On this view, the experience of scarcity has two main causes. One is maldistribution. Enough resources exist or are produced for everyone's material needs to be met, but many fail to have basic needs met because the rich get or use more than they need, and because there is huge and systematic waste in the world's agricultural and industrial (dis)organization. The second is a consequence of the way that commodification and the subsequent ideology of consumerism undermine all traditional forms of normative regulation of desire, sweeping away all local or status-bound notions of 'sufficiency' and appropriateness in consumption (see the brilliant analysis of these mechanisms in Leiss, 1978). Such anomic desire knows no bounds, but is experienced under conditions of limited and conditional (i.e. monetary exchange) legitimate access to means of satisfaction.

The second condition which is held to make the institution of rights necessary is lack of mutual benevolence. The radical critique of rights is commonly (but not always) premised on an optimistic view of human nature, such that mutual benevolence and social co-operation would be the spontaneous attributes of human sociality if it were not for the malign influence of defective social institutions, social domination and the like. Dispositions to antagonism and aggression, viewed in this sort of perspective, come from certain kinds of familial arrangements, child-rearing practices and so on, but are then reinforced and even made normative by the dominant ideology and institutional order of modern capitalist society. Competitive performance is the incessant demand at work, whilst status seeking and the competitive pursuit of 'positional goods' increasingly shapes and constrains consumption and the use of 'leisure' time. So, there are complex reinforcing linkages between the experiences of scarcity and those of individualized relations of competitive antagonism. So far as the two main rights-necessitating conditions are concerned, the radical argument is that they are not inherent in the human condition but consequences of a historically specific type of civilization – characterized by capitalism and the nuclear family. A project of radical social transformation which favoured dispositions to benevolent co-operativeness in its child-rearing practices, and institutionalized the same sentiments and dispositions in its organization of production and distribution would take us on the way to a society which had no need of rights. Concern for one another's well-being would animate social relations in ways which made authoritative imposition of restraints 'from above' unnecessary and inappropriate.

This line of argument is sometimes dismissed because it asks us to wager on an untested and utopian claim about human nature. However, it seems to me that a considerable part of the force of the argument can be sustained on the basis of everyday experience, and without any reliance on an unreasonably optimistic view of human nature. It is perfectly clear from everyday experience that people are capable of both benevolent and antagonistic dispositions, of behaving co-operatively and competitively. It is also a matter of common experience that our own dispositions to behave co-operatively or with competitive antagonism towards one another vary enormously from one institutional setting to another. Members of households often (but not always!) evolve shared norms in the division of labour and collaborate in the carrying out of agreed tasks. By contrast, motorists on congested roads, in a rush to get to work on time, are inclined to behave with a considerable degree of competitive antagonism! The policy programme of the neo-liberal right, in the ascendency in several western countries over the past two decades, has induced both cultural and institutional changes which have significantly favoured competitive antagonism as against co-operative and convivial practices across many institutional contexts. Hence, different institutional settings may favour or suppress co-operative modes of social interaction. If this is so when experienced within a few years, it does not seem such a utopian leap to expect that the settings in which deeper forms of personal identity and disposition are established over longer periods might profoundly affect the balance of co-operative and nurturative as against competitive and antagonistic dispositions.

We do not, then, need to be extravagantly optimistic about human nature to have a case for thinking that widespread dispositions to infringe one another's basic interests could be greatly reduced by suitable public policy changes and deep-level social and economic change. Whether or not antagonistic dispositions are, as proclaimed in Freud's later writings (Freud, [1930] 1985; New 1996, explores the implications of rival views of human nature for ecological politics) inherent in human nature, there can be little doubt that modern capitalism (augmented by the policy programme of the new right) profoundly exacerbates and intensifies the harmful consequences of any such dispositions. Both social order and ideological legitimacy under such conditions set up the demand for basic rights, but as we have seen, large numbers of citizens remain de facto unable to enjoy such rights as are proclaimed, and remain unprotected from significant risks and harms which fall outside the scope of liberal rights.

But, we should be clear where this partial endorsement of the radical case against rights does *not* take us. Everyday experience, as well as evidence of the huge diversity of patterns of human relationships disclosed by anthropological and historical study, justifies a view of human dispositions as openly flexible and as significantly shaped by prevailing institutional contexts. However, this is a long way from demonstrating that such flexibility and malleability is without limit, that human nature is motivationally and emotionally as well as cognitively, a 'blank sheet' until society writes its messages upon it. Not only is this view not licensed by any available evidence, but it goes against the tendency of the general argument I have so far been developing. If humans are, indeed, a part of nature, and descended, through the operation of mechanisms comparable with those which formed other species, from primate ancestors, we should expect human nature, open and 'unfinished' as it undoubtedly is, to have some positive motivational and emotional content.

In view of this it seems improbable that the psychological sources of human antagonisms and conflicts could be eliminated by radical social reform – no matter how profound. Moreover, the plausibility of a future society in which there were no institutional or socio-cultural sources of antagonism is far from being demonstrated. So, it would be unwise to ground any political project on the assumption that human relations could be fully pacified in some future social order (I leave aside here the perfectly serious question as to whether, even if possible, such a project would be desirable!). It is reasonable to suppose that relative scarcity, antagonism and conflict of interests would feature to some degree in any possible form of human society. It follows that some authoritative normative framework (for which the discourse of rights and justice is our current paradigm) would be required to regulate relationships and protect the interests of the vulnerable. Rights – or some close functional analogue – are likely to prove indispensable.

However, in spite of this crucial qualification, a great deal of the radical case against rights remains defensible. The conceptual limitations of specifically liberal views of rights can be endorsed, as can the radical claim that the proclamation of universal rights under conditions of deep social and economic inequality is little more than an ideological cloak for vested interests. Further, we do not need the utopian vision of a universally benevolent and abundant commonwealth to justify the belief that radical social and economic change might significantly reduce, if not eliminate, the sources of antagonism and conflict which give rise to the demand and need for rights under contemporary capitalist relations. Social and economic relations which fostered, rather than suppressed, co-operative and sympathetic dispositions and sentiments would offer a context in which the need for rights was much less pervasive, and in which such rights as were still required could be much more readily enforced. In other words, rights would have less work to do, and what work remained would go with, rather than against, the grain of the wider institutional setting and popular sentiments.

## Rights and the pacification of our relation to nature

The alternative to a society riven with antagonisms, attempting but generally failing to keep them in order through the institutions of rights and justice would seem to be a society built on co-operative and democratic forms of organization in which norms of care and mutual support would go with the flow of spontaneous sentiments generated by the prevailing forms of social interaction. This line of thought can be extended to address the key limitations of the rights approach to our relations with non-human nature. As recent feminist work has insisted (e.g. Donovan and Adams 1996), no matter how well reasoned the case for rights might be, changed relations between humans and animals will depend primarily on deep changes in our emotional and sentimental attachments to their well-being. But these changes, in turn, will be inseparable from transformations in the institutional contexts and power-structures which currently prevail. The largest-scale and most systematically organized abuses of non-human animals occur in intensive rearing regimes in agriculture and in research laboratories. In both contexts there is evidence of genuine human compassion for animal suffering, but it is systematically overridden by the prevailing cultural priorities, authority structures and institutional objectives of the relevant agribusiness complex or industrial or public-sector institute. This contrasts markedly with the normative order which prevails in institutions such as the keeping of 'pet' or 'companion' animals. Here, long-term and continuous interaction with the animal, and the non-instrumental normative frame within which the practice has meaning, typically generate spontaneous sentiments of care and concern for the animal's well-being. Attempts to regulate pet-keeping and protect the interests, or 'rights' of the pet remain necessary, but only to deal with particular human actions or neglect which run against the grain of the spontaneous sentiments and normative order of the practice. In the case of the meat industry, or research and development in pharmaceuticals, by contrast, attempts at regulation fly in the face of powerful institutional pressures and organized interests.

The implications seem clear: whatever the merits, as tactics within an overall strategy, of extending rights claims to non-human nature, such tactics are unlikely to be successful unless they are connected with a broader struggle to transform our relations to each other, to domesticated animals and to the rest of nature. The aim would be to generate harmonious, benevolent and co-operative spirals, as against destructive, competitive and antagonistic ones, through the establishment of new dominant patterns of interaction, experiences and spontaneous sentiments. This might include, for example, working for cultural shifts through which people gained wider and deeper experience of contact with non-human nature, through conservation work in urban sites, countryside activities, organic horticulture and so on, but perhaps even more important might be a self-reflective practice of recognition of how much the contacts and engagements with nature *which we already have* enrich and give meaning to our lives.

This is the beginning of an answer to the question: 'if not rights, what is the alternative?' This alternative would be a many-sided project for social, economic and ecological transformation inspired by spontaneous moral sentiments which flow from anxiety and horror in the face of continuing human destruction of non-human nature, and by the egalitarian, cooperative and popular democratic values inherited from earlier anarchist and socialist traditions, and now carried forward by the feminist, peace, green and other progressive social movements (see R-GSG 1995, for one attempt to spell out such a project). Of course, this is a very tall order! There are some obvious objections. I will conclude by mentioning just two. One derives from a strong sense of urgency about ecological destruction, and from the desire to do something about that and the abuse of animals in the here-and-now. My argument is definitely not intended as a rebuttal of reform measures within the existing social and political framework. The suggestion is, rather, that alternative proposals for reform should be evaluated in terms of their contribution to a longer-term strategy of deep social change. Some reforms, such as, for example, the application of neoclassical economics to measure the 'value' of environmental 'goods', and the use of market-based incentives, intensify the shift towards an ever more rationally intensive commodification of nature. Such measures are very appealing to many environmentalists, but my argument is that they take us even further from where we need to be. In general, forms of regulation based on collective decision-making, itself deriving from fully informed and inclusive dialogue, are to be favoured against measures which reduce questions of life quality to questions of technically calculable economic cost.

The second objection to my argument is that it does, after all, rely on a utopian fantasy about the human condition, if not about human nature. This would, indeed be so if it remained unqualified. I think there is good reason to believe that human societies could be far more convivial, cooperative and harmonious with their non-human contexts and conditions than the example provided by the current dominance of globalizing capital accumulation. However, this is not to deny that there may be something stubbornly present in the human condition itself which resists the final elimination of competitive antagonism and destructiveness, not only in relation to one another, but also in relation to nature. Perhaps neither our relations to one another, nor our relations to the non-human world can be fully pacified. More than 40 years ago, Marcuse (1956) addressed the question of human emancipation on the basis of his pessimistic reading of Freud's later work (most notably Freud [1930] 1985). Let us suppose that the human psyche has an irreducible component of 'instinctual' or primary aggressiveness. Let us also acknowledge the significance of Lukes's third and fourth conditions necessitating rights: that even if we are well disposed to each other, we may still harm each other by acting upon value assumptions which are not shared, or because we do not have adequate knowledge of the effects of our actions on the well-being of others. Finally, let us recognize that despite our uniqueness in our ability to transform our environments and adapt to their constraints, we remain, as Marx ([1844] 1975) put it, 'active natural beings': we cannot live without intervening in and appropriating from the world around us. There is no 'pre-established harmony' between our needs and that world. Every imaginable form of human social life, in other words, will be characterized by 'scarcity' in the sense that what we take from it, the way we take it, and what we put back will stand in need of regulation.

Put together, all these considerations point to the conclusion that the moral framework of rights and justice, together with their extension (perhaps through analogous normative concepts) to cover our relations with the non-human world can never be finally dispensed with. However, the hope might be that linking the radicalization of the discourse of rights and justice with a democratic project of social transformation would create a more favourable social setting for the institutionalizing of rights, as well as of other forms of normative regulation of our relations with non-human nature.

First, as we have seen, the hope would be that the prevailing institutional forms and moral sentiments would reduce the amount of infringement of individual rights that went on. Similarly, more extensive and ecologically benign forms of agriculture, horticulture and sylviculture, would drastically reduce the need for interventions to protect bio-diversity and landscape values. In the absence of powerful material and policy incentives favouring environmental destruction (such as prevail over these key practices today), those charged with land management in these areas could give practical effect to the respect for non-human nature which many of them already share. The legal apparatus of nature protection, like that of rights and justice would have less work to do, and so be more effective in doing it.

Second, the prevailing socio-economic inequalities which obstruct the extension and practical realization of rights in our own societies would be substantially ameliorated, if not removed. But these inequalities are also causally responsible for much current abuse of non-human nature. As we have seen, the most systematic, institutionalized and large-scale abuse of non-human animals takes place in research labs and intensive rearing regimes where powerful economic interests drive the practices. At the other end of the economic scale, the Brundtland report (WCED 1987) succeeded in demonstrating the extent to which the disparate survival strategies imposed on the world's poor and dispossessed are implicated in environmental degradation. In general, eliminating both unaccountable concentrations of economic power, and widespread poverty would be the most effective strategy for environmental protection currently available to us.

Third, in such a transformed economy and society, the normative context in which the residual enforcement of rights and nature protection took place could be expected to be much more favourable. Public regulation would be upholding and protecting what was already favoured and nurtured by everyday experience of interaction with other humans and with non-human beings and environments. Above all, it should be emphasized, a strongly institutionalized protection of universal civil liberties would still be required to offset any tendency for new forms of oppression and exploitation to emerge, or for old ones to reassert themselves.

## References

Agnew, Robert (1998) 'The Causes of Animal Abuse: A Social-Psychological Analysis', *Theoretical Criminology*, 2(2): 177–209.

Beck, Ulrich (1992) *Risk Society: Towards a New Modernity.* London: Sage.

Beirne, Piers (1998) 'For a Non-Speciesist Criminology: Animal Abuse as an Object of Study', unpublished paper.

Benton, Ted (1991) 'Biology and Social Science: Why the Return of the Repressed Should be Given a (Cautious) Welcome', *Sociology*, 25(l): 1–29.

Benton, Ted (1993) *Natural Relations: Ecology Animal Rights and Social Justice.* London: Verso.

Bookchin, Murray (1991) *The Ecology of Freedom.* Montreal: Black Rose.

Carson, Rachel (1962) *Silent Spring.* Boston, MA: Houghton Mifflin.

Commoner, Barry (1972) *The Closing Circle.* New York: Bantam.

Conway, Gordon and Jules Pretty (1991) *Unwelcome Harvest.* London: Earthscan.

Devall, Bill and George Sessions (1985) *Deep Ecology.* Layton, Utah: Gibbs Smith.

Donovan, Josephine and Carol J. Adams (eds) (1996) *Beyond Animal Rights.* New York: Continuum.

Engels, Friedrich ([18451 1969) *The Condition of the Working Class in England.* London: Panther.

Freud, Sigmund ([1930] 1985) 'Civilization and its Discontents', *Civilization, Society and Religion.* Harmondsworth: Penguin.

Giddens, Anthony (1994) *Beyond Left and Right.* Cambridge: Polity.

Gilligan, Carol (1982) *In a Different Voice.* Cambridge, MA: Harvard University Press.

Goodman, David and Michael Redclift (1991) *Refashioning Nature: Food, Ecology and Culture.* London: Routledge.

Gould, Peter (1988) *Early Green Politics.* Brighton: Harvester.

Leiss, William (1978) *The Limits to Satisfaction: On Needs and Commodities.* London: Marion Boyars.

Lukes, Steven (1985) *Marxism: and Morality.* Oxford: Oxford University Press.

Marcuse, Herbert (1956) *Eros and Civilization.* London: Routledge and Kegan Paul.

Marx, Karl ([1844] 1975) 'Economic and Philosophical Manuscripts', *Marx and Engels Collected Works. Vol. 3.* London: Lawrence and Wisharr.

Meadows, Donella and Dennis Meadows (1974) *The Limits to Growth.* London: Pan.

Naess, Arne (1989) *Ecology, Community and Lifestyle.* Cambridge: Cambridge University Press.

New, Caroline (1996) *Agency, Health and Social Survival: The Ecopolitics of Rival Psychologies.* London: Taylor and Francis.

Pepper, David (1996) *Modern Environmentalism.* London: Routledge.

R-GSG (Red-Green Study Group) (1995) *What on Earth is to be Done?* 2 Hamilton Road, Manchester: R-GSG.

Regan, Tom ([1984] 1988) *The Case for Animal Rights.* London: Routledge.

Rose, Steven (1991) 'Proud to be Speciesist', *New Statesman and Society*, 26 April, p. 21.

Shiva, Vandana (1989) *Staying Alive.* London: Zed.

Singer, Peter ([1975] 1990) *Animal Liberation.* London: Jonathan Cape.

Soper, Kate (1995) *What is Nature?* Oxford: Blackwell.

Stone, Christopher (1974) *Should Trees Have Standing? – Towards Legal Rights for Natural Objects.* Los Altos: William Kaufmann.

Stone, Christopher (1987) *Earth and Other Ethics.* New York: Harper and Row.

Thomas, Keith (1983) *Man and the Natural World.* Harmondsworth: Penguin.

World Commission on Environment and Development (WCED) (1987) *Our Common Future.* Oxford and New York: Oxford University.

# 9. For a nonspeciesist criminology: animal abuse as an object of study

*Piers Beirne*

This article considers a variety of arguments about why theory and research on animal abuse should be developed by criminologists. These include, with more or less satisfaction, the status of animal abuse as (1) a signifier of actual or potential interhuman conflict, (2) an existing object of criminal law, (3) an item in the utilitarian calculus on the avoidance of pain and suffering, (4) a violation of rights, and (5) one of several oppressions identified by feminism as an interconnected whole. The article concludes that animal abuse is an important object of study for criminology not only *sui generis* but also because its presence may indicate or predict situations of interhuman violence.

It is now just over two hundred years since the English feminist Mary Wollstonecraft (1792) published her pioneering treatise *A Vindication of the Rights of Woman*. Though her onslaught on sexist notions of rights has long been justly celebrated, another aspect of her discourse on rights and justice has been generally ignored, namely, the attempt to establish animal abuse as an antecedent of female abuse. Probably because this avenue in Wollstonecraft's thought has been ignored, so too has the criticism of her platform mounted several weeks later by the eminent Cambridge philosopher Thomas Taylor. In his satirical reply *A Vindication of the Rights of Brutes*, Taylor (1792) attacked Wollstonecraft's feminism by suggesting that if her arguments were correct, her support of equality between men and women should be extended to more brutish animals (such as magpies, oxen, and dogs) and eventually, to vegetables, minerals, and contemptible clods of earth. And that, Taylor rejoiced, was known by all to be self-evidently absurd!

Extended proposals for the attachment of rights to nonhuman animals were not made until a century after Wollstonecraft's treatise on women's rights – for example, in Henry Salt's (1892) plea for vegetarianism in his book *Animals' Rights*. But only in the past two decades has the logical conclusion of Taylor's invective itself been viewed as absurd. During this time and rapidly following the disintegration, in some circles at least, of several modernist 'isms' – and their displacement by new discourses, especially to do with gender,

---

\* From *Criminology* (1999), 37(1): pp.117–147.

race, and age – there has emerged a transformation in intellectual thought about nonhuman animals (hereinafter, 'animals'[1]) that is at once moral, ethical and epistemological. In First World countries this transformation has led to a widely publicized, loosely organized, and occasionally secretive movement whose goals and diverse activities are variously known, depending on how they are characterized and by whom and with what intent, as 'animal welfare,' 'animal defense,' 'animal protection,' 'animal liberation,' and 'animal rights.' In those cases in which the movement has successfully marshaled public pressure to bear on the polity, its gains seem to have been extraordinary, and these despite the well-financed opposition of entrenched corporate interests. Noteworthy movement successes include greater restrictions on scientific and commercial laboratory experimentation on animals; a drastic reduction in fur industry sales; the protection of endangered species, especially popular exotica such as whales, eagles, and wolves; and tighter controls on conditions in intensive rearing regimes, slaughterhouses, and animal shelters.

The theoretical heart of this movement began with, and in many key respects is still inspired by, the writings of a small group of moral philosophers (Clark 1977; Godlovitch et al. 1974; Regan 1983; Singer 1990). Their erstwhile goal has been the deconstruction and elimination of practices that promote the satisfaction of human interests at the expense of animals and, largely through the vehicles of utilitarianism and liberal-rights theory, the creation of a nonspeciesist discourse that might more justly govern our relationships with animals. To these founding philosophical statements must now be added the pioneering contributions of feminist philosophers and philosophers of science (e.g. Adams 1991 1994; Adams and Donovan 1995; Donovan and Adams 1996; Harraway 1983 1989; Midgley 1983; Noske 1997; Sperling 1991).

Much of this literature is impaled on a debate that begins with the common rejection of the Cartesian view that animals are the moral equivalent of machines, but which then fractures, sometimes bitterly so, into several camps whose answers to a number of difficult questions are respectively informed by utilitarianism, liberal-rights theory, and feminism. These questions are motivated as much by a genuine concern for animals as by perennial puzzles about the nature of the good society and of the role of a responsible citizenry within it. How do animals differ from humans? Are the interests of animals in avoiding pain of the same sort as those of humans? Are the grounds for not abusing animals the same as those for not abusing humans? To such questions the defining contributions of moral philosophy have led to a mass of theoretical and empirical studies of human-animal interaction in such diverse fields as biology, psychology, feminism, cultural history, and the history of science.

Some of the concerns of these studies have recently infiltrated sociology, which, rather nervously, has sought to escape the rigid boundaries between human and animal societies imposed by Durkheim's imperialistic declaration in *The Rules of Sociological Method* that the social and cultural realms are autonomous from the biological. Indeed, sociologists are nowadays authors of articles in new animal-centered scholarly journals such as *Anthrozoös, Between the Species,* and *Society and Animals;* in 1994 *Qualitative Sociology* (vol. 17, no. 2) devoted a special issue to 'human-animal interaction.' The achievement of a well-formed sociology of human-animal interaction is still far from secure, but clear advances have been made in the domains of feminism and ethnographic studies of face-to-face human-animal interaction (e.g., Arluke and Sanders 1996). Impressive, if sharply contrasting, accounts of the animal rights movement have been provided in Jasper and Nelkin's (1992) *The Animal Rights Crusade*, in Francione's (1996) *Rain Without Thunder*, and in Silverstein's (1996) *Unleashing Rights*. In addition, timely sociological perspectives on the notion of animal rights are contained in Tester's (1991) *Animals and Society* and in Benton's (1993; and see Pocar 1992) *Natural Relations*.

Among criminologists, however, there has as yet emerged no explicitly theorized category of animal abuse. None of the leading journals in the field has published an article on animal abuse, and the topic is altogether ignored in criminology and criminal justice textbooks. To the problem of why animal abuse has not been recognized as a worthy object of study by criminologists, despite its long-standing criminalization, a cynical response might refer to patterns of governmental and private research funding. A less tangible, though perhaps better, explanation is that criminologists naturally prefer to investigate harms committed by human offenders against human victims rather than those committed by humans against other species. Or, to put this slightly differently, perhaps criminologists instinctively attach less importance to understanding the abuse of nonhuman victims than they do to the study of harms committed against *Homo sapiens*. But neither of these explanations is sufficient because, even if correct, each is a product of the anthropocentric ways in which, by religion or by law, for example, animal abuse tends to be problematized. Thus, neither Christianity (Roman Catholicism, in particular) nor Judaism encourages a strong censure of animal abuse because at both their respective doctrinal centers is a rigid hierarchical Chain of Being, in which God sits atop humans and humans bestride animals. Moreover, anticruelty legislation does not encourage a very serious view of animal abuse because, as I will suggest later, it is less concerned with the protection of animals, as such, than it is with the upholding of community moral standards.[2]

Yet, there are signs that the lengthy scholarly neglect of animal abuse in criminology may be ending. For example, papers on animal abuse have been delivered to the British Society of Criminology (one each in 1995 and 1997), and sessions and roundtables on it took place at the annual meeting of the American Society of Criminology in 1996, 1997, and 1998. Moreover, the new journal *Theoretical Criminology* has just published a special issue on 'green criminology' (on animals see, especially, Agnew 1998; Benton 1998; and see Beirne 1994, 1995, 1997; Cazaux, in press). In trying to place animal abuse on the research agenda of criminology, these early labors seem keen to avoid the inevitable intellectual ghettoization that would ensue from approaching it only from some already-given perspective external to criminology, such as that of animal rights or of deep ecology. Agnew's (1998) well-crafted paper, for example, attempts to develop a comprehensive theory of animal abuse, and in so doing, draws on a number of existing criminological theories, including social learning theory, strain theory, and control theory, in order to explain why individuals abuse animals.

In what follows I consider a variety of arguments about why animal abuse is an important object of study for criminology and why theory and research on it should be developed.[3] Though by the order of presentation of these arguments I do not necessarily mean to convey an order of logical or intellectual priority, they include, with more or less satisfaction, the status of animal abuse as

1 a signifier of actual or potential interhuman conflict;
2 an existing object of criminal law;
3 an item in the utilitarian calculus on the avoidance of pain and
4 a violation of rights; and
5 one of several oppressions identified by feminism as an interconnected whole.

## Animal abuse as a signifier of interhuman conflict

Though animal abuse does not yet constitute a coherent object of criminological study, this is not to say that animals are never present in discourse about crime. Moreover, identifying precisely how animals are constructed in existing discourse about crime is a useful task because it forces one to recognize some of the theoretical difficulties that confront a sensitive (i.e., nonspeciesist) understanding of animal abuse. Schematically, animals currently occupy three basic discursive roles in criminology, each of which is held to signify some aspect of interhuman conflict. Each of these three roles differs from the other two not only in its empirical manifestations but also in such factors as the character of the roles assigned animals and the degree of importance accorded them. In the first role, as private property, animals appear as the contested objects of interhuman conflict; in the second, various types of animal behavior are held to parallel or to imply interhuman conflict; and in the third, certain forms of animal abuse are identified as signifiers of interhuman violence.

In their first and most commonplace role, animals typically appear as commodities that are contested objects of human ownership. Here, they can be stolen, poached, damaged, held as ransom, rustled, or otherwise misappropriated. In this guise they are visible, for example, as neatly wrapped packages of flesh that are manipulated by white-collar criminals in the meatpacking industry in the United States (Clinard 1952); as prized objects at the nexus of poaching, sport, and class struggle in eighteenth-century England (Hay 1975); and as the commodified prey of twentieth-century American cattle rustlers (Swanson et al. 1992: Ch. 18) or Canadian lobster poachers (McMullan and Perrier 1997; see further Beirne 1995: 16–19). Yet, in none of these studies are animals themselves the focus of study and none of them refers to the pain or suffering inflicted on the animal, whether that was forbidden by the law and, if it was, whether human perpetrators were arrested, prosecuted, or punished for their misdeeds.

Animals' second and far more interesting and complex role in existing criminology derives from the domain concerns of two tendencies, one the labors of natural scientists eager to apply principles of ethology and ecology to the study of human societies (e.g., Wilson 1975), the other the desire of some social scientists to abandon what they perceive as the crude antibiologism of the Durkheimian tradition (e.g., Hirst and Wooley 1982). The coincidence of these tendencies has led to the insertion of animals in criminology by evolutionary psychology and evolutionary ecology. Both of these latter perspectives begin with the Darwinian notion that all species exist, or through the process of natural selection cease to exist, in a constant struggle to reproduce as successfully as possible and to survive better and to acquire more resources than competing species. Both employ animal behavior as a site of extrapolation for generalizations about human behavior (e.g., Cohen and Machalek 1988; Daly and Wilson 1988; Ellis 1990; Ellis and Walsh 1997; Vila and Cohen 1993; Wilson and Herrnstein 1985: 508–529).

It must be stressed that it would be most extraordinary if, given that they all inhabit tiny planet Earth, species of all sorts did not share a host of environmental problems to do with the supply and quality of food, water and oxygen, and the destruction of natural habitat. Herein, in part, lies the importance of claims like those made by Daly and Wilson (1988), for example, that there are parallels between homicide among humans, on the one hand, and violence and killing among nonhuman animals, on the other; or by Cohen and Machalek (1988) that a better understanding of crime can be had by examining the genetic, developmental, and cultural strategies that might be common to such diverse species as ants, bees, chimpanzees, and humans. How various species respond to common problems, whether their respective responses are or are not the same, and whether in the search for solutions to them some species are able to impose their will and their interests on others – these questions might all be of interest to a nonspeciesist (or 'green') criminology.

While there are immense epistemological and ontological difficulties inherent in biocriminology's attempt to construct cross-species generalizations, here I must stress only that nowhere in this discourse does the abuse of animals by humans occur as an object of study in its own right (even if animals could meaningfully be said to engage in 'homicidal' behavior, for example, I take it that criminologists should not be in the business of studying and policing violence that occurs between nonhuman species).

In recent years it is in their third role, as signifiers of interhuman violence, that animals have most often entered discourse about crime. Most criminologists will have learned of this chiefly from widely circulated reports in the mass media that link animal abuse and subsequent interhuman mass murders committed by adolescent males. For example, it was reported that prior to the 'Satanic-cult' killing of two schoolgirls and the wounding of seven others by an armed teenager in a Mississippi school in October 1997, the alleged (now convicted) teenage murderer, Luke Woodham, had engaged with a friend in the gruesome torture of his own dog. According to police, the two teenagers 'repeatedly beat the dog with a club, wrapped it in garbage bags, torched it with a lighter and flammable fluid, listened to it whimper and tossed it in a pond' (New York Times, October 15, 1997:A10). After describing the sight of the dog sinking beneath the surface of the pond, Woodham added, 'it was true beauty' (p. A10).[4] In another report of mass murder (of two classmates and both his parents) in Springfield, Oregon, in May 1998, it was revealed that 15-year-old Kip Kinkel had earlier enjoyed shooting squirrels, setting off firecrackers in cats' mouths or stuffing them down gopher holes (Associated Press, May 23 1998). At a similarly anecdotal level, it has been widely reported that adult mass murderers and serial killers tend as adolescents disproportionately to have engaged in animal abuse. This maturational link has been claimed for a number of serial killers in the United States, including Thomas Lee Dillon (Anon. 1993: 17), Ted Bundy (White 1992: 6), Alberto DeSalvo and Jeffrey Dahmer (New York Times, August 7, 1991: A8). As a generalization, however, it is quite vulnerable to obvious counterfactual examples, such as the strenuous denial of its applicability in her own case by the English 'Moors murderess' Myra Hindley (The Guardian, December 18 1995), and to the thorny problem that some mass murderers have regarded themselves as long-standing 'animal lovers' (Skrapec 1996: 165) and even, in the case of some leading Nazis in Germany in the 1940s, as champions of animal rights (Arluke and Sax 1992; Lasik 1998: 288).

In psychology, psychiatry, veterinary studies, and social welfare, a growing body of research has sought to examine whether the act of animal abuse is a sign of some psychologistic defect in the character of the perpetrator. Some studies have sought to detect mental and characteriological defects in children who assault animals (e.g., Ascione 1993: 233–235; Ascione et al. 1997b; Patterson et al. 1989). 'Assaultive children' are sometimes described as having multiple personality and dissociative disorder – the American Psychiatric Association now lists cruelty to animals as a form of conduct disorder in its Diagnostic and Statistical Manual of Mental Disorders of 1994 – and their behavior has been linked to other antisocial tendencies such as nonproductive firesetting and even enuresis (see Justice et al. 1974; Wax and Haddox 1974; Wooden and Berkey 1984: 35–37, 56–57). Other studies have focused on the developmental relationship between the abuse of animals by children and adolescents and their eventual maturation into adults with antisocial, aggressive, or violent tendencies (e.g., Ascione 1993: 229–233; Felthous and Kellert 1987). While this 'escalation thesis' has become widely accepted in the literature, it has been challenged in a recent study by Miller and Knutson (1997). With the use of self-report questionnaires given to 314 inmates in the Iowa Department of Corrections and to 308 university undergraduate students, this study found either a modest association or none at all among abusive childhood environments, exposure to animal cruelty, and subsequent violent behavior. However, the methodology of this study did not permit a determination of the key question of whether the particular individuals who as children or youth frequently engaged in acts of animal abuse subsequently committed violents acts against humans (and see Miller and Knutson 1997: 79).

Animal abuse has also been identified as a signifier of a variety of forms of domestic violence. Specifically, it has been found to be disproportionately present in situations of partner abuse (Donley et al., in press; Arkow 1994; Ascione 1998; see also Patronek 1997; Ascione et al. 1997a; Browne 1987: 157; Gelles and Straus 1988: 68 119; Renzetti 1992: 21), child physical abuse (Deviney et al. 1983), child sexual abuse (Boat 1995; Friedrich et al. 1986; Hunter 1990: 214–216), and sibling abuse (Wiehe 1990: 44–45). One of the virtues of this research is the great diversity of its sources of data. Indeed, the finding of an empirical link (of whatever sort) between interhuman conflict and animal abuse is drawn not only from victimization surveys and structured interviews with battered women and abused and neglected children but also from reports of animal abuse to veterinarians, animal shelters, women's shelters, and police. At the same time, though a proper discussion of them is far beyond my scope here, numerous methodological and conceptual problems remain to be clarified in this research, including the chronological sequence of animal abuse and interhuman violence; the problem of differential recall of animal abuse in self-report studies; the use of control groups of nonrandom composition; and even the uncritical construction and employment of such basic categories as 'abuse' and 'cruelty' (see further, Beirne 1995: 19–23).

In sum, these existing discursive positions of animals in criminology clearly entail research and policy implications for the recognition of a variety of forms of interhuman conflict. As they are now constituted, however, they are no more than prefigurative markers in some still-to-be-written history of the criminological study of animal abuse because the scripts and statuses thus far assigned animals in criminology betray the predominant fact that they are not regarded as sentient beings capable of pain and suffering but as Cartesian automata that are mere appendages to humans. As in postmodernist historiography (e.g., Darnton's 1985 *Great Cut Massacre*) and in rural history (e.g., Archer 1985) so, too, only rarely in criminology is the physical abuse of animals an object of study in its own right, to say nothing of the abuse that occurs in the more contentious domains of the psychological and the emotional. When they enter existing criminological discourse, animals tend to be cast as creatures of anthropocentrism and anthropomorphism, as unproblematic objects that are only coincidentally present in some undesirable aspect of the complex web of human relationships.

Against this background, I move to a consideration of whether existing criminal law can provide an objective basis for a nonspeciesist approach to animal abuse in criminology.

## Criminal law, criminology, and animal abuse

> An animal can be made to suffer, but we would never say, in a sense considered proper, that it is a wronged subject, the victim of a crime, of a murder, of a rape or a theft, of a perjury.
>
> Derrida (1992: 18)

A comprehensive history of the extension of criminalization practices to animal abuse has yet to be written. However, it can be said with some confidence that in the United States the emergence of legal safeguards against animal abuse stretches back to an Ordinance in the Massachusetts Bay Colony. There, in 1641, Liberty 92 of the 100 Liberties to be 'respectfully, impartially and inviolably enjoyed' (Leavitt and Halverson 1990: 1) provided that cruelty to domestic animals be forbidden. Cruelty to domestic animals was also a crime explicitly forbidden in Connecticut, and fines were imposed for ill-treating animals early in the eighteenth century in Hartford, New Haven, and Fairfield counties. The first statutory protection of animals was enacted in 1821 in Maine, which provided that the cruel beating of horses or cattle was a crime punishable with a fine of up to $5 or 30 days in jail (*Laws of the State of Maine*, ch. iv, §7); in 1822, the same year that the British parliament passed the *Act to Prevent the Cruel and Improper Treatment of Cattle*, courts in New York State held that wanton cruelty to an animal was a misdemeanor at common law. During the nineteenth century, anticruelty statutes were introduced by many other states (Brooman and Legge 1997; Favre and Tsang 1993), roughly similar parallels for which can be found in the enactments of other technologically advanced societies.

In the contemporary United States, the content of animal abuse is specified in a mass of federal and state legislation, according to which animals can be personal or public property, hazards, nuisances, and victims of ecological crimes and cruelty. Current legislation includes the Federal Meat Inspection Act (1958); Humane Slaughter Act (1958); Animal Welfare Act (1966, as amended 1970, 1976, 1985, 1990); Endangered Species Act (1969); Horse Protection Act (1970); Wild Horses and Burros Act (1971); Marine Mammal Protection Act (1972); Toxic Substances Control Act (1976); Food Security Act (1985); Health Research Extension Act (1985); the Improved Standards for Laboratory Animals Act (1985); and the Pet Protection Act (1990).[5] In addition to this legislation, all 50 states have now enacted anticruelty statutes. While these latter vary somewhat in how they define crucial terms like 'animal' and 'cruelty,' they generally recognize that animals ought to be protected from cruelty, abandonment, and poisoning and that they must be provided with necessary sustenance, including food, water, and shelter (Francione 1995: 121–123).[6]

Though some uncritical notion of 'animal cruelty' is indeed criminalized by this body of law, infractions of it have so far failed to command the scholarly attention of criminologists. It might be concluded from this that the concerns of criminologists lag far behind those of criminal law. But before rushing headlong to close this gap, criminologists must enquire whether criminal law can provide an objective basis for the study of animal abuse. How are animals constituted in this legislation? How are their interests secured by it? If it is proper to regard the intentional infliction of pain on animals as a form of abuse – and there is no good reason not to do so – consider the status of the two chief legislative controls in this regard, namely, the U.S. Animal Welfare Act 1966 (as amended) and individual state anticruelty statutes. The U.S. Animal Welfare Act, first, was enacted, *inter alia*, 'to ensure that animals intended for use in research facilities ... are provided humane care and treatment' (s.1, b.3). Though long-standing controversy exists about the morality of using animals in scientific research (e.g., see Rowan 1984) and about the number of animals involved (e.g., see Rowan *et al.* 1995: i–vii),[7] the fact remains that a large number, perhaps many millions, of animals are used in experiments in which they are burned, scalded, probed and injected with substances, blinded and otherwise mutilated, often without anaesthesia (Francione 1996: 7–8). Though under the terms of the act some of this pain is excusable because it is deemed necessary for advancing knowledge of cures and treatment for diseases and injuries that affect both humans and animals, no such anthropocentric utiltarianism should be uncritically appropriated as the basis for determining what, for objective scholarly purposes, constitutes animal abuse.

Consider also the type and extent of human/animal interaction that comprise cruelty to animals as specified in anticruelty legislation in the United States. Rather than rehearse the language of each of the 50 state anticruelty statutes *seriatim*, I refer to the practices criminalized by the American Law Institute's (1980) *Model Penal Code*. The code provides that a misdemeanor is committed if any person purposely or recklessly

> (1) subjects any animal to cruel mistreatment; or (2) subjects any animal in his custody to cruel neglect; or (3) kills or injures any animal belonging to another without legal privilege or consent of the owner (§250.11).

For my purposes here, the code's anticruelty provisions harbor several difficulties.[8] First, its language and terms of reference are most vague. Thus, §250.11 of the code altogether fails to define such crucial terms as 'animal,' 'cruel,' 'mistreatment,' 'neglect,' and 'injury.' While imprecision in the term 'animal' creates no overwhelming definitional problem except for those unfortunate creatures at the lower end of the phylogenetic scale,[9] the vague character of the other language is a serious practical and analytic problem if the study of animal abuse is to be approached through the lens of criminal law. What, exactly, constitutes 'cruel mistreatment' and 'cruel neglect,' for example? Why is the term 'injury' exclusively confined to physiological harm rather than expanded to embrace other harmful conditions undoubtedly experienced by nonhuman animals – mammals, most obviously – such as prolonged suffering and psychological distress?

Moreover, while the code (and most other anticruelty statutes) excludes from its scope accepted veterinary practices and activities carried on for scientific research, it implicitly licenses any abusive treatment of animals that is not perceived as cruel by community sensibilities. In bizarre homage to Durkheim's (1893) analysis of crime and punishment in *The Division of Labour in Society*, to the code's drafters the purpose of anticruelty statutes has never been to create a direct duty to exercise care toward animals, as such, but to 'prevent outrage to the sensibilities of the community' (p. 425; and see Francione 1995: 123–133).[10] Also exempt from the code, therefore, are the branding, castration, and killing of animals for food – practices that, in the United States alone, are applied to 9 billion farm animals annually (U.S. Department of Agriculture 1996). Again, cruelty may be inflicted on animals in the course of training, governing, and disciplining them, provided that it is not 'excessive'; deadly physical force may also be used both against one's own animal, even if the death is unnecessary, providing the killing is done 'humanely,' and against the animals of others if they threaten property, however trivial. Moreover, even if particular acts of animal abuse are defined as cruel or otherwise illegal, detection of them is quite rare and prosecution and conviction very difficult (Silverstein 1996: 134).

None of the deaths or painful practices inflicted on animals by humans listed above violates anticruelty statutes. None of them therefore necessarily involves a crime, as such. But precisely because so many human practices that are harmful to animals lie outside the scope of existing criminal law, the latter is far too narrow a basis for the study of animal abuse. Ironically, so far from it being an heuristic device for the study of animal abuse, criminal law is a major structural and historical mechanism in the consolidation of institutionalized animal abuse.[11] As Benton (1998: 171) rightly complains,

> The largest-scale and most systematically organized abuses of nonhuman animals occur in intensive rearing regimes in agriculture and in research laboratories. In both contexts there is evidence of genuine human compassion for animal suffering, but it is systematically overriden by the prevailing cultural priorities, authority structures and institutional objectives of the relevant agribusiness complex or industrial or public-sector institute. This contrasts markedly with the normative order which prevails in institutions such as the keeping of 'pet' or 'companion' animals.

How, then, should one understand animal abuse? The problem is not unlike the one famously posed in Sutherland's (1949) *White Collar Crime*. To his own question, 'Is white-collar crime crime?', Sutherland answered that criminologists should study anything defined as *socially harmful* by any branch of law, that is, whether by criminal law or by administrative law. But Sutherland's conclusion is not especially helpful here since even enlightened approaches to crime, such as his own, are permeated with human exceptionalism and speciesism. Even when the concept of crime is expanded to constitute 'social harm' or 'analogous social injury,' for example, no space is allowed therein for harms and injuries committed against animals because the social totality that is the object of such analyses is traditionally construed as one that is exclusively comprised of one species, namely, humans (and see note 1 above). Animals, in other words, remain without standing in a sort of legal and moral wilderness.

### Utilitarianism: on suffering and equal consideration

If existing criminal law is an inadequate basis for the study of animal abuse, perhaps it can be secured by considering the suffering intentionally inflicted on other species by us humans. While there are various routes by which one can arrive at the conclusion that one has a duty not to cause nonhuman animals to suffer (e.g., the Buddhist doctrine of *ahimsa*, or 'no harm'), in Western societies it has been reached most often within the utilitarian calculus on the avoidance of suffering.

In its modern form, the utilitarian argument on animal abuse derives from the conjunction of two eighteenth-century Enlightenment traditions, one involving a rejection of the Cartesian view that animals are the moral equivalent of machines, the other an acceptance of the doctrine of utility established by the Italian and French *philosophes* and by the Scottish civic tradition. To the *philosophes* the key ethical principle is that righteous actions are those that maximize happiness and pleasure and that minimize suffering and pain; an ethical society is one that tries to minimize pain and suffering wherever and however they occur. Thus, in 1766, Cesare Beccaria, the principal architect of modern administrative criminology, urged 'be just with all the beings that surround you. Remember that even the smallest creatures, crushed by arrogant and cruel man, are endowed with a little ray of life' (cited in Maestro 1973: 50). Jeremy Bentham first advocated the extension of utilitarianism to the interaction between humans and animals in a passage in his *Introduction to the Principles of Morals and Legislation*. Here, he claimed that there is no good reason why humans should be allowed to torment animals or to be cruel to them (1789: 282; see also Blackstone 1769, Bk. 4, Ch. 23: 235–236). He believed that the interests of animals in the enjoyment of happiness had previously been neglected because of 'the insensibility of the ancient jurists,' who degraded animals into 'the class of *things*' (p. 236). Bentham reasoned that 'this degrading objectification' involved the same mistake as the institution of slavery, or when humans have pain inflicted upon them because of their skin color. In the same way that 'the French have already discovered that the blackness of the skin is no reason why a human should be abandoned without redress to the caprice of a "tormento,"' so too, Bentham continued, 'the day *may* come when the rest of the animal creation may acquire those rights which never could have been withholden from them but by the hand of tyranny' (p. 283):

> It may come one day to be recognized, that the number of the legs, the villosity of the skin or the termination of the *os sacrum*, are reasons equally insufficient for abandoning a sensitive being to the same fate. What else is it that should trace the insuperable line? Is it the faculty of reason, or, perhaps, the faculty of discourse? But a full-grown horse or dog is beyond comparison a more rational, as well as a more conversible animal, than an infant of a day, or a week, or even a month, old. But suppose the case were otherwise, what would it avail? The question is not, Can they *reason*? Can they *talk*? but, Can they *suffer*? (p. 283.)

Because for Bentham animals are sentient beings who can suffer and feel pain, it follows that they have an interest in avoiding pain and that, given the principle of utility, humans are obliged not to inflict it on them.

Bentham's strictures against the infliction of pain on animals have become the theoretical focus of the reformist tendency in the animal protection community known as 'welfarism.' This tendency has been nurtured by Peter Singer's (1975) widely read *Animal Liberation*, a book of consequentialist moral theory applied to animal suffering. Singer begins by pointing out that the basis of Bentham's argument about animal rights is not that animals have rights – Bentham anyway tended to deride the notion of natural rights as nonsense upon stilts – but that in respect of their avoidance of pain and their seeking of pleasure they should be allowed the same consideration as humans. In the same way that there are some males who attach greater weight to the interests of their own gender at the expense of females (sexism), Singer continues, and just as there are others who give preference to their own race at the expense of other races (racism), so there are some humans who give greater consideration to the interests of their own species than they do to those of nonhuman animals (speciesism).

In supporting the extension of utilitarian considerations to animals, Singer elevates the capacity to suffer over the capacity for language, for example, or that for mathematics. This he does because he holds that the capacity to suffer is the *sine qua non* of having interests at all. As such, neither vegetables nor minerals nor clods of earth enter his calculus because they are not sentient beings capable of feeling pain or happiness. Rather, as insentient objects they are without interests.

For Singer, then, the capacity for suffering is the essential precondition for having interests. Utilitarianism entails equality of consideration for *all* animals, both human and nonhuman. All animals have an equal interest in avoiding suffering; moral actions are those that uphold those interests. To his cardinal rule of equal consideration, Singer attaches the qualification that equal consideration does not mean that all animals should be treated in the same way. Animals of different species have different interests and to treat them the same ('equally') would therefore be to mistreat them. Singer's position that one law for the lion and the ox is oppression allows him to admit to obvious differences between humans and nonhumans while retaining the principle of equality of consideration for all animals.[12] Singer therefore enjoins us all to avoid the infliction of pain and suffering on humans and animals alike. We should make our lives as free from cruelty as possible and refuse to buy the products of modern animal farming. We must become vegetarian. We must expose and condemn the suffering involved in hunting, trapping, rodeos, zoos, circuses, and in the buying and selling of animals.

Singer's many exhortations have successfully acquired a large and quite influential following. But it must be said that his act-utilitarianism does not place the liberation of animals from suffering on a very secure footing. If the rightness or wrongness of any given action is to be judged only by its consequences, and if the criterion of this is a utilitarian calculus aimed at the maximization of pleasure and the minimization of suffering, it follows that particular acts of suffering may be justified if they serve to increase the collective good. Singer's theory of animal liberation does not condemn animal experimentation absolutely, for example, and actually supports particular instances of it if they are believed to lead to a scientific cure for illness and disease *in humans*. (One wonders if there are scenarios that would allow Singer to support experimentation on humans if so doing might lead to good health in sick animals.) In principle, there is nothing in such utilitarianism that would preclude any form of torture or suffering inflicted on a minority if the result was a decrease in the suffering of the majority.

Ultimately, therefore, while Singer's intervention has done much to draw critical attention to the extent of animals' suffering, it has done little to overcome the classical view of animal welfare that humans may (ab)use animals if they calculate that the outcome warrants it.

## Animals as subjects of rights

This difficulty with Singer's utilitarianism is the precise starting point of the non-consequentialist, deontological theory of animal rights that Tom Regan (1983) offers in his book *The Case for Animal Rights*.

To simplify greatly, Regan puts forward this theory in three stages. First, he distinguishes between legal rights and moral rights. Legal rights, on the one hand, are those that particular laws happen to classify as rights. As such, their existence and facticity depend on the society in which they are enacted. The degree of respect accorded them varies by such factors as race, class, gender, and religion. Moral rights, on the other hand, are universal rights. They apply equally to all their holders and do not flow from the creative or capricious acts of individuals (e.g., despots) or groups (e.g., legislatures). Moral rights are not acquired rights but basic ones, and everyone is obliged to uphold them. Of all moral rights the most fundamental is the right to respectful treatment. Second, Regan identifies the sort of individuals who are the bearers of rights, namely, those with a variety of sophisticated abilities whom he terms 'moral agents.' He objects that utilitarianism views individuals as 'mere receptacles' for value. To put this another way, in the utilitarian or receptacle view of value it is what goes into the cup, rather than the cup itself, that has value. On Regan's postulate of inherent value, it is the cup itself that has value – a value that is reducible neither to what goes into it nor to others' evaluations of it. Inherent value resides in those individuals who are moral agents, and it resides in them equally. If it did not, it would lead to a 'perfectionist' theory of justice, which is unacceptable because it would allow differential treatment of individuals according to the quantity and quality of various virtues that they exhibited. Because moral agents have equal inherent value, all are equally valuable, and thus, '[a] criminal is no less inherently valuable than a saint' (p. 237).

Who is a moral agent? To be a moral agent is to be more than alive and merely conscious, though it may also be less than an autonomous agent in the Kantian sense. A moral agent is a 'subject-of-a-life':

> Individuals are subjects-of-a-life if they have beliefs and desires, perceptions, memory and a sense of the future, including their own future; an emotional life together with feelings of pleasure and pain; preference- and welfare-interests; the ability to initiate action in pursuit of their desires and goals; a psychophysical identity over time; and an individual welfare in the sense that their experiential life fares well or ill for them (p. 243).

Regan argues that the moral community consists not only of moral agents but also of all those to whom moral agents owe duties, that is, other moral agents and also 'moral patients.' Moral patients are those who lack the prerequisites that would enable them to control their behavior in ways that would make them morally accountable. Moral patients include human infants, young children, the mentally ill, and the enfeebled of all ages. Even though they have the ability to harm others, moral patients can do neither right nor wrong. They are always innocent. Since moral patients are subjects-of-a-life, they have inherent value and one is required to respect them no less than one respects moral agents. To respect a moral patient means not only to revere her life but also to defend her from harm. Not to respect her would be arbitrary and unjust.

Regan claims, third, that among the leading attributes of the mental life of many animals, especially normal mammalians aged one or more, are perception, memory, desire, belief, self-consciousness, intention, and a sense of the future. Because such animals satisfy the criterion of a subject-of-a-life, they have inherent value and, therefore, they have the same basic rights as human moral patients, including the right to respectful treatment and the right not to be harmed.[13] Indeed, to treat animals with respect is to treat them not with kindness but with justice.[14] Finally, it should be recorded that Regan catalogues two ways in which animals can be harmed, namely, through inflictions and deprivations. While disdaining its utilitarian framework, Regan applauds Bentham's focus on the ability of animals to suffer because it is suffering that is the paradigm of a harm understood as an infliction. It is a form of prolonged pain of considerable intensity that diminishes the victim's satisfaction of needs and/or interests, her quality of life and her physiological and emotional welfare. Harms as inflictions would therefore seem to constitute cruelty writ large. Harms as deprivations are those harms that do not necessarily involve pain and suffering and about whose existence the harmed individual does not even have to be aware:

> That harms can take the form of deprivations, independent of considerations about suffering, and that animals can be the subjects of such harm, is readily seen if we recall that many animals have needs and attendant desires over and above the basic biological ones for food, water, rest, and the like. Humans are, we say, social animals, but we are not the only ones. The more we learn about animals, both domesticated and wild, the more we must be impressed with the social needs and arrangements that characterize their lives ... To place animals with such desires in situations in which these desires cannot be fulfilled – as is done by caging wolves in, say, roadside zoos – is to cause them *prima facie* harm, whether they suffer or not, because it is to deny them the opportunity to satisfy their desires for companionship or physical freedom of movement (p. 98).

Though deprivations need not involve pain and suffering, sometimes they do, as when a caged wolf is drugged into a stuporous state. Conversely, suffering can itself lead to deprivation, as in the case of an intensively raised farm animal who thereby suffers ulcers, which diminish her ability to fulfil a variety of her natural desires. The ultimate form of deprivation (and of suffering, if it involves pain) is death because the loss of life forecloses all possibilities of the satisfaction of desires.

To many observers Regan has provided a powerful framework for the assignment of roughly the same sort of *prima facie* rights to animals as are assigned to humans under the banner of human rights. To most anthropologists and zoologists there is little in Regan's theory that is objectionable or even especially controversial. Benton, for example, concludes that it rests on a 'defensible and ... largely convincing view of the psychological complexity, capacities and needs of at least some non-human animals ... it is also in accord with the best scientific knowledge available' (1993: 86; and see Masson and McCarthy 1995). Some theologians and philosophers actively oppose it, however, and raise with varying degrees of importance different sorts of difficulty for Regan's theory. For example, some claim that not all animals, including humans, have equal inherent worth (e.g., Edwards 1993). Others assert that the concept of animal rights devalues the notion of human rights.[15] Still others take issue with the apparently low level of consciousness attributed by Regan to nonmammals and, therefore, with the overly narrow range of animals that might have rights (see Leahy 1991: Ch. 2; Benton 1993: Ch. 4). In this vein, Susanne Kappeler (1995) has adamantly complained that though it masquerades as an antispeciesist defense of some animals (i.e., mammals), Regan's rights theory is in fact 'a form of super-speciesism, redefining a superrace of the "healthy" and "whole" with "lives worth living" ' (p. 333).

Only time and further theoretical reflection can tell whether such criticisms are less durable than those that assert that in Regan's assignation of rights to animals lies some of the same problems as those entailed in human rights. Among these problems, in particular, are that their claims to universality embody an imperialist essentialism that is vulnerable to the objections of cultural relativism and postmodernism; that once acquired both in principle and in law, they are in practice individualist notions that do little to aid the plight of all their bearers; that they are abstract and formal rights with no necessary substantive content; and that, if enacted – as in the case of civil liberties and rights for persons of color, for example – they might not be enforced or recognized. Moreover, especially in self-avowed property-owning democracies and in societies where (human) individualism is energetically encouraged and respected, the right of animals to be free from cruelty and abuse will ultimately be thwarted, if not altogether undermined, by human rights to privacy and to the enjoyment of private property.

## Feminist theory and animal advocacy

> We should not kill, eat, torture, and exploit animals because they do not want to be so treated, and we know that. If we listen, we can hear them.
>
> Josephine Donovan (1990: 375)

Singer's utilitarianism and Regan's rights-based theory are now established as the twin philosophical pillars of animal protectionism. Yet, though it is possible to see their concern with the plight of animals as identical, their arguments actually involve quite different routes to different goals. In terms of how their opposing positions are embodied in day-to-day practice, the respective adherents of utilitarianism and rights-based theories often seem to be engaged in the sort of internecine warfare typical of movements that have splintered into irreconcilable camps: passionate disagreement over tactics and strategy and charges and countercharges of selling out, of reformism, and of idealism.

However, with the emergence in the animal protection community of an antipatriarchal feminist metaethic (variously known as 'ecofeminism,' 'cultural feminism,' and 'radical cultural feminism'), it has become clear that utilitarian and rights-based theories share more common ground than was previously realized. From a feminist perspective (e.g., Harding 1991; Held 1994), a fatal problem with both theories is their masculinist adherence to scientific rationalism, which inevitably entails a politics of exclusion and a sneering dismissal of sentimentalism. Undeniably, both Singer and Regan wish to distance themselves from a purely sentimentalist or emotional attachment to animals. In the Preface to his book *Animal Liberation*, for example, Singer (1975: i–ii) relates how, when living in England, he and his wife were invited to tea by a lady who had heard he was writing a book on animals. Upon their arrival, their hostess proudly informed them that she had a dog and two cats and that she loved animals. She was therefore surprised to learn from the Singers that they themselves owned no pets. Though they were interested in the prevention of suffering and misery, they informed her that

> we were not especially 'interested in' animals ... We didn't love animals. We simply wanted them treated as the independent sentient beings that they are, and not as a means to human ends – as the pig whose flesh was now in our hostess's sandwiches had been treated (p. ii).

Singer's point here is that sentimental appeals for sympathy toward any given animal accomplishes little of positive value for the welfare of animals as a whole. As he puts it, 'the portrayal of those who protest against cruelty to animals as sentimental, emotional 'animal-lovers' has had the effect of excluding the entire issue of the treatment of nonhumans from serious political and moral discussion' (p. iii). Likewise, in the Preface to *The Case for Animal Rights*, Regan (1983: xii) enjoins his readers to make a sustained committment to nonsentimental rational enquiry:

> Since all who work on behalf of the interests of animals are more than a little familiar with the tired charges of being 'irrational,' 'sentimental,' 'emotional' or worse, we can give the lie to these accusations only by making a concerted effort not to indulge our emotions or parade our sentiments.

But feminist members of the animal protection community retort that such statements are classic exemplars of epistemological dualism because they effectively equate 'sentimental' and 'emotional' with 'irrational' and all three traits with 'less than male' and 'female' (e.g., Adams 1995a; Curtin 1991; Donovan 1990; Kappeler 1995; Kheel 1985; Luke 1992). For this reason they have derided Regan's epistemology as a masculinist rationalism that rejects the importance of emotions and sentiments both in life and in understanding. Instead, feminists have developed what Josephine Donovan (1990: 351) describes as 'more of a sense of emotional bonding with animals as the basis for their theory than is evident in the male literature.' Indeed, since for theologians, philosophers, and statesmen a clinical and unemotional rationalism has been one of the key criteria for admission to the moral community, there is an almost inevitable commonality of interests among all disenfranchised minorities.

In respect of feminist theorising about animals, this commonality of interests is evident in two distinct tendencies. First, and much more familiar, liberal feminists have attempted to transcend the subordinate position into which both they and animals have been forced by men. From the writings of Mary Wollstonecraft to Simone de Beauvoir and onward, this approach is manifest in the core claim that women are essentially unlike animals and that they should be admitted to the moral community because, like men, they are quite capable of discarding their primitive animalistic characteristics and of developing rational minds and habits. According to the logic of this first tendency, feminists should discard any common position with animals and engage in the pursuit of masculinist freedoms and rights. The reasons this shortsighted position lacks intellectual and political coherence do not need to be detailed here, though it must be pointed out, as Adams and Donovan (1995b: 2) suggest, that 'this emphasis on severing the woman-animal identification was a necessary phase in the transformation of cultural ideology about women.'

A second feminist approach to animals is largely a corrective to the limitations of the first. A decade or so in the making but still not yet a fully articulated perspective, its several strands are visible in two recent anthologies: *Animals and Women: Feminist Theoretical Explorations* (Adams and Donovan 1995a) and *Beyond Animal Rights: A Feminist Caring Ethic for the Treatment of Animals* (Donovan and Adams 1996). At root, it seeks to identify the myriad ways in which, historically and structurally, patriarchal societies oppress women and how their oppression stems from and parallels the same sources as the dominionistic treatment of all Others. Among feminism's crucial tasks are therefore to uncover how patriarchal ideologies like transcendent dualism (Ruether 1975: 195) and somatophobia (Spelman 1982) create categories of despised and disenfranchised bodies and how they aid men in their subjugation of women, slaves, persons of color, nondominant men, and animals. As Adams and Donovan stress, the recognition of these ideologies is crucial because they provide 'the context for women's oppression and the relationship it has with other forms of oppression' (1995b: 2). It would therefore be beneficial for women to seek common fellowship, for example, with those indigenous peoples who make no conceptual distinction between humans and other animals and who tend to equate all living beings, plants, earth, and water. According to Adams and Donovan,

> feminist theory must engage itself with the status and treatment of the other animals ... We believe that feminism is a transformative philosophy that embraces the amelioration of life on earth for all life-forms, for all natural entities ... All oppressions are interconnected: no one creature will be free until all are free – from abuse, degradation, exploitation, pollution, and commercialization (p. 3).

Two strategies must be pursued to realize this holistic vision. First, it is necessary to develop a feminist ethic of care for animals. This can be approached through the evolving debates on the 'morality of responsibility and caring' in Carol Gilligan's (1982) *In a Different Voice*. Crucially, her text rejects the emphasis of utilitarianism and liberal-rights theory on abstract rules, procedural consistency, and justice; instead, it embraces the particular, the connection among all beings, and an ethic of responsible caring. Second, an active engagement is needed with the ways in which all animals – both human and nonhuman – can be used and abused by men. This can be illustrated by considering for a moment the sexual abuse of animals. Adams (1995b), for example, describes how the killing, harming, and sexual abuse of animals not only violate other living beings but also represent coercive ways for a male to demonstrate that he holds the power in a household. Instances of such instrumental violations include a male's threats to kill his spouse's pet animal, the actual killing of an animal in the presence of a woman and her children, and a woman's forced sex with an animal. Similarly, I (Beirne 1997) have argued that sexual relations between humans and animals should neither be understood nor condemned – let alone tolerated – in terms of the masculinist and anthropocentric discourse of Leviticus, Exodus, and Deuteronomy. Rather, bestiality is a coercive act that often causes animals physical and emotional pain and even death. Having certain similarities to the sexual abuse of women and children, bestiality should therefore be named 'interspecies sexual assault' and censured accordingly.

In its emphasis on an ethics of caring and a politics of good fellowship with all other beings, this new feminist approach to animals is a radical alternative to both utilitarianism and rights theory. Yet, the shifting grounds on which this feminism condemns animal abuse merit closer inspection. Should animal abuse be condemned because it allegedly has the same source – white male domination – as all other forms of oppression and is therefore linked to them? I am not at all sure that there is any meaningful sense in which all oppressions, including animal abuse, can be said to stem from a unitary source. How do the hitherto neglected relations of class and race enter this feminist perspective? The question of race, for example, is an especially difficult one because feminists of color have had good reason to distance themselves from animals: As bell hooks points out about the social position of the black female, it was not so long ago that many whites 'saw her ability to endure hardships no "lady" was supposedly capable of enduring as a sign that she possessed an animalistic sub-human strength' (1981: 81–82). Moreover, given that women have a sharing of interests and a bonding with animals – or, as I have perhaps too loosely claimed elsewhere, because assaults on animals are 'structurally similar' to and 'parallel' assaults on women (Beirne 1997: 324–327) – should animal abuse be condemned because the abuse of categorical equivalents ought also to be condemned? Yet none of these connections is altogether satisfactory, not least because humans and animals are in important respects factually dissimilar and, especially in the case of domesticated animals, unequal in others. As these problems are investigated further, perhaps society will eventually reach the conclusion that animal abuse should be censured not because it is similar to the abuse of humans but because it is loathsome to animals themselves.

## Conclusion

In this article I have sought to contribute to the development of a non-speciesist criminology. I have suggested that because human-animal interaction is a pervasive aspect of human sociality and cultural practices, research on animal abuse is likely to confirm that animal abuse is a signifier of various forms of interhuman conflict, especially interpersonal violence. But this reason for studying animal abuse, provocative and sound though it might be, has been no more than briefly alluded to here. In part, this is because the existing research on the links between them – on why, and how, and how often and under what social and cultural conditions, animal abuse might signify interhuman conflict – is still very much in its infancy. Moreover, precisely because this line of research begins with or privileges a prior attachment to the centrality of *interhuman* violence, I have not been tempted to give it greater prominence in an article whose main task is to identify the need for a nonspeciesist criminology. That task must wait for another occasion.

Instead, I have outlined various arguments why, *sui generis*, animal abuse is a legitimate and important object of study. These include its status as an existing object of criminal law; an item in the utilitarian calculus on the avoidance of pain and suffering; a violation of rights; and one of several forms of oppression identified by feminists as an interconnected whole. Each of these arguments has considerable merit. In concert, they point to the compelling conclusion that a criminology that ignores animal abuse will be a speciesist discourse utterly irrelevant to the understanding of much harm and suffering inflicted by humans on nonhuman, but nevertheless valuable, forms of life. Rather than cede the study of it to other disciplines, criminologists should with confidence apply their theoretical expertise to the understanding of animal abuse. Having in mind Agnew's (1998) application to animal abuse of strain theory and social control theory, for example, criminological theory can profitably be combined with situational factors such as social position to explain why individuals engage in animal abuse. There is much else that criminologists can contribute to the study of animal abuse, including examination of the conceptual difficulties involved in its definition and measurement; the ideological and cultural processes that underpin it; how it is criminalized or otherwise censured by the state and state agencies, and with what consequences; and how its forms and severity vary from one social and cultural setting to another.

## Notes

1  In this article, I prefer the seemingly neutral juxtaposition 'human animals/nonhuman animals' to 'humans/animals' because the latter inevitably privileges humans and because we humans and our fellow creatures are all animals. But I must confess that this attempt to avoid speciesist language falls prey to another error. While the term 'nonhuman animals' is a useful reminder that the terrain of human/animal relations is marked by speciesist language, to speak of *nonhuman* animals is ironically to privilege humans for it defines all animals other than *Homo*

*sapiens* as lacking in certain qualities that allegedly inhere only in humans (see further Beirne, 1996). Moreover, as Geertrui Cazaux (in press) has rightly pointed out, this is not altogether unlike describing human females as nonmale humans.

2   Further, some might protest that the study of animal abuse should be left to vivisectionists and natural scientists or to partisans and propagandists in the animal rights movement. Is not the *social* the proper domain of sociology and criminology? However, the skeptical objection that animal abuse is not a proper object of criminology largely assumes that animals play no significant role in human societies. As such, like slaves and women, especially, animals are seen as Others who are external to the social and who are without legitimate claims to inclusion in it or recognition by it. But against such practices of exclusion, it must be pointed out that in every known society animals are and have been involved in a wide variety of social relationships with humans. Some of these relationships are exploitative, some of them commercial, and others affective. Among them are the use of animals to replace or augment human labor, to meet human bodily or organic needs, and to provide sources of entertainment and edification (Benton, 1993: 60–69). In all societies, too, animals are important items in cultural and symbolic practices. In large-scale, urbanized societies, especially where the size of the agricultural sector has been declining, they occupy significant roles as companions.

3   Though space does not allow me properly to assess competing definitions of animal abuse, in this discussion I am guided by Agnew's (1998: 178; and on companion animal abuse, see Vermeulen and Odendaal, 1993) recent definition. Somewhat to rework Agnew's definition, I define animal abuse as any act that contributes to the pain, suffering, or death of an animal or that otherwise threatens its welfare. Animal abuse may be physical, psychological, or emotional; may involve active maltreatment or passive neglect or omission; and may be direct or indirect, intentional or unintentional.

4   Describing the event, Woodham admitted,
On Saturday of last week, I made my first kill. The victim was a loved one, my dear dog Sparkle. I will never forget the howl she made. It sounded almost human. I'll never forget the sound of her breaking under my might. I hit her so hard I knocked the fur off her neck (p. A10).

5   Moreover, there now exists a considerable body of case law involving litigation on behalf of animals, including the enforcement of laws directly relating to the treatment and interests of animals. See further, the variety of case law identified by Silverstein (1996: 132–156).

6   However, a majority of state anticruelty statutes define the acts of commission and omission that constitute cruelty to animals as misdemeanors rather than felonies. Among the 16 states that define the offense as a felony, penalties for violations vary considerably. For example, while the maximum fine for cruelty to animals is $5,000 in Alaska and Pennsylvania and $10,000 in Wisconsin, it is only $50 in Missouri. Prison sentences, too, span a wide range: from nothing at all in Ohio and Virginia, to a maximum of six months in Alabama and California, three years in Maine, and five years in Oklahoma.

7   According to Rowan *et al.*, (1995: i–vii), in the United States 1.2 million dogs, cats, primates, rabbits, hamsters and guinea pigs are used annually in laboratories. Including rats and mice, total annual animal usage is 20 million.

8   A major legalistic problem of the code and many anticruelty statutes is that it is very hard to prove the necessary *mens rea* in the case of a defendant whose actions are cruel but also customary and acceptable, though this is really not of concern here. See further, Francione (1995: Ch. 7).

9   Older statutes defined 'animal' variously as 'all brute creatures' (Michigan), 'any animal in subjugation or captivity, whether wild or tame' (Oklahoma), 'every

living creature' (Arkansas) and 'any useful beast, fowl or animal' (North Carolina). In the code, as its drafters point out (p. 426), the division is between humans and all other living creatures. But should fish, birds, spiders, and worms, for example, not also count as animals?

10  Similarly, there is compelling evidence that a concern with animals' suffering per se was not the major factor in the development of anticruelty legislation in Britain. There, in a period dominated by the threat to political stability of working-class insurrection both at home and abroad, the main concerns of key early nineteenth-century reformers such as Lord Erskine, Sir William Pulteney. and Richard Martin ('Humanity Dick') lay as much with the suffering of animals as they did with the establishment of institutions to cultivate and to police orderly moral conduct among humans and to appropriate bodily and moral boundaries between humans and other species (see further, Tester, 1991: 105–111).

11  I cannot discuss here the complex historical reasons why criminal law has so firmly avoided the censure of large-scale animal abuse (see also note 9, above), but it is worth noting that in the United States and in Britain and in its former colonies, the emergence of legal safeguards against animal abuse at the beginning of the nineteenth century was associated with the growth of capitalist economic relations and with the social, ideological, and juridical processes that sustained them. In the erection of social and ideological distinction between humans and animals, property interests have always been preeminent. As Francione argues, '[the code and] the anticruelty statutes are, and always have been, limited in ways that effectively protect property interests in animals and protect nonanimal property interests as against animal interests' (1995: 134 and see Stone, 1972).

12  Especially given several ambiguous references in *Animal Liberation* to 'animal *rights,*' Singer has subsequently been careful to stress that the notion of rights plays no significant role in his utilitarianism and that it operates merely as a concession to popular rhetoric. He therefore complains, I have little to say about rights because rights are not important to my argument. My argument is based on the principle of equality, which I do have quite a lot to say about. My basic moral position is utilitarian. I make very little use of the word 'rights' in Animal Liberation, and I could easily have dispensed with it altogether. I think that the only right I ever attribute to animals is the 'right' to equal consideration of interests, and anything that is expressed by talking of such a right could equally well be expressed by the assertion that animals' interests ought to be given equal consideration with the like interests of humans (Singer, 1990: 122).

13  However, these rights are not absolute and Regan (1983) specifies two principles that might justify the overriding of rights: (1) the 'miniride principle,' whereby one should choose to harm the innocent few to save the rights of the innocent many; (2) the 'worse-off principle,' whereby one should choose to harm the many if not doing so entails that another course of action would leave some of the few worse off than any of the many; and (3) the 'liberty principle,' whereby the innocent have the right to selfdefense even if so doing overrides the rights of others (pp. 286–312).

14  To treat them thus Regan offers 'practical' advice on a number of animal related issues: for example, one must cease to dine on animals and one must not use them as receptacles of value, whether in hunting and trapping or in science and education (Ch. 9).

15  For example, in early 1995, just after the arrest of dozens of activists protesting the delivery of veal calves from Britain to the Continent, John Habgood, the Archbishop of York, published a condescending essay in The Times (February 11, 1995) in which he condemned their animal rights platform. The Archbishop

suggested that, though he believed that animals should be treated with respect and that they should be spared unnecessary suffering, it was wrong to talk of animals as having rights because only moral beings [i.e., humans – P.B.] have that capacity. Since animals are not and cannot be part of any moral community, he reasoned, they cannot be said to have rights. Those who campaign on behalf of animals using the language of 'animal rights' therefore succeed, he concluded, only in devaluing the notion of human rights and, as such, in disregarding the legitimate claims of their fellow human beings.

## References

Adams, Carol, J. (1991) *The Sexual Politics of Meat.* New York: Continuum.

Adams, Carol, J. (1994) *Neither Man Nor Beast: Feminism and the Defense of Animals.* New York: Continuum.

Adams, Carol, J. (1995a) 'Caring about suffering: A feminist exploration, in Josephine Donovan and Carol J. Adams (eds), *Beyond Animal Rights: A Feminist Caring Ethic for the Treatment of Animals.* New York: Continuum.

Adams, Carol, J. (1995b) 'Woman-battering and harm to animals, in Carol J. Adams and Josephine Donovan (eds), *Animals and Women: Feminist Theoretical Explorations.* Durham, NC: Duke University Press.

Adams, Carol, J. and Josephine Donovan (eds) (1995a) *Animals and Women: Feminist Theoretical Explorations.* Durham, NC: Duke University Press.

Adams, Carol, J. (1995b) 'Introduction, in Carol J. Adams and Josephine Donovan (eds) *Animals and Women: Feminist Theoretical Explorations.* Durham, NC: Duke University Press.

Agnew, Robert (1998) 'The causes of animal abuse: A social psychological analysis, *Theoretical Criminology,* 2(2): 177–209.

American Law Institute (1980) *Model Penal Code and Commentaries.* Philadelphia: American Law Institute. Anon.

American Law Institute (1993) 'Alleged serial killer Thomas Lee Dillon. *Animal People.* January/February: 17.

Archer, John E. (1985) 'A fiendish outrage? A study of animal maiming in East Anglia: 1830–1870. *Agricultural History Review,* 33(2): 147–157.

Arkow, Phil (1994) 'Child abuse, animal abuse, and the veterinarian', *Journal of the American Veterinary Medical Association,* 204(7): 226–247.

Arluke, Arnold and Clinton R. Sanders (1996) *Regarding Animals.* Philadelphia: Temple University Press.

Arluke, Arnold and Boria Sax (1992) 'Understanding Nazi animal protection and the Holocaust', *Anthrozoös* 5(1): 6–31.

Ascione, Frank, R. (1993) 'Children who are cruel to animals: A review of research and implications for developmental psychopathology', *Anthrozoös* 6(4): 226–247.

Ascione, Frank, R. (1998) 'Battered women's reports of their partners and their children's cruelty to animals', *Journal of Emotional Abuse* 1(1): 120–133.

Ascione, Frank R., Claudia V. Weber, and David S. Wood (1997a) 'The abuse of animals and domestic violence: A national survey of shelters for women who are battered', *Society & Animals* 5(3): 205–218.

Ascione, Frank R., Teresa M. Thompson, and Tracy Black (1997b) 'Childhood cruelty to animals: Assessing cruelty dimensions and motivations', *Anthrozoös* 10(4): 170–177.

Beirne, Piers (1994) 'The law is an ass: Reading E.P. Evans The Medieval Prosecution and Capital Punishment of Animals', *Society and Animals,* 2(1): 27–46.

Beirne, Piers (1995) 'The use and abuse of animals in criminology: A brief history and current review', *Social Justice,* 22(1): 5–31.

Beirne, Piers (1996) 'A note on speciesist language and animal abuse', *The Critical Criminologist,* 7(1): 7–8.

Beirne, Piers (1997) 'Rethinking bestiality: Towards a sociology of interspecies sexual assault', *Theoretical Criminology,* 1(3): 317–340.

Bentham, Jeremy (1789) *An Introduction to the Principles of Morals and Legislation.* 1970. Edited by J.H. Burns and H.L.A. Hart. University of London: Athlone Press.

Benton, Ted (1993) *Natural Relations: Ecology, Animal Rights and Social Justice.* London: Verso.

— (1998) 'Rights and justice on a shared planet: More rights or new relations?' *Theoretical Criminology* 2(2): 149–175.

Blackstone, William (1769) *Commentaries on the Laws of England*. Oxford: Clarendon Press.

Boat, Barbara, W. (1995) 'The relationship between violence to children and violence to animals: An ignored link?' *Journal of Interpersonal Violence*, 10(2): 229–235.

Brooman, Simon and Debbie Legge (1997) *Law Relating to Animals*. London: Cavendish.

Browne, Angela (1987) *When Battered Women Kill*. New York: Free Press.

Cazaux, Geertrui (in press) 'Legitimating the entry of the animals issue in critical criminology.' *Humanity and Society*.

Clark, Stephen (1977) *The Moral Status of Animals*. Oxford: Clarendon.

Clinard, Marshall B. (1952) *The Black Market: A Study of White Collar Crime*. New York: Rinehart.

Cohen, Lawrence E. and Richard, Machalek (1988) 'A general theory of expropriative crime: An evolutionary ecological approach', *American Journal of Sociology*, 94(3): 465–501.

Curtin, Deane (1991) 'Toward an ecological ethic of care', *Hypatia*, **6**(1): 60–74.

Daly, Martin and Margo, Wilson (1988) *Homicide*. New York: Aldine de Gruyter.

Darnton, Robert (1985) *The Great Cat Massacre and Other Episodes in French Cultural History*. New York: Vintage.

Derrida, Jacques (1992) 'The mystical foundations of authority', in Drucilla Cornell, Michel Rosenfeld and David Gray Carlson, *Deconstruction and the Possibility of Knowledge*. New York: Routledge.

Deviney, Elizabeth, Jeffery Dickert and Randall Lockwood (1983) 'The care of pets within child abusing families', *International Journal for the Study of Animal Problems*, 4(4): 321–329.

Donley, L., Gary J. Patronek and Carter, Luke (in press) 'The epidemiology of animal abuse and neglect in Massachusetts', *Society and Animals*.

Donovan, Josephine (1990) 'Animal rights and feminist theory', *Signs*, 15(2): 350–375.

Donovan, Josephine and Carol J. Adams (eds) (1996) *Beyond Animal Rights: A Feminist Caring Ethic for the Treatment of Animals*. New York: Continuum.

Durkheim, Emile (1893) *The Division of Labour in Society*. trans. W.D. Halls. 1984. New York: Free Press.

Edwards, Rem, B. (1993) 'Tom Regan's seafaring dog and unequal inherent worth', *Between the Species*, 9(4): 231–235.

Ellis, Lee (1990) 'The evolution of collective counterstrategies to crime: From the primate control role to the criminal justice system', In Lee Ellis and Harry Hoffman (eds), *Crime in Biological, Social, and Moral Contexts*. New York: Praeger.

Ellis, Lee and Anthony Walsh (1997) 'Gene-based evolutionary theories in criminology', *Criminology*, 35(2): 229–276.

Favre, David and Vivien Tsang (1993) 'The development of anti-cruelty laws during the 1800s', *Detroit College of Law Review*, 1: 1–35.

Felthous, Alan R. and Stephen R. Kellert (1987) 'Childhood cruelty to animals and later aggression against people: A Review', *American Journal of Psychiatry*, 144(6): 710–717.

Francione, Gary L. (1995) *Animals, Property, and the Law*. Philadelphia: Temple University Press.

Francione, Gary L. (1996) *Rain Without Thunder: The Ideology of the Animal Rights Movement*. Philadelphia: Template University Press.

Friedrich, William N., Anthony J. Urquiza and Robert L. Beilke (1986) 'Behavior problems in sexually abused young children', *Journal of Pediatric Psychology* 11(1): 47–57.

Gelles, Richard J. and Murray, Straus (1988) *Intimate Violence*. New York: Simon and Schuster.

Gilligan, Carol (1982) *In a Different Voice. Psychological Theory and Women's Development*. Cambridge, Mass: Harvard University Press.

Godlovitch, Stanley, Roslind Godlovitch and John Harris (eds.) (1974) *Animals, Men and Morals*. New York: Grove Press.

Godlovitch, Stanley, Roslind Godlovitch and John Harris (eds.) (1989) *Primate Visions: Gender, Race and Nature in the World of Modern Science*. New York: Routledge.

Harding, Sandra (1991) *Whose Science? Whose Knowledge? Thinking from Women's Lives*. Ithaca, N.Y.: Cornell University Press.

Hay, Douglas (1975) 'Poaching and the game laws on Cannock Chase', In Douglas Hay, Peter Linebaugh, John G. Rule, E.P. Thompson and Cal Winslow (eds) *Albion's Fatal Tree: Crime and Society in Eighteenth-Century England*. Harmondsworth: Penguin.

Held, Virginia (1994) *Feminist Morality: Transforming Culture, Society and Politics*. Chicago: University of Chicago Press.

Hirst, Paul and Penny Woolley (1982) *Social Relations and Human Attributes*. London: Tavistock.

Hooks, Bell (1981) *Ain't I a Woman: Black Women and Feminism*. Boston, Mass: South End Press.

Hunter, Mic (1990) *Abused Boys: The Neglected Victims of Sexual Abuse*. New York: Lexington.

Jasper, James M. and Dorothy Nelkin (1992) *The Animal Rights Crusade*. New York: Free Press.

Justice, Blair, Rita Justice and Irvin A. Kraft (1974) 'Early-warning signs of violence: Is a triad enough?' *American Journal of Psychiatry*, 131(4): 457–459.

Kappeler, Susanne (1995) 'Speciesism, racism, nationalism … or the power of scientific subjectivity', In Carol J. Adams and Josephine Donovan (eds) *Animals and Women: Feminist Theoretical Explorations.* Durham. N.C.: Duke University Press.

Kheel, Marti (1985) 'The liberation of nature: A circular affair', *Environmental Ethics* 7(2): 135–149.

Lasik, Alekswander (1998) 'Rudolf Höss: Manager of crime', In Yisrael Gutman and Michael Berenbaum (eds) *Anatomy of the Auschwitz Death Camp.* Bloomington: Indiana University Press.

Leahy, Michael P.T. (1991) *Against Liberation: Putting Animals in Perspective.* New York: Routledge.

Leavitt, Emily Stewart and Diane Halverson (1990) 'The evolution of anti-cruelty laws in the United States', In Emily Stewart Leavitt and Diane Halverson (eds) *Animals and Their Legal Rights.* Washington, D.C.: Animal Welfare Institute.

Lockwood, Randall and Frank R. Ascione (eds) (1998) *Cruelty to Animals and Interpersonal Violence.* West Lafayette, Ind.: Purdue University Press.

Luke, Brian (1992) 'Justice, caring and animal liberation', *Between the Species,* 8(2): 100–108.

Maestro, Marcello (1973) *Cesare Beccaria and the Origins of Penal Reform.* Philadelphia: Temple University Press.

Masson, Jeffrey Moussaieff and Susan McCarthy (1995) *When Elephants Weep: The Emotional Lives of Animals.* New York: Delacorte.

McMullan, John L. and David C. Perrier (1997) 'Poaching vs. the law: The social organization of illegal fishing', In John L. McMullan, David C. Perrier, Stephen Smith and Peter D. Swan (eds.), *Crimes, Laws and Communities.* Halifax, N.S.: Fernwood.

Midgley, Mary (1983) *Animals and Why They Matter.* Athens: University of Georgia Press.

Miller, Karla S. and John F. Knutson (1997) 'Reports of severe physical punishment and exposure to animal cruelty by inmates convicted of felonies and by university students', *Child Abuse & Neglect* 21(1): 59–82.

Noske, Barbara (1997) *Beyond Boundaries: Humans and Other Animals.* Montreal: Black Rose Books.

Patronek, Gary J. (1997) 'Issues for veterinarians in recognizing and reporting animal neglect and abuse', *Society and Animals,* 5(3): 267–280.

Patterson, G.R., Barbara D. DeBaryshe and Elizabeth Ramsey (1989) 'A developmental perspective on antisocial behavior' *American Psychologist,* 442: 329–335.

Pocar, Valerio (1992) 'Animal rights: A socio-legal perspective', *Journal of Law and Society* 19(2): 214–230.

Regan, Tom (1983) *The Case for Animal Rights.* Berkeley: University of California Press.

Regan, Tom (1987) *The Struggle for Animal Rights.* Clarks Summit. Pa: International Society for Animal Rights.

Renzetti, Claire (1992) *Violent Betrayal: Partner Abuse in Lesbian Relationships.* Newbury Park, Calif.: Sage.

Rowan, Andrew N. (1984) *Of Mice, Models, & Men.* Albany: SUNY Press.

Rowan, Andrew N., Franklin M. Loew, and Joan C. Weer (1995) *The Animal Research Controversy.* Medford, Mass: Tufts University, Center for Animals and Public Policy.

Ruether, Rosemary Radford (1975) *New Heaven/New Earth: Sexist Ideologies and Human Liberation.* New York: Seabury.

Salt, Henry (1892) *Animals' Rights 1980.* Clarks Summit, Pa.: Society for Animal Rights.

Silverstein, Helena (1996) *Unleashing Rights: Law, Meaning and the Animal Rights Movement.* Ann Arbor: University of Michigan Press.

Singer, Peter (1990) *Animal Liberation.* 2d Ed. New York: Avon.

Skrapec, Candice (1996) 'The sexual component of serial murder', In Thomas O'Reilly-Fleming (ed.) *Serial & Mass Murder.* Toronto: Canadian Scholars Press.

Spelman, Elizabeth (1982) 'Woman as body: Ancient and contemporary views', *Feminist Studies* 8(1): 109–131.

Sperling, Susan (1991) 'Baboons with briefcases: Feminism, functionalism and sociobiology in the evolution of primate gender', *Signs* 17(1): 1–27.

Stone, Christopher (1972) 'Should trees have standing? Towards legal rights for natural objects', *Southern California Law Review* 45. Spring: 450–501.

Sutherland, Edwin H. (1949) *White Collar Crime.* New Haven: Yale University Press.

Swanson, Charles R., Neil C. Chamelin and Leonard Territo (1992) *Criminal Investigation.* New York: McGraw-Hill.

Taylor, Thomas (1792) *A Vindication of the Rights of Brutes.* 1966. Gainesville, Fla.: Scholars' Facsimiles and Reprints.

Tester, Keith (1991) *Animals and Society.* London: Routledge.

U.S. Department of Agriculture (1966) *Agricultural Statistical Services,* April–September.

Vermeulen, Hannelie and Johannes Odendaal (1993) 'Proposed typology of companion animal abuse', *Anthrozoös* 6(4): 248–257.

Vila, Bryan J. and Lawrence E. Cohen (1993) 'Crime as strategy: Testing an evolutionary ecological theory of expropriative crime' *American Journal of Sociology* 98(4): 873–912.

Wax, Douglas E. and Victor G. Haddox (1974) 'Enuresis, firesetting and animal cruelty', *Child Psychiatry and Human Behaviour* 4(3): 151–156.

White, Kenneth (1992) 'The shape of cruelty', *The Latham Letter* 13(3): 6–7.

Wiehe, Vernon R. (1990) *Sibling Abuse*. Lexington.

Wilson, E.O. (1975) *Sociobiology, the New Synthesis*. Cambridge, Mass.: Harvard University Press.

Wilson, James Q. and Richard J. Hernstein (1985) *Crime and Human Nature*. New York: Simon & Schuster.

Wollstonecraft, Mary (1792) *A Vindication of the Rights of Women*. (1982) London: J.M. Dent.

Wooden, Wayne S. and Martha Lou Berkey (1984) *Children and Arson: America's Middle Class Nightmare*. New York: Plenum.

# 10. An environmental victimology*

*Christopher Williams*

## Introduction

> *I do not want to be a victim,* and all steps should be taken to guard against my victimization.
>
> *If I am a victim, I want all available help,* and expect government, industry, and community to come to my aid.
>
> *I do not want to be revictimized* by governments, companies, courts, or the medical and legal professions.

The expression of these demands from the Permanent Peoples' Tribunal on *Industrial and Environmental Hazards and Human Rights* in Bhopal (PPT 1992: 13) reflects the urgent need to address environmental victimization, not only in the form of obvious disasters as at Bhopal, but also the 'creeping disasters' such as traffic pollution. Law is one form of response, but, as is lucidly argued by Peter Yeager in *The Limits of Law* (1991), even in state-of-the-art countries such as the U.S., statutes alone can never fully address the problems posed by environmental crime. The difficulties experienced in implementing statutory compensation in Bhopal provide a poor-nation perspective (BGIA, 1992). There is an obvious need for social justice approaches to parallel formal legal processes.

## The limits of 'environmental justice'

The 'environmental justice movement' has provided the most prominent alternative in recent years, at least in the U.S. (see Bryant 1995; Hofrichter 1993; Capek 1993). Yet, although generating valuable insights and an effective basis for informed environmental activism, its broader application is limited, principally for three reasons.

---

* From *Social Justice* (1996), 23(4): pp. 16–40.

First, 'environmental justice' relies greatly on *subjective (often self-) definitions of victimization*. This may work well in relation to activism, but ultimately the development of justice perspectives, legal or social, requires objective benchmarks. Without objective definitions, how do we apply victim conceptualizations when (i) victims *will* not self-define? What of the 'manic denial' of the Mormons in Nevada, who accept the health problems resulting from nuclear testing as a necessary sacrifice for the good of the state (Gallagher 1993: 217), or the Indian who attributes lead poisoning to *karma*, not to the illegal smelter next door? How do we accord victim status when (ii) victims *cannot* self-define, for example, with the unborn child or when the outcome is severe intellectual disability from radiation or lead pollution (Williams 1996a)? How do we formally identify victims when (iii) national or community leaders will not acknowledge the victimization of those they govern? In the case of cross-border acid rain and Chernobyl, European governments did not argue for redress because they did not want to encourage precedents that might later be applied in reverse. What of the individuals among the Mescalero Apaches in New Mexico who will eventually suffer health problems because their leaders encourage the importation of hazardous toxic waste to reap the short-term cash rewards?

Second, 'environmental justice' *bases its key arguments on (i) assumptions about power relationships and (ii) group identities, which (iii) reflect the gender, class, and ethnic structures of U.S. society.*

(i) The assumption of the powerless as victim and the powerful as victimizer can lead to a stereotyped view that omits the victimization of those with power and wealth. If wealth and perpetrating environmental crime always go hand-in-hand, how do we conceptualize the Czech industries that polluted rivers then flowing through wealthy Germany, or the threat posed to Norway from Russia's decaying nuclear weapon facilities, or people in Hong Kong and Taiwan who suffer the pollution from mainland China?

(ii) When group identity is the prerequisite of analysis, this can omit the victimization of those scattered within populations who may be vulnerable because, for example, of their clinical status. The link between background radiation from nuclear testing and babies born with Down's Syndrome (Bound *et al.* 1995: 164–170) involves mothers whose only group identity is that they are over 40, and the true victim group is their unborn children. Class, wealth, race, neighborhood, and gender (of the victims) are irrelevant concepts.

(iii) North American group identities are often not applicable in other settings. For example, the link between minority ethnic groups, poor neighborhoods, and pollution is less strong in regions such as Sweden, China, or the former Soviet Union. Moscow, home to the Russian ethnic power elite, is both one of the wealthiest and one of the most polluted regions in the country. In some settings, standard assumptions about the vulnerability of minority groups seem incorrect. While U.S. research shows that minority ethnic groups suffer more from lead pollution, a study in the U.K. revealed that Asian children in a London borough suffered less than their white peers (Lansdown and Yule 1986: 115). Later in this issue [of *Social Justice* (1996), 23(4), Chapter 11 of this volume], Sharon Stephens (1996) argues that the environmental justice frame does not readily embrace a global perspective on children.

Third, because environmental justice usually adopts an activist stance, it often *lacks academic objectivity*. This puts it in a weak position to address conceptual conundra that are familiar to traditional victimology – for example, 'victim participation' in, or 'victim precipitation' of, the circumstances that cause their suffering. Truck drivers who have respiratory ailments because of particulates in exhaust emissions are an obvious case. There are limitations on how activist arguments – often reflecting what the victimologist Ezzat Fattah (1992: 12) has dubbed 'missionary zeal' – will bring about the necessary changes in thinking among hardened politicians for whom self-interest is usually the primary motivation.

Most importantly, the activist position, often manifest as 'nonviolent direct action,' leads to an avoidance of any discussion of violent victim resistance. It may be that most responses in the U.S. have been nonviolent, but that is not so within a global view. Understanding the violent spirals surrounding environmental victimization is crucial, and, as will be argued later, will probably be the most distinctive feature of a victimology perspective.

## 'Environmental victimology'

The 'environmental justice' approach has played a vital role in generating an awareness of the human dimensions of environmental change, mobilizing action, and in amassing data. However, its shortcomings propose that other, complementary perspectives now need to be developed. Although currently an unfashionable area of academic study, victimology is the obvious direction to look. The *U.N. Declaration on Victims of … Abuse of Power* (1985) provides a starting point, and appears prescient of the likely concerns of an environmental view. It relates specifically to:

> persons who … have suffered harm … through acts or omissions that do not yet constitute violations of national criminal laws but of internationally recognised norms relating to human rights (in Fattah, 1989).

An environmental perspective fits within the framework of 'Radical Victimology' (Mawby and Walklate 1994: 8, 13), which is broadly concerned with human rights, abuses of power, and human suffering irrespective of whether the circumstances are within the ambit of law.

This article therefore proposes working definitions, embraces a brief critique of the 'environmental justice' approach, consolidates an emerging epistemology, and outlines issues that could be the concern of an environmental victimology in the future. Finally, it raises the question as to whether, in the context of the scale and nature of environmental victimization, 'justice' or 'security' is the guiding principle.

## Definitions

### *Who are 'environmental victims'?*

The notions of victims in relation to the environment has been applied very loosely. The study entitled *Victims of the Environment* (Rossi *et al*. 1983) only concerns natural disasters such as tornadoes and earthquakes, in which there are no apparent perpetrators. In the headline 'Brain Damage Found in Victims of Bhopal Disaster' (*British Medical Journal* 1994: 359), meanwhile, the meaning is very different since the environmental factors were not natural and there were clearly culpable entities. Michael Reich adopts the term 'victims,' giving it the same meaning, throughout his book *Toxic Politics: Responding to Chemical Disasters* (1991). In an editorial in *Down to Earth*, India's environmental magazine, Anil Agarwal wrote recently of his experience of cancer: 'I was speaking not just as an environmental activist, but also as an environmental victim' (1995: 4). The term therefore arises naturally in discussion of contemporary environmental problems, but without sufficient precision for academic purposes.

Surprisingly, 'environment' is rarely defined clearly in law or international declarations (Birnie and Boyle 1992: 2). Through usage, it is now generally taken to comprise four components: chemical, physical, micro-biological, and psychosocial (Lee, in Bullock *et al*. 1988: 275). The importance of the latter is in relation to corporate abuses of power that manipulate the other three components. An example would be cigarette advertising aimed at children or developing countries.

When formally conceptualizing 'environmental victims,' it is helpful to exclude those more accurately described as 'environmental casualties' – those who suffer as a result of natural disasters. Implicit in the etymology of 'casualties' is the notion of *chance*, while the concept 'victims' embodies the idea of suffering caused by a *deliberate or reckless human act* (including an act of omission). Some circumstances that appear natural may, if analyzed in greater depth, be a consequence of human acts. Those killed by the flooding of the Yangtze River in 1995 may have been victims of deforestation and soil erosion that precipitated the surge (Bird 1995: 2). Environmental suffering that has affected many generations, such as iodine deficiency, might not be seen as victimization until power relationships are examined. Why are the communities that suffer iodine deficiency forced to live on land that cannot sustain human life properly? Later in this issue [of *Social Justice* (1996), 23: 4], Peter Penz (1996) and Meena Singh (1996) further develop the possibilities in relation to transnational victimization and environmental refugees.

Environmental law usually embodies the principle that the outcome of an act must have been 'reasonably foreseeable' for it to constitute an offense. So far, however, most environmental law relates to damage to the physical world, not human injury. If we are considering human injury as a specific outcome, it seems more appropriate to borrow from common law in relation to personal injury offenses, for example assault, where the principle is whether an act is deliberate *or reckless*. Reckless behavior may not embody foreseeing a *specific outcome*, simply that an act, could, by its nature, be dangerous to others. The distinction is important. Many claims for compensation for environmentally mediated injury fail because the perpetrator maintains that it was impossible to foresee a specific outcome. For example, the dumping of a particular substance may be excused because it was not known, at the time, to be hazardous (the specific negative outcome was not 'foreseeable'). Yet, in the same circumstances, it might be claimed that to dump the substance was *reckless* because it was not proven safe. In the light of the inability of science to keep up with the problems it causes, this common-sense precautionary principle seems more in accord with human well-being. It is the tradition of common law on personal injury, not environmental protection, that has at its heart the direct well-being of humans.

Intergenerational responsibility must be implicit in any conceptualization because of the time-latent nature of much environmental victimization. The U.K. *Congenital Disability (Civil Liabilities) Act 1976*, for example, embraces environmentally mediated injury causing 'predisposition (whether or not susceptible to immediate prognosis) to physical or mental defect in the future.' There needs also to be an assumption that both victims and perpetrators might be individuals *or groups*. Moreover, as will be argued later in relation to causation, it is more appropriate to phrase a definition 'consequence of' rather than 'caused by.'

The outcome of victimization is better described as 'injury' rather than 'suffering.' Injury, as an 'adverse health effect' caused by environmental factors, is neatly defined by Christiani (Chivian *et al.* 1993: 15): 'any effect that results in altered structure or impaired function, or represents the beginnings of a sequence of events leading to altered structure or function.' Implicit in the term 'injury' is a relationship between two events (cause and effect) that culminate in tangible harm; suffering implies less acute general experiences that might be tolerated without actual injury. This distinction also addresses the debate, common now in poorer countries, that people must endure some environmental suffering for the benefit of economic development, such as dam building. This is an arguable trade-off, but in no justice system is it acceptable to trade off the infliction of human *injury* (or causing death) against economic benefit.

This restriction to 'injury' therefore creates a much narrower frame of reference than that used within the environmental justice debate. Later in this issue, Peter Penz argues well for a broadening of the definition when considering transnational dimensions (1996). Pragmatically, if an aim of a victim conceptualization is to change policy, then governments are more likely to respond in relation to tight, manageable definitions, which may be stretched a little, than to 'catch all' concepts that might appear to carry a host of hidden ramifications. As to starting point; 'environmental victims' can therefore be defined as:

> those of past, present, or future generations who are injured as a consequence of change to the chemical, physical, microbiological, or psychosocial environment, brought about by deliberate or reckless, individual or collective, human act or act of omission.

The etymology of 'victim' embodies 'sacrifice,' and this underlying meaning provides a helpful insight. Environmental victims are often, in effect, sacrificed for the benefit of a more powerful entity. It is common for industrial polluters to argue that the environment of a few downstream/downwind individuals must be sacrificed for the greater good of improving national economies or providing employment. It is all interesting coincidence that we find the U.S. government talking formally of toxic no-go areas as 'environmental sacrifice zones' (Walker 1988: 8). It is even more chilling to find that the local term for children downwind of U.S. nuclear test sites in Nevada, who were born with birth defects, is 'the sacrifice babies' (Gallagher 1993: 217).

### What is an 'environmental cause' of victimization?

Arguing causation is the prerequisite of establishing victim status. Although it is convenient for an activist to talk of problems as 'environmentally caused,' a cause in relation to the definition of 'environmental victim' (above) is human interaction with the environment, not the environment itself – 'environmentally mediated' would be a more apt term, but as yet this has no legal meaning. The understanding of causation requires greater clarity.

Initially, there is a conceptual legacy within law that must be challenged – the requirement that cause and effect must be adjacent. The law is usually framed in terms such as *'proximate* cause,' *'immediate* violence,' or *'a continuing, operating,* and substantial cause' (Emmet 1984: 60), reflecting the rule of criminal jurisprudence *cause proxima non remote spectatur.* Existing law has therefore been weak at conceptualizing the indirect nature of environmental victimization. Causal understandings of 'interjacency' are needed – embracing space, time, and multiplicity and interaction of causes and effects – that reflect the 'creeping disasters' or, in the UNICEF term 'slow emergencies,' which now threaten human safety. Court judgments provide one source of evolving concepts, such as that of 'major contributory cause.' *Toxic Torts* (Pugh and Day 1992) provides a number of examples, which can inform a victimology perspective.

Another approach to the problem can derive from the philosophy of law: the importance of how the causal question is phrased. This is raised by Hart and Honore, in *Causation in the Law* (1985), who cite a judge who considered the form 'Did the injury cause X' inferior to 'Did X result from the injury' (p. 87), and argue that their own preferred form is 'Was X the consequence of Y' rather than, 'Was Y the cause of X' (p. 135).

This can be exemplified in terms of environmental victimization involving a toxic release that degraded farmland, leading to malnutrition, and then to a high incidence of disability in the local population. In this case, it is easy to argue that the toxic release did not 'cause the disability' – the direct cause was malnutrition. It is less easy to argue that the disability was 'not a consequence' of the release. How should an 'environmental cause' be defined in legal or quasi-legal terms? One approach is the recognition of environmental causes as the *presence* or *absence* of environmental factors, with each of these embracing the standard distinction in criminal and civil laws defining offenses, and therefore victimization, as stemming from human acts or omissions. Broadly, 'environmental causes' would then fall into four groups, which are exemplified in Figure 10.1. Specific instances of victimization may well fit within more than one of these four categories, or may fit better in a different category at different periods over a long time scale (i.e., in the case of 'creeping disasters').

The model is not hypothetical. Although scattered, laws and judgments already exist that acknowledge these four forms of environmental cause. For example, legislation in some Indian states redresses the *absence* of iodine in the environment by a statutory requirement that iodine is included in salt. Victimization, if iodine is not added to salt, therefore results from an *omission*. A U.K. Court of Appeal ruling in 1995 found that 'running a sewerage system in an unmaintained state is sufficient to entitle a jury to find the party responsible for the system guilty of causing pollution … failure implied and omission' (Tan 1995: 11). This provides an instance of *presence/omission*. A definition emerges from this model, that an 'environmental cause' of victimization is 'a presence or absence of chemical, physical, micro-biological, or phsycho-social environmental factors, resulting from individual or collective human act or omission, over any time-scale, of which the consequence is human injury.'


**An emerging epistemology**

'Environmental justice' naturally provides an important contribution to the emerging epistemology of a victim perspective, but mainly from a rich-nation perspective. An issue of *Social Problems* in 1993 (Perrolle) presented key papers concerning class, ethnicity, gender, and race in relation to community and workplace environmental hazards. So, too, do *Toxic Struggles* (Hofrichter 1993) and *Environmental Justice* (Bryant 1995). Later in this issue [of *Social Justice* (1996), 23(4)], Barten, Fustukian, and de Haan (1996) provide an example, however, of how rich-nation concepts need to be questioned in relation to occupational health.

The links between race and environmental victimization have been well analyzed by Robert Bullard (e.g., 1993), but when we look globally, concepts

|  | Act | Omission |
|---|---|---|
| Presence of environmental agent | E.g., the *presence* of methyl-isocyanate caused by an *act* of polluting and poisoning (Union Carbide – Bhopal) | E.g., the *presence* of excess lead in water supplies caused by an *omission* of the duty to provide safe drinking water |
| Absence of environmental agent | E.g., the *absence* of food and micro-nutrients leading to malnutrition and brain injury resulting from land degradation caused by the *act* of dumping toxic waste | E.g., the *absence* of iodine caused by an *omission* of failing to iodize salt in accordance with the law (India) |

**Figure 10.1**  Defining 'an environmental cause of victimization'

become less easy to generalize. 'Minority groups' can sometimes appear to act against their own interests. In the Solomon Islands, the Western approach of coercive environmental law fails because, although it may seem to be in the best interests of those it relates to, the perceived need for regulation is not shared culturally. A more consensual approach to implementing environmental regulation is required (ELF 1994: 19).

Cultural perspectives on *determining what constitutes*, as distinct from simply *stating the experiences of*, environmental victimization are largely missing from the environmental justice debate. An indigenous community may feel little concern over the aesthetics of massive industrial development, but might consider disturbance to a small sacred lake or shrine by minor oil pollution to be extreme eco-vandalism. Alicia Fentiman (1996) provides an example of necessary cultural understanding later in this issue [of *Social Justice*, 23(4)].

Specific problems experienced by women, particularly concerning workplace 'fetal protection policies,' are explored in the U.S. and U.K. contexts in *For Whose Protection* (Kenney 1992). Feminist concerns are more broadly discussed in relation to North-South divides in *Ecofeminism* (Mies and Shiva 1992).

However, the feminist contribution to environmental justice has yet to resolve unambiguously a central conflict: that between the rights of women over their bodies and the right to work, and the rights of unborn children not to be exposed to toxic substances. The usual conclusion is that the work environment should be made safe for everyone. Unfortunately, U.S.-oriented discussion does not then go on to consider the dilemma when the work environment is not made safe, which is the case in most poorer countries.

Conflicts between the rights of the mother and the potential unborn victim extend beyond the workplace. In the U.S., pregnant women who take drugs are being charged with 'distributing' drugs to their babies – a measure that is not accepted by most feminist academics. Should the rights of the unborn victim be subjugated to those of the mother, or is the womb the 'environment' of the fetus and thus subject to the same ethical considerations that we now apply to other human environments? Once born, most nations accept that, in a case of conflict, the best interests of the child take precedence. Why should there be any difference for the unborn child? This takes us back to the need for objective definitions of environmental victimization, and to the first aspect of the emerging epistemology, the status of the unborn victim.

### The unborn victim

In the light of the copious writings, and common rhetoric, about the need for 'intergenerational justice' over millennia (e.g., Laslett and Fishkin 1992), it is curious that very little has been said about the first stepping stone to this glorious ideal – the immediate next generation – the unborn child. Environmental medicine now provides considerable evidence of the vulnerability of the fetus to environmental toxins and genetic transfer. Yet, in general, this understanding has not been satisfactorily translated into bases for action within either formal or informal justice frames. What is the status of an unborn victim?

One of the few attempts to clarify this question was the U.K. Law Commission report, *Injuries to Unborn Children* (1973). The authors were of the view that 'where a child is born with a disability which was caused by someone's fault occurring before birth, he [sic] should be entitled to recover damages from, that person' (p. 8). In the U.K., a recent Court of Appeal ruling concluded that, although under English law an unborn child has no independent legal personality, courts will adopt the civil maxim that 'an unborn child shall be deemed to be born whenever its interests require it' (Tan 1992: 32). This derived from earlier precedents in Canada and Australia (Law Commission 1973: 5, *i*). Without the 'best interests' *caveat*, the ruling would probably have conflicted with lawful abortion in the case of an impaired or unwanted child.

The U.K. Congenital Disability (Civil Liabilities) Act of 1976 was intended to establish the rights of the unborn victim following confusion surrounding the disabilities caused by the Thalidomide drug, but it is far from ingenuous. Compensation is denied if injury to the parent preceded conception and one or both parents knew of the reproductive risk related to their job. It is unlikely that parents working in, for instance, a nuclear power station could prove that they did not know of the risk factor. In effect, employers can negate their responsibility by telling employees that their work poses a reproductive hazard (see Miller 1989). Why are the rights of unborn victims diminished by the actions or knowledge of others (their parents) over whom they have no control?

In 1992, a U.K. woman who kicked a pregnant neighbor in the stomach, causing fatal brain damage to the fetus, was charged with manslaughter. This was the first case of its kind in the U.K. (*Guardian* 1992b: 29). A later U.K. appeal ruling concluded that a man who stabbed his pregnant girlfriend, killing the unborn child, could be convicted of murder or manslaughter (Dyer 1995: 7).

These cases raise interesting questions. Could a fetus also be a direct victim of a criminal assault? Might injury from an environmental agent constitute an assault, murder or manslaughter? Could a fetus be awarded compensation for injuries following a conviction for assault against its mother or itself? In the U.K., an unborn child *could* be considered eligible for an award from the *Criminal Injuries Compensation Board* (Clark 1993). A recent decision held: 'We accept that "personal injuries" is a term which can properly be applied to injuries occurring before birth and do not regard the precise stage at which injuries occurred as relevant to our decision' (*R v. CICB ex parte P* 1993).

In the U.S., before 1946, the unborn victim was rarely recognized. Since then, the courts of every North American state have held 'as a development of the common law and despite previous decisions to the contrary,' that a child can recover damages for a prenatal injury (*Guardian* 1992a). Yet doubt lingers – only a few states will acknowledge injury resulting from events happening *before* conception (e.g., high blood lead in a mother, due to employment a year earlier, which later crosses into the fetus). This question might be clarified, however, by applying a 'man-trap' test. If a farmer set a 'man-trap' in 1990, which injured a 10-year-old child in 1995, the farmer would clearly be responsible for the injury. Yet what if the child were only three years old? Again, there seems little doubt that the farmer would he responsible, even though the child had not been conceived at the time of the act that caused the injury.

Many of the concerns of unborn victims are at present outside the remit of law, legislation varies considerably between nations, and cultural dimensions have been ignored. How would victim status for an unborn child be reconciled in some African communities, where babies do not achieve full human status until a naming ceremony at around 18 months of age? It has proved possible to agree on children already born in the *U.N. Convention on the Rights of the Child*. Is it possible to agree on the rights of the unborn child? Debates to achieve international consistency should establish three points of consensus, which already exist in isolated agreements, that:

- The unborn child has full victim status when this is in its interests, for example, in relation to criminal and civil actions and compensation schemes;
- Acts or omissions, affecting parents before conception, can constitute victimization of an unborn child;
- The rights of the unborn child cannot be diminished by the acts or omissions of others – logically, the concept of contributory negligence cannot be applied to unborn victims.

### Avoidance of liability and responsibility

Theoretical discussions of causation take us to the practical aspect – deliberate denial of causal links – the avoidance of liability and responsibility by perpetrators. Although a familiar part of mainstream victimology – concerning, for example, children, women (Fattah 1989), or disabled people (Williams 1995) – the discussion takes on new dimensions in relation to the environment, for two reasons: the *complexity* of establishing causation creates an easy escape for perpetrators, and the *scale* of remediation is usually immense and so the incentive to avoid liability is great.

At the domestic level, David Dembo, in *Abuse of Power* (1993: 142), provides an excellent synopsis of diversionary tactics employed by industrial and other corporate victimizers to avoid liability:

- Deny the problem;
- Put it in perspective;
- Blame a hysterical public;
- Blame the victim;
- Try to divide the victims; and
- When possible, settle with the government if it will be less costly.

Delaying court hearings so that victims and witnesses die, 'papering out' court proceedings by producing an excess of irrelevant data, and regular press releases providing copious information that is always the same are other common approaches. Another common tactic is for corporate polluters to accuse communities of creating the environmental problems for which they are, in the main, responsible. As discussed below, *Shell* adopted this approach in relation to Ogoniland (Slayter 1995: 16). An easy excuse for avoiding liability is provided when people migrate to a disaster area and attempt to claim compensation, as at Bhopal. Yet why should there be any surprise at such responses by people in poor communities? They are a natural consequence of the original victimization and, more significantly, of delays in admitting liability and providing redress. Environmental victimology could usefully develop understandings of these social dynamics, because although the corporate polluter may win a court case, it will certainly not win in the eyes of the global community and therefore lose that priceless asset, public trust.

Governments also become conspirators in avoidance. In the Bhopal case, special legislation *diminished* the rights of victims through giving the state absolute control over claims and denying liability for future generations (*Bhopal Gas Leak Disaster [Processing of Claims] Act 1985*). The U.S. *Radiation Exposure Compensation Act* 1990, operates similarly through excluding regions in Nevada where fallout from weapons testing was greatest, and again denying liability to future generations (Gallagher 1993: *xxvii*).

The international context provides even greater possibilities for avoidance. In some situations, time-scales mean that responsible entities will either disappear or change dramatically, and this does not just concern intergenerational responsibility over centuries. Chernobyl provides the obvious example – the responsible nation ceased to exist three years after the disaster. Russia then claimed control of the nuclear industry, but maintained it had no liability because it too was a victim. (This is akin to 'I am not guilty of assault because I hurt my fist when I hit you!') Guilty individuals were then named by the new state, without any trial; the real culprits became high-ranking officials in the new government. The government controls the courts (Fedorychyk 1994: 5). South Africa provides another unique dimension (Singh 1996). It seems unlikely that black environmental activists would hold the Mandela government accountable for environmental problems created by the former apartheid regime.

How acceptable is the claim that responsibility is annulled by an apparent change of regime? If this question is not addressed, one result might be that in the future, regimes may commonly abdicate power as a means of avoiding responsibility for environmental disasters – the nation-state equivalent of going bankrupt and setting up again under a new name. One answer would be to hold banks and other international funding agencies responsible for the environmental victimization they have financed.

Environmental problems now create land areas that have negative value, and the incentive to cut the line of responsibility is obvious. In recent years, a dilapidated oil refinery was sold for just one dollar because of its toxic legacy, and the U.S. Energy Department 'is now reconciled to writing off some nuclear factory sites as 'national sacrifice zones,' where a complete cleanup would be prohibitively expensive' (Walker 1988: 8). Thinking further, might we see large nations *force* independence on environmental disaster regions to avoid responsibility? Will we see future presidents tell local mayors that they can have 'countries' of their own, which happen to come with a decaying nuclear power station? What will be the reaction of potential environmental victims in such circumstances – 'freedom struggles' to fight *against* independence?

Our formal knowledge of corporate avoidance strategies is now quite comprehensive, although much of the work is probably of more help to perpetrators than victims. Less thought has been given to the ultimate form of avoidance – if you create an environmental problem, give it away. The approaches reflect what Michael Reich terms 'a strategy of diversion combined with a strategy of dissociation' (1991: 263). Avoidance will increase until we learn to understand and counter both these strategies *in parallel*.

### 'Victim syndrome'

Avoidance of liability leads to failures to prevent or redress victimization, and a social impact that has been dubbed the 'environmental victim syndrome.' Although considerable attention has been given to clinical or psychological outcomes, for example, cancer or post-traumatic stress (e.g., Bass *et al.* 1993), much less attention has been given to psychosocial outcomes of environmental victimization. David Marples' book, *The Social Impact of the Chernobyl Disaster* (1988), is one of the few examples of a comprehensive case study, and *Who Pays the Price: The Sociocultural Context of Environmental Crisis* (Johnston 1994) provides a more analytical, anthropological perspective.

It is possible to gain an impression of the more obvious concerns from informal accounts. Rosemary Gillespie (1994: 13) reports, from firsthand experience, that the results of industrial victimization from an RTZ copper mine in Bougainville include 'a deep sense of social malaise ... which expressed itself in clan tensions, depression, alcohol abuse, rage, traffic accidents, and incidents of violence ...' Green Cross detects in the former Soviet Union 'instability in contaminated regions, caused by the feeling of "being left alone" with the toxic threats' (GC 1994). More formal typologies arise in relation to experiences in hazardous work environments. Roberts (1993: 74) determines anxiety, fatalism, depression, lowered self-esteem, and anomie and describes exploitation, selfishness, and a loss of confidence in commercial practice, government, science, and organized labor.

Women may suffer particular problems in situations where they are especially valued for their reproductive capabilities. Any perceived threat to reproductive health can lead to alienation. Padma Prakash (1985) describes how women who were conspicuously injured in Bhopal suffered from divorce, abandonment, and violence. Myth can be as potent as fact. Madhursree Mukerjee puts the Bhopal situation bluntly: 'Because reproductive disorders are so commonplace, young women who were exposed to the gas are assumed to be infertile, and no one will marry them' (1995: 16). Children, too, may become marginalized. From Belarus, in a village where Chernobyl victims are receiving medical help, it is reported that 'there is tension between the local children and "these Chernobyl kids" who are bullied and ignored' (Barnett 1994: 9).

Migration is a common consequence of environmental problems, as Meena Singh discusses later in thus issue (1996; and see Myers 1995). The implications for a community can be subtle. Who leaves? In northwest Bohemia, where the burning of lignite coal produces severe air pollution, it is the doctors and other professionals who migrate first. Family life can be disrupted if some members wish to move from an affected region and others want to remain. This was an explanation for increased divorces among Welsh farmers in areas affected by Chernobyl fallout.

Do specific forms of environmental victimization produce specific outcomes? The problems caused by iodine deficiency are now quite well documented. Researchers from the *Programme Against Micronutrient Malnutrition* describe the situation in the Philippines: 'The result is poor productivity; a nation not up to par economically; a substandard quality of life for its citizens; and a country which cannot compete globally (PAMM 1995: 2). From a local perspective, social problems in villages in northern India are described by Hetzel (1989: 92) as 'a major block to human and social development,' including 'a high degree of apathy' (even effecting domestic animals) and 'effects on initiative and decision-making.' In one Chinese village, known locally as 'the village of idiots', 'the economic development of the village was retarded ... [N]o truck driver or teacher was available. Girls from other villages did not want to marry and live in the village.'

In north Indian villages, in which contaminated drinking water is reportedly causing a 40 per cent incidence of intellectual disability (Saxena 1991: 3), there is an absence of village headmen, the villagers cannot remember the last time they held a village meeting, and they say that statutory health and education services have disappeared, but are not motivated to complain. This appears to be a manifestation of a concern expressed by the U.N. (1991): 'learning disorders are a particular source of danger because they may affect an entire population and even impair its capacity to resist exploitation.'

Environmental factors that affect the brain and cause intellectual decline have predictable outcomes in terms of the capabilities of a community, but might less obviously affect social order. Needleman *et al.* (in Batten 1992: 15) found what appears to be an insignificant relationship between lead intake and an IQ deficit of 2 to 5 points. However, the effect trebled the number of children with IQ scores below 80 and there was a threefold reduction in the number with IQ scores above 125. An IQ of around 80 is directly related to increased criminal activity (because those concerned are vulnerable to criminal influence, but are still capable enough to carry out criminal activities). Most industrialized communities already have a skill shortage of technically able labor at around IQ 125, which would be exacerbated by this lead-related IQ deficit.

Another danger is that environmental health problems create 'false norms' within a community. The *Programme Against Micronutrient Malnutrition* reports that in the Philippines, iodine deficiency disease 'is so commonplace, that many feel it is a normal part of life' (PAMM 1995: 2). In the 19th century, in regions of Switzerland in which iodine deficiency created large numbers of cretins, families who did not have such a child were considered not to have been blessed by God. Within communities, poor health, low intelligence, and the psychosocial symptoms of victimization become an accepted part of a community's expectation of life.

Studies of communities following the Hiroshima and Nagasaki bombs provide good basis for understanding the unique outcomes of nuclear contamination. Victims suffered occupational discrimination, marriage opportunities were affected, and any minor illness gave rise to fears about genetic health problems (Lifton 1967: 106). Lifton coined the term 'nuclear numbing' to describe the form of denial among the post-bombing society in Hiroshima and Nagasaki.

Lifton's work is echoed in analyses of the Chernobyl disaster. Fedorychyk reports a 'syndrome of the victim,' which 'spreads among people and means that people consider themselves doomed':

> they don't want to have long-term plans ... [and] their life attitude is aggressively parasitical ... [P]eople have lost their confidence in the State, because it acted against people; in science, because it caused the problems which it could not solve; in medicine, because it was used as a political instrument; in world community ... people in Ukraine try to forget about Chernobyl in order not to go mad ... [T]his generation will have serious discrimination problems in getting married (1994: 2).

An awareness of 'victim syndrome' can form the basis for specific case studies and, more importantly, for remediation strategies. An affected community seems likely to display the following symptoms: family disruption; alienation, particularly of women and children; reduced marriage and employment prospects – because of a perceived genetic or health legacy; a perception that life has no future; social apathy; community and personal abandonment; loss of confidence in social institutions; 'denial' of the victimization; false norms; economic dislocation; local and domestic conflict; skills deficit; migration; increased criminality by those of low, but not clinically diagnosed IQ deficit; exploitation; and a breakdown of traditional structures for community management.

Because it arises from a quasi-clinical patient/victim outlook, the psycho-social evidence usually omits two crucial aspects. First is the *resilience* of victims, natural or assisted. Later in this issue [of *Social Justice*, 23(4)], Sharon Stephens (1996) describes how involvement in activism can change adverse outcomes among children. A similar effect was noted in relation to *Love Canal* (Stone and Levine 1986). Second, there is the possibility of violent resistance, which will be discussed later.

## Future issues

The distinction between 'epistemology' and 'issues' is, to some extent, arbitrary. However, the preceding topics have attracted sufficient attention to argue that there is at least a distinct body of knowledge and formal analysis relating to them. The following three areas of discussion exemplify concerns that are evident from general discourse and the media, but have not yet, it seems, attracted significant attention from the academic community.

### Environmental blackmail

The degree to which the environment will become a vehicle for domestic and international blackmail is difficult to predict and little thought has been given to possible responses. On the domestic level, threats equate with other forms of blackmail. The Mafia has taken an interest in toxic waste in the U.S. and Italy (Block and Scarpitti 1982; Bond 1994: 3), which extends to threats to dump waste on private land if landowners do not pay up. (This gives a new meaning to the term 'environmental protection'!). In 1994, most of Lithuania was without electricity for a day because of a Mafia bomb threat at a nuclear power station. It was not reported whether money changed hands, but the incident raises the possible specter of 'double blackmail,' in which a poor state turns to its wealthy neighbors and suggests that they might pay the sum demanded, because they are just as likely to suffer if the threat is carried out.

On an international scale, Martin Woollacott concludes of Ukraine's request that the G-7 nations fund the closure of the still-functioning reactors at Chernobyl and build new plants:

> A Chernobyl pay-off carries with it serious dangers. One is that it could be a precedent for other such payments to governments elsewhere. The idea that you can pressure the wealthier nations into giving you aid by persisting in running dangerous technologies whose effects, when they go wrong, will not be confined to your own country, is dangerously close to blackmail (1994: 22).

Paul Brown (1994: 37) describes similar circumstances surrounding the funding by the European Bank of Reconstruction and Development of new reactors at Mochovce in Slovakia. Mochovce is near the Austrian border, and Brown concludes, 'there are plenty more unfinished reactors and safety work to do in the stricken lands of the East – and the prospect of more Chernobyls is a loaded gun to hold at the head of bankers.' 'Paying up' is not necessarily the answer. European aid to assist Bulgaria to improve safety at its Kozloduy station was given on the understanding that the reactor was closed down, but in the winter of 1995 it was brought back into operation. The official EC comment was dry, but provides an indication of how crudely negotiations of this nature now operate: 'It seems they've gone back on the agreement. That raises the question of whether they should get anymore funds' (Traynor 1995: 13).

International blackmail may entail more subtle cross-border implications. Teichman and Barry reported in 1992: '... financially strapped Khazakhstan is accepting and burying South Korean nuclear waste at $1,000 per kilo and hoping to leverage its willingness to accept hazardous waste against the Ukraine for badly needed food' (Tufts 1992). Did Khazakhstan learn a trick from the Ukraine? If you do not have your own nuclear disaster to use as a threat, then import one.

Threats may well be linked to other conflicts. The firing of oil wells by Iraqi forces during the Gulf conflict demonstrates that blackmail in the form of eco-war is no longer science fiction. During the 1994 to 1995 Chechnya-Russia conflict, the Chechen President Dzhokhar Dudayev threatened terrorist attacks on nuclear power stations and weapons stores if Russian forces deposed his government. As a former high-ranking officer in the USSR Air Force, he was well placed to use such tactics.

Whatever the future scenarios for environmental blackmail, it is certain that if threats are ever carried out, there will be significant victimization of entirely innocent third parties, avoidance will be easy, and redress virtually impossible. As yet, there seem to be no policies to address environmental blackmail, as there are, for example, in relation to plane hijacks. Perhaps the starting point is for the global community to use the word 'blackmail' overtly, in response to comments such as that reported from President Leonid Kuchma of the Ukraine about the ongoing threat from the Chernobyl reactors: 'If the world, particularly Europe, is really concerned about safety, then let us look at the financial situation' (*Independent* 1995: 2).

## Violence

There has been growing interest in environmental problems as a source of conflict between nations or regions in relation to scarcity of essential resources such as water (e.g., Bächler *et al.* 1993). However, little academic consideration has been given to the violent spirals deriving from environmental victimization, a circumstance that is distinct from conflicts over natural resources.

In Bougainville (Solomon Islands), indigenous people's resistance to pollution from copper mining by Rio Tinto Zinc (RTZ) included blowing up electricity pylons, which brought about the closure of the mine (Gillespie 1994). This catalyzed an independence struggle, which has transmuted into an ongoing conflict with blockades and a shoot-to-kill policy involving local people, RTZ, the Papuan militia, and the Australian government (Pacific Research 1994: 19–30). The outcome is in no one's interests, particularly that of RTZ, which consequently experienced difficulties in attracting financial backing for other projects.

Even nonviolent popular resistance to oil pollution caused by Shell in Ogoniland (Niger Delta) provided the opportunity for widespread violence and human rights abuses by state security forces (Rowell 1995: 6; Orr 1995: 15). Environmental activism then embraced broader political aims, principally a fairer distribution of oil revenues in favor of the Delta region. One refinery was forced to close down because (according to Shell) of fears for staff safety. Four traditional chiefs were killed, it was claimed, by activists, which then led to the 'judicial murder' of Ken Saro-Wiwa and other environmental activists following a show trial and international protest in 1995. Shell also admitted importing weapons into Nigeria to help the police protect its oil installations (Duodu 1996: 1).

Shell maintains that environmental damage was not the 'cause' of the spirals of violence – an argument that probably would not hold if we apply the 'consequence' test proposed within the definition of causation outlined above. International protest against Shell suggests that public perception does make the causal link, but we still lack the necessary formal conceptualizations. The starting point is an understanding that environmental victimization can be considered, both informally and legally, as an act of violence (Williams 1996b). If this is established, it is then not difficult to comprehend that the response to corporate violence may be public violence, provoked by the initial victimization. The prevention of violence should *not*, therefore, be an implicit assumption within environmental victimology. As argued later, if it is the only option to ensure human security, it is morally defensible.

### How do victim responses evolve?

At this point, it should have become clear that an important purpose of environmental victimology will be to understand the spirals of violence associated with victimization. It is therefore important to develop an awareness of how victim responses appear to evolve over time in relation to violence. From a global perspective it is possible to hypothesize a generalized pattern (see Figure 10.2):

1 *Passive acceptance*, which seems evident in regions where people are faced with other more pressing problems, e.g., following major political transition as in Eastern and Central Europe, where pre-1989 environmental activism has nearly disappeared, and in South Africa (see Singh 1996, in this issue [of *Social Justice*, 23(4)]); then,

2 *Confrontation and litigation.* Bhopal provides a current example. As Sarangi's article in this issue (1996) records, there was the potential for violent confrontation at the mass protests in the first two years following the disaster, but activists opted instead to use legal channels for redress. That potential did not become actual violence is worthy of analysis. The promise of compensation, combined with a tradition of tolerance, may be part of the explanation. Then either:

3 *Violence*, which is often linked to other political action, as in Bougainville and Ogoniland. The link between environmental and political activism wars most evident in the Eastern bloc before 1989, and was demonstrated more recently in the response of people in Tahiti to the French nuclear tests in the South Pacific (Williams 1996b); or:

4 *Nonviolent community conflict resolution*, as exemplified by the U.S. Good Neighbor Agreements (Henkels and Lewis 1996, this issue [of *Social Justice*, 23(4)]).

The latter is obviously a desirable goal and the key to achieving this end is a public right of access to environmental information. In the U.S., where recent freedom of information legislation has led to local monitoring and publication of industrial discharges, solution-oriented community action *with* (rather than against) industrial polluters is emerging in the form of 'Good Neighbor Agreements' (GNP 1994). Pollution statistics and worst-case scenarios are appearing in local papers, and software for domestic PCs is becoming available to help with local analysis. One result is that some polluters have realized how much money they are losing through their factory chimneys in the form of expensive, retrievable substances. Henkels and Lewis (1996) later in this issue further explain both the broad principles and the details of Good Neighbor Agreements. The question raised by this approach is: How applicable is it in a poor-nation setting where community resources do not match those in the U.S.? Might Good Neighbor Agreements have prevented the violence in Bougainville or Ogoni?

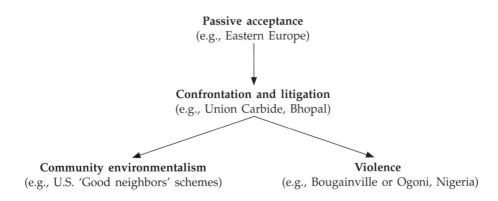

**Figure 10.2** Evolution of victim responses (in relation to current situations)

## Conclusion – justice or security?

Environmentally mediated injury is now a significant aspect of personal victimization, resulting from both conspicuous and 'creeping' disasters. Environmental law has a restricted potential to address this threat; thus the need for parallel social justice perspectives. The 'environmental justice movement' has been the most prominent alternative so far, but it is limited because of its subjective definitions, assumptions about power relationships and group identities, and an activist stance.

Traditional victimology is the obvious source of inspiration for a complementary approach but, surprisingly, it has not yet embraced an environmental perspective. The *U.N. Declaration on Victims of ... Abuse of Power* (1985) provides a clear starting point, from which definitions of 'environmental victims' and 'environmental cause' can be developed.

From diverse sources it is possible to construct an emerging epistemology in relation to environmental victims. It addresses concerns such as the status of the unborn victim, avoidance of liability and responsibility, and a 'victim syndrome.' Possible future issues, as yet largely ignored by academics, are likely to include environmental blackmail, spirals of violence, and the ways in which victim responses evolve. Other areas of concern, not discussed within this article, are cultural dimensions (e.g., Fentiman 1996), the cost consequences of victimization (e.g., Williams 1996c), theories of innovation and change (e.g., Hetzel 1989: 148; Lansdown and Yule 1986: 271), educational implications, case studies of specific outcomes (e.g., Williams 1996a), and how to conceptualize disparate victimizer groups, for example, car drivers.

### Justice or security?

The takeoff point for this view of an environmental victimology was a brief, functional critique of the environmental justice approach. Yet the scale and nature of contemporary environmental victimization prompt a deeper question: is 'justice' in any form always an adequate reference point?

Common ethics accept that individual conscience can and should, in certain circumstances, be put above the law. How else do we sanction the actions of those who fight against 'lawful,' but unjust regimes such as apartheid in South Africa, or find guilty those who commit atrocities, through following 'lawful' orders, at trials such as Nuremberg? Similarly, there is a circumstance in which the day-to-day principles of justice can be suspended for a greater good – that of *security*. The taking of human life, enforced labor in the form of military service, and the appropriation of privately owned resources are examples of justice norms that can be set aside in the interests of (usually national) military security. There is also one significant example of a shift from justice to security ethics in an environmental context: China's one-child policy. Injustice at the family level is 'accepted' (by the state, most educated Chinese, and more recently the international community) to ensure the security of a whole population through preventing ecological overload.

At what point does environmental victimization start to represent a threat to human survival sufficient to permit us to shift from the ethics of justice to those of security? In his article later in this issue, Peter Penz (1996) hints that cross-border victimization, such as pollution, may sanction military actions against another nation. This would represent a shift from a principle of international justice as the guiding ethic – the autonomy of nation-states over their territory – to the ethics of national security. How long before we see the security forces of a wealthy nation 'take out,' by force, an upstream/ upwind polluting factory in a neighboring state, which has been the basis for environmental blackmail?

The 1995 *Commission on Global Governance* seems prescient of this scenario, proposing (albeit in another context) that:

> ... in certain certain severe circumstances [fundamental human rights] must prevail over the ordinary rights of individual states ... where people are subjected to massive suffering and distress ... [T]here is a need to weigh a state's right to autonomy against its people's right to security (CGG 1995: 68, 71).

Note the compatibiliy between this assertion and the U.N. Declaration on Victims, quoted earlier. Within this new framework, security needs might prevail over justice not only between nations, but also between a state and its citizens. There are three possibilities: (1) *when a state fails to protect its citizens from domestic threats*, as in Bougainville (Australia had trusteeship) and Ogoniland – and remember that in these examples victims did in fact 'take out' the industries that threatened their security, through actual or fear of violence; (2) *when the state diminishes the rights of its victim-citizens through legislation*, as in relation to the Union Carbide (Bhopal) disaster and U.S. weapons testing; and (3) *when the state is victimizer*, such as in the case of Iraq's deliberate poisoning of the waters that sustain the life of the Marsh Arabs.

This line of thinking generates an obvious question. If, between states and between state and citizen, the need to ensure human security 'must prevail' over justice norms as reflected in international or domestic law, and we accept the inference that military force may then legitimately be used against the entity posing the threat to human security, do we then accept that the principle extends to violence by community activists against the threat posed by the lead smelter down the road? From the common law perspective on personal injury, we hardly need the commission's sanction. Morally, the notion of self-defense could appear sufficient.

To illustrate the need to rethink our response to the new environmental security threats of the post-Cold War era, Gwyn Prins remarks, 'You can't shoot an ozone hole' (1991: 12). The illustration is thought-provoking, but just one end of a spectrum – you *can* bomb a filthy factory. Understanding the spirals of violence, which appear inevitable when our ethical basis is forced to shift from justice to security, is the broader purpose of an environmental victimology, and is distinct from the remit that the environmental justice movement currently sets itself. We need urgently to develop better *and broader* understandings of environmental victimization, and through these to develop a consensus on the relationships between justice norms and the sometimes conflicting demands of human security.

## References

Agarwal, A. (1995) 'Editorial', *Down to Earth*, 31 December.

Bächler, G., Böge, V., Klötzli, S. and Libiszweski, S. (1993) *The Destruction of Nature as a Cause of Conflict*. Münster: Agenda-Verlag.

Barnett, L. (1994) 'Coping with the psychological aftermath of Chernobyl', *Global Security* (Winter).

Barten, F. (1992) *Environmental Lead Exposure of Children in Managua, Nicaragua*. Den Haag: CIP-Gegevens Koninlijke Bibliotheek.

Barten, F. (1996) 'The occupational health needs of workers: the need for a new international approach', *Social Justice*, 23(4) (Winter).

Bass, C. and Kenny, J. (1993) *Beyond Chernobyl: Women Respond*. London: Envirobook.

BGIA (1992) *Compensation Disbursement: Problems and Possibilities*. Bhopal: Bhopal Group for Information and Action.

Bird, M. (1995) 'Yangtze death toll on rise', *Independent on Sunday* (9 July).

Birnie, P.W. and Boyle, A.E. (1992) *International Law and the Environment*. Oxford: Clarendon Press.

Block, A. and Scarpitti, F. (1982) *Poisoning for Profit: The Mafia and Toxic Waste in America*. New York: William Morrow.

Bond, M. (1994) 'Poisonous trail of the toxic cowboys', *The European* (27 May).

Bound, J., Francis, B. and Harvey, P. (1995) 'Down's Syndrome: prevalence and ionising radiation in an area of north west England, 1957–1991,' *Journal of Epidemiology and Community Health*, 49.

*British Medical Journal* (1994) 'Brain damage found in victims of Bhopal disaster', *British Medical Journal*, 309.

Brown, P. (1994) 'Slovak debate sums up nuclear power struggle', *The Guardian* (31 December).

Bryant, B. (1995) *Environmental Justice*. Boston: Island Press.

Bullard, R.D. (1993) *Confronting Environmental Racism: Voices from the Grassroots*. Massachusetts: South End Press.

Bullock, A., Stallybrass, O. and Trombley, S. (1988) *Dictionary of Modern Thought*. London: Fontana Press.

Capek, S.M. (1993) 'The "environmental justice" frame: a conceptual discussion and an application', *Social Problems*, 40(1): 5–24.

CGG (1995) *Our Global Neighbourhood – The Report of the Commission on Global Governance*. Oxford: Oxford University Press.

Chivian, E., McCally, M., Hu, H. and Haines, A. (1993) *Critical Condition: Human Health and the Environment*. Cambridge, Mass.: MIT Press.

Clark, J. (1993) Private correspondence from the Criminal Injuries Compensation Board (U.K.).

Dembo, D., Morehouse, W. and Wykle, L. (1993) *Abuse of Power – Social Performance of Multinational Corporations: The Case of Union Carbide*. New York: New Horizons Press.

Duodu, C. (1996) 'Shell admits importing guns for Nigerian police', *The Observer* (28 January).

Dyer, C. (1995) 'Judge wrong over "killing" of baby', *The Guardian* (25 November).

*ELR* (1994) 'Pacific legal developments', *New Zealand Environmental Law Reporter*, 1.

Emmet, D. (1984) *The Effectiveness of Causes*. London: Macmillan

Fattah, E.A. (1992) *Towards a Critical Victimology*. London: Macmillan.

Fattah, E.A. (1989) 'On some neglected types of victimisation – victims of abuse of powers', in E. Fattah (ed.), *The Plight of Victims in Modern Society*. London: Macmillan.

Fedorychyk, S. (1994) 'Experiences of Chernobyl'. Unpublished paper presented to the Permanent Peoples' Tribunal, London.

Fentiman, A. (1996) 'The anthropology of oil: the impact of the oil industry on the fishing communities in the Niger Delta', *Social Justice*, 23(4) (Winter).

Gallagher, C. (1993) *American Ground Zero: The Secret Nuclear War*. Massachusetts: The MIT Press.

GC (Green Cross) (1994) *Green Cross – The Legacy Programme*. Geneva: Green Cross.

Gillespie. R. (1994) 'The case of Bougainville'. Unpublished paper presented to the Permanent Peoples' Tribunal, London.

GNP (Good Neighbor Project) (1994) *The Good Neighbor Handbook: A Community-Based Strategy for Sustainable Industry*. Waverly: Good Neighbor Project.

*Guardian* (1992a) 'A child disabled by pre-natal injury can sue for damages', *The Guardian* (20 May).

*Guardian* (1992b) 'Woman killed unborn baby by kicking neighbour in stomach', *The Guardian* (15 May).

Hart, H.L.A. and Honore, A.M. (1985) *Causation in the Law*. Oxford: Oxford University Press.

Henkels, D. and Lewis, S. (1996) 'Good Neighbor Agreements', *Social Justice*, 23(4) (Winter).

Hetzel, B.S. (1989) *The Story of Iodine Deficiency*. New York: Oxford University Press.

Hofrichter, R. (ed.) (1993) *Toxic Struggles: The Theory and Practice of Environmental Justice*. Philadelphia: New Society Publishers.

*Independent* (1995) 'Chernobyl may not be shut down', *The Independent* (12 November).

Johnston, B.R. (1994) *Who Pays the Price? The Socialcultural Context of Environmental Crisis*. London: Island Press.

Kenney, S.J. (1992) *For Whose Protection? Reproductive Hazards and Exclusionary Policies in the U.S. and Britain*. Michigan: University of Michigan Press.

Landsdowne, R. and Yule, W. (1986) *Lead Toxicity: History and Environmental Impact*. Baltimore: John Hopkins University Press.

Laslett, P. and Fishkin, J.S. (eds) (1992) *Justice Between Age Groups and Generations*. New Haven: Yale University Press.

Law Commission (1973) *Injuries to Unborn Children – Working Paper No. 47*. London: The Law Commission.

Lifton, R.J. (1967) *Death in Life: The Survivors of Hiroshima*. London: Weidenfeld and Nicholson.

Marples, D.R. (1988) *The Social Impact of the Chernobyl Disaster*. New York: St. Martin's Press.

Mawby, R.I. and Walklate, S. (1994) *Critical Victimology: International Perspectives*. London: Sage.

Mies, M. and Shiva, V. (1992) *Ecofeminism: Reconnecting a Divided World*. New Delhi: Kali for Women.

Miller, C.E. (1989) 'Radiological risks of civil liability', *Journal of Environmental Law*, 1.

Mukerjee, M. (1995) 'Persistently toxic: the Union Carbide accident in Bhopal continues to harm', *Scientific American* (June).

Myers, N. and Kent, J. (1995) *Environmental Exodus: An Emergent Crisis in the Global Arena*. Washington: Climate Institute.

Orr, D. (1995) 'Ogoni spirits unbroken by new repression', *The Independent* (30 November).

Pacific Research (1994) 'The failure of the Bougainville Peace Talks', *Pacific Research* (November).

PAMM (1995) 'Misconception of IDD prevalence obstacle to strong legislation', *PAMM News* (January).

Penz, P. (1996) 'Environmental victims and state sovereignty: a normative analysis', *Social Justice*, 23(4) (Winter).

Perrolle, J.A. (1993) *Social Problems – Special Issue on Environmental Justice*. Lafayette: Society for the Study of Social Problems.

PPT (Permanent Peoples' Tribunal) (1992) *Findings and Judgments*. London: Permanent Peoples' Tribunal.

Prakesh, P. (1985) 'Neglect of women's health issues', *Delhi Economic and Political Weekly* (14 December).

Prins, G. and Stamp, R. (1991) *Top Guns and Toxic whales: The Environment and Global Security*. London: Earthscan.

Pugh, C. and Day, M. (1992) *Toxic Torts*. London: Cameron May.

Reich, M.R. (1991) *Toxic Politics: Responding to Chemical Disasters*. Ithaca: Cornell University Press.

Roberts, J.T. (1993) 'Psychosocial effects of workplace hazardous exposures: theoretical synthesis and preliminary findings', *Social Problems*, 40.

Rossi, P.H., Wright, J.D., Weber-Burdin, E. and Pereira, J. (1983) *Victims of the Environment: Loss from Natural Hazards in the United States*. New York: Plenum Press.

Rowell, A. (1995) 'Trouble flares in the delta of death', *The Guardian* (8 November).

Sarangi, S. (1996) 'The movement in Bhopal and its lessons ', *Social Justice*, 23(4) (Winter).

Saxena, R. (1991) 'Excess fluoride leaves in its wake a village of cretins', *Sunday Observer* (India 15 December).

Singh, M. (1996) 'Environmental security and displaced people in Southern Africa', *Social Justice*, 23(4) (Winter).

Slayter, A. (1995) 'Why the Nigerian people can be sure of Shell (letter)', *The Guardian* (15 November).

Stephens, S. (1996) 'Environmental justice: the case of children', *Social Justice*, 23(4) (Winter).

Stone, R.A. and Levine, A.G. (1986) 'Reactions to collective stress: correlates of active citizen participation at Love Canal', *Prevention in Human Services*, 4.

Tan, Y.H. (1995) 'Unmaintained sewage system caused pollution', *The Independent* (31 January).

Tan, Y.H. (1992) 'Children have rights to sue for pre-natal injuries', *The Independent* (8 April).

Traynor, I. (1995) 'Europe faces nuclear nightmare', *The Guardian* (26 October).

Tufts (1992) *International Security – The Environmental Dimension (Tufts International Symposium)*. Massachusetts: Tufts University.

U.N. (1991) Document E/CN.Sub 2/1991/31. New York: United Nations.

Walker, M. (1988) 'Ageing atom industry in cash crisis', *The Guardian* (12 December).

Williams, C. (1996a) 'The environmental causes of intellectual injury – a victim perspective', *International Review of Victimology* (forthcoming).

Williams, C. (1996b) 'Environmental victimization and violence', *Aggression and Violent Behaviour* (forthcoming).

Williams, C. (1996c) 'Environmental victims – arguing the costs', *Environmental Values* (forthcoming).

Williams, C. (1995) *Invisible Victims: Crime and Abuse Against People with Learning Difficulties*. London: Jessica Kingsley.

Woollacott, M. (1994) 'Nuclear accidents waiting to happen', *The Guardian* (6 July).

Yeager, P.C. (1991) *The Limits of Law: The Public Regulation of Private Pollution*. Cambridge: Cambridge University Press.

# 11. Reflections on environmental justice: children as victims and actors*

*Sharon Stephens*

In *Radical Ecology*, Carolyn Merchant (1992) argues forcefully that the modern world's dominant norms of production, social relations, and ideology are resulting in an accumulation of ecological stresses on the air, water, soil, and diverse life forms, as well as on the capacity of human societies to maintain and reproduce themselves over time. Although these ecological stresses are a result of globally articulated processes, she notes, they are 'experienced differently in the First, Second, and Third Worlds and by people of different races, classes, and sexes' (*Ibid.*: 10). This is also true, she might have added – but tellingly did not – of people of different ages.

Merchant's important insights – that environmental risks are experienced differently by different groups and, moreover, that they are borne disproportionately by those groups that are already the most socially, politically, and economically vulnerable – are core concepts in the rapidly proliferating literature on 'environmental justice.' (See, for example, Bryant 1995; Bullard 1994; and Hofrichter 1993b.) The concept has been developed during the last decade by theorists and activists, largely in the United States, to describe what many regard as a qualitatively new sort of grass-roots environmental movement, linking concerns with social justice to concerns about environmental quality. This linkage has important implications for how people perceive environmental problems and for the practical responses they develop to address these problems. Here I wish to argue that the term 'environmental justice' has been developed in distinctive ways in the context of U.S. culture and politics, and that this context has significantly affected the nature of environmental justice theory and its usefulness in other contexts.

Since 1992, I have been involved in the development of an international, interdisciplinary 'Children and Environment' research program and network, based at the Norwegian Centre for Child Research in Trondheim, Norway. (See Stephens 1994.) Because of the magnitude and seriousness of environmental risks to children in Eastern Europe and the former USSR, the Centre has been particularly concerned with developing a network of relations with researchers and activists in these regions. When I first encountered the notion of environmental justice, I felt there was great potential here for providing

* From *Social Justice* (1996), 23(4): pp. 62–86.

powerful theoretical and practical tools to address the special environmental vulnerability of children and to illuminate distinctive constellations of risks in particular world regions. Significantly, however, references to children of the former USSR are almost entirely absent from the existing environmental justice literature. I suggest that the neglect of these topics can be linked to a particular construction of 'community' – one that is in some respects distinctively American and is dominant within the environmental justice movement. This is a view of community that tends to make children invisible, as a special class of victims and especially as actors. It is also a view of community that poses formidable obstacles to international coalition building.

This article begins with a brief discussion of the history of the environmental justice movement and of the reasons why race, ethnicity, class, and occupation (and, to lesser and problematic extents, geopolitical location and gender) are theorized in the literature, while age is ignored as a significant dimension of environmental justice thinking. (My focus here is on children, but this discussion could be productively extended to include the special environmental vulnerabilities of the elderly as well.) I then discuss ways in which perspectives on children as a distinctive environmental 'special interest group' offer important possibilities for developing a more inclusive and effective environmental justice movement, both within the United States and internationally.

## Environmental justice theory: the U.S. context

Historians of the environmental justice movement (for example, Bullard 1993a, 1993b; Di Chiro 1995) argue that there is a broad-based, culturally diverse grass-roots environmental movement in the U.S. today that differs in important ways from the essentially white, middle-class environmental movement they call 'mainstream environmentalism.' This mainstream movement grew out of the late 19th- and early 20th-century conservationist movement, which is mainly concerned with protecting endangered species and natural wonders from destruction and commodification in the frenetic process of U.S. industrialization and urbanization.

After World War II, the environmental movement in the U.S. became somewhat broader based. There was continuing concern with species and wilderness preservation, but there was also increasing concern with such urban issues as pollution, traffic, and density of population. Nevertheless, the main actors in the postwar environmental movement remained middle-class whites. This affected the way they viewed environmental problems and possible solutions. They tended to emphasize the importance of scientific and technical evaluations, legislative approaches, and political lobbying at the national level. Most of the important mainstream environmental groups, e.g., the Audubon Society, the National Resources Defense Council, and Friends of the Earth, have a lobbying center in Washington, D.C., aimed at influencing national regulations and policies.

During the 1970s and 1980s, however, an increasing number of grass-roots environmental groups began to form at the local community level, initially in response to specific environmental risks, such as the siting of waste disposal areas or incinerators, the building of lead smelters, the heavy use of pesticides in local agriculture, and nuclear weapons testing. Activists in these local groups tended not to be typical 'mainstream environmental activists.' They were generally *not* white, middle class, or well educated (in terms of 'mainstream' educational standards ).

They represented instead those groups most at risk from corporate and military development: people of color, the poor, and working-class populations. As Bullard (1993b: 17) notes: 'The most polluted urban communities are those with crumbling infrastructure, ongoing economic disinvestment, deteriorating housing, inadequate schools, chronic unemployment, a high poverty rate, and an overloaded healthcare system.' Because of the legacy of racism in the U.S., people of color (particularly African Americans and Latino Americans) are disproportionately represented in these troubled communities. At the heart of the environmental justice movement is the claim that certain groups have borne the greatest burden of 'development,' without proportionate access to the benefits or a chance to question the language of cost/benefit balancing itself.

Di Chiro (1995: 299) recounts the illuminating story of a 1993 encounter between mainstream environmental groups (including the Sierra Club and the Environmental Defense Fund) and the group called Concerned Citizens of South Central Los Angeles, based in a predominantly African American, low-income community that was concerned about plans to build a 1,600 ton per day solid waste incinerator in the center of their neighborhood. Members of Concerned Citizens were informed that potential contamination of an urban community by highly toxic dioxins, fluorons, and other chemicals likely to be released by the incineration facility was a 'community health issue,' not an environmental one.

Environmental justice advocates claim that grass-roots environmental groups in the U.S. are redefining the scope of the environmental movement by showing that environmental problems are inseparable from other social injustices. The quest for environmental justice thus becomes an extension of the quest for basic civil rights. Indeed, the strategies that characterize many of the new grass-roots groups show historical continuities with the Civil Rights Movement of the 1960s and 1970s. Having little access to formal structures of power, civil rights groups were dependent on mass direct actions, such as protests, street demonstrations, and grass-roots voting registration programs. Similarly, grass-roots environmental groups often employ confrontational direct action strategies, such as public demonstrations, petitions, community education hearings, and debates. Some grass-roots leaders have become adept at using the public media to help publicize what often seem to be David and Goliath struggles of disenfranchised groups against powerful corporate polluters and state and federal governments.

However, to do so more effectively, many are arguing, it is necessary to move beyond single-issue protests based in particular communities to form multi-issue, multicultural coalitions. Much of the writing on these coalitions tends, in my opinion, to be rather utopian in celebrating the potential for a national network of community activists to transform and revitalize American democracy, 'from the bottom up.' Lois Gibbs, head of the nationwide Citizens' Clearinghouse for Toxic Hazards, asserts (1993: x): 'A major goal of the grass-roots movement for environmental justice is to rebuild the United States, community by community.' Such statements seem at times to be motivated by nostalgia for the community-based 'yeoman democracy' celebrated in some versions of early American history, in contrast to the overdeveloped bureaucracies and out-of-human-scale political institutions that appear to characterize the present.

However, with an estimated 5,000 local, community-based antitoxic groups in the U.S. today, there is a real danger that community-based activism will merely shift problems around, without getting at the structural roots of the problems themselves. For example, a successful protest against high levels of lead contamination in the soil of a poor, largely Latino community in West Dallas led to a cleanup project, which resulted in the redeposition of lead-contaminated soil in a landfill in Louisiana – perhaps not surprisingly located in a predominantly African American community (Bullard 1993a: 28).

The dangers of uncoordinated community-based activism have become even more pronounced in the present era of 'flexible capital accumulation.' (See Field 1994, for discussion of distinctively 'post-Fordist' environmental problems in the U.S.) The economic recession in the last decade in the U.S. has led to concerted corporate attacks against the environmental movement and to increasing attempts to cut production costs and increase profits by paying less for labor and circumventing environmental regulations. In the name of flexibility, the state is allowing corporations to buy and sell 'pollution credits,' which means that some factories can legally exceed federal limitations on the amounts of pollutants they emit. An example is the Tennessee Valley Authority, which greatly exceeds federal limitations on sulfur dioxide emissions. Again, it should come as no surprise to learn that this is an area populated largely by African Americans. The expectation has been that this is a population not likely to be able to mount effective, sustained protests.

The hope among advocates of the environmental justice movement is that diverse groups can organize around interlinked concerns for environmental quality and social equity, with the aim of effecting significant social and institutional changes, rather than merely relocating problems from one area to another. Environmental justice advocates are calling for greater citizen participation in basic social planning for economic development, land use, and zoning. Eventually, advocates claim, the movement could lead to radically transformed relations among local citizens, corporations, and government, to the point that concerns about the quality of everyday life and sustainable communities could begin to hold their own against powerful corporate and political interests.

Evaluation of such claims is beyond the scope of this article. What I wish to argue here is that the implementation of such a radical democratic agenda would require comprehensive structural-historical understandings of integral links among the organization of capital, patterns of social inequality, and the distribution of environmental risks, not only in the U.S., but also internationally. Such a radical political program would also require developing new and innovative approaches to community mobilization and coalition building. As

I argue below, recognition of children – as both environmental victims and actors – represents an important, largely untapped, resource for mobilization in the environmental justice movement. Why then, have perspectives on children's situations and possibilities and on the international dimensions of environmental justice remained so undeveloped within this movement?

Part of the answer is that environmental justice theory was articulated initially in connection with analysis of environmental risks and activism within 'communities of color' within the United States. The considerable strengths – and limitations – of the movement need to be assessed in this light.

## Environmental racism

A case of large-scale civil disobedience that occurred in Warren County, North Carolina, in 1982 has been identified by some movement historians as the first active demonstration of an emerging environmental justice movement.

> At this demonstration, hundreds of predominantly African American women and children, but also local white residents, used their bodies to block trucks from dumping poisonous PCB-laced dirt into a landfill near their community. The mainly African American, working class, rural communities of Warren County had been targeted as the dumping site for a toxic waste landfill that would serve industries throughout North Carolina ... Unlike social activism against toxic contamination that predated this event, such as the struggle against Hooker Chemical Company at Love Canal, New York, in the late 1970s, this action began to forge the connections between race, poverty, and the environmental consequences of the production of industrial waste. The Warren County episode succeeded in racializing the antitoxics agenda and catalyzed a number of studies that would document the historical pattern of disproportionately targeting racial minority communities for toxic waste contamination (Di Chiro 1995: 303).

One such study was the influential report sponsored by the Commission for Racial Justice (1987), which showed race to be the leading factor in the location of commercial hazardous waste facilities in the U.S. Sixty percent of African Americans and Latino Americans and over 50% of Asian/Pacific Islanders and Native Americans live in areas with one or more toxic waste sites.

It is not just that politically underrepresented and economically marginalized communities are more likely to be polluted than others, but that environmental regulations are also less likely to be enforced in these areas. According to a *National Law Journal* study of civil court cases in 1991 (reported in Hofrichter 1993a: 2–3), 'penalties under hazardous waste law at sites having the greatest white population were about 500% higher than penalties at sites with the greatest minority population.'

The term 'environmental racism' was coined in 1987 by the Reverend Benjamin Chavis, executive director of the Commission for Racial Justice. Chavis (quoted in Di Chiro 1995: 304) defines environmental racism as:

racial discrimination in environmental policy making and the enforcement of regulations and laws, the deliberate targeting of people of color communities for toxic waste facilities, the official sanctioning of the life-threatening presence of poisons and pollutants in our communities, and a history of excluding people of color from leadership in the environmental movement.

The term 'environmental racism' allowed people to identify and name conjoined environmental/social forces affecting communities of color across the country and provided a conceptual foundation for uniting communities with very different cultures and histories. In 1991, the First National People of Color Environmental Leadership Summit in Washington, D.C., brought together African, Native, Latino, and Asian American delegates from the U.S., as well as a number of delegates from Canada, Central and South America, Puerto Rico, and the Marshall Islands. The aim of the conference was to develop a 'multiracial movement for change,' based on a commitment to working out from the realities of discrimination in people's everyday lives and environments to a principled critique of the power structures that were responsible for these inequalities – and that had historically kept diverse communities of color largely unaware of their common interests.

Thus, migrant farmworkers in the U.S. (of whom 95% are Latino, African American, Afro-Caribbean, and Asian) began to link their concerns about pesticide exposure and unhealthy field and living conditions to Native American concerns about the environmental and health consequences of uranium mining and nuclear waste disposal sites on reservation lands. These largely rural populations have begun to find common cause with urban communities of color. Because of the history of institutionalized racism in the U.S., linked to discriminatory practices in housing, health care, education, and employment, African Americans are seriously – and disproportionately – affected by industrial toxins, contaminated air and drinking water, and the location of hazardous waste treatment and storage facilities. Research shows that even when social class is held constant, African Americans are at significantly greater risk than whites of exposure to a wide range of toxic materials. Lead poisoning is a classic example, affecting approximately four million children in the U.S. today. Across the spectrum of income levels, African American children are two to three times more likely than white children to suffer from lead poisoning (Bullard 1993a: 36). This is largely because people of color do not have the same opportunities as whites to 'vote with their feet' – to escape unhealthy physical environments by moving.

The racialization of the grass-roots antitoxics movement in the U.S. has sparked important studies, galvanized local communities to action, provided a powerful foundation for regional and national coalition building, and at least partly succeeded in transforming mainstream environmentalism. Some organizations – for example, Greenpeace – have responded to challenges from the environmental justice movement by incorporating social justice issues into their discussions and including more people of color on their governing boards and general staff. Members of mainstream organizations have also provided expert testimony about environmental risk exposures in court cases and have provided technical assistance in monitoring exposure levels in communities of color.

We may also ask how the emphasis on race as a factor of environmental discrimination might limit the usefulness of environmental justice theory in other regions of the world, where the dominant axes of discrimination are linked to a history of colonialist relations, or to religious or ethnic affiliation. It is important to remember that American constructions of 'race' as a category of identity and a basis for political activism are far from universal. As noted above, the theory and practice of the environmental justice movement in the U.S. have been strongly influenced by its roots in the Civil Rights Movement of the 1960s. This movement was developed in opposition to U.S. structures of racial discrimination and was grounded in notions of human rights and democratic participation that are extended only with difficulty to the situations of other groups – for example, to Ukrainian and Belorussian populations in the vicinity of Chernobyl, or even to women and children in the U.S. (The question of universal human rights in relation to the special rights of particular groups is discussed more fully below.)

## Other dimensions of environmental justice: class, occupation, and geopolitical location

The contemporary literature on the theory and practice of environmental justice is marked by attempts to expand the range of groups considered to be at special risk. Some groups become particularly vulnerable because of occupation – for example, workers in hazardous oil, petrochemical, and nuclear industries, and rural farmworkers, particularly those in large 'agribusiness' regions (Noble 1993; Chavez 1993). Given the structure of American race relations, there are, of course, integral links between patterns of environmental racism and occupation and class-based environmental inequities.

Some of these links are discussed in the environmental justice literature. Yet there is little discussion of how constellations of race, class, and occupation might be very differently structured outside the U.S., making coalition building along lines of 'environmental racism' extremely difficult. This may be one reason why, despite frequent arguments for the importance of connecting grass-roots groups at national and international levels, there are very few examples of the latter.

Bullard (1993b: 19) provides a striking example of what he calls 'toxic colonialism,' whereby the First World exports its most profitable and dangerous production methods, goods, and waste disposal strategies to the Third World. Bullard refers to an internal memorandum written in 1991 by Laurence Summers, chief economist at the World Bank. This memorandum caused a minor international scandal after it was leaked to the press. Summers lists a number of reasons why the World Bank should be encouraging, rather than discouraging, the movement of dirty industries to the less-developed countries. These reasons include lower health costs and less likelihood of public opposition. Summers (quoted in Bullard 1993b: 19) observes: 'I've always thought that under-polluted areas in Africa are vastly *under* polluted:

their air quality is probably vastly inefficiently low compared to Los Angeles or Mexico City.' He goes on to speak of 'world welfare enhancing trade in air pollution and waste' to the Third World. We are certainly justified in asking more specific questions about *whose* welfare is actually being enhanced here, and in what ways.

The environmental justice literature includes important discussions of the export of industrial and military wastes to the Third World (Greenpeace 1992), the relation between nuclear weapons states and indigenous peoples (Nietschmann and Le Bon 1987), and some of the difficulties and challenges of forging a truly international environmental justice movement (Kiefer and Benjamin 1993; Peng 1993; and Buttel 1995). What is generally lacking, however, is systematic discussion of the ways in which globally significant changes in politics, economy, and culture in recent decades have affected the environmental experiences of local communities in the United States. Although there is a growing body of historical studies of the environmental justice movement in the U.S., there is little reflection about why this movement appeared when it did – in the mid-1970s. This was a period when notions of 'everyday life' and 'community' were becoming problematic in new ways, when the economic, political, and environmental situations of the poor were steadily deteriorating at the local level, and when skepticism about the efficacy of mainstream political parties and strategies was increasing.

The mid-1970s has been characterized as a transition period in the movement to 'late' or 'advanced capitalism' and a 'global regime of flexible accumulation.' (See Harvey 1989.) This shift involved changes in the international structuring of capital and finance institutions, including new and expanded roles for the World Bank, International Monetary Fund, and multinational corporations. These globally significant developments have challenged the capacities of nation-states to regulate and control their domestic economies, resulted in cutbacks and 'downsizing' of social welfare programs and institutions around the world, and rendered increasingly problematic attempts at economic and political 'renewal' and 'revitalization' that are framed primarily in local or even national terms. Since the 1970s, 'flexibility' has become a sort of corporate and fiscal mantra, leading to attacks on nationally organized labor unions and federally mandated environmental regulations, as well as to greater economic and political disenfranchisement of already marginalized communities (Harvey 1989: Martin 1990).

Chawla (1995: 71) outlines four dimensions in which global capital is currently being restructured for flexibility in order to raise industry profits:

> First, flexibility in labor processes through new technologies and forms of organization intensifies work itself, increasing its pace, the length of the work day, and supervisory control, and decreasing social relations among workers. Second, capital achieves flexibility in labor markets by subcontracting, part-time employment, and other means by which work can be quickly reallocated from one group of people to another. Third, flexible state policies allow capital to shed its social responsibilities to workers and to the communities in which it operates. Finally, computers

and telecommunications enable flexible geographic mobility, fragmenting production and administration, and giving capital the ability to effectively 'deterritorialize' itself, freeing its operations from local and national controls.

This restructuring has profound consequences for individuals, families, and communities around the world. 'It results in unemployment or job insecurity, declining wages, long work days, the privatization or loss of social services, high stress, and unraveling social networks,' as well as 'alienated and dangerous communities' (Ibid.). It also results in environmental pollution, particularly in areas where it is believed that residents lack the education and political leverage for effective protest. In the face of such assaults on the integrity of local communities, it becomes increasingly problematic to rely uncritically on notions of local community action as the primary springboard to a revitalized democracy and transformed corporate/political agenda.

Of course, it also becomes increasingly important to think about the importance of community for human growth and development, life quality, and identity, and about the many different visions of community we might draw upon in strengthening, rebuilding, and, to some extent, constructing anew the communal frameworks of our daily lives.

## Ecofeminism

Recent environmental justice writings have attempted to theorize not only race, class, and occupational correlates of environmental risk, but also gender dimensions (Epstein 1991; Kraus 1993a, 1993b, and 1994; and Rosenberg 1995). It has been estimated that over 80% of the leaders of grass-roots protests in the U.S. are women, from predominantly blue-collar and minority backgrounds. Pardo (1990) describes, for example, the Mothers of East Los Angeles, a group of Latino American women who successfully opposed the building of a hazardous waste incinerator in East Los Angeles and went on to work for improved housing, schools, and neighborhood safety – all issues they saw as being equally 'environmental.'

In Love Canal: My Story, Lois Gibbs (leader of the national organization Citizens' Clearinghouse for Hazardous Waste) describes her entry into political life, motivated by a wife's and mother's concerns about her family's health. When her daughter developed a rare blood disease and her son was diagnosed with epilepsy, Gibbs began to speak with other parents, who were increasingly concerned about their own children's health. Little by little, they pieced together an understanding of how local chemical contamination in their neighborhood might be linked to health problems in their families. Gibbs describes her increasing politicization, as she took a leading role in community efforts to gain access to information, acknowledgment of local concerns from authorities and corporate representatives, and compensation for damaged health and local environments. In the course of negotiating with predominantly white, male, middle-class business people and policymakers, she began to develop broader understandings of social inequities that determine which communities are subject to the greatest environmental risks and which groups have the power to set political agendas.

It is interesting, however, that race and class tend to be more prominent than is gender, both in the environmental justice theoretical literature and in the autobiographical accounts of women activists. One reason is the uneasy relation between the American feminist movement and the perspectives of activist women, who see concerns about children, motherhood, families, and communities as the primary motivations for their political involvement. Another reason is that Grassroots environmental campaigns grow out of local, geographically identifiable communities. Given patterns of residential segregation in the U.S., spatially identifiable communities can often be correlated with race and class, but obviously not with gender.

Capek (1993: 5) observes that the interpretive frame of 'environmental justice' was 'fashioned simultaneously from the bottom up (local grass-roots groups discovering a pattern to their grievances) and from the top down (national organizations conveying the term to local groups)' and depending upon them for their political legitimacy and momentum. This integral relation between theory and practice was much less the case with grass-roots activism and 'ecofeminism,' an intellectual development beginning in the late 1970s that attempted to bring together insights from the feminist, environmental, and peace movements (Seager 1993a, 1993b; Mies and Shiva 1993; Shiva 1994; Diamond and Orenstein 1989). The ecofeminist literature often tends to be framed in abstract language from feminist theory that working-class women find distant from their own concerns. This, together with the 'new age' spiritual bent of some prominent ecofeminist authors, tends to diminish the potential relevance of ecofeminist theories for local activists.

In my opinion, however, ecofeminism has much to offer to the environmental justice movement. This literature is particularly strong in tracing links between militarism – a project heavily infused with structurally 'male' imagery and motivations – and serious environmental problems that often put women (and children) at special risk. A U.N. report from Iraq after the Gulf War (reported in Seager 1993b: 63) notes that one important consequence of war-related environmental destruction in the area is that women and children are spending increasingly large parts of their days searching for food, fuel, and water. Many toxic agents in wide use by military forces have particularly damaging effects on the sensitive reproductive systems of women. For example, the 25 million gallons of defoliants, herbicides, and other chemicals used by the U.S. military services in Vietnam have been linked to studies indicating that Vietnamese women have the highest rate of spontaneous abortions in the world, as well as high incidences of vaginal infections, cervical cancers, and occurrences of birth defects in their offspring (*Ibid*.: 64). Gallagher (1993) documents some of the human costs, particularly in terms of reproductive abnormalities and childhood illnesses, of populations living downwind of U.S. nuclear weapons tests in the deserts of Nevada.

Despite such compelling evidence, however, the links between gender and environmental risk still remain only partially developed in the environmental justice literature. The situation is even more problematic when we turn our attention to children and the variable of age.

## Children as a special environmental interest group

It is extraordinary how little attention has been given in the environmental justice literature to the special vulnerabilities of children (with the exception of lead poisoning in children, often cited in connection with pronounced environmental risks to African American populations). The neglect of children is especially striking, when we consider that concerns about child health and welfare figure prominently among the reasons given by grass-roots activists – a majority of them women – for their own political activism. Lois Gibbs (quoted in Kraus 1993a: 113) emphasizes how action aimed at the protection of children 'brings a concrete moral dimension to our experience – they are not an abstract statistic.' At a recent conference in Ann Arbor, Michigan (December 1995), on 'The Environmental Connection: Rising Rates of Breast Cancer, Reproductive Disorders, and Children's Disease,' I was struck by how many of the talks by grass-roots activists began with personal tales of the suffering of children – their own or others'. 'Statistics,' many repeated, 'are human beings with the tears removed.' Activists resolutely defend a view of the grass-roots movement that remains close enough to people's everyday lives and experiences to keep the tears in view.

Yet even though concerns about children are clearly central to the engagement of grass-roots activists themselves, the social dimension of age remains outside the boundaries of theoretical discussion. The following statement by Mary Mellor (1993: 37) is typical of the environmental justice literature: 'Ecological fault lines follow structures of economic power: from whites to people of color, men to women, rich to poor, North to South.' She *might* also have added, 'from adults to children' – but, significantly, she did not.

We have ample evidence that the developing bodies of children are characterized by biological processes and interactive relations with the physical world that are in many respects very different from those of adults (Ebrahim 1982; World Health Organization 1986; Stephens 1994). Children have been identified as the 'canaries in the mines,' insofar as their bodies are particularly vulnerable to deteriorating environmental conditions. (This phrase refers to mining practices in the last century aimed at monitoring the quality of underground air. When canaries brought down into the mines became sick and stopped singing, it was an early warning sign that the air had become dangerous for miners as well.)

Children are also vulnerable to environmental risks because of their distinctive pathways of exposure. A dramatic example of this point may be the marked increase in childhood cancers and mysterious swollen abdomens among Iraqi children after the Gulf War (Hoskins 1993). Some scientists have argued that these health problems may be due in part to children playing with empty artillery shells made from 'depleted uranium,' a byproduct of the nuclear industry that is desirable in weapons production because it is so hard. Although the Pentagon insists that the shells are only 'very, very mildly radioactive' – not enough to be classified as 'radiological weapons' – it is unlikely that Pentagon scientists ever considered the possible consequences of children playing with the empty shells. A doctor who was part of an international medical team evaluating the postwar situation of Iraqi children reported seeing children in Basra putting empty artillery shells over their hands and using them as hand puppets.

Di Chiro (1995: 303) notes that environmental justice activists are attempting to redefine 'the environment,' away from notions of a pristine, natural environment untouched and uncontaminated by human actions and toward a community-based vision of the environment as 'the place you work, the place you live, the place you play.' In fact, there is little play going on in the environmental justice field.

We know that children do an increasingly large share of subsistence work, both in the Third World and elsewhere (Ennew and Milne 1989; Niewenhuys 1994). Children are also increasingly drawn into the wage-labor market in conditions that are often dangerous to their physical and social development. However, children not only work, they also *play*, and these activities constitute special forms of 'the environment' that are not apprehensible from an adult-centered perspective. A focus on children's experiences of environmental risks calls our attention in the most demanding ways to the micro-processes of human/environment relations. What consequences do environmental changes and regulations have for children's everyday lives, for the nature of their social interactions, for the spaces they occupy in work and play, for the very composition of the air they breathe, the food they eat, and the dirt under their nails?

Children around the world are increasingly bearing the burdens of 'development.' This may be most starkly apparent in the ways that global restructuring and increasing disparities between the 'haves' and 'have nots' are played out in the lives of poor children. As Chawla (1995: 71) notes, these processes frequently translate into 'diminished nutrition and health care, substandard schools, or schools that become inaccessible when attendance fees are imposed, alienated and dangerous communities, street work or other child labor to supplement inadequate family incomes.' They also frequently translate into deteriorating environments with particularly serious consequences for children in urban slum and squatter areas. Blanc (1994: 21–22) observes:

> children can be seen playing, washing themselves, and drinking the polluted waters of Bangkok's canals, or roaming through the uncollected garbage in Nairobi … The shortage of water, sewage, and sanitation forces parents and their children to use particularly polluted outlets. Overcrowding increases the possibility of the spread of infections and contagious diseases.

Infants and children in developing countries are several hundred times more likely to die from diarrhea, pneumonia, and measles than are children in Europe and North America (Hardoy et al. 1990).

Children's environmentally related health problems are strikingly evident in the former USSR. A recent UNICEF study on conditions in Central and Eastern Europe – entitled 'Crisis in Mortality, Health, and Nutrition' – notes that 17% of the former USSR has been declared an ecological crisis area (UNICEF 1994: 29). Children's respiratory diseases (chronic bronchitis and asthmatic diseases), allergies, retarded intellectual development, and anemia have been linked to high levels of environmental contamination (including pesticides and toxic metals in groundwater and soil, as well as sulfur dioxide, nitrogen oxides, and lead pollution in the air). There has been a striking increase in thyroid cancer among children in Belarus, Ukraine, and the Russian Federation following the Chernobyl accident (World Health Organization 1995). These environmental problems are compounded by social problems in a 'political economy of transition': 'cracks in the system' – in the form of decreasing availability of social services, increasing unemployment, family tensions, and urban violence – are widening and children are often the first to suffer the consequences (UNICEF 1994: 10).

We might ask about the consequences of global development and restructuring for the environments, health, and psychological and social welfare of more materially privileged children as well. Increasing numbers of children in the industrialized world suffer from environmentally related allergies, respiratory ailments, and immune system disturbances, linked to chemical burdens in food, air, clothing, and the indoor environments of homes and schools (Rapp 1991: 362–3 17). These problems are not correlated with class, ethnicity, or race in any simple way.

While acknowledging that childhoods around the world are very different and that children do not comprise a self-evidently unitary group (any more than do 'women' or 'people of color'), we can still see ways in which the special characteristics of children's biology and development represent a foundation for regarding children as a special category of environmental victims. This point has significant implications for national and international environmental policy formation. Consider, for example, children's special vulnerability to radiation risks, which are greatest to rapidly dividing cells and developing organs. It is noteworthy that powerful international organizations (such as the ICRP, International Commission for Radiological Protection) concerned with setting 'safe' or 'acceptable' levels of radiation exposure base these standards on risk assessments done with respect to 'normal' populations. Many of these studies are occupational studies of workers in nuclear plants. The 'normal' population thus turns out to be largely white, male, healthy Euro-Americans of working age.

'Ecofeminist' perspectives would appear to be relevant here in explaining the lack of attention to children's special vulnerabilities. The 13-member, self-appointing executive committee of the ICRP consists exclusively of male representatives from the 'hard' sciences – primarily physicists and radiation biologists. There has never been a public or community health specialist on the governing committee, or a social scientist, or a woman. Study after study shows a significant gender gap in the ways people think about radiation risks, and this gap persists even among radiation scientists themselves (Slovic 1991). This finding makes it difficult to argue, as some have tried to do, that the gap can be attributed to women's relative lack of knowledge and reliance on feelings. There are probably multiple overdetermined reasons – inflected by race and class, as well as gender – why the ICRP's executive committee has not registered significant concern with children or grass-roots public concerns about radiation safety.

Such perspectives are also potentially relevant for explaining the marked neglect of children as a special environmental interest group in the environmental justice literature. In part, this may reflect the general neglect of children in the 'macro' disciplines of sociology, economics, and political science. Despite important developments in recent years in the sociology of childhood (see James and Prout 1990), research on children, particularly in the U.S., still tends to be 'ghettoized' in the fields of child development, education, and the child welfare branch of social work.

A low priority is also given to children in American political life, despite their current ubiquity in discussions of the need for welfare reform. The 'needs of children and future generations' are cited, repeatedly, as reasons for getting tougher with unwed welfare mothers, for streamlining and 'downsizing' the welfare system, and for calling on states and local communities to take over services no longer guaranteed at the federal level. Children in these debates seem to be a sort of 'empty sign,' brought in to sweeten the bitter pill of drastic welfare cuts that are likely to have very damaging consequences for the health and wellbeing of real children, as the Children's Defense Fund and other child advocacy organizations frequently assert.

I believe, however, that the most important reason for children's neglect in the environmental justice literature is the widespread assumption that although children may be *objects of* environmental inequalities, they cannot be actors and *participants* in grass-roots activism.

**Children as environmental actors**

The environmental justice movement puts a high priority on the potential for political mobilization of groups at special risk. Children have not traditionally been seen as political actors, in this connection, it is of interest that the Warren County, South Carolina, demonstration regarded by many as the founding act of the environmental justice movement, involved 'hundreds of predominantly African American women and children' who 'used their bodies to block trucks from dumping poisonous PCB-laced dirt into a landfill near their community' (Di Chiro 1995: 303). Yet the participation of children quickly and characteristically disappears from the discussion, in favor of issues of race, class, and gender.

There is a tendency in American culture to naturalize and essentialize children as passive victims or beneficiaries of adult actions. 'They are innocent, vulnerable, and dependent, and therefore society's primary responsibility is to protect them from adult experiences, like war and work, so that they can develop in their separate spheres of school and play' (Chawla 1995: 73). We have seen, however, that the boundaries of these separate spheres of childhood worlds (which certainly never existed in the idealized ways in which they are now often nostalgically conceived) are increasingly transgressed. The everyday lives of children are increasingly subject to forces that are currently restructuring families, communities, classes, racial and ethnic groups, nations, and world regions. (See Stephens 1995, for a discussion of children's changing life conditions in 'late capitalism.')

235

Di Chiro (1995: 310) develops a perspective on the environmental justice movement as a 'political culture based on community-organized and network-oriented social organization … Community becomes at once the idea, the place, and the relations and practices that generate what these activists consider more socially just and ecologically sound human/environment configurations.' The emphasis on community has allowed movement activists to argue for integral connections between ostensibly separate realms of environmental quality and social justice. Pam Tau Lee, a board member of the National Toxics Campaign Fund, observes:

> [Environmental justice is] able to bring together different issues that used to be separate. If you're talking about lead and where people live, it used to be a housing struggle; if you're talking about poisoning on the job, it used to be a labor struggle; people being sick from TB or occupational exposures used to be separate health issues, so environmental justice is able to bring together all of these different issues to create one movement that can really address what actually causes all of these phenomena to happen and gets to the root of the problems (quoted in Di Chiro 1995: 301).

Yet insofar as the core notion of community draws on conventional ways of thinking about children's situations and interests as reflections of the situations and interests of adults, children become merely background to and passive recipients of adult actions on their behalf. It is interesting that historians of the environmental justice movement represent one of the decisive outcomes of the First National People of Color Environmental Leadership Summit in 1991 as a rejection of the old 'partnership based on paternalism' with mainstream environmentalists (Di Chiro 1995: 303). People of color, the argument goes, are taking a collective stand against being treated like children and denied participation in decision-making processes that profoundly shape their daily lives. However, we might also begin to question why children themselves continue to be 'treated like children.'

There is evidence from around the world that children are playing increasingly important roles in 'investigating, planning, monitoring, and managing the environments of their own communities' (Hart 1994: 92). (See also Bajracharya 1994; and Miljeteig 1994.) A fascinating and illuminating case in point appears to be the involvement of children and youth in grass-roots environmental activism in the former USSR.

There is growing evidence that women in the former USSR – as in the U.S., and in many other regions of the world – are taking central roles in the grass-roots environmental movement. (See, for example, Feshbach and Friendly 1992.) We have as yet only suggestive, anecdotal information about children's involvement. Zhirina (1994) describes the participation of children in environmental activities in the Bryansk region of southwestern Russia. This area suffers from considerable fallout from Chernobyl, as well as from toxic industrial chemicals. Concerned about these problems, 'Viola,' a local environmental group, carried out studies to measure levels of radiation in the soil and in local vegetation and amounts of heavy metals and organic compounds in river and local drinking water. The group then embarked on public information programs aimed at politicians and business people. 'Viola' found that even when local authorities were well informed about pollution levels and health risks, there was little practical response. The political and business communities appeared to be more concerned about immediate economic problems than about environmental and health problems.

The group then turned their attentions to 'ordinary people' – factory workers and residents of polluted towns and villages in the region. Again, there was little response. Many people found it difficult to challenge polluting industries they depended on for employment. The weight of knowledge about extensive radioactive and chemical pollution in their communities and, more generally, in the former USSR resulted in a kind of 'psychic numbing,' making people unwilling or unable to acknowledge personal dangers, either to themselves or their families.

Finally, as a last resort, 'Viola' began working with children. The group started environmental education programs, both within the schools and local communities. In the period 1986 to 1990, parents and teachers had noticed a sharp increase in depression, passivity, and aggression among young people. This situation improved markedly as children (some as young as 10 years old) became involved in monitoring local pollution – drawing up maps of the effects of acid rain and measuring levels of chemical and radioactive contamination.

One group of children found high levels of mercury in ponds and ditches where they played. They traced the chemical to a local factory producing mercury vapor lamps for the military. The children, together with 'Viola' members and some parents and teachers, then made formal protests to local authorities and factory officials. This resulted in the factory installing cleanup equipment that eliminated the runoff of mercury into local water supplies. Another group of children located radioactive hot spots on local playgrounds. Sand on the playgrounds was removed and the play area paved over with asphalt, minimizing dangers from direct contact with radioactive soil.

Admittedly, these are small actions within a very seriously contaminated area. Yet 'Viola' members also reported that mobilization of children had significant effects on adults as well as children. Children's engagement with environmental concerns helped to break through the adults' 'psychic numbing,' so that parents, teachers, and administrators became more openly concerned about environmental problems and more willing to consider environmental cleanup programs and health rehabilitation programs that do not have immediate economic payoffs.

The Norwegian Centre for Child Research and the Moscow-based Center for Independent Ecological Programs (a research branch of the Socio-Ecological Union) developed plans for a jointly sponsored workshop, held outside Moscow in June 1996 on the topic of 'Children's Participation in Community-Based Environmental Care.' Aims of the meeting were to develop plans for studying the nature and dimensions of children's participation in grass-roots environmental activism in the former USSR, to compare these activities with various sorts of children's environmental participation in the West, and to explore possibilities for international network building.

To my knowledge, no studies have yet been done of children's participation in grass-roots environmental activism in the U.S. This, it seems, is a crucial area for future research. How do concerns about children's health and well-being figure in people's motivations for involvement? How do children understand adult concerns, debates, and actions, and to what extent are children themselves actively involved in the 'new environmentalism'? How might serious considerations of children as both environmental victims and actors change the ways we envision environmental justice theory and practice'? Opening up this area of research requires a reconceptualization not only of children and childhoods, but also of community, democratic participation, and human rights.

## Children as right holders

The fact that the United States was one of the last countries to sign the United Nations *Convention on the Rights of the Child* (adopted by the U.N. in 1989 and signed by the U.S. in 1995) suggests deeply entrenched – and divided – thinking about the appropriate role of children in society. Opposition to U.S. ratification has come from two sources: conservative 'family values' groups, concerned about the ways that children's rights claims might undermine parental rights over children, and women's rights advocates, concerned that an emphasis on children's rights might deflect attention and resources away from adult women, who are more able to analyze various forms of discrimination against them and to carry out concerted political actions.

The U.N. *Convention on the Rights of the Child* is in many respects an unprecedented document in the international human rights arena (Alston *et al.* 1992; Freeman and Veerman 1992; Stephens 1995). Earlier U.N. Conventions, such as the U.N. *Convention on the Elimination of All Forms of Discrimination Against Women* (1979), were based on claims that particular collectivities have special rights because of a history of discrimination that had denied them the full range of internationally recognized human rights. The Women's Convention stresses that it is the duty of ratifying states to modify or abolish all social impediments to the formal equality of individuals – male *and* female – before the law. In contrast, the children's convention (defining the 'child' as a person up to the age of 18) puts forth a notion of children as rights holders, associated with different sorts of rights at different stages of development and with respect to the child's evolving capacities for rational consideration and moral judgment.

The U.N. *Convention on the Rights of the Child* has been characterized by the Three P's: Protection, Provision, and Participation. Children have the right to be protected from harm, to be provided with services necessary for their healthy growth and development, and to participate in decisions that affect them according to their evolving capacities. An argument can be made that the child's rights to protection and care should be foregrounded in connection with very young children, while rights to self-expression and meaningful social participation become more important in connection with older children.

One of the qualitatively new aspects of the Convention is its emphasis on the capacity of children to act at least partially independently of adults. Thus, the Convention lays down rights, such as children's rights to freedom of expression (Article 13), association (Article 15), and participation (Article 12) that are not just protective, but also enabling. The contentious 'participation clause' (Article 12) – asserting that the child shall have a right to express his or her own views 'in all matters affecting the child, the views of the child being given due weight in accordance with the age and maturity of the child' – has sometimes been narrowly interpreted to refer to parental custody cases, but is increasingly construed much more broadly (Miljeteig 1994).

There is no general consensus in international law on either the right to a decent environment as an individual human right or environmental rights as collective human rights. Nevertheless, some legal scholars (for example, Pevato 1994) have argued that a child's right to a decent environment may be found by implication through other human rights recognized in various conventions – in particular, the U.N. *Convention on the Rights of the Child*. Note, for example, articles 6 (right to life), 24 (right of the child to the enjoyment of the highest attainable standard of health), 27 (right of every child to a standard of living adequate for the child's development), and 31 (right of the child to rest and leisure and to engage in play and recreational activities). Pevato (*Ibid.*: 178) argues that the convention 'stresses that children need special safeguards, including "appropriate legal protection" and children living in "exceptionally difficult conditions" need special considerations. Such circumstances would no doubt include environmentally disastrous locations where children struggle to survive.'

Although plausible and compelling arguments may be made for arguing that ratifying states are obliged to work toward providing the quality environments. children require to enjoy their convention-guaranteed rights, much work still must be done in exploring the implications of the 'participation clause' and the levels and kinds of children's environmental participation that might be regarded as being in 'children's best interests.' (Obviously, children's age, cultural backgrounds, social situations, and specific concerns are of central relevance here.) There is a growing body of literature (for example, Chawta and Kjoerholt 1996; Edwards 1996; Miljeteig 1994; Hart 1992; King 1995; and Stephens 1994) concerned with complexities of 'children's participation' and the social possibilities – and dangers – associated with this notion. I have argued elsewhere (Stephens 1994: 14) that:

> the expectation that children have special responsibilities to identify, articulate, and propose solutions for adult-created environmental prob-lems parallels the notion that it is the Third World poor, in many respects the victims of international development policies of previous decades, who are responsible for turning the tide of global processes of environmental degradation and for initiating a new era of sustainable global development.

There is a danger of asking children to become 'small adults' and take on enormous burdens before they are ready (Elshtain 1996). Yet, in the case of the children of Bryansk, the environmental participation of even fairly young children seems to have resulted in real improvements – material, psychological, and social – in children's lives and in the community as a whole.

Debates about the desirability and consequentiality of different sorts of children's participation, and about children's rights more generally, point to changes in children's life conditions and changing social constructions of childhood that have not yet had an impact on the environmental justice literature. Capek (1993: 8) observes that 'environmental justice is premised on the notion that the rights of toxic contamination victims have been systematically usurped by more powerful social actors, and that "justice" resides in the return of these rights.' As I have argued above, the U.S. Civil Rights Movement has provided the master frame validating the struggle for environmental justice by other disenfranchised groups. We might ask how other sorts of internationally significant rights claims – such as the claims for special women's and children's rights – might challenge theorists of the environmental justice movement to reframe their discussions, and might even provide important new concepts and languages for people 'on the ground' to recognize and name injustices in their everyday lives and to forge new connections across social and geographical boundaries. The social category of children is unique in crosscutting all others (race, class, gender, ethnicity, religion, and nationality). It thus holds out the possibility for coalition building that unites special interest groups grounded in more narrowly defined localities or social conditions.

## Conclusion

There are important practical arguments for including children in the environmental justice movement. As noted above, much of the literature in this area tends to rely on somewhat romantic, or at least uncritical, assumptions about the powers of citizen democracy. Yet where do adult citizens develop these strengths? It is not enough just to hold a town meeting. It is also necessary to have people attend these meetings who have the skills and knowledge to participate in democratic institutions. We need to know much more about the ways that children are already involved in grass-roots environmental activism, both in the U.S. and elsewhere; about the possibilities and consequences for children of different types and levels of involvement in different social and cultural contexts; and about the ways in which children's participation can affect the adults around them, as well as contribute to the development of concerns and capacities with important implications for their future actions as adult citizens.

The virtual absence of discussion of children in the environmental justice literature – either as victims or actors – suggests that there may be inequities within the movement itself (as well as constraining assumptions about children and childhood on the part of people who study and write about this movement). However, opening up this field to serious considerations of children's experiences, understandings, concerns, and potentials for action is not just a matter of social equity. It also raises important theoretical issues for discussion and new possibilities for practical engagement at the community, national, and international levels.

## References

Alston, Philip, Stephen Parker, and John Seymour (eds) (1992) Children, Rights, and the Law. Oxford: Clarendon Press.

Bajracharya. Deepak (1994) 'Primary Environmental Care for Sustainable Livelihood: A UNICEF Perspective.' Childhood 2,1–2 (February-May): 41–56.

Blanc, Cristina Szanton (1994) Urban Children in Distress: Global Predicaments and Innovative Strategies. New York: Gordon and Breach.

Bryant. Bunyan (ed.) (1995) Environmental Justice: Issues, Policies, and Solutions. Washington, D.C./ Covelo, Cal.: Island Press.

Bullard, Robert D. (1993a) 'Anatomy of Environmental Racism.' Richard Hofrichter (ed.), Toxic Struggles: The Theory and Practice of Environmental Justice. Philadelphia, Penn./Gabriola Island, B.C.: New Society Publishers: 25–36.

Bullard, Robert D. (1993b) 'Anatomy of Environmental Racism and the Environmental Justice Movement.' Robert D. Bullard (ed.) Confronting Environmental Racism: Voices from the Grass-roots. Boston: South End Press: 15–11.

Bullard. Robert D. (ed.) (1994) Unequal Protection: Environmental Justice and Communities of Color. San Francisco: Sierra Club Books.

Buttel, Frederick H. (1995) 'Rethinking International Environmental Policy in the Late Twentieth Century.' Bunyan Bryant (ed.) Environmental Justice: Issues, Policies, and Solutions. Washington. D.C./Covelo, Cal.: Island Press: 187–208.

Capek, Stella M. (1993) 'The Environmental Justice Frame: A Conceptual Discussion and an Application.' Social Problems 40,1 (February): 5–25.

Chavez, Cesar (1993) 'Farm Workers at Risk.' Richard Hofrichter (ed.) Toxic Struggles: The Theory and Practice of Environmental Justice. Philadelphia, Penn/Gabriola Island. B.C.: New Society Publishers: 163–171.

Chawla, Louise (1995) 'The World Summit for Social Development: Issues for Children.' Barn/ Childhood, Norwegian Centre for Child Research No. 2: 65–80.

Chawla, Louise and Anne Trine Kjoerholt (1996) 'Children as Special Citizens.' PLA Notes 25 (Notes on Participatory Learning and Action) (February): 13–16.

Commission for Racial Justice (1987) Toxic Waste and Race in the United States: A National Report on the Racial and Socioeconomic Characteristics of Communities with Hazardous Waste Sites. New York: United Church of Christ.

Diamond, Irene and Gloria Orenstem (1989) Reweaving the World: The Emergence of Ecofeminism. San Francisco: Sierra Club Books.

Di Chiro, Giovanna (1995) 'Nature as Community: The Convergence of Environment and Social Justice.' William Cronon (ed.) Uncommon Ground: Toward Reinventing Nature. New York: W.W. Norton and Co.: 298–531.

Ebrahim, G.J. (1982) Child Health in a Changing Environment. London: Macmillan.

Edwards, Michael (1996) 'Institutionalizing Children's Participation in Development.' PLA Notes 25 (Notes on Participatory Learning and Action) (February): 47–51.

Elshtain, Jean Bethke (1996) 'Political Children.' Childhood: A Global Journal of Child Research 3,1 (February 1): 1–28.

Ennew, Judith and Brian Milne (1989) The Next Generation: The Lives of Third World Children. London: Zed Press.

Epstein, Barbara (1991) 'Ecofeminism and Grass-roots Environmentalism in the United States.' Richard Hofrichter (ed.) Toxic Struggles: The Theory and Practice of Environmental Justice. Philadelphia. Penn./Gabriola Island. B.C.: New Society Publishers: 144–153.

Feshbach, Murray and Alfred Friendly, Jr. (1992) Ecocide in the USSR: Health and Nature Under Siege. New York: Basic Books.

Field, Rodger (1994) 'Children, Community, and Pollution Control: Toward a Community-Oriented Environmentalism.' Childhood 2.1–2 (February/May): 38–41.

Freeman, Michael and Philip Veerman (eds) (1992) The Ideologies of Children's Rights. Dordrecht/ Boston/London: Martinus Nijhoff Publishers.

Gallagher, Carol (1993) American Ground Zero: The Secret Nuclear War. Cambridge. Mass.: MIT Press.

Gibbs, Lois (1993) 'Foreword.' Richard Hofrichter (ed.), Toxic Struggles: The Theory and Practice of Environmental Justice. Philadelphia. Penn./Gabriola Island, BC: New Society Publishers: ix–xi.

Gibbs, Lois (1982) Love Canal: My Story. Albany: State University of New York Press.

Greenpeace (1992) 'The "Logic" Behind Hazardous Waste Export.' Greenpeace Waste Trade Update, First Quarter: 1–2.

Hardoy, J.E., S. Cairncross, and D. Satterthwaite (eds) (1990) The Poor Die Young: Housing and Health in Third World Cities. London: Earthscan Publications.

Hart, Roger (1994) 'Children's Role in Primary Environmental Care.' Childhood 2.1 (February/ May): 103–110.

Hart, Roger (1992) Children's Participation: From Tokenism to Citizenship. U.N. Children's Fund. Innocenti Essays No. 4.

Harvey, David (1989) The Condition of Postmodernity: An Inquiry into the Conditions of Cultural Change. Oxford: Basil Blackwell.

Hofrichter, Richard (1993a) 'Introduction.' Richard Hofrichter. Toxic Struggles: The Theory and Practice of Environmental Justice. Philadelphia. Penn./Gabdola Island. B.C.: New Society Publishers: 1–12.

Hofrichter, Richard (1993b) Toxic Struggles: The Theory and Practice of Environmental Justice. Philadelphia, Penn./Gabriola Island, B.C.: New Society Publishers.

Hoskins, E. (1993) 'With Its Uranium Shells. Desert Storm May Have Sown Death.' International Herald Tribune (January 22): 4.

James, Allison and Alan Prout (eds) (1990) Constructing and Reconstructing Childhood: Contemporary Issues in the Sociological Study of Childhood. London: The Falmer Press.

Kiefer, Chris and Medea Benjamin (1993) 'Solidarity with the Third World: Building an International Environmental Justice Movement.' Richard Hofrichter (ed.) Toxic Struggles: The Theory and Practice of Environmental Justice. Philadelphia, Penn./Gabriola Island. B.C.: New Society Publishers: 226–237.

King, Donna (1995) Doing Their Share to Save the Planet: Children and the Environmental Crisis. New Brunswick: Rutgers.

Kraus, Celene (1994) 'Women of Color on the Front Line.' Robert Bullard (ed.), Unequal Protection: Environmental Justice and Communities of Color. San Francisco: Sierra Club Books: 256–271.

Kraus, Celene (1993a) 'Blue-Collar Women and Toxic-Waste Protests: The Process of Politicization.' Richard Hofrichter (ed.) Toxic Struggles: The Theory and Practice of Environmental Justice. Philadelphia. Penn./Gabriola Island, B.C.: New Society Publishers: 107–118.

Kraus, Celene (1993b) 'Women and Toxic Waste Protests: Race, Class, and Gender as Resources of Resistance.' Robert D. Bullard (ed.) Environmental Justice and Communities of Color. San Francisco: Sierra Club Books.

Martin, Emily (1994) 'Post-Darwinism.' Emily Martin. Flexible Bodies: Tracking Immunity in American Culture from the Days of Polio to the Age of AIDS. Boston: Beacon Press: 227–251.

Mellor, Mary (1993) 'Building a New Vision: Feminist, Green Socialism.' Richard Hofrichter (ed.), Toxic Struggles: The Theory and Practice of Environmental Justice. Philadelphia, Penn./ Gabriola Island, B.C.: New Society Publishers: 36–17.

Merchant, Carolyn (1992) Radical Ecology: The Search for a Livable World. London: Routledge.

Mies, Maria and Vandana Shiva (1993) Ecofeminism. London: Zed Books.

Miljeteig, Per (1994) 'Children's Involvement in the Implementation of Their Own Rights – Present and Future Perspectives.' Paper presented at the International Society for the Study of Behavioral Development, Amsterdam (June 28–July 22).

Nietschmann, Bernard and William Le Bon (1987) 'Nuclear Weapons States and Fourth World Nation.' Cultural Survival Quarterly 11: 5–7.

Niewenhuys, Olga (1994) Children's Lifeworlds: Gender, Welfare. and Labour in the Developing World. London and New York: Routledge.

Noble, Charles (1993) 'Work: The Most Dangerous Environment.' Richard Hofrichter (ed.) Toxic Struggles: The Theory and Practice of Environmental Justice. Philadelphia. Penn./Gabriola Island, B.C.: New Society Publishers: 171–179.

Pardo, Mary (1990) 'Mexican-American Women Grass-Roots Community Activists: Mothers of East Los Angeles.' Frontiers: A Journal of Women Studies 1: 1–6.

Peng, Martin Khor Kok (1993) 'Economic and Environmental Justice: Rethinking North-South Relations.' In Hofrichter (ed.): 219–226.

Pevato, Paula M. (1994) 'Do Children Have a Role to Play in Environmental Protection?' The International Journal of Children's Rights 2: 169–190.

Rapp, Doris (1991) Is This Your Child? Discovering and Treating Unrecognized Allergies in Children and Adults. New York: Quill/William Morrow.

Rosenberg, Harriet G. (1995) 'From Trash to Treasure': Housewife Activists and the Environmental Justice Movement.' Jane Schneider and Rayna Rapp (eds.) Articulating

Hidden Histories: Exploring the Influence of Eric R. Wolf. Berkeley: University of California Press: 191–203.

Seager, Joni (1993a) Earth Follies: Coming to Feminist Terms with the Global Environmental Crisis. London: Routledge.

Seager, Joni (1993b) 'Creating a Culture of Destruction: Gender, Militarism, and the Environment.' Richard Hofrichter (ed.) Toxic Struggles: The Theory and Practice of Environmental Justice. Philadelphia, Penn./Gabriola Island, B.C.: New Society Publishers: 58–67.

Shiva, Vandana (ed.) (1994) Close to Home: Women Reconnect Ecology. Health, and Development Worldwide. Philadelphia: New Society.

Slovic, Paul (1991) 'Perceived Risk, Trust, and the Politics of Nuclear Waste.' Science 254: 1603–1607.

Stephens, Sharon (1995) 'Children and the Politics of Culture in Late Capitalism.' Sharon Stephens (ed.) Children and the Politics of Culture. Princeton, N.J.: Princeton University Press.

Stephens, Sharon (1994) 'Children and Environment: Local Worlds and Global Connections.' Childhood 2,1–2 (February/May): 1–22.

UNICEF (1994) Crisis in Mortality, Health. and Nutrition: Central and Eastern Europe in Transition. Economies in Transition Studies. Regional Monitoring Report No. 2 (August). Florence. Italy: United Nations Children's Fund.

WHO (World Health Organization) (1995) 'Post-Chernobyl: Work Cut Out for Decades to Come.' World Health Organization Press Office. Press Release WHO 84,24 (November).

WHO (World Health Organization) (1986) Environmental Health Criteria 59. Principles for Evaluating Health Risks from Chemicals During Infancy and Childhood: The Need for a Special Approach. Geneva: WHO.

Zhirina, Lyudmilla (1994) 'Viola' Helps Teachers and Children Combat Pollution in Bryansk.' Surviving Together (Summer): 34–36.

# 12. Against 'green' criminology*

*Mark Halsey*

This article offers an overview of recent work on environmental crime and regulation. It demonstrates the majority of such scholarship is imbued by quite problematic ideas concerning how best to envisage the nature of environmental harm and the type of regulatory structures which should be promoted to assist in the amelioration of environmental damage. The article concludes with a very brief discussion of the kinds of theoretical tools which might be used in place of orthodox framings of environmental crime and its prevention.

Let me preface my critique of green criminology with some initial observations about environmental matters. Like previous decades, the first few years of the 21st century have heralded the notion that global depletions of biodiversity, as well as human-induced declinations in air, water and soil quality, are chronic processes rather than fleeting events. These are not, it now seems clear, the result of some inexplicable 'blip' in (supposedly predictable) weather patterns, breeding cycles, market forces or the like. Instead, they are fundamentally linked to the 'normal' operation of various political, cultural and economic practices (United Nations Environment Programme 2002). As a result, and with the possible exception of terrorism and the (in)actions of so-called 'rogue' states, investigating the causes and possible remedies of environmental harm (however defined) are now key priorities for most Western nations.[1] Environmental problems are, in short, recognized to be of a central and serious kind, such that those who trivialize or downplay the fate of the globe are increasingly being asked by governments, by law, by green groups, and by 'average' citizens to justify their (improbable/imprudent) position.

In this context – and as a discipline intimately concerned with the geographies, intensities, frequencies and visibilities of harm – it would be reasonable to assume that the vicissitudes of environmental damage and environmental crime (two very different things) would by now constitute central objects of criminological thought (Cohen 1988). For, make no mistake, environmental harms do markedly impact the capacities of particular populations to actively and benignly engage with the flows of matter–energy conducive to what might be termed 'non-toxic lives'. Sound evidence of this can be found in

---

* From *British Journal of Criminology* (2004), 44(4): pp. 833–853.

what remains the most comprehensive study on global ecosystemic health, conducted by some 175 scientists on behalf of the United Nations Development Programme, the United Nations Environment Programme, the World Bank and the World Resources Institute. The report shows that:

> Half of the world's wetlands were lost [during the twentieth century]; Logging and conversion have shrunk the world's forests by as much as half [to around 3 billion hectares]; Some 9 percent of the world's tree species are at risk of extinction; Tropical deforestation may exceed 130,000 square kilometers per year; Fishing fleets are 40 percent larger than the ocean can sustain; Nearly 70 percent of the world's major marine fish stocks are overfished or are being fished at their biological limit; Soil degradation has affected two-thirds of the world's agricultural lands in the last 50 years; Some 30 percent of the world's original forests have been converted to agriculture; Since 1980, the global economy has tripled in size and [the] population has grown by 30 percent to 6 billion people; Dams, diversions or canals fragment almost 60 percent of the world's largest rivers; Twenty percent of the world's freshwater fish are extinct, threatened or endangered. (Media Release, 17 April 2000, Washington, DC, summarizing key trends emerging from *World Resources 2000–2001: People and Ecosystems: The Fraying Web of Life.*)

Despite such disturbing trends – whose 'truth effects' will always be subject to the power of particular discourses to (re)construct the limits of harm – criminological concern for the environment is, quite demonstrably, by far and away the exception to the rule (but see Goff and Geis 1993; Edwards *et al.* 1996; Williams 1996; Beirne 1998; Halsey and White 1998; Pearce and Tombs 1998; A-Khavari *et al.* 1999; Halsey 1997a; 1997b; 1999; Seis 1999; Walters 2004). A key question, therefore, is this: why, at a time when most disciplines (e.g. politics, economics, history, cultural studies) have built or extended their oeuvres to include an analysis of environmental problems, has criminology seen fit not to do so? Alternatively, why are there so few criminologists writing about environmental harm/crime, as opposed to the multitude prepared to discuss such issues as illicit drug taking, rape, robbery, homicide and other so-called 'orthodox' crimes?

Such questions stand to generate many important insights about criminology as well as those working within (and beyond) its confines. Elsewhere, I respond to these issues and look specifically at the relationship between criminology, andro/anthropocentrism, and the marginalization of Nature as the other of 'real' criminological work (see Halsey 2005a). For the moment, though, I want to leave these questions at the rhetorical level (as events which cast a shadow over the remainder of this discussion) and move instead toward an equally pressing issue. This has to do with how criminology has talked about environmental crime/harm to date and the problematic dimensions of such discourse.

I want to argue that green criminologists have, with few exceptions, drawn implicitly or explicitly upon one or a combination of five (competing) environmental perspectives – all of which emerge within, and carry with them the kinds of shortcomings associated with, modernist thought.[2] These perspectives are *liberal ecology* (World Commission on Environment and

Development 1987; Barbier 1989; Pearce *et al.* 1989; Barde and Pearce 1991; Pearce 1991), *ecomarxism* (Bahro 1984; Castillina 1985; Dunkley 1992; Pepper 1993), *ecofeminism* (Plumwood 1986; Meis and Shiva 1993), *deep ecology* (Leopold 1970; Naess 1973; 1989; Devall and Sessions 1985; Tobias 1985), and *social ecology* (Bookchin 1986; 1987; Clark 1990; Merchant 1992).[3] My intention is to show that adherence to any of these streams of thought necessarily leads to highly questionable renderings of Nature, society, subjectivity and, concomitantly, of what causes and what might be seen to prevent environmental damage. Green criminology does not, I will argue, possess the lexicon required to move beyond modernist conceptions of harm and reparation. Moreover, I want to suggest that when criminologists engage the term 'green', they necessarily manifest the kind of political baggage which comes with dividing the world into distinct – one might say, polar – domains. Getting better at socio-ecological relations will not, I contend, be simply a matter of siding with the green or red, the anthropocentric or ecocentric, the classical view of offending or the positivist, the constructionist take on 'reality' or the essentialist (Platonic), and so forth. Rather, improved functioning of socio-ecological worlds needs to be tied to ways of thinking-acting which subvert binary modes of thought (i.e. thought which results from the habit of segmenting the world into polar opposites and unified categories).[4] Indeed, I want to suggest that *the term 'green' should be jettisoned from criminological discourse*, primarily because it does not adequately capture the inter-subjective, inter-generational, or inter-ecosystemic processes which combine to produce scenarios of harm. There are particular costs associated with thinking and writing the world in various ways, and green criminology, I will suggest, misunderstands the nature and extent of the task at hand.

## Review and critique

### The problem of anthropocentrism

Perhaps the most worrying trend emerging from recent criminological work on environmental issues is that such efforts have generally been of an uncritical kind. By this I mean that such studies support and adhere to the tenets associated with what I have termed a liberal ecological outlook – an outlook imbued by *anthropocentric* principles and practices. Very briefly, liberal ecology views environmental problems as symptoms of unchecked – but ultimately controllable – market forces. It is no surprise, then, that the solutions to environmental crime (and environmental harm, more generally) have, in the main, been posed in terms of how best to (a) modify (but not radically alter) industrial processes, (b) modify (but not radically alter) environmental law, and (c) modify (but not radically alter) the nature and limits of enforcement (see, e.g. Del Frate and Norberry 1993; Grabosky 1994; Gunningham *et al.* 1995; McDowell 1997; Grabosky and Gant 2000; Davies 2002). A closer analysis of a relevant text will illustrate my concerns.

In a recent piece by the Deputy Commissioner of the Australian Federal Police (AFP), Davies (2002) offers a brief overview of the cost and scope of the illicit trade in wildlife – 'said to exceed five million birds, thirty thousand primates and fifteen million furs per year'. He continues, 'The economic value of this trade is estimated at US$1.5 billion and throughout the world over 600 species are threatened by th[e] trade [in wildlife]' (Davies 2002: 20). These are, without doubt, statistics to be deeply troubled by. But equally troubling is the way in which enforcement agencies portray their activities along binary lines. Specifically, the limits of *real* environmental harm equate to all those activities of an ecologically damaging nature *as proscribed by law* (e.g. wildlife smuggling, illegal dumping of chemicals, etc.). For instance, Davies writes that 'Environmental criminals can include the highest level of corporations, organized crime, and as we are now well aware, terrorists' (2002: 21). Here, a definitive line is drawn between the 'inside' and 'outside' of environmental crime, and, more particularly, who counts as 'real' environmental offenders and who do not. On the inside are the illegal activities of individuals and corporations which are capable of being formally construed as 'environmental crime' in a court of law (typically, and most problematically, a court severely limited in power and jurisdiction).[5] On the outside, though, are all those actors and activities which are, for all intents and purposes, 'untouchable'. What these actors do (and do not do) may be intentional, may be harmful, and may lead to longterm deleterious effects on ecosystems, but so long as such acts occupy a sphere beyond that dealt with by enforcement agencies, they do not, indeed cannot, constitute environmental crime.

This is a highly problematic state of affairs because one of the greatest perpetrators of ecological damage is the (post-)modern state (see Goff and Geis 1993; Williams 1996; Halsey 1997b). And yet, the body of this offender will not – indeed, cannot – make it onto Davies' (nor any other liberal ecological) list of environmental criminals, due mainly to the structural constraints which attend a system geared toward exponential profit and commodification of earth. There is a serious problem, therefore, with the way in which enforcement bodies envision, speak about, and frame environmental harm.[6] The most dangerous of these is the belief that the factors which compel people to commit environmental crime are somehow logically separate from those factors and conditions which lead the state to permit environmental damage 'by other means' and at different speeds and scales from moment to moment. Put another way, it is the height of naiveté to believe that capturing environmental criminals means arresting the alliances, personal habits and institutional routines that sanction a more generalized mode of environmental decay.

In addition to the above type of text, there is, of course, a (small) body of criminological writings on environmental harm which is concerned to move beyond the problems harboured by liberal ecology. Indeed, several well known criminological and socio–legal journals have, in recent times, devoted whole issues to addressing themes such as 'The Environment and Social Justice' (Goff and Geis 1993), 'Environmental Victims' (Williams 1996), 'For a Green Criminology' (Beirne 1998), 'Interdisciplinary Perspectives on Environmental Law' (A-Khavari *et al.* 1999), 'Environmental Justice Policy' (Seis 1999) and 'Globalisation and Environmental Harm' (Shank 2002). In addition to these, several books have been published dealing with matters of ecological criminality (e.g. Edwards *et al.* 1996; Pearce and Tombs 1998). Environmental criminological texts situated beyond liberal ecology fall into two broad ecophilosophical schools of thought – *biocentrism* (deep ecology) and *ecocentrism* (ecomarxism, ecofeminism and social ecology) (for a criminologically based outline of the basic principles behind each of these ecophilosophical schools, as well as that of anthropocentrism, see Halsey and White 1998). Although the vast majority of this literature adopts a critically informed position on the structures and processes leading to environmental damage, there are a number of problems associated with such efforts, which need, I think, to be brought to light. As a means of elucidating some of the problems associated with these ecophilosophical schools generally, I will examine the biocentrically informed work of Barnett (1999) and the ecocentrically based work of Benton (1998), as well as that of Lynch and Stretesky (2003).

### The problem of biocentrism

Barnett's article, 'The Land Ethic and Environmental Crime', attempts to build an 'eco-critical' definition of, and means for dealing with, environmental offences based around the writings of Aldo Leopold – specifically, his 1947 work, *A Sand County Almanac.*[7] Specifically, the category 'environmental crime' should be reorganized around Leopold's edict that, ' [A] thing is right when it tends to preserve the integrity, stability and beauty of the biotic community. It is wrong when it tends otherwise' (quoted in Barnett 1999: 162). The failure to base definitions of environmental crime around this principle has led, according to Barnett, to a sharp 'divergence between environmental harm in fact and environmental harm as conceived in law' (1999: 182). Further, Barnett explains that Leopold's work is not some romantic call for a 'return to nature', but is, instead, the result of 'good science'. As he writes, 'Leopold's observation of ecosystem dynamics led to *his scientific understanding of sustainability.* He considers the land ethic as science-based in that it aligned ethical demands with *objective need*' (1999: 182, emphasis added). Such an ethic – grounded as it is in science – has, according to Barnett, the capacity to radically transform social relations because 'land owners [would come] to recognise the realities of interdependency and sustainability and accept [...] self imposed limits on their behaviour' (1999: 182). In addition to Leopold, the work of Edwin Sutherland is invoked by Barnett as a means of illustrating the power of group norms over law in influencing and changing behaviour – the idea being that people learn and internalize environmentally destructive rules and rationales and that they can therefore replace these with rules and rationales of an ecological kind.

From this brief summary, it should be clear that there are a number of problems with Barnett's attempts to reframe matters of environmental harm within a biocentric framework. First, the urge to identify 'right' conduct with everything that tends toward 'integrity, stability and beauty' is a decidedly modernist, not to mention dangerous, idea. For one thing, it ignores the fact that ecosystems do *not* operate around steady-state principles. Instead, the so-called 'integrity' and 'stability' of 'the biotic community' fluctuates in accordance with forces often generated from those biotic communities themselves – storms, drought, fire, volcanic eruptions, and so forth. On a second and related count, it is questionable whether it is possible to logically speak of 'the biotic community' as something existing externally to the

248

happenings of 'humanity'. Perhaps a more productive approach would be to say that there are numerous and heterogeneous interfaces between bodies and practices – some leading to monstrous crossbreeds (e.g. dioxin) and black holes (e.g. nuclear waste repositories) and some drawing lines of deterritorialization (e.g. hemp-based paper mills, nuclear-free zones) (Deleuze and Guattari 1996). Determining whether one is witnessing the former or the latter is an ongoing contestable project that cannot be brought to a halt by some casual and ontologically questionable reference to absolute beauty or integrity.

One might say, therefore, that the concept of 'ecosystemic integrity', along with that of the 'beauty' of biotic environments, are anything but an objective means of positing a socio-environmental ethic(s). Indeed, what is most apparent is the way in which state departments co-opt the concept of 'ecosystemic integrity' to justify present modes of harvesting and managing all manner of 'resources' (fibres, grains, fruits, flesh, skins, and so forth). The fact, for example, that clearfell logging and the concept of ecological integrity are made to stand as synonymous events in the eyes of most foresters should indicate that what matters in environmental conflict is not the 'harm' attached to a given state of affairs, so much as how various elements (bureaucratic, protest, etc.) bring about particular alignments between expert discourse and the cultural imaginary (see Luke 1997). By taking the concept of 'beauty' as timeless rather than discursively constructed, Barnett is unable to account for the fact that – to continue the example – forest administrators generally view a newly felled coupe as something of great beauty, since it represents the opportunity for 'new' forest structures to emerge (where each stand of trees will be incessantly managed to display the same age, height and density). This, it should be recalled, is the bureaucrat's vision of a forest, exhibiting unsurpassed levels of 'ecological integrity' and 'stability'. One might also draw attention to the way in which 'beauty' has been used to oppress, injure and restrain, not just bodies of Nature, but the bodies of women as well (e.g. the practices of Chinese foot-binding, genital mutilation, and the like). This again shows that of critical importance in environmental matters is an awareness of how words and their associated (assembled) meanings evolve with respect to configurations of power and desire.

A third problem with Barnett's work is its uncritical adherence to the Western scientific method and its ability to know or recognize 'sustainability' in all its guises. Numerous studies have shown that science holds little capacity to name or capture the combination of forces which lead to environmental damage (see Beck 1992; Lash *et al. 1996)*. Moreover, where science believes it has adequately categorized Nature, this has most often led not to benign practice, but to a range of unforeseeable deleterious effects (e.g. failure of coupes to regenerate, sedimentation of fresh water streams, declining numbers of arboreal and ground dwelling mammals, etc.). In short, there is ample reason to be highly suspicious of any theory or ethic which tries to derive legitimacy on the basis of its scientificity. Biological science, just like criminology, is a discourse which, while leading to real effects, is constituted and sustained through all manner of rhetorical manoeuvres and assumptions about the limits of knowledge and the operation of power. For this reason alone, science needs always to be subject to critique, not blind acceptance.[8]

A fourth and final problem associated with Barnett's work is his reluctance to think through the criminal-justice-oriented implications of defining environmental crime according to the tenets of the land ethic. As he admits, this approach will see a whole host of acts, presently cast as 'environmental harm in fact' (i.e. harms which fall outside the boundaries drawn by law), come under the rubric of the juridical armature. This, I would suggest, is somewhat antithetical to the project(s) of critical criminology which, as I understand it, advocates for *less*, not more, state intervention in social, economic and ecological life. Moreover, criminologists have shown time and time again that criminalizing a behaviour is a very poor way of reducing its occurrence. Admittedly, Barnett does invoke Sutherland's work as a means for suggesting that of ultimate importance in ecological matters is that ethics eventually must replace law/juridical coercion. But this does not go very far towards explaining how such an ethic might arise. Indeed, one might question whether it is in fact desirable for all persons to live by the tenets of one edict above all others. One could even say that such a plan harbours the potential for perpetuating a kind of (ecological) fascism. This is something that biocentrists do not seem to want to grasp – that there is strength in diversity of socio-ecological knowledges and practices and that the nature of Nature is not its capacity to foster an equality of relationships or some perfect symbiotic state, but its tendency toward disequilibrium and difference. Given such conditions, it is very hard to see how 'correct action' or 'best practice' could equate to rigidly adhering to the terrains and experiences mapped out by a single edict/principle. Profit, Christ, Progress and Reason have all, at one time or another (and even collectively), been touted as *the* way to a perfected state of affairs. And all, of course, have led to untold violence for countless human and non-human worlds. How logical, therefore, is it to think that the 'new' idols of Integrity, Stability and Beauty will bring an end to such violence?

### The problem of ecocentrism

Perhaps the key criminological statement to emerge around an ecocentric theme in recent times is by Ted Benton (a long-time proponent of ecomarxism), entitled 'Rights and Justice on a Shared Planet: More Rights or New Relations?' [see Reading 8, this volume]. This piece – appearing in what has become a key collection in the criminological literature on environmental harm – offers a sophisticated account of environmental protection based on an ecocentric conception of rights and obligations. It discusses and moves beyond both Peter Singer's utilitarian approach and Tom Regan's deontological (consequentialist) stance to the protection of species in order to chart a 'relational' ethical program for combating human-induced environmental decay. Benton sums up his outlook as follows: 'The aim would be to generate harmonious, benevolent and co-operative spirals, as against destructive, competitive and antagonistic ones, through the establishment of new dominant patterns of interaction, experiences and spontaneous sentiments' (1998: 171). He continues:

> This alternative would be a many-sided project for social, economic and ecological transformation inspired by spontaneous moral sentiments which flow from anxiety and horror in the face of continuing human

destruction of non-human nature, and by the egalitarian co-operative and popular democratic values inherited from earlier anarchist and socialist traditions, and now carried forward by the feminist, peace, green and other progressive social movements. (1998: 171)

To be fair, Benton is quick to admit the utopian nature of his perspective. But such a recognition does not counter other shortcomings harboured by his work. These have mainly to do with the problematic conception of 'human nature', as well as the championing of a *universal* system of human and non-human rights. On the first count, the notion of human nature deployed by Benton is one which claims that there is something that – after all is said and done – gives humanity an *essential* aspect. For Benton, this aspect waxes and wanes between the two poles of innate aggression/competition, as against cooperation/reciprocity. The very fact that he acknowledges these *two* poles should dispel any possibility of a *fixed* human nature. To posit a 'human nature' is to side with the view that humans are essentially and always x *not y*. But in his work, this tension is unresolved and it is this bipolar stance which leads Benton to call *both* for extensive state regulation *and* the maintenance of spaces/opportunities for 'spontaneous moral sentiments' which would somehow 'naturally' lead, as he terms them, to improved socio-ecological relations.

One could say that if there is a human nature, then it would exist always and absolutely, or not at all. Here, Benton – as well as anthropocentric, biocentric and ecocentric theorists generally – runs up against a highly problematic view of the human subject. This problematic revolves around placing the seeds of ecological renewal *either* at the mercy of a benevolent and essentially cooperative subject, waiting to be 'released' from systems/structures of antagonism and repression via sustained periods of mass reflection and rationally planned action, *or* such seeds are given over to the workings of an essentially malevolent and egoistic subject, doomed to entrench structures of ecological collapse. In either case, there is a failure to develop a processual view of subjectivity – one which posits that human nature (just like Nature) is produced and reproduced through the *textual machines*[9] which cut across the *assemblages*[10] (familial, pedagogical, political, leisure) each inhabits from one moment to the next. Criminologically, it is the work of Stuart Henry and Dragon Milovanovic (1996) that has come closest to outlining such a conception. I will say more on this shortly.

On the second count, problems also accompany Benton's appeal to a universal system of rights as the vehicle most capable of protecting human and non-human environments. Again, to be fair, Benton admits that 'rights may be little more than an empty formality, serving merely to legitimate persisting de facto inequalities' (1998: 162). However, he nonetheless goes on to place considerable faith in the 'inherent' emancipative powers common to movements and political creeds which draw/rely heavily upon appeals to universal rights (see Benton 1998: 171). Indeed, the conclusion to his piece – which speaks of a time when 'Public regulation would be upholding and protecting what was already favoured and nurtured by every day experience of interaction with humans and other non-human beings and environments' – is laden with all the (problematic) rhetoric of modernity and its inability to resist positing foundations for measuring the moral aptitudes of the universal human subject (1998: 173). As Benton concludes, 'Above all, … a strongly institutionalised protection of universal civil liberties would still be required [in Eco-/Utopia?] to offset any tendency for new forms of oppression and exploitation to emerge, or for old ones to reassert themselves' (1998: 173).

This, of course, would present to many as a highly logical and prudent programme. However, I would argue that such a vision is imbued by the modernist dimensions and structures which have helped to create and entrench anti-ecological networks across much of earth. For when, it might be asked, have institutions (which necessarily harbour an abstracted/reified account of 'the individual' and their circumstance(s)) ever been capable of upholding the *rights already extant* in international laws and treaties? Further, what kinds of narratives/voices would such institutions inadvertently marginalize or malign in the quest to uphold the 'Truth' of its socio-ecological vision? In short – and to draw on Foucault's sentiments in the foreword to *Anti-Oedipus* – how would such institutions learn to look for the micro fascist leanings inside each of its structures and programmes? There is, quite demonstrably, an urgent need for the emergence of a very different regulatory terrain – specifically, one which constantly puts asunder the concepts of 'nature', 'sustainability', 'culture', 'economy' and 'humanity', which pervade its aspects. Contrast this against Benton's observation that in the future world, governed by a 'relational' ethical outlook, 'Every imaginable form of human social life … will stand in need of regulation' (1998: 172). Here, the world conjured by Orwell in his *1984* seems perilously close – especially if, by 'regulation', Benton means governance of human conduct by 'external powers' (this concept, it should be noted, is never clarified in his work).

Before offering some suggestions of how one might leave the shortcomings of green criminology behind, I want to offer a brief critique of one of the latest pieces to appear in the field. The relevant work here is entitled 'The Meaning of Green: Contrasting Criminological Perspectives' (Lynch and Stretesky 2003 [see Reading 4, this volume])[11] and stands, I would argue, as one of the more thoughtful pieces to appear under the banner of green criminology.[12] The primary argument put by Lynch and Stretesky is that criminologists have a choice between two competing versions of what it is to be 'green' – the *corporate* perspective and the *environmental justice* view. The former defines environmental crime as events in contravention of the law and tends to disregard the impact of race, gender and power upon the formulation of such definitions (2003: 229–230). The latter, on the other hand, defines 'a green crime [as] an act that 1) may or may not violate existing rules and environmental regulations; 2) has identifiable environmental damage outcomes; and 3) originated in human action' (Lynch and Stretesky 2003: 227). Along with this definition goes the concern to analyse 'how forms of race, class and gender inequities affect the social construction of environmental laws' (2003: 228).

At first glance, this sounds highly promising. However, there are a number of problems that need surveying. First, Lynch and Stretesky do not clarify their position regarding the role of the state and its relationship to strategies of environmental renewal. This is an absolutely critical issue because, as Stanley Cohen reminds us, if more events are formally defined as crime, then the result will be a far wider array of acts (potentially) brought before authorities. The closest Lynch and Stretesky come to clearing up their position is their assertion that the green 'definition focuses attention on acts that, whether or not defined as illegal, *should nonetheless be considered criminal*' (2003: 229, emphasis added). If, on the one hand, they wish to argue – as they seem to do – that the capitalist state is the archetypal example of an institution suffering from chronic regulatory capture (see Paehlke and Torgerson 1990), then they need to explain how such an institution could ever see its way clear to criminalize all those events which, to put it bluntly, make capitalism work. But if, on the other hand, the (future) role of the state is to remain largely unchanged, then (and this brings me to a second point of contention) Lynch and Stretesky need to advance a far more nuanced conception of (socio-cultural) power than they do. Here, it is boldly stated that 'Power [...] is the key issue that separates the [...] opposing stances' of the corporate as against the environmental justice version of green criminology (2003: 230).

One of the great weaknesses of Lynch and Streteskys' piece is, I would submit, that they align themselves to a Marxist notion of power – a hydraulic rendering which says that there are people/groups who possess power (in the manner of an object) and those who are devoid of it (for a critique, see Foucault 1977; 1982). Indeed, Lynch and Streteskys' text is imbued by all the traditional dichotomies which flow from such a conception (equality/ inequality, powerful/powerless, corporations/citizens, First World/Third World, global/local, to name several).[13] The problem here is that such a view of power – and, specifically, the kind of stochastic modelling of the world it produces – ignores the *micropolitical* and *heterogeneous* practices, thoughts and routines which various persons/groups engage. It is, arguably, through the intra- and inter-subjective modes (doing, thinking, ritualizing) that the reproduction of the discursive frames used to justify, neutralize or normalize (environmental) harm occurs. Lynch and Stretesky are, in one sense, right to point out that the vast bulk of environmental damage stems from privileging 'the *economic sphere* over other social structures and issues' (Lynch and Stretesky 2003: 231, emphasis added). But I want to suggest that structural economic power relies for its efficacy not simply on the relations between government, law and economy, so much as on the *flows of pleasure* which invest the population at any one time. Not only is it profitable to be environmentally destructive (in the sense of mining, manufacturing cars, clearfelling forests), it *feels* good too (in the sense of purchasing a gold necklace, driving on the open road, looking at a table, chair, or house constructed from redwood, mahogany, mountain ash or the like). *Environmental damage is, in short, as much a corporeal (bodily/subjective) event as it is a corporate/state practice* and Lynch and Stretesky fail to address this situation.

A third criticism of Lynch and Streteskys' work concerns their invocation of a dialectical view of society (i.e. one that proclaims the existence of opposites ('Man'/Nature) and that the resolution of opposites is possible and necessary). A green criminology, they argue, must strive for 'the elimination of social and economic inequalities' (2003: 229). Similar to that extolled by Barnett, Benton and others, this conception of the logics of social relations is of the modernist variety. It suggests that it is possible to invent a place and time where all humans can peacefully coexist – and that universal goodwill toward one another will naturally be extended to non-human worlds as well. This, of course, is hubris.[14] To desire an end to 'social and economic inequality' may be politically correct, may make certain people feel good about their regard for others, but it ignores the issue of how one judges (not to mention *who* would judge) where *difference* ends and inequality begins. The point here is that the judgments (laws, discourses, categories) which organize the earth and its inhabitants are viewed as sufficient to their task when they in fact harbour all manner of epistemological dilemmas – such as that concerning language and its (in)ability to adequately name or convey the meaning of events (ecological, cultural, etc.). Here, one runs the very real risk of marginalizing that which gives the world its vitality. These are issues which Lynch and Stretesky neglect to address.

My fourth and final criticism relates to Lynch and Streteskys' deployment of the phrase 'environmental justice'. In this case, they write as if they know – beyond any shadow of doubt – how to recognize this brand of justice (and, presumably, injustice) wherever and whenever it might occur. There is, in other words, an alignment to an Aristotelian view of justice (and, thus, of knowledge about the world). The classically Aristotelian question is of the form: what is x? Here, one either admits of essences and absolutes – that hiding behind appearances and surfaces (of each environmentally harmful event) lies the true or hidden meaning of things, or, one admits that 'truth', just like justice' or 'freedom', is discursively produced from moment to moment. Lynch and Stretesky fall foul of the first scenario – which is curious, to say the least. For they correctly state that 'Crimes are constantly made and unmade through acts of social construction and deconstruction' (2003: 228). But, and this is critically important, they do not extend this same constructionist outlook to the concept of environmental justice. It is as if such justice is instinctual, universal, always already 'there', simply waiting to be pronounced. But this, again, is an absurd and dangerous position. What is called 'environmental justice' will be as susceptible to the forces of social, symbolic and rhetorical competition as those impacting the meaning(s) of environmental crime/harm. Justice, to be clear, is never pure or unadulterated. Instead, it arrives through the pronouncements of bodies who are themselves subject to a multitude of genealogical forces – forces which govern what it is logically possible to say about a given (criminal/harmful) event (see Foucault 1991).

### Toward an alternative terrain

In light of this critique, it is apparent that there are a number of problematic assumptions underpinning recent efforts by criminology to theorize environmental harm. These revolve mainly around: (a) the general reluctance to put into critical relief the concept of environmental damage and the associated (but manifestly distinct) category of environmental crime; (b) the inability to move beyond dialectical models of society and conflict resolution; (c) the unwillingness to do away with modernist accounts of the relationship between 'words' and 'things'; and (d) the incapacity to develop a nuanced account of human/environmental interaction. But, given the ways in which criminology has envisioned Nature throughout its history, these oversights are none too surprising. In highly schematic form, I would say that Nature – as deployed across two centuries of criminological thought from Beccaria to Lombroso, through to Becker and up to Henry and Milovanovic – functions in four main ways. First, in classical criminology, nature appears as the original or primordial sign – as that which can be read, deciphered, and mirrored by humanity in the laws it posits and the conceptions of the body it holds (rational, wilful, responsible, introspective). Here, nature presents as a *mimetic force* – it is something orderly, hierarchical, powerful and thus so should be the key institutions and principles characterizing liberal democracy. Secondly, in positivist criminology, nature presents as that which incites persons toward irrational and problematic conduct. Here, humanity loses the capacity for free and spontaneous action and is subject to the unpredictable conditions and trajectories that nature summons forth *within* the human body. In a sense, nature is cast here as a *dangerous and uncontrollable force*.

Thirdly, in critical criminology (spanning social reactionist perspectives up to and including marxist and early feminist accounts of crime), nature presents as the *external* factor which shapes and influences the capacity for benign or damaging conduct to materialize in a vast range of contexts (peer groups, families, schools, work places, neighbourhoods, states, etc.). In more detailed terms, Nature appears and disappears from the critical criminological scene in line with attempts to come to grips with the thresholds at which consciousness (the transcendental subject) and environment (enunciated not in terms of its ecological dimensions but in terms of *goods* (e.g. alcohol, drugs, guns), *services* (e.g. police, welfare, shelter, hospitals) and *external stimuli* (e.g. media, school curricula, peers, popular culture) combine to produce scenarios of conflict rather than something other. Within critical criminology, Nature, it could be said, presents as the *recurring yet discursively absent other* – as the force which constitutes the objects of the criminological terrain[15] but which has been simultaneously made, until very recently, to occupy a location at the periphery of criminology's 'real' business.

Fourthly, and finally, there marches the extension of critical criminology informed by a mixture of postmodernist and poststructuralist observations. Here, Nature has yet to be adequately theorized or discussed within criminology (but see Groombridge 1998; Lane 1998; Halsey 1999). However, I would suggest that reference to the work of poststructuralist writers, Gilles Deleuze and Felix Guattari, offers a potentially rich source for thinking through key critical issues associated with nature and its (de)regulation. For it is they (after Thales, Heraclitus, Homer, Anaximander, Cratylus, and, more recently, Nietzsche) who consistently conceive the world (Nature) as *flow* (as that which incessantly returns, despite all attempts to classify, manage and contain portions of the Earth) rather than structure (as that which has a teleology, a definitive inside, an indelible Truth). Such a conception is critical to pulling apart what Deleuze has termed 'the image of thought'[16] (or, better, the image of Nature) which has dominated both criminological work and state policies and practices on environmental issues to date. More than this, the work of Deleuze and Guattari provides a means for keeping pace with the mobility of environmental problems by considering Nature and systems of environmental regulation as always already discursively produced and contested. Significantly, they make no grand claims concerning 'solutions' or the precise conditions for long-term 'ecological sustainability'. Indeed, terms such as these (i.e. solution, sustainability, program) should be subjected to rigorous interrogation and, perhaps, ultimately effaced from the lexicon of environmental struggle. In a sense, it may be better to do to Society and Nature what Nietzsche did to God and Man. And it may be important to do this in order to better know the impact of particular subjectivities (the economic subject, the familial subject, the leisure oriented subject, the technologically embedded subject) on various arrangements of matter–energy (those which invest and make possible assemblages of work, play, education, and so forth). Deleuze and Guattari are invoked here not as environmental saviours, but as thinkers, whose lexicon may produce a new problematic of ecological damage – a problematic which, for instance, brings issues of speed, envisioning, scale and affect[17] to the fore (see Halsey 2005b, forthcoming). The claims, therefore, made by Deleuze and Guattari are decidedly modest. And, in keeping with such modesty, I want now merely to suggest several ideas that it might be useful to keep in mind when addressing problems of Nature (which are, everywhere and always, problems concerning the flows, use and blockages of matter-energy).

First, move beyond Nature toward that which Deleuze and Guattari term the *plane of consistency* (toward the place of 'pure potentials', a place prior to the production of words and things). The plane of consistency presents as an important concept for teasing out the effects of naming, dividing and dichotomizing the cosmos:

> The plane of consistency ... is opposed to the plane of organization and development. Organization and development concern form and substance: at once the development of form and the formation of substance or a subject. But the plane of consistency knows nothing of substance and form: haecceities, which are inscribed on this plane, are precisely modes of individuation proceeding neither by form nor by the subject. The plane consists abstractly, but really, in relations of speed and slowness between unformed elements, and in compositions of corresponding intensive affects. ... Spinoza, Holderlin, Nietzsche are the surveyors of such a plane of consistency. Never unifications, never totalizations, but rather consistencies or consolidations. (1996: 507)

From this passage, it can be said that Deleuze and Guattari are concerned to show the price paid for blocking/filling out the plane of consistency with particular kinds of bodies – forests, rivers, races, genders, economies, chronologies, legalities, policies. A sustained engagement with Deleuze and Guattari therefore prompts the question: *At what social, cultural and ecological cost do – indeed can – we presently name, divide, and regulate the plane of consistency?* It should not in any way be supposed that the plane of consistency resides as some kind of lost panacea for current ills. For how could, in any case, something be considered 'lost' that is always already there? Rather, the plane of consistency (the plane of supermolecular nature) is that which has the potential to radically problematize present ways of conceiving the society-economy-culture-nature nexus. More than this, it causes each rendering of 'the real' (e.g. forest), 'the proper' (e.g. function), and 'the authentic' (e.g. custodian) to be put asunder. Through its concern to map both the ambiguity of bodies and the (traditionally molar or rigid) responses levied by particular agencies to such ambiguity, Deleuze and Guattari (and, more specifically, their mode of inquiry, called schizoanalysis) stands as a technique for problematizing and perhaps even disengaging the structures of modernity (or the image of (environmental) thought). The key here is to invent concepts which allow one to escape the image of thought which governs what it is possible and not possible to do and say with respect to 'the environment'. In short, conjure an image of the acategorical[18] (of that which eludes description or capture) in order to understand anew the ethical weight which arrives with speaking and naming the limits of environmental harm.

Secondly, think in terms of lines rather than structures. That is, consider the idea that molarity (identity, unity, Truth) equates more often than not to a truncation of the possibilities associated with particular terrains. Conversely, experiment with the Real (the place beyond accepted lexicons and dispositions) in order to maximize the unsaid of each event (in order, that is, to bring to prominence minor or discounted knowledges, viewpoints, experiences) (see Foucault 1980b).

Thirdly, give thought to the juxtaposition of bodies which result from the operation of texts. Indeed, read all events as texts to be pulled this way and that, rather than as objective instruments or data waiting to be acted upon (see Halsey 2001). Here, realize that although there are no limits to the juxtaposition and ordering of bodies, there are, nonetheless, consequences and effects. It is the machines (political, scientific, legal, economic) which portray these consequences and effects as knowable and/or controllable that need to be exposed for what they are – the impossible masquerading as the normal/logical.

Fourthly, put bodies into critical relief (especially so-called 'human' bodies). Conceive bodies (one's own and each others') as projects in the making and as conduits for the flows of commodification which reach across and irrevocably transform the planet. Think about the body as one's first and last means of resisting the forces establishing a becoming-the-same from one territory to the next. Think, in other words, of the epidermis not as a container, but as a membrane, whose aspects are infused not just by sunlight, sound, water, and so forth, but also by the decisions reached on climate change, corporate investment, trade subsidies, export volumes, the value of the dollar, and the like around the globe. Treat the body as the politico-ecologically interested force par excellence (see Featherstone *et al.* 1991). In terms of instituting meaningful change, put faith in one's own body (which is, in any case, always already, subject to someone else's desires, knowledges, capacities) *before* one puts faith in bodies of laws and regulations.

Fifthly, know that the existence of humans (or various types of subjectivities) will automatically equate to some degree of socio-environmental conflict. What counts is maintaining enough room on the *plane of reference* (filled as it is with subjects, objects and Truth) such that no single solution holds sway for any length of time. To run contrary to this would be to invite the forces of fascism into the discourse(s) of environmental harm and its possible renewal. These forces, are, of course, omnipresent. But the *proliferation and diversification of environmental strategies* may help to limit their impact on day-to-day struggles. As Guattari writes, 'Rather than looking for a stupefying and infantilising consensus, it will be a question in the future of cultivating a dissensus and the singular production of existence' (2000: 50). In simpler terms, 'We must ward off, by every means possible, the entropic rise of a dominant subjectivity' (Guattari 2000: 68).

A sixth and final (although there can be no final) point for criminologists to keep in mind when dealing with the problematics of Nature would be to know that one is never totally removed from 'the action'. *Mapping the limits of environmental harm and legal intervention always already has an ethical and social dimension to its aspects.* This is why it is not enough to merely become acquainted with the machines plugged into one's own body. Instead, it is equally vital to develop a knowledge of how and where to plug one's body into the machine or machines deemed capable of delivering the desired socio-ecological effect(s).[19]

In order to avoid the charge of epiphenomenalism, I think it important to draw attention to the kind of criminological work which resonates with what I have been advocating to date. I mentioned earlier that Henry and Milovanovic (1996) are two seminal authors, concerned to advance a criminological perspective which eschews modernist as well as (some kinds of) postmodernist constraints (see also Nelken 1994; Young 1996; Pavlich 1999; 2000; 2001). Central to their work has been the formulation of a *constitutive* definition of crime – a definition that enables commentators to conceive of crime as having corporeal effects without having to rely upon notions of 'human nature' or the 'universal subject' nor upon linear conceptions of cause and effect. Although, at times, their articulation of such a definition seems imbued by an anthropocentric outlook,[20] and, further, although the very positing of a definition is, in many senses, a decidedly modernist trait (embodying the will to represent or contain events), there remains, I believe, something useful in such an attempt. In specific terms, Henry and Milovanovic assert:

> Crimes [...] are nothing less than moments in the expression of power, such that those who are subjected to them are denied their own contribution to the encounter and often to future encounters, are denied their worth, are simultaneously reduced and repressed in one or several ways. Crime [...] is the power to deny others their ability to make a difference. It is the ultimate form of reification in which those subject to the power of another agency suffer the pain of being denied their own humanity, the power to make a difference. ... (1996: 116)

Clearly, it is necessary to view 'others' as having to include non-human as well as human bodies. It is also necessary to envisage 'the power to make a difference' as denoting the literally infinite array of colours, smells, sounds, as well as geological/botanical/hydrological flows and coagulations of particular regions, which, if allowed to emerge, might meaningfully impact social, legal, political and aesthetic relations. Here, the major strength of Henry and Milovanovics' work is that they are sensitive to the fluid nature of the concept 'harm', as well as to who or what is capable of being harmed from one moment (or politico–historical juncture) to the next. As they write, 'We need to define crime and its harm in terms of specific, but historically contingent, victim categories, but *to be aware of the emerging social constructions whose relations of power are relations of harm*' (1996: 119). In this sense, the problem is not crime, but the limits placed upon who and what can count as criminal subjects and/ or criminal objects. More than this, *the problem is how to think beyond crime as a useful category of thought.*

A further strength of constitutive criminology is its understanding of the role of language in framing and producing harm – that words are, to greater or lesser degree, violent events.

> The call for universality in discourse (as in Habermas' call for a search for consensus in 'ideal speech situations') is a form of harm: it makes common that which is irregular, it homogenizes the heterogeneous. As an alternative to the legalistic definition of crime, our postmodernist definition of crime focuses on harm inflicted in all its guises and would certainly include the '"violence of language" […], particularly how the disenfranchised, disempowered, and marginalized have been denied expressive forms for their desires and yearnings…' (Henry and Milovanovic 1996: 118).

What matters here is not the 'truth' or 'falsity' of Henry and Milovanovic's conception of crime, so much as *how it might be put to work*. That is, what counts is the fact that such a definition may open up new discursive and extra-discursive pathways where other definitions have fallen short. As a means of teasing small-scale/local revolutions from overarching (seemingly fixed) situations or states of affairs, a definition of crime that puts the emphasis on inter-relatedness over and above segmentation would seem to be a good starting point. The utility of a definition of environmental crime will be the degree to which it elicits new types of existential territories, makes possible new modes of envisioning the human/earth nexus, invites a reconceptualization of the relationship between speed and damage, and, following Spinoza, asks of bodies what each can *do* rather than what each *is* (i.e. what manner of becomings are sustained or curtailed by particular decisions to use or regulate earth).

Another sign of a good definition[21] of environmental crime would be its ability to chart *multiple ethical paths* and programmes without, at the same time, falling into a hyper-relativism. Following Nietzsche, it is crucial to consider the value of current values, which means, in effect, to consider which kind of body modernity has most often aligned itself with – the body of the herd, the same, and the representative? Or the body ceaselessly transforming, reaching, and creating 'beyond itself? A crucial part of enacting a *transvaluation of all values* (Nietzsche 1968) is to see to it that one does not remain overtly and purely nihilistic – something which Henry and Milovanovic go to great lengths to reiterate.[22] Significantly, the process of de(con)struction[23] always already has an ethic or a trajectory residing within its parameters. The challenge is to discern the limits of the process of reconstruction, the limits of affirmation – the limits, in other words, of the new alignments between bodies and words that (might) emerge from critique. But, just as it is important to be affirmative, it is equally important to be aware of the logic underpinning affirmation. For, to chart a definition of crime or harm is to side with a *particular logic of accusation* (Pavlich 2000). And, to do this is to bring (back) into play at least some of the dualisms so common to the criminological terrain (harm/benign, cause/effect, culpability/incapacity, etc.). This, in turn, often leads to the appearance of bodies whose task it is to judge the moment when one side of the binary should divorce from the other. But, in a constitutive world, it will be necessary to focus not on 'environment' versus 'jobs', 'protesters' versus 'administrators', 'crime' versus 'law', or 'harm' versus 'integrity', but on the molarized structures which force particular assemblages of enunciation (such as courts, science, politics) to view these aspects as discrete points on a plane of reference rather than as becomings or intimations of the possible on the plane of consistency. And what of the role of commentary in a constitutive environment? Simply, *the task of the critic will be to draw attention to the possible by showing the contingent dimensions of the actual.*[24] More than this, the challenge is one of nurturing assemblages (academic and countless others) willing to throw the transformative weight of the acategorical behind socio-ecological struggles.

## Notes

1  See, e.g. documents emerging from the UN Commission on Sustainable Development, 11th Session, New York, 28 April–9 May 2003. Evidence of further commitment toward resolving particular kinds of environmental damage is (despite the lack of support from countries such as the US and Australia) reflected in the text, 'Kyoto Protocal – Status of Ratification, 10th July 2003' (84 Signatures, 111 Ratifications, Acceptances, Approvals and/or Accessions) (available online at http://unfccc.int/resource/kpstats.pdf).

2  Carrington (1994: 263), following the work of Hebdige, has tendered three defining characteristics of modernity: 'its essentializing conception of history, politics, society and the transcendental subject, its teleological search for origins or causes, and its utopian solutions to the problems of modern[ity].'

3  Under what I term *liberal ecology* (which is, geopolitically, the most dispersed of environmental philosophies), environmental harm tends to be reduced to problems of participatory democracy and unresponsive market mechanisms. In all instances, liberal ecology views as *compatible* both the long-term health of ecosystems *and* the maintenance of the structures inherent to liberal democratic/late-capitalist societies. For *ecomarxists* (who take, as their starting point, the few remarks made by Marx and Engels on the ecologically destructive aspects of industrialism), the primary cause of environmental degradation is capitalism or, indeed, any system based on exponential material growth and antagonistic class relations. The 'solution' to environmental degradation is, therefore, framed in terms of common ownership of the means of production and the application of 'objective' scientific data to environmental problems, like the greenhouse effect, hazardous waste and deforestation. *Ecofeminists* (coming to prominence in the 1970s and beyond in the wake of classic feminist texts by such authors as Marilyn Waring, Simone De Beauvoir, Marilyn French and Gloria Steinem) consider environmental damage to be symptomatic of entrenched patriarchal social relations. In this sense, it is *men* (specifically, the knowledges and practices that they embody and perpetuate), and not just economic *systems* per se (feudalism, capitalism, socialism, anarchism), that are held to be the catalyst of environmental destruction. By excluding women from key debates and issues, men, it is contended, can *only* reinforce androcentrism and its necessary corollary, ecocide. For *deep ecologists*, environmental damage is viewed as the product of widespread ignorance of 'the interconnectedness of all things' – particularly of the individual (or 'small' self) to the world (or 'larger' self). In an attempt to move beyond crude anthropocentric accounts, deep ecology ascribes intrinsic value and indeed moral consideration to ecosystems writ large (called 'biocentric egalitarianism'). Here, indigenous knowledges of various terrains are configured as overarching panaceas to ecological (and social) dilemmas. *Social ecology* conceives environmental problems not only as the logical

extension of the domination of women by men, but also of men by men – particularly of those men who hold and wield political and economic power over those who do not. Social ecologists argue that it is possible to read or discern from nature the 'correct' or best way of organizing social relations. Such an idea – echoing the project of Comte – goes hand in hand with the belief that the world has, beneath all its veneers, surfaces, appearances and impressions, an essential and timeless body of signs, waiting to be read and acted on by 'man'. For a detailed account of these perspectives, see Halsey (2005a, forthcoming).

4   In the final section, I offer a very brief examination of the work of Gilles Deleuze and Felix Guattari as a possible means of reinventing criminological talk about ecological matters.

5   In a three-year period, spanning 1994–6, the Victorian Environment Protection Agency (the primary regulator of a southern Australian State, composed of some 4.5 million people) prosecuted a total of 133 cases, with a conviction rate of 38 per cent. The most common penalty in this period was a fine (n = 75) and the average amount imposed was $2,750 (ranging from $40 for littering to $16,000 for breaching air-pollution statutes) (see Environment Protection Authority 1994; 1995; 1996; 1997). This situation continues to reflect national trends up to and including the end of 2002 (see prosecution data, given in the annual reports of each Environment Protection Authority). The fact that so few people receive substantial fines or go to prison for environmental offences surely cannot be an indication that all is well with humanity and various bioregions (i.e. that the harms perpetrated against earth are somehow small, discrete, unintentional or the like). Equally, the fact that the most common type of environmental crime (from an international perspective) likely to result in a prison sentence is 'exceeding bag limits' for various fish species does not mean that the damage 'caused' by such offences is the most serious environmental problem which people the world over consciously or actively perpetuate. Rather, such a circumstance is, critically, an indication of what regulators 'choose' or, more accurately, have the capacity, to name (and, where possible, enforce) as environmental crime. There are many important parallels here with the way in which formal definitions of violence are constructed in a manner to exclude much of what governments, corporations, police and armies do (see Box 1983).

6   There is, of course, a substantial criminological literature (e.g. Tappan 1947; Sutherland 1949; Schwendinger and Schwendinger 1975) dealing with what should fall within and beyond the criminological gaze. My own view is that criminology should not be constrained by a strictly delimited field of analysis. Indeed, the vitality of the discipline depends on its capacity to subject to critique events and processes which, when viewed through one lens or another, are apt to attract the label 'harm' or a closely associated term. Indeed, a key critical criminological task is to bring to light the factors which function to divide criminal from so-called normal, routine or acceptable practice. This, arguably, is what is so striking about environmental issues and their relation to the criminological purview: namely, that it is very difficult to rename and re-envision much of what we take to be pleasurable, profitable and progressive as one and the same as those events which contribute to the diminution of species and the toxic transformation of the biosphere.

7   The use of Leopold's work is, in itself, a problematic move, since it does not sit easily alongside the main tenets of eco-critical criminology (see Seis 1993). One of the key claims of eco-critical criminology is that the human capacity to colonize and dominate most if not all parts of the biosphere *distinguishes* it from *all* other species. Leopold, on the other hand, was firmly of the view that humans are, as he puts it, merely 'plain members' of the biotic community. In short, it is probably not a wise decision to call upon a biocentric theorist to fill out the tenets of an eco-critical criminology, since the latter is somewhat removed from the principle of biospheric egalitarianism (i.e. the belief in the moral equivalence and worth of all species). This said, the point of Barnett's article is to establish a new relationship between (environmental) law and ethics. Indeed, he makes the general point that law necessarily stems from an ethics of one kind or another (1999: 166). This is, of course, a fair enough contention. However, it is also important to know that much law is predicated on *moral*, not ethical, principles (where morality denotes discursive practices of right and wrong, whose form and limits are informed by religious or other transcendental narratives).

8   This thought, of course, extends to the ecological trends cited at the outset of this discussion. That is, information contained in the World Resources text produces *truth claims* (by injecting a body of data into the body of particular social and political networks) and not *the* Truth about ecosystemic deterioration.

9   Deleuze and Guattari (1996) use the term 'machine' (which should *not* be thought of as equating to the mechanical or artificial) to denote the process which brings about and often changes the relationship between words and things. 'Every machine', they write, '… is related to a continual material flow […] that it cuts into' (Deleuze and Guattari 1994: 36). These relationships can appear permanent and natural or as contestable and reworkable,

depending on the kind of machine operating at any one moment. Machines of axiomisation (e.g. the law machine) will tend toward the former whereas machines of absolute decoding (e.g, the terrorist machine) tend toward the latter. Guattari (1995: 58) writes, 'From now on the machine will be conceived in opposition to structure, the latter being associated with a feeling of eternity and the former with an awareness of finitude, precariousness, destruction and death. Beneath the diversity of beings, no univocal ontological plinth is given, rather there is a plane of machinic interfaces.' Critically, and in contradistinction to structuralist and modernist arguments, there is no single unified subject that commands or sets in train any given machine (entailing that there can be no single cause nor solution to particular kinds of dilemmas). Instead, machines have a thoroughly social dimension to their aspect (everyone or no one is implicated). Poststructuralists argue that the world is best conceived in machinic or textual terms – as replete with formed and unformed things whose meaning is continually negotiated, posited, remade, solidified and put asunder by signs which are *'differential*, not referential' in their performance (Belsey 2002, emphasis added). From a poststructuralist viewpoint, signs do not have lurking within them an essence or an eternal 'expressed'. If this were the case – and this is something which modernity is structurally bound to overlookthen there could be *no* debate over the precise signifi(c)ance of 'such processes as global warming, habitat fragmentation, bleaching of coral reefs, falling numbers of the Spotted Quoll, and the like. Without machines, though, there would be no such thing as greenhouse, habitat, coral, or Spotted Quolls (or Nature, Man, Woman, Species, Environmental Harm, or Law). Instead, and most significantly, there would pass the continual variation and return of the flow of unformed elements, unmarked by anthropomorphisms or distinctions between words and things. All of this is critically important because it enables the texts which write the world (such as government and scientifc reports, Acts of Parliament, news headlines, academic theorizing, and so forth) to be understood as machines. And they are machines precisely to the extent that they carve out and bring into relief various kinds of bodies (national parks, industrial zones, endangered species, enforcement personnel, scientists, social dissenters). The point to grasp is that most machines parade their bodies as the natural, immutable and proper state of affairs, where, in fact, such bodies are culturally contingent and politically infused. Ecologically, it is necessary to ascertain whether a text brings about a proliferation of different bodies and potentials or whether it draws a production of the same.

10   Wherever there is an arrangement or ordering of practices and concepts within a defined territory, there is, according to Deleuze and Guattari, the production of an assemblage or body. 'We will call an assemblage every constellation of singularities and traits deducted from the flow – selected, organized, stratified – in such a way as to converge [...] artificially and naturally; an assemblage, in this sense, is a veritable invention' (1996: 406, emphases removed). On such a count, 'an assemblage [or body] has neither base nor superstructure, neither deep structure nor superficial structure ...' (1996: 90). Bodies, in other words, are impermanent-but this certainly does not mean that they are without effects. Instead, each body (the body of a water catchment, the body of a national park, the body of a forest, the body of a law enforcement officer, the body of a protester) can be conceived as a zone of intensity, occupying a space between two poles or 'vectors'. Deleuze and Guattari call these poles the *stratified vector* (or stratum) and *destratified vector* (or substratum). Between these vectors (i.e. throughout a body), there is a constant tension between states of *molarity* (reaction, becoming-the-same), *molecularity* (action, becoming-other) and *supermoleularity* (hyperaction, becoming-immanent). In other words, a body is a conglomeration of volatile forces effected by numerous machines at any one time – a site of rigidities, regularities and blockages (a *territory*) but also a site of experimentation, contingency and possible escapes (a deterritorialisation). Bodies, therefore, are always already of the order of micropolitical in(ter)ventions.

11   Despite stating that their aim is to 'highlight a human-centred orientation' for green criminology (Lynch and Stretesky 2003: 218), 1 have included this text under ecocentrism because it seeks (a) to move beyond crude market forces as solutions to environmental problems (placing it outside a liberal or anthropocentric framework) and (b) views the human capacity for global ecological destruction as setting this species apart from all others (placing it outside a biocentric stance).

12   Lynch, it should be noted, was one of the first to raise the possibility of a green criminology (see Lynch 1990).

13   Perhaps the most striking (and damaging) binary in their work is that which attends the statement, '[Beyond all other definitions of environmental crime], [o]nly one viable option remains: the more radical environmental justice definition of green outlined [in our work]' (Lynch and Stretesky 2003: 233). Here, a theoretical fascism has replaced any concern for open-ended exploration of socio-ecological possibilities.

14  Derrida (1992: 28) once remarked, 'Nothing seems to me less outdated than the classical emancipatory ideal' (meaning that there can be no repressed or latent subjectivity, waiting to be released to some ideal state).

15  For example, police vehicles are linked to the production of magnesium and other metals, as much as they are a means of transport or surveillance, and prisons – in so far as they require multiple resources for their construction and day-to-day operation – are as much a drain on the earth's ecology as they are places for incapacitation or rehabilitation.

16  The image of thought – the discursive structuring and limiting of what can be said and done – rigidly marks out the thresholds dividing self from other, inside from outside, the familiar from the unfamiliar, and, importantly, the ecologically significant from the ecologically expendable. On this basis, disengaging the image of thought – or 'the figure in which *doxa* is universalized by being elevated to the rational level' – becomes, for Deleuze and Guattari, the key to rewriting the world, and thereby socio-environmental issues anew (Deleuze 1994: 134).

17  For a discussion of this concept and its place within Deleuze and Guattari's work, see Massumi (2002).

18  In an erudite review of Deleuze's *Difference and Repetition*, Foucault remarks, 'The most tenacious subjection of difference is undoubtedly that maintained by categories. By showing the number of different ways in which being can express itself, by specifying its forms of attribution, by imposing in a certain way the distribution of existing things, categories create a condition where being maintains its undifferentiated repose at the highest level. Categories organize the play of affirmations and negations, establish the legitimacy of resemblances within representation, and guarantee the objectivity and operation of concepts. They suppress the anarchy of difference, divide differences into zones, delimit their rights, and prescribe their task of specification with respect to individual beings. ... Difference can only be liberated through the invention of an acategorical thought' (Foucault 1980a: 186).

19  Indeed, this is the task I set myself in *Becoming Contested: Deleuze and the Lexicon of Ecological Struggle* (Halsey 2005a, forthcoming), where I apply the tenor of the six aforementioned suggestions to a key site of environmental struggle and regulation. In such a forum, I put, as it were, *my* criminological machine to work within the 'real' world(s) of environmental damage, protest, and state intervention.

20  For instance, at one point, these authors remark, '[C]rime is the expression of some agency's energy to make a difference on others and it is the exclusion of those others who in the instant are rendered powerless to maintain or express their *humanity*' (Henry and Milovanovic 1996: 116, emphasis added).

21  Of course, the plane of consistency knows nothing of definitions and perhaps, in an 'ideal' world, it would be best to be rid of them. But, as a means of marking out the vicissitudes of various problems – indeed, what counts *as* 'a problem' – definitions would seem to be an indispensable aspect of current states of affairs.

22  This is evident in their efforts to chart the distinction between a nihilist and an *affirmative* postmodern stance.

23  I am using this term in the Derridean sense. Pavlich (2001: 162) gives voice to this by observing that 'Deconstruction ... is concerned with experiences that dissociate, open, welcome and include; it is not concerned with attempts to gather, entrench, defend or exclude by defining the present in absolute ways'.

24  In the words of one writer, each 'becomes the watch, the witness, who flags multiple shifting dangers that attach to social formations' (Pavlich 2001: 163).

# References

A-Khavari, A., England, P. and Godden, L., eds (1999), 'Interdisciplinary Perspectives on Environmental Law', *Griffith Law Review*, Special Issue, 8/2.

Bahro, R. (1984), *From Red to Green*. London: Verso.

Barrier, E. (1989), 'The Contribution of Environmental and Resource Economics to an Economics of Sustainable Development', *Development and Change*, 20: 429–59.

Barnett, H. (1999), 'The Land Ethic and Environmental Crime', *Criminal Justice Policy Review*, 10/2: 161–92.

Barde, J. and Pearce, D., eds (1991), *Valuing the Environment*. London: Earthscan.

Beck, U. (1992), *Risk Society*. London: Sage.

Beirne, P. (1998), 'For a Green Criminology', *Theoretical Criminology*, Special Issue, 2/2.

Belsey, C. (2002), *Poststructuralism: A Very Short Introduction*. Oxford: Oxford University Press.

Benton, T. (1998), 'Rights and Justice on a Shared Planet: More Rights or New Relations', *Theoretical Criminology*, 2/2: 149–76.

Boorchin, M. (1986), *The Modern Crisis*. Philadelphia: New Society Publishers.

Boorchin, M. (1987), 'Social Ecology versus 'Deep Ecology': A Challenge for the Ecology Movement', *The Raven Anarchist Quarterly*, 1/3: 219–50.

Box, S. (1983), *Power, Crime and Mystification*. London: Tavistock.

Carrington, K. (1994), 'Postmodernism and Feminist Criminologies: Disconnecting Discourses?', *International Journal of the Sociology of Law*, 22: 261–77.

Castillina, L. (1985), 'Why 'Red' Must be 'Green' Too', in M. Nikolic, ed., *Socialism on the Threshold of the Twenty-first Century*. London: Verso.

Clark, J., ed. (1990), *Renewing the Earth: The Promise of Social Ecology*. London: Merlin Press.

Cohen, S. (1988), *Against Criminology*. New Brunswick: Transaction Books.

Davies, J. (2002), 'To Fight Environmental Crime, Together, and Win', *The Journal of the Australian Federal Police: Platypus Magazine*, 74: 20–8.

Deleuze, G. (1994), *Difference and Repetition*. New York: Columbia University Press.

Deleuze, G. and Guattari, F. (1994) *Anti-Oedipus*. Minneapolis: University of Minnesota Press.

Deleuze, G. and Guattari, F. (1996), *A Thousand Plateaus*. Minneapolis: University of Minnesota Press.

Del Frate, A. A. and Norberry, J., eds (1993), *Environmental Crime, Sanctioning Strategies and Sustainable Development*. Rome/Canberra: UNICRI/AIC.

Derrida, J. (1992), 'Force of Law: The 'Mystical Foundation of Authority', in G. Carlson, D. Cornell and M. Rosenfeld, eds, *Deconstruction and the Possibility of Justice*. New York: Routledge.

Devall, B. and Sessions, G. (1985), *Deep Ecology: Living as if Nature Mattered*. Salt Lake City: Gibbs Smith.

Dunkley, G. (1992), *The Greening of the Red: Sustainability, Socialism and the Environmental Crisis*. Leichardt: Pluto Press.

Edwards, S., Edwards, T. and Fields, C., eds (1996), *Environmental Crime and Criminality: Theoretical and Practical Issues*. New York: Garland Publishing.

Environment Protection Authority (1994), *Environment Protection Authority Annual Report 93/94*. Melbourne: EPA.

Environment Protection Authority (1995), *Environment Protection Authority Annual Report 94/95*. Melbourne: EPA.

Environment Protection Authority (1996), *Environment Protection Authority Annual Report 95/96*. Melbourne: EPA.

Environment Protection Authority (1997), *Environment Protection Authority Annual Report 96/97*. Melbourne: EPA.

Featherstone, M., Hepworth, M. and Turner, B., eds (1991), *The Body: Social Process and Cultural Theory*. London: Sage.

Foucault, M. (1977), *Discipline and Punish*. Ringwood: Penguin.

Foucault, M. (1980a), *Language, Counter-Memory, Practice: Selected Essays and Interviews by Michel Foucault*. New York: Cornell University Press. Edited by Donald F. Bouchard.

Foucault, M. (1980b), *Power/Knowledge: Selected Interviews and Other Writings 1972–1977*. New York: Pantheon Books. Edited by Colin Gordon.

Foucault, M. (1982), 'Afterword: The Subject and Power', in H. L. Dreyfus and P. Rabinow, eds, *Michel Foucault: Beyond Structuralism and Hermeneutics*. Chicago: University of Chicago Press.

Foucault, M. (1991), 'Nietzsche, Genealogy, History', in P. Rabinow, ed., *The Foucault Reader*. London: Penguin.

Goff, C. and Gels, G., eds (1993), 'The Environment and Social Justice', *The Journal of Human Justice*, 5/1.

Grabosky, P. (1994), 'Green Markets: Environmental Regulation by the Private Sector', *Law and Policy*, 16/4: 420–48.

Grabosky, P. and Gant, F. (2000) *Improving Environmental Performance, Preventing Environmental Crime*, Research and Public Policy Series, 27, Canberra: AIC.

Groombridge, N. (1998), 'Masculinities and Crimes Against the Environment', *Theoretical Criminology*, 2/2: 249–68.

Guttari, F. (1995), *Chaosmosis: An Ethico-Aesthetic Paradigm*. Sydney: Power Publications.

Guttari, F. (2000), *The Three Ecologies*. London: Athlone Press.

Gunningham, N., Norberry, J. and McKillop, S., eds (1995), *Environmental Crime*. Conference Proceedings Series, 26, Canberra: AIC.

Halsey, M. (1997a), 'Environmental Crime: Towards an Eco-Human Rights Approach', *Current Issues in Criminal Justice*, 8/3: 217–42.

Halsey M. (1997b), 'The Wood for the Paper: Old-growth forest, Hemp and Environmental Harm', *Australian and New Zealand Journal of Criminology*, 30/2: 121–48.

Halsey, M. (1999), 'Environmental Discontinuities: The Production and Regulation of an Eco-experience', *Criminal Justice Policy Review*, 10/2: 213–55.

Halsey, M. (2001), 'An Aesthetic of Prevention', *Criminal Justice*, 1/4: 385–420.

Halsey, M. (2005a, forthcoming), *Becoming Contested: Deleuze and the Lexicon of Ecological Struggle*. London: Ashgate.

Halsey, M. (2005b, forthcoming), 'Environmental Visions: Deleuze and the Modalities of Nature', *Ethics and the Environment*, Special Issue, Ethics of Seeing: Consuming Environments.

Halsey, M. and White, R. (1998), 'Crime, Ecophilosophy and Environmental Harm', *Theoretical Criminology*, 2/3: 345–72.

Henry, S. and Milovanovic, D. (1996), *Constitutive Criminology: Beyond Postmodernism*. London: Sage.

Lane, P. (1998), 'Ecofeminism Meets Criminology', *Theoretical Criminology*, 2/2: 235–48.

Lash, S., Szerszynski, B. and Wynne, B., eds (1996), *Risk, Environment and Modernity*. London: Sage.

Leopold, A. (1970), *A Sand County Almanac*. New York: Ballantine Books.

Luke, T. (1997), *Ecocritique*. Minneapolis: University of Minesota Press.

Lynch, M. (1990), 'The Greening of Criminology: A Perspective for the 1990s', *The Critical Criminologist*, 2: 11–12.

Lynch, M. and Stretesky, P. (2003), 'The Meaning of Green: Contrasting Criminological Perspectives', *Theoretical Criminology*, 7/2: 217–38.

Massumi, B. (2002), *Parables for the Virtual*. London: Duke University Press.

McDowell, D. (1997), *Wildlife Crime Policy and the Law: An Australian Study*. Canberra: AGPS.

Meis, M. and Shiva, V. (1993), *Ecofeminism*. Melbourne: Spinifex.

Merchant, C. (1992), *Radical Ecology: The Search for a Liveable World*. New York: Routledge.

Naess, A. (1973), 'The Shallow and the Deep, Long-Range Ecology Movement: A Summary', *Inquiry*, 16: 95–100.

Naess, A. (1989), *Ecology, Community, and Lifestyle*. Cambridge: Cambridge University Press.

Nelken, D., ed (1994), *The Futures of Criminology*. London: Sage.

Nietzsche, F. (1968), *The Will to Power*. New York: Vintage Books.

Paehlke, R. and Torgerson, D., eds (1990), *Managing Leviathan: Environmental Politics and the Administrative State*. London: Belhaven.

Pavlich, G. (1999), 'Criticism and Criminology: In Search of Legitimacy', *Theoretical Criminology*, 3/1: 29–51.

Pavlich, G. (2000), 'Forget Crime: Accusation, Governance and Criminology', *Australian and New Zealand Journal of Criminology*, 33/2: 136–52.

Pavlich, G. (2001), 'Critical Genres and Radical Criminology in Britain', *British, Journal of Criminology*, 41/1: 150–67.

Pearce, F. and Tombs, S. (1998), Toxic. *Capitalism: Corporate Crime and the Chemical Industry*. Brookfield, VT: Ashgate.

Pearce, D., Markandya, A. and Barrier, E. (1989), *Blueprint for a Green Economy*. London: Earthscan.

Pearce, D., ed. (1991), *Blueprint 2: Greening the World Economy*. London: Earthscan.

Pepper, D. (1993), *Eco-Socialism: From Deep Ecology to Social Justice*. New York: Routledge.

Plumwood, V. (1986), 'Eco-Feminism: An Overview and Discussion of Positions and Arguments', *Australasian Journal of Philosophy* (supplement) 64: 120–38.

Schwendinger, H. and Schwendinger, J. (1975), 'Defenders of Order or Guardians of Human Rights?', in I. Taylor, P. Walton and J. Young, eds, *Critical Criminology*. London: Routledge and Kegan Paul.

Seis, M. (1993), 'Ecological Blunders in US Clean Air Legislation', *Journal of Human Justice*, 5/1: 58–81.

Seis, M., ed. (1999), *Criminal Justice Policy Review*, Special Issue on Environmental Justice Policy, 10/2.

Shank, G., ed. (2002), *Social Justice*, Special Issue: Globalisation and Environmental Harm, 29 1/2.

Sutherland, E. (1949), *White Collar Crime*. New York: Dryden Press.

Tappan, P. (1947), 'Who is the Criminal?', *American Sociological Review*, 12: 96–102.

Tobias, M., ed. (1985), *Deep Ecology*. San Diego: Avant Books.

United Nations Environment Programme (2002), *Global Environment Outlook 3: Past Present and Future Perspectives*. Nairobi: UNEP.

Walters, R. (2004) 'Criminology and Genetically Modified Food', *British journal of Criminology*, 44/2: 151-67.

Williams, C., ed. (1996), *Social Justice*, special issue on Environmental Victims, 23/4.

World Commission on Environment and Development (1987), *Our Common Future*. Oxford: Oxford University Press.

Young, A. (1996), *Imagining Crime*. London: Sage.

# Part 2

# Dynamics of Environmental Crime

## Introduction

Broadly speaking, environmental crime is associated with harms against humans, against specific environments and against animals. Not all of these harms are illegal (such as the clearfelling of old growth forests). However, to some degree, they are all now being identified as problematic due to the work of those activists and academics who are defining harm in more expansive ways.

Recent years, for example, have seen greater legislative and judicial attention being given to the rights of the environment *per se*, and to the rights of certain species of nonhuman animal to live free from human abuse, torture and degradation. This reflects both the efforts of eco-rights activists (e.g., conservationists) and animal rights activists (e.g., animal liberation movements) in changing perceptions, and laws, with regard to the natural environment and nonhuman species. It also reflects the growing recognition that centuries of industrialisation and global exploitation of resources are (now rapidly) transforming the very basis of world ecology – global warming threatens us all, regardless of where we live or our specific socio-economic situation.

The movement from theory to practice, from conceptualisation to empirical demonstration, from abstract consideration to grounded research, is a reciprocal and continuous progression. The more we learn about the world around us, the more we think about the world; and the more we think about the world, the hungrier we get to learn more about how things work, about how life is constituted and reproduced, and about how the planet as a whole has got to be in the state it is in.

The study of environmental crime is theoretically informed by the kinds of considerations expressed in the first section of the reader. This section on the 'dynamics of environmental crime' includes readings that drill down from the lofty peaks of philosophy and at times highly convoluted spheres of theory to consider environmental crime in its more detailed, defined and concrete forms.

The section begins with several readings that provide a general summary and framing of environmental crime issues. Schmidt (Reading 13) takes the reader on a tour of various kinds of environmental crime, their costs to humanity and planetary wellbeing, their locations and their perpetrators. It is a benchmark study that provides an overview of the state of environmental crime worldwide. This is followed by White's typology describing the various ways in which environmental crime can be categorised and thought about in applied practical terms (Reading 14).

The next three readings deal in various ways with the problem of hazardous and toxic waste. Block (Reading 15) describes issues surrounding pollution and waste disposal, and highlights the criminal nature of some kinds of waste disposal (including the participation of organised criminal syndicates). Saha and Mohai (Reading 16) explore the practical ways in which environmental injustice manifests itself, and the choices and non-choices involved on the part of those who reside next to hazardous waste facilities. Santana (Reading 17) reminds us that among the most prolific of waste-producing industries is the military. Moreover, often the waste is particularly toxic (including for example, lead and radioactive substances) and dangerous to all that come into contact with it.

The notion of differential victimisation is an important aspect of the study of environmental crime, as illustrated in the work of Saha and Mohai among others in this compilation. Differential victimisation refers to the idea that some groups or classes of people are more negatively affected by environmental harms than others. This is also evident in the next group of papers. Pellow (Reading 18) provides a framework of analysis that is intended to enhance our understanding not only of the practice of illegal dumping, but the social processes and social inequalities surrounding the practice. Pinderhughes (Reading 19) continues the discussion by explicitly confronting the question of racism and environmental inequality. Much work has been done in places like the United States on how African Americans in particular suffer disproportionately poor environments compared with other cohorts of Americans. Brook (Reading 20) demonstrates that the problem also very much pertains to the indigenous peoples of North America as well.

The next few papers consider environmental harm that occurs in different places and in different industries. Tailby and Gant (Reading 21), for example, provide an overview of abalone poaching in Australia, including different kinds of perpetrators, the costs of such theft and so on. On the other side of the world, McMullan and Perrier (Reading 22) provide insight into lobster poaching in the Maritime Provinces of Canada. This paper examines the cultural processes and social networks that underlie poaching activity and generally favourable consumer responses to this. Walters (Reading 23) takes the reader to Zambia in order to consider the ways in which powerful nation-states are trying to impose genetically modified organisms (in this case, in maize) on less developed countries in ways that basically violate a number of international conventions and ethical obligations.

The final paper, by Lynch and Stretesky (Reading 24), provides important insights into how to undertake research into environmental crimes (such as distribution of toxic materials) through use of alternative sources of data. By drawing upon medical and epidemiological evidence, they demonstrate how victimisation and criminal activity can be documented without recourse or reference to crime statistics generated by criminal justice agencies. This allows for evidence to be put forward that is not dependent upon the latter agencies, many of which do not formally collect such data in the first place.

# 13. Environmental crimes: profiting at the earth's expense*

*Charles W. Schmidt*

Imagine for a moment that it's a hot summer day and you're driving; you roll up the windows in your car and turn on the air conditioning. As chilly air flows from the dashboard, you begin to feel comfortably insulated from the sweltering world outside. If your car was built in or before 1995, this soothing relief may be generated by a coolant called CFC-12, one of several chlorofluorocarbons (CFCs) implicated in the destruction of the ozone layer, a protective layer miles above the Earth that filters out carcinogenic ultraviolet rays.

In fact, CFCs are illegal under both international and domestic rules, unless they've been obtained from used equipment. But millions of cars in the United States still rely on CFC-based cooling systems, and retrofitting cars for safer alternatives is expensive: up to $500 per vehicle. The high cost of conversion has created a demand for contraband CFCs, which are conveniently delivered to the United States and elsewhere by a thriving black market. Contraband CFCs are so pervasive they have at times rivaled cocaine as among the most profitable illegal imports crossing U.S. borders. Meanwhile, illegal trade in these substances delays recovery of the ozone layer, heightening the risk of skin cancer for literally everyone under the sun.

The strong trade in CFCs is but one example of a growing international environmental crime problem. Criminal groups are making millions by trading in environmental contraband, hazardous waste, and endangered species of plants and animals. Still others profit by illegally dumping waste in the ocean or in developing countries, sometimes on behalf of companies eschewing high disposal costs at home.

## The international environmental crime threat

Although their effects can be global in nature, environmental crimes most often harm the world's poor disparately. Contraband waste, for instance, is usually dumped in underdeveloped countries that lack the legislative and technical

---

* From *Environmental Health Perspectives* (2004), 112(2): pp. A96–A103.

controls needed to protect vulnerable populations. Duncan Brack, an associate fellow at the Royal Institute of International Affairs (RIIA), a London-based international research group, says that in some countries, environmental crimes erode state authority and contribute to a culture of lawlessness.

Brack points out that certain regions of Honduras, for instance, have been abandoned to an increasingly uncivil society, with a violent culture fueled by illegal fishing and logging. 'These crimes degrade and in some cases completely destroy the natural resources that many local communities rely on for their survival,' Brack says, 'Illegal logging, fishing, and wildlife trades are almost invariably carried out at unsustainable levels, running down the natural capital from which poor people derive their livelihoods.'

International criminals have latched on to environmental contraband because it generates substantial and often easy profits. A 30-pound cylinder of colorless, odorless CFC-12 bought in China for US$40 can be sold on the U.S. black market for up to $600. Waste dumping can also be lucrative and virtually risk-free – the ocean's sheer size means dumping there can be extremely difficult to detect, and illegal waste, imports are widely thought to cross national borders easily, particularly in developing countries, where inspection systems are minimal. According to the most recent published estimates, contained in a December 2000 White House report titled *International Crime Threat Assessment*, illegal dumping generates up to $12 billion worldwide in criminal revenues annually. The endangered wildlife trade is also a financial bonanza for criminals. A single rhinoceros horn can earn one destitute poacher several hundred dollars, equivalent to a year's salary in some African countries. The same horn, ground up and used as a perceived remedy for impotence and other ailments, can fetch half a million dollars in Asia. Worldwide, illegal wildlife trading generates at least $10 billion a year, according to the U.S. Department of Justice.

Many experts now believe that international environmental crime threatens to become an even greater problem than it already is. According to Durwood Zaelke, who directs the International Network for Environmental Compliance and Enforcement (INECE), a multinational group of enforcement experts based in Washington, D.C., countries are generating more waste than ever, and disposal systems are often unable to meet growing demands. And natural resources of fish, exotic species, and timber are dwindling, which increases the street value of the stocks that remain. Thanks to the forces of economic globalization, contraband including CFCs, endangered species, and toxic waste is flowing through national borders that are disturbingly porous. Indeed, even in the United States only 2% of international cargo shipments receive any inspection at all, much less a thorough search for environmental contraband. A pervasive lack of enforcement also contributes to the growth of environmental crime, especially in developing countries where corruption, poverty, war, and other social problems are perceived as greater and more immediate threats.

Police organizations find that criminals who deal in environmental contraband often display little concern for the risk of capture. 'During our investigations, we are often faced with exuberant confidence by smugglers who feel they have nothing to fear,' says Alexander von Bismarck, a senior investigator with the Environmental Investigation Agency (EIA), a private organization based in London and Washington, D.C. 'Some of them act as if they've stumbled on a gold mine. During a recent undercover meeting, one dealer said, "This is better than drug smuggling."'

## Shortcomings of multinational treaties

Today, the battle against international environmental crime is waged through a system of multinational treaties addressing nearly every conceivable aspect of environmental protection. But despite their noble intents, nearly all of these hundreds of 'multilateral environmental agreements' (MEAs) lack effective enforcement capacity. Zaelke says that many MEA member countries – especially developing countries – don't have adequate institutional and legal frameworks to enforce treaty obligations.

Zaelke points to the Convention on International Trade in Endangered Species of Wild Fauna and Flora (CITES), which in 1973 banned the trade of thousands of plants and animals, as a case in point. Only about one-quarter of the 164 CITES member countries are thought to have even the minimum legislation to implement the treaty, Zaelke says.

Explanations for the lack of enforcement are both simple and complex, he says. 'It's simple in that it often isn't done at all, as in the case where a country doesn't even pass the national legislation needed to implement a treaty. And it's complex in that there are many reasons for these institutional failures, from a lack of funding, to a lack of political will to follow through on implementation.'

Usually, inadequate infrastructure for environmental protection is accompanied by a dearth of knowledge about the safe handling of hazardous materials. Criminals who take advantage of lax controls to illegally dump toxic waste place local populations at serious risk. In December 1998, for example, 3,000 tons of mercury-laden waste generated by Formosa Plastics of Taiwan was dumped in a field near Sihanoukville, Cambodia, allegedly sickening several villagers and sparking a rumor that the material was radioactive. In an ensuing riot, some 10,000 people fled the area, and 8 people were killed. (The waste was ultimately shipped back to Taiwan.)

Mark Measer, a criminal intelligence officer with Interpol, the international police organization based in Lyon, France, says most poor communities who handle these materials have no idea what they're being exposed to. 'They don't realize the threats they're facing, and they don't know what protective measures to take,' he explains. 'In the United States, these materials are all labeled and accompanied with safety procedures. But people in these poor communities usually handle this stuff with their bare hands and without respiratory protection.'

The task of investigating and prosecuting environmental crimes in developing countries is extremely challenging, Measer adds. Even where environmental laws exist, local police forces are often uneducated about environmental concerns or influenced by corrupt officials. Prosecution can also be held up by a lack of informed judges. The United Nations Environment Programme (UNEP) is particularly concerned about a lack of training in environmental law among the global judiciary, and has launched ongoing training efforts in this area.

But even an informed judiciary, well-trained investigators, and the political will to promote environmental enforcement can't necessarily prevent illegal trading, which will be exploited by criminals as long as they perceive a demand. CFC trades, for instance, are flourishing despite a ban imposed by the Montreal Protocol on Substances that Deplete the Ozone Layer, which is widely seen as the most successful MEA in existence, responsible for an 80% drop in CFC use since the treaty was enacted in 1989. The Montreal Protocol is currently ratified by 184 countries, including the United States, whose own vigorous efforts to enforce it have imposed $40 million in fines and 76 years of jail time.

As of the mid-1990s, some 20,000 tons of CFCs were being traded through black market channels, according to the EIA. The United States has traditionally been the biggest importer, but significant markets exist in Europe and Japan, and are emerging in some developing countries. A worldwide glut of CFCs has kept prices low and delayed efforts to replace the chemicals with nonpolluting alternatives, thereby advancing what many scientists believe is an impending ecological catastrophe – depletion of the ozone layer.

**Transit nations and illegal crime**

According to von Bismarck, 'transit nations' such as Singapore play a key role in illegal trading schemes. Transit nations are midpoints on global trade routes, places where cargo ships stop briefly en route to their final destinations. Singapore is one of the busiest transit ports in the world – nearly 40,000 containers pass through the island state every day.

The country is reputed to be efficient, reliable, and free of corruption, and yet it has emerged as a major hub for illegal CFCs and other environmental contraband. Why? 'Because transit inspections in Singapore are minimal and because the confidentiality of private business information there is highly respected,' von Bismarck says, 'brokers can unload cargo, repackage it, and reroute it to new destinations with minimal oversight from customs officials.' Thus, transit nations provide opportunities for smugglers to disguise material origins and make paper trails harder to follow.

Julian Newman, an investigator with the EIA's London office, adds that site visits to Singapore-based chemical brokers revealed CFCs were sitting out openly at the brokers' facilities. Says Newman, 'Transit controls in Singapore are totally lacking. We found these materials in yards, not in any sort of bonded areas under customs control. The brokers can do whatever they want with it.'

In November 2003, the EIA exposed the shadowy world of this illegal trade when it broke a CFC smuggling operation in Singapore. To catch the smugglers, EIA operatives established a phony company they called Hall Global Logistics that claimed to be seeking CFC-12 for South African clients. South Africa is a party to the Montréal Protocol and has enacted an import ban on CFCs. Three companies responded to the EIA's inquiry, but one – Leempeng Enterprise

– was particularly experienced in the intricacies of the trade, EIA investigators say. According to its website, Leempeng is a dealer for 'all kinds of aerosol and non-aerosol components and parts,' and its activities include the export of automotive coolants.

During a series of meetings with EIA operatives, Leempeng executives detailed precisely how illegal CFC-12 shipments to South Africa could be arranged. First, CFC-12 purchased from Chinese merchants would be repackaged in small aerosolized cans deliberately mislabeled as 'air-conditioner oil.' The cans would be concealed in legitimate shipping containers, whose accompanying documents would be falsified to trick customs agents. Finally, the CFCs would be shipped to a neighboring country and delivered to South Africa through a land border.

According to the EIA, Leempeng executives boasted of their smuggling experience, emphasizing links to personal contacts in multiple countries, including the United States, to which they have allegedly sold several CFC shipments of 25 tons each. The company is now under investigation by Singapore's National Environment Agency, which would not comment for this article.

## Disappearing hazardous waste

Perhaps no environmental contraband is as mysterious as the tons of hazardous waste that vanish every year into illicit dumps around the world. Included in this vast international waste heap are used batteries, electronic junk, old ships, toxic incinerator ash, industrial sludge, contaminated medical equipment, and military hardware. According to Zaelke, some 300–500 million tons of hazardous waste are known to be produced annually. 'Some of it is properly disposed of,' he says, 'As to the rest, we just don't know what happens to it. We are suspicious that much of it is dumped illegally.'

Citing 'Italian press sources,' the authors of *International Crime Threat Assessment* wrote that European crime groups export hazardous waste to countries throughout Europe, Asia, and Africa through a variety of 'trash for cash' schemes. According to the report, crime groups in Russia and Japan also capitalize on this illegal trade, which is often linked with money laundering, arms sales, and other illicit activities. The Italian Mafia, which has successfully infiltrated Italy's industrial waste disposal sector, is thought by several experts, including the authors of *International Crime Threat Assessment*, to be heavily involved. The report states that half of Italy's processed waste disappears annually, most of it presumably dumped abroad.

The main treaty that regulates hazardous waste trades today is the Basel Convention on the Control of Transboundary Movement of Hazardous Wastes and Their Disposal. Brokered in 1989 and now ratified by 158 countries, the Basel Convention imposes a system of informed consent on member countries, who must notify importers of impending waste shipments, and also must ensure that disposal methods minimize health and environmental impacts. Further, in 1995 the convention adopted an amendment known as the Basel Ban, which, if enacted, will ban the export of any hazardous waste for any reason from the 29 wealthiest nations of the Organization of Economic Cooperation and Development (OECD) to any non-OECD nation.

According to Jim Puckett, who cofounded and coordinates the nonprofit Basel Action Network (BAN) in Seattle, Washington, criminals can easily bypass the Basel Convention's barriers. The easiest way, and by far the most common, he says, is to simply mischaracterize the waste, for instance, by deliberately mislabeling hazardous waste barrels as containing environmentally innocuous materials. This was the tactic used by the now-defunct Japanese company Nisso, which in January 2000 was caught by the Filipino police trying to dump 2,700 tons of infectious medical waste in the Philippines, disguising it as recyclable scrap paper, when in actuality the waste was full of used needles, syringes, diapers, and other discarded hospital products. Greenpeace International subsequently found that illegal dumping of Japanese medical waste in the Philippines is a customary practice.

Like most other MEAs, the Basel Convention is stifled by inadequate implementing legislation among its members. According to the treaty secretariat, fully one-third of Basel countries are unable to enforce their treaty obligations. Some of these countries lack any ability to prevent illegal waste imports whatsoever. As reasons for noncompliance, countries cite a lack of resources, training, staff, expertise, and public awareness, in addition to lax border controls. Of course, the most noncompliant countries are typically poor and vulnerable not only to illegal waste dumps but also to highly toxic waste delivered for the purpose of 'recycling.'

**The recycling problem**

According to a 1994 Greenpeace International study, up to 90% of the waste shipped to the developing world is slated for recycling; BAN estimates that figure today may be as high as 99%. Unlike waste headed for disposal, recyclables have some economic value, typically in the form of residual metals. Spent lead-acid batteries, for instance, are a source of elemental lead, and galvanic sludges left over from electroplating activities contain nonferrous metals. Environmental problems occur when these materials aren't recycled at all, or are recycled in highly hazardous and polluting operations.

Measer says it's hard to determine if recyclable waste has been handled properly – and therefore legally – within importing countries. Developing nations don't often have the infrastructure they need to track the waste and monitor handling. If the waste is simply dumped, someone would have to report the incident to the proper domestic authorities. But if these same authorities have no ability or desire to investigate the incident, then it will likely go unpenalized, Measer says. Interpol may undertake an investigation, he adds, but only if the importing country requests it. 'We can't command the authorities to investigate. We can only respond to requests for assistance,' he explains.

In some instances, the challenge of prosecuting recycling crimes has less to do with enforcement capacity than it does with conflicting legal systems among the countries involved. China's cottage electronics recycling industry,

274

which processes much of the world's old computers and television sets, provides a case in point. According to a February 2002 report published by BAN and other advocacy groups titled *Exporting Harm: The High-Tech Trashing of Asia*, this industry poisons villagers and contaminates ecosystems. Electronics are often loaded with lead – cathode ray tubes in outmoded computer screens contain up to four pounds of the toxic metal each. Unprotected villagers are exposed to lead when they strip electronics of anything of value (for instance, copper coils), sometimes by burning the equipment or dissolving it in acidic fluids. China has banned these shipments; they are therefore illegal under both China's own domestic laws and the terms of the Basel Convention, to which China is a party. Even so, according to the report, the shipments still arrive daily, coordinated by Hong Kong brokers on behalf of Western exporters.

Roughly half this waste is thought to come from the United States, according to the Worldwatch Institute, an independent research organization in Washington, D.C. However, under U.S. law, electronics exports are legal – unlike China, the United States is not party to the Basel Convention and therefore has no binding obligation to its terms. Moreover, electronics waste is not considered hazardous under the Resource Conservation and Recovery Act; even if it were, the exports would still be legal under this domestic law because it is destined for 'recycling' rather than 'disposal.'

## A diplomatic stalemate

This confusing legal morass provides a diplomatic stalemate through which an environmental crime in China can be routinely perpetrated by the United States. Thus far, the United States has refused to ratify the Basel Convention, mainly, says Puckett, because it wants to protect its international recycling industry, which generates billions in annual revenue.

Environmental crime fighters will soon face a host of emerging challenges brought on by developments on the diplomatic front. Several important new treaties are coming into force, each of them banning trade in a host of toxic chemicals. Included among them are the Stockholm Convention on Persistent Organic Pollutants, which will require member nations to reduce or eliminate the production and use of 12 highly toxic compounds, and the Rotterdam Convention on the Prior Informed Consent Procedure for Certain Hazardous Chemicals and Pesticides in International Trade (PIC), which will seek to ensure that companies that export any of a designated set of hazardous chemicals obtain consent from importing nations before the shipments are received. Without consent, shipments of these chemicals can be denied passage through the receiving country's borders.

As they come into force, both these treaties will likely face the same difficulties plaguing MEAs in general: namely, no global enforcement provisions, inadequate border controls, and lack of political will to properly implement the treaties within domestic legislation. At the very least, says Puckett, such treaties should require mechanisms to gather the data to better understand and monitor border shipments.

Richard Emory, a senior attorney at the EPA, is strongly critical of the POPS and PIC conventions. In an article published in the 2002 *Colorado Yearbook of International Environmental Law,* Emory wrote that POPS does nothing and PIC does very little to define national measures and tools for effective shipment tracking and compliance monitoring for hazardous chemicals. Specifically, the treaties merely suggest that member countries 'take measures' to ensure that imports and exports are in compliance. What the treaties should – but do not – require, Emory wrote, are definitive documentation systems, such as manifests that identify shipments are regulated chemicals and provide the necessary information to ensure compliance. (Emory refused to be interviewed for this article.)

Jim Willis, who directs the UNEP Chemicals Unit, says some progress is being made in this area. For instance, the World Customs Organization recently announced it would establish customs codes for PIC chemicals and some key Basel Convention waste such as electronics waste, which will facilitate tracking to a degree, he says. 'We do seem to be noting progress in the ability of countries to safely manage such chemicals [through the MEA process],' he says. 'And the political priority of dealing with the chemicals seems to be increasing.' According to Willis, the best way for countries to respond to illegal trade is by ratifying the relevant conventions, implementing the necessary domestic laws, and ensuring that customs agents and other officials are adequately trained.

In May 2002, the RIIA convened a workshop on environmental black markets in London. The workshop's conclusions, contained in a November 2002 report titled *International Environmental Crime: The Nature and Control of Environmental Black Markets,* emphasize that illegal trade can be curbed if countries are willing to target flagrant violators, increase the use of sanctions and other penalties, encourage compliance through positive incentives, and mandate the use of identifying documents to flag MEA-governed shipments. Stakeholders have also suggested that countries must improve law enforcement coordination and information gathering, preferably through some sort of independent international body.

Along these lines, UNEP recently announced the creation of its 'Green-Customs' program, which was launched in June 2003. This program aims to improve coordinated intelligence gathering and training of customs agents, who are saddled with monitoring MEA-designated shipments and distinguishing them from the overwhelming volume of international cargo.

These efforts underscore the potential usefulness of international networks that link regulatory agencies, law enforcement officials, prosecutors, non-governmental organizations, and other stakeholders in an effort to more effectively police environmental crimes. Networks could make it easier to work internationally across a broad spectrum of cultures, languages, legal systems, and governments by creating acceptable environmental standards that the global community can refer to when attempting to hold a country accountable. 'A network can raise awareness about a particular enforcement issue and help channel resources to where they're most needed,' Zaelke says. 'They also can be used to assist countries to develop and implement legislation and coordinate law enforcement strategies across national borders.'

Today, environmental crime is an issue that is being intensely studied and dissected, even if efforts to fight it are still largely inadequate. Meanwhile, criminals continue to raise the ante; many of them simply incorporate penalties into the cost of doing business. Stopping these crimes will require officials to wield an ever bigger stick and increase the resources to deal with them. But boosting the capacity to fight environmental criminals is an enormous challenge, one that requires resources, determination, and political will. If environmental criminals are to be checked, then they must be fought with a level of severity at least equal to the ecological threats they pose.

# 14. Environmental crime in global context: exploring the theoretical and empirical complexities*

*Rob White*

## Introduction

Environmental issues have generated considerable public interest in recent years, and not surprisingly criminologists and other social scientists are now likewise turning their attention to how best to define and respond to environmental harm (Lynch and Stretesky 2003; White 2003). Insofar as major environmental changes are occurring on the global scale, with significant impacts at the local level, so too greater urgency and critical analysis about environmental matters has grown. Simultaneously, similar kinds of local issues are being repeated across the globe, making us realise that the global and the local are frequently intertwined and in many ways inseparable. This is often encapsulated in the term 'glocalisation' (see Crowley 1998).

The task of trying to understand, interpret and act upon matters that are often systemic, complicated and intrinsically inter-connected poses certain dilemmas for the criminologist. For instance, our interest and knowledge in this area may well be growing (albeit from a rudimentary base), but the more we know, the less secure we seem to be in the knowledge that we have. The very complexities of the issues can make it daunting to tackle them. It certainly makes things analytically challenging.

Consider, for example, the following observations. The development of a green or environmental criminology as a field of sustained research and scholarship will by its very nature incorporate many different perspectives and strategic emphases. Environmental criminology:

> deals with concerns across a wide range of environments (e.g., land, air, water) and issues (e.g., fishing, pollution, toxic waste). It involves conceptual analysis as well as practical intervention on many fronts, and includes multi-disciplinary strategic assessment (e.g., economic, legal, social and ecological evaluations). It involves the undertaking of organisational analysis, as well as investigation of 'best practice' methods of monitoring, assessment, enforcement and education regarding environmental protection and regulation. Analysis needs to be conscious

* From *Current Issues in Criminal Justice* (2005), 16(3): pp. 271–285.

of local, regional, national and global domains and how activities in each of these overlap. It likewise requires cognisance of the direct and indirect, and immediate and long-term, impacts and consequences of environmentally sensitive social practices (White 2003: 484).

One challenge for environmental criminology is to separate out different levels and kinds of analysis, and to 'make sense' of what is a very complicated whole. This is the intent of the present paper. That is, I wish to explore the conceptual and research challenges of studying environmental harm as a criminological phenomenon. In order to do so, I wish to utilise an analytical mapping exercise that covers key areas of potential interest to criminologists. This is followed by an appraisal of how environmental crime itself is socially constructed. To illustrate this we will consider issues pertaining to fishing and social regulation.

## Analytical mapping of environmental harm

To understand complexity, we need to simplify. My objective in this section is to identify some important areas for analytical consideration and to discuss these in abstract conceptual terms. Specifically, I wish to discuss environmental issues in regards to four types of perspective: focal considerations; geographical considerations; locational considerations; and temporal considerations (see Table 14.1).

**Table 14.1**  Mapping of environmental harm

| | | | |
|---|---|---|---|
| *Focal Considerations*: [Identify issues pertaining to victims of harm] | | | |
| Environmental Justice [human beings] | Ecological Justice [bio-sphere, including plants and animals] | | |
| *Geographical Considerations*: [Identify issues pertaining to each geographical level] | | | |
| International | National | Regional/State | Local |
| *Locational Considerations*: [Identify issues pertaining to specific kinds of sites] | | | |
| 'Built' Environments [e.g., urban, rural, suburban] | 'Natural' Environments [e.g., ocean, wilderness, desert] | | |
| *Temporal Considerations*: [Identify issues pertaining to changes over time] | | | |
| Environmental Effects [short-term/long-term] | Environmental Impact [manifest/latent] | Social Impact [immediate/lasting] | |

Exploration of themes and issues within each of these areas exposes the diversity of perspectives, approaches and concepts that are utilised in the field of environmental criminology.

### Focal considerations

By 'focal' considerations I refer to concerns that centre on the key actors or players who are at the centre of investigation into environmental harm. In other words, the emphasis is on identifying issues pertaining to the victims of harm, including how to define whom or what is indeed an environmental 'victim'.

How we understand the relationship between human beings and the environment is crucial to defining and responding to environmental issues (see Table 14.2). Different perspectives or eco-philosophies include: anthropocentric (or human-centred); biocentric (or species-centred); and ecocentric (socio-ecological centred). These perspectives can be assessed on the basis of how they conceive environmental problems, how they depict the role of humans in the production of such problems and how they approach the issue of environmental regulation (see Halsey and White 1998).

For many of those working on environmental issues, the question of broad philosophy translates into specific concerns with the idea of eco-human rights or ecological citizenship (see for example, Halsey 1997; Smith 1998). What does this mean in practice? It means that present generations ought to act in ways that do not jeopardise the existence and quality of life of future generations. It also means that we ought to extend the moral community to include non-human nature. By doing so, we enter a new politics of obligation:

> In ecological thought, human beings have obligations to animals, trees, mountains, oceans, and other members of the biotic community. This means that human beings have to exercise extreme caution before embarking upon any project which is likely to have the possibility of adverse effects upon the ecosystems concerned (Smith 1998: 99).

This particular notion of ecological citizenship thus centres on human obligations to all living things, and to carefully assess the impacts of human activity across the human and non-human domains.

However, such considerations are not without their problems. Thus, the conceptualisation of 'rights' is itself contentious when extended to the non-human (see Christoff 2000). For example, should environmental rights be seen as an extension of human or social rights (e.g., related to the quality of human life, such as provision of clean water), or should human rights be seen as merely one component of complex eco-systems that should be preserved for their own sake (i.e., as in the notion of the rights of the environment)? While increasingly acknowledged in international law, the environment connection with human rights continues to be somewhat ambiguous and subject to diverse practical interpretations (Thornton and Tromans 1999). Nevertheless, such ambiguities and tensions over 'rights' are essential parts of the criminological debates characteristic of the shift from eco-philosophy to conceptions of environmental crime.

280

**Table 14.2**  Eco-Philosophies

---

*Anthropocentrism*
- superiority of humans over all other living and non-living entities
- non-human nature viewed instrumentally
- humans are separate from world's ecosystem
- ideological basis for human activity is self-interest
- highly centralised organs of power: nation-states and corporations
- concern with economic interests and profits
- strategy of 'sustainable development'
- emphasis on 'management' of resources
- domination of humans by humans, and domination of non-human nature by humans

*Biocentrism*
- biocentric equality
- human beings have same moral worth as other 'species' on planet
- non-human species have intrinsic value
- ideological basis for activity is preservation and realisation of all species
- reduces the social to the biological: 'survival of the fittest'
- 'natural selection' of human beings (via war, disease, famine) is not a problem
- human pursuits should ideally be directed by an understanding of 'Gaian Truth'
- decisions concerning the environment should be made according to which outcomes are most likely to foster the widest possible diversity of life, both non-human and human
- emphasis on 'righteous management' involving mass preservation of wilderness etc.
- issue of interplay between human rights and 'biotic' rights

*Ecocentrism*
- humans and their activities are inextricably integrated with the rest of the natural world
- human have the capacity to deploy methods of production which have global consequences; therefore, they have a responsibility to ensure that such production methods do not exceed the ecospheric limits of the planet
- live simply so that others [human and non-human] may simply live
- balance between instrumental and intrinsic conceptions of non-human nature
- dialectical nature of the relationship between human action and non-human processes, interconnectedness of life
- social justice is equally important and inextricably bound to issues of ecology
- work with non-human nature, and a commitment to collective needs
- principles of participatory democracy, via bioregionalism, and constant movement between local initiative and global solidarity

---

*Source*: adapted from Halsey and White, 1998.

Within criminology there are significant issues surrounding scale, activities and legalities as these pertain to environmental harm. A strict legalist approach tends to focus on the central place of criminal law in the definition of criminality. Thus, as Situ and Emmons (2000: 3) see it: 'An environmental crime is an unauthorised act or omission that violates the law and is therefore subject to criminal prosecution and criminal sanctions'. However, other writers argue that, as with criminology in general, the concept of 'harm' ought to encapsulate those activities that may be legal and 'legitimate' but which nevertheless negatively impact on people and environments (Lynch and Stretsky 2003).

The responses of the state to environmental harm (however defined) are guided by a concern with environmental protection. This is generally framed in terms of ensuring future resource exploitation, and dealing with specific instances of victimisation that have been socially defined as a problem. Risk management in this case is directed at preventing or minimising certain destructive or injurious practices into the future, based upon analysis and responses to harms identified in the present.

Analysis of environmental issues proceeds on the basis that someone or something is indeed being harmed. *Environmental justice* refers to the distribution of environments among peoples in terms of access to and use of specific natural resources in defined geographical areas, and the impacts of particular social practices and environmental hazards on specific populations (e.g., as defined on the basis of class, occupation, gender, age, ethnicity). In other words, the concern is with human beings as the centre of analysis. The focus of analysis therefore is on human health and wellbeing and how these are affected by particular types of production and consumption.

Here we can distinguish between environmental issues that affect everyone, and those that disproportionately affect specific individuals and groups (see Williams 1996; Low and Gleeson 1998). In some instances, there may be a basic 'equality of victims', in that some environmental problems threaten everyone in the same way, as in the case for example of ozone depletion, global warming, air pollution and acid rain (Beck 1996). As extensive work on specific incidents and patterns of victimisation demonstrate, however, it is also the case that some people are more likely to be disadvantaged by environmental problems than others. For instance, American studies have identified disparities involving many different types of environmental hazards that adversely affect people of colour throughout the United States (Bullard 1994). There are thus patterns of 'differential victimisation' that are evident with respect to the siting of toxic waste dumps, extreme air pollution, access to safe clean drinking water and so on (see Chunn *et al.* 2002; Williams 1996). Another dimension of differential victimisation relates to the subjective disposition and consciousness of the people involved. The specific groups who experience environmental problems may not always describe or see the issues in strictly environmental terms. This may be related to knowledge of the environmental harm, explanations for calamity and socio-economic pressures to 'accept' environmental risk (see Julian 2004). The environmental justice discourse challenges the dominant discourses by placing *inequalities* in the distribution of environmental quality at the top of the environmental agenda (see Julian 2004; Harvey 1996).

By way of contrast, *ecological justice* refers to the relationship of human beings generally to the rest of the natural world, and includes concerns relating to the health of the bio-sphere, and more specifically plants and creatures that also inhabit the biosphere (see Benton 1998; Franklin 1999). The main concern is with the quality of the planetary environment (that is frequently seen to possess its own intrinsic value) and the rights of other species (particularly animals) to life free from torture, abuse and destruction of habitat. Specific practices, and choices, in how humans interact with particular environments present immediate and potential risks to everything within them.

In specific areas, concepts such as speciesism may be invoked. This refers to the practice of discriminating against non-human animals because they are perceived as inferior to the human species in much the same way that sexism and racism involve prejudice and discrimination against women and people of different colour (Munro 2004). However, it is important to recognise that the environmental justice discourse is critical of many mainstream environmental groups precisely because of their 'focus on the fate of "nature" rather than humans' (Harvey 1996: 386). To put it differently, taking action on environmental issues involves choices and priorities. Many communities who suffer from the 'hard end' of environmental harm feel that their wellbeing ought to take priority over 'natural environments' or specific plants and animals as such.

### Geographical considerations

Students of environmental harm have to be cognisant of the varying issues that pertain to different geographical levels. As alluded to above, some issues are of a planetary scale (e.g., global warming), others regional (e.g., oceans and fisheries), some are national in geographical location (e.g., droughts in Australia), while others are local (e.g., specific oil spills). Similarly, laws tend to be formulated in particular geographically defined jurisdictions. With regard to nation-states such as Australia, relevant laws include international law, federal laws, state laws and local government by-laws.

Intervention on environmental issues requires not only new concepts of justice and rights, they also require acknowledgement of transnational processes and responsibilities. It has been pointed out that:

> ... transnational economic processes, transcontinental cultural links and transboundary environmental impacts have generated a new democratic deficit – the remedy of which requires new forms and institutions for democratic participation which extend beyond the borders of the nation-state (Christoff 2000: 200).

The telecommunications revolution has brought the world into the lounge rooms of the advanced industrialised countries and extended the scope of our knowledge of the fate of previously unheard of places and species. It has also expanded public or commonsense knowledge of the inter-connected nature of environmental processes (and harms), which finds expression in the catchphrase 'Think globally, act locally'. Institutionally, the concern with environmental wellbeing is manifest explicitly in the priority areas of international policing.

From the point of view of international law enforcement agencies, the major issues relating to environmental crime are:

- the trans-border movement and dumping of *waste products*;
- the illegal traffic in real or purported *radioactive or nuclear substances*; and
- the illegal traffic in species of *wild flora and fauna*.

These areas have been identified by agencies such as Interpol as key subjects in relation to environmental crime. It is worth exploring the first of these in greater depth, given that much of the transfer of waste has been from advanced industrialised countries to 'third world' countries.

The biggest exporter of toxic waste is the United States. Hazardous residues and contaminated sludge are most likely to find a foreign home in a Third World country. The pressures for this are twofold. On the one hand, the US has seen the closing of many domestic landfills due to public health problems, and increasing public consciousness of the dangers posed by toxic waste. On the other hand, poor countries (and corrupt state officials) may find it financially attractive to offer their land as sites for US waste (see Rosoff, Pontell and Tillman 1998).

The problem is not only the transfer of toxic waste; it is the generation of toxic waste in other countries by companies based in advanced industrialised nations. The classic case of this are the *maquiladoras*, American-owned factories set up across the border in Mexico. Here, environmental regulation is lax, with resulting high levels of chemical pollution, contamination and exposure to toxic materials. Closer to home for Australians, is the huge environmental damage caused to the *Ok Tedi* river in Papua New Guinea by the activities of the Australian mining corporation BHP (see Low and Gleeson 1998). Because the PNG government was dependent on the earnings from the Ok Tedi copper mine it actively cooperated with BHP in the destruction of local rain forest and much of the river system. Many villagers have lost the entire environment that supported their way of life (Low and Gleeson 1998: 8).

These examples highlight the fact that to understand the overall direction of environmental issues demands analysis of the strategic location and activities of transnational capital, as supported by hegemonic nation-states on a world scale. Capitalist globalisation, bolstered via neo-liberal state policy, means that there is great scope to increase environmentally destructive activity. This is demonstrated in how the traffic in risk occurs at the global level where developing countries play the same role as the poorer communities within the developed nations (e.g., 'business-friendly' countries that accept hazardous industries and toxic wastes). The issue here is how best to respond to NIMBY [Not In My Backyard] opposition within developed countries in ways that do not simply shift the problem elsewhere.

> The structural difference of economic needs and government regulation between the developed and developing worlds, and the absence of any supra-national body to ensure consistency in environmental standards, has encouraged western industrial capital to shift unpopular and increasingly illegal hazard-producing activities and wastes across national boundaries to states which often define, and welcome, these transfers as 'investment' (Low and Gleeson 1998: 121).

For criminologists, the challenge is to incorporate notions of environmental justice into their overall analytical framework by maintaining a sense of global scale. It also requires understanding of the political economy of environmental harm (White 2002).

### Locational considerations

We can make a distinction between geographical area and 'place'. The latter refers to specific kinds of sites as described in the language of 'natural' and 'built' environment. There is considerable overlap, interconnection and interplay between these types of environments. Nevertheless, the distinction is useful, particularly when assessing which environmental issues appeal to which sections of the population and for what reasons (Tranter 2004).

In simple terms, we can describe the 'Built' environment as basically referring to significant sites of human habitation and residency. It includes urban and rural areas, and areas of cross-over between the two consisting of major regional concentrations of people, commuter suburbs and zones, and so on. The 'Natural' environment consists of wilderness, oceans, rivers and deserts. These are sites in which human beings may be present, or through which they may traverse, but which are often seen as distinctive and 'separate' from human settlement per se (however, this needs to be qualified by acknowledging different ways in which humans interact with their environments, reflecting different cultural and material relationships to the land – see Langton 1998).

What constitutes an environmental harm or environmental crime is partly a matter of visibility of the issues, partly a matter of public policy. What can be identified via personal experiences, expert representation or sectional interest group as being worthy of attention, is that which is most likely to gain recognition as a public issue (see Hannigan 1995). Meanwhile, governments have laws across a wide range of issues, relating to air, water, toxic waste, use of public lands, endangered species and the list goes on. The relationship between public policy and government strategic action is also shaped by contingency – specific events, situations and disasters tend to shake things up rapidly and with immediate effect.

The precise nature of an environmental issue is in itself linked to specific group interests and consciousness of harm. For example, environmental issues have been categorised according to three different types of harm (Crook and Pakulski 1995; Tranter 2004; see also Curson and Clark 2004). These are set out in Table 14.3.

The significance of conceptualising environmental issues in this way is that it demonstrates the link between environmental action (usually involving distinct types of community and environmental groups), and particular sites (such as urban centres, wilderness areas or seacoast regions). Some issues tend to resonate more with members of the public than others; other issues generally only emerge if an accident or disaster brings it to the fore.

The mobilisation of opinion is crucial to determination of what is or is not considered a 'crime' (or 'harm'), and how the state will in the end respond to the phenomenon in question. The complex relationship between human and non-human 'rights' is thus played out in practice through the importance of

**Table 14.3** Colouring environmental issues

---

*'Brown' issues*
- air pollution
- pollution of urban stormwater
- pollution of beaches
- pesticides
- oil spills
- pollution of water catchments
- disposal of toxic/hazardous waste

*'Green' issues*
- acid rain
- habitat destruction
- loss of wildlife
- logging of forests
- depletion of ozone layer
- toxic algae
- invasive species via human transport
- water pollution

*'White' issues*
- genetically modified organisms
- food irradiation
- in vitro processes
- cloning of human tissue
- genetic discrimination
- environmentally-related communicable diseases
- pathological indoor environments

---

'place' in the lives of diverse communities. This inevitably leads to conflicts over purposes, as each place or site is subject to competing demands – jobs (via logging), recreation (via tourism), sustenance (via settlement), aesthetics (via photography) and so on. Disputes over value and use are settled using the full range of political, ideological, legal, coercive and persuasive means available to stakeholder parties.

### Temporal considerations

Another key issue for consideration relates to issues pertaining to changes over time. To some extent, such considerations are ingrained in contemporary environmental impact assessment in the guise of the 'precautionary principle' (Harvey 1998; Deville and Harding 1997). That is, what we do with and in the environment has consequences, some of which we cannot foresee.

Temporal considerations can be distinguished in terms of environmental effects, environmental impacts and social impacts. The short-term effects of environmental degradation include such things as the release of chlorofluorocarbons into the atmosphere, the long-term effect being the accumulation of greenhouse gases and ultimately climate warming. Environmental impacts begin with global warming as a manifest consequence of planetary change, and results in the latent consequences of changes in sea levels and changes in regional temperatures and precipitation (among other things). The social impacts of environmental change are both immediate, as in the case of respiratory problems or increased probability of disease outbreak, and long-term (e.g., lower quality of life, alteration of physiological functioning).

From the point of view of eco-philosophy, the tendency has been for anthropocentric perspectives to dominate when it comes to answering the questions, *what to do, over what period of time?* And yet, protection of the environment very often requires criteria that go beyond a human-centred approach. To put it differently, the appropriate time scale for understanding resource and population stability is generally much longer than we are used to:

> Different systems move along different time scales. Geology works in the millions of years; economics in the tens of years; biology from a few minutes to a few centuries; evolutionary biology from a few years to millions of years. Appropriate time scales depend on how long it takes for things to happen in the subject area (Page 1991: 64).

The importance of temporal concerns is reflected in cultures that view the relationship between people and the environment in holistic, reciprocal terms. The concept of 'balance' in some indigenous communities, for example, remains of vital significance: 'This precarious balance still exists, and the relationship between plants, animals, the elements, the air, water, wind and earth are all equally and evenly placed within the whole' (Robyn 2002: 202). Here we see a value system and code of ethics that embodies living within one's means and living within and as part of nature (see also Langton 1998). It is an ecocentric approach to life.

The philosophy of living in and with nature is empirically reflected in two phenomena: one relating to 'place', the other to 'time'.

> The diversity of Native cultures and kinds of social organizations which developed through time represent a high degree of social/political complexity and are varied according to the demands and necessities of the environment. For example, American Indian nations organized at the band level of social/political development have used effective strategies to take advantage of marginal habitats such as the Arctic and deserts of the Americas where resources are limited (Robyn 2002: 198–199).

Importantly, such systems are usually decentralised, communal and self-reliant: 'These societies live closely with and depend on the life contained in that particular ecosystem. This way of living enabled Indigenous communities to live for thousands of years in continuous sustainability' (Robyn 2002: 1999).

The point of this discussion is that evaluation of environmental issues needs to consider the element of time: negatively, from the perspective of short- and long-term consequences of environmental harm; positively, from the perspective of 'what works' in protecting and preserving environments.

In summary, I have tried to demonstrate that there are a number of intersecting dimensions that need to be considered in any analysis of specific instances of environmental crime. These include consideration of who the victim is (human or non-human); where the harm is manifest (global through to local levels); the main site in which the harm is apparent (built or natural environment); and the time frame within which harm can be analysed (immediate and delayed consequences). While this represents a form of analytical mapping of environmental harm, that illustrates the complexities of such analysis, it remains to be seen how such mapping might assist in explaining the 'real world' of environmental criminalisation.

## Social construction of environmental issues

To some extent an abstract model or mapping of environmental harm can be useful in exposing areas of further research and consideration, beyond that dealt with formally by law enforcement agencies and the criminal justice system at present. However, it can also be used to assist in explaining why it is that some types of human activity are more likely to be subject to criminalisation than others. The theme of this section is how environmental crime is socially constructed. Specifically, the concern is to identify those elements that together result in activity being deemed harmful, and thereby worthy of investigation and prosecution.

When considering these matters, it is useful to bear in mind the following questions (see White 2004):

### What is the problem?

In order to do this we have to deal with issues of definition and evidence of harm. We have to analyse potentially competing claims as to whether or not the problem exists, and diverse lay and expert opinion on how the problem is interpreted. Does it pose a risk, and if so, to whom, and in what ways? Is the initial problem serious enough in the public's eye to warrant a social response in the form of community action or state intervention?

### Why does the problem occur?

To answer this we need to examine the social context, and to investigate the actions of key actors involved with the phenomenon.

### What are the social dynamics that allow the problem to persist or ensure that state action is taken to overcome it?

To answer this we need to tackle issues pertaining to the shaping of perceptions, interpretation of events, and intervention processes. Is the problem socially constructed as a *social problem* warranting social action? In what ways is the problem construed from the point of view of *social regulation* and what forms of state and private intervention are mobilised to contain or manage the problem? Is the problem itself to be addressed, or is the focus on how best to avoid, cover-up or manage any risk associated with the problem?

### A case study: Abalone theft

In recent years the stealing of abalone has come to prominence and, indeed, is touted as one of the key areas in which environmental crime, as crime, is being addressed in a concerted way in Australia. We want to know why this is the case, especially given that environmental harm in many other cases draws much less state attention.

The abalone industry is highly regulated, with strict quotas enforced, limited numbers of licensed divers and extensive documentation of each catch required. Part of the reason for this high level of regulation is that the industry is a major export earner, bringing in over $100 million a year. Australia produces about one-third of the global wild abalone harvest, and it has been pointed out that 'Australia's stake in global supply has increased following the decline and/or disappearance of abalone populations in other parts of the world – including Japan, Mexico, South Africa and the United States (California) – due to negative environmental conditions, limited stocks, illegal fishing and poor fisheries management' (Taiby and Gant 2002: 1). Global demand for abalone, and high profits from abalone sales, have contributed to the growth in illegal harvesting.

The illegal abalone market has been described in terms of five categories of offender (Tailby and Gant 2002). In summary, these include:

- Organised poachers who operate in crews and harvest large quantities.
- Licensed divers who engage in over-quota fishing and docket fraud.
- Shore-based divers who access certain poaching spots.
- Extended family groups who engage in double-bagging.
- Individuals who take over-bag limit.

Our main interest here is with the organised stealers of abalone (although there is some over-lap with licensed divers, who may use the same networks for processing and distributing the catch). There are several features of these groups that warranted particular attention (Tailby and Gant 2002; Leonard 2004; Little 2004). For example, organised poachers frequently have sophisticated infrastructure to facilitate the theft – boats, infrared night vision equipment, scuba gear, hired transport vehicles, light aircraft and so on. Illegal processing of the abalone may also be quite sophisticated, and involve canning, drying or cryovac (vacuum) packaging.

Abalone thieves of this kind are willing to cross state borders to harvest abalone. Increasingly, it appears that organised criminal groups are moving into the industry, including outlaw motorcycle gangs and Asian crime figures. The illicit networks extend across state boundaries (from Tasmania to Queensland, or Victoria to New South Wales, for example). They also cross international boundaries, as one of the more lucrative markets for illegally harvested abalone is Asia. It has also been suggested that there are links between trade in illegal Australian abalone and the illicit drug markets. Again, these links transcend state and national boundaries.

Given the negative impact of illegal harvesting, use and sale of abalone on the legitimate industry, on royalty/tax revenue to the state and on abalone stocks generally, concerted efforts have been made to counter the illegal industry. Illegal accessing and processing of abalone is criminalised, both in terms of the law and in terms of resources put into the law enforcement process. Thus, 'Each abalone-producing state has legislation carrying high pecuniary penalties and custodial sentences for abalone offending, and has dedicated abalone-crime investigators' (Tailby and Gant 2002: 5). In Tasmania, for example, offenders may be prosecuted under the state's Criminal Code for offences such as lying to public officials and receiving or possessing stolen property, or they may be subject to two indictable offences under the Living Marine Resources Management Act 1995 that refer to illegally taken fish and falsifying documents (Leonard 2004; Little 2004). Each area of law imputes that the illegal action is treated as a serious matter. This is also apparent in the penalties assigned to offenders. For example, as a result of the joint efforts of the National Crime Authority and Tasmania Police in 'Operation Oakum', an investigation into abalone theft, several people have been sentenced to prison, including a two-year term of imprisonment in one particular case (Australian Crime Commission 2004; see also Tasmania Police 2004).

Investigation of abalone-related criminality features the use of a broad spectrum of police powers, including phone taps, dedicated surveillance, monitoring of documentation, and surprise inspections of processing facilities (Little 2004; Leonard 2004; Tailby and Gant 2002). The cross-border elements of the crime mean that it is of interest and concern to national law enforcement agencies such as the National Crime Authority (now the Australian Crime Commission), to state police services, to relevant fisheries bodies both at the national (National Fisheries Compliance Committee) and state levels (e.g., Fisheries Monitoring and Quota Audit Unit, Tasmania), to the Australian Customs Service, and the Australian Quarantine Inspection Service. In other words, dealing with the crime necessarily involves a wide range of agencies at the local, regional, national and international levels. Cooperation amongst enforcement and monitoring agencies is essential, and agencies such as the NCA have played an important role in providing crossjurisdictional coordination, access to substantial investigatory powers and use of advanced surveillance technologies.

There are a number of interrelated reasons why abalone theft has been defined and successfully prosecuted as an environmental crime. The social construction of environmental harm, in this instance, is largely due to the complexities of the issues and, ultimately, the economic bottom line (see Table 14.4).

Analysis of the different dimensions of an environmental issue can be used to both explain why some activities are subject to criminalisation, and why some are not. A case study approach can provide useful insights into how and why this is so. The framing of abalone poaching as a 'crime' by law enforcement officials is basically achieved precisely because of strong institutional (read economic) pressures to do so. By contrast, environmental harms that are ecologically problematic but economically lucrative, such as clearfelling of old growth forests, seldom attract official sanction. In such circumstances, it is left to green activists and environmental movements to contest the master definition of the situation and to thereby call into question the political processes by which the 'legal' and the 'illegal' are determined.

**Table 14.4**  Mapping of Abalone stealing as a crime

---

*Focal Considerations*:
[Identify issues pertaining to victims of harm]

| | |
|---|---|
| **Criminalisation** | link to breaches of criminal law; criminal breaches of maritime law |
| **Anthropocentric** | link to business interests, state income and exploitation of resource for human benefit |

---

*Geographical Considerations*:
[Identify issues pertaining to each geographical level]

| | |
|---|---|
| **Cross-border** | link to national/state mobilisation of resources, facilities and powers |
| **International** | link to operational matters, international trade |

---

*Locational Considerations*:
[Identify issues pertaining to specific kinds of sites]

| | |
|---|---|
| **Ocean/Coastal** | link to nature of detection/surveillance [crime initiated] |
| **City/Factories** | link to surveillance, use of telephones, communications, transportation [crime realised] |

---

*Temporal Considerations*:
[Identify issues pertaining to changes over time]

| | |
|---|---|
| **Resource depletion** | link to immediate and longer-term impacts, especially in the light of world share of market |
| **Realisation of value in formal and informal markets** | link to current global price for abalone |

---

## Conclusion

The intention of this paper has been to acknowledge the different ways in which environmental crime can be analysed, and to identify potential dimensions that might be considered in investigations of environmental issues. The paper has discussed issues relating to focal targets (e.g., human beings and non-human nature), scale (e.g., local, regional, global), consequences (e.g., immediate, long term), and time-scale in gauging events, activities and harms. A series of charts were introduced as a means to illustrate key points and to summarise potential areas of analytical concern. By charting out the issues in this way, we are better able to signpost future research projects and to gauge what further work needs to be done to advance environmental criminology as a field of inquiry.

## References

Australian Crime Commission (2004) *Annual Report 2002-2003*, Australian Crime Commission, Canberra.

Beck, U (1996) 'World Risk Society as Cosmopolitan Society? Ecological Questions in a Framework of Manufactured Uncertainties', *Theory, Culture, Society*, vol 13, no 4, pp 1– 32.

Benton, T (1998) 'Rights and Justice on a Shared Planet: more rights or new relations?', *Theoretical Criminology*, vol 2, no 2, pp 149–175.

Bullard, R (1994) *Unequal Protection: Environmental Justice and Communities of Color*, Sierra Club Books, San Francisco.

Christoff, P (2000) 'Environmental Citizenship', in Hudson, W and Kane, J (eds) *Rethinking Australian Citizenship*, Cambridge University Press, Melbourne.

Chunn, D, Boyd, S and Menzies, R (2002) '"We all live in Bhopal": Criminology Discovers Environmental Crime', in Boyd, Chunn and Menzies (eds) *Toxic Criminology: Environment, Law and the State in Canada*, Fernwood Publishing, Halifax.

Crook, S and Pakulski, J (1995) 'Shades of Green: Public Opinion on Environmental Issues in Australia', *Australian Journal of Political Science*, vol 30, pp 39–55.

Crowley, K (1998) '"Glocalisation" and Ecological Modernity: challenges for local environmental governance in Australia', *Local Environment*, vol 3, no 1, pp 91–97.

Curson, P and Clark, L (2004) 'Pathological Environments', in White, R (ed) *Controversies in Environmental Sociology*, Cambridge University Press, Melbourne.

Deville, A and Harding, R (1997) *Applying the Precautionary Principle*, The Federation Press, Sydney.

Franklin, A (1999) *Animals and Modern Cultures: A Sociology of Human-Animal Relations in Modernity*, Sage, London.

Halsey, M (1997) 'Environmental Crime: Towards an Eco-Human Rights Approach', *Current Issues in Criminal Justice*, vol 8, no 3, pp 217–242.

Halsey, M and White, R (1998) 'Crime, Ecophilosophy and Environmental Harm', *Theoretical Criminology*, vol 2, no 3, pp 345–371.

Hannigan, J (1995) *Environmental Sociology: A Social Constructionist Perspective*, Routledge, London.

Harvey, D (1996) *Justice, Nature and the Geography of Difference*, Blackwell, Oxford.

Harvey, N (1998) *Environmental Impact Assessment: Procedures, Practice, and Prospects in Australia*, Oxford University Press, Melbourne.

Julian, R (2004) 'Inequality, Social Differences and Environmental Resources', in White, R (ed) *Controversies in Environmental Sociology*, Cambridge University Press, Melbourne.

Langton, M (1998) *Burning Questions: Emerging environmental issues for indigenous peoples in northern Australia*, Centre for Indigenous Natural and Cultural Resource Management, Darwin.

Leonard, G (2004) Personal communication, 9 November 2004 [in his capacity as Chief Investigations Officer, Fisheries Monitoring and Quota Audit Unit, Tasmania].

Little, C (2004) Personal communication, 9 November 2004 [in his capacity as Tasmania Police member of Operation Oakum].

Low , N and Gleeson, B (1998) *Justice, Society and Nature: An Exploration of Political Ecology*, Routledge, London.

Lynch, M and Stretsky, P (2003) 'The Meaning of Green: Contrasting criminological perspectives', *Theoretical Criminology*, vol 7, no 2, pp 217–238.

Munro, L. (2004) 'Animals, 'Nature' and Human Interests' in White, R (ed) *Controversies in Environmental Sociology*, Cambridge University Press, Melbourne.

Page, T (1991) 'Sustainability and the Problem of Valuation', in Costanza, R (ed) *Ecological Economics: The Science and Management of Sustainability*, Columbia University Press, New York.

Robyn, L (2002) 'Indigenous Knowledge and Technology', *American Indian Quarterly*, vol 26, no 2, pp 198–220.

Rosoff, S, Pontell, H and Tillman, R (1998) *Profit Without Honor: White-Collar Crime and the Looting of America*, Prentice Hall, Upper Saddle River, USA.

Situ, Y and Emmons, D (2000) *Environmental Crime: The Criminal Justice System's Role in Protecting the Environment*, Sage, Thousand Oaks.

Smith, M (1998) *Ecologism: Towards Ecological Citizenship*, University of Minnesota Press, Minneapolis.

Tailby, R and Gant, F (2002) The Illegal Market in Australian Abalone, *Trends and Issues in Crime and Criminal Justice*, No. 225, Australian Institute of Criminology, Canberra.

Tasmania Police (2004) *Annual Report 2002–2003*, Department of Police and Public Safety, Hobart.

Thornton, J and Tromans, S (1999) 'Human Rights and Environmental Wrongs: Incorporating the European Convention on Human Rights: Some Thoughts on the Consequences for UK Environmental Law', *Journal of Environmental Law*, vol 11, no 1, pp 35–57.

Tranter, B (2004) 'The Environment Movement: Where to from Here?', in White, R (ed) *Controversies in Environmental Sociology*, Cambridge University Press, Melbourne.

White, R (2002) 'Environmental Harm and the Political Economy of Consumption', *Social Justice*, vol 29, no 1–2, pp 82–102.

White, R (2003) 'Environmental Issues and the Criminological Imagination', *Theoretical Criminology*, vol 7, no 4, pp 483–506.

White, R (2004) 'Introduction: Sociology, Society and the Environment' in White, R (ed) *Controversies in Environmental Sociology*, Cambridge University Press, Melbourne.

Williams, C (1996) 'An Environmental Victimology', *Social Justice*, vol 23, no 4, pp 16–40.

# 15. Environmental crime and pollution: wasteful reflections[1]*

*Alan A. Block*

> The history of men is reflected in the history of sewers.... Crime, intelligence, social protest, freedom of conscience, thought, theft, all that human laws prosecuted or have prosecuted was hidden in this pit.
>
> Victor Hugo, *Les Miserables*

## Introduction

In the 1970s, a new menace became the centerpiece for a new generation of environmentally minded reformers. Organized crime, which controlled the private sanitation industry in the Northeast, moved center stage. This took place at approximately the same time that the U.S. government passed the first important toxic waste legislation in its history. The most significant legislation passed was the Resource Conservation and Recovery Act that mandated special handling of the newly recognized category of waste called either toxic or hazardous. Interestingly enough, the legislation was designed to patrol and discipline the waste disposers, not the producers. It was based on the premise that once the waste passed from its producers – chemical companies and other industrial firms – into the hands of the disposers, it ceased to be the producers' property. In any case, a great deal of needed attention was focused on the mob firms and their practices. There was some rectification of this when Superfund legislation was passed in the early 1980s. It mandated that all responsible parties (producers and disposers) would have to clean up polluted sites. It has not always worked very well. I will discuss this issue at some length using a particularly egregious organized crime waste group as a template. Concentration on waste disposers had another significant side. Around 1970, several private carting firms began a rapid process of expansion, buying dozens and dozens of small carting companies and landfills across the country. In a relatively short period, they became the waste industry's most important companies. I will spend some time explaining the methodology of expansion, for it bears a striking resemblance to the methods employed by

---

* From *Social Justice* (2002), 29(1–2): pp. 61–81.

organized criminals. Reformers particularly watched the giants, if for no other reason than their sheer size and, as I will show, their penchant to behave improperly.

By the 1990s, the giants had finally moved into the New York market on the heels of the government finally doing something significant about mob control. Once New York was gained, another period of intense consolidation took place. Two firms ended up controlling most of the New York market. This was a somewhat unexpected development, I suppose, for one of the charges against organized crime was that it had constructed a monopoly in New York. Thus, the criminal cartel monopoly was replaced with a two-firm oligopoly. I shall argue that the variance between the mob cartel and the giants when it comes to legal issues such as antitrust and pollution was not very large. I will take an in-depth look at the past practices of two large firms that were gobbled up in the last phase of consolidation in New York, for they were involved to one degree or another with illicit plans and actions to dump toxic waste in Third World countries. Finally, in the last section of the article, I will discuss other kinds of companies that routinely pollute.

## Criminal cartels in waste

In 1957, the U.S. Senate Select Committee on Improper Activities in the Labor or Management Field, chaired by Senator John McClellan, showed that organized crime had built 'business empires in the private carting industry through a system of monopoly enforced by trade associations and cooperative labor unions.'[2] This was another instance of organized crime's domination of certain working-class trades in New York, which included, at one time or another, cinders, cloth shrinking, construction, flower shops, the Fulton fish market, funeral homes, hod carrying, ice, kosher butchers, laundry services, newsstands, overall makers, paper hangers, taxicabs, waterfront workers, and window cleaners.[3] Among the McClellan Committee's findings after two investigations, one in Los Angeles, was the degree of ethnicity and kinship that bound racketeers in waste together. In Los Angeles, Armenian heritage appeared to be the primary connecting link, while in New York Italian roots were most significant. Among the owners of garbage firms who were identified as racketeers in the Greater New York area were Antony Ricci, Carmine Tramunti, Anthony Corallo, Nunzio and Vincent Squillante, Nicholas Ratteni, James Licari, Gennaro Mancuso, Alfred Toriello, Frank Caruso, Joseph Feola, and Anthony Carfano. Several had already acquired major reputations as organized crime felons.

It is not unusual to find a common heritage supported by some-times-complicated kinship patterns in trades, including those associated with waste. A survey of Paris sewermen in 1979, for example, found a persistence of 'hereditary endogamy.' Parisian sewer workers were 'more commonly introduced into the service by another relative who had been or was a sewerman – nephew, uncle, cousin, brother-in-law, and so on.'[4] Of course, Parisian sewermen did not go on to own private sewer businesses and create monopolies based on criminally coercive practices.

At the base of the private sanitation criminal domains was the principle of 'territorial rights,' later called 'property rights.' This meant that whatever garbage firm first contracted with a business to pick up its rubbish had a right to that business forever. Indeed, the right extended to the location itself, no matter what happened to the original contracting party. Naturally, it was a method of dimming competition, although sometimes it was honored more in the breach than otherwise, especially given racketeers' propensity to cheat and steal from one another.

Following the McClellan Committee's work in 1957, local, state, and federal authorities pursued garbage racketeering decade after decade. Numerous investigations took place chiefly in the five boroughs of New York City, in Nassau and Suffolk Counties on Long Island, in Westchester, Putnam, Orange, and Rockland Counties, just north and northwest of the city, in Northern and Central New Jersey, and at times in Philadelphia. Each investigation and prosecution revealed organized crime's monopolies in private sanitation work.

## The routine activities of criminal waste enterprises

All County Environmental Service Corporation and its related firms is a template for the mob-related solid and hazardous waste companies investigated over several decades in the New York Metropolitan Area. It was a transporter of septic and hazardous wastes, a hazardous waste facility, and a devotee of illegal hazardous waste disposal. The New York State Assembly Environmental Conservation Committee offered an historical account of All Country, its crimes, and corporate permutations from 1977 through most of 1984.[5]

For almost a decade, John, Robert, and Joseph Mongelli, together with brothers Frank and John Coppola, owned and operated the Warwick, New York, headquartered All County.[6] In addition, the Mongellis owned several waste disposal companies – I.S.A. of New Jersey, Inc.,[7] Tri-State Carting, Inc.,[8] Grace Disposal and Leasing, Ltd.,[9] Orange County Sanitation, Inc.,[10] and Round Lake Sanitation Corporation.[11] In testimony before the U.S. Congressional Committee on Interstate and Foreign Commerce in 1980, two detective sergeants with the New Jersey State Police, Dirk Ottens and Jack Penny, presented evidence tying the Mongelli family to Mario Giganti, one of the important leaders of a major organized crime syndicate known as the 'Genovese family.'[12] Giganti, the Mongellis' ultimate boss, was somewhat foolishly listed on the payroll of Round Lake Sanitation in New York as a solicitor. By 1986, Louis Mongelli was described as a 'reputed ... Genovese crime family member.'[13] In 1989, John Coppola became a valued member of a New Jersey gubernatorial campaign team.[14]

The Mongellis and their associates were primarily engaged in the illicit disposal of hazardous waste. In 1977, they took over the Penaluna Road landfill in Warwick, New York, and dumped toxic waste at will, thereby threatening Greenwood Lake, a source of drinking water for around one million northern New Jersey and New York inhabitants. I.S.A. trailers were spotted unloading drums of sludge composed of oil, grease, and degreasers, while a Grace Disposal worker was on hand to flatten the empty drums. Other information clearly showed industrial waste from a nearby Ford plant was also disposed of at the landfill. Finally, the *Newark Star Ledger* reported that 'thousands of gallons of 'solvents ... paint and pigment residues ... dirty thinners ... still bottoms ... glue residue' and other organic, toxic compounds were picked up from industries in New Jersey and slated for disposal at Warwick.'[15] To cover their tracks, the criminals created phony records indicating some of these wastes went to a 'safe' landfill that did not actually exist, and to another that had no record of receiving any of the toxic products, even though it probably did.

The New York Department of Environmental Conservation (DEC) ordered the Penaluna landfill closed in 1980. Grace Disposal went out of business and the site, reported Assemblyman Hinchey, 'which is 36 acres in size and 50 feet deep, is now leaching organic chemicals and the toxic metals – cadmium, lead, and mercury – into a stream and wetland that feed Greenwood Lake.' The estimated toxic leachate, according to the DEC, was 7,200 gallons per day.

In the summer of 1979, All County moved some of its operations to New Jersey, though it still maintained a significant presence in New York. It bought several storage facilities in the town of Edgewater, on the shore of the Hudson River, and another in Newark. It did not inform New Jersey authorities about the Edgewater facilities. They were discovered by New Jersey's Department of Environmental Protection (DEP) over a year later. By the spring of 1983, the Mongellis and their partners had a long list of hazardous waste violations in the State of New Jersey. From Edgewater, All County improperly disposed of hazardous waste at Mount Marion, New York. It continued its past practice with waste from the Mobil Chemical Company in Edison, New Jersey, carting it to Wayne, Pennsylvania. It also hooked up with a New Jersey firm, S & W Waste, that hobnobbed with racketeers and top state politicians.[16] In one deal, All County delivered PCBs to S & W even though it was not licensed to receive them. Other similar All County violations followed. For example, it delivered 3,338 gallons of supposedly flammable solvents to a facility in Virginia. Burned three days later, it was subsequently learned that the shipment was laden with PCBs. Once again, All County was not authorized to handle PCB wastes and the facility was forbidden to burn them.

The Coppolas severed their relationship with All County in the spring of 1983. At the same moment, the Mongellis sold All County to a former employee, James Stroin. He had first-class training in illegally disposing of hazardous waste, having worked at the notorious Kin-Buc landfill in Edison, New Jersey, the largest and leakiest chemical landfill in the Northeast. It was closed in 1977 when toxic chemicals from the site were found pouring into the Raritan River, a major drinking water supply. In this ever so slightly revamped venture, Stroin was joined by David Rosenberg, who remained at his post of vice president and operations manager for the firm. It was more of the same: principally the illegal disposal of PCBs. Stroin and Rosenberg only lasted in business about eight months because they were caught sending PCBs from the same facility to the Virginia firm that had illegally burned them for the Mongellis.

All County, under the ownership of the Mongellis and Coppola, had other criminal business associates. One was RA-MAR Waste Management, owned by another Coppola brother, Ralph. This firm specialized in septic tank cleaning and waste-oil collection. RA-MAR serviced Westchester, Orange, and Rockland Counties in New York and was headquartered in New York and New Jersey. RAMAR's operating philosophy was almost a mirror image of All County's. From the autumn of 1979 to the summer of 1981, RA-MAR was cited for 20 distinct toxic waste violations in New Jersey. RA-MAR and All County worked closely together from time to time.

There was also a strong connection between RA-MAR and two large New Jersey-based waste-oil recovery companies – Noble Oil and Oil Recovery. Between May 1983 and January 1984, RA-MAR reported taking 695,000 gallons of waste oil to Noble Oil Company alone. In May 1984, the two waste-oil firms were indicted for their participation in a 'massive operation in which hazardous chemical wastes were mixed with heating oil and then sold to the public.' The corporate officers, Christopher Grungo (Noble Oil) and Joseph Cucinotta (Oil Recovery), were charged with conspiracy, theft, deceptive business practices, and the illegal transportation and disposal of hazardous waste.[17] Nonetheless, in May 1984, RA-MAR's permit to haul waste oil to Noble Oil and Oil Recovery was renewed by New York State's environmental agency.

'Although All County Environmental Service Corporation is not presently in operation,' Assemblyman Hinchey noted back in 1984, 'the Mongellis and Coppolas still operate waste disposal businesses in New York State.' He added, 'Round Lake Sanitation collects garbage in Orange, Ulster, and Sullivan Counties,' and Round Lake and another Mongelli/Coppola business, Tri-State Carting Corporation, 'are currently permitted by DEC to transport industrial wastes.' ISA of New Jersey was still hauling garbage in Orange County, New York. Obviously, the Mongellis were not deterred by their past legal difficulties or by Assemblyman Hinchey's report.

The final section of the report contained Hinchey's suggestions. All of these facts, he wrote, establish the need for 'significant changes in the solid waste permitting program as well as further investigation of specific corporations and individuals who are chronic violators of the Environmental Conservation Law and who associate with businesses having similar backgrounds.' Hinchey wanted a tough 'permit program to regulate private garbage haulers,' an absolute 'prohibition on the approval of permits to individuals who simultaneously operate hazardous and solid waste disposal companies,' and a meaningful review of DEC's authority from the New York State Legislature to deny and revoke permits. Hinchey's ideas did not take root, at least in his estimation. His committee continued to bedevil the New York (and federal) regulators through the early 1990s with reports and hearings that proved the regulators, at least, were not paying very much attention to significant criminal polluters.[18]

In one remarkable case, Hinchey's chief investigator, Arthur John Woolston-Smith, determined that an organized crime felon, Frank Sacco, was running a landfill in the Hudson Valley town of Tuxedo, about 30 miles north of the city. Sacco had past convictions and prison sentences dating back 45 years that included an assault (stemming from an arrest for rape), extortion, loan sharking, witness tampering, robbery, dealing in stolen securities, and an escape from prison, to mention a few. The town's Justice of the Peace leased the site to Sacco. Others involved with Sacco in this deal were a former assistant district attorney, the Tuxedo police chief, and a DEC official who took bribes from Sacco and ended up as his mistress.[19] When Sacco's landfill was finally closed, shallow groundwater monitoring established arsenic, iron, manganese, and selenium at levels in violation of drinking water standards. Substantial concentrations of lead were found, as well as moderate levels of toluene, benzene, xylene, trichloroethylene, ethylbenzene, carbon disulfide, and z-butanone. The hazardous wastes at the site were attributable to 'petroleum contaminated waste soils and waste contaminated with industrial solvents.'[20] The dead body discovered in the landfill was one of Sacco's employees.[21]

The Mongellis were finally run to ground by federal authorities in the 1990s, although not because there was a structured inquiry into criminal waste firms. It began because an FBI agent used to take his morning coffee in a restaurant next to a Mongelli facility. The agent became upset with the odors wafting into the coffee shop and determined to find out who or what was causing his morning nausea. That led to several queries and those eventually led to an investigation.[22] As a result, in October 1991 the Mongellis were indicted on federal racketeering charges for paying off the 'Genovese crime family and trying to bribe a state environmental official.'[23] Also indicted were the following Mongelli companies: Round Lake Sanitation, I.S.A. in New Jersey, Orange County Sanitation, Continental Technology, Lake Region Service Garage, and AAA Recycling. The Mongelli's, according to the FBI and Otto G. Obermaier, the U.S. attorney from the Southern District of New York, 'siphoned millions of dollars in cash from their businesses' using 'a number of intermediaries to "launder funds" for them' for nefarious purposes. They were caught in an undercover operation offering bribes 'ranging as high as $500,000 for the first year and $300,000 for each succeeding year' to a detective posing as a high-ranking DEC official.[24] They wanted another landfill. It would take several years before the case was settled and the Mongellis punished.

## National firms: illicit behaviors

In the late 1960s and early 1970s, three sanitation firms, one in Boston, another in Chicago, the third in Houston, began a process of rapid expansion. Their growth took place in tandem with the full blossoming of the environmental movement in the U.S., which forced the government to create the Environmental Protection Agency in 1970 and to pass important legislation dealing with toxic waste disposal during that decade. The Boston firm, SCA Services, did not quite make it to the top. It was publicly burned for its involvement with organized criminals in New Jersey and corporate leaders with exceptionally sticky fingers.

In testimony before the U.S. House of Representatives Subcommittee on Oversight and Investigations in 1980 and 1981, a former gangster detailed SCA's complicity with organized crime. At one hearing, the Committee summed up his testimony about SCA's expansion, noting that in its expansion in the early 1970s, it bought small garbage firms and gave the owners stock in SCA and an employment contract to continue operating their former firms as before. The gangster pointed out, somewhat inarticulately, what this meant in New Jersey: 'So you have the same people that individually were controlled by organized crime into SCA.'[25] SCA's reputation took an exceptional drubbing in December 1980, six days after the subcommittee's first hearing featuring the reformed felon's dissection of SCA's ties to organized crime. This time it was tied to an organized crime homicide. On December 22, 'Crescent Roselle, general manager of Waste Disposal, Inc., one of SCA's largest New Jersey subsidiaries, was brutally murdered in a gangland-style execution,' shot numerous times while sitting in his car outside his company office.[26] In the subcommittee's May 1981 hearing, a New Jersey law enforcement official bluntly stated that SCA had other subsidiaries that were managed by mobsters.[27]

The other two national (in time, international) companies, Chicago's Waste Management Inc. (WMI) and Houston's Browning-Ferris Industries (BFI), fared far better than did SCA. Their chiefs quickly stepped to the level of the very rich. Waste Management and Browning-Ferris did have their bumpy moments. In the past three decades, each has pled either guilty or *nolo contendere* to various charges ranging from environmental malpractice to shady business activities. Each has aggressively maintained, however, that these problems were the result of simple mistakes, common industry errors, or isolated acts carried out by lower-level employees who misbehaved without the knowledge of the organization's leadership.

In a massive class-action civil case against Waste Management, Waste Management of North America, Waste Management Partners, and Browning-Ferris, filed in summer 1988, however, a far different picture emerged. There were seven named plaintiffs in this case: (1) Cumberland Farms, an operator of convenience stores throughout the United States; (2) Kirschner Brothers Oil Co., a marketer of petroleum products; (3) Dan Rosenberg, d/b/a Animal Hospital of Chester County, an individual who operates an animal hospital; (4) George Gusses, an individual who operates a business; (5) the Perry Corporation; (6) Uncle Donald's, d/b/a Huey's; and (7) Overton Pub, d/b/a East End Pub. The suit was based on alleged violations of Title 1 of the Sherman Anti-Trust Act. In it, the named plaintiffs and the class they represented, who 'have directly purchased, in the course of their business, containerized solid waste removal and disposal services from one or more of the defendants, their wholly-owned subsidiaries, affiliates, and alleged co-conspirators,'[28] were all customers of either WMI or BFI. The plaintiff's attorneys alleged that WMI and BFI 'engaged in an extensive pattern of anticompetitive activity across the United States,' engineered and directed by their 'national and regional officers.'[29] In a 111-page memorandum developed in 1990 that successfully defeated a motion by the defendants for a summary judgment, the plaintiffs' attorneys started with 10 key points:

1 George Farris, BFI's chief financial officer, met with Donald Flynn, WMI's chief financial officer, and with Harold Gershowitz, WMI's senior vice president. Flynn and Gershowitz disclosed that, in view of the fact that

'the environment for price increases is improving,' WMI planned to implement a '4–5%' national price increase over the next few years. This one meeting alone compels the denial of defendants' motion.

2  A government memorandum reported that criminal price-fixing by the defendants in Atlanta 'can be attributed to more than overly aggressive local managers' and was 'probably directed by corporate officials from the company headquarters.'

3  A sworn declaration from a BFI sales manager describes how John Drury, then BFI's executive vice-president, orchestrated price-fixing activities in Atlanta.

4  A former BFI executive testified that BFI's national director of labor relations told him to 'get together with Waste Management' and end a price war in Ohio.

5  Ed Drury, BFI's national vice president, directed price fixing in the Arrowhead region (Colorado, Nebraska, Iowa, Wisconsin, Minnesota, North and South Dakota, Wyoming, Montana, and several Canadian provinces).[30]

6  John Drury, BFI's president, personally appointed John Pinto as vice president to head BFI's northeast region. Pinto had clear ties to organized crime and was subsequently indicted and pled guilty to bid rigging, price fixing, and bribery of officials.

7  John Drury, BFI's president, assigned a new district manager to Pittsburgh with instructions that the sales manager report directly to him. The district manager proceeded to engage in price-fixing and bid rigging, and periodically delivered suitcases of cash generated from these activities to Houston for use as payoffs to public officials.

8  A BFI salesperson testified that she was not permitted to solicit WMI customers and when she attended sales meetings with salespersons from other districts, learned that it was a company-wide policy.

9  Both BFI and WMI encouraged price-fixing by actively promoting employees who engaged in it. Bruce Ranck, for example, was a principal target of a state antitrust prosecution (which BFI settled for $350,000) and federal antitrust prosecution (to which BFI pled guilty and paid a one million dollar fine). Notwithstanding his involvement in illegal activity, Ranck was promoted and now holds the position of executive vice president of BFI, with responsibility for all of BFI's North American solid waste operations.

10  BFI's vice chairman and national director of marketing, Norman Myers, paid a bribe to defeat a competitor's landfill application, and then attempted to conceal this payment.[31]

Plaintiffs' attorneys went into the history of WMI, pointing out that WMI's predecessor firms belonged to the Chicago Suburban Refuse Disposal

Corporation (CSRDC) through the 1960s and into the early 1970s. Nearly all the private waste companies in Chicago were part of CSRDC and operated under a system called the 'Chicago Rules,' which added up to precisely the same system of 'property rights' discovered by Senator McClellan in his New York racketeer investigation.[32] Furthermore, it was asserted that as soon as WMI was formed in 1968 and BFI in 1969, they started to buy CSRDC companies. 'As members of the Chicago families became absorbed into WMI and BFI,' the plaintiffs' memorandum holds, 'the 'Chicago rules' became a national code of conduct.'[33] In terms of the structure of waste malfeasance, the mobsters in New York and New Jersey ruled through the 'property rights' system and, importantly, through their control of private landfills (although illegal entry to municipal landfills through bribes has been a constant as well).[34] The Pennsylvania case alleges that WMI and BFI did the same. 'The defendants have gone to extraordinary lengths to obtain control of landfills,' the plaintiffs' counsel argued, 'including the bribing of state officials.'[35]

The plaintiffs' claims were further buttressed by a detailed and damning series of cases that included examples from the 1970s and 1980s. There were bribery and price-fixing cases, including a 1987 case in Ohio that alleged BFI and WMI subsidiaries engaged in price-fixing and 'customer allocation' in violation of the Sherman Anti-Trust Act. The companies pled guilty and each paid a one million dollar fine.[36] In the five-year period before the filing of the Pennsylvania case, it was pointed out that 'federal prosecutors convened grand juries to investigate anticompetitive conduct by BFI or WMI subsidiaries in Rochester, New York; Toledo, Ohio; Orange County, California; San Diego County, California; Memphis, Tennessee; Birmingham, Alabama; Orlando, Florida; Jacksonville, Florida; Phoenix, Arizona; Kansas City, Missouri; Oahu, Hawaii; Pittsburgh, Pennsylvania; and Columbus, Ohio.'[37] Most of the fines were below one million dollars and had no effect on the companies' earnings.

In fact, from 1977 to 1989, WMI's gross income went from $60 million to $850 million, and BFI's zoomed from $33 million to $423 million. The chief operating officers' earnings were spectacular. From 1987 to 1989, WMI's chief executive officer, chief operating officer, and treasurer received compensation packages of $12.8 million, $16.3 million, and $25.1 million respectively. In 1989, their personal holdings in WMI stock had a value of $117 million, $38 million, and $33 million.[38]

To drive home the plaintiffs' point that the price-fixing conspiracy was national, the memorandum claims to have 'hard, documentary evidence that the highest ranking officers at BFI and WMI met to exchange information regarding future pricing.'[39] Supposedly, they met under the guise of what they called 'The Splinter Group of the New York Society.' In their summation, plaintiffs' attorneys noted that WMI's chief financial officer and its senior vice president, and BFI's senior vice president attended these meetings. There they shared information on 'future marketing plans ... bids on future projects, expansion plans, anticipated capital expenditures, profit margins, and dividend policies.'[40]

There is little doubt that the plaintiffs' suit had merit and it established that at least part of organized crime's methodology of control in the waste arena, so strongly and repeatedly condemned, has likely been common waste industry practice. At the center nestled 'property rights/Chicago rules.' Corporate expansion, on the other hand, was engineered through 'predatory pricing' practices designed to drive uncooperative small firms to the wall. As Professor Howard Smith describes it, 'a price is predatory if it is below the seller's otherwise profit maximizing price and is charged for the purpose of eliminating competition in the short run and reducing competition in the long run.'[41] Once that is accomplished and a monopoly, or more likely, an oligopoly achieved, prices rocket up. On October 30, 1990, Waste Management agreed to pony up $19.5 million and Browning-Ferris $30.5 million to settle the antitrust case.[42]

## Cumberland farms: sins of the plaintiff

The above discussion should not be taken to mean that the first named plaintiff in the case, Cumberland Farms, was itself a 'clean' company. The company started life in 1938 as a roadside milk and egg business in Cumberland, Rhode Island. A Greek immigrant, Vasilios Haseotes, owned the stand and turned it into a convenience store. It eventually became the nation's third-largest convenience store chain, and the largest independent gasoline retailer in the 1980s. It reached the top after buying most of Chevron's and Gulf's northeast marketing facilities for around $350 million. This purchase gave Cumberland an additional 3,373 jobber and dealer supply contracts, and 20 terminals.[43] Clearly, this was its high point. On January 7, 1991, Cumberland was sued by the Department of Justice and the Environmental Protection Agency for 'unlawfully filled wetlands.'[44] More bad news came that summer. The *Philadelphia Inquirer* reported that Cumberland Farms coerced 'its convenience-store employees to confess to thefts they had not committed.'[45] In the spring of 1992, Cumberland filed for Chapter 11 protection.[46] Several years later, Cumberland lost a suit to Goldman Sachs for stealing three million barrels of oil from Goldman's trading unit, J. Aron. This was the culmination of years of legal wrangling and payouts by Cumberland to Goldman. Earlier, Goldman had recovered approximately $41 million from Cumberland, which it accused of 'unauthorized blending, burning, and outright theft of about 5% of the 57 million barrels that J. Aron processed.'[47] More dreary environmental news was still to come, including Cumberland's neglectful running of an air polluting refinery in Newfoundland.[48]

## The changing New York market and waste consolidation

During the 1990s, New York prosecutors, particularly Robert Morgenthau, the New York County (Manhattan) district attorney, finally took on the task of busting organized crime's dominance in the private New York waste market. They successfully prosecuted some and sued others from the underworld of waste and their trade associations (including The Greater New York Waste

Paper Association, The Kings County Trade Waste Association, the Association of Trade Waste removers of Greater New York, and The Queens County Trade Waste Association).[49] In this complicated and long investigation, BFI played an undercover role in the demise of the organized crime cartel. With BFI's permission, Morgenthau placed an agent into its New York operation. Evidence was gathered on the mob's tactics in an attempt to chase the firm from the city. BFI trucks were tailed, stolen, and disabled. Executives endured threatening phone calls and letters.[50] In June 1995, Morgenthau's 114-count indictment ended the siege. Almost two years later, BFI bought the Manhattan routes and trucks of one of the mob outfits, Five Bros. Carting Co, whose owner, Michael D'Ambrosio, was secretly recorded telling Morgenthau's undercover agent that BFI was 'a bug that needed to be crushed.'[51] D' Ambrosio pled guilty to 'enterprise corruption.' He was fined one million dollars and sentenced to prison.

The giants (BFI and WMI) had finally broken into the New York solid waste market, the nation's largest. Joining them in New York were a fast-rising firm named USA Waste Services and a smaller conglomerate, Eastern Environmental Services, with deep ties to the largely criminal New Jersey scene. Though some in New York talked about *stasis* in the newly consolidated market, remarkable changes were on the way.

The most stunning development was a merger between WMI and USA Waste. In 1998, 'old' WMI was 'acquired by smaller rival USA Waste Services Inc. for stock valued at about $13.5 billion.' Although the new company would still be called Waste Management, it would be run by the leaders of USA Waste, with its main corporate office in Houston.[52] The result of the logic of consolidation, cost reductions were achieved by consolidating routes and sacking 'redundant' employees.[53] The move was carried out by USA Waste's chairman, John Drury, the former BFI president who was identified as a key director of the long price-fixing conspiracy with WMI in the *Cumberland Farms et al.* case.

## Consolidation's odd twists and turns: the return of the irrepressible

In 1990, Drury quit BFI in a disagreement over policy issues. Three years later, he was asked to head USA Waste. He took the post in 1994 and mandated 'no recycling, no overseas ventures.'[54] Under Drury, USA Waste was on the prowl for other waste companies. In 1995, it gobbled up Chambers Development, 'which had 50 collection operations in eight Atlantic seaboard states.' The following year it bought out a California-based firm that also operated in Texas, Louisiana, Arkansas, Colorado, and Florida. Around the same time, USA Waste announced it would buy another waste conglomerate, United Waste Systems, based in Connecticut. The Connecticut firm had purchased five waste collection businesses and two transfer stations in Wisconsin, Minnesota, and Pennsylvania the year before.[55] On the last day of 1998, Drury bought out Eastern Environmental Services.[56] Now only two major competitors remained 'in the multibillion-dollar trash disposal market in New York City and … in cities in Pennsylvania and Florida,' said a somewhat concerned Justice

Department, which nevertheless allowed the deal to go through after Eastern and Waste Management shed some companies in several states.[57] Eastern had just acquired several allegedly 'former' mob trash firms in New Jersey, and two Florida firms. One beneficiary of the Waste Management-Eastern deal was an emerging trash conglomerate, Republic Services, headed by Wayne Huizenga, who was responsible for the original creation of Waste Management in Chicago. Huizenga, like Drury, had taken time off from garbage. However, he spent his off time creating Blockbuster Video, the nation's largest video rental company, and buying a professional sports team or two, a stadium here and there. Republic picked up some of the discarded firms and was well on its way to becoming another major player in the wildly consolidating waste world.

## USA waste: two sleazy background issues

USA Waste was pushed into the very big leagues of waste, before its deal with Waste Management, through its purchase of United Waste Systems, which came to life in 1989 under the aggressive leadership of its 33-year-old chairman and CEO, Bradley S. Jacobs.[58] By 1992, United had landfills and composting and recycling centers in West Virginia, Pennsylvania, Massachusetts, Kentucky, Mississippi, Michigan, and Connecticut. Despite these activities, it had lost $4.5 million since 1990. Nonetheless, some observers thought its prospects were promising, for United raised $36 million in new capital in 1992 through an Initial Public Offering (IPO) of its stock. It planned to spend the money on five new acquisitions.[59]

### I. The Meditative Bradley Jacobs

Chairman Jacobs' background was somewhat baffling. According to the *Hartford Courant* (Connecticut) newspaper, Jacobs' CEO experience started in 1979, at the age of 23, with Amerex Oil Associates, which had its corporate offices in Morristown, New Jersey.[60] From 1984 to July 1989, he headed up an international trading company based in England, Hamilton Resources (UK) Ltd.[61] What Jacobs did for, or with, Amerex or Hamilton Resources is not noted in any published account of his background. It seems there was much to hide, for he had worked with a cast of Europeans and Americans suspected of illicitly selling toxic waste to the impoverished West African country of Benin, making night runs of toxic waste to other West African countries, and likely selling oil to South Africa while the U.N.-sponsored embargo of oil to Pretoria was running.

To attempt to unravel this suspected misbehavior and place it into perspective, one must go back to a company called Pan Ocean Oil, which started in 1970 with $16 million in cash. Six years later, after it finally hit pay dirt drilling in the North Sea, Marathon Oil bought it for $260 million.[62] In the extremely complex structure of an oil major, Pan Ocean's ownership had been in the hands of Marathon's wholly owned subsidiary, Interocean Oil. This entity became, or was subdivided into a firm called Interocean Oil

(Nigeria). On November 1, 1982, all of Interocean's stock was sold and its interest in what was by then Pan Ocean Oil (Nigeria) was 'transferred' to Impex Ltd., a firm incorporated in Anguilla, a small and somewhat notorious island nation in the British West Indies.[63] Anguilla's notoriety is based on its penchant for allowing a host of criminals, many in the narcotics business, to establish phony banks, some no more than trailers in goat pastures.

Pan Ocean next turned up as a series of interrelated firms: Panoco Group, PNOcean (supposedly with offices in New York and Houston), Panoco International, Panoco (Geneva), Panoco (Nigeria), and Panoco (Benin). To muddy the waters a little more, a Panoco entity was affiliated with the United States Oil Co., based in New York, whose director also ran Panoco (Geneva), which, it was reported, 'operates in Nigeria through Pan Ocean Oil (Nigeria).[64] The Geneva based Panoco, and I presume all the rest including Impex in Anguilla, were directed by an Italian, Vittorio Fabbri, who had an office at 375 Park Avenue, New York. Standing behind Fabbri as the owner of most of the above entities was supposedly another Italian named Bellini.

British journalists from Box Television tie Bradley Jacobs to this group, since Fabbri supposedly introduced him to the pleasures and potential profits of selling European and American hazardous waste to Benin. In 1985, Panoco (Geneva) persuaded the Benin authorities to scuttle a contract with Saga Petroleum, a private Norwegian oil company, and instead to contract with Panoco (Benin).[65] It was the beginning of a very convoluted series of deals, unraveled principally by Box reporter Adam Kemp, that ultimately led to Jacobs. Kemp found that the Republic of Benin agreed to receive about five million tons of toxic waste a year for 10 years for a 'mere two dollars and 50 cents a ton.' The contact was signed with a Gibraltar company named SESCO. Looking for SESCO led Kemp to London's elegant Eaton Square and Hamilton Resources, which was listed in the phone directory as a 'Local Listening Post for Crude Oil Market.' A little sleuthing turned up an item from Greenpeace, which accused Hamilton of involvement in a 'possible dumping deal' with impoverished Guinea Bissau. Hamilton issued a denial stating, 'our company has never made any attempt to build a landfill' there. Kemp went to Companies House in London, where he discovered that almost all the shares of Hamilton Resources were owned by Hamilton Resources (Gibraltar). Moreover, Hamilton and SESCO used the same registered office, Finsbury Management, in Gibraltar. Documents showed that SESCO and Hamilton (Gibraltar) had appointed, at the same time, two other firms as directors – 'Amwell Servicing and Tikka Overseas Amwell Services, in the British Virgin Islands.' A check of documents in Washington, D.C., revealed SESCO correspondence signed by Josephine Mandel, apparently a company director. She subsequently appeared as the company secretary of Hamilton Resources UK Ltd. Hamilton's records listed her address as 'Lima, Peru.' Not unexpectedly, inquiries in Lima to find her were fruitless.

London's Hamilton Resources listed a Jill Aldridge as another director. She had an address in Holland that turned out to be a Transcendental Meditation study center run by followers of Maharishi Mahesh Yogi. Aldridge had lived there, but left a few months before Kemp arrived in Holland looking for her. Box Television reportedly found her working at Roydon Hall, the 'cult's headquarters' in Kent. Bradley Jacobs was also known as a devotee of Transcendental Meditation. Kemp called Jacobs, who admitted he knew the name Jill Aldridge and then rang off.

Benin was the last stop in this puzzling investigation. Benin's self-styled Marxist President, Mathieu Kerekou, had signed a contract with SESCO's representative, Lamia Catche, for a 10-year toxics deal. In other Benin government documents, however, Mme. Catche is 'named as Executive Vice President of the Group Hamilton Resources.' Kemp gathered increasing evidence that proved Bradley Jacobs had put together a three-part transnational toxic waste dumping scheme. First, a network of waste brokers was created to scour factories in Europe for product; second, SESCO was formed to do the same in the United States; and third, MJ Carter Associates was retained to help plan a huge landfill in Benin.

The waste intended for Benin was described as 'very, very volatile solvents, which would fairly readily burst into flame.' There were also herbicides, methylene chloride, and degreasing solutions made of 'organo-chloride compounds' that were guaranteed to evaporate under the African sun and thus pose a serious health hazard to landfill workers and the many people living on the perimeter of the site. Benin's alarmed health minister, Andre Atchade, wrote the following to President Kerekou: 'These schemes are disastrous for our country and constitute a threat to the safety of our land and people.... We should remember Chernobyl.' The president fired him and then placed him under house arrest for his audacity. Jacobs first denied having anything to do with the project. He told Kemp, 'you know, it's a farce; it's like a total farce.' Later, however, he admitted his involvement.

## 2. Eastern environmental: the saga of the unwelcome ash

Another USA Waste purchase, Eastern Environmental, had a problem stemming from the dumping of toxic waste in the Third World. In 1988, between 2,000 and 5,000 tons of Philadelphia's toxic incinerator ash were dumped on the beaches of the Haitian coastal town of Gonaives.[66] The ash was the property of a waste disposal outfit, Joseph Paolino and Sons. That firm had taken over a six million dollar contract to dispose of Philadelphia's ash, which 'contained lead, cadmium, barium, arsenic, mercury, dioxin, and cyanide.'[67] Paolino hired Amalgamated Shipping of the Bahamas, which engaged the ship *Khian Sea* to carry the ash somewhere in the Caribbean. The ship left port in August 1986 with approximately 14,000 tons of ash. It tried to unload in the Bahamas but failed. Then it spent almost two years in limbo trying to find some Caribbean country that would make the deal. In the last week of October 1987, Haiti's Department of Commerce granted permission for the ship to unload on the beach at Gonaives. Within a few days, however, the Haitian government, in particular the Minister of Commerce, announced a change in policy and wished to cancel the permit. It was too late. The ship was gone and part of Philadelphia's ash lay on the beach.[68]

About 10,000 tons remained on board when the *Khian Sea* slipped out of Haitian waters. The ship tried repeatedly to find a country to accept the cargo. It underwent suspicious name changes and sailed to the Mediterranean to try several spots, including Suez. Finally, somewhere between Suez and Singapore, it offloaded the rest of Philadelphia's ash.

Years later, the New York Trade Waste Commission, a new regulatory agency put in place by Mayor Rudolph Giuliani to help combat mobster control of the waste industry, found a connection between Eastern Environmental and Joseph Paolino and Sons, and thus the toxic ash. The head of Eastern and its largest shareholder is Louis D. Paolino, one of Joseph's sons. The old man had died in 1984, but the firm continued. In 1991, it was charged with various crimes related to cheating its workers out of wages and benefits. In 1995, it was fined by the Nuclear Regulatory Commission for having radioactive material without a permit. After that, it seems to have disappeared. The Trade Waste Commission determined that Eastern would not be licensed to operate in the city until it helped to clean up Gonaives. Although everyone involved seems to deny a connection between the Paolino company and Eastern Environmental, beyond the genetic, Eastern finally agreed to pay two-thirds of the costs to remove the ash from Haiti.[69]

### 3. Serious strains in the marriage

The waste industry is so volatile that centralization soon began to crack a bit. At the turn of the millennium, the new Waste Management filed a lawsuit concerning its $1.3 billion purchase of Eastern Environmental, which it was alleged, 'overstated its profits.'[70] John Drury, who by August 1999 had become Waste Management's former chairman and CEO, was also named in the suit, as was Rodney Proto, WMI's former president, sacked at the same time Drury retired. Drury, who was quite ill, and Proto were thought to have 'personally' benefited from 'deals with Eastern's chairman, Louis Paolino.' In this alleged scam, in the autumn of 1995, Paolino, then a vice-president of USA Waste, joined with several others to buy out Eastern Environmental; they took control of Eastern in 1966 and began 'a systematic accounting fraud which caused the operating performance of Eastern to be regularly and materially overstated.'[71]

### Reflections

Two main methodologies have long characterized the U.S. waste industry: property rights and predatory pricing.[72] Nearly all the firms, from those controlled by organized crime to the Giants, have been guilty of one or both of these offenses. In addition, they have all been guilty of recklessly dumping toxic waste into leaky landfills and faulty incinerators.[73] Every one who understands the waste industry knows this. Even a generally sympathetic story in *Fortune* magazine about BFI noted that its reputation in the 1980s was odious. The magazine described the company as 'entangled in price-fixing and pollution cases from Louisiana to Niagara Falls.' A New York State congressional report held BFI's methods to be virtually the same as those used by 'organized-crime Garters.'[74] This statement was only partially accurate, however, The Giants were addicted to national and international expansion –

Waste Management operated in Saudi Arabia as early as the 1970s – while the sway of the various crime cartels in waste was local or regional. The few mob firms seeking landfills much further afield were usually knocked about by citizen's environmental groups and, from time to time, state law enforcement. Local papers, often in rural Midwestern or Appalachian counties, had a field day printing stories about how the New York Mafia was invading their town or county. The value of a 'bad reputation' was not very useful when it came to expansion outside the Northeast, with an occasional exception.

The organized crime companies did not go public; they sold no stock. Their companies were, to put it mildly, closely held. This was at least partially done to keep their books from the prying eyes of outsiders. Although some profited greatly from their business acumen, they also had a penchant for stealing worker's benefits from their controlled Teamster locals. Thus, they could never match the kind of capital that the Giants routinely raised. Waste Management and BFI were public companies; their stock was traded on the Exchange. The gangsters' forte was more along the line of extortion, and they lived in a perilous environment of their own.

The Giants were ruthless in their zeal for growth. They were very aggressive when accused of criminal behavior and were not at all reluctant to sue critics for besmirching their good names. Their executives did not have 'rap sheets.' Predatory pricing was their main methodology and that meant antitrust violations. No one, except the victims, equated those sorts of activities as examples of real racketeering. Even in the two examples of the past flirtations of USA's affiliates with Third World despots to unload their toxic products at bargain basement prices, little reaction was aroused. Indeed, scarcely anyone in the U.S. knew anything about Jacobs' activities in Benin, his Gibraltar company, or his alter ego SESCO. Moreover, no one in authority raised much of an eyebrow over what must have been significant connections between Eastern's current officers and the firm that dumped ash in Haiti, so long as Eastern paid a large portion of the cleanup.[75]

## Notes

1  Originally presented at the Second International Conference for Criminal Intelligence Analysis, 'Assessing Tomorrow's Challenges Today,' sponsored by the Royal Institute of International Affairs, National Criminal Intelligence Service, Interpol, London, England, March 1999.
2  U.S. Senate Select Committee on Improper Activities in the Labor or Management Field, *Hearing: Organized Crime in the New York Private Carting Industry* (Washington, D.C.: Government Printing Office, 1957: 6672).
3  Alan A. Block and William J. Chambliss, *Organizing Crime* (New York: Elsevier, 1981: 1415).
4  Donald Reid, *Paris Sewers and Sewermen: Realities and Representations* (Cambridge, Mass.: Harvard University Press, 1991: 169–170).
5  Maurice D. Hinchey, Chairman, the New York State Assembly Standing Committee on Environmental Conservation, *Criminal Infiltration of the Toxic and Solid Waste Disposal Industries in New York State* (Albany, NY: September 13, 1984); also Alan A. Block (ed.), *The Business of Crime: A Documentary Study of Organized Crime in the American Economy* (Boulder, CO: Westview Press, 1991: Chapter 7; 175–196).
6  John R. Coppola, Vice President, All County Service Corporation, 'Application to Dispose of Solid Waste at the Orange County Solid Waste Disposal Facilities' (October 24, 1974).
7  New York State, Senate Select Committee on Crime (July 7, 1980: 518); Robert Mongelli, I.S.A. in New Jersey, Town of Wallkill, 'Application for Garbage and Refuse Permit' (December 13,

1981, January 16, 1984); Joseph Mongelli, I.S.A. in New Jersey, Town of Wallkill, 'Application for Garbage and Refuse Permit' (1983).

8   See Vic Wehnan, Environmental Conservation officer, to David Archibald, New York State Department of Environmental Conservation, Memorandum (May 12, 1980).

9   Robert A. Mongelli, Grace Disposal and Leasing, Ltd., New York State Department of Environmental Conservation, 'Application for the Operation of a Solid Waste Management Facility' (February 18, 1978).

10   Robert Mongelli, Orange County Sanitation, Town of Wallkill, 'Application for Garbage and Refuse Permit' (December 22, 1980, December 17, 1981, 1983, January 16, 1984).

11   Joseph Mongelli, President, Round Lake Sanitation Corporation, 'Application to Dispose of Solid Waste at the Orange County Solid Waste Disposal Facilities' (August 2, 1974); Robert Mongelli, Round Lake Sanitation Corporation, New York State Department of Environmental Conservation, 'Application for Septic Tank Cleaner and Industrial Waste Collector Permit' (July 22, 1983).

12   U.S. Congress, House of Representatives, Committee on Interstate and Foreign Commerce (December 16, 1980: 63–64).

13   See 'The Tuxedo Story: A Report from Chairman Maurice D. Hinchey on Illegal Disposal of Wastes in the Hudson Valley, Pre-Hearing Report of August 30, 1989' (p. 4).

14   *Ibid.*: 3.

15   Gordon Bishop, *Sunday Star-Ledger* (April 8, 1979, Section 1: 18).

16   See my testimony on S & W in 'On the Need for the Waste Industry Disclosure Law' (Pennsylvania House of Representatives, the Conservation Committee, *Hearings on House Bill 2228, The Waste Industry Disclosure Law*, February 15, 1990).

17   Superior Court of New Jersey, Burlington County, *State of New Jersey v. Chrisroper R. Grungo et al., Defendants, Criminal Action XXVII*, Law Division Docket No. SGJ-114-83-3, Burlington County Courthouse, Mount Holly, New Jersey (April 22, 1985).

18   A few of the many investigations Hinchey conducted can be found in 'A Public Hearing into the Illegal Disposal of Wastes in the Hudson Valley' (September 19, 1989); 'A Private Hearing into the Involvement of Organized Crime in the Waste Disposal Industry' (September 6, 1989); 'A Public Hearing into the Illegal Disposal of Wastes and Landfill Problems in the Columbia County Area' (March 14, 1990); and 'Illegal Dumping in New York State: Who's Enforcing the Law' (February 6, 1991).

19   See the report from Chairman Maurice D. Hinchey to the New York State Assembly Committee on Environmental Conservation Concerning Illegal Disposal of Wastes in the Hudson Valley (February 6, 1991, Appendix C) for Sacco's arrest record, and 'The Tuxedo Story:' Pre-Hearing Report of August 30, 1989 (p. 7).

20   *Ibid.*: 53–54.

21   *Ibid.*: 6.

22   Author's interviews with FBI Special Agent Jerry W. Hanford, the coffee drinker, working out of the Bureau's White Plains Office.

23   Lisa W. Foderaro, 'New York Trash Haulers Charged with Bribery and Payoffs to Mob' (*New York Times*, October 9, 1991).

24   United States Attorney, Southern District of New York, 'Outline of Indictment: *United States of America v. Mongelli*' (Press Release, October 8, 1991).

25   U.S. House of Representatives, Committee on Energy and Commerce. Subcomittee on Oversight and Investigations, *Report: Hazardous Waste Enforcement* (Washington, D.C.: Government Printing Office, December 1982: 21).

26   *Ibid.*: 22.

27   *Ibid.*: 24.

28   United States District Court for the Eastern District of Pennsylvania, *Cumberland Farms, Inc. et al. v. Browning-Ferris Industries, Inc. et al.*, Master File Civil Action No. 87-3717, 120 F. R. D. 6421 1988 U.S. Dist. LEXIS 7484; filed July 21, 1988.

29   United States District Court, Eastern District of Pennsylvania, *Cumberland Farms, Inc., et al., Plaintiffs v. Browning Ferris Industries, Inc., et al., Defendants, Plaintiffs' Memorandum in Opposition to Defendants' Motion for Summary Judgment*, Master File, No. 87-3717, page 1.

30   *Ibid.*: 53.

31   *Ibid.*: 2–3.

32   *Ibid.*: 6.

33   *Ibid.*: 7.

34   See, for example, Brian Larkin, 'Probers Charge Bribes Opened Landfill's Gates,' *Staten Island Advance* (June 16, 1994: 1).

35   United States District Court, Eastern District of Pennsylvania, page 22.

36   *Ibid.*: 13.

37   *Ibid.*: 15.

38  *Ibid.*: 16.
39  *Ibid.*: 23.
40  *Ibid.*: 94.
41  Howard Smith, 'Hidden Graves: Predatory Pricing and Organized Crime' (Ph.D. dissertation, Pennsylvania State University, 1999: 107).
42  Larry Carpenter, Undersheriff, Ventura County, California, Sheriff's Department, 'Waste Management Report' (Attachment 4, September 20, 1991: 5).
43  J. Richard Shaner, 'Cumberland Farms: Is It Changing Identities?' (*National Petroleum News* 80,1 1, October 1988: 66).
44  'Justice Department Sues Cumberland Farms for Wetlands Violations' (*Business Wire*, January 7, 1991).
45  Associated Press (August 20, 1991).
46  *National Petroleum News* (April 1993).
47  James Norman, 'Goldman Wins $21 Mil Suit over Cumberland Theft' (*Platt's Oilgram News* 75,98, May 21, 1997: 1).
48  Peter Gullage, 'Come-By-Chance Refinery Vows to Cut Emissions' (*Platt's Oilgram News*, August 5, 1998).
49  Superior Court of the State of New York, County of New York, Robert M. Morgenthau, District Attorney of New York County, Plaintiff-Claiming Authority, against Frank Alloca. VA Sanitation Inc., *et al.*, *Order to Show Cause and Temporary Restraining Order with Supporting Papers* (CPLR ART. 13-A), June 19, 1995.
50  Philip S. Angell, 'Cleaning Up New York' (*Infrastructure Finance*, May 1, 1997).
51  Steve Daniels, 'BFI Purchases Midsize New York City Hauler' (*Waste News*, March 17, 1997: 2).
52  'Houston-Based USA Waste Services to Acquire Waste Management' (*Duluth News Tribune*, March 12, 1998).
53  *Ibid.*
54  *Forbes* (June 2, 1997).
55  *Solid Waste Report* (May 11, 1995).
56  'Waste Management Completes Eastern Deal' (*Greenwire*, January 4, 1999).
57  See the *Miami Herald* and the *Associated Press* (January 1, 1999).
58  Jim Roberts, 'Investors Welcome Micro Warehouse, United Waste IPOs' (*Fairfield County Business Journal*, December 28, 1992, Sec. 1: 1).
59  *Ibid.*
60  State of Delaware, 1982 Annual Franchise Tax Report, Amerex Oil Associates, Inc., File Number 8590-38, filed February 3, 1983.
61  'Corporate Facts: United Waste Systems Inc.' (*Hartford Courant*, September 25, 1995, Business Weekly Section: 4).
62  'Nigeria' (*Platt's Oilgram News*, February 28, 1983: 3).
63  'Companies' (*Oil and Gas Journal*, March 7, 1983: 46).
64  *Journal of Commerce* (December 28, 1987).
65  'Saga Protests Benin Ouster: Creditors Losing $60 Million in Offshore Venture' (*Platt's Oilgram News*, September 16, 1985: 1).
66  James Ridgeway, with Gaelle Drevet, 'Dumping on Haiti: How Thousands of Tons of Philadelphia's Toxic Waste Ended Up on a Haitian Beach and What the City of New York Is Doing About It' (*The Village Voice*, January 13, 1998).
67  *Ibid.*
68  *Ibid.*
69  *Ibid.*
70  'Waste Management Lawsuit Alleges Fraud by Acquired Firm' (*Philadelphia Inquirer*, January 1, 2000, at www.phillynews.con/inquirer/2000/JanOllbusiness/EASTERNOI.htm).
71  *Ibid.*
72  In a twist, BFI's fear of predatory pricing actually haunted its first attempt to enter the Greater New York market. In Suffolk County, Long Island, three towns – Babylon, Huntington, and Islip – joined together in the 1970s to create the Multi-Town Solid Waste Authority. The goal was to develop a resource-recovery facility. BFI applied to construct the facility and made the short list in 1980. BFI's inclusion likely stemmed from the activities of Anthony A. Boccaccio, who was an engineer with Grumman at the same time he worked in 'public relations' for Multi-Town. The Grumman connection was important, for Grumman's Energy Systems held the license for the German VKW mass-buming technology system. Grumman decided to close down this division and sold the license to BFI. The royalty agreement gave Grumman the right to receive a fixed percentage on any contract BFI successfully negotiated using the license. Had this project worked, Grumman would have earned over two million dollars. In 1982, Multi-Town selected BFI's subsidiary, Energy Systems, to build the plant.

The entire project was destroyed by political corruption in various quarters, although it took Anthony Noto, who became a Babylon Town supervisor in 1982, to finally do it in. Without bothering to notify anyone, Noto hired an Albany firm with no prior experience to provide the technology for the plant. Noto failed at every important task and made BFI 'spend thousands of dollars in overtime for engineers, attorneys, and accountants.' There is no doubt that Long Island's organized crime carters were afraid of BFI's reputation for predatory pricing, which they believed had just been employed in upstate New York. They made sure it would not get any kind of a stake on Long Island. State of New York, Commission of Investigation, *The Multi-Town Solid Waste Management Authority and the Crisis of Solid Waste Management* (270 Broadway, New York, NY, October 1984: 60, 73).

73  See Alan A. Block, 'Into the Abyss of Environmental Policy: The Battle over the World's Largest Commercial Hazardous Waste Incinerator Located in East Liverpool, Ohio' (*Journal of Human Justice*, November 1993).

74  Richard Behar, 'Talk About Tough Competition: How Bill Ruckelshaus is 'Taking on the New York Mob' (*Fortune*, January 15, 1996: 93).

75  Many other toxic waste polluting companies exist beyond those mentioned here. The oil industry seems to breed them. Some important waste oil firms, fuel oil distributors, retail gas and diesel station owners, and owners of fuel terminals have been major-league polluters. Many sell product laced with flammable toxics, while others pollute through negligence or deliberately to keep costs down. Additionally, ship-based oil pollution spreads a host of toxic chemicals. There are some 100 to 200 identified carcinogens in every 10,000 pounds of oil released into the oceans. Spills have the immediate effect of killing waterfowl and mammals. Even more insidiously dangerous, the carcinogens disrupt the food chain because oil pollution kills the coastal phytoplankton that feed commercial fish, thereby causing a reduction in harvests. The organisms that survive 'introduce the oil toxins into the food chain as they are consumed.' See Paul S. Dempsey, 'Compliance and Enforcement in Environmental Law: Oil Pollution of the Marine Environment by Ocean Vessels' (*New Journal of International Law and Business* 6, 1984: 459–1160).

Cruise ships are notorious oil polluters. Their crimes were uncovered this decade. In 1994, the U.S. Coast Guard detected a huge oil slick trailing after the world's largest cruise ship, Royal Caribbean's *Sovereign of the Seas*. A four-year investigation determined 'a fleet-wide conspiracy within Royal Caribbean Cruises Ltd. to save millions of dollars by dumping oily wastes into the sea' (*Ibid.*). Even after Royal Caribbean paid a nine million dollar fine in June 1998 and said it would never happen again, it did happen one month later. Royal Caribbean's *Nordic Empress* dumped oily wastes and attempted to hide the fact by creating false records. To defend itself, Royal Caribbean's lawyers boldly claimed, 'a private company doing business in the United States was immune from criminal prosecution because its ships fly foreign flags' (Douglas Franz, 'Gaps in Sea Laws Shield Pollution by Cruise Lines,' *New York Times*, January 3, 1999: 1). Royal Caribbean's ships are registered in Liberia. Helping Royal Caribbean make this case were former U.S. Attorneys General Benjamin R. Civiletti and Elliot L. Richardson. Royal Caribbean also took on board William K. Reilly, a former head of the Environmental Protection Agency. He was hired, Royal Caribbean said with a straight face, to help implement a new environmental compliance program (*Ibid.*). Civiletti and Richardson should have been chagrined when the *Nordic Express* discharge was discovered, as it followed their courtroom performances in defense of Liberian registry (*Ibid.*).

# 16. Historical context and hazardous waste facility siting: understanding temporal patterns in Michigan*

*Robin Saha and Paul Mohai*

This article tests the proposition that, beginning in the 1970s, historic growth of public environmental concern and opposition to waste facilities, as well as changes in the policy environment increasingly encouraged hazardous waste facilities siting to follow the path of least (political) resistance and resulted in environmental inequities. Our longitudinal analysis of sitings in the State of Michigan from 1950 to 1990 reveals a distinct temporal pattern supporting our hypotheses. Whereas significant racial, socioeconomic, and housing disparities at the time of siting were not in evidence for facilities sited prior to 1970, patterns of disparate siting were found for facilities sited after 1970. Thus, we call for environmental justice studies employing longitudinal methods to understand the processes and factors contributing to environmental inequalities with greater consideration to changes in historical context.

Environmental justice research largely has been devoted to examining social inequalities in the geographic distribution of environmental hazards such as waste facilities and other pollution sources (Brown 1995; Bullard 1983, 1990; Mohai and Bryant 1992; Ringquist 2005). Environmental justice scholars only recently have begun to examine inequitable distributions over time. Longitudinal studies focus on the temporal sequence of events that result in present day environmental inequalities by assessing social and demographic characteristics of host neighborhoods at the time noxious facilities are sited and by analyzing subsequent changes (Been 1994; Been and Gupta 1997; Krieg 1995; Oakes, Anderton, and Anderson 1996; Pastor, Sadd, and Hipp 2001; Stretesky and Hogan 1998; Szasz and Meuser 2000). This literature asks generally whether minority and low-income neighborhoods 'attract' noxious land uses and whether localized negative impacts (e.g., on property values, neighborhood pride, health, and safety) lead to disproportionate demographic changes (Baibergenova *et al.* 2003; Freudenberg 1997; Nelson, Genereux, and Genereux 1992; Vrijheid *et al.* 2002). By going beyond merely asking whether environmental inequalities exist, these studies take an important step toward understanding environmental inequity formation processes and associated factors (Pellow 2000). This article tests the proposition that, beginning in the

---

*From *Social Problems* (2005), 52(4): pp. 618–648.

1970s, historic growth of public environmental concern and opposition to waste facilities, as well as changes in the policy environment increasingly encouraged hazardous waste facilities siting to follow the path of least (political) resistance and resulted in disparate siting in low-income and minority neighborhoods.

## Explanations of hazardous facility location

Environmental justice theory currently is under active development, as researchers consider the myriad factors that may account for disparities in the distribution of environmentally hazardous sites by race and socioeconomic status. Rational choice, sociopolitical, and racial discrimination models have been offered to explain discriminatory siting decisions and post-siting demographic changes that may occur in the surrounding neighborhoods (Saha and Mohai 1997). These models have often been treated as competing explanations, but in fact they may be complementary.

Rational choice models emphasize market rationality in industry site-selection decisions and in household residential-location decisions. Low-income and minority neighborhoods provide the most efficient locations for industry because land prices and compensation costs are relatively low, and industrial zones often coincide with where low-income and minority residents live (Portney 1991a). Neighborhood transition subsequent to siting occurs in response to the siting of noxious facilities and other locally unwanted land uses as relatively high-income residents vote with their feet. Their departure and the subsequent downward pressure on housing costs provide ample affordable housing for disproportionately low-income minorities, thereby creating new disparities or worsening ones that exist at the time of siting (Been and Gupta 1997).

Sociopolitical models focus on social group differences in the ability to resist siting proposals and force the clean-up of contamination (Schlosberg 1999). For example, Robert D. Bullard (1983, 1990) argues that siting follows the 'path of least political resistance' because low-income and minority communities lack the power to influence siting decisions. Community resistance may also be lowered by the promise of jobs and tax revenues (Bohon and Humphrey 2000; Bullard and Wright 1987). At the same time, disadvantaged groups are underrepresented in industry and government where siting decisions are made and approved (Mohai and Bryant 1992). Thus, because of their political and economic vulnerability, low-income and minority neighborhoods are less likely to defeat siting proposals and are more likely to receive proposals deflected from more politically powerful (i.e., affluent, white) areas.

Racial discrimination models posit that minority communities are targeted intentionally for reasons of prejudice, beliefs in racial superiority, or a desire to protect racial group position (Pulido 2000). Racial discrimination also can take an institutionalized form not necessarily directly related to racist ideologies; for example, informal or formal land use and siting decision rules of industry and government that might appear race neutral, nevertheless, might lead to racially disparate outcomes (Feagin and Feagin 1986). Moreover, discrimination in various institutional domains, such as housing, education employment, and health care, and interactions thereof, can disadvantage minorities and limit their social and physical mobility (Mohai and Bryant 1992; Pellow 2002; Stretesky and Hogan 1998).

A common assumption underlying all these models is that the undesirability of hazardous waste and polluting industrial facilities and social, economic, and political factors affecting their placement have been constant over time. Testing of these models has produced mixed results. Some studies have reported evidence of racial and socioeconomic siting disparities (Been 1994; Hurley 1997; Pastor *et al.* 2001). Some have found evidence of post-siting demographic change (Mitchell, Thomas, and Cutter 1999; Stretesky and Hogan 1998). Still others have found evidence supporting neither (Been and Gupta 1997; Oakes *et al.* 1996).

We believe that part of the ambiguity of these studies relates to inconsistencies produced by relying on census tracts of widely varying sizes and with boundaries that shift from decade to decade (Mohai and Saha 2003). Recently, the problem of shifting tract boundaries, and hence of the shifting size of neighborhoods around hazardous sites, has been overcome by examining consistent geographic areas around such sites using Geographic Information Systems (GIS) technology (e.g., see Pastor *et al.* 2001). Another possible explanation for the ambiguous results may be the different temporal scopes of these studies. Despite implicit assumptions that the social, economic, and political factors affecting siting decisions are constant over time, factors in one historical period may have been more or less influential than in another. In this article we argue that the historical context of hazardous waste facility siting, in fact, has been changing significantly over the last 50 years, as public concerns about toxic contamination have grown and as industry and government responses have evolved.

By historical context, we mean the sociopolitical conditions at any given time that may affect siting outcomes. These include public attitudes and behaviors regarding hazardous waste, institutional arrangements of siting decision-making authority, and political opportunity structure for public participation in siting decisions. We argue that the latter two factors largely have been shaped by the policy environment (i.e., the laws governing the siting process, which in turn have been shaped by the emergence of mass environmental concern).

Our purpose then is to explain how and why the historical context of hazardous waste facility siting has been changing and to explore the consequences of these changes for racial and socioeconomic disparities in siting. We do so through an empirical analysis of temporal patterns of commercial hazardous waste siting in Michigan from 1950 to 1990. As Manuel Pastor, Jr., Jim Sadd, and John Hipp (2001) have done, we attempt to remove spatial ambiguity across census decades by mapping precise facility locations and controlling the geographic areas examined around their locations by using GIS methods. In considering the various factors influencing siting decisions that have changed over time, we analyze the historical development of environmental concern about waste facilities and the anti-toxics and environmental justice movements (Gottlieb 1993; Szasz 1994). We also examine changes in the political opportunity structure (in the narrow sense of 'proximate' or 'policy specific opportunities') for potential host communities (Tarrow 1996: 42). Thus, we consider how changes in federal-state-local institutional arrangements, brought about by the Resource Conservation and Recovery Act (RCRA), channeled and constrained social group participation in governmental siting decisions. We suggest that consideration of historical context can improve the explanatory value of environmental justice research models.

## Historical context and siting of hazardous waste facilities

We provide below an historical account of the development of public environmental concern about solid and hazardous wastes and the associated Not-in-My-Backyard (NIMBY) phenomenon. We delineate three distinct periods relevant to understanding public attitudes and anxieties about hazardous waste, social group political participation in siting decisions, and their effects on facility siting outcomes. These periods include: (1) the pre-NIMBY/pre-RCRA era (pre-1970); (2) the early NIMBY era (1970–1980); and 3) the post-Love Canal era (post-1980). We hypothesize that disparate siting patterns did not exist for facilities sited in the pre-NIMBY/pre-RCRA era, but that such patterns emerged in the early NIMBY era, and increased in severity in the post-Love-Canal era.

### Pre-NIMBY/pre-RCRA era (pre-1970)

The unprecedented growth in public awareness and concern during the 1960s and early 1970s about a wide range of environmental issues likely had a primary influence on the siting process. In addition to growing public concern about air and water pollution, population control, and natural resource protection, concern about waste disposal also developed during the 1960s, and would later expand in the 1970s (Dunlap 1992; Kanagy, Humphrey, and Firebaugh 1994). To address concerns about adverse health and environmental impacts of evergrowing amounts of solid waste, Congress passed the Solid Waste Disposal Act of 1965 and the Resource Recovery Act of 1970, which together created a limited federal role in solid waste management. These laws encouraged states and municipalities to shift from open dumping to sanitary landfills by providing grants, training programs, and technical standards. Prior to 1965, few states participated in waste management activities (Blumberg and Gottlieb 1989).

Although solid waste issues were squarely on the public agenda, hazardous wastes were not, and would not be until the Love Canal story broke in 1979 (see below). Prior to the enactment of RCRA of 1976 and the Hazardous and Solid Waste Amendments of 1984 no national policies regulated the siting of hazardous waste facilities. A similar situation existed at the state level. For example, in Michigan, no specific state policies provided oversight of hazardous waste facility siting until the passage of the state Hazardous Waste Management Act (Act 64) of 1979. The so-called Superfund Act (Comprehensive Environmental Remediation, Compensation, and Liability Act of 1979, or CERCLA) and its list of abandoned, contaminated sites are testimony to prior decades of unregulated handling of hazardous waste.

For waste facilities sited prior to RCRA and Act 64, governmental siting decisions rested with the appropriate local governmental approval bodies (e.g., city building departments and planning offices or zoning boards), which assured that standard building code, zoning requirements, and the like were met. Even in areas where zoning may have precluded siting in certain locations, zoning could be changed or variances issued. For example, Detroit was known for the 'flexibility' of its ordinances (Sugrue 1996). There were typically no specific requirements pertaining to design safety, operating conditions, or public participation in siting decisions beyond those required for any other industrial facility. Due to the lack of public awareness of the risks of hazardous waste and a similar lack of development of environmental and health sciences, public and governmental involvement in siting decisions was minimal, and many facilities 'functioned with an absolute minimum of technical safeguards or provisions for community input or oversight of facility management' (Rabe 1994: 28). Prior to the NIMBY phenomenon and RCRA, pollution was more generally accepted as a necessary price of economic prosperity, local approvals were routine, public opposition was rare, and the legal or regulatory context allowed little democratic deliberation in siting decisions (Davy 1997).

### Early NIMBY era (1970–1980)

Although sanitary landfills offered a significant improvement over open dumping in protecting public health and the environment, growing concern over the risks of old dump sites (many that were later to be designated Superfund sites) transferred to the new landfills and other disposal facilities, such as incinerators. According to the U.S. Environmental Protection Agency (EPA), community opposition to the siting of waste facilities grew throughout the 1970s and threatened to undermine governmental efforts to improve solid waste management (Bacow and Milkey 1982; U.S. EPA Office of Water and Waste Management 1979). Thus, public concern about waste facilities appears to have contributed to widespread growth of community organizing as environmental concern became expressed through local citizen action. This phenomenon became widely recognized and somewhat pejoratively labeled as the Not-In-My-Backyard (NIMBY) syndrome, fueled by highly visible events such as the Three-Mile Island nuclear accident of 1979.[1]

Despite the early emergence of mass environmental consciousness and growth in concern and citizen activism regarding solid waste facilities, accounts suggest that specific concern related to hazardous waste did not develop until around the time of Love Canal. These concerns centered around potential health risks, the impact on property values, the inability to keep out other undesirable land uses, and overall declines in the quality of life in a host community (Edelstein 1988). Environmental public opinion surveys by the EPA in 1973 and by the Council on Environmental Quality and Resources for the Future in 1980 show a shift in attitudes during the 1970s from disinterest and acceptance to extreme concern and opposition in regard to the local placement of hazardous waste facilities (Lindell and Earle 1983). Thus, in the late 1970s, public environmental concern over hazardous waste appears to have been increasing.

In the late 1970s and early 1980s, public concern about hazardous waste and grassroots organizing against new facility siting was generated by several well-publicized and controversial cases such as those in Love Canal, New York, and in Times Beach, Missouri (Kasperson 1986). Peter M. Sandman (1985) asserts that prior to Love Canal 'citizens were not very involved in, nor knowledgeable about, the siting of landfills and other hazardous waste disposal practices' (p. 439). The significance of Love Canal in catapulting public awareness (and fear) about hazardous waste does not mean that concern did not exist beforehand (Morell and Magorian 1982; U.S. EPA Office of Water and Waste Management 1979).[2] However, what distinguishes the early 1970s from the late 1970s and, more so, from the early 1980s is the extent of social embeddedness of hazardous waste concern. Andrew Szasz (1994) explains that

> As recently as 1976, 'toxic waste' was not yet a well-formed social issue. There was no clear public opinion concerning it, no crystallized mass perception that it is a serious threat to people's health. Hazardous waste became a true mass issue between 1978 and 1980, when sustained media coverage made *Love Canal* and *toxic waste* household words. By 1980, the American public feared toxic waste as much as it feared nuclear power after Three Mile Island. (p. 5)

Thus, any public opposition to hazardous waste facilities that existed in the early-NIMBY era might have related more to the type of facility. Local opposition to hazardous waste landfills and incinerators might have stemmed from their being similar technologies to familiar solid waste management facilities, rather than the hazardous wastes themselves. But that would soon change.

### Post-Love Canal era (post-1980)

Love Canal is a town near Niagara Falls where a residential neighborhood had been built on hazardous wastes dumped by a chemical company and covered with a thin layer of soil. Because of growing health concerns among residents, Lois Gibbs, a mother and housewife, led a lengthy campaign that captured the national spotlight. Her efforts eventually led to government action culminating in a federal buy-out of homes, President Carter visiting the site, and Congress enacting the 'Superfund Act' (see Gibbs 1982; Levine 1982). Love Canal heightened public fears that other communities were also unknowingly at risk of exposure to hazardous wastes and, more importantly, added new fuel to the NIMBY phenomenon.

According to Szasz (1994), public opposition to the siting of hazardous waste facilities was 'sporadic and isolated' prior to Love Canal but became widespread and vigorous afterward. Those who share this view note that public opposition grew steadily after the late 1970s and early 1980s (Mazmanian and Morell 1994). Studies of local reactions to hazardous waste sites document the emergence of increasing numbers of community groups organized around hazardous waste issues in the early 1980s (Freudenberg 1984; Quarantelli 1989). Concern about hazardous wastes paralleled that of pesticides and

318

other forms of toxic contamination (Brown 1981). For example, in Michigan, contamination of cattle feed with a flame retardant (PBB) heightened concerns about toxic chemicals and food safety in the late 1970s and early 1980s (Reich 1991). In 1984 came news coverage of the Union Carbide (now part of Dow Chemical) factory accident in Bhopal, India, which led to community right-to-know provisions of Superfund Amendments and Reauthorization Act of 1986 (i.e., creation of the Toxic Release Inventory [TRI]).

The growth of groups organized around toxics issues was so sudden and dramatic that a popular social movement with a formal infrastructure developed (Cable and Benson 1993). The emergence of an anti-toxics movement in many middle- and working-class neighborhoods reflected a change in societal views regarding the role of citizen involvement in siting decisions (Portney 1991b). The expansion of the movement is evidenced not only by the explosive growth in the number of grassroots groups during the 1980s, but also by national networks and international organizations such as the Citizen's Clearinghouse for Hazardous Waste (recently renamed the Center for Health, Environment, and Justice), the now-defunct National Toxics Campaign, and Greenpeace (Gottlieb 1993). Dorceta E. Taylor (1998) reports that, although localized opposition existed in the 1970s, throughout the 1980s grassroots organizations increased in number by over three-fold and grew in sophistication (see also Davy 1997).

Various accounts indicate that political mobilization around hazardous waste siting proposals from the 1970s to the 1990s progressively moved from white middle-class, to white working-class, to minority communities (Hurley 1995; Morrison 1986; Taylor 1993, 1997). In fact, surveys of citizens' groups from the early 1980s did not report involvement of minority and low-income populations in opposition campaigns, but noted participation primarily from the white-collar middle class and sometimes the 'working class' (Freudenberg 1984; Quarantelli 1989). Nevertheless, mobilization in communities of people of color in the late 1970s and early 1980s has been documented, such as the widely publicized Warren County protests in North Carolina. However, the emergence of a coherent grassroots people of color movement (i.e., the environmental justice movement) does not appear to have occurred until the late 1980s and early 1990s (Taylor 2000), suggesting that minority and poor communities were initially politically vulnerable to waste facility sitings.

The impact of public opposition has been significant, especially regarding the siting of new hazardous waste facilities (Dinkins 1995; Freudenberg and Steinsapir 1991). In the 1980s, some analysts considered public opposition 'the single most critical factor in developing new hazardous waste management facilities' (Furuseth 1989: 358; see also Daly and Vitaliano 1987). The role of public opposition in unsuccessful siting proposals is well-documented (O'Hare, Bacow, and Sanderson 1983; Rabe 1994). The difficulty of siting new facilities in the face of nearly universal public opposition was cited as evidence of the failure of RCRA (Mazmanian and Morell 1994) and prompted calls for new approaches to siting (NGA 1981; Rabe 1994). Thus, the historic growth of public concern about hazardous waste and resulting growth in grassroots activism has changed fundamentally the sociocultural context in which facility siting occurs.

There are some important implications regarding (1) the steady and increasing environmental concern in response to increasing recognition of the seriousness of environmental problems, and (2) the explosive growth of citizen opposition to siting of environmental hazards, which appeared to have occurred relatively late in minority and working-class communities. These developments suggest that facility siting increasingly followed the path of least resistance throughout the 1970s and 1980s. As middle-class, upper-class, and (later) working-class communities became involved in citizen opposition groups, new facilities were increasingly likely to be deflected or directed to minority and low-income neighborhoods and communities, which were seen as the paths of least resistance due to their need for jobs and their political vulnerability associated with limited access to resources and allies in government (Bullard and Wright 1987). Because the environmental justice movement did not develop in earnest until the 1990s (see Taylor 2000), siting in minority and low-income communities may have increased throughout the 1970s and 1980s. Although mobilization of people of color has been significant in the 1990s, with the subsequent prominence of 'success stories,' their ability to resist unwanted facilities appears limited (Cole and Foster 2001; Hurwitz and Sullivan 2001; Moss 2001), suggesting that disparate siting persisted in the 1990s, though perhaps to a lesser degree.

## The legal context of siting

Public environmental concern also resulted in RCRA of 1976, the Hazardous and Solid Waste Amendments (HSWA) of 1984, and corresponding state legislation (Davis 1993). These laws fundamentally altered the playing field of siting contestation, particularly in the post-Love Canal era when the laws took effect. We argue below that these changes in the legal and regulatory context of siting, by changing the dynamics of NIMBY-ism, further contributed to racial and socioeconomic siting disparities. We explain how siting laws served as an additional factor to encourage sitings to follow the path of least resistance by shifting authority from the local level to state and federal agencies. By shaping the political opportunity structure for public participation in siting decisions (Tarrow 1996), thereby leading to discriminatory outcomes, these institutional arrangements constitute an indirect form of institutional discrimination.

In enacting RCRA and HSWA, Congress sought for states, rather than the EPA, to administer their own hazardous waste programs. States were encouraged to pass their own legislation modeled after RCRA and to develop programs at least as stringent as the EPA's. Since passage of RCRA and Michigan's corresponding legislation, Act 64, decision-making authority in Michigan shifted from local government to the Michigan Department of Environmental Quality (DEQ).[3] Local government authority under Act 64 is minimal, and merely consists of verifying that siting proposals comply with local zoning. At the same time, Act 64 gives preemptive decision-making authority to the DEQ to override local opposition to siting. This authority also exists in the majority of other states managing RCRA programs (Rabe 1994).

State siting decisions are made through permitting systems prescribed under RCRA. The purpose of permitting programs is to ensure government oversight and protection of human health and the environment in the construction, operation, and closure of facilities. In Michigan, waste facility developers must obtain a permit from the DEQ before construction can begin. Although developers can be denied a permit, the DEQ is obligated to approve a permit if a proposal meets legal and technical requirements (Davy 1997). Prior to issuance of a final permit, the agency issues a draft permit, which starts a 45-day public comment period. In Michigan, if a public hearing is requested (they are not required), a Site Review Board oversees them and subsequently advises the DEQ (Fletcher 2003). The draft permit signals imminent state approval provided that no 'substantial new questions concerning the permit are raised' (U.S. EPA Office of Solid Waste 1990: III-79). Thus, public participation in siting decisions under RCRA occurs essentially after the decision has been made (Cole and Foster 2001; Kraft and Kraut 1988). Nevertheless, the provisions provide limited access points for the public to influence final permitting decisions, and these changes and state pre-emption alter the political opportunity structure for collective action in proposed host communities (McAdam 1982).

Public participation rules allow certain communities to delay or curtail the siting process. Administrative and legal challenges at the state and federal levels, and even local zoning disputes, may also stall the process, thereby encouraging facility sponsors to withdraw their applications and to seek more receptive locations (Cerrell Associates, Inc. 1984; Daly and Vitaliano 1987). For facilities such as incinerators that also must obtain Clean Air Act (CAA) permits, citizen groups may file CAA appeals or law suits. However, bringing such challenges or delaying permit approvals by taking advantage of the public participation provisions of Act 64, RCRA, or other environmental laws requires considerable technical, legal, and financial resources that often are available only to affluent, politically well-connected communities. This policy environment, in disadvantaging minority and low-income communities and leading to disparate outcomes, is a form of indirect institutional discrimination (Feagin and Feagin 1986; Lake 1996; Stretesky and Hogan 1998). In fact, Thomas H. Fletcher (2003) documents affluent white communities' effective use of delay strategies to oppose hazardous waste facility siting in Michigan during the 1980s. However, less empowered communities tend to lack the political clout and resources needed to mount effective public opposition campaigns (Hurwitz and Sullivan 2001). In fact, evidence such as a report commissioned by the California Waste Management Board, entitled 'Political Difficulties Facing Waste-to-Energy Conversion Plant Siting,' indicates that opposition from low-income and minority neighborhoods might be less likely than from other areas (Cerrell Associates 1984; Portney 1991a).

In summary, we posit that a historical convergence of several interacting factors has contributed to disparate siting in recent decades. These developments include the growth of public concern about hazardous waste, laws to manage it, growth in local opposition to the placement of it, as well as concern about the failure to successfully site new facilities. Changes in the historical context of siting in the 1970s and 1980s contributed significantly to sociopolitical conditions in which the siting of new waste facilities followed the path of least resistance that allowed patterns of disparate siting of hazardous waste facilities during the early NIMBY era (in the 1970s). Conversely, facilities sited in the pre-NIMBY/pre-RCRA era (prior to 1970) would not necessarily have been sited disproportionately in areas least able to resist them. Furthermore, the consequences of new siting laws and policies favoring affluent communities, along with the progressive growth of environmental concern and NIMBY behaviors ignited by public fears about hazardous waste in the wake of Love Canal, suggest that disparate siting has been more prevalent and severe in the 1980s than in the 1970s.

## Temporal patterns revealed by previous studies

Although not explicitly considering the role of historical context, at least six empirical studies have examined the past demographics of hazardous waste sites to determine whether minorities or low-income persons were overrepresented, relative to the wider community, in areas near these facilities around the time of siting (Been 1994; Been and Gupta 1997; Hamilton 1993; Hurley 1997; Oakes et al. 1996; Pastor et al. 2001). The temporal spans examined by these studies vary considerably, as do the methodologies employed. For example, all but two of the studies essentially examined individual host census tracts, zip codes, townships, or counties, and thus did not necessarily geographically standardize the host areas into consistent areas over time or among facilities (Mohai and Saha 2003). Despite these limitations, the findings can be used to assess temporal patterns in disparate siting. This is accomplished by examining siting disparities in the pre-NIMBY/pre-RCRA, early NIMBY, and post-Love-Canal eras as delineated above.

Vicki Been (1994) conducted two longitudinal studies that were extensions of a 1983 U.S. General Accounting Office (GAO) study of four hazardous waste landfills in the Southeast and Bullard's 1983 study of ten municipal waste facilities and mini-incinerators in the Houston area (Harris County, Texas). Three of four facilities examined in the GAO study (U.S. GAO 1983) sited in neighborhoods with disproportionately high percentages of African Americans were sited in the 1970s. Of the 10 facilities from the Bullard study, two were sited in the 1950s and the remaining eight in the 1970s. Been found five of the eight facilities sited in the 1970s were sited disproportionately with respect to race. None of the facilities sited in the pre-NIMBY/pre-RCRA era (pre-1970) evidenced disparate siting.

Similarly, in a national study, James T. Hamilton (1993) found minority percentages to be a positive predictor and mean housing values to be a negative predictor of counties that received new commercial hazardous waste facilities sited in the 1970s. In a more refined zip code area study, Hamilton (1995) found that facilities that expanded their capacity between 1987 and 1992 were disproportionately located in zip codes with higher percentages of minorities, lower housing values, and, to a lesser extent, lower incomes. In both studies, Hamilton's multivariate analyses showed an independent and significant effect (as predicted) relative to measures of public opposition. Although expansion plans are different than new sitings, Hamilton's findings are consistent with the supposition that the emergence of vigorous public opposition influenced siting decisions in the early-NIMBY and post-Love-Canal eras.

Andrew Hurley (1997) used census tracts within one mile of 56 hazardous waste sites in St. Louis, Missouri. The sites included abandoned toxic waste sites, waste recycling facilities, and other facilities that posed known health risks. A distinct historical pattern was found. Prior to 1975, African-Americans were underrepresented or proportionally represented in hazardous waste tracts compared to the metropolitan area, but after 1975, waste sites were located in predominantly African-American neighborhoods. Pastor and associates (2001) examined census tracts within one-quarter mile and one mile of 38 high-capacity hazardous waste facilities sited in the 1970s and 1980s in Los Angeles County. These host neighborhood tracts had significantly higher minority percentages (of both African Americans and Latinos) and lower incomes, housing values, and educational attainment levels prior to siting than other tracts in the county. Both Hurley (1997) and Pastor and associates (2001) show siting disparities in the early-NIMBY and post-Love-Canal eras.

Social and Demographic Research Institute (SADRI) researchers at the University of Massachusetts (Oakes *et al.* 1996) conducted a national study of commercial hazardous waste facilities sited in the 1960s 1970s, and 1980s. The SADRI researchers limited their analysis to metropolitan areas with at least one facility and examined socioeconomic and housing conditions during the decade of siting. They found tracts with facilities did not have significantly higher minority percentages, poverty rates, or housing values than tracts without facilities in 'areas with significant industrial employment' (Oakes *et al.* 1996:137). In a previous analysis of the same facilities, SADRI researchers compared host tracts to census tracts without facilities, regardless of levels of industrial and manufacturing employment (Anderson, Anderton, and Oakes 1994). As in the subsequent study, they found no significant differences in minority percentages or poverty rates, but they did find significant housing value disparities for facilities sited in the 1970s and 1980s as well as differences in levels of industrial and manufacturing employment.

Vicki Been and Francis Gupta (1997) conducted another national study that made comparisons using single host tracts but a slightly different universe of commercial hazardous waste facilities than SADRI. Been and Gupta found race, poverty, and housing disparities in the early-NIMBY era, and poverty and housing disparities in the post-Love-Canal era (see Table 16.1). However, they did not examine siting disparities in the pre-NIMBY/pre-RCRA era.

Another study that used counties and incorporated areas as the unit of analysis examined the location of 73 facilities on the EPA's Toxic Release Inventory sited in South Carolina from the 1930s through the 1980s (Mitchell *et al.* 1999). In separately examining urban, suburban, and rural areas, compared to overall state averages, Mitchell and associates (1999) found that host areas did not have significantly higher minority percentages, regardless of the decade sited. Host areas of rural facilities sited in the 1970s and 1980s did, however, exhibit disproportionately lower income levels.

Table 16.1 summarizes the results of this review of previous studies. Table 16.1 shows that racial, socioeconomic, and housing disparities at the time of siting have not been in evidence for noxious facilities sited in the pre-NIMBY/pre-RCRA era. However, in the early-NIMBY era the phenomenon appears in national-, regional-, county-, and city-level studies. Although disparities have also been found for facilities sited in the post-Love Canal era, the results appear to be less robust. Nevertheless, despite the methodological variations, a clear pattern is evident. Siting disparities appear subsequent to the emergence of widespread public environmental concerns, the concomitant rise of public opposition to waste facility siting, and changes in the policy environment of siting.

## Temporal analysis of TSDF siting in Michigan

A more purposeful assessment of the importance of historical context to the incidence of disparate siting was conducted by examining commercial hazardous waste treatment, storage, and disposal facilities (TSDFs) sited in Michigan from the 1950s through the 1980s. We tested the hypothesis that discriminatory siting patterns did not exist for facilities sited in the pre-NIMBY/pre-RCRA era (pre-1970), but that such patterns emerged in the early NIMBY era (1970s), and increased in severity in the post-Love Canal era (post-1980).

### Methods

Siting conditions were examined for 23 commercial hazardous waste TSDFs operating in Michigan in 1989. The TSDFs were identified from lists obtained from the EPA Resource Conservation and Recovery Act Information System (RCRIS) under a Freedom of Information Act request. The TSDF names and locations from RCRIS were compared to lists obtained from the Michigan Department of Natural Resources (DNR). Opening dates were either obtained from or confirmed by the DNR (Sliver 1993). The TSDFs were sited throughout the state in both metropolitan and non-metropolitan areas. Appendix A lists the geographic locations and current status of the facilities, and shows that some facilities have ceased operations since 1989.[4] No new commercial TSDFs have been sited from 1989 to the time of our analysis.

The locations of facilities were digitally mapped by making site visits and using Topographically Integrated Graphic Encoding and Referencing System (TIGER) files and Geographic Information Systems software (ArcView GIS v. 3.2). This was accomplished by using the street layer of the TIGER files as a guide (GeoLytics Inc. 1999; Wessex Inc. 1995). Standardized host neighborhood areas were created with circular 'buffers' of a 1.0-mile radius centered at the TSDF locations, and demographic and housing characteristics of these areas were estimated through area-weighting procedures described below.[5] Delineating consistently sized circular host neighborhood areas served to control for proximity between the TSDFs and nearby populations and surmounted the difficulties of managing census tract boundary changes across multiple decades. For 1950, 1960, and 1970, high quality digitized census tracts were not available. Therefore, these were created by using printed maps as a

**Table 16.1** Review of existing quantitative studies of racial, socioeconomic, and housing disparities at time of siting

| ERA | Decade | Study | Scope/Area | Race/Income/Housing | | |
| --- | --- | --- | --- | --- | --- | --- |
| | | | | Ethnicity | Poverty | Costs |
| PRE-NIMBY/PRE-RCRA ERA | 1930s and earlier | Mitchell et al. 1999 | South Carolina | No | No | n/a |
| | 1940s | Hurley 1997 | St. Louis, MO | No | n/a | n/a |
| | | Mitchell et al. 1999 | South Carolina | No | No | n/a |
| | | Hurley 1997 | St. Louis, MO | No | n/a | n/a |
| | 1950s | Mitchell et al. 1999 | South Carolina | No | No | n/a |
| | | Been 1994; Bullard 1983 | Harris Co., TX | No | No | n/a |
| | | Hurley 1997 | St. Louis, MO | No | n/a | n/a |
| | 1960s | Oakes et al. 1996 | U.S. | No | No | No |
| | | Mitchell et al. 1999 | South Carolina | No | No | n/a |
| | | Hurley 1997 | Gary, Indiana | No | n/a | n/a |
| EARLY NIMBY ERA | 1970s | Hamilton 1993 | U.S. | Yes | No | Yes |
| | | Oakes et al. 1996 | U.S. | No | No | No |
| | | Been and Gupta 1997 | U.S. | Yes | Yes | Yes |
| | | Been 1994; GAO 1983 | Southeast U.S. | Yes | Yes | Yes |
| | | Mitchell et al. 1999 | South Carolina | No | No | n/a |
| | | Pastor et al. 2001 | Los Angeles Co., CA | Yes | Yes | Yes |
| | | Hurley 1997 | St. Louis, MO | Yes | n/a | n/a |
| POST-LOVE CANAL ERA | 1980s | Hamilton 1995 | U.S. | Yes | Yes | No |
| | | Oakes et al. 1996 | U.S. | No | No | No |
| | | Been and Gupta 1997 | U.S. | No | Yes | Yes |
| | | Mitchell et al. 1999 | South Carolina | No | No | n/a |
| | | Pastor et al. 2001 | Los Angeles Co., CA | Yes | Yes | Yes |
| | | Hurley 1997 | St. Louis, MO | Yes | n/a | n/a |
| | 1990s | Been and Gupta 1997 | U.S. | No | Yes | n/a |

guide and by 'dissolving' the boundaries of sets of 1990 census blocks such that digital shapes produced corresponded to each of the 1950, 1960, and 1970 tracts. In some cases, it was necessary to adjust vertices of the 1990 blocks to correspond precisely to 1950, 1960, or 1970 tract boundaries. For 1980 and 1990, commercially available digitized block groups were used (GeoLytics Inc. 1998). These smaller constituent units of census tracts allowed more accurate estimation of population and housing characteristics in circular host-neighborhood areas. Block groups were not used for earlier censuses because data were not sufficiently reported at that level.

To estimate the demographic composition of host neighborhoods 1.0-mile radius circular buffers were 'intersected' with the digitized census tracts or block groups corresponding to the census immediately preceding and following siting, using the Xtools extension for Arc- View GIS (v. 3.2) and a Lambert's Conformal Conic Projection.[6] The percentage of each tract's (or block group's) area within the buffers was computed, and raw census data were weighted according to the proportion of area within each circle. For example, demographic and housing data for blocks groups 10 or 50 percent within the circle were weighted (multiplied) by 0.10 and 0.50. Thus, if a block group had a population of 3,000 and was 30 percent within the 1.0-mile buffer, its contribution to the population of the 1.0-mile host neighborhoods would be 900. If an entire tract or block group was contained within the buffer, then a weighting factor of 100 percent was used (i.e., the demographic and housing characteristics for the entire tract or block group were used). Using this area-weighting method, raw data for all 1950, 1960, and 1970 tracts, and 1980 and 1990 block groups that were completely or partially intersected by the 1.0-mile circles were aggregated. These values were used to calculate percentages and means for host neighborhoods (see Appendix B).[7]

Some areas within the circular buffers were not 'tracted' because they were not designated by the Census Bureau as census tracts. For areas not covered by tracts, the same area-weighting procedures were applied to Minor Civil Divisions (MCDs), which are the primary incorporated and unincorporated political divisions of a county, including cities, towns, and townships. On average, MCDs are larger than census tracts, but smaller than counties. Area-weighted MCD data for untracted areas within circular buffers were aggregated with those of tracted areas to compute estimated population and housing characteristics of all areas (tracted and untracted) within a 1.0-mile radius. These steps were required for three facilities located in or near untracted areas – one sited in the 1970s and two sited in the 1980s.

The area-weighting method was employed to test two basic propositions: (1) disparate siting was less prevalent and severe prior to 1970, and (2) the severity of disparate siting (i.e., the magnitude of racial, socioeconomic, and housing disparities) were greater for TSDFs sited in the 1980s than for TSDFs sited in the 1970s. Racial, socioeconomic, and housing disparities were assessed by examining demographic conditions at or near the time of siting to determine whether disparate siting occurred. Socioeconomic conditions in host neighborhoods were assessed by examining mean family incomes, poverty rates, and employment variables such as unemployment rates and labor force participation rates.[8] These data also served as an indicator of household- and neighborhood-level economic conditions. Housing disparities were assessed by examining mean owner-occupied housing values, homeownership rates, and housing vacancy rates. In addition, changes in the size of the housing stock and new residential housing construction rates were examined (see Appendix B for a list of data sources and construction of the variables). These data provided insights into neighborhood investment, housing quality and demand, shifts in residential land use patterns, and the overall economic vitality of host neighborhoods. These analyses were done separately for TSDFs sited in each decade before 1970 and after 1970.

Because census data are reported in ten-year intervals corresponding to the beginning of each decade, it was only possible to assess demographic conditions at the exact time of siting for those facilities that were sited at the turn of a decade (i.e. 1950, 1960, 1970, etc.). Although it could be argued that decennial data might be appropriately used for facilities sited within a year or two before or after a census date, facilities sited in the middle of the decade would pose a problem in determining from which census data should be considered. The approach taken was to examine conditions for the census immediately preceding siting and the census immediately following siting. By doing so, demographic and housing conditions at or near the time of siting were assessed. For example, if a facility was sited in 1962 or 1965, then data from the 1960 and 1970 censuses were used. If disparities were noted in the location in both 1960 and 1970, then it could be reasonably assumed that disparities existed at the time of siting, since it would be highly unlikely that the disparities in 1960 would disappear in 1962 or 1965 and then reappear in 1970.

Disparities were assessed by comparing the demographic and housing conditions in 1.0-mile host neighborhoods to all areas beyond 1.0 mile in the host metropolitan areas and non-metropolitan host counties. Alternate assessments were made using the entire State of Michigan as the comparison area, but these data were not reported for a few reasons. First, many areas in Michigan, especially remote regions, were likely not suitable for siting TSDFs because, for example, they were located far from the centers of hazardous waste production and lacked necessary transportation infrastructures. These areas are not appropriate to include in the comparison area when the objective is to assess demographic and housing disparities between areas that reasonably could have received TSDFs. Second, the entire state has lower minority percentages and higher percentages of persons of low socioeconomic status than host metropolitan areas and non-metropolitan host counties, making the likelihood of finding racial and socioeconomic disparities greater. Thus, the most conservative comparison area, least likely to yield disparities, was used.

## Results

Two facilities were sited in the 1950s, five in the 1960s, eight in the 1970s, and eight in the 1980s (see Appendix A). To determine whether historical context has influenced siting as hypothesized, we first consider TSDFs sited before 1970.

*Pre-NIMBY and Pre-RCRA Era Sitings (Prior to 1970).* Racial, socioeconomic, and housing disparities at the time of siting were assessed for Michigan TSDFs sited in the 1950s and 1960s, prior to the time during which significant changes occurred in the sociocultural and legal context of siting. Table 16.2 shows demographic and housing data in the censuses before and after siting for TSDFs sited in the 1950s. These TSDFs were sited in the Detroit metropolitan area, which at the time included Wayne, Oakland, and Macomb counties. Table 16.2 shows that during the decade of siting, the total population in 1.0-mile host neighborhoods of TSDFs sited in the 1950s decreased slightly (about 5 percent) from 43,209 to 41,072. The relatively high population density indicates that these TSDFs were located in or near residential areas in urbanized areas of metropolitan Detroit.

Table 16.2 also shows that host neighborhoods of TSDFs sited in the 1950s were nearly entirely white. The percentage of nonwhites in the 1.0-mile host neighborhoods was less than 1 percent in both 1950 and 1960, while areas beyond 1.0 mile in the Detroit metropolitan area were 12 percent and 15 percent nonwhite in 1950 and 1960, respectively.[9] Because TSDFs that were classified as being sited in the 1950s for this study were sited in 1948 and 1952, the 1950 Census data corresponds to conditions closest to the time of siting. Regardless, nonwhites were underrepresented in these host neighborhoods at the time of siting, and during the entire decade of siting.

In 1950, mean family income in 1.0-mile host neighborhoods was 11 percent greater than that in areas beyond 1.0 mile in the Detroit metropolitan area: $4,472 vs. $4,036, respectively (see Table 16.2). Thus, mean family income in host neighborhoods of TSDFs sited in the 1950s was disproportionately high at the time of siting. Employment conditions in host neighborhoods of TSDFs sited in the 1950s also appeared relatively good. In 1950, labor force participation rates in the host neighborhoods were slightly higher than those in areas beyond 1.0 mile (58 percent vs. 56 percent). Table 16.2 also shows lower civilian unemployment rates in host neighborhoods than in more distant non-host areas (4.0 percent vs. 6.2 percent). The 1960 data show that employment conditions remained robust throughout the 1950s.

Mean housing value in host neighborhoods, however, appeared to decline relative to the comparison areas. For example, in 1950, mean owner-occupied housing value within 1.0 mile ($9,531) was 5 percent lower than that in areas beyond 1.0 mile ($10,007). However, in 1960 the mean within 1.0 mile was 21 percent lower than in the comparison areas. Although housing value was not disproportionately low at the time of siting, neighborhood changes occurred in the decade of siting that appear to have had an adverse impact on housing values. Appreciation and new home building in other parts of the county can also explain the increasing housing value disparity. Nevertheless, homeownership rates remained relatively robust throughout the 1950s, while housing vacancy rates in host neighborhoods stayed relatively low (see Table 16.2). In addition, the number of housing units increased 14 percent, from 12,895 to 14,663. Growth in the housing stock indicates that TSDFs sited in the 1950s were in thriving residential areas.

In fact, overall economic, employment, and housing conditions in host neighborhoods of TSDFs sited in the 1950s appear to have been relatively good

**Table 16.2** Racial, socioeconomic, and housing disparities for pre-NIMBY, pre-RCRA (pre-1970) TSDFs[a]

| Variable | Sited in 1950s | | | | Sited in 1960s | | | |
|---|---|---|---|---|---|---|---|---|
| | 1950 Census | | 1960 Census | | 1960 Census | | 1970 Census | |
| | 1.0 Mile Circle | Beyond 1.0 Mile | 1.0 Mile Circle | Beyond 1.0 Mile | 1.0 Mile Circle | Beyond 1.0 Mile | 1.0 Mile Circle | Beyond 1.0 Mile |
| Total population | 43,209 | 2,972,988 | 41,072 | 3,721,288 | 21,423 | 4,104,124 | 31,232 | 4,579,743 |
| Number of housing units | 12,895 | 845,132 | 14,663 | 1,138,580 | 5,975 | 1,260,409 | 8,769 | 1,444,513 |
| Population density (persons per square mile) | 6,912 (4.66) | 1,483 | 6,570 (3.54) | 1,856 | 1,381 (0.96) | 1,434 | 2,014 (1.26) | 1,600 |
| Percent black | 0.54% (0.04) | 12.0% | 0.46% (0.03) | 15.0% | 1.14% (0.08) | 14.0% | 1.06% (0.06) | 16.8% |
| Percent nonwhite | 0.62% (0.05) | 12.2% | 0.78% (0.05) | 15.2% | 1.25% (0.09) | 14.2% | 1.58% (0.09) | 17.2% |
| Mean family income | $4,472 (1.11) | $4,036 | $7,513 (0.95) | $7,887 | $7,499 (0.96) | $7,836 | $12,890 (0.96) | $13,400 |
| Percent persons 14 years and over in labor force | 58.3% (1.04) | 56.2% | 56.0% (1.00) | 56.0% | 56.9% (1.01) | 56.1% | 62.9% (1.07) | 58.9% |
| Percent unemployed civilians 14 years and over | 3.97% (0.64) | 6.15% | 6.36% (0.82) | 7.79% | 6.71% (0.89) | 7.56% | 4.82% (0.85) | 5.70% |
| Mean owner-occupied housing value | $9,531 (0.95) | $10,007 | $11,641 (0.79) | $14,656 | $13,101 (0.90) | $14,531 | $22,712 (1.03) | $22,073 |
| Percent owner-occupied housing units | 68.8% (1.11) | 61.7% | 67.7% (0.95) | 71.1% | 84.7% (1.19) | 71.5% | 81.0% (1.12) | 72.4% |
| Percent vacant housing units | 1.92% (0.56) | 3.43% | 5.36% (0.85) | 6.31% | 4.80% (0.76) | 6.32% | 2.96% (0.71) | 4.14% |

[a]Numbers in parentheses are ratios of values within 1.0-mile host neighborhoods to values in areas beyond 1.0-mile in host metropolitan areas.

during the entire decade of siting. The only remarkable finding regarding these host neighborhoods was the extremely low representation of minorities.

Siting conditions were remarkably similar for TSDFs sited in the 1960s, all but one of which were also sited in the Detroit metropolitan area (see Appendix A). In 1960, the nonwhite percentage in 1.0-mile host neighborhoods was about 1 percent, compared to 14 percent in areas beyond 1.0 mile in the host metropolitan area (see Table 16.2). In 1970, the nonwhite percentage in these host neighborhoods was still less than 2 percent, while in comparison areas it was 17 percent.

In 1960 and 1970, mean family income in host neighborhoods was similar to (only 4 percent lower than) that in comparison areas. Thus, no pattern of income disparities at the time of siting could be discerned. Although mean housing value in 1960 within 1.0 mile was approximately 10 percent lower than the mean value in areas beyond 1.0 mile ($13,101 vs. $14,531), it rebounded by 1970, when it was 3 percent higher ($22,712 vs. $22,073). Thus, neither a strong nor consistent pattern of housing value disparities is evident. Table 16.2 shows that host neighborhoods of TSDFs sited in the 1960s had relatively high homeownership rates and low housing vacancy rates, indicating relatively good housing conditions in these neighborhoods. In addition, from 1960 to 1970, the number of housing units increased 47 percent, compared to a 15 percent increase in comparison areas. These findings are generally consistent with those of TSDFs sited in the 1950s.

Employment conditions in host neighborhoods of TSDFs sited in the 1960s were also favorable relative to the rest of the host metropolitan area. For example, Table 16.2 shows that labor force participation rates in 1.0-mile host neighborhoods were 57 and 63 percent in 1960 and 1970, respectively, compared to 56 and 59 percent in areas beyond 1.0 mile. Unemployment rates were also slightly lower in host neighborhoods than in comparison areas in 1960 and 1970.

Overall racial, socioeconomic, and housing conditions in host neighborhoods of TSDFs sited in the 1960s were very similar to those of TSDFs sited in the 1950s. Minorities were underrepresented in host neighborhoods of TSDFs sited in both decades. These facilities were sited disproportionately in non-minority or white areas. Using mean income as an indicator, overall socioeconomic status in host neighborhoods of pre-1970 TSDFs sited was comparable to those in more distant areas in the host metropolitan area. Parity in employment conditions and relatively high homeownership rates demonstrate that host neighborhoods of TSDFs sited in the 1950s and 1960s were not economically depressed. Housing vacancy rates and increases in the number of housing units also indicate relatively high housing demand. Thus, in nearly all respects, neighborhoods of TSDFs sited before 1970 appear to have been vibrant, affordable, and desirable places to live when the hazardous waste facilities were sited.

Population density data show some differences between the TSDFs sited in the 1950s and 1960s. Table 16.2 shows a much higher population density in the decade of siting in host neighborhoods of TSDFs sited in the 1950s than those sited in the 1960s (6,912 vs. 1,381 persons per square mile, respectively). These data are consistent with the more urban location of TSDFs sited in the 1950s (see Appendix A). Table 16.2 also shows that, during the 1950s, population density decreased in host neighborhoods of TSDFs sited during the 1950s, whereas population density increased rapidly during the 1960s in host neighborhoods of TSDFs sited during the 1960s. Thus, during the decade of siting, there appear to be inherent demographic differences between host neighborhoods of TSDFs sited in the 1950s and 1960s, the former showing population decline and the latter exhibiting population growth.

These changes suggest that host neighborhoods of TSDFs sited during the 1950s underwent a slight economic decline during the decade of siting, whereas host neighborhoods of TSDFs sited during the 1960s did not. This conclusion is reinforced by data on rates of home ownership (i.e., the percentage of owner-occupied housing). Table 16.2 shows that the homeownership rate in 1.0-mile host neighborhoods of TSDFs sited in the 1950s was greater than that in non-host areas beyond 1.0 mile in 1950 (69 percent vs. 62 percent). However, during the 1950s homeownership rate remained static in these host neighborhoods, but increased dramatically elsewhere, such that the homeownership rate became slightly lower than that in non-host areas in 1960 (68 percent vs. 71 percent). In contrast, the homeownership rate in host neighborhoods of TSDFs sited in the 1960s was much higher (85 percent) and remained consistently above rates in non-host areas throughout the decade of siting (i.e., in both 1960 and 1970; see Table 16.2). A similar pattern can be noted with regard to mean family income changes.

Despite these differences, Michigan TSDFs sited before 1970 exhibited no consistent or strong racial, income, or housing disparities at the time of siting. However, if our proposition that historical context is important to the incidence of disparate siting is correct, then disparities will be in evidence with respect to TSDFs sited after 1970.

*Early NIMBY Era Sitings (in the 1970s).* Eight TSDFs were sited in Michigan during the 1970s, four in the Detroit area, three in the Grand Rapids-Muskegon-Muskegon Heights area, and one in a non-metropolitan area. Because TSDFs sited in the 1970s were located in two different metropolitan areas and a non-metropolitan county (Allegan), areas beyond 1.0 mile in the host metropolitan areas and non-metropolitan host county were used as the comparison area. For TSDFs sited in the 1970s, Metropolitan Statistical Area boundaries (MSAs) as defined in 1970 were used to ensure that comparison areas consisted of the same geographic areas for the 1970 and 1980 censuses. The Detroit MSA included, Macomb, Oakland, and Wayne counties. The Grand Rapids and Muskegon MSAs included Kent, Muskegon, and Ottawa Counties.[10] For TSDFs sited in the 1980s, MSA boundaries were used as defined in 1980. This entailed adding Lapeer and St. Clair counties for the Detroit MSA and substituting a different non-metropolitan county (Alpena).

Table 16.3 shows that host neighborhoods of TSDFs sited in the 1970s had a disproportionately high percentage of nonwhites at or near the time of siting. In 1970, the nonwhite percentage in 1.0-mile host neighborhoods was 2.9 times greater than that in areas beyond 1.0 mile in the host MSAs and non-metropolitan host county (46 percent vs. 16 percent). In 1980, the nonwhite percentage within 1.0 mile was 3.4 times greater than that in areas beyond

1.0 mile (67 percent vs. 20 percent). Thus, large racial disparities at the time of siting are evident.

Table 16.3 also shows that income disparities existed at the time of siting for TSDFs sited in the 1970s. In 1970, mean family income in 1.0-mile host neighborhoods was 23 percent less than that in areas beyond 1.0 mile ($10,167 vs. $13,289). In 1980, mean family income within 1.0 mile was 35 percent less than that beyond 1.0 mile ($17,681 vs. $27,110). Thus, there were not only substantial income disparities, but the magnitude of these disparities increased during the decade of siting. Table 16.3 shows a similar pattern for family poverty rates in 1970, which in 1.0-mile host neighborhoods were 2.0 times greater than those in the area beyond 1.0 mile (18 percent vs. 9.1 percent). In 1980, the family poverty rate was 2.6 times greater (18 percent vs. 6.7 percent). These data show that the poverty rate in host neighborhoods of TSDFs sited in the 1970s remained static, while it decreased in comparison areas. Disparities were also found with respect to employment conditions. In 1970, the unemployment rate in host neighborhoods was 1.4 times greater than that in comparison areas (8.1 percent vs. 5.7 percent). However, by 1980 the unemployment rate was 1.8 times greater in the same host neighborhoods (20 percent vs. 11 percent). A similar pattern can be noted with respect to labor force participation rates. The above data demonstrate that socioeconomic conditions in host neighborhoods of TSDFs sited in the 1970s were disproportionately low.

These host neighborhoods exhibited housing value disparities that increased during the decade of siting. Table 16.3 shows that mean housing value in 1.0-mile host neighborhoods in 1970 was 37 percent less than values in areas beyond 1.0 mile ($13,767 vs. $21,831). By 1980, mean housing value had become 54 percent less in host neighborhoods ($22,489 vs. $48,961). The homeownership rate was also consistently lower in host neighborhoods. For example in 1970, the homeownership rate was 65 percent, compared to 73 percent in non-host areas. In 1980, the homeownership rate in host neighborhoods declined considerably to 57 percent, while in comparison areas it had declined very slightly to 72 percent. Table 16.3 shows that host neighborhoods of TSDFs sited in the 1970s also had a higher housing vacancy rate. In 1970, the vacancy rate in host neighborhoods was lower than that in nonhost areas (7.1 percent vs. 4.1 percent). In 1980, the vacancy rate in host neighborhoods was 9.1 percent, but only 4.9 percent in comparison areas. Because housing vacancy rate in host neighborhoods grew much more rapidly during the decade of siting than in non-host areas, the magnitude of disparities increased during this period.

The lower housing values, lower homeownership rates, and higher housing vacancy rates as well as worsened employment conditions indicate that household- and neighborhood-level economic conditions were relatively depressed in host neighborhoods at the time of siting. The depressed economic conditions in host neighborhoods of TSDFs sited in the 1970s also are evidenced by the loss of population and residential housing. Table 16.3 shows that, from 1970 to 1980, the population in 1.0-mile host neighborhoods declined by over 22,000 persons (18 percent). The number of housing units also declined by 3,853 (9.1 percent) during the decade of siting. These declines occurred while the population remained stable and the number of housing units

**Table 16.3** Racial, socioeconomic, and housing disparities for early NIMBY and post-Love Canal eras (post-1970) TSDFs[a]

| | Sited in early NIMBY era (1970s) | | | | Sited in post-love-canal era (1980s) | | | |
|---|---|---|---|---|---|---|---|---|
| | 1970 Census | | 1980 Census | | 1980 Census | | 1990 Census | |
| Variable | 1.0 Mile Circle | Beyond 1.0 Mile | 1.0 Mile Circle | Beyond 1.0 Mile | 1.0 Mile Circle | Beyond 1.0 Mile | 1.0 Mile Circle | Beyond 1.0 Mile |
| Total population | 124,754 | 4,838,403 | 102,711 | 4,782,397 | 71,724 | 4,213,715 | 52,709 | 4,110,950 |
| Total housing units | 42,234 | 1,515,866 | 38,381 | 1,747,245 | 29,880 | 1,537,803 | 22,850 | 1,615,757 |
| Population density (persons per square mile) | 5,083 (5.03) | 1,010 | 4,179 (4.19) | 999 | 4,490 (4.24) | 1,058 | 3,300 (3.20) | 1,032 |
| Percent black | 45.1% (3.08) | 14.6% | 65.6% (3.60) | 18.2% | 50.6% (2.50) | 20.2% | 52.8% (2.38) | 22.2% |
| Percent nonwhite | 45.6% (2.93) | 15.6% | 67.3% (3.36) | 20.0% | 53.3% (2.43) | 21.9% | 55.9% (2.27) | 24.6% |
| Mean family income | $10,167 (0.77) | $13,289 | $17,681 (0.65) | $27,110 | $17,155 (0.62) | $27,570 | $26,725 (0.55) | $48,414 |
| Percent families below poverty level | 17.9% (1.97) | 9.1% | 17.7% (2.64) | 6.7% | 22.4% (3.23) | 6.9% | 34.2% (3.27) | 10.5% |
| Percent 16 years old and over in civilian labor force | 57.9% (0.98) | 58.8% | 56.0% (0.89) | 62.6% | 49.2% (0.79) | 62.1% | 49.7% (0.77) | 64.2% |
| Percent unemployed civilians 16 years old and over | 8.05% (1.42) | 5.65% | 19.52% (1.81) | 10.78% | 22.0% (1.89) | 11.6% | 21.4% (2.41) | 8.9% |
| Mean owner-occupied housing value | $13,767 (0.63) | $21,831 | $22,489 (0.46) | $48,961 | $24,059 (0.48) | $49,675 | $39,295 (0.47) | $83,468 |
| Percent owner-occupied housing units | 65.0% (0.89) | 73.2% | 57.1% (0.80) | 71.7% | 41.9% (0.59) | 71.6% | 40.9% (0.59) | 69.7% |
| Percent vacant housing units | 7.1% (1.74) | 4.1% | 9.1% (1.86) | 4.9% | 11.4% (2.33) | 4.9% | 10.1% (1.80) | 5.6% |

[a]Numbers in parentheses are ratios of values within 1.0-mile host neighborhoods to values in areas beyond 1.0-mile in host metropolitan areas and non-metropolitan host counties.

increased over 16 percent in the comparison areas. This finding suggests that housing units in some residential areas were falling into disrepair and being demolished. It appears that TSDF host neighborhoods were being converted to other land uses, such as industrial, or were just outright abandoned. In fact, little new housing construction occurred in host neighborhoods of TSDFs sited during the 1970s: 6.5 percent of all housing units in 1.0-mile host neighborhoods were built during the 1970s, compared to nearly 20 percent of those in areas beyond 1.0 mile. The loss of housing and low rates of new housing construction indicate that these host neighborhoods were undergoing residential decline in the decade of siting. Moreover, the finding of racial, socioeconomic, and housing disparities at the time of siting for TSDFs sited in the 1970s supports the hypothesis that siting disparities would be found for TSDFs sited after 1970 and the advent of mass environmental concern and the NIMBY phenomenon.

*Post-Love Canal Era Sitings (in the 1980s).* Racial, socioeconomic, and housing disparities were also evident at the time of siting for the eight TSDFs sited in Michigan during the 1980s. Six were sited in the Detroit metropolitan area, and five of these were sited in the City of Detroit. Two were located in the City and County of Alpena in the northeast lower peninsula of Michigan.

The nonwhite percentage in 1.0-mile host neighborhoods of TSDFs sited in the 1980s was consistently higher than that in non-host areas. Table 16.3 shows that, in 1980, the nonwhite percentage in 1.0-mile host neighborhoods was 2.4 times that in non-host areas beyond 1.0 mile (53 percent vs. 22 percent). In 1990, the nonwhite percentage in these host neighborhoods was 2.3 times greater than that in comparison areas (56 percent vs. 25 percent). Although the nonwhite percentage increased slightly in both host neighborhoods and comparison areas during the 1980s, the magnitude of racial disparities did not increase; rather, it actually decreased slightly. These findings indicate that the minority percentage in host neighborhoods of TSDFs sited in the 1980s was not growing rapidly or disproportionately during the decade of siting, in contrast to host neighborhoods of TSDFs sited in the 1970s. In fact, racial disparities for more recent sitings appear to be slightly smaller in magnitude than for those sited in the 1970s, running contrary to the hypothesis that disparities would increase from the 1970s and 1980s. Nevertheless, the high percentage of nonwhites in host neighborhoods suggests that racial transition occurred prior to the decade of siting. These host neighborhoods were well-established African-American areas, which is consistent with the preponderance of these TSDFs being located in the City of Detroit.

Income disparities at the time of siting are also in evidence for TSDFs sited in the 1980s. Table 16.3 shows that in 1980 mean family income in 1.0-mile host neighborhoods was 38 percent lower than that in areas beyond 1.0 mile ($17,155 vs. $27,570). In 1990, mean income was 45 percent lower in host neighborhoods than in comparison areas ($26,725 vs. $48,414). Poverty rates appear to follow a similar trend. Thus, income disparities appeared to be increasing during the decade of siting, suggesting that host neighborhoods were undergoing relative economic decline. In fact, the magnitude of these disparities was greater than that for TSDFs sited in the 1970s.

Similarly, disparities in employment conditions were greater for TSDFs sited in the 1980s. For example, unemployment rate disparities were greater for TSDFs sited in the 1980s than in the 1970s: 1.9 to 2.4 times greater in host neighborhoods of the 1980s-sited TSDFs, compared to 1.4 to 1.8 times greater for the 1970s-sited TSDFs. In both 1980 and 1990, the unemployment rate for 1980s-sited TSDFs exceeded 20 percent. In addition, disparities in the labor force participation rate were considerably greater for TSDFs sited in the 1980s than for TSDFs sited in the 1970s. In fact, the labor force participation rates for censuses immediately preceding and following siting in host neighborhoods of 1980s sitings (49–50 percent) were much lower than those of 1970s sitings (56–58 percent). Thus, socioeconomic conditions in host neighborhoods of TSDFs sited in the more recent decade were less favorable than those in host neighborhoods of TSDFs sited in the 1970s. These results provide additional evidence that the magnitude of disparities at the time of siting has increased over time, despite the aforementioned findings regarding racial disparities.

Table 16.3 also reveals housing value disparities. For example, in 1980, mean owner-occupied housing value in host neighborhoods was 52 percent less than that in areas beyond 1.0 mile ($24,059 vs. $49,675). These disparities are far greater in magnitude than those of TSDFs sited in the 1970s, for which values for the pre-siting census were 37 percent lower in host neighborhoods. In 1990, the magnitude of housing value disparities for the 1980s TSDFs remained virtually unchanged. The homeownership rate was also relatively low. The 1980 homeownership rate in host neighborhoods was 42 percent, compared to 72 percent in non-host areas. In 1990, these disparities persisted. The homeownership rate in host neighborhoods was 41 percent versus 71 percent in comparison areas. These homeownership rates were considerably lower than analogous pre-siting and post-siting rates for host neighborhoods of TSDFs sited in the 1970s, which were 65 percent and 57 percent in 1970 and 1980, respectively (see Table 16.3).

The lower mean housing value and homeownership rate relative to those of TSDFs sited in the 1970s suggest that TSDFs sited in the 1980s were located in declining residential neighborhoods with relatively low housing demand. In fact, the population in these host neighborhoods decreased more than 20 percent during the decade of siting, while population in non-host areas decreased 2.4 percent. Housing vacancy rate data reinforce this conclusion. Table 16.3 shows extremely elevated vacancy rates in both 1980 and 1990 in host neighborhoods of TSDFs sited in the 1980s. In 1980, the vacancy rate of 11 percent was 2.3 times greater than the 4.9 percent rate in areas beyond 1.0 mile. Housing vacancy rate disparities can also be noted in 1990. In contrast, host neighborhoods of TSDFs sited in the 1970s had a vacancy rate of 9.1 percent in 1980, or 1.9 times greater than areas beyond 1.0 mile. In fact, of the vacant housing units in host neighborhoods of TSDFs sited in the 1980s, 14 percent were boarded up in 1990 and, therefore, were uninhabitable.

These data suggest that many housing units had fallen into disrepair during the 1980s. Table 16.3 also provides evidence of the abandonment of residential housing during the decade of siting: 24 percent of the housing units within 1.0 mile of TSDFs sited in the 1980s were lost from 1980 to 1990. This severe housing loss occurred against the backdrop of a 5.1 percent housing unit increase in the comparison areas. In contrast, 9.1 percent of housing units were lost during the decade of siting within 1.0 mile of TSDFs sited in the 1970s. This finding provides additional support for the hypothesis that TSDFs would be sited in increasingly impoverished and declining neighborhoods over time as public opinion and opposition regarding new facility siting increasingly galvanized and the policy environment of siting evolved. Overall, disparities among economic indicators increased in magnitude between the 1970s and 1980s, while the magnitude of racial disparities did not. Possible reasons are explored below.

## Discussion

Models of environmental injustice tend to assume that public opposition, attitudes that drive the NIMBY phenomenon, and government and industry responses have been constant over time; therefore, they predict siting disparities regardless of the historical context of siting. However, we found evidence of disparate siting in the early NIMBY and post-Love Canal eras, but not in the pre-NIMBY/pre-RCRA era. This finding is consistent with the proposition that growth of environmental concern, public opposition, and changes in the policy environment – and thus the political opportunity structure – prompted hazardous waste facilities sitings to follow the path of least resistance. Although widespread concern about hazardous waste did not develop until the late 1970s, general public awareness in the late 1960s and early 1970s about waste facilities, pollution, and other environmental issues may have spilled over to siting of hazardous waste facilities. Following Love Canal, specific concern about hazardous waste, hazardous waste facilities, and related NIMBY behaviors expanded greatly, particularly in the 1980s when RCRA provided new opportunities for neighborhoods with high levels of political clout and technical know-how necessary to influence siting decisions. Industry, in turn, altered its site-selection strategy through the permitting process; as the antitoxic movement emerged and public opposition posed a serious threat to siting, minority and low-income neighborhoods were increasingly attractive locations (Bruelle 2000; Cerrell Associates, Inc. 1984; Daly and Vitaliano 1987). Thus, the basic factors driving the sociopolitical and rational choice explanations have changed dramatically over recent decades. While it is less clear how factors underlying racial discrimination explanations have changed over time, institutional discrimination may have been relatively constant in its presence, if not its exact character or causal mechanisms (see discussion below).

The increased magnitude of economic disparities from the 1970s to 1980s supports the hypothesis that the burgeoning NIMBY phenomenon and new opportunities for public participation in siting decisions, coupled with the assertion of pre-emptive state authority, increasingly encouraged disparate siting. Although the magnitude of racial siting disparities did not increase from the 1970s to 1980s, they remained significant. Host neighborhoods of TSDFs sited in the 1980s were predominantly African-American. Sitings in both the 1970s and 1980s exhibited signs of progressively worsening economic and housing conditions, as new commercial hazardous waste facilities were increasingly located in the deteriorating urban core of Detroit. Consequently, host neighborhoods exhibited increasingly lower housing values, lower new home construction rates, and larger and more pervasive losses of population and housing. In fact, in these recent decades, neighborhood demographic and housing changes took place prior to and during the decade of siting.

The Detroit metropolitan area includes a highly segregated central city and smaller African-American enclaves (such as parts of the City of Pontiac), which appear to have been targeted for new TSDFs sited in the 1980s, by a process very similar to that which Laura Pulido, Steve Sidawi, and Robert O. Vos (1996) describe in detail regarding the Mobil refinery and other industry in Torrance, California. The siting of new TSDFs in older residential areas with aging and deteriorating housing occurred at a time when Detroit experienced de-industrialization and white flight, processes that further concentrated people of color and the poor in the central city (Sugrue 1996; Wilson 1992). Host neighborhoods of TSDFs sited in the 1970s underwent dramatic racial transition and economic decline during the 1970s, whereas host neighborhoods of TSDFs sited in the 1980s already had undergone such changes. By reducing neighborhood social cohesion and political capacity, as Pastor and associates (2001) also observed, demographic instability could make such neighborhoods particularly vulnerable to new facility sitings. While this last observation is consistent with sociopolitical models, racial discrimination explanations also apply.

For example, a history of industrial and residential development in the East Los Angeles area similarly notes how housing segregation and disinvestment helped to concentrate minorities in areas with the least desirable types of land uses (Pulido *et al.* 1996). The limited redevelopment options of blighted areas, the courting of polluting industry, and the establishment of industrial zoning in minority enclaves paved the way for siting of waste and other polluting facilities – a case of siting following the 'path of most assistance' rather than the path of least resistance. Christopher Boone and Ali Modarres (1999), Robert Hersh (1995), Hurley (1995), Chad Montrie (2005), David N. Pellow (2002), and Andrew Szasz and Michael Meuser (2000) have documented similar examples of how racial segregation, economic decline, uneven redevelopment, and industrial zoning concentrated low-income populations and segregated minorities where environmental hazards were then located in Commerce, California; Pittsburgh, Pennsylvania; Gary, Indiana; Memphis, Tennessee; Chicago, Illinois; and San Jose, California, respectively. The racial disparities and increasing magnitude of disparities in economic and housing conditions associated with TSDFs sited in Michigan supports a similar conclusion. In fact, nationwide, factors increasing such vulnerability to siting were particularly virulent in the 1970s and 1980s (Jargowsky 1997; Massey and Denton 1993; Wilson 1987). Because the breadth of social forces contributing to these temporal patterns have a decidedly institutional character, disparate siting can be viewed as a form of indirect institutional discrimination.

The slight decrease in the magnitude of racial disparities in the 1980s is consistent with the early emergence of the environmental justice movement and growth in the capacity of minority and low-income communities to oppose new facility siting effectively. However, because no new commercial hazardous waste facilities were sited in Michigan during the 1990s, the decade in which the movement came to the fore, this possibility was not assessed.

## Conclusions

Our longitudinal study of disparate siting in Michigan reveals temporal patterns that correspond to historic changes in sociopolitical conditions (i.e., pubic attitudes and actions, institutional arrangements, and the policy environment of siting). Pre-NIMBY/pre-RCRA era facilities were located in economically vibrant neighborhoods with relatively good housing and employment conditions. In contrast, host neighborhoods of TSDFs sited in the early NIMBY and post-Love Canal eras exhibited progressively more depressed economic and housing conditions. Furthermore, host neighborhoods of these TSDFs, sited in the 1970s and 1980s, had increasingly severe income and poverty disparities, low housing demand, and high rates of residential housing decline at the time of siting. These findings are generally consistent with the review of previous studies of disparate siting and facility expansion plans (e.g., Hamilton 1995; Hurley 1997).

However, to firmly establish the role that historical context plays in disparate siting, more longitudinal studies are needed. These studies should examine other states and regions and the nation as a whole, as well as other types of locally unwanted land uses. If possible, they should extend their temporal scopes to before 1970, and assess effects of the environmental justice movement on siting decisions since 1990. We also suggest that future environmental justice studies, both cross-sectional and longitudinal, not assume that sociopolitical conditions and policy environment in the past were the same as they are today or that conditions in previous periods were uniform. Better understanding is also needed of how changes in the types of racial discrimination – overt and subtle, individual and institutional – have influenced siting decisions over time. Finally, we encourage greater exploration than was possible in this study of ways to integrate rational choice, sociopolitical, and racial discrimination models, for example, by further understanding how they may be mutually reinforcing, or interacting, over time (Pulido 1996).

Over the past several decades, siting decisions have occurred in a highly contested political landscape. Our findings support the argument that siting increasingly has followed the path of least resistance as a result of unprecedented growth in public environmental concern and citizen action. Institutional factors also are likely to have contributed to the historical patterns. As state and federal agencies assumed responsibility for approving siting proposals of industry, legislatively mandated permitting processes have provided new political opportunities for public involvement, both administrative and judicial. Distributional politics appear to have prevailed such that those segments of the population with fewer political, organizational, and technical resources have borne a disproportionate share of the society's environmental burdens.

Moreover, the historic patterns found in this study suggest that discriminatory siting is here to stay, given the current sociopolitical and legal terrain. As long as the most polluted and disempowered communities are seen and remain as paths of least resistance, attention to post-siting neighborhood changes that may exacerbate siting disparities might only serve as a diversion from the difficult task of addressing institutional forms of discrimination that pervade industry and governmental siting decisions. Government and industry policies that equalize the playing field and pay attention to the racial and socioeconomic composition and existing pollution burden of proposed host neighborhoods could help. Also helpful would be reform of economic development policies and practices by which local officials court or assist polluting industries in locating in already overburdened areas and overlook such areas for more benign forms of redevelopment.

## Notes

1  The apparent parochial nature of NIMBY does not suggest that participants in NIMBY campaigns all view the siting of facilities in other communities besides their own as acceptable. The term NIMBY is used here mainly for convenience to refer to the recent historical period in which vigorous opposition has been prevalent. NIMBY groups have grown in their sophistication and understanding of the broad context of hazardous waste problems (Szasz 1994). Some groups redefine the problem of 'where to put it' by advocating, instead, for more comprehensive solutions such as source reduction and recycling (Bryant 1995).

2  The U.S. EPA Office of Waste and Waste Management (1979) report, produced by Centaur Associates, provides examples of successful public opposition from early 1970s, including the IT Corporation facility in Brentwood, California; Padre Juan facility in Ventura County, California; and Resource Recovery Corporation in Pasco, Washington. Other unsuccessful campaigns included Wes-Con in Grandview and Bruneau, Idaho; and Calabasas, in Los Angeles, California. The vast majority of cases (16 of 21) met substantial public opposition in the late 1970s.

3  This state agency was created in 1996 as a result of a reorganization of the Department of Natural Resources (DNR). Functions related to Act 64 that were previously carried out by the DNR are now performed by the DEQ. To avoid confusion, the subsequent discussion refers only to the DEQ.

4  Three other TSDFs were excluded from the analyses because they were sited at the same location as existing facilities. These TSDFs were not treated as separate sitings, since they were essentially on-site expansions.

5  Circular areas within 2.0 miles were also examined, but the results were not substantially different than those for the 1.0-mile host neighborhoods. Therefore, the results for the 2.0-mile areas are not reported, but can be requested from the authors.

6  See Oregon Department of Forestry (2003) for documentation about Xtools.

7  This method is becoming widely accepted. Other studies that have employed this type of technique include Chakraborty and Armstrong 1997; Glickman 1994; Glickman, Golding, and Hersh 1995; Hamilton and Viscusi 1999; Mohai and Saha 2003; Sheppard et al. 1999; and U.S. GAO 1995.

8  Reliable poverty rates were not available for the 1950 and 1960 censuses and thus could not be used to assess socioeconomic disparities for TSDFs sited in the 1950s and 1960s. However, for TSDFs sited after 1970, family poverty rates were available. Educational attainment levels were also examined for TSDFs sited in all decades, but their analysis did not alter the basic conclusions. These data, therefore, are not reported.

9  Nonwhites are nearly entirely African-American, but include all persons who did not identify as white on the race question of census questionnaires. Therefore, nonwhites may also include Asians, Pacific Islanders, and Native Americans. Because some Hispanics, or Latinos, might identify as whites, only some Hispanics are included in the nonwhite total. However, because Hispanics were only a very small percentage of the total, nonwhite percentages would not have differed if all Hispanics could be counted among the nonwhites. Making this correction was not possible prior to the 1990 Census.

10  Livingston County was excluded from the Detroit MSA because it became part of the Ann Arbor Primary MSA (PMSA) in 1990. To be consistent, only counties in 1980 MSAs that were

also part of an MSA in 1990 were used. As a result, Oceana County was excluded from the Muskegon MSA.

## References

Anderson, Andy B., Douglas L. Anderton, and John Michael Oakes. 1994. 'Environmental Equity: Evaluating TSDF Siting over the Past Two Decades.' *Waste Age* 25(7): 83–100.

Bacow, Lawrence S. and James R. Milkey. 1982. 'Overcoming Local Opposition to Hazardous Waste Facilities: The Massachusetts Approach.' *Harvard Environmental Law Review* 6: 265–305.

Baibergenova, Akerke, Rustam Kudyakov, Michael Zdeb, and David O. Carpenter. 2003. 'Low Birth Weight and Residential Proximity to PCB-contaminated Waste Sites.' *Environmental Health Perspectives* 111:1352–57.

Been, Vicki. 1994. 'Locally Undesirable Land Uses in Minority Neighborhoods: Disproportionate Siting or Market Dynamics.' *The Yale Law Journal* 103: 1383–1422.

Been, Vicki and Francis Gupta. 1997. 'Coming to the Nuisance or Going to the Barrios? A Longitudinal Analysis or Environmental Justice Claims.' *Ecology Law Quarterly* 24: 1–56

Blumberg, Louis and Robert Gottlieb. 1989. *War on Waste: Can America Win Its Battle with Garbage.* Covelo, CA: Island Press.

Bohon, Stephanie A. and Craig R. Humphrey. 2000. 'Courting LULUs: Characteristics of Suitor and Objector Communities.' *Rural Sociology* 65: 376–95.

Boone, Christopher G. and Ali Modarres. 1999. 'Creating a Toxic Neighborhood in Los Angeles County: A Historical Examination of Environmental Inequality.' *Urban Affairs Review* 35: 163–87.

Brown, Michael H. 1981. *Laying Waste: The Poisoning of America by Toxic Chemicals.* New York: Washington Square Press.

Brown, Phil. 1995. 'Race, Class, and Environmental Health: A Review and Systemization of the Literature.' *Environmental Research* 69: 15–30.

Brulle, Robert J. 2000. *Agency, Democracy, and Nature: The U.S. Environmental Movement from a Critical Theory Perspective.* Cambridge, MA: The MIT Press.

Bryant, Bunyan, ed. 1995. *Environmental Justice: Issues, Policies, and Solutions.* Washington, DC: Island Press.

Bullard, Robert D. 1983. 'Solid Waste Sites and the Black Houston Community.' *Sociological Inquiry* 53: 273–88.

———. 1990. *Dumping in Dixie: Race, Class, and Environmental Quality.* Boulder, CO: Westview Press.

Bullard, Robert D. and Beverly Hendrix Wright. 1987. 'Blacks and the Environment.' *Humboldt Journal of Social Relations* 14(1/2): 165–84.

Cable, Shari and Michael Benson. 1993. 'Acting Locally: Environmental Injustice and the Emergence of Grassroots Environmental Organizations.' *Social Problems* 40: 464–77.

Cerrell Associates, Inc. 1984. 'Political Difficulties Facing Waste-to-energy Conversion Plant Siting.' Report prepared for California Waste Management Board, Los Angeles, CA.

Chakraborty, Jayajit and Marc P. Armstrong. 1997. 'Exploring the Use of Buffer Analysis for the Identification of Impacted Areas in Environmental Equity Assessment.' *Cartography and Geographic Information Systems* 24(3): 145–57.

Cole, Luke W. and Sheila R. Foster. 2001. *From the Ground Up: Environmental Racism and the Rise of the Environmental Justice Movement.* New York: New York University Press.

Daly, John B. and Eric N. Vitaliano. 1987. *Hazardous Waste Facility Siting: A National Survey.* Albany, NY: Legislative Commission on Toxic Substances and Hazardous Wastes.

Davis, Charles E. 1993. *The Politics of Hazardous Waste.* Englewood Cliffs, NJ: Simon & Schuster.

Davy, Benjamin. 1997. *Essential Justice: When Legal Institutions Cannot Resolve Environmental and Land Use Disputes.* New York: Springer-Verlag Wien.

Dinkins, Carol E. 1995. 'Impact of the Environmental Justice Movement on American Industry and Local Government.' *Administrative Law Review* 47: 337–53.

Dunlap, Riley E. 1992. 'Trends in Public Opinion toward Environmental Issues: 1965–1990.' Pp. 89–116 in *American Environmentalism*, edited by Riley E. Dunlap and Angela G. Mertig. Washington, DC: Taylor and Francis New York Inc.

Edelstein, Michael R. 1988. *Contaminated Communities: The Social and Psychological Impacts of Residential Toxic Exposure.* Boulder, CO: Westview Press.

Feagin, Joe R. and Clarece B. Feagin 1986. *Discrimination American Style: Institutional Racism and Sexism.* 2d ed. Malabar, FL: Kriege Publishing Co.

Fletcher, Thomas H. 2003. *From Love Canal to Environmental Justice: The Politics of Hazardous Waste on the Canada-U.S. Border*. Peterborough, Ontario: Broadview Press.

Freudenberg, Nicholas. 1984. 'Citizen Action for Environmental Health: Report on a Survey of Community Organizations.' *American Journal of Public Health* 74: 444–48.

Freudenberg, Nicholas and Carol Steinsapir. 1991. 'Not in Our Backyards: The Grassroots Environmental Movement.' *Society and Natural Resources* 4: 235–45.

Freudenberg, William R. 1997. 'Contamination, Corrosion, and the Social Order: An Overview.' *Current Sociology* 45(3): 19–39.

Furuseth, Owen J. 1989. 'Community Sensitivity to a Hazardous Waste Facility.' *Landscape and Urban Planning* 17:357–70.

GeoLytics Inc. 1998. *CensusCD+Maps* Version 3.0. New Brunswick, NJ: GeoLytics Inc.

———. 1999. *StreetCD 98*. New Brunswick, NJ: GeoLytics Inc.

———. 2001. *CensusCD 1970*. New Brunswick, NJ: GeoLytics Inc.

Gibb, Lois M. 1982. *Love Canal: My Story*. Albany, NY: State University of New York Press.

Glickman, Theodore S. 1994. 'Measuring Environmental Equity with GIS.' *Renewable Resources Journal* 12(3): 17–21.

Glickman, T.S., D. Golding, and R. Hersh. 1995. 'GIS-Based Environmental Equity Analysis – A Case Study of TRI Facilities in the Pittsburgh Area.' Pp. 95–114 in *Computer Supported Risk Management*, edited by G. E. G. Beroggi and W. A. Wallace. Dordrecht, Netherlands: Kluwer Academic.

Gottlieb, Robert. 1993. *Forcing the Spring: The Transformation of the American Environmental Movement*. Washington, DC: Island Press.

Hamilton, James T. 1993. 'Politics and Social Costs: Estimating the Impact of Collective Action on Hazardous Waste Facilities.' *RAND Journal of Economics* 24(1): 101–25.

———. 1995. 'Testing for Environmental Racism: Prejudice, Profits, Political Power?' *Journal of Policy Analysis and Management* 14(1): 107–32.

Hamilton, James T. and W. Kip Viscusi. 1999. *Calculating Risks? The Spatial and Political Dimensions of Hazardous Waste Policy*. Cambridge, MA and London: The MIT Press.

Hersh, Robert. 1995. *Race and Industrial Hazards: An Historical Geography of the Pittsburgh Region 1900–1990*. Discussion Paper 95–18. Washington, DC: Resources for the Future.

Hurley, Andrew. 1995. *Environmental Inequities: Class, Race, and Industrial Pollution in Gary, Indiana 1945– 1990*. Chapel Hill: University of North Carolina Press.

———. 1997. 'Fiasco at Wagner Electric: Environmental Justice and Urban Geography in St. Louis.' *Environmental History* 2: 460–81.

Hurwitz, Julie H. and E. Quita Sullivan. 2001. 'Using Civil Rights Law to Challenge Environmental Racism: From Bean to Guardians to Chester to Sandoval.' *The Journal of Law in Society* 2: 5–70.

Jargowsky, Paul A. 1997. *Poverty and Place: Ghettos, Barrios, and the American City*. New York: Russell Sage Foundation.

Kanagy, Conrad L., Craig R. Humphrey, and Glenn Firebaugh. 1994. 'Surging Environmentalism: Changing Public Opinion of Changing Publics?' *Social Science Quarterly* 75:804–19.

Kasperson, Roger E. 1986. 'Hazardous Waste Facility Siting: Community, Firm, and Governmental Perspectives.' Pp. 118–44 in *Hazards: Technology and Fairness*. Washington, DC: National Academy Press. Krieg, Eric J. 1995. 'A Socio-Historical Interpretation of Toxic Waste Sites: The Case of Great Boston.' *The American Journal of Economics and Sociology* 54(1): 1–14.

Kraft, Michael E. and Ruth Kraut. 1988. 'Citizen Participation and Hazardous Waste Policy Implementation.' Pp. 63–80 in *Dimensions of Hazardous Waste Policy*, edited by Charles E. Davis and James P. Lester. New York: Greenwood Press.

Lake, Robert W. 1996. 'Volunteers, NIMBY, and Environmental Justice: Dilemmas of Democratic Practice.' *Antipode* 28:160–74.

Levine, Adeline. 1982. *Love Canal: Science, Politics, and People*. Lexington, MA: Lexington Books.

Lindell, M. and T. Earle. 1983. 'How Close Is Close Enough: Public Perception of the Risks of Industrial Facilities.' *Risk Analysis* 3: 245–53.

Massey, Douglas S. and Nancy A. Denton. 1993. *American Apartheid: Segregation and the Making of the Underclass*. Cambridge, MA: Harvard University Press.

Mazmanian, Daniel A. and David Morell. 1994. 'The 'NIMBY' Syndrome: Facility Siting and the Failure of Democratic Discourse.' Pp. 233–50 in *Environmental Policy in the 1990s: Toward a New Agenda* 2d ed., edited by Norman J. Vig and Michael E. Kraft. Washington, DC: Congressional Quarterly Press.

McAdam, Doug. 1982. *Political Process and the Development of Black Insurgency 1930–1970*. Chicago: University of Chicago Press.

Mitchell, Jerry T., Deborah S. K. Thomas, and Susan L. Cutter. 1999. 'Dumping in Dixie Revisited: The Evolution of Environmental Injustices in South Carolina.' *Social Science Quarterly* 80: 229–43.

Mohai, Paul and Bunyan Bryant. 1992. 'Environmental Racism: Reviewing the Evidence.' Pp. 163–76 in *Race and the Incidence of Environmental Hazards: A Time for Discourse*, edited by Bunyan Bryant and Paul Mohai. Boulder, CO: Westview Press.

Mohai, Paul and Robin Saha. 2003. 'Reassessing Race and Class Disparities in Environmental Justice Research Using Distance-based Methods.' Paper presented at the Annual Meeting of the American Sociological Association, Atlanta, GA, August 16–19.

Montrie, Chad. 2005. 'From Dairy Farms to Housing Tracts: Environment and Race in the Making of a Memphis Suburb.' *Journal of Urban History* 31(2): 219–40.

Morell, David and Christopher Magorian. 1982. *Siting Hazardous Waste Facilities: Local Opposition and the Myth of Preemption*. Cambridge, MA: Ballinger.

Morrison, Denton. 1986. 'How and Why Environmental Consciousness Has Trickled Down.' Pp. 187–220 in *Distributional Conflicts in Environmental and Resource Policy*, edited by Allan Schnaiberg, Nicholas Watts, and Klaus Zimmerman. Aldershot, UK: Gower Publishing Company Limited.

Moss, Kary L. 2001. 'Environmental Justice at the Crossroads.' *The Journal of Law in Society* 2: 71–108.

National Governors' Association (NGA). 1981. 'Siting Hazardous Waste Facilities.' *The Environmental Professional* 3: 133–42.

Nelson, Arthur C., Michelle Genereux, and John Genereux. 1992. 'Price Effects of Landfills on House Values.' *Land Economics* 68: 359–65.

Oakes, John Michael, Douglas L. Anderton, and Andy B. Anderson. 1996. 'A Longitudinal Analysis of Environmental Equity in Communities with Hazardous Waste Facilities.' *Social Science Research* 23: 125–48.

O'Hare, Michael, Lawrence Bacow, and Debra Sanderson. 1983. *Facility Siting and Public Opposition*. New York: Van Nostrand Reinhold.

Oregon Department of Forestry. 2003. 'XTools Description.' *Oregon Department of Forestry*. Salem, OR: Oregon Department of Forestry. Retrieved May 17 2005 (http://www.odf.state.or.us/divisions/ management/state_forests/GIS/Documents/xtools.htm).

Pastor, Manuel, Jr., Jim Sadd, and John Hipp. 2001. 'Which Came First? Toxic Facilities, Minority Movein, and Environmental Justice.' *Journal of Urban Affairs* 23: 1–21.

Pellow, David N. 2000. 'Environmental Inequality Formation: Toward a Theory of Environmental Injustice.' *American Behavioral Scientist* 43: 581–601.

———. 2002. *Garbage Wars: The Struggle for Environmental Justice in Chicago*. Cambridge, MA: MIT Press.

Portney, Kent E. 1991a. *Siting Hazardous Waste Treatment Facilities: The NIMBY Syndrome*. New York: Auburn House.

———. 1991b. 'Public Environmental Policy Decision Making: Citizen Roles.' Pp. 195–215 in *Environmental Decision Making: A Multidisciplinary Perspective*, edited by Richard A. Chechila and Susan Carlisle. New York: Van Nostrand Reinhold.

Pulido, Laura. 1996. 'A Critical Review of the Methodology of Environmental Racism Research.' *Antipode* 28:142–59.

———. 2000. 'Rethinking Environmental Racism: White Privilege and Urban Development in Southern California.' *Annals of the Association of American Geographers* 90: 12–40.

Pulido, Laura, Steve Sidawi, and Robert O. Vos. 1996. 'An Archaeology of Environmental Racism in Los Angeles.' *Urban Geography* 17: 419–39.

Quarantelli, E. L. 1989. 'Characteristics of Citizen Groups which Emerge with Respect to Hazardous Waste Sites.' Pp. 177–95 in *Psychosocial Effects of Hazardous and Toxic Waste Disposal on Communities*, edited by Dennis L. Peck. Springfield, IL: Charles C. Thomas.

Rabe, Barry G. 1994. *Beyond NIMBY: Hazardous Waste Siting in Canada and the United States*. Washington, DC: The Brookings Institute.

Reich, Michael R. 1991. *Toxic Politics: Responding to Chemical Disasters*. Ithaca, NY: Cornell University Press.

Ringquist, Evan. 2005. 'Assessing Evidence of Environmental Inequalities: A Meta-analysis.' *Journal of Policy Analysis and Management* 24: 223–48.

Saha, Robin and Paul Mohai. 1997. 'Explaining Racial and Socioeconomic Disparities in the Location of Locally Unwanted Land Uses: A Conceptual Framework.' Presented at the Annual Meeting of the Rural Sociological Society, Toronto, Canada, August 15–17.

Sandman, Peter M. 1985. 'Getting to Maybe: Some Communications Aspects of Siting Hazardous Waste Facilities.' *Seton Hall Legislative Journal* 9: 437–65.

Schlosberg, David. 1999. *Environmental Justice and the New Pluralism: The Challenge of Difference for Environmentalism*. New York: Oxford University Press.

Sheppard, Eric, Helga Leitner, Robert B. McMaster, and Hongguo Tian. 1999. 'GIS-based Measures of Environmental Equity: Exploring Their Sensitivity and Significance.' *Journal of Exposure Analysis and Environmental Epidemiology* 9: 18–28.

Sliver, Steven. 1993. Hazardous Waste Program Officer, Michigan Department of Natural Resources, Phone Interview, n.d.

Stretesky, Paul and Michael J. Hogan. 1998. 'Environmental Justice: An Analysis of Superfund Sites in Florida.' *Social Problems* 45: 268–87.

Sugrue, Thomas J. 1996. *The Origins of the Urban Crisis: Race and Inequality in Postwar Detroit.* Princeton, NJ: Princeton University Press.

Szasz, Andrew. 1994. *EcoPopulism: Toxic Waste and the Movement for Environmental Justice.* 2d ed. Minneapolis: University of Minnesota Press.

Szasz, Andrew and Michael Meuser. 2000. 'Unintended, Inexorable: The Production of Environmental Inequalities in Santa Clara County, California.' *American Behavioral Scientist* 43: 602–32.

Tarrow, Sidney 1996. 'States and Opportunities: The Political Structuring of Social Movements.' Pp. 41– 60 in *Comparative Perspectives on Social Movements: Political Opportunities, Mobilizing Structures, and Cultural Framing*, edited by Doug McAdam, John D. McCarthy, and Mayer N. Zald. Cambridge: Cambridge University Press.

Taylor, Dorceta E. 1993. 'Environmentalism and the Politics of Inclusion.' Pp. 53–61 in *Confronting Environmental Racism: Voices from the Grassroots*, edited by Robert D. Bullard. Boston: South End Press.

———. 1997. 'American Environmentalism: The Role of Race, Class, and Gender in Shaping Activism 1820–1995.' *Race, Gender & Class* 5: 16–62.

———. 1998. 'Mobilizing for Environmental Justice in Communities of Color: An Emerging Profile of People of Color Environmental Groups.' Pp. 32–67 in *Ecosystem Management: Adaptive Strategies for Natural Resource Organizations in the 21st Century*, edited by Jennifer Alley, William R. Burch, Beth Canover, and Donald Field. Philadelphia, PA: Taylor & Francis.

———. 2000. 'The Rise of the Environmental Justice Paradigm: Injustice Framing and the Social Construction of Environmental Discourse.' *American Behavioral Scientist* 43:508–80.

U.S. Bureau of the Census. 1950a. *Census of Population, Census Tract Statistics, Detroit, Michigan and Adjacent Area.* Vol. III. Washington, DC: U.S. Government Printing Office.

———. 1950b. *Census of Population.* Vol. II, Part 22, 'Characteristics of the Population.' Washington, DC: U.S. Government Printing Office.

———. 1961a. *Census of Population and Housing 1960, Census Tracts, Detroit, Michigan, Standard Metropolitan Statistical Area.* PHC(1)-40. Washington, DC: U.S. Government Printing Office.

———. 1961b. *Census of Population and Housing 1960, Census Tracts, Grand Rapids, Michigan, Standard Metropolitan Statistical Area.* PHC(1)-54, Washington, DC: U.S. Government Printing Office.

———. 1961c. *Census of Population and Housing 1960, Census Tracts, Muskegon-Muskegon Heights, Michigan, Standard Metropolitan Statistical Area.* PHC(1)-98. Washington, DC: U.S. Government Printing Office.

———. 1961d. *Census of Population 1960.* Vol. 1, Part 24, 'Characteristics of the Population, Michigan.' Washington, DC: U.S. Government Printing Office.

———. 1970. *Census Users Guide.* Washington, DC: Government Printing Office.

———. 1984a [1982]. *Census of Population and Housing 1980* (United States): Summary Tape File 3A. Washington, DC: United States Department of Commerce, Bureau of the Census.

———. 1984b [1982]. *Technical Documentation, Census of Population and Housing 1980* (United States): Summary Tape File 3A. Washington, DC: United States Department of Commerce, Bureau of the Census [producer]. Ann Arbor, MI: Inter-university Consortium for Political and Social Research [distributor].

U.S. EPA Office of Solid Waste. 1990. *RCRA Orientation Manual: 1990 Edition.* EPA 530-SW-90-036. Washington, DC: U.S. Government Printing Office.

U.S. EPA Office of Water and Waste Management. 1979. *Siting of Hazardous Waste Management Facilities and Public Opposition.* EPA SW 809. Washington, DC: Government Printing Office.

U.S. General Accounting Office (U.S. GAO). 1983. *Siting of Hazardous Waste Landfills and Their Correlation with Racial and Economic Status of Surrounding Communities.* RCED-83-168. Washington, DC: U.S. General Accounting Office.

———. 1995. *Hazardous and Nonhazardous Waste: Demographics of People Living near Waste Facilities.* RCED-95-84. Washington, DC: U.S. General Accounting Office.

Vrijheid M., H. Dolk, B. Armstrong, G. Boschi, A. Busby, T. Jorgensen, and P. Pointer. 2002. 'Hazard Potential Ranking of Hazardous Waste Landfill Sites and Risk of Congenital Anomalies.' *Journal of Occupational and Environmental Medicine* 59:768–76.

Wessex Inc. 1994 [1992]. *1990 Census of Population and Housing.* Summary Tape Files 1A and 3A. Washington, DC: U. S. Bureau of the Census [producer]. Winnetka, IL: Author [distributor].

Wessex Inc. 1995. *1990 TIGER Files* [CD-ROM]. Winnetka, IL: Wessex Inc.

Wilson, Carter A. 1992. 'Restructuring and the Growth of Concentrated Poverty in Detroit.' *Urban Affairs Quarterly* 28:187–205.

Wilson, William J. 1987. *The Truly Disadvantaged.* Chicago, IL: University of Chicago Press.

**Appendix A** Geographic location and current operating status for commercial TSDFs operating in Michigan in 1989, by decade opened

| # | Decade Opened | Closed or Closing as of 2002 | Metropolitan Area | County Census Division (CCD) | Urbanized Area in 1990 | Central City Location |
|---|---|---|---|---|---|---|
| 1 | 1950s[a] | No | Detroit | Detroit | Yes | Yes |
| 2 | 1950s | Yes | Detroit | Dearborn | Yes | No |
| 3 | 1960s | No | Detroit | Van Buren Township | No | No |
| 4 | 1960s | No | Detroit | Romulus | Yes | No |
| 5 | 1960s | Yes | Detroit | Roseville | Yes | No |
| 6 | 1960s | No | Detroit | Brownstown Township | No | No |
| 7 | 1960s | No | Grand Rapids-Muskegon | Grandville | Yes | No |
| 8 | 1970s | No | Detroit | Detroit | Yes | Yes |
| 9 | 1970s | Yes | Grand Rapids-Muskegon | Grand Rapids | Yes | Yes |
| 10 | 1970s | Yes | Detroit | Inkster | Yes | No |
| 11 | 1970s | Yes | Grand Rapids-Muskegon | Muskegon Heights | Yes | No |
| 12 | 1970s | No | Detroit | Detroit | Yes | Yes |
| 13 | 1970s | No | Detroit | Van Buren Township | No | No |
| 14 | 1970s | No | Non-metropolitan | Plainwell | No | No |
| 15 | 1970s | No | Grand Rapids-Muskegon | Dutton | No | No |
| 16 | 1980s | Yes | Detroit | Detroit | Yes | Yes |
| 17 | 1980s | Yes | Detroit | Pontiac | Yes | No |
| 18 | 1980s | No | Detroit | Detroit | Yes | Yes |
| 19 | 1980s | No | Detroit | Detroit | Yes | Yes |
| 20 | 1980s | No | Non-metropolitan | Alpena | No | No |
| 21 | 1980s | No | Detroit | Detroit | Yes | Yes |
| 22 | 1980s | No | Non-metropolitan | Alpena | No | No |
| 23 | 1980s | Yes | Detroit | Detroit | Yes | Yes |

[a]Sited in 1948, but treated as 1950s siting.

**Appendix B** Census Data Sources by Census Year and Geographic Area

| Year | Variable | Geographic Area | Source | Census Table(s) |
|---|---|---|---|---|
| 1990 | Total population | Metropolitan Areas (MAs); counties; block groups | [a] | Table P 1: Persons |
| 1990 | Black and white population | MAs; counties; block groups | [a] | Table P-8: Persons by Race |
| 1990 | % black and % nonwhite | MAs; counties; block groups | Calculated[a] | From Table P-8: Persons by Race |
| 1990 | Mean family income | MAs; counties; block groups | Calculated[a] | From Tables P-108: Aggregate Family Income and P-4: Families |
| 1990 | Family poverty rates | MAs; counties; block groups | Calculated[a] | From Table P-123: Poverty Status in 1989 by Family Type and Presence and Age of Children |
| 1990 | % unemployed in civilian labor force | MAs; counties; block groups | Calculated[a] | From Table P-70: Sex by Employment Status for Persons 16 Years and Over |
| 1990 | % in civilian labor force | MAs; counties; block groups | Calculated[a] | From Table P-70: Sex by Employment Status for Persons 16 Years and Over |
| 1990 | Mean value of owner-occupied housing units | All areas | Calculated[a] | From Tables H-24: Aggregate Value, Specified Owner-Occupied Housing Units |
| 1990 | Total number of year-round housing units | All areas | [a] | Table H-1: Housing Units |
| 1990 | Vacant housing units | All areas | [a] | Table H-2: Occupancy Status Housing Units |
| 1990 | Vacancy rate | All areas | Calculated[a] | From Table H-1 Housing Units and H-2: Occupancy Status |
| 1990 | Owner-occupied housing units | All areas | [a] | Table H-9: Tenure by Race of House-holder, Occupied Housing Units |
| 1990 | Percentage of owner-occupied housing units | All areas | Calculated[a] | From Tables H-1 Housing Units and H-3: Tenure, Occupied Housing Units |
| 1990 | % housing structures built 1980–1989 | All areas | Calculated[b] | From Table H-25: Year Structure Built |
| 1990 | % boarded up or vacant units | All areas | Calculated[a] | From Table H-6: Boarded-up Status, Vacant Housing Units and Table H-22: Occupancy Status |

| Year | Variable | Geographic Area | Source | Census Table(s) |
|---|---|---|---|---|
| 1980 | Total, black and white Populations | MSAs (Metropolitan Statistical Areas); counties; Municipal Civil Division (MCDs); block groups | c | Table 2: Persons, Urban and Rural and Table 22: Persons by Race |
| 1980 | % black and % nonwhite | MSAs; counties; MCDs; block groups | Calculated[c] | From Table 22: Race |
| 1980 | Mean family income | MSAs; counties; MCDs; block groups | Calculated[c] | From Table 9: Families and Table 77: Aggregate Family Income by Race of Householder in 1979 |
| 1980 | Family poverty rates | MSAs; counties; MCDs; block groups | Calculated[c] | From Table 86: Family Type by Poverty Status in 1979 by Presence and Age of Related Children |
| 1980 | % unemployed in civilian labor force | All areas | Calculated[c] | From Table 55: Race by Sex by Labor Force Status |
| 1980 | % in civilian labor force | All areas | Calculated[c] | From Table 55 (see above) |
| 1980 | Total year-round housing units | All areas | c | Table 21: Occupancy Status, Year-round Housing Units |
| 1980 | Mean value of owner-occupied housing units | All areas | Calculated[c] | From Table 240: Aggregate Value of Specified Owner-Occupied Non-condominium Housing Units and Table 238: Mortgage Status and Year Householder Moved into Unit for Specified Owner-Occupied Non-condominium Housing Units |
| 1980 | % owner occupied housing units | All areas | Calculated[c] | From Table 21 (see above) and Table 97: Tenure of Occupied Housing Units |
| 1980 | Vacancy rate | All areas | Calculated[c] | From Table 21 (see above) |
| 1980 | % housing units built 1970–80 | All areas | Calculated[c] | From Table 209: Tenure and Occupancy Status by Year Structure Built, Year-round Housing Units |
| 1980 | % boarded up housing units | All areas | Calculated[c] | From Table 96: Vacancy Status, Vacant Housing Units |
| 1970 | % black and % nonwhite | MSAs; counties; MCDs; tracts | Calculated[d] | From Table P-105: Race |

| Year | Variable | Area | Source | Description |
|---|---|---|---|---|
| 1970 | Mean family income | MSAs; counties; MCDs; tracts | Calculated[d] | From Table P-1: Aggregate Family Income of Families, and Table P-19: Families by Type, Presence and Age of Own Children |
| 1970 | Family poverty rate | MSAs; counties; MCDs; tracts | Calculated[d] | From Table P-19: Families by Type, Presence and Age of Own Children and Table P-84: Families by Presence of Related Children Under 18, Type of Family, and Poverty Status |
| 1970 | % unemployed in civilian labor force | All areas | Calculated[d] | From Table P-54: Population 16 Years Old and Over by Labor Force Status, Selected Characteristics, and Sex |
| 1970 | % in civilian labor force | All areas | Calculated[d] | From Table P-54 (see above) |
| 1970 | Total housing units | All areas | [d] | Table H-7: Total Housing Units |
| 1970 | Mean value of owner-occupied housing units | All areas | Calculated[d] | From Table H-1: Aggregate Housing Value for Units for Which Value is Tabulated and Table H-52: Value, Occupancy Status, and Race of Head |
| 1970 | % owner-occupied housing units | All areas | Calculated[d] | From Table H-8: Year Structure Built, Tenure, and Race of Head |
| 1970 | Housing vacancy rate | All areas | Calculated[d] | From Table H-35: Occupancy/Vacancy Status of Occupied and Vacant Year-round Housing Units |
| 1970 | % housing units built 1960–1970 | All areas | Calculated[d] | From Table H-8 (see above) |
| 1960 | % black and % nonwhite | MSAs; counties | [e] | Table 38: Characteristics of the Population, for Counties |
| 1960 | % black and % nonwhite | Tracts | [f, g, h] | Table P-1: General Characteristics of the Population, by Census Tracts |
| 1960 | Mean family income | MSAs; counties | Calculated[e] | From Table 86: Income in 1959 of Families and Persons, and Weeks Worked in 1959, for Counties |
| 1960 | Mean family income | Tracts | Calculated[f,g,h] | From Table P-1: General Characteristics of the Population by Census Tracts: 1960 |

| Year | Variable | Geographic Area | Source | Census Table(s) |
|---|---|---|---|---|
| 1960 | Total housing units | MSAs; counties | c | Table 27: Financial Characteristics and Duration of Vacancy for SMSAs, Constituent Counties, Places of 50,000 Inhabitants or More, Urban Balance, Rural Total, and Urbanized Areas |
| 1960 | Total housing units | Tracts | f, g, h | Table H-1: Occupancy, Structural Characteristics of Housing Units, by Census Tract |
| 1960 | Mean value of owner-occupied housing units | MSAs; counties | Calculated[e] | From Table 27 (see above) |
| 1960 | Mean value of owner-occupied housing units | Tracts | Calculated[f,g,h] | From Table H-2: Year Moved into Unit, Automobiles Available, and Value or Rent of Occupied Housing Units, by Census Tracts |
| 1960 | % owner-occupied housing units | MSAs; counties | e | Table 22: Tenure, Vacancy Status, and Conditional Plumbing Facilities for SMSAs, Constituent Counties, Places of 50,000 Inhabitants or More, Urban Balance, Rural Total, and Urbanized Areas and Table 27 (see above) |
| 1960 | % owner-occupied housing units | Tracts | f, g, h | Table H-2 (see above) |
| 1960 | Vacancy rate | MSAs; counties | c | Tables 12 and 17 (see above) |
| 1960 | Vacancy rate | Tracts | f, g, h | Table H-2 (see above) |
| 1950 | % black and % nonwhite | MSAs; counties | i | Table 42: General Characteristics of the Population for Counties |
| 1950 | % black and % nonwhite | Tracts | j | Table 2: Characteristics of the Population, by Census Tracts: 1950 |
| 1950 | Mean family and unrelated individuals income | MSAs; counties | Calculated[i] | From Table 45: Income in 1949 of Families and Unrelated Individuals, for Counties |
| 1950 | Mean family and unrelated individuals income | Census tracts | Calculated[j] | From Table P-1: Characteristics of the Population, by Census Tracts: 1950 |

| Year | Variable | Geography | Source | Source description |
|---|---|---|---|---|
| 1950 | Total housing units | MSAs; counties | i | Table 2: Summary of Selected Housing Characteristics for the State (Urban and Rural, Standard Metropolitan Statistical Areas, Urban Places of 10,000 or More, and Counties |
| 1950 | Total housing units | Tracts | j | Table 4: Characteristics of Dwelling Units, by Census Tract |
| 1950 | Mean value of owner-occupied housing units | MSAs; counties | Calculated[i] | From Table 38: Financial Characteristics of Urban and Rural-Nonfarm Dwelling Units, for Counties |
| 1950 | Mean value of owner-occupied housing units | Tracts | Calculated[j] | From Table 4: Characteristics of Dwelling Units, by Census Tract |
| 1950 | % owner-occupied housing units | MSAs; counties | Calculated[i] | From Tables 1 and 28 (see above) |
| 1950 | % owner-occupied housing units | Tracts | Calculated[j] | From Table 4: Characteristics of Dwelling Units, by Census Tract |
| 1950 | Vacancy rate | MSAs; counties | Calculated[i] | From Tables 1 and 28 (see above) |
| 1950 | Vacancy rate | Tracts | Calculated[j] | From Table 4: Characteristics of Dwelling Units, by Census Tract |

a  Wessex, Inc., 1994: File 3.
b  Wessex, Inc., 1994: File 1.
c  U.S. Bureau of Census 1984b.
d  Geolytics 2001: File 4.
e  U.S. Bureau of the Census 1961d.
f  U.S. Bureau of the Census 1961a.
g  U.S. Bureau of the Census 1961b.
h  U.S. Bureau of the Census 1961c.
i  U.S. Bureau of the Census 1950b.
j  U.S. Bureau of the Census 1950a: Ch. 17.

# 17. Resisting toxic militarism: Vieques versus the U.S. Navy*

*Déborah Berman Santana*

Environmental justice activists and scholars have frequently condemned toxic capitalism's poisoning of communities of color as criminal in nature (Simon 2000). However, rarely is their critique specifically directed at the United States military. Indeed, the military sees itself as the country's 'oldest, largest, busiest, and most successful company,' whose 588 'plants' (bases) and \$270 billion in budget revenues during 1999 – growing to \$400 billion by 2003 – dwarfed all other U.S. corporate giants (Department of Defense 2000). Patricia Hynes (1999: 49) observed that 'the Pentagon is the largest sole consumer of energy in the United States, and very likely, worldwide.' By its own admission, the military burns enough gas per day to drive a car 13,000 times around the world, operates 550 public utilities, uses one-quarter of U.S. hydropower capacity, and generates most of the nuclear waste in the U.S. Moreover, the Defense Department's generation of over 750,000 tons of toxic waste per year dwarfs the combined toxic production of the top three chemical companies (St. Clair and Cockburn 2001). It seems clear that the toxic legacy of this biggest of 'big businesses' deserves much more attention.

Although the U.S. government has attempted to sanction some polluters, its preferential treatment of the worst polluters – the largest and most powerful corporations – reveals Washington's complicity in toxic capitalism. The military, as the largest corporation and most egregious polluter, has been subject to less oversight, regulation, and sanction than any other toxic criminal has. Before 1980, the military was not subject to any environmental regulations and rarely documented toxic or hazardous waste disposal (Zito 2002). Not until 1988, for example, was the military required to take into account how endangered species might be affected by its activities. In 1999, Congress shielded the military from requirements to pay fines for breaking environmental laws, but the Pentagon still complained that 'encroachment' – the expanding protection of areas to benefit ecological or social health – was harming military readiness. Therefore, peace and justice activists were hardly surprised when the 'war against terrorism' was invoked to justify a proposed total military exemption from environmental laws.

---

\* From *Social Justice* (2002), 29(2): pp. 37–47.

Among its many contradictions, the purported military mission to protect society is violated by its activities, which endanger human and environmental health. Moreover, as befits a rigidly hierarchical institution charged with assuring global dominance by the U.S. elite, these activities disproportionately threaten communities where peoples of color live and work: urban ghettoes, tribal lands, and colonized countries. If corporate criminals all too often get off with a mere slap on the wrist, the military is literally getting away with murder. By contrast, resistance to such criminal abuses is criminalized; activists engaging in peaceful civil disobedience to block threatening military activities are often punished with stiff fines and prison sentences. If those who try to stop abuse of colonized and oppressed peoples and lands are punished, while the criminals go free, then the legal system is facilitating toxic capitalism in its most lethal form: militarism.

Anti-military movements among peoples of color, linked to struggles for environmental and social justice and self-determination, are growing stronger and building networks across the globe. The Pentagon has acknowledged its fear of a 'domino' effect from such movements, which could restrict its hold on power and corporate patrons' dollars. Challenging militarism should be central to any critique of 'toxic capitalism.' It is particularly helpful to study and support movements that articulate the criminal nature of U.S. military activities and the toxic nature of capitalism, while working toward community-controlled use and protection of resources. There is probably no clearer example than the grass-roots struggle to oblige the U.S. Navy to stop bombing Vieques, Puerto Rico, and clean up and return the lands for community directed, ecologically and socially sustainable use. A brief introduction to the land, the people, and the struggle illuminates militarism's key role in toxic capitalism, while offering guidelines to help replace such destructive 'dominoes' with life-affirming alternatives.

## Vieques: the land and the people

The hilly island of Vieques, known affectionately as 'isla nena' (little girl island), lies six miles off the southeastern coast of Puerto Rico and comprises some 33,000 acres. Its ecology is known for considerable diversity and its fertile soils have historically supported a wide variety of crops. Some of the earliest human remains found in the Caribbean – more than 4,000 years old – were discovered on Vieques. Although archaeologists believe that Vieques holds an important key to understanding Caribbean pre-Columbian history, the military occupation of the island has severely restricted its study (Rodriguez 1999). At the time of Columbus, Arawak-speaking Tainos ruled Vieques (literally, 'little island'). Although the Spanish killed their leaders in battle and scattered the population, for centuries the 'little island' resisted full Spanish control.

During the 19th century, Spain officially began settling Vieques, offering land to Spanish and other Europeans for agricultural development. The settlers brought workers – enslaved and free people of African descent – to provide labor in the expanding plantation economy. These laborers continued Vieques' tradition of resistance by protesting poor working conditions. Though titled land ownership was concentrated in the hands of relatively few families, by law workers had inheritable usufruct rights over homes and lands; abundant fishing also lessened dependence upon the wealthy. By the early 20th century, more than 10,000 residents were counted, and several thousand more traveled to nearby islands to work – or escaped notice in many isolated settlements. After the U.S. invaded and occupied Puerto Rico in 1898, land concentration increased in sugar cane regions such as Vieques; by the 1930s, the local elite was joined by a U.S.-based corporation in owning 70% of the little island's acreage. Existing race, class, and gender inequities were exacerbated by the new colonial regime and helped set the stage for the Navy's occupation of the island (Ayala 2001).

## The Navy's war against Vieques

Long before 1898, the U.S. Navy had been interested in establishing bases in Puerto Rico, including the strategically located islands of Vieques and Culebra (Berman Santana 1998). The Navy began bombing practice in Culebra in 1901 and field maneuvers in Vieques as early as the 1920s. In 1938, Admiral William Leahy wrote the first draft of a bill that would allow the Navy to acquire land in the U.S. and its territories for new bases and training areas; the following year he was named governor of Puerto Rico. In March 1941, Congress approved a sweeping bill allowing military expropriation of vast expanses of land; another law, passed in August, allowed the Navy to take immediate possession of targeted lands in Vieques. In effect, Washington's plan to build a giant base to shelter the British fleet plunged Vieques into World War II even before the United States was officially at war. Between 1941 and 1943, the Navy took over 21,000 of the island's 33,000 acres. The entire western portion of the island – where most of the rural settlements were located – was expropriated, along with 10,000 acres in the sparsely settled eastern section, but the Navy takeover also included 2,500 acres in the central part of the island.

The two largest landowners were fairly well compensated, but dozens of small property owners – and thousands of residents who had use rights, but no title – were given scant hours' notice, offered $25 to $100 for their belongings, and warned they would be bulldozed along with their homes if they didn't move fast enough. The displaced were offered lots in the lands taken by the Navy in the island's center, on condition that they sign a contract recognizing that they could be ordered to vacate 'Navy property' on short notice. These lands were generally rough brush lands lacking services or buildings; several women gave birth in the fields because there was no time to build shelters for them (Cordero Ventura 2001). In time, people built homes in the parcels, but despite promises did not receive titles to those lands after the war. Over the years, community land invasions helped force the Navy to transfer these central lands to the local government. Even today, however, most Viequenses lack affordable access to title.

Organized opposition to the Navy was at first blunted by fear of political persecution, strong support for the Allied war effort, and the many jobs created to build the giant base. Work included constructing a giant pier that was to stretch all the way to Puerto Rico. Among the other projects were flattening and removing land and vegetation to make way for hundreds of underground bunkers and weapons storage facilities, operating rock and sand quarries for building materials, and building roads and bridges to accommodate tanks throughout the western end, including in sensitive mangroves and wetlands. However, by 1943 it became clear that the British Navy would not need the shelter and work on the base was abandoned. Not surprisingly, the first major anti-Navy protest took place in 1943, because Vieques would soon be left without land and jobs (Ayala 2001: 36).

Opposition was also tempered by the expectation that after the war the lands would be returned. In 1945, the Navy leased thousands of acres to the Puerto Rican government, which began a series of agricultural projects that rehabilitated lands and created over 600 jobs (Bonnet Benitez 1977: 121–126). In 1947, though, the Navy dropped another bombshell: they announced that they would retake the lands they had leased and expropriate over 4,000 additional acres. Although a local group called 'Sons of Vieques' organized protests, the Navy ended up with 26,000 of Vieques' 33,000 acres – over 76% of the island – with civilians squeezed in the middle, imprisoned in a reservation (Melendez L6pez 1982).

The eastern half of Vieques became Camp Garcia, a base that often housed thousands of U.S. Marines. Their 'Eastern Maneuver Area' forms part of the Atlantic Fleet's premierbombing, training, and weapons testing facility; it has also been used for joint maneuvers with NATO and OAS forces, and has been rented out to other countries and weapons manufacturers. In 1948, the Navy held its first large-scale war games in Vieques, in which 60 ships, 350 planes, and 50,000 troops from all branches of the U.S. military participated. The games displayed the racism underlying the Vieques occupation: invading forces (the U.S. troops, called 'Blues' and given English names) attacked and conquered the island, which was defended by the Puerto Rico National Guard, called 'Blacks' and given Spanish names (*Ibid.*: 78–79). The western lands housed the Naval Ammunitions Supply Depot (NASD), which stored all kinds of weapons and explosives. Open burning and detonation of munitions and other toxic substances has been a common practice, even without the required permits. Training over the years has included documented use of 'non-conventional' (biological, chemical, nuclear) arms such as 'depleted' uranium and napalm (Lindsay-Poland and Berman Santana 2001). Additionally, millions of hair-sized aluminum- or lead-covered glass fibers known as 'chaff' are routinely dispersed during exercises.

The Navy proposed numerous times to remove the entire civilian population from Vieques, and even the dead from the cemetery in a plan known locally as 'Plan Dracula.' Each time popular resistance defeated the plans. Unlike many military bases in the U.S., after the early 1940s the Navy was never a primary source of employment for Vieques. Even indirect economic activity, such as the proliferation of bars and laundry services, was offset by the loss of small businesses serving the needs of a shrinking civilian-focused society; moreover, the new businesses became flashpoints for alcohol- and sex-related conflicts (Ayala 2001: 35). Tensions rose over the years, when military personnel – often thousands of Marines let loose in the civilian sector–engaged in sexual assaults on women and children and drunken brawls with local men. Although a number of Viequenses were killed in such altercations, as well as in accidents from explosives, no military personnel ever faced criminal charges. Local resistance grew to the extent that sailors and Marines were often attacked with bottles and stones; finally, in the early 1980s the military stopped allowing off-duty personnel to enter the civilian sector.

An intense round of anti-military activism in the 1970s forced the Navy out of Culebra, but not from Vieques. In fact, in 1979 several key leaders were given federal prison terms for holding a religious service in the restricted area. One, Angel Rodríguez Cristóbal, was murdered in prison (Meléndez López 1982). After losing Culebra as a bombing range, the Navy intensified its use of Vieques for bombing, land maneuvers, and weapons testing. Interestingly, U.S. Marines were no longer stationed in large numbers in Camp García once destructive practices were intensified. When toxic contamination grew exponentially, many patrolling and security duties were contracted out to a firm that hired Viequenses.

Today, Vieques is an island and people fighting against extinction. Between 1983 and 1998, the Navy dropped 17,783 tons of bombs on Vieques.[1] The 'Live Impact Area' – 900 acres at the eastern end of the island where ships and planes practice bombing – contains more craters per square inch than the moon does (Seguinot 1994: 114). Parts of the rock substrata are damaged and much of the soil has been pulverized. Navy-contracted 'experts' have minimized the importance of indigenous sites, and many have been destroyed. Far from demonstrating concern, a recent Navy document claimed that since bombing has destroyed so many of the cultural resources, little probably remained, so continued bombing would have no significant negative impact (U.S. Navy 2001: 4.13–14). Around the bombing zone, key plants and animals in the local food chain show dangerous amounts of heavy metals, particularly components of weapons and targets such as arsenic, barium, cadmium, chromium, cobalt, copper, cyanide, lead, nickel, tin, vanadium, and zinc (Massol Deya and Diaz 2001). The prevailing easterly trade winds carry contaminated dust from the impact area directly into the civilian zone, where the same contaminants show up in excessive amounts in vegetation and residents. Civilian water supplies have also shown traces of military explosives since at least the late 1970s. Cancer, heart disease, and kidney, reproductive, respiratory, and skin ailments linked to the same heavy metals have increased dramatically since the 1970s and now occur at higher rates in Vieques than in Puerto Rico, particularly among children (Nazario et al. 2002). If the higher than average mortality rate in Vieques cannot be explained by significant differences in age distribution or lifestyle – both of which are similar to other rural municipalities – then environmental contamination must be considered. Since so little polluting economic activity occurs in Vieques, the most obvious contamination source is the Navy.

Because the giant Roosevelt Roads Navy Base blocks the shortest sea route to Puerto Rico, people and goods must travel to Vieques from Fajardo, which is 17 miles and over an hour away. The local clinic has been so badly under-funded that most medical needs – including prenatal care and childbirth

– must be met by going to the big island. Not surprisingly, the island suffers from higher rates of low birth weight and infant mortality than is the case in the rest of Puerto Rico. Fishing suffers from damage to marine habitats, which for years have evidenced degradation related to bombing and other military activities; the many days when Navy maneuvers severely limit fishing (more than half the year during the 1990s) also hurt the industry. For years, the Navy opposed attempts to strongly develop the tourism or manufacturing industries, preferring instead to limit traffic in and around Vieques. Over the years, thousands of Viequenses were forced to migrate in search of work, so that the population steadily declined to seven or eight thousand, and has only recently grown to just over nine thousand. The island's small tourism industry is dominated by a growing settler community of more than 1,000 white North Americans and Europeans, who drive up real estates prices (properties often advertised only among themselves), build walled villas and rental condos, disparage the locals, and dream of separating Vieques and Culebra from Puerto Rico to create the 'Spanish Virgin Islands.' Young people in Vieques have few alternatives to leaving; some take jobs that will allow them to retire early, hoping to return with a pension, but others never return. More than one Viequense has described their community as an 'endangered species' and referred to the ongoing colonization as 'Hawaii-zation.'

**Vieques fights back: struggle for peace and justice**

Since the 1940s, local resistance has had its periods of organized activity, such as the broad-based campaign that prevented further military expropriations in the 1960s and the fishermen-led disruptions of Navy exercises during the 1970s. Such periods of open resistance were frequently followed by political buyouts or repression and a less active interlude. Besides grass-roots organizing to oppose the Navy, the municipal assembly passed resolutions during each decade since the 1950s that called for the Navy to leave and return the lands to the people. In the early 1990s, activists in Vieques formed the Committee for the Rescue and Development of Vieques (CRDV) and continued protesting Navy activities there. They also offered *'la protesta con la propuesta'* (the protest with the proposal) for the island's biggest ecological, economic, and social challenges, advocating 'the four D's: Demilitarization, Decontamination, Devolution (of lands), and (community-based, sustainable) Development.' In 1995, CRDV testified in the U.S. Congress in favor of a bill to return the western lands to Vieques' control; they also put forth an integrated land use plan that included some urban growth to ease overcrowding, integrated development of fishing, small-scale tourism and agriculture, and conservation of sensitive and historic sites. They also called for a 'community land trust' to manage the returned lands and a 'community extension program' for research, education, and training. Unfortunately, Congress shelved the bill and the land-use plan got little attention. Then on April 19 1999, two 500 pound bombs killed a civilian guard named David Sanes, igniting a major anti-Navy movement that captured world attention.

Activism since 1999 has included rallies in Puerto Rico – such as a February 2000 march by over 150,000 people in San Juan – and wherever Puerto Ricans live, including major protests in New York and the 2000 Democratic Convention in Los Angeles. Fundraising efforts feature concerts, plays, and films, fueled by a Vieques-inspired cultural explosion. There have also been ongoing commitments from labor unions and other organizations. Regular efforts to educate and lobby Congress included a visit by hundreds of Viequenses and Puerto Ricans to Washington, D.C., during March 2001, when some legislators expressed surprise that Vieques was inhabited! By far, the most powerful activism has been militant, nonviolent civil disobedience. Two days after David Sanes was killed, Puerto Rican environmental activist Alberto de Jesus ('Tito Kayak') decided to stay on the bombing range to prevent more Navy bombing. Thousands of Puerto Ricans and others followed his example, and within a year 14 protest camps had been established, representing teachers, fishermen, church groups, and others.

Since May 4, 2000 – when the U.S. government sent in federal marshals, the FBI, and the military to remove the protesters – over 1,500 people have been arrested for continuing to enter whenever the Navy sends its battle groups for bombing practice. Hundreds have served prison sentences of up to six months for the misdemeanor offense of trespassing. Well-known arrestees such as the Reverend Al Sharpton and Robert Kennedy, Jr., helped bring attention to the Vieques struggle, but ordinary people from all segments of Puerto Rican society, who risk their lives for peace, form the backbone. The Navy has failed to neutralize the movement through offers of base employment, cash payments, and other gifts, as well as a heavily financed public relations campaign. This was evidenced by a July 29, 2001, vote in which 70% of Viequenses voted for the Navy to leave. Not even the repressive post-September 11 atmosphere, along with increasingly harsh treatment of protesters-including physical abuse of arrestees and indiscriminate tear-gassing of peaceful demonstrators on the civilian side – has dampened popular dedication to peace for Vieques. Finally, the Vieques struggle has linked up with a growing international network against U.S. militarism, featuring reciprocal visits and sharing of strategies with activists from Korea, Okinawa, Hawaii, San Francisco's Bayview-Hunter's Point, and elsewhere.

No one can doubt the difficulty involved in challenging the world's most powerful military, but an even greater challenge is what will happen to Vieques after the Navy leaves. The exquisite beauty of the 'isla nena' has attracted attention from numerous resort developers, who have cultivated connections to North American settlers and Puerto Rican politicians. Some of the Navy's strongest congressional allies have vowed never to let the lands leave federal hands, Accordingly, they have fought to ensure that, should the Navy leave Vieques, the lands would be transferred to the Department of the Interior, where they would be closed to the public as a 'wilderness reserve' and left uncleaned.[2] If carried out, Viequenses would be punished for opposing the Navy by again squeezing them in their reservation between contaminated and restricted federal 'conservation' lands.

Considering Puerto Rico's colonial political status, San Juan is obviously vulnerable to pressure from Washington. Nearly every governor has attempted to end the bombing of Vieques, only to end up making a deal. The pro-statehood government – in power from 1992 until the end of 2000 – allowed its Planning Board to work with the Navy on the Land Use Plan. In August 2000, the Planning Board held a required public hearing in Vieques on the first draft. Among its features were: building three new factories tied to the military, building a large new port for cruise ships and commercial traffic near the new resort and far from town, having the Navy run the local clinic, and attracting 10,000 new settlers to Vieques, mainly from military families. Despite limited availability, 35 members of Vieques community groups and supporting technical experts reviewed the draft and signed up to address the hearings. The hearings played to a packed house and lasted over six hours. Speaker after speaker denounced the plan in detail, and hundreds of Viequenses held a spirited protest outside. Finally, at midnight the mayor rejected the draft land-use plan.

The revised version, reviewed in November 2000, chose a 'Navy-free Vieques' as the preferred option, but still contained serious problems (Puerto Rico Planning Board 2000). For example, it was assumed that agriculture, fishing, and nonmilitary factories were not viable and that Vieques would have to depend almost entirely on foreign tourism. Second, all three land areas – the two military properties and the civilian sector in between – were treated as separate entities, instead of as one island. Third, it ignored the need to shorten travel time between Vieques and the big island – which must be between the closest points. Most troubling was that there was nothing about land tenure or protection from outside speculation. Nonetheless, in January the new mayor of Vieques announced that he would work to revise the plan and incorporate proposals that activists had worked on for years.

In 1999, a large group of San Juan-based professionals responded to a call from Vieques activists for ongoing technical assistance. The Technical and Professional Support Group (known as GATP in Spanish) includes planners, attorneys, health professionals, ecologists, economists, and other individuals with the expertise needed to assist the Viequenses in making their own development and conservation plans. This group has worked on a voluntary basis for over three years to flesh out the details of a community-directed, ecologically and socially sustainable land use and development plan. From the start, work has included dozens of meetings and workshops in Vieques to learn what the people themselves see as their most pressing problems and possible solutions. The first volume of their work, completed during summer 2000, presented a detailed picture of present economic, social, and environmental challenges, including analyses and suggestions given in dozens of community workshops. In the winter of 2001 to 2002, they worked on the community land-trust proposal; a second volume would detail specific strategies for responsible and integrated development, some of which received attention from the local government.

Recent declarations by high Navy officials that other training areas may better serve their needs indicate that they may be preparing a face-saving explanation for their expected departure from Vieques. Accordingly, some activists are attempting to shift their focus to the more contentious – and potentially more divisive – problems of cleanup and control of the lands.

Whether they can successfully apply the experiences of the demilitarization phase (the 'first D') to the rest of the struggle remains to be seen. Nonetheless, the struggle has had a transformative effect, not only on Viequenses, but also on other Puerto Ricans, who see Vieques as a workshop for learning to successfully challenge powerful forces of division, domination, and exploitation that have long ruled this colonized Caribbean nation.

Vieques is a powerful case study of a life-affirming struggle that stood up to the world's most powerful, violent, and destructive force and offered an alternate vision of security based on a culture of peace, cooperation, and community control. Environmental and social justice advocates everywhere can apply the 'four D's' – demilitarization, decontamination, devolution, and development – to their own struggles to protect their environments and sustain their communities. Support for this struggle against the world's most serious environmental criminal, the U.S. military, is therefore vital. A victory for Vieques – and for Puerto Rico – will offer hope for the future of us all.

## Notes

1 By comparison, the Hiroshima and Nagasaki atomic bombs dropped 12,500 and 22,000 tons, respectively.
2 The Floyd D. Spence National Defense Authorization Act for Fiscal Year 2001 (P.L. 106–398) was signed by President Clinton on October 30 2000. Sections 1503 to 1508 concern Vieques.

## References

Ayala, César (2001) 'From Sugar Plantations to Military Bases: The U.S. Navy's Expropriations in Vieques, Puerto Rico 1940–45.' *CENTRO Journal* 13,1 (Spring): 22–41.

Berman Santana, Déborah (1998) 'Puerto Rico's Operation Bootstrap: Colonialist Roots of a Persistent Model for 'Third World' Development.' *Revista Geográfica* 124: 87–116.

Bonnet Benrtez, Juan A. (1977) *Vieques en la historia de Puerto Rico.* San Juan: F. Ortiz Nieves.

Cordero Ventura, Cruz (2001) *Vieques: Sesenta Anos de Bombardeos en Tiempos de Paz.* Published by the author.

Hynes, H. Patricia (1999) 'Taking Population out of the Equation: Reformulating I=PAT.' Jael Silliman and Ynestra King (eds.), *Dangerous Intersections: Feminist Perspectives on Population, Environment, and Development.* Cambridge: South End Press: 39–73.

Lindsay-Poland, John and Ddborah Berman Santana (2001) *Environmental Impacts of Military Training.* Vieques Issue Briefs. No. 1. San Francisco: Fellowship of Reconciliation Task Force on Latin America and the Caribbean.

Massol Deyá, Arturo and Elba Díaz de Osbourne (2001) *Ciencia y Ecologia: Vieques en Crisis Ambiental.* Adjuntas: Publicaciones Casa Pueblo.

Melendez, Arturo (1982) *La Batalla de Vieques.* Río Piedras: Editorial Edil.

Nazario, Cruz María, John Lindsay-Poland, and Deborah Berman Santana (2002) *Health in Vieques: A Crisis and Its Causes.* Vieques Issue Briefs, No. 3. San Francisco: Fellowship of Reconciliation Task Force on Latin America and the Caribbean.

Puerto Rico Planning Board (2000) *Plan de Ordenacion Territorial.* San Juan: Commonwealth of Puerto Rico.

Rodríguez, Miguel (1999) '*La Marina y el patrimonio arqueológico de Vieques.* Testimony presented at the Government of Puerto Rico Special Commission on Vieques (June 15).

Seguinot, José (1994) *Geografía, Ecología y Derecho de Puerto Rico y el Caribe.* San Juan: First Books Publishing of Puerto Rico.

Simon, David R. (2000) 'Corporate Environmental Crimes and Social Inequality.' *American Behavioral Scientist* 43,4 (January): 633–640. At http://lbss.sfsu.edu/naff/PA748/simon.htm.

St. Clair, Jeffrey and Alexander Cockburn (2001) 'The Military's Toxic Timebombs.' *Nature & Politics* 5 (May 9): 18. At http://eatthestate.org/05-18/NaturePolitics.htm.

United States, Department of Defense (2000) *DoD 101*. At http://www.defenselink.mil/pubs/dod101/largest.html.

United States, House of Representatives (2002) 'Hearings Before the Military Readiness Subcommittee of the House Armed Services Committee.' March 14. At www.house.gov/liasc/schedules/ 2002.htm1.

United States, House of Representatives, Armed Services Committee (1981) 'Report of Panel to Review the Status of Navy Training Activities on the Island of Vieques.' Ninety-sixth Congress 2nd Session (February).

United States Navy (2001) *Programmatic Environmental Assessment (EA) for Continued Use with Non-Explosive Ordnance of the Vieques Inner Range*. Prepared for the Commander in Chief, U.S. Atlantic Fleet, in compliance with Section 102(2)(c) of the National Environmental Policy Act of 1969 (February 14).

— (1999) The National Security Need for Vieques. Prepared for the Secretary of the Navy by Conunander, U.S. Second Fleet, and Commander, U. S. Marine Corps, Forces Atlantic.

Zito, Kelly (2002) 'What Lies Beneath: Hamilton Homes on Hold as Developer, Army Deal with Methane Gas Buildup at Former Landfill Site.' *The San Francisco Chronicle* (Sunday, June 2): H1-7.

# 18. The politics of illegal dumping: an environmental justice framework*

*David N. Pellow*

Studies of the intersection between environmental hazards and community demographics have concluded that environmental inequality is prevalent in communities across the United States. While these studies offer persuasive indicators of environmental inequality, we still have little understanding of the social forces involved in the production of these unequal outcomes. Drawing on a case study of a community of color facing illegal dumping, I propose an environmental justice framework to explain the social dynamics that produced this outcome.

**Key Words** environmental inequality • environmental justice • environmental racism

## Introduction

Numerous studies of the intersection between ecological hazards and social inequality have concluded that environmental inequality and environmental racism are prevalent in communities across the United States (Krieg 1998; Mohai 1996; Pastor, Sadd and Hipp 2001). That is, communities of color and low-income neighborhoods are disproportionately burdened with a range of environmental hazards, including polluting industries, landfills, incinerators, and illegal dumps. Researchers have supported this conclusion with analyses of census data and case studies of contaminated communities where poor persons and people of color are the residential majority. Significant attention has also focused on the environmental justice (EJ) movement that has emerged with the aim of reducing the level of environmental risk in communities across the U.S. (Bullard 2000).

In this article, I argue that while these studies offer persuasive indicators of environmental inequality, we have little understanding of the complexity involved in the decision-making that produces or otherwise influences these unequal outcomes. Specifically, few if any studies have proposed a conceptual framework for understanding how environmental inequality emerges in

---

\* From *Qualitative Sociology* (2004), 27(4): pp. 511–525.

communities. I propose an 'environmental justice framework' to address these questions. In the remainder of the article, I review the relevant literature on environmental inequality/racism; I then develop an environmental justice framework, and apply it to a case study of illegal dumping in communities of color in Chicago, Illinois.

## Studies of environmental inequality: origins and processes

### Place-specific explanations for environmental inequality

While environmental racism and inequality are national, even global, phenomena, they unfold and impact people differently across space, depending on any number of factors. In their recent study of the state of Massachusetts, Faber and Krieg (2001) argue that a combination of white and middle-class flight to the suburbs, a rise in the number of people of color in the central cities, and increases in illegal dumping and the siting of incinerators produced environmental inequalities in that state. In a case study of the US Steel Corporation in Gary, Indiana, Hurley (1995) found that Latinos and African Americans faced disproportionately high levels of exposure to environmental toxins on the job and in their neighborhoods as a result of local racial discrimination.

Roberts and Toffolon-Weiss (2001) argue that the primary cause of environmental inequalities in the state of Louisiana is an alliance among business, the state, and other 'growth machine' interests to create a 'good business climate' that favors private profits over public and environmental health. The authors conclude that each particular EJ struggle may reveal driving factors that are unique to that specific context. For African Americans, Vietnamese, and Native American communities in the state, the process by which environmental inequalities emerged was distinct. For example, in the case of some African Americans in Louisiana, they face environmental racism not only as a result of contemporary racist environmental policies, but also because many polluting corporations occupy land that was once the site of slave plantations, land where the descendants of slaves and sharecroppers now live. Thus context, place, and history matter a great deal.

In a study of Torrance, California, Sidawi (1997) demonstrated that, as a result of racially biased urban planning during the last century, Chicanos faced the highest levels of exposure to industrial pollution in that city, when compared to Anglos. Similarly, Boone and Modarres (1999) argue that in Commerce, California, although hazardous industry was sited in close proximity to Latino populations, zoning and urban planning practices had as much, if not more, to do with industrial location decisions as did demographics and racial politics. As they state, 'demographics alone are not responsible for the concentration of manufacturing in Commerce' (ibid., p. 165). They emphasize the importance of 'place-specific analysis' to determine the root causes of environmental inequalities.

## Macro-level explanations for environmental inequality

While discriminatory zoning practices and laws certainly contribute to environmental inequality, Bullard (1990, 1996, 2000) demonstrates that all of the city of Houston's municipal landfills are located in African American neighborhoods, *despite the absence* of any zoning laws. In this case, he maintains that there was *de facto* zoning by Houston's powerful white city leaders, who apparently viewed African American neighborhoods as appropriate sites for waste disposal. In other words, Bullard concludes that racism is a general organizing principle of city and county politics in the U.S.

Compounding the institutional racism in politics, Pastor, Sadd, and Hipp (2001, p. 19) argue that a lack of 'pre-existing racially based social capital' also places communities of color at a disproportionately higher environmental risk than white communities. Communities with low levels of voting behavior, home ownership, wealth, and disposable income are more vulnerable to high concentrations of polluting facilities than are other communities. Unfortunately, for communities of color, these characteristics are often highly correlated with race. Bullard's (1990) classic study *Dumping in Dixie* supported this claim more than a decade ago with evidence that polluters follow the 'path of least resistance' when seeking cost-effective dumping sites. In Bullard's estimation, the basis for these choices is institutional racism, which, in turn, 'influences local land use, enforcement of environmental regulations, industrial facility siting, and, where people of color live, work, and play' (Bullard 1996, p. 449). Those communities most capable of mounting effective collective resistance tend to be better educated, have higher income levels, and have fewer people of color. Building on this record of evidence, Lake concludes that environmental inequalities 'arise from the unequal power relations controlling the organization of production in capitalist societies' (Lake 1996, p. 169).

Thus, on one hand, we can cull from this literature particular factors that have produced environmental inequalities in certain case studies: local growth machine politics, discriminatory and insensitive zoning (or lack thereof), residential and occupational segregation, and white flight. On the other hand, a number of scholars point to a range of interrelated macro-level factors believed to be the general cause of environmental inequality: racism, social inequality, a lack of social capital, and the limited capacity to engage in collective action in the face of powerful political economic institutions. I argue that, while both groups of studies are helpful for understanding the nature of environmental racism, a new framework is needed to address both the generalities and complexities of this phenomenon, a framework that acknowledges both the macro-level themes of institutional inequality and the more micro-level motivations of particular organizations and actors involved in EJ struggles. In order to capture these factors that define many EJ struggles I propose an 'environmental justice framework.'

## An environmental justice framework

The framework I propose is organized around four dimensions relevant to most EJ conflicts. First is the importance of viewing environmental inequality as a sociohistorical process rather than as a discrete event. A focus on the history of an EJ conflict opens a window into the processes by which hazards are created and distributed. Second is a focus on the complex roles of the many people and organizations (stakeholders) involved. Environmental inequality impacts many actors and institutions with often contradictory and crosscutting allegiances (the state, workers, environmentalists, residents, private capital, and neighborhood organizations). These stakeholders are engaged in struggles for access to valuable resources (clean and safe working and living environments, natural resources, power, and profit). Third is the effect of social inequality on stakeholders. Institutional racism, class and gender inequalities, political hierarchies, and other forms of stratification play decisive roles in EJ struggles. Specifically, those populations of workers and residents lower on the social hierarchy are generally low-income and/or people of color and are therefore more likely to suffer environmental injustices. Fourth is agency – the power of populations confronting environmental inequalities to shape the outcomes of these conflicts. That is, marginal groups can sometimes create openings in the political process to mitigate environmental inequality. Through resistance they can shape environmental inequalities.

I refer to this as an environmental *justice* framework because, although it underscores the causes and nature of environmental *inequalities*, I view the absence of environmental justice (EJ) as the central problem. In this study, I focus on a case in which a community of color faces an ecological threat. By drawing on the environmental justice framework, I seek to explain the social dynamics that produced this outcome.

## Methods

I collected data from 1997 through 1999 – as part of a larger project – employing archival, interview, and participant observation methods. I collected numerous newspaper articles and government documents on EJ conflicts in Chicago during the 1990s. Data were also culled from hundreds of memos, reports, internal documents, and studies from various grassroots and environmental advocacy organizations involved in these struggles. I conducted forty face-to-face semistructured interviews with residents, environmentalists, and government officials active in Chicago's solid waste conflicts. Interviews ranged from thirty minutes to two hours and were audiotaped, transcribed, and analyzed with a thematic coding system. Thus, through observation, interviews, and documentary analysis, I have triangulated data sources to provide the most accurate and complete presentation of the case study as possible (Denzin 1970).

## History and process: Chicago, a hotbed of environmental justice conflict

Operation Silver Shovel was an illegal dumping scandal that occurred in Chicago's West Side Latino and African American communities during the 1990s. Thousands of tons of debris from construction, demolition, and residential remodeling projects were dumped in these neighborhoods, creating small mountains of waste, over the objections of local residents. Unfortunately, this case was not without precedent.

On November 19, 1913, Mary McDowell addressed the City Club of Chicago. McDowell, an activist associated with Jane Addams' Hull House, was widely known as 'the Garbage Lady.' She and other reformers were leading a battle against the city's unhealthful and exploitative practice of concentrating garbage dumps in immigrant neighborhoods. McDowell and her colleagues were, without question, early environmental justice activists, fighting against environmental injustices directed at European immigrant populations in their ward, but also speaking out against violence and discrimination directed at African Americans. The City Club requested that she address its members about 'Chicago's garbage problem.' Her remarks that day in 1913 are illuminating with regard to EJ struggles of nearly a century ago as well as today:

> Finally, let me say that here in Chicago the people in the 'back yard' of the city are awake. We can never go back to the old outrageous conditions. The old attitude of mind was represented by a lawyer before the Finance Committee in the City Hall when he said: '*Gentlemen, in every great city there must be a part of that city segregated for unpleasant things, and, of course, you know that people in that part of town are generally not sensitive.*' Now, Chicago dare not have that attitude. We must take a new attitude of mind toward these other districts because the people are thinking in those districts and the standard is growing higher every day ... We must make it so that it will not be tolerable to the citizens even on the edge of town (McDowell 1913; emphasis added).

That powerful leaders and institutions behave in ways that create environmental injustices is rarely a question. However, many activists and scholars speculate as to whether or not those stakeholders actually *intend* to do so. This quote suggests a conscious, even nonchalant, ideological framework that supports the production of environmental injustices as an inherent necessity of urban life and politics.

Groups involved in Chicago's early garbage wars included Hull House, the City of Chicago, private waste haulers and dumpers, and the immigrant ethnic groups living in the wards and neighborhoods where dumping was occurring. These stakeholders were in conflict over *the* seminal environmental justice issue: the distribution of solid waste in neighborhoods populated by less powerful socioeconomic or racial/ethnic groups. McDowell's very presence at the City Club of Chicago indicates that the protests that emerged over this crisis had caught the attention of the media, policymakers, and influential institutions. She also noted that the system was being changed precisely because of local neighborhood consciousness of environmental injustices, thus creating a 'standard [that] is growing higher every day.' In short, McDowell's statement nicely illustrates the *environmental justice framework*. She demonstrated that the history and process of waste management and dumping were in transformation; that multiple stakeholders were involved in this drama, not just waste dumpers and community residents; that longstanding practices of institutional racism and classism were at work in these communities; and that ordinary people, residents targeted by these practices, were changing the very face of these environmental injustices by challenging them.

Chicago is a city frequently rocked with environmental justice battles, as evidenced by its continual 'garbage wars,' wherein residents struggle to keep solid waste out of their communities and, by extension, inside other communities. More than eighty percent of the city's formal garbage disposal occurs in landfills on the mostly working-class, African American, Latino, and European ethnic Southeast side. Chicago hosts the most landfills per square mile in the nation. But formal waste disposal practices are only one dimension of Chicago's garbage wars. Less visible is the *informal* practice of illegal, or 'fly,' dumping.

Chicago has a long history of conflicts over illegal waste disposal. At the end of the nineteenth century in the immigrant enclave of the twenty-ninth ward, Alderman Tom Carey made a fortune creating large pits in the neighborhood to make bricks for his own construction company and then receiving payment from the city to fill them in with garbage (Hull House 1895, ch. VII). In 1910, the Superintendent for the Department of Health was dismissed after an investigation concluded that several incidents involving graft and extortion at a waste dump had occurred on his watch (Citizens' Association of Chicago 1910). In 1914 the City Council of Chicago passed an ordinance outlawing unregulated dumping. But since that time, there have been frequent scandals over the illicit trade in garbage for favors and cash.

This phenomenon also reflects the problem of environmental inequalities. A study during the 1990s by the Chicago Department of Streets and Sanitation revealed that, of the ten city neighborhoods with the most illegally dumped garbage, all are at least sixty percent African American or Latino. And wards where people of color are the majority account for seventy-nine percent of all illegally dumped garbage in the city (Cohen 1992). This is the historical context in which Operation Silver Shovel must be viewed.

## Operation silver shovel

### A multi-stakeholder view of illegal dumping: politicians, firms, and residents

John Christopher was a businessman. Since the late 1980s, he was in the business of 'recycling' construction and demolition (C&D) waste and finding places to dump it at the lowest possible cost. The vast majority of the waste Christopher was dumping originated from highway construction projects and remodeling firms across the mostly white North Side of the city and suburbs. John Christopher began dumping his waste in working-class and low-income African American and Latino communities on Chicago's West Side, particularly Lawndale and Austin. In order to ensure that he could commit these crimes without detection by the police or City Hall, he paid local aldermen cash bribes. For example, Christopher later admitted to paying bribes in the late 1980s of approximately $5,000 per month to Alderman William Henry of the 24th Ward 'in return for Alderman Henry's agreement to assist [Christopher] in using and operating the site … without interference from the City of Chicago' (Plea Agreement 1995). Christopher's deals intensified the close links that normally exist between political institutions and economic organizations in the urban political economy (Schnaiberg 1994).

Every community where Christopher dumped his waste was primarily African American or Latino, as was each alderman whom he bribed. The KrisJon company claimed to be recycling the C&D waste for use in future construction operations. However, KrisJon was not actually recycling the waste. Instead, the company was crushing large rocks and concrete blocks and simply piling them up – creating dumps in the neighborhoods. Local activists soon discovered that KrisJon had no permits for this operation and was therefore in violation of several city ordinances. KrisJon was engaged in illegal dumping.

Communities confronting environmental inequalities in the U.S. typically respond in a variety of ways. Public protests, petitioning and targeting political leaders, and negotiating directly with polluting firms are just a few methods commonly found in EJ groups' tactical repertoires (Gottlieb 1993; Hurley 1995). Resident stakeholders on Chicago's West Side were no different.

Local neighborhood groups in Lawndale and Austin protested against the illegal dumping operations early on. In 1990, residents held public hearings to discuss a site that was being proposed for a dump that KrisJon was to operate. A short while later, when the site was operational and producing a large volume of dust, an organization called Concerned Parents of Sumner, Frazier, and Webster Elementary School Children (schools located within blocks of the dump) sent letters to John Christopher requesting a number of environmental improvements. Christopher never responded. His dumpsites, however, were bustling and receiving waste from ninety-six different locations around metropolitan Chicago. The noise and vibrations from trucks delivering the waste was so extensive that it cracked the streets and sidewalks, damaged the foundations of nearby homes, and kept residents awake at night. Residents believed that the dust from the operation was linked to severe respiratory problems in these African American and Latino communities. One man reported that he had experienced

> … coughing, wheezing, short of breath, headache, sinus and I have been hospitalized six times since the dump been on Kildare [Street]. I had to remove carpet from floors because of dust and dust flares up my asthma (Interview 1997).

Another resident, Doreen Jenkins, wrote of her son's medical problems:

> … including a trip to the emergency room in January for headaches, dizziness and difficulty breathing. The emergency services report attached to Ms. Griffin's letter describes that the 'community is quite polluted by trucks that dump dirt into the air.' Ms. Griffin pleaded to 'please stop this illegal operation in our neighborhood' (Vinik and Harley 1997).

While perhaps not scientifically conclusive, these residents' claims resonate strongly with the testimonies of other persons living near polluting facilities in numerous communities across the nation (Brown and Mikkelsen 1990; Kroll-Smith and Floyd 1997).

Although the Illinois State's Attorney has the authority to bring legal action against a company when there is 'substantial danger to the environment or to the public health,' the community received only a noncommittal letter from an Assistant State's Attorney. By this time, one of the dumpsites was measured at eighty feet high. Residents began to refer to it as 'the mountain' and successfully urged the City of Chicago to file a suit against John Christopher's operation as a common law public nuisance and as a violation of the Municipal Code prohibiting open dumping. In fact, the Illinois Environmental Protection (IEP) Act expressly prohibits both open dumping and the operation of unpermitted waste storage, treatment, or disposal facilities. There are also requirements in the IEP Act concerning dust minimization and permits. However, the court denied the plaintiffs' motions, allowing dumping operations to continue. Despite the fact that Christopher's facility violated all of these regulations, the Illinois Environmental Protection Agency issued no citations. This official sanctioning of direct violations of city and state laws in a community of color stunned local activists.

The community meetings and protests continued. In February 1992, more than six hundred people signed a petition demanding the closure of KrisJon's two major sites at Kildare and Kostner Avenues. The South Lawndale Community Block Club wrote letters to city and state environmental regulators, stating:

> KrisJon is receiving more consideration and respect by the courts than the residents who live and own property in this area. This is an insult to our community ... We are still appalled that this company has been allowed to operate in our area next to our homes, residents and schools with no regard to the rights of the people who reside in our area.

The resident-activist stakeholders were fighting what appeared to be either a case of near total insensitivity by the state or an alliance between government and polluters to allow the dumps to remain in these communities of color.

But not everyone in the community was opposed to the dumping operations. Some residents joined John Christopher and participated in neighborhood 'beautification projects' wherein he provided them with grass, flower, and vegetable seeds for landscaping and gardening. He also received the support of one of the strongest institutions in the African American community – the church. In 1991, a local pastor wrote a public letter applauding Christopher's efforts to 'give back' to the community, and thirty residents signed a petition indicating they '... welcome the KrisJon Construction Company into the community and are grateful that the company is involved in a beautification project that will benefit the community and its residents.' Hence even under these particularly pernicious circumstances, there were local leaders willing to publicly support even the most egregious violations of community sentiment.

While local leaders and politicians were involved in this struggle, the federal government was also well aware of the illegal dumping operations and used them as an opportunity to launch an investigation of political corruption. In 1992 the Federal Bureau of Investigation (FBI) secretly secured John Christopher's cooperation in what became known as Operation Silver Shovel. Christopher became a 'mole,' working undercover for the U.S. Attorney's Office and the FBI in an effort to uncover political corruption associated with the disposal of solid waste in Chicago. So, just as he had done in the 1980s, Christopher bribed African American and Latino aldermen to allow him to dump waste in their wards; the only difference was that in 1992 he was secretly videotaping the transactions. The public was not informed about this sting operation until 1996 when the media broke the case.

Residents who had already been protesting the dumping were incensed that the government had sanctioned this process. The Reverend Jesse Jackson and his organization Operation PUSH joined local activists and exhorted community members to take action:

> These dump sites must be removed. They bring property value down with rats and roaches ... They're health hazards. If you live in those areas call PUSH and fight back or they'll keep doing it (Walls 1996).

Despite this persistence on the part of activists, it would be many more months before any positive changes would result from their protests. This is in large part because these communities possess few economic and political resources.

### Inequalities: race, class, and political power

While local aldermen were receiving bribes to allow dumping to continue unabated, activists were aware of the environmental inequality/racism dimensions of this struggle. One resident wrote a letter to the Cook County State's Attorney about KrisJon:

> The company operates only in minority areas. We also know that the company poses health hazards, damages our buildings and houses, and decreases our property values.

Echoing this sentiment, a local newspaper in the Austin community referred to the dumping practices as

> ... 'environmental racism'... in poor areas of Chicago where toxic dumpers, solid waste treatment companies and others see large profits to be made from garbage and industrial waste [and they] attempt to gain footholds with the cooperation of greedy, corrupt, and stupid elected officials. Apparently, the first battle-ground is North Lawndale (Austin Voice 1994).

This writer makes two major points. The first is that the dumpsites are in poor communities; the second is that certain elected officials facilitated this process. I will address both issues because they underscore the nature of social inequality in these communities.

The two largest illegal dumpsites on the West Side were on Kostner and Kildare Avenues. The level of class and racial inequality evident at these sites is remarkable. For example, the neighborhood surrounding the Kostner dump (based on a one-square-mile radius from the site) had a median household income of $20,469 compared to a citywide median income of $26,301 (U.S. Census Bureau 1990). The majority of residents in this community are people of color, with Latinos comprising 46.3 percent and African Americans 40.2 percent. Citywide, African Americans comprise 39.1 percent of the population and Latinos 19.6 percent. Thus the median household income in this neighborhood is well below both the national poverty level and the citywide median, and the percentage of people of color is higher than the citywide percentage. The figures for the Kildare site are even starker. For example, the neighborhood surrounding the Kildare dump (based on a one-square-mile radius from the site) had a median household income of $15,113. The majority of people in this community are also people of color, with African Americans comprising 89.6 percent and Latinos 6.6 percent. Both of these communities are what William Julius Wilson (1996) has called 'new poverty areas,' where the majority of people live in deep poverty and most adults are either unemployed or underemployed. Thus, the majority of the residents in these neighborhoods experienced a significant degree of poverty, economic instability, and relative deprivation.

With regard to the role of corrupt elected officials, this dimension of inequality requires analysis but should also include a consideration of activities by residents who themselves accepted bribes and facilitated illegal dumping practices. The relative lack of status and political influence over citywide politics among Chicago's African American and Latino aldermen is rivaled only by the political powerlessness among their constituents. Poor and working-class residents of color in Chicago are not particularly influential in local politics and therefore offer polluters easy targets. The attendant lack of economic stability that characterizes many of these neighborhoods only reinforces their political powerlessness and the diminished status of their elected officials. This subjugated position also renders these groups particularly vulnerable to efforts by polluting firms to 'divide and conquer' residents over potential economic benefits that may accompany industrial activity.

Frequently, when communities confront environmental threats, they are beset by internal fractures surrounding family conflicts, fear of job losses, and loyalties to various neighborhood institutions and firms involved. These tensions generally intensify the pain and anxiety that normally develop during conflicts over environmental contamination (Brown and Mikkelsen 1990; Hurley 1995; Roberts and Toffolon-Weiss 2001). Chicago's West Side was characterized by a particularly intense array of divisive wedges that rendered these working-class, polluted communities of color quite vulnerable.

Foremost among these fractures was the abuse – by aldermen – of their political positions to allow waste dumping in return for cash. But in addition to this, John Christopher had to build broader community support for his operation to ensure its survival. One strategy was to bribe residents who had complained about his facilities. One resident reported:

The [truck] running up and down the street shaking the building so bad it cracked the front of the building and the roof have come loose. . . My son has shortness of breath especially when the wind is coming from the west. I told John [Christopher] that his dust was a problem covering my cars every day. So he gave me $20. I told him that wouldn't pay for a whole year. Earlier he had sent $15 (Interview 1997).

For some observers fifteen or twenty dollars may seem outrageously small for a 'pay-off.' However, in some West Side neighborhoods in Chicago, including Lawndale and Austin, the unemployment rate among African American residents has exceeded 50 percent in the last decade (Wilson 1996). Given this context, the low price for compliance is not so surprising.

While some segments of the community were united against illegal dumping, the fractures remained. The divisions and betrayals within the West Side communities went much deeper than the misdeeds of corrupt politicians, immoral businessmen, and the occasional resident in need of cash. In fact, local street gangs in the Austin community were discovered regulating the fly dumping trade and were said to have charged as low as five dollars per ton of waste dumped on vacant lots. In another instance, in December of 1997, a number of Austin residents employed by a North Side remodeling company were cited for illegally dumping debris in their own community. 'You have companies and residents, bringing garbage from the suburbs back into their own neighborhoods,' one observer commented (McNeil 1998).

Austin and Lawndale are two communities in desperate need of sustainable economic development, so politicians and residents were easy prey to bribes, temporary jobs, or a range of cash-producing activities associated with illegal waste dumping. This dynamic illustrates the depths of economic despair in many communities of color, which have become so desperate for development that garbage – or one's willingness to accept it – is viewed as one of the only marketable resources available. In the next section I consider these communities' ability to produce real change and challenge environmental injustices.

### Agency: shaping and reducing environmental inequalities

West Side neighborhood activists were ultimately successful at urging the city, the state EPA, and the federal EPA to take action in the Operation Silver Shovel case. The three levels of government have begun to develop a comprehensive 'strategy to address the problem of illegal solid waste disposal in Chicago' (Vinik and Harley 1997, p. 32). Some of the concrete steps taken include: developing a community policing program specifically for illegal dumping; training police officers on illegal dumping surveillance techniques; strengthening the city ordinance regulating dumping; inspecting dumpsites and testing them for hazardous and chemical waste; and beginning waste clean-ups at the sites. New or modified city ordinances in Chicago include penalties such as jail time for illegal dumpers, the seizure and impoundment of all vehicles used for fly dumping, and the barring of contractors convicted of illegal dumping from future eligibility for city contracts. The city also introduced a new surveillance system near many illegal dumpsites and vacant lots and began vigorously prosecuting and fining dumpers (*Chicago Defender* 1997).

One West Side activist wrote a letter to a public interest lawyer about the community's success:

> We won the case and a law was changed because we fought so persistently to stop the illegal operation in our community ... Removal efforts just started after the recent publicity. Officials that we appealed to for years are now appearing to help since Operation Silver Shovel hit the news.

Crediting her own organization's activism and the news media coverage, this activist acknowledged that it often takes many stakeholders several years to create an opening in the local political process.

The community fought back repeatedly and, despite years without official support, was able to initiate governmental action, regulatory enforcement, and a clean-up of the waste. Angry constituents also later voted out of office one of the aldermen who accepted bribes. At the national level, as a result of the Operation Silver Shovel scandal, U.S. Representative Cardiss Collins of Illinois (an African American woman) introduced a House bill intended to outlaw environmental racism. Although the bill later died, this was evidence that grassroots activists were able to put the issue of environmental racism on the public agenda. In this way, even the most dispossessed and disenfranchised communities on Chicago's West Side shaped the discourse around – and even reduced the impacts of – environmental racism.

## Discussion and conclusion

### *Illegal dumping and the environmental justice framework*

Operation Silver Shovel was a case of environmental inequality/racism and can be analyzed using the framework I introduced earlier. First, a historical analysis reveals that Operation Silver Shovel was not an isolated instance of environmental racism without precedent. Illegal dumping in Chicago's communities of color and immigrant neighborhoods is more than a century old and it has been one of the key battlefronts in that city's garbage wars. Hence, the fly dumping in the Lawndale and Austin communities was part of a longstanding and larger pattern of environmental inequality around the city. Second, many stakeholders with a host of complex motives were involved in this conflict. While most residents opposed the waste dumpers, many locals were facilitating the waste trade, including aldermen, neighbors in need of cash, and gang members. The other key stakeholders were the various levels of government, each of which was complicit in allowing these acts of environmental injustice to go unchallenged, despite their obvious illegality. Third, Operation Silver Shovel is largely rooted in institutional racism and class inequalities in that this type of locally unwanted land use is likely to appear only in low-income neighborhoods and communities of color. KrisJon and the FBI targeted these communities because of their vulnerability, their lack of political power, and the presence of politicians willing to accept bribes for favors. Finally, this was a defining moment for the power of the grassroots to exercise agency – to challenge powerful actors and institutions. Community groups persisted in their efforts to bring public attention to the problem of illegal dumping and to get the courts and government agencies to enforce the law and, despite virtually no assistance, were able to implement real changes. These formerly powerless networks of ordinary citizens placed the issue of environmental racism on the city's agenda and successfully reduced the level of environmental hazards in their neighborhoods.

Environmental inequality/racism occurs, therefore, when historical and contemporary social forces intersect to position various stakeholders in a state of power imbalance with regard to environmental resources. These conflicts are, in turn, shaped by all affected groups, and can be mitigated or exacerbated when the power imbalances are reduced or increased. Drawing on the environmental justice framework and the case of illegal dumping, three things are clear: 1) Environmental inequality/racism is not just about correlations between hazards and populations. It is about the power dynamics that produce these inequalities and the power of the grassroots to challenge and reverse them; 2) environmental inequality/racism is not just about communities of color versus white communities. While racism may play a persistent role in these conflicts, the range of motivations among stakeholders – including the desire for political power – and intraracial divisions across a range of community interests matter a great deal; and 3) until we understand why certain interests in communities of color are willing to support environmentally harmful practices we will never truly understand environmental racism and will therefore be ill-equipped to move toward environmental justice. It is my hope that future studies will take these findings into account.

## References

*Austin Voice.* (1994, October 18). Alderman Miller & Flood Bros. trying to sneak dump into Lawndale. p. 1.

Boone, C., & Modarres, A. (1999). Creating a toxic neighborhood in Los Angeles County. *Urban Affairs Review*, 35, 163–187.

Brown, P., & Mikkelsen, E. (1990). *No safe place: Toxic waste, leukemia and community action.* Berkeley: University of California Press.

Bullard, R. (1990). *Dumping in Dixie* (1st ed.) Boulder, Co: Westview Press.

Bullard, R. (1996). The legacy of American apartheid and environmental racism. *St. John's Journal of Legal Commentary*, 9, 445–474.

Bullard, R. (2000). *Dumping in Dixie* (3rd ed) Boulder, Co: Westview Press.

*Chicago Defender.* (1997, December 17). City swats down illegal fly dumpers. p. 5.

Citizens' Association of Chicago. (1910, June). Bulletin No. 25. Chicago.

Cohen, L. (1992, April). Waste dumps toxic traps for minorities. *The Chicago Reporter*, p. 2.

Denzin, N. (1970). *The research act.* Chicago: Aldine.

Faber, D., & Krieg, E. (2001). *Unequal exposure to ecological hazards: Environmental injustices in the Commonwealth of Massachusetts.* Northeastern University, Boston, MA.

Gottlieb, R. (1993). *Forcing the spring.* Washington, DC: Island Press.

Hull House (1895). *Hull-House maps and papers.* New York: T. Y. Crowell.

Hurley, A. (1995). *Environmental inequalities.* Chapel Hill: UNC Press.

Krieg, E. (1998). The two faces of toxic waste. *Sociological Forum*, 13, 3–20.

Kroll-Smith, S., & Floyd, H. H. (1997). *Bodies in protest: Environmental illness and the struggle over medical knowledge.* New York: New York University Press.

Lake, R. (1996). Volunteers, NIMBYs, and environmental justice. *Antipode*, 28, 160–174.

McDowell, M. (1913, December 20). *The City Club Bulletin*, Chicago, p. 331.

McNeil, B. (1998, June 4). City tries to trash illegal dumping in Austin. *Austin Weekly*, p. 4.

Mohai, P. (1996). Environmental justice or analytic justice? *Social Science Quarterly*, 77, 500–507.

Pastor, M., Sadd, J., & Hipp, J. (2001). Which came first? Toxic facilities, minority move-in, and environmental justice. *Journal of Urban Affairs*, 23, 1–21.

Plea Agreement. (1995, December 27). U.S. Attorney, Northern District, Illinois and J. Christopher.

Roberts, T., & Toffolon-Weiss, M. (2001). *Chronicles from the environmental justice frontline*. New York: Cambridge University Press.

Schnaiberg, A. (1994). The political economy of environmental problems. *Advances in Human Ecology*, 3, 23–64.

Sidawi, S. (1997). Planning environmental racism. *Historical Geography*, 25, 83–99.

U.S. Census Bureau. (1990). *Census of the population: 1980*. Washington, DC.

Vinik, N., & Harley, K. (1997). *Environmental injustice*. January. Chicago: Chicago Legal Clinic.

Walls, S. (1996, February). Rev. Jackson plans dump site clean up. *Chicago Weekend*, p. 4.

Wilson, W. J. (1996). *When work disappears*. New York: Random House.

# 19. The impact of race on environmental quality: an empirical and theoretical discussion*

*Raquel Pinderhughes*

## Abstract

The toxic pollution problem is composed of several interrelated parts which are involved in the process of production, use, and disposal of chemicals and products considered necessary for society. Each day, millions of pounds of toxic chemicals are used, stored, disposed of, and transported in and out of communities throughout the United States. Most Americans assume that pollution and other environmental hazards are problems faced equally by everyone in our society. But a growing body of research shows that the most common victims of environmental hazards and pollution are minorities and the poor. Disproportionate exposure to environmental hazards is part of the complex cycle of discrimination and deprivation faced by minorities in the United States. This article examines social science empirical research on the relationship between race, class, and the distribution of environmental hazards and the theoretical perspectives which have emerged to explain environmental inequities. The article also discusses the link between the environmental justice movement, which seeks to confront the causes and consequences of environmental inequities, and social science research on environmental inequity.

## Introduction

Many toxic substances threaten the health and well being of people in the United States.[1] Human exposure to toxins occurs through various pathways – pesticides in the food, heavy metals, synthetic chemicals, plastic residues, pesticides and other chemical products in the water, and toxic chemicals in the air and soil (Freudenberg 1984: 21). When individuals are exposed to environmental hazards, the substances often behave synergistically, creating more dangerous effects than those expected by exposure to the hazards individually (Nader, Brownstein, and John 1981; Cohen and O'Conner 1990). Cancer, heart disease, diseases of the respiratory system, neurological damage, birth defects and genetic mutations, miscarriage, lowered sperm count, and

---

\* From *Sociological Perspectives* (1996), 39(2): pp. 231–248.

sterility are some of the adverse health effects associated with exposure to environmental hazards.

The toxic pollution problem is composed of several interrelated parts which are involved in the process of production, use and disposal of chemicals and products considered necessary for society. Each day millions of pounds of toxic chemicals are used, stored, disposed of, and transported in and out of communities throughout the United States (Takvorian 1993). U.S. corporations use about 65,000 different chemicals, and introduce over 5,000 new chemicals, each year (Halperin, Ratcliffe, Frazier, Wilson, Becker and Schulte 1986). The majority of these chemicals have not undergone extensive testing to indicate whether they cause long-term health effects such as cancer and reproductive damage (Draper 1993). Over 560 million tons of hazardous waste are generated by American industry annually – more than two tons for every resident (Goldman 1991). The Environmental Protection Agency (EPA) has identified over 30,000 uncontrolled toxic waste sites in the United States.

Most Americans assume that pollution and other environmental hazards are problems faced equally by everyone in our society (Mohai and Bryant 1992). But a growing body of research shows that the most common victims of environmental hazards and pollution are minorities and the poor.[2] A strong association between non-white and poor communities and the location of hazardous waste sites has been demonstrated (U.S. Government Accounting Office 1983; Anderson 1986; United Church of Christ 1987; *National Law Journal* 1992). Studies on air quality have documented that minorities and the poor face higher levels of air pollution than other groups (Freeman 1972; Zupan 1973; Asch and Seneca 1978; Golobter 1993). Public health studies show that minorities are more severely affected by environmental hazards than whites (Harding and Greer 1993).

While all people are threatened by environmental hazards and pollution, toxic chemicals, hazardous substances, and industrial pollutants are disproportionately located in non-white communities and people of color are more severely impacted by these hazards than their white counterparts. Disproportionate exposure to environmental hazards is part of the complex cycle of discrimination and deprivation faced by minorities in the United States (Golobter 1993; Bullard 1993).

For the most part, studies of discrimination and inequality have focused on structural and economic inequality in the housing and labor markets, the impact of discrimination on infrastructure development and land use patterns, political participation and representation, racial attitudes, prejudice, racial and ethnic conflict, the psychosocial impact of oppression, and issues related to criminal justice. A review of the literature reveals that the issue of environmental quality has only recently been included in social science analyses of racial discrimination and inequality in the United States.

Recent, pioneering studies provide compelling evidence that environmental quality is mediated by race and socioeconomic status, directly linked to dynamics of discrimination and racial inequality in America, and cannot be separated from issues of equity (Bullard 1983, 1990a, 1990b, 1993; Bullard and Wright 1986, 1991; Bryant and Mohai 1992; Center for Third World Organizing 1986; Freeman 1972; Gianessi, Peskin and Wolff 1979; Golobter 1993; Russell

1989; Mann 1991; Taylor 1989, 1993; United Church of Christ 1987; U.S. Government Accounting Office 1983; Werette and Nieves 1992; Capek 1993; Pefia and Gallegos 1993; Takvorian 1993).

This article focuses on the relationship between race and environmental quality. It examines social science research on the relationship between race, class, and the distribution of environmental hazards and the theoretical perspectives which have emerged to explain the existence of environmental inequities. The article also discusses the link between the environmental justice movement, which seeks to confront the causes and consequences of environmental inequity, and social science research on environmental inequities.

## Theoretical perspectives

The dominant theoretical perspective which is advanced in the disparate studies on the relationship between race, class and environmental quality is that environmental inequities are the result of institutionalized racism.[3] Feagin and Eckberg's (1980) formulation on the dimensions of discrimination provide a framework for understanding how housing discrimination, redlining, residential segregation, market forces, discriminatory practices of federal agencies and local governments, and lack of political and economic power in minority communities produce environmental inequities in American society. They describe an interactive system which has seven dimensions: (a) motivation, (b) discriminatory action, (c) effects, (d) the relation between motivation and action, (e) the relation between action and effects, (f) the immediate organizational (institutional) context, and (g) the larger societal context.

There are two main formulations of this theoretical perspective; both explain how institutionalized racism results in minority communities being targeted as sites for environmentally hazardous industries and facilities. The first perspective emphasizes the functional link between racism, poverty and powerlessness. Minority communities are targeted for siting because they are poorer, less informed, less organized, and less politically influential (Bullard 1983, 1993; Takvorian 1993). To save time and money, companies seek to locate environmentally hazardous industries in communities which will put up the least resistance, which are less informed and less powerful politically, and are more dependent upon local job development efforts. Richard Lazarus (1992: 6), Professor of Law at Washington University Law School, states:

> It is clear that the environmental statutes promise a great deal. But everyone knows that these laws are not self-enforcing. Those who complain, who have greater access, who know how to tweak their Congress-people to do something, are more likely to get the attention of very busy people. And the people with greater know-how are generally those with greater political and economic resources, who tend to be white.

A report written by the Cerrell Associates, for the Waste Management Board of California, confirms this. It describes the people most likely to express opposition to environmentally hazardous projects as liberal, college-educated, young or less than middle-aged, middle- and high-income groups in large urban areas, particularly those in the Northeast and West. Consequently, Cerrell advised companies to, 'locate sites in lower socioeconomic neighborhoods where they will meet with less opposition' (Cerrell Associates 1984).

The second perspective focuses particularly on how the link between race and environmental inequity is essentially forged by segregated housing patterns which confine blacks, and other people of color, to poor communities over burdened by environmental risks (Godsil 1991; Bullard 1983, 1993; Bullard and Feagin 1991). According to sociologist Robert Bullard (1993: 18):

> Income alone does not account for these above-average percentages (of the most polluted communities). Housing segregation and development patterns play a key role in determining where people live. Moreover, urban development and the 'spatial configuration' of communities flow from the forces and relationships of industrial production which, in turn, are influenced and subsidized by government policy.

In contrast to blacks, poor whites are more able to live in economically varied areas and, therefore, benefit from the clout of other (white) middle-class residents with whom they reside or live close to (Godsil 1991). As a result of residential segregation, redlining, discriminatory land use, and zoning regulations, there is a disproportionate location of environmental hazards in minority communities and people of color face a disproportionate impact on their health and well-being from pollution and environmental hazards:

> The dynamics of segregation, by allowing poor whites to benefit from middle-class resistance to hazardous waste facilities, and lowering land values in minority neighborhoods, may cause disproportionate sitings in predominantly minority areas. The current political climate in middle- and upper-income areas is hostile toward waste facilities generally and hazardous waste facilities particularly (Godsil 1991: 400).

Both perspectives recognize that institutionalized racism is at the heart of environmental quality and that problems related to poor environmental quality are compounded by a series of problems also attributed to institutionalized racism:

> On top of ... unequal housing opportunities, poor health care, drugs and violence in neighborhoods and other daunting obstacles to their right of pursuit of happiness, minorities are having to live with bad air and tainted water that damages their health and sometimes takes their lives (Newton and Ortega 1991: 100).

A central question in the debate over the causes of environmental inequality is whether the differential levels of environmental quality are the result of class factors or racial dynamics – whether the bias of distribution of environmental hazards is a function of poverty rather than race (Mohai and Bryant 1992).

Are not minorities disproportionately targeted and impacted because they are disproportionately poor?

Clearly, poverty plays an important role. First, because of limited income, poor people cannot buy their way out of polluted neighborhoods (Mohai and Bryant 1992). Second, because land values are lower in most poor neighborhoods, polluting industries seeking to reduce the costs of business are attracted to poor neighborhoods. Third, wealthier communities can use their political clout and resources – time, money, contacts and knowledge – to pressure city governments not to grant permits to polluting industries, in classic NIMBY fashion.[4] Fourth, because minorities are underrepresented in governing bodies, they tend to be less aware of policies which are being implemented and lack critical resources necessary to pressure government to protect their communities from hazards and threats (National Law Journal 1992). But a growing number of studies on the distribution of specific environmental hazards and environmental quality by race and income show that race is an independent factor, not reducible to class, in predicting the distribution of environmental hazards:

> Environmental inequities cannot be reduced solely to class factors ... race and class are intricately linked in our society. However, race continues to be a potent predictor of where people live, which communities get dumped on and which are spared. Racial bias creates and perpetuates unequal environmental quality in communities of color and white communities (Bullard 1993: 11).

## Empirical studies

A review of the empirical literature on the distribution of environmental hazards reveals that minorities and poor people bear the brunt of environmental dangers. Studies on the distribution of outdoor air pollution indicate that pollution is regressively distributed by income and race (Asch and Seneca 1978; Freeman 1972; Golobter 1993; Mann 1991). A study conducted on the distribution of air quality in the New York region showed that air quality decreases with income group (the lower the income group, the lower the air quality it is exposed to) and that air quality improvements have benefitted the poor the least (Zupan 1973). Commenting on the study, Robert Knox – Chief Ombudsman in the U.S. Environmental Protection Agency and later Deputy Director of the EPA's new office of Environmental Equity, stated, 'race and class are so strongly related that identifying one variable or the other as the root of public health problems may not be necessary' (Knox 1993). Further, although government agencies and legislators have implemented more effective regulations to control air pollution, minority communities are not significantly benefiting from these new policies. A recent study on the distribution of air pollution by income and race (Golobter 1993) concluded that although the quality of air for many Americans continued to improve in the 1970s and 1980s, there remains a persistent and widening set of inequities, related to race and class, in the distribution of both ambient air pollution and the benefits from the implementation of the Clean Air Act.

In 1987 the United Church of Christ's Commission on Racial Justice released a landmark report which examined the relationship between race and the location of hazardous wastes sites across the nation (United Church of Christ 1987). The UCC study showed that race is the strongest factor related to the presence of hazardous wastes in residential communities throughout the United States, more significant than socioeconomic indicators, such as household income or the average value of homes. The report revealed that three out of five African Americans live in communities with uncontrolled toxic waste sites. Three of the five largest landfills in the nation, which account for over 40% of the nation's total capacity for commercial hazardous waste disposal, are located in predominantly black and Latino communities. More than 15 million blacks and 8 million Latinos live in communities with one or more uncontrolled toxic waste sites. African Americans are heavily overrepresented in the populations of the cities with the largest number of uncontrolled toxic waste sites, which include (in order) Memphis, St. Louis, Houston, Cleveland, Chicago, and Atlanta. Los Angeles has more Latinos living in communities with uncontrolled toxic waste sites than any other metropolitan area in the United States; the higher the concentration of Latinos in an area of the city, the higher the concentration of uncontrolled toxic waste sites in the same area. About half of all Asian/Pacific Islanders and Native Americans live in communities with uncontrolled waste sites (United Church of Christ 1987; Lee 1993).

A study conducted by the U.S. General Accounting Office (GAO) in 1983 examined the racial demographics of hazardous waste sites located in the southeastern part of the United States. The GAO study of the socioeconomic and racial composition of communities surrounding the four major hazardous waste landfills in the South, revealed that three out of four off-site landfills were located in communities whose residents were predominantly black (GAO 1983).

A systematic review of fifteen studies on the distribution of environmental hazards led its authors to conclude that, taken together, the findings from these studies indicate clear and unequivocal class and racial biases in the distribution of environmental hazards (Mohai and Bryant 1992). A follow-up study, on the location of major environmental hazards in Detroit, revealed that blacks are clearly overrepresented in communities located near commercial hazardous waste facilities. Based on their research the authors concluded that race was a better predictor of resident's proximity to such facilities than income – the closer a neighborhood is to a hazardous site, the higher the percentage of African American residents: 'If you are black, your chances of living within a mile of such a facility are about four and half times greater than if you are white' (Mohai and Bryant 1992: 12).

A study conducted in Houston, Texas found that six out of eight municipal incinerators and five city landfills are located in predominantly African American neighborhoods; almost all of the city owned municipal landfills and garbage incinerators in Houston are located in African American communities (Bullard 1990). A study funded by the National Science Foundation revealed that in a number of major Southern cities African American residents are burdened with a disproportionately large share of urban pollution and hazardous landfills when compared to their white counterparts (Bullard and Wright 1987).

Research conducted by the Environmental Health Coalition in San Diego documented that businesses that generate, use, store and dispose of toxics are concentrated in the county's low income communities of color (Williams and Takvorian 1990). In addition to repeated incidents of illegal dumping and release of toxics from companies operating in mixed residential/industrial communities, the study found that the largest quantity of toxic materials in the county were located in Barrio Logan, a community which is 99 percent Latino. A study of environmental hazards in Richmond, California found that 300 industrial facilities located in predominantly African American and Latino low-income neighborhoods are routinely discharging at least 210 different toxics into the air and water, and as solid waste, or are present at unsafe industrial storage sites (Belliveau, Kent and Rosenblum 1989). The greatest concentration of hazardous waste sites in the United States are located in the predominantly African American and Latino sections of South Chicago (Newton and Ortega 1991).

Native American lands have become prime targets for waste disposal proposals. A report released by Greenpeace states that there is 'a concerted effort to turn Indian lands into the dumping grounds for America's poisons' (Angel 1992). The study concluded that intense grass-roots opposition and complex permitting procedures in communities across the United States have motivated the waste disposal industry to turn its attention to the segment of society it believes is the most vulnerable as a result of unemployment, pervasive poverty, and sovereign status – Indian people and Indian land. More than three dozen reservations have been targeted for landfills and incinerators because of the special quasi-sovereign status of Indian nations. Fifteen of the 18 federal research grants for Monitored Retrievable Storage Facilities for nuclear wastes were done on Indian reservations (Sierra Roundtable 1993).

## The effects on health

A review of the public health and environmental health studies on the distribution of hazardous waste production and disposal sites in the United States found that studies basically ignored the selective health risks of minority communities located in neighborhoods where exposures to hazardous substances from these sites are most likely to occur (Harding and Greer 1993). The few existing studies which are attentive to issues of race document that people of color suffer disproportionately from occupational and residential exposure to environmental hazards.

A study conducted by the Navajo Nation found that children growing up in uranium mining areas, such as Grants Uranium Belt in New Mexico, are developing ovarian and testicular cancers at rates 15 times higher than the national average (Taliman 1992). Uranium-contaminated Navajo land and water are believed to contribute to an organ cancer rate among

380

Navajo teenagers which is 17 times the national average (Bryant and Mohai 1992).

Gilbert (1991) found higher rates of cancer, chronic respiratory illness, and reports of neurological disorders in non-white Tennesseans who live in Memphis as compared to white Tennesseans; the area has more uncontrolled hazardous waste sites (173 in 1987) than any other city in the United States.

A study of health risks associated with hazardous landfills in Southeast Chicago found that 150,000 residents in a housing project live near 50 active or closed commercial hazardous waste landfills and 103 abandoned toxic waste sites. The residents, almost all of whom are either African American or Latino, have abnormally high levels of cancer and infant mortality (Nadakavukaren 1991).

Research on the health of residents in Lake Charles, Louisiana revealed that the eye irritation, constant nosebleeds, nausea, and cramps experienced by African American residents were related to contaminated groundwater and windblown chemical fumes which leaked from an industrial dumpsite in the area (Center for Third World Organizing 1986).

An investigative report of abnormally high rates of adult cancer and severe neurological disorders in newborns in Southside Tucson, Arizona revealed that extremely high levels of trichloroethylene (TCE) had been released into the drinking water supply by an industrial waste dump located near the predominantly Latino community. In a one block area, 30 homes were hit with cancer and at least five women gave birth to babies with anencephaly (De La Pefia 1991). Preliminary investigation of newborns with similar neurological problems in towns along the U.S./Mexican border link these disorders to water their mothers are drinking which is contaminated by chemicals from the maquiladora industries along the border. A study of ground water contamination found that areas with the highest levels of contamination were, 'more rural, more Hispanic, and of lower income and education level' (Newton and Ortega 1991: 101).

## Environmental policy and practice

Examination of federal agency policy and practices yields evidence of racial inequity in the federal Government's clean up of hazardous sites and in its pursuit of polluters – agency policy and practice consistently favor white communities over minority communities under environmental laws meant to provide equal protection to all the nation's residents. A 1992 study conducted by the National Law Journal, which analyzed census data, EPA civil case dockets, and the agency's performance at 1,177 Superfund toxic waste sites, found that penalties for hazardous waste sites in areas with large white populations were about 500 percent higher than penalties at sites with large minority populations, averaging $335,566 for the white areas compared to $55,318 for minority areas.[5] A comprehensive analysis of every U.S. environmental lawsuit revealed that in the past seven years, penalties against pollution law violators in majority white areas tend to be higher than those in majority non-white areas. Further, the government takes longer to address hazards in minority communities and it accepts solutions less stringent than those recommended by the scientific community in those areas when it does not do so in majority white areas (National Law Journal 1992). Specifically, the study revealed that the population which benefited from the 352 Clean Air Act cases brought to bear in the seven-year period was 78.7 percent white, 14.2 percent black, and 8.2 percent Hispanic. The investigation also showed that under the Superfund cleanup program, abandoned hazardous waste sites in minority areas take 20 percent longer to be placed on the national priority action list than those in white areas. Further, in minority areas the EPA chose 'containment,' the capping or walling off of a hazardous waste dump site, seven percent more frequently than the preferred method, called 'treatment' which permanently eliminates the waste and rids it of its toxins. At sites in white communities, the EPA ordered 'treatment' 22 percent more often than 'containment.'

The study also revealed how industries located in low income minority communities are fined considerably less than those located in high-income white communities in EPA court cases. Violators in minority communities were fined 506 percent less than those in white areas under the Resource Conservation and Recovery Act (RCRA). One of the largest RCRA fines ($350,000) was lodged against Laidlow Environmental Services in Cleveland, Ohio, a 91 percent white area with a low median income of $19,921. One of the lowest fines ($60,000) was lodged against Quemetco Inc in Industry, California for similar violations. The population in Industry is predominantly Latino but the median income is $33,572: According to the investigators:

> This racial imbalance, the investigation found, often occurs whether the community is wealthy or poor. … The life-threatening consequences of these policies are visible in the day-to-day struggles of minority communities throughout the country. These communities feel they are victims three times over – first by polluters, then the government, and finally the legal system (National Law Journal 1992: 2).

## The environmental justice movement

Obtaining environmental protection and improving environmental quality are inherently political issues, directly linked to the political process (Davies and Davies 1975). Since the 1960s, the mainstream environmental movement has been one of the most visible and powerful social movements within the spectrum of political activism in the United States. It has built an impressive political base for environmental reform and has been instrumental in getting regulations and legislation passed to improve the environment. Since the 1970s environmental regulation has been one of the most important areas of U.S. domestic politics (Gottlieb 1993).

Communities of color have long been involved in the struggle for safe and healthy residential and occupational environments. Local level protest against inadequate sanitation and municipal service delivery, lead poisoning in urban dwellings, asbestos in schools and workplaces, rodents, and environmental pollutants ranging from agricultural pesticides to industrial chemicals are among those issues which have been of concern to communities of color and were consistently on the agenda of the Civil Rights Movement.

African Americans, Latinos, Asians, and Native Americans have long been concerned about environmental issues, but they have conceptualized their concerns as community, labor, economic, health, and civil rights issues rather than as 'environmental' issues. At a roundtable organized by *Sierra* magazine, Carl Anthony, director of Urban Habitat, explained, 'We've [people of color] all been involved in the struggle for environmental justice for a very long time, even if we didn't call it that.'

Efforts to build links between civil rights activists and environmental activists date back to at least the 1960s. In 1968, the U.S. National Advisory Commission on Civil Disorders discovered that systematic neglect of garbage collection and sanitation services in African-American neighborhoods con- tributed to the urban disturbances in the 1960s (Bullard 1993). In 1970, U.S. Senator Philip Hart (D-MN) facilitated a meeting among representatives from labor unions, environmental groups, and minority organizations to address problems concerning the urban environment. In 1976, the United Auto Workers brought together leaders from unions, environmental groups, economic justice, and church organizations at a conference on the urban environment in Black Lakes, Michigan. That same year, the Urban League began its environmental action with Project Que: Environmental Concerns in the Inner City. In 1977, the Urban Environment Conference (UEC) funded eleven nationwide conferences to build coalitions among environmentalists, minorities and occupational health organizers. In 1978, the Urban League, UEC, and Sierra Club co-sponsored a conference in Detroit entitled City Care: A Conference on the Urban Environment which drew 700 participants (Sierra Roundtable 1993). But these events did not convince mainstream environmental organizations to seriously consider the causes and consequences of the disproportionate location of environmental hazards in communities of color or support struggles for environmental quality in these communities.

The event which focused national attention on environmental inequities and galvanized people of color and environmental activists to focus on the relationship between environmental hazards and minority communities occurred in 1982. That year, residents of Warren County, North Carolina protested the dumping of more than 32,000 cubic yards of soil contaminated with highly toxic polychlorinated biphenyl (PCBs) in their community (Geiser and Waneck 1983).[6] Several years earlier, in 1978, the contaminated soil had been illegally dumped along 210 miles of roadway which stretched into fourteen North Carolina counties. When the federal EPA and the state began clean up activities, the Governor decided to bury the contaminated soil in the city of Afton in Warren County. Warren County has the highest percentage of blacks in North Carolina (84%) and is one of the poorest counties in the state. Dr. Charles Cobb, of the United Church of Christ's Commission for Racial Justice, called the decision to bury the contaminated soil in Afton 'attempted genocide' because the water table of Afton was only 5–10 feet below the surface and the residents of the community derived all of their drinking water from local wells.

When residents learned that PCBs from the landfill were likely to enter their drinking water supply they worked with the United Church of Christ and Southern Christian Leadership Conference to organize a massive protest against the siting. There was widespread protest, including nonviolent civil disobedience protest against the siting. Protesters came from all over the country and 500 people were arrested. The protest marked the first time anyone in the country had been jailed trying to halt a toxic waste landfill.

Although the campaign to halt the siting failed, the protest produced at least five significant outcomes. First, it caught the attention of activists in communities of color throughout the nation. Second, it brought about a convergence of civil rights and environmental rights. Third, it mobilized a nationally broad-based group to protest environmental inequities. Fourth, it marked the emergence of the environmental justice movement.[7] Reverend Ben Chavis, then director of the United Church of Christ Commission on Racial Justice, recalled:

> While we were marching, we got letters from communities all around the country, saying the same thing was happening to them. The white community is also exposed, but our point is the disproportionality of the exposure and the enforcement effort between white communities and communities of color (National Law Journal 1992: 32).

Fifth, it led the Commission on Racial Justice to undertake its landmark study of the link between race and the location of hazardous waste sites in the United States which showed that race is the strongest factor related to the presence of hazardous wastes in residential communities throughout the United States (United Church of Christ 1987; Lee 1993).

The Commission's findings prompted Reverend Ben Chavis, then director of the UCC Commission, to use the term 'environmental racism' to describe both the intentional and unintentional disproportionate imposition of environmental hazards in communities of color. Subsequently, the Commission formally defined the term to mean:

> ... racial discrimination in environmental policymaking. It is racial discrimination in the enforcement of regulations and laws. It is the deliberate targeting of communities of color for toxic waste disposal and the siting of polluting industries. It is racial discrimination in the official sanctioning of the life-threatening presence of poisons and pollutants in communities of color. And, it is racial discrimination in the history of excluding people of color from the mainstream environmental groups, decisionmaking boards, commissions, and regulatory bodies (Bullard 1993: 3).

Until the emergence of the environmental justice movement, the mainstream environmental movement's agenda was largely focused on protecting the natural world – endangered forests, nearly extinct species, polluted streams, global warming, and natural resource conservation – rather than on what Taylor (1993) has called 'human interest ecology' (Krieger 1970).[8] A survey conducted by the Sierra Club, in 1978, revealed that its members were most concerned about wilderness preservation, wildlife, and alternative energy. According to Bullard and Wright, 'the issues and concerns that Black neighborhood residents saw as priorities were not high on the agendas of environmentally oriented organizations' (Bullard and Wright 1986: 3). According to environmental scientists Wilbert Wilson and Kwamena Ocran (1991: 24):

> Environmental and conservation interests have traditionally sought the protection of resources, habitats and species which are of little direct interest to minorities, often ignoring the environmental plight of the poor who are concentrated in urban centers.

In order to enhance their ability to effect policy at the local and national levels, leaders of the environmental justice movement challenged the mainstream environmental movement to address the causes and consequences of injustice in the environmental arena. Pat Bryant, Director of Gulf Coast Tenants Leadership Development Project explained:

> No political movement in the United States can claim to be national and progressive until it addresses the question of race. Environmental organizing, the area that holds the most progressive potential of any movement in the last two decades, is caught up in its failure to respond convincingly to this question. In order to move from isolated local victories to real national impact, the environmental movement has to confront its own whiteness (1989: 48–52).

In 1990, staff at the Southwest Organizing Project (SWOP), a grassroots community organization which exists to empower the disenfranchised in the Southwest to realize racial and gender equality and social and economic justice, sent a letter to the nation's largest environmental organizations, called the 'Group of Ten.'[9] The letter, which was signed by over one hundred individuals from churches, unions, universities, and community groups in the Southwest, demanded change in the organizational composition and agendas of these organizations:

> Although environmental organizations calling themselves the 'Group of Ten' often claim to represent our interests, in observing your activities it has become clear to us that your organizations play an equal role in the disruption of our communities. … Your organizations continue to support and promote policies that emphasize the cleanup and preservation of the environment on the backs of working people in general and people of color in particular. In the name of eliminating environmental hazards at any cost, across the country industrial and other economic activities which employ us are being shut down, curtailed, or prevented while our survival needs and cultures are ignored. We suffer from the end results of these actions, but are never full participants in the decision-making which leads to them. … We … call upon you to cease operations in communities of color within 60 days, until you have hired leaders

from those communities to the extent that they make up between 35 and 40 percent of your entire staff. ... Also provide a list of communities of color to whom you furnish services, or Third World communities in which you have organizing drives or campaigns (SWOP, March 1990).

In October 1990, the Congressional Black Caucus sent a letter to Environmental Protection Agency (EPA) chief William Reilly urging the government to do something about increased environmental risks to minorities. Reilly reacted by outlining a plan to establish a work group to study environmental risk and low-income communities. Subsequently, environmental justice activists challenged Reilly to prove that the EPA's plans were more than just a token gesture designed for public consumption (Newton and Ortega 1991).

In October 1991, activists in communities of color, working with members of the Commission for Racial Justice, organized the First National People of Color Environmental Leadership Summit. The Summit had three purposes. First, to provide a forum and venue for minority leaders in organizations which are challenging environmental injustice or whose communities are disproportionately impacted by environmental injustice. Second, to provide the opportunity for dialogue between community leaders and the heads of national environmental organizations, from a perspective framed by communities of color. Third, to impact the decision making process in public policy around the environment at federal, state, and municipal levels. The overall goal of the Summit was to initiate an ongoing multi-faceted process to develop a comprehensive and tangible national agenda that would help reshape and redirect environmental policy in the United States to embrace the concerns of minority Americans.

Today, the environmental justice movement, which emerged to directly confront environmental racism, is composed of a national alliance of church, labor, civil rights, community groups, academics, and others. It is a community based movement led by people of color. According to Ben Chavis:

> Our guiding principle is that our work must be done from a grassroots perspective, and it must be multi-racial and multicultural ... we're being inclusive, not exclusive. We're not saying to take the incinerators and the toxic waste dumps out of our communities and put them in white communities – we're saying they should not be in anybody's community ... It's not a movement of retribution it is a movement for justice. You can't get justice by doing an injustice on somebody else. When you have lived through suffering and hardship, you want to remove them, not only from your own people but from all people (Sierra Roundtable 1993: 52).

## Conclusion

A review of the literature on race and environmental quality reveals that there is a strong association between race and the distribution of environmental hazards in the United States. Environmental hazards are disproportionately located in communities of color. As a result, people of color are more at risk for adverse health risks which result from exposure to environmental hazards. Decisions about where to locate environmentally hazardous industries and facilities, and about how and whether to clean them up, are also mitigated by race. These phenomenon are part of the complex cycle of discrimination faced by people of color in the United States.

The environmental justice movement grew out of grassroots struggles to confront environmental inequities at the local level. Activities have been organized to confront local and regional hazards, challenge federal regulations and policies, get federal and local officials to clean up hazardous areas and push the mainstream environmental movement to focus on the causes and consequences of environmental inequities. More recently, the environmental justice movement has been strengthening its relationship to activists struggling for environmental justice outside the United States.

Research on the link between race, class, power, and environmental inequity has contributed to the emergence of the environmental justice movement. Social science research has provided important data on the distribution of environmental hazards, the extent of inequities and the importance of symbolic resources. Research has expanded the theoretical analysis of environmental inequity as a form of institutionalized racism.

The concepts of 'discrimination' and 'institutional racism' are central to social science research on racial and ethnic relations and conflict in the United States. Scholars engaged in research on the relationship between race, class, and environmental quality have utilized these concepts to inform our understanding of environmental inequities in the United States (Taylor 1993; Bullard 1993). They have also developed new concepts, like 'environmental racism,' 'environmental blackmail,' and 'environmental equity,' which need to be incorporated as central elements in future research on environmental quality, race relations and racial inequality in America.

The concept of 'environmental equity' refers to the right of all individuals and communities to have an equal opportunity to live and work in healthy environments; no one group or sets of groups should have to pay a disproportionate price for the nation's environmental hazards and problems. Environmental inequity can be attributed to several factors: First, the inequity in political and economic power to influence the siting of hazardous industries results in a higher concentration of hazards and toxins in communities of color and poor communities. Second, the inequity in exposure to hazards exists as a result of a set of structural conditions which include barriers that reduce residential and occupational alternatives and restrict or eliminate opportunities for mobility for people of color, working class and poor people. These structural conditions are part of the web of institutional racism which results in inequities in virtually all facets of life including wages, job opportunities, housing options, standard of living and the quality of the residential and work environments. Just as housing discrimination and employment discrimination reduce the options for settlement and employment, environmental racism reduces the options for living and working in a healthy environment. Third, unequal enforcement of environmental regulations results in a widening of the gap in environmental quality.

The emergence of the environmental justice movement and the development of research on environmental inequity have broad implications for the future of the analysis of the effects of racial and class inequality and for future social movements in this country. Research on the relationship between race, class, and environmental quality has established environmental inequity as a significant consequence of racial and class inequality. Future research on race relations and poverty must incorporate the concepts of environmental equity and environmental justice as central elements in any analysis of race and class relations.

Future research on environmental equity needs to bridge different disciplines to produce a more comprehensive picture of the scope, character, and effect of environmental inequity. There is a need for more research on national, regional and local patterns of environmental inequity. Comparative interdisciplinary research on a number of communities needs to be conducted linking the economics of the location of industrial hazards, related health factors and outcomes, social-psychological effects of exposure to hazards, distribution patterns of toxics and hazards, detailed accounts of the political process which resulted in siting, and an analysis of the enforcement and regulating role of governmental agencies and political representatives.

In the area of community action, social movements, and social policy, the articulation of environmental inequity as a significant national concern has infused local grassroots movements with a new level of legitimacy and potential political power. The elevation of environmental justice to a core issue within the civil rights movement and the incorporation of concerns about environmental inequity into the agenda of mainstream environmental groups enhances the resources, exposure and efficacy of local grassroots movements against environmental hazards. On a national level, these developments provide the potential for a social movement of major proportions linking the civil rights movement, grassroots environmental justice movements, mainstream environmental organizations, and public health community in the United States and around the world.

## Notes

1. The Green Index, which measures and ranks each state's environmental health along 256 indicators, includes the following criteria: air and water pollution; toxic chemical waste and hazardous solid waste storage and disposal; agricultural pollution; public water systems that violate the Safe Drinking Water Act; contaminated groundwater; toxic chemical air emissions; and military bases and industrial sites with substantial hazardous wastes.
2. In this article, the terms 'minority,' 'non-white,' and 'people of color' are used interchangeably to refer to people of African, Latino, Native American, and Asian-Pacific Island descent living in the United States.
3. The concept was first used by Carmichael and Hamilton (1967). For reviews of the concept, see Feagin and Eckberg (1980), Bullard and Feagin (1991), and Bullard (1993).
4. The term 'NIMBY' refers to Not In My Back Yard.
5. In 1978, Congress passed the Resource Conservation and Recovery Act (RCRA). RCRA is designed to address the 'treatment, storage, and disposal of hazardous waste not discharged directly in the air, water, or sewer systems.' In 1980, Congress passed the Comprehensive Environmental Response Compensation and Liability ACT (CERCLA), commonly known as 'Superfund.' CERCLA authorizes the federal government to finance the cleanup of hazardous waste sites from a trust fund established with tax moneys levied on certain products

(petrochemicals, inorganic raw materials, domestic crude oil, and imported petroleum products). Superfund permits the federal government to require parties responsible for causing the release, or creating the uncontrolled hazardous waste site, to finance cleanup. It also requires states to participate in any cleanup action within their borders; either they may cooperate with the Environmental Protection Agency or they may take the lead on cleanup projects themselves. For more information on Superfund, see Wolf (1992) and Russell, Colglazer, and Tonn (1992).

6   For information on the dangers PCBs pose to public health, see Geiser and Weneck (1983).

7   Capek (1993) suggests that a social constructionist perspective is particularly useful for understanding the emergence and development of the environmental justice movement. Capek analyzes the environmental justice frame as a claims-making activity – a form of interaction wherein demands are made by one party to another that something be done about a punitive condition. Defining a situation as unjust is more than just an act of categorization, it implies a strategy for action.

8   Scholars such as Krieger (1970) and Bullard and Wright (1987) argue the mainstream environmental movement emerged with agendas focused on natural resources, ecology, wilderness, wildlife preservation, wildlife conservation, and pollution abatement and did not take up concerns affecting people of color until very recently. In contrast, Taylor (1993) traces the environmental movement's interest in 'human interest ecology' to the 1950s and 1960s. Davies and Davies (1976) trace the historical roots of the mainstream environmental movement's interest in human ecology to concerns about the proper handling of waterborne sewage in ancient Rome and cite examples from the 13th century, when Edward I banned the burning of sea coal in London to alleviate air pollution, and to 1388, when Richard II forbade river pollution.

9   The Group of Ten includes the Sierra Club, the Sierra Club Legal Defense Fund, Friends of the Earth, the Wilderness Society, National Audubon Society, Natural Resources Defense Council, Environmental Defense Fund, National Wildlife Federation, Isaak Walton League, and the National Parks and Conservation Association.

# References

Anderson, J.E. 1986. 'U.S. Population Distribution and the Location of Hazardous Waste Sites.' Paper presented at the Annual Meeting of the Population Association of America, U.S. Centers for Disease Control, Atlanta, GA.

Angel, Bradley. 1992. *The Toxic Threat to Indian Lands: A Greenpeace Report*. San Francisco, CA: Greenpeace.

Asch, Peter, and Joseph J. Seneca. 1978. 'Some Evidence on the Distribution of Air Quality.' *Land Economics* 54(3): 278–297.

Belliveau, Michael, Michael Kent, and Grant Rosenblum. 1989. *Richmond at Risk: Community Demographics and Toxic Hazards from Industrial Polluters*. San Francisco, CA: Citizens for a Better Environment.

Bryant, Bunyan, and Paul Mohai. 1992. *Race and the Incidence of Environmental Hazards*. Boulder, CO: Westview.

Bullard, Robert D. 1983. 'Solid Waste Sites and the Black Houston Community.' *Sociological Inquiry* 53(2–3): 273–288.

Bullard, Robert D. 1990a. 'Ecological Inequities and the New South: Black Communities Under Siege.' *Journal of Ethnic Studies* 17(4): 101–115.

Bullard, Robert D. 1990b. Dumping in Dixie: Race, Class and Environmental Quality. Boulder, CO: Westview.

Bullard, Robert D. 1990c. 'Housing Barriers-Trends in the Nation's 4th Largest City.' *Journal of Black Studies* 21(1): 4–14.

Bullard, Robert D. 1993. *Confronting Environmental Racism*. Boston, MA: South End Press.

Bullard, Robert D., and Joe R. Feagin. 1991. 'Racism in the City.' Pp. 55–76 in *Urban Life in Transition* edited by M. Gottdiener and C.V. Picvance. Newbury Park, CA: Sage.

Bullard, Robert D., and Beverly H. Wright. 1986. 'The Politics of Pollution: Implications for the Black Community.' *Phylon* 47(1): 71–78.

Bullard, Robert D., and Beverly H. Wright. 1987. 'Blacks and the Environment.' *Humboldt Journal of Social Relations* 14: 165–184.

Bullard, Robert D., and Beverly H. Wright. 1991. 'The Quest for Environmental Equity: Mobilizing the African American Community for Social Change.' *Society and Natural Resources* 3(4): 301–311.

Capek, Stella M. 1993. 'The 'Environmental Justice' Frame: A Conceptual Discussion and an Application.' *Social Problems* 40(1): 5–24.

Carmichael, S., and C. Hamilton. 1967. *Black Power*. New York: Random House.

Center for Third World Organizing. 1986. *Toxics and Minority Communities*. Oakland, CA: Center for Third World Organizing.

Cerrell Associates, Inc. 1984. *Political Difficulties Facing Waste-to-Energy Conversion Plant Siting*. Los Angeles, CA: California Waste Management Board, Technical Information Series.

Cohen, Gary, and John O'Conner. 1990. *Fighting Toxics*. Washington, DC: Island Press.

Davies, Clarence J., and Barbara S. Davies. 1975. *The Politics of Pollution*. Indianapolis, IN: Pegasus.

De La Pena, Nonny. 1991. 'Fighting for the Environment.' *Hispanic* (March): 18–23.

Feagin, Joe R., and Douglas Lee Eckberg. 1980. 'Discrimination, Motivation, Action, Effects, and Context.' *Annual Review of Sociology* 6: 1–20.

FitzSimmons, Margaret, and Robert Gottlieb. 1988. 'A New Environmental Politics.' In *Reshaping the U.S. Left: Populist Struggles in the 1980s*, edited by M. David and M. Spencer.

Freeman, Myrick A. 1972. 'The Distribution of Environmental Quality.' In *Environmental Quality Analysis*, edited by A.V. Kneese and B. T. Bower. Baltimore, MD: Resources for the Future/ Johns Hopkins University.

Freudenberg, Nicholas. 1984. *Not In Our Backyards*. New York: Monthly Review Press.

Gelobter, Michel. 1993. Race, Class and Outdoor Pollution: The Dynamics of Environmental Discrimination from 1970-1990. Unpublished Ph.D. dissertation, University of California at Berkeley.

Geiser, K., and G. Waneck. 1983. 'PCBs in Warren County.' *Science for the People* (Summer): 13–17.

Godsil, Rachel D. 1991. 'Remedying Environmental Racism.' *Michigan Law Review* 90: 394–425.

Gianess, Leonard P., Henry M. Peskin, and Edward Wolff. 1979. 'The Distributional Effects of Uniform Air Pollution Policy in the U.S.' *Quarterly Journal of Economics* (Summer): 281–301.

Gilbert, D. 1991. 'Environmental Racism: Why Hazardous Waste Has Become a Civil Rights Issue.' *Memphis Flyer* (Tennessee Environmental Council, Memphis, TN) (Fall).

Goldman, Benjamin. 1991. *The Truth About Where You Live: An Atlas for Action on Toxins and Mortality*. New York: Random House.

Gottlieb, Robert. 1993. *Forcing the Spring: The Trans-formation of the American Environmental Movement*. Washington, DC: Island Press.

Halperin, William, J. Ratcliffe, M. Frazier, L. Wilson, S. Becker, and P. Schulte. 1986. 'Medical Screening in the Workplace: Proposed Principles.' *Journal of Occupational Medicine* 28: 547–552.

Harding, Anna, and Marsha Greer. 1993. 'The Health Impact of Hazardous Waste Sites on Minority Communities: Implications for Public Health and Environmental Health Professionals.' *Journal of Environmental Health* 55: 6–9.

Knox, Robert. 1993. 'Environmental Equity.' *Journal of Environmental Health* 55: 32–34.

Kraft, Michael E., and Bruce B. Clary. 1989. 'Citizen Participation and the NIMBY Syndrome: Public Response to Radioactive Waste Disposal.' *The Western Political Quarterly* (August): 299–327.

Lee, Charles. 1993. 'Beyond Toxic Wastes and Race.' Pp. 41-52 in *Confronting Environmental Racism*, edited by Robert Bullard. Boston, MA: South End Press.

Mann, Eric. 1991. *L.A.'s Lethal Air*. Los Angeles, CA: Labor/Community Strategy Center.

Mohai, Paul. 1985. 'Public Concern and Elite Involvement in Environmental Conservation.' *Social Science Quarterly* 66: 820–838.

Mohai, Paul. 1990. 'Black Environmentalism.' *Social Science Quarterly* 71: 744–765.

Mohai, Paul, and Bunyan Bryant. 1992. 'Race, Poverty, and the Environment.' *EPA Journal* 18: 1.

Nadakavukaren, A. 1991. 'People Living with Pollution.' *Greenpeace* (Fall): 8–13.

Nader, Ralph, Ronald Brownstein, and John Richard. 1981. *Who's Poisoning America: Corporate Polluters and their Victims in Chemical Age*. San Francisco, CA: Sierra Club Books.

National Law Journal. 1992. 'Unequal Protection: The Racial Divide in Environmental Law.' *National Law Journal*.

Newton, Kathy Cone, and Francis Ortega. 1991. 'Beyond Ankle Biting: Fighting Environmental Discrimination Locally, Nationally, and Globally.' *The Workbook* 16(3): 98–123.

Peia, Devon, and Joesph Gallegos. 1993. 'Nature and Chicanos in Southern Colorado.' Pp. 141–160 in *Confronting Environmental Racism*, edited by Robert Bullard. Boston, MA: South End Press.

Russell, Dick. 1989. 'Environmental Racism: Minority Communities and Their Battle Against Toxics.' *Amicus Journal* 11: 22–32.

Russell, Milton, William Colglazier, and Bruce Tonn. 1992. 'The U.S. Hazardous Waste.' *Environment* (Summer): 12–39.

Sierra Roundtable on Race, Justice, and the Environment. 1993. 'A Place at the Table.' *Sierra Magazine* (June): 50–96.

Southwest Organizing Project. 1990. 'Letter to Big Ten.' Albuquerque, NM: Southwest Organizing Project.

Taliman, V. 1992. 'The Toxic Waste of Indian Lives.' *Covert Action* 40: 16–22.

Taylor, Dorceta E. 1989. 'Blacks and the Environment: Toward an Explanation of the Concern and Action Gap Between Blacks and Whites.' *Environment and Behavior* 21: 175–205.

Taylor, Dorceta E. 1993. 'Environmentalism and the Politics of Inclusion.' Pp. 53–62 in *Confronting Environmental Racism*, edited by Robert Bullard. Boston, MA: South End Press.

Takvorian, Diane. 1993. 'Environmental Equity: Toxics and Neighborhoods Don't Mix.' *Land Use Forum* (Winter): 28–31.

United Church of Christ Commission for Racial Justice. 1987. *Toxic Wastes and Race in the United States: A National Report on the Racial and Socio-Economic Characteristics of Communities with Hazardous Waste Sites*. New York:

United Church of Christ. U.S. General Accounting Office. 1983. *Siting of Hazardous Waste Landfills and Their Correlation with Racial and Economic Status of Surrounding Communities*. Washington, DC: GAO/RCED.

Wernette, Dee R., and Leslie A. Nieves. 1992. 'Breathing Polluted Air.' *EPA Journal* 18(1): 16–17.

Wilson, W., and K. Ocran. 1991. *Human Ecology Bulletin*.

Williams, and Diane Takvorian. 1990. *Communities at Risk: Your Right to Know About Toxics*. San Diego, CA: Environmental Health Coalition.

Wolf, Frederick. 1992. 'Superfund.' *Journal of Environmental Health* (January/February): 18–22.

Zupan, Jeffrey M. 1973. *The Distribution of Air Quality in the New York Region*. Baltimore, MD: Resources for the Future/Johns Hopkins Press.

# 20. Environmental genocide: Native Americans and toxic waste*

*Daniel Brook*

## Abstract

Physical and cultural genocide have been practiced against Native Americans for half a millennium. In the modern era, these forms of genocide have been superseded by a more insidious, and ultimately more destructive, form. Environmental genocide is perpetrated by the U.S. government and by private corporations alike; some of their methods are legal, while others are not. Against this harsh backdrop, Native Americans are more unified and are becoming better organized than ever, and they are fighting back for their very survival.

Genocide against Native Americans continues in modern times with modern techniques. In the past, buffalo were slaughtered or corn crops were burned, thereby threatening local native populations; now the Earth itself is being strangled, thereby threatening *all* life. The government and large corporations have created toxic, lethal threats to human health. Yet, because 'Native Americans live at the lowest socioeconomic level in the U.S.' (Glass, n.d., 3), they are most at risk for toxic exposure. All poor people and people of color are disadvantaged, although '[f]or Indians, these disadvantages are multiplied by dependence on food supplies closely tied to the land and in which [toxic] materials ... have been shown to accumulate' (*ibid.*). This essay will discuss the genocide of Native Americans through environmental spoliation and native resistance to it. Although this type of genocide is not (usually) the result of a systematic plan with malicious intent to exterminate Native Americans, it is the consequence of activities that are often carried out on and near the reservations with reckless disregard for the lives of Native Americans.[1]

One very significant toxic threat to Native Americans comes from governmental and commercial hazardous waste sitings. Because of the severe poverty and extraordinary vulnerability of Native American tribes, their lands have been targeted by the U.S. goverment and the large corporations as permanent areas for much of the poisonous industrial by-products of the dominant society. 'Hoping to take advantage of the devastating chronic unemployment,

---

* From *American Journal of Economics and Sociology* (1998), 57(1): pp. 105–113.

pervasive poverty and sovereign status of Indian Nations', according to Bradley Angel, writing for the interational environmental organization Greenpeace, 'the waste disposal industry and the U.S. goverment have embarked on an all-out effort to site incinerators, landfills, nuclear waste storage facilities and similar polluting industries on Tribal land' (Angel 1991, 1).

In fact, so enthusiastic is the United States government to dump its most dangerous waste from 'the nation's 110 commercial nuclear power plants' (ibid., 16) on the nation's '565 federally recognized tribes' (Aug 1993, 9) that it 'has solicited *every* Indian Tribe, offering millions of dollars if the tribe would host a nuclear waste facility' (Angel 1991, 15; emphasis added). Given the fact that Native Americans tend to be so materially poor, the money offered by the government or the corporations for this 'toxic trade' is often more akin to bribery or blackmail than to payment for services rendered.[2] In this way, the Mescalero Apache tribe in 1991, for example, became the first tribe (or state) to file an application for a U.S. Energy Department grant 'to study the feasibility of building a temporary [*sic*] storage facility for 15,000 metric tons of highly radioactive spent fuel' (*Akwesasne Notes* 1992, 11). Other Indian tribes, including the Sac, Fox, Yakima, Choctaw, Lower Brule Sioux, Eastern Shawnee, Ponca, Caddo, and the Skull Valley Band of Goshute, have since applied for the $100,000 exploratory grants as well (Angel 1991, 16–17).

Indeed, since so many reservations are without major sources of outside revenue, it is not surprising that some tribes have considered proposals to host toxic waste repositories on their reservations. Native Americans, like all other victimized ethnic groups, are not passive populations in the face of destruction from imperialism and paternalism. Rather, they are active agents in the making of their own history. Nearly a century and a half ago, the radical philosopher and political economist Karl Marx realized that people 'make their own history, but they do not make it just as they please; they do not make it under circumstances chosen by themselves, but under circumstances directly found, given and transmitted from the past' (Marx 1978, 595). Therefore, '[t]ribal governments considering or planning waste facilities', asserts Margaret Crow of California Indian Legal Services, 'do so for a number of reasons' (Crow 1994, 598). First, lacking exploitable subterranean natural resources, some tribal governments have sought to employ the land itself as a resource in an attempt to fetch a financial return. Second, since many reservations are rural and remote, other lucrative business opportunities are rarely, if ever, available to them. Third, some reservations are sparsely populated and therefore have surplus land for business activities. And fourth, by establishing waste facilities some tribes would be able to resolve their reservations' own waste disposal problems while simultaneously raising much-needed revenue.

As a result, '[a] small number of tribes across the country are actively pursuing commercial hazardous and solid waste facilities'; however, '[t]he risk and benefit analysis performed by most tribes has led to decisions not to engage in commercial waste management' (*ibid.*). Indeed, Crow reports that by 'the end of 1992, there were no commercial waste facilities operating on any Indian reservations' (*ibid.*), although the example of the Campo Band of Mission Indians provides an interesting and illuminating exception to the trend. The Campo Band undertook a 'proactive approach to siting a commercial solid waste landfill and recycling facility near San Diego, California. The Band informed and educated the native community, developed an environmental regulatory infrastructure, solicited companies, required that the applicant company pay for the Band's financial advisors, lawyers, and solid waste industry consultants, and ultimately negotiated a favorable contract' (Haner 1994, 106). Even these extraordinary measures, however, are not enough to protect the tribal land and indigenous people from toxic exposure.

Unfortunately, it is a sad but true fact that 'virtually every landfill leaks, and every incinerator emits hundreds of toxic chemicals into the air, land and water' (Angel 1991, 3). The U.S. Environmental Protection Agency concedes that '[e]ven if the … protective systems work according to plan, the landfills will eventually leak poisons into the environment' (ibid.). Therefore, even if these toxic waste sites are safe for the present generation – a rather dubious proposition at best – they will pose an increasingly greater health and safety risk for *all* future generations. Native people (and others) will eventually pay the costs of these toxic pollutants with their lives, 'costs to which [corporate] executives are conveniently immune' (Parker 1983, 59). In this way, private corporations are able to externalize their costs onto the commons, thereby subsidizing their earnings at the expense of health, safety, and the environment.

Sadly, this may not be the worst environmental hazard on tribal lands. Kevin Grover and Jana Walker try '[t]o set the record straight' by claiming that 'the bigger problem is not that the waste industry is beating a path to the tribal door [although it is of course doing so]. Rather, it is the unauthorized and illegal dumping occurring on reservations. For most Indian communities the problem of open dumping on tribal lands is of much greater concern than the remote prospect that a commercial waste disposal facility may be sited on a reservation' (Haner 1994, 107).[3]

There are two major categories of people who illegally dump waste on tribal land. They have been called 'midnight dumpers' and 'native entrepreneurs.' *Midnight dumpers* are corporations and people who secretly dump their wastes on reservations without the permission of tribal governments. *Native entrepreneurs* are tribal members who contaminate tribal land, without tribal permission, for private profit or personal convenience. Both midnight dumpers and native entrepreneurs threaten Native American tribes in two significant ways: tribal health and safety, and tribal sovereignty.

First, toxic waste poses a severe health and safety risk. Some chemical agents cause leukemia and other cancers; others may lead to organ ailments, asthma, and other dysfunctions; and yet others may lead to birth defects such as anencephaly. Toxic waste accomplishes these tragic consequences through direct exposure, through the contamination of the air, land, and water, and through the bioaccumulation of toxins in both plants and animals. And because of what Ben Chavis in 1987 termed 'environmental racism,' people of color (and poor people) are disproportionately affected by toxic waste. Native Americans are especially hard hit because of their ethnicity, their class, and their unique political status in the United States.

A second problem that Native Americans must confront when toxic waste is dumped on their lands is the issue of tribal sovereignty, and more specifically the loss of this sovereignty. 'Native American governments retain all power not taken away by treaty, federal statute, or the courts. As an extension of this principle, native governments retain authority over members unless divested by the federal government' (Haner 1994, 109–110). Jennifer Haner, a New York attorey, asserts that illegal dumping threatens tribal sovereignty because it creates the conditions that make federal government intervention on the reservations more likely (*ibid.*, 121). The federal government can use the issue of illegally dumped toxic waste as a pretext to revert to past patterns of paternalism and control over Native American affairs on the reservations; Native Americans are viewed as irresponsible, the U.S. government as their savior.

Less abstract examples of threats to sovereignty include the experience of the Kaibab-Paiute Tribe. The Waste Tech Corporation 'wanted to restrict the Kaibab-Paiute Tribe from having full access to their own tribal land … [and also wanted] the unilateral right to determine where access roads would be built, and the unilateral right to decide to take any additional land they desired' (Angel 1991, 3). Another concrete example is Waste Management, Inc.'s attempt to curtail the powers of the Campo Environmental Protection Agency and to dilute other tribal regulations. Amcor officials at the Pine Ridge Reservation in South Dakota, as a further example, sought exemption from any environmental laws mandated for tribal lands after the contract was signed. All of these acts are threats to the sovereignty of Native American tribes and contribute to the genocidal project.

Tribal lands are detrimentally affected through other external and unwanted environmental influences, as well. Indeed, '[o]ff-site pollution is [also] a major problem for Native Americans' (Lewis 1994, 189). There are many examples, and each one is a very significant tragedy:

> When tankers like the Exxon *Valdez* spill their cargoes of crude oil, they pollute thousands of miles of coastline … Pollutants from mining and processing plants migrate into reservation air and water. Cyanide heap-leach mining in Montana is polluting water on the Fort Belknap reservation. Radioactive pollution and toxic waste from the Hanford nuclear weapons plant threaten all tribes who depend on the Columbia River … The Mdewakanton Sioux of Prairie Island, Minnesota, fear the health impacts of a nuclear power plant built on the edge of their small reservation, while the Western Shoshones protest the use of their land as a nuclear test site. Industrial waste dumps surround the St. Regis Indian Reservation, fouling the St. Lawrence River. Poorly treated urban waste and agricultural effluent threatens nearby reservation environments (*ibid.*).

Deadly environmental threats also emanate from uranium and coal mining, U.S. military target practice and war games, spent ammunition shells, discarded batteries, and asbestos. Sadly, this is only a partial list. In fact, a survey of only 25 Indian reservations revealed 'that 1200 hazardous waste generators or other hazardous waste activity sites were located on or near … [those] reservations selected for the survey' (Williams 1992, 282). The issue is serious, the scope is wide, and the results are disastrous.

Native Americans have always altered their environment, as well as having it altered by others. The environment, like culture, is inherently dynamic and dialectical. Native Americans 'used song and ritual speech to modify their world, while physically transforming that landscape with fire and water, brawn and brain. They did not passively adapt, but responded in diverse ways to adjust environments to meet their cultural as well as material desires' (Lewis 1994, 188). However, the introduction of toxic waste and other environmental hazards, such as military-related degradation, have catastrophically affected the present and future health and culture of Native Americans.

Yet, Native Americans and other people of color, along with poor people, women, and environmentalists, have been organizing against toxic waste and fighting back against the government and the corporations. Indeed, 'the intersection of race discrimination and exposure to toxic hazards', according to Andrew Szasz, Professor of Sociology at the University of California, Santa Cruz, 'is one of the core themes of the [anti-]toxics movement' (Szasz 1994, 151).[4] In spite of the often desperate poverty of Indian tribes, 'a wave of resistance has erupted among Indian people in dozens of Indian Nations in response to the onslaught of the waste industry' (Angel 1991, 5). Sporadic resistance has also developed into organized and sustained opposition. Facing the threat of a toxic waste facility on their land in Dilkon, Arizona, in 1989, the Navajo formed a group called Citizens Against Ruining our Environment, also known as CARE. CARE fought the proposed siting by educating and organizing their community, and their success inspired other similarly situated Native Americans. (CARE later merged with other Navajo groups fighting for the community and the environment, to create a new organization, called Dine CARE). The following year, in June 1990, CARE hosted a conference in Dilkon called 'Protecting Mother Earth: The Toxic Threat to Indian Land', which brought together 'over 200 Indian delegates from 25 tribes throughout North America' (ibid.).

The following year's conference in South Dakota included '[o]ver 500 Indigenous delegates from 57 tribes' (ibid., 6). It was at this second annual conference that the delegates created the Indigenous Environmental Network. The IEN states that it is 'an alliance of grass roots peoples whose mission is to strengthen, maintain, protect and respect the traditional teachings, lifestyles and spiritual interdependence to the sacredness of Mother Earth and the natural laws' (Aug 1993, 7). This is wholly in concert with 'the most enduring characteristic of American Indians throughout the history of the continent: the ability to incorporate technological, natural, and social changes while maintaining cultural continuity' (Crow 1994, 593). Therein lies the natural affinity between Indian opposition to toxic waste and the broader environmental justice movement. 'Environmental justice,' according to the journal of the Citizens' Clearinghouse for Hazardous Waste, *Everyone's Backyard*, 'is a people-oriented way of addressing "environmentalism" that adds a vital social, economic and political element ... When we fight for environmental justice, we fight for our homes and families and struggle to end economic, social and political domination by the strong and greedy' (Szasz 1994, 152–153).

Fighting for environmental justice is a form of self-defense for Native Americans. As the *Report of Women of All Red Nations* declared, 'To contaminate Indian water is an act of war more subtle than military aggression, yet no less deadly ... Water is life' (February 1980, in Collins Bay Action Group 1985, 4). Toxic pollution – coupled with the facts of environmental racism, pervasive poverty, and the unique status of Native Americans in the United States – 'really is a matter of GENOCIDE. The Indigenous people were colonized and forced onto reservations ... [Native Americans are] poisoned on the job. Or poisoned in the home ... Or forced to relocate so that the land rip-offs can proceed without hitch. Water is life but the corporations are killing it. It's a genocide of all the environment and all species of creatures' (Bend 1985, 25; emphasis in original). In effect, toxic pollution is a *genocide through geocide*, that is, a killing of the people through a killing of the Earth.

Environmental threats are, unfortunately, not new. In the mid-1800s, Chief Seattle of the Suquamish tribe reportedly stated that '[t]he Earth does not belong to [human beings]; [humans] belong to the Earth. This we know. All things are connected like the blood which unites one family. All things are connected. Whatever befalls the Earth befalls the [children] of the Earth. [Human beings] did not weave the web of life; [they are] merely a strand in it. Whatever [they do] to the web, [they do to themselves]' (Chief Seattle 1987, 7). In this vein, genocide is ultimately also suicide.

Five hundred years after the commencement of colonialism and genocide, 'the exploitation and assault on Indigenous people and their land continues. Instead of conquistadors armed with weapons of destruction and war, the new assault is disguised as 'economic development' promoted by entrepreneurs pushing poisonous technologies. The modern-day invaders from the waste disposal industry promise huge amounts of money, make vague promises about jobs, and make exaggerated and often false claims about the alleged safety of their dangerous proposals' (Angel 1991, 1). Yet, also 500 years later, Native Americans are still resisting the onslaught and are still (re)creating themselves and their cultures. And increasingly, Native Americans are better organized and more united than ever in their struggle against environmental racism and for environmental justice.

## Notes

1 Under the statutory law of many states, for example, murder is defined by either a premeditated intent to kill or *an extremely reckless act that would reasonably be believed to cause serious bodily harm or death*. The latter definition is referred to as 'depravity of heart'.
2 For similarities with Mexico's treatment by the U.S. government and transnational corporations, see my 'Toxic Trade' in *Z Magazine* (Brook 1992).
3 Like much of Native American history, this phenomenon, too, is mirrored in the experiences of many Third World countries, as well as minority communities within First World countries. See, for example, *Economist* 1992a, 66; *Economist*, 1992b, 18–19; Ross 1992, 5; Medoff and Sklar 1994.
4 See also my review of this book in the *Journal of Political Ecology* (Brook 1994).

# References

*Akwesasne Notes* [1978] 1981. *Basic Call to Consciousness*. Mohawk Nation via Rooseveltown, N.Y.: Akwesasne Notes.

——. 1992. 'Application for Study Grant Is First under Energy Dept. Program'. *Akwesasne Notes* 23 (3) (Midwinter).

Angel, Bradley. 1991. *The Toxic Threat to Indian Lands: A Greenpeace Report*. San Francisco: Greenpeace.

Aug, Lisa. 1993. 'The Nuclear Carrot'. *Turtle Quarterly* 5 (Spring-Summer).

Barry, Tom. 1979. 'Bury My Lungs at Red Rock'. *The Progressive*, February.

Bend, Jill. 1985. 'Northern Saskatchewan: Behind the Uranium Curtain'. *Akwesasne Notes* (Summer).

Brook, Daniel. 1992. 'Toxic Trade.' *Z Magazine* 5 (9) (September).

——. 1994. 'Review.' *Journal of Political Ecology*, vol. 1.

Chief Seattle. [1854] 1987. 'Chief Seattle's Message'. In Robert Cooney and Helen Michalowski, eds. *The Power of the People: Active Nonviolence in the United States*. Philadelphia: New Society Publishers.

Collins Bay Action Group. 1985. *Earth Communique*. Mimeo, 15 May.

Crow, Margaret. 1994. 'U.S. Indians and the Environment'. Duane Champagne, ed. *The Native North American Almanac*. Washington, D.C.: Gale Research.

Dmitryev, Franklin. 1995. 'Rising Community Struggles Fight Toxic Environmental Racism'. *News & Letters*, July.

Economist. 1992a. 'Let Them Eat Pollution'. *The Economist*, 8 February.

——. 1992b. 'Pollution and the Poor'. *The Economist*, 15 February.

Glass, Ron. N.d. *By Our Own Lives: Moving the Foundation Stone of Racism*, Mimeo.

Haner, Jennifer Smith. 1994. 'Tribal Solutions to On-Reservation Environmental Offenses: Jurisdictional Parameters, Cultural Considerations, and Recommendations'. *American Indian Law Review*, 19 (1).

Marx, Karl. [1852] 1978. 'The Eighteenth Brumaire of Louis Bonaparte.' In Robert C. Tucker, ed. *The Marx-Engels Reader*, 2d ed. New York: W.W. Norton.

Lewis, David Rich. 1994. 'Environmental Issues'. In Mary B. Davis, ed. *Native America in the Twentieth Century: An Encyclopedia*. New York and London: Garland Publishing.

Medoff, Peter, and Holly Sklar. 1994. *Streets of Hope*. Boston: South End Press.

Parker, Vawter. 1983. 'Sierra Club Forces Action on Radioactive Tailings'. *Sierra* (November/December).

Ross, John. 1992. 'Mexico's Disappearing Toxic Wastes'. *Latinamerica Press*, 20 (August).

Szasz, Andrew. 1994. *EcoPopulism: Toxic Waste and the Movement for Environmental Justice*. Minneapolis and London: University of Minnesota Press.

Taliman, Valerie. 1994. 'Saving Native Lands: One Woman's Crusade against Environmental Racism'. *Ms.* (January/February).

Williams, Teresa A. 1992. 'Pollution and Hazardous Waste on Indian Lands: Do Federal Laws Apply and Who May Enforce Them?' *American Indian Law Review*, 17 (1992): 269–290.

# 21. The illegal market in Australian abalone*

*Rebecca Tailby and Frances Gant*

For some time there has been growing concern about the illegal trafficking of Australian abalone (a highly prized shellfish delicacy). As global populations of the resource decline, increased pressure is placed on Australia's abalone fishery to meet ongoing international demand. This strong demand, which is not being fully met through the legitimate trade, creates incentives for people to supply the black market with stolen or 'poached' abalone. Abalone has become an attractive criminal commodity, and reports suggest that a profitable illegal market exists alongside the legitimate market. While abalone poached from Australian waters may find its way into the domestic market, the majority is destined for overseas export. The first question always asked is 'what is the size and value of the illegal market?' On the basis of information currently available, the Australian Institute of Criminology has not been able to answer this question. The AIC has a strong research interest in illicit markets and this paper explores the nature of the illicit market in Australian abalone. It examines the various players involved in this illegal trade, vulnerabilities in the legitimate industry, and potential options for disrupting the illicit market.

Adam Graycar
Director, Australian Institute of Criminology

Abalone is a gastropod mollusc found on rocky reefs along the Australian coastline but mainly harvested off the colder waters of the southern states. The meat of these shellfish is regarded as a delicacy in certain cultures and is highly sought after, particularly in Asian markets. Australia currently produces around one-third of the global wild abalone harvest, with national export earnings from fresh, chilled and frozen abalone rising from $86.7 million in 1998–99 to $102.5 million during 1999–2000 (ABARE 2002). Australia's stake in global supply has increased following the decline and/or disappearance of abalone populations in other parts of the world – including Japan, Mexico, South Africa and the United States (California) – due to negative environmental conditions, limited stocks, illegal fishing and poor fisheries management.

---

* From *Trends & Issues in Crime and Criminal Justice No. 225* (2002). Canberra: Australian Institute of Criminology.

The increasing scarcity of abalone-producing reefs overseas and the growing pressure on Australia's abalone fishery to meet global demand have placed Australian abalone at a premium. While total allowable catch (TAC) limits on abalone harvesting have been set by each abalone-producing state in Australia to protect this resource, ongoing demand from consumers, coupled with high profits to be made from abalone sales, are providing the incentive for further amounts to be harvested illegally. The purpose of this paper is to explore such illegal harvesting and, more specifically, the illicit market in Australian abalone.

## Methodology

This paper is based on research undertaken by the Australian Institute of Criminology on behalf of the Marine and Freshwater Resources Institute of Fisheries Victoria. The project involved analysis of fisheries-related intelligence and compliance data in order to derive an estimate of the scale of illegal abalone catches in Australia. Although a quantitative exercise, much qualitative information came to light during the course of the project and forms the basis of the following discussion.

Information was obtained through three principal means:

- discussions with a range of stakeholders, including fisheries officers from all Australian jurisdictions, personnel from other law enforcement agencies responsible for fisheries compliance (such as Tasmania Police and the Australian Customs Service) and a range of abalone industry representatives;

- a comprehensive review of abalone-related intelligence and compliance data holdings in all jurisdictions; and

- a review of media and other literature.

### Regulation in the abalone industry

To ensure protection of Australia's abalone fishery and avoid over-exploitation, there is strong regulation of the abalone industry in Australia. In addition to TAC limits, there is an abalone licensing system which restricts the number of people who can legally harvest abalone. Abalone dive licenses are a valuable commercial asset, realising up to $2 million when traded.

Respective state fisheries agencies undertake continuous assessment, monitoring and management of the abalone fishery. Each state has legislation and associated regulations outlining permitted and prohibited activity in the abalone fishery. Although certain regulatory controls pertain across all abalone fishing in Australia (such as minimum size limits and closed fishing seasons, which apply to commercial and recreational fishers alike), regulation is heavily focused on the commercial sector.

All commercial abalone divers must complete catch records upon landing their daily take of abalone. From this point on (that is, from catch through to sale) abalone must at all times be accompanied by conforming documentation (docketing) as proof of its legitimacy (see National Fisheries Compliance Committee 1999). This docketing system allows abalone to be tracked through the market. It also permits comparison of declared amounts along the chain (that is, from landing to delivery to processor to subsequent consignment) to enable detection of any discrepancies. Detailed quota-management systems exist in each state fisheries agency which enable reconciliation of diver, processor and export records, and the tracking of catch against quota limits.

Compliance monitoring by fisheries agencies encompasses the above aspects in relation to the licensed sector, and also includes policing of unlicensed poachers. Customs and the Australian Quarantine Inspection Service (AQIS) also have a role in compliance monitoring at the border.

## The illegal market

Despite the extensive regulatory framework governing Australia's abalone fishery, illegal abalone harvesting and trading does occur. The capacity of individuals to enter the legal market is restricted by the limited availability of abalone dive licenses and the high costs of purchasing a license and associated set-up fees. When considered alongside the potential profits to be made through illegally harvesting and trading abalone, this combination of factors may motivate the entry of individuals to the illegal market. Figure 21.1 shows the stages in the illegal abalone market while Figure 21.2 shows the different ways in which abalone may be illegally caught, processed and either used by or sold to the end consumer. It should be noted that the methods used by those operating outside legal channels do not differ greatly to those used by legitimate divers and processors.

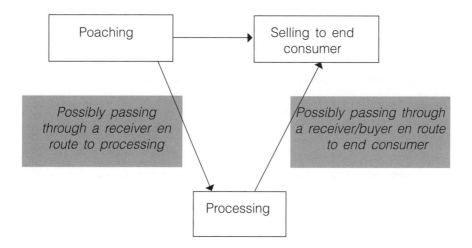

**Figure 21.1**  Stages in the illegal abalone market

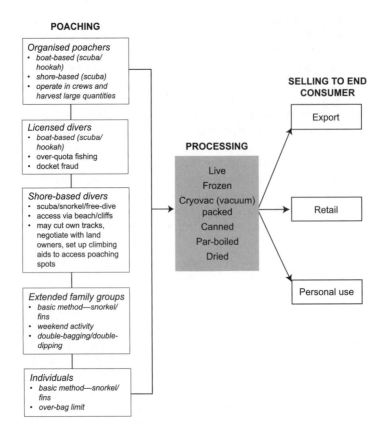

**POACHING**

Organised poachers
- boat-based (scuba/hookah)
- shore-based (scuba)
- operate in crews and harvest large quantities

Licensed divers
- boat-based (scuba/hookah)
- over-quota fishing
- docket fraud

Shore-based divers
- scuba/snorkel/free-dive
- access via beach/cliffs
- may cut own tracks, negotiate with land owners, set up climbing aids to access poaching spots

Extended family groups
- basic method—snorkel/fins
- weekend activity
- double-bagging/double-dipping

Individuals
- basic method—snorkel/fins
- over-bag limit

**PROCESSING**

Live

Frozen

Cryovac (vacuum) packed

Canned

Par-boiled

Dried

**SELLING TO END CONSUMER**

Export

Retail

Personal use

**Figure 21.2**  Methods used in each stage of the illegal abalone market

Abalone poachers can be loosely categorised into five types of offenders, varying in their levels of sophistication and method. Of course, these are neither exclusive nor exhaustive categories but rather provide a general overview of the different ways abalone is taken from the water.

### Organised poachers

Organised poachers share some characteristics with commercial licensed divers in that many work from boats and/or the shore, mostly using surface-supplied air ('hookah equipment') or scuba (self-contained underwater breathing apparatus), and are generally proficient divers who are able to harvest large quantities of abalone efficiently. Many organised poachers operate in 'crews' incorporating divers, deckhands, lookouts and couriers. Unlike licensed divers, poachers generally shuck their abalone (that is, remove the meat from the shell) under the water, returning only with the meat. This reduces the weight of the catch and makes the abalone easier to manage.

In order to avoid detection and maximise the size of catches, organised poachers are willing to:

- dive under the cover of darkness;
- dive in areas which are remote and/or difficult to access;
- use sophisticated technology to assist poaching (for example, infra-red night vision equipment) and to track or report the presence of compliance officers in the area through radios and scanners;
- cross state borders to harvest abalone; and
- fish for days at a time.

Many organised poachers have developed elaborate methods for concealing and moving illegally caught abalone. These include:

- hiding their catch either close to the beach or at sea, often submerged in a known location and/or with some form of beacon or buoy to mark the site for later pickup;
- building secret compartments in boats to conceal poached abalone;
- creating makeshift abalone storage receptacles in cars (for example, converting additional petrol tanks) to avoid detection during transit from the beach;
- hiring small planes to drop off divers in remote areas, returning later to collect and transport large catches of illegally caught abalone; and
- using hire vehicles to transport stolen catches to avoid asset forfeiture provisions if the authorities intercept the vehicle.

The majority of organised poachers make the greater part of their income through illicit means. It is estimated that one of the more well-known abalone poachers in Australia made in excess of $1 million per year from the harvest and sale of illegal abalone (Neales 1997). The lucrative nature of the abalone trade is reportedly beginning to attract the interest of some organised crime figures. There are suggestions that outlaw motorcycle gangs and Asian crime figures have entered the market, acting as buyers and distributors and establishing illicit networks extending overseas to the consumer markets in Asia (Morgan and Papps 1996; Neales 1997; Nicholl 1999).

These trends are perhaps not surprising, given reports that organised criminal groups grew to dominate the illicit abalone market in some other abalone-producing countries such as South Africa (Gastrow 2001). It has been suggested that illegal Australian abalone is being traded for heroin and marijuana overseas (Coffey and Hart 1999). Within Australia, anecdotal evidence from several jurisdictions suggests links between the trade in illegal abalone and local illicit drug markets. The growing evidence of serious criminality, both in terms of the calibre of criminals taking up key roles in the distribution of illegal abalone, and the links between the illegal abalone trade and other established transnational and local criminal markets, provides reason for concern.

### Licensed divers

While the majority of licensed divers operate legitimately within their industry, there may be a few who exploit their position by engaging in quota fraud. This is done either by harvesting catches which are not declared (that is, fishing 'over their quota'), or by 'fudging' catch weight records to misrepresent the true amount of abalone caught. Excess abalone may be supplied directly to consumers or to processors for illegal preparation and sale. Unlike organised poachers, licensed divers supplement their legitimate income with illicit activity.

### Shore-based divers

As the name suggests, shore-based divers generally poach abalone close to the beach. Rather than using a boat and hookah, shore-based divers prefer to use scuba equipment and enter the water via the beach or cliff faces. If not intending to harvest a large catch, shore-based divers may free-dive for abalone using mask, fins and snorkel. As with organised poachers, abalone is generally shucked under the water and bagged. Bags are either carried to shore or left under the water to be picked up at a later time. While shore-based divers tend not to be as active as organised boat-based poachers in terms of the length of time spent poaching, they may still harvest significant catches. Shore-based divers have been known to cut their own walking tracks and trails to access abalone-rich coastal reefs, to negotiate with private land owners for access to certain cliffs/beaches, and to set up ropes and climbing aids to access poaching spots.

### Extended family groups

Although not considered to be classic poachers, extended family groups also pose a threat to scarce abalone resources, particularly those within the intertidal zone. These groups – which can consist of up to 20 people – often operate on weekends. Groups typically harvest abalone to the cumulative recreational bag limit (usually with only a few members of the group actually doing the harvesting) and stockpile the goods. The methods used to poach abalone are generally basic, and most often involve wading in shallow water or using a snorkel and fins.

Having collected the combined bag limit, family groups will either:

- continue to harvest over the bag limit, hiding excess catch in and around poaching areas for later pick-up to avoid detection; or

- take the catch home, then return to harvest a second and sometimes a third time – this is known as 'double-bagging' or 'double-dipping'.

Much of the abalone taken by extended family groups is for personal use, although it has been suggested that excess amounts of abalone are used to supply local restaurants and other illicit buyers.

### Individuals

Individuals may also take over-the-bag-limit abalone and stockpile, as well as hide, the fish. These people tend to be opportunistic offenders who poach as the need arises, whether for personal use or to earn some easy money. Again, the methods used are relatively basic.

*Illegal processing*

Processing of abalone may be quite minimal, requiring the abalone to be shucked, frozen or parboiled; some abalone are even shipped 'live'. Alternatively, processing may be more sophisticated and involve canning, drying or cryovac (vacuum) packaging.

Illegal processing encompasses the processing of illegally caught abalone either by registered processors or by non-registered 'backyard' processors. Legitimate processors may collude with licensed divers to disguise quota fraud activity and/or may accept illegally caught abalone from unlicensed divers for illegal processing. Registered processors may disguise the movement of illicit abalone by:

• manipulating the amounts of abalone recorded on official fish transfer dockets in order to disguise the processing of off-quota abalone;

• over-packing export consignments, enabling some illicit abalone to be moved with legitimate consignments; or

• overstating 'recovery rates'.

In South Australia and Western Australia, where abalone are permitted to be shucked prior to landing, recovery rates refer to the actual weight of abalone meat that remains after the loss of fluid (water) which occurs during transit from the beach to the processing factory. In the south-eastern Australian states, where abalone must be landed and transported whole to processing facilities, recovery rates refer to the proportion of the meat that remains after removal

---

**Case study: Tat Sang Loo**

In *Tat Sang Loo* (unreported judgment of the Dandenong Magistrates Court, 17 March 1999), Loo represented the highest link of a Victorian network that facilitated the collection, payment, processing and distribution of illegally caught abalone into New South Wales and Queensland. Illegal abalone received by Loo was processed at his residence, half of which had been converted to an illegal processing factory. The 'factory' comprised ceilings equipped with exhaust fans, three washing machines and bathtubs to wash abalone, and seven gas stoves and large cooking pots to cook the abalone. Three cryovac machines were also used to vacuum-seal the product and an entire room had been purpose-built as an abalone-drying kiln. Raids at this and additional premises resulted in the seizure of 31,004 abalone which had an estimated street value of $750,000. Extensive records seized during the raids revealed that between October 1997 and September 1998, Loo had processed and consigned 9.8 tonnes of abalone to New South Wales and Queensland (wholesale value of $1.35 million). The abalone were destined for wholesalers, Asian food markets and duty-free shops in Sydney and Surfers Paradise. Loo pleaded guilty to 14 charges of possessing, receiving and consigning excess abalone without a licence, and was sentenced to 18 months' imprisonment. He has also been subject to various financial penalty orders totalling more than $1 million.

of the shell and viscera. Unscrupulous processors may claim an artificially high recovery rate in order to supplement the legal catch with illicit abalone, laundering it in the process. It is difficult to assess the level of illegal abalone being moved through registered processing premises, or the proportion of registered processors engaging in illegitimate activity.

As for processing by non-registered operators, fisheries officers report that abalone offenders have sometimes been caught processing abalone in makeshift rooms in private residences, using rather unsophisticated methods. Certainly in the case of live, frozen or cryovac abalone, preparing the product for sale is not necessarily a complicated process. However, a recent operation in Victoria highlights the level of organisation and sophistication that some illegal abalone processors are willing to adopt (see case study).

*Consumers*
There is no one identifiable pathway for the movement of illegal abalone from ocean to end consumer, and indeed abalone may move through a number of hands before reaching the end consumer. For example, illegal abalone may move straight from a diver to a processor to a consumer. Alternatively, illegal processors may sell to receivers or direct to a network of buyers, many believed to be based in Melbourne, Sydney and the Gold Coast. Poached abalone may then be sold to restaurants and retail outlets over the counter or through consignment. Of course some illegal abalone never enters the market but is directly consumed by the poacher.

Legal and illegal abalone is predominantly intended for export, yet is usually first sold domestically to buyers. Within Australia, illegal abalone is generally transported via private means, such as air or road couriers. Occasionally, interstate transport may be as unsophisticated as a number of large eskies of abalone packed in ice and put in the back of a car or light plane. The majority of illegal Australian abalone gets marketed for sale and export, either direct to consumer markets in Asia, or indirectly via sale to Asian tourists and tour groups visiting Australia.

In the case of export, abalone may be concealed:

- through false labelling of export consignments, such as labelling canned abalone as some other product (for example, vegetables), or exporting small amounts of dried abalone through the post and misdeclaring the contents;

- by mixing abalone with other product in export packaging so it passes undetected on cursory inspection – for example, placing a layer of lobster on top of a bin of abalone, and declaring the entire consignment as 'lobster'; or

- in hand and/or cargo luggage of out-bound passengers, many of whom are tourists – there is evidence of organised tour scams where members of tour groups each carry out of Australia the legal limit of abalone (10kg) but on arrival at the destined country stockpile the goods for sale.

## Intersection between legal and illegal markets

As stated, the majority of illegal abalone activity is believed to occur outside the licensed sector, with those involved tending to poach, process and sell abalone to other like-minded people. It is possible, however, for poached abalone to enter the legitimate market, knowingly or otherwise. This can occur when:

- legitimate processors are willing to accept and process over-quota or 'off-the-ticket' abalone from licensed divers – in other words, abalone not declared by the diver;

- registered processors accept poached abalone from unlicensed divers;

- retailers and end consumers are willing to buy it – retailers purchasing illegally caught and processed abalone may do so knowingly, attempting to disguise the purchase by 'reusing' documentation from a legitimate abalone purchase; or

- consumers purchase poached abalone unknowingly – this occurs particularly as poached abalone can easily blend in with legitimate stock.

Essentially, those who are willing to purchase illegal abalone do so because it is cheaper than legitimately harvested abalone. In other cases, it may be an issue of scarcity.

## Disrupting the market for illegal abalone

The illicit trade in Australian abalone has a number of negative effects on the legitimate industry. Due to the clandestine nature of its harvest and subsequent handling, poached abalone may be of poor quality and a subsequent risk to human health. It can therefore adversely affect the image of Australian abalone on the international market. As is the case in other types of markets, illegal operators who have few overheads and accept lower prices for their abalone undercut legitimate operators in price. The presence of poachers supplying abalone to local buyers/restaurants at reduced prices can restrict the potential for sales in local legal markets. At a more fundamental level, large-scale sustained illegal fishing has the potential to threaten the very sustainability of Australia's abalone stocks.

Recognising the serious impact which abalone poaching may have on Australia's legitimate industry, numerous measures have been taken to deter criminal activity within Australia's abalone fishing industry. Each abalone-producing state has legislation carrying high pecuniary penalties and custodial sentences for abalone offending, and has dedicated abalone-crime investigators. In addition, some state courts are empowered to impose control orders on recidivist abalone offenders.

As with all markets, whether legal or illegal, the illicit market in abalone is characterised by a chain of distribution from the source of the product to the end consumer. As discussed, this chain is not an absolute progression from point A to B to C; goods may move through a number of market players. Having identified these players, as well as the law enforcement measures in place to deter offending within the industry as a whole, there are additional measures which can be put in place to disrupt the market for illegal abalone at each stage. This is principally achieved by making it more difficult for people to illegally access, process and sell abalone.

### Accessing abalone

In the case of unlicensed abalone divers or those licensed divers who may fish in excess of their quota, it is difficult to monitor and police illicit catches. Unless unlicensed offenders are caught coming out of the water with over-the-bag-limit abalone, or licensed divers are caught in possession of undocumented or over-quota abalone, large quantities of abalone may be poached from Australian waters and moved from the beach undetected. It is here, however, that strategies aimed at disrupting the illicit market in abalone would be most beneficial, as they would reduce the offender's ability to access abalone stocks. Prevention of illicit harvesting is also the best outcome in terms of protecting the fishery and maintaining fish stocks.

To enable the detection and interception of unlicensed fishing activity, and to ensure licensed divers are complying with docketing and quota requirements and size restrictions, a law enforcement presence on the coast is critical. While a crucial point at which the flow of illegal abalone through the market can be prevented, the ability to enhance beach detection is problematic due to a number of factors, including:

- constraints on the level of resources committed to monitoring abalone-related activity;
- occupational health and safety regulations restricting the activities of fisheries officers in some jurisdictions; and
- difficulties associated with surveillance of the vast Australian coastline.

As well as policing by law enforcement, other avenues can be used to learn about and respond to potential illegal activity at the beach. Initiatives such as Fishwatch, a toll-free government service, encourage members of the community to report any suspicious activity relating to marine life – including abalone – to fisheries agencies. Such programs currently operate in several Australian states. Those within the licensed sector are also in a good position to pass on any information about illegal operators and activity that they may come across. Industry should be encouraged to report this information through safe and effective reporting programs.

### Processing abalone

Fisheries agencies are responsible for auditing registered abalone processors. To assist the audit process, mandatory labelling of all legitimate processed abalone has recently been introduced. This initiative complements more traditional auditing procedures that include documentation checks using the quota management system and surprise inspections of processing facilities. These measures can be effective in monitoring the amounts of abalone moving through such factories, and detecting discrepancies in the paper trail suggestive of illicit product. However, inspections may be compromised by the fact that once incoming catches of abalone are combined with existing stock at the processing facility it becomes virtually impossible to determine whether abalone have been caught legally and by whom.

Another opportunity for auditing registered processors occurs when the product leaves the premises. Inspections of the amount of outgoing abalone, to ensure that consignments are declared and that the weight of the consignment is correct, are important to enable 'in–out' reconciliation of stock.

Intervention at this stage of the chain is more straightforward in the case of backyard processors as the entire establishment is illegitimate, therefore any discovery of such facilities indicates illicit activity. The difficulty in such cases is that unsophisticated processing can be performed almost anywhere. Such establishments are typically discovered only after tip-offs from the public or informers, or through surveillance of divers engaged in illegal harvesting. This reinforces the importance of maintaining intelligence and effective policing strategies.

Agencies other than fisheries and police services can play a part in policing operations that involve the illegal processing of abalone – particularly from private/backyard premises. These might include environment protection agencies, local councils and the Australian Taxation Office. Environmental protection agencies and local councils can monitor compliance with environmental regulations and by-laws such as waste disposal, noise pollution and zoning, while the Tax Office can be used to flag any discrepancies between employment, assets and income. These agencies also have the authority to inspect business premises, issue infringement notices, impose fines and investigate business records and financial accounts.

By applying this type of pressure on illegitimate traders to comply with regulations, these agencies increase the cost of illicit activity as well as the risk of detection and apprehension. In other words, they can assist fisheries and law enforcement services in disrupting the activity of those involved in the illicit abalone market.

### Export and sale

There are a number of measures that can be implemented at the final point in the Australian market (that is, where poached abalone is exported to overseas destinations). The majority, if not all, of the abalone intended for overseas export passes through an airport, whether in cargo, hand luggage, on a person, through the mail or by consignment. The Australian Customs Service therefore has an invaluable role through the inspection of luggage and passengers at airports, as well as in monitoring export consignments. AQIS has a similar role insofar as officers may conduct quality control inspections to ensure abalone product intended for export is fit for human consumption. Any detections and seizures of illegal abalone at this point pose significant obstacles to the supply of abalone to lucrative international markets.

While illegally obtained abalone bound for export can be detected through random searches and scans of luggage, passengers and consignments, Customs is also in an ideal position to play a proactive role should sufficient resources be available to follow leads provided by fisheries and other law enforcement agencies concerning the suspected movement of illegal abalone out of Australia. Given competing enforcement and policing priorities for Customs in terms of other illicit goods, however, the interception of illegal or suspect abalone at the border may not be as high a priority. Furthermore, the above-mentioned strategies may do little to disrupt the domestic market in poached Australian abalone and that product which is not bound for overseas.

Timely intelligence sharing from state fisheries and police concerning illegal product headed for export serves to facilitate border interceptions. This information exchange between key stakeholders could be strengthened by the development of national information and reporting systems for fisheries intelligence. Recent progress has been made towards prohibiting the export of any abalone except for AQIS-approved product and domestic sales complying with the National Docketing System. Similarly, consideration of the inclusion of abalone as a scheduled export item under Customs legislation may provide additional legislative backing for the interception of illegal abalone exports.

To date there have been a number of multi-jurisdictional operations targeting the Australian black market in abalone which have succeeded due to strong cooperation between fisheries, state police and federal agencies such as Customs and AQIS. However, jurisdictional and cross-agency coordination issues can serve to hamper efforts to disrupt both the domestic and international black market trade in abalone. These factors, as well as differences in state legislation, are likely to pose ongoing difficulties for countering the illicit market across jurisdictions. In these cases, the Australian Fisheries Management Authority may have a role to play in coordinating responses to domestic abalone trafficking.

## Conclusion

While some researchers have explored the involvement of criminal actors in illegal abalone markets overseas (Gastrow 2001; the National Crime Authority has also done some recent Australian research in this area), very little research has been conducted into the illicit abalone market in Australia. This paper sought to fill some of this gap by providing an overview of the illicit Australian abalone market based on fieldwork and discussions with key stakeholders. The illegal market in poached abalone is a lucrative one which involves a variety of players ranging from suppliers, handlers, buyers and distributors. The difficulties inherent in policing illegal activity within the industry are numerous and stem from the fact that illegal harvesting takes place offshore and can occur at any number of sites along Australia's extensive southern coastline. Illegal processing can likewise occur almost anywhere, and there are possibilities of cross-border movement of stolen product. Continued assessment, monitoring, regulation and policing of the licensed and unlicensed abalone sectors are key strategies that must be used to address the threat of unsustainable harvesting from Australia's abalone fishery.

## Acknowledgment

Funding for this national Marine and Freshwater Resources Institute project was provided by the Fisheries Research and Development Corporation.

## References

Australian Bureau of Agricultural and Resource Economics (ABARE) 2002, *Australian Commodities*, vol. 9, no. 1, p. 285.

Coffey, M. & Hart, B. 1999, 'Beaches of fear', *Herald Sun*, 22 June 1999.

Gastrow, P. 2001, *Triad Societies and Chinese Organised Crime in South Africa*, occ. paper no. 48, Institute for Security Studies, South Africa, <http://www.iss.co.za/Pubs/PAPERS/48/48.html>.

Morgan, H. & Papps, N. 1996, 'Abalone poachers fund drug trade', *The Advertiser* (Adelaide), 13 May 1996.

National Fisheries Compliance Committee 1999, *From Boat to Buyer: National Docketing System – A Strategy to Protect our Seafood Resource* (brochure).

Neales, S. 1997, 'The big steal', *Good Weekend*, 11 October 1997.

Nicholl, J. 1999, 'Cutting Asian organised crime: Blade National Task Force', *Australian Criminal Intelligence Digest*, no. 16, July 1999, Australian Bureau of Criminal Intelligence, pp. 12–13.

# 22. Lobster poaching and the ironies of law enforcement*

*John L. McMullan and David C. Perrier*

This article studies law in action as it relates to organized lobster poaching in Canada. It examines the distinct pattern of relationships that constitutes poaching as a business enterprise and analyzes how 'living law' operates as an ironic facilitative form for that which it tries to control. We argue that business poachers evade, avoid, and neutralize fishery laws and regulations by creatively using and manipulating the legal boundaries and organizational resources at their disposal. In effect, the law is an enabling structure for blue water illegality. We analyze business poaching activities as a type of workplace crime, and we account for regulatory failure in the lobster fishery.

## Introduction

This article studies 'law in action' as it relates to poaching in the lobster fishery of Southwest Nova Scotia, Canada. For decades, tensions between fishers and the state have been escalating. Conflicts over quotas, regulations, licenses, procedures, and enforcement have been widespread and volatile. Poaching has become what Scott (1986: 18) terms 'a routine form of everyday resistance,' part of the ongoing process of testing and negotiating the terms of lobster harvesting and merchandizing. Central to the development of poaching have been a series of legal changes whereby informal, community-based property rights, local management strategies, and folk forms of resource knowledge and use have been displaced and outlawed by new state property rights and claims and by new social regulations about harvesting, development, and management (Hanson and Lamson 1984; Apostle, Kasdan, and Hanson 1984; Barrett 1987; Clement 1986; Davis and Thiessen 1988; Sutinen and Gauvin 1989; Sutinen, Rieser, and Gauvin 1990).

This regulatory explosion has resulted in a climate of uncertainty for fishers, social divisions among them, and conflicts between fishing communities and the state. The media characterization is one of 'lobster wars,' 'black market

* From *Law & Society Review* (2002), 36(4): pp. 679–720.

fisheries,' 'piscatorial piracy,' and 'coastal communities on trial.' Indeed, the prosecution records of the Department of Fisheries and Oceans (DFO) reveal the seriousness of business poaching. Of the 531 reported lobster offenses we studied, three-quarters of them were committed by commercial fishers and involved offenses such as using illegal gear and fishing undersize lobsters (McMullan, Perrier, and Okihiro 1993: 128–30). Of course, these statistics tell only part of the story. We found that there is also a large hidden figure of unrecorded illegality in the fishery. While prosecution files provide useful information about the age, location, attitudes, and behavior of offenders and about the methods of law enforcement, they do not provide a coherent understanding of either the social organization of poaching or the legal relations and enforcement strategies surrounding the translation of law into social practice.

Our concern in this article is to examine the distinct pattern of relationships that constitutes business poaching in Southwest Nova Scotia and to analyze how law operates as an ironic facilitative form for that which it tries to control. We study how and why business poachers creatively use and manipulate the legal boundaries and organizational resources at their disposal to effectively evade, avoid, and neutralize fishery laws and regulations. We examine how lobster fishing is an encapsulated operation within a larger system that renders it susceptible to insider illegality and illicit organization as a business racket. 'Living law,' in this instance, combines lawful and unlawful behavior and demonstrates that rules and regulations may be exploited by small independent producers to support their interests even though they do not possess much power or enormous wealth.

This article is organized as follows. First, we discuss our research methods. Second, we outline the regulatory regime governing the lobster fishery and discuss how this has contributed to social conflict between fishers and the Department of Fisheries and Oceans. Third, we define business poaching as one type of poaching organization. Next, we describe the system of law enforcement as it relates to poaching. Then we examine the relationship that business poaching has with the state's law enforcement apparatus: opportunities for illegalities, methods of detection and surveillance, apprehension and preventive capabilities, prosecution, and deterrence. We compare poaching with other forms of workplace crime and show how poaching organizations have effectively mediated law as a field of rules, regulations, and sanctions and have transformed it into an 'enabling structure' for successful illegal or extra-legal activities. Finally, we conclude by discussing the implications that our research has for understanding social crime, the hidden economy, regulatory compliance, and law in action.

## Research methods

Our research is based on the following methods: a historical analysis of government legislation and regulation, an archival study of the DFO prosecution records and legal documents over a ten-year period, a social survey of the entire population of fishery officers and administrators (n = 57) in Southwest Nova Scotia, and a random survey of lobster fishers (n = 100) located in three distinct regions of that same area.

Our research strategy was to obtain information from government sources first and then to obtain the cooperation of local lobster fishers. We gained the assistance of the DFO by meeting with the regional director and explaining our research objectives to him. After some deliberation and meetings with his staff in Halifax and Ottawa, he arranged for us to gain access to sensitive prosecution data, provided they were treated confidentially and reported without attribution. This allowed us to compile a trend analysis of violations in the lobster fishery which documented the following: name, age, sex, and address of offender; type of offense; date and place of offense; offender behavior; law enforcement action; court date; location and name of judge; pleas and dispositions; and dollar value of dispositions. The regional director also contacted area managers under his authority and they in turn arranged for us to gain access to field supervisors and fishery officers. With their cooperation, we conducted detailed interviews with enforcement officers at ten offices in Southwest Nova Scotia. All participants enthusiastically endorsed the research process, and no questions went unanswered. Indeed, we were surprised by the volume of information provided and by the candor with which fishery officers volunteered information to us. They were especially forthright about the organization of illegal fishing and about the capacity of their own organization to enforce the laws against poachers.

The interview schedule for fishery officers consisted of both closed and open-ended questions. Interviews were taped and transcribed and lasted for approximately two hours. Each interview focused on the following: (1) demographic background characteristics; (2) work history and work roles; (3) danger and violence on the job; (4) relations with communities, fishers, and poachers; (5) relations with regulatory bodies and the legal system; and (6) internal organizational relations. The information was collected over a two-year period in accordance with officers' work schedules. The data were then coded, and a ranking index was constructed that measured cooperation and conflict between fishery officers and fishers. We discussed our initial findings, which documented the capacity of the enforcement regime, with senior officials in the DFO and then presented them at the DFO's annual convention. The feedback from this meeting encouraged us to refocus our research on lobster poaching and to include data from the fishers themselves.

We decided to revisit our interviews with fishery officers to determine whether the qualitative information would allow us to map the organizational dimensions of poaching and explain how laws and regulations were transformed into social practices. The data from the interviews were especially detailed and complete. We extracted specific information from each interview, clustered and compared responses according to communities, and developed a typology of poaching organizations. Furthermore, the qualitative data permitted us to piece together a relatively coherent picture of how 'unofficial law' and 'living law' operated at sea, on public wharves, in government offices, and in coastal communities. In particular, it afforded insight into the paradoxes and gaps between law 'in text' and law 'in action' and about how law functioned as a 'facilitative form' for specific poaching enterprises (McBarnet 1993).

While the data collected from official government sources provided a perspective on poaching and law enforcement, they did not include narratives from those who were either fishers or poachers. Obtaining data from fishing communities, however, was not straightforward or easy. Suspicion of outsiders, mistrust of researchers in general, and the continuing conflict between government and fishing communities made access difficult. We solicited support from the Maritime Fishermen's Union (MFU) to overcome these problems. We outlined our project to their research officer and shared our preliminary findings on law enforcement with the union executive. We asked for their participation in the study and assured them that all information would be collected confidentially and reported anonymously. The MFU was relatively receptive to our research endeavor. They were especially concerned about overfishing in the lobster sector and about problems their members were having with law enforcement officials. After a period of deliberation, they endorsed our study. They arranged for us to obtain a list of all registered lobster fishers in Southwest Nova Scotia from the DFO. They identified specific clusters of communities where fishing was intense and overfishing was common. We catalogued these clusters into three distinct areas of Southwest Nova Scotia and employed the services of a research institute to draw a random sample from each area and to arrange for personal interviews with 100 fishers.[1]

Because of enmity between fishing communities and previous researchers, we decided to use interviewers from the local communities to conduct the interviews. We employed the services of the Gorsebrook Research Institute (GRI), an inter-university agency, to help us select interviewers who had research experience in fishing communities. After we designed an interview schedule, we went to Southwest Nova Scotia and held a one-day training session with the three GRI interviewers. We reviewed the questionnaire with them and counseled them on interview skills, techniques, and etiquette. The interviewers were assigned to one area, and each interviewer pretested the interview schedule in communities in his or her area. After the pretest, we returned to Southwest Nova Scotia, analyzed the results, and modified our final interview schedule accordingly.

The interviewers (two females and one male) administered the questionnaire over a four-month period when fishers were not at sea. Relations with the research team were generally cordial and cooperative. Fishers seemed especially interested and eager to state their views on fishing laws, regulations, enforcement, and illegalities. Interviews were conducted in their homes and lasted approximately one hour. Many respondents, however, were reluctant to have their comments tape-recorded. Only one-third agreed to this arrangement; the remainder allowed us to record their answers on the questionnaire schedule.

Each interview contained closed and open-ended questions and focused on the following: (1) demographic background characteristics; (2) work history in the lobster fishery; (3) cooperation and competition in harvesting the resource; (4) the regulations and laws governing lobstering; (5) the organization of poaching; and (6) the capacity of the state to detect, apprehend, charge, convict, and sanction illegal fishing.

The data from these interviews added enormously to our portrayal of poaching organizations. In particular, they allowed us to detail the illegal techniques of poaching; the size of poaching teams; the economic value of business poaching; the relations between front-line suppliers and background operators in the organization of business poaching; the modus vivendi that business poachers have with the state, the community, and other fishers; and the capacity of business poachers to either neutralize the law or use it to their advantage.

## Regulation and social conflict in the lobster fishery

The commercial lobster fishery was founded in the mid-nineteenth century and managed by a laissez-faire approach. Few regulations governed the commons, and community customs structured the rights of access, management, and stock protection. Informal norms among fishers set the fishing boundaries, defined the shares of the commons, and limited the harvesting effort. Fishers established informal property rights to territoriality, community exclusivity, and local fish stocks (Acheson 1975, 1987, 1988; Martin 1979). Relatively stable moral economies, organized on a harbor-by-harbor basis, established definite insider/outsider rules and provided mutual welfare and folk wisdom about the sea and its resources that amounted to a code of fishing conduct (Davis and Kasdan 1984; McCay 1978, 1984; Mathews and Phyne 1988; Miller and Van Maanen 1979). This code guarded territory closely and punished interlopers informally and at times severely. Sanctions were quick, and transgressors were forced out or put out of business. In the end, common use rights to piscary were not open to all, but they were exclusive to community-defined groups that cooperatively managed the resource (Ciriacy-Wantrup and Bishop 1975; Davis and Kasdan 1984). By the mid-1880s, lobster fishing began to undergo a major transformation. Markets expanded, canneries proliferated, and landings, landed values, and fish prices escalated. Technological innovations in the form of gas engine boats and closed-end hoop nets increased fishing capacity and allowed for more efficiency and effectiveness. Stocks were heavily fished inshore as well as in the near shore. Capitalization of the resource eroded the communal use rights of lobster fishers. Privatization controlled by cannery operators 'established implicit property rights over particular fishing grounds' (Scott and Tugwell 1981: 26). The state, for its part, sought to manage the commons by introducing regulatory measures: district controls, seasonal closures, lobster size restrictions, trap size capture rules, and prohibitions on harvesting egg-bearing lobsters (DeWolf 1974; Scott and Tugwell 1981). From 1873 to 1927, the federal government used legislation, commissions, and regulations to diminish the informal comanagement responsibilities of fishers and to gradually establish itself as *the* sole manager of the resource.

The years between 1927 and 1960 were ones of further state intervention. Legislation and regulations calibrated the carapace length size, restricted lobster fishing to one season a year, reterritorialized lobster fishing grounds, and regulated the use of gear and vessels more intensively. As Scott and Tugwell (1981: 27) note, 'Capital, vessel and gear mobility were drastically restricted by the introduction of a regulation which stated that no one could use in lobster fishing any boats, traps, or other lobster fishing equipment that had been used during that year in lobster fishing operations in any other lobster district.' Furthermore, the post-World War II period ushered in state-supported financial and social welfare plans and policies for fishers, including trap insurance schemes; guaranteed low-interest loans for gear, boats, and engines; subsidies for new vessel construction; assistance for storage, equipment, maintenance, and bait; and unemployment insurance premiums.

The period from 1960 to the present refined and reconfirmed these measures and added new regulations that prohibited possession of lobsters out of season, prevented vessels from transporting lobsters without permission, outlawed hauling lobster traps on Sundays, and forbade fishing by means other than lobster traps. Most important, the panoply of regulations was accompanied by an extensive and controversial tag trap limitation program and an ambitious, limited-entry licensing program. These programs were designed to control fleet capacity, size, and mobility in what had become a lucrative corporate fishery with large vessels possessing sophisticated engines, radar, depth sounders, and parlor traps. Southwest Nova Scotia trap limits ranged over the years from 250 to 375 to 425 per boat, per fisher (McEachern 1969).

Trap limits were immediately followed by the implementation of *boat* licensing rather than *fisher* licensing. Class B licenses were issued to all boats with less than 100, 75, or 50 traps. Class A licenses were issued to 'all boats with a number of traps greater than the upper limit for Class B licenses' (Scott and Tugwell 1981: 29). When a Class B boat was no longer used for lobster fishing, the license was not renewed. When a Class A boat stopped lobster fishing, the boat as well as the license was sold and the government reserved the right to buy back boats and to retire licenses (Scott and Tugwell 1981:29). The effect of this policy was to phase out 'moonlighters' and part-time fishers, but not to eliminate the number of Class A lobster boats that accounted for most of the harvesting effort (DeWolf 1974: 26). As a result, incomes for lobster fishers stayed low and capture capacity remained high. By 1977, the government reconsidered its boat licensing policy and reverted to licensing fishers; however, the previous trap limits for boats were carried forward and allocated to individual fishers. Thus A-licensed fishers were designated as full-time, B-licensed holders were considered part-time, and the new category C-licensed fishers was created for those who had acquired a registered lobster fishing vessel after 1968 but were not eligible for either A or B licenses.

By 1980, regulations were legion and complex. To many fishers, these state interventions were confusing, cumbersome and a curb on their rights to harvest the resource. As Hanson and Lamson (1984: 5) note, '[t]his resulted in a climate of uncertainty with rules applied and quotas assigned in a manner not clearly perceived by all participants as being either equitable or efficient.' Furthermore, the declaration of a 200-mile offshore economic zone by the federal government in 1977 rapidly capitalized the already competitive primary and secondary fishing sectors in the lobster industry. Fishers in the in-shore and nearshore small-boat sector were encouraged to invest in better equipment and larger vessels. At government behest, they borrowed large amounts of money from loan boards to finance these ventures. More and more fishers became dependent on financial institutions and government programs for the acquisition for their capital outlay and fishing technologies (Stiles 1972; Davis and Kasdan 1984: 113). Although these programs were designed to rationalize capacity and increase incomes, they ultimately created a severe debt-dependent situation for fishers. As Davis and Kasdan (1984: 112) put it, this relationship was 'a tightening noose from the fishermen's perspective.'

These government initiatives contributed to the restructuring of property relations in the lobster fishery. The communal use right to piscary was usurped and replaced with private property and state property rights (MacPherson 1978: 4–5, 201). By creating a system of selective licensing and establishing a *privilege* to fish, the right to the commons was transformed into the private property of the fisher, albeit a highly restricted right to access and harvest the resources. Indeed, private ownership was strengthened when the government sanctioned the transfer of the right to fish to others for profit. Thus one could 'buy out of' and 'buy into' the lobster fishery. However, the rights of owners did not include management rights normally associated with property. According to Marchak (1987: 5), '[f]ishers do not make the crucial decisions with respect to the resource, control of habitat and water ways, allocation of licenses, and limitations on capture capacities.' These were claimed by the state and bureaucratically imposed on the private user. But unlike the community, governments are institutionally committed to manage not one resource but many, not one use but many; and they are required to balance, negotiate, and decide about conflicting interests outside of the fishery such as logging and mining (Marchak 1989: 10). Thus, for most resources, the issue for government is not conservation in perpetuity, or comanagement for communities, but administration for profits and long-term fiscal success.

In effect, these legal tools and regulatory instruments were used to exercise social control over customary productive and local management practices, and they quickly produced collision, conflict, and disorder between fishers, communities, and the state.[2] In legal terms, this privilege to fish conveyed inclusion and exclusion and constituted categories of violators that were previously nonexistent but that were increasingly subject to sanctions: the communal poachers, who had no license to fish or fished out of season; the outlaw poachers, who fished as they pleased and were a law unto themselves; and the business poachers, who did not abide by the rules or regulations about lobster size and trap limits.

## Poaching organizations

Poaching then includes acts committed by noncommercial and commercial fishers who violate seasonal and area closures, trap and gear restrictions, lobster size restrictions, and licensing rules. In previous research, we analyzed communal, outlaw, and business poaching organizations in considerable detail.[3] *Communal poaching*, we found, is a steady, routine activity perceived as a 'natural' event in many maritime communities. As one fishery officer put it, '[i]f poaching is not repeated every day or night and the proceeds not sold, the poachers are left alone by the community. That is a policy that has been here for hundreds of years ... and before regulations.' Communal poachers are not, then, normally rich or strangers. They are known to neighbors, family, and kin. They poach for subsistence or to supplement a low income or wage. The primary method of social control, therefore, is containment – to keep their poaching activity within community traditions and to integrate their deviant activities into an acceptable norm (Netboy 1968; Hay 1977; Howkins 1979; Taylor 1981, 1987). The division of labor is elementary – usually a small team of two or three people, although single poachers are not uncommon. Poaching work of this type is regular and unhurried. Communal poachers use nonviolent techniques of stealth, accept small returns, and poach for personal or family consumption.

*Outlaw poaching*, we discovered, is 'troublesome' to commercial fishers and to many fishing communities. These poachers cannot rely on communal goodwill to avoid detection or censure (Kuperan and Sutinen 1998). Like communal poachers, most outlaw poachers are not commercial fishers. But unlike the former, their poaching is for profit. The principal method of social control is usually exclusion. Outlaw poaching functions on the margins of a community or in the spaces between them. Even though outlaw poachers have access to vast, remote, and nonpoliced fishing spaces and the equivalent of safe havens or sanctuaries, they still need to interact with the communities against which they are poachers. They require equipment, supplies, and accomplices to dispose of their illegal catch. To emerge safely from these face-to-face encounters, outlaw poachers make use of superior technology (better boats, equipment, and communications), superior force (violence or the threat of collective violence), and superior strategic planning (nocturnal fishing, fishing in remote areas, appropriating licensed traps, and calibrating escape techniques to evade the law).

So outlaw poachers are in a precarious position. They have to be ready to take flight to evade detection, yet they have to devise routine practices of poaching. They cannot be constantly on the move, nor can they afford a high-risk game of capture and reprisal. Unlike other types of rural or maritime deviants who are 'open' about what they do, outlaw poachers devise deceitful techniques to minimize their personal risk (Hobsbawm 1969; Hay 1977; O'Malley 1979; Best 1980; Taylor 1981; McCay 1984; Peace 1996).

Their division of labor is more complex than communal poaching. Typically, outlaw poaching involves fairly permanent teams of between three and six people largely drawn from family or kin relations. Their organization requires positions for tacticians and strategic planners who ensure security of operations and merchandising of catches to local and regional markets. However, outlaw poachers are more likely to resort to coercion in managing relations with other fishers and law enforcement officers (Cressey 1972; McIntosh 1975; Best and Luckenbill 1982; Jones 1982; Sharpe 1984: 121–31).

Poaching as a *business enterprise*, however, is conceived of, planned and carried out by full-time, licensed commercial fishers who supply illegal catches as part of their lawful fishing activities. Organizationally, it overlaps with other forms of commercial and regulatory practices and procedures that are structured by normative activities such as fishing for a livelihood, interacting with other resource users, responding to the regulatory requirements of sea-level bureaucrats, cooperating with law enforcement people, and so on. Business poaching, which is essentially a violation of trap quotas or carapace length requirements, is embedded within the social relations that make up normal lobstering. The full-time, routine working relationships of fishing provide the environment for conducting illegal activities. Business poachers are not full-time miscreants; unlike outlaw poachers, illegal lobstering is not their major occupational role.

Business poaching, then, is not a separate illicit organization; it is a subterranean one whose illegal activities blend into the normal intersecting processes of fish harvesting, production, and distribution. Victims – that is, other fishers and members of the community – know what is occurring. The compliance literature suggests that about 10% of fishers persistently violate major regulations around trap and gear allocations, quotas, seasonal closures, catch size, and, in the case of the lobster fishery, carapace length and egg-bearing lobsters. The other fishers generally comply, exhibiting lower violation rates, but they rarely intervene to prevent overfishing (Sutinen and Kuperan 1989; Feldman 1993; Sutinen, Rieser, and Gauvin 1990; Kuperan and Sutinen 1998). So in the short run, the burden of prevention falls on the state, and business poachers are chiefly in conflict with the state rather than with communal entities, although they are concerned to contain their rival – the outlaw poacher. Insofar as they wish to develop a sideline operation into a poaching business, they must garner support and cultivate cooperation *within* the existing institutions with which they constantly interact. In McIntosh's (1973:40) words, '[a] racket operates almost like a legal business.'

## Law enforcement practices, communal poaching, and outlaw poaching

The task of enforcing the law against poaching in Southwest Nova Scotia is in the hands of unarmed fishery officers and their supervisory and administrative staff, who have to police about 1,700 registered fishers located in approximately 185 communities spread out over 2,500 miles of coastline.[4] Resource management and conservation is organized by an area concept. At the apex of this scheme is an area manager who reports directly to a regional director of fisheries operations. The area manager's responsibilities include consulting with fishers and processors regarding changes and amendments to fishery regulations. The staff consists of an administrative assistant, a senior advisor of policy program and development, a statistical coordinator, and a licensing liaison administrative officer, as well as a chief enforcement officer and an area inspection chief who report directly to the area manager. Four field supervisors, in turn, report directly to the chief enforcement officer, and each has a staff consisting of licensing clerks, operations officers, statistical officers, and fishery officers. Southwest Nova Scotia has 49 officers engaged in frontline enforcement.

The chief methods of law enforcement in the lobster fishery are boat patrols, wharf checks, stakeouts, informants, community watch programs, and special task forces. Boat patrols are used to survey harbors, bays, inlets, and easily accessible open waters. Boats are not standardized, and the fleet consists of

14- and 16-foot aluminum vessels, 20-foot skiffs, small speed boats, Boston whalers, Cape Island vessels, and the occasional 42-foot vessel with a captain and engineer aboard. These boats are used to check licenses, fishing locations, trap quotas, tagged gear in the water, safety equipment, and illegal catches. Boat patrols occur primarily in the spring and are conducted 1 to 3 miles from shore. According to one fishery officer, 'We all take our turn on the boats … and we pretty well work the whole area depending upon what fishery is dominant.' However, the fleet is rarely deployed in offshore waters, and it lacks both the personnel and the capacity to tow boats and haul traps on trawls. In the words of one field supervisor,

> You are going to hear the same complaint from everyone, and that is the lack of personnel and equipment to do the job. Right here all we have are small patrol boats … skiffs up to 20 feet, and we have no capability for hauling gear that is out there and no capability to go far out to sea. … I have four fishery officers here and I need a minimum of six.

Not surprisingly, dock checks at public wharves are the primary tool of law enforcement. They are used to regulate seasonal openings and closures, verify licenses and registrations, monitor gear before it is set in the water, seize illegal traps and tags, manage landed catches and, where appropriate, issue warnings for violations. One fishery officer recounted,

> Prior to November 30 (opening day of the lobster season), about a month and a half we are busy issuing new tags, registering vessels, and so on … and then through the first two or three days we are looking mainly for untagged gear. … We more or less show the flag on the wharf, and hopefully discourage a few people who may think about using untagged gear or are thinking of getting a jump on others in leaving early for the fishing grounds.

Fishery officers also charge most fishers on or near the wharf for violations of the Fisheries Act.

> You get a guy with short lobsters on board the boat and if they are segregated when he comes into port there is definite intent. If the short lobsters are found in his truck and you know they came off his boat … you're going to get a conviction. … Once you get away from the high tide mark, you are going to get a conviction.

Stakeouts, where officers conceal their presence, are additional investigative and enforcement techniques that either anticipate where illegal activity will occur or allow apprehension in the act. General stakeouts involve setting up proactive checkpoints on either sea or land. Undercover tactics include dressing as civilians, using unmarked vehicles, and deploying unknown vessels to survey, approach, and apprehend poachers. As one officer remarked, 'With outlaw poachers, I try to apprehend them on the water because there is no way they are going to be apprehended on the wharf. If I do that I'm going to have a big fight on my hands.' Stakeouts are often difficult to organize. They are costly, time-consuming, and labor-intensive. They involve overtime, night work, backup, and planning, yet they only cover specific incidents and limited coastal areas. As one officer stated, 'It takes a special time, you might go in there 12 hours early and just lie there and wait or you have to go in the middle of the night.' Communication equipment is described as 'the peanut system.' It is either absent or antiquated with limited range, poor transmission quality, and no central operating node. Two other officers observed,

> There is one night scope within the whole district and when you need it, try and find it! ... If I get down on the eastern side of —— bay below the granite outcrop I can't reach anyone by radio ... We have no 24-hour monitoring system so if you are working up in —— at 2 o'clock in the morning and you need help or assistance, you can't get it. You're just by yourself, so you can be in a pretty bad situation.

So general stakeouts are relatively ineffective in detecting violations, apprehending poachers, enabling prosecutions, and registering convictions. Indeed, it is not uncommon for stakeouts to be 'staked out' by poachers who monitor officers' movements and communications on scanners. While driving to a stakeout, one officer almost struck a deer on the highway. He radioed his fellow officers about the incident and later that evening three local fishers asked, 'How big was that buck that almost struck you?' All in all, stakeouts result in charges less than half the time they are used.

Informants are also used to control poaching. Typically, information is offered individually and secretly, and is shared in the normal course of work activities. From time to time fishers pass on information anonymously by telephone or through third parties. In rare cases where violations cannot be managed by community persuasion, formal collective reporting may occur. One officer noted, 'I had at least fifty fishermen come in here and tell me about one fellow who was setting well over his limit on trawl and they went so far as to offer their boats to me to see for myself.'

In some areas where poaching is low, informants account for the discovery of four out of every five cases of illegal activity. 'We need the eyes of the fishers and the communities ... Without them we might not hear about violations until two or three months later,' stated one regional supervisor. So the majority of informants are usually fishers and fish plant managers who are cultivated as regular 'snitches' by fishery officers.

> You seldom stumble across a poacher. You stake them out. ... I received word on Saturday from a fisherman that poachers had illegal lobsters and were going to take them out of the water. So we set up a stakeout ... in plain clothes and no government vehicles. It was strictly a dropoff situation. You drop officers off at various places along the shore where you suspect something is going to be happening and where you have good visibility. You watch the poachers go out, do their poaching, and come in. ... You have maintained continuity of that vessel that hauled the traps until you get to the beach. Then you move in!

However, in other areas where poaching is intense and communities are close-knit, there is little information exchange. One officer explained,

> The people around here are very closed-mouth and they won't tell you a great deal ... They won't complain like in other areas. ... If you are not aware of the problem, you can't do very much about it. You can't identify a problem if there are no complaints.

In these communities, informants are typically members of the general public and not from the fishing industry. Another officer emphasized, 'There is a lot of fear of reporting poachers ... I find the people who complain to me are not fishermen. ... Out of fifty-five fishermen maybe, just maybe, three or four report things.' Taken together, the use of informants is a commonplace enforcement practice whose success varies from one community to another.

The difficulty in acquiring reliable and systematic information about poaching has led the DFO to institute a formal 'Report a Poacher' program. This anonymous telephone exchange initiative operates 24 hours a day and offers financial rewards for information that leads to convictions. This information, in turn, has enabled fishery officers to enhance surveillance and organize specific stakeouts. One officer explained,

> A lot of time people won't give you information directly, but will hint at something ... you have to almost read between the lines and figure out who is doing what ... they tell you maybe you should drive in there, or maybe you should ask where so and so was last night at 7 o'clock.

Ironically, many telephone calls have directed fishery officers to sites where no illegalities have occurred or were made by disputing parties to enact revenge for past grievances. The program has been more symbolic than instrumental and has been the least effective law enforcement tool in detecting and apprehending violators. According to one officer, 'No information came from calls on the Zenith number ... to me a fishery officer has to be in a community at least five years before he develops any rapport and a system is up that he can actively use to get information.'

Finally, the government deploys an operational task force to patrol, survey, and assist law officers in apprehending poachers. As the area manager reported, 'The idea is to centralize resources in one office and create an organization that is designed to support everyone else.' The tactical unit is composed of about thirty people and is equivalent to a mobile strike force. Typically, the task force draws four or five officers from its registry and moves them from one area to another. It is equipped with the latest advanced technology and equipment, including 42-foot patrol vessels, helicopters, night scopes, and communication devices. The task force gathers intelligence, conducts aerial surveillance, bolsters normal law enforcement routines, and manages periodic social crises in the fishery (Perrier and McMullan 1996; Arai 1990, 1994; Phyne 1992: 529, 530). It is primarily deployed in the ground fishery and is only used for lobster enforcement when there are collective mobilizations by angry fishers and their organizations. It is most effective as a reactive mechanism to anticipated disorder, but it is an uncertain method to proactively enforce lobster regulations on a daily basis. The unit takes too much time to assemble and plan its activities, and task force members have to overcome their lack of familiarity with the target areas before they can be effective in translating law into an enforcement practice.

All three types of poaching organizations have shown a remarkable capacity for survival and for avoiding and evading the law enforcement regime. Fishing out of season without a license and with untagged gear are violations of the Fisheries Act. If they are not careful, communal poachers can attract the attention of fishery officers. However, evading the law is not too difficult because the law is seldom there to be evaded in the first place. As Sutinen and Gauvin (1989) and Furlong (1991) observe, the typical odds of being caught violating fishery regulations are below 1% and often at or near zero. There are so many coastal communities to regulate that the state can have only a distant and indirect connection to most of them. Furthermore, the community often operates to shield the communal poacher from law enforcement techniques. The presence of the fishery officer is typically greeted with warnings – car horns, radio alerts, and the like. Poaching simply desists until the coast is clear. The small scale and non-threatening nature of communal poaching means that it is often undetected. Commercial fishers are unlikely to sanction or betray local communal poachers to the state because they poach for personal use and do not threaten the commercial fishery (Martin 1979; Phyne 1990). Law enforcement agencies, for their part, cannot rely on good information from the community to track down leads, develop surveillance, or plan stakeouts. Even wharf checks and sea patrols have only a limited impact on communal poachers. They easily avoid the public docks where fishery officers are likely to be stationed. They effectively land their illegal catches at many points along the shore. They escape detection while fishing illegally by monitoring the whereabouts of fishery officers and scrupulously avoiding them, and by skillfully concealing, even destroying incriminating evidence in order to poach another day.

Outlaw poachers also keep away from law enforcement officers who are interested in bringing them to account. Not only do they fish covertly at night, or in out-of-the-way places and at irregular times of the year, but they also evade detection while they are at work. They fish outside the limited geographical and tactical reach of the DFO. As one officer remarked, 'We really don't have the capacity to inspect and apprehend; our equipment is still in the dark ages ... it is like having an RCMP [Royal Canadian Mounted Police] constable in a four-cylinder car try to catch speeders.' Nor is it easy to secure evidence against outlaw poachers. The L Flag procedure, which required all vessels to cease fishing and make ready for boarding and inspection, no longer applies to domestic vessels. 'Poachers see us coming,' declared one officer, and 'they just outrun us or they throw everything overboard.' A fisher from one community summed up the difficulties: 'We talk about it, we swear about it, but you can't catch them guys. We did report them. The fishery officers tried, couldn't catch them.'

Outlaw poachers also use superior force in evading the law. 'The outlaws are poaching all the time,' complained one officer. 'We've been rammed by them, and in one case they tried to sink us.' Another fishery officer recounted a similar episode:

> One night on a stakeout, we saw two fellows fishing illegally. I had a night scope with me and we came to arrest this guy. He tried to kick me in the groin. I deflected the kick. ... On another occasion ... this guy had untagged gear on board and I tried to seize the trap as evidence but he got a hold of the other end. He told me ... in no uncertain terms that the trap was going to stay with him and it was his property, and there was no way I was going to get it, even if it meant a fistfight.

Nor is violence restricted to the act of poaching. It can occur against law enforcement officials away from the job. One officer had all the windows in his house smashed, a second had his tires slashed three times, a third received harassing phone calls, a fourth faced an arson threat, and a fifth was warned to watch out for his safety. As one officer stated, 'Outlaw poachers are a different breed ... with the commercial fishermen, they are more sophisticated ... you don't have the violent confrontations.'

In sum, enough people are ready and able to form a 'subculture of resistance' within which techniques of outlaw poaching can be refined and passed on from generation to generation. One senior fishery officer put it as follows:

> In these harbors there are strong cultures ... and it is part of the local culture ... they have much less tolerance of the law. ... They think they have a right to fish even if they do not hold a license. ... I think it has a lot to do with the grandfather, the father, and the son who always fished as they pleased.

## Business poaching and law enforcement

The business poacher cannot evade state control by working stealthily, counting on the quick escape, or directly confronting enforcement officers, as do outlaw poachers. Because the techniques for obtaining illegal lobsters are often a series of 'insider work crimes,' such as exceeding conventional gear limits; manipulating government tags on lobster traps; overstating trap losses due to bad weather, frigid temperatures, and routine hauling; and concealing illegal gear in the water (i.e., untagged traps), business poachers use and manipulate the law rather than avoid or evade it.

## Lobstering and insider illegality

Two major factors underpinning lobstering render it susceptible to insider illegality. First, the entire process occurs in a context whereby actions and settings are privatized. Self-regulation is the preferred method of harvesting the resource and preserving law and order in the fishery. Little control from above is exerted over the structure of fishing activity. The bureaucratic organization of the state is less than a coherent and integrated system. Overall coordination and oversight are lacking. Gaps between 'on the water' enforcement and administrative centers and between state policies and their implementation are many and easily exploited by fishers. A large variety of innovative rules, shortcuts, and legal neutralizations occur at the interstices of law enforcement and fishing activities. These legal maneuvers result in the formation of discrete informal lines of action, communication, influence, and control that both enable and routinize business poaching (Chambliss 1973: 353–80, 1978). As Kuperan and Sutinen (1998:310) observe, '[p]assion, inadvertence and accident rarely cause a fishery violation; most are the result of deliberate choice.'

Second, not only is lobstering an 'encapsulated system' – operating with its own set of rules within a larger system – it is also a relatively solitary activity (Acheson 1987). Most lobster fishers fish alone or in small work crews (two to three people) from diesel-powered boats equipped with depth sounders, hydraulic haulers, ship-to-shore radios, and compasses. Lobsters are caught in wooden traps or 'pots' about three or four feet long and made of oak frames covered with hardwood slats or vinyl-covered wire. Typically, lobster fishers have 350 to 425 legal traps each. On a calm day a lobster fisher might haul 100 to 200 traps (Acheson 1987).

Work activities, however, vary greatly from season to season. In winter months lobstering is much more difficult, distant from the shore, dangerous, and unprofitable. Spring and late fall are unquestionably the busiest months of the year, when traps are near shore, more plentiful, and pulled frequently. Although most lobster fishers move their traps according to this general pattern, they are not all equally productive. Experience, as well as ability and willingness to work, greatly affect catches and income. As Acheson (1987: 39) notes, '[I]n some instances skilled fishermen catch more than twice as many lobsters as unskilled fisherman with the same number of traps in the same territory.'

While licensing, seasonal closures, and trap quotas regulate the work habits of lobster fishers, territoriality also limits production. Competition for fishing bottom has resulted in diverse territorial arrangements ranging from relatively open, nucleated, and mixed fishing patterns to closed, exclusive, perimeter-defended patterns (Acheson 1987: 42–45). This has led to the formation of 'harbor gangs,' who carefully guard fishing space, regulate resource ecology, monitor boundary disputes, and limit newcomers. Most conflicts, regardless of their size and intensity, are resolved informally and privately, although not always peacefully. Suspicion of outsiders is strong among many lobster fishers, as is the feeling that they do not need added mediators to control competition or manage the commons. Silence and secrecy are the preferred methods of coping with trouble. Even the victims of territorial disputes remain mum. The immediate working team and the harbor community are the basic units of loyalty, friendship, and policing (Acheson 1987, 1988).

Processes of boundary maintenance and change, as well as the seasonal movement of gear and the daily routines of setting and hauling traps, occur without much direct state supervision or oversight. While this allows for a regime of self-regulation for and by fishers, it also permits the modification of rules and procedures independent of local, state overseers (Acheson 1987: 39). Fishers can step outside their formally mandated work relations and techniques, acquiring in the process enormous non-delegated and unofficial powers. As one fisher observed, 'Poachers that are licensed fishermen … they are proud of it … the only reason they do it is because they know they can get away with it … nobody checks … the officers are not around when you set them (traps) or when you haul them in.' It is these very features of lobstering – encapsulation, isolation, silence, suspicion of outsiders, and an absence of supervision from above – that contain the possibilities for routine, self-righteous, illegal profiteering by insiders.

## Poaching as a business organization

Poaching as a business racket includes skippers, family members, crew, fish buyers, and other distributors who operate informally and loosely in a network of common interest and purpose. A conservative estimate places the number of involved participants in any given setup at five to seven. They compose a rather flexible organizational unit, and their power is local and shapeless. The rackets are small, relatively discrete units, infiltrating and operating parallel to established spheres of harvesting and distribution, and any given community has multiple operators and multiple competitors. As one officer noted, 'The problem of poaching for profit is not restricted to any one community … it is spreading all along the coast … you have more boats, more gear, more traps on the boats, and the attitude out there among fishermen seems to be to hell with the regulations.'

Lobster pounds and fish plants in coastal communities are very much part of the racketeering networks. They link the illegal supply brought about by overfishing to a legitimate marketplace. Illegal catches are often logged and certified as legal inventories and then transported by air or by road to cities like Halifax, Boston, and Montreal. One fishery officer noted,

> Buyers tend to overlook the illegal activities of fishermen because they have nothing to lose by being caught with lobsters that were caught in untagged lobster traps. Once the lobsters are in the plant, who is to know … you don't have to doctor records, the more for them [fish buyers] to take to the United States and the more profit for everyone.

The overall operation requires few expenditures. Expensive items such as labor, capital, expertise, equipment, and technology are not needed. Legitimate lobstering activities and associations provide the know-how, contacts, material outlay, and legitimations. Financial arrangements mirror those of the normal market. They are backed by a continuous organization with local and national agents who are experienced in finding purchasers (Mack 1972; Cohen 1977; Munsche 1981; Sharpe 1984: 127–31).

Social ties in the poaching organization are instrumental, and recruitment to this form of poaching is relatively open – a form of controlled friend/kin sponsorship. Some skippers, crews, and fish plants run tight operations. For others, the circle of accomplices is wider and more flexible. The production of illegal catches in some communities is constant, while in others it is intermittent. For example, many ports in Digby County and the northern portion of Yarmouth County report catches that are within the lawful limit, while many ports in the southern regions of Yarmouth County and in the northern part of Shelburne County report trap usage that is on average 100 to 200 traps above the 400-trap limit (Kearney 1988: 7–8). This system of deteriorating compliance is consistent with Gauvin and Bean's estimates that about 10% of the fishers in the Massachusetts lobster and Rhode Island clam fisheries are frequent violators and that 30 to 40% are occasional violators (cited in Kuperan and Sutinen 1998: 330, 311).

Insofar as fish plant owners and managers are involved in the illegal businesses, they work regularly and normally. Most fishers, as well as other community members, know what buyers are up to and cooperate with them over a period of time. For example, collusion between small draggers, trucking firms, and fish buyers is not uncommon. Class C draggers and scallop boats periodically drag the lobster areas to supplement their income, then off-load the crates onto trucks and move them to different fish plants for merchandising. As one fishery officer observed,

> The problem is catching them ... the commercial crime section of the RCMP is checking local fish plant records but they supply false documents when caught ... and we charged the manager and owner of this plant, and by the way the fish was trucked from a small dragger that had landed in Lunenburg. The plant had their truck there to pick up the load, but they lied to us ... I think the skipper will pay the fine as will the fishing company. After all, what's $5,000 ... they can make up the loss later.

While this illegal fishing certainly aggravates relations between lobster fishers and the small boat ground-fish fleet, it also demonstrates the desire to make illicit profiteering part and parcel of known regularized enterprises. Unlike rackets that surround small-time embezzlement or blackmail, where restricted customers get to hear of the illegal businesses and where the scale of the racket is severely limited, the lobster rackets strive to be organized on a permanent and continuous business basis.

The collaboration of the victim is crucial to the organizational potential of business rackets (McIntosh 1973: 35–69). This raises the question of why those with a self-interest in compliance are unwilling or unable to betray the poacher to the state and support stronger law enforcement. In many coastal communities, noncompliance is not a major problem. Even though violations are hard for officials to observe and act upon, most fishers in these communities live within the limits of the law. However, in the resource-rich lobster fishing areas of Southwest Nova Scotia, the pattern of compliance is different and problematic, for three compelling reasons.

First, many fishers claim a cognizance of business poaching and for a time at least tolerate it because they do not see violations as causing immediate and obvious harm to the fish stocks. One fishery officer remarked,

> The lack of control exercised by fishers over lobster poachers and licensed fishers infringing the regulations ... reflects the abundance of the resource over the past few years.

Appeals to community loyalty, tradition, and knowledge; to local trust and cooperation; and to the need to stay competitive further seduce the reluctant ones to participate in overfishing or at least to stay silent about it. As one fisher stated,

> The worst problem we get is poaching by fishermen ... when you abide by the law and you see a fellow coming in with twice the catch and nothing happens, what can you do? How can you remain honest? ... So you just shut up about it and go about your own business.

Indeed, the social reputation of a lobster fisher is not likely to be affected if the fisher poaches in communities where large numbers of fishers are also poaching and where communities acquiesce to this type of behavior (Kuperan and Sutinen 1998: 321–22).

Second, fishers are often reluctant to report illegal overfishing because they have little confidence that the state can do anything about it (Taylor 1987: 295, 303, 304; Furlong 1991; Sutinen, Rieser, and Gauvin 1990). As Kearney (1988:9) notes, '[t]he vast majority of fishermen are in favor of a trap limit and strict enforcement of that limit ... however when faced with competition from the fishermen who do not respect the limit and who are not likely to be charged by the DFO the average fisherman feels forced to put more traps in the water in order to remain competitive.' Nonviolators must compete with violators for fish resources, and when the outcome of the regulation 'favors one group against another it erodes the legitimacy the individuals in that group grant to the institutions enforcing the regulation, thus increasing non-compliance' (Kuperan and Sutinen 1998: 325). The process of illegal fishing as a business racket then spirals upward and outward from that mistrust of state power. Furthermore, the fishers involved in business poaching actually possess a perceived level of legitimate power that exceeds that of the state. One fishery officer put it astutely:

> Overfishing has a lot to do with the culture of the area. ... The people that are held up as heroes in their community are the people who catch the most fish, the people who spend the most money, and those who fight for the most or talk the loudest. Their lifestyle is one of 'fight back.'

Finally, threats and intimidation are also present in coastal communities where business poaching thrives. Most fishers in these communities also know that illegal entrepreneurs can resort to strong sanctions to ensure silence and support for their poaching activities. 'Semi-isolation and intolerance of the law,' according to one area manager, 'breeds the Wild West spirit.' This contributes to what another DFO official called the 'fear factor.' 'There is a lot of fear reporting poachers ... that gear will be damaged or their boats, or [that] the heads of their traps will be cut off.' This in turn discourages communal betrayal of poachers to the state. As one fisher put it,

> I say 75 percent of us would ignore them. It isn't worth the risk of squealing on one. I got an investment in my boat and lobster gear of $150,000, he [the business poacher] could damage that.

So the self-regulation regime among lobster fishers seems to accommodate the illegal violations of the business poacher, provided, of course, that the illegalities do not destroy the commons for everyone.

### Using, manipulating, and neutralizing laws

Poaching operations on this scale, of course, cannot remain unknown to state agencies, so the possibility of this kind of lawbreaking flourishing depends not only on secrecy and invisibility but also on the inability of the state to suppress it. To start, the law is often confusing and confounding. The Fisheries Act, the specific lobster regulations, and the variation orders add up to a complex, bewildering, and ever-changing amalgam of legal rules, programs, and procedures (Phyne 1990; Arai 1994; Perrier and McMullan 1996). What is a regulation or a rule one day may not be the next, and officers at any given time may not know what is appropriate or inappropriate conduct. As one area supervisor observed,

> The system has become so complicated that it feeds itself on paper. ... It is difficult for one or any fishery officer to do our jobs now ... this year the sum total of changes in variation orders has been around thirty. Changes in some fisheries, changes in the quotas, changes in vessel quotas, and changes in the season; every time a variation order comes in now it is to correct something in the regulations ... the system is now sort of consuming itself.

If regulations and rules are complicated and ambiguous, then procedures required to determine guilt are no more obvious. In the lobster fishery, it is illegal to catch undersize lobsters. Fishers are supposed to measure their catch immediately upon removal from a trap and return immature and egg-bearing lobsters to the sea. But a legal decision of due diligence (R v. Belliveau 1986) now exempts them from having to do so until the first appropriate opportunity. This has made charging for undersize lobsters a virtual impossibility. As one officer stated, 'Judges felt it wouldn't be logical to measure their lobsters immediately because of poor weather conditions and so unless a fisherman segregates his 'shorts,' he has no fear of interference from us at sea, and even if he lands them at the wharf and can drum up a good enough story, he walks.' The due diligence decision also makes it hard to enforce regulations regarding untagged traps. A fishery officer has to prove intent to use the traps

430

illegally. Business poachers easily claim that they did not know that the gear was untagged when it was in the water, or that the tags were removed by normal wear and tear. In the words of one senior officer, 'It is really difficult to establish strict liability ... we are now in a situation that unless you're with the boat from the time a fisherman leaves until he comes back, you can't really prove in court that he caught fish illegally.' The DFO is losing 4 out of 5 cases brought to court. 'It is a free-for-all,' reported a fishery officer, 'Chances are fishermen are going to be found not guilty.'

Moreover, the nature of much fishery law and regulation is administrative and thus similar to tax laws, drug legislation, and environmental regulations (Department of Fisheries and Oceans 1990). The state is the primary victim, and fishery officers seldom obtain testimony from others to lay a charge. They rarely seek convictions unless they have actually witnessed an infraction, and so they are slow to follow up on information received from the community (Grimshaw and Jefferson 1987: 52). This gives rise to the perception among fishers that the government is unable to properly manage the commons and police poachers. Fishery officers, as a result, have low public credibility. They possess a weak and ambiguous authority. Their self-presentation at sea creates discrepant definitions. Unable to exert their duties forcefully, they are often denounced or disbelieved (Arai 1994; Phyne 1988, 1990, 1992; Perrier and McMullan 1996). One fisher remarked, 'I don't know how they can enforce them [sic] lobster regulations. I haven't seen a fishery officer on the wharf in God only knows how long ... over two years.' By contrast, fishery officers are the objects of surveillance by fishers. Their routines and whereabouts are tracked by walkie-talkies, ship-to-shore radios, telephones, and vehicles. As one fisher stated, 'We know where the fishery officers are at all times because there ain't enough of them ... it is told on the radio that they are out (on patrol at sea).'

For fishery officers, more and more enforcement work is bureaucratic report writing – weekly work plans, monthly accounts, violation reports, boat registrations, daily schedules, licensing records, and so on. About 35% of all fishery officers' time is taken up with managing the flow of clerical information, activities, and duties, and this directly and drastically limits the amount of time officers spend in field activities implementing their work plans. Monday, for example, is commonly known as 'office day,' and one seldom finds fishery officers on the water or on the wharves. Report writing, of course, is initiated and responded to by supervisors who monitor daily routines and then assign or reassign priorities. As one officer observed, 'The whole system is driven from above ... it is a paper chase, chasing itself.'

Offenses under the Fisheries Act and violations of lobster regulations are neither prioritized nor ranked by seriousness, so management decisions effectively impose a semblance of order on a rather complex compendium of laws, policies, and procedures. Indeed, enforcement work is often directly decided by department policy and administrative objectives and is therefore highly controversial (Arai 1994; Phyne 1990). At the beginning of the lobster season, for example, officers are ordered to devote almost their entire time to this fishery. They neglect other sectors and do not attend to habitat and conservation matters. Similarly at the start of the ground fishery, all other fisheries are left nonpoliced. As one supervisor explained, 'I am constantly shifting people into those areas that need it the most ... but frankly it is a political maneuver ... all we are really doing is fire fighting.'

The DFO increasingly takes counsel from advisory groups composed of fishers and other state personnel. On one occasion these groups were instrumental in convincing government policy makers to allow lobster fishers to set traps 24 hours before the opening of the season. This, it was thought, would reduce congestion on the wharves and allow for a more orderly setting and hauling of gear. But it also meant that fishery officers could not enforce any regulations since they had no authority to charge individuals for trap offenses before the beginning of the season. As one officer commented,

> Everything was nonenforceable. All we could do was stand there, as they set all the untagged lobster pots they wanted to. ... The advisory group came up with a plan that beat the regulations, and our people went along with it.

So the laws, regulations, and procedures are often imprecise guides to action (McBarnet 1978, 1981, 1993; Jones and Levi 1983; Manning 1977; Ericson 1982; Shearing 1981). They are also not easily enforceable on the open sea. Budgetary restrictions and staff shortages ensure that contacts between law officers and business poachers are infrequent and entirely predictable. About 1 in 4 fishery officers is now a seasonal employee, hired from May to September and so unavailable to police lobster violations during peak lobster season. Contacts between regulators and regulated occur mainly in government offices, where licenses and records are monitored, or at public wharves, where catches are intermittently invigilated by fishery officers (Perrier and McMullan 1996).

The condition of the government fleet is such that many vessels cannot patrol in rough seas more than a few miles from shore. They have aging boats that can barely handle tidal currents, let alone pursue sophisticated poaching operators. Many vessels do not have hydraulic haulers on board, so the process of inspection is laborious and time-consuming. 'It's a joke,' quipped one officer, 'Right now most of us can only catch poachers if fishermen let us on their boats.' Communication equipment is similarly ineffective. Business poachers have UHF and portable radios that are superior to those used by government officials. 'We tune into their channels and monitor them right on their boats,' declared one poacher. Day scopes and night scopes are also limited in range and highly cumbersome to carry on stakeouts. 'Our communication system is always breaking down,' noted one officer. 'We have lost poachers simply because we couldn't talk to our partner who was a mile away. We could not intercept ... hell, I could be assaulted by fifteen people with machetes and the last words that would go over the system would be 'Is anyone on the air?''

Fishery officers lack many of the resources to routinely patrol at sea or conduct effective surveillance or undercover work. They have the ability to mount periodic trap hauls and to dispense special task forces to 'trouble areas,' often to quell disorder after the fact, but they are only rarely able to exact a uniform compliance through their enforcement regime. Not surprisingly, only 10% of those charged with fishing out of season, 20% of those charged with fishing undersize lobsters, and 33% of those charged with overfishing beyond the trap limit were apprehended at sea (McMullan, Perrier, and Okihiro, 1993: 139; Phyne 1992; Arai 1994).

Finally, law enforcement officials are not able to count on sustained support from the judiciary in convicting and punishing business poachers. Prosecuting lawyers are not especially experienced, effective, or predictable in obtaining convictions. In addition, most judges are reluctant to find business poachers guilty because severe penalties, such as license suspensions and seizures of fishing equipment, deprive fishers and those dependent upon them of an economic livelihood. The courts tend to impose sanctions on only the most blatant offenders as measured by the illegal gains or social harm caused by the *detected* and *proven* violations (Sutinen, Rieser, and Gauvin 1990; Sutinen and Gauvin 1989). The following is a typical observation:

> We get a lot of help from judges when the poaching is committed by outsiders or those who do not have a license. But fishermen can do what they want. ... Every time you make a case the judges find a reason to dismiss it ... their loyalties are with the fishermen because they make a living from the resource.

Moreover, penalties do little to deter business poachers. They generally are not large relative to illegal gains. Blewett, Furlong, and Toews's (1987) analysis of Canadian fisheries enforcement, Furlong's (1991) study of regulatory enforcement in the Quebec fishery, and Sutinen, Rieser, and Gauvin's (1989) research in the northeastern United States found that most penalties have no deterrent effect on violations. An average fine of $500 and even those as high as $3,000 do not prohibit persistent and organized lobster poaching. A fisher put it as follows:

> Look, a fine of $1,000 is nothing. It is bullshit. You know, if I go out and catch four or five loads of fish and make good money off it, the most you can burn me for is $5,000. OK, if you catch me, and 90% of the time you won't ... then it is just the cost of doing business.

So the organization of business poaching does not require corruption. There is no evidence that front-line or background operators purchase immunity from the state by bribing or influencing public officials. Fishery officers are not 'on the take.'[5] Nor do poaching rackets have positions for enforcers who control rivals and discipline nonconforming members. There is no evidence that these sideline businesses coordinate their activities into any confederation or cartel. Nevertheless, business poachers do plan strategically for long-term matters such as safety, and they do share market contacts. They develop tactics to eke out illegitimate businesses under cover of their legitimate work roles. They organize the immediate act of poaching rationally, risk-free, and relatively successfully (Cressey 1972; Cohen 1977; Munsche 1981; Best and Luckenbill 1982; Jones 1982). The organization of business poaching is larger in scale and more complex and continuous than the other two kinds of poaching. Its security of operations is ensured because it depends, in a way that no other poaching organization does, on relationships with legitimate sections of society that have been built up interactively over time.

## Social crime, workplace crime, and regulatory failure

These findings raise questions about the role of poaching and its status as either a social crime or a type of borderline crime. Hay's (1977) work on poaching and the English game laws suggests that poaching then was a collective action whereby the poor poached game with some notion of a common right to the resource. This sense of an organized, nonmonetary use right gave the commoners a feeling of solidarity and an idea of shared values within which poachers were often tolerated. People breaking such laws and hence defying the authority of the propertied class and the state were, in effect, asserting popular attitudes in defense of customary rights to access and harvest all natural resources. Gleaning, wrecking, smuggling, rioting, and exerting the right to traditional perquisites at work were all social crimes that were regarded as normative or at least justifiable on quasi-legal grounds by large sections of the population, even though they were increasingly classified as 'real crimes' by the courts and the statute books (Winslow 1977; Rule 1977; Thompson 1977; Sharpe 1984; Linebaugh 1991).

In our study, communal poaching is certainly motivated by claims to rights of piscary, based on an alternative moral defense of community resource access and conduct. Licensing and enforcement of trap limitations do go against customs of the commons in that they restrict access to the resource, limit the size of lobster catches, disturb gear once it is set on the ocean bottom, and prevent the neighborly exchange of lost or damaged traps to their rightful owners. As Kearney (1984:50) observes, these practices have 'transformed community traditions and services into illegal acts liable to prosecution in a court of law.' Indeed, fishing illegally has a lengthy history in Southwest Nova Scotia. Divergent attitudes to property rights have resulted in routine evasion, avoidance, and noncompliance with fisheries law throughout much of the twentieth century. Lobster fishers do not easily or willingly recognize the state-based constitutional right of jurisdiction over the resource as either valid or sensible (Prince 1899; Department of the Environment 1975; Department of Fisheries and Oceans 1975). As noted, this has led to two distinct approaches to fish harvesting and organization: one based on traditional communal practices and the 'right of access,' and the other based on state control, property relations, and the ascribed 'privilege to fish.' These in turn are often in conflict, and communal poaching has emerged as a form of everyday resistance to state regulation. It continues to receive local tolerance and support and to preserve, in part, the onstage theater of power that characterizes social relationships between fishers, state law, and their communities.

However, something else is also at play. Outlaw and business poaching are primarily concerned with profiting from the provision of legal goods in an illegal manner. Their candidacy for inclusion as a 'social crime' is undermined by the fact that they have been organized to supply a black market in illegal lobster and not to ensure immediate subsistence or to defy state property management. In this regard, these two types of poaching organizations are not unlike 'gentlemen' poaching enterprises of the eighteenth and nineteenth centuries, many of which poached for profit and were not composed of the rural poor. As Sharpe (1984:130) observes of this type of poaching, '[t]he game trade existed in a 'legal twilight' ... not only was the poacher able to find someone willing to buy game from him, but the purchaser would often encourage the poacher to take yet more.' Poaching then was thus more of a commercial enterprise than a subsistence activity, and this was largely responsible for the legal conflict and violence that surrounded it (Munsche 1981; Jones 1982).

This suggests that business poaching may be better appreciated as a form of 'borderline crime,' such as fiddling or pilfering. Studies of small businesspeople, salespersons, dock workers, garage mechanics, bartenders, supermarket and retail clerks, bakers, and amateur traders in illegal goods, for example, indicate that the type of job is largely irrelevant to whether a hidden economy actually operates (Ditton 1977; Henry 1978; Henry and Mars 1978). Mars (1984: 136–59) suggests that some social factors favor workplace crime: 'passing trade,' which refers to the transitory nature of patron-client relations; 'exploiting expertise,' which refers to the imbalance of power and knowledge between goods and service providers and customers; 'gatekeepers,' which refers to the management of imbalances between supply and demand; 'triadic occupations,' which refers to the complex of alliances that can be made by any two parties against a third, and 'special efforts/skills,' which refers to work situations where economic returns are directly related to individual effort or skill and where economic pressures exist for extra rewards. In addition, four supplementary functions interact with and reinforce the social factors: control systems, ambiguities surrounding goods and services, the ease of converting and smuggling goods to private use, and the anonymity arising from the work organization itself. The main social factors, Mars says, are concerned with power, while the supplementary functions are concerned with the nature of goods and services and the social exchanges between them and the people who produce, handle, and buy them. Together the supplementary functions, acting in concert with one or more main social factors, facilitate what Mars (1984: 137) terms *workplace crime*, or *fiddle-proneness*.

While Mars (1984:152) recognizes that a hidden economy is growing and likely to expand in the personal service sector of the economy, he neglects to consider how workplace crime operates in the primary resource sector. Our data suggest that gatekeepers, triadic relationships, and special efforts/ skills factors are critical to explaining business poaching. With regard to the imbalance between supply and demand, we find that lobster fishing is a competitive business, where the consumer exerts influence and where there is a surplus of supply relative to demand. Poachers who supply illegal lobsters are not required to work for background patrons. Rather, they are in a relatively autonomous relationship with merchandisers and, if anything, the economy of poaching is in a state of vertical malintegration. This, we suggest, allows for widespread outlaw and business poaching to supply both the legal demand for lobster and the hidden economy. While power is vested in the hands of background operators like fish processors, competition and rivalry over shares and markets are also common. Unlike rackets in the construction business, in the provision of laundry and sanitation services, or in historic forms of gambling, where suppliers and customers are prevented from selecting other competitive services and must be made to conform to a monopolistic agenda, lobster poaching is a relatively independent and mostly nonviolent enterprise that has community support and does not require official corruption.

Ditton (1977) points out that many forms of workplace crime also involve triadic relations, where two parties form alliances to cheat or fiddle a third party. In his study of the baking industry, he describes the collusive training whereby managers teach their staff how to overcome bureaucratic restrictions by learning to fiddle customers. Of course, fiddling does involve situations where employees and customers form alliances to cheat corporate employers. But the triadic fiddle frequently makes a victim of the state. Not only is it common in the catering industry and in the building construction trades for both management and employees to cheat government taxation systems, but it is also common for resource workers in the forestry and fishing sectors to collude with corporate actors to deceive governments of rightful revenue (Royal Commission of Pacific Fisheries Policy 1982; Marchak 1984; Marchak, Guppy, and McMullan 1987).

This is precisely the situation with regard to lobster poaching! Outlaw poachers enter into alliances with hotels, restaurants, community groups, and private citizens to dispose of their illegal catches, and business poachers sell their illegal catches through the normal distributors and retailers. These arrangements amount to an underground economy, in that restaurants and hotel operators, for example, buy lobsters cheap from outlaw poachers and sell them at a greater profit. Lobster pounds and fish companies purchase lobsters from business poachers on a cash-only basis without providing official receipts. Business poachers thus acquire both legal (declared) and illegal (undeclared) incomes. Retailers for their part profit by selling off their unofficial, unrecorded illegal inventory to buyers without government knowledge. Taken together then, outlaw poachers, business poachers, fish plants, and other purchasers receive an invisible, illegal income and governments, both federal and provincial, are shortchanged of tax revenue.

Lobstering is a fishing practice where levels of skill and effort vary immensely (Clement 1986; Acheson 1987, 1988; Davis 1991). Economic return is directly related to individual commitment or ability. However, carapace size regulations, licensing and registration systems, trap quotas, and seasonal closures place severe limits on the economic rewards that the market might otherwise permit. These regulations function to bureaucratically and collectively fix formal rewards for all resource harvesters. But the real market price of the resource increases economic pressure for the financial rewards to be calibrated with the market demand for lobster. This, we suggest, encourages individual and insidious arrangements, including outlaw poaching networks that operate at the interstices of law, community, and marketplace and business poaching rackets that are essentially the fiddling activities of employed, aggressive, and skilled fishers, whom Mars (1984: 40) calls 'hawks.' These fishers overcome the bureaucratic impediments that limit differential payments and use the collusion of communities and private capital to 'moonlight' in order to match supply to fluctuating demand. Knowledgeable and experienced fishers' real earnings, then, are based, in part, on their participation in the hidden economy.

These three main factors explaining borderline crime are augmented by supplementary functions (Mars 1984: 154–59). As noted above, control systems in the lobster fishery are very expensive and complicated to install. Instead, the regulatory regime operates according to a compliance model that favors persuasion, education, negotiation, avoidance, and cooperation, resulting in a 'watch' style of law enforcement that is reluctant, reactive, remote, and symbolic (Lundman 1980: 45–49). In many harbors, the imbalance between supply and demand, the vertical malintegration in the industry, the collusive relations between suppliers and buyers, and the economic pressures for overfishing combine with this difficulty of control to make lobster poaching a virtual certainty.

Ambiguity over the quantity and quality of lobsters and the ease in converting and smuggling them for private use also enhances the development of poaching. As in the building business or in amateur trading, where materials and goods delivered to a site may not easily be quantified (Henry 1978; Mars 1984), lobster catches sold to processing companies, hotels, restaurants, and private civic clubs are not always properly recorded, or in some instances, not even recorded at all. At busy times and especially in a sellers' market during December, May, and June, ambiguity is increased. Traps are unaccounted for, tags go missing, short lobsters get mixed into legal catches, suspicious landings go unobserved, illegal catches disappear into community institutions, and 'poached' lobsters are converted into legal trade by fish processors. Furthermore, fishers who harvest lobsters easily overfish them because they operate with little oversight at sea and can land at private wharves all along the coastline because there is little concerted control on shore. Ambiguity of quantity and category is especially exploited when the state cannot physically account for the accumulative value of the hidden economy in 'fiddled fish' and when the state lacks enforcement expertise and is itself one of a triad. Lobster pounds and outlaw poachers easily move illegal lobsters into the local economy, sell them under the table, and bypass the government's system of declared earnings.

A common facilitator of workplace crime is the anonymity and scale of organization. Mars (1984) emphasizes the size and impersonality of larger organizations. He argues that bigger is not always better because moral attachments and property rights are inversely related to organizational complexity. This may be true when fiddling is a form of 'theft' victimizing larger corporate actors. We find, however, that lobster poaching does not require impersonal and large-scale organizational structures to be successful. The fact that lobstering is autonomous, relatively solitary, and a territorially bound and insular, in-group work activity means that it contains many possibilities for routine illegal profiteering by insiders. The decentralized relations between suppliers, purchasers, and government actually allow illegal activities to overlap and intersect with licit fishing activities. The relations between the many scattered front-line suppliers and the less numerous background intermediaries are not relations in which the latter administer the former. There is no tendency toward a centralizing business type of poaching organization. Nevertheless, there is a viable hidden economy where small-scale producers and their employees, as well as outsiders to the industry, can earn dishonest wages by 'fiddling the state.'

Our discussion of the role of poaching, the tragedy of the commons, and the hidden economy raises the issue of negotiated noncompliance, or regulatory failure. The socio-legal regulatory literature enumerates different styles of enforcement. Some writers favor dichotomous distinctions such as persuasion versus punishment or deterrence versus conciliation, while others see three polar types rather than two: deterrence, persuasion, and education (Hawkins 1984; Hopkins 1994; Pearce and Tombs 1997; Hutter 1999; Winter and May 2001). Grabosky and Braithwaite (1986) develop an even more elaborate schema of seven different identifiable enforcement types that they locate along two axes: detached command-and-control regulation versus cooperative self-regulation, and enforcers versus nonenforcers. Indeed, existing research strongly suggests that national differences exist between regulatory regimes. The United States, for example, tends to employ a more proscriptive, deterrence-oriented style of regulation resulting in ambitious regulatory rules, strict legalistic enforcement, frequent and larger regulatory sanctions, and the production of detailed records and reports as well as evidence of compliance. In Canada and in other countries such as Australia, New Zealand, Denmark, Japan, and the United Kingdom, the preferred style of regulatory enforcement is more cooperative and negotiated in nature and relies heavily on persuasion, standard-setting, and the circulation and dissemination of information. The regulated populations in these studies comprise industrial sectors, individual corporations, small businesses and employers, managers, and employees. Some of these groupings are complex, well organized, and transnational, whereas others are simple, small-scale, and local (Bardach and Kagan 1982; Braithwaite 1985, 1993; Snider 1990; Hutter 1999; Aoki, Kagan, and Axelrad 2000; Kagan, Gunningham, and Thornton 2001).

Not surprisingly, some regulatory programs achieve their basic objectives, at least to some degree, and some do not, and of course, the reasons for compliance and noncompliance are various and numerous (Bardach and Kagan 1982; Gunningham 1987; Hutter 1999). We find that the reasons for regulatory noncompliance are four-fold. To start, self-interest, which is a major reason for compliance, especially corporate compliance, is not compelling in the case of small-scale lobster producers. Lobster fishers do not view strict compliance as necessary for the viability of their work or for the long-term future of the resource because they believe that they are able managers. Nor are they particularly concerned with protecting their image among their peers or in their communities. Communal and business poaching are not perceived as susceptible to external pressures from consumers, distributors, retailers, or other fishers. In addition, moral suasion that provides powerful reasons to comply with the law out of a genuine concern for protection, conservation, and security of the resource is minimal. The fishery officers we researched believed that fishers can be divided into two groups: those that feel an obligation to comply with the law and those who feel that the spirit and the letter of the law are unfair because the regulatory regime goes against communal, customary practices. For the latter group, the commitment to comply with the law is low. They question the state's need for a regulatory regime and are skeptical of the experts who claim to be able to better manage the resource.

Cost, which includes factors such as profit maximization, financial needs, working conditions and equipment, and worker morale is also a much-cited reason for regulatory compliance and noncompliance (Gunningham 1987; Snider 1990; Hopkins 1994; Pearce and Tombs 1997). The fishers we interviewed believed that they were caught in a contradictory policy. As a result of government programs to capitalize the fishing industry, fishers in the small boat sector have borrowed large sums of money to finance investments in new equipment and vessels. They became dependent on financial institutions and government loan boards for capital outlay. Although these programs were initially designed to rationalize the 'right to fish,' they have ultimately forced fishers into a severe debt-dependent position. This is complicated by the regulatory restrictions that, in effect, have restructured property relations in the lobster fishery and made the state the custodian of the resource by creating a system of selective access and control. Fishers have found themselves on the horns of a dilemma. On the one hand, capitalization has created overcapacity and the problem of too many fishers chasing too few fish. On the other hand, regulations have restricted fishing effort. Complying with the rules is a costly proposition. Fishing outside the rules has been one way for licensed fishers, in particular, to maintain flexibility in a restrictive fishery where debt loads have skyrocketed and bankruptcies and repossessions have grown.

Other authors, notably Bardach and Kagan (1982), mention intraorganizational pressures such as internal audits and inspections, task forces, expert planners, and labor management committees as reasons for compliance. We found that these pressures are rather weak. As noted earlier, little administrative control is exercised over the harvesting process. Fish companies do not set work standards or production quotas. In fact, this dispersed situation is exploited by both fishers and buyers to form a hidden economy based on negotiated noncompliance. Industrywide agencies, local advisory committees, and representative associations of producers, retailers, fishers, and governments do not function to produce an industry that is highly motivated to comply with DFO regulations. Similar to companies where the size of the firm, the work site, and the labor force are small, we have found that fishers are primarily reactive in their attitudes toward promoting compliance and controlling workplace deviance. These intraorganizational groups tend to promote minimalist standards, rules, and inspections.

The question that is fundamental to this research is the extent to which knowledge of the law and enforcement of it affects compliance. The socio-legal research suggests that knowledge of the law may be unclear for both regulators and regulated (Bardach and Kagan 1982; Hutter 1999). We found that neither the law nor its interpretations are clear to many fishery officers, area managers, and regional directors. Front-line regulators feel that knowledge of the legal system used to enforce fisheries policy is patchy and poorly understood and resourced by area managers and regional supervisors. This is perceived rather widely as symbolic of disinterest among the higher echelons of the DFO. If the threat of formal legal sanction is necessary for legal regulations to be effective and for compliance to be achieved, then the rules must be clear and the sanctions certain. We found that regulators in the lobster fishery are uncertain of laws, puzzled by the frequency and complexity of amendments and variation orders, and convinced that the sanctions are paltry and symbolic. The regulated, for their part, perceive the enforcement and implementation of fisheries law as occasional, uncertain, and aggravating. They define much fishery regulation and enforcement as 'bureaucratic schemozzel,' where officers with ambiguous authority have the unenviable task of enforcing many laws perceived as irrelevant and inconsistent by those being regulated. Indeed, poachers who are allegedly subjected to the legal process in theory often subject the law to their own use in practice. They manage the 'edges of illegality' to their own advantage. They play with, work on, and in some instances even invent boundaries to law-breaking. However, an important finding is that the subjected, 'the officially labeled,' may from time to time be in control of the labeling process. Laws, regulatory statutes, and variation orders are not only a mechanism of social control but are also a mechanism for escaping it. In defining what is to be controlled, law also defines the limits of control and the limits of its power. Business poaching is especially dynamic and creative. It subverts the power of the state by clever and rational means. When the due diligence decision is invoked, the consequence is the erosion of strict liability. Fishers avoid the regulations by claiming that tags on traps have been 'removed' by nature (i.e., climatic conditions), and that 'tinkers' (undersize lobsters) could not be measured at sea because oceanic conditions have prevented it. Law at sea is more a fiction than a reality. More complex adaptations to state power are also commonplace. These include the routine surveillance of fishery officers at their places of work and in their communities as well as the promotion and development of nonenforceable rules and procedures governing how and where fishing can occur.

One way to limit maneuvers at the boundaries of the licit and the illicit, of course, is to remove the boundaries or refuse to say where they are demarcated. This is precisely what occurred in the due diligence case (*R v. Belliveau* 1986) brought by fishers against the DFO. The judge interpreted fishery laws and regulations by looking beyond the specific violation to its real social purpose. The legal judgment, which was widely criticized by the DFO, invoked the ideology of the rule of law to actually restrict regulatory control over fishers. It argued against retrospective law by insisting on certainty and clarity before the law; insofar as intent was concerned boundaries were made clear, but no exact precedents for the future were established since the law was said to be still evolving. In short, this legal decision short-circuited the law enforcement regime and unwittingly facilitated illegal fishing.

Of course, the opportunity to creatively use and manipulate legal boundaries is not equally available to all poachers. Communal and outlaw poachers, who are not normally registered fishers, have little scope or recourse to fiddle with the law in this manner. Their choices are deceptive, evasive, and quick-escape schemes. At an elementary level the difference is not what they do, but how they do it. Unlike outlaw poachers, business poachers stay on the 'right side of the law' because they have the opportunities and resources to manipulate the law to escape control and yet remain legitimate. This they accomplish in two ways. First, they play on problems of enforcement by making themselves 'invisible' and by calculating the presence, or rather the absence, of law enforcement personnel and technology. Second, they work creatively on the fabric of law itself so that enforcement officers are confronted with the paradox of trying to secure compliance under the law when the literal requirements of the law and its regulations are already being met.

An implication of this research, contra those who say that only 'corporate elites' or 'high net worth individuals' can creatively mediate and manipulate the law, is that immunity from the law may be more widespread (McBarnet 1993). Our research shows that laws and regulations can be 'bent' by small independent producers to support their interests even though they do not possess much power or enormous wealth. Ironically, in this instance, law is translated into the very practices that it seeks to control. Law in action, we suggest, is an aid to the organization of business poaching and a practice that is easily evaded and avoided.

## Notes

1  The sample size of fishers was restricted to 100 due to our limited funding support. We recognize that this is not a representative sample. However, we tried to stratify our sample so that we obtained interviews from diverse communities where licensed fishers were highly concentrated. We are reasonably confident that our qualitative data accurately reflect the fishers' perspective.
2  For a more detailed analysis of illegality and social conflict in the Nova Scotia lobster fishery, see McMullan, Perrier, and Okihiro (1993: 121–46).
3  See McMullan and Perrier (1997) for a detailed discussion of these three types of poaching organizations.
4  The Coast Guard can board vessels and arrest fishers, but it usually turns over the cases to the DFO for prosecution. The Navy mainly provides material and logistical aid to the other two agencies.
5  However, Kuperan and Sutinen (1998: 328), in their study of 'blue water crime,' suggest that detection and conviction of violators may be low because syndicates try to 'influence enforcement personnel' or obtain information on surveillance activities from 'insiders who warn fishermen of the Department's planned surveillance activities so that they can avoid detection and arrest.' But the authors admit that the evidence is not compelling.

## References

Acheson, J. M. (1975) 'The Lobster Fiefs: Economic and Ecological Effects of Territoriality in the Maine Lobster Industry,' 3 *Human Ecology* 183–207.
—— (1987) 'The Lobster Fiefs Revisited,' in B. J. McCay & J. M. Acheson, eds., *The Questions of the Commons*. Tuscon, AZ: Univ. of Arizona Press.
—— (1988) *The Lobster Gangs of Maine*. Hanover, NH: Univ. Press of New England.
Aoki, K., R. A. Kagan, & L. Axelrad (2000) 'Industrial Effluent Control in the United States and Japan,' in R. A. Kagan & L. Axelrad, eds., *Regulatory Encounters: Multinational Corporations and American Adversarial Legalism*. Berkeley: Univ. of California Press.
Apostle, R., L. Kasdan, & A. Hanson (1984) 'Political Efficacy and Political Activity Among Fishermen in Southwest Nova Scotia: A Research Note,' 19 *J. of Canadian Studies* 157–65.
Arai, B. (1990) 'The Enforcement Practices of Fishery Officers: A Case Study from the Scotia – Fundy Region.' Presented at the Atlantic Association of Sociologists annual meeting.
—— (1994) 'Policy and Practice in the Atlantic Fishers: Problems of Regulatory Enforcement,' 20 *Canadian Public Policy* 353–64.
Bardach, E., & R. A. Kagan (1982) *Going by the Book: The Problem of the Regulatory Unreasonableness, A Twentieth Century Fund Study*. Philadelphia, PA: Temple Univ. Press.

Barrett, G. (1987) *Uneven Development, Rent and the Social Organization of Capital: A Case Study of the Fishing Industry of Nova Scotia, Canada.* D. Phil. Diss., Univ. of Sussex, Brighton, England.

Best, J. (1980) 'Licensed to Steal,' in R. W. Love, ed., *Changing Interpretations and New Sources in Naval History.* New York: Garland.

Best, J., & D. F. Luckenbill (1982) *Organizing Deviance.* Englewood Cliffs, NJ: Prentice-Hall.

Blewett, E., W. Furlong, & P. Toews (1987) 'Canada's Experience in Measuring the Deterrent Effect of Fisheries Law Enforcement,' in J. Sutinen & T. Hennessey, eds., *Fisheries Law Enforcement: Programs, Problems and Evaluation.* Marine Technical Report 93, Univ. of Rhode Island.

Braithwaite, J. (1985) *To Punish or Persuade: Enforcement of Coal Mine Safety.* Albany: SUNY Press.

—— (1993) 'The Nursing Home Industry,' in M. Tonry & A. J. Reiss, Jr., eds., *Beyond the Law: Crime in Complex Organizations.* Chicago: Univ. of Chicago Press.

Chambliss, W. J. (1973) 'Vice, Corruption, Bureaucracy and Power,' in W. J. Chambliss, ed., *Sociological Readings in the Conflict Perspective.* London: Addison-Wesley.

—— (1978) *On the Take: From Petty Crooks to Presidents.* Bloomington: Indiana Univ. Press.

Ciriacy-Wantrup, S. V., & R. Bishop (1975) 'Common Property as a Concept in Natural Resource Policy,' 15 *National Resources J.* 713–27.

Clement, W. (1986) *Struggle to Organize: Resistance in Canada's Fishery.* Toronto: McClelland & Stewart.

Cohen, A. K. (1977) 'The Concept of Criminal Organization,' 17 *The British J. of Criminology* 97–111.

Cressey, D. R. (1972) *Criminal Organization: Its Elementary Forms.* London: Heinemann.

Davis, A. (1991) 'Insidious Rationalities: The Institutionalization of Small Boat Fishing and the Rise of the Rapacious Fisher,' 4 *Maritime Anthropological Studies* 13–31.

Davis, A., & L. Kasdan (1984) 'Bankrupt Government Policies and Belligerent Fishermen Responses: Dependency and Conflict in the Southwest Nova Scotia Small Boat Fisheries,' 19 *J. of Canadian Studies* 108–24.

Davis, A., & V. Thiessen (1988) 'Public Policy and Social Control in the Atlantic Fisheries,' 15 *Canadian Public Policy* 66–77.

Department of the Environment (1975) *Lobster Fishery Task Force Report.* Ottawa: Fisheries and Marine Services.

Department of Fisheries and Oceans (1975) *Preliminary Report – Lobster Fisheries Task Force.* Ottawa: Department of Fisheries and Oceans.

—— (1990) An Overview of Proposed Amendments to the Fishers Act. Ottawa: Department of Supply and Services.

DeWolf, A. G. (1974) 'Lobster Fishery of the Maritime Provinces: Economic Effects of Regulations,' Fisheries Research Board of Canada, Bulletin 187, Environment Canada, Ottawa.

Ditton, J. (1977) *Part-Time Crime: An Ethnography of Fiddling and Pilferage.* London: Macmillan.

Ericson, R. (1982) *Reproducing Order: A Study of Police Patrol Work.* Toronto: Univ. of Toronto Press.

Feldman, P. (1993) *The Psychology of Crime.* New York: Cambridge Univ. Press.

Furlong, W. J. (1991) 'The Deterrent Effect of Regulatory Enforcement in the Fishery,' 67 *Land Economics* 116–29.

Grabosky, P., & J. Braithwaite (1986) *Manners Gentle: Enforcement Strategies of Australian Business Regulatory Agencies.* Melbourne, Australia: Oxford Univ. Press.

Grimshaw, R., & T. Jefferson (1987) *Interpreting Police Work.* London: Allen & Unwin.

Gunningham, N. 'Negotiated Non-Compliance: A Case Study of Regulatory Failure,' 9 *Law and Policy* 69–87.

Hanson, A., & C. Lamson (1984) *Fisheries Decision-Making: Perspectives on East Coast Canadian Policy Setting and Implementation.* Halifax: Dalhousie Univ.

Hay, D. (1977) 'Poaching and the Game Laws on Cannock Chase,' in D. Hay, P. Linebaugh, J. G. Rule, E. P. Thompson, and C. Winslow, eds., *Albion's Fatal Tree: Crime and Society in Eighteenth Century England.* Middlesex: Penguin Books.

Hawkins, K. (1984) *Environment and Enforcement.* Oxford: Clarendon.

Henry, S. (1978) *The Hidden Economy: The Context and Control of Borderline Crime.* Oxford: Martin Robertson.

Henry, S., & G. Mars (1978) 'Crime at Work: The Social Construction of Amateur Property Theft,' 12 *Sociology* 245–63.

Hobsbawm, E. (1969) *Bandits.* London: Widenfeld & Nealson.

Hopkins, A. (1994) 'Compliance with What? The Fundamental Regulatory Question,' 34 *British J. of Criminology* 431–43.

Howkins, A. (1979) 'Economic Crime and Class Law: Poaching and the Game Laws, 1840-1880,' in S. B. Burman & B. E. Harrell-Bond, eds., *The Imposition of Law.* New York: Academic Press.

Hutter, B. M. (1999) 'Controlling Workplace Deviance: State Regulation of Occupational Health and Safety,' 8 *Research and the Sociology of Work* 191–209.

Jones, D. (1982) 'The Poacher, A Study in Victorian Crime and Protest,' in D. Jones, ed., *Crime, Protest, Community and Police in 19th Century Britain*. London: Routledge & Kegan Paul.

Jones, T., & M. Levi (1983) 'The Police and the Majority: The Neglect of the Obvious,' 56 *Police* 4.

Kagan, R. A., N. Gunningham, & D. Thornton (2001) 'Regulatory Regimes and Variations in Corporate Environmental Performance: Evidence From the Pulp and Paper Industry,' Paper presented at the Annual Meeting of the Law and Society Association, Budapest, Hungary, July.

Kearney, J. F. (1984) *Working Together: A Study of Fishermen's Response to Government Management of the District 4A Lobster Fishery*. Pointe-de-l'Eglise, Nova Scotia: Presses de l'Universite Sainte-Anne.

—— (1988) 'The Lobster Trap Tag in Fishing Area 34 (Southwest Nova Scotia): The Technical, Legal and Management Problems Associated with Tag Design,' Research Document, Maritime Fishermen's Union, Yarmouth.

Kuperan, K., & J. G. Sutinen (1998) 'Blue Water Crime: Deterrence, Legitimacy and Compliance in Fisheries,' 32 *Law and Society Rev.* 309–30.

Linebaugh, P. (1991) *The London Hanged: Crime and Civil Society in the Eighteenth Century*. London: Allen Lane, Penguin Press.

Lundman, R. J. (1980) *Police and Policing: An Introduction*. New York: Holt, Rinehart & Winston.

Mack, J. (1972) 'The Able Criminal,' 12 *British J. of Sociology* 44–55.

MacPherson, C. B. (1978) *Property: Mainstream and Critical Positions*. Toronto: Univ. of Toronto Press.

Manning, P. K. (1977) *Police Work: The Social Organization of Policing*. Cambridge, MA: MIT Press.

Marchak, P. M. (1984) *Green Gold: The Forest Industry in British Columbia*. Vancouver: British Columbia Univ. Press.

—— (1987) 'Uncommon Property,' in P. Marchak, N. Guppy, & J. McMullan, eds., *Uncommom Property: The Fishing and Fish-Processing Industries in British Columbia*. Toronto: Methuen.

——(1989) 'What Happens When Common Property Becomes Uncommon?' 80 *B.C. Studies* 3–24.

Marchak, P. M., N. Guppy, & J. L. McMullan, eds. *Uncommon Property: The Fishing and Fish-Processing Industries in British Columbia*. Toronto: Methuen.

Mars, G. (1984) *Cheats at Work: An Anthropology of Workplace Crime*. London: Unwin Paperbacks.

Martin, K. D. (1979) 'Play by the Rules or Don't Play at All: Space Division and Resource Allocation in a Rural Newfoundland Fishing Community,' in R. Anderson, ed., *North Atlantic Maritime Culture*. The Hague: Mouton Publishers.

Mathews, R., & J. Phyne (1988) 'Regulating and Newfoundland Inshore Fishery: Traditional Values versus State Control in the Regulation of a Common Property Resource,' 23 *J. of Canadian Studies* 158–75.

McBarnet, D. J. (1978) 'The Police and the State: Arrest, Legality and the Law,' in G. Littlejohn, ed., *Power and the State*. London: Croom Helm.

—— (1981) *Conviction: Law, the State and the Construction of Justice*. London: Macmillan.

—— (1993) 'Legitimate Rackets: Tax Evasion, Tax Avoidance and the Boundaries of Legality,' 3 *J. of Human Justice* 56–74.

McCay, B. J. (1978) 'Systems Ecology, People Ecology and the Anthropology of Fishing Communities,' 6 *Human Ecology* 397–422.

—— (1984) 'The Pirates of Piscary: An Ethnohistory of Illegal Fishing in New Jersey,' 31 *Ethnohistory* 17–37.

McEachern, D. B. (1969) *Progress Report on the Trap Limit and License Control Survey*. Ottawa: Department of the Environment, Maritimes and Newfoundland Lobster Fisheries, Economics Branch, Fisheries Service.

McIntosh, M. (1973) 'The Growth of Racketeering,'' 2 *Economy and Society* 35–69.

—— (1975) *The Organization of Crime*. London: Macmillan.

McMullan, J. L., & D. Perrier (1997) 'Poaching vs. the Law: The Social Organization of Illegal Fishing,' in J. L. McMullan, D. Perrier, S. Smith, & P. Swan, eds., *Crimes, Laws and Communities*. Halifax: Fernwood.

McMullan, J. L., D. Perrier, & N. Okihiro (1993) 'Regulation, Illegality and Social Conflict in the Nova Scotia Lobster Fishery,' 33 *J. of Legal Pluralism and Unofficial Law* 121–46.

Miller, M. L., & J. Van Maanen (1979) 'Boats Don't Fish, People Do: Some Ethnographic Notes on the Federal Management of Fisheries in Gloucester,' 38 *Human Organization* 377–85.

Munsche, P. B. (1981) *Gentlemen and Poachers: The English Game Laws 1671–1831*. Cambridge, England: Cambridge Univ. Press.

Netboy, A. (1968) *The Atlantic Salmon: A Vanishing Species?* Boston: Houghton Mifflin.

O'Malley, P. (1979) 'Class Conflict, Land and Social Banditry,' 26 *Social Problems* 271–83.

443

Peace, A. 'When the Salmon Comes: The Politics of Summer Fishing in the Irish Community,' 52 *J. of Anthropological Research* 85–107.

Pearce, F., & S. Tombs 'Hazards, Law and Class: Contextualizing the Regulation of Corporate Crime,' 6 *Social and Legal Studies* 79–107.

Perrier, D., & J. L. McMullan (1996) 'Enforcement and Illegality in the Southwest Nova Scotian Lobster Fishery,' unpublished report.

Phyne, J. (1988) *State Regulation of the Inshore and Inland Fisheries of Newfoundland: A Study of the Role of Federal Fishery Officers.* Ph.D. Diss., McMaster Univ., Hamilton.

—— (1990) 'Dispute Settlement in the Newfoundland Inshore Fishery: A Study of Fishery Officers' Responses to Gear Conflicts in Inshore Fishing Communities,' 3 *Maritime Anthropological Studies* 88–102.

—— (1992) 'Changes from Compliance to Deterrence among Federal Fishery Officers: An Atypical Case of Regulatory Policing?' 29 *Canadian Rev. of Sociology and Anthropology* 524–34.

Prince, E. E. 'Report of the Canadian Lobster Commission 1898,' in *31st Annual Report, Supplement 1.* Ottawa: Department of Maritime Fisheries.

Royal Commission of Pacific Fisheries Policy (1982) *Turning the Tide: A New Policy for Canada's Pacific Fisheries.* Ottawa: Queen's Printer.

Rule, G. J. (1977) 'Wrecking and Coastal Plunder,' in D. Hay, P. Linebaugh, J. G. Rule, E. P. Thompson, & C. Winslow, eds., *Albion's Fatal Tree: Crime and Society in Eighteenth Century England.* Middlesex: Penguin Books.

Scott, J. (1986) 'Everyday Forms of Peasant Resistance,' 13 *J. of Peasant Studies* 5–35.

Scott, A., & M. Tugwell (1981) 'Public Regulation of Commercial Fisheries in Canada – The Maritime Lobster Fishery,' Technical Report No. 16. Ottawa: Economic Council of Canada.

Sharpe, J. A. (1984) *Crime in Early Moder England 1550–1750.* London: Longman Group Ltd.

Shearing, C. (1981) 'Subterranean Processes in the Maintenance of Power: An Examination of the Mechanisms Coordinating Police Action,' 18 *Canadian Rev. of Sociology and Anthropology* 3.

Snider, L. (1990) 'Cooperative Models and Corporate Crime: Panacea or CopOut?' 36 *Crime and Delinquency* 373–90.

Stiles, G. (1972) 'Labour Recruitment and the Family Crew in Newfoundland,' in R. R. Anderson, ed., *North Atlantic Maritime Cultures.* The Hague: Mouton Publishers.

Sutinen, J. G.,& K. Kuperan (1989) *Compliance and Enforcement in Northeast Fisheries.* Saugus, MA: New England Fishery Management Council.

Sutinen, J. G., & J. R. Gauvin (1989) 'An Econometric Study of Regulatory Enforcement and Compliance in the Commercial Inshore Lobster Fishery of Massachusetts,' in P. A. Neher, R. Arnason, & N. Mollet, eds., *Rights-Based Fishing.* Boston: Kluwer Academic Publishers.

Sutinen, J. G., A. Rieser, & J. R. Gauvin (1990) 'Measuring and Explaining Noncompliance in Federally Managed Fisheries,' 21 *Ocean Development and International Law* 335–72.

Taylor, L. (1981) 'Man the Fisher: Salmon Fishing and the Expression of Community in a Rural Irish Settlement,' 8 *American Ethnologist* 774–88.

—— (1987) 'The River Would Run Red with Blood: Community and Common Property in an Irish Fishing Settlement,' in B. J. McCay & J. M. Acheson, eds., *The Question of the Commons: The Culture and Ecology of Communal Resources.* Tucson: Univ. of Arizona Press.

Thompson, E. P. (1977) *Whigs and Hunters: The Origin of the Black Act.* Middlesex: Penguin Books.

Winslow, C. (1977) 'Sussex Smugglers,' in D. Hay, P. Linebaugh, J. G. Rule, E. P. Thompson, & C. Winslow, eds., *Albion's Fatal Tree: Crime and Society in Eighteenth Century England.* Middlesex: Penguin Books.

Winter, S. C., & P. J. May (2001) 'The Role of Information and Interest-Organizations in Fostering Environmental Regulatory Compliance,' Paper presented at the Annual Meeting of the Law and Society Association, Budapest, Hungary, July.

## Case cited

*R. v. Belliveau* (NSCA) Nova Scotia Judgements (1986) NSJ No. 432, Action SCC No. 01553.

# 23. Crime, bio-agriculture and the exploitation of hunger*

*Reece Walters*

The rapid expansion of biotechnology during the past decade has created widespread debate and concern within the agricultural sector and consumer groups. This article examines the monopolization of bio-technology and the political economy of genetically modified food. It further explores the ways that powerful governments and corporations seek to dominate global food markets whilst exploiting, pressuring and threatening vulnerable countries. In doing so, it provides a detailed examination of Zambia, which has experienced significant political and economic pressure from Western governments and corporations to accept genetically modified maize. Finally, it explores 'eco-crime' within frameworks of state and corporate crime, international environmental law and emerging discourses in green criminology.

## Introduction

Discourses in state-corporate crime continue to examine the complex relationships between harm and economic, political and social power (Tombs and Whyte 2003).

The introduction of genetic or living modified organisms to the world's food chain is an issue involving state and corporate power that has polarized governments, consumers, scientists, farmers and, most importantly, the world's hungry. Emerging from international discourses on genetically modified organisms (GMOs) are issues of commerce and trade, health and safety, environment and biodiversity, politics and international relations, science and technology, and, as this article argues, illegal, unethical and harmful practices. Central to the argument in this article is that the commercialization of GM food and the aggressive trade policies of governments and corporations in pursuit of capital accumulation is, to adopt Green and Ward's (2004: 29) analytical framework, a 'highly criminogenic force' involving acts of organizational deviance and breaches of international law. Moreover, acts of environmental harm or 'eco-crime' have emerged within discourses on crimes of the powerful

---

* From *British Journal of Criminology* (2006), 46(1): pp. 26–45.

(see Tombs and Whyte 2003; Kauzlarich and Kramer 1998; Pearce and Tombs 1993) and will be further examined within developing debates of 'green criminology' (see South 1998; Lynch and Stretesky 2003; White 2003).

Millions of people worldwide suffer from malnutrition and starvation (Food and Agriculture Organisation of the United Nations 2004). For some, international hunger is a humanitarian crisis; for others, it is a commercial opportunity. The political economy of food and hunger is a long-established debate (see Harle 1978; Dreze *et al.* 1995) and the emerging discourses about GM food and its development and consumption must be seen as an extension of the politics of humanitarian relief, free trade and sustainable development. Within these discourses are issues of economic hegemony and the politics of world trade, as Mulvany (2004) argues: '... those with power, particularly the United States, have used hunger as justification for trade supremacy and the promotion of genetically modified (GM) crops owned by northern multinational corporations – much to the delight of pro-GM advocates.' The production and sale of GM food remains an issue of intense conflict in global trade, as issues of health, the environment, economics and consumer protection are widely contested.

The relationship between criminology and GM food has been explored in the Winter 2004 edition of *The British Journal of Criminology,* notably that 'the scientific biotech world of GM foods must be placed on the criminological agenda where the reported harms, risks and inequalities are examined with social and political narratives that challenge the existing priorities of governing bodies' (see Walters 2004: 165). This article seeks to further the criminological debate by exploring the issue within state–corporate crime complexes and emerging debates within 'green criminology' through a case study of Zambia. Why Zambia? The concerns over GM food safety received international headlines when the Zambian President, Mr Mwanawasa, condemned it as 'poisonous' (Plaut 2002). Zambia is one of six southern African nations that, for most of its 40-year independence, has faced food shortages. However, despite this, the Government continues to reject GM food in fear of potential harm to its population and biodiversity. For some American geneticists, the stance adopted by the Zambian president was 'incomprehensible – unless one views it from an economic point of view', claiming that the Zambian Government was protecting its future trade in Europe (see Fedoroff and Brown 2004: 310). Controversially, Pringle (2003: 189) has argued that 'the Zambian incident also refocused attention on the developing world as a new front line in the biotech wars'. What could be learned from visiting one of the so-called biotech 'war zones' and examining how the majority world had become embroiled in the politics of global trade and GM food? This article draws on 18 semi-structured interviews conducted in Zambia during September 2004. In addition, visits were undertaken to organic and commercial farms outside Lusaka and discussions held with small-scale farmers, the farmer's union and consumer groups. The interviews with senior government personnel including the Minister of Agriculture, as well as scientists, academics, trade investors, conservation association representatives and regulatory agencies, sought to understand the Zambian Government's position and its political and economic ramifications. For example, why would a nation with 'millions of people facing starvation' reject GM food aid? What reasons could explain the international political and economic pressure placed on Zambian authorities, businesses, scientists and farmers? Were such actions in breach of newly enacted international environmental law, namely the Cartagena Protocol on Biosafety and the International Treaty on Plant Genetic Resources for Food and Agriculture? And what are the challenges facing biosafety and regulation when powerful governments and corporations wilfully neglect or violate international treaties?

Walters (2004: 165) has noted that a social and political analysis of the complex debates involving GM food requires a 'criminological knowledge capable of transcending disciplinary boundaries in order to critique the multifaceted dimensions of international biotechnology'. This research necessitated an engagement with international trade law and environment law, environmental and trade politics, discourses on the political economy of hunger and food, debates about biotechnology, food science and agriculture, as well as an understanding of the sociology of development.

## Case study: Zambia

Zambia is a Southern African landlocked country, bordered by seven other nations (Angola, Democratic Republic of Congo, Tanzania, Malawi, Zimbabwe, Mozambique, Namibia) with a population of 10.5 million people. Previously known as Northern Rhodesia and subject to South African and British rule, it became a republic under its existing name in 1964 and, unlike many of its African nations, has not experienced civil war. It is rich in natural resources, including copper, zinc, gold and gemstones; however, its external debt of $US5 billion and an unemployment rate in excess of 50 per cent of the population makes it one of the United Nations' Highly Indebted Poor Countries (HIPC). Alongside disturbing economic trends, Zambia continues to tackle intense social problems. These include an HIV rate of 16.5 per cent of the entire population, a national life expectancy of 38 years and upwards of 90 per cent of its people living below the poverty line, including 65 per cent having no access to safe drinking water, electricity or sanitation (World Health Organisation 2004). That said, a 23 per cent rise in exports in 2003, a stable inflation and an increased domestic gross product in what the Government refers to as the 'longest period of sustained growth since independence' provide reason for optimism (Magande 2004; cf. World Bank 2004). Along with mining, one of the best-performing sectors is agriculture. For the first time in Zambia's 40-year independence, it is exporting surplus grain to neighbouring Malawi and Angola. Agriculture is an essential part of the social and economic fabric of Zambian society. Zambia has more than 800,000 farmers (Simwanda and Mwila 2004a) and an estimated 85 per cent are 'small-scale or peasant farmers' who own less than one hectare of land and produce 80 per cent of the nation's crops (Simwanda and Mwila 2004b).

### The Zambian Government's rejection of GM food

Grain is a cornerstone of Zambian society, especially cassava and maize, which are staple foods in the north and south, respectively. While fulfilling dietary needs, it also holds substantial social and political value, as one interviewee said 'if you can't manage maize then you cannot be a President of Zambia, it is our lifeblood'. The cultural significance of food is a relatively recent discourse in Western societies (see Ashley *et al.* 2004); however, in Southern Africa, it is has played an essential role in ceremony, worship and social structure for thousands of years.

As mentioned above, the concerns over GM food safety received international headlines when the Zambian President referred to it as 'poison'. The introduction of genetic technology into the food chain has posed a perceived danger to their staple food that has generated a discourse of fear and moral panic among many Zambians who are united behind their President's opposition to GM food. In Lusaka, for example, the colloquial name for a prostitute (most of whom are HIV-positive) is a 'GMO'. The use of language that seeks to demonize GM food as morally repugnant, diseased and harmful must be contextualized within the social value of maize in Zambia and within contemporary discourses of risk and moral panic.

Not only is GM maize considered harmful to human health, but the Zambian authorities interviewed for this research had reason to believe that unmilled US grain donations were being strategically transported to Zambia to permit illegal growing of GM crops that would contaminate natural maize varieties, in what was perceived as a strategic attempt to pollute biodiversity and create economic dependence (cf. Nottingham 2003).

The Zambian Government has been hailed as leading the African opposition to GM food. It rejected GM grain during its food deficit of 2002 and prompted other nations at the September 2002 World Earth Summit, including Ethiopia, Mozambique and Zimbabwe, to oppose US Government claims that they were 'letting people starve through misplaced concern over GM food' (Martin 2002). The Zambian Government called a national debate on 10 August 2002 on the safety of GM food. This meeting recommended a Zambian-led 'fact finding mission' involving leading scientists and medical experts' travelling overseas with a specific remit to comment on the Government's adoption of the precautionary principle. It concluded that the safety of GM food was uncertain, that GM maize would contaminate indigenous Zambian maize varieties, that the export industry of maize and organic foods was jeopardized and that the 'government should maintain the current stand of not accepting GM Foods by employing the precautionary principle' (Banda *et al.* 2002: 38). This fieldwork resulted in the Zambian Government's maintaining its cautious approach and moving towards the drafting of biosafety legislation. The Ministry of Science encapsulated the Government's position in the publication of its 'Biosafety Strategy':

> While biotechnology is often promoted by agri-business as an answer to the world's food problems, real food security problems are caused not by food shortages, but inequity, poverty and the concentration of food production. Therefore, unless regulated, biotechnology is likely to further consolidate control of the seed industry in the hands of a few large firms. (Ministry of Science, Technology and Vocational Training 2003: 7)

It should be noted that the Zambian Government is not opposed to biotechnology per se. The National Institute for Scientific Research continues to conduct experiments using genetic technologies that aim to reduce animal disease as well as exploring medicinal benefits. A senior scientist with the Ministry of Science, Technology and Vocational Training dismissed allegations that Zambia was anti genetic technology, claiming 'of course we are exploring developments in genetic science but our resources are limited. We have various laboratories and experiments conducting research into genetic possibilities ... But to suggest that Zambia is opposed to genetic technology is simply not true, we are opposed to GM food and we are opposed to the pressure to accept it' (Zambian scientist 2004). As Paarlberg (2001) argues, the politics of precaution across developing countries is not simply 'thumbs up or thumbs down on a single issue', but a variety of ways that countries are responding to intellectual property laws, risk assessment and management, biotechnology research and regulation. The debate surrounding the refusal of GM food is, therefore, not one-dimensional; indeed, there are several reasons for adopting the precautionary principle. For example, the Minister of Agriculture stated that 'we are adopting the precautionary principle on GM food and until we have more accurate scientific facts that clearly show that it is safe, we will not introduce it to our environment ... I am wanting to explore the potential of our biodiversity before we destroy what we already freely have, what God has given us for free. How can we accept GMO's when I know that such technology could destroy our biodiversity, the possibilities of which are still unknown' (Sikatana 2004) – a reasonable argument; however, the expansion of bio-agriculture in Southern Africa is not subservient to ecological dangers or risks to biodiversity. As the following section explores, the production and sale of GM food are driven by the economic imperatives of 'free trade' and an aggressive political economy that seeks new markets in fragile, vulnerable and 'at risk' societies.

### Political and economic pressure to accept GM food

In 2003, despite having a clear understanding of Zambia's explicit opposition to GM food, the United States has continued to distribute food aid through the United Nations' World Food Programme that contains GM maize. When the Zambian Government called for an immediate withdrawal of all the contaminated food, a riot broke out among some starving people in southern Zambia. The Zambian minister for Agriculture, Mr Mundia Sikatana, accused the United States of 'promoting food riots in order to force Zambia to accept GM maize' (quoted in Jonathan 2004).

Moreover, US authorities continue to place intolerable pressure on African nations to accept what is now a surplus of GM food from US farmers. For example, the US Ambassador to the United Nations, Mr Tony Hall, suggested that Zambia's political leaders be convicted as criminals, by stating that 'people that deny food to their people, that are in fact starving people to death, should be held responsible ... for the highest crimes against humanity in the highest courts in the world' (quoted in Reuters 2002). Other sources in the international press were claiming that 'millions' were dying in Zambia (see Laidlaw 2002) and Minister Sikatana explained that this was all part of the political pressure placed on his Government by US authorities:

Food is a weapon of mass destruction. It is used by some countries to control and pressure the poorer African nations. Western leaders have accused my President of untruths. In 2002 when we had a food deficit, they said that 4 million people were starving. This was all propaganda. No one in Zambia died from starvation. The food deficit was isolated to Southern regions where people eat maize. In the north we had a surplus of cassava, if the US Government really wanted to help Zambians why not transport our surplus cassava from the north to hungry people in the south, but no. So you must understand how lies and manipulation are used to exploit the hungry. But this year we have a surplus of maize. For the first time in Zambia's 40 year independence we have a surplus of grain, and we are now exporting grain to Angola and Malawi, and we've done it without GMOs. (Sikatana 2004)

Other Government interviewees also placed the above comments of US Ambassador Hall within its political and economic contexts, arguing that it 'served to endorse US food aid policies. … African countries experience this sort of political pressure from the west all the time whether it be in health, education or whatever. And why? Because there are more and more business opportunities emerging in Africa in engineering and development and western countries are all competing for the profits'.

The US Government has also been accused of dumping unwanted GM food on starving African countries and using Africa as a 'human experiment' (Townsend 2002). In addition, it has been alleged that the US Government and biotech industries are using the UN food aid programme as a 'covert subsidy for US farmers' (Vidal 2002). This criticism has further deepened the scepticism of sub-Saharan nations and stiffened their resolve to reject GM foods from the United States. One Zambian scientist explained:

The US oversupply of GM grain creates a danger for the North American market. Too much grain drives prices down which effects local American markets. Food aid to Africa provides an option to rescue local markets while scoring international political points as a donor of food. But then again, it is never simply donated, it always comes with a debt of some kind. But it must be remembered that the US are not motivated by a sincere humanitarian desire to help people who are hungry, they are motivated by their own local economies and their own local markets.

Government, non-governmental organizations and farmer groups in Zambia interviewed for this research reported that starvation was exaggerated by the West to optimize commercial opportunities. That said, there is no doubting that Southern Zambia experienced a six-month food shortage in 2002, but reports of widespread famine and death were untrue and exploited. For example, US President, George Bush, claimed that US efforts to reduce hunger in Africa were 'impeded' by European nations that 'have blocked all new bio-crops because of unfounded, unscientific fears'. As a result, President Bush argued that African countries 'avoid investing in bio-technologies for fear that their products will be shut out of European markets' (see BBC News 2003).

Yet, it is clear that the politicization of hunger serves to mask the economic priorities of the US administration. Take for example, the non-food industries of cotton and tobacco.

Zambia has a very productive and thriving cotton industry. Indeed, cotton has been hailed as the 'one unquestioned success of Zambia's turn towards a market economy' since the country's liberalization policies in 1994 (Tschirley *et al*. 2004). Like other Zambian industries that have proven commercially and internationally fruitful, such as copper, gold and gemstones, cotton has also attracted offshore corporate interests. Several interviewees reported that US and UK cotton corporations were growing and testing GM cotton without the Zambian Government's knowledge. Again, a growing and lively market economy for cotton in Zambia has attracted corporate interests with a pro-GM position for increasing yields and maximizing profits. Of course, the proposed bt cotton for the Zambian market (which has been prohibited by current Zambian authorities) would have seen offshore corporate industries patent cotton plantations and increase their profit share in crop production.

Interestingly, while US officials have put pressure on Zambia to accept biotechnologies with food and cotton, the opposite is true for tobacco. Philip Morris USA, the largest tobacco company in the United States, with cigarette brand varieties consuming 49.9 per cent of the US retail markets, refuses to purchase GM tobacco from international growers (Philip Morris USA 2004). GM technologies in cigarette production are used solely by US-based Vector Group Limited, which also produces a nicotine-free cigarette. Vector claims that it is committed to helping people quit smoking and their research demonstrates that one in three smokers using its Quest nicotine-free cigarette ceases smoking within four weeks (Tobacco.org 2004). As one Zambian interviewee from the tobacco industry stated: '... if GM technologies are so good, as the US keeps saying with food and cotton, why not for tobacco? It's simple, GM tobacco is less addictive and therefore it's not wanted, now what does they say about the US' motivation?' This contradiction serves to briefly illustrate that the propagation of GM technologies by the US Government and bio-corporations is more about exploitation for economic growth than humanitarian relief and poverty reduction.

This exploitation of hunger is a violation of the 1999 United Nations Food Aid Convention, to which the United States is a signatory. Article 1 stipulates that 'food aid provided is aimed particularly at the alleviation of poverty and hunger of the most vulnerable groups, and is consistent with agricultural developments in those countries'. Food shortages and hunger are not intended to be commercial opportunities and signatories of the Food Aid Convention agree to reduce poverty and famine through aid and not advance their own agricultural industries or exploit new trade agreements. Moreover, the US Government's insistence that Zambia accept GM food and the subsequent pressure that was exerted (discussed further below) was a clear breach of Article 1. In addition, the US Government refused to provide food grants or cash to Zambia for non-GM aid – a position that violates the 'terms of aid' defined in Article 9 of the Food Aid Convention.

## World trade wars and the promotion of GM technologies

The economic imperatives of US agricultural and foreign policy are further highlighted in relation to the so-called 'US trade wars'. In addition to verbal pressure from international diplomats, the US Government has also launched a case with the World Trade Organisation (WTO) in an attempt to seek a ruling that prevents an anti-GM trade stance currently adopted by the European Commission. In May 2003, the Bush administration began its case in the WTO against the European Commission, seeking billions of dollars damages for lost revenue, arguing that the EU violated its WTO obligations with a moratorium on GM food that constituted a 'trade barrier' (Schifferes 2003). Since the commencement of the proceedings, the US Government has argued that the EU moratorium on GM food was not only harming international trade, but was also preventing developing countries from importing biotechnology. The United States seeks an international ruling that would force countries to accept GM food and its associated biotechnology products. This has raised serious concerns by governments and agricultural groups around the world that the WTO is an inappropriate place to make a judgment confined by narrow trade rules. The WTO is due to report its findings in July 2005.

The outcome of the WTO ruling will clearly influence governments and international trade. That said, the legal and political pressure exerted throughout its proceedings is already having an impact on international governing bodies. For example, in March 2004, the European Commission approved the trial planting of NK603 maize – a herbicide-resistant crop – owned by bio-tech giant Monsanto (Engdahl 2004). Moreover, in May 2004, 60 organizations from 15 African countries forwarded an open letter to the United Nations' World Food Programme, criticizing that the (WFP) and US Agency for International Development (USAID) were misleading African nations by presenting them with a 'no choice option' but to accept GM food (Ash and Mayet 2004). Further condemnation of the United Nations followed with the UN Food and Agriculture Organization (FAO) releasing its report, 'Agricultural Biotechnology: Meeting the Needs of the Poor?', which was criticized for being 'biased against the poor, against the environment and against food production in general'. It prompted a second open letter, signed by representatives from 80 countries angered by the United Nations' support of biotech companies, stating 'The report turns FAO away from food sovereignty and the real needs of the world's farmers, and is a stab in the back to the farmers and rural poor FAO is meant to support' (quoted in Grain 2004).

Within the Zambian context, these international pressures and 'trade wars' have clearly influenced the local WFP as well as USAID. In 2004, the US Government provided an estimated US$66 million in financial assistance to Zambia, through USAID. Its Strategic Plan for Zambia for 2004 to 2010 focuses on five key objectives of 'increased private sector competitiveness', 'improved quality of basic education for more school-aged children', 'improved health status of Zambians', 'Government held more accountable' and 'reduced impact of HIV/AIDS through multi-sectoral response' (US Department of State 2004).

The Zambian's Government rejection of US GM food has reportedly produced ramifications for funding. An interviewee for this research who sits on various official committees stated 'USAID has reduced funding for projects in social and health type projects. This is a silent or unspoken penalty for rejecting GMO's'. It appears, however, that USAID remains committed to its first objective in Zambia, namely providing business opportunities for US-based companies, as one scientist stated: 'USAID champion western ideals whilst creating opportunities for US business' ... business is number one and if research starts saying that GM food is harmful then it will effect US business ... so the research doesn't get done unless it can produce positive results.'

Another scientist interviewed for this research stated that his organization received substantial funding from USAID (as many organizations in Zambia do) and that USAID 'actively dissuaded us from doing research on GM food'. Indeed, scientific research into GM technology in Zambia has received substantial funding from biotech companies and pro-GM lobbies. As one senior Government scientist interviewed for this research stated: '... we have Monsanto funding research people like academics and other scientific projects to promote GMO's. ... It's more promotion and public relations than what I'd call real research, but it still has a lot of important people listening to it both in Zambia and in other countries.'

Therefore, in addition to international political and legal pressure, there is evidence of governments and corporations adopting an orchestrated campaign to suppress or prevent research in Zambia that criticizes GM food, and, instead, to actively promote pro-GM technologies.

### US Government pressures the Vatican

In addition to political, economic and legal pressures, the US Government has been actively engaged in exerting diplomatic pressure, notably within the Vatican City.

With millions of followers of the Catholic faith, an endorsement of GM food from the Holy See would create substantial business opportunities and revenue for the US Government and its biotech corporations. Moreover, it is worth tracing some of the events involving the Holy See, as Jesuit Priests in Zambia have been actively opposing the aggressive trade policies of GM corporations and, as a result, have been severely criticized by US Government authorities and pro-GM scientists (see Apel *et al.* 2002).

During September–December 2002, following the Zambian Government's rejection of GM food, US authorities began meeting with senior archbishops at the Vatican. The US ambassador to the Holy See and a strong advocate of biotechnology, Mr Jim Nicholson, held several meetings with Archbishop Leonardo Sandri, Monsignor Celestino Migliore and Jesuit Superior General Peter-Hans Kolvenbach to obtain 'a clear and unambiguous' statement that affirmed the 'the safety of biotech foods' that would 'neutralise anti-propaganda in Africa' (Cardinale 2003). Such meetings did not achieve their objective; instead, the Holy See reaffirmed the right of developing countries to adopt the precautionary principle regarding the acceptance of food aid. As a result, the United States intensified its pressure on the Vatican, with the US Secretary of State, Colin Powell, receiving an audience with the late Pope John Paul II on 2 June 2003 (Independent Catholic News 2003). Mr Powell is reported to have said to the Pope 'Look at me, Sir. I eat genetically modified products every day; all in all, I'm not doing too badly, am I?'

The US delegation to the Vatican clearly influenced the Holy See and within five months, a conference was organized on 10–11 November 2003, in the offices of the Pontifical Council for Justice and Peace 'to gather a great amount of information about GMOs, studying their implications in the fields of nutrition, commerce, the environment, and health care, as well as humanitarian and ethical aspects' (Catholic World News 2003). The conference had a clear pro-GM agenda, yet its outcome failed to produce a definitive Vatican position on GM food. In early 2004, US authorities maintained diplomatic pressure on the Vatican through the release of a book written by the Ambassador of the United States to the Holy See, Mr Jim Nicholson. This book celebrates 20 years of diplomatic relation between the Holy See and the United States. In doing so, it provides a substantial discussion about GMOs. In this book, Nicholson (2004: 108) makes the US case for GM food in Africa and, in so doing, identifies the rationale for the US pressuring the Vatican: '... we believe the Holy See's moral voice on food consumption safety and on the potential of such food to end world hunger and malnutrition may help diminish myths about biotech foods in underdeveloped countries. Moreover, the Holy See can discourage the spread of erroneous information, which jeopardize the lives of persons, through prominent Church personalities or groups associated with them' (cf. Magister 2004). Furthermore, he criticized certain individuals in Zambia, notably a 'Jesuit priest' for spreading misinformation about GMOs, paralysing 'the World Food Programme's efforts in Zambia, and placing 'millions of lives at risk' (Nicholson 2004: 109). These disparaging remarks were directed at Dr Peter Henriot, the Director of the Jesuit Centre for Theological Reflection in Lusaka, who has been critical of biotechnology and its potential deleterious effects on developing societies. More recently, Henriot has criticized a further conference convened at the Vatican on 24 September 2004 entitled 'Feeding a Hungry World: The Moral Imperative of Biotechnology'. This conference was funded and organized by the US Embassy to the Holy See and included six plenary speakers, most with affiliations to biotech companies in the United States (see Turnley 2004). Father Henriot and a senior researcher in agriculture in Lusaka, Dr Roland Lesseps, suggested that the conference was seriously flawed, concluding that the Vatican should be extremely cautious that it is not seen to be compromised through linkages with known promoters of only one position on this issue: 'When ethical and religious issues such as food security are being discussed, there is no place either for one scientific view to be heard or only one political force to be recognised' (Lesseps and Henriot 2004). Others severely criticized the conference for an unquestioning belief in GM technology and for being 'hopelessly stacked in favour of the controversial new technology' (Hitchen 2004). These 'outspoken' voices may have influenced the Pope, who had recently intimated a rejection of GM food by stressing the rights of farmers, the need to preserve biodiversity and protect indigenous communities 'whose vast patrimony or culture and knowledge linked to biodiversity, run the risk of disappearing because of a lack of adequate protection' (Pope John Paul II, quoted in Independent Catholic News (2004)). This case serves to illustrate the various dimensions to the 'biotech wars' in Zambia.

## Monopolies and the politics of GM food

The first question that arises from the above case study is why have US officials and corporations placed so much pressure on Zambia? There are several dimensions to this question's answer. First, an anti-GM stance in Europe and a growing consumer rejection of GM technologies is reportedly costing the US Government millions per year in exports (Alden and Man 2002). In addition to EU and most African countries rejecting GM foods, governments in China, Japan, Indonesia and Thailand have also decided to temporarily halt GM crop planting (Puttajanyawong 2004). It is essential that with European and Asian markets closed, new markets are found for the world's surplus GM food – securing Africa as a future GM market is essential to the sustainability of bio-agriculture. Secondly, the acceptance of US GM grain as African food aid is both politically and economically important. Food aid is a multi-million dollar industry, with significant diplomatic advantages for international negotiations. Thirdly, Zambia has become strategically important for the pro-GM movement. Zambia's outspoken and internationally reported opposition to GM food has unintentionally asserted its agricultural significance in the sub-Saharan region. Neighbouring countries look to Zambia for direction in relation to biodiversity. As a result, to win Zambian support for GM food is a political and economic coup, as other nations that are sceptical of bio-agriculture may embrace the technology. Fourthly, developing nations are biodiversity rich and their genetic resources are of substantial commercial value to northern industrialized countries. It is therefore important for Western economic growth that trade routes with African nations remain open and prosperous (cf. Biggs 1998).

It is important to contextualize the above reasons within the politics of GM food and shared monopolies. The overwhelming majority of GM food and its accompanying fertilizers, seeds and herbicides are produced from four chemical corporations, namely Monsanto, Syngenta, Du Pont and Bayer (see Nottingham 2003). Clearly, GM food and genetic engineering remain big business. Yet, free-trade ideologies espoused by the WTO to enhance notions of competitive capitalism are compromised by a status quo of monopoly capitalism. The costs to consumers and industries when market dominance is controlled by a select number of large conglomerates has been examined in discourses of corporate or 'elite' deviance for some time (Simon and Eitzen 1990; see also Tombs and Whyte 2003). Such discourses remain important for understanding the inherent dangers of market control, particularly in developing societies where economic vulnerabilities create opportunities for eco-plunder and corporate exploitation. The lucrative global trade for governments and the four GM giants is essential for understanding pressures, unethical and illegal actions discussed in relation to Zambia. As Winston (2002: 174) argues, 'genetically modified organisms would be only an interesting academic sideline if there was no money to be made. The heavy investments in research that have driven corporate biotechnology would not have been forthcoming without the product protection provided by patents'. The monopolization of four biotech companies in what is commonly referred to as 'bio-imperialism' (see Engdahl 2004) continues to mount concerns and fears within agricultural and consumer groups. Farmers, for example, remain sceptical of the motivations and tactics of corporations that attempt to control and profit from food production through the laws of patent and intellectual property.

In addition, the aggressive and unlawful business practices of the GM giants have heightened widespread anxiety about the technology. For example, public relations have reportedly entered the fray by representing biotech companies in the promotion of GM food technologies. Allegations of fraud have been pitted against Bivings Group, hired by Monsanto to discredit the findings of research that criticized GM maize in Mexico. It was alleged that Bivings invented bogus citizen movements and phantom corporations to challenge environmentalists and independent scientific research that criticized GM food technologies. Bivings have denied the allegations but not pursued the matter legally. The evidence of anti-GM hostilities from fake people and companies, bogus websites and fraudulent emails, all linked to the computers of the Bivings Group, may explain their lack of legal intervention (see Monbiot 2002; cf. Engdahl 2004). In addition, the reputation of the biotechnology industry will be further damaged by Monsanto's $US1.5 million fine for bribery. The US bio-agricultural giant admitted that one of its senior executives orchestrated the payment of various bribes to Indonesian officials during 1997–2002 to suppress anti-GM activists and to receive preferential government treatment for its GM products (BBC News 2005).

Moreover, Clapp (2003) outlines how biotech corporations play an increasingly influential role in environmental policy making and global environmental governance. This is achieved through the presence of bio-technology representatives who are actively involved in lobbying at international negotiations. As a result, transnational corporations are not simply reacting to the decisions of environmental governing bodies and protocols, but 'increasingly engaged directly in public debates to maximise industry profit' (Clapp 2003: 3). Hence, industry lobby groups strongly opposed the strict regulations over GMOs proposed in the negotiations of the Cartagena Protocol in favour of 'free trade'. Of course, the duplicitous and unethical involvement of corporations in environmental politics is not new. The use of green media campaigns and corporations rebranding themselves as environmentally friendly while, at the same time, polluting the environment and lobbying politicians and environmental groups for commercial opportunities has been widely reported (see Karliner 1997). However, as deGrassi (2003: 51) argues, the manipulation of the GM debate serves to exploit vulnerable societies, stating that 'governments and corporations have mobilized funding as part of high-stakes international dispute over biotechnology, in essence rendering African agricultural research – and our understanding of poverty dynamics on the continent – pawns in the conflicts of the powerful'.

The monopolization and manipulation of governing bodies stated above are of considerable concern with relation to risk assessment. There is no democratization of risk assessment in GM foods but a corporate hegemony over science, with claims to 'absolute or scientific truth'. As Wales and Mythen (2002) argue, 'despite recognized social and political dimensions of risk, science, as a totalizing discourse still regulates the production of "truth"'. This is clearly problematic on various fronts, not least because the science of biotechnology and GM organisms remains fraught with ambiguities, uncertainties and complications (see Ahmed 2004).

The actions of GM corporations and the negative press that accompanied it, coupled with the reported reality of GM gene transfer in the environment and risks to the human body (see Pollack 2004; Rieger *et al.* 2002; World Health Organisation 2000), has Plant Biotechnology, according to Lurquin (2002: 138), facing 'possibly more opposition today, at least in some segments of society than nuclear power plants'. Moreover, in the United States, recent reports indicate that two-thirds of all crops are contaminated with GMOs, 'dooming organic agriculture and posing a sever future risk to health' (Lean 2004). As a result, the majority of Americans are now opposed to GM. A 2003 food and biotechnology agriculture survey revealed that 58 per cent were 'unwilling to eat genetically modified (GM) food' (see Fedoroff and Brown 2004: 313). This growing groundswell against GMOs has been castigated by biotechnology companies in the United States who claim that Americans have contracted 'the European disease' (Collins 2004; cf. Baker and Burnham 2002).

In September 2004, 60 per cent of Britons stated that they were opposed to GM foods and feared that they were consuming GM products 'unknowingly' (Lawrence 2004). The International Consortium on Biotechnology Research (ICBS) identifies that media reporting of scientific testing of GM food in the United Kingdom and United States highlights the negative aspects of research and has contributed to consumer rejection of GM products (see Marks *et al.* 2002a). In a separate piece, Marks *et al.* (2002) claim that the agro-biotechnology scientists have contributed to the communication problem by not publishing their work in peer-reviewed journals. Moreover, pro-biotech organizations such as ICBS have developed economic models and marketing strategies to enhance consumer and business confidence in GM foods (see Santaniello *et al.* 2002b). This identifies the importance of discourses on risk, fear and moral panic within the politics of GM food and its impact on global trade, consumer attitudes and corporate responsibility – such issues are not explored here. Attention is now turned to international environmental law and the emerging concept of 'eco-crime'.

## Eco-crime, green criminology and international environmental law

### Eco-crime

Eco-crime is illegal and/or harmful behaviour, including threatening, damaging or destroying the natural environment, and is a term often used synonymously with 'environmental crime' or 'green crime', which has recently emerged as a key issue in debates about globalization, sustainable development and conservation (see Carrabine *et al.* 2004, of Westra 2004). It is defined in various international protocols as 'an unauthorised act or omission that violates the law and is therefore subject to criminal prosecution and criminal sanction' (Situ and Emmons 2000: 3). Many such violations are reflected in the growing number of domestic laws, as well as international environmental protocols, treaties and conventions that provide legal mandates that prohibit a range of activities identified as hazardous and deleterious to global ecosystems (see Soyland 2000). Moreover, discourses in organizational deviance and human rights that place eco-crime within analyses of state-corporate crime provide useful analytical pathways beyond the boundaries of international law (see White 2003; Green and Ward 2004).

Eco-crime is also a unifying term that incorporates a range of terms, including 'ecocide', 'geocide', 'geo or eco terrorism' and 'environmental and green crime' (see Berat 1993; Odek 1994; Gray 1996; Broswimmer 2001). Many such acts are reflected in the growing number of treaties. Two recently enacted international laws, namely the Cartagena Protocol on Biosafety and the International Treaty on Plant Genetic Resources for Food and Agriculture, are crucial for exploring emerging eco-crimes committed by states and corporations described above.

### Developments in international environmental law

For more than five years, the negotiations that have lead to the Cartagena Protocol were hotly contested, frequently on the brink of collapse and fraught with manipulation. As Nijar (2002: 263) identifies, every step of the way, 'the biotechnology industry and its governmental protagonists in the negotiating process fought to prevent the protocol from coming into existence'. Bail *et al.* (2002) provide a detailed insight into the often bitter debate that transpired between negotiating groups that were polarized by vested interests.

The Protocol came into force on 11 September 2003, exactly 90 days after the 50 signatories had ratified it. The protocol provides a mandate for the safe transfer, handling and use of 'living modified organisms resulting from modern biotechnology that may have adverse effects on the conservation and sustainable use of biological diversity, taking also into account risks to human health, and specifically focusing on transboundary movements' (Article 1). Countries that plan to introduce living modified organisms into another country will be required to submit an application notifying exact details of content (Articles 7 and 8) and all products intended for food or feed must be labelled (Article 18). The importation of all GMOs to nations that are party to the Protocol will require risk assessments and the express written approval of the receiving country (Articles 11, 15 and 16). No signatory to the Protocol can be forced to accept GMOs without their consent, thus preserving sovereign rights – an issue that is being contested by the United States in the WTO. Moreover illegal movement of GMOs, notably contravention of the protocol (Article 25), provides for liability and redress that includes financial penalties (see Articles 27 and 28).

Moreover, the Protocol is consistent with the Convention on Biological Diversity and adopting the precautionary principle 15 of the Rio Declaration which states 'that where there is threat of significant reduction or loss of biological diversity, lack of full scientific certainty should not be used as a reason for postponing measures to avoid or minimize such a threat'. Therefore the Cartagena Protocol (notably Articles 1, 10 and 11) encourage parties to incorporate precautionary measures into their national framework. In doing so, it grants a right to take precaution based on national or internal risk assessments. A lack of scientific evidence confirming 'potential adverse effects' cannot be asserted to force any country to accept GMOs. This principle has been strongly adopted by developing countries such as Zambia that currently lack the infrastructure to categorically and scientifically deduce the risks posed by GMOs. The Cartagena Protocol permits all parties to self-determine their acceptance or rejection of GMOs based on their own mechanisms of risk assessment. This principal creates tensions with notions of free trade and international trade law. The US-led case in the WTO against the European Union's so-called moratorium on GM food has been premised on the assumption that anti-GMO stances based on unscientific and inconclusive evidence constitute illegal trade barriers (see Falkner 2004).

The Cartagena Protocol has recently been strengthened with the ratification of the International Treaty on Plant Genetic Resources for Food and Agriculture that officially became law on 29 June 2004. This agreement has been reached in harmony with the Convention on Biological Diversity and has two distinct objectives. The first is the 'conservation and sustainable use of plant genetic resources for food and agriculture' and the second is the 'fair and equitable sharing of the benefits arising out of their use' (Article 1). As a result, the treaty aims to address acts of bio-piracy and bio-prospecting. The commercial use of genetic resources must result in equitable sharing (information exchange, access to technology, capacity building and financial payments) to the country of genetic origin (Article 13). Moreover, the treaty identifies the important role of farmers and indigenous knowledge in the preservation of genetic resources and establishes a set of 'farmers' rights' that includes the 'right to equitably participate in sharing benefits arising from the utlization of plant genetic resources for food and agriculture' and 'the right to participate in making decisions, at the national level, on matters related to the conservation and sustainable use of plant genetic resources' (Article 9).

Both of the above laws provide substantial stepping stones in safeguarding the autonomy of biological diversity of individual nation states and protection from the exploitation and aggressive trade policies of powerful Western states. They grant rights of sovereignty to individual parties and provide a legal mandate for developing countries to reject GM food. In doing so, it is now illegal to distribute and trade in GM food products without the express written consent of the receiving government. Moreover, it is a requirement to label all GM food products and for countries to base decisions on importing GM products based on their own risk-assessment processes. Importantly, the use of threats and intimidation (discussed in the case study above) through political, diplomatic or legal pressure to accept GM food is a breach of the Protocol that grants specific rights of self-determination over food and biodiversity to all signatories.

Like all treaties and international agreements, mechanisms of compliance, liability and redress especially against powerful non-party countries (such as the United States) remain an ongoing issue of concern – and perhaps a weakness of the Protocol. That said, the Cartegena Protocol and the Treaty on Genetic Resources have served to promote eco-sovereignty and preserve biodiversity. In doing so, bio-rich developing countries have been given both a voice and a forum to develop their economic opportunities while preserving their cultural heritage. Moreover, new international environmental laws provide nation states with the mandate to develop their own legislative frameworks and the confidence to resist the aggressive tactics and practices of powerful corporations and governments. As mentioned above, Zambia has continually been pressured by US authorities for its anti-GM stance. In 2005, Zambia will pass its Biosafety Legislation for the protection and preservation of its biological resources. It does so with the full backing of the international community and environmental law.

### The greening of criminology

The diversity of subject matter covered under both international environmental laws has necessitated the integration of diverse expertise and knowledge, including criminology.

Green criminology [first coined by Lynch (1990)] is a useful paradigm for analysing 'eco-crime' and provides an umbrella under which to theorize and critique the emerging terminology related to environmental harm. Green criminology is a hybrid of state–corporate crime analyses and must integrate concepts of power, governance, globalization and capital within a model of environmental justice. Moreover, the greening of criminology provides an interface with social movements, green politics and disciplines in law, environmental science and human rights to examine issues of environmental harm and ecological preservation.

A criminological scholarship committed totally to the environment is long overdue, as it seeks to explore issues of environmental deviance by utilizing a range of analytical tools in the production of a knowledge that is theoretical, empirically grounded and politically active. The production and trade of GM food are important issues for green criminology that provide a mandate for broadening the critical gaze and opening up the debate to alternative avenues of analysis that examine the issues within social, cultural and political frameworks.

Carrabine et al. (2004: 28) identify that green criminology in its 'early stage of development has four main tasks (a) to document the existence of green crimes in all their forms and to evolve basic typologies and distinctions such as that between primary and secondary green crimes; (b) to chart the ways in which the laws have been developed around this area, and to assess the complications and political issues generated; (c) to connect green crimes to social inequalities; (d) to assess the role of green social movements (and their counter-movements involved in a backlash) in bringing about social change'.

Halsey (2004: 835) provides an argument 'against' green criminology, claiming that it has failed to move beyond 'modernist conceptions of harm and reparation' that focus on anthropocentric concepts and practices. As a serious theoretical enterprise, green criminology must be reviewed, critiqued and challenged in order for it to develop into a dynamic and viable discourse. That said, Halsey's attempt to 'sound the closing bell' is a little premature when green criminology remains a new critical narrative that continues to develop and find its way. Halsey offers what could be called a form of 'post-structuralist green criminology' that seeks to deconstruct modernist notions of nature in favour of a constitutive criminology (see Henry and Milovanovic 1996) that moves beyond dualisms and 'truisms' to a reflexive and malleable environmental lexicon, capable of transcending the polarized, politicized and reductionist discourses within eco-marxism, eco-feminism, eco-critical theory and social ecology. The poststructuralist green position must be an extension of existing social and political thought within criminological scholarship and not a replacement. For example, Foucault's discourse analysis is capable of understanding the politics of GM food, notably the ways in which governments, corporations and interest groups have established 'regimes of truth' about the risks and uses of GM food (see Toke 2004).

However, debates about GM food that include the exploitation of hunger described in the above Zambian case study require an interdisciplinary and multifaceted green criminology where power and economy are indeed important aspects to the debate. Halsey's argument that 'structural economic power relies for its efficacy not simply on the relations between government, law and economy, so much as the *flows of pleasure* which invest the population at any one time' (p. 844) is interesting, yet devoid of the necessary understandings that influence the lives, economies and polities of the developing world. The exploitation of the world's hungry and the biotechnology industry's pressure on the world's poor is less about 'flows of pleasure' and more about power and profit. That said, a postmodern green perspective may offer a useful way forward to disentangle contested notions of 'eco-sovereignty', 'eco-plunder', 'ec-autonomy' and 'sustainable development' that are central to the GM food debate.

Finally, Newburn and Sparks (2004) identify the ways in which crime-control policies travel internationally and examine the need for transnational justice to extend beyond domestic borders to form international networks of policing and prevention. The global reach of environmental harm and actions defined above as 'eco-crimes' must also be addressed beyond national domains. Green criminology has the potential, for example, to assert environmental justice within emerging debates of a newly created International Environment Court (see Pirro 2002). Such critical engagement at an international level with scholars and practitioners from diverse fields seeks to integrate notions of ecological harm within frameworks of state crime, corporate responsibility and conservation. In doing so, it may serve to harness the growing amount of international environmental law and policy, and provide leadership through the impasse created by polarized debate of trade and environmentalism. Yet, these and others remain some of the challenges facing a 'green criminology' if it is to provide an alternative or something new within debates about environmental crime and justice.

## Conclusion

The monopolization of biotechnology in the past five years and the expansion of GM products have produced aggressive, unethical and illegal corporate actions in the name of free trade that necessitate criminological involvement. The ongoing pressure on countries such as Zambia to accept GM technologies violates international environment law and serves to remind us how states and corporations exercise and exploit law, international relations and power for political and economic gain. This research identifies that emerging eco or green crimes within GM food are issues that influence human and environmental safety and require a criminological agenda that transcends disciplinary boundaries and engages with diverse narratives in commerce and law, as well the natural and social sciences. The regulation, prevention and prosecution of eco-crimes require an engagement with both the local and the global. Therefore, criminology must deploy multiple approaches in addressing the increasing risks and harms posed by governing bodies within the politics and trade of GM food. Such a perspective requires a holistic approach that draws upon multiple narratives and is attentive to political and social movements in conservation and environmentalism. The exploitation of the majority world by powerful Western corporations and governments also requires an action-led criminology, capable of responding to the realities of those affected. Bio-agriculture and GM food provide important examples of how criminology must continue to develop in order to embrace the challenges posed by technological advancement and global trade.

## References

Ahmed, F., ed. (2004), *Testing of Genetically Modified Organisms in Foods*. Binghamton, NY: Food Products Press.

Alden, E. and Man, M. (2002), 'US Shifts Tactics in GMO Clash with EU: Washington Hopes Diplomatic Efforts Would Isolate Europe and Change Global Attitude', *Financial Times*, 15 October 2002.

Apel, A., Conko, G., Defez, R., Ederle, D., Kershen, D., Morandini, P., Parrott, W. and Prakash, C. (2002) *To Die or Not to Die: This Is the Problem*. Agbioworld: Tuskegee Institute.

Ash, B. and Mayet, M. (2004), 'African Groups Accuse WFP and USAID of Denying Africa's Right to Choose to Reject GM Food Aid', Africa Centre for Biosafety and Earthlife Africa, 4 May 2004, available online at: www.connectotal.com/gmfoof/ac040504.txt.

Ashley, B., Hollows, J., Jones, S. and Taylor, B. (2004), *Food and Cultural Studies*. London: Routledge.

Bail, C., Falkner, R. and Marquard, H., eds (2002), *The Cartagena Protocol on Biosafety: Reconciling Trade in Biotechnology with Environment and Development*. The Royal Institute of International Affairs, London.

Baker, G. and Burnham, T. (2002), 'The Market for Genetically Modified Foods: Consumer Characteristics and Policy Implications', *The International Food and Agribusiness Management Review*, 4: 345–50.

Banda, M., Mwenya, W., Bolla, G., Chale, P., Aongola, A., Mwila, G. and Lewanika, M. (2002), *Report of the Fact Finding Mission on Genetically Modified Crops and Food Products*. Lusaka: USAID.

BBC News (2003), 'Bush: Africa Hostage to GM Fears', *BBC News UK Edition*, 22 May 2003, available online at: www.news.bbc.uk/l/hi/world/americas/3050855.stm.

BBC News (2005), 'Monsanto Fined $1.5 m for Bribery', *BBC News UK Edition*, 7 January 2005, available online at: http://news.bbc.co.uk/l/hi/business/4153635.stm.

Berat, L. (1993), 'Defending the Right to a Healthy Environment: Toward a Crime of Genocide in International Law', in N. Passas, ed. (2003), *International Crimes*. Dartmouth: Ashgate.

Biggs, S. (1998), 'The Biodiversity Convention and Global Sustainable Development', in R. Kiely and P. Marfleet, eds, *Globalisation and the Third World*, 113–40. London: Routledge.

Broswimmer, F. (2001), *Ecocide: A Short History of Mass Extinction of Species*. London: Pluto Press.

Cardinale, G. (2003), 'For a Fistful of Biotech Grain', *30 days in the Church and the World, International Monthly*, available online at: www.30giorni.it/us/articolo.asp?id =1057.

Carrabine, E., Iganski, P., Lee, M., Plummer, K. and South, N. (2004), *Criminology: A Sociological Introduction*. London: Routledge.

Catholic World News (2003), 'Vatican to Host Conference on Genetically-Altered Food Products', available online at: www.cwnews.com/news/viewstory.cfm?recnum =25799.

Clapp, J. (2003), 'Transnational Corporate Interests and Global Environmental Governance: Negotiating Rules for Agricultural Biotechnology and Chemicals', *Environmental Politics*, 12: 1–23.

Collins, S. (2004), 'Anti-GM Views Growing in the US', *New Zealand Herald*, 8 June 2004.

Convention on Biological Diversity (2004), 'Ratification of the Cartagena Protocol on Biosafety and its Entry into Force', available online at: www.biodiv.org/biosafety/ratification.asp (accessed 4 October 2004).

Degrassi, A. (2003), Genetically *Modified Crops and Sustainable Poverty Alleviation in Sub-Saharan Africa: An Assessment of Current Evidence*. Penang: Third World Network.

Dreze, J., Sen, A. and Hussain, A., eds (1995), *The Political Economy of Hunger*. Oxford: Clarendon Press.

Engdahl, F. W. (2004), *Bio-Imperialism: Why the Biotech Bullies Must be Stopped*. Little Marais: Organic Consumers Association.

Falkner, R. (2004), 'Trading Food: The Politics of Genetically Modified Organisms', in B. Hocking and S. McGuire, eds, *Trade Politics, Second Edition*. London: Routledge.

Fedoroff, N. and Brown, N. (2004), *Mendel in the Kitchen: A Scientist's View of Genetically Modified Foods*. Washington, DC: Joseph Henry Press.

Food and Agriculture Organisation of the United Nations (2004), The *State of Food and Agriculture: Agricultural Biotechnology, Meeting the Needs of the Poor*. Rome: United Nations.

Grain (2004), 'FAO Declares War on Farmers, Not on Hunger', Press Release, available online at: www.grain.org/go/fao-en.

Gray, M. (1996), 'The International Crime of Ecocide', *California Western International Law Journal*, 26: 215–71.

Green, P. and Ward, T. (2004), *State Crime: Governments, Violence and Corruption*. London: Pluto Press.

Halsey, M. (2004), 'Against "Green" Criminology', *British Journal of Criminology*, 44: 833–53.

Harle, V., ed. (1978), *The Political Economy of Food*. Westmead: Saxon House.

Henry, S. and Milovanovic, D. (1996), *Constitutive Criminology: Beyond Postmodernism*. London: Sage.

Hitchen, P. (2004), 'Critics Slam Vatican-US Promotion of GM Foods', *The Tablet*, 2 October 2004, available online at: www.connectotal.com/gmfood/ta021004.html.

Independent Catholic News (2003), 'Colin Powell Visits Pope', 2 June 2003, available online at: www.indcatholicnews.com/colin.html.

Independent Catholic News (2004), 'Pope Hints at Rejection of GM Food', 19 October 2004, available online at: www.incatholicnews.com/pogmfd.html.

Jonathan, A. (2004), 'Zambia Refuses GM Foods', 21 June 2004, available online at: www.news24.com/News24/Africa/News/0,,6619,2-11-1447_1545602,00.html.

Karliner, J. (1997), *Corporate Planet*. San Francisco: Sierra Publishing.

Kaularich, D. and Kramer, R. (1998) *Crimes of the American Nuclear State: At Home and Abroad*. Boston: Northeastern University Press.

Laidlaw, S. (2002), 'Grappling with GM Conundrum: Millions Dying as Zambia Rejects Food Aid in Bid to Protect Economy', *The Toronto Star*, 10 November 2002.

Lawrence, F. (2004), 'Concern at GM Crops Increases', *The Guardian*, 2 September 2004.

Lean, G. (2004), 'Genetically Modifies Strains Have Contaminated Two-Thirds of all Crops in US', *The Independent*, 7 March 2004.

Lesseps, R. and Henriot, P. (2004), 'Serious Flaws in a Conference on Moral Imperative of Biotechnology', Press Release, Jesuit Centre for Theological Reflection, Lusaka, Zambia, 20 September 2004.

Lurquin, P. (2002), *High Tech Harvest: Understanding Genetically Modified Food Plants*. Colorado: Westview Press.

Lynch, M. (1990), 'The Greening of Criminology: A Perspective for the 1990s', *The Critical Criminologist*, 2: 11–12.

Lynch, M. and Stretesky, P. (2003), 'The Meaning of Green: Contrasting Criminological Perspectives', *Theoretical Criminology*, 7: 217–38.

Magande, N. (2004), 'Minister of Finance and National Planning, Republic of Zambia', in World Report International Limited, *Zambia: 40 Years of Independence. Stability, Growth and Hope for the Future*. London: WRI.

Magister, S. (2004), 'The Multiplication of Loaves Has a New Name: GMO', *L'espresso la Repubblica*, available online at: http://213.92.16.98/ESW_articolo/0%2C2393%2C42098%2C00.html.

Marks, L., Mooney, S. and Kalaitzandonakes, N. (2002a), 'Quantifying Scientific Risk Communications of Agrobiotechnology', in V. Santaniello, R. Everson and D. Zilberman, eds, *Market Development for Genetically Modified Foods*, 205–16. New York: CABI Publishing.

Marks, L., Kalaitzandonakes, N., Allison, K. and Zakharova, L. (2002b), 'Time Series Analysis of Risk Frames in Media Communication of Agrobitechnology', in V. Santaniello, R. Everson and D. Zilberman, eds, *Market Development for Genetically Modified Foods*, 217–26. New York: CABI Publishing.

Martin, P. (2002), 'Greenpeace, Zambia Reject US Claim', *The Washington Times*, 31 August 2002.

Ministry of Science, Technology and Vocational Training (2003), *National Biotechnology and Biosafety Strategic Plan: 2003–2007*. Republic of Zambia, Lusaka.

Monbiot, G. (2002), 'Corporate Phantoms: The Web of Deceit Over GM Food', *The Guardian*, 29 May 2002.

Mulvany, P. (2004), 'The Dumping Ground: Africa and GM Food Aid', *Open Democracy*, 29 April 2004.

Mundia, S., Permanent Secretary (Marketing and Co-operation), Ministry of Agriculture, Republic of Zambia. Interviewed in Lusaka on 24 September 2004.

Newburn, T. and Sparks, R. (2004), *Criminal Justice and Political Cultures. National and International Dimensions of Crime Control*. Devon: Willan.

Nicholson, J. (2004), *The United States and the Holy See: The Long Road*. Vatican City: US Embassy.

Nijar, G. (2002), 'Third World Network', in C. Bail, R. Falkner and H. Marquard, eds, *The Cartagena Protocol on Biosafety: Reconciling Trade with Environment and Development*. London: Earthscan Publications.

Nottingham, S. (2003), *Eat Your Genes: How Genetically Modified Food is Entering Our Diet*. London: Zed Books Ltd.

Oder, J. (1994), 'Bio-Piracy: Creating Propriety Rights in Plant Genetic Resources', *Journal of Intellectual Property Law*, 2: 141–81.

Paarlberg, R. (2001), *The Politics of Precaution: Genetically Modified Crops in Developing Countries*. Baltimore: The John Hopkins University Press.

Pearce, F. and Tombs, S. (1993), 'US Capital versus the Third World: Union Carbide and Bhopal', in F. Pearce and M. Woodiwiss, eds, *Global Crime Connections: Dynamics and Control*. London: Macmillan.

Philip Morris USA (2004), 'Company Information', available online at: www.pmusa.com/ about_ us/company_information.asp.

Pirro, D. (2002) 'Project for an International Court of the Environment: Origins and Development', available online at: www.biopolitics.gr/HTML/PUBS/VOL8/html/Pirro.htm.

Plaut, M. (2002), 'Zambia Furious Over GM Food', BBC World Edition. 6 November 2002, available online at: www.bbc.co.uk/2/hi/africa/241603.stm.

Pollack, A. (2004), 'Genes from Engineered Grass Spread for Miles, Study Finds', *The New York Times*, 21 September 2004.

Pringle, P. (2003), *Food Inc. Mendel to Monsanto: The Promises and Perils of the Biotech Harvest*. New York: Simon and Schuster.

Puttajanyawong, T. (2004), 'Thai Cabinet Overturns GMO Approval', *Reuters*, 31 August 2004.

Reuters (2002) 'US to give hungry Zambia food despite GM spat', 9 December 2002.

Rieger, M., Lamond, M., Preston, C., Powles, S. and Roush, R. (2002), 'Pollen-Mediated Movement of Herbicide Resistance Between Commercial Canola Fields', *Science*, 296: 2386–8.

Santaniello, V., Evenson, R. and Zilberman, D., eds (2002), *Market Development for Genetically Modified Food*. Oxon: CABI Publishing.

Schifferes, S. (2003), 'US Launches GM Trade War', *BBC News UK Edition*, 13 May 2003, available online at: www.bbc.co.uk/1/hi/business/3025217.stm.

Sikatana, M. (2004), The Hon. Minister of Agriculture, Republic of Zambia. Interviewed in Lusaka, Zambia at Mulunguishi House on 22 September 2004.

Simon, D. and Eitzen, D. (1990), *Elite Deviance: Third Edition*. Needham Heights, MA: Allyn and Bacon.

Simwanda, L. and Mwala, J. (2004a), *Fact Finding Mission on GMOs by Zambian Delegation to South Africa*. Lusaka: Zambia Trade and Investment Enhancement Project.

Simwanda, L. and Mwala, J. (2004b), 'Access to Genetic Resources in Zambia', *African Perspectives to Law: Access to Genetic Resources*. London: Environmental Law Institute.

Situ, Y. and Emmons, D. (2000), *Environmental Crime: The Criminal Justice System's Role in Protecting the Environment*. Thousand Oaks, CA: Sage.

South, N. (1998), 'Corporate and State Crimes Against the Environment', in V. Ruggiero, N. South and I. Taylor, eds, *The New European Criminology: Crime and Social Order in Europe*, 443–61. London: Rouledge.

Soyland, S. (2000), Criminal *Organisations and Crimes Against the Environment*. Turin: UNCRI.

Tobacco.org (2004), 'DJ Vector Group Seeks Guidance from FDA on Smoking Cessation Claim', 6 October 2003, available online at: www.tobacco.org/articles/org/vector/?&total count_ 194&starting_at=50.

Toke, D. (2004), *The Politics of GM Food. A Comparative Study of the UK, USA and EU*. London: Routledge.

Tombs, S. and Whyte, D., eds (2003) *Unmasking the Crimes of the Powerful: Scrutinizing States and Corporations*. New York: Peter Lang Publishing.

Townsend, M. (2002), 'UK Chief Scientist Slams US GM 'Aid' to Africa as a 'Massive Human Experiment', *The Observer*, 1 September 2002.

Tschirley, D., Zulu, B. and Shaffer, J. (2004), *Cotton in Zambia: An Assessment of Its Organisation, Performance, Current Policy Initiatives, and Challenges for the Future*. Lusaka: Food Security Research Project.

Turnley, A. (2004), 'Feeding a Hungry World: The Moral Imperative of Biotechnology Conference Program Schedule', Unpublished Conference Schedule. Public Affairs Coordinator, US Embassy to the Holy See.

Vidal, J. (2002), 'US Dumping Unsold Food on Africa', *The Guardian*, 7 October 2002.

United States Department of State (2004), 'Background Note: Zambia', Bureau of African Affairs, September 2004, available online at: www.state.gov/r/pa/ei/bgn/2359/htm.

Wales, C. and Mythen, G. (2002), 'Risky Discourses: The Politics of GM Foods', *Environmental Politics*, 11: 121–44.

Walters, R. (2004), 'Criminology and Genetically Modified Food', *The British Journal of Criminology*, 44: 151–67.

Westra, L. (2004), *Ecoviolence and the Law (Supranational Normative Foundations of Ecocrime)*. Ardsley, NY: Transactional Publishers Inc.

White, R. (2003), 'Environmental Issues and the Criminological Imagination', *Theoretical Criminology*, 7: 483–506.

Winston, M. (2002), *Travels in the Genetically Modified Zone*. Cambridge, MA: Harvard University Press.

World Bank (2004), 'Zambia Data Profile', 19 August 2004, available online at: www.worldbank.org/data.

World Health Organisation (2000), *Safety Aspects of Genetically Modified Foods of Plant Origin*, Report of a Joint FAO/WHO Expert Consultation on Foods Derived from Biotechnology. Geneva: United Nations.

World Health Organisation (2004), 'Zambia', www.who.int/countries/zmb/en/.

# 24. Toxic crimes: examining corporate victimization of the general public employing medical and epidemiological evidence*

*Michael J. Lynch and Paul Stretesky*

## Abstract

This article examines the issue of corporate harm and violence using evidence from medical literature and related studies that focus on the health consequences associated with toxic waste, pesticide and dioxin exposure. These studies provide a useful alternative measure of the harms produced by corporate crimes of violence that are unmeasured in more traditional sources of data. Further, the kinds of health consequences associated with modern industrial production of toxic waste products can be thought of as 'criminal' in the broadest sense since alternative, nontoxic methods of production are often available. Examples of these alternative methods of production are provided, along with a discussion of the impact current practices have on minority health.

Recently, criminologists have expressed increased interest in toxic crimes and harms committed by corporations through the production, distribution, storage, and disposal of hazardous chemicals and wastes (Pearce and Tombs 1998, 1997; Lynch *et al.* 2001). In some cases, these actions violate regulatory law (Clifford 1998); in others, the 'harms' are not illegal but are morally questionable, socially unacceptable, or widely debated (Pearce and Tombs 1998). In either case, controversy exists over the risks and benefits to humans. This article examines medical and related health research on the human health risks associated with three main categories of toxic chemicals: pesticides, dioxin, and hazardous waste. The goal is to demonstrate ways criminologists can employ medical evidence to identify toxic harms where other forms of data (e.g. standardized measures like the UCR) do not exist.[1] This article also addresses issues of responsibility and culpability for toxic crimes employing scientific evidence on human health effects and the neglect of alternative, nonpolluting productive practices and alternative technologies. To provide some background for our study, we begin with a brief discussion of the deviance and legal definition of toxic crime.

---

\* From *Critical Criminology* (2001), 10: pp. 153–172.

## Defining crime

The definition of crime has been widely debated and emphasizes two views: legal and deviance models (Burgess 1950; Schwendinger and Schwendinger 1970; Sutherland 1940, 1945; Tappan 1949; Henry and Lanier 2001). Criminologists who employ a deviance model must provide their own justifications for the harms they study, while those employing a legal standard rely upon assumptions rooted in the law making process.

The legal aspects of defining toxic harms are contentious and pits governmental, corporate, and public interest against one another. In some cases, the government takes the lead in protecting citizens from harm. In others, the government and corporations misrepresent the harmful effects of toxin exposure (Fagin and Lavelle 1996; Karliner 1998), leading to a lack of protective legislation. In cases where public health laws fail to satisfy citizens' demands, grass-roots political activism (Bullard 1993; Gibbs 1995) and moral crusades (Friedrichs 1996: 17–19) sometimes emerge to alter public health laws. Each of these efforts affects whether legal rules apply to toxic hazards. The question of whether these laws adequately reflect harms can be clouded by the nature of the law-making process. Consequently, it is necessary to assess the question of harm independently of definitions provided by law. The deviance model provides criteria useful to this effort.

The deviance perspective identifies three conditions useful for identifying egregious behavior. First, evidence that the products/processes in question are reasonably expected to harm human health must be presented.[2] Second, toxic harms can be placed in context by comparing them to other harms society considers serious (i.e., street crimes). As an example, Montague (1996) compared harm from assault rifles and pesticides to legislation trends. In 1994, there were an estimated 250 assault rifle homicides in the U.S., which caused Congress to ban the sale of assault rifles. In contrast, pesticide[3] exposure kills 10,400 people each year, yet Congress is reluctant to pass legislation restricting pesticide use and production (for other examples see: Frank and Lynch 1992; Reiman 1998; Simon 1999). Third, evidence that corporations have knowledge of the risks they create, or are indifferent to these risks, should be provided. This evidence is often difficult to obtain because corporations employ elaborate mechanisms to conceal the harms they produce (e.g., destruction and falsification of records and scientific results; misinformation campaigns) (see for example, Fagin and Lavelle 1996; Stauber and Rampton 1995; Lappe 1991). Nevertheless, research has revealed corporate knowledge that their products and practices cause harm (Fagin and Lavelle 1996; Gibbs 1995; Glantz et al. 1996; Karliner 1998; Stauber and Rampton 1995). Corporations demonstrate indifference to toxic risks when they evade laws designed to prevent human harm, such as when they dump pesticides banned in the US in foreign nations lacking legal restrictions (Ruttenburg 1985; Silverman and Lydecker 1982; Waldo 1985; Weir and Schapiro 1982). Indifference is evident when corporations act to increase environmental and workplace maximum toxin exposure standards (Castleman and Ziem 1989, 1988; Roach and Rappaport 1990) or when corporations avoid using safe alternatives (e.g., solar energy, organic farming, rototilling) to polluting and harmful technologies.

The criteria discussed above are part of law making processes directed at defining toxic harms. Law making processes that define toxic harms are heavily influenced by corporate interests expressed in corporate sponsored research (Colburn *et al.* 1997; Erhlich and Erhlich 1996; Fagin and Lavelle 1996) and public relations campaigns (Karliner 1998; Stauber and Rampton 1995). Independent scientists sometimes refute corporate claims and state policies designed to protect public health (Carson 1962; Erhlich and Erhlich 1996; Steingraber 1998). In the long run, however, industry interests have held greater sway, resulting in laws favoring corporate profit making over public health interests.

To promote an understanding of these issues, we review medical literature that attributes cancer to individual level lifestyle explanations. This paradigm does not fully explain larger patterns of disease, and ignores important effects based on social class, gender and race. This literature also ignores the role that increased exposure to a host of toxic industrial chemicals plays in cancer causation and trends. To explore these alternatives, we review medical literature on toxic exposure outcomes in three areas: pesticides, dioxin, and hazardous waste.

## Understanding cancer trends and causes

Like social science research, medical research emphasizes a paradigm that promotes individual level analysis and explanation (Foucault 1975). Medical research resembles criminological research to the extent that both seek the causes of problems within individuals and take as their starting point the abstract individual – a being detached from her or his connections to the social, political, and economic order. Cancer disease models, for example, begin with cell pathology. This focus, coupled with an emphasis on individualized, reactive treatments, generated the popular 'lifestyles' approach to cancer that relates cancer's causes to an individual's dietary (high fat, low fiber) or other (smoking) choices (for review and critique see, Lappe 1991). In this view, responsibility for cancer is individualized and there is little reason to address social contributions (e.g., pollution, pesticide use, and the relationship between race, class and exposure to pollution) to cancer rates. While lifestyle factors may contribute to the probability that an individual contracts cancer, they fail to explain the long-term rise in cancer rates across the population.

Increasingly, research is moving toward exploring the environmental dimensions of illness and discounting genetic explanations (Colborn *et al.* 1997). Birth defects, for example, have been specifically linked to exposure to environmental toxins. A Norwegian study of subsequent births by mothers who had a first child with birth defects discovered that such mothers were 11.6 times more likely than a control group to have a second child with a birth defect. This finding appeared to support biological/genetic explanations for the presence of birth defects; however, researchers found an unexpected result: women who had previously given birth to a child with a birth defect and moved away from the municipality in which they lived during their first birth saw a significant decline in the rate of birth defects among second children (to 5.1 times; Terje *et al.* 1994). This difference could only be attributed to environmental factors. In sum, 'there is abundant scientific evidence that birth defects in laboratory animals and in humans have occurred as a result of exposure to five classes of pollutants: radiation; pesticides; metals ...; solvents; and dioxin-like chemicals including PCBs' ... (Montague 1994a; see also, Clarkson 1985; Kristensen *et al.* 1993).

Lifestyle explanations also fail to account for race and class effects. For example, African-Americans have a greater than expected share of cancer problems, whether measured by incidence rates (new cancer cases per 100,000 population), mortality rates (deaths per 100,000 population) or 5-year survival rates. Furthermore, over time, the cancer situation for African-Americans has deteriorated relative to whites (Montague 1994b). Consistent with the medical model, many argue that these data speak to racially-linked, genetic predispositions for cancer, or to differences in diet or smoking patterns. These might be reasonable explanations if all African-Americans were genetically and culturally undifferentiated – which they are not. Genetic explanations also have a difficult time explaining why Black women's breast cancer rate increased much more rapidly (18%) than for all women (2.7%) between 1973 through 1989 (Miller *et al.* 1992; Beardsley 1994).[4] References to biological differences or evolution cannot explain such short-term, abrupt patterns. The relationship between race and cancer may be better explained by examining correlates affecting proximity to hazardous waste sites. Recent studies show an association between community race and class characteristics and distance to hazardous waste sites (Stretesky and Hogan 1998). They also support an argument that exposure to pesticides, dioxin, and hazardous waste explains long-term cancer trends (Colborn *et al.* 1997; Steingraber 1998) and the race and class dimensions of this issue (on Native Americans see, Montague 1994d). This recognition moves away from singling out individuals for making poor lifestyle choices and towards examining social responsibility for controlling the harms that may drive the cancer rates.

**Categories of toxic threats**

Landrigan (1992) noted that toxic chemicals are a significant source of illness and death in the U.S. On a daily basis, Americans are exposed to numerous toxic chemicals, both directly and indirectly. For example, a 1995 study of drinking water quality estimated that 14 million people were exposed to herbicide-contaminated drinking water (Wiles *et al.* 1995). Other research reveals that most pesticides (97%) never reach their intended targets, pests, and end up becoming a significant source of environmental damage, pollution, human illness, and death (Montague 1991b). Some suggest we might be better off without pesticides, which are applied at a rate of about 4 pounds per person in the U.S. (Montague 1991b; for opposing opinions see: Higley and Pedigo 1996). Responsibility for this high level of production and use of pesticides can be traced to numerous factors, including over-reliance on pest controlling chemicals on farms, public lands (Schultz 1989), and homes (Grossman 1995). Farm over-reliance is encouraged here and abroad by pesticide manufacturing contracts that require minimum purchases and applications (Weir and Shapiro 1982). Governmental agencies such as the Forestry Service over-apply pesticides to federal lands (Wargo 1996). Like big-chemical manufacturers, lawn services often compel customers to sign contracts requiring a minimum number of pesticide applications, whether or not they are needed, while manufacturers stimulate consumer reliance on inorganic lawn care products through advertising. Many homeowners are deceived (a term used in a General Accounting Office study of pesticide advertising and safety claims, see, Hembra *et al.* 1990) into believing that pesticides are safe and nontoxic. Government efforts to control such false claims making by regulating the pesticide/herbicide industry have been unsuccessful (Hembra *et al.* 1990).

Broadly understood, people are aware that pesticides can be unsafe; however, they believe they are protected by governmental regulations, and trust warning labels, though most people cannot read them. A study of pesticide labels published in *Journal of the American Optometric Association* (1994) noted that it requires 11th-grade reading skills to understand a pesticide label. The study concluded that 40 to 50 percent of the general population cannot read and understand pesticide product labels, even if they had the 20/30 vision needed to read the label (Montague 1995). Advertising and federal regulations encourage the belief that pesticides are safe. Numerous studies, however, contradict this contention.

### Cancer, herbicide and pesticide studies

The first category of dangerous toxic chemicals is herbicides and pesticides, which have a strong relationship with long-term or persistent exposure and cancer (Ritter 1997). The first successful inorganic herbicide, 2,4-D or Dichlorohenoxyacetic Acid, was introduced in 1946. It is the most widely used herbicide both historically and cross-culturally, and 600 million pounds – 6 pounds per square mile of land – are used in the US annually (Montague 1991a). Despite its widespread use, exposure to 2,4-D is believed to cause cancer, especially soft-tissue malignant and non-Hodgkins lymphomas (Hardell and Erikson 1988). Studies of farm and railroad workers in Nebraska, Kansas, Saskatchewan, and Sweden exposed to 2,4-D reported higher rates of cancer when compared to unexposed workers (Axelson *et al.* 1980; Blair 1990; Eriksson *et al.* 1990; Hardell and Eriksson 1988; Hoar *et al.* 1990, 1986). In the long run, these cancers have increased along with increased use of 2,4-D on forest acreage and lawns (Cantor *et al.* 1980). Supporting this contention, a National Institute of Occupational Safety and Health (NIOSH) study revealed a 46% higher cancer rate among workers in factories manufacturing 2,4-D herbicides (Montague 1991a). Research on dogs exposed to 2,4-D in backyards supports human research results (Hayes *et al.* 1991).

Exposure to pesticides has also been associated with increased breast cancer rates among women. A study of women from Long Island, N.Y., discovered that those who grew up within one mile of a chemical production plant had higher rates of breast cancer than other women (Melius *et al.* 1994; on cancer rate differences for other nations and nationalities see, Kohlmeier, Rehm and Hoffmeister 1990; Westin and Richter 1990). Pesticides exposure also has detrimental influence on pregnant women, whose children experience increased birth defects and prenatal mortality rates (Zhang *et al.* 1992).

Despite this evidence, industries and corporations that produce pesticides and promote their widespread use continue to deny a role in causing illness and death in American society. Instead, headed by powerful, multinational corporations, the chemical industry presses for the increased use of dangerous pesticides and herbicides that also produce dioxins (see below). Monsanto stands out as an example of this tendency in marketing genetically altered plant seeds that produce super-plants that are disease and pesticide resistant. Monsanto sells both genetically engineered seeds and the pesticides they resist. Rifkin (1998) noted that Monsanto's (and other company's) seeds are so specialized that they resist only that company's specific pesticides (e.g., Monsanto seeds resist theMonsanto herbicide, Roundup). In short, people are increasingly exposed to carcinogenic, life and health threatening chemicals so that multinational corporations can expand their markets and incomes.

Corporations have also looked the other way when it comes to public and worker health and safety. This is nowhere more clear than in the debate over maximum exposure levels to toxins, where corporations have demonstrated an ability to have their interests reflected in governmental standards. Many medical researchers believe this tendency has increased health risks for the rest of the public (Castleman and Ziem 1989, 1988; Colborn *et al.* 1997; Roach and Rappaport 1990; Wargo 1996).

### Preventable harm: the myth of living in modern society

A typical response to the evidence of the harm posed by pesticides is that the risks are exaggerated, unavoidable, necessary, and beneficial in a broader sense. These beliefs are false. Speaking to these issues, Wargo (1996: 6) asks, given imperfect knowledge, 'why would policy makers presume that pesticides – intentionally toxic substances – pose no significant threat to human health?' With respect to necessity, consider the following: a 1993 National Academy of Sciences study found that organic farms appear more profitable than inorganic farms. Further, between 1945 and 1989, chemical use on US farms increased 10 fold with no increase in arable land. During this 'chemical war' on pests, food losses to insects doubled (Wargo 1996). For particular crops, the story was even worse: despite 'a thousand fold increase in the use of insecticides on corn, losses to insects have increased 400 percent' (Wargo 1996: 7). Pest resistance causes escalating use of pesticides and a search for more powerful, broad-spectrum products.

Research and development of safe pesticide alternatives lags behind or is frustrated in other ways. For example, for centuries, sap from India's Neem tree has been regarded as a 'cure to all ailments' like skin rashes, and gum disease (Shiva 1997). It is also a natural pesticide that repels over two hundred different insects (Rifkin 1998). Research has confirmed that Neem is not only safe, but as effective as pesticides such as DDT and Malathion in protecting crops (National Research Council 1995; Stone 1992). W. R. Grace, a multinational corporation, recently obtained a patent on Neem and now markets it along side its synthetic pesticides (Rifkin 1998; Shiva 1997). Because of this patent, Neem is no longer freely available without paying a subsidy to W.R. Grace.

Also, in 1990, Cuba was cut-off from agrochemicals due to embargos and deteriorating relations with socialist block nations. Facing farming without pesticides, many feared the worst for Cubans, including famine. The famine, however, never happened. Cuba experienced the 'largest … conversion from conventional agriculture to organic … farming in human history' (Rosset and Benjamin 1994: 82), relying on predatory insects and microbial antagonists. Organic farming methods have proven effective in Cuba, and represent 'a savings, after costs, of 15.6 million dollars per year' (Rosset and Benjamin 1994: 37). Increased reliance on natural pesticides has also enhanced the potency of synthetic pesticides, when needed as a supplemental control, because insects do not develop resistance.

Many examples of inexpensive, effective pesticide alternatives could be provided. Moving toward such alternatives is a necessary part of protecting people's health and well-being. Yet, exposure to pesticides is just the tip of the iceberg of hazardous chemicals to which people are exposed on a daily basis (on drinking water exposure, see EPA 1991).

### Dioxin: the modern industrial nightmare

A second toxic threat comes from dioxin, a controversial chemical with outspoken critics (Gibbs 1995) and staunch corporate safety claims. Dioxin is the generic name for a family of chemical waste by-products that results from chlorine, pesticide, and polyvinylchloride (PVC) production, as well as paper-milling, bleaching, and waste incineration (Gibbs 1995; Erhlich and Erhlich 1996). Dioxin exposure is widespread in the US and world population. Many believe dioxin to be one of the most toxic human-waste products encountered in our environment (Colborn et al. 1997; Gibbs 1995).

Dioxin is relatively rare in nature. Studies of natural sediment demonstrate the first widespread manifestations of dioxin in the 1940s (Czuczwa and Hites 1985; Czucwa et al. 1984), meaning that dioxin is a modern by-product. Dioxins are persistent chemicals that biodegrade slowly and generally only under direct exposure to sunlight, so they possess the ability to steadily accumulate in the environment. In addition, dioxins are fat-soluble and are easily stored in fatty deposits in animals where they remain intact and become part of the food chain (Gibbs 1995).

There are dioxins all around us – some result from the cooling of gases following incineration. Airborne dioxin particles may travel thousands of miles before settling on land, in waterways, or on biota where they are consumed as part of the food chain and become more concentrated (Colborn et al. 1997). Dioxins are also found in waste sites where incinerator ashes are dumped. Dioxins are not water-soluble; thus, when they leach from waste sites into ground water, they are carried by solvents and oil-based products that may also have carcinogenic properties, enhancing the effects of dioxin exposure.

Human exposure to dioxin occurs primarily through the consumption of meat, chicken, fish, and dairy products. Clean fruits and vegetables are considered 'dioxin safe' because plant intake of dioxin through soil and water is minimal. According to the EPA, about 90 percent of a 'daily allowable dose' of dioxin[5] comes from meat, fish and dairy products (DeVito *et al.* 1995). The average person ingests approximately *280 times the EPA standard for dioxin.* Once ingested, dioxins attach to Ah receptors, and are stored in fatty tissue (on dioxin toxicology see, DeVito and Birnbaum 1994). The more fat a body has, the more dioxin it is capable of storing. Because dioxins are fat- and not water-soluble, normal routes of toxin excretion from the body (e.g., perspiration, urination) are ineffective in reducing dioxin concentrations. In addition, dioxin has a half-life of between seven and eleven years (Pirkle *et al.* 1989), meaning that, after two decades, 12.5 to 25% of the original ingested amount remains.

Over the past 15 years, only a handful of epidemiological studies – all of which are reported below – have examined the consequences of dioxin exposure on humans. All found significant increases in cancer rates among exposed populations (Bertazzi *et al.* 1998, 1997, 1993, 1989; Hardell *et al.* 1981, 1979; Fingerhut *et al.* 1991; Saracci *et al.* 1991; Pesatori *et al.* 1998; Flesch-Janys 1995). These results are supported by long-term animal studies showing that dioxins cause a variety of cancer types (Della *et al.* 1987; Kociba *et al.* 1978; Roa *et al.* 1988; for overview see, Gibbs 1995: 93).

Following concerns raised by dioxin-associated illnesses, large dioxin generating companies, Monsanto, BASF, and Dow initiated reanalysis of dioxin effects studies of previously exposed populations in West Virginia and West Germany that showed negative health outcomes (increased mortality and cancer rates; Suskind and Hertzberg 1984). Corporate researchers, however, manipulated sample data and eliminated statistically significant differences in death and illness rates (see, Gibbs 1995, 2–11; on similar null findings and unethical practices affecting Dow Chemical's Agent Orange, see Erhlich and Erhlich 1996). Chemical manufacturers used these data to successfully defend themselves from tort suits *until* plaintiffs proved these studies were manipulated (Gibbs 1995).

Further, as Colborn *et al.* (1997: 117) point out: 'Dioxin might be more dangerous than anyone had suspected, but contrary to what many had thought, its greatest threat was not cancer. The newly emerging hazard was its power to disrupt natural hormones.' Dioxin is an endocrine disrupter, and thus prevents normal development in animals and humans. For example, even a small dose of dioxin equivalent to exposure levels in the US, Japan, and Europe can drastically affect pre-natal development, causing reduced fertility and diminished intelligence (Colborn *et al.* 1997). Research has also shown high levels of dioxin in mothers' breast milk – a significant source of dioxin contamination in infants (Schester *et al.* 1994b). Dioxins have also been connected to immunological diseases in both animals (Fernandez-Salguero *et al.* 1995; Ross *et al.* 1995) and humans (Hoffman *et al.* 1986; Reggiani 1980, 1978; for other health consequences see, Colborn *et al.* 1997; Gibbs 1995; Steenland et al. 1999; McGregor *et al.* 1998).

### Reducing dioxins in the environment

The paper pulp industry, which uses chlorine to bleach paper, is one of the largest dioxin producers in the world. Significant reductions in dioxin could be achieved if paper producers would simply use existing chlorine free paper technology (Erhlich and Erhlich 1996; Gibbs 1995; O'Brien 1997). Some segments of the paper industry have move toward chlorine-free production and admit that dioxin is a health risk (O'Brien 1997). Most, however, have lobbied against the movement to chlorine free technologies and actively participated in the dissemination of misinformation concerning the dangers of dioxin (Erhlich and Erhlich 1996). Contrary to paper industry claims, chlorine free technologies are also less expensive than older paper technologies (Gibbs 1995). The federal government has attempted to reduce dioxin through demand-side economics by requiring the use of chlorine free paper (e.g., in EPA Region 10), again with great resistance from the paper industry.

### Hazardous waste

The third category of toxic chemicals is hazardous waste, which reaches the public in many ways. As noted, many chemicals used in agriculture and in yards contain active ingredients that are known or suspected carcinogens (see Stretesky and Lynch 1998), and many leach into the American water supply (EPA 1991). Many pesticides and fertilizers also include 'inert ingredients' that are a trade secret under federal regulations, which also allow manufactures to include hazardous chemical waste as inert ingredients in pesticides if these ingredients make the target more susceptible to active poisons (Hollingsworth 1998).

Further, more than 41 million Americans live within 4 miles of 1,134 documented Superfund waste sites – and millions more live near unlisted waste sites. Health hazards associated with exposure to chemicals found in these sites have been widely studied and demonstrate the human risks. For example, a study of 593 sites in 339 U.S. counties with hazardous waste ground water contamination revealed increased levels of lung, stomach, intestinal, bladder, and rectum cancer (Griffin et al. 1989; Osborne et al. 1990). Ground water contamination has also been associated with higher rates of spontaneous abortion (Aschengrau at al. 1989) and birth defects (Goldberg et al. 1990). Research demonstrates numerous other health issues associated with proximity to hazardous waste cites and consumption of contaminated drinking water: increased rates of birth defects (Geschwind et al. 1990; Najem and Voyce 1993); abnormal liver function (Meyer 1983); chronic kidney disease, stroke, hypertension, heart disease, anemia, and skin cancer in populations exposed to toxic metals (Neuberger et al. 1990); increased rates of leukemia among children (Byers 1988; Cutler et al. 1988; Lagakos et al. 1986); and other lesser problems (Baker et al. 1988; Hertzman et al. 1987; Ozonoff et al. 1987). Many of these health effects have been known for over a decade.

Studies have also shown that proximity to hazardous waste sites have a variety of health effects (Najem and Voyce 1993), including reproductive health concerns for women (Goulet and Goldberg 1993). Women with breast cancer have elevated levels of DDT, DDE, and PCBs – a group of chlorinated hydrocarbons (Falck et al. 1992; Wolff et al. 1993; Colborn et al. 1997). Mortality studies of workers exposed to chlorinated hydrocarbons – chemists, pharmaceutical workers, chemical engineers, and petrochemical employees

– show they are significantly more likely to die from cancers than those from other occupations (Ames *et al.* 1987; Arnetz 1991; Hagmar *et al.* 1986; Hoar and Pell 1981a, b; Li *et al.* 1969; Olin 1978; Olin and Ahlbom 1980; Searle *et al.* 1978; Thomas and Decoufle 1979; Walrath *et al.* 1985).

## Alternative to old polluting technologies

Despite the evidence reviewed above, industries and corporations continue to deny a role in causing illness and death in American society and the rest of the world (Karliner 1998; Weir and Schapiro 1982). Instead, chemical industries continue to press for the increased use of pesticides that produce toxic wastes such as dioxins. Also, corporations support incineration of toxic waste because it reduces the volume of solid waste, is assumed safe, and has fewer disposal requirements. But problems associated with incineration of pesticides and the production of dioxin are evident at numerous governmental facilities in the US. For example, one government facility in Jacksonville, Arkansas routinely failed to meet government air quality standards, emitting 400 times more dioxins than law allows (Costner 1992a). Research also indicates troubling waste incineration problems at other government facilities (Costner 1992b; on related effects of incinceration see, Hardy *et al.* 1987a, b; Cross *et al.* 1987). While incineration reduces waste, it is not a safe post-production solution. Changing how we produce things is a more effective strategy for controlling waste.

For example, one way to reduce waste and incineration is to implement 'design for environment' (DFE) ideas and technology that, in some cases, eliminate waste by allowing products that are normally land-filled to be reclaimed (Hart 1997). Xerox has become a leader in DFE technology, which it uses in the production of Lakes copiers. This production process generates zero waste – all materials are used or reclaimed. Further, Xerox requires that all manufacturers who contribute parts to Lakes copiers use DFE technology and produce zero waste. Buildings can be designed along similar lines to minimize environmental impact employing recycled materials and passive solar energy (Van der Ryn and Cowan 1996). Some of these buildings are so efficient they produce excess energy that is sold back to the electric company. As Van der Ryn and Cowan (1996) demonstrate, it is possible to change the way we produce things, minimizing and reclaiming waste, and reducing energy use associated with pollution through fundamental ecological engineering.

Further, in Cologne, Germany, a company with a monopoly on garbage disposal incinerated all recyclable organic garbage (approximately 40% of all garbage; Mies 1993: 297–324). A new technology that made compost out of organic wastes and transformed garbage into useful products – compost and heat – for no additional costs was implemented in place of incineration. The Cologne project not only prevented environmental contamination, but also reduced the need for chemical fertilizers. While the incineration company opposed the recycling project, it was so successful and received such extensive public support that it was adopted throughout the city.

## Conclusion

This review of environmentally induced, health-related illness and disease has explored only a portion of the literature available on these issues. This literature establishes that it is reasonable to assume that corporate products and practices threaten public health. There is a likely relationship between increasing rates of illness and disease, especially cancer, and increased exposure to chlorine based inorganic chemicals and wastes. Further, this review shows that the industries that produce the products responsible for increasing levels of pesticides, herbicides, PCBs, and resultant dioxin waste seem to know these products and by-products have human health consequences. As was the case with the tobacco industry (Glantz *et al.* 1996), pesticide, herbicide, and PCB manufacturers manipulated scientific data to influence conclusions concerning the safety of their products and by-products, and hid important findings from the public/consumers.

These findings are enough to establish that corporations and industries that produce pesticides and dioxins show a blatant disregard for the effects of their products and by-products on human and animal populations. The fact that corporations continue to choose to produce commodities and waste that generate such a potential threat is a sign of their disregard for life that can only be equated with ordinary acts of crime such as robberies, muggings, assaults, and homicides.

Finally, this review has importance through its connection to studies in the area of environmental justice. That literature suggests a class and race bias in the location of hazardous waste facilities (United Church of Christ 1987). To some extent, the kinds of harms caused by the chemicals discussed here are so elusive that they escape attempts to associate the locations of classes and races with hazardous waste deposits. In this respect, the broader political and economic organization of society has set into motion a process that is equally capable of victimizing everyone in the U.S., regardless of race or social class. Many studies, however, find that there is a relationship between race and increased rates of those diseases and illnesses associated with herbicide, pesticide, and dioxin production. At this time, this race relationship should continue to be taken seriously, and be given attention along side political and economic perspectives focusing on corporate threats to the health and well-being of all citizens.

## Acknowledgements

We would like to thank John Cochran, Amory Starr, Christine Stretesky, Paul Leighton and three anonymous reviewers from *Critical Criminology* for their encouragement, comments, and suggestions.

## Notes

1  This review does not represent a scientific sample of this research, nor does it report results for *all* human risk studies in these areas. It excluded results from corporate sponsored research – research produced directly by corporate scientists or indirectly through association and institute grant programs funded by corporations (e.g., the Chemical Manufacturers Association) – because the results are likely to be biased.

2  The medical evidence reviewed below addresses this issue with respect to pesticides, dioxin and toxic waste. Due to space limitations, the remaining criteria receive less attention.

3  Scientifically, the class of chemicals called pesticides, include chemicals that are destructive of life forms, such as insecticides, rodenticides, herbicides, etc. This article uses the term pesticides to refer to all these classes of chemicals, and is more specific where necessary.

4  One of the interesting differences that also needs to be explained is the higher survival rates for white women than for black women (Montague 1994c). Survival rate differences indicate the possibility of racially biased delivery of health care (which, in part, is explicable due to the connection between race and class in America).

5  The daily allowable dose of dioxin is 0.0006 picograms or $6 \times 10^{-17}$ grams per kilogram of body weight; or 0.42 picograms for the average man. The average person ingests approximately 119 picograms of dioxin a day – 280 times the EPA standard – and would have a 'dioxin burden' (fat disolved dioxin) of 9000 picograms/kilogram of body weight (Gibbs 1995, 75). The EPA estimates that 14000 picograms/kilogram of body weight cause human harm (on human exposure estimates see, Orband 1994; Patterson *et al.* 1994; Schester 1994a; for Germany, see, Beck *et al.* 1994; on native populations exposure, see, DeWaily *et al.* 1994).

## References

Ames, B. *et al.* (1987). Ranking possible carcinogenic hazards. *Science* 236, 236–271.

Arnetz, B.B. (1991). Mortality among petrochemical science and engineering employees. *Archives of Environmental Health* 46, 237–248.

Aschengrau *et al.* (1989). Quality of community drinking water and the occurrence of spontaneous abortion. *Archives of Environmental Health* 44, 283–290.

Axelson, O. *et al.* (1980). Herbicide exposure and tumor mortality. *Scandinavian Journal of Work, Environment and Health* 6, 73–79.

Baker, D.B. *et al.* (1988). A health study of two communities near the stringfellow waste disposal site. *Archives of Environmental Health* 43, 325–334.

Beardsley, T. (1994). A war not won – trends in cancer epidemiology. *Scientific American* 270, 130–138.

Beck, H., Dross, A., and Mathar,W. (1994). APCDD and PCDF exposure and level in humans in Germany. *Environmental Health Perspectives* 102(s), 173–185.

Bertazzi, P. (1998). The Seveso studies on early and long-term effects of dioxin exposure. *Environmental Health Perspectives* 106(52), 625–633.

Bertazzi, P. *et al.* (1997). Dioxin exposure and cancer and cancer risk: A 15 year mortality study after the Seveso accident. *Epidemology* 8(6), 646–652.

Bertazzi, P., Pesatori, A., Consonni, D., Tironi, A., Landi, M., and Zocchetti, C. (1993). Cancer Incidence in a Population Accidentally Exposed to 2,3,7,8-tetrachlorodibenzo-PARA-dioxin. *Epidemiology* 4, 398–406.

Bertazzi, P., Zocchetti, C., Pesatori, A., Guercilena, S., Sanarico, M., and Radice, L. (1989). Ten-year mortality study of the population involved in the Seveso incident in 1976. *American Journal of Epidemiology* 129, 1187–1200.

Blair, A. (1990). Herbicides and non-Hodgkin's lymphoma: New evidence from a study of Saskatchewan farmers. *Journal of the National Cancer Institute* 82, 544–545.

Bullard, R. (1993). Confronting Environmental Racism: Voices from the Grassroots. Boston: South End Press.

Burgess, E.W. (1950). Comment. *American Journal of Sociology* 56, 32–33.

Byers, V.S. (1988). Association between clinical symptoms and lymphocyte abnormalities in a population with chronic domestic exposure to industrial solvent contaminated domestic water supply and a high incidence of Leukaemia. *Cancer Immunology and Immunotherapy* 27, 77–81.

Cantor, K.P. *et al.* (1980). Distribution of Non-Hodgkin's lymphomas in the United States between 1950 and 1975. *Cancer Research* 40, 2645–2652.

Carson, R. (1962). *Silent Spring*. New York: Houghton-Mifflin.

Castleman, B.I. and Ziem, G.E. (1989). Toxic pollutants, science, and corporate influence. *Archives of Environmental Health* 44(2), 68, 127.

Castleman, B.I. and Ziem, G.E. (1988). Corporate influence on threshold limit values. *American Journal of Industrial Medicine* 13(5), 531–559.

Clarkson, T.W. (1985). Reproductive and developmental toxicity of metals. *Scandinavian Journal of Work, Environment and Health* 11, 145–154.

Clifford, M. (1998). *Environmental Crime*. Gaithersburg, Maryland: Aspen.

Colborn, T., Dumanoski, D., and Myers, J. (1997). *Our Stolen Future*. New York: Plume.

Costner, P. (1992a). *The Incineration of Dioxin in Jacksonville, Arkansas*. Washington, D.C.: Greenpeace Toxics Campaign.

Costner, P. (1992b). *Chemical Weapons Demilitarization and Disposal*. Washington, D.C.: Greenpeace.

Cross, J. *et al.* (1987). Contaminant concentrations and toxicity of sea-surface microlayer near Los Angeles, California. *Marine Environmental Research* 23, 307–323.

Cutler, J. *et al.* (1988). Childhood Leukemia in Woburn, Massachusetts. *Public Health Reports* 101, 201–205.

Czuczwa, J.M. and Hites, R.A. (1985). Historical record of polychlorinated dioxins and furans in Lake Huron sediments. In L.H. Keith, C. Rappe and G. Choudhary (eds.), *Chorinated Dioxins and Dibenzofurans in the Total Environment*. Boston: Butterworth.

Czuczwa, J.M., B.D. McVetty, and Hites, R.A. (1984). Polychlorinated dibenzo-p-dioxins and dibenzofurans in sediments from Siskiwt Lake, Isle Royale. *Science* 226, 568–569.

Della P.G., Drgani, T.A., and Sozzi, G. (1987). Carcinogenic effects of long-term 2,3,7,8-tetrachorodibenzo-p-dioxin treatment in the mouse. *Tumori* 73, 99–107.

DeVito, M.J. *et al.* (1995). Comparisons of estimated human body burdens of dioxinlike chemicals and TCDD body burdens in experimentally exposed animals. *Environmental Health Perspectives* 103(9), 820–831.

DeVito, M.J. and Birnbaum, L.S. (1994). Toxicology of dioxins and related chemicals. In A. Schecter (ed.), *Dioxins and Health*. New York: Plenum.

DeWailly, E. *et al.* (1994). Exposure of remote maritime populations to co-planer PCBs. *Environmental Health Perspectives* 102(s)(1), 205–209.

Environmental Protection Agency (U.S.) (1991). *National Survey of Pesticides in Drinking Water*. Office of Water. Washington, D.C.: US. EPA.

Erhlich, P. and Ehrlich, A. (1996). *Betrayal of Science and Reason*. Washington, D.C.: Island Press.

Eriksson, M. *et al.* (1990). Exposure to dioxins as a risk factor for soft tissue sarcoma: A population-based case-control study. *Journal of the National Cancer Institute* 82, 486–490.

Fagin, D. and Lavelle, M. (1996). *Toxic Deception: How the Chemical Industry Manipulates Science, Bends the Law, and Endangers Your Health*. Birch Lane Press.

Falck, F., Ricci, A., Wolff, M.S., Godbold, J., and Dreckers, P. (1992). Pesticides and polychlorinated biphenyl residues in human breast lipids and their relation to breast cancer. *Archives of Environmental Health* 47(2), 143–146.

Fernandez-Salguero, P. *et al.* (1995). Immune system impairment and hepatic fibrosis in mice lacking the dioxin-binding ah receptor. *Science* 268, 722–726.

Fingerhut, M.A. *et al.* (1991). Cancer mortality in workers exposed to 2,3,7,8-tetrachlorodibenzo-p-dioxin. *New England Journal of Medicine* 324, 212–218.

Flesch-Janys, D. *et al.* (1995). Exposure to polychlorinated dioxins and furans (PCDD/F) and mortality in a cohort of workers from a herbicide-producing plant in Hamburg, Federal Republic of Germany. *American Journal of Epidemiology* 142(11), 1165–1175.

Foucault, M. (1975). *The Birth of The Clinic*. New York: Vintage.

Frank, N. and Lynch, M.J. (1992). *Corporate Crime, Corporate Violence*. Albany, New York: Harrow and Heston.

Friedrichs, D.O. (1996). *Trusted Criminals*. Belmont, California: Wadsworth.

Geschwind, S.A. *et al.* (1990). Risk of congenital malformations associated with proximity to hazardous waste sites. *American Journal of Epidemiology* 135, 1197–1207.

Gibbs, L.M. (1995). *Dying From Dioxin*. Boston: South End Press.

Glantz, S. *et al.* (1996). *The Cigarette Papers*. Berkeley: University of California Press.

Goldberg, S.J. *et al.* (1990). An association of human congenital cardiac malformations and drinking water contaminants. *Journal of the American College of Cardiology* 16(1), 155–164.

Goulet, L. and Goldberg, M. (1993). Reproductive outcomes among women living near a sanitary landfill site in Montreal, Quebec, Canada, 1979–1989. *American Journal of Epidemiology* 138, 8.

Griffin, J. *et al.* (1989). Cancer mortality in U.S. counties with hazardous waste sites and ground water pollution. *Archives of Environmental Health* 44(2), 69–74.

Grossman, J. (1995). Dangers of household pesticides. *Environmental Health Perspectives* 103(6), 550–554.

Hagmar, L. *et al.* (1986). Mortality and cancer morbidity among workers in a chemical factory. *Scandinavian Journal of Work, Environment and Health* 12, 545–551.

Hardell, L. *et al.* (1981). Malignant lymphomas and exposure to chemicals, especially organic solvents, chlorophenols, and phenoxy acids: A case-control study. *British Journal of Cancer* 43, 169–176.

Hardell, L. *et al.* (1979). Case-control study: soft-tissue sarcomas and exposure to phenoxyacetic acids or chlorophenols. *British Journal of Cancer* 39, 711–717.

Hardell, L.H. and Eriksson, M. (1988). The association between soft tissue sarcomas and exposure to phenoxyacetic acids. *Cancer* 62, 652–656.

Hardy, J. *et al.* (1987a). The sea-surface microlayer of puget sound: Part I. Toxic effects on fish eggs and larvae. *Marine Environmental Research* 23, 227–249.

Hardy, J. *et al.* (1987b). The sea-surface microlayer of Puget sound: Part II. Concentrations of contaminants and relation to Toxicity. Marine Environmental Research 23, 251–271.

Hart, S. (1997). Beyond greening: Strategies for a sustainable world. *Harvard Business Review* 75(1), 66–78.

Hayes, H.M. *et al.* (1991). Case-control study of canine malignant lymphoma: positive association with dog owner's use of 2,4-dichlorophenoxyacetic acid herbicides. *Journal of the National Cancer Institute* 83, 1226–1231.

Hembra, R.L. *et al.* (1990). *Lawn Care Pesticides.* Governmental Accounting Office (RCED-90-134). Gaithersburg, Maryland: U.S. GAO.

Henry, S. and Lanier, M. (2001). *What is Crime?* Boston: Rowman and Littlefield.

Hertzman, C. *et al.* (1987). Upper Ottawa Street landfill site health study. *Environmental Health Perspectives* 75, 173–195.

Higley, L. and Pedigo, L. (eds.) (1996). *Economic Thresholds for Integrated Pest Management.* Lincoln, Nebraska: University of Nebraska Press.

Hoar, S. *et al.* (1990). A case-control Study of non-Hodgkin's lymphoma and the herbicide 2,4-dichlorophenoxyacetic acid (2,4-D) in Eastern Nebraska. *Epidemiology* 1, 349–356.

Hoar, S. *et al.* (1986). Agricultural herbicide use and risk of lymphoma and soft-tissue sarcoma. *Journal of the Americal Medical Association* 256, 1141–1147.

Hoar, S. and Pell, S. (1981a). A retrospective cohort study of mortality and cancer incidence among chemists. *Journal of Occupational Medicine* 23, 485–494.

Hoar, S. and Pell, S. (1981b). A retrospective cohort study of disability among chemists. *Journal of Occupational Medicine* 23, 495–501.

Hoffman, R.E. *et al.* (1986). Health effects of long-term exposure to 2,3,7,8-tetrachlorodibenzo-p-dioxin. *Journal of the American Medical Association* 255, 2031–2038.

Hollingsworth, J. (1998). Toxins infiltrate farm fertilizers. *Tampa Tribune,* March 27, 1, 13.

Karliner, J. (1998). *The Corporate Planet.* SF: the Sierra Book Club.

Kociba, R.J. *et al.* (1978). Results of a two-year chronic toxicity and oncogenicity study of 2,3,7,8-tetrachlorodibenzo-p-dioxin in rats. *Journal of Toxicology and Applied Pharmacology* 35, 553–574.

Kohlmeier, L., Rehm, J., and Hoffmeister, H. (1990). Lifestyle and trends in worldwide breast cancer rates. In D.L. Davis and D. Hoel (eds.), *Trends in Cancer Mortality in Industrialized Countries.* New York: New York Academy of Sciences.

Kristensen, P. *et al.* (1993). Perinatal outcome among children of men exposed to lead and organic solvents in the printing industry. *American Journal of Epidemiology* 137(2), 134–144.

Lagakos, S.W. *et al.* (1986). An analysis of contaminated well water and health effects in Woburn, Massachusetts. *Journal of the American Statistical Association* 81, 583–196.

Landrigan, P.J. (1992). Environmental disease – A preventable epidemic. *American Journal of Public Health* 82, 941–943.

Lappe, M. (1991). *Chemical Deception.* SF: The Sierra Club.

Li, F. *et al.* (1969). Cancer mortality among chemists. *Journal of the National Cancer Institute* 43, 1159–1164.

Lynch, M.J., Stretesky, P., and McGurrin, D. (2001). Toxic crimes and environmental justice. In G. Potter (ed.), *Controversies in White Collar Crime.* Cincinnati, Ohio: Anderson.

McGregor, D.B. *et al.* (1998). An IARC evaluation of polychlorinated dibenzo-p-dioxin and polychlorinated dibenzoflurans as risk factors in human carcinogenesis. *Environmental Health Perspective* 106(52), 755–760.

Melius, J. *et al.* (1994). *Residence Near Industries and High Traffic Areas and the Risk of Breast Cancer on Long Island.* Albany, New York: State of New York Department of Health

Mies, M. (1993). The need for a new vision: The subsistence perspective. In M. Mies and V. Shiva (eds.), *Ecofeminism.* Zed Books, Ltd.

Meyer, C.R. (1983). Liver dysfunction in residents exposed to leachate from a toxic waste dump. *Environmental Health Perspectives* 48, 9–13.

Miller, B.A. *et al.* (1992). *Cancer Statistics Review, 1973–1989.* Washington, D.C.: National Institutes of Health. Publication No. 92-2789.

Montague, P. (1996). The pesticide failure. Rachel's *Environment & Health Weekly*, 482. http://www.envirolink.org/pubs/rachel.

Montague, P. (1995).Many pesticides, little knowledge. *Rachel's Hazardous Waste News*, 469. http://www.envirolink/org/pubs/rachel.

Montague, P. (1994a). Birth defect – Part 2: why birth defects will continue to rise. *Rachel's Environment & Health Weekly*, 411.

Montague, P. (1994b). Cancer injustice: Part I. *Rachel's Hazardous Waste News*, 386. http://www.envirolink/org/pubs/rachel.

Montague, P. (1994c). Cancer injustice: Part II. *Rachel's Hazardous Waste News*, 387. http://www.envirolink/org/pubs/rachel.

Montague, P. (1994d). Violence in Indian country over waste. *Rachel's Hazardous Waste News*, 404. http://www.envirolink/org/pubs/rachel.

Montague, P. (1991a). Pet dogs get cancer from weed killers. *Rachel's Hazardous Waste News*, 250. http://www.envirolink.org/pubs/rachel.

Montague, P. (1991b). The false promise of pesticides. *Rachel's Hazardous Waste News*, 247. http://www.envirolink.org/pubs/rachel.

Najem, R.G. and Voyce, L.K. (1993). Health effects of a thorium waste disposal site. *American Journal of Public Health* 80, 478–480.

National Research Council (1995). *Neem, A Tree for Solving Global Problems*. National Research Council Report. Washington, D.C.: National Academy Press.

Neuberger, J.S. *et al.* (1990). Health problems in Galena, Kansas: A heavy metal mining superfund site. *The Science of the Total Environment* 94, 261–272.

O'Brien, M. (1997). Alternatives to risk assessment: The example of dioxin. In C. Levenstein and L. Wooding (eds.), *Work, Health and Environment*. New York: The Guilford Press.

Olin, R.G. (1978). The hazards of a chemical laboratory environment – a study of the mortality in two cohorts of Swedish chemists. *American Industrial Hygiene Association Journal* 39, 557–562.

Olin, R.G. and Ahlbom, A. (1980). The cancer mortality among Swedish chemists graduated during three decades. *Environmental Research* 22, 154–161.

Orband, J.E. *et al.* (1994). Dioxins and dibenzofuran in adipose tissue of the general U.S. population and selected subpopulations. *American Journal of Public Health* 84, 439–445.

Osborne, S.J., Shy, C.M., and Kaplan, B.M. (1990). Epidemiologic analysis of a reported cancer cluster in a small rural population. *American Journal of Epidemology* 132(1), S87–S95.

Ozonoff, D. *et al.* (1987). Health problems reported by residents of a neighborhood contaminated by a hazardous waste facility. *American Journal of Industrial Medicine* 11, 581–597.

Patterson, D.G. *et al.* (1994). Levels of nonortho-substituted polychlorinated biphenyls, dibenzo-p-dioxins, and dibenzofurans in human serum and adipose tissue. *Environmental Health Perspective* 102(s)(1), 195–204.

Pearce, F. and Tombs, S. (1998). *Toxic Capitalism*. Aldershot; Brookfield, Vermont: Ashgate.

Pearce, F. and Tombs, S. (1997). Hazardous, law and class: contextualizing the regulation of corporate crime. *Social and Legal Studies* 6, 79–107.

Pesatori, A.C. *et al.* (1998). Dioxin exposure and non-malignant health effects: A mortality study. *Occupational and Environmental Medicine* 55(2), 126–131.

Pirkle, J.L., Wolfe, W.H., and Patterson, D.G. *et al.* (1989). Estimates of the half-life of 2,3,7,8-TCDD in Vietnam veterans of operation ranch hand. *Journal of Toxicology and Environmental Health* 27, 165–171.

Rao, M.S., Subbararo, V., Prasad, J.D., and Sarpelli, D.C. (1988). Carcinogenicity of 2,3,7,8-tetrachlorodibenzo-p-dioxin in the Syrian Golden Hamster. *Carcinogenesis* 9(9), 1677–1679.

Reggiani, G. (1980). Acute human exposure to TCDD in Seveso, Italy. *Journal of Toxicology and Environmental Health* 6, 27–43.

Reggiani, G. (1978). Medical problems raised by the TCDD contamination in Seveso, Italy. *Archives of Toxicology* 40, 161–188.

Reiman, J. (1998). *The Rich Get Richer and the Poor Get Prison*. Boston: Allyn and Bacon.

Rifkin, J. (1998). *The Biotech Century*. New York: Putnum.

Ritter, L. (1997). Report of a panel on the relationship between public exposure to pesticides and cancer. *Cancer* 80, 2019–2033.

Roach, S.A. and Rappaport, S.M. (1990). But they are not thresholds: A critical analysis of the documentation of threshold limit values. *American Journal of Industrial Medicine* 17(6), 727–753.

Ross, P. *et al.* (1995). Contaminant-related suppression of delayed-type hypersensitivity and antibody responses in harbor seals Fed Herring from the Baltic Sea. *Environmental Health Perspectives* 103, 162–167.

Rosset, P. and Benjamin, M. (1994). *The Greening of the Revolution: Cuba's Experiment with Organic Agriculture*. Melbourne, Australia: Ocean Press.

Ruttenberg, R. (1985). Hazard export: Ethical problems, policy proposals and prospects for implementation. In J. Ives (ed.), The Export of Hazard: Transnational Corporations and Environmental Control Issues. Massachusetts: Routledge and Keegan Paul.

Saracci, R., Kogevinas, M., Bertazzi, P.A., Bueno de Mesquita, B.H., Coggon, D., Green, L.M., Kauppinen, T., L'Abbe, K.A., and Lynge, M. (1991). Cancer mortality in workers exposed to chlorophenoxy herbicides and chlorophenols. *Lance* 338, 1027–1032.

Schester, A., Ryan, J.J., Masuda, Y.P., Brandt-Rauf, J., Constable, D.C., Hoang, C.D., Le, T., Hoang, Q., Nguyen, T.N., and Pham, H.P. (1994a). Chlorinated and brominated dioxins and dibenzofurans in human tissue following exposure. *Environmental Health Perspectives* 102(s)(1), 135–147.

Schester, A., Ryan, J.J., Masuda, Y. Brandt-Rauf, P., Constable, J., Hoang, D.C. Le, T., Hoang, Q., Nguyen, T.N., and Pham, H.P. (1994b). Polychlorinated biphenyl levels in the tissue of the exposed and nonexposed humans. *Environmental Health Perspectives* 102(s)(1), 149–158.

Schultz, W. (1989). *The Chemical Free Law*n. Emmaus, Pennsylvania: Rodale Press.

Schwendinger, H. and Schwendinger, J. (1970). Defenders of order or guardians of human rights? *Issues in Criminology* 7(1), 71–81.

Searle, C.E. *et al.* (1978). Epidemiological study of the mortality of British chemists. *British Journal of Cancer* 38, 192–193.

Shiva, V. (1997). *Biopiracy*. Boston: South End Press.

Silverman, M., Lee, P.L. and Lydecker, M. (1982). *Prescription for Death: The Drugging of the Third World*. Berkeley: University of California Press.

Simon, D. (1999). *Elite Deviance*. Boston: Allyn and Bacon.

Stauber, J.C. and Rampton, R. (1995). *Toxic Sludge is Good For You!* Monroe, Maine: Common Courage Press.

Steenland, K. *et al.* (1999). Cancer, heart disease and diabetes in workers exposed to 2,3,7,8 tetrachhlorodibenzo-p-dioxin. *Journal of the National Cancer Institute* 91(9), 779–786.

Steingraber, S. (1998). *Living Downstream: A Scientist's Personal Investigation of Cancer and the Environment*. New York: Vintage.

Stone, R. (1992). A biopesticidal tree begins to blossom. *Science*, Feburary 28, 1070.

Stretesky, P. and Hogan, M. (1998). Environmental justice: An analysis of superfund sites in Florida. *Social Problems* 45, 268–287.

Stretesky, P. and Lynch, M.J. (1998). Corporate environmental violence and racism. *Crime, Law and Social Change* 30, 163–184.

Suskind, R.R. and Hertzberg, V.S. (1984). Human health effects of 2,4,5-T and its toxic contaminants. *Journal of the American Medical Association* 251, 2372–2380.

Sutherland, E.H. (1945). Is white collar crime? *American Sociological Review* 10, 132–139.

Sutherland, E. (1940). White collar criminality. *American Sociological Review* 5, 1–12.

Tappan, P.W. (1949). Who is the criminal? *American Sociological Review* 12, 96–102.

Terje, R. *et al.* (1994). A population-based study of the risk of recurrence of birth defects. *New England Journal of Medicine* 331(1), 1–4.

Thomas, T.L. and Decoufle, P. (1979). Mortality among workers employed in the pharmaceutical industry: A preliminary investigation. *Journal of Occupational Medicine* 21, 619–623.

United Church of Christ (1987). *Toxic waste and race in the United States*. New York: United Church of Christ.

Van der Ryn, S. and Cowan, S. (1996). *Ecological design*. Washington, D.C.: South End Press.

Wargo, J. (1996). *Our children toxic legacy: How science and law fail to protect us from pesticides*. New Haven, Connecticut: Yale University Press.

Waldo, A. (1985). A review of US and international restrictions on exports of hazardous substances. In J. Ives (ed.), *The Export of Hazard: Transnational Corporations and Environmental Control Issues*. Boston: Routledge and Kegan Paul.

Walrath, J. *et al.* (1985). Causes of death among female chemists. *American Journal of Public Health*, August, 883–885.

Weir, D. and Shapiro, M. (1982). *Circle of Poison*. San Francisco: Institute for Food and Development Policy.

Westin, J.B. and Richter, E. (1990). The Israeli breast-cancer anomaly. In D.L. Davis and D. Hoel (eds.), *Trends in Cancer Mortality in Industrialized Countries*. New York: New York Academy of Science.

Wiles, R. *et al.* (1995). *Herbicides in Drinking Water*. Washington, D.C.: Environmental Work Group and Physician for Social Responsibility.

Wolff, M.S. *et al.* (1993). Blood levels of organochlorine residues and risk of breast cancer. *Journal of the National Cancer Institute* 85, 648–652.

Zhang, J. *et al.* (1992). Occupational hazards and pregnancy outcomes. *American Journal of Industrial Medicine* 21, 397–408.

# Part 3

# Environmental Law Enforcement

## Introduction

Environmental crime is studied for a reason; namely, we need to understand the genesis and dynamics of such crime so that we can adequately respond to it. More work needs to be done to understand the nature and scope of environmental harm, and unfortunately, much the same can be said when it comes to addressing it.

There is a huge and growing literature on environmental laws and environmental regulation. A concern with ecological wellbeing and sustainability has spawned a wide spectrum of governmental responses as well as new areas of professional intervention. These initiatives range from the funding of climate change research institutes whose brief is to engage in futures planning, through to development of systematic tools of environmental and social impact assessment. There are lot of people doing a lot of work on environmental issues.

However, from a criminological viewpoint, there is actually relatively little being done when it comes to the 'hard end' of the compliance and enforcement continuum. For a variety of reasons (relating to commercial interests, powerful lobby groups, electoral cycles and so on), dealing with environmental harms as crimes has not generated the same passion, urgency or funding support.

As the readings in this section on 'environmental law enforcement' demonstrate, generally speaking the response to environmental crime by criminal justice agencies has been light-handed and grossly inadequate up to this point in time. The occasional prosecution and imprisonment of an environmental offender is the exception that only reinforces the general rule – environmental crime is not treated seriously by the formal institutions of criminal justice.

The first few papers in this section are concerned with the issue of whether environmental crime is being taken seriously and if so, what avenues for action there might be. Brack (Reading 25) provides an overview and introduction to various measures that could be taken to combat environmental crime. Part of the problem, however, is that environmental crime is not necessarily prioritised by governments, even where issues of national security are involved (with the notable exception of ecosabotage, which is being defined in some jurisdictions as a form of terrorism). This lack of prioritisation is discussed by Elliot (Reading 26) in her chapter on transnational environmental crime in the Asia Pacific.

The police clearly have an important – if not always central – role in tackling environmental crime. Tomkins (Reading 27) discusses the levels and types of police intervention on such matters, drawing upon examples from around the world. Moving from identification of different jurisdictional services to assessment of actual practices, Akella and Cannon (Reading 28) provide an evaluation of environmental law enforcement in four different countries. They examine common problems confronting police in Brazil, Mexico, Indonesia and the Philippines as local officials attempt to address different types of environmental issues.

One way in which to forestall environmental harm is to implement good crime prevention measures and strategies. Bartel (Reading 29), for example, writes about the use of satellites in uncovering illegal land clearances. Technologies such as this and the use of DNA testing are fast becoming an integral part of environmental law enforcement. So too, lessons learned from dealing with traditional (street) crimes, such as burglaries, are being applied to the environmental crime area. Schneider (Reading 30) presents an illustration of this in a discussion of how the illicit trade in endangered wildlife can be reduced by adopting a market reduction approach. The limits of certain kinds of policing and crime prevention are exposed by Stretesky's examination of the viability of and problems associated with corporate self-policing measures as these pertain to environmental issues (Reading 31).

Once an offender has been charged, the next question relates to how the criminal law is applied within the courts. The reading by Du Rees (Reading 32) provides a sociological account of how criminal laws are variously, and unevenly, applied by agencies and personnel that have some mandate to prosecute environmental offenders. These observations are further supported by Prez (Reading 33), who points to the ritual trivialisation of environmental prosecution. A wide variety of excuses are made, and accepted, in court that basically diminish the importance of the offence and thus allow offenders to escape penalty. A discussion paper by the UK House of Commons (Reading 34) provides additional confirmation that magistrates and judges require support, training and education when it comes to apprising environmental crimes and dealing with environmental offenders. Fortney (Reading 35) suggests that part of the solution to adequate prosecution lies in the adoption of tailored enforcement measures. That is, if we want to convict and penalise offenders in the most meaningful fashion, then we need to tailor the response to their specific situation and circumstances.

This section concludes with a discussion of policy, law and practical intervention. Dorn, Van Daele and Vander Beken (Reading 36) provide a discussion of the waste management industry and the issues arising from pressures and changes occurring within this industry. This reading highlights the importance of both ongoing research into specific environmental harms, and the need for strategic thinking around matters that are constantly changing, institutionally and in substance.

Research, policy and practice are always intertwined – and the effectiveness of environmental law enforcement very much depends upon how environmental problems are conceptualised, how the nature and dynamics of harm are understood, and how resources are mobilised in response to specific environmental crimes.

# 25. Combatting international environmental crime*

*Duncan Brack*

## Introduction

'Environmental crime' occurs when individuals and companies deliberately flout environmental laws and regulations for profit or power. Where these activities lead to acknowledge transboundary or global environmental impacts, they can be termed 'international environmental crime'. The most commonly known examples of this type of criminal activity are as follows. In the area of *biodiversity*, the best-known instance is the illegal trade in endangered species of wild flora and fauna and their products, i.e. evasion of the controls instituted under the 1973 Convention on International Trade in Endangered Species (CITES). Other examples include illegal whaling and biopiracy, the illegal use of genetic resources or information – for example development and commercialisation as pharmaceutical products – removed from indigenous habitats without permission or licensing. There is also the future possibility of illegal trade in genetically modified products, in breach of the provisions of the 2000 Cartagena Protocol to the Biodiversity Convention (agreed but not yet in force), which establishes a system for regulating such trade.

*Natural resources-related crime* covers two main areas. Illegal fishing – for example, banned driftnet catches, or fishing beyond quota – is a relatively recent phenomenon. As 60% of the ocean fisheries are currently being exploited at or beyond their sustainable yield, it is also a matter of growing economic and social concern. Illegal logging and trade in timber and timber products is widespread and represents not only a threat to biodiversity, but also a major loss of revenue to many developing economies.

In the areas of *wastes*, the illegal movement of hazardous wastes – in breach of the 1989 Basel Convention – is probably the newest area of international environmental crime. Rising standards of waste disposal in many industrialised countries are leading to rising costs and hence a growing incentive for illegal disposal. The illegal disposal of nuclear waste is a closely related topic; the dumping of waste oil at sea, in breach of the International Maritime Organisation's Marine Pollution (Marpol) Convention, is a matter of concern to many countries with long coastlines.

* From *Global Environmental Change* (2002), 12: pp. 142–147.

Environmental crime related to *banned substances* currently has one example, the illegal trade in ozone-depleting substances (ODS), in breach of the controls required by the 1987 Montreal Protocol on Substances that Deplete the Ozone Layer. There are in addition, however, possible future candidates, including evasion of the 1998 Rotterdam Convention on chemicals and pesticides, and the 2001 Stockholm Convention on persistent organic pollutants (POPs Convention), which have both been agreed but are not yet in force.

## The causes of black markets

There are several drivers behind the emergence of international environmental crime and environmental black markets. The first is differences in costs or values, where illegal activities are driven by regulations creating cost differentials between legal and illegal products, by differential compliance costs in different countries, by demand for scarce products for which substitutes are not available or accepted and by a lack of concern for or valuation of the environment.

The second cause is regulatory failure, where illegal activities result from a lack of appropriate regulation, including failures to determine and/or protect property rights (open access problems).

The third is the failure to enforce existing laws, where illegal activities exist because of problems with enforcement, including suitability of regulation/enforcement methodology and costs of compliance, regulatory capture, lack of resources and infrastructure, political will and/or expertise, corruption, and political and economic disruption.

The reported incidence of illegal environmental activities has undoubtedly grown in recent years, partly because the formal implementation of new multilateral environmental agreements (MEAs) has provided new opportunities for evasion, and partly because greater public and governmental awareness has led to more investigation into the issues. Other contributory factors include the general trend towards trade liberalisation and deregulation, which makes border controls more difficult; the growth of transnational corporations and activities, amongst whom regulations are often difficult to enforce; the transformation of the Comecon bloc, and the associated difficulties of law enforcement; the growth of organised transnational crime; and the growing involvement of developing countries in MEAs, but – in many of them – a lack of adequate resources to implement their provisions effectively. For all these reasons, it seems very likely that international environmental crime will continue to expand in the coming decades.

## How much environmental crime is there?

The availability and quality of data on all forms of international environmental crime is – virtually by definition – extremely poor. Not only it is difficult to acquire information, but in many instances, there is a reluctance amongst enforcement agencies (e.g. customs), who in general are not familiar with these problems, to investigate them. However, partial data and anecdotal evidence are available in many cases. This section focuses on three examples.

### Endangered species

Total international trade in animals, plants and their products is estimated to generate an annual turnover well in excess of $20 billion, including 40,000 primates, several million animal pelts, several million birds, 10 million reptile skins, 500 million tropical fish, and 9–10 million orchids. It is believed that a quarter of this trade might be unlawful, although as noted above this figure is no more than a guess. Interpol estimates place illegal trade in endangered species as likely to be the second largest criminal activity world-wide, after narcotics (though the illegal timber trade is probably larger). Poaching and smuggling of ivory, tiger skins and other body parts, and rhino horns, in particular, has threatened the existence of all or some populations of the species in question.

The illegal trade arises mainly because of the demand for exotic pets and flowers, for certain luxury foodstuffs (e.g. caviar), and for traditional purposes (e.g. rhino horn for traditional East Asian medicine or ivory for personal *hanko* seals). There are three main methods of illegal trade:

- Failure to implement CITES controls. Of 81 countries examined in an IUCN study in 1994, only 15 possessed legislation meeting all the requirements for CITES implementation; 27 met none of the requirements.

- Abuse of the controls, including counterfeit documents, fraudulent applications for genuine CITES permits and false declarations to customs officials (helped by the fact that many endangered species are very difficult to distinguish from similar but nonendangered species). The existence of pre-CITES stockpiles (e.g. of ivory) in some countries also complicates control efforts, as do various categories of legal trade (non-commercial, captive-bred, personal effects, etc.). Limited resources, both of money and personnel, and lack of awareness and political will, mean that enforcement of the legislation that exists is often inadequate.

- Concealment of the specimens in consignments of other goods or in personal effects or diplomatic baggage (which also contributes to a high mortality rate, though even legal trade suffers from this problem).

### Logging and the trade in timber

Of all the different varieties of international environmental crime, illegal logging and the illegal trade in timber and timber products is almost certainly the most economically significant. Some estimates suggest that the illegal timber trade may comprise over a tenth of a global business worth about US$100 billion. It seems likely that at least half of all the logging activities in particularly vulnerable regions – the Amazon Basin, Central Africa, Southeast Asia and the Russian Federation – is illegal (Brack and Hayman (2001) summarise current estimates). As the World Bank's review of its global forest policy observed:

countries with tropical moist forest have continued to log on a massive scale, often illegally and unsustainably. In many countries, illegal logging is similar in size to legal production. In others, it exceeds legal logging by a substantial margin ... poor governance, corruption, and political alliances between parts of the private sector and ruling elites combined with minimal enforcement capacity at local and regional levels, all played a part (World Bank, 1999, p. xii).

Illegal logging is not confined to developing countries, but the problems there are much worse, as resources are limited, international companies which offer investment are proportionately more powerful, and civil society is weaker. Allocation of timber concessions has often been used as a mechanism of extending patronage. Accordingly, timber companies may evade national regulations with relative impunity. State forestry institutions may be subject to regulatory capture, becoming clients of industrial interests and exercising their powers as a form of private property rather than as a public service.

A joint UK–Indonesia study of the timber industry in Indonesia in 1998 suggested that about 40% of throughput was illegal, with a value in excess of US$365 million. Similarly, over 80% of logging in the Amazon may not be compliant with government controls. A World Resources Institute comparison of import and export data for Myanmar in 1997 revealed substantial under-declaration, accounting for foregone revenue of US$86 million, equivalent to almost half of official timber export revenues. Studies in Cambodia in 1997 by Global Witness and the World Bank suggested illegal extraction may be over 4 million $m^3$, at least 10 times the size of the legal harvest, worth between US$0.5 and 1 billion. If this level of extraction continues, the country would be logged out in just 10 years from when the industry officially began.

The scale of illegal logging represents a major loss of revenue to many developing economies and can lead to widespread associated environmental damage; it is also a threat to biodiversity, and in some cases a breach of controls under CITES. The substantial revenues from illegal logging sometimes fund and thereby exacerbate national and regional conflict, the strongest recent example being Cambodia, where Khmer Rouge forces were sustained primarily by logging revenues for several years in the mid-1990s.

The illegal trade may also distort and devalue the entire global marketplace, making it difficult for sustainable management – which has to endure additional costs from good husbandry and proper tax declaration – to survive. As the World Bank reported, 'widespread illegal extraction makes it pointless to invest in improved logging [practices]. This is a classic case of concurrent government and market failure'.

### Ozone-depleting substances

The emergence of illegal trade in ozone-depleting substances (ODS) is a good example of a problem springing directly from the negotiation and implementation of an international treaty, the 1987 Montreal Protocol on Substances that Deplete the Ozone Layer. The Protocol is one of the most effective MEAs in existence, but one of its remaining weaknesses is the emergence of illegal trade in ODS, primarily in the US and EU, but also now in developing countries. In 1994–95, CFCs were the second most valuable contraband smuggled through Miami, after cocaine. Government and industry estimates suggest a global total of 16,000–38,000 tonnes in the probable peak year, 1995. The higher figure is equivalent to 15% of consumption world-wide, worth more than $0.5 billion. CFC smuggling appears to have declined since then, particularly in the US and probably in the EU, and in general CFCs seem to be in shorter supply, as they should be in the absence of illegal material.

The incentive for illegal use arises not from the higher cost of the ODS alternatives – they have often proved to be cheaper and more effective than the ODS they replaced – but from the cost of adaptation or replacement of the machinery in question, which can be relatively high. Since most refrigeration and air-conditioning equipment has relatively long lifetimes, this implies a continued incentive for illegal use in the short and medium-term.

The main source of the illegal material now entering the EU appears to be China, and for the US, probably China and Mexico. The Russian Federation continued to produce in breach of its commitments after 1995, though Russian production ceased at the end of 2000. It is also possible that some ODS illegally entering the EU and US may in fact have been legally produced there, exported and then clandestinely re-imported.

There are five major methods of illegal trade:

- Mislabelling of containers (for example, as HFCs or hydrocarbons or as recycled ODS) and of accompanying documentation (including the use of false customs codes); ODS are colourless, odourless gases at room temperature, and chemical analysis is needed to determine precisely what substances are present.

- Concealment of material, for example by constructing cylinders with hidden compartments containing illegal material, or, more simply, by concealing cylinders in the midst of legitimate cargo.

- Disguise: virgin CFCs can be deliberately contaminated, for example with water vapour, to make them appear as recycled material.

- Diversion of material destined for legal markets in developing countries into domestic markets in nondeveloping countries, with false documentation. This was a common problem in the US, with Miami an important source as a major trans-shipment port.

- Diversion of material from legal uses (feedstock, essential use exemptions, etc.) into illegal uses. This is probably the least likely of the five routes examined here, particularly for essential use exemptions, where purity requirements imply strict monitoring.

## Tackling environmental crime

Serious though all these problems are, they are at least beginning to be addressed. Some effective enforcement has taken place in several countries, including control of the illegal trade in wildlife and wildlife products, and of smuggling of ODS. These experiences provide useful lessons to be learned for the control of such activities more widely.

G8 summits have, since 1996, called for more effective and better coordinated action to combat international environmental crime. The first meeting of the G8 Nations' Lyon Group Law Enforcement Project on Environmental Crime took place in July 1999, aiming to improve information exchange, data analysis and investigative cooperation among law enforcement agencies, regulators and international organisations. Options for the control of illegal logging are being considered under the G8 Forestry Initiative, due to report next year. Interpol, the World Customs Organisation (WCO) and UNEP have all begun to work on the issue, and are establishing cooperative frameworks between themselves and MEA secretariats. The International Network for Environmental Compliance and Enforcement (INECE) and the European Network on the Implementation and Enforcement of Environmental Law (IMPEL) are but two of a number of networks of enforcement agencies also being established.

There are many policy options available for combating international environmental crime. They can be considered under three broad headings.

### Reducing demand

ODS crime is the exception here, as the one area in which demand will eventually disappear of its open accord, as all ODS-using equipment is eventually phased out. In all other areas, two factors are necessary if the demand for the illegal products is to be successfully curtailed.

First, there must be some means of identifying illegal material, probably through some kinds of licensing or certification systems; CITES already provides this for endangered species. The growth of certification systems based on sustainability criteria (such as the Forest Stewardship Council certificates for timber) offers one possibility for discriminating against illegal products, though it may be easier in some cases simply to identify legality. This requires effective means both of issuing and verifying the certificates, implying separate systems for administration and monitoring, and also a legal framework which allows material lacking a valid licence to be seized at the border, or when put on sale. This is a particular problem for areas of criminal activity where a global MEA is not in existence (such as fishing or logging), and there may be a case for the negotiation of global agreements on illegal activity (possibly starting at a smaller, regional, scale). There are also possible complications with WTO regulations which could usefully be explored.

Second, consumers, retailers and importers of the products need to be educated to look for and demand the certificate, and to refuse products which lack it. Often ignored in many discussions of enforcing environmental crime, public awareness campaigns have proved of value in some cases (e.g. in enforcement of CITES) and could usefully be extended. Central and local government procurement programmes can also play an important role.

### Reducing supply

Strategies aimed to reduce the supply of illegal materials need to concentrate on the underlying economic, social and political drivers behind the illegal activity – and are accordingly difficult and complex to implement. Once again, ODS crime is the 'easy' area, where supply will be phased out in any case under the Montreal Protocol. In other areas, including wildlife, fishing and logging, policy options include reform of the systems for granting exploitation rights, taxes, subsidies and regulation, and the involvement of local communities and the availability of alternative forms of employment and economic activity.

### Controlling the illegal trade

Most discussions of controlling international environmental crime tend to concentrate, not unnaturally, on improving enforcement, and there is indeed a wide range of policy options available. They include:

- Greater cooperation between environment and enforcement agencies at the international, regional and national levels. Intelligence gathering, information exchange, guidance (such as codes of best practice) and training can all be coordinated and delivered effectively at international or regional level. In some cases, there may be a need for new legal instruments such as MEAs. At national level, there is a strong case for establishing environmental crime units or working parties, as recommended by Interpol, involving all relevant agencies, NGOs, and industry. Some harmonisation of relevant legislation (for example, in terms of penalties) would be helpful.

- Enhanced means of tracking and identification, including more research and effort in collecting data; the development of independent verification of data reported under MEAs; possible extension of the WCO's Harmonised System of customs classification; greater investment in tracking mechanisms, identification of country/factory/area of origin, requirements for export and import licences, pre-shipment inspections, certification systems, etc.; the establishment of registers of licensed traders; and the greater use of new technology. The Montreal Amendment to the Montreal Protocol, agreed in 1997 after mounting concern over the size of the illegal trade, established such a system of import and export licences for ODS. The development of 'extra-territorial' legislation aiming to regulate the overseas activities of domestically based companies. The OECD Anti-Bribery Convention is relevant here, and the US Lacey Act, which provides for action against imports of species obtained illegally in foreign countries (e.g. those covered by CITES or by domestic legislation such as the US Endangered Species Act), is also a useful model.

- The allocation of greater resources, in terms of finance and personnel, to tackling the problem. This includes a higher priority for environmental issues within police and customs agencies (which is often about awareness raising as much as anything else); greater resources devoted to implementing and monitoring MEAs; and financial, technical and capacity-building assistance for developing countries and transition economies. As many cases of environmental crime may involve unpaid taxes or charges, however, investment here can reap financial as well as environmental dividends.

## Conclusions

The growth of environmental crime is a serious side effect of the development of policies aimed at protecting the environment. Unlike most other kinds of crime, it harms not just individual victims, but society as a whole. *International* environmental crime potentially damages the *global* environment.

The total value of the illegal activities involved in international environmental crime may be in the order of $20–40 billion a year, about 5–10% of the size of the global drugs trade. Compared to the 'war on drugs', however, the resources and political will devoted to tackling the international environmental crime are derisory – yet the problem threatens every citizen of the world, and undermines several key environmental treaties.

There is no shortage of policy options available for improving the enforcement of environmental regulations and controlling illegal activity. What is still lacking is political will and resources.

## References

Brack, D., Hayman, G., 2001. Intergovernmental Actions on Illegal Logging: Options for Intergovernmental Action to Help Combat Illegal and Illegal Trade in Timber and Forest Products. Royal Institute of International Affairs, London.

World Bank, 1999. Forest Sector Review. World Bank, Washington.

# 26. Transnational environmental crime in the Asia Pacific: an 'un(der)securitized' security problem?*

*Lorraine Elliott*

## Abstract

While other forms of transnational crime in the Asia Pacific have been securitized – that is, represented by policy elites and security actors as crucial or existential threats to national and regional security – transnational environmental crime has been un(der)securitized. It warrants little mention in regional security statements or the security concerns of individual countries. Yet the consequences of activities such as illegal logging and timber smuggling, wildlife smuggling, the black market in ozone-depleting substances and dumping of other forms of hazardous wastes and chemical fit the (in)security profile applied to other forms of transnational crime. This article surveys the main forms of transnational environmental crime in the Asia Pacific and assesses the 'fit' with a 'crime as security' framework. It shows that transnational environmental crime generates the kinds of 'pernicious effects ... on regional stability and development, the maintenance of the rule of law and the welfare of the region's people' that the ASEAN Declaration on Transnational Crime identified as matters of serious concern. The analysis draws on securitization theory to understand the lack of a 'securitizing move' and to explain why security elites do not believe the problem warrants serious attention. The possibilities explored here include intellectual inertia, confusion about referent objects, institutional incapacity, mixed policy signals and the exclusion of environmental expertise from a closed community of security elites.

**Key Words** Securitization theory • transnational crime • environmental crime • illegal logging • wildlife trafficking • ODS smuggling.

## Introduction

Environmental degradation and resource decline are important policy challenges for the Asia Pacific. While the economic, social and ecological consequences usually dominate policy discussions, there is a growing

---

* From *The Pacific Review* (2007), 20(4): pp. 499–522.

recognition that environmental challenges complicate security issues as well. Most commentaries on regional security make some reference to non-military or transnational security concerns and most make a passing reference to environmental degradation. The literature on 'environmental security' as a conceptual addition to the security lexicon and an admittedly contested policy issue in the Asia Pacific is well established.[1] The debates about the tensions between a soft-realist variant of environmental security and a more critical security studies inspired model that takes people or communities or societies (or even ecosystems) as the referent for insecurity and challenges the adequacy of state-centric models need not, therefore, be rehearsed in any depth here.[2]

Rather than revisit the existing literature about environmental security, this article focuses on one aspect of the environmental security challenge – transnational environmental crime (TEC) – that has fallen out of regional security debates or, more to the point and somewhat surprisingly, was never there in the first place. Commentary on the security consequences of other forms of transnational crime is now incorporated in regional security declarations and agreements. Transnational crime has, in effect, been 'securitized' – declared to be a security issue – although this is uneven in breadth (the range of issues) and depth (the extent to which making security claims about transnational crime translates into actual policy responses).[3] Yet the problem of transnational *environmental* crime and illegal resource activity in the Asia Pacific is rarely mentioned in this context.[4] In comparison with other forms of transnational crime, TEC has not been securitized. One purpose of this article is to ponder why this might be so.

Exploring the 'why' requires some prior attention to the 'what' of environmental crime and its security consequences. This article therefore begins with an overview of the main forms of transnational environmental crime in the region. To counter the argument that TEC has not been securitized because there are *no* (in)security consequences similar to those alleged for other forms of transnational crime, the second section then considers the possible security impacts of such activity. The approach to securitization used here focuses mainly on the 'speech act' or the 'securitizing move' – the discursive step by which actors offer up an issue area in security terms – rather than the full gamut of what Buzan *et al.* (1998) call 'successful securitisation' that involves claims for emergency or extraordinary measures and acceptance of these claims by the 'relevant audience' (which could be elites or the wider public). The discursive concern is not whether a referent object is *actually* threatened such that its continued existence in its present form is brought into doubt but whether problems are conceptualized or presented in those terms by actors who are in an authoritative position to do so, most commonly 'political leaders, bureaucracies, governments, lobbyists and pressure groups' (Buzan *et al.* 1998: 40–1). However, an empirical investigation of the nature and insecurities of actual threats is important for two reasons. First, the declaration that something is a security problem is more likely to be accepted, and therefore lead to successful securitization, when the securitizing actors can support and legitimize their claims with 'evidence'. Second, the securitization of other forms of transnational crime in the region has relied on this evidentiary mode of argument. Using a metric drawn from the 'transnational crime as (in)security' literature, the second section shows that the security consequences of illegal and criminal cross-border environmental and resource activity are, by most measures, as serious as those of other forms of transnational crime in the region. The third section canvasses regional security responses and demonstrates that transnational environmental crime has been 'undersecuritized' by regional elites, compared with other forms of transnational crime, and offers some preliminary thoughts about why this might be so.[5]

## Transnational environmental crime: global and regional

Environmental crime and illegal resource activity constitute a particular dimension of the non-compliance and enforcement problem that is central to the global politics of the environment. Where an activity is regulated or prohibited under the terms of a multilateral environmental agreement (MEA) – such as the trade in protected species or hazardous waste – signatory governments are expected to enact legislation that gives effect to that agreement and establishes penalties and sanctions for violation of that legislation. Other forms of illegal resource and environmental activity are defined primarily by domestic legislation and may well, therefore, be illegal or prohibited in one country but not in another – the use of genetically modified organisms is one such case. Still others – and illegal logging is perhaps the best example here – have become internationally 'criminalized' in normative terms through soft-law declarations, private international regulation and national legislation which establishes categories of illegality in individual jurisdictions.[6]

As the discussion below shows, environmental crime has become increasingly transnationalized in the terms suggested by the UN Convention against Transnational Organized Crime which defines transnational criminal activity in jurisdictional and process terms. A crime is transnational if it is committed in more than one state; is committed in one state but a substantial part of its preparation, planning, direction or control takes place in another state; is committed in one state but involves an organized criminal group that engages in criminal activities in more than one state; or is committed in one state but has substantial effects in another state (United Nations General Assembly 2000: article 3).[7] The main areas of environmental crime are:[8]

- the smuggling of plants and animals (dead or alive) or parts thereof in contravention of the 1972 Convention on International Trade in Endangered Species (CITES);

- the illegal extraction, exploitation and smuggling of natural resources including timber resources and oceans resources;

- the illegal movement and dumping of hazardous and other wastes (sometimes referred to as 'waste tourism' (van der Meer 1992)) in contravention of agreements such as the 1989 Basel Convention and the 1972 London Dumping Convention;

- the smuggling of illegal pollutants, including those specified under the 1987 Montreal Protocol on ozone-depleting substances (ODS), the 1998 Rotterdam Convention on Prior Informed Consent which covers various hazardous chemicals, and the 2001 Stockholm Convention on Persistent Organic Pollutants;

- the illegal use of genetic resources which are removed from indigenous habitats without permission or licensing and the possibility of a black market in genetically modified products or genetic materials such as those stored in tissue banks.

TEC is most often conceptualized as a form of enterprise crime in pursuit of profit, characterized by high returns and low risk, or as a means of avoiding excise, taxes and high disposal costs. It is increasingly systematic; the most lucrative areas of environmental crime are marked by official corruption, money laundering and the involvement of organized crime groups.[9] TEC serves also to generate 'venture capital' for other illicit activities such as drugs and arms, and often involves parallel trafficking, that is using the same smuggling routes for different goods, combining illegal shipments, or using ostensibly legal shipments such as wildlife to conceal other forms of illegal goods.[10]

There is little doubt that TEC is one of the fastest growing areas of illegal activity and one which now constitutes a significant proportion of the trade in resources and environmental goods. Approximately 25 per cent of all trade in wildlife is thought to be illicit. Illegally harvested and smuggled timber is an increasingly significant component of the international timber trade. Some figures suggest, for example, that over half the tropical timber imported annually into the European Union alone has been logged illegally (International Centre for Trade and Sustainable Development 2004: 2). At the height of the global black market in ODS in the mid-1990s, between 16,000 and 30,000 tonnes of illegal CFCs (chlorofluorocarbons) were traded each year in contravention of the Montreal Protocol (UNEP 2001: 3). Overall, the illegal environmental trade is estimated to be worth US$22–31 billion a year (or more) to criminal syndicates around the world (Lauterback 2005). Interpol and the G8 have valued the global illegal wildlife trade alone at US$10–20 billion a year, ranking with drug smuggling and arms trafficking as major black markets in production terms. The profits can be high even for small-scale operations. Individuals of some species (ranging from exotic parrots to rare orchids and snowdrops) fetch large sums on the black market. Ounce for ounce, for example, rhino horn can be more valuable than gold or class A drugs (Anon. 2002b).[11] Contraband CFCs have been described as 'rivalling cocaine as among the most profitable illegal imports crossing US borders' (Schmidt 2004: A97). As well as generating profit for organized crime, TEC results in revenue losses for legitimate producers. The World Bank calculates, for example, that timber-producing countries in the developing world lose something between US$10–15 billion a year because of illegal logging on public land (World Bank 2006: xi). This pattern of scope and reach, smuggling, corruption and organized criminal activity applies as much to the Asia Pacific as to other parts of the world, as the discussion below reveals.

496

## Illegal logging in the Asia Pacific

Illegal logging in the region involves a range of 'chain of custody' practices: extraction and harvesting crimes, processing crimes, and transportation crimes. Extraction crimes – which include harvesting in contravention of national law, logging without a licence or with a fraudulent licence, or logging inside protected areas – may well outstrip legal harvesting. Between 51 and 80 per cent of timber taken in Indonesia is thought to be illegally logged: the equivalent of 33 million cubic metres of illegally harvest round wood is smuggled out of Indonesia a year and about 300,000 cubic metres of merbau logs are smuggled from Papua *each month*. In Cambodia, the proportion of illegal harvesting could be as high as 94 per cent of all logging (Brack 2005: 29). As much as 95 per cent of wood exported from Burma to China may come from illegal sources (GlobalWitness 2006). Illegal logging is also extensive in Laos, Thailand and the Philippines. Timber is smuggled from source countries to major regional hubs such as Singapore, South Korea and China (the largest consumer of stolen timber in the world), processed or relabelled as legally harvested product (timber laundering) and then often re-exported outside the region to the United States and Europe among other destinations.[12] Customs seizures of illegal timber have increased since the hardwood species ramin was made subject to import and export controls under appendix III of CITES but the impact has not been extensive. The 155,000 cubic metres of smuggled timber seized by Indonesian officials in 2005 makes only a minor dent in the trade compared with the 3.6 million cubic metres of round wood alleged to be moved illegally from Papua alone each year (Anon. 2006).[13]

The illegal timber trade is supported by other forms of illicit and criminal activity: bribery and fraud; money laundering; violence and at times murder.[14] The extent of the trade would be impossible without a well-organized network of shipping companies and agents, brokers and middlemen in places such as Singapore, Malaysia, Hong Kong and China who support relabelling, processing and transportation crimes. 'Several major syndicates' are thought to be in operation (see Newman and Lawson 2005: 17), involved in chartering cargo vessels, faking documents, issuing letters of credit and forging connections between buyers and sellers.[15] The attraction for criminal gangs is that, despite the size of the product, timber smuggling is easier than drug smuggling.[16] The returns are high, the risk of capture low, and the penalties often minimal. Corruption is also endemic in the illegal timber trade. This ranges from petty corruption of police and customs officials who might destroy evidence or knowingly issue false transportation documents through to financial involvement at the highest levels of political elites and military forces in countries such as Indonesia (see EIA/Telapak 2002; International Crisis Group 2001), Burma and Laos (Siem Bok 1999) and Cambodia (Global Witness 2007).[17]

## Wildlife trade in the Asia Pacific

Wildlife trade constitutes a second substantial illegal economy in the Asia Pacific, with Southeast Asia alone thought to be responsible for about a quarter of the world's illegal wildlife trade (Lin 2005: 201). Customs seizures give evidence of the range of wildlife smuggled into and through the region: ivory, marine turtle eggs, pangolins, freshwater turtles among others. While there is some opportunity poaching, wildlife smuggling syndicates are now active in most areas of the trade. Some of this involves stealing to order for private collectors, zoos, and medical and research laboratories. The trade is also driven by the demand for exotic meats in niche markets such as Japan, South Korea and Thailand and by a sustained market for traditional Asian medicines (TAM) even though, as Hayman and Brack (2002) point out, animal products constitute less than 10 per cent of the components of TAMs (and endangered species less than 3 per cent).

The expansion of the region's transport infrastructure has provided more opportunities for the movement of illegally sourced wildlife. High levels of illegal cross-border trade in wild species have been recorded in the tri-border area of Cambodia, Laos and Vietnam (see Thomson 2002: 11). Singapore and Hong Kong have become major transit points. There is a growing illegal trade from China into the countries on its Himalayan borders – Nepal, India and Pakistan – involving threatened species such as the Tibetan antelope, the giant panda and the Saker Falcon (Li et al. 2000). Rhino horn and tiger parts are traded across the Sino-Burma border. Bear populations in East Asia have been the victim of the demand for bear gall bladder in the TAM pharmacopoeia.[18] The black market extends to even larger species. Live Indo-Chinese tigers as well as tiger parts are smuggled through Thailand (EIA 2001). Documentation is forged or altered in cases where concealment is clearly difficult, with elephants and komodo dragons being traded illegally from Indonesia to countries such as Argentina, China, Germany, France and Mexico.

Smuggling regional wildlife can be a profitable business. For example, Chinese three-striped turtles (used in TAM as well as favoured as pets) can be purchased in Laos for as little as US$75–260, exchange hands in Hong Kong for US$1,000 and sell in the United States via the Internet for US$2,200 a pair (Cook et al. 2002: 18). A Chinese alligator can fetch up to US$15,000. The aggregate figures are staggering. To take just one example, the revenue and profits for wildlife smuggled through Vietnam are estimated at US$66.5 million and US$21 million a year, respectively (cited in Lin 2005: 203).

### The trade in hazardous pollutants and waste

The region has become a hub for the black market in ODS. China is a major source of counterfeit CFCs and Southeast Asia a major trade route. Illegal CFCs can be moved easily through Singapore, for example, to countries outside the region – to Nepal as a staging post for smuggling CFCs into India, or to South Africa (see EIA/Telepak 2003: 2). The profits can be high. A 30-pound cylinder of CFCs can be bought in China for approximately US$40 and sold on the US black market for up to US$600 (Schmidt 2004: A97). As with other forms of transnational environmental crime, it seems highly likely that organized criminal groups are involved in pollutant smuggling in the region.

The extent of the illegal waste trade in the region is less clear than the evidence for ODS, but the documentation of individual cases suggests that there is regular illicit activity. In December 1996, used lead acid batteries were exported from Australia through Singapore for recycling and recovery operations in the Philippines in contravention of both the Basel Convention and Australian domestic legislation (although the subsequent court case determined that this was a negligent contravention rather than criminal activity). In 1998, between 3,000 and 4,000 metric tonnes of toxic waste from a Taiwanese petrochemical company were found in an open dump in Sihanoukville, Cambodia.[19] In January 2000, Japanese industrial waste-processing company Nisso Ltd was caught trying to dump 2,700 tons of infectious medical waste in the Philippines (see Schmidt 2004: A101).[20] Other kinds of wastes are also traded illegally, or at least dubiously, into the region. China, for example, remains a centre for recycling e-waste even though such shipments into the country are banned and are illegal under the Basel convention. Schmidt (2004: A101) suggests that European, Russian and Japanese crime groups have established an illegal market for hazardous waste in Asia, often in conjunction with money laundering and arms sales.

## Transnational (environmental) crime as a security threat?

Serrano suggests that, as a general phenomenon, 'transnational crime has risen to new stardom in the wars of international security rhetoric' (Serrano 2002: 13). For some, 'international organized criminal activity poses a threat to world security ... analogous to acts of aggression' (Guymon 2000: 56). While few commentators go quite that far, except perhaps in their claims about terrorism, most argue that transnational crime, and organized crime in particular, should be taken seriously on the security agenda to the extent that 'the struggle against ... transnational crime [is argued to be] the defining security concern of the twenty-first century' (Galeotti, cited in Emmers 2003: 421). While the focus on the speech act in securitization theory suggests that security is socially constructed through discursive claims by elites or authoritative actors, in practice much of the security/securitized discourse in the region also involves claims about the actual security consequences that arise from particular 'threats'. One important question for this article, therefore, is whether transnational environmental crime generates the *same or similar kinds* of security concerns that elites in the region have claimed for other forms of transnational crime. There are two steps here: first, identifying the security 'metric' that has been attached to transnational crime and, second, assessing whether TEC fits this metric. The literature on transnational crime draws on two approaches to non-traditional security although in practice the boundaries are sometimes blurred. The first – widening – explores the threat posed to the state and, by extension, to societies from sources other than military ones (a non-traditional threat to a traditional referent object). The second approach – deepening – introduces non-traditional referents by considering the consequences for economic and human security and, in the case of TEC, ecological security.

From a statist perspective, transnational crime can constitute an alternative, albeit illicit, form of authority. Guymon suggests that three components of state sovereignty and authority are either challenged or made vulnerable by transnational crime: the 'control of borders, the monopoly on the use of violence for enforcement, and the power to tax economic activities within state borders' (Guymon 2000: 56). Castle adds to this the 'maintenance of the core values of a society' including the rule of law and the existence of a fair and open marketplace (Castle 1997: 6). Security is undermined, he argues, in situations where the state is 'unable to enforce its own laws in particular regions' or where a region is 'beyond effective state control' (Castle 1997: 6). In effect, transnational crime, and organized crime in particular, undermines a government's ability to govern.

Transnational criminal activity takes advantage of 'weak governments, corruption and nepotism' (McFarlane 2001: 5). Widespread corruption undermines the credibility and functioning of law enforcement agencies, the judiciary and the legal system. The state is also made insecure when the agents of the state are either unable to resist or are actively involved in organized crime and illegality. The involvement of politicians and business, bureaucratic and military elites and lesser officials in sustaining illicit markets constitutes 'shadow states' (see Duffy 2005) that subvert the usual practices of state-based governance. In the most extreme cases of high-level corruption and personal patronage, the state itself no longer functions in the Weberian sense as a provider and guarantor of public goods but as a 'protection racket' that sustains private appropriation and rent-seeking.[21]

Transnational crime is implicated in the deepening of non-traditional insecurities, although the connection between transnational crime and human (in)security is a complex one. In already vulnerable societies and polities, criminal groups and the victimization and violence that can accompany activities such as drug smuggling, arms smuggling and people trafficking can pose a serious threat to individual security and to the security of local communities. Individuals and communities are also the victims of the effects of illegal commodities such as drugs or arms and, for women and children in particular, of human trafficking. Yet, at the same time, some forms of illegal activity may be the only means of survival for some in the face of poverty. As Peter Andreas suggests, 'in many places ... the criminalized economy has been a crucial source of both revenue and employment' (Andreas 2002: 37–8), although this can also increase vulnerability to the more organized and systematic forms of criminal activity.

In the Asia Pacific, regional declarations attest to these concerns. The authoritative statements that are adopted in both official and second-track contexts constitute a form of discursive securitization of transnational crime by policy elites over time.[22] In the Joint Communiqué of the 29th ASEAN Ministerial Meeting in July 1996, ministers identified transnational crime as a possible threat to the political, societal and economic security of the ASEAN nations. The ASEAN Declaration on Transnational Crime adopted a year later referred more specifically to the 'pernicious effects ... on regional stability and development, the maintenance of the rule of law and the welfare of the region's people'. The Declaration proclaimed that transnational crime 'undermines civil society, distorts legitimate markets and destabilizes States' (ASEAN Secretariat 1997: preamble). The 1999 Plan of Action to Combat Transnational Crime publicized the region's concerns about the potential for transnational crime to undermine the ASEAN objective of making Southeast Asia a prosperous and peaceful community. The Chairman's statement following the 8th meeting of the ASEAN Regional Forum (ARF) advised that 'Ministers recognised that the transnational crimes could not only have potentially serious impacts on regional peace and stability, but also pose a threat to the national economic development and social well-being of all states' (ASEAN Regional Forum 2001: para 26) although most of the ARF's work has focused on counter-terrorism. In sum, as Hernandez and Pattugalan put it, 'transnational crime [is now seen as] a major threat to domestic security, inter-state relations and global security' (Hernandez and Pattugalan 1999b: ii).

Is this framework of threat and insecurity that invokes state, economic and human referents also relevant to transnational environmental crime? Some of the insecurities are specifically environmental. The longer-term impacts of illegal resource extraction and smuggling of prohibited or regulated goods (whether wildlife or chemicals) are as much environmental as they are economic or political. Illegal logging takes place in some of the region's most vulnerable forests and is a major driver of deforestation which is occurring at a rate far higher than elsewhere in the world. The ecological consequences include soil erosion, changes to local climate and water retention patterns, and increased susceptibility to flooding and landslides. Timber smuggling and the illegal trade in wildlife destroy habitats, exacerbate species endangerment and contribute to loss of biodiversity. Smuggling CFCs and other prohibited or regulated pollutants undermines global attempts to manage problems such as ozone depletion or chemical pollution. Dumping hazardous and toxic wastes poisons water tables, river systems and local ecosystems. The (in)security consequences of TEC are not, however, limited to the environmental sector. Rather, they play out against the same kinds of concerns articulated in regional claims about other forms of transnational crime.

## State security

The most orthodox of the concerns with state security remains the potential for conflict between countries. Actual conflict over transnational environmental crime is unlikely. Political dispute, sometimes accompanied by an occasional military deployment or show of force, is much more likely. China and Indonesia, for example, found themselves in dispute following Indonesian Navy seizures of consignments of illegal logs en route to China. Malaysia and Indonesia have had a number of disagreements over illegal logging and problems of cross-border incursions. Troops have been deployed in mainland Southeast Asia to protect borders regions against illegal logging and timber smuggling. While illegal fishing has not been explored extensively in this article, it is perhaps the exemplar case in which disputes over access to and authority over resources are 'interactive with … threat perceptions' (Ganesan 2001: 520).[23] Transnational environmental crime has also generated funds to sustain regional conflict. Illegal logging and smuggling across the Thai–Cambodian border was a major source of funding for the Khmer Rouge, and control of logging concessions and illegal logging remains a major source of income for both the Burmese regime in its fight against insurgency and for those insurgency (or liberation) groups as well.[24]

The kinds of illegal transnational environmental trade documented above challenge the extent to which states in the region are able to control transactions across their borders. This is a threat to the condition of *effective* sovereignty that Buzan and Wæver define as central to the existence of a state (Buzan and Wæver 1997: 242). These are not occasional movements of goods: smuggling of timber and wildlife is a daily occurrence with large quantities of contraband being moved by truck, barge and ship. Indeed, border control over these shipments is often non-existent for both land and sea borders. The incursions involve not only the smuggling of commodities. Chainsaw operators or wildlife poachers themselves move across borders (from China into Burma, or from Malaysia into Indonesia) to 'steal' timber or endangered species.

Criminal gangs and the 'chain of custody' syndicates involved in transnational environmental crime in the Asia Pacific also threaten the state through challenging techniques of governance. As with other forms of transnational crime, the patterns of bribery and corruption associated with transnational environmental crime undermine good governance, corrode the institutions of the state and compromise core values such as democratic processes and the rule of law. Local crime groups or (otherwise) legitimate companies that are heavily involved in illegal environmental activity are able to establish effective control over local communities. They constitute an alternative form of authority that 'take[s] advantage of corrupt officials and politicians as well as weak governmental institutions and law enforcement agencies' (Emmers 2002: 6). Violence in support of transnational environmental criminal activity often functions at a local level to intimidate villagers into compliance or, occasionally, to eliminate those who resist environmental exploitation. Where the illegal resource industry is 'protected and sometimes even organized by corrupt elements in the civil service, security forces and legislature' as the International Crisis Group has reported for Indonesia (2001: 1) or Global Witness (2007) for Cambodia, the 'shadow-state' syndrome is well advanced.

### Economic security

In the framework outlined above, the power to tax economic activities, generate revenue and minimize economic externalities is a feature of both state and economic security. Environmental crime and illegal resource activity threaten legitimate companies, impede the development of free markets and can undermine investment. Governments and communities are robbed of revenues, resources and benefits. The Indonesian government estimates that illegal logging results in an annual loss in revenue of about US$3 billion (Anon. 2006). The direct losses from illegal logging and unreported timber processing to East Kalimantan alone are counted at US$100 million a year (Anon. 2004: 1). The National Resilience Institute estimates that all forms of illegal environmental activity in Indonesia resulted in losses to the Indonesian treasury of more than US$8 billion a year in 2003, representing almost 40 per cent of the expected domestic revenue for the year and three times the amount allocated to servicing foreign debt (cited in Guerin 2004). It is not just that revenue is lost to government coffers. As suggested above, often it becomes a source of private gain for ruling elites and creates a shadow economy that competes with and distorts the legitimate economy.

As well as these direct costs to economic security, transnational environmental crime generates indirect, intangible and hidden costs through the loss of future resource revenue, the costs of soil erosion, loss of biodiversity and water services, or the financial impacts of floods that are the side-effects of extensive and so-often illegal deforestation and resource exploitation. The free functioning of the market which, in neo-liberal economic terms at least is also crucial to economic security, is also compromised by illegal environmental activity. For example, the sale of cheap (because illegal) timber from Kalimantan and Sumatra into China, Malaysia and Hong Kong has depressed the value and quantity of official timber exports by as much as one million cubic metres a year according to the Indonesia wood panel industry association APKINDO (see EIA/Telapak 2000: 7). Legitimate and legal timber companies simply cannot compete.

### Human security

The human security consequences of transnational crime are usually expressed in rather generic concerns about the 'welfare of the region's people' (as the ASEAN Declaration on Transnational Crime put it). Individuals and communities are made insecure in a number of ways by illegal resource extraction or the illegal dumping of pollutants and waste – through the direct impact of environmental destruction, through the loss of livelihoods and income associated with resource loss, and through the practices of exploitation and intimidation that often accompany transnational environmental crime. The extensive destruction of forest lands from illegal logging undermines the lives and life-choices of communities that rely on the forests for shelter, for food, for medicines and for cultural and spiritual identity. Indigenous communities are often particularly vulnerable to the kinds of human rights abuses that come with the involvement of outsiders in illegal and legal resource extraction, whether timber or wildlife. Hazardous and toxic wastes, including e-waste, expose local communities and those working in the recycling industry to levels of contaminants which bring high and often long-term health risks. The involvement of criminal groups or the military in illegal resource extraction and transnational environmental crime often goes hand in hand with violence, threats or other forms of coercion that create insecurity not just for individuals but for local communities. Local communities are often induced into complicity in illegal logging at source, either through being forced to relinquish community forestry concessions or work as illegal chainsaw operators, although they rarely share in the economic profits. A cubic metre of illegal merbau at point of import into China is worth US$240, for example, but local loggers receive just US$11 a cubic metre. Illegal logging also depresses wages and working conditions for workers in the legal industry and workers involved in the illegal industry are often in an even worse position because of their weak or non-existent bargaining power.

## Regional responses: securitization and (under)securitization

The adoption of policy initiatives on transnational environmental crime and illegal resource activity has generally been an ad hoc and uneven process, characterized by problems of institutional incapacity and policy lag. Nevertheless, there is a slowly growing network of national policies and nascent regional programmes that focus on both the law enforcement and environmental dimensions of illegal resource activity. For the most part, however, these policies have not been incorporated into regional programmes on transnational crime of the kind referred to above.

National initiatives have included the establishment of enforcement units and the adoption of various kinds of action plans. The Philippines government now has a 'forestry czar' with a mandate to address illegal logging. The Malaysian government has established a logging task force. In February 2005, the Indonesian government established a joint operation, codenamed Hutan Lestari, to crack down on illegal loggers in Papua, Kalimantan and Sumatra (although as this joint operation involves the police, military, prosecution service and investigators from the forestry ministry, all of whom have at some stage been involved in the illegal trade, questions have been raised about its long-term likelihood of success). At the CITES meeting in Bangkok in 2004, then Thai Prime Minister Thaksin Sinawatra called for a crime-fighting initiative in the Asia Pacific region to combat the illegal wildlife trade and to complement the work of the national CITES management authorities. His pledge to create such a unit in Thailand was fulfilled by the Thai Central Investigation Bureau in February 2006. A wildlife crime unit has also been established in Taiwan. Despite these policy initiatives, environmental crime does not attract the same kinds of criminal penalties as other forms of illegal activity involving commodities such as drugs or arms.[25]

Some bilateral agreements have been adopted in an attempt to manage the cross-border aspects of illegal resource and environmental trade. China and Indonesia, for example, signed a Memorandum of Understanding on timber trafficking in 2002 although implementation has been slow. Japan and Indonesia have adopted a similar Memorandum. The need for multilateral and multi-sector responses to problems that have regional reach is also now being given some practical effect in programmes and initiatives designed to deal specifically with the cross-border crime-fighting and law enforcement aspects of problems such as illegal logging and the wildlife trade. The East Asia Forest Law Enforcement and Governance (FLEG) process, part of a global multi-stakeholder initiative, was initiated in Bali in 2001. The Bali Declaration sought immediate action to 'intensify national efforts, and to strengthen bilateral, regional and multilateral collaboration to address violations of forest law and forest crime', in particular 'illegal logging and associated illegal trade and corruption and their negative effects on the rule of law' (FLEG 2001: 1).[26] The ASEAN Regional Action Plan on Trade in Wild Fauna and Flora 2005– 2010, announced after the 13th meeting of CITES in Bangkok in October 2004, set out to develop effective and enforceable legislation to implement the CITES agreement. It calls for the establishment of national inter-agency committees and for better networking among law enforcement authorities in ASEAN. The

Plan also anticipated an ASEAN CITES Enforcement Taskforce (now established as the ASEAN Wildlife Enforcement Network) to exchange information and to coordinate regional participation in Interpol's Wildlife Crime Working Group.[27] ASEAN's Strategic Plan of Action on Forestry for 2005–2010 established two cooperation programmes that address, respectively, the trade in illegal wood products and CITES wildlife issues, although neither programme uses the words 'transnational crime'. In April 2005, UNEP's Regional Office for Asia and the Pacific (UNEP/ROAP) and the Regional Intelligence Liaison Office of the World Customs Union (RILO/AP), currently based in Beijing, signed an agreement to enhance coordination on environmental crime and implement Green Customs initiatives in the Asia Pacific with a particular focus on the black market in ODS and other prohibited chemicals. In August the same year, the multi-stakeholder Asian Environmental Compliance and Enforcement Network (AECEN) was established, as a component of the International Network on Environmental Compliance and Enforcement (INECE), to enhance national compliance capacity.

While the criminal, law enforcement and border management problems of TEC have clearly reached the public policy agenda, environmental crime is almost never mentioned in regional programmes and declarations on security and transnational crime. The 29th ASEAN Ministerial Meeting (AMM) in 1996 did include environmental crimes among a list of crimes to which attention *should* be given. Despite this injunction, the various communiqués, agreements, action plans and work programmes that come from ASEAN's Senior Officials Meeting on Transnational Crime (SOM-TC) and Ministerial Meetings on Transnational Crime (AMM-TC) contain almost no reference to transnational environmental crime. The December 1997 ASEAN Declaration on Transnational Crime does not include environmental crime among those crimes with whose 'pernicious effects' it is concerned. TEC does not feature in the ASEAN Manila Declaration on the Prevention and Control of Transnational Crime (1998). Nor does it seem to have been on the agenda of the ASEAN Chiefs of Police (ASEANAPOL) conferences. The ASEAN Plan of Action to Combat Transnational Crime notes that the region has had to deal with 'many new forms of organised crimes that transcend national borders and political sovereignty' (ASEAN Secretariat 1999) but does not include environmental crimes among them. The Work Programme to Implement ASEAN's Plan of Action to Combat Transnational Crime, adopted by the second annual ASEAN Senior Officials Meeting on Transnational Crime in Kuala Lumpur in May 2002, addresses eight types of crime that fall under the Plan of Action – environmental crime is not among them.[28] The 2002 Declaration on the Conduct of Parties in the South China Sea anticipated cooperation among the parties on transnational crime problems such as trafficking in drugs and arms. There is no specific reference to environmental trafficking. Track II processes such as the Council for Security Cooperation Asia Pacific (CSCAP) have also paid little attention to environmental crime, despite a long-standing concern with 'significant transnational crime trends which affect security in the Asia Pacific region as a whole'.[29]

There are some occasional examples of cross-referencing between environ-mental crime and other forms of transnational crime, or between environmental crime and regional security. Indonesia's money-laundering legislation, for example, explicitly refers to tracking funds from illegal logging (Anon. 2006: 74). The Indonesian government included the illicit trade of illegally logged timber in its contribution to the Annual Security Outlook prepared for the 12th ASEAN Regional Forum meeting in 2005 but was the only country to do so. In its section on conflict prevention, ASEAN's Vientiane Action Programme (VAP) refers to the importance of regional cooperation to combat transnational crime and other transboundary problems, but makes no mention of any particular crimes. The programme does point to the importance for building a strong socio-cultural community of environmental sustainability, protecting species and managing forests. The detailed programme areas of the VAP suggest also that combating illegal logging and tackling illegal traffic of dangerous wastes is central to developing an *economic* community but falls short of making claims about what this might mean for security.

For the most part, then, transnational environmental crime has not been securitized in the way that other forms of transnational crime in the region have. In terms of the securitization literature, there are few 'speech acts', despite the fact that the insecurity consequences are at least as challenging as those that are claimed by elite 'securitizing actors' for other forms of cross-border illegal activity.

### Explaining (under)securitization: some possibilities

If, as John McFarlane points out, 'many countries [in the Asia Pacific] now regard transnational crime ... as a national security issue' (McFarlane 2001: 3), why is transnational environmental crime undersecuritized in the Asia Pacific compared with other transnational crime sectors? Some general thoughts are offered here, in anticipation of further research into this puzzle. Transnational environmental crime is not '[brought] into being as a security situation' (Williams 2003: 513) because no one is *successfully* representing it as such. The first step in this process of representation requires that the relevant (securitizing) actors believe that a problem requires urgent attention or that it constitutes an existential threat to some recognized security referent. Despite official commitment to comprehensive security and despite the securitization of other forms of transnational crime, security actors in the Asia Pacific are generally wary of incorporating non-traditional considerations such as environmental ones into the security agenda. To the extent that it is recognized as a form of *transnational* criminal activity at all, it is likely that environmental crime is not perceived to be of the same gravity as other forms of transnational crime. While these are serious forms of transnational crime, they are rarely taken seriously by relevant security actors.

One reason is that these are new and poorly understood policy challenges compared with other forms of transnational crime. Indeed, McFarlane points out that the whole issue of transnational crime was 'considered marginal to the regional security agenda' (McFarlane 2005: 301) until the mid-1990s, so perhaps it is not surprising that environmental crime remains undersecuritized. There is also confusion among security actors about the referent object of TEC compared with other forms of transnational crime such as arms smuggling, drug trafficking or people trafficking where the security impact on individuals, communities and the state appears more straightforward. This intellectual inertia and confusion is compounded further by problems of institutional capacity. Agencies involved in law enforcement, border control and intelligence have been hard pressed to deal with other aspects of transnational crime, let alone add one more issue area to their responsibilities. Perceiving these problems primarily in environmental rather than security terms also tends, as Lin points out, 'to reduce its importance on national policy-making agendas … resulting in fewer resources and less attention being committed to it' (Lin 2005: 192).

Securitization is also 'structured by the differential capacity of actors to make socially effective claims about threats' (Williams 2003: 514). This capacity relies, in turn, on the ability to mobilize expert knowledge into the security sector and, as van Munster argues, 'on the social position and authority of the securitizing actor' (van Munster 2005: 3). Successful securitization requires that the claims of existential threat are accepted by the relevant audience. Elite perceptions dominate the Asia Pacific security landscape. The regional experience of discursive securitization confirms that 'something is [constructed as] a security problem when *elites* [the securitizing actors] declare it to be so' (Wæver 1995: 55; emphasis added). In line with Hansen's prediction for non-democratic systems, the relevant audience is also unlikely to be 'the entire population … [but] much smaller, restricted to the power elite' (Hansen 2000: 289). Three relevant points arise from this issue of elite dominance. First, those who might seek to 'speak' the security of TEC and to identify threats that arise from it (existential or otherwise) are not part of this particular security elite in the Asia Pacific. Those who are most knowledgeable about these challenges are found in resource and environmental ministries, in non-governmental organizations, in regional organizations and, to some lesser extent, in those agencies responsible for customs and border control. Despite their expert knowledge in the environmental sector, they are either not taken seriously or authoritatively within the community of security actors or there is simply insufficient interaction between the two communities of policy actors. The intellectual wariness works both ways: those who pursue improved public policy responses to transnational environmental crime may well be reluctant to use the language of security which is associated with the intrusion of security agencies into society. Second, securitization 'presupposes the existence of a situation in which speech is indeed possible' (Hansen 2000: 285). Those who are most affected by the insecurities of environmental crime – the poor in both rural and urban areas, women, and indigenous peoples – are those who are least in a position to 'speak' the security impact of environmental crime, either because they are marginalized from political decision making and from security elites or because they are physically intimidated and prevented from expressing their concerns. Third, there is also the possibility of active elite resistance or attempts to keep the issue off the policy agenda, including the security agenda. Securitizing environmental crime could 'inject urgency into [the] issue and lead to a mobilisation of political support and a better deployment of resources' (Emmers 2002: 6). The extent of ruling elite, business and military involvement in illegal resource and environmental trade (and its adjacent activities such as money laundering), suggests that there might be little incentive among those who could influence the securitization of TEC to do so.[30]

This confusion and resistance is not helped by what could be characterized as policy incoherence at the international level. As well as the relevant Conventions explored above (CITES, Basel, Rotterdam and Stockholm) there is a range of international, multilateral and multi-stakeholder (public–private) initiatives on illegal environmental trade and resource activity.[31] Compared with international law in other areas of transnational crime such as drug smuggling or people trafficking, most fall outside a law enforcement framework.[32] Rather, they rely on procurement, certification, import/export controls and monitoring. Other processes send mixed messages on how seriously the international community takes transnational environmental crime. CITES, for example, does not impose criminal sanctions but relies on states parties to do so. The preamble to the UN Convention against Transnational Organized Crime suggests that the Convention should constitute an effective tool against criminal activities such as illicit trafficking in endangered species of wild flora and fauna. However, transnational environmental crimes fall outside the serious crimes framework defined in the Convention. National legislation rarely imposes the penalties of four or more years imprisonment for activity such as timber smuggling or wildlife smuggling that are required to count as a 'serious crime' under the Convention. Even then, few countries in the region are parties to the Convention although a number have signed but not yet ratified.[33]

## Some concluding notes

The discussion in this article was initiated by a particular puzzle about the apparent non-securitization or, at very least, undersecuritization of transnational environmental crime in the Asia Pacific. The puzzle arises because other forms of transnational crime which generate similar patterns of insecurity have been taken up by security elites and represented as matters of concern for states in the region. The possible explanations for this situation explored in the third section of the paper focus on understanding one step only of the securitization process, the discursive step in which relevant actors represent or construct a particular problem in security terms. This phase of what is a much larger project generates at least three consequent research purposes. The first derives from some of the limitations of securitization theory itself – it focuses primarily on theorizing successful securitization and deducing, from this, the necessary conditions for such outcomes. Non-successful securitization is assumed, therefore, to arise because these conditions are lacking. That, in effect, is the interpretive approach applied here to TEC. The next step is to conduct a more detailed empirical study of security elite perceptions of transnational environmental crime in the Asia Pacific to verify, adjust or reject such hypotheses.

The second research theme focuses on regional policy responses to the challenges of transnational environmental crime, irrespective of whether or not these have been securitized. Theoretical propositions about discursive securitization – the speech act – are basically agnostic on the *effectiveness* of actual policy responses. Given the serious nature of the problems, more research needs to be done to conceptualize, map and assess regional governance on transnational environmental crime. The third research purpose links these theoretical and policy considerations. While the focus here is on showing how TEC generates security concerns and pondering why, therefore, such activities have not been securitized, further work is required on whether securitization of TEC on such terms is to be recommended. Critics of securitization as a process (rather than of the theory itself) have noted that it anticipates a suspension of democratic practices and a privileging of particular forms of expert knowledge that runs counter to policy making that is open, measured and allows space for debate and contestation (see, for example, Aradau 2004; Williams 2003). Despite the 'tactical attractions' of securitizing an issue (Buzan *et al.* 1998: 29), the move from normal politics to security politics runs the risk of narrowing the policy focus to one of defence against threat rather than one which seeks to address the causes of insecurities. Such a narrowing may well be counter-productive in responding to the challenges of transnational environmental crime in the Asia Pacific.

## Acknowledgements

An earlier version of this paper was delivered to a workshop on Re-envisioning Asia-Pacific Security at the Australian National University in August 2006. This article was completed during a Visiting Professorship at the Institute for Environmental Studies at the Free University of Amsterdam, and a Visiting Fellowship at the Research Institute for Law, Politics and Justice at Keele University. Thanks are due to both institutions for their support, and the Department of International Relations at the Australian National University for supporting the author's sabbatical leave. Thanks are also due to Katherine Morton, Ralf Emmers, Graeme Cheeseman, John McFarlane, Andreas Schloenhardt and the journal's anonymous referees for their comments and helpful suggestions.

## Notes

1   See, for example, Dupont (1998, 2001), Elliott (2002a, b, 2007a) and Barnett (2001).
2   See Haque (2001) and Elliott (2007b).
3   For more, see Emmers (2002, 2003), McFarlane (2005) and Hernandez and Pattugalan (1999a).
4   The exception is illegal, unregulated and unreported (IUU) fishing and poaching which is usually raised in the context of maritime cooperation.
5   An important caveat applies to this investigation. The discussion here makes no particular claims about whether TEC *should* be securitized. Nevertheless, there is an interesting debate to be had about whether the logic of exceptionalism that accompanies the emergency measures associated with full securitization is appropriate for dealing with transnational environmental crime.
6   Some endangered timber species are listed under CITES appendices.
7   Other approaches to TEC rely on a consequentialist definition. Duncan Brack (2002: 143) suggests that environmental crime is international or transnational when the deliberate

flouting, by individuals and companies, of environmental laws and regulations for power and profit has transboundary or global *impacts*. A third body of literature defines eco-crimes not in terms of law enforcement but in terms of harm and particularly harm to the environment (in effect, crimes against the environment); see, for example, Walters (2006) and Halsey (2004).

8   Although it is not covered here, other more localized forms of cross-border environmental crime would include problems such as sand smuggling between Indonesia and Singapore, which allegedly involves organized crime syndicates; see Anon. (2002c).

9   See, for example, Cook *et al.* (2002), Zimmerman (2003), Warchol (2004) and G8 Environment Ministers (1999). TRAFFIC International, on the other hand, has suggested that organized criminal activity within the illegal wildlife trade is relatively rare (Anon. 2002a).

10  For example, smuggled turtles and marijuana have been found in the same illegal shipments (*BBC News* 1998). Live snakes have been found stuffed with condoms full of cocaine (Anon. 2002b). For other examples see also van Note (2002), Zimmerman (2003), Cook *et al.* (2002) and Hayman and Brack (2002).

11  A kilo of rhino horn can trade for as much as US$30,000 on the Asian market; see Warchol (2004: 59).

12  The Environmental Investigation Agency has identified China as the largest consumer of stolen timber in the world; see Newman and Lawson (2005).

13  There have been some suggestions that Indonesian Navy seizures of illegal timber ships have as much to do with underpaid bribes, or trumping bribes to disrupt competing operations, as they do with genuine interdiction (Newman and Lawson 2005: 8).

14  Bribery and corruption sometimes go to the highest levels. Ferdinand Marcos is reported to have accepted payoffs of more than US$1 billion from Japanese timber companies when he was president of the Philippines (see van Note 2002).

15  An Indonesian forestry ministry official has referred to the powerful businessmen involved in the timber smuggling industry as 'slippery as eels in a pond of lubricating oil' (cited in Guerin 2004).

16  Undercover operations conducted by the London-based Environmental Investigation Agency and Jakarta-based Telapak have caught smugglers and brokers on tape making such claims on more than one occasion.

17  Otherwise legitimate timber companies – such as Asia Pulp and Paper – are also reported to be involved in illegal harvesting; see Yoon (2004) or any of the reports produced by EIA/Telapak or by GlobalWitness.

18  While some of the bear populations in Asia – the Sun Bear, the Sloth Bear, the Asiatic Black Bear and the Brown Bear (as well as the Giant Panda which is not relevant for TAM) – are banned from international trade under CITES, hunting them or farming live bears in not always illegal in East Asia.

19  Following rumours that the material was radioactive, 10,000 people sought to flee the region and eight were killed in a subsequent riot.

20  The shipment involved 122 containers. The cost of repatriation for the Japanese government was estimated at over 100 million yen (the company president had reportedly gone missing); see Anon. (2000).

21  For an explanation and examples of the 'shadow state', see Le Billon (2000), Nest (2002), Reno (2000) and Global Witness (2007).

22  In practice some issues such as drug smuggling, arms smuggling and terrorism attract more policy attention than adjacent issues such as corruption which go to the heart of domestic governance.

23  The Indonesian government has cited illegal fishing (and the economic losses associated with this) as a major reason for seeking to strengthen its naval capabilities. Illegal fishing is a continuing source of tension between Thailand and its neighbours, particularly Malaysia, involving naval and border patrol activity on both sides. Shots have, on occasion, been fired.

24  The evidence is mixed on what happens when conflict is contained by ceasefire agreements. There is some evidence that illegal logging and smuggling actually increases in Burma because both sides are more easily able to access forest lands for illegal harvesting (see Talbott and Brown 1998: 54). On the other hand, Global Witness (2006) has reported a near standstill in logging in regime controlled areas and those controlled by Kachin state ceasefire groups in northern Burma.

25  An attempt by the government of President Megawati Sukarnoputri to bring illegal logging into the serious crimes category failed because making it a capital offence, punishable by death, was thought a step too far by parliamentarians and NGOs alike.

26  The FLEG East Asia process involves a Task Force and an Advisory Group and periodic meetings with the support of international partners such as ASEAN and APEC. Not all

countries in the region are part of the FLEG process: Malaysia, Singapore and Thailand are notable non-participants.

27　This is helped by the fact that all ten ASEAN countries are parties to CITES.

28　The eight areas of transnational crime are: drug trafficking, trafficking in persons, sea piracy, arms smuggling, money laundering, terrorism, international economic crime, and cyber-crime.

29　The report of the 2nd meeting of what was then a CSCAP Study Group identified a number of areas of transnational crime but environmental crime was not among them.

30　Buzan *et al.* refer to these as the 'functional actors' in the securitization process – those who can affect the dynamics of a sector without being its agents or referents (Buzan *et al.* 1998: 36).

31　Examples include the Forest Law Enforcement and Governance (FLEG) initiative, the Voluntary Partnership Agreements established by the European Union, the OzonAction Network, the Coalition Against Wildlife Trafficking (CAWT), and the Global Forest & Trade Network, to name just a few.

32　In 1994, Interpol established an environmental crimes committee with two working groups, one on wildlife crimes and one on pollution crimes, and developed the 'ecomessage' reporting system to generate a database on international environmental crime.

33　China, Malaysia, the Philippines, Lao PDR, Cambodia and Burma are parties to the Convention; Japan, South Korea, Indonesia, Vietnam, Singapore and Thailand have not yet ratified the Convention. North Korea, Mongolia and Brunei have not signed.

# References

Andreas, Peter (2002) 'Transnational crime and economic globalization', in Mats Berdal and Mónica Serrano (eds) *Transnational Organized Crime and International Security*, Boulder: Lynne Rienner, pp. 37–52.

Anon. (2000) 'Govt begins unloading batch of waste returned from R.P', *Yomiuri Shimbun*, 21 January 2000; accessed at http://ban.org/ban news/japan2.html, 18 October 2007.

—— (2002a) 'Eco-crooks outwitting law agencies', April; accessed at http://www. envirocrime. com/forum/ disc5/00000017.htm, 7 February 2007.

—— (2002b) 'Organised criminal gangs deal wildlife and drugs', *Environment News Service*, 19 June.

—— (2002c) 'Navy foils sand smuggling to Singapore', *The Jakarta Post*, 29 July.

—— (2004) 'East Kalimantan loses US$100 million annually in timber revenue', *CIFOR News* No. 35, p. 1.

—— (2006) 'Down in the woods', *The Economist*, 25 March, p. 74.

Anstill, James (2002) 'Tusks of 600 elephants make up record haul of smuggled ivory', *Guardian*, 13 July, p. 20.

Aradau, Claudia (2004) 'Security and the democratic scene: desecuritization and emancipation', *Journal of International Relations and Development* 7(4): 388–413.

ASEAN Regional Forum (2001) Chairman's Statement: Eighth Meeting of the ASEAN Regional Forum, Hanoi, 25 July.

ASEAN Secretariat (1997) ASEAN Declaration on Transnational Crime, Manila, 20 December.

—— (1999) *ASEAN Plan of Action to Combat Transnational Crime*, Jakarta: ASEAN Secretariat.

Barnett, Jon (2001) *The Meaning of Environmental Security*, London: Zed Books.

BBC News (1998) 'Environmental crime – a global problem', 5 April; accessed at http://news.bbc. co.uk/2/hi/in_depth/74317.stm, 7 February 2007.

Brack, Duncan (2002) 'Combating international environmental crime', *Global Environmental Change* 12(2): 143–7.

Buzan, Barry and Wæver, Ole (1997) 'Slippery? Contradictory? Sociologically untenable? The Copenhagen School replies', *Review of International Studies* 23(2): 241–50.

Buzan, Barry, Wæver, Ole and de Wilde, Jaap (1998) *Security: A New Framework for Analysis*, Boulder: Lynne Rienner.

Castle, Allan (1997) *Transnational Organized Crime and International Security*, Working Paper No. 19, Vancouver: Institute of International Relations, University of British Columbia.

Charma, Charu (2003–04) 'Enforcement mechanisms for endangered species protection in Hong Kong: a legal perspective', *Vermont Journal of Environmental Law* 5: 1–34.

Cook, Dee, Roberts, Martin and Lowther, Jason (2002) *The International Wildlife Trade and Organized Crime: A Review of the Evidence and the Role of the UK*, Godalming: WWF-UK.

Duffy, Rosaleen (2005) 'Global environmental governance and the challenge of shadow states: the impact of illicit sapphire mining in Madagascar', *Development and Change* 36(5): 825–43.

Duncan, Brack (2005) 'Controlling illegal logging and the trade in illegally harvested timber: the EU's Forest Law Enforcement Governance and Trade Initiative', *RECIEL* 14(1): 28–38.

Dupont, Alan (1998) *The Environment and Security in Pacific Asia*, Oxford: Oxford University Press.

—— (2001) *East Asia Imperilled: Transnational Challenges to Security*, Cambridge: Cambridge University Press.

EIA (2001) *Thailand's Tiger Economy*, London: EIA.

EIA/Telapak (2000) *Illegal Logging in Tanjung Puting National Park: An Update on the Final Cut Report*, London and Jakarta: EIA/Telapak.

EIA/Telapak (2002) *Above the Law: Corruption, Collusion, Nepotism and the Fate of Indonesia's Forests*, London and Jakarta: EIA/Telapak.

EIA/Telapak (2003) *Singapore's Illegal Timber Trade and the US–Singapore Free Trade Agreement*, London and Jakarta: EIA/Telapak.

Elliott, Lorraine (2002a) 'Environmental security in East Asia; defining a common security agenda', in Paul G. Harris (ed.) *International Environmental Cooperation: Diplomacy and Politics in East Asia*, Boulder: University Press of Colorado, pp. 31–52.

—— (2002b) 'Secur(itiz)ing the environment: unravelling environmental security in Pacific Asia', in Bruce Vaughn (ed.) *The Unraveling of Island Asia: Governmental, Communal and Regional Instability*, Westport, CT: Praeger, 191–206.

—— (2007a) 'Globalization and political violence: the environmental connection', in Christopher Hughes and Richard Devetak (eds) *The Globalization of Political Violence*, London: Routledge.

—— (2007b) 'Harm and emancipation: making environmental security "critical" in the Asia Pacific', in Anthony Burke and Matt McDonald (eds) *Critical Security in the Asia Pacific*, Manchester: Manchester University Press.

Emmers, Ralf (2002) *The Securitization of Transnational Crime in ASEAN*, IDSS Working Paper No. 39, Singapore: Institute for Defence and Strategic Studies.

—— (2003) 'ASEAN and the securitization of transnational crime in Southeast Asia', *The Pacific Review*, 16(3): 419–38.

Environmental Investigation Agency (2000) Actions needed at the 12th Meeting of the Parties of the Montreal Protocol to combat illegal trade in ODS; accessed at http://www.eia-international.org/cgi/reports/reports.cgi?t=template&a=30, 7 February 2007.

Forest Law Enforcement and Governance [FLEG] (2001) Ministerial Declaration of the East Asia Ministerial Conference, Bali, 11–13 September; accessed at http://abc.net.au/4corners/content/2002/timber mafia/resources/balideclaration.pdf, 7 February 2007.

G8 Environment Ministers (1999) Communiqué of the meeting in Schwerin, Germany, March 1999; accessed at http://www.g7.utoronto.ca/environment/1999schwerin/communique.html, 7 February 2007.

Ganesan, N. (2001) 'Illegal fishing and illegal migration in Thailand's bilateral relations with Malaysia and Myanmar', in Andrew T. H. Tan and J. D. Ken Boutin (eds) *Non-traditional Security Issues in Southeast Asia*, Singapore: Institute of Defence and Strategic Studies/Select Books, pp. 507–27.

Global Witness (2006) 'China border logjam: the beginning or the end of action against illegal timber exports in Northern Burma?, Press Release, 23 January; accessed at www.globalwitness.org/press releases/display2.php?id=327, 7 February 2007.

—— (2007) *Cambodia's Family Trees: Illegal Logging and the Stripping of Public Assets by Cambodia's Elite*, Washington, DC: GlobalWitness.

Godson, Roy and Williams, Phil (1998) 'Strengthening cooperation against transnational crime', *Survival* 40(3): 66–88.

Guerin, Bill (2004) 'Illegal loggers: shoot them', The Asian Times, 7 July; accessed at http://www.atimes.com/atimes/Southeast Asia/FG07Ae03.html, 7 February 2007.

Guymon, Carrielyn Donigan (2000) 'International legal mechanisms for combating transnational crime: the need for a multilateral convention', *Berkeley Journal of International Law* 18(1): 53–101.

Halsey, Mark (2004) 'Against "green" criminology', *British Journal of Criminology* 4(6): 833–53.

Hansen, Lene (2000) 'The little mermaid's silent security dilemma and the absence of gender in the Copenhagen School', *Millennium: Journal of International Studies* 29(2): 285–306.

Haque, M. Shamsul (2001) 'Environmental security in East Asia: a critical view', *Journal of Strategic Studies* 24(4): 203–34.

Hayman, Gavin and Brack, Duncan (2002) *International Environmental Crime: The Nature and Control of Environmental Black Markets*, London: Royal Institute of International Affairs.

Hernandez, Carolina G. and Pattugalan, Gina R. (eds) (1999a) *Transnational Crime and Regional Security in the Asia Pacific*, Quezon City, Manila: Institute for Strategic and Developmental Studies.

—— (1999b) 'Foreword', in Carolina G. Hernandez and Gina R. Pattugalan (eds) *Transnational Crime and Regional Security in the Asia Pacific*, Quezon City, Manila: Institute for Strategic and Developmental Studies.

International Centre for Trade and Sustainable Development (2004) *BRIDGES: Trade Bio Res* (Special Issue), 20 November.

International Crisis Group (2001) *Indonesia: Natural Resources and Law Enforcement*, Asia Report No. 29, Jakarta and Brussels: ICG.

Lauterback, Andrew (2005) Statement of the Chairman, Interpol Environmental Crimes Committee, 5th International Conference on Environmental Crime, Lyon, 2–3 June; accessed at http://www.interpol.int/Public/EnvironmentalCrime/Meetings/LyonJune2005/Default.asp, 7 February 2007.

Le Billon, Philippe (2000) 'The political ecology of transition in Cambodia 1989–1999: war, peace and forest exploitation', *Development and Change* 31(4): 785–805.

Li Yi-ming, Gao Zenxiang *et al.* (2000) 'Illegal wildlife trade in the Himalayan region of China', *Biodiversity and Conservation* 9(7): 901–18.

Lin, Joeline (2005) 'Tackling Southeast Asia's illegal wildlife trade', *Singapore Yearbook of International Law* 9: 191–208.

McFarlane, John (2001) 'Transnational crime: response strategies', paper presented at the 4th National Outlook Symposium on Crime in Australia – New Crimes or New Responses, Australian Institute of Criminology, Canberra, 21–22 June.

—— (2005) 'Regional and international cooperation in tackling transnational crime, terrorism and the problem of disrupted states', *Journal of Financial Crime* 12(4): 301–9.

Nest, Michael (2002) *The Evolution of a Fragmented State: The Case of the Democratic Republic of Congo*, Working Paper No. 11, New York: International Center for Advanced Studies, New York University.

Newman, Julian and Lawson, Sam (2005) *The Last Frontier*, London and Jakarta: EIA/Telapak.

Reno, William (2000) 'Shadow states and the political economy of civil wars', in Mats Berdal and David M. Malone (eds) *Greed and Grievance: Economic Agendas in Civil Wars*, Boulder: Lynne Rienner, pp. 43–68.

Schmidt, Charles W. (2004) 'Environmental crimes: profiting at the Earth's expense', *Environmental Health Perspectives* 112(2): A96–A103.

Siem Bok (1999) 'The fight against illegal loggers', *The Economist*, April, p. 24.

Talbott, Kirk and Brown, Melissa (1998) 'Forest plunder in Southeast Asia: an environmental security nexus in Burma and Cambodia', *Environmental Change and Security Project Report* No. 4 (Spring): 53–60.

Thomson, Julie (2002) 'Tiger protection gets a boost in Central Indochina', *TRAFFIC Dispatches* No. 19 (March): 11.

UNEP (2001) 'Illegal trade in ozone depleting substances: is there a hole in the Montreal Protocol?', in *OzonAction Newsletter* (Special Supplement), No. 6, Paris: UNEP Division of Technology, Industry and Economics.

United Nations General Assembly (2000) Convention against Transnational Organised Crime, A/RES/55/25.

Van der Meer, Y. A. (1992) 'Combating environmental crime in an international context', in *Proceedings of the Second International Conference on Environmental Enforcement*, Vol. 2, Washington, DC: International Network on Environmental Compliance and Enforcement.

Van Munster, Rens (2005) *Logics of Security: The Copenhagen School, Risk Management and the War on Terror*, Working Paper 10/2005, Odense: University of Southern Denmark Political Science Publications.

Van Note, Craig (2002) 'Global crime, corruption and accountability', presentation to the Lecture Series on World Sustainablility, Ramopo College; accessed at http://www.geocities.com/profwork/ws/van note.html, 7 February 2007.

Wæver, Ole (1995) 'Securitization and desecuritization', in Ronnie D. Lipschutz (ed.) *On Security*, New York: Columbia University Press, pp. 46–86.

Walters, Reece (2006) 'Crime, bio-agriculture and the exploitation of hunger', *British Journal of Criminology* 46(1): 26–45.

Warchol, Greg L. (2004) 'The transnational illegal wildlife trade', *Criminal Justice Studies* 17(1): 57–73.

Williams, Michael C. (2003) 'Words, images, enemies: securitization and international politics', *International Studies Quarterly* 47(4): 511–31.

World Bank (2006) *Strengthening Forest Law Enforcement and Governance: Addressing a Systemic Constraint to Sustainable Development*, Report No. 36638-LB, Washington, DC: World Bank.

World Rainforest Movement (2005) WRM Bulletin No. 98 (September).

Yoon Szu-Mai (2004) 'Storm over Asian-Pacific timber trade', CorpWatch, 5 March 2004; reproduced at Global Policy Forum, www.globalpolicy.org/socecon/envronmt/2004/0305asiatimber.htm, 7 February 2007.

Zimmerman, Mara E. (2003) 'The black market for wildlife: combating transnational organized crime in the illegal wildlife trade', *Vanderbilt Journal of Transnational Law* 36(5): 1657–89.

# 27. Police, law enforcement and the environment*

*Kevin Tomkins*

## Introduction

Enforcing environmental laws and regulations is an important ingredient in protecting the environment and reducing environmental harm. This is generally achieved by various environmental law enforcement agencies operating from a global to local level. For instance, some environmental law enforcement agencies operate only at an international level whereas others only operate at the local level. Furthermore, environmental law enforcement agencies utilise various enforcement methods to ensure compliance to environmental legislation. In some cases enforcement agencies rely on coercive powers to demand compliance to environmental laws, generally labelled 'command and control' strategies; others rely on conciliatory and educational strategies to persuade individuals, organisations and governments to comply with environmental laws and regulations.

The aim of this paper is to identify police services operating in environmental law enforcement from the global through to the local level. The role that police services play in the enforcement of environmental laws and regulations requires analysis and understanding if better enforcement policies are to be developed. However, before such analysis is possible there is a need to identify 'who does what' in the field of environmental law enforcement at an institutional level. Identifying the different levels of environmental law enforcement involves considering all police institutions from the international to the local level. The identification of environmental law enforcement institutions is also important in that many of the law enforcement institutions are increasingly cooperating at the international, regional, national, state and local levels.

Before discussing the police institutions involved in environmental law enforcement, certain terms need to be defined. Policing is generally about space and territory (see Herbert 1997). In other words, police services have a prescribed geographic territory, which they defend from activities prohibited by law, defined as crimes. In this instance, environmental crime is an 'unauthorised act or omission that violates the law and is therefore subject to criminal prosecution and criminal sanctions' (Situ and Emmons 2000: 3).

* From *Current Issues in Criminal Justice* (2005), 16(3): pp. 294–306.

For the purposes of this paper international policing institutions are those that operate across the globe at an international level, while regional police services have a number of police services from separate sovereign countries operating within a geographic area of the globe. National police services operate within the territorial boundaries of a sovereign country and state or provincial police services operate in delineated territorial boundaries of a nation. Local police services operate within a delineated geographic area, city or a state.

## Police differences and similarities

Implementation of environmental legislation has involved considerable cooperation between diverse policing institutions through international multilateral agreements, regional political or legal blocks, and national, state or local laws (see Birnie and Boyle 2002). For example, similar environmental laws and their methods of enforcement have, to some extent, been incorporated into the domestic laws of many member states of the European Community (EC) and indeed some member states allow the EC to legislate in a qualified manner on environmental matters (Birnie and Boyle 2002: 9). Consideration of regional political systems such as the EC requires understanding of how environmental laws are enforced by police services across diverse policing jurisdictions.

Police services, typically, are the legitimatised state apparatus that have the power to enforce the laws of the land, by coercive methods if necessary (see Reiner 1985: 2; Freckelton 1988). Traditionally, police services were seen as a 'crime fighting' or a 'crime prevention' force (Waddington 1999). However, modern police services now provide a variety of services to the community beyond these traditional concerns (White and Perrone 1997: 10–32).

Modern police organisations perform many different functions that cover a myriad of administrative, regulatory, social welfare and law enforcement roles in civil society. For example, police in many jurisdictions are responsible for the licensing of firearms, provision of motor vehicle licenses and registration, providing social services and, importantly, enforcing environmental laws. The increased participation of the police in civil society has become the subject of considerable investigation and research (see for instance, Waddington 1999: Finnane 1994; Bolen 1997; Bryett and Harrison 1994). Indeed, there has been a significant amount of research into policing practices, procedures, tactics and the roles that police now play in society.

Policing and social control systems across many jurisdictions have thus attracted considerable research attention (see for example, Morgan and Smith 1989; Waddington 1999; Uglow 1988, McCulloch 2001). However, many of these studies are country specific and, in many cases, focus on a particular police service, tending not to engage in cross-national comparisons. One of the reasons that these studies have not compared policing systems in different countries has been the concern that the differences in cultural and societal structures of the police services being studied are too wide to develop an understanding of policing at a comparative international level (Bayley 1999:

3). The general objection to comparative international studies of policing is that the differences '... are perceived to be so great as to bear no relation to one's own national or local [policing] experience' (Bayley 1999: 3).

Debate over the study of policing at an international level has also been linked to debate about whether the countries that are being compared are similar in legal, cultural and political terms. The issue is one of cultural dimensions – that is, the political and social context of the policing services being compared must be similar in socio-political perspectives and in spatial and temporal dimensions to be of any value to social science (Bayley 1999). However, as will be affirmed here, comparisons between police services from different countries are possible and indeed necessary '... for the scientific insight that policy-making requires' (Bayley 1999:11). Appreciation of differences is as important as acknowledgement of similarities when it comes to the development of insight into what works best in particular social settings.

The law enforcement organisations involved in enforcing environmental laws are varied and have many different operational principles dealing with and responding to environmental crimes. Specifically, law enforcement agencies can be divided into two main categories. The first is general law enforcement agencies or police services, and the second is specific environmental law enforcement agencies. General law enforcement agencies can be described as traditional law enforcers who mainly deal with conventional crimes such as street crime. Environmental law enforcement agencies are more specialised enforcers dealing mainly with environmental crimes.

## International environmental law enforcement organisations

Recent years have seen a proliferation of international, regional and national law enforcement organisations working together at an international level. One of the main international law enforcement institutions is the International Criminal Police Organization (Interpol), which in its present form was created in 1956. It is the largest international police organisation in the world with 181 member countries spread over five continents. Every member country has a local Interpol office called a National Central Bureau, which is staffed by police officers from the member country and which works to coordinate Interpol goals within their borders.

The mission of Interpol is 'To be the world's pre-eminent police organisation in support of all organisations, authorities and services whose mission is preventing, detecting, and suppressing crime' (International Criminal Police Organization 2004). Interpol advocates that this is achieved by:

- Providing both a global perspective and a regional focus;
- Exchanging information that is timely, accurate, relevant and complete;
- Facilitating international co-operation;
- Co-ordinating joint operational activities of its member countries;
- Making available know-how, expertise and good practice (International Criminal Police Organization 2004).

Interpol supplies national law enforcement services with information on international crimes committed in other member countries and has developed databases on persons, organisations and businesses of interest that may be involved in international criminal activities. However, environmental crime is a relatively new challenge for law enforcement agencies worldwide and although administrative/civil actions are often an effective response to environmental violations, criminal enforcement is also now seen as an essential factor in preventing and deterring environmental crime. Interpol has been actively involved in this area since 1993 when the first meeting on environmental crime was organised upon the request of some member countries. In particular, the two key areas of environmental law enforcement that Interpol are involved in are the illegal shipment of hazardous waste and the illegal trade in endangered species (Klein 1994).

Interpol also works in cooperation with the United Nations Environmental Program (UNEP). This cooperation includes the UNEP providing resources for implementation and compliance efforts, facilitating communication and data exchange through liaison with Secretariats to the Multilateral Environmental Agreements (MEA) and the World Customs Organization.

Some of the MEAs that require enforcement include, for example:

- Those covering biodiversity and wildlife, including the 1946 International Convention for the Regulation of Whaling; the 1971 Ramsar Convention on Wetlands of International Importance; the 1973 Convention on International Trade in Endangered Species (CITES); the 1979 Bonn Convention on the Conservation of Migratory Species; the 1992 UN Convention on Biological Diversity and its protocol, the 2000 Cartagena Protocol on biosafety; and the 1994 International Tropical Timber Agreement.

- Those designed to protect the atmosphere, including the 1979 UN Economic Commission for Europe (UNECE) Convention on Long-Range Trans-boundary Air Pollution (together with five protocols on particular pollutants: nitrogen oxides, volatile organic compounds, sulphur, heavy metals and persistent organic pollutants); the 1985 Vienna Convention for the Protection of the Ozone Layer, and its protocol, the 1987 Montreal Protocol on Substances that Deplete the Ozone Layer; and the 1992 UN Framework Convention on Climate Change, and its protocol.

- Those dealing with the marine environment, including the 1972 London Convention on the Prevention of Marine Pollution by Dumping of Wastes and other Matter; the 1973 Convention for the Prevention of Pollution from Ships, and its protocol, the 1978 Marpol Protocol; and the 1982 UN Convention on the Law of the Sea, together with an implementing agreement.

- Those regulating the use of chemicals, including the 1998 Rotterdam Convention on the Prior Informed Consent Procedure for Certain Hazardous Chemicals and Pesticides in International Trade.

- Those dealing with waste, including the 1989 Basel Convention on the Control of Trans-boundary Movements of Hazardous Wastes and their Disposal.

- Others, including the 1991 Espoo Convention on Environmental Impact Assessment; the 1992 UN Convention to Combat Desertification; and the 1998 Aarhus Convention on Access to Information, Public Participation in Decision-making and Access to Justice in Environmental Matters (for full discussion on international environmental agreements see, Birnie and Boyle 2002).

Multilateral Environmental Agreements are based on Principle 12 of the Rio Declaration 1992, which suggests that international environmental agreements are clearly preferable to unilateral action in tackling trans-boundary or global environmental problems. Well over 200 MEAs now exist, with memberships varying from relatively small groups to over 180 member countries.

*Case example*

In Nigeria, it became known that since August 1987 huge consignments of toxic waste had been imported from Italy and illegally dumped in a small port called 'Koko Town' on the outskirts of Warri delta region of the country. It was suspected that an Italian national, working for a construction company in Nigeria, was the main offender. Through a Nigerian accomplice the Italian managed to obtain a permit to import chemicals and other substances into the country. Interpol investigations revealed extensive irregularities in clearing the toxic waste consignments from Italy. Shipping documents described the toxic waste as items listed in a pharmaceutical permit allowing importation. Investigations at the dumping site revealed that the waste was highly toxic, radioactive and harmful to humans and the environment. Some of the drums containing the harmful waste were damaged due to inappropriate handling, storage and corrosion. Consequently, the hazardous waste contaminated the soil, the ground water supplies and a river in Koko (Klem 1994: 337).

International agencies and experts were mobilized to clean up the toxic spills. 4000 tons of hazardous and radioactive waste were eventually taken back to Italy and the Italian government took over the responsibility for cleaning up and decontaminating the dumping site in Nigeria.

## Regional law enforcement organisations

### Europe

There has been considerable cooperation between national law enforcement organisations in Europe. This has resulted in a regional law enforcement organisation being created. The European Law Enforcement Organisation (Europol) aims at improving the effectiveness and cooperation of the competent authorities in the member states in preventing and combating terrorism, unlawful drug trafficking, and other serious forms of organised crime. On 12 November 2001, the European Parliament approved an initiative for a framework extending Europol's mandate to include environmental crime. The objective of this was to enhance the effectiveness of co-operation within the scope of the Europol Convention by giving Europol the means to carry out its tasks in relation to all aspects of international organized crime, particularly environmental crime.

In further developments in Europe, the Baltic Sea Region Task Force falls under the umbrella of the Helsinki Convention, which entered into force on 17 January 2002. The contracting parties to the convention include Denmark, Estonia, European Commission, Finland, Germany, Latvia, Lithuania, Poland, Russian and Sweden. The objectives of the task force are to facilitate trans-national understanding of the incidence of environmental crime in the member states and develop cooperative enforcement structures to combat organised environmental criminals (Secretariat of the Task Force on Organised Crime in the Baltic Sea Region 2002: 4).

On 1 May 2002, the European Commission supported Article 40 of the 1990 Schengen Convention, which will enable cross-border surveillance of friends, family, accomplices and victims of suspects being investigated. The Commission suggested that increasing the opportunities for police offcers to continue surveillance operations in other member states who are party to the convention, would represent progress towards developing police cooperation and boosting the success of judicial inquiries.

*Case example*
Although Europol is not actively engaged in policing environmental laws in member states of Europe at present, the following example highlights the types of enforcement operations in which Europol will be engaged. The Bundesgrenzschutzamt See (German Sea Frontier Police) in January 1999 observed an oil tanker with Maltese registration discharging oil in the Danish Exclusive Economic Zone (EEZ). A few days later, oil from the tanker drifted ashore on the coastline in five locations around Skagerrak. The investigation involved searches at Wilhelmshaven, Germany, where the cargo of crude oil was unloaded, and at Muuga, Estonia, where a new cargo of fuel oil was loaded. In addition, searches were conducted of the, owner and manager's residences in Malta, Italy and Greece. Investigations involving interrogations and searches for documents in other European countries were carried out in accordance with the European Convention of 1959 on mutual assistance in criminal investigations (Wandall 2002: 12).

**Federal environmental law enforcement**

A number of countries have national law enforcement agencies to protect the integrity of their national borders. In particular, the increased threat from terrorism and the increased occurrence of environmental crimes within national territories have created the need for much greater cooperation between national and state police organisations. For example, countries like the USA, Australia, Germany and Indonesia all have federal police services that are responsible for investigating crime in their respective countries. Many of these federal police organisations also cooperate with internal state police services to help deal with crime at a national and state level. The Environmental

520

Protection Agencies/Authorities (EPA) are other law enforcement bodies that are mandated to enforce environmental laws and regulations.

## USA

### Federal Bureau of Investigation

The Federal Bureau of Investigation (FBI) is the investigative arm of the US Department of Justice. To combat environmental crime in 1996 the FBI created the Hazardous Materials Response Unit to respond to the threat of terrorism involving chemical, biological, and nuclear weapons and to increases in environmental crimes within the USA. The Unit responds to criminal acts and incidents involving hazardous materials and develops the FBI's technical proficiency and readiness for crime scene and evidence-related operations in cases involving chemical, biological, and radiological materials and wastes. This is accomplished through an integrated effort involving specialised response teams, a national training program, interagency liaison, technical assistance to FBI field and Headquarters divisions, and the development of field response programs. The Unit also trains, equips, and certifies FBI field office personnel for hazardous materials operations (Federal Bureau of Investigation Hazardous Materials Response 2000).

### USA Environmental Protection Agency (Federal)

In the USA the Environmental Protection Agency is required to ensure that all states implement the minimum standards of the various federal environment protection laws. The EPA has particular enforcement roles to play in ensuring that industries, individuals and governments adhere to minimum environmental standards and prosecute any violations of these laws. The EPA's Criminal Investigation Division (CID) Special Agents are sworn federal law enforcement officers with statutory authority to conduct investigations, carry firearms, make arrests for any federal crime and to execute and serve warrants (United States Environmental Protection Agency 2004b).

It is of note that there are considerable differences between the USA EPA and the activities of similar Australian agencies, such as the New South Wales Environmental Protection Authority (see below). For example, the NSW Environmental Protection Authority does not engage in coercive methods of environmental law enforcement, unlike the USA Environmental Protection Authority. Rather, the NSW Environmental Protection Authority acts as the. main prosecutorial service of environmental offences in New South Wales (New South Wales Environmental Protection Authority Prosecution Guidelines 2004), but rely upon police for coercive interventions as required.

### Case example

On May 17, 2004 a private contractor from Mobile, Alabama, pleaded guilty to two counts of violating the Resource Conservation and Recovery Act (RCRA). The contractor was contracted by the Escambia County Utility Authority in Florida to transport and dispose of wastes from its wastewater treatment facility. The wastes included oils, tar, paint wastes, hydraulic fluid and solvents, which are required under RCRA to be disposed of by a licensed hazardous waste disposal facility. Instead, the contractor dumped the waste chemicals at separate locations throughout Southern Alabama. The Jacksonville Area Office of EPA's Criminal Investigation Division, EPA's Emergency Response Branch and the FBI investigated the case. The prosecution was brought by the U.S. Attorney's Office in Mobile and the Environmental Crimes Section of the U.S. Department of Justice in Washington, D.C. (United States Environmental Protection Agency 2004a)

### Australia

#### Australian Federal Police (AFP)

The AFP enforces Commonwealth criminal laws, and protects the national interests from crime in Australia. The AFP is Australia's international law enforcement and policing representative, and the principal source of advice to the Australian Federal Government on policing issues. In responding to offences that are committed against the environment the AFP federal agents work with the assistance of other state police forces and such environmental regulatory agencies as the Australian Maritime Safety Authority (AMSA) as part of the investigation process. For example, in the event that a ship travelling in Australian waters discharges oil, the investigation process may include identifying the ship and taking samples from various parts of the ship and investigating the circumstances surrounding an alleged oil spill (see Davies 2002).

#### Case example

As Davies (2002) notes, in Australia offences such as the presentation of false documentation to the Commonwealth, are in themselves not an environmental offence. However, offences like falsifying documentation can and have been used to prosecute offenders for environmental harms. In one such case professional fishermen were catching Orange Roughy fish well in excess of the legal quota then disguising the fact by incorrectly identifying the fish on documentation presented to the relevant fishing authorities. The Orange Roughy is a slow growing and breeding deep-sea fish and has considerable commercial viability that is easily threatened by fishing practices that exploit the fish stock. The falsified documentation presented to fishing authorities became the basis for the prosecution of the fisherman (Davies 2002:26).

In another investigation, AFP agents issued a summons to the operators of the Club Med Lindeman Island Resort following a joint investigation with the Great Barrier Reef Marine Park Authority (GBRMPA). The investigation followed a complaint by the Queensland Environmental Protection Authority that the resort had pumped raw sewage into an area of the ocean that is located within the marine park. Federal agents and investigators from GBRMPA executed search warrants at the resort. The investigation found that between 700,000 and 1,000,000 litres of raw sewage was pumped into the ocean after an underground pipe burst. Holiday Villages (Australia) Pty Ltd trading as Club Med Lindeman Island Resort were convicted with negligently discharging waste in the Marine National Park 'A' Zone of the Great Barrier Reef Marine Park between 30 November and 7 December 2000 and were fined $6000.00 plus court costs (Australian Federal Police 2003)

## State/provincial environmental enforcement

Many countries have policing organisations that are responsible for law enforcement at the state or provincial level (Waddington 1999). For example, Australia, the USA and Germany all have state police services with specific territorial jurisdiction. The realms of responsibility range from controlling traffic to the apprehension of offenders within their geographical borders. Generally, most state police services do not enforce environmental laws or regulations and have far less effect on the control of industry or business activities. When state police services do become involved with environmental crimes, it is normally the result of other investigations. However, there are some state law enforcement services that have specialised environmental law enforcement units that respond to environmental crimes.

### USA: Massachusetts

The Environmental Strike Force (ESF) is an interagency unit comprised of law enforcement officials from the Massachusetts Department of Environmental Protection, Environmental Police officers from the Department of Fisheries, Wildlife and Environmental Law Enforcement, state police, and prosecutors from the Office of the Attorney General. The Strike Force gathers evidence during investigations against alleged environmental offenders. The Massachusetts Environmental Strike Force is responsible for enforcing environmental laws, and for licensing and registering boats and recreational vehicles. These environmental police officers work in the seven inland and coastal regions of the state and are responsible for enforcing a wide variety of laws and regulations relating to the environment. Environmental law enforcement officers also investigate cases of illegal waste disposal, wetlands violations, and assist in search and rescue efforts (Massachusetts Environmental Strike Force 2004).

### Case example

In December 2001, a demolition contractor pleaded guilty to forty counts of violating the notification requirements under Massachusetts's environmental laws. The guilty plea resulted from an investigation by ESF after several Department of Environmental Protection staff working at a landfill became ill after being exposed to a polycyclic aromatic hydrocarbons (PAH) contaminated road base product delivered by the contractor. The 2 year investigation determined that the source of the contaminated material was a stockpile of material processed by the contractor at a quarry. Records revealed that contractor sold or shipped the contaminated material to two residential developments and numerous commercial locations. After pleading guilty the contractor was ordered to pay a $1 million criminal fine and another $400,000 in restitution to DEP and to Massachusetts Highway Authority for cleanup and response costs incurred during the investigation. The contractor also agreed to clean up three additional sites that had received the contaminated material, to remove two corporate officers who held management positions at the time of the incidents, to hire an independent onsite environmental auditor, and to implement an environmental management system to help prevent future incidents (*Commonwealth v MRP Site Development, Inc*).

### Australia: New South Wales (NSW) Environmental Protection Authority

The Environment Protection Authority (EPA) is the primary NSW environmental law enforcement organisation responsible for protecting the environment. The EPA works in partnership with business, industry, government and community organisations. The regulatory functions of the EPA require it to be active in environmental education, environmental economics, environmental research and monitoring, and regular reporting on the state of the environment to the government and NSW community. As a general principle, when a serious breach of the environment protection laws comes to the attention of the EPA, the authority will lead any investigation and take any appropriate action. This suggests that because of the functions, powers, objectives, and the legal and specific expertise within the organisation, the EPA is generally better equipped than other law enforcement agencies to investigate and prosecute serious breaches of NSW environmental laws (New South Wales Environmental Protection Authority 2004: 1–2).

### Case example
An unauthorised discharge of up to 70,000 litres of wastewater effluent from a pig farm on 3–4 October 1999 resulted in contaminated effluent entering and progressing down a watercourse on a neighbour's property. Sampling results suggested that the effluent entered a nearby waterway. The concentrations of nutrients in the discharge channel on the neighbour's property and downstream in the creek were well in excess of the Australian and New Zealand Environment Conservation Council (ANZECC) guidelines. As this was the third incident the defendant was convicted of the offence and fined $30,000. The defendant also had to pay the costs of the prosecutor, which was a further $5,920 (*EPA v Larkray Pty Ltd [2001] NSWLEC 92*).

### Australia: Tasmania Police

The Tasmanian Police Service does not have a specialist environmental enforcement unit. However, Tasmania Police have been involved in investigating some types of environmental crimes, such as abalone poaching. Another associated area of environmental law enforcement has been the Bush Watch initiative. Bush Watch is similar to Neighbourhood Watch programmes operating in many cities and towns across Australia. The focus of Bush Watch is in the rural areas of Tasmania, where it is designed to prevent livestock theft, and to protect native fauna and flora (Tasmania Police 2003).

### Case example
Tasmania Police's Oakum Task Force has investigated the involvement of criminal organisations in the systematic theft of abalone from Tasmanian state waters, and its subsequent processing and export from the state. Their investigations culminated in 169 charges relating to either serious criminal matters such as drug trafficking, or significant matters under the Living Marine Resources Management Act (1995), being preferred against 17 individuals from four separate syndicates involved in illegal abalone operations (Tasmania Police 2003: 43–44).

## Local law enforcement

There are varied enforcement agencies dealing with the implementation and enforcement of environmental laws at a local level. Enforcement agencies include county sheriffs departments in the USA or municipal police services such as the Toronto Police Service in Canada. These police organisations have very restricted territorial boundaries and enforce national, state and local laws within these areas. These police services are different from state police services in that the officers, particularly the sheriffs in the USA, can be elected officials.

### *El Paso County Sheriff's Department Environmental Crimes Unit, Texas*

The El Paso County Sheriffs Department Environmental Crimes Unit in Texas is an example of a local enforcer of environmental laws. Many of the incidents that the Environmental Crimes Unit deal with are small and isolated cases of building waste or rubble dumping and illegal dumping of light industrial or household waste (El Paso County Sheriffs Department Environmental Crimes Unit 2004).

*Case example*
On 5 August 2001 a caravan park owner intentionally pumped out sewage from a septic tank at 9 a.m. in the morning for over twenty-five minutes. The sewage ran back underneath a caravan owned by a resident forming a pool of sewage for the following three days. The liquid contained particles of human waste, was black in colour, and smelled for three to four days. The offender was found guilty of a charge laid by the El Paso County Sheriff's Department Environmental Crimes Unit and was sentenced to one year jail time, probated two years, was fined $20,000 and placed on $18,500 probation with sentences to run concurrently (*Winfried Heiringhoff v State of Texas*).

## Environmental crime: the local to the global

Environmental crimes, whether committed by organised criminal gangs, corporations or individuals can affect environs outside the immediate area where the offence occurs. For example, an environmental crime committed in one location may not adversely affect that specific area, particularly if the pollution or harmful substances released are carried by air or water. However, it may do considerable damage to the environment some distance from the source of the pollution.

The effects of environmental crime or harm can manifest in ways that cut across international, national, state and local borders. In response, different police services may be required to collaborate in order to counter the problem. Identifying policing institutions at the different levels of intervention raises important issues about what role police organisations are to play in combating environmental crimes that involve different political and policing jurisdictions. In particular, we need to know what kind of structures and strategies are needed to facilitate cooperation between different police services dealing with this type of crime to ensure efficiency and effectiveness in protecting the environment.

Police cooperation from the local to international level raises important questions about how policing organisations view other policing institutions whom they may work with in investigating environmental crime. The levels at which policing organisations are involved in enforcing environmental laws are indicated in Table 27.1. The very existence of different levels of police involvement highlights the fact that environmental crime can and does cut across borders and different jurisdictions. Moreover, the type of intervention in policing environmental crimes can move from one level to another in either direction. For example, in the case of Operation Oakum in Tasmania, state police became involved in a multi-level policing operation that included state, federal and international police organisations; in the Nigerian case the investigation moved from the international to the local law enforcement arena.

**Table 27.1** Operational levels of police organisations

| Operational level | Examples of police organisations |
|---|---|
| International | Interpol |
| Regional | Europol |
| National | Australian Federal Police |
| State | Tasmania Police |
| Local | The El Paso County Sheriff's Department Environmental Crimes Unit |

The way in which police and governments respond to incidents of environmental crime requires considerable cooperation by diverse police institutions to ensure that the environment is protected.

The issue of police cooperation in combating environmental crime requires considerable research to understand how police services from different jurisdictions understand the legal systems of other police services that they may have to cooperate with. This is particularly relevant in combating not only environmental crime but also other international crimes such as terrorism. Given the international and trans-border nature of some environmental crimes, police services will have to become global in their outlooks towards their counterparts in other countries. Knowledge of and familiarity with the strategic and operational approaches taken by diverse enforcement bodies would also be useful in enhancing cooperation across jurisdictional boundaries.

## References

Australian Federal Police (2003) *AFP Annual Report 2002–2003*, Canberra.
Bayley, D H (1999) 'Policing the World Stage' in Mawby, R I (ed) *Policing Across the World. Issues for the Twenty-first Century*, University College London Press, London.
Birnie, P and Boyle, A (2002) *International Law and the Environment*, 2nd Edition, Oxford University Press, London.

Bolen, J (1997) *Reform in Policing: lessons from the Whitrod era*, The Institute of Criminology Monograph Series, Hawkins Press, Sydney.

Bryett, K and Harrison, A (1994) *An Introduction to Policing: Trends and Procedures in Policing*, Vol 4, Butterworths, Sydney.

Davis, J (2002) 'To fight environmental crime together and win', *Platypus Magazine*, No 74, pp 20–28.

El Paso County Sheriffs Department Environmental Crimes Unit (2004), accessed 23 October 2004, <http://www.co.el-paso.tx.us/ca/ca-environ,btm>.

Faure, M G and Heine G (2002) *Criminal Penalties in EU Member States' Environmental Law*, Maastricht European Institute for Transnational Legal Research, Faculty of Law.

Maastricht University and the Institute for Criminal Law and Criminology, Faculty of Law, University of Berne, Maastricht, The Netherlands.

Federal Bureau of Investigation Hazardous Materials Response (2000), accessed 20 July 2004, <http://www.fbi.gov/hq/lab/org/hmru.htm>.

Finnane, M (1994) *Police and Government: Histories of Policing in Australia*, Oxford University Press, Melbourne.

Freckelton, I and Selby, H (eds) (1988) *Policing in Our Society*, Butterworths, Brisbane.

Herbert, S (1997) *Policing Space Territoriality and the Los Angeles Police Department*, University of Minnesota Press, Minneapolis,

International Criminal Police Organization (2004), accessed 12 June 2004 <http://www.interpol.int/Public/Icpo/default.asp>.

Klem, S (1994) 'Environmental Crime and the role of ICPO-Interpol', paper presented at the *Third International Conference on Environmental Enforcement*, April, Oaxaca, Mexico.

Massachusetts Environmental Strike Force (2004) <http://www.mass.gov/dep/esf/aboutesf.htm>.

McCulloch, J (2001) *Blue Army: Paramilitary Policing in Australia*, Melbourne University Press, Carlton South.

Morgan, R and Smith, D (eds) (1989) *Coming to terms with policing: perspectives on policy*, Routledge, London.

New South Wales Environmental Protection Authority (2004) *Prosecution Guidelines*, Environmental Protection Authority, Sydney.

Reiner, R (1985) *Politics of the Police*, Wheatsheaf Books, Sussex.

Secretariat of the Task Force on Organised Crime in the Baltic Sea Region (2002) *Report On Environmental Criminality*, The Task Force Secretariat National Commissioner of Danish Police, Copenhagen.

Situ, Y and Emmons, D (2000) *Environmental Crime: The role of the criminal justice system in protecting the environment*, Sage, Thousand Oaks California.

Tasmania Police (2003) *Annual Report 2003, Tasmania Department of Police and Public Safety*, Hobart, Tasmania.

Uglow, S (1988) *Policing the Liberal Society*, Oxford University Press, Oxford.

United States Environmental Protection Agency (2004a) 'EPA Press Advisory', received 1 Sep 2004.

United States Environmental Protection Agency (2004b), 'Criminal Enforcement', <http://www.epa.gov/compliance/criminal/investigations/index.html>.

Waddington, P A J (1999) *Policing Citizens*, University College London Press, London.

Wandall, P (2002) *Task Force on Organised Crime In the Baltic Sea Region*, Seminar on Environmental Criminality 22 April in Copenhagen, National Commissioner of Police, A Department Forensic Division, Flying Squad Denmark.

White, R and Perrone, S (1997) *Crime and Social Control: An Introduction*, Oxford University Press, Melbourne.

## Cases

*Commonwealth v MRP Site Development, Inc.* (Suffolk Superior Court), accessed 20 September 2004 at <http://www.mass.gov/dep/esf/esfacts.htm>.

*EPA v Larkray Pty Ltd* [2001] NSWLEC 92.

*Winfried Heiringhoff v State of Texas*, no 08-02-00230-CR Court of Appeals of Texas Eighth District El Paso, 130 S.W.3d 117; 2003 Tex. App. LEXIS 7197.

# 28. Strengthening the weakest links: strategies for improving the enforcement of environmental laws globally*

*Anita Sundari Akella and James B. Cannon*

## Introduction

Poor enforcement in the environmental realm affects a diverse range of victims. Entire societies are affected when countries lose important sources of revenue that would have accrued from legitimate commerce in natural resources, or when overall governance is undermined by lawlessness in the natural resources sector. The livelihoods of traditional resource users are destroyed by illegal loggers and fishers. Those lawbreakers exploit forests and oceans with no regard for future productivity. Downstream communities are devastated by flash floods from debris coming out of illegally logged forests that protect watersheds, with the poor often being affected disproportionately.

Biodiversity conservation efforts are also severely compromised by poor enforcement. In the absence of enforcement, both traditional and more innovative solutions for countering biodiversity loss may not be successful. Creation of protected areas, measures to protect endangered species, tradable development rights, and ecosystem services markets alike may fail if people cannot be held to the agreements they make. Despite the efforts of conservationists over time, the quality and effectiveness of enforcement still fall far short of where they need to be.

Although weak enforcement is generally acknowledged as a widespread and significant problem, the full complexity of the underlying causes of this weakness is often not understood. Consequently, the most commonly applied solutions are overly simplistic. If systematic analysis is not done, then raising fines, investing in more cars, or hiring more detection agents may seem appropriate strategies for improving enforcement performance. However, those investments may not be the most effective or cost-effective strategies. Identical investments in another aspect of enforcement – for instance, offering specialized training to prosecutors who argue environmental cases in court – might yield a stronger deterrent against environmental crime. Even where investments in stronger detection are needed – as is often the case – such

*Strengthening the Weakest Links: Strategies for Improving the Enforcement of Environmental Laws Globally* (Washington, DC: Center for Conservation and Government), 2004, 1–34.

528

investments may underperform unless other weaknesses in the enforcement system are addressed at the same time.

Identifying weaknesses in an enforcement regime and devising investments that yield the best returns in enforcement performance can be challenging. Enforcement economics[1] provides a simple, yet elegant, theoretical framework for analyzing each component of the 'enforcement chain' so that weaknesses can be pinpointed and addressed. This holistic approach is rooted in the understanding that enforcement does not consist of detection alone. Rather, enforcement is a 'chain' that also includes the subsequent steps of arrest, prosecution, and conviction. For an enforcement system to effectively deter environmental crime, each of those steps must happen efficiently. The system is only as strong as the weakest link in this chain.

In 2000, with support from the U.S. Agency for International Development (USAID), we at Conservational International (CI) began analyzing the quality of enforcement in four priority biodiversity-rich countries. In each country, our objective was to determine why enforcement was not working, and then to contribute to development of cost-effective investment strategies for strengthening enforcement performance. Our adaptation of an enforcement economics methodology that had been developed for the fisheries context[2] proved a useful analytical tool for this work.

In each country, our work resulted in developing strategic action plans that would improve enforcement performance and were tailored to suit each site. Those plans were designed in collaboration with enforcement agency officials, civil society representatives, and other key stakeholders.

For multiple reasons, the enforcement economics analyses were carried out in close dialogue with enforcement agencies in each site. First, this collaboration allowed us improved access to sensitive enforcement data. Second, by incorporating the agencies into our efforts, we hoped to build awareness of key enforcement problems in the agencies, and to increase their understanding of how the system worked as a whole. Third, working with multiple agencies allowed us to facilitate and encourage interagency dialogue. Fourth, the relationships with senior enforcement agency officials provided researchers with additional personal protection as they did their field work. Finally, through our collaboration, we ensured that the agencies themselves helped lead the process of developing the enforcement-strengthening action plans, thereby increasing ownership and the likelihood that the plans would be implemented.

Key actors and decisionmakers in enforcement agencies and government are most effectively drawn into a discussion about improving an enforcement system when the arguments are presented clearly and rigorously and are complemented by supporting evidence about where and why weaknesses exist. When robust proposals for investments that can increase the system's effectiveness are proffered and when the proposals use a clear analytical framework, opportunities for collaboration with agencies to design, finance, and implement improvement strategies become evident.

While this approach has many advantages and makes a useful contribution, it also suffers the drawback that it emphasizes the technical reasons for weak enforcement. However, this is valuable since enforcement agencies are generally dealing with symptoms, and rarely analyze or concern themselves with addressing the root causes for illegal activities. This approach may also downplay the importance of factors such as unfair laws, lack of alternative legal incomes, corruption, and lack of political will. However, carrying out parallel investigations of and responses to the other issues can neutralize that drawback. The common understanding and trust built up by using this approach to strengthen enforcement also provides a sound basis for more difficult and delicate political and governance discussions regarding corruption and political will.

In this study, synthesizing the problems identified in each site will allow us to develop a set of overall lessons learned. The synthesis will reveal a number of enforcement challenges that were common across countries. The lessons learned will point to a set of priority investment areas for improving enforcement performance. This piece will briefly discuss site-level results, but it will focus primarily on the common themes that emerged from synthesis of the results that have been drawn from the participatory site-level work. We believe that the lessons learned can contribute significantly to efforts toward developing a global agenda of priority actions that will strengthen implementation of both natural resource legislation and protected area boundaries.

This report will begin by putting the discussion of enforcement in its proper context. After describing the enforcement economics methodology, we will present an overview of results from the four country case studies. We will then identify and discuss common weaknesses that are prevalent across sites. Finally, we will detail a clear set of technical investment priorities for enforcement.

## Enforcement in context

For the purposes of this paper, 'enforcement' is defined as the system comprising detection, apprehension, prosecution, and conviction of lawbreakers. Strengthening enforcement is a means to an end, not an end in itself. The end goal of improving enforcement is to eliminate illegal activities or to reduce them to tolerable levels – in other words, to improve compliance. Enforcement contributes to that goal by directly suppressing criminal activity and by creating a deterrent effect.

Enforcement strengthening is only one of a number of ways of contributing to the end goal of improving compliance. Other ways include preventative measures such as developing alternative legal sources of income, improving public awareness and support for the laws, reducing the opportunity to break the law, lowering the demand for illegal products, reducing the profits of illegal activities relative to legal ones, and reforming the law to legalize hitherto illegal activities.

### Ways to improve compliance

Considerable debate takes place over the best ways to improve compliance with particular natural resource and environmental laws. The answer will vary according to the type and scale of crime, the market for the product, the identity of the perpetrators, and the reasons for which they act illegally. For instance, traditional hunting of endangered and newly protected species by indigenous peoples requires a response different from that for professional wildlife poaching or commercial-scale illegal logging by organized criminal gangs. Co-management approaches may often be the most just and efficient approach for the former type of illegal activity, but the assistance of government enforcement agencies is likely required for the latter. Co-management approaches involve local communities in enforcement activities in a way highly tailored to local issues. Whether illegal activities are practiced for cultural reasons or are key to livelihoods, co-management approaches often combine enforcement with developing alternative activities that are culturally acceptable.

The best way to improve compliance will also vary depending on why enforcement against a particular crime is inadequate. Some causes, such as inadequate financial or human resources, or poor training, can be relatively easier to rectify. Others – particularly those where the solution may lie outside the control of enforcement agencies – are far harder to rectify. Problematic causes include lack of support for laws widely viewed as unjust, political uncertainty, lack of political support for stronger enforcement, and ingrained corruption.

Compliance is usually best improved by implementing a mix of preventative and enforcement-strengthening measures together. It is generally accepted that stand-alone efforts to strengthen enforcement are rarely the most effective way forward. However, this actuality does not mean enforcement strengthening can be ignored. A certain level of increased enforcement is necessary to improve compliance in most situations and will be a crucial element, for instance, when combating organized, commercial-scale illegal activities.

### Unjust laws and unfair enforcement

A key concern over strengthening enforcement in isolation is the risk of enforcing unjust or counterproductive laws. For instance, traditional users may be unfairly criminalized when government forest policy and laws fail to respect the rights and concerns of indigenous peoples or local communities, as has often occurred during the creation of logging concessions or protected areas by colonial or central governments. The answer to unfair or counterproductive laws is legal reform and – depending on the circumstances – compensation for 'regulatory takings' by government. The answer is not weak enforcement. In general, enforcement-strengthening efforts should not be applied to disputed laws that are undergoing reform, although such thinking has been exploited, for instance, in Papua, by illegal loggers, who argue that they are acting in community interests so they can escape enforcement efforts.

Enforcing disputed laws will likely rouse opposition to enforcement strengthening, particularly from essentially pro-reform allies. This opposition would be unfortunate, because weak enforcement of other, undisputed laws is often identified as one of the reasons that local and indigenous groups are harmed by illegal activities. One way forward is to focus initial enforcement-strengthening efforts on noncontentious laws that are generally seen as legitimate. Ideally, those laws would be the ones governing crimes that have the largest economic, social, and environmental effect. Reinforcing enforcement to combat crimes that are having direct negative effects on local populations could also help build local confidence in and support for law enforcement. Strengthening environmental and natural resource laws that protect the rights and livelihoods of the poor is also a key element of poverty-reduction strategies.

In some cases, the laws may not be at issue, but their application is viewed as illegitimate by local stakeholders because the stakeholders are not adequately involved in decisionmaking. In such situations, co-management approaches – for instance, of natural resources or protected areas – may be necessary to build local support.

In other cases, the laws may be generally accepted as appropriate and fair, but enforcement may be applied unequally, with the rich and powerful – or the enforcement agency staff members themselves – avoiding justice. Again, this circumstance is not a reason for weak enforcement but rather for increased efforts to ensure that laws are enforced more fairly. Unequal application of enforcement may simply indicate that the rich can afford better lawyers. In such cases, the main need may be for legal assistance for those who are unable to afford lawyers themselves. However, unequal application of the law may also be a symptom of corruption.

### Ways to reduce corruption

The different types of corruption – petty or grand, collusive or noncollusive – pose many challenges to the various approaches for improving compliance. Enforcement strengthening itself can help reduce corruption, both directly by detecting it and indirectly because better enforcement makes corruption more expensive and more difficult. Corruption itself undermines all parts of the enforcement system, and efforts to combat corruption, therefore, need to be integral to enforcement-strengthening programs. Enforcement-strengthening efforts should start by cleaning up the enforcement and licensing agencies themselves. Greater confidence and trust in government agencies is necessary as a base for strengthening broader public respect for the law and its institutions. Anticorruption efforts include supporting nongovernmental organization (NGO) or civil society watchdogs, as well as various efforts within the enforcement system, such as introducing appropriate checks and balances, ensuring pay and bonus structures to create appropriate incentives, revising staffing procedures, and making public the enforcement information needed to evaluate performance. Those efforts must include the judiciary. A clean and effective judiciary that hears cases fairly will encourage well-intentioned enforcement agents and prosecutors so they know there is a point to doing their jobs well. A clean and effective judiciary can also lead reform efforts within the enforcement system, thereby rooting out and punishing corrupt officials.

In extreme cases, high levels of corruption can call into question whether investing in stronger enforcement is really worthwhile until corruption is brought under some semblance of control. While it is likely that corruption will reduce the effectiveness of investments in enforcement strengthening, it is unlikely that the benefits will be nullified completely. In fact, strengthening the rule of law is generally viewed as an essential part of anticorruption efforts. As a special case, the rigorous analyses of enforcement systems of the type described here promote transparency and understanding and are generally considered a useful component of efforts to reduce corruption.

Another issue generally linked to corruption is military involvement in illegal activities. The commonly accepted long-term answer is to 'get the soldiers back in the barracks' and create a 'modern' army, meaning one that is fully funded by central government, is under its full control, and fulfills only regular military functions. In the short term, the answer may be to seek agreement that some questionable parts of the military's business operations be legalized. However, the agreement would be conditional on not engaging in any illegal activities such as resource extraction in particular areas, particularly protected areas and indigenous lands. While some parts of the military may often be engaged in illegal activities, either directly or through corrupt practices, the military in general may need to be engaged directly in finding solutions. In many countries, for instance, the cooperation of the military is required to combat illegal logging carried out on a large scale by organized crime, particularly when elements in the military are involved in the illegal logging.

### Ways to raise public awareness

In other cases, both the laws and their implementation may be fair, but public understanding and support for the laws may be low. Under those circumstances, awareness raising and education efforts are a priority. In other cases, a law may be fair in theory, but the absence of other livelihood options may make its application extremely punishing in practice. The answer is not weak enforcement, but additional assistance and support to develop alternative income opportunities, along with possible legal reform.

Legal and procedural reform, compensation, legal aid, public outreach, innovative co-management, anticorruption efforts, and support for alternative legal livelihoods can improve compliance directly and can ease the enforcement challenge. Balanced compliance-improvement efforts that include such measures and enforcement strengthening are likely to be more cost-effective than efforts that overemphasize one measure at the expense of investments in the others.

Efforts that recognize and address the legitimate concerns of various stakeholders are also likely to be most successful in building and maintaining political will for action. Opposition from elites defending their entrenched interests is often blamed for lack of political will for enforcement strengthening. However, unless laws are seen to be fair and to be applied fairly, then opposition from those supporting community rights and grassroots reform may undermine the political will for stronger enforcement. Building and maintaining the political will for improving compliance will generally require building and maintaining a broad pro-reform alliance.

For many good reasons, therefore, enforcement-strengthening efforts should not proceed as stand-alone activities. Rather, their success is augmented if they are carried out together with a package of activities that fall into two general classes: (1) preventative activities that directly improve compliance while reducing enforcement challenge and (2) activities designed to ensure that the laws and their enforcement are workable and fair. The most effective package of activities will vary from place to place and should be developed by local experts and stakeholders.

## Enforcement economics – theoretical underpinnings

### Description of the quantitative model

Economists focusing on the question of enforcement have suggested that the economic deterrent 'value' of an enforcement regime can be determined as follows:

$$\text{Enforcement Disincentive} = P_d \times P_{a|d} \times P_{p|a} \times P_{c|p} \times \text{Fine} \times e^{-rt}$$

Where:

$P$ = probability
$d$ = detection
$a|d$ = arrest given detection
$p|a$ = prosecution given arrest
$c|p$ = conviction given prosecution
$e$ = a mathematical constant, the exponential function of 1
$r$ = interest rate
$t$ = time from detection to fine

In this model,[3] the frequency and intensity of illegal behavior are assumed to be proportional to the net profits from illegal behavior. If the gross profits of illegal behavior are greater than the expected value of the enforcement disincentive – that is, if violators of environmental laws believe that their profit will be greater than what they will have to pay for breaking the law – then the net profits of illegal activity are positive, and violators will choose to commit the crime. By the same token, if the expected value of the enforcement disincentive is high enough to make the net profits of illegal activity negative, they will decide not to commit the crime.

As shown in the equation above, the value of the disincentive to commit an environmental crime is equivalent to the probabilities of each step in the legal process happening, multiplied by the amount of the fine, and discounted for the time between detection and paying the fine. According to this logic, an enforcement system can be considered 'effective' only if it generates an enforcement disincentive (ED) that is larger than the financial incentives (profit) motivating the illegal behavior. For this analysis, 'effectiveness' will be defined as such.

The assumptions underpinning this economic framework are closest to reality in the case of commercial illegal activities that are being run on a rational profit-making basis. The underlying assumptions are less well suited to illegal activities that occur as part of subsistence livelihoods or that are driven by cultural objectives. Nonetheless, the model structure is still a useful framework for analyzing the performance of enforcement of noncommercial crimes.

This model offers four particularly interesting insights into enforcement systems:

1 If the probability – or even the perceived probability – of any one of the elements in the enforcement chain is zero, then the value of the entire chain is reduced to zero. The enforcement regime presents no disincentive to breaking environmental laws.

2 By this logic, enforcement systems are holistic in nature and must be conceived of and dealt with as such. The disincentive value generated by an enforcement regime relies not only on how well the agencies responsible for each element of the enforcement chain do their individual piece but also on how well those agencies work together as a system. The system is only as strong as its weakest link.

3 An element-by-element examination of the enforcement system will help pinpoint exactly where in the process – and within which agencies – weaknesses are being generated.

4 The time element is an important one, because discounting[4] for each year between detection and payment of the fine will significantly reduce (a) the value of the fine to the violator, (b) the overall value of the disincentive provided by the enforcement regime, and (c) the disincentive to commit an environmental crime.

Determining the disincentive created by an enforcement regime, therefore, requires calculation of the probabilities of detection, arrest, prosecution, and conviction. Either observed probabilities or perceived probabilities can be used in this determination – using the former gives an actual value to the enforcement disincentive, while using the latter tells us what the expected value of the enforcement disincentive is to the violator. Observed probabilities can be determined by collecting data from official records on incidence of detection and so forth. Perceived probabilities are determined through the use of socioeconomic surveys or questionnaires.

Perceived probabilities may be a better indication of disincentive value than observed probabilities, because violators of the law act on their perception of how effective an enforcement system is. In other words, the deterrent effect of an enforcement system will vary depending on how its effectiveness is communicated to violators and to the public at large.

As experience with and information about the enforcement system develops, transparency increases. Thus, observed and perceived values might be expected to become closely correlated or to converge. Having both pieces of information is ideal, because it facilitates analysis of both where the weaknesses in the enforcement chain lie and how people's perceptions of the enforcement regime will affect their behavior. Furthermore, in instances in which a lack of data precludes the calculation of an observed probability, perceived probability can reasonably be used as a proxy. Only rarely, however, are both pieces of information available.

In many instances, getting the data necessary to run the quantitative model may be difficult. Enforcement agencies may prohibit access to official enforcement records because those records are seen as sensitive, potentially embarrassing, or even damaging to the agencies. Or official enforcement records may be so poorly maintained that collecting accurate data that can be used to calculate observed probabilities is virtually impossible. The difficulty of designing surveys and questionnaires that accurately capture information for calculation of perceived probabilities makes that alternative equally challenging.

Nonetheless, even where the collection of quantitative data is not possible, the enforcement economics model can provide an excellent analytical framework. The underlying premise of the model – that the overall success or failure of the enforcement system relies on the effective execution of each step in the enforcement chain – can guide a process of gathering expert opinion and anecdotal evidence for a qualitative analysis. A methodical examination of the performance of each step in the system – using information from key informants such as field agents, prosecutors, and other experts – will not yield a numeric calculation of the enforcement disincentive but will provide precise insights into how effective an enforcement regime is in deterring environmental crime.

### Determinants of the quality of enforcement

Although the quantitative enforcement economics model identifies which probabilities in the enforcement chain are low, it does not answer the question of why probabilities are low. The determinants of the quality of enforcement are factors that influence how efficiently enforcement activities are carried out and, therefore, affect the probabilities of detection, arrest, prosecution, conviction, and penalty. For instance, the probability of detection is determined not only by obvious factors such as numbers of park guards or availability of equipment but also by less-obvious factors such as pay and reward structures to environmental protection agents.

Each successive link in the enforcement chain can be analyzed similarly to identify factors that are contributing to poor performance for that aspect of the chain. By way of example, a partial listing of the determinants of the quality of enforcement, as applied specifically to each link in the enforcement chain, follows:

- Probability of detection is correlated to the incentives given to park guards, rangers, and forest and fishery environmental protection agents (e.g., pay levels and other rewards); to availability of equipment; to number of personnel charged with detecting environmental crimes; and to technical knowledge and skill of personnel.

536

- Probability of arrest given detection is correlated to police pay and reward structure, to availability of equipment, to quality of evidence, and to social perceptions about the crime.

- Probability of prosecution given arrest is correlated to rewards for prosecutors, to capacity of the justice system and those in it to prosecute environmental crimes, to whether the illegal act is a criminal or civil offense, to social attitudes toward the crime, and to quality of evidence.

- Probability of conviction given prosecution is correlated to rewards for judges and magistrates, to capacity of the justice system, to nature of the crime, to social attitudes toward the crime, and to quality of evidence.

Weaknesses that often undermine all steps in the enforcement chain are generated when enforcement agents, police officers, prosecutors, or judges fear negative repercussions from doing their jobs properly or when they are intimidated or co-opted by those breaking the law. Analysis of the determinants of the quality of enforcement clarifies why enforcement is weak, thus complementing quantitative analysis of where weaknesses exist in the enforcement chain.

## Overview of country case study results

From 2000 to 2004 the Center for Conservation and Government (CCG) used the enforcement economics methodology as an analytical framework for assessing the effectiveness of enforcement in four countries: Brazil, Indonesia, Mexico, and the Philippines. In each country, we examined enforcement of a specific crime in a part of the country where biodiversity was under substantial threat. To make the analyses site specific, we modified the generalized form of the ED model to accurately reflect the steps composing the enforcement chain in each country. The type of environmental crime examined varied in each site, thereby reflecting the most pressing threat identified in each country or region. Finally, depending on the handling of the crimes studied in each country, we determined whether to analyze administrative or judicial enforcement processes.[5]

In each site, the analysis of enforcement effectiveness was used to develop strategic action plans for strengthening key weaknesses in partnership with local enforcement agency[6] officials and other stakeholders.[7]

Because we worked closely with enforcement agencies in executing the site-level analyses, we intentionally did not focus on the issue of corruption. In interviews and other discussions, corruption was identified as an important factor contributing to weak enforcement in all four countries. However, we did not further examine this issue in all case studies. Therefore, although corruption was a major challenge in each site, we will offer no specific commentary on corruption.

In this section, we will present a short background on each site, as well as the quantitative results and some key points of interest about the results from each site. This overview of site-level quantitative findings is limited and is not a full reflection of the very detailed systemic analysis done in each site. However, the overview will serve as the basis for in-depth exploration of lessons learned from the synthesis of results across those sites.

As a group, the case studies gave quantitative validation of one thing that most conservationists already know: Enforcement of natural resource and biodiversity laws and regulations is abysmal in these biodiversity-rich countries. The existing enforcement regimes in the countries we studied are weak, and not one of them provides an adequate disincentive to offset the incentives that are driving illegal environmental activities. While some of their failings are caused by resource limitations, myriad other factors contribute significantly to the agencies' poor performance. The issues that make enforcement ineffective do not lie in any one step of the enforcement chain or in any single agency, but are pervasive throughout the systems.

## Case Study I: Bahia, Brazil – The Atlantic Forest

**Environmental Violation Analyzed**: Illegal logging and deforestation

**Scale of Crime**: Small-scale extraction of logs, or clearing for agricultural purposes

**Administrative or Judicial**: Judicial

**Components of the Enforcement Chain**: Detection, citation, prosecution, conviction, and penalty

**Agencies Analyzed**: Brazilian Institute for the Environment and Renewable Resources (Instituto Brasileiro do Meio Ambiente e dos Recursos Naturais Renováveis – IBAMA) (detection and citation), Ministério Público (prosecution), judiciary (conviction and penalty)

The Atlantic Forest is one of the world's hotspots of plant and animal endemism and diversity. Currently, less than 8 percent of the original Atlantic Forest is still standing (Galindo-Leal and Câmara 2003). The fragments of primary forest found in a roughly 14,000-square-kilometer area of Southern Bahia make it one of the richest centers of endemism in the Atlantic Forest. It is also the only remaining habitat for a variety of plant and animal species, including the endangered primates *Leontopithecus chrysolmelas* (golden-headed lion tamarind) and *Cebus xantosthernos* (golden-breasted capuchin).

This ecosystem has long been under threat from a variety of actors. Originally, cocoa farmers were the primary engine of ecosystem degradation. More than 400,000 hectares of this region were converted from forest to cocoa between 1960 and 1980 (Alger and Caldas 1994). As cocoa production has declined, beginning in the early 1990s, the degradation of primary and secondary forest fragments in Southern Bahia has intensified. With the decline, cocoa farmers have switched into even more destructive economic activities like raising full-sun coffee, cattle ranching, and logging (their perennial fallback activity). Deforestation of forested areas on private lands or in protected areas has also risen because of the increased numbers of landless peasants who

538

were formerly employed on cocoa plantations. The combined factors have contributed to the ongoing high-level threat to Southern Bahia's remaining forest fragments.

Logs illegally extracted from this region are generally processed in local sawmills and are used domestically – in Bahia itself and in states such as Rio de Janeiro and Minas Gerais, where demand for wood is high (Mesquita 1997). Deforested areas are generally converted to other uses – poor farmers may use the land for subsistence farming, whereas larger farmers often convert it to one of the more destructive activities described earlier.

In Southern Bahia, our analysis focused on cases of illegal logging and deforestation that had occurred in a 72-municipality region between the years of 1995 and 2002. While there are state agencies charged with detection, our effort focused on cases originating with detection by IBAMA, the federal environmental agency that has had the longest-standing responsibility for enforcement in the region. The enforcement process analyzed in this case was a judicial process, so we also tracked the cases through the hands of public prosecutors and into the courts.

According to research done by the Instituto de Estudos Socioambientais do Sul da Bahia (Institute for Social and Environmental Studies of Southern Bahia – IESB), the profits to illegal logging from harvesting as little as one tree in the biodiversity-rich forests of this region are $75.[9] Using the enforcement economics methodology, we found the value of the disincentive generated by the enforcement system in this region was only $6.44.

Qualitative analysis demonstrates that the primary factors contributing to ineffective enforcement in Southern Bahia[10] are the following:

- Budgetary constraints
- Jurisdictional confusion
- Procedural inefficiencies
- Low technical capacity
- Lack of interagency cooperation

In calculating the ED for Southern Bahia, we had to make two generous assumptions. Data limitations[11] precluded the calculation of precise quantitative

**Table 28.1 Case Study 1**: Atlantic Forest, Bahia, Brazil

| Probability | | Value[8] | Cumulative Probability |
|---|---|---|---|
| Probability of detection given illegal logging/deforestation | $P_d$ | 1 | |
| Probability of citation given detection | $P_{a/d}$ | 1 | |
| Probability of prosecution given citation | $P_{p/a}$ | 0.51 | 0.51 |
| Probability of conviction given prosecution | $P_{c/p}$ | 0.16 | 0.082 |
| Average value of penalty | | $100.91 | |
| Average time elapsed (days) | $t$ | 451 | |
| Enforcement disincentive | $ED$ | $6.44 | |
| Profits to illegal logging/deforestation | | $75.00 | |

values for probability of detection and probability of citation upon detection. For this analysis, therefore, we assumed both those probabilities to be 100 percent. However, detailed qualitative analysis previously conducted in the region (Akella, Orlando, Araujo, and Cannon 2004) has clearly demonstrated that the probabilities are not that high in either case. The probability of detection is quite low owing to a number of factors including lack of public willingness to report environmental crimes, jurisdictional confusion, and lack of equipment and personnel. Likewise, probability of citation upon detection is low because detection agents often give warnings rather than writing up citations and, in some instances, may be bribed into 'overlooking' a detected illegal act. If calculated using the true probabilities of detection and citation upon detection, the ED would undoubtedly be much lower than the already paltry $6.44 calculated through this work.

These data show that the cumulative probability of an illegal act being penalized is only 0.082. However, this cumulative probability is also artificially high because we assumed the probabilities of detection and citation upon detection were both 1. In reality, the ultimate probability of a crime being penalized is far less than 0.082.

In this case, even with (assumed) 100 percent detection, the enforcement system is ineffectual at countering the incentives to log or deforest. In Bahia, only half of all detected offenses are prosecuted, and an even lower percentage of offenders are convicted. Penalties are relatively low, and the slow functioning of the system ensures that violators, even if sanctioned, do not 'pay' for their offenses until well after a year has passed – during which time they can continue to violate the law. In such circumstances, having outstanding detection would make very little difference. This case study validates the assertion that detection alone is not enforcement and that investments across the enforcement chain are necessary to make the system more effective.

The government's instinct has often been to spend any enforcement-strengthening money that becomes available on acquiring more cars and hiring more people for detection efforts. While those additions are undoubtedly important, our analysis suggests that the Bahian system's effectiveness would improve more through concurrent investments in other elements of the enforcement chain – training prosecutors and judges, for instance.

## Case Study 2: Chiapas, Mexico – The Selva Maya

**Environmental Violation Analyzed**: Illegal wildlife hunting and trade

**Scale of Crime**: Subsistence-level hunting

**Administrative or Judicial**: Administrative

**Components of the Enforcement Chain**: Detection, inquiry, processing, sanction, and penalty

**Agency Analyzed**: Federal Prosecutorial Service for Environmental Protection (Procuraduría Federal de Protección Ambiental – PROFEPA) (administrative process encompassing all steps)

540

The Mesoamerica Hotspot is the second richest global hotspot, in part because of its geographic position at the interface between North America and South and Central America and the Caribbean. The Selva Maya forms the northern part of the Mesoamerica Hotspot, occupying southeastern Mexico, northern Guatemala, and Belize. The Selva Maya is a unique mosaic of tropical ecosystems resulting from hundreds of years of management by the ancient Mayans. Its biodiversity significance stems from the presence of two major classes of tropical ecosystems: montane tropical forests and lowland rain forests. Those ecosystems incorporate populations of key endangered species, including the major remaining populations of *Tapirus bairdii* (Baird's tapir), the *Ara macao cyanoptera* (scarlet macaw), the *Agriocharis ocellata* (ocellated turkey), and a subspecies of the *Tayassu pecari ringens* (white-lipped peccary).

Wildlife biodiversity in the Selva Maya (including the above-named species) is severely threatened by hunting for bush meat and commercial trade. Mexico has an active internal trade in native wild parrots and other species. Mexican reptile and bird species are often exported illegally. Intense demographic pressure and poverty in the region are the primary underlying causes of wildlife hunting. The main focus of current conservation strategies in Selva Maya is on habitat conservation. However, hunting levels are giving rise to increasing concerns about the emergence of 'empty forests.'

In the Selva Maya, we hoped to focus on the activities of both small- and large-scale wildlife hunters and traders, using data on violations detected between 1999 and 2001. However, the records we found of wildlife hunting and trading cases that were initiated by PROFEPA during this time period were only for small-scale, subsistence-level hunting. Although large-scale commercial hunters and traders are quite active in the region, case records for commercial-scale wildlife hunting and trading activities were not found in local PROFEPA offices.

PROFEPA, a federal agency, is the primary authority dealing with wildlife violations in the Selva Maya. Mexican law allows for environmental violations to be handled through either a judicial process or an administrative process. In the judicial process, PROFEPA does the initial detection and inquiry and then passes the case on to the prosecutors of the Ministério Público (MP),

**Table 28.2 Case Study 2**: Selva Maya, Chiapas, Mexico

| Probability | | Value[12] | Cumulative Probability |
|---|---|---|---|
| Probability of detection given illegal wildlife hunting/trade | $P_d$ | 1 | |
| Probability of inquiry given detection | $P_{i/d}$ | 0.58 | 0.58 |
| Probability of processing given inquiry | $P_{p/i}$ | 0.69 | 0.4 |
| Probability of sanctions given processing | $P_{s/p}$ | 0.03 | 0.012 |
| Average value of penalty | | $545.47 | |
| Average time elapsed (days) | $t$ | 263 | |
| Enforcement disincentive | $ED$ | $5.66 | |
| Profits to illegal wildlife hunting/trade | | $191.57 | |

who process it and try it in court. However, our analysis found that the local PROFEPA office sends only 2 percent of wildlife hunting and trade cases on to the MP (i.e., the probability of prosecution[13] given detection is only 0.02). The reason, PROFEPA personnel suggest, is that the majority of the cases they handle have insufficient evidence to be useful to the MP (Conservation International – Selva Maya 2003).

Given the low percentage of cases that go through the judicial process, we focused our analysis on the administrative process instead. This administrative process – from detection through sanction – occurs wholly within PROFEPA, through its Judicial Area Sub-Delegation. Because PROFEPA chose to process the bulk of the wildlife violations in our sample administratively, this process was the most relevant one to analyze.

Averaging PROFEPA's data on the value of confiscations, we estimated the profits to illegal wildlife hunting and trade in the Selva Maya at $191.57 per trip. On the basis of available data, we found that the value of the enforcement disincentive generated by PROFEPA's administrative system is only $5.66.

Qualitative analysis showed that the main causes of ineffective enforcement in Selva Maya are the following:

• Inadequate and unclear laws governing wildlife hunting and trade
• Lack of technical capacity
• Scarcity of necessary equipment
• Poor collaboration among environmental enforcement agencies

Given the data constraints, we again made the generous assumption in this case that the probability of detection was 1. Again, qualitative research has demonstrated that this probability is most likely very low. The single fact that no files for cases of large-scale commercial wildlife hunting and trade were found exemplifies this. Even assuming perfect detection, analysis shows that the system does a very poor job of offsetting the incentives driving illegal hunting and trade.

Sadly, this assumption of perfect detection also means that the very low 0.012 cumulative probability of a crime resulting in sanctions is artificially high. In reality, given that the probability of detection is not really 1, the probability of sanction is even lower than 0.012.

It is evident that the most serious problems are at the point of sanctioning violators and imposing penalties. Only 0.03 of the cases that make it through the processing stage results in any sanction. When offenders know that – even if they are detected, investigated, and processed – the chances of their being sanctioned is so low, they are unlikely to take the threat of enforcement very seriously.

The particularly low probability of sanction given processing in this case may reflect a deliberate policy of weak enforcement, given the fact that those responsible for small-scale subsistence hunting are the poor and disadvantaged people who have few alternatives.

However, if this probability also applies in more serious cases, it is very troubling. The limitations of PROFEPA's data made it impossible to determine whether this same low rate of sanctions is prevalent in cases of commercial-scale wildlife hunting and trade. The low rate of detection of large-scale wildlife operations, combined with a low rate of sanctions, could mean that this system presents virtually no deterrent to lucrative commercial wildlife hunting and trade.

## Case Study 3: Indonesia – Papua Province

**Environmental Violation Analyzed**: Mostly the shipment of illegal logs

**Scale of Crime**: Average nearly 2,000 m³ of logs per crime

**Administrative or Judicial**: Judicial

**Components of the Enforcement Chain**: Detection, investigation, police review, prosecution, conviction, and penalty

**Agencies Analyzed**: Provincial Office for Natural Resources Conservation (Balai Konservasi Sumber Daya Alam – BKSDA) (detection and investigation); Provincial Forestry Service (Dinas Kehutanan) (detection and investigation); military (detection); customs (detection); police (detection, investigation, and review); Ministry of Forestry (detection, investigation); Attorney General (prosecution); Ministry of Justice (conviction and penalty)

Papua Province, Indonesia, is the western half of the island of New Guinea. The island forms one of the world's last three mega-diversity tropical wildernesses and, as such, is a global priority for biodiversity conservation. Papua Province also has the largest remaining forest areas in Indonesia and is the source of an increasingly significant amount of Indonesia's logs and timber products. However, it is now one of the major areas of commercial-scale illegal logging in Indonesia.

**Table 28.3 Case Study 3**: Papua Province, Indonesia

| Probability | | Value[14] | Cumulative Probability |
|---|---|---|---|
| Probability of detection given illegal logging | $P_d$ | 0.032 | |
| Probability of investigation given detection | $P_{i/d}$ | 0.68 | 0.022 |
| Probability of police review given investigation | $P_{r/i}$ | 0.684 | 0.018 |
| Probability of prosecution given police review | $P_{p/r}$ | 0.41 | 0.007 |
| Probability of conviction given prosecution[15] | $P_{c/p}$ | 0.85 | 0.006 |
| Average value of penalty | | $1,197.00[16] | |
| Average time elapsed (days) | $t$ | 269 | |
| Enforcement disincentive | $ED$ | $6.47[17] | |
| Profits to illegal logging | | $91,967.36 | |

Commercial-scale illegal logging comes in various forms and is carried out by a variety of actors. The illegal activity of greatest concern occurs in areas where logging is not permitted (e.g., watershed protection forests, protected areas) and is linked to companies with licenses to log areas nearby. Those companies may carry out the logging themselves, subcontract to smaller local companies, or simply buy logs without obtaining appropriate papers to demonstrate legality.

Although large-scale illegal logging is taking place, little evidence was found of enforcement efforts in the forest. This absence is largely because of the low numbers of rangers available to carry out patrols. Instead, most enforcement efforts are targeted at interdicting large shipments of logs that are not accompanied by the correct paperwork (either because the logs were illegally cut or because they were being smuggled out to avoid taxes and fees). Hence, the example presented here generally concerns the enforcement of shipping large quantities of illegal timber out of Papua on large ships.[18] Because of the large volumes involved, the values in this example are a few orders of magnitude larger than those in earlier examples. Although such illegal acts can be considered either crimes or administrative violations, most were treated as criminal cases. Our analysis shows that although the profits to logging in this case are close to $100,000, the value of the disincentive presented by the enforcement regime is under $7. Put one way, if only the fine is considered, the incentives are approximately 14,000 times larger than the disincentives to illegally log in Papua.[19]

Qualitative analysis demonstrated that ineffective enforcement in Papua can be largely attributed to the following:

• Overlapping and inconsistent laws governing logging
• Lack of coordination between agencies and between local, provincial, and central offices of single agencies
• Inadequate budgetary resources
• Insufficient numbers of trained forest investigators
• Lack of incentives for effective performance

While corruption and lack of political will are major reasons for poor compliance with forestry and nature conservation laws in Indonesia, this study focused on the technical reasons for poor enforcement (for reasons explained earlier).

The cumulative probability of being convicted of illegal timber shipping in Papua is only 0.006. This number is more realistic than the cumulative probabilities calculated for the Bahia and Selva Maya sites, because the probability of detection was not assumed to be 1 in this site.

The probability of detection in this case appears extraordinarily low in comparison to the other probabilities associated with steps in the enforcement system. If our estimate of total quantity of illegal logging is correct, then improving detection is the topmost priority in this case.[20] Detection is low because of the lack of rangers, as noted previously, but also because few people are willing to appear as witnesses or inform enforcement authorities when they detect forest crime. People are hesitant to come forward because enforcement agencies do not do enough to protect witnesses and informants from suspects. Furthermore, people believe the enforcement agencies are corrupt or incompetent and will not use the information properly or effectively

Relatively speaking, investigation, police review, prosecution, and conviction are being done well, although there is still room for improvement. It is important to remember that the other probabilities, while higher, are still too low for the system to function effectively even if detection is improved significantly, given the size of penalties imposed. Hence, it is not appropriate to focus all available resources on improving detection alone. Raising the probability of detection to 1 in this case would bring the enforcement disincentive[21] only up to roughly $200 – larger than the current disincentive, but still an inadequate deterrent. Without larger penalties, confiscation of logs and equipment, and improvements in the other enforcement steps, illegal logging will continue to be lucrative.

It is commonly suggested that raising fines can fix poor compliance, because it is thought that if the fine is higher, violators will be deterred from breaking the law. While it is true that higher penalties do present a greater deterrent, the effects of increasing penalty size are diminished by the low probability of actually being penalized. Three findings emerge from this observation. First, weaknesses in the enforcement system need to be fixed if large penalties are to translate into effective deterrents. Second, when the probability of actually being penalized is low, the size of the penalty required to create a deterrent becomes very large (in this case the penalty would need to be raised to many millions of dollars). Third, the required size of penalty can quickly exceed what is politically or culturally viable, meaning other enforcement steps must be strengthened for realistically sized penalties to create an effective deterrent.

### Case Study 4: Palawan, Philippines – The Calamianes Islands

**Environmental Violation Analyzed**: Illegal fishing with dynamite and cyanide

**Scale of Crime**: Small-scale illegal fishing by local communities and seasonal fishermen in municipal waters and areas of ancestral domain

**Administrative or Judicial**: Judicial

**Components of the Enforcement Chain**: Detection, arrest, filing, prosecution, conviction, and penalty

**Agencies Analyzed**: Philippines National Police (PNP) Maritime Unit (detection, arrest, filing, sometimes prosecution); Philippines National Coast Guard (detection, arrest, filing); public prosecutors (prosecution); municipal and regional courts (conviction and penalty)

Northern Palawan's marine environment is particularly rich in biodiversity. The region's Calamianes Islands form part of the 'coral triangle,' which supports the world's richest coastal marine biodiversity. The productivity of the waters of Northern Palawan was once incredibly high. However, those fishing grounds are now considered depleted because of overfishing. With the reported dwindling catches and high international demand for the live reef fish trade (LRFT), many fishers have shifted to more destructive methods.

Cyanide and dynamite fishing for the LRFT have resulted in the deterioration of critical coral reef habitat. Illegal trade of live fish species such as the *Cheilinus undulatus* (Napoleon wrasse) and the *Cromileptes altivelis* (barramundi cod) seriously threatens their survival. Although fisheries jurisprudence in the Philippines is considered good, effective enforcement of fisheries laws has remained a pronounced challenge.

While local villagers often identify seasonal fishermen and neighboring villages for illegal fishing, interviews with key informants have revealed that community members also participate in cyanide and dynamite fishing. High international demand for live fish makes destructive fishing a lucrative source of income for fishermen (Mayo-Anda, Dalabajan, and Lasmarias 2004).

In Palawan, CI worked closely with a local partner, the Environmental Legal Assistance Center (ELAC).[23] Our work focused on cyanide and dynamite fishing cases that had occurred between 1999 and 2002. Thus, we examined the effectiveness of the judicial process that began with detection by the PNP Maritime Unit or the Coast Guard,[24] then passed through the public prosecutors or chiefs of police acting as prosecutors, and ended with final resolution in the courts system.

Detailed economic and livelihood analysis of the LRFT conducted by Conservation International (Conservation International – Philippines 2002) calculated the profits to cyanide and dynamite fishing at $70.57 per trip. The enforcement economics analysis demonstrates that the value of the disincentive generated by the enforcement regime is only $0.09, or virtually zero.

Qualitative analysis identified the following factors as being the primary causes of ineffective enforcement in the Calamianes:

- Low infrastructure capacity
- Low technical capacity
- Procedural inefficiencies
- Lack of interagency coordination
- Lack of incentives for effective performance

**Table 28.4 Case Study 4**: Calamianes Islands, Palawan, Philippines

| Probability | | Value[22] | Cumulative Probability |
|---|---|---|---|
| Probability of detection given cyanide/ dynamite fishing | $P_d$ | 0.062 | |
| Probability of arrest given detection | $P_{a/d}$ | 0.003 | 0.00019 |
| Probability of filing given arrest | $P_{f/a}$ | 0.85 | 0.00016 |
| Probability of prosecution given filing | $P_{p/f}$ | 0.62 | 0.0001 |
| Probability of conviction given prosecution | $P_{c/p}$ | 0.24 | 0.00002 |
| Average value of penalty | | $4,463.32 | |
| Average time elapsed (days) | $t$ | 210 | |
| Enforcement disincentive | $ED$ | $0.09 | |
| Profits to cyanide/dynamite fishing | | $70.57 | |

The cumulative probability of someone being convicted of illegal dynamite or cyanide fishing in the Calamianes is very low at only 0.00002. As in the Papua case, the fact that no assumption was made about the probability of detection makes this cumulative probability more realistic.

The numbers for probability of arrest given detection and probability of filing given arrest merit some specific attention, because they are particularly interesting. Examination of the two probabilities demonstrates the importance of gathering qualitative information that can help interpret and judge the accuracy of the quantitative results. The very low probability of arrest upon detection is troubling not only because it is so low but also because the system's corruption appears to be embedded in this low probability. Many detection records indicated that a violator had been caught at sea and his equipment and catch had been confiscated but that the violator had escaped before an arrest could be made. Given the confiscation of equipment – including the boat – escape would seem implausible. It seems more likely that this low rate of arrest reflects bribery of arresting officers by dynamite and cyanide fishers. If we consider this information, the relatively high probability of filing given arrest, seems less impressive. While the 0.85 probability calculated from our sample may lead to the conclusion that filing does happen a majority of the time, the number of cases making it past arrest to the filing stage is minimal. Furthermore, qualitative data indicate that the filing process is so rife with issues that filing generally does not happen within the time frame prescribed by law.

One of the enforcement-strengthening strategies developed in the Palawan case is worth mentioning, because it is different from the strategies developed through our work in other places. In the rest of our sites, we focused on fixing the existing enforcement system. In the Philippines, this was not our focus. In our discussions with enforcement personnel from PNP Maritime Unit and the Coast Guard, as well as with prosecutors, it became clear that enforcement of illegal fishing was not viewed as a top priority for those agencies. Their multiple responsibilities – which encompass not only environmental issues but also customs and immigration issues, as well as generally maintaining peace and order – made it difficult to justify devoting additional personnel and resources to enforcement against destructive fishing in local waters.[25] In that situation, it was questionable whether funneling resources into those agencies would improve the enforcement system.

However, we found that local governments and communities had a strong interest in ensuring that illegal fishing rules were enforced in municipal waters or in areas of ancestral domain. Therefore, it seemed that dedicating resources to developing a co-management approach to fisheries enforcement would be a more appropriate and successful means of achieving better enforcement in the Calamianes.

Philippines federal law allows for (1) citizens' arrest of environmental violators and (2) establishment of administrative adjudication bodies at the municipal level, which are empowered to handle such violations administratively – confiscating equipment, holding offenders, and charging small fines. In the fishing municipalities of the Calamianes, politicians and citizens alike have an interest in seeing the productivity of their waters protected. They also share an interest in seeing outsiders and other violators punished for destructive fishing practices.

Rather than trying to improve the judicial process that has handled these cases to date, we decided to invest in helping establish detection, apprehension, and adjudication functions within the municipalities. Our partner ELAC is currently working with local authorities in three municipalities to write and pass municipal fishing ordinances; training community members and citizens groups in detection and apprehension; and working with municipal authorities, civil society groups, NGOs, and community leaders to form municipal adjudication bodies comprising representatives from each of those sectors.

National-level policy work will also be necessary to ensure the effectiveness of the adjudication bodies. For instance, current laws dictate that the maximum monetary penalty that a municipal adjudication body can charge is PhP 2,500 (US$50). Furthermore, the law mandates that any fines collected by the adjudication bodies are not remitted to the municipality but rather go into the Philippines National Treasury. The effectiveness of municipal adjudication bodies will be augmented if (1) they are allowed to assign higher administrative penalties to offenders, and (2) if collected penalties, or some percentage of them, are retained locally to finance municipal-level enforcement efforts.

The value of this example is that it suggests that in some instances – when enforcement performance is poor and there is little support for fixing it – it may be useful to explore the viability of alternative enforcement systems.

## Synthesis of results and global lessons learned

A number of site-specific problems were found in each country where the enforcement economics analysis was conducted. Site-specific action plans were developed to address them. Those action plans are currently being used to help implement enforcement-strengthening activities in those countries.

Another contribution of the enforcement economics case studies – and the one discussed here – was that they allowed us to identify five key weaknesses that were present across the four sites. Our discussions with global enforcement experts have confirmed that the common challenges identified in our work exist in many countries of biodiversity importance. Understanding the lessons learned in a generalized sense can be a useful way to begin incorporating enforcement strengthening into global conservation strategies.

This section will present the five most important common challenges that we found in our sites:

1 Poor interagency cooperation
2 Inadequate budgetary resources
3 Technical deficiencies in laws, agency policies, and procedures
4 Insufficient technical skills and knowledge
5 Lack of performance monitoring and adaptive management systems

As noted earlier, carrying out this work in close partnership with the enforcement agencies themselves has resulted in a focus on largely technical measures. However, successfully tackling the challenges will have a positive effect on other challenges not explicitly listed, such as corruption (e.g., through improving agency resources, streamlining procedures, promoting interagency cooperation and supervision). While not all necessary enforcement-strengthening activities are captured, the ones discussed here are all essential if enforcement is to be strengthened successfully.

Each issue will be described in detail and discussed as we draw on site-level examples, as well as on information gathered by talking to global enforcement experts.

### Challenge 1: poor interagency cooperation

In the countries studied, we found that the multiple agencies charged with enforcement rarely communicate nor are they mandated (by policy or law) to do so. This lack of integration is both horizontal and vertical – that is to say, the various agencies involved in a single step of the enforcement chain do not coordinate with one another, much less with agencies responsible for other steps of the enforcement chain. For instance, prosecutors make little effort to work with detection agents in building cases, even when their own understanding of environmental law or detection agency procedures is limited. And judges do not consult with any other agencies to gather information on damages caused that might help assess appropriate penalties.

This poor coordination occurs in part because individual agencies have little incentive to work more closely together. Individual agencies most often perform their function in the enforcement chain in isolation. If their performance is checked at all, it is also in isolation. The effectiveness of the enforcement system as a whole is rarely considered. Although overall performance is greatly enhanced when agencies collaborate and act as a system, this collaboration rarely happens. Getting agencies to collaborate in this way may often require formal instructions to do so from local and national political leaders. Even when individual agencies fully understand the holistic nature of enforcement or their role in the system, their authority is limited to their own function. The inefficiencies that result from poor coordination are significant, as the following examples demonstrate. For this reason, persuading agencies to think and act holistically, as a system, is a useful step forward.[26]

#### Jurisdictional confusion

The enforcement economics analyses revealed that jurisdictional confusion is common among detection agencies, prosecutorial services, and even courts. With respect to detection, this jurisdictional confusion often results in important areas having no routine detection activities. In Southern Bahia, the federal and state detection agencies were unclear on which areas and which types of crimes were within whose jurisdiction. As a result, each agency tended to decide that the other agency was most likely responsible. Thus, some of the most important repositories of biodiversity in the region were largely ignored.[27]

The same failure happened in Palawan, where both the Philippines National Police Maritime Unit and the Coast Guard insisted that the same areas fell under the jurisdiction of the other agency. The failure of detection agencies to clarify jurisdictional confusion and coordinate activities so that priority areas are patrolled has a substantial effect on quality of detection. Detection is weak for many reasons, but the contribution of jurisdictional confusion between detection agencies is often overlooked.

Similar problems exist in prosecutorial services and courts. Because detection agencies have a limited understanding of how prosecutors are organized, citations or case files are often misdirected. In Brazil, for instance, we found that case files that should have gone to state prosecutors were being sent to federal prosecutors, and vice versa. Because federal and state prosecutors have little interaction, no efficient procedure existed for getting case files to the right prosecutor. The result was that case files would remain in limbo and unprocessed for long periods of time, sometimes exceeding the statute of limitations.

In the Philippines, this same type of situation occurred because detection agents and prosecutors were uncertain as to which courts should handle which cases,[28] and they would frequently file cases in the wrong courts. This misfiling either would delay prosecution of the case or would result in files being mishandled or lost.

Jurisdictional confusion causes poor detection, failure to prosecute, and lengthy delays in the time it takes for cases to get through the system. This lack of clarity is not the result of some great complexity in how jurisdiction is assigned; it comes from a simple lack of information. It seems likely that such situations could be easily resolved if agencies communicated better and reached a working consensus on questions of jurisdiction and collaboration.

*Procedural inefficiencies*

The lack of interagency cooperation generates procedural inefficiencies that undermine the effectiveness of enforcement. Agencies that rarely interact cannot develop strategies for streamlining their handling of environmental violations. As a consequence, procedural issues can compromise the proper and timely functioning of the enforcement system.

In Papua Province, Indonesia, the political processes of decentralization and special autonomy have reorganized the reporting lines that used to connect local-level forestry services to the Ministry of Forestry. Regardless of the merits of such a process, one unintended result has been the breakdown of information flows between regency (local), provincial, and central forestry units. The result is that the provincial forestry department is often unaware of many of the cases being handled at the regency level, and the Ministry of Forestry is unaware of many of the cases of illegal logging that have been detected in Papua. This lack of information can greatly impede the probability of arrest in cases of, for instance, illegal log shipments, given that the Ministry of Forestry still finances joint operations with the navy and needs information to decide where to carry out operations. In a few cases, local enforcement agencies were not aware of the illegal logging cases that were identified by the Ministry of Forestry.

Also in Papua Province, efforts to reduce some time-consuming procedural inefficiencies have been compromised by agency politics. Standard forest rangers are not qualified to carry out investigations and must call in the police. For all crimes, the police are the primary investigation agents who collect the evidence and present it to prosecutors. Given the workload of the police, there are often delays in investigating forest crime cases. In the interest of improved efficiency, a mechanism was set up whereby forest rangers could undertake investigations as Forest Civil Investigators (FCIs). To become an FCI, a forest ranger must undergo special training from the police in carrying out investigations, must get a decree that is from the Ministry of Forestry and is endorsed by both the police and attorney general headquarters in Jakarta, and must submit that decree to the Ministry of Justice in order to receive an FCI license. A ranger qualified as an FCI can, in theory, investigate forest crimes under the supervision of regency police and can work directly with prosecutors. However, the police have not been entirely comfortable with the new arrangements and have sought to retain their role as primary investigators and intermediaries between forest rangers and prosecutors. Although many rangers have received training to become an FCI, few have successfully gotten their license from the Ministry of Justice. If the FCI mechanism cannot be made to work, then some alternative is needed for reducing delays in investigations.

The situation in Southern Bahia provides another example of procedural inefficiency. In that region, upon detecting a violation and writing up a citation, the detection agency IBAMA – rather than directly handing over the case to the prosecutor in the locale of the crime – would send the citation to IBAMA's nearest regional office. The regional office would, in turn, send the file to IBAMA's state headquarters in the capital, Salvador. IBAMA in Salvador would then send it to the MP's state headquarters in Salvador, who would send it to the appropriate regional MP office,[29] who would then pass it on to the prosecutor in the locale of the crime. The case began in the locale of the crime and ended there – yet, in between, it would pass through as many as six offices in three cities. The results of this time-consuming voyage were significant – cases would get 'lost' (unintentionally or intentionally); prosecution would be delayed; and, in some instances, the three-year statute of limitations was exceeded, making prosecution impossible.

Again, the convoluted or unclear procedures are not necessary; they simply have not been clarified or improved upon. Simple discussion among upper management of agencies across the enforcement chain could result in more efficient procedures that would improve the effectiveness and timeliness of the enforcement system.

### Weak cases

Poor collaboration between agencies charged with different enforcement functions often precludes prosecutors from building effective cases and prosecuting them successfully. Analysis showed that often prosecutors – even those with little understanding of environmental law and environmental crime – would not consult with detection agents or inspectors to inform themselves of the details of the case. For their part, detection agents and investigators, if they fail to consult with prosecutors, are often unaware of what information or evidence is necessary for building strong cases. Weak cases are unlikely to result in convictions and present a serious obstacle to enforcement effectiveness.

In Brazil, we found that many cases are never prosecuted for lack of adequate evidence to support the charge being made. In issuing citations, detection agents are required to record name of the offender, locale of the crime, and nature of the crime. However, they often fail to provide important supporting information – reports from witnesses, photographic evidence, and the like – making it difficult or even impossible for prosecutors to argue cases successfully. In both Indonesia and Mexico, inadequate quality of evidence was commonly cited as a reason for police not sending cases to prosecutors or for prosecutors deciding not to submit cases to court. Although lack of technical capacity (training in quality of evidence) is certainly partly to blame, so too is the lack of interagency communication, which means detection and investigation agencies are not aware what the next agency up the 'chain' is looking for.

Lack of information on the prosecutor's part can lead to poorly argued cases. In one case from the south of Bahia, IBAMA agents detected trucks that were illegally transporting logs, confiscated the equipment and timber, and filed citations with the appropriate prosecutor's office. Unfortunately, the public prosecutor allegedly did not know that a notice of equipment confiscation is usually accompanied by a citation for an environmental violation. The defense attorneys appeared in court with only the confiscation notices, the prosecutor did not link the confiscation to an environmental violation, and the judge returned the trucks with no penalty.

The anecdotal evidence from all four countries and from people working on enforcement globally is full of stories of cases that were unsuccessful because of insufficient evidence or poor prosecution. Many cases might have turned out differently had the detection agents or investigators known what evidence a prosecutor would need, and had the prosecutor understood what information the detection agency could provide. But in the countries we studied, this type of consultation is not required and is unlikely to happen organically. As a result, cases that may have otherwise served as enforcement success stories have ended up being examples of what not to do.

### Challenge 2: inadequate budgetary resources

In each of the case study sites, inadequate resources compromise the ability of detection and investigation agencies, prosecutorial services, and the judiciary to fulfill their enforcement responsibilities effectively. The personnel and infrastructure issues generated by persistently low levels of funding can be observed across the enforcement chain.

Low salaries for detection and investigation positions make them unappealing to highly qualified applicants. As a result, the education level of many agents is quite low. While limited schooling does not necessarily preclude them from being excellent field agents, it may lead to inefficiencies in the handling of paperwork or the preparation of cases. The low salaries, combined with a lack of recognition or reward structures, may also contribute to high incidence of corruption or bribe-taking among field agents. As described, the enforcement economics analyses did not explicitly address corruption. However, anecdotal evidence from all four sites indicates that corruption is considered a major obstacle to effective enforcement.

The personnel and equipment shortages that result from budget limitations also affect enforcement quality. A lack of human resources makes it difficult for detection and investigation agencies to adequately cover critical ecosystems. In Bahia, for instance, two detection agents with one car between them were charged with all detection activities in a critical 72-municipality, 200-square-kilometer area at the time of our study.

In Papua Province, the police are the lead agency charged with investigating forest crimes. The police are overworked and do not have the necessary training in forestry law to be able to investigate the more technical infringements effectively. The advent of forest rangers trained as investigators could remedy both capacity and training problems, but too few such trained FCIs are currently in Papua. During the time this research was being carried out, there were only three FCIs in the whole province (approximately 1 for every 15 million hectares).

This issue affects the likelihood and success of prosecution and conviction. In Palawan, biodiversity-rich municipalities – by virtue of being remote – do not have full-time prosecutors or judges. Proceeding with a case, therefore, implies filing cases with the prosecutor in Puerto Princesa. Because reaching Puerto Princesa requires either a lengthy boat journey or an expensive plane journey, we found that many cases were not being filed at all. Detection agencies, already low on equipment, could not spare their limited boats, and financial resources for flying were unavailable. As a result, cases either were falling out of the system altogether or were being poorly handled by undertrained chiefs of police acting as prosecutors.

In Southern Bahia, budget shortfalls have led to the closure of many rural prosecutorial offices and courts in municipalities of conservation importance. Consequently, environmental cases from those municipalities cannot be processed or judged until substitute prosecutors and judges pass through once every six months or longer. Because substitutes must handle all types of cases when they arrive, environmental cases are often not prioritized and go unprocessed during the substitute's rotation. If this omission happens more than once, the likelihood is high that the three-year statute of limitation will be exceeded so that the case can no longer be prosecuted. In the rural offices and courts that have remained open, the lack of basic infrastructure such as computers has complicated efforts to handle and track cases efficiently. In the Selva Maya, PROFEPA reports that its limited number of PROFEPA prosecutors are severely overworked, each handling an insurmountable number of case files. According to the agency, this major factor contributes to the poor performance of prosecutors in building and presenting cases.

Another important consequence of insufficient budgets is that enforcement agencies are unable to provide the specific environmental training or ongoing capacity-building programs that could significantly improve enforcement performance of their personnel. The effects of poor capacity, as well as field-based examples of those effects, are more amply discussed in subsequent sections.

Perhaps the most important overarching consequence of inadequate budget resources is that shortfalls make implementing new strategies to improve enforcement performance very difficult. While it is certainly true that the resources available to enforcement agencies are not always being used efficiently, it is equally true that any concerted overhaul of enforcement performance will require far more funding than what is currently available. Without greater financial resources, therefore, it seems unlikely that lasting change in enforcement systems will be possible.

### Challenge 3: technical deficiencies in laws, agency policies, and procedures

The legitimacy of environmental laws and the fairness of their enforcement are key factors that affect the weakness of enforcement and the success of strengthening activities, as discussed previously. This study, however, did not assess the legitimacy or fairness of laws. Rather, it focused on technical failings of the laws themselves (i.e., lack of clarity in the laws being enforced, disproportionately low penalties, or ambiguity in sentencing guidance). This study also examined technical weaknesses in the laws and procedures governing how the enforcement system operates.

Effective enforcement is undermined when the laws the system is meant to uphold are unclear. Likewise, when internal enforcement agency policies do not support effective enforcement, the action of those agencies is bound to be less than optimal. Analysis of the enforcement systems in our case study sites demonstrates that although clear laws and good policies are fundamental to guaranteeing the deterrent value of an enforcement regime, these laws and policies are often lacking.

*Legal framework*
Weak legislation can take many forms. In some instances, the law may not clearly define what constitutes an environmental crime, or it may be inconsistent in its treatment of comparable violations (illegal hunting vs. illegal fishing, for instance). The Selva Maya case study provides a telling example of this type of weakness. '[Mexico's] General Law on Ecological Balance and Environmental Protection (LGEEPA) defines wild flora and fauna, in sections XVII and XVIII. However, due to the lack of definition of wild flora and fauna in the constitution and the fact that no clear definition of species exists, their legal standing is not clear. This lack of clarity is important given that clearly defined concepts indicating to which goods the regulations apply are key ... [to determining the] appropriation and [use] of these resources. If this clarity does not exist, there is room for diverse interpretations of the law and regulations, which creates legal loopholes that make enforcement efforts difficult' (Reuter and Habel 2004).

Brazil's progressive Law of Environmental Crime of 1998, although poorly implemented, provides a positive example of a strong national environmental law. This law consolidates legislation regarding most environmental violations – which had previously been scattered in diverse special laws – under one legal statute, thereby ensuring internally consistent treatment of diverse

554

violations. Furthermore, because this federal law explicitly characterizes which acts constitute 'environmental crimes,' it provides a much stronger basis for legal action than the prior penal structure.

Clear roles and mandates for agencies charged with enforcement of environmental legislation may not be established in the law. This situation can compromise the enforcement agencies' ability to execute their functions or, to the contrary, can provide them with legal cover to avoid their responsibilities. In Bahia, for instance, the division of enforcement responsibilities between federal and state detection agencies was established in a 'Federative Pact.' Although the pact was agreed to by all parties, it did not carry the weight of law. As a result, when the federal and state agencies – whose activities it was meant to govern – did not deliver on their enforcement responsibilities, they did so without facing any substantial penalty or sanctions. The successful use of the Philippines' law allowing for citizens' arrests of environmental violators provides a positive example of how a clear mandate can empower agencies or even civil society to enforce natural resource regulations.

Laws established at different levels (i.e., federal, state, and local) may be overlapping or contradictory, thereby undoing one another. In Papua Province, Indonesia, the political legislative processes of decentralization and special autonomy handed the powers over production forests to the provincial and regency (local) governments. Although the law decentralizing power did require that local laws conform with various national laws, the Ministry of Forestry did not do enough to make local authorities fully aware of all aspects of the new laws. Consequently, the newly empowered local officials drafted legislation and issued permits largely as they saw fit, often failing to comply with the requirements of national laws. The result is logging operations that are legal according to local permits, but illegal under national law. This confusion creates a significant 'gray area' in the law that must be reformed (Patlis 2002).

Either the penalty structures for environmental crimes may not be clearly defined by law or the penalties prescribed by law may be so low that they neither compensate for damages nor contribute to a credible deterrent. Weaknesses in the penalty prescriptions were found across the countries studied. As described earlier, Philippines law allows for establishing municipal-level adjudication bodies to handle environmental violations administratively. But it then limits the effectiveness of those administrative adjudication bodies by setting the maximum fine they can charge at PhP 2,500, or US$50. Brazil's Law of Environmental Crime is explicit in describing the appropriate penalties for violations of different magnitudes. However, it also allows judges to apply 'alternative sentences,' but it provides no clear guidelines for how alternative sentences should be set. In Bahia, that lack of clarity results in judges applying extremely low alternative penalties or penalties that are not commensurate with the level of damage done to the environment.

*Internal Agency Policies*
Of course, even strong laws cannot be effectively enforced when internal enforcement agency policies do not support good performance.

For instance, budget allocation policies contribute significantly to weaknesses in overall enforcement. The effects of persistent low levels of funding on the performance by detection and investigation agencies, prosecutors, and judges have already been described. In the sites studied, the lack of good policies regarding periodic training, interagency collaboration, or performance monitoring was also troubling. The absence of such policies underscores the point that enforcement agencies fail to incorporate these important components of effective enforcement into their operations.

### Challenge 4: insufficient technical skills and knowledge

One factor hampering the effectiveness of the enforcement regimes studied was inadequate technical capacity across the enforcement chain. Although personnel shortages caused by budget shortfalls were often lamented, enforcement agencies in the sites studied were relatively less concerned with the technical skills of existing personnel. As noted earlier, greater budgetary resources might permit more training or salaries high enough to attract higher-caliber employees. However, when the training offered to staff members is insufficient, having more insufficiently trained staffers is unlikely to improve performance. Although having more enforcement agency staff members would no doubt help, increasing their individual technical skills and knowledge is also critical.

Detection agents, investigators, prosecutors, and judges in the study sites all had limitations in their individual skills and knowledge that might have been remedied through periodic or even one-time intensive training, but had not been. Instead, detection agents receive limited training at the beginning of their careers, if at all, and prosecutors and judges are rarely up-to-date on environmental law or policy. If and when some training was given, each agency generally trained its own, without the benefit of cross-fertilization that incorporating other enforcement agencies in the capacity-building process might have provided. The effect of this weak capacity is self-evident – when the enforcement actors do their jobs poorly because they lack the skills they need, the enforcement system cannot function effectively.

#### Detection agents and investigators

Effective detection requires a variety of skills, and the job of a detection agent or investigator can be challenging. Individual agents must know enough law to identify an environmental violation, must be able to accurately assess the nature of a crime as well as the species and ecosystems involved, and must be adept at collecting evidence and doing paperwork so that prosecutors are well equipped in court. The detection and investigation agencies must also know how to plan patrols, mount proactive investigations, and help prosecutors build strong cases.

Sadly, because of a lack of investment in human capital, detection agents and investigators in the countries we studied lacked many skills. In Bahia, we found various citations on which detection agents had made errors – for instance, in describing the crime or assessing the nature of the crime – that made prosecution impossible. In Selva Maya, detection agents had difficulty telling the difference between endangered and not endangered wildlife, and they could not identify violations as a consequence. This limitation affected success in latter steps of the enforcement chain. For instance, PROFEPA investigators work primarily on forest crime but have limited understanding of wildlife issues. Even though wildlife hunting and trafficking are major threats, very few capacity-building opportunities are offered for these themes. Interviews revealed that PROFEPA inspectors who had been working five to seven years had received at most two training courses in that time, not necessarily on these topics. Because there is inadequate wildlife expertise, when specialists' reports on wildlife are requested by the MP, they are often written by forestry experts. In many instances, the resulting reports either are poorly formulated or incorrectly identify species, making their utility to MP prosecutors negligible.

In many instances, quality of evidence gathered initially was very poor. By the time a case got to prosecution, there was no longer any way to prove the crime. In Bahia, public prosecutors recounted instances in which the evidence submitted by IBAMA was insufficient, but it could not be improved by the time of prosecution because, for instance, (1) a deforested virgin forest patch would already be grown over with secondary vegetation, or (2) a sawmill would have been dismantled and moved elsewhere, leaving no evidence.

Detection agents often lacked the skills to think strategically about optimizing use of limited resources to ensure targeted efforts focused on priority areas and threats. For instance, the fact that PROFEPA in the Selva Maya shows a number of subsistence hunting cases but no wildlife trafficking cases, when wildlife trafficking is known to be a major problem in the region, is telling. Unless PROFEPA agents are able to act strategically to make linkages from the 'subsistence' hunters they encounter to the real drivers of the wildlife trade, their work will be ineffectual in stemming biodiversity loss. This study indicates that they currently lack the technical skills necessary to work at this level and, consequently, are having little effect on the most damaging problem.

Detection and investigation agencies are not giving their personnel the training that they need to be highly effective in their jobs. Clearly, there are many reasons: limited financial resources, restricted internal technical expertise, and so on. When people think about fixing detection of illegal forest clearing, for example, they most often argue for high-tech solutions involving satellites and remote sensing capacities. While remote sensing can be a cost-effective way of detecting infringements across large regions (and of special value when the areas are remote and not patrolled), it is not sufficient for strengthening enforcement unless the resources and capabilities to use the information effectively are available. Our work indicates that complementary investments are needed to build the capacity of enforcement agencies' human capital. In some – perhaps most – situations, investments in training the existing staff members could have an equally impressive effect on quality of detection. Furthermore, the work of capacitated detection agencies and investigators would surely guarantee better success in the latter steps of the enforcement system, further contributing to systemic effectiveness.

*Prosecutors*

Capacity issues compromise the quality of environmental crime prosecution. In most of the countries we studied, there are no specific prosecutors for the environment. Rather, prosecutors are expected to handle all types of cases – from heinous crimes to petty theft to environmental violations. They receive little training in environmental law and are, therefore, unable to handle environmental cases well. To be effective, prosecutors require more than just a sound understanding of environmental law and its advances. They must also be knowledgeable about detection agency procedures and capabilities, so that they can maximize the information they have to work with. Furthermore, they must be able to determine what evidence is needed to make a strong argument in an environmental crime case, so that they can instruct detection agents and investigators who are helping build the case. Finally, they must understand the concept of compensation of environmental damages, so that they can make appropriate penalty recommendations to judges.

Examples demonstrating that prosecutors neither understand detection agency procedure nor have the skills necessary to guide the process of evidence collection have already been presented. The effect of prosecutors' limited capacity to build and present strong cases is clearly demonstrated by results from the case study sites. For instance, in Selva Maya, one of the major factors contributing to lengthy processing times in PROFEPA's administrative process is poor prosecutorial performance. Even though PROFEPA assigns specific prosecutors to handle environmental cases exclusively, they are responsible for all different types of environmental crimes. They also lack the environmental law training necessary to execute this responsibility effectively.

Analysis shows that case arguments and penalty recommendations sent by PROFEPA prosecutors to the Judicial Area Subdelegate for final approval are frequently returned to the prosecutors without approval because of inadequacies in how the cases are presented. In many instances, cases were returned because the subdelegate felt that the arguments written were not well founded in legislation, that the cases had been poorly drawn up, or that suggested sanctions were inadequate. When a case would be returned to the prosecutors, their excessive workload would result in those cases falling to the bottom of the list of priorities, delaying proper presentation and final approval of the sanction by the subdelegate.

Poor training and lack of prosecutorial technical capacity significantly undermine the performance of an enforcement regime. In the prevailing climate in the countries studied – where prosecutors have limited training on environmental law and are responsible for handling cases related to every type of crime – improving prosecutor performance will prove difficult. However, dedicating specific effort to building a core base of capacitated prosecutors who can work with detection agencies to build strong cases, and who can present compelling cases and appropriate sentencing recommendations to judges, could measurably improve the performance of enforcement overall.

*Judges*

Like the other agencies involved in the enforcement system, the judiciary's capacity deficit on environmental issues compromises the quality of enforcement performance. In part, this weakness results from the fact that, like prosecutors, judges are responsible for hearing all types of cases, and they receive no special training in environmental law. This issue may even be more pronounced among the members of the judiciary than among prosecutors. In Brazil, for instance, while the Ministério Público (the ministry that houses public prosecutors) has made some effort in recent years to draw attention to environmental law issues, the magistracy has made no such strides. As a result, a judge is unlikely to improve his or her environmental knowledge through institutional means and can do so only through personal interest (Tessller 2001). The outcome of this lack of capacity is predictable – judges often consider environmental crime to be less serious than other forms of crime, fail to convict environmental offenders, and frequently apply penalties that do not compensate for damages when they do convict. While specific environmental courts presided over by judges with specific environmental training might be more effective, such systems rarely exist in practice.

In Brazil, our work showed that the penalties being applied by judges were insufficient and were not in keeping with the spirit of that country's Law of Environmental Crime. Although the law is fairly explicit about what types of penalties (including jail time) are allowable for environmental crimes of different magnitudes, it also allows for the application of alternative penalties that can keep offenders from spending time in jail. Even in the case of alternative penalties, penalties should be commensurate with the severity of the crime. However, our sample showed that in many instances, major cases of deforestation were being punished with very light penalties – such as (1) volunteering with the local university's parks and garden corps or (2) donating a basket of food to a charitable institution. Whether those penalties were the result of judges either underestimating the importance of environmental crime or not understanding the penalty prescriptions of the law is unclear. With better training in environmental law, however, both issues might have been resolved.

The role of the judge in the enforcement process is extremely important. Appropriate sentencing and penalties are critical to the effectiveness of an enforcement regime. Even when detection and prosecution are done perfectly, a judge whose understanding of environmental law is limited and who sentences and applies penalties inappropriately may easily undo the good work of the agencies that handled the case earlier in the enforcement chain. Even when detection and prosecution are weak, an effective and fair judge may prove to be a catalyst in encouraging those agencies to improve their performance. But in the absence of specific training on environmental law and on application of penalties in environmental cases, judges are more likely to contribute to a system's failure to present a substantial deterrent to environmental violations.

As this section demonstrates, capacity issues are not limited to one agency or one component of the enforcement chain. Rather, they permeate the system, creating inefficiencies and compromising effectiveness across the system. Efforts must be made to build the technical knowledge and skills of personnel in agencies throughout the enforcement system, if low technical capacity is to be removed as an obstacle to weak enforcement.

## *Challenge 5: lack of performance monitoring and adaptive management systems*

An overarching problem found consistently across sites and across agencies was the failure to monitor performance or to make any systematic, routine efforts to measure effectiveness and to develop action plans for improving performance. In each site, we found that the enforcement agencies had never done the type of systematic analysis of their performance that we have presented here.

The complexity of gathering data for the quantitative case study analyses highlighted the fact that agencies involved in the enforcement chain – detection agencies, prosecutorial services, and the judiciary – do not maintain uniform case tracking systems and do not calculate performance data or monitor their performance in any systematic fashion. No individual agency appears to monitor its own performance or even manage its case data in a way that would be conducive to doing such monitoring. Perhaps more important, the agencies as a group do not work together to monitor the overall effectiveness of the system, which comprises all of them. As a result, those agencies are unable to adapt their enforcement activities to improve effectiveness – either individually or as a system.

Although most agencies do keep some records, there is little consistency in the content or quality of the records that are kept. Electronic case files are rare; when paper case files do exist, they are not managed or organized in any systematic way. Tracking the progress of a case from the early stages of detection through conviction and penalty can be virtually impossible, because each agency that handles a case file numbers it differently.

This weak system of data collection and management demonstrates that no effective efforts to review past performance are made by the detection agencies. Because they do not assess their own performance, those agencies are unable to identify where the weaknesses in their overall system may lie. As a result, they do not understand the complex causes of those weaknesses and are unable to work jointly to develop adaptive management strategies to improve performance.

## Investment priorities for strengthening enforcement performance

The preceding synthesized analysis demonstrates how numerous and complex the problems are that plague enforcement systems. However, the analysis also shows how methodical examination of an enforcement system can make understanding the problems easier. Once the problems and their diverse causes are understood, some very commonsense solutions for strengthening enforcement performance become obvious.

Efforts to improve enforcement of environmental laws have frequently relied on making large investments in detection. In the few places where weak detection is the only major problem in the enforcement system, such investments will be highly effective. However, the holistic vision of the enforcement economics framework makes one thing clear. Solutions that focus on only one step of the enforcement chain, or that fail to address the many issues contributing to a weak step, will have little effect on the overall quality of enforcement in situations where enforcement is weak for a number of reasons. To be most effective, investments must be directed at improving multiple facets of the problem simultaneously. In that way, scarce conservation dollars spent on enforcement will be spent wisely.

Numerous organizations provide international technical assistance on environmental enforcement issues to biodiversity-rich countries. Many offer highly specialized training in one component of the enforcement system. Such organizations can greatly increase their effect by ensuring that their technical assistance packages are part of a broader comprehensive strategy for strengthening enforcement performance.

Using the findings of our enforcement work in the four case study sites, we have identified three technical enforcement-strengthening priorities that we think should be part of a global conservationist strategy for strengthening enforcement of natural resource legislation and protected areas. The priorities, which are aimed at strengthening specific enforcement weaknesses, are also intended to serve the additional purpose of augmenting interagency collaboration.

These recommendations are made at a fairly general level. The full potential breadth of the recommendations is best defined through broader consultation with international experts in environmental legislation, in monitoring enforcement performance, and others. Similarly, site-specific enforcement-strengthening programs should be designed in consultation with local experts and enforcement practitioners.

All the recommendations are derived from the work described here and, hence, are technical in nature (as noted earlier). However, as previously described, technical enforcement-strengthening efforts should not proceed as stand-alone activities. Rather, it is essential for success that they be carried out as part of a package of activities that fall into two general classes: (1) preventative activities that directly improve compliance and reduce the enforcement challenge and (2) activities designed to ensure that the laws and their enforcement are workable and fair. The most effective package of activities will vary from place to place and should be developed by local experts and stakeholders.

### Investment priority 1: reform enforcement policy

Without an underlying framework of environmental legislation that is consistent and clear, an enforcement system cannot be effective. When laws are weak in their language, or limited in their coverage, they become open to interpretation and legal loopholes, making them difficult to enforce. Similarly, in the absence of internal policies that promote good performance, the activities of enforcement agencies are unlikely to be optimal.

Any global effort to strengthen enforcement of environmental laws must dedicate substantial resources to improving the quality of environmental legislation and of enforcement agency policies. Specifically, the efforts should focus on the following reforms, among others:

- Increase budget allocations to agencies across the environmental enforcement chain. Funding should be earmarked within the agencies' budgets for specific enforcement-strengthening activities.

- Strengthen, clarify, and consolidate legislation. Particular attention should be paid to clearly defining environmental violations, developing guidelines for applying penalties, and ensuring that penalties prescribed by law are internally consistent and sufficient to compensate for environmental damages.

- Establish guidelines for interagency cooperation and annual performance reporting. Building the provisions into either law or internal agency policies not only will allow enforcement agencies to be more mindful of their performance but also will force them to think like a system.

- Create the legal framework for alternative enforcement systems to operate. Because official enforcement systems may be ineffective, establishing the legal bases for community-based or other supplementary systems can augment the likelihood of a credible deterrent.

### Investment priority 2: build enforcement capacity

The poor capacity of detection and investigation agents, prosecutors, and judges presents a daunting challenge to effective enforcement. When enforcement personnel lack the training necessary to perform their duties, all elements of the enforcement chain, and hence the deterrent value of the overall enforcement regime, are compromised.

Any global effort to improve enforcement performance in countries of high biodiversity importance must devote substantial resources to building the capacity of these enforcement actors. Providing comprehensive training programs that can be adapted to different sites, as well as running those programs, is likely one of the most cost-effective ways to improve performance across the enforcement chain. Capacity-building efforts should incorporate the following elements, among others:

- Improve performance of detection agents, prosecutors, and judges through periodic training. Given the fact that legislation and agency policies and procedures are consistently being updated or modified, it is critical that training – both in the classroom and through on-the-job training – be offered to those audiences on a continuing basis.

- Involve all agencies in the enforcement chain in the process of designing curricula for each audience. Although each agency responsible for a component of the enforcement chain claims that it can train its own personnel, efforts to date have been either insufficient or of limited availability. If representatives from across these agencies worked together to determine what training each set of actors needs, training programs could be much more effective. Integrated training programs would provide trainees with a clearer vision of how the overall system works. By so doing, they could ensure that the efforts of one agency or institution would bolster the efforts of the later agencies and institutions that handle environmental cases.

- Take advantage of existing technical assistance partnerships with donor government agencies. A number of international aid agencies have existing technical assistance and capacity-building programs with enforcement agencies in biodiversity-rich countries. For instance, U.S. agencies, including the Forest Service, State Department, Environmental Protection Agency, and Fish and Wildlife Service, often have bilateral capacity-building activities in countries of biodiversity importance. Intergovernmental agencies such as the United Nations, Organization for Economic Cooperation and Development, and World Conservation Union also have some capacity to provide this type of support. Consolidating the ongoing work of multiple agencies into strategically designed capacity-building efforts can increase their impact. Furthermore, maximizing the use of existing means of capacity building can substantially reduce the additional costs of expanded training programs.

- Incorporate specialized local NGOs, think tanks, and institutes in capacity-building efforts. Enforcement training programs should not be developed only with government enforcement agencies. Many countries have strong local organizations or institutes whose expertise in the fields of environmental legislation, biological priority setting, and capacity building is very strong and can help make training efforts locally relevant. Such groups should be incorporated into the process of designing and executing training programs.

### Investment priority 3: implement performance monitoring and adaptive management systems

When enforcement agencies do not monitor their individual performance or do not work together to assess the whole system's effectiveness in deterring environmental violations, they cannot implement the changes vital to improving the system. In many developed countries, enforcement agencies are required to periodically calculate performance indicators, which are made publicly available. But the poor collection and management of data by enforcement agencies in biodiversity-rich countries makes this type of regular performance evaluation very difficult and expensive.

Investments in other enforcement-strengthening efforts must be complemented by investments in developing enforcement performance monitoring and adaptive management systems. It is only with such systems that the success or failure of the other investments can be gauged. The design of performance monitoring and adaptive management systems should incorporate the following elements:

- Develop standardized data management systems for use across agencies. Integration of case-tracking databases makes observing the progress of cases as they move through the enforcement chain feasible, which it currently is not in many places. Tracking cases from beginning to end is a basic use of information – but even that information can be used to calculate basic performance indicators such as the enforcement economics model's probabilities. Developing a simple multiagency case-tracking system can lay the groundwork for future interagency efforts to develop more complicated systems for managing data and calculating performance statistics.

- Reach agreement on enforcement statistics (indicators) to be produced annually. Given the variety of enforcement statistics and the different purposes they serve, it is important for enforcement agencies across the chain to agree to a set of indicators to be produced annually. The process of developing indicators agreed to by all agencies can be complicated and may take a few years. While that process is under way, the enforcement economics model's probabilities, which measure the success rate of each step in the enforcement chain, can serve as basic indicators of enforcement performance.

- Train key staff members in data collection and management, analysis of enforcement statistics, and development of strategic enforcement-strengthening plans. To successfully implement performance monitoring and adaptive management systems, an integrated corps of technical staff members with the capacity to develop, generate, and interpret enforcement indicators must be created. To be highly effective, this group's members must understand both the broad enforcement system and the operations of individual agencies. This knowledge will allow members to work with senior management of the enforcement agencies to understand the reasons behind identified weaknesses and to develop strategic solutions.

- Require annual publication and public disclosure of enforcement performance reports. Informed civil society can be a strong engine for reform. Evaluating performance of individual agencies and the overall system annually, in addition to making evaluation results transparently available, is critical to ensuring that enforcement agencies continually work to perform effectively.

## Conclusion

The poor enforcement of natural resource laws in countries of high biodiversity importance is widely acknowledged, but its underlying causes are often poorly understood. The primary innovation of the enforcement economics analyses detailed here is that they present a rare quantitative measure of exactly how bad enforcement is. In sites where a probability of detection could be estimated, the cumulative probability of a case resulting in a conviction was less than 0.01. In other words, less than 1 percent of environmental crimes result in a conviction.

What the numbers reveal is stunning. In all sites studied, the deterrent generated by the enforcement regime was grossly insufficient to offset the incentives that drive illegal environmental activity. We believe that this result is not particular to the countries that we analyzed, but rather that enforcement of environmental laws is abysmal in most countries of biodiversity importance.[30] This finding does not bode well for biodiversity conservation efforts, because many innovative approaches to conservation require adequate enforcement if they are to be effective.

Clearly, enforcement of environmental laws should not be seen as an end unto itself. Ultimately, improving enforcement is only one of the elements necessary to ensure compliance. For enforcement strengthening to contribute to increasing compliance, the laws to be enforced must be just and equitable. Furthermore, enforcement must be part of a package that also includes two other types of actions: (1) preventative activities that directly improve compliance and reduce the enforcement challenge and (2) activities designed to ensure that the laws and their enforcement are workable and fair.

The underlying causes of poor enforcement are many, and problems often permeate every step of the enforcement chain. Our work in the field points to five common challenges that impede effective enforcement. First, poor interagency cooperation makes it difficult for the enforcement system to run smoothly and to work effectively as a system. Second, inadequate budgetary resources cause personnel and infrastructure weaknesses that compromise quality of enforcement. Furthermore, this lack of budget makes any concerted overhaul of the enforcement system impossible and makes lasting change difficult. Third, technical deficiencies in the laws and agency policies that support effective enforcement – which are fundamental for the system's proper functioning – make performance less than optimal. Fourth, insufficient technical skills and knowledge of personnel from across the enforcement chain lead to poor execution of enforcement responsibilities, thus reducing the likelihood that violators will be sanctioned. Finally, the lack of performance monitoring and adaptive management systems means that neither enforcement agencies nor the public at large have any concrete indication of how effective the system is in deterring environmental crime. Without a precise understanding of where the system's weaknesses are and why they exist, strategic plans to improve performance cannot be designed and implemented.

Because enforcement systems are holistic in nature, a system can be only as strong as the weakest element in the chain. That being the case, investments in improving one element in the chain will be ineffective if other elements remain weak. While raising fines and investing in detection capacity are common solutions to weak enforcement, the enforcement economics logic clearly demonstrates that such investments in isolation are unlikely to be effective in most cases. However, the investment priorities presented in this analysis fit the profile of the type of efforts that are likely to result in significant improvement of enforcement performance. Improving the quality of environmental legislation and enforcement agency policies is critical to ensuring that the foundation for enforcement efforts is solid. Building capacity of personnel across the enforcement chain is vital to effective enforcement, because lack of capacity frequently contributes to inefficiencies in the functioning of the system. Capacity-building efforts should be implemented using jointly developed training programs that are executed in partnership with local expert institutions and with those international technical assistance providers that are already working with enforcement agencies. Finally, investments in other enforcement-strengthening efforts must be complemented by investments in developing enforcement performance monitoring and adaptive management systems. Such systems will allow the success or failure of the other investments to be gauged.

If scarce conservation dollars are to be spent on strengthening enforcement, they must be spent in ways that will guarantee the maximum improvement in performance. The challenges noted here demonstrate that while the factors contributing to weak enforcement are complex, understanding those factors is simple if the right analytical framework is used. Once they are understood, effective and efficient solutions for addressing the challenges become apparent. Strengthening the weakest links in this way is an indispensable part of any package whose aim is to successfully achieve biodiversity conservation.

## Notes

1  Defined as a vein of behavioral economics that sprang from efforts to understand the factors influencing the decision whether or not to commit a crime (Becker 1968).
2  Sutinen 1987.
3  Developed from Sutinen 1987.
4  The quantitative analyses that are presented here used a 20 percent discount rate.
5  An administrative process occurs entirely within the detection agency generally, does not involve appearing in court, and can result in sanctions like confiscation or a fine. A judicial process begins in the detection agency and ultimately ends up in the courts system, where sentence is assigned by a judge.
6  For this report, 'enforcement agency' refers not only to detection agencies and investigators but also to prosecutorial services and the judiciary – namely, all the agencies involved in the enforcement chain.
7  The detailed findings on factors affecting performance in each site, as well as the strategic action plans developed to improve performance, are published separately.
8  Note that these probabilities translate into likelihoods of 100, 100, 51, and 16 percent.
9  This value is based on 1997 data from IESB (Mesquita 1997), corrected to calculate an equivalent 2004 value.
10  Although corruption was also identified as a contributing factor, no specific analysis of corruption was conducted.
11  Per IBAMA procedure, records of complaints and overall detections are not kept, and the first record of a case is the citation that is filled out by IBAMA.
12  Note that these probabilities translate into likelihoods of 100, 58, 69, and 3 percent.
13  Please note that probability of prosecution is different from probability of processing; the former refers to the judicial process and the latter refers to the administrative process that was the focus of this study.
14  Note that these probabilities translate into likelihoods of 3.2, 6.8, 84, 41, and 85 percent.
15  Probability of conviction is for cases heard in regency (local) courts. The probability of conviction presented here does not include the results of appeals to higher courts.
16  The average value of the penalty and confiscated timber is $164,706 (rupiah to US$ exchange rate of 9.383 rupiah to US$1 for the period of 2001–2003. Source: Pacific Exchange Rate Service at the Sauder School of Business, University of British Columbia).
17  The enforcement disincentive including the value of confiscated timber is $890.43.
18  There were a few cases of logging without a permit.
19  All information is from Suryadi , Cannon, and Widjayanto (2004). The value of the disincentive climbs to nearly $1,000 when the value of confiscated timber is included.
20  The probability of detection was obtained by dividing the quantity of illegal timber by the estimated total quantity of illegal logging. The quantity of illegal timber detected was obtained from the case information. The estimated total quantity of illegal logging was based on information from the Provincial Forestry Service.
21  Considering the penalty alone.
22  Note that these probabilities translate into likelihoods of 6.2, 0.3, 85, 62, and 24 percent.
23  Local data collection in the Calamianes was done by ELAC. Analysis was done jointly.
24  Both of which are provincial branches of a federal agency.
25  For instance, the Philippines Coast Guard is mandated to enforce 'all applicable laws upon the high seas and territorial waters of the Philippines including all ports, custom zones, waterways, and other inland waters' (Mayo-Anda, et al. 2004).
26  Analyzing and explaining the performance of the whole enforcement system can also provide incentive to cooperate more closely – a point that will be explored in subsequent sections.
27  Ironically, when licensing powers are unclear, agencies are more likely to fight for the right to do the licensing – because the licensing agency receives licensing fees.

28 Municipal Trial Court, Municipal Circuit Trial Court, or Regional Trial Court.
29 Either the state prosecutor's or federal prosecutor's office, but files often would be sent to the wrong one.
30 These often are developing countries. Although enforcement is often poor in developed countries, the lower opportunity cost of not acting illegally in these richer countries makes environmental rule-breaking less pervasive.

## References

Akella, A. S., H. Orlando, M. Araujo, and J. B. Cannon. (2004). 'Enforcement Economics and the Fight against Forest Crime: Lessons Learned from the Atlantic Forest of Brazil.' Washington, DC: Conservation International – Center for Conservation and Government, September 2004.

Alger, K., and M. Caldas. 1994. 'The Declining Cocoa Economy and the Atlantic Forest of Southern Bahia, Brazil: Conservation Attitudes of Cocoa Planters.' The Environmentalist 14, no. 2: 107–19.

Becker, G. S. (1968). 'Crime and Punishment: An Economic Approach.' Journal of Political Economy 76, no. 2: 169–217.

Conservation International – Philippines. (2002). 'An Analysis of the Live Reef Food Fish Trade in the Calamianes, Palawan, Philippines.' White paper, Manila: Conservation International – Philippines.

Conservation International – Selva Maya. (2003). 'Cacería e tráfico de fauna silvestre en la Selva Maya y la Sierra Madre del Sur de Chiapas.' White paper, Tuxtla Gutierrez, Mexico: Conservation International – Selva Maya, September 2003.

Galindo-Leal, C., and I. G. Câmara. (2003). The Atlantic Forest of South America: Biodiversity Status, Threats, and Outlook. Conservation International – The Center for Applied Biodiversity Science. Washington, DC: Island Press.

Mayo-Anda, G., D. Dalabajan, and N. Lasmarias. (2004). 'Deterrent Value of Law Enforcement on Dynamite and Cyanide Fishing: An Enforcement Economics Study of the Calamianes Group of Islands, Palawan, Philippines.' White paper. Puerto Princesa, Philippines: Conservation International – Philippines, Environmental Legal Assistance Center, August 2004.

Mesquita, C. A. B. (1997). Indústria Madeireira no Sudeste da Bahia: Aspectos Sócio-Econômicos e Ambientais. Ilhéus, Brazil: Instituto de Estudos Sócio-Ambientais do Sul da Bahia, November 1997.

Patlis, J. (2002). 'Mapping Indonesia's Forest Estate from the Lawyer's Perspective: Laws, Legal Fictions, Illegal Activities, and the Gray Area.' White paper, Washington, DC: World Bank–WWF Alliance, October 2002.

Reuter, A., and S. Habel. (2004). 'Brief Assessment on Wildlife Enforcement Related Topics in Mexico.' Consultant's report. Mexico City: Conservation International – TRAFFIC North America, July 2004.

Suryadi , S., J. Cannon, and A. Widjayanto. (2004). 'Combating Illegal Logging and Wildlife Trade in Papua, Indonesia: Priorities for Enforcement Strengthening.' Jakarta, Indonesia: Conservation International Indonesia and Conservation International Center for Conservation and Government, September 2004.

Sutinen, J. G. (1987). 'Enforcement of the MFCMA: An Economist's Perspective.' Marine Fisheries 49, no. 3: 36–43.

# 29. When the heavenly gaze criminalises: satellite surveillance, land clearance regulation and the human-nature relationship*

*Robyn Luise Bartel*

## Introduction

'Whenever there are men competent for the task, let them be given forest to cut down in order to improve our possessions' (Charlemagne).[1]

Many changes wrought by humanity on the environment have involved not only a dramatic change in its physical appearance and composition, but also cultural and institutional changes, for example in the view of the value of property as expressed in the extract above. In countries such as Australia, higher prices and commodity values have usually been placed on privately owned production landscapes with only the extraordinarily exquisite, or discarded leftovers remaining in public ownership. In the latter, limits have been placed on human activities and, at the same time, the purpose for exclusion is expressed in terms of the benefits to humanity. The world's first reserve, Yellowstone National Park in the United States, was declared in 1872 with the objective of preservation 'for the benefit and the enjoyment of the people'.

Similarly, the earliest known conservation laws which criminalised activities that harmed the environment in some way, were enacted to further the desires of humanity, or at least those of a privileged group. For example in the 11th Century, the habitat of game species were preserved by prohibitions against tree-felling in the New Forest (Mannion 1997). The law was limited to protecting recreational hunting by the elite from the interference of poaching by the poor. These forests were viewed as premium resources by feudal owners who recognised the impact of over-use and the importance of controlling allocation. Such utilitarian justifications continue to underpin most of the interactions that humanity has with the landscape. However, while humans may be excluded from nature as understood as 'wilderness' or 'native', by laws of public reservation and prohibition on use, in most areas of the landscape it is nature that has been excluded by human action. One of the most obvious and dramatic ways in which nature has been excluded from the landscape is by land clearance. This changes both the nature of the

---

* From *Current Issues in Criminal Justice* (2005), 16(3): pp. 322–339.

landscape and the culture of the humans living in the landscape. In some areas humans have come to consider themselves as the sole occupiers, rights-holders and beneficiaries of nature. It is perhaps ironic then that the activity of land clearing has proved itself, due to the consequent decline in biodiversity, the enhanced greenhouse effect and the degradation and desertification of the land, to be offering fewer and fewer benefits to humanity and risking our long-term environmental security.

Satellite remote sensing, which is data about the earth, captured from space-borne sensors, has contributed greatly to the scientific understanding and popular awareness of the effects that human activities have on the landscape. The exposure of the decline in native vegetation cover has been especially significant in Australia. Through the 1970s and 1980s land clearing attracted widespread concern, and institutional responses, such as land clearance regulations, were introduced to criminalise unauthorised clearance of native vegetation on private land.[2] Monitoring of land clearance by satellites has since been used as an evaluation tool to look at whether or not these legislative and policy attempts to affect land usage have been materially effective in reducing the rates of land clearance. Satellite remote sensing shows that these measures have been ineffective (Bartel 2004). Implementation strategies are slowly receiving greater political attention and the extension of the role of satellite remote sensing to surveillance and policing, previously once only mooted (Bartel and Leach 2000), is now becoming real.

Satellite remote sensing is beginning to be used in Queensland and South Australia to identify compliance or transgression to land clearance restrictions, and forensically as evidence in prosecutions. Considering the degree of early advancements in this technology, its utilisation in detection and enforcement is long overdue. However, the technology has a unique surveillance capacity and only in very limited cases has there been similar types of continuous or semi-continuous surveillance implemented, for example in situational crime prevention with closed circuit television camera monitoring in public areas. Satellite images showing Indonesian forest fires have been suggested as sources of evidence for use by Malaysia, Singapore and Brunei to take Indonesia to the International Court of Justice, however this is an isolated case (Anon 1999). The closest and best-established precedent is in Europe where satellite imagery is used to monitor compliance to subsidy claims under the Common Agricultural Policy (Pederson 2000). In Australia, however, the technology is being used to support regulations that are far more controversial amongst the regulated community. While satellite monitoring for data gathering purposes (for example mapping of landcover, farm planning and crop yield estimates) may be widely accepted, the surveillance capacities of satellite imagery have not gone unchallenged. The bases for these challenges are similar to the objections to the land clearance laws themselves. Is it right to criminalise a land usage activity that has long been seen as productive and desirable? Is there perhaps a more basic question about our appreciation of the nature of human activities or their 'unnaturalness' that deserves further consideration? And how can the utilisation of satellite imagery help or hinder us in this endeavour?

## Land clearance legislation in Australia and the role of satellite surveillance

Australia ranks ninth among the world's top land clearing nations for the last decade. Nine of the top 20 (including Australia) are classified as mega-diverse in their biodiversity. Between 1990 and 2000 Brazil cleared at a rate of 2,226,000 ha/yr, Indonesia 1,312,000, Sudan 959,000, Zambia 851,000, Mexico 631,000, Democratic Republic of the Congo (Zaire) 532,000, Burma/Myanmar 517,000, Nigeria 398,000, Zimbabwe 320,000, Argentina 285,000, Peru 269,000 and Cote d'Ivoire 265,000 (FAO 2001). Australia's land clearing rate for the period was 378,000 ha/yr.[3] This dramatic land cover change continues an historic trend in Australia. The National Land and Water Resources Audit (ANVA 2001) has estimated that 30% of the open forests nationwide have been cleared since European settlement, 30% of the woodlands, 25% of the open woodlands, 15% of the acacia forests and woodlands, 35% of the mallee, 45% of the heath and 30% of the rainforest. The amount of change varies regionally, clearance being concentrated in the areas of longest settlement, with an estimated 90% of all native vegetation types lost from the eastern temperate zone. Few areas have been left completely unaffected by some level of use. Of Kirkpatrick's (1994) estimate of 43 million hectares of native bush remaining 25 million hectares have been affected by logging and 61% by grazing.

Human-induced landcover change is not new. Flannery (1994; 2001) argues that the arrival of humans to North America and to the Antipodes resulted in major extinctions and major changes to the distribution of ecosystems due to hunting and the use of fire. The arrival subsequently of more significant numbers of humans bringing more advanced technology has resulted in far more rapid rates of change. Concern for human-induced landcover change and its consequences has been raised by the development of one of these technologies, that is satellite remote sensing. For the last 30 or so years, satellite remote sensing imagery has depicted great swaths of forested areas in Asia, Africa, the Amazon and Australia turning from green to brown. Much of the change in Australia has been due to the increasing use of land for agricultural production. Between 1990 and 1995 close to 80% of the land cleared in the major agricultural zones of Australia was for pasture development, mainly for cattle. This land clearance mainly occurred in the state of Queensland (Barson *et al.* 2000: 65).

The introduction of legislative measures and the subsequent criminalisation of land clearance, which primarily affects private landholders, have been due in part to the high rates of land clearance on private land made evident by satellite remote sensing studies. Government commissioned reports utilising imagery in South Australia in the 1980s and Woodgate and Black's (1988) study of Victoria both led to legislative changes in the respective states (Kestel Research 1990).

Over the last two decades all state and territory jurisdictions in Australia have either introduced or strengthened existing administrative licensing requirements for clearing private land, with civil and criminal penalties to follow unauthorised clearance.[4] Compliance may also involve revegetation and on-going management responsibilities that may be registered with the land title. Implementation of these laws requires monitoring and satellite remote sensing may be seen as an ideal surveillance tool as it 'looks into' everyone's backyard and can determine the land usage being carried out there.

## A short survey of technical capacities in satellite surveillance

Satellite imagery consists of pictures of the earth taken at a distance, that is remotely. Skidmore's (1998) definition of satellite remote sensing is that it is '(A) record of the Earth's features obtained from reflectance or emittance of electromagnetic radiation'. Early pictures of the Earth from space made resonant, as few descriptions could, the vulnerability of our planet. They provided powerful illustrations of the concept that our planet and its resources are finite. The earth in space became a symbol of fragility, powerfully linked with our responsibility for it. A well-known 'greenie' poster depicts the Earth against an endless sea of black universe with the tag: 'Ignore it and it will go away'.

The Earth has been far from ignored. Satellite imagery has become ubiquitous in studies monitoring change at the global and local level. From space, weather systems are continually tracked, the extents of sea ice measured and landcover change observed. Programmes such as NASA's Global Land Cover Characterisation Project, the World Climate Research Programme, the International Geosphere-Biosphere Programme and the global vegetation monitoring undertaken by Earth Observation's Space Applications Institute (Europe) all incorporate remote sensing from satellites as part of their data gathering and research.

Different satellite sensors provide different types of ground data, or imagery. Unlike conventional photography, satellite imagery is in a digital raster or grid format in which the size of each square or pixel in the grid is determined by the spatial resolution of the sensor. Military 'Keyhole' satellites have very fine spatial resolution and are therefore usually able to detect and precisely locate very small objects. Satellites used for assessing large-scale weather and landcover patterns however, do not need to 'see' everything in such great detail and have a much coarser view. The 1.1 kilometres × 1.1 kilometres pixel size of AVHRR data from the NOAA satellite (and its affordability) mean that it is often used for monitoring of continental scale landcover change. It is unsuitable for applications requiring high locational accuracy and greater detail, since these require higher spatial resolution. Carterra imagery from the IKONOS satellite (launched September 1999), has a panchromatic band with a spatial resolution of 0.82 m, and multispectral spatial resolution of 3.28 metres in four bandwidths.[5] Satellites carry a number of detectors for each bandwidth and the surface reflectance of electromagnetic radiation is selectively measured within these bandwidths and recorded as area weighted averages for each pixel.[6]

Change in land cover is detected by the change in spectral message or signature received for each bandwidth, or band. There are no unique spectral signifiers for specific land cover types (only water can be unfailingly detected, by its inability to reflect the infra-red spectrum). However, through experimental use and examination of spectral relationships, many land cover types can be identified using semi-automated techniques. The Landsat satellites, with a spatial resolution of around 30 metres, have been used for most of the data gathered on Australian land clearance and have provided the most reliable continuous record of land cover change in Australia. The Landsat 7 satellite was launched in April 1999, providing similar data to that of its predecessor Landsat 5. Data from Landsat 5 has been available since 1983 and from its predecessor from 1972. It was the early data from the older Landsat satellites that led to the regulatory response which criminalised unauthorised land clearance in South Australia.

The interpretation of satellite imagery for the purposes of mapping and for surveillance is a process of categorisation; the Earth's diverse surface is simplified into land cover types to reduce the complexity. This also makes it easier to assess a change in conditions.[7] For ongoing compliance, repeat surveillance is important as land use is an ongoing activity. Evidence of a contravention related to land cover change lasts longer than evidence of pollution, which may be blown or washed away. In the future an element of 'rapid response' may be instituted by real-time monitoring, which is essentially shortening, via systemic and automated processing techniques, the turn around time between data acquisition and identification of clearance locales. Timely discovery is also important to ensure that statutory limitation periods do not run out.[8] From past patterns of land clearance it may also be possible to identify areas at risk, for example if a remnant of a once larger size has been diminished, further loss may also be likely. Vulnerability may also be graded according to spatial relationships, for example areas closest to existing production and areas that are unfenced or inadequately fenced may be at greater risk from stock grazing than other areas. Private tenure is also a causative and therefore predictive factor for unauthorised land clearance.

One of the biggest problems with the current time-efficient methods of satellite monitoring is that by 'ignoring' the clearance of grasslands, sparser woodlands, shrublands, wetlands and heathlands, and patch clearance of areas smaller than 1 hectare, the area of clearance is underestimated. Legislative protection as well as monitoring has been very much 'on the side of the trees'. The popular perception of native vegetation is tree-centred, as are the aims of projects for addressing salinity and land degradation. In Queensland the law only covers trees. In the future, national and state policies and market forces that favour the planting of exotic and non-local native trees in monocultures, may achieve greenhouse targets without however, accomplishing the aims of biodiversity protection. Land clearance is also often referred to merely as deforestation and the absurdity of this term's focus on trees is made apparent by comparing it to its appropriation for other vegetation types: 'degrassation', 'deheathation'.

The New South Wales State of the Environment report (NSWEPA 2000: 6.3) criticised the current amount of information concerning native vegetation, stating that: 'There is a paucity of data on the condition of native vegetation communities ... The range of clearing rates varies widely depending on the methodology used'. The greater resolution provided by alternative data sources such as Carterra increases the processing time, by creating more information than is required which then needs to be filtered out. Although increased resolution is unsuitable for monitoring larger areas, it is eminently suitable for monitoring urban restrictions and to track the fate of individual trees, which are protected by local planning laws and decisions, significant trees legislation and the South Australian land clearance legislation.

## Current and future challenges for satellite surveillance

One necessary condition for a regulatory implementation strategy to be effective is sufficient monitoring, at least to assess compliance. As Grabosky (1995:360) observes, lack of monitoring can weaken regulation. This should not however, be assumed to be a serious consideration for those 'concerned with image rather than substance [of law] … But for those seeking to effect genuine change, some kind of monitoring system is essential'. Detection is essential for deterrence. In a classical conceptualisation of deterrence, most famously stated by Bentham, observance and compliance with law is principally generated by the threat of punishment. For such a threat to operate as a disincentive the probability of detection, apprehension and prosecution must be high and the likely penalty outweigh the benefit of contravention. Detection is also important for an appreciation of the merits or demerits of that behaviour and its consequences. In the area of land clearance regulation, harm is inchoate but evidence of the extent of the actual harm caused by the offence is essential in sentencing, especially where proportional sentencing policies are favoured, for example in New South Wales. Satellite remote sensing can assist in determining factors important in sentencing, such as the size of the area of the land cleared, the vegetation type cleared and the replacement land usage.

Satellite surveillance monitoring of adherence to land clearance regulation is technically an ideal solution for the disparateness of the regulated community and the lack of point source or point impact style of damage. Another advantage of the broad field of view provided by satellite remote sensing is that all landholders are brought within it, not just those who bring attention to themselves by applying for a permit. By comparison, detection of 'traditional' criminals is a reactive process, relying heavily on reporting by victims, informants and witnesses. In the traditional policing of criminal law, the criminal can rarely be apprehended whilst carrying out the criminal activity and is only apprehended if there is evidence of a conspiracy. The success of policing, or the achievement of the 'order' side of the law and order question, is measured in terms of reported crimes solved. However, there is no way of knowing how many crimes are actually committed. Declining crime rates therefore may or may not reflect successful crime prevention. The number of crimes reported serves as an indicator, but is not an absolute measurement, of the safety of social conditions or the deterrence effect of law and order. Satellite remote sensing surveillance differs from traditional policing and other environmental monitoring in its capacity to be employed as an all-seeing eye, to firstly identify all regulated behaviour, whether it be beyond compliant, compliant or transgressive, and secondly to serve as an evaluator of the regulators by monitoring implementation strategies.

Queensland is now using remote sensing in a systematic way to identify illegal land clearance, by matching the locations of vegetation loss apparent in imagery to the areas in the Department of Natural Resources and Mines' permit register. Over 2000 and 2001, the Statewide Landcover and Tree Survey (SLATS) has identified 61,000 hectares of possibly illegal or exempt clearance, that is clearance that did not appear in the register. As a result over 3,000 sites are being investigated by the Department's prosecution branch (Sullivan 2003). Satellite mapping also assists in building the databases upon which the Department administers and decides permit applications. There has already been criticism (for example by rural lobby group Agforce in Queensland) that satellite maps are insufficiently accurate to be used as a basis for granting permits, as some vegetation and property boundaries have been found to have been misplaced, leading to permits being granted over inappropriate areas (Robbins 2001). The claimed scientific accuracy of remote sensing must be able to withstand cross-examination in the court where, for example, expert witnesses are used.

In South Australia satellite imagery trials have led to several prosecutions. However, there remains a reliance on public reporting of breaches, which effectively outsources the detection aspect of policing to the public. Reporting of clearance therefore, is concentrated according to population densities and is dependent upon awareness of, and presumably support for, the legislation. Over half of the reports received each year between 1999 and 2001 were from highly urbanised areas, such as metropolitan Adelaide, the Yourke and Fleurieu Peninsulas, and Kangaroo Island. The fewest number of reports arose in the north and west of South Australia, where there is less conflict over land use, less sympathy perhaps for the legislation and fewer pairs of eyes due to the lower population density. Greater clearance of vegetation occurs in the south-east of the State and it is also more noticeable because the vegetation being cleared is more 'obvious' vegetation such as woodland. It is far more difficult for humans, and satellites, to detect degradation of grassland by over-grazing, which is prohibited by South Australian law.

In Victoria, where the policing of land clearance is the responsibility of each local council's enforcement officer (who may also call on police and authorised officers of the Department of Sustainability and Environment, formerly DNRE), councils have very few resources for monitoring and are reliant on community reporting. The Municipal Association of Victoria (MAV 2000) proposed that a random checking system be instituted which involved sending letters to people asking them whether they had conformed to land clearing permit conditions and 'those that have not, or that do not reply would be monitored and prosecuted if they do not abide by the controls'. This type of monitoring is limited to those who have already placed themselves within the system by making an application. In a survey of staff from 45 councils conducted by the MAV in November 2000, 32 out of the 45 interviewed said that there was a lack of resources and/or staff and 14 complained about the reliance on community reporting. Survey respondents also wanted information about all vegetation cover, not just trees. One respondent said that the lower and middle storeys of vegetation were often forgotten in monitoring and enforcement, and another said that the knowledge of grasslands was particularly poor (MAV 2000: 10, 17).

In New South Wales, officers from the Department of Infrastructure Planning and Natural Resources (formerly DLWC) are at present totally reliant on reports of illegal clearance from the general public. The Department received over 2000 reports in 2000 and 2001, which is four times the number received in 1995 and 1996 after SEPP 46 was introduced. As the Department's draft compliance policy notes however, although '(R)eports from the community are highly valuable, systematic programs are also needed to detect alleged breaches'. The policy states that random audits are conducted to track compliance, therefore those already in the system (by applying for a permit) may be more likely to be exposed. The Auditor-General's Performance Audit Report (2002:44) however, found that the Department 'conducted few formal compliance audits and little systematic compliance monitoring', noting that on-site property checks may only be made at the time of permit application, and only for large applications or when Crown pastoral leases (in the west of the State) were transferred.

Policing of land clearing regulations in most states appears to be hampered by a lack of systematic monitoring and lack of commitment to employing satellite technology to detect infringements.[9] With the exception of Queensland, policing in Australia continues to be 'outsourced' to the public. Where clearance is likely to be greater, such as in expanding rural areas informer reluctance may be high.

The deployment of remote sensing in its 'big-brother' mode, that is to police landholder behaviour at the property and paddock level, may be feared to be politically unpalatable. It is this, rather than any technical deficiencies, that has led to its slow uptake. It may be politically unpalatable for a number of reasons. The general public appear largely unaware of the capacities of present public and private satellites. Ikonos2, the satellite that provides Carterra data, has been likened to Big Brother in a front-page newspaper article, which showed an image of the city of Melbourne (Mascall and Dare 2000). Few people are aware that their backyards are routinely mapped by several satellites and most would be unaware that military satellites such as the Keyhole can 'see' in resolutions of centimetres (Richelson 1998). Concerns range from being 'spotted' in one's backyard pool to having competitors monitoring one's production levels (Phillips 1999). As the utilisation of satellite surveillance increases one can predict that intentional evasion may become a concern. Studies of pollution have shown that enforcement strategies involve both the regulatees and the regulators, who both utilise counter-strategies, including delaying tactics, intimidation and evasion (Hawkins 1984:120). Satellite signals may be distorted by manipulating ground conditions, for example 'adding' spurious cover to approximate vegetation when it has actually been removed or by degrading the vegetation to prevent it being classed as deserving of conservation (Binning and Young 1997: 28).

The potential exists for the policing of landcover change to be far more intrusive than regular reactive policing. Although remote sensing saves resources and inspectors' time, it may be the case that landholders themselves would prefer a knock at the door rather than a camera in the sky. Satellite surveillance may also be objected to on the grounds that the land clearance restrictions themselves have been opposed. For example, the discontent about private costs being incurred as the boundary between private production and public conservation is blurred, and the criminalisation of traditionally productive activities. Satellite surveillance may be viewed as unreasonable in policing generally but perhaps more specifically in the context of land clearance regulation, which lacks widespread ground-based support amongst the regulated community and has suffered from a low degree of voluntary compliance.

## Satellite surveillance: sensing a division between humans and nature

'New World countries, such as Australia, New Zealand, USA and Canada, are typified by a strong functional and symbolic separation of nature and culture. Visions of ecological integrity and cultural integration seek to blur this distinction, creating patchy landscapes in which in situ nature conservation occurs as an integral part of commercial land use activities' (Hamblin 2000: 1).

Satellite pictures demarcate areas of human habitation and use, from other areas. Labelling an area as a certain land use by definition excludes other uses that may exist in the same location. For example, one major satellite study concluded that about 40% of Australia is intensively used for agricultural production (cropping, pasture etc), plantations and urban and residential purposes. In total 60% of Australia is used for agriculture (Graetz et al. 1995). The implication is that some areas are solely used to produce for and house humanity, and the areas remaining are unproductive. By categorising the world as such, satellite imagery divides the world often according to the boundaries of private and public ownership and traditional production and preservation. This division obscures the fact that nearly every landscape on earth has been or is used and modified by humans. It hides the fact that areas of native vegetation are also production landscapes for humans: they are used by humans for recreation and amenity, to produce filtered water and air, to preserve biodiversity and for other ecosystem purposes. In some areas the history of inhabitancy and modification by First Peoples runs for millennia and to such an extent that the ecosystems viewed as natural by the invading conquerors can arguably be described as cultural artefacts. Traditional production landscapes are not exclusively human. They house native flora and fauna and indeed the 'human' production carried out in an area is entirely dependent on the pre-existing 'nature' in the area. Enforcing the 'us and them' dichotomy of human versus nature, that has grown from our self-awareness and perhaps the distancing effects of technology and industrialised living, obscures important facts that may impair our cultural development and therefore our interactions with the landscape.

In many areas of Australia production is now criminalised and conservation enforced on private land. Historically, the act of clearing was considered part of the definition of ownership, for example Locke's (1690) notion of ownership arising from a 'mixing of labour with land'. In Australia clearing was often a condition of leasehold and freehold land grants: land purchase agreements required it and land selection laws from the mid-1800s demanded that settlers improve their land by clearing. This liberal and capitalist history of property ownership has often caused considerable resistance to the fettering of what are perceived as inalienable rights of land use. However, the idea that landholders are also land-stewards is also part of the culture. The idea of environmental stewardship arises from a Biblical notion that has a variety of interpretations; from warranting a form of benevolent custodianship to authorising patriarchal domination. Environmental stewardship also has ecocentric roots, in the idea that humans are ecological actors holding responsibilities and duties to and for nature. The legal recognition of these responsibilities and duties links them to property and therefore to property owners only. In the South Australian case of *Backhouse v Judd* Justice Napier observed that '(T)here is nothing novel in the idea that [ownership of] property is a responsibility as well as a privilege'.[10] According to Baden and Stroup (1990:132) '(I)t is important to understand that ownership does not entail the right to use that property in a way that is costly to others'. Young (2000) predicts that the role of satellite technology will extend beyond surveillance by 'putting the onus back onto landholders', for example an environmental-loading based tax for the impact of individual properties' production on the environment could be calculated and charged to the landholder.

The boundaries between public and private have been blurred by land clearance regulations but they still effect a strong spatial demarcation at the property level. The boundary between conservation and production imposed on private land is felt by many landholders as a cost. It may be that costs should be imposed beyond the farmgate. Unsustainable farming practices cause public harm, because native vegetation produces public goods such as ecosystem benefits. According to a user pays philosophy, land stewardship is not just the landholders' duty but that of all beneficiaries: of the broader society. The Victorian Government (DNRE 2000) recognises that 'the permanent care of our natural environment is one of the most important duties of government'. Presently the broader community obtain a benefit at no cost, if landholders produce public goods such as ecosystem preservation. Rather than criminalising traditional agriculture, the users of benefits arising from the native vegetation could be made to pay through government introduced taxation, or via the market. Presently, there are some market forces towards sustainable farming in its production sense but there is little accountable value in preserving vegetation for the landholder: 'Some of the harm caused to the environment is due to the absence of markets for certain natural resources and environmental amenities ...' (Industry Commission 1998). Privatisation is presently seen as hollow in dollar terms for the landholders, as they receive no identifiable financial benefit from their ownership of in situ native vegetation. The only benefits landholders accrue occur in the possibility of conversion, that is land clearance releasing the land to a more profitable use. While the situation may be seen as a market failure that has required the current move toward criminal legal intervention, it has also been argued that the market can offer a solution.

## A market view to provide environmental justice: the solution or the same problem?

Agriculture contributes over 3% to Australia's $600 billion Gross Domestic Product and accounts for $16 billion (22%) of Australia's export earnings. Agriculture also provides over 300,000 jobs mainly in the grain, sheep, beef and fruit industries (ABS 2002). These figures fail to take into account the full costs and benefits of production. A traditional criticism of the market, often used to justify regulatory intervention, is the failure of the market to account for externalities in pricing goods. This includes the under-valuation of the on- and off-site and out-of-time costs of production and the use of natural resources and services (including benefits foregone). The following definition of externalities describes their creation by market failure: 'An externality arises when production or consumption by one party entails uncompensated costs or benefits that are not paid for, by others' (Industry Commission 1998:72). Since the costs of degradation and rehabilitation, and the benefits of in situ vegetation, are unbudgeted for in agricultural production valuations, primary producers do not at present bear the full costs of production, there is a hidden subsidy. Users do not pay either because the products are not priced or paid for appropriately, or, in the case of public goods, paid for at all. The under-valuation and non-inclusion of externalities skews a cost-benefit analysis even further. For example, the discounting of land prices gives an artificial comparative advantage to most commercial endeavours and makes scientific research and conservation measures difficult.

It has been argued that ecosystem benefits are not marketable commodities and their production has never been paid for as there is no way of excluding non-paying users. Randall (1994) says it is possible to create a more inclusive accounting of environmental benefits. Randall suggests triple bottom line accounting as a way of accounting for social and environmental costs and benefits, as well as those costs and benefits that are more ostensibly economic. However, there are few operational precedents of this type of accounting. Most accounting of this kind has been theoretical only, for example in Australia the PM's Science, Engineering and Innovation Council (2002) made an account of the future costs of environmental damage, including species extinctions and salinity. Lockwood et al. (2000) have estimated the value of remnant vegetation to landholders and Costanza et al. (1997) have made a global assessment of the value of ecosystem services. A new bottom line may drive acceptance and appreciation of the presence of nature in landscapes hitherto regarded as human, as well as the effect humans have on all landscapes, even those hitherto regarded as wilderness. However, economic analysis remains fundamentally focussed on valuing everything in purely monetary terms, whereas there are other values that are attached to the landscape and land use. Further privatisation and commodification may merely attach pricetags to the landscape and there are equity issues around entry into the market and the distribution of wealth. Furthermore, the identification of ecosystem services presumes human beneficiaries. Similarly the early conservation and preservation laws, arguments for biodiversity's material benefits, and even aesthetic contributions (depending on how wide one wishes to cast the anthropocentric net), are limited to the instrumentalist or consequentialist and therefore utilitarian sphere. These arguments ignore the 'for own sake' intrinsic value or essentialist arguments.[11] Intrinsic value arguments recognise the inherent and inalienable right of living beings to exist, irrespective of their value to humanity.

A more inclusive valuation of the effects of consumption may require the expansion of a monetary estimation to include the 'fragile, intangible, or unquantifiable' (Tribe 1974), the 'incommensurables' (Hardin 1968), the 'non-use/intrinsic/existence' (Industry Commission 1998: 76) values and absolute goods. In many cases it is difficult to give an accurate (for the purposes of assessment) monetary value to environmental resources and the costs generated by their use, and it may be entirely impossible to assess the monetary worth of non-use values such as the intrinsic value of environmental resources independent of human existence. There may be some things, like sanctity of life and the freedom to evolve, that are priceless. These values and costs are hard to account for when a product's value is usually only recognised, and recognised as having its greatest value, in relation to the price that will be paid for its ownership or consumption. Fully internalising these externalities requires that a monetary value be assigned to things whose value is difficult to estimate in dollar terms. This is even more difficult when looking at future monetary estimations of value. Intergenerational equity requires that costs to future generations are included, however future benefits are often discounted, and may actually be incalculable if they really are priceless.

Economic analysis is limited because it recognises only monetary value, only assessment by comparison, and therefore only one means of assessing the quality of life and assessing good. The only 'good' attainable (at best) via the traditional market is to achieve the efficient allocation of scarce resources, which itself assumes that there must be a type of optimal resource use and does not envisage no use. Economic analysis is limited as it exists within an enduring growth paradigm, without acknowledging that there are limits to growth. Broader economic accounting retains 'capitalism's leitmotiv' (Low and Gleeson 1998: 163) of commodifying resources. Commoditisation or monetising may be unpalatable ideologically and inclusive pricing does not necessarily lead to conservation if the costs are still outweighed by the benefits of consumption. As with the deterrent effects of law, the costs must be so great that no benefit will outweigh them. This may require government intervention if the market fails to produce this outcome.

Environmental accounting, satellite surveillance and criminalization, may be seen as institutional technofixes akin to Hardin's (1968) 'technical solutions' for resource degradation and scarcity, solutions which he saw as requiring '... a change only in the techniques of the natural sciences, demanding little or nothing in the way of change in human values or ideas of morality'.[12] If neither criminalization nor the market can offer a solution, what type of change may be required?

**Seeing ourselves in nature, nature in ourselves: a reconciliation solution?**

The change in values attempted by some legislation, from describing human action on private land as desirable to designating it as criminal, is a dramatic one. This change reflects a view that, problematically, extends beyond human actions that have negative consequences. Much of the current system of legislation, impacts only on those who have existing native vegetation remaining and does not impact upon those who have already cleared their land. Regrowth or offsets however, may become a condition for successful clearing applications in Victoria and New South Wales. Restoration orders could also be included as penalty for illegal land clearing in South Australia and New South Wales. The results of these restorative attempts have been argued to be merely gardens that are not really 'natural' because of their human origins (Elliot 1997). Benson (1999) refers to intentionally re-established areas as 'designer' ecosystems. While it is desirable that natural ecosystems not be viewed as 'renewable' to justify their destruction, it seems odd to discount human attempts to restore an environment that has been degraded by unsustainable management. According to the 'garden' view, humans can do no right. At its most extreme, the view would result in a policy of non-intervention even if this intervention is only to address the harm caused by past interference. Retention alone, like more formal reserve systems, may only offer the ad hoc preservation of vegetation in areas that have been historically too hard to clear or have proved unviable. For practical reasons it may never be possible to reserve or restore all ecosystems.[13] However, it would be irresponsible, given the present state of awareness, not to make the attempt at restoration, and unfair to require only those with un-cleared land to bear the full responsibility for reparation. The costs of sourcing, planting and ongoing management would make such ventures unfeasible for most private landowners and outside assistance would in all likelihood be essential.

Arguably, the question of whether environments that are intensively managed or where certain conditions for their development have been instigated by humans, are so divorced from nature that they are no longer part of nature, remains to be more cogently addressed. Perhaps nature should not be so narrowly defined so as to exclude humanity, especially in Australia where many ecosystems may owe part of their evolution to Aboriginal land management practices such as firestick farming. Glazebrook (2003) argues that something natural may result in ecological restoration where humans work with rather than against nature.[14] There are some landscapes that may equally belong both to nature and to culture. Rose (1996: 85) quotes an Australian Aboriginal woman as saying '(T)his earth has an Aboriginal culture inside'. It is possible that this perspective may be extended, the arcadian or bucolic paradise created by a combination of human and nature, may not be just a product of the imagination. The harvest used to be seen as a time of richness and of bounty, the fruits of the earth and of human toil to be celebrated. The harvest, in some ways, is now seen as something that occurs at the expense of non-human nature: salinising and acidifying the soil, if not eroding it completely; destroying organisms rather than husbanding them; and making the environment more harsh and extreme rather than more habitable and hospitable.

How did this picture of agriculture as universal despoiler emerge? There have been many connections made between agriculture and desertification. Perhaps most portentously the crucible of agriculture, the Fertile Crescent, no longer supports the production that fostered its name. Human mismanagement on a gross scale continues to be evidenced by excessive and dangerous agrichemical inputs, the declining diversity in agricultural landscapes and cultivars, poor animal welfare and the effects of unsustainable practices such as excessive water use and overstocking. Given this track record it is not surprising that there are serious concerns surrounding genetically modified foods. In Australia, unsustainable land management practices have caused dramatic declines in water quantity and quality, salinisation, soil acidification, deterioration of soil structure and erosion. This has led to billions of dollars in lost productivity. The cost of reparation in Australia has been estimated to be in the billion dollar range and in some cases farm retirement and industry restructuring have been recommended (Madden *et al.* 2000; Wentworth Group 2002). However, without resorting to romanticism, there are alternative stories, for example in Southern Australia there is considerable evidence that some pastoral areas have developed a self-supporting nature of their own (Smith 2000). Humans have developed sustainable systems, sometimes even within industrialised agriculture, and agriculture may support and be part of natural systems and thus part of nature (Altieri 1987). Agroecologists view people as part of evolved ecosystems that have both natural and human elements. The challenge we face at present is to overcome the human-nature dichotomy. It may be time to acknowledge that some landscapes modified by humans, whether by First Peoples, by activities intended to restore nature or perhaps by agriculture may be accepted not only as part of nature but as essential for securing our environmental future. Ongoing management of areas that are a combination of culture and nature may then be recognised as a valuable contribution.

## Conclusion

The early images from space were of the whole Earth, we were all 'in it together'. Satellite imagery has revealed extensive information about land cover change. The use of satellite imagery has made the extent of land clearance blatantly apparent, exposing the degree of land clearance and the degree of non-compliance with land clearance prohibitions. However, what is appreciated about the imagery owes much to the values held by the observer. The processing of satellite imagery categorises the landscape so that it is split between agriculture defined by private tenure, commercial production, human occupation and impact, and nature defined by public tenure, preservation and the exclusion of humans. There is great force and naming-power in categorisation, which tells us what something is and in doing so implies what it is not and therefore important complexities may be concealed. By dividing the landscape according to tenure and function, satellite imagery alternatively commodifies and criminalises, and both ways of seeing fail to recognise other functions and values. By introducing conservation as a function of private land management, land clearance regulations have crossed this tenure boundary while maintaining the division between the natural and the human. However, the divide between human and nature is an artificial one, since areas that have been preserved in some way from human impact often have a history (and prehistory) of human influence and are presently maintained by humans. The divide also fails to recognise that natural landscapes are productive: they produce much that we consume and much that is necessary for ecosystem functioning. These same functions may be performed in private areas where humans live as part of agricultural systems or in rehabilitated ecosystems that operate according to ecological principles. In some environments the human elements of the landscape may be indistinguishable from the parts considered 'natural'. The human-nature demarcation has allowed for the homelands of First Peoples to be redefined as wilderness. While they have been held up as trophies of so-called pristine nature, untouched by human hand, they have nevertheless been used both before and after the act of reservation. Indeed in reservation they have been described as commodities that have been saved from being consumed by humanity. Few measures however, have recognised any use of nature which is independent of human benefit even when benefits have been more broadly considered so as to include ecosystem services. Arguably, we need to go beyond seeing the environment, whether intensively modified or 'natural', as merely a factory for products that humans can consume and we need to see humans as more than mere consumers or criminals.

Ecocentric policies, such as the Commonwealth of Australia's Biodiversity Strategy (1996) and the Victorian Government's Native Vegetation Management Framework: A Framework for Action (2002), recognise the intrinsic value of native vegetation. However the message contained here may be based on a view that nature and humans are distinct entities with interests of their own that are inevitably in conflict. Seeing landscapes as either dichotomies of wilderness versus production or wilderness versus destruction devalues the complex human-nature relationship. One way of recognising the productive value in natural systems as well as the natural value of agricultural systems, is environmental accounting. This, however, still serves only to emphasise consumption and to commoditise. It provides a price to be exchanged between a provider and a buyer. Labelling human and nature in this way and denying commensuration of other values in dollar terms, blocks other ways of seeing, for example from seeing ourselves as a part of, rather than apart from, nature.

Satellite surveillance may entrench existing ways of seeing the human-nature relationship, for example seeing the landscape as a consumable. It may also reinforce the wilderness boundary that exists between most conservation and production, that is the conception of a division between 'virgin' land unspoiled by human action and that which is a victim of, rather than being improved by, human action. Inadequate conceptions of the human element in landscapes are presently circumscribing the development of effective institutional responses to land clearance and land management. Without new ways of envisaging the relationship between humans and nature it is unlikely that any attempt to criminalise land clearance behaviour will be seen as a just and effective solution.

Satellites may be used to unmask the material consumption of the landscape and to define it as criminal. However, to do so may conceal, as do the land clearance regulations themselves, other relationships that exist between humans and nature. The fact that humans are themselves at risk because they have caused their environments to be at risk, is a potent signal of these relationships. Halsey (2004b: 838) discusses the work of Deleuze and Guittari and argues that 'it is questionable whether it is possible to logically speak of "the biotic community" as something existing externally to the happenings of "humanity". Perhaps a more productive approach would be to say that there are numerous and heterogenous interfaces between bodies and practices ...'.

Defining human activity in the landscape as simply criminal, destructive, consumptive or unnatural, simply because it is human, ignores the fact that human-modification has not always compromised or been at the expense of the natural values of landscapes, just as nature is not always beneficial. The culture of humans in any landscape plays an important role in determining the environmental outcomes of that landscape and therefore solutions to mismanagement will need to be socially sustainable to be environmentally sustainable. This may not be easily achieved if the role of humans is restricted to that of consumer, despoiler or criminal. Since 1872 the effective boundaries of Yellowstone National Park have been extended to cover the natural ranges of wildlife rather than just scenic values for humans. In Australia land clearance regulation has blurred the line between private-and-production and public-and-preservation. The boundaries may have to be obscured even further for a truer picture of our role and interconnection with nature to emerge. Should we not extend the boundaries of nature to include ourselves? In division we obscure the humanity in the 'other' (nature) as well as the 'other' in ourselves.

## Notes

1   Charlemagne, *Capitulare Aquisgranense*, art 19, 77, in 'Monumenta Germaniae Historica', vol 2 p 172, 8th Century, Boretius, A (ed) (1897) cited in Glacken, C J (1967) *Traces on the Rhodian Shore: Nature and Culture in Western Thought from Ancient Times to the end of the Eighteenth Century*, University of California Press, Berkeley, p 763, 334.

2   The following decade also saw continuing enactments and re-enactments in all state and territory jurisdictions. As responsibility for the environment under the Constitution (by omission) is in the hands of the states, each state and territory has its own version. For e.g. s 21(2) of the *Native Vegetation Conservation Act* 1997 (NSW) states that '(A) person must not clear native vegetation on any land except in accordance with a development consent that is in force or a native vegetation code of practice' and applies Part 4 of the *Environmental Planning and Assessment Act* 1979 (NSW) to the clearing of native vegetation. Offences constitute breaches of the s 76(2) of the *Environmental Planning and Assessment Act* 1979 (NSW) prohibition of development without consent and are therefore offences under s 125(1) of the *Environmental Planning and Assessment Act*. The maximum penalty for unauthorised clearance in New South Wales is $1.1 million. Protections also extend to public authorities and public land and incarceration is also possible under other legislation in some jurisdictions. In Queensland a timbercutter was sentenced to 12 months imprisonment by a District Court (upheld on appeal *R v Dempsey* [2002]) for felling 25 trees, including a 100 to 300 year old Queensland Maple, Maple Silk Wood, Northern Silky Oak and Black Walnut between 20 December 2000 and 2 January 2001, contrary to s 56(1) of the *Wet Tropics World Heritage Protection and Management Act* 1993 (Qld).

3   The figure for Australia used by FAO was 282,000 ha/yr, placing us eleventh but this more recent figure places Australia in 9th position. The more recent figure is from Barson, M, Randall, L and Bordas, V (2000) *Land cover changes in Australia 1990–1995. Results of the collaborative Bureau of Rural Sciences – State agencies' project on remote sensing of agricultural land cover change*, Bureau of Rural Sciences, Canberra, p 92.

4   For a recent review see Productivity Commission 2004, *Impacts of Native Vegetation and Biodiversity Regulations*, Report No 29, Melbourne.

5   Carterra data has recently been purchased by the NSW Government for landcover monitoring purposes.

6   Other satellites with higher resolution capabilities are the French Spot satellite which produces 10 m square pixels in black and white (panchromatic) and 20 m square pixels in four electromagnetic wavelength ranges, or bandwidths and the DigitalGlobe's QuickBird satellite has a similar range of multispectral and panchromatic data to that of Carterra.

7   The Landsat bands most useful for identifying the presence or absence of vegetation are the red and near infra red bands (Bands 3 and 4). These bands are often related in ratios or indices as 'greenness' indicators; to detect areas of higher vegetation relative to lower. A thresholded greenness indicator may be used to categorise cover types or all cover types may be classified according to their spectral signature, by categorising the relative reflectance or spectral signals of the surface into (for example) areas of forest cover, urban areas and bare land.

8   For example the limitation period for enforcement in South Australia is 3 years (6 with the approval of the Minister, see sections 33 and 35 of the *Native Vegetation Act* 1991 (SA)).

9   Restrictions in Tasmania were only introduced in 2002 and Western Australia has only recently strengthened earlier legislation to bring it into comparable line with the other states discussed here, see further Bartel, R L (2004) 'Satellite Imagery and Land Clearance Legislation: A Picture of Regulatory Efficacy?' *The Australasian Journal of Natural Resources Law and Policy*, vol 9, no 1, pp 1–31.

10   [1925] SASR 395.

11   The utilitarian have been described by Eugene Hargrove as the 'bread and medicine' arguments, 'The Paradox of Humanity: Two Views of Biodiversity and Landscapes,' in Kim, K C and Weaver, R D (eds) *Biodiversity and Landscapes: A paradox of humanity* (1994), Cambridge University Press, New York, pp 173–86.

12   See Halsey (2004a:37) for an illuminating discussion of the effects technology has had on our ways of seeing and the limitations of these resultant ways of seeing and proposed techno-institutional fixes for human-induced environmental harm, see further Halsey, 2004b: 836.

13   Nor desirable to keep them like museum pieces.

14   Glazebrook, T (2003) 'Art or Nature? Aristotle, Restoration Ecology, and Flowforms,' *Ethics and the Environment*, vol 8, no 1, pp 22–36.

## References

ABS (Australian Bureau of Statistics) (2002) *Agriculture, Australia*, Cat No 7113.0, Australian Bureau of Statistics, Canberra.

Altieri, M A (1987) *Agroecology: The Scientific Basis of Alternative Agriculture*, Westview Press, Boulder, p 227.

Anon (1999) 'Greens say Jakarta must answer for annual smog', *The Age*, Reuters, AP, 8 August, p 12.

ANVA (Australian Native Vegetation Assessment) (2001) *Australian Native Vegetation Assessment 2001*, National Land and Water Resources Audit, Land and Water Australia, Commonwealth of Australia, Canberra, available on-line at <http://audit.ea.gov.au/ANRA>, accessed December 2004.

Auditor-General of New South Wales (Sendt, R J) (2002) *Performance Audit Report: Department of Land and Water Conservation: Regulating the Clearing of Native Vegetation*, The Audit Office of New South Wales, available on-line at http://<www.audit.nsw.gov.au/perfaud-rep/Year-2002-2003/LandClearing-Aug2002/LandClearing-Contents.html>, accessed December 2004.

Baden, J and Stroup, R L (1990) 'Natural Resource Scarcity, Entrepreneurship, and the Political Economy of Hope,' *Economics and the Environment: A Reconciliation*, Walter Block, ed, Fraser Institute, Vancouver, B.C. pp 117–136.

Barson, M, Randall, L and Bordas, V (2000) *Land cover changes in Australia 1990–1995. Results of the collaborative Bureau of Rural Sciences — State agencies' project on remote sensing of agricultural land cover change*, Bureau of Rural Sciences, Canberra, pp 92, 65.

Bartel, R L (2004) 'Satellite Imagery and Land Clearance Legislation: A Picture of Regulatory Efficacy?', *The Australasian Journal of Natural Resources Law and Policy*, vol 9, no 1, pp 1–31.

Bartel, R L and Leach, J H J (2000) 'Big Brother and the Law of the Land: The Role of Satellite Surveillance and GIS in the Regulation of Land Clearance', *Proceedings of the Spatial Information Research Centre's 12th Colloquium*, SIRC2000, University of Otago, New Zealand, pp 267–277.

Benson, J S (1999) *Setting the scene: The native vegetation of New South Wales*, Native Vegetation Advisory Council of New South Wales, Sydney, available on-line at <http://www.rbgsyd.nsw.gov.au/__data/page/228/settingthescene.pdf>, accessed December 2004.

Binning, C E and Young, M (1999) *Conservation Hindered: The impact of local government rates and State land taxes on the conservation of native vegetation*, National Research and Development Program on Rehabilitation, Management and Conservation of Remnant Vegetation, Research Report 3/99, Environment Australia, Canberra.

Costanza, R, d'Arge, R, de Groot, R, Farber, S, Grasso, M, Hannon, B, Limburg, K, Naeem, S, O'Neill, R, Paruelo, J, Raskin, R, Sutton, P. and van den Belt, M (1997) 'The value of the world's ecosystem services and natural capital,' *Nature*, (1997) 387, pp 253–260.

DNRE (Department of Natural Resources and Environment, Victoria) (2000) *Restoring our Catchments: Draft Native Vegetation Management Framework, DNRE*, Land and Water, Melbourne.

Elliot, R (1997) *Faking Nature: the ethics of environmental restoration*, Routledge, London and New York, p 177.

FAO (United Nations Food and Agriculture Organization) (2001) *Global Forest Resources Assessment 2000*, available on-line <http://www.fao.org/documents/show_cdr.asp?url_file=/DOCREP/004/Y1997E/Y1997E00.HTM>, accessed December 2004.

Flannery, T (1994) *The Future Eaters: An ecological history of the Australasian Land and Peoples*, Reed Books, Port Melbourne, p 423.

Flannery, T (2001) *The Eternal Frontier: an ecological history of North America and its people*, Text Publishing, Melbourne, p 404.

Glacken, C J (1967) *Traces on the Rhodian Shore: Nature and Culture in Western Thought from Ancient Times to the end of the Eighteenth Century*, University of California Press, Berkeley, p 763.

Glazebrook, T (2003) 'Art or Nature? Aristotle, Restoration Ecology, and Flowforms,' *Ethics and the Environment*, vol 8, no 1, pp 22–36.

Grabosky, P (1995) 'Counterproductive Regulation,' International *Journal of the Sociology of Law*, vol 23, pp 347–369.

Graetz, D R, Wilson, M A and Campbell, S K (1995) 'Landcover disturbance over the Australian Continent: A contemporary assessment,' *Biodiversity Series Paper No 7*, Department of the Environment, Sport and Territories, Canberra, p 86.

Halsey, M (2004a) 'Environmental Visions: Deleuze and the modalities of nature,' *Ethics and the Environment*, vol 9, no 2, pp 33–64.

Halsey, M (2004b) 'Against "Green" Criminology,' *British Journal of Criminology*, vol 44, pp 833–853.

Hamblin, A (2000) 'Executive Summary,' in *Visions of Future Landscapes, Fenner Conference on the Environment 1999*, Bureau of Rural Sciences, Canberra, pp 1–2.

Hardin, G (1968) 'The tragedy of the commons,' *Science*, vol 162, pp 1243–1248.

Hargrove E (1994) 'The Paradox of Humanity: Two Views of Biodiversity and Landscapes,' in Kim, K C and Weaver, R D (eds) *Biodiversity and Landscapes: A paradox of humanity*, Cambridge University Press, New York, pp 173–86.

Hawkins, K (1984) *Environment and Enforcement: regulation and the social definition of pollution*, Clarendon Press, Oxford, p 253.

Industry Commission (1998) *A full repairing lease: Inquiry into ecologically sustainable land management*, Report No 60, available on-line at <http://www.pc.gov.au/ic/inquiry/60eslm/finalreport/index.html>, accessed December 2004.

Kestel Research (Hibberd, J and Wilson, B) and Victorian Department of Conservation and Environment (Goodson, P and Woodgate, P) (1990) Report to the Resource Assessment Commission on Forest Clearing in Australia, *Resource Assessment Commission Forest and Timber Inquiry Consultancy Series* No. FTC91/02. Stage 1 Report.

Kirkpatrick, J (1994) *A Continent Transformed: Human Impact on the Natural Vegetation of Australia*, Oxford University Press, Melbourne, p 133.

Locke, J (1690/1967) *Two Treatises of Government*, Peter Laslett Critical (2nd) Edition, Cambridge University Press, London, p 525.

Lockwood, M, Walpole S and Miles, C (2000) *Economics of Remnant Native Vegetation on Private Property*, National Research and Development Program on Rehabilitation, Management and Conservation of Remnant Vegetation, Research Report 2/00: Land and Water Resources Research and Development Corporation, Canberra, p 59.

Low, N and Gleeson, B (1998) *Justice, Society and Nature: an exploration of political ecology*, Routledge, London and New York, p 257.

Madden, B, Hayes, G and Duggan, K (2000) *Repairing the country: A national scenario for strategic investment*, Report prepared for the Australian Conservation Foundation, National Farmers Federation and the Land and Water Research and Development Corporation, 2000, available on-line at <http://www.nff.org.au/pages/pub/rtc.pdf>, accessed December 2004.

Mannion AM (1997) *Global Environmental Change: A Natural and Cultural Environmental History*, Longman, New York, p 404.

Mascall, S and Dare, P (2000) 'Our 800 km eye in the sky,' *The Age*, 9 April, p 1.

MAV (Municipal Association of Victoria) (2000) Submission to Victoria's Draft Native Vegetation Management Framework, p 28.

NSWEPA (New South Wales Environment Protection Authority) (2000) *New South Wales State of the Environment 2000*, NSWEPA, Sydney.

Pederson, B F (2000) 'Controlling Area Based Subsidies within the European Union using Web-Based GIS', *Proceedings of the 10th Australasian Remote Sensing and Photogrammetry Conference*, pp 703–710.

Phillips, G (1999) 'Big Brothercam: eyes in the sky, office and home,' *The Age*, 4 September.

PM's Science, Engineering and Innovation Council (2002) *Sustaining our Natural Systems and Biodiversity Report*, Commonwealth of Australia, Canberra, Available on-line at <http://www.dest.gov.au/science/pmseic/documents/Sustaining_our_Natural_Systems_and_Biodiversity_Working_Group_Paper.doc>, accessed December 2004.

Productivity Commission 2004, *Impacts of Native Vegetation and Biodiversity Regulations*, Report No 29, Melbourne.

Randall, A (1994) 'Thinking about the value of biodiversity,' in Kim, K C and Weaver, R D (eds) *Biodiversity and Landscapes: A paradox of humanity*, Cambridge University Press, Cambridge, pp 271–285.

Richelson, J T (1998) 'Scientists in Black,' *Scientific American*, vol 278, no 2, pp 38–45.

Robbins, M (2001) 'Felling trees by satellite "flawed",' *The Australian*, Wednesday 3 October, p 7.

Rose, D B (1996) *Nourishing Terrains: Australian Aboriginal Views of Landscape and Wilderness*, Australian Heritage Commission, Canberra, p 95.

Skidmore, A (1998) 'Worlds Apart,' *ITC Journal: International Journal of Aerospace Survey and Earth Sciences*, vol 3–4, pp 240–245.

Smith, D F (2000) *Natural Gain in the Grazing Lands of Southern Australia*, University of New South Wales Press, Sydney, p 225.

Sullivan, G (2003) 'Enforcing Queensland's Vegetation Clearing Laws', paper presented to Queensland Environmental Law Association Seminar, *Clearing Vegetation in Queensland, Mapping, Prosecutions and Legal Aspects for Landholders and Developers*, 11 August 2003.

Tribe, L H (1974) 'Ways not to think about plastic trees: new foundations for environmental law,' *Yale Law Journal*, vol 83, no 7, pp 1315–1348.

Wentworth Group (2002) *Blueprint for a Living Continent, A way forward from the Wentworth Group of concerned scientists* (World Wildlife Fund Australia, 2002), available on-line at <http://www.ccsa.asn.au/Blueprint_for_a_Living_Continen.pdf>, accessed December 2004.

Woodgate, P and Black, P (1988) *Forest cover changes in Victoria 1869–1987*, Department of Conservation, Forests and Lands, East Melbourne, p 31.

Young, M (2000) *First or second-best solutions? Looking back on Australasian agrienvironment policy from 2020*, paper presented at the Australian Agricultural and Resource Economics Society Annual Conference.

# 30. Reducing the illicit trade in endangered wildlife: the market reduction approach*

*Jacqueline L. Schneider*

The market reduction approach is a crime reduction strategy that aims to reduce and disrupt stolen goods markets, in addition to reducing theft levels by making it more risky for thieves to sell stolen property. Initially, the concept has shown promise in England with regard to reducing traditional forms of property-related crime as well as disrupting certain types of stolen goods markets. Additionally, strides have been made using property as a unit of analysis rather than traditional foci of attention when examining crime patterns and designing tactical responses. In line with the 2005 United Nations program of work on transnational and organized crime, this article uses the specific example of the illegal trade of endangered flora and fauna to explore how the market reduction approach can be expanded beyond its current use into the realm of nontraditional types of property crime.

**Key Words** endangered species • illicit markets • market reduction approach • illegal wildlife trade

Historically, criminological research has examined offender motivations, patterns of offending, or general causes of criminality. For example, research has focused on criminal careers to see what patterns of criminality exist (see Farrington, 1999; Shover, 1996; West 1996). Correlations between specific types of offenses have been demonstrated (see Schneider, 2005a, for the burglary–shoplifting link, and for the drugs–crime link, see Jarvis and Parker, 1989; Bennett, 1998, 2000; and Gossop, Marsden, and Rolfe, 2000). Research explains burglars' decision-making process (see Bennett and Wright, 1984; Palmer, Holmes, and Hollin, 2002; Wright and Decker, 1994), the impact of illegal markets in general (see Reuter, 1984, 2004), and how stolen goods markets operate (see Allen, 2000; Frieberg, 1997; Sohneider, 2005b; Stevenson, Forsythe, and Weatherbum, 2001; Sutton 1995, 1998;[1] Sutton, Schneider, and Hetherington, 2001). Until relatively recently, evidence that depicts accurately the contributing role that macrolevel factors play in keeping theft levels high has been lacking in the literature. This is in spite of the fact that discussions pertaining to the importance of traditional stolen goods markets have been

* From *Journal of Contemporary Criminal Justice* (2008), 24(3): pp. 274–295.

evident in the literature as early as the 1700s (see Colquhoun, 1796/1976; Henry, 1977) through to modern times, when Chappell and Walsh (1974) and Klockars (1974) demonstrated clearly the crucial role these markets played. Research, albeit in its infancy, has begun to examine the nature of traditional stolen goods markets and the extent to which they help to maintain theft levels (see Allen 2000; Frieberg 1997; Schneider, 2003, 2005a, 2005b; Stevenson *et al.* 2001; Sutton 1993, 1998). Although strides are being made to better understand traditional stolen goods markets, very little is being done to explore less traditional property markets, such as endangered wild flora and fauna.[2]

Research on and relating to the illegal trade in endangered wildlife is insufficient in terms of both quantity and quality. Very little scientific evidence exists that (a) describes the nature and characteristics of the markets that deal in endangered species, (b) explains how these specific markets operate, (c) explores what function they serve in the proliferation of criminal activity revolving around these illegal markets, or (d) explores the relationship, if any, that exists between the illegal trade in wildlife and other types of illegal commodities and their markets, such as drugs, weapons, or – even as distasteful as it is – humans and/or their body parts. Going beyond the simple notion that thieves steal to make money, preliminary market-level analyses reveal that thieves steal because they know there are ways for them to sell the goods they steal. In other words, the crime of handling is supported by a structure that allows thieves the opportunity to sell stolen property either to people who use the items themselves or to those who sell it on to others. This assertion is mainly thought of in terms of traditional forms of property, such as televisions, DVD players, and cell phones, and traditional forms of crime, such as shop theft, burglary, and theft of or from motor vehicles. It is proposed here that theft of more exotic property, such as endangered plants, animals, and their parts, occurs as a result of these same dynamics – thieves, poachers, and handlers trade these items because somewhere there is a handler who has people ready and willing to purchase the ill-gotten goods. Therefore, the aim of this article is to demonstrate how a crime reduction strategy that targets traditional thieves, handlers, and stolen property can be expanded to redress less traditional property and theft-related crime, such as the illicit trade in endangered species. By applying the data-driven concept of the market reduction approach (MRA), a more thorough and systematic understanding of these practices can begin to develop.

## The MRA

The foundations of the MRA, in terms of policing strategies, rest on pro-active, intelligence-led, and zero-tolerance policing, whereas its theoretical underpinnings rely on routine activity theory to guide the model. The original work by Cohen and Felson (1979) specifically examined incidents or events rather than individuals, who were considered merely objects who had 'inclinations' to engage in these events (see Clarke and Felson, 2004). Routine activity theory proposed that three basic elements must exist for a crime event to occur: likely offender, suitable target, and the absence of a capable guardian (see Clarke and Felson, 2004; Felson, 2002; Felson and Clarke, 1998).

The overall aims of the MRA are to disrupt and reduce stolen goods markets by discovering what property is stolen, how thieves acquire the property in terms of both location and technique, how goods are recycled back into the community, and who the consumers of these goods are. Once these patterns are identified, specific policing interventions can be developed based on existing data. Public information through various media outlets is disseminated to keep citizens apprised of operational results and for general crime prevention purposes.[3]

There are two dimensions on which success can be measured. The first is connected to changes in the type of stolen goods market operating, and the second centers on the type of property stolen. MRA tactics must be evidence led; therefore, interventions should aim to reduce and/or disrupt the specific type of market operating locally, as identified through analyses. The monitoring process reveals the impact of those interventions. So a change from the targeted stolen goods market to a different type of market would show disruption. For example, if initial analyses showed that particular goods were traded via residential fences, interventions ought to target residential fences. Postintervention, if goods are then found to be traded via a network of associates rather than residential fences, a change has occurred, hence a disruption. A related indicator of success would be a change in the amount of time it takes a thief to sell the stolen goods. The longer it takes for the goods to exchange hands, the more risky it is for the thieves because of the increased probability of police's detecting the thief with goods. Furthermore, increases in disposal times might also indicate the unwillingness of handlers to take the goods, suggesting awareness that authorities are indeed targeting the illegal activities.

The second indicator of successful tactical interventions relates to the property itself. Again, once hot property is identified through analyses, interventions targeting that type of property are undertaken. If successful, shifts from the demanded property to another type of property would indicate that operations were having an effect. Additionally, significant fluctuations in the reported number of stolen items of the same property or, finally, changes in the types of crimes that generated the theft of demanded property would all be evidence of success. This highlights the importance of constant monitoring so that changes in either method of disposal or hot products can be observed.

In England, crime and disorder partners, including police, appeared to know very little about the process by which stolen goods exchange hands once they are removed from their rightful owners (see Schneider 2005b; Sutton 1993, 1995, 1998; Sutton et al. 2001). Furthermore, research points out that research examining methods for disposing stolen goods is meager, leaving anecdotal evidence to steer police practice rather than the preferred research-based evidence. Stolen goods markets, because of their very nature, are difficult to investigate; thus intervention with the aim of disrupting or reducing them has taken a backseat to other policing priorities and key performance indicators. Obviously, police investigate cases involving stolen goods and their markets in the absence of the MRA. However, investigations and interventions are executed generally on a case-by-case basis and are done in isolation of other types of offenses. The MRA sought to redress this gap in knowledge and practice, thus providing a more systematic and routine tool for intervention.

From 1999 to 2002, funding was made available to crime and disorder partners via the U.K. Home Office's Crime Reduction Programme,[4] a £250 million investment by government with the aim to implement and test empirically innovative crime reduction strategies. The MRA was one of the many targeted policing initiatives funded under the program.[5] Initial findings from the funded projects revealed that the concept had promise (for details of the evaluations of these funded projects, see Hale, Harris, Uglow, Gilling, and Netten, 2004), and in 2004, the MRA was put forward as best practice, suggesting that it should be adopted by crime and disorder partners throughout the United Kingdom.

The independent evaluations of the MRA crime reduction program projects demonstrated some degree of impact on stolen goods markets and acquisitive crime;[6] however, it has never been applied or tested on markets whereby the traded goods are nontraditional or extremely uncommon. At the United Nations Crime Congress 2003, the author presented the concept of the MRA as a possible intervention tool for illegal markets covered under the UN Convention on Transnational and Organized Crime, which includes cultural or heritage items, weapons and ammunition, flora and fauna, and humans and their parts. The following section puts into context the program of work outlined by the UN, followed by a discussion of illegal trade in wild flora and fauna. Finally, recommendations are made for a body of work to begin on this underdeveloped area of work.

It is acknowledged here that the other illegally traded goods in the convention, for example, cultural items, fine art, weapons, and human beings and their body parts, could be potentially affected by the use of the MRA. However, the scope of this article is limited to the area of endangered species, as there is an extreme void in that literature. Also, the trafficking in humans is so complex that the subject demands separate examination of the practicalities of the application of the concept. Finally, this article contains no data analyses. The data needed to support the implementation of the MRA with regard to endangered species are in need of development before the actual concept can be used. Data that do exist are not organized sufficiently to permit the level of analysis that the MRA demands. Rather, this article discusses the fragile nature of existing data and offers suggestions on how future study and the collection of the particular type of necessary MRA data the can take place. Therefore, this article demonstrates clearly how conceptually the MRA can be used to disrupt and reduce the illegal trade in flora and fauna as a starting point for investigation and for a way to introduce policy makers to the idea.

The MRA, as applied to the illicit endangered species trade, seeks to identify the routine patterns of those involved: poachers, handlers, and consumers – those who hunt, transform, transport, and buy the wildlife (the likely offenders); the precise wildlife being hunted, transformed, transported, and purchased (the suitable targets); and those whose remit is to actually conserve and protect these species (conservators, police, customs, and wildlife officers). The invisible nature of this trade, coupled with its underresearched and underpoliced status, results in a basic void of knowledge about the very routines necessary to affect it. This article hopes to bring to the attention of conservators and policy makers a new tool that could assist them in their efforts to affect or redirect their interdiction work with illegal trade in endangered flora and fauna.

As previously stated, the concept relies on the systematic and routine analyses of data for the purpose of guiding police operational tactics.[7] In essence, the MRA is a crime reduction strategy that offers practitioners a methodology or a framework that seeks to synthesize the analyses of various forms of official and interview data to identify the exchange relationship between thieves and handlers of stolen goods (the markets) and the property that is most in demand (the 'hot products').[8]

Table 30.1 pits traditional foci of attention in terms of how data are created by police against that of the MRA, which uses differently the existing crime data to better address the stolen goods markets. The table is divided into three columns. The first describes what types of data are traditionally collected when examining theft-related offenses. For example, police collect information on what types of crime are driving the theft, such as burglary, shop theft, or theft from motor vehicles, with the aim of linking crimes to a specific individual offender. The second column describes how the MRA would approach traditional forms of theft. The unit of analysis shifts from offender to property and subsequently to the process by which stolen property moves from point of origin (residence, shop, car) through to those who purchase the goods. The final column illustrates how the MRA is applied to endangered species trafficking. Rather than focusing on whether the property is a specific electronic device, investigators would need to collect data on what plants or animals or their by-products are being targeted. For example, if black bears are found killed, investigators need to identify what body parts are removed to determine if the market is being fueled by the demand for gall bladders or for pelts or claws. There are only a few regions worldwide that host the black bear, including North America. With the decline in numbers of bears in Asia, poachers are turning to North America to fill the demand, which remains high in several Asian countries. Therefore, in terms of the MRA, investigators need to be able to track incidents occurring in range countries (countries of species' origin) to those countries where the parts are consumed (in the case of bear gall bladders, Japan, South Korea, Taiwan, and China). This expands our understanding of 'location,' as the MRA does not situate the crime in merely one stationary location; rather, it looks at the totality of the crime as a way to intervene at all points in the illicit goods' life cycle. Gathering information about stolen goods markets requires police and partner agencies to expand their sources of data as well as to change the unit of analysis from the person to that of property (items stolen).[9] By doing so, the chances of disrupting and reducing stolen goods markets are enhanced greatly.

## United Nations – a program of work

Crime congresses are organized by the UN Economic and Social Council

**Table 30.1** Focus of attention

| Focus | Traditional | MRA | MRA/Wildlife |
|---|---|---|---|
| Who | Individual offender | Thief, handler, consumer | Hunter, poacher, handler, consumer |
| What | Individual crime (burglary, shop theft, theft from motor vehicle) | Specific types of property | Animals, plants, and/or by-products |
| Location | Individual address | Type of location (house, shop, shed, school, business) | Country of origin (range area), country of consumption |
| Date | Date of victimization | Seasonality | Seasonality, mating season |
| How | Individual modus operandi of offender | How things are bought and sold (type of stolen goods market) | How things are harvested, processed, shipped |
| Why | Drugs, poverty, greed, abuse | Demand | Demand |

Note: MRA = market reduction approach.

(ECOSOC) every 5 years, as provided by Article 62 of the UN Charter and General Assembly (GA) Resolution 415(V) of 1950 (see Clark, 1994; Fasulo, 2004; United Nations, 2004a). The congresses have a number of purposes. They provide a forum for views pertaining to crime and justice to be shared among and between member states, intergovernmental agencies, nongovernmental agencies (NGOs), and individual experts. Research findings and experiences with use and implementation of various laws as well as policy are also shared during these meetings. Emergent trends and issues in crime prevention and criminal justice are identified and discussed. Advice, comments, and suggestions on crime prevention and criminal justice are prepared for submission to the Commission on Crime Prevention and Criminal Justice for possible inclusion in its program of work.

The agenda for crime congresses is set in advance by member states of the UN crime commission, which meets annually. The Commission on Crime Prevention and Criminal Justice is composed of 40 member states that are selected and serve on a rotating basis; however, other nations can attend. The crime commission is a functional body of the ECOSOC whereby member states introduce, debate, and adopt resolutions for consideration by the ECOSOC and/or UNGA. These resolutions provide the framework for a course of action with regard to international policies on crime prevention and criminal justice, thus mandating member states to a specific course of action or program of work. Through the crime program, the UN Office of Drugs and Crime (UNODC) carries out the mandates established by the commission and therefore is responsible for crime prevention, criminal justice, and criminal law reform.[10] UNODC pays particular attention to transnational organized crime, corruption, terrorism, and the trafficking in humans by supporting the development of international legal instruments on global crime, including the UN Convention Against Transnational and Organized Crime and its three protocols, which entered into force in September 2003.

In 2005, the 11th UN Congress on Crime Prevention and Criminal Justice took place in Bangkok, Thailand. Five areas of substantive areas of work were included on the agenda: effective measures to combat transnational and organized crime, international cooperation against terrorism, corruption, economic and financial crimes, and making standards work.[11]

Most relevant to the current discussion is the first item on the agenda, transnational and organized crime. Property-based issues in the UN Convention Against Transnational and Organized Crime and its protocols center on firearms; protected species of wild flora and fauna; cultural property; persons, especially women and children; smuggling of migrants; and finally, human organs.[12] According to Zimmerman (2003), the convention is a guiding document that has two goals. The first is to eliminate differences between national legal systems that have previously prevented mutual assistance, and the second is to set standards of national legislation that will enhance efforts to combat effectively organized crime. Claims have been made linking the illicit trade in flora and fauna, as well as the trafficking of humans, to organized crime, thus situating firmly this activity alongside other organized criminal activity as outlined in the convention.[13] However, the evidence linking the illegal trade in cultural items to organized crime is much less definitive. The data on which the authors' claims are made remain elusive and ambiguous. The suppositions are indeed made but with no supporting evidence. For obvious reasons, this presents to researchers methodological concerns, on one hand, and, on the other, an opportunity to conduct more scientific research to substantiate these claims. Particularly, interviews with poachers and handlers of endangered wildlife are essential and part of the overall MRA model.

Moreover, the Convention on International Trade in Endangered Species of Wild Fauna and Flora (CITES) and the Convention on Biological Diversity provide the foundation for the UN's call to protect wild flora and fauna.[14] Member states are encouraged to adopt protective and preventative measures against the illegal trafficking for a variety of endangered species. It is acknowledged here that the illegal trade in protected and/or endangered species is a low priority for many member states, mainly because of competing interests, such as trafficking in persons or weapons. Finally, some member states have domestic laws that run counter to both the Convention Against Transnational and Organized Crime and CITES, which confounds issues greatly, thus making intervention, interdiction, and prevention efforts exponentially more difficult.

## Illegal trade in endangered species

Although there is minimal literature available to help further our understanding of stolen goods markets, there is even less scientifically based literature that relates to the illegal trade of endangered wildlife. Agency reports provide the vast majority of information on this topic.[15] Although these reports contain information about trade routes, types of activities, and impact on natural habitat (see Cook, Roberts, and Lowther, 2002; Cowdrey, 2002), missing from them are detailed explanations about scientific methodology and data collection and interrogation procedures, thus leaving the findings open to obvious scrutiny in terms of validity and reliability. The information contained in these reports is reported here, as there is a dearth of other available information on topic among the social scientific literature. Other academic research tends to focus on legislation, treaties, or one species at a time, making generalizations or inferences about activities about overall practices virtually impossible.

### The extent of the illegal trade

According to agency reports, most of the trade in wildlife is legal and provides much-needed revenue to range areas or source countries, many of which are located in developing countries or countries with economies in transition. However, according to Zimmerman (2003), 'The black market in illegal wildlife is now the second largest in the world-ranking only behind the trade in illegal drugs' (p. 1659). Therefore, the illegal trade, according to Cook et al. (2002), not only threatens survival and conservation of endangered species but also offers high rewards and low risks to those involved.

Calculating the costs of the illegal trade is fraught with difficulty, but as a way to illustrate both the scale of the problem and the frailty of the data, existing figures are reported here. Cook et al. (2002) estimate US$159 billion annual trade based on declared import values of commodities.[16] However, the Metropolitan Police (United Kingdom) estimate that 350 million animals and plants are traded every year, with a market value of US$25 billion, of which one quarter is from illegal trading.[17] And still another estimate puts the illegal, international trade of environmentally sensitive material, which includes wildlife and ozone-depleting substances, at nearly US$8 billion (see Rubin and Stucky, 2004). Cowdrey (2002) estimates that US$25 million worth of caviar left the United Arab Emirates (UAE) illegally for destinations in the United States and United Kingdom but offers no mention of total global costs across all types of illegal activities.

Although is it obvious that no standardized formula exists to calculate the costs of legal or illegal revenues, three additional things are evident. First, loss of wildlife extends well beyond monetary values; for example, the depletion of rainforests is said to contribute to global climate changes in addition to the destruction of natural habitats that sustain plants, animals, and humans. Second, the trade in endangered species, if it is truly second only to that of illegal drugs trafficking, must be extremely lucrative – presenting traders with opportunities to earn vast amounts of money while remaining relatively invisible to authorities. Third, the limitations placed on the legal wildlife markets provide a fertile environment for illegal markets to develop and thrive. Illegal markets, as with any strongly demanded commodity, will bypass legal trade regulations, such as quotas, permits, and documentations required, for example, by CITES signatory countries.[18] Moreover, an item included on the World Conservation Union's (IUCN) Red List of Threatened Species might well increase the desirability of the item among certain collectors.[19] The greater the scarcity of the plant or animal, the greater the desirability as well as the costs in terms of acquisition from the wild, preparation of goods for processing, and subsequently, transportation to final consumer destinations. The amount of effort it takes to obtain the item coupled with the level of protection levied at it will no doubt be reflected in the final price.

The lack of social science on this topic is conspicuous by its absence. Given the level of criminality, the extent of potential illegal profits, the level of damage incurred as a result of the trade, and the seriousness of the damage, it is surprising that social scientists have neglected the field of work.

### The Activities

According to Cook *et al.* (2002), there are five distinct types of illegal activities with regard to the trade in flora and fauna. These include the illegal timber trade; caviar trafficking; activities related to drug trafficking; skins, furs, and traditional Asian medicines (TAM); and specialist specimen collection. Each of these activities are said to have their own highly organized methods, markets, and trade routes. However, this finding contradicts Cowdrey (2002), whose work espoused that trade routes for these run parallel not only to each other but with illegal trade routes of drugs and weapons.

According to Cowdrey (2002), items or goods flow from range or source areas, which are countries or regions of natural habitat, through to consumer areas, often-times using intermediate destinations. These serve several important functions. They act as a funnel for long-haul trips where items are packed in bulk. Intermediate destinations can serve as a stopover place where shipments or modes of transportation can be switched. The port can function as a processing area where items are altered from their raw form to a finished product; for example, elephant tusks can be carved into a variety of smaller ivory items, which would be much more difficult to detect. Destinations operate as transshipment centers or free-trade areas, which are normally countries with weak borders, legislation, and enforcement. Intermediary stops can provide the opportunity to serve as regional distribution centers, where bulk shipments are broken down into smaller, less conspicuous ones.

However, there is a complicating factor of captive-bred or artificially propagated specimens that are farmed in nonrange areas and then are traded in the international arena. The level of skill required in terms of trade and shipment is product dependent, with illegal timber and caviar trafficking requiring the most sophisticated level of organization. Furthermore, illegal shipments are categorized by the skill level needed in production and, in ascending order, include processed parts (carved ivory, TAM, sawn timber), unprocessed parts (bones, tusks, skins), dead animals and plants, and live animals and plants (Cowdrey, 2002).

Data about the participants involved in illegally traded wildlife is extremely scarce although crucial to the MRA. Although very little hard data exist, there is a 'commonly held view that most wildlife crime offences are committed by a hard-core of habitual offenders, many of whom operate within organised gangs and have a lengthy history' (Cook *et al.* 2001, p. 25). Sweeping statements such as these are unhelpful unless there is some reference made to existing data. Indeed, they are particularly problematic when situated alongside a crime reduction concept, such as the MRA, that relies on the systematic analysis of data to guide tactical interventions.

Swanepoel (1998) conducted an exploratory study that examined the illegal trade in rhino horns in South Africa. Analyses of criminal cases involving poaching and/or trading in rhino horns demonstrated that outlets for the horns were located in the Far East, North Yemen, and India. Traders in the property were identified as poachers who were local residents familiar with the terrain. Runners acted as middlemen between the poachers and the wholesalers, who ensured that the horns found their way to their final destinations. Offenders had a mean age of 35 (range 20–65) with higher-than-average educational levels to the general population in South Africa. Swanepoel's study offered no evidence demonstrating a connection to organized crime groups or gangs.

## A route into the data

The number of regulatory, conservation, and enforcement agencies involved in monitoring the illegal trade in endangered flora and fauna might well be confounding policing and research efforts. In conjunction with the UN Convention Against Transnational and Organized Crime, recommendations to assess data capturing techniques within each member nation's jurisdiction, along with the manner in which seizure data are recorded, probably are in order. Indeed, Interpol's Wildlife Working Group as early as 1994 emphasized the need to collect accurate and detailed data on wildlife crime, specifically calling for the creation of a global database that would aid countries in their efforts to combat the illegal trade.[20] This, coupled with a recommendation made here to redirect the way existing Red List data are analyzed, might assist efforts to implement the MRA.

CITES is an international treaty that aims to ensure that the international trade in wild plants and animals does not endanger their survival.[21] In 1963, a resolution of the IUCN needed agreement on cross-border trade pertaining to wildlife; therefore, CITES establishes a permit system for importing and exporting regulated wildlife. Currently, there are approximately 30,000 species of animals and plants protected to varying degrees by the convention. In three appendices, the plants and animals are categorized by the degree to which their survival is threatened. For example, flora or fauna that are listed in Appendix 1 are threatened by extinction; therefore, trade is permitted only in exceptional circumstances. Those listed in Appendix 2 are not threatened with extinction, but trade is controlled strictly to prevent transfer to the more protective category. Appendix 3 species are protected in at least one country that has asked other CITES signatories for assistance in their preservation. The treaty itself does not make the trade in protected species criminal; however, penalties in the form of trade sanctions can be levied against a member party that does not enact corresponding national legislation.

IUCN, through its Species Survival Commission, determines what species are endangered, with the aid of governments and scientists.[22] IUCN produces the Red List, which provides taxonomic and conservation status of species to determine the relative risk of extinction and to highlight those taxa facing higher risks of global extinction. The Red List for 2006 contains 16,119 (7,725 animals; 8,394 plants) species threatened with extinction,[23] including one in three amphibians, one in four mammals, one in eight birds, and approximately 50% of freshwater fish.

Red List data are presented in a number of tables that depict data in various forms. For example, one table is provided that gives the numbers of threatened species by major groups across several years. Generally speaking, animals are categorized and subcategorized as vertebrates (mammals, birds, reptiles, amphibians, fishes), invertebrates (insects, mollusks, crustaceans, others), and plants classified as mosses, ferns and allies, gymnosperms, dicotyledons, and nonocotyledons. These very broad categories serve as the basis for all other Red List tables. The numbers included in each taxonomic group, as above, are listed for each country; for example, the 2006 Red List showed the following taxonomic groups for Cameroon:[24] 43 mammals, 18 birds, four reptiles, 53 amphibians, 39 fishes, one mollusk or crustacean, one other type of invertebrates, and 355 plants, for a total of 514 threatened species. Further tables show the status of animals and plants, again by country.[25]

What is not apparent from these tables are the specific species in each category that are endangered, meaning it is not obviously evident what specific mammals make up the 43 in Cameroon or what specific birds make up the 18. Therefore, it is difficult to identify precisely what animals and plants are under threat or are prime for targeting in terms of policing intervention. If specific species can be identified more easily and readily, individuals or groups who hunt and/or harvest the animals and plants can be sought out as well as the mechanisms by which they move the species through the trade routes to their final consumer destinations. By tracing the movement of the animal or plants, investigators will be able to focus on the manner by which the species are handled, thus identifying the illegal markets. In essence, analysis for each country will yield a species profile in terms of exactly what is endangered, what specific species of animals and plants are most demanded, how they are bought and sold, and routes of trade. From these profiles, linkages based on the hot products can be possibly identified, thus providing a more complete picture of how each of the demanded animals and plants and/or their by-products is taken from range areas and transported to consumer areas. Investigators will also be able to discover if all species are handled in the same or different manners, thus specifying a typology of markets, as was done with traditional stolen goods.

The ambiguous nature of existing data pertaining to endangered species complicates the analyses needed to identify hot products as well as their illegal, 'stolen' markets. However, some other data appear to be available. These include seizure data from related agencies. For example, in the United Kingdom, Her Majesty's Customs and Excise (HMC&E) records seizure data of all CITES- and EU-listed species where illegal consignments are detected. The agencies mainly responsible in the United States at the federal level for similar data are Customs and Border Protection Service, Department of the Interior's Fish and Wildlife Services, Department of Commerce's National Marine Fisheries Services, Coast Guard, and Department of Agriculture.[26] Determination as to which U.S. agency has jurisdiction is dependent on the nature of the species involved, thus making interrogation of data complicated if not impossible. Additionally, the quality of data remains elusive. It is not clear if each of these agencies collects the same general category of information or if each operates independently, which is often the case.

## Similarities and differences between the traditional and exotic stolen goods markets

As a way to move forward in applying the MRA to less traditional forms of property, theft, and 'stolen' goods markets, it is helpful to compare similarities and differences between them and the illicit trade in less traditional types of goods, such as endangered wildlife. Similarities include the invisible nature of the crime or activity, supply and demand of goods, the type of data and the manner in which they are used by officials, and connection, if any, to the drug trade. Although there may be many differences between traditional stolen goods markets and the illegal trade in endangered species, the main ones discussed here include the global scale of the trade, the commodities themselves, their impact on the environment, and the potential for profit. Each is significantly serious enough to warrant further study.

Perhaps the most obvious similarity is that the activities in each of these types of illegal markets are highly invisible to authorities. For traders in traditional stolen goods markets and those involved in the illegal trade of endangered wildlife, the obscure nature of their criminality shields them from official notice. Whether done under cover of darkness on a housing estate in England or in the rural villages of Indonesia, crimes involving the illegal taking of property, be it an iPod or a Javan tiger, to fulfill demand elsewhere remains underpoliced.[27] Obscurity, along with the fact that these activities are an extremely low priority at all government levels, ensures that illegal trade in wildlife will continue to thrive.[28]

Additionally, the lucrative nature of each type of trade makes it such that cooperation with the police, if and when an offender is charged, is not in the best, long-term interest of participants. Moreover, if the trade in flora and fauna is indeed connected strongly to organized crime, fear of retribution will no doubt weigh heavily with those involved who are contemplating cooperation with authorities. Therefore, participants in each of the types of illegal markets encounter extremely low risks in terms of detection, arrest, and prosecution while enjoying potentially high rewards and large monetary returns.

A second similarity is that of demanded goods, which are, or should be, according to the MRA, the focus of analyses in terms of both patterns and interventions. As previously mentioned, whatever illegal property is demanded, illegal suppliers will strive to fulfill that demand. Schneider (2005b) found that thieves often steal to order or steal particular items because they know there exists willing buyers, thus suggesting that some illegal markets are demand driven. Whether it is the latest handheld computer, mobile phone, rare statue of Buddha, *shahtoosh* shawl,[29] or TAM made from rhino horn or bear gall bladder, the aim is to deliver the coveted items to those who are willing to pay for them. In other words, as hypothesized earlier, thieves (or poachers) acquire the goods because they know there are avenues through which they can sell them – there is an opportunity to sell the demanded property to those who either use it themselves or are willing and able to sell it on to their final consumers. The key is to understand and identify exactly what is demanded and what property is driving the thefts. Alternatively, in terms of endangered wildlife, what is driving the hunting and harvesting of plants and animals or their by-products? Once that is determined, the nature of the exchange relationship can begin to take shape. Are they legitimate zoo owners who are 'ordering' protected Thai birds of prey? Or are there special-interest shops that import illegal TAM to supply consumers who see no illegality in their use? Or are people placing orders so that their private collections contain impressive, rare breeds? Determining what goods are in demand and how those goods find their way from range areas to consumer areas is the job of wildlife task forces worldwide.

Third, reliable data that describe the true extent of handling conventional forms of property, as well as more exotic goods, are lacking. Although some jurisdictions are better equipped to collect data than others, the authorities tend to rely only on either reported stolen items or seized property. In their raw form, neither of these is necessarily used for analyses or is conducive for it.

Police property databases, as mentioned previously, are used rarely for crime pattern analyses. These data are frequently difficult to obtain and are deficient in terms of completeness and/or accuracy. Property categories are extremely broad in their descriptions, thus providing very limited use in terms of identifying hot products or trends and hence yielding limited tactical use. For example, one police database in England classified all forms of property into 57 main categories.[30] From this, property was broken down further into subcategories, which contained manufacturers' and model descriptions. To illustrate how inefficient the categorizations were, the general descriptor for one type of property was 'electric/gas appliances, including power tools'; included in this were more than 900 items including gas stoves, batteries, DVD players, and electric lawn mowers. Because of the data warehousing and processing system, there were not practical ways of calculating the actual count of products stolen at a sufficient microlevel so that hot products could be determined. Analyses could, however, be easily calculated to know rankings of 'electric/gas appliances, including power tools' in relation to other categories. It was also found that these categories were not mutually exclusive, nor were they exhaustive, thus rendering the calculations futile.

Seizure data pertaining to wildlife seem to suffer from many of the same ambiguities and deficiencies. According to Cook *et al.* (2002), data are categorized as live animals, animal products and derivatives, animal products for food (not fish), live wild ornamental plants, nonwood forest products, fisheries food products, and timber. Furthermore, Cowdrey (2002) analyzed seizure data further to '*clarify*' [italics added] the information. In his analysis of HMC&E data, live animals included 47% reptiles and 18% parrots and macaws; dead animals consisted of 26% TAM, 17% reptile skins, and 21% corals and seashells; products included both processed and raw ivory and caviar; and finally, plants accounted for only 7%o of seizures, mainly consisting of orchids from Thailand. Data at this level of detail are not conducive to assisting in the analyses of stolen or illegal goods markets. Rather, details of what exact type of reptile or coral is needed to frame tactical decisions as well as to develop a more thorough understanding of the nature of traded goods and markets.

A final similarity between the two types of illegal markets is the relationship that exists with the trafficking in drugs. Research conducted on traditional stolen goods markets revealed an intimate connection between drugs markets and stolen goods (see Schneider 2003, 2005b). Specifically, drug dealers will trade stolen goods as payment for drugs. When this occurs, the drug dealer takes on the role of handler, thus providing police with additional intervention opportunities, such as execution of search warrants for stolen property at drug dealers' residences. With regard to the illegal wildlife trade, the connection to drugs is threefold. First, trafficking and/or smuggling routes run parallel for both commodities; second, legal shipments of wildlife are used to conceal drug consignments; and finally, wildlife is traded for drugs as part of the laundering process of proceeds (see Cook *et al.* 2002). Some caution must be used here. Cook *et al.* (2002) never explain on what these conclusions are based. There is no mention of the methodology used; therefore, we really do not know if researchers collected data from the field or through interviews with offenders or police officials or if they relied solely on library resources. Therefore, the relationship between drug and wildlife trade is claimed, but it is not substantiated.

Perhaps the most striking feature of the unlawful trade in endangered flora and fauna that distinguishes it from traditional stolen goods markets is its global nature. Those who make up the components of these illegal markets may be thousands of miles apart. In other words, the consumers could be separated from the poachers and/or handlers by incredible distances. The types of exotic plants and animals that make up the endangered species trade literally come from any part of the world – depending on exactly what is demanded or desired. For example, Thailand seems to be a primary source for certain birds and orchids, and the majority of illegally obtained caviar stems from the UAE.

Research demonstrates that most thieves and handlers of traditional stolen goods operate near where they live (see Rengert and Wasilchick, 2000; Wiles and Costello, 2000); therefore, property in traditional stolen goods markets could originate as close as your next-door neighbor. Stolen electronic and other durable goods are widely available to those who partake in the illicit trade. Methods for transporting them from their source (house, shop, vehicle) can be measured in yards or miles, not hundreds or thousands of miles. Although stolen goods markets no doubt exist in cities, towns, and villages worldwide, the goods are traded locally. For the wildlife trade, the tactical complexities of moving illicit goods across vast distances require sophisticated coordination of efforts between those at the source country and those at the final destination, including the various intermediary routes along the way. A thief can provide his or her customers with the latest electronic device from local suppliers (victims), but a poacher or handler in endangered plants and animals has to be in or near the source region of the desired commodity, then make arrangements to transport it to the final destination. Because of the nature of illegal flora and fauna, markets may well expand beyond local areas – making this crime a truly global one.

The commodities that serve as the foundation for the illicit wildlife markets are markedly different from those. traded in traditional stolen goods markets. By their nature, endangered species are indigenous plants and/or animals that are removed from their country of origin either dead or alive, depending on the consumer's need. To illustrate, a bear's gall bladder, which necessitates the killing of a bear, may be the desired product to be used in TAMS in one instance, whereas another customer may simply want to own the endangered Schreiber's fringe-fingered lizard.[31] Obtaining the animals requires knowledge of habitat, tracking, hunting, and preserving the specimens. Harvesting plants, too, calls for this specialized knowledge. Source regions are often-times tropical with extremely dense vegetation-knowing where to go and how to store the plants so a viable shipment is delivered mandates that poachers demonstrate a particular know-how. Securing traditionally stolen goods can be much less complicated, sometimes only requiring a brick thrown through the shop or house window. Finally, although both types of markets require handlers, those who deal in traditionally stolen goods can be easy to find. Given that we know that thieves operate locally, the handlers are not far afield. The literature on markets involving endangered species is so understudied that we simply do not know how convoluted the process of handling is or how difficult it is for poachers to find handlers to move their products onward. It is proposed here that the trade in flora and fauna is a complicated one that involves numerous people from source to destination regions – covering thousands of miles and a multitude of countries in between.

Disruption to or destruction of the environment is a serious consequence of the illegal trade in flora and fauna. Removing indigenous species from their natural habitat can affect negatively other species in that area in terms of food sources, natural cover, and vegetation. This invasion into natural areas is said to have a negative overall effect on global health; for example, shrinking of the rainforests of Brazil has contributed to global warming as well as the destruction of various species, plant and animal. Goods that fuel traditional stolen goods markets may well disrupt the quality of life of those from whom the goods were taken and even disrupt certain neighborhoods; however, the potential for traditional stolen goods markets to obliterate an entire species is not a reality. Once driven to extinction, the plants and animals under threat cannot be repropagated. Additionally, the effect of their disappearance must be recognized as having an effect on their human counterparts. The scale of potential disruption to human life as a result of the destruction of wildlife is such that intervention and interdiction efforts must be raised.

Because of the purported size, scope, and global nature of the illicit trade in flora and fauna, the potential profits are enormous. Even though the figures provided previously regarding the costs of this trade are inconsistent and fragile, what is evident is that the potential for profit is significant. Although we do not know exactly how much tiger skins or the pelts of the chiru cost those who demand them, we can surmise that they simply cannot be as inexpensive as a stolen iPod. The networks that require the acquisition, processing, and transportation of these commodities must expand beyond several nation-state boundaries, thus requiring detailed coordination between actors. Intuitively this sounds like a reasonable conclusion to make; however, without MRA-like research findings, we cannot possibly know the extent to which these types of markets operate independently or if they live off other illicit goods' established trade routes and markets. What is not known is if those who make the profits are organized and if the trade in one species is managed by specific handlers or if handlers are more generalists – meaning that they deal in any endangered species.

## The way forward: application of the MRA to illegal wildlife trafficking

Although our understanding about conventional stolen goods markets is still under construction, there are, nevertheless, lessons that can to be applied to the rather opaque trade in endangered species. As evidenced, commonalities do indeed exist between customary and unconventional types of criminal activities. The nature of the differences also compels us to begin work swiftly, as the consequences of allowing the proliferation of this trade can be tragic. Because of these shared traits, it is believed that the MRA can be extended beyond its current use into the realm of illegal trafficking in protected species. However, the process of applying the crime reduction strategy will most likely be a lengthy, and perhaps complicated, one, as it was with traditional stolen goods markets.[32] Although the problem of trafficking in endangered species expands well beyond any one country's geopolitical boundary, tackling the crime can be made more manageable by breaking it down into its analytical parts: the property and the process through which it changes hands from thief, poacher, or hunter through to consumers.

The first challenge is to rethink the way the data are presented and used. For example, Red List data provide a service to the conservation societies by showing what species are at risk of extinction. The list also shows what countries host the most endangered categories of species. However, as with police property data, the categorizations of species and the manner in which they are organized do not easily lend themselves to crime reduction analysis. This is not surprising, as the data were not compiled for that purpose. However, a more thorough interrogation of existing data may prove useful. Using the previous example of Cameroon, details of the exact species of the 43 mammals under threat or protection would be needed, as would all the other animals and plants. By amassing these data, Cameroon would have a much clearer picture of what is endangered not only in terms of survival but also for being illegally traded. This process, in the ideal, would be done by and for all signatory countries.

Additionally, a database relating to the markets themselves has to be developed. This really cannot take place until a critical mass of offenders who are willing to be interviewed is achieved. Systematic, in-depth, qualitative interviews with those who hunt and gather the plants and animals are needed to gain an understanding as to (a) the types of wildlife they hunt or harvest, (b) the length of time it takes to dispose of their products, (c) the amount of profit made by specific types of plants or animals they hunt or harvest, (d) how they came to engage in the activity, (e) how they became connected to those who are able to sell the goods, (f) how they actually dispose of the plants or animals once they are harvested, and (g) whether markets are product specific or more generalized.[33]

Rather than focusing solely on an individual offender, all participants in the chain are targeted, especially handlers and consumers, as they drive the demand. As demonstrated previously, handlers have been shown to play an important role in keeping theft levels high simply by giving thieves (or in the case of wildlife, poachers and hunters) an outlet for the goods. Officials seem to be reluctant to focus on consumers of stolen goods, as they do not fit the stereotypical images of the criminal underworld. Research shows that in addition to drug-addicted people, young people, legitimate businesses, and those with lower incomes have all been shown to purchase conventional stolen goods (see Allen, 2000; Sutton, 1998). Authorities fear the risk of a political backlash if 'law-abiding' citizens are arrested and/or prosecuted for buying stolen goods. However, if demand is to be reduced, the impact of buying illegal goods must be made known to those who seek to own the items.

Keeping with the example of the bear gall bladders and the plight of the black bear, the following is a brief and simplistic description of how the MRA might be used to intervene. Enforcement and/or conservationists' data reveal that the number of carcasses is increasing whereby gall bladders, paws, and/or claws are missing. The MRA process necessitates that information be collated regarding (a) who is tracking, killing, and dissecting the bears for their parts; (b) how the poachers are moving the parts from the range area to the area of consumption; (c) the process by which these two parties exchange the goods; (d) the process by which the goods reach the final consumer; and (e) the reasons for which the gall bladders are demanded by consumers. Because the gall bladders are used for medicinal products and aphrodisiacs in countries throughout Asia, processing and transshipment may very well occur in several countries. It is through coordinated efforts between CITES signatory countries that information can be collected and used to affect the trade. Additionally, the MRA uses media to educate people regarding the plight of the bear, alternative choices for use, and intervention efforts; therefore, efforts must be aimed at consumers.

However, an alternative strategy to implement the MRA can be taken. Starting with Red List data, crime reduction experts could partner with scientists and conservationist to identify exactly what species are endangered. In other words, they can work together to drill down into the data to discover what species of mammals or plants or fish a specific country is reporting. Once the 'property' is known with certainty, the partners can begin to collect data through interviews and analyses of other related official data with the aim of developing a market profile of how the endangered species are bought and sold and are moved from range country to consumer country.

The challenge here is to structure a coordinated effort in how the illegal trade in endangered flora and fauna is approached. For example, if a series of protocols are put in place, either through CITES or the UN Convention Against Transnational and Organized Crime (2004b), signatory countries could begin to systematically and routinely collect, analyze, and disseminate data that pertain specifically to their hot property or products as well as to their corresponding endangered species markets. The development of an international clearinghouse of data, predicated on uniformly categorized and collected data, would prove invaluable when trying to see how different products in various countries are linked or how the markets themselves operate within and between countries. The development of this clearinghouse would provide an excellent opportunity for police practitioners and conservationists to work alongside crime reduction experts, who could provide the technical assistance in designing the database so that analytical potential could be maximized.

Once the specifics are known about which plants and animals are under threat of being trafficked, and the process by which they are bought and sold, countries would be better equipped to prioritize policing interventions as well as conservations initiatives. Although there are admittedly other global policing priorities that fall under the guise of the UN Convention Against Transnational and Organized Crime, such as trafficking in humans, smuggling of migrants, and trafficking in human organs, the effect of the illegal trade in endangered species is far-reaching. Damage goes well beyond the loss of a particular breed of animal or plant. Local economies, habitats, and the livelihood of entire populations of people are at risk of demise until and unless systematic interventions are taken against the practice. The MRA provides a way forward with the trafficking of protected flora and fauna but also shows promise with any property-demanded illegal practices.[34]

## Notes

1 Sutton (1998) identifies five types of exchange relationships or stolen goods markets. See his report for a more complete description of each.
2 The following terms are used interchangeably in this article: *endangered flora and fauna, endangered wildlife,* and *endangered species.* They ail consist of flora and fauna that have been identified as endangered.
3 For details of the actual market reduction approach (MRA) model, see Figure 1 in Sutton, Schneider, and Hetherington (2001, p. 7).
4 This money was invested in England and Wales, with Northern Ireland and Scotland having separate funding programs.
5 The author has worked previously with Sutton to further develop the MRA and has also worked as the action researcher on one of the government-funded MRA projects.
6 See Hale, Harris, Uglow, Gilling, and Netten (2004).
7 See Sutton *et al.* (2001).
8 See Clarke (1999) for a complete discussion of hot products.
9 Historically, property data remain untapped as a source for analyses. Property information is often collected merely for insurance purposes. The MRA *stretches existing* databases well beyond their capacities to identify which property is most in demand, thus fueling the stolen goods markets.
10 See United Nations (2004a) for more detailed discussions of the purpose of the UN Office of Drugs and Crime.
11 See United Nations (2005).

12   See United Nations (2001, 2004b, 2005).
13   See Cowdrey (2002); Cook, Roberts, and Lowther (2002); and Zimmerman (2003).
14   See http://www.cites.org.
15   TRAFFIC (http://www.traffic.org), World Wildlife Fund (WWF; http://www.worldwildlife.
     org/ endangered), and World Conservation Union (http://www.iucn.org).
16   Cowdrey (2002) reports this figure as an export value. Although both are agency reports for
     TRAFFIC-WWF, it remains unclear on what exactly the figures are based, thus adding to the
     confusion.
17   See http://www.met.police.uk/wildlife.
18   The Convention on International Trade in Endangered Species of Wild Fauna and Flora
     (CITES) is considered to be one of the most successful international treaties; however, the
     illegal trade in wildlife threatens its continued success (see Zimmerman, 2003).
19   Simply known as Red List.
20   See http://www.interpol.int/Public/EnvironmentalCrime/Wildlife/Default.asp.
21   The convention was agreed in 1973 and in force by 1975 with 80 nations participating.
     Currently there are 167 signatory parties.
22   See http://www.iucn.org for details.
23   According to the World Conservation Union (IUCN), this is an extreme underestimation, as
     only 3% of the 1.9 million worldwide species are assessed by the Red List.
24   I think it is safe to say that not many crime reduction officers or criminologists would be
     equipped to analyze the data as listed by their scientific annotations. Biologists, zoologists,
     and botanists may well have to lend a collaborative hand for the data to be interrogated to
     an optimum degree.
25   Categories include extinct, extinct in wild, critically endangered, endangered, vulnerable,
     lower risk or conservation dependent, near threatened, least concerned, and data deficient.
26   Importantly, each of the 50 U.S. states has similar agencies that may or may not collect the
     same data as its federal counterparts.
27   *Pantkera tigris* ssp. *sondaica* is listed as extinct on the Red List, as there are diminishingly
     small numbers of the animal capable of breeding still alive in the wild.
28   See Lowther, Cook, and Roberts (2002) for a review of sanctions applied in the United
     Kingdom and United States.
29   *Shahtoosh* is manufactured from the underfieece of Tibetan antelope (also known as chiru),
     which is killed in the process.
30   Although the list is extensive, it cannot possibly be exhaustive to include all types of property
     in existence.
31   *Acanthodactylus schreiberi* is classified as endangered by IUCN for many reasons, one of
     which is human disturbance.
32   In one U.K. police force, it took nearly 9 months of assessing and subsequently restructuring
     property databases so that they could be used for the purposes of crime pattern analyses.
     However, the efforts resulted in the successful implementation of the MRA, which resulted
     in a disruption in stolen goods markets (see Schneider, 2005b).
33   Decker (2005) is an excellent source for those who use offender interviews as part of their
     research agenda. He provides details and strategies on how to conduct properly these
     often-overlooked sources of information.
34   Articles are in preparation by the author that illustrate the manner in which the MRA
     can be used to combat (a) human trafficking and (b) cultural items, antiquities, and fine
     arts.

## References

Allen, J. (2000). *Community survey of willingness to receive stolen goods* (Contemporary Issues in
     Crime and Justice No. 51). Sydney, Australia: NSW Bureau of Crime Statistics and Research.
Bennett, T. (1998). *Drugs and crime: The results of research on drug testing and interviewing arrestees*
     (Home Office Study 183). London: Home Office; Research, Development and Statistics
     Directorate.
Bennett, T. (2000). *Drugs and crime: The results of the second developmental stage of the NEW-ADAM
     programme* (Home Office Study 205). London: Home Office; Research, Development and
     Statistics Directorate.
Bennett, T., and Wright, R. (1984). *Burglars on burglary.* Aldershot, UK: Gower.
Chappell, D., and Walsh, M. (1974). Receiving stolen property: The need for systematic inquiry
     into the fencing process. *Criminology,* 11, 484–497.

Clark, R. S. (1994). *The United Nations Crime Prevention and Criminal Justice Program: Formulation of standards and efforts at their implementation.* Philadelphia: University of Pennsylvania Press.

Clarke, R. V. (1999). *Hot products: Understanding, anticipating and reducing demand for stolen goods* (Police Research Series Paper 112). London: Home Office; Research, Development and Statistics Directorate; Policing and Reducing Crime Unit.

Clarke, R. V, and Felson, M. (2004). Introduction: Criminology, routine activity, and rational choice. In R. V Clarke and M. Felson (Eds.), *Routine activity and rational choice: Advances in criminological theory* (Vol. 5, pp. 1–14). New Brunswick, NJ: Transaction.

Cohen, L. E., and Felson, M. (1979). Social change and crime rate trends: A routine activity approach. *American Sociological Review*, 44(4), 588–608.

Colquhoun, P (1976). *A treatise on the police of the Metropolis.* London: Dilley. (Original work published 1796)

Cook, D., Roberts, M., and Lowther, J. (2002). The international wildlife trade and organised crime: A review of the evidence and the role of the UK. Wolverhampton, UK: WWF-UK.

Cowdrey, D. (2002). *Switching channels: Wildlife trade routes into Europe and the UK. A WWF/Traffic report.* Wolverhampton, UK: University of Wolverhampton.

Decker, S. (2005). *Using offender interviews to inform police problem solving* (Problem-Oriented Guides for Police Problem Solving Tools Series No. 3). Washington, DC: U.S. Department of Justice, Office of Community Oriented Policing Services.

Farrington, D. (1999). Measuring, explaining, and preventing shoplifting: A review of British literature. *Security Journal*, 12(1), 9–27.

Fasulo, L. (2004). *An insider's guide to the UN.* New Haven, CT: Yale University Press.

Felson, M. (2002). *Crime in everyday life* (3rd ed.). Thousand Oaks, CA: Sage.

Felson, M., and Clarke, R. V. (1998). *Opportunity makes the thief: Practical theory for crime prevention* (Police Research Group Paper 98). London: Home Office; Research, Development and Statistics Directorate.

Freiberg, A. (1997). Regulating markets for stolen property. *Australian and New Zealand Journal of Criminology*, 30(3), 237–258.

Gossop, M., Marsden, J., and Rolfe, A. (2000). Drug misuse and acquisitive crime amongst clients recruited to the national treatment outcome research study (NTORS). *Criminal Behaviour and Mental Health*, 10, 10–20.

Hale, C., Harris, C., Uglow, S., Gilling, L., and Netten, A. (2004). *Targeting the markets for stolen goods – two targeted policing initiative projects.* (Home Office Development and Practice Report No. 17). London: Home Office; Research, Development and Statistics Directorate.

Henry, S. (1977). On the fence. *British Journal of Law and Society*, 4, 124–133.

Jarvis, G., and Parker, H. (1989). Young heroin users and crime: How do the 'new users' finance their habits? *British Journal of Criminology*, 29(2), 175–185.

Klockars, C. (1974). *The professional fence.* New York: Free Press.

Lowther, J., Cook, D., and Roberts, M. (2002). *Crime and punishment in the wildlife trade.* Wolverhampton, UK: WWF-UK.

Palmer, E. J., Holmes, A., and Hollin, C. R. (2002). Investigating burglars' decisions: Factors influencing target choice, method of entry, reasons for offending, repeat victimisation of a property and victim awareness. *Security Journal*, 15(1), 7–18.

Rengert, G., and Wasilchick, J. (2000). *Suburban burglary: A tale of two suburbs* (2nd ed.). Springfield, IL: Charles C. Thomas.

Reuter, P. (1984). Social control in illegal markets. In D. Black (Ed.), *Toward a general theory of social control* (pp. 29-58). New York: Academic Press.

Reuter, P (2004). *The organization of illegal markets: An economic analysis.* Honolulu, HI: University Press of the Pacific.

Rubin, J., and Stucky, S. (2004). Fighting black markets and oily water: The Department of Justice's national initiatives to combat transnational environmental crime. *Sustainable Development Law and Policy*, 21, 21–26.

Schneider, J. L. (2005a). The link between shoplifting and burglary: The booster burglar. *British Journal of Criminology*, 45(3), 395–401.

Schneider, J. L. (2005b). Stolen goods markets: Methods of disposal. *British Journal of Criminology*, 45(2), 129–140.

Schneider, J. L. (2003). Prolific burglars and the role of shoplifting. *Security Journal*, 16(2), 49–59.

Shover, N. (1996). *Great pretenders: Pursuits and careers of persistent thieves.* Boulder, CO: Westview.

Stevenson, R. J., Forsythe, L. M. V., and Weatherburn, D. (2001). The stolen goods markets in New South Wales, Australia. *British Journal of Criminology*, 41, 101–118.

Sutton, M. (1993). *From receiving to thieving: The market for stolen goods and the incidence of theft* (Home Office Research Bulletin No. 34). London: Home Office; Research, Development and Statistics Directorate.

Sutton, M. (1995). Supply by theft: Does the market for second-hand goods play a role in keeping crime figures high? *British Journal of Criminology,* 35(3), 400–416.

Sutton, M. (1998). *Handling stolen goods and theft: A market reduction approach* (Home Office Research Study 178). London: Home Office; Research, Development and Statistics Directorate.

Sutton, M., Schneider, J., and Hetherington, S. (2001). *Tackling theft with the market reduction approach* (Crime Reduction Research Series Paper 8). London: Home Office; Research, Development and Statistics Directorate; Policing and Reducing Crime Unit.

Swanepoel, G. (1998). The illegal trade in rhino horn: An example of an endangered species. *International Journal of Risk, Security, and Crime Prevention,* 3(3), 207–220.

United Nations. (2001). UN *convention against transnational organized crime* (AIRES/55/25). New York: Author.

United Nations. (2004a). *Basic facts about the United Nations.* New York: United Nations Department of Public Information.

United Nations. (2004b). *United Nations convention against transnational organized crime and the protocols thereto.* New York: United Nations Office on Drugs and Crime.

United Nations. (2005). *Discussion guide* (A/CONF.203/pm.l). New York: Author.

West, W. G. (1996). The short-term careers of serious thieves. In D. F. Greenberg (Ed.), *Criminal careers* (Vol. 2, pp. 3–24). Aldershot, UK: Dartmouth.

Wiles, P, and Costello, P (2000). *The 'road to nowhere': The evidence for travelling criminals* (Home Office Research Study 207). London: Home Office; Research, Development and Statistics Directorate.

Wright, R. T., and Decker, S. H. (1994). *Burglars on the job: Streetlife and residential break-ins.* Boston: Northeastern University Press.

Zimmerman, M. E. (2003). The black market for wildlife: Combating transnational organized crime in the illegal wildlife trade. *Vanderbilt Journal of Transnational Law,* 36, 1657–1689.

# 31. Corporate self-policing and the environment*

*Paul B. Stretesky*

The U.S. Environmental Protection Agency's Self-Policing Policy (more commonly referred to as the Audit Policy) waives or reduces penalties when regulated entities voluntarily discover, disclose, and correct environmental violations. This study draws upon a rational choice model of corporate crime to determine if traditional regulatory efforts such as inspections and enforcement actions are associated with the odds of disclosing an environmental violation under the Audit Policy. A case control design is used to compare companies that self-police to companies that do not self-police. The event group consists of all 551 companies that disclosed at least one environmental violation under the Audit Policy between October 1 1998 and September 30 2000. The control group consists of a simple random sample of 551 companies that did not use the Audit Policy but were discovered to have violated at least one environmental law during the same time period as the event group. There is no evidence that inspections and enforcement increase Audit Policy use. However, the results do suggest, first, that the Audit Policy is more likely to be used by large companies than by small companies and, second, that it is likely to be used for reporting violations as opposed to more serious emissions or permit violations. In terms of public policy these findings suggest that regulatory agencies such as the EPA can do relatively little to increase the self-policing of environmental violations.

**Key Words** corporate crime • corporate environmental behaviour • effectiveness of government interventions • pollution prevention • self-regulation • voluntary initiatives

The issue of corporate self-policing has interested criminologists for some time (for example, Braithwaite and Fisse 1987). Despite this curiosity, corporate self-policing has yet to be empirically studied. Self policing occurs when a company is offered an economic incentive to report its administrative, civil, and criminal violations to the proper authorities.[1] The idea that self-policing can prevent crime is becoming increasingly popular among policy makers (Freeman 2000; Rosenbaum 2000). Self-policing is characteristic of the general trend in

---

*From *Criminology* (2006), 44(3): pp. 671–708.

regulatory policy toward market-based incentives and away from traditional enforcement.[2] In an incentive system, the state offers rewards to companies to promote the least expensive, most flexible methods for achieving compliance (Freeman 2000: 197). In an enforcement system, the state determines the rules and regulations and establishes punishment for administrative, civil, and criminal violations. The move from traditional enforcement to market-based incentives means that corporate crime research will increasingly focus on reasons companies do not use incentives rather than on why they violate the law in the first place (Braithwaite 2002; Braithwaite and Fisse 1987).

This research focuses on one particular incentive, a self-policing act adopted by the Environmental Protection Agency in 1995. The 'Incentives for Self-Policing: Discovery, Disclosure, Correction, and Prevention of Violations' (Audit Policy) emphasizes market-based incentives and voluntary compliance (EPA 1995). The policy was adopted to persuade companies to improve their environmental performance by disclosing and correcting environmental violations in exchange for the elimination or reduction of gravity-based penalties and the promise not to initiate a civil or criminal investigation of the violation. It is market-based in that it increases regulatory efficiency and improves environmental performance when compared to forms of traditional enforcement because environmental violations are detected and corrected more quickly. This study draws on a rational choice perspective of corporate behavior to determine whether variations in inspections and enforcement (that is, traditional regulatory mechanisms) are associated with the disclosure of an environmental violation to the EPA using the Audit Policy (that is, a market-based incentive).

### Rational choice, deterrence, corporate crime

Research suggests that a rational choice perspective may be useful in understanding corporate crime (Block, Nold, and Sidak 1981; Braithwaite and Makkai 1991; Jamieson 1994; Paternoster and Simpson 1996; Piquero, Exum, and Simpson 2005; Simpson and Koper 1992). Rational choice suggests that a crime will occur when the anticipated benefits of committing the crime outweigh the perceived costs (Zimring and Hawkins 1973). The overarching theme of a rational choice perspective can often conjure images of people's behavior as being driven by a cost-benefit calculator. There are, nevertheless, a number of cultural and structural constraints on rational choice that suggest that cost-benefit calculations are not always identical (Simpson 2002). In the case of corporate crime, deviations in organizational culture may change an employee's perceptions of the costs and benefits of engaging in corporate illegality (Vaughan 1998). Personality may also affect decisions about whether to engage in corporate crime (Piquero, Exum, and Simpson 2005). Overall, the research on rational choice and corporate crime suggests that the perceptions of the costs and benefits of engaging in criminal behavior can vary across firms and across employees. Despite variation among individuals and organizations many regulatory agents continue to believe that illegal corporate behavior can be deterred though more traditional regulatory mechanisms such as inspections and enforcement (Mintz 1995).

Deterrence theory has clearly developed within the framework of rational choice (Tittle and Paternoster 2000: 510). The idea behind deterrence is that people are likely to obey the law because they fear legal sanctions. The greater the certainty, severity, and celerity of punishment, the more likely it is that crime will be prevented (Zimring and Hawkins 1973). According to the corporate crime literature, individuals employed by corporations may be more prone to deterrent messages than the general public. Paternoster and Simpson (1996) note:

> It has long been thought that a deterrence/rational choice theory would be especially useful in understanding corporate crime, because both corporate crime and corporate offenders were thought to be particularly amenable to sanction threats. (550)

Likewise, Braithwaite and Makkai (1991) point out that 'deterrence is supposed to affect organizations because top management of organizations are paid to protect the interests of those organizations; accordingly, they act to do so' (10). Finally, Vaughan (1998) suggests that many people believe that

> [punishment and the threat of punishment] is considered an important tool for the social control of organizations because of institutionalized beliefs that the ultimate cause of organizational offending is rational actors who will include the costs of punishment in their calculations and be deterred from violative behavior. (24)

Few empirical studies of corporate crime draw on a deterrence perspective. In the early 1980s, Block and his colleagues (1981) published the first study of the relationship between deterrence and corporate crime by looking at antitrust violations in the white bread industry. They measured deterrence messages by counting antitrust enforcement actions against a bread producer and by counting the enforcement actions that took place in the surrounding cities in the same Department of Justice enforcement region where the bread producer was located. What Block and colleagues (1981: 439) found was that 'a price-fixing case against bakers in one city induced bakers in neighboring cities to reduce markups.' They also point out that known colluders 'remedy their price fixing by reducing their markups in the following year' (439). It is interesting to point out that they report that a successful federal prosecution often produced minor fines but signaled to consumers that a class action suit is possible. The researchers believed that these class action civil suits had a greater corporate deterrent effect on antitrust behavior than traditional criminal enforcement.

Simpson and Koper (1992) also looked at the potential deterrent effect of corporate sanctions on antitrust behavior. Unlike Block and colleagues (1981), Simpson and Koper conducted a longitudinal study of a group of corporate anti-trust offenders to determine how those firms 'responded to legal sanctions over time [while controlling for] changes in the economy, the regulatory environment, and corporate size and profitability' (351). The researchers approximated sanction certainty by estimating the number of previous annual minor antitrust cases initiated against a firm; measured sanction celerity by estimating the amount of time between the firm's commission of the offense and the case outcome; and measured sanction severity by rank ordering case outcomes according to outcome seriousness. They found only modest empirical support for a corporate deterrent effect. Past guilty verdicts appear to decrease future offending. They also observe that a change in the way anti-trust offenses were handled (that is, handled as felonies rather than misdemeanors) appeared to reduce firm recidivism. Other deterrence related variables were not associated with corporate recidivism, or appeared to increase rather than decrease rates of recidivism (Simpson and Koper 1992).

Block and colleagues (1981) and Simpson and Koper (1992) focused on the concept of objective deterrence in their analyses of corporate crime. In the literature, studies of objective deterrence focus on the actual level of punishment by, for example, looking at observed rates of inspections and enforcement actions (Simpson 2002; Tittle and Paternoster 2000: 511). More recent studies, however, have tended to focus on subjective deterrence – people's perceptions of punishment. Braithwaite and Makkai (1991) conducted one of the first quantitative studies of subjective deterrence in a corporate setting by studying chief executives of organizations in the Australian nursing home industry. Looking at 'whether management perceptions of deterrence have any effect on organizational compliance' (8), they measured subjective deterrence by asking nursing home administrators several questions, including each employee's perceptions of the probability that commonwealth or state government would: detect violations, sanction violations, and apply a specific type of sanction such as 'cutting of commonwealth funding' or 'withdrawal of home's license to operate' (1991: 13). The investigators find partial support for the proposition that the estimated probability of detection is positively associated with compliance (see also Makkai and Braithwaite 1994). No evidence, however, suggests that measures of sanction certainty and sanction severity deter corporate crime. In a follow-up study of the nursing home industry Makkai and Braithwaite (1994), significantly, find evidence that supports the position that 'emotions of guilt among managers predict the subsequent compliance of their organizations' (347). The importance of this finding is that deterrent messages are perceived differently depending upon the individual personality traits of organizational actors.

In a more recent study of corporate crime, Paternoster and Simpson (1996) examined the notion of rational choice by drawing on their subjective expected utility theory. They tested their theory by looking at the relevance of formal and informal sanctions among a set of ninety-six graduate students who were enrolled in masters of business administration programs. Each student answered questions about four fictitious scenarios that were designed to resemble the crimes of price fixing, bribery, manipulation of sales statistics, and environmental dumping. The corporate manager was described as the main actor in each scenario. The students were asked to approximate the probability that they would do the same thing as the hypothetical manager if in the same situation. The students' estimates of the probability that they would violate the law formed the dependent variable in Paternoster and Simpson's analysis. The independent variables in the analysis measured each individual's perceived probability that he or she would be detected and punished. The perceived costs of offending included both formal sanctions such as regulatory, civil, and criminal sanctions and informal sanctions such as 'loss of occupation position, social censure, personal embarrassment, and shame' (580). Paternoster and Simpson found 'respondents were more likely to report an intention to commit the act when it was described as being a common practice within the firm' (580). The researchers also found an interaction effect between deterrence and morality. When moral inhibitions are high, deterrence does not matter. When moral obligations are weak, individuals base their decisions on perceived incentives and costs. Thus, deterrence is more likely to be effective when moral inhibitions are weak.

Piquero, Exum, and Simpson (2005) also recently examined deterrence theory and corporate crime by taking individual personality 'constraints' that shape decision-making processes into account. The researchers integrate desire-for-control (DC) into a rational choice model of corporate crime (see also Burger 1992). There was an interaction between sanction threats and levels of DC among the forty-six students Piquero and her colleagues (2005) studied: 'High levels of DC were, as expected, positively related to individual informal sanction certainty (short- and long term), individual informal sanction severity (long term); firm formal sanction severity, individual morality and shame' (272).

Together studies of deterrence and corporate crime suggest that corporate behavior may not be influenced to any great degree by traditional enforcement efforts. Still, because there are few empirical studies of corporate crime, the issue of the impact of deterrence messages on corporate behavior is left open to considerable debate. This study can be viewed as an effort to provide more information on corporate crime and deterrence by examining the relationship between traditional enforcement mechanisms and the corporate decision to use the Audit Policy. Before describing the methods and data used to examine that relationship, I give an account of and explain the policy.

**Audit policy background**

To best understand the policy's purpose, it is important to distinguish between self-policing and self-auditing (Stafford 2003: 3). Self-auditing occurs when a company actively assesses its compliance with environmental regulations on its own and does not forward the assessment results to authorities, such as the EPA in the case of environmental audits. Self-policing occurs when a company reports the violations it discovers to authorities. The development of the policy relates directly to the increased use of self-audits by regulated entities. According to Pfaff and Sanehirico (2004),

> If a firm wishes to be in compliance with environmental regulations – in light of the penalties for noncompliance, including fines, civil liability, and consumer dissatisfaction – it often has no choice but to devote substantial resources to self-investigation. (415)

Because the quantity and complexity of environmental regulation have grown, firms engage increasingly in self-audits. The advantage, of course, is that environmental violations may be discovered and corrected before environmental regulatory agencies discover the violation. The disadvantage is that 'discovering a [violation] through such an investigation may *increase* the chance that the [violation] will be detected by a regulator,' which may lead to fewer self-audits than would otherwise be initiated (Pfaff and Sanchirico 2004: 416). Despite this disadvantage, Moriandi (1998) found that nearly 75 percent of all firms conduct environmental audits.

Before the EPA adopted the Audit Policy, Price Waterhouse conducted a self-audit survey of 369 companies. They found that 20 percent of the firms in their sample did not perform self-audits because they believed that any negative information obtained could be used against them by regulatory agencies in a civil or criminal enforcement action (Chemical Week 1995: 66). Moreover, nearly 9 percent of companies reported that their voluntary self-audit data had actually been used by a regulatory agency in an enforcement action (Chemical Week 1995). Finally, 30 percent of all firms reported that they would expand their use of self-audits if the civil and criminal penalties associated with the discovery of violations by those audits were eliminated. It should not be surprising, then, that such reports by industry have led to the following sorts of observations on the part of corporate executives:

> Responsible, regulated companies pay an additional price for their vigilance. When they self-report the problems, as many laws now require, EPA enforcers routinely hand out large fines, even though EPA acknowledges that the violations were inadvertent, self-corrected, and harmless. Meanwhile, regulated competitors who never search for problems in the first place avoid these penalties and appear responsible by comparison. In other words, EPA's enforcement policy actually discourages environmentally protective behavior that focuses on prevention. (*Washington Report* 1995: 5)

Pfaff and Sanchirico (2004) report that several highly publicized cases in the early 1990s created even more tension between companies and environmental regulators over self-audits. One example is the Adolph Coors case. That company conducted a voluntary self-audit and found that the air emissions at its Colorado headquarters were higher than allowable under EPA guidelines. When Coors voluntarily disclosed that self-discovered violation and developed a plan for compliance, it was fined nearly $1 million by the Colorado Department of Health and the Environment. Many pro-business policy makers argued that cases like Coors demonstrate that 'by aggressively prosecuting those who seek to identify their own pollution problems, the regulators discourage self-audits' (Powers 1996: 6).

At the federal level, the tension between regulating and regulated entities over self-audits was addressed by the EPA's Audit Policy in 1995.[3] The policy waives or reduces gravity-based penalties, but does not impact penalties that may result from the economic benefits resulting from the noncompliant behavior.[4] Gravity-based penalties may be reduced by 75 percent or 100 percent, depending on the circumstances of the discovery. If the firm discloses the violation during a systematic self-audit without prompting by the government or third party plaintiff the gravity-based portion of the penalty may be reduced by 100 percent. If the firm discloses a violation discovered in a nonsystematic way (for example, the violation was discovered by happenstance by a company employee), the penalty is reduced by 75 percent. The idea behind the difference in penalty reductions is to encourage corporate environmental self-audits. To qualify for the penalty reduction a firm must not only self-police, but do so in a timely and cooperative fashion, simultaneously working to correct the violation. Thus, according to the Audit Policy, companies must report discovered violations to regulators within 21 days, correct it within 60 days, take steps to prevent the violation from occurring again, and cooperate fully with the EPA.

## Data and methods

The unit of analysis in this study is the company. The decision to study companies rather than facilities or geographic areas such as states or counties is largely based on theoretical and practical concerns. From a policy standpoint, the study of companies is desirable because they are the entities that make the decision to disclose environmental violations under the Audit Policy (Rebovich 1998). In other words, the Audit Policy implies a rationality that is typically associated with company-level decisions. Thus, from a rational choice perspective, Simpson argues that companies are economic entities that are 'rationally constructed, chartered, and owned by stockholders. Their overriding goals are economic, that is, profitability and market share expansion' (1986: 860).

### Sample and study design

To assess whether variables that measure inspections and enforcement are related to self-policing, one must compare companies that use the Audit Policy to companies that could, but do not, use the Audit Policy. A case-control design is used to make that comparison. Case-control designs are cross-sectional and 'though infrequently used ... offer tremendous logistical efficiency in the study of rare events, such as divorce, joining a religious cult, or committing a crime' (Lacy 1997: 129). Case-control designs are typically used to identify factors that help differentiate a population of all known cases that experience an event (the event group) from a random sample of cases that do not (the control group). That is, case-control designs stratify disproportionately on the dependent variable. In this study, a case-control approach is useful because many companies violated environmental regulations during the 2 years under investigation, but only a handful of these companies reported their violations to the EPA using the Audit Policy.

The event group is composed of all companies that reported an environmental violation of the Clean Air Act (CAA), Clean Water Act (CWA), Comprehensive Environmental Response, Compensation and Liability Act (CERCLA), Resource

Conservation and Recovery Act (RCRA), Toxic Substances Control Act (TSCA), and Emergency Planning and Community Right to Know Act (EPCRA) under the Audit Policy during the 1999 and 2000 fiscal years (October 1 1998 through September 30 2000). EPA's Office of Regulatory Enforcement provided a list of all the names of companies (N = 551) that used the Audit Policy during the 1999 and 2000 fiscal years.[5]

In this study, the control group should ideally be composed of companies that could have used the self-policing policy. Thus, the ideal controls will have violated at least one environmental law during FY1999 or FY2000 but not used the Audit Policy. The problem is, of course, that identifying ideal controls is not possible because there is no way to know about environmental violations that have not been discovered by the state. For the purposes of this study, then, a control group could be selected in one of two imperfect but different ways. First, a sample of all companies could be compared to companies that use the Audit Policy. The problem with this approach is that most control companies could not use the policy during FY1999 and FY2000 because those companies did not violate an environmental law. Thus, the comparison between cases and controls would be problematic to the extent that companies violating environmental laws are different from companies not doing so.

Second, the control group could be constructed to consist only of companies identified as violating an environmental law. The problem with this approach is that it also may introduce selection bias into the study: undiscovered violators may be different from discovered violators. For instance, undiscovered violators may not be inspected as frequently as companies discovered to have violated criminal laws.

Although either strategy for selecting a control sample may introduce selection bias into this study, the second method was chosen because there are likely to be smaller differences between discovered and undiscovered violators than between violators and nonviolators. For this reason, the control group consists of 551 companies, obtained by means of a simple random sample of the thousands of companies that the EPA discovered to have violated a federal environmental law (that is, CAA, CWA, CERCLA, RCRA, TSCA, and EPCRA) during the same period as the event group (Scalia 1999). In this study, the control group is selected from a population of companies that might have used the Audit Policy but did not because the company did not want to report the violation, was unaware of the EPA's self-policing policy, or was unaware of the violation. To be consistent with the case-control literature the sampling frame constructed to select the controls was constructed from a list of all companies that had civil and administrative actions as identified in the EPA's Integrated Data for Enforcement Analysis (IDEA) system. IDEA was developed in response to a need for integrated data on facilities that were potentially involved in enforcement or compliance actions. It is now a major data retrieval mechanism for accessing multimedia enforcement and compliance data and the primary system that informs the EPA's Online Tracking Information System (OTIS), which nearly all regulatory personnel use to track facility compliance, make enforcement decisions, and create annual reports.[6]

### Dependent variable

The dependent variable, Audit Policy use, is dichotomous and indicates whether a company self-disclosed or was discovered to have violated an environmental law (that is, CAA, CWA, CERCLA, RCRA, TSCA, or EPCRA) at any time during the 1999 to 2000 fiscal year. If a company disclosed a violation to the EPA it was assigned a score of 1. If a company was investigated and found to have violated an environmental law at any of its facilities it was assigned the score of 0.

### Independent variables

Variables measuring inspections and enforcement were created using the IDEA system, which was accessed though the National Computing Center's IBM mainframe. The variable measuring threat of inspections was obtained from EPA staff. Control variables were also created to determine whether a potential relationship between inspections or enforcement variables and Audit Policy might be spurious. Independent variables were created from information obtained from three sources. First, the *American Business Discs* (1998, 1999) were used to obtain financial and organizational information about companies in the sample. Data from the 1998 and 1999 disc are used to ensure that company information is collected prior to the discovery or disclosure of an environmental violation. Second, the *Dun and Bradstreet/Gale Industry Reference Handbooks* (McConnell and Hall 1998) are used to create variables that tap into the financial state of a particular industry in which the company broadly operates. Third, case information regarding the location of violation, number of violations, and nature of violation was obtained from the Office of Compliance and Assistance at the EPA. A summary of variable descriptions, descriptive statistics, and data sources are listed in appendix A.

*Inspections and Threat of Inspections.* The Audit Policy is more likely to be used by companies when inspection rates are high (Scholz and Gray, 1997; Stafford 2002, 2003). The idea that inspections can influence compliance is based on rational choice assumptions about the fear of apprehension or future apprehension. For example, Laplante and Rilstone (1996) find that inspections have a strong positive effect on how a company reports required environmental data. Dasgupta, Hettige, and Wheeler (2000) discovered that perceived regulatory pressure increased the likelihood that firms would adopt unilateral, voluntary environmental initiatives. Thus, the more certain it is that a violation will be discovered and subsequently punished, the less likely it is that an offender will violate the law. Although a relatively high inspection rate may be interpreted as increasing the probability that any existing violation will be detected, a relatively low inspection rate may be interpreted as decreasing the probability that any existing violation will be detected. Indeed, past research on self-reporting suggests that when facilities are inspected they are more likely to submit EPA-required discharge monitoring reports (Magat and Viscusi 1990: 354).

To examine the potential impact of inspections on the Audit Policy, three variables are created to tap different dimensions of the concept of certainty of apprehension. First, in the case of specific deterrence where past inspections at company facilities could lead to sanctions, a company inspections variable is created to indicate the average number of inspections at company facilities 2 years before the disclosure or discovery of a violation. The company inspections variable represents the sum of the number of Reporting for Enforcement and Compliance Assurance Priorities (RECAP) inspections at all company facilities (estimated by IDEA) divided by the number of company facilities eligible for inspection.[7]

Second, in the case of general deterrence where a company may look to the likelihood of apprehension based on the inspection rate of similarly situated actors, a regional industry inspections variable is created and represents the average number of inspections at similar facilities within the same industry and EPA region 2 years prior to the disclosure or discovery of an environmental violation.[8] Again, regional industry inspections is calculated by adding the number of RECAP inspections of all companies operating in the same region and industry together and then dividing by the number of company facilities eligible for inspections. Regional and industry effects were taken into account in order to best get at the company's reference group (Block, Nold, and Sidak 1981). There is good reason to believe that a company will pay greater attention to trends within their industry and geographic region than trends in other industries and other EPA regions that may have different economic and enforcement climates (GAO 2000).

Third, the EPA has tried to encourage companies to disclose environmental violations under the Audit Policy through initiatives targeted at specific industries. It does so by disseminating the Audit Policy and the potential for future inspections and enforcement actions against companies within particular industries – typically in a mailed letter, informing companies that they can participate in the Audit Policy by conducting a self-audit and reporting any discovered violations to the EPA within a set period. If companies do not participate in the initiative they are told that there is a high likelihood of being inspected in the near future to determine if operations are in compliance with environmental regulations. In exchange for participation in the program (that is, conducting self-audits and reporting results), however, companies may gain 'low inspection priority' and are less likely to be inspected in the future (typically 1 to 2 years). Following the logic that the threat of inspections may increase the fear of apprehension for an environmental violation, companies that receive a letter asking them to participate may be more likely to follow the policy. Thus, a dichotomous audit letter variable is created and coded 1 when a company is operating in an industry that was targeted by an Audit Policy letter and 0 when a company was not operating in such an industry.

*Enforcement Actions.* The Audit Policy is more likely to be used by companies when they have been the target of an enforcement action. This assumption is based on the notion that corporations are rational actors whose fear of punishment will cause them to ask the EPA to waive that punishment under the Audit Policy. Earnhart found that 'enforcement related specific and general deterrence significantly may induce better environmental performance' (2004: 399). In this study, the idea that enforcement actions may increase the likelihood of participation in voluntary programs is examined in terms of both specific and general deterrence. A company's experiences with past punishment (specific deterrence) is measured by creating a variable that counts the number of formal enforcement actions by the EPA against the company 2 years before the discovery or disclosure of an environmental violation.[9] If past enforcement has a specific deterrent impact on corporate behavior such that companies are more willing to turn themselves in as opposed to trying to beat the regulatory system, then the company enforcement variable should be positively related to the dependent Audit Policy variable.

To tap the notion of general deterrence and a company's observations regarding another's punishment, a variable is created to measure the rate (per facility) of formal enforcement actions in the company's same industry and region 2 years prior to the discovery or disclosure of the policy. If the general levels of enforcement in a company's industry and region influence corporate behavior such that companies are more likely to use the policy when a significant portion of those companies around them are being punished for environmental violations, then the regional enforcement levels variable should be positively related to the dependent Audit Policy variable.

*Company Size.* In general, research indicates that larger companies are more likely to participate in voluntary environmental initiatives (Arora and Cason 1995; DeCanio and Watkins 1998). To measure company size, a company size factor is created to represent the principal component index of company sales and the number of employees in the year prior to the year of self-disclosure or discovery of an environmental violation. The company size factor was constructed from information available in the *American Business Discs* (1998 1999), which lists eleven categories of company sales and number of employees. EPA data are notorious for being incomplete – especially with regard to company financial indicators where rates of missing data have been found to be on the order of 30 percent (Grant, Jones, and Bergesen 2002). Therefore, data on company size and employees were collected by manually looking up each company in the *American Business Discs*. In addition, the size component was highly consistent and all component loadings exceeded 0.8.

*Public Ownership.* In addition to company size, a dichotomous public ownership variable is created to measure whether a company is publicly owned (coded 1) or not publicly owned (coded 0). Existing research on privately versus publicly held corporations indicates that the behavior of publicly held companies is likely to be partially governed by 'stock-market induced pressures for consistency' (Trostel and Nichols 1982: 59). Davidson, Worrell, and Lee (1994) also point out that the stock market may react negatively to some types of corporate crime. Thus a financial interest on the part of public investors hopes to ensure that a company is acting to protect short-term investments. Moreover, managers of publicly held companies must respond to a variety of stakeholder interests that managers of private companies do not, including a large number of public investors who may demand that companies operate in environmentally responsible ways. Public investors may see the potential negative publicity associated with the discovery of an environmental violation and the potential gravity-based penalty as a threat to the stability of a company's stock prices that may signal financial problems or inept management. Public ownership was also determined by information available in the *American Business Discs*.

*Credit Rating.* To examine the concept of company strain a credit rating variable is created that estimates each company's credit rating. The *American Business Discs* rank companies according to their credit rating, in terms of 'satisfactory,' 'good,' 'very good,' and 'excellent.' Very few companies had credit ratings in the top or bottom categories, so the credit rating variable is dichotomous. Companies with satisfactory and good credit were assigned a score of 1, while companies with very good or excellent credit ratings were assigned a score of 0. It may be that a company with a relatively low credit rating is more likely to experience economic strain and therefore take a chance and commit an environmental violation in the hopes that the violation will never be detected.

*Industry Sales.* An alternative measure of economic strain, as suggested by the compliance literature, can be determined by estimating a company's market share. Companies with a lower market share may be operating in a more competitive market and therefore be less likely to pay the costs associated with maintaining counsel to advise them on regulatory matters such as the existence of the Audit Policy or the economic and regulatory benefits of using the policy. Some researchers believe that companies operating in competitive markets are more likely to engage in voluntary programs that can save the company money (Arrow 1962). To capture a company's market share, a variable (percentage industry sales) is created that measures company sales as a percentage of total industry sales. Total industry sales are derived from the *Dun and Bradstreet/Gale Industry Reference Handbooks* (McConnell and Hall 1998). Each company's primary industry is estimated using the four digit primary industry standard industrial classification (SIC) code listed in the *American Business Discs*.[10]

*Violation Characteristics.* Characteristics of the violation may also be an important predictor of environmental self-policing (Pfaff and Sanchirico 2004). The two characteristics of violations that may be important are the number of violations and the type of violation.

Companies are probably better at detecting environmental violations through self-audits than regulatory personnel, who do not constantly inspect facilities or may miss violations during routine inspections. However, the EPA will closely examine the violation once a company reports it to the agency. It is therefore probably in the company's best interests to disclose all potential violations. Such behavior protects the company from having additional violations discovered at a later date during an investigation of Audit Policy claims. The discovery of additional violations may prompt traditional enforcement actions. It is likely, then, that the policy encourages companies to report all violations rather than a single violation. Companies, then, are likely to self-disclose multiple violations to reduce their liability (Rebovich 1998). Although most companies in the sample violated one environmental law, several violated more than one. For instance, it was not uncommon to encounter cases in which the Clean Air Act and the Resource Conservation and Recovery Act were simultaneously violated. For this reason, a multiple law violated variable is created to indicate whether a company's actions resulted in the violation of more than one environmental law.

To construct this variable, companies discovered or reported to have violated more than one environmental statute (such as EPCRA or CAA) during fiscal year 1999 or 2000 were assigned a score of 1. Companies that violated only one were assigned a score of 0. It is important to point out, however, that a single violation may be illegal under multiple statutes or even multiple statutory sections. Thus, this variable does not adequately represent crime seriousness, but instead represents discretion by the EPA or company reporting environmental violations. Just as with traditional street crimes, where the prosecutor has a great amount of discretion in deciding what charges to file, environmental violations are likely to be based on the discretion of the actors determining the charges. With the Audit Policy, companies are likely to anticipate and report every possible charge associated with a particular violation to fully cooperate with the EPA. In the case of EPA-discovered violations, the state may be most concerned with presenting enough charges to negotiate a successful consent decree.

The type of environmental violation may also be an important predictor of Audit Policy use. According to Pfaff and Sanchirico (2004), companies typically use the policy to disclose violations relating to a failure to comply with EPA mandatory reporting requirements. For example, several companies in this sample were charged with a violation of the EPCRA section 313 because they did not submit a toxic chemical release inventory (TRI) form to the EPA. The TRI form notifies the EPA and the public about chemical releases and other waste management practices. Pfaff and Sanchirico show that nearly 70 percent of all Audit Policy cases report violations as opposed to more serious emissions and permit violations. For this reason a dummy reporting violation variable is created. A company was assigned the score of 1 if at least one of its environmental violations was identified as a reporting violation and a score of 0 if all violations fell under another category (for example, permit and/or emissions violation). Information on violation type was obtained from the EPA's Administrative, Civil, and Criminal Docket.

*EPA Region.* The EPA influences environmental enforcement by issuing various policies and memoranda to guide enforcement policy. However, differences in philosophies and other factors such as budget constraints can result in significant variations in enforcement practices for similar cases in different EPA regions (GAO 2000). The GAO recently found extreme variations in facility related inspections across EPA regions that ranged from a low of 27 percent of all facilities inspected to a high of 74 percent. To control for potential regional variation in enforcement practices, a series of dummy variables were used to represent the EPA region in which the company facilities are located (Region 1–CT, MA, ME, RI, NH, and VT; Region–2 NJ, NY, PR, and VI; Region 3–Washington DC, DE, MA, PA, VI, and WV; Region 4–AL, FL, GA, KY, MS, NC, SC, and TN; Region 5–IL, IN, MI, MN, OH, and WI; Region 6–AR, LA, NM, OK, and TX; Region 7–IA, KS, MO, and NE; Region 8–CO, MT, ND, SD, UT, and WY; Region 9–AZ, CA, HI, and NV; Region 10–AK, ID, OR, and WA). Region 1 is the reference category.

## Analysis

This quantitative analysis examines whether inspections and enforcement are related to Audit Policy use. Table 31.1 begins to address these questions and contains the mean values for the variables used in this analysis, by policy use.

Table 31.1 suggests that several of the variables used to distinguish between the cases and controls are important predictors. First, the company inspections and regional industry inspections variables have a greater mean for companies that use the Audit Policy than companies caught by EPA traditional enforcement mechanisms. For instance, the average 2-year facility inspection rate among the companies that used the Audit Policy is .89, whereas among companies caught violating environmental laws it is .37 ($p < .01$). Also, companies in industries that received an Audit Policy letter informing them that they would likely be the target of future inspections use the Audit Policy at a much greater rate than companies that had their violations discovered by the EPA (31 percent versus 7 percent; $p < .05$). Finally, company enforcement actions occurred more frequently among those companies that used the Audit Policy than among those companies that did not use the Audit Policy.

**Table 31.1** Comparison of companies

| Variable | Discovered (mean) | Self-Disclosed (mean) | Diff. | SE of Diff. (t-score) |
|---|---|---|---|---|
| Company inspections | .37 | .89 | .52 | .11 (4.70)*** |
| Regional industry inspections | .78 | .93 | .15 | .05 (3.01)** |
| Audit letter | .07 | .31 | .24 | .02 (10.46)*** |
| Company enforcement actions | .11 | .25 | .14 | .05 (.06)** |
| Regional enforcement levels | .04 | .03 | −.01 | .01 (−.35) |
| Company size factor | −.53 | .56 | 1.09 | .05 (21.88)*** |
| Public ownership | .05 | .19 | .14 | .02 (7.40).*** |
| Credit rating | .49 | .24 | −.25 | .03 (−9.09)*** |
| % industry sales | 3.70 | 13.00 | 9.30 | 1.32 (7.04)*** |
| Number of laws violated | 1.00 | 1.20 | .20 | .03 (6.66)*** |
| Reporting violation | .24 | .62 | .38 | .03 (14.02)*** |
| EPA region | | | | |
| Region 1 | .05 | .05 | −.00 | .01 (−.44) |
| Region 2 | .04 | .08 | .04 | .02 (2.68)** |
| Region 3 | .11 | .11 | −.00 | .02 (−.05) |
| Region 4 | .08 | .10 | .02 | .02 (1.22) |
| Region 5 | .05 | .18 | .13 | .02 (6.67)*** |
| Region 6 | .31 | .12 | −.19 | .02 (−8.30)*** |
| Region 7 | .11 | .08 | −.03 | .02 (−1.98)* |
| Region 8 | .09 | .03 | −.06 | .01 (−4.19)*** |
| Region 9 | .10 | .04 | −.06 | .02 (−3.77)*** |
| Region 10 | .03 | .05 | .02 | .01 (1.72) |
| Multiple regions | .01 | .16 | .15 | .02 (9.26)*** |
| n | 551 | 551 | | |

Mean difference is statistically significant (*t*-test).
*$p < .05$ **$p < .01$ *** $p < .001$

As indicated in Table 31.1 both the company size variable and the public ownership variable help distinguish between the two groups of companies. Specifically, larger companies and companies that are publicly owned are more likely to use the Audit Policy than the smaller companies and companies that are privately owned. Consistent with the voluntary compliance literature, companies with lower credit ratings are less likely to use the Audit Policy than companies with higher credit ratings. Also interesting is the finding that companies with larger shares of the market in their industry are more likely to use the policy than companies with less of a market share in their industry. In terms of case characteristics, companies that used the Audit Policy were more likely, on average, to report violating more environmental laws when compared to companies that had their violations discovered by EPA regulators.

Phaff and Sanchirico (2004) discovered that Audit Policy cases were likely to be reporting violations. Table 31.1 suggests that the group of companies that used the Audit Policy were more likely, on average, to self-disclose a reporting violation (as opposed to a permit or emissions violation) than the group of companies that had their environmental violations discovered by the EPA. Finally, as the GAO suggested (2000), variations in Audit Policy exist according to the EPA region in which a company's facilities operate.

Table 31.1 helps illustrate the potential differences between companies that self-police and those caught by traditional EPA enforcement mechanisms. The results suggest that company-specific inspections and enforcement and general regional inspections are related to corporate self-policing such that increasing traditional enforcement mechanisms will also increase rates of corporate self-policing.

The results in Table 31.1 are not conclusive, however, because they fail to adjust for competing explanations of Audit Policy use. It may be that inspection and enforcement variables that appear to differentiate between the cases and controls in the bivariate analysis are irrelevant in multivariate analysis. It is important, then, to determine whether the results in Table 31.1 can be replicated in the context of competing explanations for Audit Policy use. To make those comparisons, logistic regression analysis is used to estimate the odds of Audit Policy use among the two groups of companies for several independent variables simultaneously. Logistic regression is an appropriate and typical statistical method for analyzing case-control designs (Lacy 1997).

Industry variation may be an important consideration in this analysis. The complexity and nature of industry variation often mean that studies of corporate compliance focus on a single industry rather than several simultaneously. The companies in this study represent seventy-three industries (appendix B). To ensure that industry variation is not responsible for the associations observed in this analysis, fixed-effects logistic regression is used to estimate odds ratios in addition to ordinary logistic regression (StataCorp 2001). These models enable us to examine the possibility that the apparent effect of independent variables reflect those of another group of variables correlated with the industry in which the company operates. The regression thus helps ensure that the effects of the independent variables are not the result of variation in factors associated with company industry. One drawback of using this method, however, is that the procedure relies on variation within the matched sets (that is, variation on Audit Policy reporting within each industry). Industries with no variation on the dependent variable are not informative. For this reason, the sample sizes for the fixed effects analyses are less than 1,102 because they represent only the number of cases in industries with variation in Audit Policy use, not the total number of cases. When EPA region is fixed, there are 1,033 cases in the analysis.[11] Two digit SIC codes were used to identify the general industry within which a particular company operates.[12] This system assigns codes to facilities based on the products they produce or the services they render. These codes were easily obtained from company financial reports in the *American Business Discs* and represent companys' primary lines of business.

Table 31.2 displays the results of the multivariate analysis of Audit Policy use. Model 1 (Table 31.2) presents the results in ordinary logistic regression and model 2 (Table 31.2) presents the results when company industry is fixed.

When controlling for all variables thought to influence policy use, inspection and enforcement variables no longer appear to be statistically significant predictors. The results appear relatively consistent between models 1 and 2 (except as noted), indicating that industry variation has little impact on the variable examined in this analysis.

To determine if multicollinearity might be a problem, the bivariate correlations of the independent variables included in the model in table were examined. That analysis suggests that most of those correlations are relatively modest (appendix C). In fact, the largest correlation between any of the independent variables was .36, between company inspections and company enforcement actions. To determine if that relationship might pose a problem in the models, two additional models were estimated (results not shown) and either the company inspections or company enforcement actions variable was removed from the model. This procedure resulted in very small changes in standard errors of the variables remaining in the model, which suggests that multicollinearity is not a problem. Finally, variance inflation factor (VIF) scores were estimated for the models presented in Table 31.2, in view of the fact that VIF scores greater than four may be indicative of harmful multicollinearity (Fox 1991). The highest observed VIF score was for the variable Region 6 (4.1). Again, removing Region 6 from the model had little impact on the standard errors of the variables remaining in the model; none of the other variables had VIF scores that exceeded 3.1 and the average VIF score for all variables in the model was a modest 1.9.

There are three notable differences between models 1 and 2 (Table 31.2). First, in model 1 the regional industry inspections variable is statistically significant. Unlike the bivariate analysis (Table 31.1), the regional industry inspections variable is associated with a decrease in the odds of policy use (OR = 0.72; $p < .05$). This relationship is opposite of what deterrence theory would predict. However, the regional industry inspections variable changes sign in model 2 (OR = 1.12; $p < .58$) and is no longer statistically significant, indicating that model misspecification may have been the reason for the unusual relationship in model 1. Second, audit letter (OR = 2.65; $p < .001$) is statistically significant in model 1 (ordinary logistic model), but not statistically significant (OR =

**Table 31.2** Logistic regression and fixed effects (SIC Code) logistic regression of audit policy use

| Variable | Model 1 Ordinary LR | | Model 2 Fixed Effects LR | |
|---|---|---|---|---|
| | OR[a] | 95 percent CI | OR[a] | 95 percent CI |
| Company inspections | 1.04 | (.93, 1.17) | 1.04 | (.95, 1.17) |
| Regional industry inspections | .72 | (.56, .93)* | 1.12 | (.75, 1.65) |
| Audit letter | 2.65 | (1.63, 4.31)*** | 1.38 | (.62, 3.05) |
| Company enforcement actions | .86 | (.68, 1.10) | .92 | (.68, 1.25) |
| Regional enforcement levels | .61 | (.08, 4.98) | .06 | (.00, 17.5) |
| Company size factor | 3.25 | (2.50, 4.21)*** | 2.67 | (1.96, 3.65)*** |
| Public ownership | .71 | (.38, 1.33) | .74 | (.35, 1.52) |
| Credit rating | .69 | (.46, 1.04) | .66 | (.42, 1.04) |
| % industry sales | 1.00 | (.99 1.00) | 1.00 | (.99 1.01) |
| Number of laws violated | 1.83 | (1.06, 3.17)* | 1.93 | (1.03, 3.60)* |
| Reporting violation | 6.70 | (4.66, 9.63)*** | 5.33 | (3.53, 8.04)*** |
| EPA region (versus region 1) | | | | |
| Region 2 | 3.47 | (1.33, 9.03)* | 2.48 | (.80, 7.70) |
| Region 3 | 2.09 | (.88, 4.96) | 1.32 | (.46, 3.78) |
| Region 4 | 1.32 | (.58, 3.06) | .89 | (.33 2.35) |
| Region 5 | 4.51 | (1.92, 10.59)*** | 2.83 | (1.07, 7.49)* |
| Region 6 | .74 | (.34, 1.60) | .69 | (.28, 1.70) |
| Region 7 | .89 | (.39, 2.09) | .68 | (.26, 1.83) |
| Region 8 | .36 | (.14, .97)* | .29 | (.09, .95)* |
| Region 9 | .30 | (.12, .75)** | .30 | (.10, .84)* |
| Region 10 | 2.28 | (.82, 6.33) | 2.00 | (.63, 6.34) |
| Multiple regions | 6.30 | (2.00, 19.87)** | 3.40 | (.99, 11.68) |
| Constant | .24 | (.09, .60)** | | – |
| Pseudo (Cox and Snell) $R^2$ | | .42 | | .31 |
| −2 log likelihood | | 893.97 | | 646.44 |
| n | | 1,102 | | 1,033 |

*$p < .05$ **$p < .01$ ***$p < .001$

Odds ratios are determined by taking the exponentials of the regression coefficients. For example, in model 1 the Audit letter coefficient is .975 and the Audit letter odds ratio is e$^{.975}$ or 2.65. To transform odds ratios and odds ratios confidence intervals to coefficients and standard errors use the natural logarithm. For example, to determine the Audit letter coefficient in model 1 take the natural logarithm of the Audit letter odds ratio, or ln(2.65), which is equivalent to .975.

1.38; $p < .42$) in model 2 (fixed effects model). Again, this may be the result of model misspecification in model 1, where primary industry was not fixed. Moreover, because audit letters were targeted at companies within several industries, this result is not surprising. Finally, many of the regional controls that were statistically significant in model 1 are insignificant or only marginally significant in model 2, suggesting that what has often been interpreted as regional differences may actually be the result of industry related variation. Other than these three differences, models 1 and 2 are relatively similar.

Three variables stand out as important in the multivariate analysis. First, company size appears to matter. That is, large companies are more likely to use the Audit Policy than small companies (OR = 2.67; $p < .001$ [model 2]). This finding is interesting as it implies – at least on this environmental indicator – that large companies are more environmentally responsible than small companies. Combined with the indication that large companies are more likely to emit higher levels of pollution (Grant, Jones, and Bergesen 2002), the finding that large companies are more likely to use the Audit Policy has interesting implications in the area of environmental responsibility. Specifically, large may be bad in terms of pollution emissions but good in that large companies are also more likely to identify, fix, and report violations to the EPA. This is also consistent with observations that firms with the highest chemical releases were more likely to participate in the EPA's voluntary 33/50 program (Khanna and Damon 1999; see also Khanna 2001).

Company size may also be important because it has implications for market competition. Because companies may use the Audit Policy to 'get in good' with regulators and reduce regulatory costs, it may mean that smaller companies are disproportionately disadvantaged economically. That is, relative to company size, larger companies that use the policy more may gain an advantage over smaller companies relative to the cost of regulatory compliance. The EPA has recognized this issue as problematic and has therefore implemented a small business initiative within the Audit Policy framework. However, as indicated in these data, the small business initiative has been used very infrequently.

Second, Table 31.2 (models 1 and 2) indicates that case characteristics matter. Multivariate results suggest that a company is 5.3 ($p < .001$) times more likely to self-police a reporting violation than a more serious emissions or permit violation. This may reflect the fact that regulatory agencies typically ignore reporting violations when going about traditional enforcement and instead focus on more serious emissions violations. Pfaff and Sanchirico (2004) have also suggested that companies are more likely to use the Audit Policy to report minor violations because there are low transaction costs for doing so: penalties would not be severe in the event that the Audit Policy did not apply. Company personnel, then, may believe that the Audit Policy is useful because it helps foster regulator goodwill at relatively low transaction costs. Goodwill may be translated in the form of lower levels of future enforcement related activities such as costly inspections.

Finally, net of other factors, it appears that companies that violate multiple laws are much more likely to use the Audit Policy than those that violate only one (OR = 1.93; $p < .05$). If the variable Multiple Laws Violated is simply an indicator of superior detection of environmental violations, this finding would imply that companies that use the Audit Policy do a better job of detecting and determining environmental violations than regulatory agencies such as the EPA. This finding may also indicate that companies that violate more than one law are more likely to see a benefit in reporting those violations to EPA than companies that only violate one environmental law.

**Discussion and conclusion**

This analysis addresses a general question about the impact of traditional enforcement mechanisms (that is, inspections and enforcement actions) on the use of self-policing that has yet to be addressed in the corporate crime literature. These findings are important because of their implications for both corporate crime research and criminal justice policy. In terms of corporate crime research, the belief that corporations may be more prone to deterrent messages than the general public has recently been questioned (Simpson 2002). This work is consistent with recent studies finding that the association between objective deterrence messages and corporate crime is inconsequential (Braithwaite and Makkai 1991). That there is not an association between inspection rates, enforcement rates, and self-policing in this study, however, does not necessarily mean that deterrent messages are unimportant. There are two reasons why this study cannot definitively rule out the importance of objective deterrence in the study of corporate behavior. First, traditional enforcement mechanisms may be relevant to self-policing to the extent that those messages influence levels of subjective deterrence-which may be related to patterns of corporate self-policing. Indeed, corporate crime research has already begun to find that subjective deterrence is more strongly associated with corporate behavior than with objective deterrence (Paternoster and Simpson 1996).

Second, because this is a study of offenders, it may therefore represent companies that are least likely to respond to sanctions and incentives. That enforcement mechanisms are not statistically significant predictors of self-policing, then, may have more to do with the focus of the study than with the true absence of an association between enforcement mechanisms and corporate behavior in general. For this reason, broad generalizations about corporate deterrence cannot be derived from this research.

In terms of criminal justice policy, some policy makers believe that companies are more likely to engage in self-policing when they are threatened with governmental regulation (see Maxwell, Lyon, and Hackett 2000; Videras and Alberini 2000). Again, this belief relies on general and possibly inaccurate assumptions about deterrence and rational choice theories. This study suggests, at least in the case of environmental self-policing, that variations in actual levels of enforcement related behavior do not increase Audit Policy use. It therefore suggests that the EPA is not likely to improve Audit Policy efficiency by merely altering the frequency and targets of inspection and enforcement mechanisms.

Related to criminal justice policy, Pfaff and Sanchirico (2004) suggest that the Audit Policy might be harmful to the environment because it will ultimately expand the total number of environmental violations that become known to regulatory agencies. Because many of the violations are relatively minor (that is, reporting violations) the use of the Audit Policy could force more regulatory resources to be devoted to less serious violations at the cost of resources currently devoted to more serious violations. Pfaff and Sanchirico argue that 'just as a prosecutor may have less time to investigate serious crimes if she must respond to every confession that is brought to her attention, the cases that result from the policy could in principle cause a less than beneficial reallocation of regulatory funds' (2004: 428). This trend to use the Audit Policy for less serious violations needs to be closely monitored in the future.

However, at this time it is clear that corporate self-policing is relevant to the extent that reported environmental violations are rather minor.

There are three major drawbacks to this study. The first is that the reason that no association between traditional enforcement mechanisms and self policing exists is related to the fact that company level inspections and enforcement actions are not adequate indicators of deterrent messages. That is, company inspections and enforcement may also be a measure of corporate culture. Companies with good environmental track records (and thus, relatively few violations) may be more likely to use the Audit Policy than those with poor records. In a recent Audit Policy user survey, a company employee was asked if he believed his company would still have self-reported a violation to the EPA even if the Audit Policy did not exist. The employee said, 'Yes, our corporate culture is to do the right thing' (EPA 1998: 4). Indeed, this employee may not be alone in his view: almost 44 percent of all companies using the Audit Policy argue that they would self-disclose a discovered violation even if the policy did not exist (EPA 1998). That is, the corporate culture of these companies simply may be such that employees (who may be dedicated to environmental compliance within the organization) constantly work to seek out potential violations and fix violations that are discovered. Companies with a pro-compliance culture may, for obvious reasons, have fewer previous enforcement actions and be more likely to use the Audit Policy only because it is 'the right thing to do.' Thus, the deterrent and culture effects of inspections and violations may be offsetting and may explain why inspections and enforcement are not related to Audit Policy use.

Related to the notion of corporate culture, the EPA and state agencies have tried to reward companies with good environmental track records by reducing the number of routine regulatory efforts, such as routine inspections, which are often costly to the company. This type of regulatory behavior is not unusual. For instance, the EPA recently developed a Performance Track program to encourage companies to go beyond mandatory environmental compliance by offering incentives for improved performance.[13] The EPA's Office of Policy, Economics, and Innovation argues that Performance Track permits the agency to focus traditional enforcement efforts on other facilities that necessitate closer supervision (2004). Companies that participate in the program are given low priority for future inspections. Although the companies identified in this research did not participate in Performance Track, it is still reasonable to assume that EPA regulatory personnel use their discretion in regulatory decisions such that they are more likely to inspect poor performing facilities than facilities that perform relatively well. Thus, companies that are known as good corporate actors are more likely to use the Audit Policy and less likely to be inspected by the EPA than those known as poor corporate actors.

Companies that have good environmental track records may be more likely to use the Audit Policy than companies with poor environmental track records. Vaughan (1998: 53) suggests that corporate culture can work to produce violations in a way consistent with employee 'incompetence, misunderstanding of laws, or improper attention to regulatory requirements.' If Vaughan (1998) is correct it might be expected that companies with poor environmental track records are less likely to be able to adequately assess their prospects for using the Audit Policy even when such use might mitigate punishment costs and significantly reduce future corporate liability. Further research (such as studies conducted by Paternoster and Simpson 1996) in this area might look to see if enforcement actions and voluntary initiatives are indeed related to corporate culture.

The second major drawback of this study is that the control group is composed only of companies known by the EPA to have violated an environmental law. The assumption is, of course, that violators that go undiscovered by the EPA could not use the Audit Policy. This assumption may be problematic. There are certainly companies that violate environmental laws and are not caught by the EPA. In this analysis, these companies are excluded from the control group. If the undiscovered violators are no different than the discovered violators (or the relative proportion of undiscovered to discovered violators is relatively small), then excluding undiscovered violators from the sampling frame is not problematic. However, the impact that doing so may have on the results should be open to debate. It is not unreasonable to assume that the discovered violators are inspected more often than their undiscovered counterparts. If unknown violators were significantly underrepresented in the control group, the overall inspection rate in the control group might be much too high. Such a condition would weaken the relationship between company inspections and Audit Policy use – possibly to the extent that no relationship between the two variables is observed when one in fact exists. Because company inspections are almost certainly related to detection rates, the finding that company level inspections are not related to Audit Policy use should not go permanently unquestioned.

The third major drawback is that regional inspections and regional enforcement actions do not capture the potential impact of sanction severity on self-policing. It is difficult to examine sanction severity in this study because offenders are rarely incarcerated for environmental crimes. Thus, including a variable that measures incarceration would not be useful in this analysis (Scalia 1999). Moreover, most EPA cases are settled through consent decrees, which are not judicial decisions but instead negotiations between defendants and government. Consent decrees, by nature, tend not to measure sanction severity in environmental crime. Instead, penalties are often imposed by the EPA based on the defendant's ability to pay (Mintz 1995). Moreover, EPA fines are supposed to recover the economic benefit of noncompliance (that is, the amount of savings for not complying with environmental violations) and impose an additional penalty for violating the law. Unfortunately, these two types of fines are often combined and it is therefore not possible to determine the true severity of the penalty. Atlas (2001) for example, argues that

> in comparing penalties of $50,000 and $100,000, against two defendants, for example, one might assume that the latter was punished more severely. In reality, the first defendant may have gained no economic benefit from noncompliance, while the second defendant may have saved $80,000 from noncompliance, with that amount being included in its penalty. Thus, the true punishments imposed on the defendants were $50,000 and $20,000.(639)

In sum, for the purposes of this study it is not feasible to construct a general deterrence measure that taps severity of punishment since most cases are solved through consent decrees, because the defendant's ability to pay is a consideration, and because the punishment portion of the penalty is often unknown.

These potential concerns raise additional questions about self-policing and suggest that more research is needed. This research, though unique, provides some insight into the relationship between inspections, enforcement, and Audit Policy use. Because self-policing is becoming more pervasive as a regulatory approach, the results should be viewed as a starting point which may guide future criminological research in the area of self-policing as an approach to regulatory violations. Clearly, the importance of the policy shift from direct regulation to market-based incentives at the national and state level justifies such attention.

## Notes

1 In this study corporate crime is defined according to Braithwaite and Fisse as the 'conduct of a corporation, or employees acting on behalf of a corporation, which is proscribed and punishable by law' (1987: 221). According to Simpson, this definition of corporate crime 'not only includes acts in violation of criminal law, but civil and administrative violations as well' (2002: 7).

2 Mazurek (1998: 6) estimates that between the years 1991 and 2000 the number of companies participating in various U.S. Environmental Protection Agency (EPA) market based voluntary programs, like the Audit Policy, increased from 400 to 13,055.

3 The final revised Audit Policy took effect on May 11, 2000 and is published in the April 11, 2000 *Federal Register* (EPA, 2000).

4 Penalties that the EPA assess are comprised of two elements: the economic benefit component and the gravity based component. The economic benefit component reflects the economic gain derived from a violator's illegal competitive advantage. Gravity based penalties are that portion of the penalty over and above the economic benefit. They reflect the egregiousness of the violator's behavior and constitute the punitive portion of the penalty (EPA, 1999).

5 A total of 797 Audit Policy cases, representing 551 companies, were received from the EPA. The number of cases and number of companies are not equal for two reasons. First, the same company appeared in the Audit Policy database multiple times. Second, no useful information could be located for four of the cases. If more than one facility or law was reported, the information on that facility and the type of environmental violation committed was retained as an important characteristic of the company's self disclosure.

6 The IDEA system contains facility level data on inspections, enforcement actions, penalties assessed. and toxic chemicals released. A more detailed description of IDEA is available for review on the EPA website (http://www.epa.gov/compliance/data/systems/multimedia/idea/index.html). The original data sources imported into IDEA are also widely used by researchers as a source of environmental data and include: (1) AFS (CAA – AIRS Facility Subsystem); (2) PCS (Clean Water Act – Permit Compliance System); (3) RCRAInfo (Resource Conservation and Recovery Act Information System); (4) the Federal Enforcement Docket; (5) TRI (Toxics Release Inventory); and (6) NCDB (the National Compliance Database).

7 Reporting for Enforcement and Compliance Assurance Priorities (RECAP) inspections were used because they count as the official performance measure for the EPA's office of Enforcement and Compliance Assurance. A list of RECAP inspections can be obtained from the EPA website (http://www.epa.gov/echo/ dfr data_dictionary.html).

8 The EPA calculates region and industry inspection rates in The Sector Notebooks, which are available online at http://www.epa.gov/compliance/resources/publications/assistance/sectors/notebooks/index.html. Although these notebooks could not be used to estimate the variable Regional Industry Inspections used in the current analysis because dates and industries covered were not complete. For example, the EPA produces thirty three Industry Sector Notebooks, and the companies in this study represent approximately seventy three separate industries. When comparisons could be made between the two estimates, the EPA

estimates were remarkably similar to the estimates used in this study. Indeed, the bivariate correlation between the EPA estimates and this study's estimates for relatively comparable cases was .72 (n = 88). Minor discrepancies between EPA estimates and the estimates used in this study are likely due to the fact that different time periods were used across Sector Reports.

9 Typical formal enforcement actions against the companies in our sample include notices of noncompliance, consent decrees, and administrative orders. One potential problem with calculating enforcement actions using IDEA is that some enforcement actions are linked to more than one company facility. For example, in one case, a civil judicial enforcement action included violations at ten facilities. In order to avoid counting an enforcement action several times for a single company, an action that appears at more than one company facility is only counted once.

10 In many instances the EPA listed standard industrial classification (SIC) codes matched the *American Business Disc* listed in the primary company SIC codes. However, SIC codes were taken from the *American Business Discs* when EPA SIC codes did not match *American Business Disc* SIC codes or when EPA SIC codes were missing. Only primary company SIC codes were used to determine the markets in which companies compete.

11 Ordinary logistic regression is run on 1,102 cases while fixed effects logistic regression is run on 1,033 cases. While fixed effects regression is preferred to ordinary logistic regression in this case, both sets of regression results are presented to demonstrate consistency. Even though a different procedure and subset of cases were used to analyze these data, the results were remarkably similar.

12 Four digit SIC codes were also used in a fixed effects logistic regression but resulted in the loss of 459 (or 41 percent) of the cases in the analysis because of a lack of variation in the dependent variable within industry. Results of the four digit SIC code model does suggest consistency. Similar to the results presented in tables 1 and 2, the three variables that were statistically significant in the four digit SIC code models were company size (OR = 2.1; 95 percent CI = 1.6, 3.9), multiple laws violated (OR = 2.3; 95 percent CI = 1.1, 4.7), and reporting violation (OR = 3.4; 95 percent CI = 1.9, 6.1).

13 Performance Track is a voluntary EPA program that encourages companies to exceed mandatory environmental performance requirements. The focus of the program is on environmental outcomes rather than processes used to attain those outcomes. Companies that participate in Performance Track are offered a variety of incentives, including low priority for routine inspections (EPA, 2004).

# References

*American Business Disc.* (1998). Omaha, NE: InformUSA.

*American Business Disc.* (1999). Omaha, NE: InformUSA.

Arora, Seema, and Timothy Cason. (1995). An experiment in voluntary environmental regulation: Participation in EPA's 33/50 program. *Journal of Environmental Economics and Management* 28: 271–86.

Arrow, Kenneth. (1962). Economic welfare and the allocation of resources for invention. In *The Rate and Direction of Inventive Activity,* ed. Richard Nelson. Princeton, NJ: Princeton University Press.

Atlas, Mark. (2001). Rush to judgment: An empirical analysis of environmental equity in U.S. Environmental Protection Agency enforcement actions. *Law and Society Review* 35: 633–82.

Block, Michael Kent, Frederick Carl Nold, and Joseph Gregory Sidak. (1981). The deterrent effect of antitrust enforcement. *Journal of Political Economy* 89: 429–45.

Braithwaite, John. (2002). Rewards and regulation. *Journal of Law & Society* 29: 12–26.

Braithwaite, John, and Brent Fisse. (1987). Self-regulation and the control of corporate crime. In *Private Policing,* eds. Clifford Shearing and Philip Stenning. Newbury Park, CA: Sage Publications.

Braithwaite, John, and Toni Makkai. (1991). Testing an expected utility model of corporate deterrence. *Law & Society Review* 25: 7–10.

Burger, Jerry M. (1992). *Desire for Control: Personality, Social, and Clinical Perspectives.* New York: Plenum Press.

Chemical Week. (1995). Auditing to rise? Chemical Week April 19, 66.

Dasgupta, Susmita, Hemamala Hettige, and David Wheeler. (2000). What improves environmental compliance? Evidence from Mexican industry. *Journal of Environmental Economics and Management* 39: 39–66.

DeCanio, Stephen, and William Watkins. (1998). Investment in energy efficiency: Do the characteristics of firms matter? *Review of Economics and Statistics* 80: 95–107.

Davidson, Wallace, Dan Worrell, and Chun Lee. (1994). Stock-market reactions to announced corporate illegalities. *Journal of Business Ethics* 13: 979–87.

Earnhart, Dietrich. (2004). Panel data analysis of regulatory factors shaping environmental performance. *The Review of Economics and Statistics* 86: 391–401.

Freeman, A. Myrick. (2000). Economics, incentives, and environmental regulation. In *Environmental Policy: New Directions for the Twenty-First Century*, eds. Michael Kraft and Norman Vig. Washington, DC: CQ Press.

Fox, John. (1991). *Regression Diagnostics*. Quantitative Applications in the Social Sciences Series (07-079). Newbury Park, CA: Sage Publications.

Grant, Don Sherman, Andrew Jones, and Albert Bergesen. (2002). Organizational size and pollution: The case of the U.S. chemical industry. *American Sociological Review* 67: 389–407.

Jamieson, Katherine M. (1994). *The Organization of Corporate Crime*, vol. 11. Thousand Oaks, CA: Sage Publications.

Khanna, Madhu. (2001). Nonmandatory approaches to environmental protection. *Journal of Economic Surveys* 15: 291–324.

Khanna, Madhu, and Lisa Damon. (1999). EPA's voluntary 33/50 program: Impact on toxic releases and economic performance of firms. *Journal of Environmental Economics and Management* 37(1): 1–25.

Lacy, Michael. 1997. Efficiently studying rare events: Case-control methods for sociologists. *Sociological Perspectives* 40: 129–54.

Laplante, Benoit, and Paul Rilstone. (1996). Environmental inspections and emissions of the pulp and paper industry in Quebec. *Journal of Environmental Economics and Management* 31(1): 19–36.

Magat, Wesley, and Kip Viscusi. (1990). Effectiveness of the EPA's regulatory enforcement: The case of industrial effluent standards. *Journal of Law and Economics* 33: 331–60.

Makkai, Toni, and John Braithwaite. (1994). The dialectics of corporate deterrence. *Journal of Research in Crime and Delinquency* 31: 347–73.

Maxwell, John, Thomas Lyon, and Steven Hackett. (2000). Self-regulation and social welfare: The political economy of corporate environmentalism. *Journal of Law and Economics* 43: 583–617.

Mazurek, Janice. (1998). *The Use of Voluntary Agreements in the United States: An Initial Survey*. CAVA Working Paper No. 98/11/1. Paris: Organization of Economic Cooperation and Development, Working Party on Economic and Environmental Policy Integration.

McConnell, Stacy A., and Linda D. Hall, eds. (1998). *Dun and Bradstreet/Gale Industry Reference Handbooks*. Detroit, MI: Gale Group.

Mintz, Joel. (1995). *Enforcement at the EPA: High Stakes and Hard Choices*. Austin: University of Texas Press.

Morandi, Larry. (1998). *State Environmental Audit Laws and Policies: An Evaluation*. Washington, DC: National Conference of State, Legislatures.

Paternoster, Raymond, and Sally Simpson. (1996). Sanction threats and appeals to morality: Testing a rational choice model of corporate crime. *Law & Society Review* 30: 549–83.

Pfaff, Alexander, and Chris Sanchirico. (2004). Big fields, small potatoes: An empirical assessment of EPA's self-audit policy. *Journal of Policy Analysis and Management* 23: 415–32.

Piquero, Nicole Leeper, Lyn Exum, and Sally Simpson. (2005). Integrating the desire-for-control and rational choice in a corporate crime context. *Justice Quarterly* 22: 252–80.

Powers, Ray. (1996). Self-audits and the environment. *Journal of Commerce*, January 19, 6.

Rebovich, Donald. (1998). Environmental crime research: Where we have been, where we should go. In *Environmental Crime: Enforcement, Policy, and Social Responsibility*, ed. M. Clifford. Gaithersburg, MD: Aspen Publishers.

Rosenbaum, Walter. (2000). Escaping the `battered agency syndrome': EPA's gamble with regulatory reinvention. In *Environmental Policy: New Directions for the Twenty-First Century*, eds. Michael Kraft and Norman Vig. Washington, DC: CQ Press.

Scalia, John. (1999). *Federal Enforcement of Environmental Laws (1997)*. Washington, DC: U.S. Department of Justice, Office of Justice Programs.

Scholz, John, and Wayne Gray. (1997). Can government facilitate cooperation? An informational model of OSHA enforcement. *American Journal of Political Science* 41: 693–717.

Simpson, Sally. (1986). The decomposition of antitrust: Testing a multi-level, longitudinal model of profit-squeeze. *American Sociological Review* 51: 859–75.

Simpson, Sally. (2002). *Corporate Crime, Law, and Social Control*. New York: Cambridge University Press.

Simpson, Sally, and Christopher Koper. (1992). Deterring corporate crime. *Criminology* 30: 347–75.

Stafford, Sarah. (2002). The effect of punishment on firm compliance with hazardous waste regulations. *Journal of Environmental Economics and Management* 44: 290–308.

Stafford, Sarah. (2003). Does self-policing help the environment? EPA's Audit Policy and hazardous waste compliance. Unpublished manuscript. Williamsburg, VA: College of William & Mary, Department of Economics.

StataCorp. (2001). *Stata Statistical Software: Release 7.0*. College Station, TX: Stata Corporation.

Tittle, Charles R., and Raymond Paternoster. (2000). *Social Deviance and Crime: An Organizational and Theoretical Approach*. Los Angeles: Roxbury Publications.

Trostel, Albert, and Mary Nichols. (1982). Privately-held and publicly-held companies: A comparison of strategic choices and management processes. *Academy of Management Journal* 25: 47–62.

U.S. General Accounting Office (GAO). (2000). *Environmental Protection: More Consistency Needed among EPA Regions in Approach to Enforcement*. GAO/RCED-00-108. Washington, DC: U.S. Government Printing Office.

U.S. Environmental Protection Agency (EPA). (1995). Incentives for selfpolicing: Discovery, disclosure, corrections, and prevention of violations. *Federal Register* 60: 66705–712.

U.S. Environmental Protection Agency (EPA). (1998). *Audit Policy User Survey Results*. Washington, DC: U.S. Government Printing Office. http://www.epa.gov/compliance/resources/publications/incentives/programs/ audit-results.pdf.

U.S. Environmental Protection Agency (EPA). (1999). Evaluation of incentives for self-policing, discovery, disclosure, correction and prevention of violations policy statement, proposed revisions and request for public comment. *Federal Register* 64(94): 26745–756.

U.S. Environmental Protection Agency (EPA). (2000). Incentives for self policing: Discovery, disclosure, correction and prevention of violations. *Federal Register* 65(70): 19617–627.

U.S. Environmental Protection Agency (EPA). (2001). EPA Releases FY 2000 Enforcement and Compliance Assurance Data. News Media Release, January 19. Washington, DC: U.S. Government Printing Office. http://www.epa.gov/compliance/resources/reports/endofyear/eoy2000/eoyfy2000release-rpt.pdf.

U.S. Environmental Protection Agency (EPA). (2004). *National Environmental Performance Track: Basic Information*. Washington, DC: U.S. Government Printing Office. http://www.epa.gov/performancetrack/about.htm.

Vaughan, Diane. 1998. Rational choice, situated action, and the social control of organizations. *Law and Society Review* 32: 23–61.

Videras, Julio, and Anna Alberini. (2000). The appeal of voluntary environmental programs: Which firms participate and why? *Contemporary Economic Policy* 18: 449–61.

Washington Report. (1995). Reap the rewards of self-audits. *Washington Report* 209(8): 5.

Zimring, Franklin E., and Gordon Hawkins. (1973). Deterrence: *The Legal Threat in Crime Control*. Chicago: University of Chicago Press.

## Appendix A. Variable descriptions, descriptive statistics, and data sources

| Variable | Description | Mean | SD | Source |
|---|---|---|---|---|
| **Dependent Variable** | | | | |
| Self-Policing | Dichotomous variable that indicates whether a violation of the CAA, CWA, CERCLA, RCRA, TSCA, and/or EPCRA was disclosed by the company (coded 1) or as discovered by the EPA (coded 0). Data represent FY1999 & FY2000. | .5 | .5 | EPA Office of Regulatory Enforcement (self-disclosures) and IDEA[a] (EPA discovered violations). |
| **Independent Variables** | | | | |
| Company Inspections | Average number of RECAP inspections at company facilities 2 years prior to disclosure or discovery of an environmental violation (FY1999 & FY2000). A company that violated the CAA on 5/2/00 and had its seven facilities inspected 14 times between 5/1/98 and 5/1/00 would have a company inspection score of .50. | .62 | 1.82 | IDEA |
| Regional Inspections | Average number of RECAP inspections for facilities operating in the same EPA region and industry as the study company's facilities 2 years prior to that company's discovery or disclosure of an environmental violation. If a study company's facilities operated in more than one EPA region the inspection rates were averaged. A company in the paper and allied products industry (SIC 26) operating in EPA Region 4 would have a regional inspection rate of 1.5 if the 320 facilities operating in paper and allied products industry in Region 4 were inspected a total of 480 times 2 years prior to the discovery or disclosure of an environmental violation. | .85 | .81 | IDEA |
| Audit Letter | Dichotomous variable that indicates whether a company operated in an EPA region and industry that received a letter asking them to use the EPA Self Policing policy if they discovered an environmental violation. Data for audit letters cover FY1999 and FY2000. | .19 | .39 | EPA Office of Regulatory Enforcement |

| Variable | Description | Mean | SD | Source |
|---|---|---|---|---|
| Company Enforcement | Number of formal environmental enforcement actions initiated against company 2 years prior to disclosure or discovery of the environmental violation that defined the company as a case or control. Enforcement actions that covered more than one company facility were only counted one time. | .18 | .89 | IDEA |
| Regional Enforcement | Average number of formal environmental enforcement actions for facilities operating in the same industry and EPA region 2 years prior to that company's discovery or disclosure of an environmental violation. If a study company's facilities operated in more than one EPA region the enforcement rates were averaged. A company in the paper and allied products industry (SIC 26) operating in EPA Region 4 would have a regional enforcement rate of 1.0 if the 320 facilities operating in paper and allied products industry in Region 4 had a total of 320 violations 2 years prior to the discovery or disclosure of an environmental violation. | .04 | .19 | IDEA |
| Company Size Factor | Principal component index of company sales and number of company employees. Data are based on company information gathered in 1998. | 0 | 1 | *American Business Discs* 1998 and 1999 |
| Public Ownership | A dichotomous variable that indicates whether a company is privately held (coded 0) or publicly traded (coded 1). | .12 | .32 | *American Business Discs* 1998 and 1999 |
| Credit Rating | A dichotomous variable that indicates whether a company had 'excellent' or 'very good' credit (coded 0) or 'satisfactory' or 'good' good credit (coded 1). | .36 | .48 | *American Business Discs* 1998 and 1999 |
| Industry Sales | Company sales as a percentage of total sales in company's primary industry. | 8.28 | 22.30 | *Dun and Bradstreet /Gale Industry Reference Handbooks* (1998) and *American Business Discs* (1998) |

| Variable | Description | Mean | SD | Source |
|---|---|---|---|---|
| No Laws Violated | Disclosure or discovery was for multiple environmental laws (coded 1) as opposed to only one environmental law (coded 0). For example, a company that disclosed a violation of the CAA and CWA was given a score of 1 and a company that disclosed a violation of the CAA was assigned a score of 0. | 11.1 | .45 | EPA Office of Regulatory Enforcement (self-disclosures) and IDEA (EPA discovered violations). |
| Reporting Violation | Environmental violation was a reporting violation (coded 1) as opposed to a more serious violation such as an emissions violation (coded o). | .33 | .47 | EPA Office of Regulatory Enforcement (self-disclosures) and IDEA (EPA discovered violations). |

[a]IDEA is an acronym which stands for the Integrated Data for Enforcement Analysis system. The IDEA database can be accessed through the EPA's Office of Environmental Information (https://trex.rtpnc.epa.gov/epahome/trex-webaccess.htm).

## Appendix B. Number of companies by primary industry (n =1102)[a]

| Primary Co. Industry | # Companies |
| --- | --- |
| Chemicals and allied products | 101 |
| Electric, gas, and sanitary services | 88 |
| Wholesale trade, durable goods | 79 |
| Wholesale trade, nondurable goods | 79 |
| Fabricated metal products, except machinery & transport equip. | 59 |
| Food and kindred products | 54 |
| Automotive dealers and gasoline service stations | 44 |
| Industrial and commercial machinery and computer equipment | 37 |
| Primary metal industries | 37 |
| Real estate | 34 |
| Executive, legislative & general government, except finance | 31 |
| Oil and gas extraction | 30 |
| Electronic, electrical equip. & components, not computer equip. | 28 |
| Construction – special trade contractors | 24 |
| Food stores | 22 |
| Transportation equipment | 20 |
| Educational services | 19 |
| Building construction, general contractors & operative builders | 17 |
| Engineering, accounting, research, management & related svcs | 17 |
| Communications | 16 |
| Paper and allied products | 16 |
| Air transportation | 16 |
| Petroleum refining and related industries | 15 |
| Agricultural production, livestock, and animal specialties | 13 |
| Automotive repair, services, and parking | 13 |
| Watches/clocks | 12 |
| Miscellaneous manufacturing industries | 12 |
| Stone, clay, glass, and concrete products | 11 |
| Hotels, rooming houses. camps, and other lodging places | 10 |
| Miscellaneous retail | 10 |
| Rubber and miscellaneous plastic products | 10 |
| Lumber and wood products, except furniture | 9 |
| Personal services | 8 |
| Administration of environmental quality and housing programs | 7 |
| Business services | 7 |
| Heavy construction, except building construction-contractors | 7 |
| Motor freight transportation | 6 |
| Other[b] | 84 |

[a]Primary company industry is one that best characterizes company listed in the *American Business Disc (1998)*.
[b]Thirty-six additional industries not listed but represent between one and five companies each.

## Appendix C  Correlations among Independent Variables

| | 1 | 2 | 3 | 4 | 5 | 6 | 7 | 8 | 9 | 10 | 11 |
|---|---|---|---|---|---|---|---|---|---|---|---|
| 1. Company inspections | 1.00 | | | | | | | | | | |
| 2. Regional industry inspections | .15 | 1.00 | | | | | | | | | |
| 3. Audit letter | .09 | .17 | 1.00 | | | | | | | | |
| 4. Company enforcement actions | .36 | .08 | .10 | 1.00 | | | | | | | |
| 5. Regional enforcement levels | .01 | .19 | .04 | .02 | 1.00 | | | | | | |
| 6. Company size factor | .22 | .16 | .33 | .15 | .03 | 1.00 | | | | | |
| 7. Public ownership | .11 | .04 | .23 | .13 | .00 | .51 | 1.00 | | | | |
| 8. Credit rating | -.10 | -.04 | -.10 | -.09 | .00 | -.49 | -.26 | 1.00 | | | |
| 9. % industry sales | .14 | .10 | .04 | .12 | .00 | .43 | .22 | -.20 | 1.00 | | |
| 10. Number of laws violated | .07 | .03 | .17 | .13 | .02 | .27 | .20 | -.10 | .03 | 1.00 | |
| 11. Reporting violation | .05 | .10 | .16 | .03 | .01 | .19 | .04 | .01 | .09 | .00 | 1.00 |
| 12. Region 1 | .00 | -.08 | .00 | -.03 | .00 | -.03 | -.05 | .02 | .00 | -.04 | .05 |
| 13. Region 2 | .00 | .21 | .10 | .01 | .16 | .05 | -.06 | .00 | .03 | -.02 | .00 |
| 14. Region 3 | .12 | .34 | -.10 | -.01 | .00 | -.01 | .01 | .04 | .03 | -.03 | .00 |
| 15. Region 4 | .03 | .01 | .00 | .02 | .00 | .02 | -.06 | .00 | .01 | -.05 | .07 |
| 16. Region 5 | .07 | .05 | .06 | -.04 | .00 | .11 | .01 | .00 | .06 | -.04 | .08 |
| 17. Region 6 | .00 | -.12 | -.10 | -.05 | .00 | -.18 | -.04 | .07 | -.10 | -.04 | -.20 |
| 18. Region 7 | .00 | -.16 | -.10 | -.04 | .00 | -.08 | -.04 | .00 | .00 | .00 | .00 |
| 19. Region 8 | -.10 | -.06 | .00 | -.04 | .03 | -.10 | -.02 | .01 | .00 | -.02 | .02 |
| 20. Region 9 | -.10 | -.11 | .01 | -.01 | .01 | -.04 | .03 | .02 | .00 | -.05 | .10 |
| 21. Region 10 | .00 | -.11 | -.10 | .01 | .00 | .03 | -.02 | .04 | .02 | .02 | .00 |
| 22. Multiple regions | .02 | .00 | .19 | .20 | .01 | .30 | .24 | -.10 | .08 | .28 | .12 |

| | 12 | 13 | 14 | 15 | 16 | 17 | 18 | 19 | 20 | 21 | 22 |
|---|---|---|---|---|---|---|---|---|---|---|---|
| 12. Region 1 | 1.00 | | | | | | | | | | |
| 13. Region 2 | -.06 | 1.00 | | | | | | | | | |
| 14. Region 3 | -.08 | -.09 | 1.00 | | | | | | | | |
| 15. Region 4 | -.07 | -.08 | -.11 | 1.00 | | | | | | | |
| 16. Region 5 | -.08 | -.09 | -.13 | -.11 | 1.00 | | | | | | |
| 17. Region 6 | -.12 | -.13 | -.19 | -.16 | -.19 | 1.00 | | | | | |
| 18. Region 7 | -.08 | -.09 | -.12 | -.10 | -.12 | -.17 | 1.00 | | | | |
| 19. Region 8 | -.06 | -.07 | -.09 | -.08 | -.09 | -.13 | -.08 | 1.00 | | | |
| 20. Region 9 | -.06 | -.07 | -.10 | -.09 | -.10 | -.14 | -.09 | -.07 | 1.00 | | |
| 21. Region 10 | -.05 | -.05 | -.07 | -.06 | -.07 | -.10 | -.07 | -.05 | -.06 | 1.00 | |
| 22. Multiple regions | -.07 | -.08 | -.11 | -.10 | -.11 | -.16 | -.10 | -.08 | -.08 | -.06 | 1.00 |

# 32. Can criminal law protect the environment?[1]*

*Helena Du Rées*

## Abstract

This article examines the question of whether criminal law can protect the environment by functioning as a means of controlling environmentally hazardous activities. The concept of general prevention today dominates in the context of criminalization, and has been particularly emphasized in relation to criminalizations whose objective is environmental protection. The article discusses the conditions for general prevention in the context of environmental criminal law. These conditions include the regulatory acumen of those applying the law, the likelihood of being sanctioned for offences and the severity of sanctions imposed. Further, the article identifies problems faced by the agencies whose task it is to apply environmental criminal law. The most conspicuous of these problems is the dual role of the supervisory agencies, which function both as advisers and enforcers in relation to the operations that they monitor. Police and prosecutors are primarily faced with problems of a legal–technical nature, such as difficulties proving offences have been committed and investigating the question of responsibility, and problems of competency. These competency issues include difficulties applying the regulatory framework of the criminal law and a lack of expertise in the area of natural science. Finally, explanations are sought for the problems experienced in applying environmental criminal law. The article concludes that the fundamental causes of these problems lie in the way the environmental crime legislation is based on the weighing of competing interests against one another, and the unclear role of the supervisory authorities that constitute the first link in the judicial chain. This lack of clarity gives rise to an uneven application of the legislation and causes problems for those applying the law at higher levels within the justice system.

**Key Words** Environmental crimes • Environmental criminal law • Environmentally hazardous activities • Means of control • Supervisory agencies • Techniques of neutralization

---

* From *Journal of Scandinavian Studies in Criminology and Crime Prevention* (2001), 2: pp. 109–126.

Criminal law research must always 'move with the times'. { } Pondering how a Swedish shepherd boy should be punished for bestiality (this was one of the major crime policy issues of the 18th century) is of considerably less interest today than an analysis of whether, and how, international environmental pollution can be prevented by means of the criminal law (Per Ole Träskman, Lund University, Professorial inauguration 8/3 1996).

In Sweden today, the activities of approximately half a million enterprises are classified as constituting an environmental hazard.[2] Comprehensive regulations have been introduced with the objective of ensuring that these enterprises are operated in such a way that they give rise to no unnecessary harm, or risk of harm, to people or the environment. Environmental criminal law constitutes one part of this system of regulation, and it is the part that should ultimately ensure that those engaged in various forms of environmentally hazardous activities conform to the environmental regulations. The use of penal legislation to protect the environment is a relatively new phenomenon. In Sweden, the *Environmental Protection Act* of 1969 was the first piece of integrated legislation with the objective of protecting the environment. Over recent decades, however, both in Sweden and the rest of Europe, the political focus has been directed increasingly at the use of criminal law as a means of controlling environmentally hazardous activities (SOU 1987: 32:408 ff, McLoughlin and Bellinger 1993: 105, Faure and van der Wilt 1997). The question remains, however, whether criminal law is capable of protecting the environment. One often hears in this context, for example, that environmental crime is financially rewarding, and that environmental offenders usually 'get away with it' (see, for example, Expressen 010829:18 ff, Metro 980923:24 ff, Göteborgsposten 960915:2, 'Striptease' SVT 960918).

## Research objective and data

This article is based on a study whose main objective has been to investigate the possibilities for environmental criminal law to function as a means of controlling environmentally hazardous activities (see du Rées 2001). The study examines the conditions necessary for environmental criminal law to serve a general preventive purpose. It also investigates the problems experienced by various supervisory agencies in connection with the application of environmental criminal law and looks into possible causes of these problems. The agencies studied comprise the county administrative boards, the local authority supervisory agencies, the police and prosecutors. The empirical material primarily consists of data collected using the following four questionnaires.

### My own questionnaire

A questionnaire was sent to the environmental offices of every third local authority in the country, to the largest local authority in each county, to all of the county administrative boards, to the police in each county with responsibility for the relevant forms of environmental crime, and to the offices of all those prosecutors who at the time of the study dealt with environmental offences of this kind. Table 32.1 presents the size of the relevant populations and samples, and the total response frequencies.

### Questionnaires formulated by the Prosecutor General and the National Police Board

The study has also made use of two questionnaire surveys conducted by the Office of the Prosecutor General and one conducted by the National Police Board.[3] The first of the surveys conducted by the Prosecutor General included all county administrative boards and local authority supervisory agencies, while the other included the offices of the public prosecutor. All the country's 21 county administrative boards and 95% of local authorities (272 authorities) completed the Prosecutor General's questionnaire, as did 18 public prosecutors covering all the country's seven public prosecutor's offices. The survey conducted by the National Police Board included Sweden's 21 police authorities and was completed by all of them. The Prosecutor General has done no more than carry out a simple quantitative compilation of the data collected in the questionnaires. I have re-examined the data and carried out my own analysis, which includes a qualitative categorization of the material (du Rées 2001).

### Additional material

Besides the questionnaires described above, material from the Environmental Protection Agency, the Swedish Association of Local Authorities and the National Council for Crime Prevention has also been employed. See references included in the presentation below.

### Criminal law as a means of control

The legislator conceives of criminal law as controlling people's behaviour through general prevention, i.e. in the first instance by means of deterrence, but also in the longer term by affecting the public's moral sensibilities (Wennberg

**Table 32.1** My own questionnaire. Total population, sample and response frequencies

| Agency | Population | Sample | Response frequency, % (number) |
|---|---|---|---|
| County administrative boards | 21 | 21 | 86 (18) |
| Local authorities | 286 | 116 | 73 (85) |
| Police authorities and districts | 36 | 35 | 83 (29) |
| Public prosecutor's offices | 28 | 25 | 80 (20) |
| Total | 371 | 197 | 77 (152) |

1996: 11 ff, Jareborg 1994: 41, SOU 1986: 14:67, Riksåklagaren 1998:60 ff). In the case of environmental criminal law, conditions are felt to be particularly well-suited to achieving a general preventive effect. This is because environmental crimes committed in the context of various types of enterprise are assumed, unlike many other forms of criminalized behaviour, to be determined by rational calculation and are generally the result of a premeditated decision. The threat of sanctions in this context is directed at groups of people of high social standing who feel considerable loyalty towards the legal system at the general level. Their professional operations are to a large extent dependent on reputation and goodwill. Direct general preventive effects are therefore expected to be considerable (Riksåklagaren 1998: 7, SOU 1987: 32:440 SOU 1986: 14:41).

For a general preventive effect to be achieved, however, certain conditions must be fulfilled. This is the case irrespective of the kind of behaviour that criminalization is intended to control. The three essential conditions are regulatory acumen in the actors whose job it is to apply the legislation, a certain probability that offences will result in sanctioning, and sanctions that are sufficiently severe to deter potential offenders (Tråskman 1992: 10).

## Regulatory acumen[4]

It is often contended that the environmental legislation, *inter alia* as a result of its size, is difficult to apply in practice and that the officials involved at the various supervisory agencies lack the necessary expertise and experience. My own study indicates that when it comes to applying environmental criminal law, levels of regulatory acumen at the agencies concerned do not appear to constitute a major problem (du Rées 2001). Even before the introduction of the Environmental Code in 1999, the majority of officials involved had received special training and had experience from working with environmental legislation over a long period of time. Nearly all the respondents from the county administrative boards reported that they had received environmental training, although in one-third of cases this training had taken no more than a week. In addition, the responses indicate that the majority of these respondents had also undergone some form of training in environmental law. The majority of respondents from the county administrative boards described themselves as environmental protection directors. Most of the respondents from local authorities described themselves as environmental and health inspectors. A majority of these had received over a year's environmental training. Almost half the officials from the local authority agencies had undergone a higher education course in environmental and health protection, while the other half had some other form of education that included environmental law.

A majority of the police had received between 1 and 3 months' training in environmental law, while a quarter had not received any form of environmental training. A majority of the prosecutors had received at most a week's training in environmental law, with a third replying that they had not received any form of environmental training[5] (see Table 32.2).

Table 32.2 shows that a third (32%) of officials at the county administrative boards had received at most a week's environmental training while a quarter (25%) had received over 1 year of training.

Regulatory acumen is built up through experience. The questionnaire therefore asked how much experience the environmental officials had of working with questions of environmental protection and environmental legislation. Virtually all the officials at the county administrative boards had worked with environmental protection for at least 6 years. Most of those working for the local authorities' supervisory agencies also had a great deal of experience of environmental protection work. The majority of police and prosecutors also had experience of working with cases related to environmental protection, although this experience did not extend over such a long period as that of the supervisory agencies. It should be mentioned in this context, however, that work with environmental offending comprises only a small part of the workload of the supervisory agencies to which the questionnaires were sent. At the time of the survey, a large majority of the police and prosecutors also devoted the majority of their working time to quite different categories of crime (see Table 32.3).

Table 32.3 shows that none of the environmental officials at the county administrative boards had less than 1 year's experience of working with environmental protection cases, with a majority (61%) reporting at least 10 years' experience.

The survey also asked officials at the various agencies to assess seven common environmental offences according to whether they constituted a breach of the law and whether this should be reported for indictment. All the cases described, except one which was constructed especially, were taken from district court judgements passed between 1995 and 1998. They were chosen as examples of the types of offence that lead most commonly to prosecution and conviction for environmental crimes committed in the context of economic activity. The results show a substantial level of agreement among officials from the different agencies regarding how the norms of environmental criminal law ought to be applied, at least in cases of the kind included in the

**Table 32.2** Length of environmental training for environmental officials at various agencies. Proportions in % (numbers in parentheses). The most common alternative for each agency has been highlighted

| | Agency | | | | |
|---|---|---|---|---|---|
| Training | County boards | Local auth. | Police | Prosecutors | All |
| None | 6 (1) | 5 (4) | 24 (7) | 35 (7) | 13 (19) |
| At most 1 week | 32 (5) | 9 (7) | 7 (2) | 20 (4) | 13 (18) |
| 1 week–1 month | 12 (2) | 4 (3) | 3 (1) | 30 (6) | 8 (12) |
| 1–3 months | 6 (1) | 4 (3) | 63 (18) | 10 (2) | 17 (24) |
| 3 months–1 year | 19 (3) | 15 (12) | 0 | 5 (1) | 11 (16) |
| Over 1 year | 25 (4) | 63 (49) | 3 (1) | 0 | 38 (54) |
| Total | 100 (16) | 100 (78) | 100 (29) | 100 (20) | 100 (143) |

**Table 32.3** Experience of environmental protection work possessed by environmental officials at various agencies, measured in units of time. Proportions in % (numbers in parentheses). The most common answer for each agency has been highlighted

| Experience | Agency | | | | |
|---|---|---|---|---|---|
| | County boards | Local auth. | Police | Prosecutors | All |
| None | 0 | 0 | 0 | 5  (1) | 1  (1) |
| Less than 1 year | 0 | 4  (3) | 7  (2) | 15  (3) | 5  (8) |
| 1–5 years | 6  (1) | 21 (18) | 59 (17) | 60 (12) | 32 (48) |
| 6–10 years | 33  (6) | 26 (22) | 34 (10) | 10  (2) | 26 (40) |
| More than 10 years | 61 (18) | 49 (42) | 0 | 10  (2) | 36 (55) |
| Total | 100 (18) | 100 (85) | 100  (29) | 100 (20) | 100 (152) |

survey. The survey also showed that the agencies themselves do not regard levels of relevant expertise as being among the most important problems affecting the chances of convicting environmental offenders. There was also agreement among the respondents that the greatest levels of expertise reside in the supervisory agencies, compared with the other agencies included in the survey (du Rées 2001).

## The likelihood of being sanctioned

Many environmentally hazardous operations are not subject to any form of supervision, and of those that are the frequency of inspections, particularly unannounced inspections, is low (Naturvårdsverket 1996: 24, cf. Svenska Kommunförbundet 2000: 13). Further, environmental crimes do not usually generate a concrete victim in the form of a physical person (as is the case in assault offences, for example), or one that can be represented by a physical person (as in frauds committed against an insurance company), who is able to report the offence. The number of environmental crimes that are discovered is thus dependent on the activities of the supervisory agencies. In combination with the low level of inspections, this means that the risk of being caught in connection with an environmental offence is likely to be low. In addition, few of the environmental offences that are reported lead to an indictment. Of the reported violations of the *Environmental Protection Act* (the central piece of environmental legislation prior to the introduction of the Environmental Code) an average of 12% resulted in an indictment over the course of the period 1990–8 (see the crime statistics produced by the National Council for Crime Prevention). The average proportion of all reported offences that lead to an indictment lies at present at over 50%. This proportion is usually higher for offences whose discovery depends on official efforts to uncover crime. As an example, the proportion of reported breaches of narcotics legislation that led to an indictment lay at approximately 70% in the year 2000. The proportion of reported motoring offences that led to an indictment lay at approximately 80% (see Riksåklagaren 2001, Brottsförebyggande rådet 2001). The fact that the risk of discovery is likely to be low, in combination with a low risk of conviction, means that the likelihood of receiving some form of sanction in connection with environmental crime is also going to be low.

## The severity of sanctions

Finally we come to the question of the severity of sanctions. During the period covered by this study, the sanctioning scale for environmental ounces ranged between fines at the one end and a prison term of 6 years at the other. For offences against the most commonly used legal provision, paragraph 45 of the *Environmental Protection Act*, the maximum sanction was a prison term not exceeding 2 years. The majority of officials working at the various agencies included in the study had no major objections to the sanctioning scales. On the other hand, a clear majority of these officials felt that the sanctions actually passed were too mild. The most common form of sanction for those convicted of environmental offences is a fine, which up until 1998 meant day-fines[6] over a period of between 30 and 50 days. Prison sentences are very rare. Between 1992 and 1998, only two people were sentenced to a prison term for offences against the *Environmental Protection Act*. During the same period, seven persons received a suspended sentence. Thus, up to now the gravity of environmental crime has in practice been deemed to be relatively low. This suggests that the severity of sanctions is also relatively low. This becomes even clearer when one compares the size of fines with the costs that firms have avoided having to pay, or the increases in income that have accrued, in connection with the offences in question, as can often be seen from an examination of court pronouncements in cases of environmental offending.

Figure 32.1 shows that the number convicted of crimes against the *Environmental Protection Act* peaked in 1992 and dropped thereafter. Fines dominate among the sanctions. In 1983, two people were sentenced to prison. In 1995, prosecutorial fines were issued for the first time in connection with environmental offences.

## Problems applying the legislation

The results presented above indicate that the levels of regulatory acumen at those agencies that apply environmental criminal law is not a major problem. There does, however, appear to be a problem with both of the other prerequisites for achieving a general preventive effect, i.e. the likelihood of sanctioning and the severity of the sanctions imposed. The questionnaires issued by the Prosecutor General and the National Police Board have been examined in an attempt to develop an idea of the problems that the agencies themselves experience in connection with the application of environmental criminal law. The responses from police and prosecutors describe four different categories of problem: legal–technical problems, such as difficulties in proving environmental offences have taken place, and in investigating the

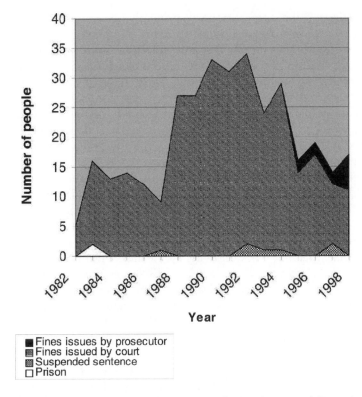

**Figure 32.1** Number of convicted crimes against the *Environmental Protection Act*

question of responsibility; technical problems, such as difficulties measuring and analysing suspected offences; problems of competency, such as difficulties handling obscure legislation and the unfulfilled need for access to expertise in specific areas; and organizational problems both within the respondents' own organizations and in the context of collaborations with other agencies. Problems related to the application of environmental regulations, i.e. legal–technical and competency problems, are by far the most dominant among the responses (du Rées 2001). I will therefore begin by examining possible reasons why the environmental legislation is regarded as difficult, and which lead to problems in applying the law.

## The foundations of environmental criminal law

Environmental law can reasonably be regarded as a relatively new area of the law. One might say that we are at present at a stage where we are attempting to adapt environmental law to new objectives, materially, processually and organizationally (Christophersen 1997: 19). However, this adaptation is taking place within the framework of established law. In Sweden this is illustrated by the way in which the regulations contained in the *Environmental Protection Act* were transferred to the new Environmental Code for the most part completely unchanged, while at the same time new objectives such as 'sustainable development' and the 'precautionary principle' have been introduced. In addition, a whole new organisational structure has been introduced in order to combat environmental crime. The new objectives and the new organisation have to work within the framework of the established system, however, a system which has evolved since the early days of industrialisation in interaction with the economic liberalism that has dominated since the 1840s and whose principle task has been to protect the rights of ownership and contractual freedom (Christophersen 1997: 83). The *Environmental Protection Act*, like today's regulations, was based on the idea of weighing competing interests against one another (see Westerlund 1975: 7 on the subject of the *Environmental Protection Act*). The question of what is and is not permitted is regulated by means of the issuance of permits specific to each enterprise whose content is based on weighing the interests of environmental protection against whatever is regarded as economically reasonable. A certain level of environmental damage is accepted in modern society since it serves to provide for other social interests. The following quote taken from the Bill that would become the *Environmental Protection Act* illustrates this relationship rather well: '{ } one of the fundamental ideas in the proposed legislation {is} namely that environmentally harmful phenomena are generally speaking to some extent unavoidable in a modern society, but that the law aims to prevent such harm to the extent that this is practically and economically feasible '(Prop. 1969: 28:252). In chapter 5, paragraph 3 of the *Environmental Protection Act*, this is formulated in the following way: 'When different interests are weighed against one another, particular attention is to be paid to on the one hand the condition of the area that may be exposed to disruption and the significance of the effects of this disruption, and on the other hand to the utility of the operations in question, the cost of protective measures and other economic effects of relevant precautionary measures.' The formulation included in the Environmental Code 2:7 provides no clearer guidance: 'The requirement of consideration {for the environment} applies to the extent that its fulfilment cannot be regarded as unreasonable. In the context of this assessment, particular attention should be paid to the utility of protective and other precautionary measures as compared to the costs of such measures.' The formulation of the environmental protection regulations, which involve the weighing up of competing interests in each concrete case, provides of course no clear guidance for the agencies whose job it is to apply the law. In the case of breaches of the environmental protection legislation, the problems are intensified in practice by the fact that permit conditions for different operations, which manifest the concrete weighing of environmental against economic interests, are not formulated with the intention of being usable in a possible court case. It is thus not difficult to see how the regulations of environmental criminal law provide very unclear guidelines as to which concrete acts are to be regarded as punishable offences.

**The role of the supervisory agencies**

In addition to the problems associated with the legislation itself, the path environmental cases must follow through the legal system is also problematic. In the context of environmental crime, the supervisory agencies play a key role in the flow of cases through the justice system. It is these agencies that uncover and report environmental offences. In addition, the way the agencies act in their contacts with companies suspected of environmental crime will often have a substantial impact on any subsequent judicial assessment of the company's possible offences.

To begin with, the focus of the supervisory agencies' work in controlling environmental harmful activities should be directed at the provision of advice and not at monitoring and repression (Prop. 1969: 28:155). The legislators felt that it was important for the supervisory agencies to be in agreement with the target group of environmental criminal law as regards what are to be considered reasonable environmental protection measures (Prop. 1969: 28:224). Thus rather than having a pure policing role, the supervisory agencies have a double role in relation to the enterprises that are to be supervised. The agencies are both to collaborate with these enterprises, and to function as their supervisor. This, of course, gives rise to particular problems.

The questionnaire survey of local authority supervisory agencies and county administrative boards, conducted by the Prosecutor General in 1998, included a question on whether the respondents reported all suspected environmental offences for indictment. Two-thirds of the supervisory agencies did not report all such suspected offences (Riksåklagaren 1998: 39).[7] This was often to do with the fact that the offences in question were regarded as very minor but almost as many supervisory agencies stated that the reason they refrained from reporting environmental offences was that they felt it was pointless to do so, because even when an offence is reported, this does not lead to any form of response (du Rées 2001).

The third most common explanation given for why supervisory agencies did not report suspected offences was that they chose to prioritize collaboration with the enterprise in question as a means of resolving any problems rather than reporting crimes to the police (du Rées 2001). This illustrates the problems involved in the supervisory agencies' dual role as both advisers and supervisors. The agencies rely on the co-operation of the enterprises concerned and it is not difficult to see that reporting offences is not the best way to maintain an environment that fosters such co-operation. Control of pollutant discharges, for example, is based to a large extent on reports from the companies themselves regarding various difficulties they may experience in avoiding excessive emissions etc.

This role confusion has been particularly apparent in those cases where the supervisory agencies have refrained from reporting offences as a result of political considerations. Seventeen local authority agencies reported that they refrained from reporting environmental offences if such a report was regarded as politically controversial. The responses show that local authorities neglect to report suspected environmental offences as a result of pressure placed on the supervisory agencies by the political leadership, or that the political leadership may arrive at a decision on the question of reporting offences that goes against the assessment of the supervisory agency that such a report should be made (du Rées 2001). In this case the problems relate to the way the control of environmental crime is organized. In part the problems have to do with the way the supervisory agencies are involved in a dependent relationship with politicians that affects their ability to carry out their duties; in part the problems have to do with the fact that in certain local authorities, decisions on whether or not to report offences are made by politicians. Table 32.4 presents an overview of numbers of responses compiled under various themes.

The table shows that 63 respondents do not report environmental offences that they consider to be minor and that 51 respondents do not report offences because they consider it pointless. Forty-nine respondents have given several reasons for not reporting all suspected environmental offences. This leaves 44 respondents associated with two of the themes, four associated with three themes and one respondent associated with four of the themes presented in the table.

### Neutralization techniques

Sociological theory contains a model that is often used in contexts where alternative normative systems compete with a dominant system of norms. This model is employed as a means of understanding why norm-breaking behaviour is maintained and repeated by individuals who in other contexts may be assumed to respect general norms (Slapper and Tombs 1999: 119). The model is used to analyse the explanations, referred to as neutralizations or rationalizations, employed by individuals in breach of the dominant norm system to justify their norm-breaking behaviour (Sykes and Matza 1957, Scott and Lyman 1968, cf. Sutherland 1949). This perspective has a wide area of application and is equally suited to describing the activities of young offenders, middle-aged white-collar criminals or officials at agencies involved in the practical application of legislation.

This model has been used *inter alia* in the analysis of embezzlement offences (Cressey 1953), juvenile crime (Sykes and Matza 1957/1993, Emerson 1969), economic offending (Coleman 1994), human rights violations (Cohen 1996) and the failure of police officers to report assaults on women (Lundberg 2001). It is also mentioned in an analysis of the norms guiding the activities of public sector agencies and entrepreneurs in connection with the tunnelling operations at Hallandsåsen in Sweden, which resulted in a number of legal investigations (Hydén and Baier 1998).

The article by Sykes and Matza (1957), seen as the central work for this theoretical perspective, examines the question of why youths who embrace the norms of the dominant culture none the less break the law on occasion. By means of various categories of explanations, referred to by Sykes and Matza as techniques, the youths neutralize their norm-breaking behaviour in order to avoid both their own and others' disapproval. The disapproval that the young offender experiences, which may arise both from his own internalized norms and from others in his surroundings, is either neutralized, turned against conformist behaviour or diverted. As a result, the social control that normally checks or prevents the motivation for norm-breaking behaviour is negated.

The youth is thereby able to participate in crime without damaging his self-image. Sykes and Matza argue that techniques of neutralisation constitute an extended interpretation of generally valid defences of norm-breaking behaviour (Sykes and Matza 1993: 235). One example of a generally accepted defence of this kind is the right to self defence. Assaulting a person as a result of a homosexual proposition is not a generally accepted form of behaviour, but may be regarded as a form of self defence by a homophobe. An assailant who neutralizes his behaviour in this way perceives such an extended interpretation of the rules of self-defence as reasonable, an interpretation that is not shared by the legal system in general. Sykes and Matza also assume that techniques of neutralization constitute an important component in what Sutherland in his analysis of 'white-collar crime' refers to as 'definitions favorable to the violations of law' (Sykes and Matza 1993: 236, cf. Sutherland 1949: 234 ff.).[8]

## The neutralizations employed by supervisory agencies

The above study of the conditions necessary for successful general prevention showed that levels of regulatory acumen did not appear to be a major problem in the context of environmental crime. Further, the agencies responsible for applying the legislation were agreed that it was the supervisory agencies that possessed the most regulatory acumen in the area of environmental crime. The analysis also showed that in spite of this, the supervisory agencies do not always report suspected environmental crimes. In this section, the neutralisation approach will be employed to analyse the supervisory agencies' praxis of not always reporting suspicions of environmental offences.

An examination has been conducted of the explanations given by supervisory agencies, i.e. the local authorities and county administrative boards, for not always reporting suspected offences. The objective has been to see which techniques of neutralization may be identified.

The first category may be termed 'denial of the victim and/or injury'. In Sykes and Matza's analysis this category is split into two different techniques. In the case of environmental crime, however, separating a denial that the offence has a victim from a denial that the offence has been harmful is more or less impossible. It is often claimed that environmental crimes have no direct victim or clearly defined group of victims. It may be difficult, for example, to connect a specific discharge of a prohibited substance to a specific form of damage to the environment or to people's health. The explanations that would be included in this category are those that have been placed under the themes ' Crime resulted in no injury or victim' and 'Crime of very minor character'.

The technique of 'shifting the blame' is a variant of what Sykes and Matza refer to as 'condemning the condemners'. Here the officials at the supervisory agencies claim that the responsibility for non-conviction lies outside the agency concerned. The explanations included in this category are those under the themes 'Crime difficult to prove', 'Reporting offence is pointless' and 'Decision not to report taken after contacts with prosecutor or police'.

The third technique of neutralisation is 'denial of the company's responsibility'. The officials at the supervisory agency report that an offence has occurred but that the enterprise concerned cannot be made liable because the act was committed unintentionally. The explanations included here are those noted in Table 32.4 under the themes 'Act should not be categorized as a crime', and 'Crime not intentional/result of ignorance on part of perpetrator'.

A fourth neutralization technique is referring to 'higher loyalties'. The officials at the supervisory agencies feel that they cannot report the suspicion of a crime as a result of political considerations, such as potential effects on the attractiveness of a local area, for example, or potential effects on job opportunities. The explanation that it is better to co-operate with an enterprise rather than reporting it for indictment is another example of this technique. The explanations that would be included here are those noted under the themes 'Supervisory agency prioritises co-operation with enterprise' and 'Politically controversial to report suspected offences' (Table 32.5).

The most common technique of neutralization employed by officials at the supervisory agencies is 'shifting the blame'. For the most part, these are explanations based on the supervisory agencies' lack of confidence in the capacity of the legal system to deal with breaches of law in a satisfactory manner. In certain cases, the officials at the supervisory agencies claim that they ask the police or prosecutor to make an assessment of the case in advance, i.e. before any form of investigation has been conducted. This technique could be seen as a means whereby officials, on the basis of an assessment of the case, look to avoid putting work into something that is not going to lead to an indictment (see Lundberg 2001: 114). The officials have adopted a form of organisational perspective that places the case in a wider context. They think in terms of what the legal system looks like and the prospects a specific case has of advancing through this system (Lundberg 2001: 119).

The next most common technique is 'denial of the victim/injury'. In this case, although the officials perceive that the breaches constitute criminal offences according to existing norms, they feel that the acts in question have not resulted in direct harm and/or are not to be regarded as serious, and that these breaches should therefore not be dealt with by the justice system. Another frequently used technique is to refer to 'higher loyalties'. Here the officials feel they have to safeguard their relationship with the enterprises in question and/or with local authority politicians. Administrative and practical tasks are of primary importance to the supervisory agencies, as is their advisory role. It may be difficult for officials to draw the line between the activities associated with this role and those associated with the role of combating crime, which requires a more repressive approach. A similar situation has arisen in connection with the implementation of the public health legislation in the United States, which has in part been unsuccessful as a result of the fact that the supervisory agencies' traditional collaborative role does not legitimate the use of criminal justice measures (Hutter 1993: 465 f, cf. Slapper and Tombs 1999: 178 f).[9] Officials also use the neutralization technique referred to as 'denial of the company's responsibility', but not to the same extent as the others.

**Table 32.4** Supervisory agencies' explanations[10] for not reporting environmental crimes, compiled into groups and themes (numbers of responses relating to different themes in parentheses). The three most common responses have been highlighted

| Group | | |
| --- | --- | --- |
| Characteristics of the offence | Characteristics of the perpetrator | Characteristics of the control system |
| Crime resulted in no injury or victim (6) | Crime not intentional/result of ignorance on part of perpetrator (7) | Supervisory agency feels reporting once is pointless (51) |
| Act should not be categorized as a crime (10) | Crime the result of an accident (1) | Agency prioritizes co-operation with enterprise in attempts to resolve problem (32) |
| Crime of very minor character (63) | | Agency regards reporting suspected offence as politically controversial (17) |
| Crime difficult to prove (16) | | Agency's decision not to report taken after contacts with prosecutor or police (10) |
| | | Agency prioritizes other tasks (3) |
| | | Agency regards administrative controls as more effective (3) |
| Total          95 | 8 | 116 |

**Table 32.5** Number of responses from supervisory agencies where certain neutralization techniques have been identified

| Denial of the victim/ injury | Shifting the blame | Denial of the company's responsibility | Higher loyalties |
| --- | --- | --- | --- |
| 69 | 77 | 17 | 49 |

The neutralization techniques employed most commonly by officials at the supervisory agencies are all connected in some way to the structure and/or functioning of the legal system in relation to environmental crime. The officials feel that reporting offences leads nowhere. It thus makes no difference what an individual supervisory agency does as the officials feel that the rest of the legal system does not work. The supervisory agencies also state that they do not report breaches of regulations that they consider ought not to be regarded as crimes. They also permit criminal law to become negotiable in the context of specific decisions, by allowing extra-legal considerations such as their relationship to enterprises and politicians to effect the outcome. Explanations of this last type may mean that the supervisory agencies are not quite clear as to their own role in the legal system, and of the requirements of a legalistic application of environmental criminal law.


## Conclusion

The above discussion has presented a number of problems associated with the application of environmental criminal law. This area of the law is subject to the same conditions as general criminal law as regards evidential requirements, the establishment of liability and so forth. The problems associated with environmental criminal law discussed above have been ascribed to conditions that differentiate this area of the law from the traditional, more general criminal legal tradition. In part it is a question of the way environmental criminal law has been constructed as a form of legislative balancing act, which involves making compromises between different interests, i.e. economic factors and environmental considerations. In part it has to do with the fact that the agencies whose task is to apply the law and report suspected offences have a dual role whose two sides are in competition with one another. Their task involves both helping companies to follow the environmental laws, and prosecuting their breaches of the law. This unclear role gives rise to an uneven application of the law which expresses itself *inter alia* in large differences in the frequency of reported offences in different parts of the country (du Rées 2001). The ambivalent attitude of the supervisory agencies also creates difficulties for the agencies and actors 'higher up' in the justice system when it comes to proving intent or negligence on the part of the offender. A further problematic factor is that the environmental control apparatus is directed at the companies as organizations, whereas questions of criminal liability are directed at physical people.

The conclusion is thus that while personnel resources, the competence of officials and a lack of co-operation between different agencies all constitute strategic problems affecting the chances of achieving convictions for environmental crime, the inadequate control mechanisms contained in environmental crime legislation constitute a much more fundamental problem. This problem is intensified by the fact that the supervisory agencies that constitute the first link in the judicial chain have an unclear role in relation to the companies they have to monitor. This leads to a vicious circle in the application of the law. The ambivalent and/or tolerant attitude of the supervisory agencies in the face of crimes affects the assessments of prosecutors and courts towards a more lenient view of these offences. This leniency on the part of prosecutors and courts then has repercussions for the way the supervisory agencies deal with environmental crime in that they cannot see any point in reporting such offences for criminal prosecution. In summary, the material presented describes the difficulties involved in using criminal law as a means of controlling environmentally hazardous activities.

In Sweden, most of the legislation relating to environmental protection has recently been brought together in an Environmental Code that came into force on 1 January 1999. In addition, a new prosecutor organization has been established for dealing with environmental crime. The new Code does not involve any major changes in relation to the area on which the above study is focused, however. The introduction of the Environmental Code has been described as a 'reprint' of the regulations previously included in the *Environmental Protection Act* (Lindblom 2001; 808). The responsibility for discovering and reporting environmental crimes remains with the local authorities' supervisory agencies. One change that should, however, be noted is that the obligation incumbent upon the supervisory agencies to report offences has been clarified in the Environmental Code. The frequency of such offence reports has increased dramatically as a result, but still varies substantially between different local authorities (Östgöta Correspondenten 2002-02-28).

The available information indicates that the problems associated with the local authorities' supervisory agencies remain. The Association of Scientists, the trade association that organizes the majority of environmental and health inspectors in Sweden, recently conducted a questionnaire survey. This indicated the existence of serious problems with the working environment at the environmental offices, a failure to observe the Environmental Code on the part of many local authorities and a deep mistrust of the local authorities regarding their supervisory responsibilities in relation to the local environment (press release, Naturvetareförbundet 2001-12-13). The substantial differences in the frequency of reported offences has been ascribed to varying levels of supervisory resources across different local authorities. Certain local authorities contend that a lack of staff prevents them from working actively to uncover environmental crimes and that those offences which are discovered are the result of random factors. The need for resources is also interpreted differently by local authorities of different political complexions (Södermanlands nyheter 2001-07-17 and 2001-09-20). The difficulties experienced by the officials involved as a result of the competing interests of local authorities to work to provide both a favourable climate for business and a good level of environmental supervision remain (Nerikes Allehanda 2002-01-19 and 2002-01-23).

Since the introduction of the environmental code, a number of cases have come to light where politicians on environmental committees have been charged with official misconduct as a result of having failed to report environmental offences. One chairman of an environmental committee for example was fined for wilful misconduct for failing to do just this (Court judgement passed in Skellefteå district court, 22 June 2000, case no. B 250-00, effective 14 July 2000). A further example is provided by the case of seven politicians from a single environmental committee who were all charged with official misconduct for failing to report environmental crimes. The politically appointed officials were found not guilty by a discordant county court which felt that while the actions of the politicians had clearly been at fault, they could not be deemed to have acted with intent because the legislation was new and would have been difficult for part-time politicians to interpret correctly (Court judgement passed in Enkoping district court, 7 February 2002, case no. B 853-00). The prosecutor has appealed against the verdict.

A possible repeat of the study presented above in order to analyse the way the legislation is applied following the introduction of the new Environmental

Code would not be meaningful at the present time. The substantial amount of time taken by the justice system to process environmental crimes means that a sufficient number of cases tried in accordance with the new legislation will not have made their way through the system for another couple of years. In addition, the major problems still being experienced by the agencies whose task is to apply the environmental criminal law have led to calls for changes. These are at present being investigated by the Environmental Code Committee which is to present its report on 1 July 2002 (Dir. 1999; 109 Department of the Environment). Further changes to Swedish environmental criminal law are therefore to be expected in the near future.

## Notes

1  This article is a revised version of a paper presented at the conference 'Environmental crime in theory and practice' in Sollentuna, Sweden on 27 and 28 September 2001. The conference was organized by the Department of Criminology, University of Stockholm, the environmental crime division of the Office of the Prosecutor General and the National Council for Crime Prevention, Sweden.
2  Based on the number of enterprises that are the object of environmental monitoring at the local authority level. See Svenska Kommunförbundet 2001. 11.
3  See Riksåklagaren 1998.
4  The term 'regulatory acumen' refers here to a combination of two factors: first the officials' awareness of the content of the norms in force, and secondly their knowledge of how these norms should be applied in practice.
5  This state of affairs has probably changed quite substantially, however, as a result of the new efforts being made at providing training for police and prosecutors in connection with the new organisational structure for combating environmental crime that was brought in with the Environmental Code on January 1 1999.
6  i.e. fines set in proportion to the offender's income.
7  All the country's 21 county administrative boards, and 95% of local authorities (272 authorities) completed the questionnaire.
8  Sutherland uses the term rationalizations (Sutherland 1949: 240).
9  In the context of research into corporate crime, Bowles (1991) has identified mechanisms that lead to officials in large corporations subordinating personal principles and ethics in the service of the requirements of the organization. This phenomenon may be termed a 'subculture of structured immoralities' (Mills 1956), compared with a 'subculture of delinquency' (Matza 1964).
10  Seventeen respondents have given other explanations that are unrelated to any of the themes and five respondents have not given any explanation of why they do not always report suspected environmental offences.

## References

Bowles ML (1991). 'The organization shadow'. Organization Studies 12: 387–404.
Brottsförebyggande råder (2001). Brottsstatistik. www.bra.se
Christophersen AB (1997). På vei mot en grønn rett? Miljörettens utvikling i lys av den økologiske erkjennelse {Towards a green law? The development of environmental law in the light of ecological knowledge}. Oslo: Ad notam Gyldendal.
Cohen S (1996). Mänskliga rättigheter och statens brott. Förnekelsens kultur {Human rights and crimes of the state. The culture of denial}. In: Åkerstrom M (ed.). Kriminalitet, kultur, kontroll {Crime, culture, control}. Stockholm Carlssons.
Coleman JW (1994). The Criminal Elite. The Sociology of White-Collar Crime. New York: St. Martins Press.
Coleman JW (1998). The criminal elite. Understanding white-collar crime, 4th edn. New York: St Martins Press.

Cressey DR (1953). Other peoples' money: a study in the social psychology of embezzlement. Illinois: Glencoe Free Press.

du Rées H (2001). Kan straffrätt skydda miljön? En studie av samhällets reaktion pá miljöbrott {Is criminal law able to protect the environment? A study of society's reaction to crimes against the environment}. Unpublished stencil. Institute of Criminology, University of Stockholm.

Emerson RM (1969). Judging Delinquents: Context and Social Process in Juvenile Court. Chicago. Aldine.

Faure MG, van der Wilt H (1997). Environmental criminal law in Europe. Maastricht, METRO, Institute for Transnational Legal Research University of Maastricht.

Hutter BM (1993). Regulating employers and employees; health and safety in the workplace. Journal of Law and Society 20: 452-70.

Hydén H, Baier M (1998). När kunskapen blir onödig – om normativ asymmetri i fallet Hallandsásen {When knowledge becomes superfluous – on normative asymmetry in the Hallandsásen case}. Appendix in Miljö i grund och botten – erfarenheter frn Hallandsásen {Environment, fundamentally – experiences from Hallandsásen}. Final report of the Tunnel task force. SOU 1998: 137.

Jareborg N (1994). Defensiv och offensiv straffrättspolitik {Defensive and offensive criminal law policy}. Nordisk Tidskrift for Kriminalvidenskab, 8: 41–53.

Lindblom PH (2001). In dubio pro natura! Nágra civilprocessuella frágor inom miljördtten {Some problems of civil procedure in environmental law}. Juridisk tidskrift 12: 805–45.

Lundberg M (2001). Vilja med förhinder. Polisers samtal om kvinnomisshandel {Will with obstacles. Conversations of police about assaults against women}. Stockholm/Stehag: Brutus Östlings Bokförlag Symposium.

Matza D (1964). Delinquency and drift. New York: Wiley.

McLoughlin J, Bellinger EG (1993). Environmental pollution control. An introduction to principles and practice of administration. London Graham & Trotman.

Mills CW (1956). The power elite. Oxford: University Press.

Naturvårdsverket (1996). Myndigheternas arbete enligt miljöskyddslagen 1995 {Authority activities according to the 1995 law on protection of the environment}. Rapport 4590 Naturvärdsverket.

Riksdagens proposition 1969:28 om miljöskyddslag {Parliamentary proposition 1969:28 of law for the protection of the environment}.

Riksåklagaren (1998). Effektivare miljöbrottsbekämpning {Combating environmental crime more effectively}. Rapport frán Riksáklagaren {Report of the Prosecutor General}, December 1998. Stockholm: Riksáklagaren.

Riksåklagaren (2001) Statistik om áklagarorganisationen {Statistics on the prosecutor organisation). www.aklagare.se

Scott MB, Lyman SM (1968). 'Accounts'. American Sociological Review 33: 46–62.

Slapper G, Tombs S (1999). Corporate crime. Edinburgh: Longman.

Statens offentliga utredningar (1986). Páföljd för brott. Om straffskalor, påföljdsval, straffmätning och villkorlig frigivning mm, del 2 motiv {Sanctions for crimes. On punishment scales, choice of punishment, measurement of punishment, and conditional release etc, part 2, line of argument}. Huvudbetänkande av Fängelsestraffkommittén {The main report of the Task Force on Imprisonment}. SOU 1986: 14.

Statens offentliga utredningar (1987). För en bättre miljö. Betänkande av utredningen om miljövårdens organisation {For a better environment. Report of the Task Force on organising the protection of the environment}. SOU 1987: 32.

Sutherland E (1949). White collar crime. New York: The Dryden Press.

Svenska Kommunförbundet (2000). Miljö- och hälsoskydd i kommunerna, en enkätundersökning 2000 {Protection of the environment and health in municipalities, a survey study 2000). Svenska Kommunförbunden.

Sykes G, Matza D (1957/1993). Techniques of neutralisation: a theory of delinquency, American Sociological Review 22: 664–670. Reprinted in Williams III FP, McShane MD (eds). Criminology theory, selected classical readings. Cincinnati: Anderson Publishing Co.: 231–40.

Träskman PO (1992). Miljöbrott och kontroll av miljöbrottslighet {Environmental crime and control of crimes against the environment}. Helsingfors: Institutionen för straff- och processrätt.

Wennberg S (1996). Introduktion till Straffrätten {Introduction to criminal law}, 4th edn. Stockholm: Juristförlaget.

Westerlund S (11975). Miljöfarlig verksamhet {Activity that endangers the environment}. Lund: Studentlitteratur.

# 33. Excuses, excuses: the ritual trivialisation of environmental prosecutions*

*Paula de Prez*

## Introduction

The Environment Agency ('the Agency'), as a regulator responsible for the development and enforcement of standards, is a vehicle of social change. Arguably, an unwritten goal of the Agency's enforcement function is to drive a progressive shift in attitudes against activities which prejudice the environment, in order that it can be better protected.[1] In order to secure progressive change in attitudes, the Agency uses regular court action as a means of reinforcing current values which condemn environmentally threatening activities. Provided the courts respond by imposing substantial penalties in cases of serious failure, the view that environmental offences are 'wrongs' and ought to be treated seriously is likely to gather strength.[2] Conversely, consistently low penalties are likely to perpetuate the view that these infringements are trifling; not deserving of society's condemnation, and inappropriately designated as unlawful.

During a study of Environment Agency enforcement, 25 environmental prosecutions were observed in order to assess how corporate defendants sought to impose their own meaning on the offences with which they were charged.[3] This article draws and builds on a court based study conducted by Croall in the 1980s, in the analogous context of consumer protection prosecutions.[4] Croall's general conclusions were that the styles of defence and mitigation used by defendants perpetuated a 'trivialisation' of their offences. It is argued in this article that, despite the common belief that environmental concerns are no longer taken for granted, routine trivialisation of environmental offences still occurs in the lower courts.

The approach taken in this article is firstly, to provide an outline of the typical form of environmental offences, and secondly, to describe and examine the prominent forms of mitigation observed during the course of this research. Comment should perhaps be made at the outset on the significance to be attached to styles of defence and mitigation. The arguments of mitigation used in court are, generally, devised by the legal profession because it is defence counsel, and not the defendants themselves who formulate mitigation arguments[5]

---

* From *Journal of Environmental Law* (2000), 12(1): pp. 65–77.

(although there are times when counsel have to follow instructions). In this respect, it is not the tactics used by defendants to combat prosecution which are detailed in this study, but those of the legal representatives employed by them. The choice of terminology and style of mitigation surely demonstrates, however, what the legal profession and its clients have assumed to be most likely to influence the bench. They may be unconvinced themselves by the sentiment of their assertions, but nevertheless believe in the persuasive value of the argument. Such arguments are therefore clearly important in analysis of the social construction of these offences, for they are designed to refute and neutralise the criminalisation of the defendant's activities. In their role as prosecutors, Agency lawyers are however bound by convention and guidance from the Bar Council and Law Society to present their case in a firm but dispassionate way. The defence therefore have the upper hand in being able to reinforce their favoured view of environmental offences.

As the majority of these cases are dealt with by the magistrates' courts and, exceptionally, the crown courts, written transcripts of judgments are exceedingly rare. It is therefore impossible to gauge with any certainty the relative success of various mitigation arguments. This limitation is, however, unimportant, for here we are concerned more with the approaches to mitigation in these cases, and how these may affect the social construction process.[6]

## Outline of the prosecutions

While the nature of many unlawful business practices is of an ongoing operation, environmental offences often take the form of a 'snapshot', requiring evidence which relates only to a specific time-frame. Substantive environmental offences have developed into a recognisable shape, largely unchanged in form from those drafted in the River Pollution (Prevention) Act of 1876. The typical characteristics of these offences, are as follows:[7]

- The offences generally prohibit an activity, for example, a deposit or a discharge of a substance which is loosely defined, although reference is made to its possible characteristics.[8]
- Offences are inchoate, requiring no specific harm to be proven but rather contemplating the possibility or risk of harm.[9]
- Liability is imposed in the first instance on those who have 'caused or knowingly permitted' the prohibited act, or in the case of waste regulation, persons who 'knowingly caused or knowingly permitted the prohibited act'.[10]
- Most offences are triable either way and currently invite a maximum penalty on summary conviction of £20,000 and/or a term of imprisonment of either three or six months. On indictment, the offences may be punishable by an unlimited fine and imprisonment of up to three years.[11]

The circumstances in which the 25 cases detailed here came to court lends support to the usual conclusions of literature on regulatory enforcement,[12] one of which is that prosecution, even of strict liability offences, was largely used as a last resort, for example where offending was flagrant or where other special circumstances warranted it. In most of these cases, for example, this was not the defendant's first offence and the offender had perhaps been cautioned on an earlier occasion, or the offence had been continued for some time and the defendant had been unresponsive to the Agency's use of other enforcement mechanisms. In all the other cases excepting one,[13] there were further 'special circumstances', for example, the abusive obstruction of Agency officers, a high-level of public interest in the incident, potential hazards to human health or tampering with evidence.[14]

The prevalent style of mitigation observed in these cases can be discussed under two broad headings; 'denying culpability' and 'trivialisation of the breach'.


## Denial of culpability

The majority of environmental offences do not require the prosecution to show the defendant acted negligently or wilfully.[15] This strict liability acts as a cloak for many defendants, for as the prosecutor is not required to prove 'fault', this leaves defence counsel plenty of room to deny culpability in order to attract the sympathy of the bench. This strategy took the form of blaming misfortune and third parties for the offence or asserting that, given that the offence was not deliberate, enforcement was an unreasonable restriction on the right to trade.

### Blaming misfortune and third parties

Whilst accepting the strict liability nature of many of the offences, defence counsel would often seek the court's sympathy by describing the incident as 'accidental' and therefore unavoidable, a 'fact of life' or an offence which 'goes on all the time'. Counsel defending a detergent spillage[16] emphasised the absence of a concrete explanation for the incident. It was suggested that a pump had started working in the middle of the night on its own; a high-level switch which would turn off the pump when detergent reached a critical level, had failed to operate; and the incident occurred late at night which meant the pump had been operating for two hours before the spillage was discovered. The defence labelled these 'facts', an 'inexplicable occurrence', and an 'unfortunate series of coincidences'. Two other defence counsel noted the 'misfortune' arising out of the coincidence of their clients' pollution and the Agency's routine inspection of the river he had polluted, on the same date.[17] A solvents manufacturing company asserted that the explosive release of pollutant could not have occurred but for the simultaneous over-pressurisation of the defendant's pipeline and an ill-fitting seal. A number of defendants made much of the fact that a release from their site had occurred at night, at the weekend, or on a 'Bank Holiday Sunday'.

Rather than highlight the improbability of the incident, other defendants attempted to excuse themselves by pointing to the fact that the regulatory regime had not specifically instructed them on how to prevent the incident.

In an IPC prosecution,[18] the defence attempted to refute that the pollution incident which had occurred was foreseeable: 'There is no industry standard requiring an alarm at this point in the process. There was no breach of an industry standard.' The judge was clearly unmoved and indicated that the degree of foreseeability required could extend far beyond common practices:

> (I)f there had been a meeting in which the possibility of such an alarm had been discussed, the conclusion would probably have been it should have been installed – a great degree of foresight is necessary.[19]

Defence counsel's regular insistence on 'inevitability' or 'unavoidable accident' as the explanation for the offence is at odds with the views of Agency officers. A survey of Agency officers conducted in early 1998[20] showed officers ranked inevitability/unavoidability very low as a cause of environmental breaches (14%). Rather, the primary reasons behind offences in the officers' views were incompetence (39%) and profit seeking (38%). It seems likely then that site and management failures are being masked in the courtroom as morally neutral incidents of misfortune.

Whilst accepting legal liability, a number of defendants sought to deflect moral responsibility for the incident by blaming a third party. In a prosecution of an unlicensed waste transfer station, the defendants relied in mitigation on the fact that for eighteen months of their unlicensed activities, the Agency had dealt solely with their director, who had now retired.[21] The intended inference here[22] was that the cause of the problem was now gone, therefore, it was inappropriate to punish the defendants as an organisation.[23] This defendant was, in effect, seeking to capitalise on the relative absence of conceptualisations of collective fault in our law.[24] Yet, the acts of the corporate defendant must be identified with those of its employees, whether past *or* present. The argument outlined above clearly makes a mockery of corporate responsibility and seeks to undermine judicial sentiment that corporate responsibility extends to its employees' acts of pollution because of the company's capacity to educate and control:

> (T)o make an offence an effective weapon in the defence of environmental protection, a company must by necessary implication be criminally liable for the acts or omissions of its servants or agents during activities being done for the company.[25]

When it appeared that the intervening act of another had become an accepted defence against water pollution charges,[26] third party intervention became a popular theme to attempt avoidance of liability. In a waste management prosecution from the West Midlands, the flytipping of eight drums of cellulose thinners had been traced back to the defendants' site. They pleaded not guilty on the grounds that these drums had been stolen from them. Their defence failed as there were no police reports consistent with this claim.[27] The need to substantiate claims of third party interference and to be able to classify them as 'extraordinary' has led to the intervention of third parties diminishing as a formal defence.[28]

Nevertheless, fault of another remains a common mitigation argument. One prosecuted pollution incident was suspected to have arisen from the 'accidental' spillage of detergent which would normally have drained into the foul sewer. Instead, the detergent had found its way to a rodding-hole which had been left open. This hole, intended only to carry roof-water, led straight to a river. The defence blamed the designers that the company had employed to redesign their factory for the proximity of the rodding-hole to the foul sewer drain. Despite clear authority to the contrary,[29] the defendants implied that the responsibility of another meant that they could not also be responsible. Another case where blame was deflected, involved the prosecution of a waste management company for a violet plume which was discharged from the defendant's high-temperature incinerator. The defendants, who disposed of waste from a range of pharmaceutical clients, refuted responsibility for the incident on the basis that:

> (T)he technology does not exist for full analysis of the drums for every constituent. Sadly, we must rely on industry and the customer – they should know best what's in their waste.

Another waste management defendant who had accumulated excavation waste, mattresses, asbestos, putrescible wastes and other wastes on his land (some ten feet high and close to a watercourse), sought to cast doubt on his personal responsibility by saying the accumulation was out of his control. Due to its position, the land was 'vulnerable to flytippers', and it was alleged that passers-by had thrown mattresses onto the field and drivers allowed onto the land had dumped unwanted materials there, although no evidence was offered to this effect. This style of mitigation tends to undermine the principles of liability which state that the concurrent responsibility of 'others' or the intervention of 'others' do not lessen the offence.[30]

There is some evidence, however, that the superior courts are becoming increasingly resistant to arguments which refute culpability. Judicial rationalisations of strict liability offences have tended to emphasise the need for 'efficient enforcement'.[31] Strict liability provisions are 'efficient' in the sense that they alleviate the burden of the prosecution from having to prove negligence or fault on the part of the operator, an impossible task given that the relevant evidence is generally behind the site boundary and under the exclusive control of the operator.[32] There is now, however, a perceptible shift in the House of Lords decision in *NRA v Empress Car*[33] from the rationale of efficient enforcement to the rhetoric of the 'duty' imposed by these provisions. The rhetoric of 'duty' portrays the defendant as, although not overtly 'negligent', nevertheless, 'failing' to prevent the incident and being in breach of a legal obligation. According to this perspective, the offender is no longer to be seen as a victim of draconian provisions designed to ensure the prevalence of environmental protection, but is portrayed as culpable and deserving of reprimand. This form of culpability is not one of 'negligence', in which the benchmark of the reasonable person is often defined by reference to a common practice,[34] but represents a higher standard defined by a failure to achieve best practice. It seems then that the courts are developing a resilience to arguments which tend to deny moral responsibility for the polluting event. These judgments may be indicative of a shift in the social construction of environmental offences, from infringements of prosecutor-friendly legislation towards breach of environmental 'duty'.[35]

Further evidence of the shift in judicial values toward absolute responsibility for acts causing environmental damage can be detected in the repeated acknowledgement that there is a foreseeable risk of escape and contamination associated with the large scale use or storage of hazardous substances. This was made explicit in the House of Lords' judgment in *Cambridge Water Co v Eastern Counties Leather*[36] where the storage of dangerous chemicals was assumed to be a 'non-natural' use for the purposes of liability under the rule in *Rylands v Fletcher*.[37] While this was a civil court judgment, a similar sentiment was echoed by a judge in an Agency prosecution:

> I am trying to find a logical basis for penalty and it must be in inadequate risk assessment, in that a small risk was not dealt with. Someone who has control of dangerous substances must deal with small risks.[38]

### Unreasonable restriction of the 'right' to trade

Another strategy of mitigation deserving of comment drew attention to the effort required to comply with existing regulation. On a charge of breaching the waste management duty of care[39] by failing to check the credentials of a waste carrier, one defendant complained that the legislation was weighty and the codes of practice too involved.[40] The manager of a hazardous waste incinerator complained that while an authorisation condition prohibited the release of visible plumes, water droplets or persistent mist from its plant, other industries, such as power stations, were allowed to lawfully discharge a visible plume from their stacks. This theme of mitigation was used across the scale of defendants. One multi-national corporate defendant emphasised the size of its undertaking and asked the court to imagine the number of licences and conditions it had to comply with.

Counsel in a waste management prosecution referred to planning permission as 'one of the many confusing pieces of legislation in force', and complained that the defendant had been confused by the number of authorities involved in the regulation of his site (including the Agency, the waste regulation authorities (prior to the Agency) and the local planning authorities). In a further case, the defence team pointed out that liability was personal and this was not a wealthy company but an individual struggling to operate a business which was legitimate except for the control provisions, and that the defendant saw himself as 'struggling against bureaucracy to make a living'.[41] Companies often emphasised the community benefit provided by the number of local people they employed, or the utility they provided by being one of the few UK manufacturers of this particular substance. Once again, it can be said that mitigation is seeking to undermine legal principle, for in the context of the law of nuisance, beneficial employment has come to be condemned as irrelevant to liability. This principle represents judicial refusal to accord privilege to commercial values in the determination of responsibility.[42]

The theme of this style of mitigation implicitly alleges that the right to engage in legitimate business activities enjoys supremacy over considerations of environmental protection. The assertion is that prosecution of this strict liability offence encroaches on the right for a business to survive and to maintain profitability, and the suggestion appears to be that enforcement is 'unfair' unless it can be done consistently with continued levels of profitability. The statutory regime of environmental protection under the Environment Act 1995 lends a degree of support to this view in the form of the Agency's duty to make a contribution to sustainable development.[43] The accepted meaning of this term appears to contemplate at least a parity of importance as between environmental and industrial interests.[44]

## Trivialisation of the breach

Trivialisation is the form of mitigation which is, perhaps, most detrimental to the ideological role of the criminal prosecution. We have seen that judicial values and the social construction of environmental offences seem to be moving away from perceptions of pollution incidents as unavoidable accidents. The Agency's prosecution practice of highlighting some 'failure' by the defendant to meet an expectation may well have played some part in this.[45] Where the contested issue relates to the severity of the incident new difficulties arise.

### Just another tear in a salted sea

Environmental offences are generally 'inchoate', that is, conviction does not require proof of harm caused by the offence. The offences merely contemplate the possibility or risk of harm:

> One looks at the nature of the discharge and one says, is that discharge *capable* of causing harm to a river, in the sense of causing damage to uses to which a river might be put; damage to animal, vegetable or other – if there is such other life which might live in a river, or damaging that river aesthetically?[46]

In a prosecution for an unauthorised 46-hour discharge of raw sewage to a brook caused by a blocked sewer, defence counsel questioned the common perceptions of sewage content as 'what is *flushed* away'. She preferred to describe sewage as including much clean water from washing machines, sinks and rainwater. In the cases observed, this style of mitigation (alleging that despite the 'escape' or 'breach', the substance concerned was relatively innocuous) was extremely popular. The views of prosecuting and defence counsel, of course, invariably differed on this issue. The test of ingestion was frequently used by defendants to persuade the court of the inert nature of the substance involved: 'Didrazoic acid is a radiographic agent and is drunk prior to X-ray.' In one water pollution case, defence counsel repeatedly emphasised that the pollutant, maize starch, was 'an edible product, not a toxic substance'. They relied on a statement that maize starch could cause no hazard to human health when in water,[47] and suggested it could not be compared to 'toxic' substances such as oil and manure. This preoccupation with public health implications and man's resistance to the contaminant aims to distract the court from the true scope of environmental regulation – a scope which embraces releases with the potential to interfere with *any* living organism or ecosystem.[48]

It was also common for defendants to refer to background pollution already present in the environment in order to measure, for the benefit of the court, the impact of the incident. A particularly incisive argument to this effect sought to undermine the need for regulation of the release of trichloroethylene,[49] and to persuade the court to reflect this in sentencing. It was shown that the substance, 56 tonnes of which had been released to the atmosphere from the plant in which it was manufactured, would evaporate in any case in the course of normal use by its consumer. Ultimately, therefore, the total volume of the substance authorised to be produced at the site, was destined to evaporate to the atmosphere. How serious then could the release of 56 tonnes of trichloroethylene be, if the total 250,000 tonnes of trichloroethylene produced at the site was anticipated as ultimately evaporating to the environment with the Agency's consent?[50] This argument, of course, seeks to distract the court from the Agency's concern which must have been about the *concentrations* released during the incident.

The practice of trivialisation extended on one occasion beyond the court room. A defendant prosecuted for unauthorised burning of waste sought to express his objections by getting an Agency witness reprimanded by the court clerk for smoking in the waiting area. His complaint was that the smoker was 'polluting the air' with his 'toxic substances' and should be appearing in the dock alongside him to answer the court for his 'crime'. Although these comments were not intended for the ears of the bench, this anecdote is a clear demonstration of the ambivalence with which pollution offences are sometimes still treated.[51]

### 'Fishes and swallows': semantics of seriousness

In the cases observed, the court was frequently asked to choose between two contrasting interpretations of the severity of a spill or escape. In the words of one High Court judge:

> (S)ewage remains sewage notwithstanding that the water authorities treat it so as to turn it into potable water. The argument at times reminded me of those black and white lithographs of Escher which depict fishes or swallows depending on whether one is concentrating on the black or the white. Some would say the picture was of fishes; others would say it was of swallows. The right answer is that it is both fishes and swallows.[52]

Some frustration was felt by Agency officers that the magistrates often did not understand the complex issues being discussed or the significance of a particular incident.[53] In one crown court case, the judge showed signs of his own frustration and admitted that he found the geological evidence presented by the prosecution 'somewhat difficult'. In most cases, the Agency's legal representative made clear attempts to present data such as 'biochemical oxygen demand' (BOD), 'parts per million' (PPM) and 'suspended solids', in a way which the court would understand, for example:

> One point two billion cubic litres of water would be needed to dilute this substance to drinking water quality. In other words four times the capacity of Lake Ullswater in the Lake District.[54]

and then again:

> It is useful to consider the dilution ratio. 84,000 litres were lost to water. It would require half a million Olympic swimming pools of water to dilute it to drinking water standard.

In an IPC prosecution,[55] the Agency solicitor described the loss of 56 tonnes of trichloroethylene, a substance toxic by inhalation, as an amount which equated to the 'volume of 4,200 household buckets'. The defence solicitor, snorted that this analogy was 'absurd', despite the fact that this phraseology had been 'borrowed' from previous proceedings in which the same solicitor had trivialised the level of an earlier spill as amounting to only 'two-and-a-half-bucketfuls'. The formal reply of the defence was that the substance was: '... not flammable, not carcinogenic, not harmful to the unborn child, and of low toxicity.' Once again, contrary to the scope of the Environmental Protection Act, the implications of the spill considered here relate largely only to their proven impact on man.

The Agency provided photographic evidence wherever possible and, in recognition of the potency of visual aids, provided photographs of similar incidents where none were available from the incident itself. In response, many defendants would convert Agency evidence into different modes of measurement, intended to appear smaller and less significant. In an IPC prosecution, the Agency described levels of chlorinated hydrocarbons in an underground pit as having reached eighteen times the permitted level. The defence responded by arguing that the amount actually discharged into the canal from the pit was '0.5% of that which the Agency permitted the defendant to discharge per year'. An indignant waste management defendant compared the single incident for which it had been prosecuted with its entire operating history of incinerating more than one million drums of waste and patted itself on the back for what it described as a '99.9998% effectiveness rate'. In a separate water pollution prosecution, defendant counsel in an attempt to diminish the importance of the case retorted to an Agency witness: 'You call it controlled water, I call it a ditch.'[56] He later referred to the prosecution's case as '... a rather desperate attempt to make a ditch a watercourse'. This defendant was acquitted by the magistrates, although the Agency were successful in obtaining a conviction on appeal.[57]

Evidence on the purported severity of the incident is always conflicting and undoubtedly confuses the court. It is impossible to gauge precisely the impact this negotiation of the 'severity' of the case has on the court's assessment on the appropriate penalty. The generally low levels of fines in environmental prosecutions[58] certainly suggest that these offences are being trivialised, and that these forms of mitigation are likely to be a contributing factor in the courts' understanding of the severity of pollution incidents.

## Conclusions

The styles of defence and mitigation used in these cases provide an insight into the style of argument which defence counsel perceive as likely to win judicial favour. If successful in influencing the court's view as to the severity of the matter, such mitigation can be seen to reinforce the social construction of environmental offences as not truly criminal and not deserving of condemnation.[59] A successful mitigation by which seriousness and culpability are ritually disguised is likely to result in reluctance by the court to implement tougher sentencing.[60] This problem is exacerbated by the current lack of guidance issued to the courts on appropriate sentencing levels.[61] Such reluctance will further reinforce views in society that environmental cases are unimportant. Mitigation can therefore play an important part in the cultural reproduction of the view that environmental offences are not 'serious'.

Many of the mitigation arguments used here potentially undermined the criminalisation and stigmatisation of the offences, which in many respects is the cornerstone of the Agency's attempts to promote deterrence. The contortions of mitigation described here are an inevitable product of the adversarial court process. The thrust of this article is, therefore, not necessarily to argue that the venue of these cases should be changed, but rather to add testimony to the powerful forces of 'trivialisation' which the Agency faces. It has been assumed that large corporate defendants are deterred from non-compliance by the adverse publicity and stigma associated with conviction rather than the fine.[62] Trivialisation of environmental offences can only serve as an impediment to enforcement as a whole, for if the implications of criminalisation are neutralised, then for the large scale operators, so is the threat of prosecution.

These suggested implications of trivialisation for the deterrence of large scale defendants was borne out by the fact that these defendants, in particular, tended to employ an aggressive style of defence and mitigation. This confrontational style of advocacy often led to detailed analysis of scientific or technical issues relating to the impact of a pollutant or the reliability of the Agency's evidence. Such an investigation is inappropriate for the lower courts, where there is a non-specialist bench. Given that the likely purpose of strict liability provisions was to be, partly, to avoid the technical argument which culpability would involve and thereby maintain the magistrates' courts as an appropriate and low cost venue for prosecution, aggressive, technical mitigation tends to undermine the efficiency of adjudication by a non-specialist bench.

If environmental enforcement discretion is to continue becoming increasingly complex, perhaps now is the time for serious consideration of an environmental division of the High Court, as recommended in 1994 by the Labour Party Policy Commission.[63] Such a court with a specialist bench would be better equipped to deal with the technical matters often raised in environmental disputes, and would perhaps have a better idea of what is reasonable or feasible to expect of industry in terms of pollution abatement. Yet, the costs of using High Court resolution with any regularity would surely be prohibitive, and it would seem more practicable to create a specialist tribunal of local court level, for example the suggestion by Bates of appointing specialist stipendiary magistrates.[64] A specialist bench would also perhaps be less susceptible to the trivialisation of environmental offences and to attempts to mask the severity of the incident which are practised by defendants in the magistrates' courts. Such reform could contribute conversely to a further trivialisation of offences. Why should these cases need a separate court structure, unless they are indeed distinct from traditional crimes?

The decision to change the venue of these cases, is clearly one in which the implications would have to be very carefully weighed and assessed. Whilst a change in venue may appear to be a sensible solution to the increasing complexity in both environmental law and science, it may compound existing problems of trivialisation by confirming environmental offences as different in nature from those 'crimes' dealt with by a bench of magistrates, making prosecution a great deal more difficult.

## Notes

1 Progressive stigmatisation is a precondition to effective enforcement of regulatory crimes, see I. Paulus, 'The Search for Pure Food' in M. Robertson (ed), *Law In Society Series* (1974) at 135.

2 M. Feeley, *The Process is the Punishment* (Russell Sage Foundation, 1979). The author states that the lower courts respond to their environment (at 20). Surely social attitudes also respond to court rulings in that increased judicial condemnation promotes a view that these offences are to be treated seriously, particularly in the minds of the offending population.

3 Most of these cases were from the Agency's North West region, that stretches from Carlisle to South Manchester, although a few were from the Midlands region. The environment of the North West region features the Mersey Basin (once labelled the most polluted major river catchment in the UK), poor sewage and sewerage facilities, a quarter of Britain's chemical plants, intensive agriculture in parts of Lancashire and Cumbria and several nuclear licensed sites. The North West region can therefore be expected to offer a reasonable cross-section of typical case profiles. Details of the individual cases may be obtained by contacting the author.

4 H. Croall, 'Mistakes, Accidents and Someone Else's Fault', *Journal of Law & Society* (1988) p 293.

5 In only one of the 25 cases did the defendant not have legal representation and even here the manager representing her company's interests had legal training. This compares with Croall's study where 42% of the defendants had no legal representation. All of these were small businesses (ibid at 297).

6 Croall also felt that the Magistrates' silence in the majority of prosecutions meant that effectiveness could not be properly assessed, ibid at 309.

7 For instance, s 5 states: 'A person commits an offence punishable under this section if he causes or knowingly permits to enter into a stream any poisonous, noxious or polluting matter.'

8 For example, the deposit of 'controlled waste', the discharge of 'poisonous, noxious or polluting substances', subsections 33(1) EPA 1990 and 85(1) respectively.

9 See particularly W. Howarth, 'Poisonous, Noxious or Polluting: Contrasting Approaches to Environmental Regulation', *Modern Law Review* (1993) 56, p 171.

10 See s 33(1) EPA 1990 and s 85 WRA 1991.

11 See subsections 85(6) Water Resources Act 1991, 33(9) and 23(2)–(4) Environmental Protection Act 1990.

12  W.G. Carson. 'Some Sociological Aspects of Strict Liability', *Modern Law Review* (1970) 33, p 396; K. Hawkins, *Environment and Enforcement* (Clarendon, 1984); and R.G. Singer, 'The Resurgence of Mens Rea – The Rise and Fall of Strict Criminal Liability', *Boston College Law Review* (1989) 30, pp 337–408.

13  The prosecution of a farmer for a water pollution incident. The prosecutor did not allege any carelessness on the part of the farmer and admitted that his conduct on discovery of the incident had been 'exemplary'.

14  These aggravating factors which seem to have featured in prosecuted cases, correspond very closely to the Agency's presumptions of prosecution in its revised prosecution policy. See *Enforcement and Prosecution Policy*, Environment Agency, November 1998. The Agency's recently revised Enforcement and Prosecution Policy will soon appear on its website.

15  Integrated Pollution Control, a statutory regime which regulates the operating conditions of sites handling 'prescribed processes'. Processes are 'prescribed' under Part I of the Environmental Protection Act 1990.

16  Rochdale Magistrates' Court.

17  Knowsley Magistrates' Court.

18  See Part I, Environmental Protection Act 1990.

19  Warrington Crown Court.

20  One hundred Environment Agency field officers participated in this research by completing an attitude survey. The survey was designed to assist discussion of enforcement cultures and strategies which exist within the Agency.

21  This argument is a common one, also used in mitigation in a recent prosecution against *British Nuclear Fuels Limited* for six years' failure to repair a bridge carrying radioactive waste-pipeline. See further 'BNFL fined £20,000 for disregarding safety', *Guardian*, 5.4.97, p 6.

22  As understood by the researcher and as commented upon by a Waste Regulation Officer present at the court.

23  The defendant was fined £4,000 for its three years of operation without a licence.

24  G. Wells, *Corporations and Criminal Responsibility* (Clarendon, 1993) at 62. See generally on the concept of corporate responsibility, B. Fisse, 'Recent Developments in Corporate Criminal Law and Corporate Liability', *University of New South Wales Law Journal* (1990) 13, p 1; C.M.V. Clarkson. 'Kicking Corporate Bodies and Damning Their Souls', *Modern Law Review* (1996) 59(4), p 557; and M. Levi, 'Business Regulatory Offences and the Criminal Law', *Company Lawyer* (1984) p 251.

25  *NRA v Alfred McAlpine* QBD [1994] 4 All ER 286 at p 300, per Morland J.

26  *Impress (Worcester) v Rees* (1971) 2 all ER 357.

27  Prosecution Memo: West Midlands Upper Trent Area, prosecution of December 1996.

28  *NRA v Empress Car* [1998] 1 All ER 481 (HL).

29  *NRA v Wright Engineering* [1994] 4 All ER 281.

30  The cases cited above at ns 20 and 21. See also, *CPC(UK) v NRA* [1995] Env LR 131; *NRA v Yorkshire Water Services* [1994] 3 WLR 1202; and more recently, *Environment Agency v Brock plc* [1998] JPL 968 (QBD).

31  See Singer's discussion of *R v Woodrow* 14 M & W 404, 153 Eng Rep 907; R.G. Singer, 'The Resurgence of Mens Rea – The Rise and Fall of Strict Criminal Liability', *Boston College Law Review* (1989) 30, pp 337–408.

32  A consideration mentioned in G. Richardson, 'Strict Liability for Regulatory Crime: The Empirical Research', *Crim LR* (1985) p 295, at p 303. The rhetoric of efficient enforcement has sometimes been accompanied by the view that environmental protection was so important as to trump considerations of criminal justice (see *Alphacell*, op cit, n 21 at 490–1; and *NRA v Alfred McAlpine* [1994] 4 All ER 286 at 300).

33  Op cit, n 20 at 489.

34  Failure to follow common practice makes it more difficult for a civil defendant to show he was not negligent; *Morton v William Dixon* (1909) SG 807; *Morris v West Hartlepool Steam Navigation Co Ltd* [1956] AC 552.

35  The rhetoric of 'rights' and 'duties' in the context of environmental protection is prevalent in the dialogue of human rights and the environment. See for example, the 1994 Draft Declaration of Principles on Human Rights and the Environment, particularly paras 5 and 21.

36  [1994] 1 All ER 53 at 79.

37  An independent tort arising out of the case of *Rylands v Fletcher* (1868) LR 3 HL 330, which imposes liability on parties who allow 'things likely to do mischief' to escape from their control, which cause damage to other parties.

38  See P. de Prez, 'Environment Agency v ICI Chemicals & Polymers', *Environmental Law & Management* (1998) 10(4), pp 187–9. Legislative rccognition of the inevitable risks associated

with chemical storage is provided by a measure now contained in s 110 of the Water Act 1989, giving the Secretary of State power to regulate such storage, and the enactment of the Hazardous Substances Act 1990. The need for such a power has existed since Control of Pollution Act 1974 but has yet to be exercised.

39  Section 34(1) Environmental Protection Act 1990. This provision requires that persons who deal with waste should take all reasonable steps to ensure; no other person commits a waste related offence, to prevent the escape of waste, to ensure that the transfer of waste is only to authorised persons and that such transfer is accompanied by a written description of the waste.

40  Prosecution Memo: West Midlands Upper Trent Area, November 1996.

41  Preston Crown Court.

42  This type of argument was successful in avoiding liability in *British Celanese v Hunt* [1969] 2 All ER 1252, but in the 1990s Lord Goff refused to allow a use to be considered ordinary or natural by virtue of its creation of employment and being a small industrial community worthy of support (see the *Cambridge Water case* [1994] 1 All ER 53 at 79).

43  Section 4 of the Act.

44  '(D)evelopment that meets the needs of the present without compromising the ability of future generations to meet their own needs.' Taken from *Our Common Future*, Brundtland Report (1987).

45  For example, Agency prosecutors referred to: 'failure to have a system for supervising pumping operations', 'failure to identify substances in drums as containing iodine', 'failure to ensure pipework running across their land was secure', 'failure to make themselves familiar with their own pipework', 'failure to install overflow alarms', 'failure to take action to prevent a downstream flow of pollution', 'delay in reporting a pollution incident to the Agency' and evidence of previous pollution.

46  Bryant J in *NRA v Egger* (1992) Newcastle Upon Tyne Crown Court, reported at Burnett Hall (1995) pp 351–4.

47  Knowsley Magistrates' Court.

48  Sections 1(3) and 1(4) EPA 1990.

49  A solvent often used for degreasing fabricated metal parts.

50  Widnes Magistrates' Court.

51  K. Hawkins, *Environment and Enforcement* (Clarendon, 1984) at 11.

52  *R v Rotherham MBC & Safety Kleen UK Ltd ex parte William Rankin*, Journal of Environmental Law (1990) 250, at 254.

53  In *civil* cases involving scientific/technical matters, the case may be heard in the Official Referee's Court (a specialist panel forming part of the High Court).

54  Widnes Magistrates' Court.

55  Ibid, n 17.

56  Chester Magistrates Court.

57  This case was subsequently heard on appeal in the High Court where a conviction was obtained.

58  The Chief Executive of the Agency said recently: 'Even the largest fines represent negligible costs for the largest companies. The Agency's largest fine last year represented the equivalent of a £15 fine on someone earning £30,000 a year.' Quoted in *Environment Action*, Environment Agency (bimonthly newsletter, October/November 1997) p 3. See also M. Hornsby, 'Watchdog seeks tougher fines for big polluters', *Guardian*, 3.9.98, p 3; and 'Get Tough Courts Told', *Environment Action* (October/November 1998) 16, p 6. Although two recent heavy penalties may help to offset this. See, op cit, n 38 where a fine of £300,000 was imposed and the £4 million fine imposed in the *Sea Empress* prosecution, January 1999 (see '£4 million fine for oil spill may put port jobs in jeopardy', *The Times*, 16.1.99).

59  A fundamental difficulty with criminal law enforcement in this area, as identified by A. Ogus, *Regulation: Legal Form and Economic Theory* (Oxford University Press, 1994) at 79.

60  H. Croall, 'Sentencing the Business Offender', *Howard Journal* (1991) 30(4), 280 at 290.

61  Although this is probably about to change given that the Home Secretary has asked the Sentencing Panel created by the Crime and Disorder Act 1997 to give guidance to the Court of Appeal on sentencing in environmental cases. In the sibling area of health and safety regulation, the Court of Appeal has issued sentencing guidelines (see *R v Howe & Sons (Engineers) Ltd* (1998) (CA) unreported) and may do the same for environmental offences as a result of the current appeal against sentence in the *Sea Empress* case (see '£4 million fine for oil spill may put port jobs in jeopardy', *The Times*, 16.1.99).

62  For a recent example, see A. Mehta and K. Hawkins, 'IPC and Its Impact: Perspectives from Industry', *Journal of Environmental Law* (1998), 10(1), 61–77.

63  *In Trust for Tomorrow*, Labour Party Commission Report on the Environment (1094) p 50. Comparison can be drawn with the Companies Court as part of the Chancery Division. A

model from which to develop our court structure may be the Land and Environment Division of South Australia's Supreme Court. See further, J. Minor, 'Environmental Court of Justice 1991', *Journal of Environmental Law* (1992), 4(1) 159; and W. Upton, 'Environmental Courts – The South Australian Initiative', *Env Law* (1994), 8(1/2) 12.

64 J. Bates, 'Examining Water Pollution Law and Regulation in Light of Current Government and EU Policy', (1997). Paper presented at Water Law Conference, London, February 1998.

# 34. Environmental crime and the courts

*House of Commons, Environmental Audit Committee*

## Conclusions and recommendations

1 We are concerned that the general level at which fines are imposed neither reflects the gravity of environmental crimes, nor deters or punishes adequately those who commit them. This is clearly unsatisfactory. (Paragraph 16)

2 For many forms of environmental crime, compulsory remediation work on the sort of blight for which the offender was himself responsible would be a more appropriate sentence than a fine. (Paragraph 17)

3 We consider it unfortunate that community sentences have for so long been tied inflexibly to custodial sentences. This has markedly reduced the ability of courts to pass appropriate sentences for environmental offences. (Paragraph 17)

4 It is clear that, given the current paltry range of sentences available, there is simply insufficient scope to properly tailor sentences to offenders. (Paragraph 18)

5 It appears to us that the profits made from crimes form too little a part in decisions as to the size of fine or sentence to be given. Courts – and prosecutors – need to bear in mind that unless the polluter pays substantially more than the sum he profits by from his crime there will be no real deterrent or punishment value to the sentence given. (Paragraph 21)

6 Both the low level of payment of fines and their indiscriminate destination are unsatisfactory. It is evidently far too easy to avoid payment: and even were 100% of fines to be paid, it would be of no benefit to those leading the fight against these crimes. This is hardly a just situation. (Paragraph 22)

---

*From House of Commons, UK (2004) *Environmental Crime and the Courts*. London: Environmental Audit Committee, 1–24.

7 We believe that there may be grounds for establishing guidance that crimes against the environment merit an automatic aggravation before the court – in other words, that one of the aggravating factors included as guidance for magistrates or judges is damage to the environment or threat to local sustainability. (Paragraph 24)

8 The current sentencing system is just not flexible and imaginative enough adequately to punish corporate bodies or those in senior managerial positions within them. It is disgraceful that some companies openly boast about their crimes as though they manifested some sort of commercial talent or marketing genius. The Government must adopt a much tougher stance with businesses – regardless of their size and nationality – which flagrantly flout the law. (Paragraph 26)

9 It is noteworthy that sections 43-7 of the Anti-Social Behaviour Act 2003 have recently come into force which assist prosecutors and sentencers in dealing more flexibly – thus effectively – with local environmental crime, particularly graffiti and fly-posting. This is very much to be welcomed. (Paragraph 27)

10 Investigating and prosecuting bodies must be congratulated for continuing to bring cases before courts when the chances of a satisfactory outcome realistically appear so slight. (Paragraph 28)

11 Preventing the common-or-garden fly-tipper, 'the man with the white van', from owning or driving a van is more useful than fining him a negligible amount which he will more than make up with his next 'job'. (Paragraph 30)

12 We expect DEFRA to move on from its welcome consultations over fly-tipping to consider wider and more detailed changes that will assist the Environment Agency and local authorities in particular in ensuring that those they detect and prosecute successfully will receive sentences that are robust and appropriate to the crimes committed and to the type of offenders involved. (Paragraph 32)

13 We acknowledge that there may be little scope for increasing the custodial maxima, but expect the Government to look into the limits on traditional sentencing across the range of environmental crimes to see where benefit may accrue from appropriate increases. (Paragraph 33)

14 The Government should seek to assist the Judicial Studies Board (JSB) to commit judicial training to environmental impacts and the principles of sustainable development. Government has a duty to encourage all engaged bodies to assist in tackling environmental crime as seriously as other crimes which blight lives: it would be wrong for government to consider this duty as one which does not extend to the judiciary. (Paragraph 36)

15 Information is key to fighting crime, and all those dealing with environmental offences, whether they be sentencers, prosecutors, investigators, or those dealing with clean-up or with prevention, require a

good corpus of information on which to build effective strategies. We look to the Government, in co-operation with other engaged bodies, to examine practical means to set up a comprehensive database of environmental crime to improve information in this area. (Paragraph 38)

16 We expect the Government to ensure that those agencies who handle community sentences are sufficiently resourced to cope with what we hope will be an increasing number of such sentences. (Paragraph 39)

17 We call on the Home Office and the Environment Agency to look again at these proposals to deal more effectively with corporate or business environmental crime; and to ensure that such proposals are quickly cast in a legislative shape upon which Parliament can then come to a decision. (Paragraph 41)

18 DEFRA should look at the possibilities of granting to environmental bodies a power similar to that the Health and Safety Executive (HSE) possesses in the form of the issuing of prohibition notices. (Paragraph 42)

19 If the Government believes that extending those powers to impose fixed penalty notices currently available in most places only to police officers or their equivalent to agents of the Environment Agency or local authorities is a good idea and will assist in tackling environmental crime then it ought to do something about it. Government inaction in the first instance led to the private legislation the precedent of which the Government now cites as reason not to act. (Paragraph 43)

20 The Government and other appropriate bodies must look seriously at the proposals for such specialist training on environmental crime and for the establishment of teams of dedicated magistrates. It is clear that without such concentrated experience and expertise the courts will continue to be a lottery often unfavourable to deterrence and proper punishment. (Paragraph 45)

21 The Government has shown itself to be sufficiently joined-up to begin to tackle antisocial behaviour. It now needs to ensure that it works in a co-ordinated fashion, and with other bodies, to tackle the currently poor sentencing record for offences against the environment. Only by doing so will it effectively begin to deal with the blight that is environmental crime. (Paragraph 46)

**Introduction**

1. During the late summer of 2003 we decided to set up a Sub-committee on environmental crime. We had been increasingly aware over that year of concerns expressed about prosecutions and sentencing in this area, and we were interested in the overlap between environmental crime and local environmental aspects of the anti-social behaviour agenda being highlighted by Government and local authorities across the country, largely in response to

public concern. We were also aware of some discrete areas within the broad scope of environmental crime, such as wildlife crime, which were continually prominent in the media and in the concerns of members of the Committee. It was decided to confine the Sub-committee's work to England and Wales on account of the different legal system in Scotland and Northern Ireland.

2. The Sub-committee on environmental crime was established on 12 November 2003. At its first meeting on 10 December, the Sub-committee decided to pursue a number of different inquiries beneath the umbrella of environmental crime. As its first inquiry, the Sub-committee decided to look into the matter of environmental crime and the courts, in the light of anxieties prevalent in the environmental media and anecdotally passed on to the Committee by agencies and bodies dealing with such crimes that there were problems with the proportion of crimes dealt with by the courts, and with the level of sentences given. It was argued that, given the low level of sentences handed out for the few cases that were successfully prosecuted, the courts were not providing the necessary deterrent to those engaged in environmental crime nor adequate punishment for their activities.

### Scope of inquiry

3. The Sub-committee announced this first inquiry on 10 December 2003. It wished in particular to hear views on:

- the scale and nature of sentences for environmental crimes, and whether or not they were commensurate with the seriousness of the crimes for which they were given;
- whether sentences were appropriately set to act as a deterrent;
- whether sentencing for environmental crimes was sufficiently flexible to allow appropriate sentencing;
- whether the guidance currently available for magistrates' courts was sufficient – and whether or not it was being used; and
- to what extent the principle of sustainable development, or other broad environmental principles, was seen by practitioners as the basis for sentencing decisions.

4. Twenty-three memoranda were received, some also relevant to inquiries that the Sub-committee intends to cover following this first inquiry. Oral evidence was heard from seven witnesses. We are grateful for all the evidence given to the Sub-committee and for the co-operation extended to it during its inquiry.

5. We are aware that there have been a number of recent developments in the area of environmental crime, not least on account of the recent enactment of anti-social behaviour legislation. Some of these developments promise to answer some of the concerns expressed to us before the Sub-committee commenced its inquiry. We are likewise aware of a number of developments that are to be expected during the remainder of this calendar year. On 23 February of this

year, the Department for the Environment, Food and Rural Affairs (DEFRA) released two consultation papers dealing with fly-tipping which will hopefully result in a strengthening of the due process of law.[1] There is increasing governmental concern, local and national, and there is now more than just that – there is also action to deal with some of the problems manifest in this area.[2] We are however concerned at the rate and extent of this improvement: it is slow, sometimes unnecessarily so, also uncertain and patchy. This rate of improvement also sadly falls within the context of environmental crime not having been taken seriously enough for many years, during which time it has festered, leading some people to become habitual offenders and others to accustom themselves reluctantly to predictable and seemingly inescapable blight. It is also clear that, despite the praise due for progress made recently by Government and many local authorities in particular, environmental crime still remains in some areas far from the priority it ought to be.

## What is environmental crime?

### Statute

6. Environmental crime includes all offences either created by statute or developed under the common law that relate to the environment. The environment is, in simple terms, the surroundings in which we live. Section 1 of the Environmental Protection Act 1990 defines the environment as 'all, or any, of the following media, namely the air, water, and land'. That Section also defines pollution of the environment as pollution 'due to the release, into any environmental medium from any process of substances which are capable of causing harm to man or any other living organisms supported by the environment.' Successive governments have legislated to give powers to executive agencies to protect the environment and enforce environmental legislation. International environmental law and principles have been transposed into national law to ensure compliance with state commitments. Environmental crime has not been codified or consolidated into a single Act but is found in a range of separate pieces of legislation. Some of the most frequently used criminal sanctions are found in the Environmental Protection Act 1990 (as amended) and the Water Resources Act 1991.

### Key organisations

7. The main organisations for securing environmental protection in England and Wales are the Environment Agency (hereafter, the Agency) and the environmental health teams of local authorities. The main aim of the Agency is to prevent or minimise harm to the environment and it has a range of enforcement and other powers available. It manages significant environmental impacts such as waste management, water pollution, the integrated pollution prevention and control regime and radioactive substances. Local authorities have powers and responsibilities for looking after the well-being of their communities. They manage local air pollution, land use, trees and open spaces and matters relating to anti-social behaviour including noise, dog fouling and

fly posting. There is overlap in responsibilities between the Agency and local authorities, particularly in relation to waste, which is governed by a protocol defining the key roles. This protocol is currently the subject of one of the DEFRA consultations referred to above. In terms of environmental crime, each agency has investigation and prosecuting powers and must comply with investigating and prosecuting codes of practice. Aside from the Agency and local government, other bodies involved in investigation include the police who are responsible for investigating wildlife crime and certain cases of criminal damage. The Crown Prosecution Service is the prosecuting agency for the police. Other prosecuting bodies in this area include HM Customs and Excise, the Pesticide Safety Directorate and the Health and Safety Executive.

### Uniqueness of environmental crime

8. It is estimated that there are up to 10,000 environmental prosecutions annually. This number is comparatively small. There were in total 1.93 million offenders proceeded against in the year 2002-03 with 33,000 for burglary alone.[3] This might suggest that, in comparative terms, environmental crime should be given less attention than many other crimes. However, Dr Leith Penny, Director of Cleansing at Westminster City Council, suggested to us that, roughly speaking, only 10% of all known environmental offences end up in court.[4] The bald statistics fail to reflect the unique nature of environmental crime. It is distinct from other aspects of law because of the potential impact of any given incident on a large sector of the community, wildlife and habitats. There may also be long-term adverse effects on the environment and future generations, effects that go way beyond simple visual blight, and loss of amenity. With reference to the local environment, there is also increasing evidence that there is a connection between local environmental degradation and increasing incidences not only of environmental but of other crimes. Whereas many other crimes involve the concept of risk of harm – drink-driving for example – that risk in environmental crimes can often be less evident at first sight but the harm more pervasive. Environmental offences also may have significant health implications.

### Relevant principles of criminal law

9. All criminal cases begin in magistrates' courts. If a defendant pleads not guilty to the charges the case will proceed to trial and may transfer to the Crown Court. Magistrates hear over 95% of all criminal cases. This proportion is even higher for environmental cases: in most environmental cases, the defendant will plead guilty. This is often because the majority of environmental offences are 'strict liability': in other words, the offences do not require proof of *mens rea*, or guilty mind, in respect of one or more elements of the offending act, but simply proof that the relevant act has been committed, unlike, say, murder which requires intention to kill the victim. Once a defendant has been convicted or has pleaded guilty to the offences, the court will pass sentence.

### Sentencing

10. Section 142 of the Criminal Justice Act 2003 has introduced new statutory

purposes of sentencing which include the punishment of offenders, the reduction of crime, the reform and rehabilitation of offenders, the protection of the public, and the making of reparation by offenders.[5] These sentencing purposes are supported by a range of sentencing options including imprisonment, suspended sentences, community service orders, fines, conditional and absolute discharges. For companies, excluding directors or the controlling minds of a company, fines are often the only option. Courts decide sentences by taking into consideration both the aggravating and mitigating factors of each particular case. Before imposing a fine the court is also under a duty to consider the offender's financial circumstances. In 2000, the Sentencing Advisory Panel issued guidance to the Court of Appeal in environmental cases.[6] It stated that for most environmental offences the starting point should usually be a fine and this should then be adjusted to take into account any aggravating or mitigating factors.

11. Many environmental offences carry exceptional summary maxima that allow magistrates to impose fines of up to £20,000 per offence. This is four times the value of the current statutory maximum fine on summary conviction for most other crimes (conviction in the magistrates' court). A few environmental offences have exceptional summary maxima of £50,000 and in one instance £250,000 (for the discharge of oil in UK waters).[7] Many environmental offences also attracted unlimited fines if sentenced in the Crown Court. At present, DEFRA is consulting on whether the maximum summary sentence for certain waste offences should be increased from £20,000 to £50,000.[8]

### Sentencing guidelines and guidance

12. In 2001, the Magistrates Association issued guidance entitled: *Fining of Companies for Environmental and Health and Safety Offences*. It issued guidance on wildlife crimes in 2002 entitled: *Wildlife Trade and Conservation Offences* as well as guidance for sentencers entitled: *Costing the Earth*. The Court of Appeal has declined to issue guidelines on environmental sentencing. In the case of *R v Anglian Water Services* (2003) it endorsed the Magistrates' Association guidance but stated that sentencing should be considered on a case-by-case basis.[9] In the absence of any more rigorous guidance there is inevitably a great diversity of sentences given for broadly similar crimes across the country.

### Environmental crime: the challenges

### Infrequency of environmental crimes

13. Environmental crime, being a broad and diffuse area of offence whose gravity is not at first always evident, presents many challenges to those authorities tasked with dealing with it. In its first inquiry, the Sub-committee chose to focus in particular upon sentencing because it was clear that here the broad nature of such crimes, and the comparative infrequency of their coming before a court, was causing the greatest problems for practitioners in terms of setting sentences appropriate for punishment and/or deterrence.

As Mr Ric Navarro, Director of Legal Services to the Environment Agency, explained to the Sub-committee, 'we know on average that only once in seven years a magistrate will have an environmental crime case'.[10] While this may somewhat overstate the infrequency with which magistrates consider environmental crimes in reality, it is clear that this lack of practical experience underpins many of the problems we will touch upon on during this Report. It is also worth noting that, as Mr Navarro went so to say, 'judges who are sitting day after day dealing with normal crime [...] find it difficult to know where to pitch environmental crime'.[11] We will come later to the matter of guidance that might assist in addressing this difficulty.

14. This infrequency is not just a problem afflicting magistrates and judges. Some of those prosecuting are also less than well-practised. In 2000, the Sentencing Advisory Panel in advice to the Court of Appeal pointed out that the standard of prosecution in environmental cases was often deficient.[12] For local authorities this may indeed have been down to lack of experience and expertise, and many local authorities have begun to take steps to address this problem. Some local authorities, of course, have always prosecuted environmental cases well. For the Environment Agency, whose prosecutors could be expected to be both experienced and properly trained, it is clear that standards were lower than they should have been. At the time that the Sentencing Advisory Panel made its comments about standards of prosecution, the Agency began a new rolling training scheme for prosecutors and investigators, and since then the EA has assured us that standards have risen.[13]

### Level of sentences

15. In broad terms, one of the principal concerns that confronted us was the fact that the level of sentences given in courts – principally magistrates' courts – for environmental crimes was too low for them to be effective either as punishment or as deterrent. This was particularly the case with repeat offences. As Councillor Sir David Williams from the Local Government Association explained to us: 'When you get somebody going to court for flytipping for the third or fourth time and they get the same standard fine which is a small fraction of the amount of money they have gained from fly-tipping... that is not only wrong in principle but very frustrating for local councils, and only encourages the crime'.[14]

16. Many different reasons were cited for this phenomenon of low sentences. Some proffered the view that magistrates were unsympathetic to the idea that environmental crime was real crime. Others felt that they were sympathetic but lacked the proper guidance or the necessary experience. It was also suggested that the higher maxima involved in many environmental crimes dissuaded the practitioner from using the full scope of sentencing available by dint of their very rarity: a magistrate used to sentencing by fines of no more than £5,000 will baulk at going higher, even when permitted, in an area in which he feels he has little experience.[15] Although we were told that 'prosecutors are reporting a perception of a greater confidence, understanding and awareness by sentencers',[16] almost all witnesses agreed that sentences were generally too

low, the maxima were not being taken advantage of, and that consequently the punishment for environmental crimes was slight and no real deterrent. **We are concerned that the general level at which fines are imposed neither reflects the gravity of environmental crimes, nor deters or punishes adequately those who commit them. This is clearly unsatisfactory.**

### Nature of sentences

17. For the vast majority of current environmental crimes, the only options open to a court until now have been to fine, or, for more serious crimes – and more serious criminals – to imprison. Only in the case where a prison sentence would be given can the option of a community sentence for some crimes be used instead. In 2002, we were told, 'something like 30 people received a community sentence [for all environmental crimes prosecuted]… and a handful went into custody'.[17] Given the breadth and unique nature of environmental crimes, this restricted choice of substantive sentences is particularly problematic. It has been suggested that, regardless of the severity of fines, financial penalties are a blunt instrument and often inappropriate both for the sorts of crimes that fall within this category and for the sorts of offenders who commit them. **For many forms of environmental crime, compulsory remediation work on the sort of blight for which the offender was himself responsible would be a more appropriate sentence than a fine.** As Mr Simon Baxter, Chief Enforcement Officer of the London Borough of Southwark, told us: 'if a child is caught doing graffiti, they should be made to go and clear that graffiti off for the next six weekends…the magistrates and the judicial system need to be creative in how they punish individuals'.[18] However, as noted above, at the moment, for most crimes, such work, in a community service order, can only be given if the offender had committed a crime serious enough or been thought deserving of imprisonment. For the vast majority of environmental crime cases brought before the courts neither of these factors applies. **We consider it unfortunate that community sentences have for so long been tied inflexibly to custodial sentences. This has markedly reduced the ability of courts to pass appropriate sentences for environmental offences.**

### Appropriateness of sentences to offenders

18. As we have seen, it is commonly felt that environmental criminals are best punished, and their sentence best put to use, by practically mitigating the ugly face of other environmental crimes – whether by cleaning up graffiti, fly-tipped waste or by making restitution to some environment damaged by crime. However, there is a further dimension to this: the extent to which the sentence should fit not just the crime but also the criminal. Clearly, one-off offenders and those with a record of repeat offences should be dealt with in different ways. Likewise, someone in a large corporation sentenced on account of an environmental crime (organised flyposting, for example) perpetrated in order to further his business interests should be dealt with differently to an employee who through negligence allowed some small environmental damage to occur. In the instance of a company where the identity of the real individual culprit is unknown or unknowable, fines are the only sentence currently available. **It**

**is clear that, given the current paltry range of sentences available, there is simply insufficient scope to properly tailor sentences to offenders.**

19. There are two particular areas where this is most of all a problem. A significant proportion of offenders who are presented before courts in environmental cases receive as sentences fines which verge on the derisory in the context of the seriousness of the crime. In *R v James, James and James & Gilbert Gardens Nurseries*, thousands of tonnes of waste was dumped in 18 separate offences between 1999 and 2000. The individuals concerned were fined only £750 and the company £80 at Cardiff Crown Court.[19] Sometimes they are discharged without any fine at all. In many instances this is because the offenders claim that they are without sufficient means to pay a more appropriate level of fine, as they are on benefit or income support.[20] Offenders also claim that substantial fines would harm their business and may perhaps result in commercial insolvency.[21] The inability of the sentencing system to deploy a punishment other than an insignificant fine in these instances is self-evident and deeply unsatisfactory. Magistrates are compelled to take account of an offender's means and of the ability to pay off a fine within one year.[22]

20. There is also a proportion of offenders who come before a magistrate who find even a significant fine derisory in terms of their ability to pay. Often there are commercial bodies or companies whose monthly turnover dwarfs the size of even the maximum possible fine from a magistrates' court. Magistrates of course have the option of transferring the case upwards to the Crown Court where some crimes attract an unlimited fine as sentence, but this happens very rarely.[23] Moreover, when cases have been transferred to the Crown Court and received very substantial fines, these fines have been reduced, often to a very marked degree, upon Appeal. One example of this is the case of the Milford Haven spillage of some 72,000 tonnes of crude oil which damaged 38 Sights of Special Scientific Interest (SSSIs), where a fine of £4 million was reduced to £750,000 on appeal, despite the fact that the Agency costed the remedying of the damage to between £49 and £58 million.[24]

### Polluter does not pay enough

21. It is a further problem that many of those who claim to have insufficient means to pay a reasonable and appropriate level of fine are nonetheless making significant profits from their crimes. Bodies involved in prosecuting environmental offences, such as the Environment Agency, are aware of many individuals who claim poverty or near insolvency yet who regularly offend and who can make substantial amounts of money from their offences. This seems to apply in particular to fly-tippers, although there are instances where individuals concern themselves in a variety of areas of environmental offence within a short period of time – they appear to have a portfolio of environmental and other contraventions which they can pursue and profit from (including dealing in red diesel, the dumping of construction waste, fisheries poaching, &c.,).[25] This is clearly unsatisfactory, and reinforces the sense that environmental crimes pay and that the polluter does not pay sufficiently if at all. Repeat offenders in particular need to be given more than just a slap

on the wrist in the form of a very low fine which they will probably not pay anyway and which will have no impact upon their habit of lucrative offending. **It appears to us that the profits made from crimes form too little a part in decisions as to the size of fine or sentence to be given. Courts – and prosecutors – need to bear in mind that unless the polluter pays substantially more than the sum he profits by from his crime there will be no real deterrent or punishment value to the sentence given.**

### Non-payment of fines

22. The Department for Constitutional Affairs (DCA) reported that only 55% of fines in 2002-03 (in terms of total monies) was actually collected.[26] The Department has no information as yet on what proportion of individual fines this represents because individuals who have been fined a number of times have an accumulated financial total to their names rather than a number of individual fines. Clearly, many of those fined do not pay – this represents an even clearer signal that fines as sentences are not just low, insufficient as punishment and as deterrent, but ineffectual even in wringing a pitiful amount of money from offenders' hands. In addition to this, magistrates take account of likely payment or non-payment when giving fines as sentences. This again tends to reduce the level of the fine given.[27] Furthermore, what money is collected goes into the Central Fund and at the moment – unlike monies from fixed penalty notices – cannot be poured back into prosecuting or investigating environmental crime, or into the environment in general, which is clearly what those involved in this area would most like to see. The Environment Agency stressed to us that it would very much like to retain these monies, 'to go on increasing [the] enforcement effort... or on projects to benefit the environment'.[28] Mr Keir Hopley, Head of Sentencing Policy and Penalties Unit in the Home Office, in evidence to us suggested hopefully that there was movement in central government in that direction.[29] **Both the low level of payment of fines and their indiscriminate destination are unsatisfactory. It is evidently far too easy to avoid payment: and even were 100% of fines to be paid, it would be of no benefit to those leading the fight against these crimes. This is hardly a just situation.**

### Mitigating and aggravating factors in sentencing

23. Courts are obliged to follow guidelines on factors which may mitigate or aggravate the severity of the sentence being considered. We have already touched upon sentences being reduced upon account of an offender's ability to pay. This is an example of a mitigating factor. There are a number of other grounds for similarly reducing sentences. It appears that mitigating factors are applied more freely than aggravating factors and this may lead to an imbalance in sentencing. The principal reason for this imbalance, leaving aside the frequency of questionable recourse to mitigation on account of insufficient means to pay, may be that most environmental offences are of strict liability and do not require a proof of intent, only that the criminal activity has been carried out by the offender. The absence of the need to demonstrate intent

appears to assist mitigation in that some crimes may not be considered *real* crimes because the offender did not intend to commit them.

24. It is arguable that prosecuting authorities could do better in putting aggravating factors before the courts with greater energy. Investigating authorities could also do more than expose the bare minimum – that an offence was committed by a particular person or body – and to look into the intention behind the crime. Was there malice, or design to avoid cost or to benefit from gain? This would of course eat up more resources, take longer and perhaps lead to fewer prosecutions with prosecutors trying to prove more than they currently need to. We consider it unfortunate that the lack of need to prove intention means that the level of fines is more likely to go down than up as crimes are assessed more on strict liability grounds rather than in the context of malice or clearly culpable negligence. Risk of harm in crimes is already taken into account where appropriate: perhaps a factor that recognises the uniqueness of environmental crime and its peculiarly wide effects should be placed before the courts so as to ensure a more balanced outcome to trials. **We believe that there may be grounds for establishing guidance that crimes against the environment merit an automatic aggravation before the court – in other words, that one of the aggravating factors included as guidance for magistrates or judges is damage to the environment or threat to local sustainability.**

### Corporate offences

25. While many environmental crimes are caused by lazy, negligent or malicious individuals, some of the worst instances of such crimes are the responsibility of companies or – in the most flagrant cases – are deliberately carried out by commercial bodies. Such bodies range in size from very small organisations, employing two or three individuals, to very large multi-national businesses. Their turnover and profitability also range across a very large spectrum, and in the case of the latter does not necessarily have any connection with the size of the business concerned. In other words, it may be unjust to fine a large company which is seldom very profitable or whose profits are necessarily slight in comparison to its size more than a smaller company which makes much more in terms of profit for its business, perhaps because it habitually commits environmental offences in order to avoid greater costs. Much of the evidence presented to us was directed at problems in dealing effectively with corporate crime: prosecuting the most appropriate individual in a business (the formally guilty party) rather than whoever is easiest to connect materially with the crime; finding any responsible individual in a business at all when intention does not have to be discerned and the company just wishes to pay the relevant fine, no questions asked; adjudging the appropriate level of fine when there is often no evidence of the general profitability of a company or its turnover, and no evidence as to the financial weight (avoided cost or earned profit) of the offence itself; and dealing forcibly with companies who deliberately and repeatedly flout the law for reasons of commercial profit.

26. It would appear from the evidence we received that prosecuting bodies spend more time and more resources on such corporate environmental crimes than their frequency would proportionately entail. Whether the form of corporate crime be the posting up of prostitutes' cards in a telephone box or the spilling of oil which blights an entire regional coastline, some of the problems outlined above seem in most instances to apply. In both the above, the person most easily prosecuted – the individual posting up the cards or who allowed the oil to spill – is not necessarily the only person who ought to be punished. It is very difficult to get behind the crime to the principal offender. Cases in which intrusive investigation to establish who is at greatest fault is clearly most necessary when an offence results from culpable negligence or deliberate intent. Examples of the latter include flyposting campaigns approved of by companies involved – Sony Records, for example, or Ansell, the owners of the Mates condoms range, whose business development manager was quoted in *Mediaweek* as saying that fly-posting gave the Mates brand 'more street credibility'.[30] In such cases, where the offence may result in considerable profits for the company involved, prosecutors rightly think it almost beside the point to deal only with a lesser individual carrying out the crime for which a senior executive is effectively responsible. Even putting aside the often extreme difficulty of finding and successfully prosecuting the individual behind the decision that led to an environmental crime, **the current sentencing system is just not flexible and imaginative enough adequately to punish corporate bodies or those in senior managerial positions within them. It is disgraceful that some companies openly boast about their crimes as though they manifested some sort of commercial talent or marketing genius. The Government must adopt a much tougher stance with businesses – regardless of their size and nationality – which flagrantly flout the law.**

### Recent developments

27. In the light of these anxieties, we are therefore pleased to see that with regard to flytipping, one of the most prevalent and significant of environmental crimes, DEFRA has, in its recent consultation, proposed increasing the fines for fly-tipping offences to take into account, in particular, repeat offending. It is clear that magistrates must be encouraged to pass higher sentences, and that higher maxima are appropriate. It is however not certain that the option to give a higher sentence alone will lead to higher sentences, since at the moment the average fine for fly-tipping is under one half of the current maxima. **It is also noteworthy that sections 43-7 of the Anti-Social Behaviour Act 2003 have recently come into force which assist prosecutors and sentencers in dealing more flexibly – thus effectively – with local environmental crime, particularly graffiti and fly-posting. This is very much to be welcomed.**

### Summary of the existing challenges

28. Given all of these factors it is remarkable that prosecuting bodies have the determination to prosecute as many cases as they do. Justice must often appear to be a lottery, and a lottery that costs the authority pursuing the case more than it is likely to receive in costs and more than the offender is likely

to receive in terms of any fine. **Investigating and prosecuting bodies must be congratulated for continuing to bring cases before courts when the chances of a satisfactory outcome realistically appear so slight.**

29. In conclusion, fines are too low and community sentences are not used frequently enough, despite their particular appropriateness. Current sentencing, even taking into account these three alternatives, is still too inflexible, especially when it comes to offenders who claim insufficient means – at one end of the scale – or those whose means are very great – at the other. Current guidelines for the mitigation of sentences work in favour of the offender and fail to recognise the peculiar nature of environmental crime and its gravity. In terms of fines, minima are probably inappropriate – for custodial sentences clearly so: maxima for fines in magistrates courts are not high enough for some offenders and offences, but there is also no sign that anywhere near the limit is commonly being given anyway.

30. The use of custodial sentences at all for environmental crime is rare and probably should remain that way. More scope needs to be given to the application of community and alternative sentencing at this level and at the lower level of crimes. In particular, the Government needs to look at enabling courts to deal more practically with criminals in this area – in particular, with repeat criminals. **Preventing the common-or-garden fly-tipper, 'the man with the white van', from owning or driving a van is more useful than fining him a negligible amount which he will more than make up with his next 'job'.** While the current guidance for magistrates on environmental crimes is good it is not necessarily being used as much as it might be. Training for magistrates is infrequent and often superseded by training which relates to more common crimes.[31] The general problem remains that the exposure of magistrates to these crimes is infrequent and most therefore lack experience and expertise. The current situation is clearly unsatisfactory and has been so for a number of years. That it is beginning to improve is welcome, but it is too late, and progress is still too slow. Habits of environmental crime that would not have formed but for the inadequacy of sentencing now have to be broken.

31. In one sense there appears to have been collective failure to deal effectively with environmental crime once they reach the courts. The failure of such crimes to be considered as any sort of priority was made to clear to us by Mr Keir Hopley, Head of the Sentencing Policy and Penalties Unit at the Home Office, when he said 'to be absolutely honest in terms of my day-to-day job and life, environmental crime is not at the forefront of my agenda'[32]: DEFRA however has to accept principal responsibility for not having addressed what it must have known to be an unsatisfactory position with regard to sentencing for environmental crimes. The Agency has certainly before now made DEFRA aware of the problems it faces. Local authorities also, once they – late in the day – decided that environmental crime was a real problem, passed on their concerns. It is the job of DEFRA to present those concerns to the Home Office whose interest in crime is so broad – necessarily – that it cannot be expected

to have any special consideration for one area of crime over another. Yet DEFRA appears to have been a lacklustre agent for positive change. It may be significant that the Department neither sought to give oral evidence during this inquiry nor, until one was directly sought, submitted a written memorandum – and that memorandum treats environmental crime almost entirely within the narrower scope of wildlife crime. It is perhaps unsurprising, given DEFRA's seeming absence from the environmental crime debate that took place during the course of the Sub-committee's inquiry, that so little was done earlier. Only the Government's concern with anti-social behaviour, a sadly euphemistic term that covers a variety of local environmental and other crimes (no less serious for their being local), seems to have kick-started any real interest in DEFRA with the crime and punishment agenda.

32. DEFRA must seize the initiative and push forward a bold and radical agenda to implement whatever changes are necessary to progress this unsatisfactory area of sentencing. Without deterrence and real punishment it cannot be expected that the incidence rate and gravity of environmental crimes will reduce. It is a problem that needs to be tackled not stroked into submission. **We expect DEFRA to move on from its welcome consultations over fly-tipping to consider wider and more detailed changes that will assist the Agency and local authorities in particular in ensuring that those they detect and prosecute successfully will receive sentences that are robust and appropriate to the crimes committed and to the type of offenders involved.**

### The way forward: suggestions and solutions

Increase in level of environmental sentences

33. Historically, sentences have been financial or custodial. In a simple world, raising the maxima for environmental crimes in either or both of these areas might have the desired effect of deterring and properly punishing offenders. As we have seen, however, the world of environmental crime is far from simple. That is not to say that there is no scope for increasing maxima for some crimes. DEFRA is consulting on just such increases for repeated fly-tipping offences. While it is clear that maxima are properly seen as caps on sentencing rather than as targets, higher maxima gives greater scope to the sentencer and may well lead to greater average sentences.[33] We believe an upwards drift in the level of sentences for some environmental crimes following the imposition of increased maxima to be desirable. Moreover, increased maxima send out an important signal to sentencers, prosecutors, offenders and the public at large that environmental crimes are to be understood as serious matters. A little bit of such understanding can do a lot of good. **We acknowledge that there may be little scope for increasing the custodial maxima, but expect the Government to look into the limits on traditional sentencing across the range of environmental crimes to see where benefit may accrue from appropriate increases.**

## Achieving higher sentencing in environmental crime

34. Raising formal limits for sentences can only be one part in the battle against environmental crime. Sentencers need to be encouraged to make proper use of the full existing range of fines and custodial sentences, encouraged in particular to consider higher fines across the board, especially for repeat offences. If this is not done, then the question of whether or not to raise maxima will remain an academic one. While environmental prosecution is only one part of better environmental protection and sustainable development, it is a key part and, as it is largely a regulatory system underpinned by the criminal law it must be robust. Prosecutors also must be encouraged to press persuasively for higher sentences, and to use all the means at their disposal to call for tougher sentencing. Prosecutors will hold back from this if they feel that their arguments will be set aside by the courts. Likewise, courts will not apply tougher sentences unless a good case for it is put by a professional and determined prosecutor. The stagnancy that results from this impasse must be overcome.

### Training and raising awareness

35. One way to encourage those involved in environmental cases to treat them more appropriately and more seriously is through training and raising awareness. There have been efforts to raise the profile of environmental sentencing by the Magistrates Association including publishing guidance for magistrates and running workshops and seminars for prosecutors. However, there is still some way to go. Recent research by Environmental Resources Management[34] found that less than a quarter of all magistrates surveyed were reasonably aware of environmental sentencing guidelines published in 2001. There is the opportunity to encourage and support further training of magistrates. Both the Agency and local authorities stressed the importance of this to us in evidence: and the former is currently helping to train magistrates in environmental crime.[35] There is also concern that there has been no comparable training or guidance issued for the Crown Court or appellate courts and although the Judicial Studies Board (JSB) have been approached by the Environment Agency to offer training in environmental matters, the offer has not yet been taken up.[36] To an extent this is a 'chicken and egg' situation. Until the JSB and the appellate courts are aware of the broader impacts of pollution and environmental harm, they will not place it sufficiently high on the agenda. However, until it is on the agenda, raising awareness will be difficult. It is evidence that there is good will towards proper and due consideration of environmental crime that the first thing that the Sentencing Advisory Panel did when it was set up was to consider and deliver guidance for environmental crime.[37] This goodwill needs to be encouraged.

36. The Government has a duty to see that the Judicial Studies Board takes to heart the centrality of environmental crime to other areas of crime and to problems faced by the sustainable development agenda. The new statutory purposes of sentencing should assist in environmental protection, for example, in making sure that reparation fits squarely with the polluter pays principle

The well-understood 'broken windows' theory, that small environmental crimes easily lead on to more major ones, which can in turn lead on to crimes of a different sort and different degree, should also be cause enough for the JSB to realise that dealing satisfactorily with environmental crime will reduce the possible incidence of other crimes. The Government should seek to assist the JSB to commit judicial training to environmental impacts and the principles of sustainable development. Government has a duty to encourage all engaged bodies to assist in tackling environmental crime as seriously as other crimes which blight lives: it would be wrong for government to consider this duty as one which does not extend to the judiciary.

37. There is also a continuing need to train prosecutors. The Agency stated that, following the report of the Sentencing Advisory Panel in 2000, it began a more substantial rolling programme of regular training for its prosecutors. There was little evidence that all local authorities have taken the same approach yet, although no doubt standards vary widely across the country. The recognition by local authorities that better training is needed may have great potential in eventually securing increased and more appropriate sentences in the courts. In addition, there is no doubt greater scope for local authorities, especially those which neighbour upon each other, to share experience and expertise in dealing with this area of crime. While many such crimes can be local, some of the effects of these crimes cross boundaries very easily, as do many of the individuals committing these offences. Cooperation is essential; and current levels of co-operation must improve if the fight against growing trends in particular in some areas of environmental crime – fly-tipping, for example – are to be combated.

*Information*

38. Curiously, less is known about environmental crime than is often supposed. One reason for this is that it covers a very broad range of offences. Another is that it is dealt with by many different bodies, some national (such as the Agency) but most (such as local authorities) regional or local. The idea of maintaining a national public database of environmental prosecutions to publicise offenders and provide more consistency in sentencing was raised by us in evidence. This received a subdued response from the Agency despite the publication of their annual name and shame publication *Spotlight on the Environment*.[38] The Agency is co-operating with local authorities to establish a flytipping data-base, *Flycapture*, which will be used by them to fight this particularly serious and widespread offence. However, because of the nature and scope of environmental crime, and the diversity of those dealing with it each reporting offences in a different way, it appears unlikely that any time soon there will be established a broader 'envirocrime' database, public or otherwise, to assist in consistency in sentencing and in supplying relevant information to prosecutors unless it receives direct central government assistance. We consider this to be unfortunate. **Information is key to fighting crime, and all those dealing with environmental offences, whether they be sentencers, prosecutors, investigators, or those dealing with clean-up or with prevention, require a good corpus of information on which to build**

**effective strategies. We look to the Government, in co-operation with other engaged bodies, to examine practical means to set up a comprehensive database of environmental crime to improve information in this area.**

*Options in sentencing*

39. Even were higher fines to result from better training and guidance, and more resort be made to custodial sentences, there would still be instances when fines or imprisonment were simply not as appropriate and therefore not as effective as other possible sentences or punishments. There would similarly be instances when increased fines or custodial sentences were clearly inappropriate and therefore subject to a level of mitigation that rendered them of negligible effect. With the coming into force of Part 12 of the Criminal Justice Act 2003 community sentences will now be able to be imposed in lieu of fines rather than, as before, in lieu of imprisonment.[39] This ought to make such sentences more frequently used to punish offenders. This is very much to be welcomed as community sentences are particularly appropriate, and, we believe, effective, in dealing with environmental crimes. This will however, require support from other criminal justice agencies, such as the probation service, to help enforce and implement community service orders. There is concern that, even with the existing options for community penalties, there is too much pressure on the probation service.[40] **We expect the Government to ensure that those agencies who handle community sentences are sufficiently resourced to cope with what we hope will be an increasing number of such sentences.**

40. The Agency in its memorandum and in evidence to us stated that it had put forward a number of proposals for sentences that it felt would be effective in dealing with the crimes it faced on a day-to-day basis. A number of these were general proposals, such as the confiscation of a vehicle used for repeated criminal activity such as, for example, the illegal dumping of waste; or remediation orders that would require an offender to remedy the environmental harm to the satisfaction of the Agency within a specified time. The majority of these proposals were however focussed on the commercial end of environmental crime. They included equity share issues that would enable a court to require companies to issue shares for a specified sum related to the avoided costs or benefits obtained through the commission of the offence; corporate rehabilitation orders where the court would grant an order that for a specified period, for example, two years, the company would have to undertake specific activities and actions; corporate bonds whereby a corporate offender either pays funds into court for a finite period or is ordered to obtain compulsory insurance to a specific value; and means whereby, in addition to any sentence imposed, the court could order that a notice be placed about the offence in the local or national media, and in the company's annual report for the benefit of shareholders.[41]

41. The Agency told us that it had been in discussions with the Home Office over some of these proposals, but that the discussions had ended at the last General Election. The Agency also admitted that the fault for not attempting

to resuscitate these talks lay as much with them as with the Home Office. It is clear that neither side considered them a priority. While fines hit companies in the pocket, that pocket is often very deep indeed, and alternative sentences may prove a better punishment and a stronger deterrent. **We call on the Home Office and the Agency to look again at these proposals to deal more effectively with corporate or business environmental crime; and to ensure that such proposals are quickly cast in a legislative shape upon which Parliament can then come to a decision.** Corporate crimes may represent a minority of environmental crimes, but these offences are often at the more serious end of the spectrum. The same sort of prominence should be given to these sorts of offences as has been given to those at the lower end of the spectrum through recent anti-social behaviour legislation.

### Alternatives to prosecution

42. One of the main alternatives to prosecution is the use of civil penalties whereby the regulator imposes a financial penalty on an offender instead of initiating a formal prosecution. Such a system is used widely in several European countries, in the United States and in Australia. The Agency suggested to us that civil penalties would provide a useful additional tool for dealing with non-intentional and less serious offending but added that it would wish to reserve the right to pursue prosecutions where appropriate.[42] In the United States of America, this system is accompanied by one where enormous penalties attach to those offences which are actually brought before a court. In October 2003, Chevron Texaco paid a $3.5 million civil penalty for air emissions. Unless a similar scale of penalties could be applied here, such a system would prove ineffectual. Nonetheless, serious thought needs to be given to those areas where the Agency considers the system may have some benefits. While we believe that courts have a central role to play in tackling environmental crime it may be that there is scope for dealing with certain crimes by civil penalty. After all, it is clear that what is paramount to tackling these crimes is what works and not any necessary recourse to the courts.

43. There may be the possibility of adapting how the Health and Safety Executive (HSE) deal with companies or organisations which regularly contravene health and safety regulations. The HSE has the power to place a prohibition notice on such bodies which forbids them to carry out their business from which the contraventions result. Clearly, this sort of power, prohibiting a business from operating on account of repeated breaches of regulations, would be directly applicable to certain areas of environmental offence and would have significant impact on such contravening businesses without the costly and time-consuming need to go to the courts. Likewise, an analogous power to this might permit a body such as the Agency summarily to confiscate a vehicle or other instrument which had repeatedly been used in environmental offences. **Clearly, DEFRA should look at the possibilities of granting to environmental bodies a power similar to that the HSE possesses in the form of the issuing of prohibition notices.**

44. One obvious existing alternative to prosecution, issuing fixed penalty notices (which currently applies for certain litter and dog-fouling offences), is not as effective as it might be due to the restricted authority of enforcement officers: they are currently often unable to secure the correct identification of offenders. This difficulty is being dealt with by a number of local authorities through private legislation for their local authority areas, to empower local authority officials to demand confirmation of an individual's stated identity and prosecute an individual who refuses to give his identity or provides a false identity [the London Local Authorities Bill, clause 29; currently before the House of Commons]. Bizarrely, the Government is citing the passage of this private legislation into law as reason to hold back from passing public legislation to this effect for the whole country. In fact, this legislation was only proposed in the first place by local authorities when the Government declined, despite much lobbying from local authorities, to propose its equivalent in public legislation for the country as a whole. This seems utterly unreasonable and counterproductive. **If the Government believes that extending those powers to impose fixed penalty notices currently available in most places only to police officers or their equivalent to agents of the Agency or local authorities is a good idea and will assist in tackling environmental crime then it ought to do something about it. Government inaction in the first instance led to the private legislation the precedent of which the Government now cites as reason now not to act.**

### An Environmental Court

The idea of specialist environmental tribunals or courts was raised in written and oral evidence.[43] The Magistrates Association did not support the idea of an environmental court, believing that environmental matters were best dealt with at the most local level (a species of judicial subsidiarity). As Ms Rachel Lipscomb, Chair of the Association, explained: 'That ...[creates] a very strong link in that people who are dealing with cases in their own area are also more aware of dangers, difficulties and prevalence [of environmental crime] than they might be, doing it on a specialist basis'.[44] Given that the level of sentencing is currently so low as to suggest that magistrates do not find the local nature of the crime that they are considering sufficiently strong a motive to attach to it a robust penalty, we are somewhat sceptical of this point. However, we do accept that there would be very considerable cost involved in establishing a nation-wide environmental court or tribunal – it would also require primary legislation.[45] While it would give welcome national prominence to the issue of environmental crime, it would not necessarily deal practically with such crimes any more effectively than other proposed alternatives.

### Specialist environmental magistrates

45. Another idea put before the Committee by a number of bodies was that there should be a corps of specialist environmental magistrates as there are for health and safety offences, or crimes involving children, for example. Given that so few magistrates encounter environmental offences in court

more than very rarely it seems only sensible to consider the establishment of specialist magistrates in each region to deal with such crimes. They would then build up expertise and experience both of which would cascade down into a more appropriate and flexible use of sentencing, and would assist in local and regional deterrence and accountability. Indeed, the idea of nominated specialists tends to find support from the London-wide specialist Health & Safety magistrates currently in operation. It is still far from certain whether the number of environmental crimes taken to court in each area would provide a sufficient body of work for such specialists, if they were to deal with such crimes exclusively. The Agency suggested that two specialist environmental magistrates in each court area could hear all environmental and health & safety cases.[46] **The Government and other appropriate bodies must look seriously at the proposals for such specialist training on environmental crime and for the establishment of teams of dedicated magistrates. It is clear that without such concentrated experience and expertise the courts will continue to be a lottery often unfavourable to deterrence and proper punishment.**

## Endnote

46. It seems to us that the key to ensuring that environmental crime is properly and effectively dealt with in courts, so that offenders are robustly punished and deterred from repeat offences, is co-operation: co-operation between Government departments, agencies and local authorities in sharing expertise and in assisting each other wherever possible; co-operation between those prosecuting and those sentencing to ensure that all are aware of relevant and practical guidance that explains the gravity of environmental offences; and co-operation between DEFRA and, in particular, the Home Office in giving environmental crime the prominence it deserves and the legislation it needs to be effectively tackled. **The Government has shown itself to be sufficiently joined-up to begin to tackle anti-social behaviour. It now needs to ensure that it works in a co-ordinated fashion, and with other bodies, to tackle the currently poor sentencing record for offences against the environment. Only by doing so will it effectively begin to deal with the blight that is environmental crime.**

## Notes

1 Fly-tipping Strategy and Consultation on statutory directions to the Environment Agency and waste collection authorities on the unlawful disposal of waste, DEFRA, February 2004.
2 see *Living Places: Cleaner, Safer, Greener*, 11th Report of the Select Committee on the Office of the Deputy Prime Minister, Session 2002–03.
3 Criminal Statistics in England and Wales 2003, Cm6054.
4 Q197.
5 Q243.
6 Q32; Sentencing Advisory Panel (2000) – Advice to the Court of Appeal, page 4.
7 Ev58.
8 Ev59.
9 Ev96.

10  Q5.
11  Q6.
12  Ev70, para 17.
13  Q19–20.
14  Q177.
15  Q23.
16  Ev4.
17  Q234.
18  Q184.
19  Ev2.
20  Q170.
21  Q29.
22  Q138.
23  A222.
24  Ev65; also *R v Anglian Water Services Ltd (EWCA Crime 2243)*.
25  Evidence given to the Sub-committee by the Environment Agency, 25 March 2004, A95: not yet printed.
26  Q265–7.
27  Q138.
28  A46.
29  Q276.
30  Ev34.
31  Q147–8.
32  Q297.
33  Q222.
34  Ev71, para 32.
35  Q6.
36  Q26.
37  Q32.
38  Q37 & Q41.
39  Q235.
40  Q121.
41  Ev17.
42  Ev16.
43  For example, Ev91.
44  A144.
45  Q238.
46  Q27.

# 35. Thinking outside the 'black box': tailored enforcement in environmental criminal law*

*David C. Fortney*

## 1. Introduction

A longstanding debate in environmental law centers around the best way to achieve corporate compliance with the many complicated provisions of environmental statutes and regulations. Effective enforcement of environmental laws against corporations is vital to any environmental-protection regime: by virtue of their size and industrial nature, corporations are often among the largest producers of pollutants. Yet corporations are not always 'polluters' in a derogatory sense; some amount of polluting byproducts are inevitable in any industrial enterprise, and American business cannot completely eliminate its emissions and effluents. Therefore, environmental enforcement must walk a fine line between being overly harsh and overly lax if it is to accomplish its goals.

In the early days of environmental regulation, violations carried largely insignificant civil fines as penalties.[1] Under this initial regime, corporations had little incentive to comply with environmental laws: it was more cost-effective to continue to pollute more than the law allowed and simply pay the fine (if the corporation was actually caught violating the law).[2] Somewhat perversely, corporations actually had a *disincentive* to comply. Compliance generally raises operating costs, which means that corporations trying to obey the law – whether out of a sense of legal duty or public obligation – lose a competitive edge to lawbreakers and consequently may suffer in the marketplace.[3] In any event, absent some guilt for breaking the law, corporate officers likely lost little sleep over their continued violations.

Over the course of the 1980s, Congress, the Department of Justice (DOJ), and the Environmental Protection Agency (EPA) realized that a harsher enforcement regime was necessary to ensure compliance with environmental laws.[4] To achieve this goal, Congress increased the complexity of the regulatory regime and raised many violations from misdemeanors to felonies.[5] The DOJ established an Environmental Crime Section, and the EPA was allowed dramatically to increase the number – and legal powers – of its environmental investigators.[6] The theory was, and remains, that without criminal sanctions,

* From *Texas Law Review* (2003), 81(6): pp. 1609–35.

including heavy fines and occasionally the imprisonment of corporate officers, corporations would continue to treat environmental violations as a 'cost of doing business.'[7] Indeed, the DOJ and EPA were very successful even in the formative years of criminal enforcement. From 1983 to 1990, the DOJ assessed a total of $57,358,404 in criminal penalties and obtained sentences of imprisonment for fifty-five percent of criminal defendants.'[8] Corporate officers could no longer sleep quite as soundly with the knowledge of continued environmental violations.

Public reaction toward environmental crime increased the pressure to obtain stiffer penalties. Images of 'midnight dumpers' and other heartless, profit-driven businessmen portrayed in books like *A Civil Action* raised awareness among members of the public. Indeed, in one survey of public perception of the severity of various crimes, environmental crime ranked seventh – above armed robbery and other serious crimes.[9] Thus, for nearly two decades, the prevailing viewpoint (and prosecutorial standard) has been to punish the corporation as a criminal. Increasingly this has also entailed the use of criminal sanctions against individual officers of these corporations.[10]

However, the increased deterrence of criminal penalties has not been achieved without a price. Critics of corporate criminal liability in environmental law point out as particularly problematic the erosion of the *mens rea* required for corporate liability, the artificial nature of 'guilt' imputed to corporate officers, and the unfairness engendered by virtually unlimited prosecutorial discretion enjoyed by the DOJ's Environmental Crimes Section.[11] In addition, these critics highlight the enormous complexity of environmental laws, noting that it is often unclear whether or not a violation has actually occurred.[12] The combination of these factors means that the sting of criminal prosecution is increasingly more widely felt in the business community. Corporate officers are being held criminally liable on thinner and thinner evidence, and smaller corporations or 'Mom and Pop' businesses are more often the target of prosecution than are large, sophisticated companies.[13] Even for those not personally prosecuted, the constant threat of draconian penalties creates an enormous emotional drain on large sections of the business community, resulting in massive social costs.[14]

This Note argues that the critics of the current regulatory regime are largely right in arguing that (at least in environmental law) criminal liability introduces more problems than it solves. The current regime of environmental criminal enforcement is unfair and inefficient because it relies on outdated models of organizations and incompatible areas of law. This Note argues that one valuable reform within environmental law is a scheme of enforcement that accounts for the type of actor in question and adjusts incentives, penalties, and even standards of proof accordingly.[15] Following the usage of 'tailored regulation,'[16] I call this theory of enforcement 'tailored enforcement.'

Part II uses a recent case to illustrate some of the problems with the current regulatory and prosecutorial regime. It focuses primarily on the different results of enforcement that are obtained depending on the type of actors involved, and preliminarily asserts that the reasons for the discrepancy are an outmoded theory of organizational liability and the current regime's lack of prosecutorial flexibility. Part III explores the debate over criminal enforcement of environmental laws and develops the argument that the current regime is fatally flawed. Part IV proposes a new regime of organizational liability that addresses the practical differences between types of organizations. This new paradigm should make the enforcement of environmental laws more fair as well as more efficient – and therefore ultimately more effective.

## II. The view from within (a prosecution)

This Part introduces the plight of one company in order to illustrate problems faced by a corporate defendant during an investigation by the EPA and prosecution by the DOJ. This case study is real: it is drawn from the experience of Koch Industries in its fight against a ninety-seven count indictment for one incident that violated emissions requirements under the Clean Air Act. The goal of this Part is twofold: first, to demonstrate, from both sides, the problems encountered by investigation and prosecution of environmental violations; and second, to explain the vast difference in results sought and eventually obtained by the DOJ. The consequences of both the problems raised and results obtained will be explored at the end of this Part and in more detail in Part III.

### A. United States v. Koch Industries

In September of 2000, the DOJ indicted Koch Industries and four of its corporate officers on ninety-seven counts of violating federal and state environmental laws. Koch's primary offense involved the release of ninety-one metric tons of the carcinogen benzene, about fifteen times the federal limit, from a refinery in Corpus Christi, Texas.[17] The DOJ's thirty-three page indictment alleged that Koch and its officers had engaged in a conspiracy to violate the law and to cover up the violations, all in the name of corporate profitability.[18] Media reports generally painted Koch as a corporation that thought of itself as 'above the law,' spewing harmful chemicals into the atmosphere while thumbing its nose both at the government and the public.[19]

Koch's version of the story was, predictably, very different. According to Koch, the company tried to comply with federal regulations. As part of that effort, it installed a thermal oxidizer to convert the benzene into carbon dioxide and water.[20] The equipment did not operate properly, however, and Koch claimed that an employee had concealed that information from the company.[21] Unaware of the problem, Koch submitted reports to federal and local officials stating that the plant was in compliance with the regulations. When Koch discovered the employee's actions, the employee was fired immediately.[22] The four officers charged in the indictment claimed no knowledge of the violations, insisting that they had no idea that the factory was not in compliance, and furthermore, that they had no way of knowing that the thermal oxidizer was not functioning properly.[23] Koch maintained that the public health was never endangered and that tests showed that benzene in the atmosphere remained within safe levels.[24]

The DOJ's lawsuit set the stakes extremely high. Koch Industries faced maximum civil fines of $48.5 million and federal criminal fines up to $352 million.[25] Moreover, each of the corporate officers individually faced fines of at least one million dollars and between twenty to thirty-five years in prison under the responsible corporate officer doctrine and for violations of state environmental statutes.[26]

However, the lawsuit was not the smashing success for which the DOJ had hoped. After months of legal wrangling by both sides, District Judge Janis Jack ordered the counts reduced from ninety-seven to nine.[27] She accused the DOJ of doubling up on many of the counts and expressed frustration with the government's case, doubting whether the government could convince a jury of Koch's wrongdoing.[28] Other critics accused the DOJ of political retribution, citing Koch's contributions to Republican Texas Governor George W. Bush and pointing out the rarity of harsh criminal prosecutions for environmental violations.[29] Citizens of Corpus Christi – those in the position most likely harmed by the violation – generally supported Koch and wondered why it had been singled out for prosecution.[30]

The resolution of the case came the morning trial was scheduled to begin. In the end, the DOJ accepted a settlement in which Koch would pay $20 million: $10 million in fines and $10 million in compensation to Corpus Christi.[31] In return, the DOJ agreed to drop all charges against the corporate officers.[32]

The *Koch Industries* case represents many of the contemporary problems in environmental criminal law. From the government's point of view, no corporation or individual should be able to get away with the extreme environmental violations that Koch committed at the Corpus Christi plant. Often, these violations are even more worthy of prosecution than other crimes because the entire public is harmed by the acts of corporations – acts that otherwise would go unpunished and thereby encourage more harmful violations.[33] However, from Koch's and its corporate officers' points of view, no one person or entity should be fined or imprisoned for acts of which they were unaware and unable to control, especially when no demonstrable harm was caused.[34] Koch and its officers could not have prevented a rogue employee's actions under the best of circumstances, yet they were held accountable for what amounted to insider sabotage.

For the illegal discharge of benzene (which was never contested by Koch) in violation of many environmental laws and regulations, no one was punished, and the corporation at fault received only a minor slap on the wrist (which bore no relation to the profits collected during the time of the violations).[35] How did the case go from one extreme of hypersensitive prosecution and draconian penalties to a soft-handed reprimand and complete exoneration of all persons responsible for the crime?

### B. Problems raised by the Koch case

The *Koch* case is troubling in several respects. First and foremost, a preventable act of environmental pollution occurred, endangering the surrounding community and further contributing to this country's air-quality problem. Yet attempts to deter this behavior raise their own difficult questions. From Koch's perspective, the prosecution was unfair; Koch was singled out for especially harsh treatment, given that most large corporations suspected of environmental violations are not even criminally prosecuted.[36] The officers also saw the case as unjust; each faced the possibility of receiving enormous fines and lengthy jail sentences for the acts of another – acts of which they may well have been completely ignorant. From the DOJ's perspective, the prosecution was politically necessary, and the threatened use of criminal sanctions was simply an expedient choice of weapons in their legal arsenal.

Finally, from society's perspective, questions arise regarding the efficacy of the current 'command and control' or 'prohibit and punish' regulatory regime. That is, given the outcome of the *Koch* case, might society be better served by another enforcement regime that is more realistic and therefore more effective? The DOJ spent millions of taxpayer dollars prosecuting the *Koch* case, only to arrive at a settlement that may well have been negotiated much more cheaply in advance or imposed as a strict liability penalty for emissions: a 'pollution tax.'[37] Koch spent millions more defending itself and its officers against charges that most likely could not be proven. Those costs will eventually be passed on to the consumer. Yet the citizens of Corpus Christi will ultimately pay the highest price, in the form of an increased risk of cancer from benzene discharges, without receiving adequate compensation or any means of cleaning up the city's air.[38]

1. *Koch's concerns: fairness, best efforts, and agent liability.*   From Koch's point of view, the company had been unfairly singled out for prosecution.[39] As anyone in the industrial world knows, perfect compliance with environmental laws is nearly, if not completely, impossible.[40] Koch believed that the violation was a relatively minor pollution incident that occurred because of a deviant employee, not because of any wrongful motive on the corporation's part.[41] Thus, Koch felt that the ninety-seven count indictment was a clear example of a vindictive DOJ 'throwing the book' at them. The enormity of the indictment did indeed have the feel of political retribution – the investigation and prosecution were conducted during the last year of President Clinton's second term, and Koch Industries was a major donor to then-Texas Governor George W. Bush's presidential campaign.[42]

It is not out of the question that the action was indeed political retribution. The DOJ's Environmental Crimes Section has complete prosecutorial discretion over the cases it chooses to pursue.[43] Many other acts of corporate pollution routinely go unprosecuted.[44] Indeed, the vast majority of cases brought by the DOJ are against smaller businesses, and few cases against large industrial corporations are prosecuted with such zeal and high stakes.[45]

None of this is to suggest that large corporations that commit environmental crimes should not be prosecuted, either because they are 'important to American business' or because the DOJ has in the past shown greater deference to large corporations. However, it does raise an issue as to the political legitimacy of allowing the DOJ's hit-or-miss prosecution of large companies.[46] This issue becomes even more important when the driving force behind decisions whether or not to prosecute appears to be driven by political, and not legal, imperatives.

The second concern for Koch is that criminal liability could be imposed on the entire organization for the rogue acts of one employee. Of course.

American law has a long tradition of holding employers responsible for the torts of their employees committed in the course of employment.[47] However, this is a doctrine of civil, not criminal, liability.[48] Criminal law generally requires proof of *mens rea*, or a 'guilty mind;' this requirement seeks to ensure that only morally culpable persons will receive the state's harshest sanctions.[49] Over the course of the twentieth century, some exceptions to this general rule have been carved out by the judiciary in order to respond to corporate crime.[50] One of the most notable of these is the responsible corporate officer doctrine, through which the requisite criminal knowledge may be imputed to corporate officers in a supervisory role.[51] Whether or not these exceptions are fair in the context of environmental law is a topic addressed in Part III.

Finally, Koch also has a right to be concerned about the relationship of the prosecution to the overall quality of the corporation's conduct. Koch has long been regarded as a good corporate citizen of Corpus Christi.[52] Furthermore, the violation was the result of a failed attempt to comply with environmental regulations. Koch had installed a thermal oxidizer, a benzenecontrol device, which later was shown to be insufficient for the volume of benzene generated.[53] Under current regulations, best efforts to comply and to promptly report any violations *may* be factored into a reduced penalty, but a lengthy checklist of factors must be satisfied. Ultimately, a reduction in penalty is largely up to EPA and DOJ discretion.[54]

2. *Koch's officers' concerns: imputed knowledge and actual culpability.* Perhaps the most pressing of any concerns addressed in this Note is that of the three Koch officers who faced individual criminal charges. The threat of one to two million dollars in fines and twenty to thirty-five years in prison would cause anxiety in anyone. However, facing such penalties based solely upon one's position within an organization – that is, facing criminal sanctions for someone else's wrongdoing, not your own – would induce not only anxiety but justifiable anger as well.

While the Koch officials fortunately did not receive those sanctions, the DOJ nevertheless threatened to impose them – and under several theories of corporate criminal liability, they could have.[55] Criminal prosecutions of individual corporate officers for corporate environmental crimes are on the rise;[56] while some of those cases likely involve officers who knew of or directed wrongful violations, there is no requirement that the individual officer knew of the violation at all.[57]

The notion that individual persons could be required to pay a two million dollar fine and spend thirty-five years in a federal penitentiary for an act they neither committed nor knew about violates the most basic premise of American criminal law – that the criminal sanction be applied only to those persons who have a guilty mind (*mens rea*).[58] Combine that fact with the vast complexity of environmental law – one EPA employee joked that 'only five people [at the EPA] understand what 'hazardous waste' is'[59] – and the result is a blanket of potential criminal liability over thousands of American corporate officers for acts they do not even realize are happening.[60]

3. *The DOJ's concerns: political imperatives and limited resources.* So far, this Note has been fairly critical of the DOJ. However, it is important to point out that (with the exception of the possible political motivation behind the *Koch* case) the Environmental Crimes Section is simply doing its job. The environmental laws, and corporate officers' liability under them, are not of the DOJ's making; they are rather charged only with enforcing those laws, regardless of their fairness. The criticism this Note aims to make is that the job the DOJ is being forced to perform is simply not the best or most fair use of governmental law-enforcement resources.

After environmental laws were strengthened in the late 1980s and the early 1990s,[61] the DOJ began seeking tougher criminal sanctions against corporations as well as individuals.[62] However, individual criminal liability generally was assessed only against small business owners (who presumably knew much more about daily environmental violations committed by their businesses) and corporate officers found guilty of ordering employees to commit violations.[63] Gradually the DOJ began to cast a wider net, prosecuting corporate officers in cases where actual intent was either absent or available only by inference.[64] Given the rising tide of public opinion against corporate polluters,[65] this is hardly surprising, if unfortunate.

The DOJ must also deal with the fact that as a government agency, its resources are limited and spread thinly over a wide spectrum of enforcement activity. The agency simply cannot prosecute all possible cases and therefore must choose which ones it will pursue. Given that some cases will be dropped and others pursued, there is no mechanism to ensure that the most 'meritorious' or 'socially important' cases get prosecuted.[66] When combined with the political pressure to 'get tough on environmental crime,' the DOJ may be forced to pursue an agenda that focuses too much on simply increasing the number of 'victories' or scoring big verdicts. The first agenda leads to increased convictions in the 'easy' cases – violations by small businesses – and the second leads to aggressive pursuit of politically appropriate 'deep pocket' corporate defendants and their 'greedy' corporate officers.[67]

4. *Societal concerns: prevention, punishment, and efficiency.* At a highly generalized level, society is also affected by the results of the *Koch* case. First and foremost, the public has an interest in a program of environmental regulation and enforcement that will encourage prevention over punishment.[68] The reason is obvious: environmental harms, while compensable and in some cases reversible, are generally permanent. Most of the damage from environmental disasters is immediate, and the only way to reduce the damage is to stop the disaster from ever happening.[69] Any environmental regime should therefore be judged not according to how many violators can be caught and punished, but by how many violations can most efficiently be prevented.

Society does have an interest in punishment, however. Any regulatory regime, no matter how incentive- or market-based, will still not stop willful polluters who attempt to cut every possible corner to reduce costs, or who perhaps simply do not care to bring themselves into compliance. Punishment is necessary for its moral component as well as its deterrent effect.[70] Given the low regard in which the American public holds environmental criminals. it would be a mistake to abolish all criminal prosecution of environmental offenders.[71]

Finally, society has an interest in the efficient use of public tax money. In order to justify the expense of litigation, the end result of that litigation should be a substantial reduction in environmental crime.[72] As consumers, the public also has a right to expect that the means of forcing environmental compliance can accomplish their goal without unreasonably burdening businesses with unwarranted or exorbitant costs. Environmental protection is an admirable and necessary policy goal, but it should not be achieved at the cost of bankrupting either American business or American consumers.

## III. Deficiencies in environmental criminal law

This Part first explores two series of critical arguments that have been made against criminal liability in environmental law. The first objects to the general principle of penalizing the violation of environmental regulations by imposing criminal liability, asserting that the goals and assumptions of environmental and criminal law are fundamentally irreconcilable. The second, narrower argument cautions against imposing criminal liability upon individual officers absent a strict showing of their willful violation of the law. This Part then examines why *mens rea* standards for individual corporate officers have eroded over the second half of the last century – a trend that continues unabated. Finally, this Part argues that while the problems of the current scheme spring in part from a fundamental incompatibility between environmental and criminal law, the larger problem is an imperfect understanding of organizational behavior, which necessarily begins to strip important protections from this portion of criminal law.

### A. General criticisms: environmental vs. criminal law

Many critics contend that basic differences between environmental and criminal law render the two disciplines fundamentally incompatible.[73] Professor Richard Lazarus, perhaps the most prolific and vocal critic of the current regulatory scheme, has identified three unique qualities of environmental law that distinguish it from virtually every other branch of law. Environmental law, he argues, is *aspirational, dynamic,* and *complex.*[74]

Environmental law is *aspirational* in the sense that it sets enormously optimistic goals with the hope of forcing dramatic changes in behavior in order to bring about substantial and rapid change.[75] For example, the original Clean Air Act of 1970 mandated that the new (and ambitious) national air quality standards be met by 1975.[76] Achievement of these standards was patently ridiculous even at the time of enactment.[77] Similarly, the Clean Water Act of 1972 sought to eliminate the discharge of pollutants into U.S. waters by 1985.[78] Needless to say, the United States is nowhere near achieving this goal, even now, eighteen years after the deadline has passed.[79] This aspirational quality is certainly responsible to some extent for the positive changes we have experienced – but 'it does not inexorably follow that [such] laws are equally well suited to civil and criminal enforcement.'[80]

Second, environmental law is *dynamic* in the sense that it is constantly changing in response to scientific discoveries.[81] Statutes and regulations are regularly revised as scientific knowledge advances. Indeed, much of the science underlying environmental law 'is tentative and uncertain'[82] and creates an atmosphere of instability within the law. Combine this scientific dynamism with the changing of political winds in different administrations, and the result is a body of law that changes so much and so fast that no one is ever truly sure what the current status of a substance, procedure, or level of discharge is.[83]

Finally, environmental law is *complex* because, among other things, it is technical, obscure, indeterminate, and extremely detailed.[84] Statutes and regulations are packed with scientific jargon and cover literally tens of thousands of pages. Mastery of them all is impossible, and even knowing where to find a regulation can be troublesome.[85] Even in the event that a compliance officer or other company employee is aware of a relevant law, it is often unclear whether or not the company is actually in violation of it, as there are rarely clear lines laid out to distinguish between acceptable and non-acceptable levels of pollution.[86] However, as Lazarus points out, 'the legal implications of being barely on one side of the law rather than barely on the other side can nonetheless be tremendous.'[87]

In contrast to environmental law, criminal law relies heavily on stability and notice.[88] Crimes such as murder, assault, and theft have been a part of law since time immemorial. Changes in the criminal law are generally made slowly, and the overall framework has not changed dramatically in hundreds of years.[89] Because of this stability, criminals are assumed to be on notice of what behavior will or will not be tolerated.[89]

Perhaps more importantly, criminal law employs *sanctions* (heavy monetary fines and imprisonment), whereas civil law employs *damages* (which may also be expensive, but are limited to the amount needed to compensate the injured party).[91] Criminal law relies on sanctions for its efficacy, and the sanction represents the moral condemnation of the community.[92] The traditional justification for criminal law's use of the sanction is that the criminal law reflects a community's moral standards of what is right and wrong; all members of the community know the standards and can therefore be held accountable for breaking them.[93] It is only once these conditions are met – clarity, stability, and notice – that the use of a sanction is justified. As Lazarus asserts, 'absent clarity, criminal law cannot serve well its deterrent function. Nor does societal retribution in the form of a criminal sanction seem fair when society has not given fair notice of what conduct warrants such extreme sanction.'[94]

These points highlight important and unresolved problems in the intersection of environmental and criminal law theory and raise serious doubts about the appropriateness of using criminal sanctions for environmental violations. Nevertheless, strong arguments can be made for the use of such criminal sanctions in this area of law. While too broad in scope to address in this Note, the basic position shared by advocates of criminal sanctions in environmental law is that without them, corporations do not change their behavior and simply write the costs of penalties into their budgets.[95] Certainly when specific intent is provable and individuals willfully have violated environmental laws, thereby knowingly endangering others, criminal sanctions are appropriate.[96] It is the harder cases, where individual officers of corporations are held liable, in the absence of knowledge or intent, that are troubling, and to which we now turn.

## B. Corporate officer liability and the erosion of mens rea

The crucial question in environmental crime is not whether environmental crime should exist at all, but what necessary factors – what level of *mens rea*, what standard of proof, what amount of demonstrable harm to others – should precede use of the criminal sanction. If it should turn out to be the case that those factors, whatever they should be, are realistically unattainable in most (if not all) actual cases, then the regulatory and enforcement model should change, rather than relaxing the conditions precedent to criminal liability for expediency's sake. However, as will be demonstrated, the history of environmental regulation shows just the opposite trend.

1. *The erosion of* mens rea. Since the Clean Air Act Amendments of 1990, corporate officers increasingly have been held personally liable under the criminal law for environmental offenses.[97] Some of those convicted showed clear intent to violate the law, and their culpability was not really in question.[98] However, a fair number of cases – a number that continues to increase as a percentage of all environmental prosecutions – see corporate officers held criminally liable in the absence of any actual knowledge of criminal violations.[99] Most often these convictions are secured under modified versions of the doctrine of respondeat superior, in which the knowledge and *mens rea* of an employee is imputed to officers in the company's management (generally the supervising officer).[100]

Yet another trend in environmental criminal law is the use of the responsible corporate officer doctrine.[101] This doctrine is an even sharper weapon in the hands of prosecutors: all that needs to be shown is that the individual charged with a crime committed by an employee was in fact in a position of ultimate (or nearly ultimate) authority within a corporation.[102] The responsible corporate officer doctrine is nothing more than a theory of strict criminal liability – making it one of only a tiny handful of strict liability offenses punishable as crimes.[103] From its earliest use in *New York Central & Hudson River Railroad*[104] and later elaboration in *United States v. Dotterweich*,[105] the responsible corporate officer doctrine has generally been applied to cases involving public safety regulation.[106] However, some commentators and regulators have begun advocating for its increased application in environmental criminal law as well, arguing that at its most fundamental level, environmental law is the same as public safety regulation.[107]

In reality, corporate decisionmaking is not nearly as coherent as these modified doctrines of respondeat superior would imply:

> Knowledge and decisionmaking authority within [corporations] can be both widely diffuse and fragmented, sometimes by the nature of these entities and sometimes by design. It is therefore difficult to identify any one individual within the institution who possessed and exercised the authority to control the polluting activities, while simultaneously having knowledge of the environmental consequences of those actions.[108]

Given the reality of corporate knowledge and decisionmaking, we should hesitate before applying strict liability criminal sanctions to corporate officers for the malfeasance of their employees, whether intentional or careless. This is because, in short, aggregate corporate knowledge does not exist.[109]

*2. Evolution of doctrines as practical necessity.* The impetus behind the evolution of criminal respondeat superior and the responsible corporate officer doctrine has nothing to do with reality but rather everything to do with making otherwise impossible applications of environmental laws possible. The doctrines emerged as a judicial solution to a gap in proof that could never be overcome.[110] A solution to this evidentiary hurdle had to be put forward if congressional mandates – whether regarding public safety or environmental protection – were to be given any effect whatsoever.[111]

In environmental crime cases, the DOJ faces a crucial problem: how to prove intent or knowledge, which is normally required for a felony conviction. Without establishing a felony-level *mens rea*, offenders may only be convicted of a misdemeanor.[112] The penalties available for misdemeanor violations are much less severe, and in the case of corporate offenders, hardly even amount to a slap on the wrist.[113] Therefore, criminal sanctions against corporate polluters can only be meaningful if they are felony sanctions.

Courts created the criminal respondeat superior and responsible corporate officer doctrines in order to overcome the obvious disconnect between the fiction of the corporate 'person' and the reality of an entity composed of many multiple decisionmakers.[114] Corporations *had* to be able to be criminally liable since they were treated in most other respects as individual rational actors within society.[115] Furthermore, courts could not allow crimes to be committed with impunity behind 'the corporate veil,' and yet it was impractical to 'pierce' that veil in all but the most extraordinary of circumstances.[116] In short, because of the theory of the corporation as a rational individual actor within society, the courts had to find a corresponding legal fiction applicable to that entity's crimes.[117]

Corporations, though, can still only be held liable for fines,[118] and this raises once again the problem of corporations writing off penalties as 'a cost of doing business.' Both the EPA and the DOJ (as well as the general public) gradually began to see that prosecuting corporate officers was the only true way to make corporations pay attention.[119] Once this realization was made, the application of strict-liability doctrines to corporate officials became not only a legal possibility but also a practical necessity.

Therefore the realities faced by the DOJ in prosecuting environmental crimes committed by corporations has led to the erosion of *mens rea* applicable to corporate officers.[120] At a basic level, this raises concerns about the degeneration of protections (constitutional and traditional) granted to individual criminal defendants. Moreover, strict liability for corporations (not including individual officers) makes sense because corporations can only be fined – they cannot go to jail. The fiction of 'imputed knowledge' or 'aggregate knowledge' may be false,[121] but at least it corresponds to the falsehood of the corporation as a 'person.' Applying that same fiction to actual individuals, who have only actual knowledge of facts, results in the possibility of people going to jail (often for a long time) based on a fiction that has no corresponding relationship to that person.

3. *Impossibility of compliance and fairness concerns.* The application of strict criminal liability to corporate officers for policy reasons such as public safety might make sense and even be acceptable if it were the case that such liability would apply fairly narrowly or only for crimes of exceptional magnitude. However, the reality of environmental law is that violations are widespread – through no intentional action on the part of corporations, but rather because of the enormous reach and complexity of environmental laws.[122] Accepting strict corporate officer liability will subject a large number of citizens to potential criminal liability for violations that have none of the hallmarks of bad faith or unlawful intention.

As discussed above, environmental law's unique qualities render it qualitatively different from other areas of law.[123] The combination of over-reaching (through its aspirational motives), instability (from its dynamic evolution), and incomprehensibility (from its extreme complexity) forms an unholy trinity that leads to a hydra-like legal regime. Environmental law imposes unrealistic goals and deadlines, constantly changes the means and standards used to reach those goals, and enumerates details in enormous volume. It is no wonder that nearly seventy percent of corporate officers acknowledged in a 1993 survey that they had been in violation of environmental requirements within the previous year, and that many corporate officials (and some officials at the EPA) maintain that they simply 'cannot comply' with the enormous number of requirements.[124]

Given this complex web of law, it is accepted that corporations will often be in violation of at least some environmental standards and regulations.[125] Accepting strict criminal liability for violations – and allowing harsh sanctions such as imprisonment – seems unfair against this legal background. Since we *know* corporations will commit violations (wittingly or unwittingly), imposing criminal sanctions on some – those that the EPA and DOJ happen by chance to catch – allows society's harshest penalties to be meted out almost at random, with no correlation to the gravity or culpability of the act itself.[112] To use an analogy from elementary school, it is like selecting one child for harsh punishment for talking in class as an example to others – even though every child is talking. The ultimate result is a 'blanket of anxiety' covering an increasing percentage of the American populace, which may be held strictly liable for criminal violations based on the actions of others.[127]

Not only is this random punishment of corporate officers unfair according to traditional notions of criminal law, it also presents a more troubling systemic problem. Strict liability within the current pervasive environmental law regime offers corporations and their officers absolutely no incentive to curb their violations or improve their environmental behavior. If punishment is certain, but only if you are caught, and if violations are certain because perfect compliance is impossible, then it makes no sense to impose the higher costs incurred by strengthened compliance measures. It makes more sense to take a chance that you will not be caught.[128] Therefore, increased strict criminal liability for environmental violations does not actually toughen environmental enforcement at all; rather, it acts unfairly to punish a few corporate officials and to remove incentives towards improving compliance. Not only are the 'poor corporate officers' the victims in such a regime – so is the public at large.

### C. 'Black-box' model of the corporation as the fundamental problem

The fundamental contradiction underlying corporate officer criminal liability is not the incompatibility of environmental and criminal law, but rather the regulatory and enforcement 'superstructure' that has been built upon a shaky foundation: the 'black-box' model of the corporation as a single rational actor. We have seen above that the judicial innovations of criminal respondeat superior and the responsible corporate officer doctrine were created in order to cope with the legal fiction of the corporation. Understanding this legal fiction is essential for the purpose of proposing environmental law reforms that will be more responsive to reality.

The corporate form has developed in part to give business entrepreneurs limited personal liability in their business ventures.[129] Both as a theoretical convenience and practical necessity (to eliminate the need to constantly conceive of a corporation as an aggregated group of individual decisionmakers), a model of corporate firm behavior emerged that characterizes an organization as 'a monolithic entity that essentially makes decisions as a natural individual would.'[130] This notion of the corporation as a fictional 'person' is well known; in the literature of behavioral theory, it is called the 'black-box' theory of the firm.[131] For purposes of simplicity, a corporation's decisions and actions are conceived of as being just as unitary and rational as a normal individual human's.[132]

Naturally, this model requires at least a moderate suspension of belief – no one with any experience in or around a corporation would ever argue that corporate decisionmaking processes and actions are unitary (or even rational in the traditional sense). However, given the necessity of the corporate form, this suspension of belief has been justified as expedient, and any detriment to the corporation has been offset by the enormous advantages gained by the corporation's status as a legal fiction.[133]

However, the black-box model of the corporation has come under harsh criticism in the latter half of the twentieth century, not only for being disconnected from reality, but also for failing to accommodate accurate predictions of corporate behavior.[134] In particular, some commentators claim that the 'unitary rational actor model' directly contradicts empirical evidence of firm decisionmaking behavior.[135] According to a black-box model line of argument, environmental criminal sanctions against corporations are often justified on the basis that corporations are 'rational polluters' who perform simple cost-benefit analyses and violate environmental laws if a violation proves to be more cost-effective.[136]

This justification is based on shaky assumptions, however. Empirical evidence shows that corporate decisionmakers (although not unitary, they can at least be conceived of as a board of directors or upper management) often do take into account non-monetary factors such as the desire to obey the law, the desire to be a good corporate citizen, and the potential reputational damage from environmental accidents.[137] Moreover, as mentioned above, total compliance with the regulatory scheme is often impossible.[138] Those making corporate decisions may be completely unaware of the fact that their planned course of action will violate environmental regulations, or decisions to contravene such regulations may even represent a choice between the less harmful of two (unavoidable) violations.[139]

This unrealistic black-box model of firm behavior is the root cause of the current flaws of American environmental criminal law. The solution to the fiction of the corporate actor was to impose strict liability; this liability was then extended to the corporate officers when initial criminal deterrence failed to influence corporate behavior. But if corporate officer liability is unfair and counterproductive, what can replace it? Or must we accept that corporations can act with relative impunity? Rather than accept a false binary between draconian individual penalties and corporate immunity, environmental criminal law should develop a new theory of enforcement based upon the realities of corporate behavior.

## IV. Thinking outside the 'black box': tailored enforcement

As we have seen above, individual liability under the responsible corporate officer doctrine and other similar near-strict liability doctrines is a necessary byproduct of current regulatory thinking: without the fiction of aggregate corporate knowledge that can be imputed to those in authority, corporations would essentially be immunized from truly deterrent criminal sanctions. However, this individual liability is often unfair and counterproductive. Moreover, it is a sanction premised on a faulty model of the regulated subject – the corporation as a 'black box.'

The solution is not to dispense with corporate criminal sanctions on the grounds that such sanctions are either unattainable or drastically unfair. Criminal penalties are essential to a coherent and effective scheme of environmental regulation. However, after understanding that the root cause of current contradictions is the black-box theory of the rational corporation, it makes more sense to alter regulatory and enforcement regimes to accommodate more realistic models of the regulated community. As different types of organizations are controlled and motivated by different forces, any effective regulatory and enforcement regime should be crafted to respond to these differences rather than force distinct types of actors to conform to a 'one-size-fits-all' paradigm.

### A. Tailored enforcement: distinct regulatory and prosecutorial standards

By 'tailored enforcement,' I mean to describe an enforcement regime that assigns different penalties to offenders for the same offense according to their organization type. Essentially, a regime of tailored enforcement is based on the assumption that different organizations have fundamentally divergent motives, organizational structures, and decisionmaking processes, so they each respond to different incentives and sanctions.[140] It is not based on the argument that corporations deserve lighter treatment than other actors in society. Indeed, it accepts the argument that corporate activity must be regulated and, when appropriate, punished. Tailored enforcement simply recognizes that imposing different types of penalties addresses the reality of the corporate entity in a more efficient manner than the current 'command and control' model of regulation.

Starting with the recognition that a vast range of organizational forms behave in a vast variety of different ways, tailored enforcement seeks to exploit those differences and 'target' enforcement strategies to organization type.[141] This Note has touched upon the disproportionate amount of criminal enforcement against small business owners and has argued that the reason – other than the political reason of boosting the DOJ's criminal-enforcement scorecard – is that generally the *mens rea* required for felony convictions is easier to prove in a small or close corporation setting, without resort to judicial strict liability constructs.[142] While unfair, the disproportionate prosecution of small businesses highlights the key tension that tailored enforcement seeks to relieve: faced with limited resources, the EPA and DOJ will more likely use those resources to fight cases they have a better chance of winning. To occasionally score a large political victory, they will seize on unpopular or otherwise vulnerable large corporations and use strict liability tactics to force large judgments or settlements. However, these large verdicts will be rare, because a criminal prosecution against wealthy and sophisticated defendants is extremely costly.

The result is that a few corporate officials are randomly and unfairly threatened with or sentenced to jail time, while the lion's share of the penal burden is borne by smaller, easier-to-convict companies.[143] This is true even though large corporations are presumably responsible for the vast majority of environmental violations (and pollution by volume)[144] and are subject to the harsh penalty of individual strict liability for corporate officers, because the penalty, as we have seen, acts neither as an effective deterrent of violations nor as an incentive for innovation and heightened compliance.

Tailored enforcement would replace the current one-size-fits-all regime with a stratified approach to enforcing environmental regulations. While it is beyond the scope of this Note to propose a comprehensive scheme of tailored enforcement, the following suggestions may provide a helpful starting point. First of all, environmental enforcement should proceed according to organization type. Large, publicly held firms have far more complex decisionmaking processes and widespread corporate authority among personnel than small, closely held companies. As demonstrated above, this leads either to increased convictions and jail time for smaller companies' 'officers' or to the occasionally unfair threat or imposition of huge fines and jail time on corporate officers of large companies. If environmental laws are to lead to increased compliance, the penalties for violating those laws should bear some relation to the actor involved. For instance, large fines (on the order of those in the *Koch* litigation) may serve as a deterrent for large firms but are likely to bankrupt smaller companies. Incarceration will likely act as an effective deterrent for most people, but the threat is much more real to persons operating smaller businesses – those who may not have the legal resources to know the complexities of environmental laws or to wage an effective defense against the DOJ.

Tailored enforcement would assess penalties based upon organization type in order to ameliorate these disparities. Fines might be assessed not only according to the offense but also on the basis of company value or market capitalization. This would help ensure that the penalties serve the same deterrent function regardless of a firm's ability to pay. Hopefully, it would eliminate the fact that for some violations, small companies go bankrupt while others factor the fine into their annual budgets.

Along the same lines, penalties should increase for second- and third-time violators. While ignorance of the complex environmental regulations may practically (and legitimately) be an excuse for initial violations, a conviction or judgment against a company puts that company on notice that it is engaging in illegal behavior. Further offenses are therefore less justified and should incur larger penalties. A fine-multiple system similar to that used in antitrust cases would work very well in environmental crime.

Finally, a regime of tailored enforcement would also delay the use of strict liability constructs until repeat violations are shown. Under such a 'multiple offender' system, responsible corporate officers would not face draconian penalties for offenses they possibly knew nothing about or that were truly 'administrative offenses.' However, as above, an initial judgment puts corporate officers on notice not only that their company is in violation of the law, but would also serve as notice that they might be held personally liable for future offenses. For such future offenses, criminal prosecution and incarceration are more justified because the traditional notice requirement of criminal law is satisfied. Allowing criminal penalties to be imposed at this stage also serves environmental enforcement's goal of eliminating violations thought to be 'a cost of doing business.'

### B. Basis in existing distinctions

Arguments can be made that requiring different punishments for crimes committed by different types of organizations somehow denies organizations equal rights or unfairly benefits some to the detriment of others. However, granting all organizations the same procedural protections and threatening them with the same sanctions has practically the same effect: large corporations are treated more lightly *overall* because they have more resources to fight the DOJ. The converse of that light-handed treatment is that when singled out, corporate officers of large corporations enjoy substantially fewer procedural rights than their counterparts in small businesses, through the application of criminal respondeat superior or the responsible corporate officer doctrine.

A further counterargument to the 'equal treatment' argument is that we routinely accord different organization types special treatment. Corporations are legal 'persons' but are denied certain constitutional rights.[145] Close corporations are treated differently from publicly-held corporations in myriad ways, an important one being the rights given to and duties owed to shareholders.[146] Corporations, partnerships, and individuals are all taxed differently.[147] Close corporations may be pierced occasionally, but this will never happen to large public corporations.[148] These are just a few of the ways in which we discriminate among organizational actors based on the practical differences between each. Similarly, tailored enforcement could be arranged among any number of variable factors, including size, closely- or publicly-held status, tax status, permit status, and industry sector. The ultimate determinants should not be arbitrary lines, but rather distinctions based on relevant differences in organizational behavior.

### C. Benefits of tailored enforcement

Tailored enforcement would allow the EPA and DOJ to accomplish their jobs more effectively with their limited resources. Under the current regime, too many resources are spent sending small polluters to jail, while large polluters generally go unscathed. By adjusting standards of proof (in prosecutions) and regulatory methods (in ordinary business) to organization type, the EPA and DOJ will be able to deliver the type of incentive or sanction most effective against that type of entity. Large enough monetary fines can – or at least should – dissuade corporate polluters. For continued violators or for particularly egregious acts, criminal sanctions will be available to rid the corporation and society of the offending officer – but the application of those harsh sanctions will be fair.

Tailored enforcement also dovetails nicely with contemporary proposals for reform elsewhere in environmental law, such as tailored regulation.[149] By adjusting environmental laws to be more responsive to the behavior of corporations, environmental protection can become an effective system, as opposed to a monolithic, impossibly complex, and overburdensome bureaucracy.

### V. Conclusion

We have examined the deficiencies of the current 'command and control' environmental regulatory and enforcement paradigm and found it to be unfair to the actors involved and inefficient in achieving social goals of greater environmental protection. The root cause of this problem is not, as some commentators argue, a fundamental disjunction between environmental and criminal law, but rather an insufficient theory of organizational behavior upon which we have built an elaborate but ineffective system of regulation and enforcement. By abandoning the black-box theory of organizations in favor of more contemporary, dynamic, and accurate models, we will be able to structure incentives and penalties according to organization type. This system of tailored enforcement should both increase justice and decrease environmental crime.

## Notes

1 On the early history of environmental regulation, see Richard J. Lazarus, *Meeting the Demands of Integration in the Evolution of Environmental Criminal Law: Reforming Environmental Criminal Law*, 83 GEO. L.J. 2407 (1995).

2 Robert W. Adler & Charles Lord, *Environmental Crime: Raising the Stakes*, 59 GEO. WASH. L. REV. 781, 782 (1991). The limited amount of government resources, and the low priority granted to the Environmental Protection Agency generally, practically guaranteed a low chance of detection of a violation. Lazarus, *supra* note 1, at 2410–12.

3 Lazarus, *supra* note 1, at 2446–53, 2455–65 (describing the preventive actions of Congress, the Department of Justice, and the Environmental Protection Agency in the 1980s).

4 *Id.* at 2415–16.

5 The Clean Air Act Amendments of 1990, for example, were several orders of magnitude longer than the original Clean Air Act. *Id* at 2426 n.78: *see also* WILLIAM H. RODGERS. ENVIRONMENTAL LAW § 3.1A (Supp. 1 2002) (discussing the enactment of the Clean Air Act Amendments of 1990).

6 *See* Judson W. Starr, *Turbulent Times at Justice and EPA: The Origins of Environmental Criminal Prosecutions and the Work That Remains*, 59 GEO. WASH. L. REV. 900 (1991) (describing the inception of environmental criminal enforcement at the two agencies and the coordinated effort between them). The number of EPA investigators continued to increase even after this initial time period. *See* Pollution Prosecution Act of 1990. 42 U.S.C. § 4321 (2000) (increasing the EPA staff of investigators to at least 200 (from approximately 50) by 1995).

7 G. Nelson Smith, Iii, *No Longer Just a Cost of Doing Business: Criminal Liability of Corporate Officials Violations of the Clean Water Act and the Resource Conservation and Recovery Act*, 53 LA. L. REV. 119, 122 (1992); *see also* David B. Spence, *The Shadow of the Rational Polluter: Rethinking the Role of Rational Actor Models in Environmental Law*, 89 CAL. L. REV. 917, 918 (2001); Lazarus, *supra* note 1, at 2452.

8 OFFICE OF ENFORCEMENT, U.S. ENVTL. PROT. AGENCY, ENFORCEMENT ACCOMPLISHMENTS REPORT, FISCAL YEAR 1993, 2–2 and app. (1994); Starr. *supra* note 6 at 901 nn.3–4.

9 Kathleen Brickey, *Environmental Crime at the Crossroads: The Intersection of Environmental and Criminal Law Theory*, 71 TUL. L. REV. 487, 489 n.5 (1996); *see also* Susan F Mandiberg, *Moral Issues in Environmental Crime.* 7 FORDHAM ENVTL. L.J. 881 (1996) (discussing the moral calculus of environmental law and the public rights at stake).

10 *See* Starr, *supra* note 6 (detailing the history of prosecuting individual corporate officers for company crimes).

11 A more detailed discussion of these and other criticisms of corporate criminal liability in environmental law will be provided in Part III.

12 Lazarus, *supra* note 1, at 2421–22.

13 Brickey, *supra* note 9, at 490–91.

14 John C. Coffee, Jr., *Does 'Unlawful' Mean 'Criminal'?: Reflections on the Disappearing Tort/ Crime Distinction in American Law*, 71 B.U. L. REV. 193, 219–20 (1991) (contending that harsh environmental sanctions entangle a large proportion of the American workforce with criminal law and create undesirable levels of anxiety); *see also* Stuart P. Green, *Why It's a Crime to Tear the Tag Off a Mattress: Over-criminalization and the Moral Content of Regulatory Offenses*, 46 EMORY L.J. 1533, 1535 (1997) (positing that the over-criminalization of regulatory crimes undermines the efficacy of punishment, wastes enforcement resources, and invites selective prosecution).

15 There is an increasing amount of legal scholarship on various reforms to the current archaic system of regulation and enforcement. Among these reforms are emissions trading, resource-allocation models, incentive-based regulation, and research and development subsidies. While many of these reforms are admirable ideas, they are all beyond the scope of this Note.

16 For one brief discussion of tailored regulation, see Timothy F. Malloy, *Regulating by Incentives: Myths, Models, and Micromarkets*, 80 TEXAS L. REV. 531, 539 (2002) (remarking that environmental regulators have employed tailored regulation, albeit in very rare instances).

17 *See* Carol Cole, *Koch Slapped with Astronomical Indictment: Prison, Fines, Are Possible.* OCTANE WK., Oct. 2, 2000, *available at* 2000 WL 4312570. Benzene is a colorless liquid that vaporizes

quickly. It is a natural component of crude oil and is produced as a byproduct when oil is refined. Andrea Jares, *Koch. 4 Employees Indicted*, CORPUS CHRISTI CALLER-TIMES. Sept. 29, 2000, at A1.

18  Jeremy Schwartz, *Koch Covered Up Its Violations*. CORPUS CHRISTI CALLER-TIMES. Sept. 30, 2000, at Al.

19  *See Id.*

20  *Id.*

21  Press Release, Koch Petroleum Groups, All Charges Against Koch Industries, Koch Petroleum and Employees Dropped (Apr. 9, 2001), *available at* http://www.Kochind.com/articles/372. asp [hereinafter Koch Petroleum Groups].

22  *Id.*

23  *Id.*

24  Cole, *supra* note 17.

25  *Id.*

26  *Id.* Statutory liability for responsible corporate officers is established in the Clean Air Act, 42 U.S.C. § 7413(c)(6) (2000), and the Clean Water Act, 33 U.S.C. § 1319(c)(6) (2000). For elaboration of the responsible corporate officer doctrine, see *United States v. Park*, 421 U.S. 658, 673–74 (1975) (noting that, to be liable, an employee need only have a position that conferred him the authority to either have prevented or corrected the violation).

27  James Pinkerton, *Koch Goes to Trial This Week in Pollution Case*, HOUS. CHRON., Apr. 8, 2001, at B1.

28  *Id.*

29  *Id.*

30  *Id.*

31  Koch Petroleum Groups, *supra* note 21.

32  *Id.*

33  *See, e.g.,* Adler & Lord, *supra* note 2, at 787–88 (noting that, from an ethical point of view the threat of widespread public harm justifies stronger penalties for environmental crimes than for many other crimes).

34  Koch maintained that benzene levels remained safe, and the Justice Department claimed that it would not introduce evidence that the community had been harmed or placed at risk. Pinkerton.supra note 27.

35  Koch Petroleum Groups, *supra* note 21.

36  Adler & Lord, *supra* note 2, at 795–96.

37  For further discussion of penalties as 'taxes,' see Robert Cooter, *Prices and Sanctions*, 84 COLUM. L. REV. 1523, 1550–52 (1984).

38  Koch claimed throughout the litigation that the levels of benzene in the air throughout the time of the violations were never dangerously high. Jares, *supra* note 17. Prosecutors, perhaps because a showing of harm under the Clean Air Act is unnecessary, did not plan on introducing evidence of benzene's hazardous effects at the trial. Dan Parker, *Koch Jurors to Be Chosen*, CORPUS CHRISTI CALLER-TIMES, Apr. 9, 2001, at B1. Nevertheless, a discharge of fifteen times the level of benzene deemed to be safe, regardless of its effects in this particular instance, is still a major cause of concern for the public health.

39  Pinkerton, *supra* note 27.

40  *See* Lazarus, *supra* note 1, at 2429–40; Brickey, *supra* note 9, at 501–04; Kevin A. Gaynor, *A System Spinning Out of Control*, ENVTL. F., May–June 1990, at 28–29 (all discussing the vast labyrinth of environmental regulations and noting that by the EPA's own admission, full compliance is not realistic). For further discussion of this issue, see *infra* subpart III(A).

41  *See* Koch Petroleum Groups, *supra* note 21.

42  Tara Copp. *Koch Industries Indictment Indicative of More Aggressive Justice Department*. CORPUS CHRISTI CALLER-TIMES, Sept. 30, 2000, at A1.

43  Lazarus. *supra* note 1, at 2456–65.

44  *See, e.g.,* Adler & Lord, *supra* note 2, at 810–15 (discussing the under-enforcement of criminal violations of major U.S. companies).

45  Kathlyn Brickey reports that, especially during the formative years of the Environmental Crimes Unit, cases against smaller, 'Mom and Pop' businesses were prosecuted far more often than cases against large companies. Often the cases against the larger companies were more meritorious both on the facts of the cases and the amount of harm done to the community. Brickey, *supra* note 9, at 496.

46  *See* Andrew S. Hogeland, *Criminal Enforcement of Environmental Laws*, 75 MASS. L. REV. 112, 116–17 (1990) (discussing the 'sporadic and decentralized' enforcement of federal environmental crimes); Lazarus, *supra* note 1, at 2456–65 (criticizing the current level of prosecutorial discretion given to the Environmental Crimes Unit). *But see* Lois J. Schiffer & James F. Simon. *The Reality of Prosecuting Environmental Criminals: A Response to Professor*

*Lazarus*, 83 GEO. L.J. 2531 (1995) (offering a rebuttal to Professor Lazarus from staff attorneys of the Environmental Crimes Unit and addressing the 'reality' of environmental prosecutions).

47  This is, of course, the doctrine of respondeat superior. *See* W. PAGE KEETON ET AL., PROSSER & KEETON ON THE LAW OF TORTS §§ 69–71 (5th ed. 1984) (discussing vicarious liability in the employment relationship).

48  *Id.* § 2 (distinguishing tortious liability from criminal liability).

49  *See* WAYNE R. LAFAVE & AUSTIN W. SCOTT, CRIMINAL LAW § 3.4a (2d ed. 1986) ('The *basic premise that for criminal liability some* mens rea is required is expressed by the Latin maxim *actus not facit reum nisi sit rea* (an act does not make one guilty unless his mind is guilty).').

50  See, e.g., N.Y. Cent. & Hudson River R.R. v. United States, 212 U.S. 481, 494–95 (1909) (holding that corporations can commit crimes that consist of purposely doing things prohibited by statute, and in such case they can be charged with the knowledge of acts of their agents who act within their authority); United States v. Dotterweich, 320 U.S. 277 (1943) (holding a pharmaceutical company president responsible for the shipment of adulterated drugs in interstate commerce); United States v. Park, 421 U.S. 658 (1975) (holding a grocery chain president liable for filthy warehouse conditions).

51  *See Park*, 421 U.S. at 658.

52  Andrea Jares, *Koch Gets OSHA Safety Award*, CORPUS CHRISTI CALLER-TIMES, Nov. 17, 2000, at C9 (reporting that Koch's Corpus Christi sites were two of only thirteen refineries in the country designated as star sites by OSHA).

53  Jeremy Schwartz, *supra* note 18, at A1.

54  *See, e.g.*, Environmental Protection Agency, Final Policy Statement, Incentives for Self-Policing: Discovery, Disclosure, Correction and Prevention of Violations, 60 Fed. Reg. 66, 706–12 (Dec. 22, 1995) (detailing a plan for penalty reductions conditioned upon prompt compliance with a list of eight factors; reductions range from 0% to 75% of the initial penalty).

55  Use of the responsible corporate officer doctrine is on the rise in environmental case. Steven Zipperman, Comment, *The Park Doctrine – Application of Strict Criminal Liability to Corporate Individuals for Violation of Environmental Crimes*, 10 UCLA J. ENVTL. L & POL'Y 123. 166 (1991); Smith, *supra* note 7, at 122–27.

56  Spence, *supra* note 7 at 923.

57  *See*, e.g.. Clean Water Act, 33 U.S.C. § 1319(c)(1) (2000); Clean Air Act, 42 U.S.C. § 7413(c)(4) (1994) (both allowing criminal liability to be imposed on 'responsible corporate officers').

58  LAFAVE & SCOTT, *supra* note 49, §§: 1.2, 3.1. Public welfare and other strict-liability offenses are obvious exceptions to this general principle. However, strict-liability offenses are rare and generally disfavored. *Id.* § 3.8. Furthermore, most strict-liability offenses carry relatively light penalties such as fines. Heavy penalties, including jail time, generally indicate a requirement of fault. *Id.* at 3.8, 3.9.

59  Lazarus, *supra* note 1, at 2434.

60  For a discussion of the complexity and wide-ranging scope of environmental law, see *infra* subpart III(A).

61  *See supra* notes 3–8 and accompanying text.

62  Mark A. Cohen, *Environmental Crime and Punishment: Legal/Economic Theory and Empirical Evidence on Enforcement of Federal Environmental Statutes*, 82 J. CRIM. L. & CRIMINOLOGY 1054, 1056 (1992); Starr, *supra* note 6, at 901.

63  Brickey, *supra* note 9, at 490–91.

64  Smith, *supra* note 7, at 154–56.

65  *See supra* text accompanying note 9.

66  Adler & Lord, *supra* note 2, at 792–94, 795–96.

67  *Id.* at 795–97.

68  Commentators have put forward a number of strategies to improve on the 'command and control' model of environmental regulation. *See generally* Malloy, *supra* note 16 (discussing incentive-based regulation as a means of increasing front-end prevention of environmental problems); Robert W. Hahn & Robert N. Stavins, *Incentive-Based Environmental Regulation: A New Era from an Old Idea?*, 18 ECOLOGY L.Q. 1 (1991) (arguing for market-based mechanisms to encourage compliance and innovation). Of course, incentive-based regulation is not without its *critics. See* Rena I. Steinzor, *Reinventing Environmental Regulation: The Dangerous Journey from Command to Self-Control*, 22 HARV. ENVTL. L. REV. 103, 151–52 (1998) (suggesting that corporations are not good candidates for self-regulation and that empirical data on incentive-based regulation are lacking).

69  Lazarus, *supra* note 1, at 2421.

70  *See* Susan Hedman, *Expressive Functions of Criminal Sanctions in Environmental Law*, 59 GFO. WASH. L. REV. 889, 889 (1991) (pointing to the 'expressive capacity of criminal law – and]

its unique ability to give force and symbolic representation to moral values by conveying condemnation and disgrace').

71 Mandiberg, *supra* note 9; *see also* Christopher H. Schroeder, *Cool Analysis Versus Moral Outrage in the Development of Federal Environmental Criminal Lax,* 35 WM. & MARY L. REV. 251 264–68 (1993) (tracing the development of environmental law and detailing periods of 'outrage' at violations followed by periods of 'cool analysis' for developing policy). Schroeder does note, however, that at times the moral outrage colors the cool analysis and results in overreaction. *Id.* at 268.

72 While there probably has been some reduction in the amount of environmental crime, any generalization about the effect of criminal sanctions may be premature (or even impossible) given the low rate of detection of environmental violations. See Lazarus, *supra* note I, at 2513 (discussing the 'great difficulty' of such detection).

73 Brickey, *supra* note 9, at 487, 490.

74 Lazarus, *supra* note 1, at 2424.

75 *Id.*

76 *See, e.g.,* Pub. L. 91–604, § 202(b)(1)(a), 84 Stat. 1676, 1690 (1970) (requiring a 90% reduction in certain automobile emissions by 1975).

77 Indeed, the EPA itself 'acknowledged that meeting the Clean Air Act requirements in the Los Angeles area 'would impose requirements so draconian as to remake life in the South Coast Basin … [The EPA] would have to prohibit most traffic, shut down major business activity, curtail the use of important consumer goods, and dramatically restrict all aspects of social and economic life.' Lazarus, *supra* note I, at 2425–26 (quoting the EPA statement at 53 Fed. Reg. 49,494, 49,495 (Dec. 7, 1988)).

78 Pub. L. 92–500, § 101(a)(1), 86 Stat. 816, 816 (1972).

79 *See, e.g.,* ENVTL. PROT. AGENCY, PROGRESS IN WATER QUALITY: AN EVALUATION OF THE NATIONAL INVESTMENT IN MUNICIPAL WASTEWATER TREATMENT, *available at* http://www.epa.gov/owm/wquality/execsum.pdf (positing that '[s]erious ecological problems remain to be solved for many of the nation's waterways').

80 Lazarus, *supra* note 1, at 2426.

81 *Id.* at 2426–27.

82 *Id.* at 2427.

83 Brickey, *supra* note 9, at 500–01.

84 Lazarus, *supra* note I, at 2429.

85 *Id.* at 2436. There are approximately 4,000 pages of regulation under the Clean Air Act alone. *Id.*

86 *Id.* at 2431.

87 *Id.*

88 *Id.* at 2440-45; Coffee, supra note 14, at 208; John C. Coffee, Jr., *Paradigms Lost: The Blurring of the Criminal and Civil Law Models – And What Can Be Done About It.* 101 YALE L.J. 1875, 1875–76 (1992).

89 William J. Stuntz, *The Pathological Politics of Criminal Law,* 100 MICH. L. REV. 505, 512–13 (2001).

90 Paris Adult Theatre I v. Slaton. 413 U.S. 49, 86 (1973): LAFAVE & SCOTT. *supra* note 49 § 1.2(b).

91 Henry M. Hart, *The Aims of the Criminal Law,* 23 LAW & CONTEMP. PROBS., Summer 1958, at 401.

92 *Id.* at 404–05.

93 *Id.*; Brickey, *supra* note 9, at 505; Coffee, *supra* note 14, at 201.

94 Lazarus, *supra* note 1, at 2444.

95 *See. e.g.,* Daniel R. Fischel & Alan O. Sykes, *Corporate Crime,* 25 J. LEGAL STUD. 319 (1996) (offering an overview of some responses to corporate crime); Smith, *supra* note 7, at 122 (responding to the felony amendments to the Clean Water Act and the Resource Conservation and Recovery Act and arguing that criminal liability means that violations are no longer just a 'cost of doing business'); Lawrence Friedman, *In Defense of Corporate Criminal Liability,* 23 HARV. J.L. & PUB. POLY 833 (2000) (arguing that without criminal liability corporations have no adequate incentive to obey some laws).

96 Kathleen Brickey, for instance, notes the high level of public support for strong environmental penalties, especially in the case of intentional wrongdoers such as the hypothetical 'midnight dumper.' Brickey, *supra* note 9, at 488–89.

97 Ruth Ann Weidel et al., *The Erosion of Mens Rea in Environmental Criminal Prosecutions,* 21 SETON HALL L. REV. I 100, 1104–05, 1123 (1990); Gaynor, *supra* note 40, at 28–29.

98 For an interesting example, see the discussion of the Pozsgai case in Adler & Lord. *supra* note 2 at 784–86.

99  Gaynor, *supra* note 40, at 28–29; see also Coffee, *supra* note 14, at 210 (noting that *mens rea* is becoming less important to finding a criminal violation).

100 Weidel et al., *supra* note 97, at 1101; Eric Colvin, *Corporate Personality and Criminal Liability*, 6 CRIM. L.F. 1, 6–8 (1995): *see also* Kenneth A. Hodson et al., *The Prosecution of Corporations and Corporate Officers for Environmental Crimes: Limiting One's Exposure for Environmental Criminal Liability*, 34 ARIZ. L. REV. 553 (1992) (offering a practicing white-collar criminal defense attorney's perspective on ways to avoid environmental criminal liability).

101 Jennifer Arlen & Reiner Kraakman, *Controlling Corporate Misconduct: An Analysis of Corporate Liability Regimes*, 72 N.Y.U. L. REV. 687, 689–90 (1997); Coffee, *supra* note 14, at 213–15.

102 United States v. Park, 421 U.S. 658, 673–74 (1975); *see also* United States v. Weitzenhoff, 35 F.3d 1275 (9th Cir. 1994) (holding senior corporate officers liable even when they did not know that their actions constituted a violation of environmental law). *See generally* Zipperman, *supra* note 55, at 129–34 (discussing the *Park* doctrine and advocating its widespread use against corporate environmental crime).

103 *See generally* Zipperman, *supra* note 55. Arlen & Kraakman, *supra* note 101, at 689–90.

104 212 U.S. 481 (1909).

105 320 U.S. 277 (1943).

106 *See Weitzenhoff*, 35 F.3d at 1283–86 (discussing the history of the responsible corporate officer doctrine).

107 *See* Zipperman, *supra* note 55, at 123 (arguing that '[i]mposing criminal sanctions upon corporate officers in response to a corporation's unlawful disposal of hazardous waste' is in accord with the traditional application of strict liability in criminal law where 'risk of injury to the public has superior importance to and is unrelated to the violator's intent').

108 Lazarus, *supra* note 1, at 2422.

109 *See* Thomas A. Hagemann & Joseph Grinstein, *The Mythology of Aggregate Corporate Knowledge: A Deconstruction*, 65 GEO. WASH. L. REV. 210 (1997) (arguing that the overwhelming complexity of modern organizations renders the notion of an aggregate corporate knowledge nearly absurd).

110 LAFAVE & SCOTT, *supra* note 49, § 3.10.

111 *See* Stan, *supra* note 6 (discussing the need for a tool to ease the burden of proof in cases of organizational crime).

112 *See* Clean Water Act. 33 U.S.C. § 1319(c)(3)(A) (Supp. 2000); Clean Air Act, 42 U.S.C. 7413(c) (1994) (both establishing a dichotomy between misdemeanor and felony violations based on willfulness or knowledge).

113 Most fines are in the $1,000 to $2,000 range.

114 Annie Geraghty, *Corporate Criminal Liabiliby*, 39 AM. CRIM. L. REV. 327, 328 (2002).

115 *Id.*

116 Public corporations are rarely, if ever, 'pierced.' Rebecca J. Huss, *Revamping Veil Piercing for All Limited Liability Entities: Forcing the Common Law Doctrine into the Statutory Age*, 70 U. CIN. L. REV. 95, 111 (2001). Moreover, piercing the corporate entity results generally in the dissolution of the corporation; therefore, even for fairly heinous environmental crimes, it is unlikely that courts would apply this penalty to a large corporation over one criminal charge.

117 Geraghty, *supra* note 114, at 328.

118 There are exceptions, such as the 'corporate death penalty' under the Federal Sentencing Guidelines. U.S. SENTENCING GUIDELINES MANUAL § RCIA (2002) (stating that 'if the court determines that the organization operated primarily for a criminal purpose or primarily by criminal means, the fine shall be set at an amount (subject to the statutory maximum) sufficient to divest the organization of all its net assets').

119 *See* Judson W. Starr, *Countering Environmental Crimes*, 13 B.C. ENVTL. AFF. L. RFV. 379, 374–80 (1986) (stating that Congress responded to public concern about environmental enforcement by instituting substantial criminal penalties, including incarceration); Starr. *supra* note 6, at 900–01 (describing the increasing incidence and duration of criminal sanctions due to public pressure for environmental compliance): Schroeder, *supra* note 71, at 263–65 (detailing periods of public outrage at corporate environmental violations and the corresponding increases in enforcement actions and criminal prosecutions of individuals and entities).

120 See generally Weidel et al., *supra* note 97, at 1101 (attributing the erosion of the traditional requirement of mens rea to legislative fiat and judicial interpretation in response to society's heightened environmental awareness and attendant emphasis on criminalizing polluters' conduct). Unfortunately, the emphasis on criminal liability over civil liability – in order to show that environmental law has 'teeth' and to increase the total number of 'criminal convictions' secured by the Environmental Crimes Section – has also led to an increased number of prosecutions of small, 'Mom and Pop' businesses. See discussion *supra* note 13 and accompanying text. Naturally, in a small business it is much easier to prove the *mens*

*rea* of business owners or managers because there are fewer employees and each is subject to greater supervision. It is also obvious that small businesses rarely have the resources to fight protracted court cases with the DOJ.

121 Hagemann & Grinstein, *supra* note 109, at 211.

122 See Brickey, *supra* note 9, at 500 ('By mandating unattainable goals, environmental laws impose extraordinarily high standards and simultaneously assure the inability of the regulated community to comply.').

123 See discussion *supra* subpart III(A).

124 Marianne Lavelle, *Environment Vise: Law, Compliance; Companies Stuff Up and Struggle to Stay Ahead of the Green Machine.* NAT'L L.J., Aug. 30, 1993, at S 1.

125 Brickey, *supra* note 9, at 500.

126 *See* Jennifer Arlen, *The Potentially Perverse Effects of Corporate Criminal Liability*, 23 J. LEGAL. STUD. 833. 835 (1994) (observing that many violations of corporate crimes, including environmental crimes, are not easily detected by the government).

127 *See generally* Coffee, *supra* note 88, at 1881, 1887–90 (describing the ill effects of overcriminalization primarily in terms of a regime of liability that encompasses far too broad a sector of the population, and specifically noting that among the ill effects of overcriminalization is the fear and anxiety of those regulated of committing an unintentional violation).

128 Cf Arlen, *supra* note 126, at 843 (suggesting that self-policing by corporations may even decline under strict liability if such measures increase the risk of the undeterred violator being caught).

129 MELVIN ARON EISENBERG, CORPORATIONS AND OTHER BUSINESS ASSOCIATIONS 219 (8th ed. unabr. 2000).

130 Malloy, *supra* note 16, at 533.

131 *See* Michael C. Jensen & William H. Meckling, *Theory of the Firm: Managerial Behavior, Agency Costs and Ownership Structure*, 3 J. FIN. ECON. 305, 306-07, 310 (1976) (describing and criticizing the black-box theory of firm behavior).

132 See *Id.* at 306–09.

133 *See* JESSE H. CHOPER ET AL., CASES AND MATERIALS ON CORPORATIONS 1–3 (5th ed. 2000) (discussing the benefits of the corporate form: limited liability, perpetual existence, transferability of ownership, and centralized management).

134 See Malloy. supra note 16 at 534–35 (describing the literature criticizing the black-box model): Spence, supra note 7, at 960–77 (concluding that the traditional view fails to explain the behavior of many regulated films).

135 *See* Spence, *supra* note 7, at 960 ('[I]t is clear that for many firms. the complexity critique offers a more accurate description of their relationship with the regulatory system than does the rational polluter model.').

136 *Id.* at 919–21.

137 *Id.* at 970.

138 *See* Lavelle, *supra* note 124; *see also* Lazarus, *supra* note 1.

139 *See* Spence, supra note 7, at 972 ('[N]oncompliance may be due to industry ignorance of the existence of regulatory requirements, or misunderstanding, or disagreements about their meaning.').

140 A regime of tailored enforcement also takes for granted a wider use of tailored regulation, which makes the same assumptions about organizational behavior. While tailored enforcement would theoretically work in a simple command and control regulatory regime, such a system of enforcement would be vulnerable to the criticism that for the same set of rules, legally equivalent actors are treated differently. The essence of tailored regulation, by contrast, is that different rules should apply to different actors so that rules may be crafted to obtain optimal results. Malloy, *supra* note 16, at 535–36; see also Colin S. Diver, *The Optimal Precision of Administrative Rules*, 93 YALE L.J. 65, 67–76 (1983) (describing a sliding scale of rules for three variables-transparency, accessibility, and congruency-and arguing that the optimal precision will be some combination of the three, but will change according to circumstance and the actors involved).

141 It is beyond the scope of this Note to propose a comprehensive scheme of tailored enforcement. Rather, this Note is meant as a proposal for further study – theoretical as well as empirical – of the effect that certain enforcement strategies have on corporate behavior.

142 See *supra* note 13 and accompanying text.

143 Adler & Lord, *supra* note 2, at 796–97, 795 96.

144 *Id.* at 796.

145 Corporations are not entitled to all 'personal guarantees' granted to natural individuals under the Constitution. First Nat'l Bank of Boston v. Bellotti, 435 U.S. 765, 779 n.14 (1978), This includes, for instance, the denial of the Fifth Amendment right against self-incrimination.

Wilson v. United States, 221 U.S. 361 (1911), and the right to privacy, United States v. Morton Salt Co.. 338 U.S. 632 (1950).

146 Galler v. Galler, 203 N.E.2d 577, 584 (Ill, 1964).

147 For example, Subchapter C of the Internal Revenue Code provides that corporations are taxed directly (of course, dividends to shareholders are taxed as well), whereas Subchapter K of the Code provides for pass-through taxation of partnerships.

148 *See, e.g.*, Robert B. Thompson, *Piercing the Corporate Veil: An Empirical Study*, 76 CORNELL L. REV. 1036, 1044, 1055 tbl.7 (1991) (stating that of approximately 1,600 reported veil-piercing cases, none were of publicly held corporations, and all of the cases involved corporations with fewer than ten shareholders).

149 *See generally* Malloy, *supra* note 16 (discussing the resource-allocation model as a basis for tailored regulation).

# 36. Reducing vulnerabilities to crime of the European waste management industry: the research base and the prospects for policy*

*Nicholas Dorn, Stijn Van Daele and Tom Vander Beken*

### Introduction: looking for problems

Illegal dumping of waste, sometimes involving its transport from the European Union to developing countries, is an issue becoming more visible in the public consciousness and in the political conscience. This is largely due to the efforts of NGOs which, over the years, have not only provided information on otherwise neglected scandals, but also sometimes indulge in high-profile public actions – forcing the administrative and enforcement agencies to 'do something'. The European Commission has, moreover, become more willing to be moved, as the following press report illustrates.

Illegal Waste Shipment: European Environment Commissioner Stavros Dimas travels to Estonia on 28th of September to support the investigation of an illegal waste shipment to the Ivory Coast by the Probo Koala. Commissioner Dimas is on a fact-finding mission to Paldiski harbour, where Greenpeace blocked the ship's departure, followed by a search of the Estonian authorities which revealed the presence of highly toxic substances on board. 'It is shocking that toxic waste from Europe reached the Ivory Coast causing so much human suffering and damage to the environment. We have European waste shipment regulations which ban such export, but apparently the law was broken.'[1]

In the European Union, the boarder policy background to the escalation of interest is the prospect that environmental policy may have become a lever through which criminal law can be advanced at a European level, rather than being a matter only for Member States. This prospect has recently been brought closer, quite recently and perhaps controversially, by a decision of the European Court of Justice.

> The Court of Justice upheld today the Commission's claim that the European Community, and not just the European Union, could prescribe criminal punishments in a Community directive or other measure. The Court handed down its judgment in *Case C-176/03 Commission v. Council*.

---

* From *European Journal of Crime, Criminal Law and Criminal Justice* (2007), 15(1), 23–36.

[…] This judgment is the first time the Court has expressly stated that the Community has the power to require member States to adopt criminal legislation.[2]

In the light of the judgement it was no surprise when, in early 2007, the Commission submitted (or rather re-submitted) a directive along those lines.[3] The directive forms part of a wider package through which the Commission seeks to use criminal laws to provide proportionate disincentives and effective deterrence. On both fronts – specific media publicity and broader European policy making – the waste management industry therefore quite suddenly finds itself rather more the centre of attention than it is used to. Understandably, the industry, through its industrial associations, seeks to counter any impression that it is criminalised in any structural sense. Equally, however – as with any other branch of the economy – it strains credibility to suggest that there are no problems. Nor would it be credible to suggest that current problems are just the result of a few 'rotten apples', or the result of penetration of the industry by criminals from outside. The very nature of the industry – getting rid of sometimes dangerous substances at a competitive price – clearly opens up the prospect of wrongdoing. What, then, are the specific vulnerabilities of waste management in relation to illegal and criminal activities? This paper reports on aspects of a recent study, independently conducted and funded by the European Commission, which examines vulnerabilities in the waste management industry. In this paper, first the existing literature is briefly reviewed. Studies on environmental crime have variously described its manifestations (descriptive studies, exposés, etc); focused on the criminal groups and individuals involved (case studies, threat or perpetrator profiles); or explored possible risks in terms of vulnerabilities of the waste business itself. The paper introduces and applies a method of scanning for criminal vulnerabilities in industrial sectors. Vulnerabilities are found in relation to regulation, the international context, and the high costs of legal waste management. Finally, the conclusion is drawn that some current and quite contingent events – in relation to European regulation, international trade and intra-regional competitiveness – may be opening up the prospects for higher standards and for a reduction in illegal behaviour in waste management.

## The literature on waste-related environmental crimes: regulatory aspects, international trade, business costs

Perhaps the most obvious type of crime in the waste management business is improper disposal of waste, sometimes involving breach of permit conditions.[4] Moreover, some companies commit not only environmental crimes (reflecting the special nature of their business) but also other forms of corporate and economic crime (reflecting the fact that they are companies). A clear example of this can be found in the Dutch TCR case.[5] This tank-cleaning company was able to secure substantial government subsidies, through powerful lobbying and opportunistic contracting. It took on contracts which could not be executed properly and, once into difficulties, criminal solutions were found. Employers who balked at the regulatory violations were ridiculed at meetings and those who participated in rule-breaking were rewarded.

Offences against competition and anti-cartel law by waste collection firms have been widely reported in the literature. Price-fixing arrangements have occurred as a result of monopolies, facilitated by trade associations and by labour unions, being established. Price fixing leads to increased costs for customers and to higher profits for the companies.[6] Carter states that it is only possible due to price inelasticity.[7] Price inelasticity refers to the fact that an increase in price does not equally reduce demand for the service. Because of the unclear nature of waste and of the various factors taken into account in pricing waste disposal services, some customers have little idea about a normal or market price. If companies work together and systematically raise their price, customers have no choice than to pay it.[8] Trying to get a better price, some customers may seek out other operators who are more accommodating. Cheapness, however, can come at a price in waste disposal, if licensed landfill operators are bribed to sign documents stating they have taken in waste shipments that in fact they have not received, the waste itself being dumped illegally.[9]

Additionally, as in any other industry, other forms of corporate crime may arise: insurance fraud, subsidy fraud, VAT fraud and other fiscal and employment offences.[10] These crimes are encountered especially with rather small companies that have been founded very recently (higher chance of financial difficulties) or, on the contrary, exist for a very long time (often family companies that have a tradition of 'pragmatic', less formalised, waste management).[11] Not only environmental crimes, but also insurance fraud, subsidy fraud, VAT fraud and other fiscal offences were committed by TRC.

Who is responsible for such crimes – some 'mafia'-type criminals who manipulate and subvert licit firms, or firms' own owners and managers? When discussing the Italian situation, the term 'ecomafia' is sometimes used, referring to the involvement of mafia groupings in the area of environmental crimes. In 2002, about 72.5 million tons of 'special wastes' (industrial, medical and construction waste) have been generated in the country. About 11.2 million tons appear to have vanished from the legal market. This equals a mountain of a surface area of three hectares and a height of 1,120 meters. This has been dumped on approximately 4,866 illegal dumping sites, while Italy contains only 1,385 legal waste disposal sites.[12] Whilst this may be labelled mafia by police and media, the fact remains that owners and managers of licit waste management firms may find themselves embroiled in controversy, as illustrated by the quotation which introduced this paper.

In the wider global perspective, substantial amounts of illegal waste have been transported from industrialised regions to developing countries, this sometimes being referred to as 'waste colonialism'.[13] With the establishment of the Basel Convention,[14] these exports of waste should have come to an end. However, international waste transports still occur, under several disguises. Domestic goods may be exported as second hand goods.[15] Also certain forms of waste disposal processes can be exported (or, should be said, 'outsourced') in their entirety, for example ship-breaking very often occurs in developing countries and can be considered as export of waste.[16]

Massari and Mozzini identify three main causes of environmental crime.[17] In the first place, there is legislation. Control is something of a double-edged sword: legislation that is weakly enforced can stimulate evasion. Adoption of new laws increases waste management costs, making it more attractive to act illegally. Differences in levels of enforcement between countries certainly plays a part – developing countries often lack the means to protect themselves from unwanted waste imports. While this problem used to arise in relation to Central and Eastern European countries at the end of the 1980s and the beginning of the 1990s,[18] it has shifted to African and Asian countries. Gilbert and Russell pay more attention to the international context, pointing to low wages, weak economy and ineffective controls as conditions for environmental crime.[19]

On an economic level, the savings made possible by illegal disposal are considerable: official reports from the Netherlands estimate the savings for illegal waste management at about 200–300%;[20] Massari and Mozzini mention 400%. The waste producers play a role in this. Business ethics may be of varying standards, contracts sometimes being struck with the lowest bidders, even if these bidders can be expected to act illegally. Brack pinpoints this issue, differentiating between, on the one hand, high costs and regulatory failure or gap, and on the other hand, difficulties at the level of enforcement.[21] Enforcement difficulties include insufficient resources and expertise; corruption as such – differentiating this from a broader sympathy towards companies faced with high costs of compliance; and a wish to avoid political and economic disruption. Regulatory failure or gap may arise in the form of inadequate clarity over what constitutes ownership of (and hence responsibility for) waste. Carter pinpoints an absence of clear and comprehensive legislation as causing environmental crime.[22] Also Szasz focused on the absence of appropriate regulations, for example in defining wastes as hazardous,[23] while Van Duyne mentioned certain regulatory loopholes.[24] One of these loopholes can be found in the poor regulation of waste brokers (see below).[25]

Situ[26] paints a similar picture. Criminal behaviour is driven by profit-making or cost-saving, reflecting the higher costs of legal modes of waste management. Situ's second cause, conflicts in belief, is in other studies referred to as a lack of business ethics or a corporate culture prone to crime. His third aspect, crime as a decision in particular circumstances,[27] refers to the physical surroundings and also to operators' judgements about the risks involved. These risks include enforcement issues.

## Specific vulnerabilities

As can be seen from the brief review of literature about, studies of crime risk in waste management have focused upon some quite broad themes, such as regulatory aspects, international trade, and business costs. No doubt such considerations help to paint a vivid descriptive picture, and have broad value – but how easy is it to move on, from an appreciation of such broad-brush and contextual consideration, to specific and concrete proposals for prevention, whether by the public authorities or by the private sector? Is there a way in which specific points of vulnerability in waste management can be identified, so that action can be taken in the short term in order to increase compliance and to reduce environmental and broader corporate crime within the industry?

It was in order to try to answer this sort of question – how to pinpoint specify vulnerabilities in economic sectors (as distinct from broad contextual considerations) – that a method of scanning sectors for their criminal vulnerabilities has been developed. MAVUS (methodology for assessing the vulnerability of sectors), is a method which has been developed to perform vulnerability studies on economic sectors is based on economic and criminological theories.[28] Economic aspects, for example PEST-analysis and the theories of Porter[29] and of Smith,[30] are employed to describe the sector and its environment. This description takes place on various levels and provides information on the sector itself (meso-level), the cluster around it (macro-level) and the business activity within the sector (micro-level). Building on some specific criminological models, notably Albanese[31] and Rozenkrans and Emde[32], some vulnerability indicators have been developed.

An application of this method in 2006 to the waste management industry resulted in the following: one of the vulnerable indicators is the 'nature of the product', as crime risks vary according to the type of product.[33] Waste is a product with an inelastic price. This makes it interesting for organised crime groups and could in particular conditions result in price fixing, as has been the case in the past in New York.[34] Although the modus operandi consisted of bribery, racketeering,[35] deceit and illegal dumping,[36] the huge profits would not have been possible if the service would have been characterised by flexible pricing, as high prices would then have resulted in demand reduction.[37]

Alongside that, the low level of integrity of the product, 'waste', creates crime opportunities. Here, 'integrity' refers to the degree to which the quality or the physical nature can be manipulated with the aim of deception.[38] Hazardous wastes can easily be mixed with non-hazardous wastes. So-called mirror entries[39] provide opportunities to hide the proportions of hazardous and non-hazardous wastes. These mirror entries refer to waste streams that are considered as hazardous only when their presence exceeds a certain level of concentration. Also, the second hand market serves as a cover for illegal waste transports. Stability constitutes a vulnerability issue as well. Waste does not perish in the short term but, considering potential environmental impacts, proper conservation and treatment methods are important – waste has to be deposited safely in its resting place. The costs of guaranteeing that waste is kept safe and stable create incentives to avoid these costs by misrepresentation and illegal dumping.

Clearly, regulation, covering many aspects of waste management, creates some risks. So do lacunae in regulation. Because legislation mainly regulates possession of waste, it mostly does not apply to waste brokers. Waste brokers were brought into being by the need for the industry to cope with environmental regulations.[40] Although brokers have to fulfil licensing conditions, waste does not legally become their property. So, in important respects, they escape direct legislative control.[41] Further critical issues of regulation are national differences concerning waste classifications,[42] the indistinctness between waste and related materials (such as quarrying and soil regulations),[43] re-use and recycling[44] and problems concerning liability for environmental crimes.[45] Further details of these vulnerabilities are given in our fuller report.[46]

The nexus of law enforcement, administrative controls, industrial self-regulation and surveillance by NGOs is characterised by formal complexities and practical difficulties. Law enforcement (including customs) controls mainly deal with transport of waste, while administrative controls focus on various other activities, such as licensing and site inspection. Informal controls are performed by federations (economic controls) and NGOs (environmental controls). Both penal and administrative controls are oriented nationally, whilst the market has increasingly opened up towards an international business. Bottlenecks are encountered during investigations and also during prosecution and trial.[47] One dilemma is the balance to be found between penalising companies and penalising employees.[48]

Administrative and penal enforcement bodies have different areas of operation and cooperation can be non-optimal. In short, the bifurcation of administrative law and penal law may hamper environmental crime investigations.[49] Furthermore, both administrative and penal law have their weaknesses. Administrative bodies often issue permit conditions and are responsible for compliance. This, together with the private nature of their procedures, makes them vulnerable towards corruption. Criminal law enforcement agencies can hardly cope with the complexity, ideology and dynamics of environmental regulations,[50] anyway the waste management business may not be near the top of their list of priorities! This complex set of actors is further elaborated by the presence of informal controls by means of federations and NGOs.

Increasing competition in the waste market provides opportunities for newcomers to enter the waste disposal business. The principles of proximity and self-sufficiency may sometimes conflict with the principles of economic efficiency.[51] This is particularly true for companies close to national borders, for which it is prohibited to export wastes to nearby foreign sites.

As the municipal waste market is less strictly regulated and the most open, various possibilities for creative waste management exist. Yet, the profits that can be achieved are less excessive. In the hazardous waste market, a combination of competition and cost reduction creates incentives for unfair competition. In the nuclear waste market, competition is much more reduced or even absent, creating a sector which is less driven by economic considerations.

The waste market has also been characterised by merger activity.[52] This has resulted in a situation of market concentration, a small club of companies accounting for most of the market share. The market share of the small players is decreasing.[53] This puts competitive pressure on the smaller companies, making them more vulnerable to infiltration by illegal entities.

The second-hand market is often used as a cover for international waste shipments to third world countries.[54] This has been made possible because of lower wages, living standards and administrative safeguards. As a legal – or semi-legal – alternative, this provides opportunities to circumvent waste management regulations.[55] Although strictly not illegal, the trademark of 'second hand goods' is often being used or abused, making it an important focal point and a vulnerable aspect. Further advancements will be needed in the management of end-of-life products[56] in order to reduce these risks. Maximisation of recovery and recycling requires legislative and regulative changes.[57]

At the level of business processes, 'nature and content of the executed service can be distinguished as most vulnerable. The main reason for this is the conflict between economic and environmental interests, creating incentives for illegal profit maximisation. Estimates indicate that profits through illegal waste management are about three to four times higher than for legal activities.[58] This could lead to creative cost reduction beyond what is allowed and to a corporate culture that considers the protection of the environment to be less important than profits. By using subcontractors, transparency can be decreased, reducing the risks of detection of illegal waste management.

Finally, concerning business processes, the central administration of waste management firms may be considered as vulnerable to some extent. Over the years, there have been increases in regulatory requirements and overhead costs falling upon waste management companies. This can have two consequences. A growing number of companies consider these costs as inevitable, and seek to turn them to their advantage, presenting environmental care and investment as part of their 'brands'. In this way, seek to differentiate themselves in the market and to justify increased prices. This is mostly the case for larger companies, who see possibilities for investing in their public image. For other, mostly smaller companies, however, these costs turn out to be an additional burden in a market characterised by high levels of competition. For some of them, lower costs, 'cutting corners' and shorter business lives (possibly associated with new start-ups under different names) may be the strategy adopted.

### Conclusion: the added value of vulnerability studies

Sector vulnerability studies belong to the wider 'family' of criminal opportunity approaches, all of which aim to identify areas of current risk and future prevention. Opportunities approaches are best known for their application at local community level (burglary, etc),[59] on product vulnerability (anything small and expensive),[60] and legislation.[61] Sector vulnerability studies extend the range, by bringing in economic sectors, scanning them in some detail. This approach absorbs the macro-level, 'environmental' contexts and concerns that have been identified in the existing literature – crime opportunities produced by the normal business drive for cost-reduction and profit-maximisation, international and other inequalities, and the often uneven effects of regulation – following these and other themes through the intermediate or meso level of particular sectors, and down to the micro level of the firm. Vulnerability studies provide a comprehensive scan for criminal opportunities.

### *Waste industry vulnerabilities today*

On the macro-level, consideration must be paid both to legislation 'in the books' and to controls *in practice*. In relation to legislation, the waste management business is beset by vulnerabilities arising from loopholes in regulation, national differences and a lack of integration. Weak and uneven controls, and the bifurcation between administrative and penal controls, prove to be particularly problematic, hampering effective regulation/enforcement.[62] The regulation – or, rather, the lack of it – of second-hand goods transported to third world countries provide cover for international waste transports. Alongside that, unstable political situations make it difficult to control certain transports, emphasising the responsibility of policymakers in the industrialised countries.

Concerning the dynamics of the industry, one could say that although barriers to entry are low in relation to bulk waste, such barriers have been rising generally. A new firm needs contacts, technological competences and capacities, the ability to fulfil safety requirements, adequate administrative capacity to deal with licensing systems and more. In theory (for those who comply), these demands result in higher levels of transparency. An exception to this general evolution is the case of the waste brokers, whose operations are characterised by a low level of transparency. Also the transparency of the small and new market players is less clear. This study brings together these factors and in doing so it makes an important claim: waste brokers are particularly important for those small and new companies that have insufficient contacts to completely fulfil the needs of the business. By bringing together those two risk elements, vulnerability is deepened.

Many studies mention the role of high costs of legal waste management as risk-producing. The present study divides these costs in two main subheadings. There is the cost of waste management *per se*. Recycling and incineration technologies are expensive and even the price for dumping has increased, because of stricter environmental regulations and licensing. There is the cost of compliance, which has increased in step with regulatory burdens: traceability, labelling, automation and book-keeping procedures have generated higher overhead costs for licit waste management companies. All such burdens give competitive advantages to illegal operators. Those waste streams that can be mixed and that can easily be transported – for example barrels of liquid hazardous wastes – are highly vulnerable to criminal activity. The inelasticity of waste disposal pricing constitutes a more general crime opportunity.

### Triggers for action?

The European Union may see some progress concerning the international transport of end-of-life infrastructure, machinery and non-recyclable products to developing countries, in which they are broken up or simply dumped. Of course, when the authorities take action (sometimes pushed into it by NGOs), then this makes good material for the news media, and for statements of condemnation by politicians (see our introduction).

Such condemnations may possibly link up with two other set of circumstances. The first of these is the pressure from the European Court of Justice (also mentioned above), to shift criminal law-making from the EU's third pillar to its first pillar (or to 'share' the issues between pillars). The possibility of policy-making in the sphere of environmental protection becoming both more politically controversial, with both and its content *and its mechanisms* become more discussed at European level, may in the long run be good for effective law making in relation to environmental crime generally. It might turn out that some governments – not wishing to be backed into a corner on the wider questions of EU competencies, crime and allocation of competences in accordance with the pillars – might seek to head off such issues by taking early and firmer action on waste or other environmental issues.

One might add to this possibility a consideration about competitive advantage (to use Michael Porter's terminology). It must be in the economic interests of European firms, and of employment, to ensure that safer (and more expensive) means of disposal are found within the EU. An increase in the vigour of enforcement of waste regulation generally, and of export controls in particular, would increase standards of recycling and disposal, would require more sophisticated waste management within the geographical boundaries of Europe, and would push up prices – hence benefiting European industry and employment. An ad-hoc European alliance between sovereigntists, big commercial interests, trade unions, NGOs and media could be one of those contingencies capable of moving mountains.

In conclusion, changes in the attentiveness of politicians and the public, developments in the European legal environments, and the interests of the waste management industry, argue for improvements in regulatory compliance and the closing off of criminal opportunities. Such improvements can be supported by sector scanning, pinpointing specific areas of criminal vulnerability within regulation, markets and firms. By identifying critical aspects, vulnerability studies can help industry, policy makers and other interested parties to reduce vulnerabilities to crime within local, national, regional and international contexts.

## Notes

1  European Commission, 2006, Illegal Waste Shipment: European Environment Commissioner Stavros Dimas travels to Estonia on 28th of September to support the investigation of an illegal waste shipment to the Ivory Coast by the Probo Koala, Press Release, IP/06/1272, 28 September, Brussels: Europe Press Releases, <http://europa.eu/rapid/pressReleasesAction. do?reference=IP/06/1272&format=HTML&aged=o&language=EN&guiLanguage=en>.
2  EU criminal law blog, 2005, September 13, Criminal penalties for environmental offences, <http://eulaw.typepad.com/eulawblog/2005/09/criminal_penalt.html>.
3  Commission of the European Communities, 2006, Proposal for a Directive of the European Parliament and of the Council on the Protection of the Environment through Criminal Law, 9.2.2007, COM(2007) 51 final, 2007/0022 (COD), SEC(2007) 160 and 161, Brussels: European Comssion, pp  17, <http://eur-lex.europa.eu/LexUriServ/site/en/com/2007/com2007_0051en01.pdf>.
4  M.J.J. Van den Anker and A.B. Hoogenboom, *Schijn bedriegt: overheid, bedrijfsleven en gelegenheidsstructuren voor criminaliteit op de hergebruikmarkt* ('s Gravenhage 1997), pp. 267–270.
5  J. Gobert and M. Punch, *Rethinking corporate crime* (London 2003) pp. 27–28.
6  J.B. Jacobs, C. Friel and R. Radick, *Gotham unbound: how New York City was liberated from the grip of organized crime* (New York 1999) pp. 86–95 and A.A. Block, *Perspectives on organizing crime: Essays in opposition* (Dordrecht 1991) pp. 78–115.
7  T.S. Carter, 'Ascent of the corporate model in environmental-organized crime', 31 *Crime Law and Social Change* (1999) p. 2.

8   J.B. Jacobs, C. Friel and R. Radick, *op. cit.*, pp. 86–95.
9   J.S. Albanese and R.D. Pursley, *Crime in America: some existing and emerging issues* (Englewood Cliffs 1993) pp. 325–326.
10  J. Gobert and M. Punch, *op. cit.*, 379p.
11  E.A.I.M. Van den Berg, *Afvalcriminaliteit*, WODC, <http://www.wodc.nl/images/afval_Volledige%20tekst_tcm11–9148.pdf>, 10p.
12  G. Di Lello Finuoli, 'Crime envrionnemental organisé: l'exemple de l'Italie', in F. Comte and L. Krämer, eds., *Environmental Crime in Europe: rules of sanctions* (Groningen 2004) pp. 103–109.
13  G. Porter, J.W. Brown and P. Chasek, *Global environmental politics* 3rd ed. (Boulder 2000) p. 105.
14  Basel Convention on the Control of Transboundary Movements of Hazardous Wastes and Their Disposal, United Nations – Treaty Series 1673 (1992) I-28911, pp. 126–161.
15  R. Agarwal and P. Sarkar, *The globalisation of waste* (New Delhi 2002).
16  K. Paul, 'Exporting responsibility: shipbreaking in South Asia: international trade in hazardous waste', 34 *Environmental Policy and Law* (2004) pp. 73–78.
17  M. Massari and P. Monzini, 'Dirty businesses in Italy: a case-study of illegal trafficking in hazardous waste', 6 *Global Crime* (2004) pp. 285–304.
18  D. Earnheart, 'Environmental crime and punishment in the Czech Republic: penalties against firms and employees', 28 *Journal of Comparative Economics* (2000) p. 379.
19  M.J. Gilbert and S. Russell, 'Globalization of criminal justice in the corporate context', 38 *Crime Law and Social Change* (2002) pp. 211–238.
20  G. Bruinsma, 'De afvalverwerkingsbranche', in G. Bruinsma and F. Bovenkerk, F., eds., *Inzake opsporing: enquêtecommissie opsporingsmethoden, Deel II onderzoeksgroep Fijnaut: branches* (The Hague 1996) pp. 261–310.
21  D. Brack, 'The growth and control of international environmental crime', 112 *Environmental Health Perspectives* (2004) pp. 80–81 and D. Brack, D., 'Combating international environmental crime', 12 *Global Environmental Change: Human and Policy Dimensions* (2002) p. 144.
22  T.S. Carter, 'The failure of environmental regulation in New York: the role of cooptation, corruption and cooperative enforcement approach', 26 *Crime Law and Social Change* (1997) p. 41.
23  A. Szasz, 'Corporations, organized crime and the disposal of hazardous waste: an examination of the making of criminogenic regulatory structure', 24 *Criminology* (1986) pp. 1–27.
24  P.C. Van Duyne, 'Organized crime and business crime enterprises in the Netherlands', 19 *Crime Law and Social Change* (1993) pp. 123–127.
25  S.A. Wright (book review), 'Dangerous grounds: the world of hazardous waste crime, Rebovich D.J.', 74 *Social Science Quarterly* (1993) pp. 452–453.
26  Y. Situ, 'Public transgression of environmental law: a preliminary study', 19 *Deviant Behavior* (1998) pp. 137–155.
27  Y. Situ, *op. cit.*, p. 150.
28  T. Vander Beken, M. Defruytier, A. Bucquoye and K. Verpoest, 'Road map for vulnerability studies', in T. Vander Beken, ed., *Organised Crime and Vulnerability of Economic Sectors: The European Transport and Music Sector* (Antwerp 2005) pp. 7–56.
29  M.E. Porter, Competitive Advantages of Nations (New York 1990).
30  D.C. Smith, 'Paragons, pariahs and pirates: a spectrum-based theory of enterprise', 26 *Crime and Delinquency* (1980), pp. 358–386.
31  J. Albanese, 'Predicting the incidence of organised crime: a preliminary model', in T. Bynum, ed., *Organised Crime in America: Concepts and Controversies* (New York 1987).
32  R. Rozenkrans and E.J. Emde, 'Organized crime: towards the preventive screening of industries: a conceptual model', 7 *Security Journal* (1996), pp. 169–176.
33  R.V. Clarke and G. Newman, *Secured by Design: A Plan for Security Coding of Electronic Products* (Jill Dando Institute of Crime Science 2002) p. 31.
34  J.B. Jacobs, C. Friel, and R. Radick, *op. cit.*, pp. 86–95.
35  T.S. Carter, *loc. cit.* (1999) pp. 1–30.
36  D.R. Simon, 'Corporate environmental crimes and social inequality: new directions for environmental justice research', 43 *American Behavioural Scientist* (2000) p. 635.
37  T.S. Carter, *loc. cit.* (1999) p. 2.
38  T. Vander Beken, M. Defruytier, A. Bucquoye and K. Verpoest, 'Road map for vulnerability studies', in T. Vander Beken, ed., *Organised Crime and Vulnerability of Economic Sectors: The European Transport and Music Sector* (Antwerp 2005) p. 34.
39  Council Decision 94/904/EC establishing a list of hazardous waste pursuant to Article 1(4) of Council Directive 91/689/EEC on hazardous waste, Official Journal L226, 06/09/2000,

1–32.

40  S.A. Wright, *loc. cit.*, pp. 452–453.

41  G. Bruinsma, loc. cit., pp. 283–284 and M.J.J. Van den Anker and W.C.E. Snels, *Wie betaalt, bepaalt: over intermediaire organisaties, milieucriminaliteit, organisatiecriminaliteit en integriteit in het complexe milieuveld* ('s Gravenhage 1999) pp. 36–38.

42  F. Ermaroca, 'Community legislation and jurisprudence in the area of waste management: recent developments', 7 *Reciel* (1998) pp. 274–282.

43  G. Amendola, 'Need for a strengthening of criminal environmental law? The Italian case', in F. Comte and L. Krämer, eds., *Environmental Crime in Europe: Rules of Sanctions* (Groningen 2004) pp. 177–195.

44  J. Puckett, *The Basel Plan: A Triumph over Business-as-usual* (Basel action network 1997) p. 4.

45  G. Bandi, 'Liability and sanctions, criminal liability in Hungary', in F. Comte and L. Krämer, eds., *Environmental Crime in Europe: Rules of Sanctions* (Groningen 2004) pp. 127–142.

46  S. Van Daele, T. Vander Beken and N. Dorn, 'The European waste disposal sector', in T. Vander Beken, ed., *The European Waste Industry and Crime Vulnerabilities* (Antwerp, in press).

47  A.M.E. Veldkamp, 'Grensoverschrijdende overbrenging van afvalstoffen', in L.E.M. Hendriks, G.A. Biezeveld and H.F.M.W. Van Rijswick, eds., *Strafrechtelijke aanpak van grensoverschrijdende milieucriminaliteit, capita selecta* (Zwolle 1996) pp. 56–58.

48  D. Earnhart, *loc. cit.*, pp. 379–399.

49  M.G. Faure and G. Heine, *Criminal Enforcement of Environmental Law in the European Union* (The Hague 2005) pp. 89–90.

50  D.C. Fortney, 'Thinking outside the 'black box' tailored enforcement in environmental criminal law', 81 *Texas Law Review* (2003), pp. 1609–1635.

51  N. Buclet and O. Godard, 'Municipal Waste Management in Europe: a comparison of national regimes' in N. Buclet and O. Godard, eds., *Municipal Waste Management in Europe: A Comparative Study in Building Regimes* (Dordrecht 2000) p. 222.

52  A. Cooke and W. Chapple, 'Merger activity in the waste disposal industry: the impact and the implications of the Environmental Protection Act', 32 *Applied Economics* (2000), pp. 749–755.

53  Waste Market Council, *Waste Market: Public Companies and Developments* (Utrecht 2003) pp. 8–9.

54  Dutch ministry of housing, spatial planning and the environment, *Twintig procent afvaltransporten illegaal*, VROM, 16/07/2004.

55  G. Porter, J.W. Brown and P. Chasek, *op. cit.*, p. 107.

56  M.W. Toffel, 'The growing strategic importance of end-of-life product management', 45 *California Management Review* (2003), no. 3, 102–129.

57  R. Lisney, K. Riley and C. Banks, 'From waste to resource management', 47 *Management Services* (2003), no. 12, 8–14.

58  G. Bruinsma, *loc. cit.*, p. 266.

59  T. Bennett and R. Wright, *Burglars on Burglary: Prevention and the Offender* (Aldershot 1984).

60  R.V. Clarke and G. Newman, *Secured by Design: A Plan for Security Coding of Electronic Products, Draft Produced for the Foresight Crime Prevention Panel by the Jill Dando Institute of Crime Science* (UCL 2002).

61  E.U. Savona and A. Di Nicola (2002), *Assessing the Risk of Organised Crimes: a User-friendly Methodology for Law Enforcement Agencies and Policy-makers*, paper presented at the Workshop on A European Strategy on Crime and Terrorism Proofing and the Assessment of the Threat from Organised Crime (Brussels 2002).

62  From the points of view both of dry analysis and of policy effectiveness, there is much to be said for convergence between the concepts of regulation and policing. See for example P. Gill, 'Policing and Regulation: What is the difference', 11 *Social and Legal Studies* (2002), pp. 523–546.

# Index

Note: 'n' following a reference denotes an endnote and 't' denotes a table 2,4-Dichlorophenoxyacetic 470